OXFORD
UNIVERSITY PRESS

Great Clarendon Street, Oxford, OX2 6DP,
United Kingdom

Oxford University Press is a department of the University of Oxford.
It furthers the University's objective of excellence in research, scholarship,
and education by publishing worldwide. Oxford is a registered trade mark of
Oxford University Press in the UK and in certain other countries

© Alisdair Gillespie and Siobhan Weare 2021

The moral rights of the authors have been asserted

Fifth Edition 2015
Sixth Edition 2017
Seventh Edition 2019
Impression: 1

Public sector information reproduced under Open Government Licence v3.0
(http://www.nationalarchives.gov.uk/doc/open-government-licence/open-government-licence.htm)

Published in the United States of America by Oxford University Press
198 Madison Avenue, New York, NY 10016, United States of America

British Library Cataloguing in Publication Data
Data available

Library of Congress Control Number: 202193495

ISBN 978–0–19–886899–6

Printed in Great Britain by
Bell & Bain Ltd., Glasgow

Eighth edition

THE ENGLISH LEGAL SYSTEM

Alisdair A. GILLESPIE

LL.B.(HONS), M.JUR., M.A.(ED), D.LITT.
PROFESSOR OF CRIMINAL LAW AND JUSTICE
AT LANCASTER UNIVERSITY

Siobhan WEARE

LL.B.(HONS), PH.D.
SENIOR LECTURER IN LAW AT LANCASTER UNIVERSITY

OXFORD
UNIVERSITY PRESS

This book is dedicated to:
Suzanne, Lily, Matthew, and Elin
(AAG)
and
James
(SW)

Preface

The book has been written for you, the student. It is likely that you are just starting to learn about law and so this textbook is designed to provide an engaging and varied introduction to the English Legal System. It will allow you to understand the key aspects of the English Legal System and help you to question why the law has evolved in this way. Each chapter includes questions for you to reflect upon what you are learning and provides suggested further reading at the end so that you can increase your knowledge and understanding

This textbook is only one part of the learning experience; there are also online resources that accompany this book. There are extra reading resources to take you even further; links to many of the specific documents discussed in the book so that, rather than relying on our interpretation of what a document says, you can read it yourself and come to your own conclusions; and there are multiple choice questions and activities that will allow you to test and develop your knowledge.

The eighth edition was written during the summer and autumn of 2020 and the Covid-19 pandemic. The everchanging nature of the restrictions, and the impacts this had both legally and socially presented somewhat of a challenge when updating the textbook. However, we have tried our best to capture the impact (both current and future) of Covid-19 on the English Legal System in a new chapter 20, 'The future in a post-Covid world'. We have also introduced some substantial changes in this eighth edition to reflect recent developments and increase accessibility. Chapter four 'International Sources of Law' has been re-written to take account of changes in the UK-EU relationship in a post-Brexit world, and minor amendments have been made in other chapters to take account of Brexit. The funding of access to justice is now a chapter is in its own right (chapter eleven) and covers the funding of both civil litigation and criminal defence costs. By bringing all elements of funding access to justice together in this way we hope that you are more easily able to engage with and understand the complexity of funding civil and criminal cases, and see the similarities and differences between the current funding arrangements. Other changes include substantial re-writes around legal education and training to take account of recent reforms and updates in relation to the roles of those in court.

As usual, thanks are due to a number of people in respect of this edition. We acknowledge the assistance of the Crown Prosecution Service, HM Courts and Tribunal Service, and the Ministry of Justice. We also would like to thank our anonymous reviewers, who have provided invaluable feedback, and helped us to ensure the book is as valuable as possible to the widest number of students studying a range of English Legal System courses. Thanks also to the team at Oxford University Press for their support of this new edition and our editor Carlotta who has been with us for both this edition, and the seventh edition (which must nearly be a new record given Alisdair's track record of losing editors).

In a post-Brexit and post-Covid world there is undoubtedly going to be significant developments within the English Legal System. We have incorporated as much of this as we can in this new edition, and with ensure that further updates will be added to the online resources over the coming weeks and months.

We hope you find this book interesting and that you find it a useful addition to your legal studies. As always, we welcome your feedback on anything that can be improved.

AAG and SW
Lancaster (virtually)
January 2021

New to this Edition

- The chapter 'International sources of law' has been extensively rewritten to include a fuller discussion of international law and its impact on UK law, and to consider the changes to the UK's relationship with the EU post-Brexit.
- A new chapter, 'Funding access to justice' combines and expands the coverage of civil and criminal legal aid to reflect recent developments and to increase accessibility.
- Full consideration of the future challenges of reforms to legal education in the chapter on the legal professions.
- 'The future in a post-COVID world' chapter looks at the impact of COVID-19 on the English legal system and considers what the future is likely to bring.

Outline Contents

Detailed Contents

ix

x

xix

Guide to the Book

The English Legal System is enriched with a range of features designed to help support and reinforce your learning. This guided tour shows you how to fully utilize your textbook and get the most out of your study.

Learning outcomes

Each chapter begins with a bulleted outline of the main concepts and ideas you will encounter. These serve as a helpful signpost to what you can expect to learn by reading the chapter.

By the end of this chapter you w

- Understand why the pressure for A
- Define ADR and explain the three
- Identify how the courts are able to
- Appreciate some of the advantage

⊟ Example

Bernard asked Wreckers Ltd to install a swir
is not fit for purpose as it leaks, meaning th
Bernard has been told it will cost £11,000 to
   Realistically Bernard's claim will be for
£10,000. However, if both Bernard and Wre

Examples

Everyday scenarios explain and illustrate how a particular law or legal practice would apply in a real-life situation.

Questions for reflection

Why was a particular decision reached in a certain case? Is the law on this point rational and coherent? Is the English Legal System fit for purpose? Questions for reflection encourage you to think about contentious issues and critique the law.

↻ QUESTION FOR REFLECTION

Should the English Legal System recognize
Is this not permitting religious law to enter
However, if arbitration—and indeed most A
disputes on their own terms, why should it
dispute according to the religious principles

◀)) LISTEN TO THE PODCAST

For guidance on how to answer this que
to the author's podcast on the online res
www.oup.com/he/gillespie-weare8e/

Listen to the podcast

Selected questions for reflection are supported by audio podcasts by the authors which appear on the accompanying website. These outline the contrasting viewpoints you may wish to consider and offer advice on how to answer the questions.

Case boxes

Real-life cases demonstrate the way in which legal concepts are used in practice: the facts and decisions are presented to assist you in understanding why the court reached its decision and what the wider implications are.

III Case Box *Sweet v Parsley*

The leading case that discusses the absen[ce] was the tenant of a farm but sublet rooms[.] appellant did not live at the farm. The polic[e] was charged with the offence of, inter alia, [b]ises used for the purpose of smoking cann[abis]

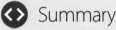

⚡ CONCILIATION

Conciliation is often used in industrial disput[es] and employers disagree over work conditi[ons] to settle disputes before strike action take[s] disputes or litigation being brought where[...] or where the trade union seeks declaration[...]

Key terms and concepts

Some key concepts and important legal terms are highlighted, using both real cases and fictitious examples to illustrate and explain.

Chapter summaries

The central points and concepts from each chapter are distilled into succinct summaries. These help you to reinforce your understanding and can also be used as a revision tool.

‹› Summary

This chapter has introduced some of the c[oncepts] a case proceeds through the small claims c[ourt/County] Court. It has also:

- Identified that a single set of rules now go[verns]

❓ End-of-chapter questio[ns]

1. Should a court discount an award to take a[...] kind of investment should they base their [...] est rates have been stagnant for the past f[...]

2. Read Penny Darbyshire, *Sitting in Judgmen[t]*

End-of-chapter questions

Problem questions and essay-type questions at the end of each chapter will help to develop your analytical and problem-solving skills.

Further reading

Suggestions for further reading are included at the end of each chapter as a springboard for reliable further study. Each source is accompanied by an explanation of its relevance to your study, guiding you to the key academic literature in the field.

≣ Further reading

Davies G, 'Civil Justice Reform: Why We Need t[o...]' *Justice Quarterly* 32–51.

This an excellent article by a former Aus[t...] premises over the place of ADR in civil lit[igation...]

Guide to the Online Resources

www.oup.com/he/gillespie-weare8e/

The book is accompanied by a range of online resources to support teaching and learning:

- Students can check their progress using a **test bank of 300 self-test questions,** offering immediate answers and feedback A selection of **annotated web links** facilitate further research in areas of particular interest

- A **flashcard glossary** provides a useful one-stop reference point for key words and terms used within the text

- Suggestions for **practical activities** are provided to help take learning further

- **Audio podcasts** by the author outline opposing viewpoints on controversial topics in this area, encouraging critical thinking and debate

Table of Cases

Court of Justice of the European Union Cases

European Court of Human Rights Cases

Table of Legislation

xxxi

Table of UK Statutory Instruments

EU Primary Legislation

EU Treaties

EU Secondary Legislation

European Directives

European Regulations

International Instruments

1

The English Legal System

By the end of this chapter you will be able to:

- Define the United Kingdom.
- Identify how many legal systems exist in the United Kingdom.
- Begin to understand the concept of law and how laws differentiate from mere rules.
- Begin to think about 'systems' and understand the key issues within the English Legal System.

Introduction

In this introductory chapter the words 'English', 'Legal', and 'System' will be discussed. These words are often used but it is not always clear why they are used in this phrase and why so many modules now refer to the English Legal System. This chapter will also prepare you for the later chapters as it will help put them into context.

1.1 England

The first word to examine is that of 'England'. The question of identity is something that appears to be raised perpetually in the media, and countries are given numerous different wordings. In this country, it is common to refer to living in 'Britain', 'the UK', or the 'United Kingdom'. The country does have a formal legal title, that of the *United Kingdom of Great Britain and Northern Ireland*. The Queen, as sovereign, has many other titles representing many of the dependent territories that exist but the title is as already stated—*United Kingdom of Great Britain and Northern Ireland*. The latest version of the title became relevant in 1920 when Ireland was partitioned and twenty-six counties were given independence, forming the Republic of Ireland.[1] The title also

---

1. It is often erroneously said that the twenty-six counties constitute 'Southern Ireland', presumably as the opposite of 'Northern Ireland'. However, this is both legally incorrect (the formal name of the state is The Republic of Ireland (in English) or Eire (in Gaelic)) and geographically incorrect since the County of Donegal is as northerly as the six counties that constitute Northern Ireland.

demonstrates that 'Britain' or, more correctly, 'Great Britain'[2] is actually the main island grouping of which England is one part.

1.1.1 The constituent parts

The United Kingdom of Great Britain and Northern Ireland consists of four countries (although one was originally a principality). The countries are England, Wales, Scotland, and Northern Ireland. The status of Wales differs from England, Scotland, and Northern Ireland. Traditionally Wales was a principality (a province ruled by a prince) and this is a term that continues to be used by some, not least because the Crown Prince of the United Kingdom is known as the *Prince of Wales* and thus the logic, to some, is that it follows that Wales is a principality. Others disagree and argue that Wales is a country and should be accorded that title. In reality the distinction between principality and country is moot and either title could be used although it would seem that many in Wales itself dislike the term principality. Wales does differ from the other constituent countries in that it has not had its own legal system since the sixteenth century, although this is beginning to change.

1.1.1.1 England and Wales

Wales does not, as yet, have its own legal system (see, however, the *Government of Wales Act 2006* discussed later—see 'Welsh legislation') and following the *Laws of Wales Act 1535*, Wales in effect became legally 'annexed' by England and ensured that the laws of England would apply in Wales too. This Act was passed by an English-only Parliament but part of its purpose was to ensure that there could be Welsh representation in the (then) English Parliament. A further *Laws of Wales Act* was passed in 1543 and gave further effect to the governance of Wales and the long title of the Act makes express reference to its status as a principality. This was followed by the *Wales and Berwick Act 1746* that defined 'England' as including all of Wales. This Act was repealed by the *Interpretation Act 1978*, but prior to this, its extent had been limited by the *Welsh Language Act 1967*,[3] which re-introduced the concept of Wales as a country in its own right.

The effect of this is that this book, along with every other book on this topic, and most modules, is technically wrong. It is not the *English* Legal System; it is technically the Legal System of *England and Wales*. That this is correct can be seen when one examines the main legal institutions. The senior courts are technically known as the *Superior Courts of England and Wales*.[4] The body for solicitors, known as the Law Society, is actually the *Law Society of England and Wales* and the body for barristers, known as the Bar Council, is actually the *General Council of the Bar for England and Wales*. This extends to judicial offices with the Lord Chief Justice technically being the *Lord Chief Justice for England and Wales*. This was perhaps most obvious when Lord Thomas of Cwmgiedd became Lord Chief Justice and chose an obviously Welsh location for his barony.

---

2. Since the term is derived from Brittany, a French region, what we understand to be Britain is 'Great' (meaning large) Britain.
3. *Welsh Language Act 1967*, s 4.
4. *Constitutional Reform Act 2005*, sch 15.

Welsh legislation

As noted earlier, the *Government of Wales Act 2006* (GoWA 2006) granted Wales a limited form of legislative powers. Initially this was through 'Assembly Powers' which were, in essence, a form of secondary legislation since each power required the approval of the Privy Council[5] but following a referendum in 2011 (which was required under s 103) the Welsh Assembly was permitted the right to pass 'Acts of the Assembly'.[6] These legislative instruments are primary legislation in Wales and, unlike measures, do not require the approval of the Privy Council (although they do, as with UK legislation, require Royal Assent). However, it would be wrong to say that Wales has yet reached the status of either Scotland or Northern Ireland in terms of devolved legislative powers, not least because its legislative competences are somewhat restricted.[7]

A number of Acts of Assembly have been passed, including the *Schools Standards and Organisation (Wales) Act 2013*, the *National Health Service Finance (Wales) Act 2014*, and the *Renting Homes (Wales) Act 2016*. Despite the introduction of these Acts of Assembly, realistically it will be some years before the laws of England and Wales differ dramatically, and even then it will not affect the legal system since courts and both civil and criminal procedure are not devolved matters (cf the position in both Scotland and Northern Ireland).

The COVID crisis in 2020 saw, for the first time, considerable difference between the laws of England and Wales. This will be considered more fully in Chapter 20.

Commission on Justice in Wales

Lord Thomas of Cwmgiedd was Lord Chief Justice of England and Wales from 2013 to 2017. Upon his retirement, the Welsh government asked him to chair a commission that reviewed the justice system in Wales. It reported in 2019,[8] recommending that the justice system in Wales and England should be separated. They found that, for example, the use of the Welsh language was inconsistent across courts in Wales, and there was a lack of understanding of local issues.

The Commission believed that Wales should have responsibility for the justice system, including its prisons, police, and the judiciary. It noted that the Welsh Assembly was starting to produce its own laws, and, therefore, it was time for the Laws of Wales to be recognized as distinct from those in England, even if they were largely the same. More importantly, they noted that it was inappropriate that the professions and courts were administered in England.

While the UK government has not formally responded to the report, in part because it is a Welsh government report, the current Secretary of State for Justice and Lord Chancellor, Robert Buckland MP, has stated that his (and, presumably, the government's) view is that the legal systems of England and Wales are best shared.[9] Accordingly, it does not seem that there will be formal separation any time soon.

---

5. *Government of Wales Act 2006*, s 93.
6. ibid, s 107.
7. ibid, s 108.
8. See https://gov.wales/commission-justice-wales.
9. Monidipa Fouzder 'Buckland: united Wales and England "best for the law"' (2020) *Law Society Gazette*, 9 October (https://www.lawgazette.co.uk/news/buckland-united-wales-and-england-best-for-the-law/5105950.article).

3

1.1.1.2 **Scotland**

Scotland is a country and joined the United Kingdom as a result of an Act of Union. The history of England and Scotland is probably well known to most readers and involved numerous battles between the two countries, sometimes with England winning, sometimes with Scotland winning. Indeed some of the battles occurred after the union with perhaps the most notable being the uprising led by 'Bonnie Prince Charlie'[10] who believed that he was the rightful heir to the throne.

Prior to the countries uniting, England and Scotland shared a sovereign, when King James VI of Scotland assumed the throne of England as King James I. This continued even through the 'Glorious Revolution' of 1688 when King William III and Queen Mary II jointly ruled both thrones. The countries were joined by the *Act of Union 1707*. In fact two statutes were passed as both the English and Scottish Parliaments had to pass the Act. The effect of the Act was to extinguish the Parliaments of *both* England and Scotland and create a Parliament of the United Kingdom. This can be contrasted with the position with Wales where Welsh members simply joined the English Parliament. The seat of Parliament was Westminster and this continues to be the case regardless of devolution (see 1.1.2).

Perhaps one of the most important aspects of the Act was the preservation of Scots law. Title 19 of the Act expressly preserved the Scottish Legal System and governed how appointments to the senior judiciary would be made. The principle of a separate legal system has continued throughout and devolution has merely altered the mechanics of this. That is not to say that Westminster does not have power to create Scottish laws since it clearly does—it is the Parliament of the United Kingdom—but there is no *automatic* assumption that laws passed will extend to Scotland (see 1.1.2).

Despite the continuing existence of the *Act of Union*, there has always been a question of whether Scotland should gain independence. Following the formation of the Scottish government after the 2011 parliamentary election, in which the Scottish National Party won a clear majority, an agreement was signed between the Scottish First Minister Alex Salmond and Prime Minister David Cameron on the holding of a referendum on Scottish independence. In September 2014, the Scottish referendum took place. The question on the ballot paper was 'Should Scotland be an independent country?' Over 3,500,000 Scots voted in the referendum, with the 'no' vote winning a majority of 55%, with over 2,000,000 votes. Despite the continued union of the United Kingdom, following the vote the Smith Commission was set up to oversee the devolution of additional powers to the Scottish Parliament.

Whilst the Smith Commission was not strongly welcomed by the Scottish National Party, it attracted considerable support from the three main parties at Westminster at that time.[11] As promised, new legislation was brought before the Houses of Parliament and the *Scotland Act 2016* was given Royal Assent on 23 March 2016. The *Scotland Act 2016* delegates more powers to the Scottish Parliament, including the power to pass laws in areas that were otherwise reserved to Westminster.

At the time of writing, the response to the vote to leave the EU in the UK-wide referendum (see Chapter 20, 'The Future in a Post-COVID World') has led to calls for another independence referendum. Scotland voted overwhelmingly to stay within the

---

10. More properly known as Charles Edward Stuart.
11. The general election of 2015 led to the *Scottish National Party* becoming the third-largest party in Westminster. The 'three main parties' prior to 2015 were the Conservatives, Labour, and the Liberal Democrats.

EU and the First Minister has suggested that the 2014 referendum result has been set aside because voters, at that time, voted to remain within a United Kingdom in Europe. Whilst the Scottish Parliament has unveiled a draft Bill for a further referendum, this would not be sufficient as Westminster must give consent for a referendum to be held. Nevertheless, it would be politically difficult for Westminster to refuse if such a Bill were to be passed by the Scottish Parliament.

1.1.1.3 Northern Ireland

Northern Ireland is the most recent addition to the United Kingdom, it being created in 1920. Prior to that Ireland was a whole country and it was a member of the United Kingdom as a result of the *Act of Union 1801*. There were many similarities between the *Acts of Union 1707* and *1801* and it was intended that it would be a merger: Ireland did not become part of the United Kingdom of Great Britain but transformed it into a new body, the United Kingdom of Great Britain and Ireland. The merger was political expediency: the two countries had shared the same King since the sixteenth century and there was close cooperation between the Parliaments but it was believed more appropriate to create a single country. Like Scotland, Ireland retained its own legal status and although there were United Kingdom laws (ie laws that applied across the entire United Kingdom) there were also individual Irish laws.

Throughout the nineteenth and twentieth centuries pressure grew for Ireland to have more responsibility for its own actions, in part as a reaction to injustices carried out by the British; a series of 'Home Rule' Bills (in effect devolution) failed but pressure grew for full independence following a series of insurrections. Eventually the United Kingdom Parliament passed the *Government of Ireland Act 1920* which would partition Ireland. Twenty-six counties would become 'Southern Ireland' and six counties would become 'Northern Ireland'. The division was broadly upon religious grounds with Ulster (which included the six counties)[12] being mainly Protestant and the twenty-six counties being mainly Roman Catholic. Of course this is a very crude approximation and there was a significant Protestant population in what was to be 'Southern Ireland' and vice versa.

'Southern Ireland' never came into existence because the twenty-six counties declared independence, forming the Republic of Ireland (Eire). The United Kingdom recognized independence but felt that Ulster was the remainder of the previous Ireland, and, therefore, the UK became the United Kingdom of Great Britain and Northern Ireland. The 1920 Act was eventually repealed by the *Northern Ireland Act 1998* which was part of the devolution process (see 1.1.2) but also in pursuance of the *Good Friday Agreement*, an agreement between the Irish and UK governments to deal with the question of Irish unification. The current position is that both Eire and Northern Ireland remain two separate countries within the island of Ireland. The government of Northern Ireland is unique within the United Kingdom in that it is based on power-sharing.

The leadership of Northern Ireland is held in the First Minister and Deputy First Minister. While the latter sounds as though it subservient, both are equally ranked. They are elected on a joint ticket, requiring a majority of members of the Northern Ireland Assembly, but also a majority of the Ulster and Nationalist representatives. The First Minister has traditionally been held by the leader of the largest party (who has

---

12. Although 'Ulster' is commonly now thought of as being Northern Ireland, it technically includes the counties of Cavan, Donegal, and Monaghan.

been a Unionist politician), with the Deputy First Minister being the leader of the largest nationalist party.

This book cannot consider the specifics of Northern Ireland political arrangements, but it is worth noting the significant differences between Northern Ireland and the rest of the United Kingdom.

1.1.2 **The United Kingdom**

Whilst this book is about the *English Legal System* (but really the Legal System of England and Wales) it is necessary to pause briefly to consider the United Kingdom. The election of a Labour government to the Westminster Parliament in 1997 led to the process of devolution. Theoretically devolution does not affect purely English matters; the law continues to be passed by the Parliament at Westminster. Devolution principally affects Northern Ireland and Scotland and this is outside the scope of this book although it is likely you will discuss them in *Constitutional Law* or similar modules.

Westminster remains the Parliament of the United Kingdom and the devolution instruments expressly preserve the right of Westminster to pass legislation that affects both Scotland and Northern Ireland. This is known as 'extent'. Both prior to and following devolution, the convention is that if an Act of Parliament is silent as to its extent (ie there is not a section within the Act of Parliament that discusses its extent) then it applies only to England and Wales. If the Act is to apply to either Scotland or Northern Ireland then a section within the Act will expressly state this and also the provisions that apply.

⚡ SEXUAL OFFENCES ACT 2003

The Sexual Offences Act 2003 was a major piece of legislation that reformed the criminal law relating to sexual offending. Section 142 states:

142 Extent, saving etc.

  (1) Subject to section 137 and to subsections (2) to (4), this Act extends to England and Wales only.

  (2) The following provisions also extend to Northern Ireland—

    (a) sections 15 to 25, 46 to 54, 57 to 60, 66 to 72, 78 and 79,

    (b) Schedule 2,

    (c) Part 2, and

    (d) sections 138, 141, 143 and this section.

  (3) The following provisions also extend to Scotland—

    (a) Part 2 except sections 93 and 123 to 129 and Schedule 4, and

    (b) sections 138, 141, 143 and this section.

By reading this section (don't worry about the language used within it, this is explained in Chapter 2) it can be seen that the whole of the Act applies to England and Wales but that only certain parts of the Act apply to Northern Ireland (those mentioned in subsection (2)). So, for example, ss 1–5 which are not mentioned would not apply in Northern Ireland and even less of it applies to Scotland (principally only Part 2 of the Act and even then ss 93 and 123–9 do not apply).

1.2 **Legal**

The second word to examine is 'legal' which is the adjective for 'law' but what is 'law'? One of the first things to note is that we talk about a 'body of law' meaning that there is more than one law. Indeed those of you who are studying for a law degree can find that out from your degree title. Most of you will be reading for the degree of LLB (Hons) but do you know what that stands for? It is the abbreviation for *Legum Baccalaureus* which means Bachelor of Laws. Why is it that there are two 'L's? It is because in Latin the abbreviation for a plural is to repeat the first letter (whereas we use 's', ie Law becomes Laws).

1.2.1 **Classifying law**

Before considering what law is (which will require a brief examination of the philosophy of law) it is worth reflecting on the types of law that exist. Law can be classified in various ways and the approach that is taken to the law will be governed by its classification.

1.2.1.1 **Substantive or procedural**

The first division that perhaps has to be discussed is that which exists between substantive and procedural law. It will be seen later that some theorists, most notably Hart, argue that law can be classified into primary and secondary rules. Primary rules are considered to be laws that set out rights, duties, and obligations. Secondary rules determine how the primary rules are to be recognized, interpreted, and applied. Whilst this can be considered relatively simplistic it does assist in our understanding of the distinction between substantive and procedural laws.

What is the first thing you think about when you think of law? There is a reasonably high chance that it will be crime (see 1.2.1.3). This is not uncommon because it is one of the few areas of law that most people know something about but also because it is an interesting area of law and one that the media deal with on a daily basis. The actual crime is *substantive* law, in other words substantive law is that which sets out the rule which must be followed. Where someone is suspected of breaching this substantive law, there has to be an investigation, prosecution, and trial. All of these areas are also governed by laws so that an individual is protected against arbitrary interference by the state. These laws differ from the rule that says a person cannot commit a crime but they are nonetheless laws, and must be followed. These rules are *procedural* law and they set out the framework by which the substantive law will be determined.

Substantive and Procedural Law

Section 1 *Theft Act 1968* states:

(1) A person is guilty of theft if he dishonestly appropriates property belonging to another with the intention of permanently depriving the other of it; and 'thief' and 'steal' shall be construed accordingly.

This is a substantive law. It, in combination with s 7 (which prescribes the punishment for theft), states that a person must not steal.

Section 24 *Police and Criminal Evidence Act 1984* states:

(1) A constable may arrest without a warrant—

    (a) anyone who is about to commit an offence;

    (b) anyone who is in the act of committing an offence;

    (c) anyone whom he has reasonable grounds for suspecting is about to commit an offence;

    (d) anyone whom he has reasonable grounds for suspecting to be committing an offence.

(2) If a constable has reasonable grounds for suspecting that an offence has been committed, he may arrest without a warrant anyone whom he has reasonable grounds to suspect of being guilty of it.

This is procedural law. It sets out the circumstances when a police officer may arrest someone, those being (approximately) that a person has committed, or is about to commit, a breach of the substantive law.

1.2.1.2 Private or public law

The next distinction that needs to be drawn is between private and public law. This is a more subtle distinction as it straddles both substantive and procedural law; ie both substantive and procedural law could be either private or public law. A crude but effective separation is to suggest that private law concerns disputes that exist between citizens, and public law is disputes that exist between the state and the individual. It is perhaps the definition of 'public' that is more relevant since certain disputes between public bodies may actually give rise to private law matters.

☰ Example Private and public law

PRIVATE LAW

Rhiannon agrees with Alison to purchase twenty-four bottles of red wine for the price of £150. When Rhiannon comes to collect them, there are only twenty bottles and yet Alison wants the full £150. If not resolved amicably it is quite possible that this dispute will end up before the courts, with Rhiannon suing Alison for breach of contract.

    This is a classic example of private law as it is a dispute between two parties and does not involve the state in its sovereign capacity.[13]

PUBLIC LAW

Jack, a (fictitious) media commentator made derogatory statements about accountants in a newspaper. Sarah runs a campaign group that attempts to raise the profile of accountants. Sarah wishes to lead a march through Jack's home town but the local police force refuses permission.

    This is a good example of public law. Sarah may think that the police force is acting unreasonably and may wish to apply to the courts to challenge this decision. This would be done through the process known as judicial review (considered at 17.3) and is a public law matter because it involves the relationship between a private citizen (Sarah) and the state (the police).

---

13.   If the dispute existed between two councils, this would remain a private law matter even though it now involves two public (state) bodies. This is because the dispute is not with the state acting in its capacity as the state, ie the sovereign.

AV Dicey, a nineteenth-century jurist, and someone who is considered to be one of the pre-eminent authorities on constitutional law, stated that there was, in England and Wales, no such thing as 'administrative' law. By this he meant to contrast the position with the continental-based systems (see 1.3) which have always believed that there is a distinction between public and private law matters. Indeed the continental system created separate courts and legal processes to resolve administrative disputes. Dicey argued that this was not the position within England and Wales because everyone was equal under the law, ie the state was bound by the same law as the citizen.

Whilst, during the nineteenth century, this may have been true it is extremely difficult to continue this approach today. The legal system has now created a specific court to deal with administrative law (called the Administrative Court) although it is, theoretically, within the ordinary court system since it merely constitutes part of the Queen's Bench Division of the High Court of Justice. However, there is no doubt that the system has now become a body of law in its own right and there is now an express and specific procedure that governs administrative disputes.[14]

1.2.1.3 Civil or criminal law

It may seem that one of the more obvious distinctions to make is between civil and criminal law but, as we will see, this is not always a simple distinction. The distinction does not, as is sometimes believed, necessarily follow the private and public split.

Civil law is effectively anything that is not criminal. This may appear a trite statement but to an extent it is easier to say this than to suggest that a crime is anything that is not civil. This is because it is generally easier to identify what is criminal rather than civil. The civil law encompasses many different bodies of law mixing both private and public law. Ordinarily criminal matters can be categorized as public law in that the state is becoming involved in its sovereign capacity in relation to a citizen. In criminal matters the state will ordinarily be the prosecutor (for offences that take place in the Crown Court this will normally be through the sovereign (known as Regina when the sovereign is female and Rex when the sovereign is male) and in magistrates' courts ordinarily through the *Director of Public Prosecutions* or *Crown Prosecution Service* (13.1.1)). Whilst many crimes will have a victim, who will almost certainly be a citizen, it is not necessarily a private dispute between citizens. Indeed the state can, if it so wishes, bring a prosecution regardless of the views of the victim (13.1.2.1). This would make it a public law matter.

However, criminal law can, under certain circumstances, be a private law matter too. Although the state sets out the legal framework and will ordinarily prosecute, there remains in England and Wales the right to undertake a 'private prosecution'. This will be discussed elsewhere (13.1.5) but in essence means that a private citizen acts as the prosecutor and brings court proceedings. Whilst the state can intervene it need not do so, and accordingly in that guise it would appear to be private law (because the state is not present); but the laws are made on the assumption that the state will be the prosecutor so is this not still public law merely instigated privately? This is confusing but does demonstrate an important point: there are no clear answers in law and thus the divisions noted in this chapter will always be somewhat imprecise in practice.

What then is a crime? An example of a crime was noted earlier (1.2.1.1) and theft (*Theft Act 1968*, s 1) is a good example of a simple crime. It is a law that prohibits

---

14. *Civil Procedure Rules*, pt 54.

something and carries with it a sanction for breaching the law. The courts have traditionally linked punishment with the idea of a crime[15] but this can in itself cause difficulty. There are many examples of situations where a person may appear to receive a punishment but it would not amount to a crime. A good example would be tax. If you need to complete a self-assessment tax form (to let the government know how much tax you must pay) there is a deadline by which you must submit it. If you miss this deadline then a surcharge (which is sometimes even called a 'fine') is payable. Is this a punishment? The person who receives it probably thinks so but a person surcharged in these circumstances is not considered to have a criminal record or to have committed a crime.

The European Court of Human Rights (ECtHR) has always adopted its own approach of what amounts to a 'crime' when adjudicating upon the *European Convention on Human Rights*.[16] In considering whether a matter is a crime the ECtHR said that domestic labelling (ie whether the state considered it to be a crime) was important but not conclusive. Other factors would include the purpose of any sanction and, in particular, its severity. As a general rule the stricter the 'punishment' the more likely it is that it will be considered a crime.

1.2.2 **What is law?**

Trying to define what law is, is a question that has taxed jurists and philosophers for centuries and will undoubtedly continue to do so. Some jurists, most notably Hart, never answered the question, appearing to suggest that it was the wrong question[17] and that the more appropriate question would be to consider what distinguishes law from other regulations or what the purpose of law is.

It is beyond the scope of this introductory text to consider this question in detail and you should (eventually) refer to texts on legal theory, philosophy, or jurisprudence to consider (note I am not suggesting you will ever be able to answer) this question. Some of you will have the opportunity to study modules on jurisprudence or legal theory and this will be at the heart of the module.

Law has to be more than just a simple set of rules and regulations. Every society has rules and regulations; most families will have a series of informal rules that must be obeyed. Would anyone categorize these as laws? Every university has a set of rules and some will even refer to the documents holding these rules as statutes. There may be a punishment for breaching some of these rules, but again can it be suggested that a university rule is a law? It is sometimes said that a law must be of general application but this need not be the case. In Chapter 2 the concept of *Private Acts of Parliament* will be discussed and these are of limited application. The simplistic answer is to say that a law is something that is handed down from the state, and that in the United Kingdom it is a rule set out by the Crown to which we, the subjects of the Crown, are bound. Are there limits to law, or where laws come from, however? It is necessary, at least briefly, to introduce some of the philosophical debates.

1.2.2.1 **Positivism**

One of the more important theories of legal governance is known as positivism. There are a number of positivist theorists but the most important are Bentham and Austin, both nineteenth-century philosophers, and Hart, a twentieth-century jurist. Positivism

---

15. John Adams and Roger Brownsword, *Understanding Law* (4th edn, Sweet & Maxwell 2006) 147.
16. See, most notably, *Welch v United Kingdom* (1995) 20 EHRR 247.
17. Brian Bix, *Jurisprudence: Theory and Context* (7th edn, Sweet & Maxwell 2015) 6.

focuses on what the law *is* rather than what it *should* be. It is often criticized as suggesting that even evil laws are valid and should be followed but this is a misunderstanding of positivism,[18] not least because positivism is not concerned with whether a law should be followed but simply what law is.

Austin believed in the premise of commands. He believed that an action would either be mandated, prohibited, not mandated, or not prohibited.[19] In other words, he believed that there was an imbalance in the state and that the Sovereign Head of State had the power to issue commands that detailed how a citizen could act, and that any other principles (eg commands from God, individual commands of employers) were not laws but merely moralistic or private requirements.[20]

Hart disagreed with this contention. He preferred the notion of rules rather than commands as he believed the notion of 'command' was problematic.[21] A significant problem with the idea of commands is that it relies on an unfettered sovereign, ie nobody can command the sovereign. Yet this is not the case in many states where there are limits on what the state can do—sometimes referred to as the 'Rule of Law'. Another key difficulty Hart had with the command theory is that a command requires a sanction, but does every law have a sanction? If one thinks of procedural law especially it is not easy to think of what a sanction would be. Hart argued that the basis of law was rules and that there were two types of rules: primary rules and secondary rules.

This, to an extent, mirrors the 'substantive' and 'procedural' rules that were discussed earlier. Hart also believed that these rules had to be set within a context of societal norms, ie that it was not just a fear of sanction that led people to follow the rules but the fact that they believed that it was 'normal' to do so.

11

⚡ PRIMARY AND SECONDARY RULES

Primary rules are those that apply directly to citizens. They are the rules that provide what our rights, duties, and obligations are.

Secondary rules are those that govern the operation of the primary rules. They put them into effect.

1.2.2.2 **Natural law**

It has been noted already that a particular criticism of positivism is the belief that moral judgements have little to do with law. Natural-law theorists believe that law is not simply that which our rulers create but that there is a 'higher law' that constrains laws. The concept of natural law dates back millennia, probably first appearing in ancient Greek philosophies[22] and was certainly strong in the early years of the Christian Church with Aquinas, who later was made a saint, being one of the principal proponents of natural law. The influence of the Church in natural law is perhaps not surprising since to someone of faith, the 'higher' law will be their God.

18.　ibid, 34.
19.　James W Harris, *Legal Philosophies* (2nd edn, Butterworths 1997) 29.
20.　ibid, 31.
21.　Brian Bix, *Jurisprudence: Theory and Context* (7th edn, Sweet & Maxwell 2015) 38.
22.　ibid, 70.

Aquinas believed that there were four types of law: eternal law, natural law, divine law, and human law.[23] He believed that human law derived from natural law, so that natural law requires a law of murder and accordingly society must create such a law. Aquinas also believed that human law had to be compatible with natural law. For a human law to be valid and enforceable it must be consistent with natural law, that being the requirements of the common good.[24] Where a law is incompatible then Aquinas believed that it was unenforceable and unjust.

A criticism of natural law is that it is not necessarily practicable. Austin, a positivist, suggested that if a crime was punishable by death it meant very little whether it was an unjust law or not since it would, in all probability, be followed leaving the 'criminal' dead but apparently secure in the knowledge that he has become a martyr. The argument of natural lawyers, however, is that it empowers judges not to follow the law. In a common-law-based system (see 1.3.1) it is accepted that judges are the guarantors of law and indeed they can create law. The suggestion is that where a law is incompatible with natural law it should not be followed by judges.

Modern natural-law theorists, most notably Finnis, argue that natural law can be equated with ethical conduct and that it is about the creation of laws that are necessary for man to live ethically.[25] This is an interesting approach and demonstrates one advantage of natural law, that it acts as a valid justification for the creation of many of the most fundamental laws (on murder, theft, marriage, and property), since without these basic laws society could not operate.

Natural law is, to an extent, considered to be the main opponent of positivism and yet there are a number of similarities between them. Both assume the concepts of rules and both accept that a state can produce the rules that surround us. Where the two appear to deviate is that natural law goes beyond positivism and seeks to discuss what the law *should* say. There is constantly a benchmark against which human laws will be measured, that of the 'higher' law.

1.2.2.3 Interpretative/rights theory

One of the more recent philosophical theories on law is referred to as the 'rights thesis' and is propagated by Dworkin, a twentieth-century jurist. Dworkin rejected the principles of positivism because he believed that law was not simply based on a series of rules but on principles, policies, and more general standards.[26] Some of these standards will include morality and it has been suggested that this can be equated, to an extent, with parts of natural law[27] but it is different in that Dworkin did not believe that there is a 'higher' law, merely that the community has institutional morality, ie a common base of principles to which its members adhere.

The centre of Dworkin's criticism is that law is based on the difference between rights (principles) and policy (goals).[28] The importance of policy was that it was a decision for the public good, a decision that influenced the community. This interplays with principles that give rise to individual rights and these may be contrary to the policy goal

---

23. ibid, 71.
24. ibid, 71–2.
25. ibid, 77.
26. James Penner and Emmanuel Melissaris, *McCoubrey and White's Textbook on Jurisprudence* (5th edn, OUP 2012) 83.
27. ibid, 94.
28. ibid, 88–94.

albeit for appropriate reasons. More than this, however, he argues that judges are obligated to decide matters on the basis of principles (rights) and not policy. This distinction is based on a similar premise to the distinction between politics and the law.

He later sought an interpretative approach to law. This is not interpretation as we understand it (ie reviewing a statute and deciding what it means) but has a more philosophical abstract sense. Dworkin believes that the law is a series of constructive interpretations, that in order for a judge to adjudicate on a problem he must look for a pattern that is discernible in the rights and policies relevant to the issue.[29] This theory of law fits the common-law system (1.3.1) because precedent is an important part of the interpretative approach. The previous decisions of judges help identify a pattern that could lead one to determine what the legal solution to a problem is. Alongside these principles, however, are the moral policies and Dworkin believed that a judge should attempt to make the law as 'good' as it can be, meaning that, where there are different alternatives, the one closest to the moral norm may be best.[30] This is also a response to the argument that positivism neglects amoral laws, whereas in the rights-based approach the amoral law is unlikely to ever be the 'best' solution to a given problem and thus the judge will reinterpret the matter.

1.3 System

The final word to examine is that of 'System'. Identifying precisely what a system is can be open to debate but it is probably more than the individual rules or laws and is instead the concept of how law is administered. In the same way that law can be divided into civil and criminal law (1.2.1.3), there are two systems, the criminal justice system and the civil justice system. Thus the system is how the law is to be applied and envelopes some procedural law together with the courts etc.

1.3.1 Common law

The English Legal System is an example of a common-law-based system. This can be contrasted with the other principal system which is sometimes known as the civil system (which can be confusing as it does not mean civil as in the distinction between civil and criminal law) and more readily understood as the continental system. These two legal systems can be found throughout the world and their use reflects the geopolitical influence of Britain, Spain, and France. Accordingly, those areas of the world that were parts of the British Empire (eg the United States of America, Canada, Australia, New Zealand, and certain African states) have all tended to follow the common-law-based system of law whereas those that formed part of the French and Spanish empires (eg Continental Europe, Latin America, and certain parts of Africa) have adopted the continental approach.

1.3.1.1 Common-law system

The principal hallmark of the common-law system is, as its name suggests, the recognition of something called 'common law'. In England and Wales law is not only passed by

13

---

29. Brian Bix, *Jurisprudence: Theory and Context* (7th edn, Sweet & Maxwell 2015) 95.
30. ibid, 98.

Parliament (known as statutory law) but also can develop from the previous decisions of courts. It is for this reason that precedent (which is explained in further detail in Chapter 3 but may be summarized here as the basis upon which certain courts set out rulings which they and other courts must follow) is so important to the common-law system.

The origins of the common law are contested. However, there is broad agreement that it emerged following the Norman Conquest and that King Henry II played a pivotal role in its development. Before the Conquest, and indeed for a period afterwards, different areas of England were governed individually by local laws and customs, rather than by a national legal system. Local courts were governed by the King's stewards, with the King himself (perhaps unsurprisingly) presiding over the King's Court (the *Curia Regis)*, which followed him as he travelled around the country. The *Curia Regis* was the origin for the development of the Court of the Exchequer and the Court of Common Pleas, as well as the Court of King's Bench.

When Henry II came to the throne (1154–89) he introduced a series of reforms which sowed the seeds of the common-law system. In 1166 at the Assize of Clarendon, Henry II ordered the non-King's Bench judges to travel around the country's circuits and establish the 'King's peace' by deciding cases. In doing so, rather than applying the piecemeal laws found in local areas, the judges applied the new laws of the state which were 'common' to all. In 1178, he appointed five members of the *Curia Regis* to sit permanently at a court in Westminster 'to hear all the complaints of the realm and to do right'. This court was the origin of the Court of Common Pleas. Eventually the court separated into two, and the Court of the King's Bench emerged, continuing to follow the King around the country. By the 1170s it was also possible to distinguish the work of the Exchequer from that of the rest of the *Curia Regis*, dealing with financial litigation and some matters of equity, eventually leading to the creation of the Court of the Exchequer. Thus, by the thirteenth century three senior courts existed, those of the Common Pleas, the Kings Bench, and the Exchequer. The judicial decisions in these cases produced 'common' law, applicable to all in the country.

The term 'common law' was used to distinguish between law that was decided by the Royal Courts in London and which was applied throughout the kingdom (thus a 'common' approach to the law), ecclesiastical (Church) law (which remained an important source and application of law until the nineteenth century), and local customary law. Eventually the common law took over the other sources of law, especially as the reporting of decisions became more ordered and it was thus easier to see how judges were applying the law.

The common law remains strong today and, whilst it is comparatively rare for the courts to create a new legal principle, there continues to be a significant amount of law that exists without statutory definition.

⚡ COMMON-LAW CRIME

Perhaps the best example of a common-law crime is that of murder. The crime of murder is not defined in statute.[31] The definition has evolved through the common law with its basis in the definition given by Coke, an eighteenth-century judge. The definition has been amended by statute[32] but its definition continues to be a matter of the common law.

---

31. Although its punishment now is: see *Murder (Abolition of Death Penalty) Act 1965*.
32. See *Law Reform (Year and a Day Rule) Act 1996*.

Where there is a 'gap' in the law the superior courts will sometimes continue to rely on their common-law powers. A good example of this is in respect of the protection of the vulnerable (particularly children) where the Family Division of the High Court of Justice claims an 'inherent jurisdiction' which means that it has the power to draw upon the common law to act in the best interests of the vulnerable person.

Common law v equity

Whilst we now refer to the system in England and Wales being a common-law system it is also necessary to refer to the place of equity. Prior to the *Judicature Acts* of 1873 and 1875 equity was considered a parallel system to the common-law courts. It is not true to think of it as being separate to the common law as its jurisdiction was inextricably linked to the common law but the common-law courts were restricted to granting damages and so if somebody could not petition the court, or wished something other than damages, the common-law courts could not assist. There was also a belief that the common-law courts were too mechanistic and that the strict rules of law sometimes created unfairness. People began to petition the King (as Sovereign) for justice and he began to delegate these matters to the Lord Chancellor and eventually created a separate series of courts, the courts of Chancery, to resolve such matters. The courts of Chancery proceeded not on the basis of the strictures of common law but on the principles of justice and they could dispense equitable rather than legal resolutions, something based on fairness, and which incorporated other remedies, including injunctions and the ability to recognize beneficial, and not just legal, interests.

Equity introduced a series of new and innovative resolutions but it became quickly apparent that in many instances a dispute could be resolved either under the common law or equity and the two parallel systems often conflicted. In the *Earl of Oxford's case*[33] the courts were called upon to decide whether common law or equity took priority. It is not necessary to consider the facts of this case in depth and you will probably read about it in *Equity & Trusts* but, in essence, there was an allegation that a judgment of the common-law courts had been obtained by bribery. The Chancery court issued an injunction preventing the common-law order being enforced and this led directly to a conflict between the two jurisdictions. It was ultimately resolved by it being ruled that in a dispute between the common law and equity, equity would prevail.

The *Judicature Acts* of 1873 and 1875 resolved this tension by unifying the jurisdictions and creating one supreme court of judicature (now embodied by the Senior Courts of England & Wales). All courts—not just the courts of Chancery—were able to exercise the equitable remedies and hence now the part of the High Court that is seen as the successor to the common-law courts (the Queen's Bench Division) readily issues equitable remedies such as injunctions or mandatory orders. It is important to note the jurisdictions did not merge and it is possible today to distinguish equity from the common law (and indeed you will do so when you study the module *Equity and Trusts*). Equity is based on a series of principles—known as equitable maxims—which continue to be used and which were considered to encapsulate the inherent fairness of equity.

33. (1615) 1 Rep Ch 1.

1.3.1.2 **Continental system**

The continental system differs from a common-law system in that it is based on the primacy of written laws. Continental systems tend to be codified, meaning that the laws are all set out in a document. This is not only the hallmark of the continental system since in many common-law countries (most notably America) they have a codified criminal law whereby all of the crimes and procedural rules relating to the criminal justice system are set out in one document, commonly referred to as a Penal Code.

The codification system means that judges are not 'creating' new laws or rights but simply interpreting the laws set out by the legislature. Accordingly, if there is a 'gap' in the law then it cannot be filled by the judges. However, of course, in practice the concept of 'interpretation' is almost as fluid as the idea of judicial creations and the fact that many courts will 'follow' the decisions of other judges (even though they arguably do not have a formal system of precedent *per se*) means that the law will develop in the way that the judges desire.

1.3.2 **An adversarial system**

The second hallmark of the English Legal System (and indeed all common-law systems) is that it is an adversarial system. This refers to how cases are adjudicated upon and can be distinguished from the inquisitorial system that is frequently found within the continental system.

1.3.2.1 **Adversarial approach**

The adversarial approach to law is where the adjudication is seen as a contest between two or more sides and it is fought out before a neutral umpire (the judge and/or jury). The judge, whilst able to ask questions, should not seek to become an investigator and should rather concentrate on ensuring that both sides are obeying the procedural rules governing the presentation of their case.[34]

A central plank of the adversarial process is the fact that the parties, not the court, call witnesses. Both parties will gather their evidence, including asking witnesses to give statements. The parties will then decide which witnesses they are going to call to give evidence in court. The opposing party is able to challenge this evidence in two ways. The first is through calling their own witnesses who may provide an alternative viewpoint on the issues. The second, and more combative, method is to allow witnesses to be cross-examined. Cross-examination is where a party directly challenges the witnesses' evidence and puts the contrary case to them.

The other key principle of the adversarial system is that of the importance of orality. In both the criminal and civil systems of justice there is still the assumption that providing live oral evidence is the best way of arriving at the facts. Indeed in a criminal trial where there is no dispute between the parties as to what the witness will say (ie there will be no cross-examination) then the statement given by that person will be tendered as evidence. The way it is tendered is that it is read out aloud. It is quite possible, or indeed likely, that giving it to the jury to read would be at the very least as effective but the tradition of oral evidence continues.

---

34. *Jones v National Coal Board* [1957] 2 QB 55.

It will be seen later in this book that changes are being made to the adversarial system in order to take the edge off some of its harshness (see in particular Chapters 17 and 19). However, these are only minor modifications and it is not a shift towards a purely inquisitorial system.

1.3.2.2 Inquisitorial approach

The continental system tends to adopt an inquisitorial approach. In this sense the court becomes the investigator itself. Rather than the judge being a neutral umpire, he is given the authority to seek out the truth by asking questions of the witnesses. The respective lawyers seek to control this questioning by reference to the procedural rules and to this extent it can be argued the roles of counsel and the judiciary are almost mirrored. It has been suggested that one advantage of this model is that it ensures that all relevant witnesses are heard[35] whereas in the adversarial system, if a witness's evidence is not helpful to a side, he or she may not be called.

Consideration was given to whether the English Legal System should move towards an inquisitorial approach but the *Royal Commission on Criminal Justice* argued that this would be a significant cultural shift.[36] Arguably this is correct and it cannot be accidental that common-law systems tend to be adversarial with continental systems being inquisitorial, suggesting that any shift to either model may involve a rethink of the legal system as a whole.

 Summary

In this chapter we have noted that:

- There is a United Kingdom of Great Britain and Northern Ireland. Whilst this is our formal state, it is constituted from four parts; England, Scotland, Wales, and Northern Ireland.

- Historically England annexed the law of Wales and so when we refer to the English Legal System we are actually including Wales too.

- Scotland and Northern Ireland have separate legal systems, these being retained as part of the Acts of Union that created the United Kingdom.

- It is difficult to identify what precisely law is and it is probably a philosophical rather than a practical problem. Law is probably a collection of rules governing rights, duties, and obligations but the extent of these rules and where the authority comes from to use them is more open to debate.

- Law can be divided into different classifications including substantive and procedural, public and private, and civil and criminal. These classifications affect how we think about law and what the law does.

- The English Legal System is based on the common law, meaning that judges are able to progress the law themselves. Decisions from previous court hearings still form part of our law.

- The English Legal System is an adversarial system meaning that a case is adjudicated by two competing sides presenting their evidence with a neutral judge or jury deciding which case they prefer.

35. Michael Zander, *Cases and Materials on the English Legal System* (10th edn, OUP 2007) 375.
36. ibid, 377.

PART I

SOURCES OF LAW

2

Domestic Sources of Law: Parliamentary Material

By the end of this chapter you will be able to:

- Understand the primary sources of domestic law.
- Differentiate between primary and secondary sources of law.
- Differentiate between primary and secondary legislation.
- Identify, and use, the different approaches to statutory interpretation.

Introduction

You are studying the law but how do you know what the law is? Where do you find law? The skill of being able to find law and the knowledge of knowing how to interpret law are two of the most important abilities of any lawyer. Indeed it is possible to go so far as to say that these are the two most important abilities of a lawyer and of a law student. If you are able to find and interpret law then you can apply those skills to any law—it does not matter whether you have studied the subject or not because all law has the same basic components in it.

Sources of law are an important (and arguably *the* most important) part of legal study since a proper grounding in the subject will allow you to access any substantive legal issue. Chapters 2, 3, and 4 will introduce you to this knowledge but reference should also be made to Legal Skills texts that will help you put this knowledge into practice. This chapter examines parliamentary material, that is to say laws passed by the Houses of Parliament, and Chapter 3 examines material produced by the courts through cases. Chapter 4 will introduce you to international sources of law.

2.1 Domestic law

This chapter discusses the sources of domestic law and we need to be clear at the very beginning of this chapter what that means.

2.1.1 International relations

As has already been noted the United Kingdom consists of four countries (England, Scotland, Northern Ireland, and Wales) and there are three legal systems (England and Wales,[1] Scotland, and Northern Ireland) each of which approaches its sources of law in similar (although not exactly the same) ways. However, the United Kingdom is also a signatory to a number of treaties, most notably the *European Convention on Human Rights* (ECHR) and, until its withdrawal from the European Union, the *Treaty of Rome* (now known by another title: see Chapter 4) which led to the UK joining what was the European Economic Community (EEC) and is now the European Union (EU).

The ECHR is directly relevant because the *Human Rights Act 1998* created a situation where it was deemed that all public bodies would abide by the Convention and provided authorities to the domestic courts to hear challenges to any breach. This chapter will look at how the *Human Rights Act 1998* has altered the way courts approach domestic legislation but will not discuss the sources of the jurisprudence surrounding the ECHR as this will be discussed in Chapter 4 (International Sources of Law). The individual rights established within the ECHR will be examined in Chapter 5 as will some of the effects of the *Human Rights Act 1998*.

The relationship with the EU is more complicated. This is partly because the withdrawal agreement requires Northern Ireland to follow some EU laws. The rest of the United Kingdom ceases to automatically follow EU law after 1 January 2021. That is a significant shift from the position while we were a member, where a considerable amount of law automatically formed part of domestic law, although that was because domestic law expressly required this.[2]

While EU law will now no longer automatically form part of English law, it remains relevant. Most EU law was automatically translated into English law, allowing it to remain in force until it is amended or repealed by domestic legislation.[3] While judges are no longer bound to follow the decisions of the Court of Justice of the EU (discussed further in Chapter 3), the decisions will remain an important source of interpretation. Similarly, the original text of the EU legislation will be an important source of what the intention behind the law was. This will be explored more fully in Chapter 4.

2.1.2 Constitution

This text is not a textbook on the constitution of the United Kingdom and those of you who are studying law as an undergraduate programme will almost certainly study the constitution of the United Kingdom in a specific module, sometimes called *Constitutional Law* and sometimes known as *Public Law*. However, it is necessary to summarize some aspects of the constitutional law so as to understand the sources of domestic law.

---

1. Although it will be remembered from Chapter 1 that Wales is starting to develop its own system of laws.
2. *European Communities Act 1972*, s 2(1).
3. *European Union (Withdrawal) Act 2018*, s 2(1).

Every country must have a constitution, which can be defined as a series of legal and non-legal rules that define how a country is governed.[4] However, the term 'constitution' in many countries means a document that enshrines the fundamental rules of governance. Perhaps the most obvious example of this is the Constitution of the United States of America which quite clearly sets out the machinery of governance, expressly creating three instruments of state: the executive (President of the United States of America), the legislature (Congress), and the judiciary (Supreme Court of the United States of America). The American Constitution is not static in that it can be changed (and indeed there are currently twenty-seven amendments, the last having been passed in 1992).[5]

Most constitutions will enshrine the laws in their constitution, ie they will require a special resolution to amend the instrument. Most democracies will normally operate on a simple majority system to pass legislation but constitutions will require a higher standard to ensure that the constitution, which will normally also prescribe the rights and freedoms of citizens, cannot be abused by rogue governments. In the United States of America any amendment to the Constitution requires Congress to pass an amendment by a two-thirds majority *and* for three-quarters of the individual state legislatures to pass the amendment.

2.1.2.1 Does the United Kingdom have a constitution?

The United Kingdom does not have a written constitution:

> There is no document in the United Kingdom equivalent, say, to the United States Constitution . . . Nor, for that matter, is there a set of statutes clearly indicated by their titles as 'Constitutional' or 'Basic' laws.[6]

However, this is no longer strictly true as the *Constitutional Reform Act 2005* obviously contains the word 'constitutional' in it, but the basic point remains intact; within the United Kingdom the legislature rarely expressly refers to pieces of legislation as constituting part of a formal constitution. That is not to say that measures do not exist because quite apart from the 2005 Act, the *Acts of Union 1707* and *1801* which created the United Kingdom (see 1.1.1) must be considered constitutional, as must the *Human Rights Act 1998*, and the *European Communities Act 1972*, until its repeal, would have also met the criterion. However, the presumption is that so-called 'constitutional' pieces of legislation are no different from any other piece of legislation and could be amended or repealed by a simple majority. The *European Communities Act 1972* is a good example of this. It was ultimately repealed by another statute.[7] While a referendum was held to determine whether to leave the EU or not, it was ultimately a statute of the UK Parliament that led to its repeal.

2.1.3 Primary and secondary sources

When locating law it is important to draw a distinction between primary and secondary sources of law. Primary sources of law are authoritative sources of law, ie they are statements of what the law is. Secondary sources are not strictly speaking statements of what the law is but rather interpretations of the law. In other words whilst they are useful in helping us understand the law (including its development) they do not, strictly speaking, say what the law *is*. Whilst you will use secondary sources quite frequently through your law studies you should not misunderstand their place and should cite primary sources where possible (see Figure 2.1).

4. Eric Barendt, *An Introduction to Constitutional Law* (OUP 1998) 2.
5. Which protects the 'compensation' (salary) of senators and congressmen.
6. Eric Barendt, *An Introduction to Constitutional Law* (OUP 1998) 26.
7. *European Union (Withdrawal) Act 2018*, s 1.

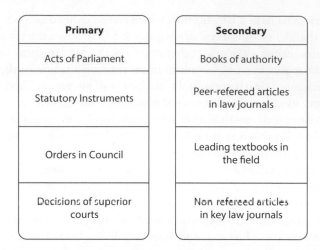

Figure 2.1 Primary and secondary sources

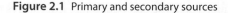

≣ Example Primary v secondary

The definition of property for the purpose of theft is contained in s 4 *Theft Act 1968*. If you were asked to define property you would refer to that section and not, for example, the pages in your criminal law textbook. However, if you wanted to discuss *why* the definition of property excludes, for example, 'wild flowers' (see s 4(3) *Theft Act 1968*) then resorting to the primary source will not help. It just tells you what the law is, not why that is the case. However, your textbook may explain it as may some academic articles.

Figure 2.1 demonstrates that within each division of sources there are different subcategories and this chapter will discuss which sources should be cited when.

2.1.3.1 **Primary sources**

It was discussed earlier that there is no enshrined specific constitutional law and thus primary sources of law can be separated into two general parts. The first is legislation, ie measures that come from the legislature (Parliament) and this is known as 'statutory law', and the second is from the decisions of courts and this is what has tended to be referred to as 'common law' but is perhaps more accurately referred to as 'case law' nowadays. The interaction between these forms of law will be discussed in this chapter but statutory law is supreme. The United Kingdom is a monarchy. The formal Head of State is the Queen (which can be contrasted with the President of the United States of America or the President of France) but at the same time we are a democracy and the head of the executive is the prime minister.[8] Sovereign power in the United Kingdom

---

8.   Although interestingly there is no *legal* rule that states that the prime minister is the head of the executive and until comparatively recently the office did not even necessarily legally exist as it was not mentioned in statutes. It is a *convention* that the prime minister is the head of the executive and this demonstrates the importance of conventions (unwritten rules of custom and practice).

resides in the Queen in Parliament. This means that all legislation requires the approval of the monarch (see 'Royal Assent' at 2.2.1.1) but that subject to this Parliament may pass such laws as it wishes. There are different types of democracies but the UK version of parliamentary democracy means that rather than citizens taking votes on issues (known as referendums) the convention is that we elect Members of Parliament who have the right to pass laws subject to their being voted out of office at the next election. There are, of course, exceptions but these are usually provided for by statutory law itself. For example, the *European Union Referendum Act 2015* provided that the UK would hold a referendum on the continued membership of the EU.[9] Technically the Act did not require Parliament to obey the result of the referendum, but politically Parliament found itself required to do so.

As the Queen in Parliament is supreme then this means that where a statute conflicts with a decision of the court, the statute (legislation) prevails. Unlike, for example, the Supreme Court of the USA, the courts of England and Wales have no power to declare a statute unlawful. Similarly, Parliament can overrule the courts. There are examples of situations where Parliament has passed legislation with the specific intention of overturning a decision of the courts[10] and the courts have had to accept that version of the law.

2.1.3.2 Secondary sources

It can be seen from Figure 2.1 that secondary sources are largely academic material, although other material (eg government policy papers) may also come within this band. The use of the material will be discussed later but it should be noted at the outset that whilst you may use secondary sources frequently in your studies (either to find primary sources or to complete an essay) they are still comparatively rarely mentioned in court. The courts do appear to be citing academic material more often than they ever did and the breadth is increasing: at one point authors would only be cited when they were dead and could not change their mind! Perhaps the growth in academic writings over recent years has led judges to consider that it can be useful to see how others have interpreted the law. However, caution should always be used when citing contemporary academic sources. You should be clear that the academic writing is an opinion on what the law *probably* is. It is not a definitive statement of the law, regardless of how distinguished the person writing it is. This is important to bear in mind when the person writing it is a senior judge. Sometimes judges will make speeches or write an article for a learned journal (known as 'extrajudicial' speeches or writing) and this will include statements of what the law may be. However, this remains a secondary rather than primary source because it is their personal view of the issue and not the ruling of a court.

2.2 Statutory law

The first source to discuss is statutory law, that being law passed by Parliament. It was noted earlier that statutory law is a primary source of law but, to confuse matters, statutory law itself is divided into primary legislation and secondary legislation with primary legislation itself being divided into two! Figure 2.2 may assist.

9. *European Union Referendum Act 2015*, s 1.
10. For example, the *Sexual Offences Act 2003* states that the test for whether an offender believed a rape complainant was consenting is an objective test whereas the courts had traditionally said that it was a subjective test.

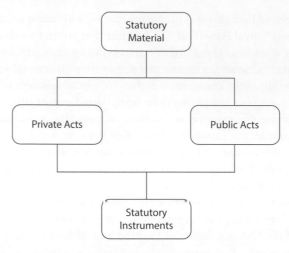

Figure 2.2 Legislation

Figure 2.2 shows that primary legislation is that which is known as an Act of Parliament and that these may exist as either a Public or Private Act. Whilst all forms of parliamentary legislation are statutory, an Act of Parliament is often referred to as a 'statute'. The statutes that you will encounter most of the time are known as Public Acts and these are measures that apply to all of society. Private Acts are those that are limited to a particular company or organization that requires powers beyond those prescribed by the normal law. They tended to be used for the creation of docks, transport links, or other major building programmes.

⚡ PRIVATE ACT

The *University of Wales, Cardiff Act 2004* is a Private (sometimes referred to as 'local') Act. Its purpose was to merge the University of Wales Medical School with the University of Wales, Cardiff. Universities can be divided into two groups: those that existed before 1992 and those that gained university status after 1992. The former were generally established by Royal Charter whereas the latter acquired their authority from the *Further and Higher Education Act 1992* and articles of governance approved by the Privy Council. Universities are independent bodies but are limited to the powers set out in either the Royal Charter or the 1992 legislation. In 2004 it was decided that the University of Wales Medical School would be incorporated into the larger University of Wales, Cardiff but neither institution had the power to do this as their status was regulated as already described. They petitioned Parliament and the *University of Wales, Cardiff Act 2004* gave the institutions the power to merge and become a single unit.

The Act thus provided one institution a power that it did not previously have and doing so did not involve it granting any wider power to either that institution or any other institution, the essence of a Private Act.

⚡ PUBLIC ACT

The *Education Act 2005* is a Public Act. Its purpose is to reform the way in which failing schools are identified and required to reform. The Act is of general importance as it applies not to a specific school or authority but to all schools in England.[11] It creates an Inspectorate for Schools in England and provides specific powers and duties for that body.

As the Act provides a general power that applies beyond a single company or authority it is a Public Act and applies as a general law of the land subject to the limitations contained within its drafting.

Secondary legislation is slightly easier to define although it is normally referred to as *statutory instruments*. An Act of Parliament will generally provide the general scope of a law and its powers but it will commonly leave some consequential matters out. Such matters could include when a piece of legislation comes into effect (a majority of Acts of Parliament do not come into effect immediately so that preparations can be made for any requisite training or public awareness campaigns) or the precise application of a law (eg what grade a person must be to exercise a power).

The balance between what goes in primary and secondary legislation is a delicate one. Parliament only has a finite amount of time to debate legislation and so if every detail of a law was placed in primary legislation then any changes (eg an organization changes its name) would require another piece of primary legislation to permit this. This would quickly lead to a situation where Parliament would have no time to discuss any other legislation. However, if too much is placed into secondary legislation then Parliament as a whole could lose control of how the law is being implemented because it is far easier for secondary legislation to be passed (see 2.2.1). To put this all into context if we look at the figures for 2018, Parliament passed thirty-four Public Acts of Parliament while 1,387 pieces of secondary legislation were passed. It is inconceivable that each piece of secondary legislation could have been passed in the same way as primary legislation or had the same level of scrutiny.

⚡ SECONDARY LEGISLATION

Part II *Regulation of Investigatory Powers Act 2000* permits certain public bodies the right to undertake covert surveillance. The Act does not say who these public authorities are or who within the organization may authorize surveillance to be carried out. These details are provided for in the *Regulation of Investigatory Powers (Directed Surveillance and Covert Human Intelligence Sources) Order 2010*.[12] The order lists each organization that may undertake surveillance (the police, local authorities, etc) and who within each organization may authorize its use (police inspector, director of housing, etc). The advantage of this is that where a new public agency requires the right to conduct surveillance Parliament need only pass a new statutory instrument rather than amend the 2000 Act.

---

11.   The *Education Act 2005* is also unusual in that it provides a general application for just England rather than England and Wales because education is a devolved matter for Wales (see 1.1.1.1).
12.   SI 2010/521.

The manner in which legislation is passed, reviewed, and treated depends on whether it is primary or secondary legislation, as will be seen.

2.2.1 **Primary legislation**

The most important type of legislation is primary legislation. Although noting the existence of Private Acts of Parliament earlier, the remainder of this chapter will focus on Public Acts of Parliament as these are the more important and also the pieces of legislation that you are more likely to encounter.

It was noted that the Queen in Parliament is the sovereign body in this country and in practice this means Parliament through its Acts of Parliament. There are (theoretically) no limits to the power of Parliament and it could legislate to do anything it wishes,

---

Example Smoking in Paris

A common example that is used when discussing the supreme nature of Parliament is that of smoking on the streets of Paris. If Parliament wished to do so it could pass a law that states it is illegal to smoke on the streets of Paris. Could this be enforced? Possibly not but it does not matter because whether a law can be enforced is not relevant to its validity. A statute banning smoking in Paris would be valid and assuming that evidence existed to show that D had smoked in Paris then if D ever set foot in England he could be arrested, tried, and convicted.

The fact that Parliament can legislate for anything has not been compromised by the constitutional changes that have taken place in recent years. It was noted in Chapter 1 that Scotland, Northern Ireland, and (to a much more limited extent) Wales have devolved authority whereby they can create their own law. However, Parliament could as easily choose to withdraw this power and centralize all legislation again. Indeed, an Act of Parliament could repeal the devolution legislation. Even without doing this, however, we can see that the UK Parliament remains supreme because the legislation expressly states that the devolution legislation does not preclude the UK Parliament from legislating over devolved areas.[13]

The *Human Rights Act 1998* (HRA 1998) is also compatible with this convention that Parliament can legislate to do anything. Whilst there is a presumption that all legislation will be compatible with the ECHR the statute expressly preserves the power of Parliament to legislate in a way that is *not* compliant with the ECHR.[14] This also serves as an example of the second principal convention that exists on the sovereignty of Parliament, which is that Parliament cannot bind its successors. In other words, the present Parliament in any current session may not pass a law that is not subject to repeal. This convention is also likely to ensure that Parliament cannot enshrine legislation as although this would not prevent Parliament from repealing it (enshrining legislation merely raises the threshold for repeal) the setting of a threshold would restrict the competency of Parliament and accordingly all statutes have (theoretically) the same status as each other.

---

13. See, for example, *Scotland Act 1998*, s 28(7).
14. See *Human Rights Act 1998*, s 19(2).

2.2.1.1 **Process of creating an Act**

We now know what an Act of Parliament is but how are they created? Reference should be made to your constitutional-law/public-law texts which will describe this process in more detail, but it is necessary at least to summarize the parliamentary process in order to understand the impact of statutes.

The general process can be represented in diagrammatic form as shown in Figure 2.3.

For the purposes of Figure 2.3 a Bill has been introduced into the House of Commons but a Bill can begin its parliamentary life in either House. While a Bill is progressing through Parliament it is easy to identify where it originated as the letters '[HL]' are appended to those Bills that start in the House of Lords. Where this happens the boxes in Figure 2.3 listed 'House of Commons' and 'House of Lords' would simply be switched. Each substantive stage will be detailed in brief.

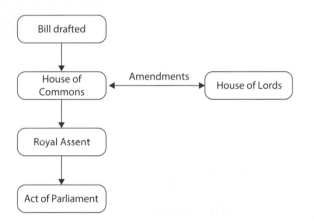

Figure 2.3 The parliamentary process

Table 2.1 The legislative stages

First Reading	Title of the Bill is read out and the Bill is printed
Second Reading	Debate on the general principles of the Bill. Vote taken on whether to proceed
Committee Stage	Passes to a Committee of the House[15]
Report Stage	Amended Bill is reprinted and voted on
Third Reading	Final amendments and vote. Passed to House of Lords if relevant

House of Commons

Regardless of whether the House receives the Bill first or second the same format is always adopted (see Table 2.1).

The matter will only not return to the House of Lords if either the Parliament Act is used (see 2.2.1.2) or the two Houses have agreed the content of the Bill following the process described.

---

15. Where this is a constitutional Bill or part of the Finance Bill ('the budget') then it would normally be a committee of the whole House, otherwise it is more likely that an ad hoc committee of up to fifty MPs is established according to party strength.

House of Lords

The process adopted in the House of Lords is virtually identical but the committee is normally a committee of the whole House and the rules relating to the choice and content of the amendments are not as regulated as they are in the House of Commons. The other significant difference is that by convention a Finance Bill is never defeated in the House and a government Bill that was included in an election manifesto is never defeated at second reading (although it may be later on).

Consideration of amendments

In many cases it is likely that the second House to consider the Bill will produce a slightly different Bill than that which was handed to them not least because members of the second House have had the opportunity to table amendments. Assuming that this happens then the matter returns to the originating House (so in our example the House of Commons) where that House must consider the amendments. If they do not agree to them (and therefore make further amendments themselves) then the matter returns to the other House and the process is repeated in a 'ping-pong' fashion until one of three things happens:

- the two Houses agree the content of the Bill
- the Houses cannot agree and parliamentary time runs out in which case the Bill is normally lost[16]
- the Parliament Act is invoked (see 2.2.1.2).

Royal Assent

Assuming that the two Houses manage to agree the content of the Bill then the Bill is sent to the Queen for Royal Assent. The date on which the Royal Assent is given is also marked on the Act and it becomes itself part of the Act (see 'Date of Royal Assent'). The constitutional position of Royal Assent is often debated but it is usually accepted that the sovereign no longer has power to decline assent.[17]

2.2.1.2 Parliament Act

The normal process by which an Act will be established is as discussed earlier but an important exception to this is when the Parliament Act is invoked. In fact there are two Parliament Acts, the first is the *Parliament Act 1911* and the second is the *Parliament Act 1949* which amended the 1911 Act. The 1911 Act was created to solve an impasse between the House of Commons and House of Lords whereby government business was being rejected by the upper House. The prime minister of the day, Herbert Asquith, sought to introduce legislation that would limit the right of the House of Lords to reject the wishes of the (democratically elected) House of Commons. If the legislation was not passed then Asquith had gained the support of the King to create sufficient new peers to ensure that the government would have a majority in the upper House, which would have been disastrous in terms of the authority and efficiency of the upper House. With that threat the House of Lords passed the 1911 Act.

---

16.   However, since 1998 the House of Commons can, in certain circumstances, agree that a government Bill can be held over to the next session (see House of Commons Factsheet L1: *Parliamentary Stages of a Government Bill*, 6–7).

17.   See, for example, Eric Barendt, *An Introduction to Constitutional Law* (OUP 1998) 41.

The main provisions of the 1911 Act are to be found in ss 1 and 2 of the Act. Section 1 states that the House of Lords may only delay a money Bill for one month and that after this has elapsed the Bill may receive Royal Assent without the authority of the House of Lords. Whether a Bill is a 'money Bill' will depend on whether the Speaker of the House of Commons certifies it as such under s 1(2). The certificate of the Speaker cannot be subject to review by any court of law.[18] This severely restricts the powers of the upper House and was imposed because one of the Bills that was rejected in Asquith's Parliament was the Finance Bill (the government budget).

The second, and more important, part of the 1911 Act is provided for in s 2. This also limits the time in which the upper House can delay a Bill. When it was originally enacted the Bill had to be rejected on the third occasion before s 2 could be used (ie the Bill had failed to gain parliamentary support in at least two successive parliamentary sessions (years)) and the rejection had to be for virtually identical Bills (subject to amendments to reflect the passage of time). If the criterion was met—and the Speaker certified the criterion as being met (s 2(4) with s 4 applying to deny the opportunity to review this certificate)—then after its rejection for the third time the Bill could receive Royal Assent without the House of Lords approving it. The only exceptions to this were money Bills (covered by s 1) and any provision that purported to lengthen the duration of Parliament.[19]

The *Parliament Act 1911* has only been used seven times, twice in 1914[20] and four times in the last twenty-five years,[21] but its most controversial use was when it was used to pass the *Parliament Act 1949* which amended the 1911 Act itself. The principal purpose of the 1949 Act was to reduce the threshold in s 2 to one year, meaning that a Bill must merely fail after it has been entered in two consecutive Parliaments and would be passed after the second, rather than third, defeat.

One important point to note about the *Parliament Act 1911* is that it applies only to legislation introduced to the House of Commons. If a Bill introduced into the House of Lords is amended by the House of Commons and the Lords refuse to accede to these amendments over two consecutive years then the Act cannot be invoked.[22]

Validity of the *Parliament Act 1949*

There has for a number of years been a debate over the validity of the *Parliament Act 1949*. The sole purpose of this Act was to amend the 1911 Act and two criticisms have been made of the 1949 Act. The first, as Loveland notes, is that some consider it unconstitutional because the 1911 Act was not designed to limit further the power of the upper House,[23] but from a legal standpoint this argument carries little weight due to the competency of Parliament to legislate in any manner. The second argument is that legislation under the 1911 Act is not primary legislation *per se* but delegated legislation

31

---

18.   *Parliament Act 1911*, s 4.

19.   Ensuring that a rogue government could not legislate to continue in power where it had a majority but knew it was unlikely to be re-elected.

20.   To legislate for the disestablishment of the Church of Wales (*Welsh Church Act 1914*) and once to legislate for home rule in Ireland (*Home Rule Act 1914*) although this Act was never implemented.

21.   To legislate for war crimes (*War Crimes Act 1991*), European parliamentary elections (*European Parliamentary Elections Act 1999*), to legalize certain homosexual acts and to reduce the age of consent for sexual activity (*Sexual Offences (Amendment) Act 2000*), and to ban hunting (*Hunting Act 2004*).

22.   Hilaire Barnett, *Constitutional & Administrative Law* (9th edn, Routledge 2011) 354.

23.   Ian Loveland, *Constitutional Law, Administrative Law, and Human Rights: A Critical Introduction* (7th edn, OUP 2015) 70.

(the delegation being the 1911 Act permitting law to be made in a way contrary to the usual parliamentary process), and that delegated legislation cannot be used to alter primary legislation without express permission to do so.

The debate about the validity of the Act had been played out in the pages of academic books and journals but in 2005 it became a real proposition when it formed the basis of a case before the courts. The *Hunting Act 2004* was arguably one of the most controversial statutes in recent years and it banned certain types of hunting with live animals. The debate in Parliament was acrimonious and the House of Lords refused to pass the legislation. The government used the Parliament Act to force the provision through but the *Countryside Alliance*, an organization created to lobby against the Act, sought to challenge the ruling.

The challenge was rejected by the High Court and the matter proceeded to the Court of Appeal (*R (Jackson and others) v Attorney-General*[24]) who needed to consider the status of the 1949 Act. The court agreed that legislation under the 1911 Act was delegated legislation rather than true primary legislation. The court argued that this conclusion was inevitable because delegated means the authority arises from another piece of legislation and this is what happens when the Parliament Act is invoked. The Bill which is to become an Act can only do so because of the authority vested in the 1911 Act. If the 1911 Act was repealed then a Bill rejected by the House of Lords could not become an Act of Parliament.[25] However, the court also rejected the suggestion that because it was delegated legislation it was somehow not as effective as an Act of Parliament and held that the legitimacy of an Act passed under the Parliament Act was present. In terms of the 1949 Act the court held that although the 1911 Act could not be used to bring further significant constitutional change (as it did not expressly so provide) the 1949 Act could not be so categorized. The court also made the important point that the amended Act had been used three times already without challenge and that the sovereign, Parliament, and the courts had acted on that Act implicitly acquiescing to the validity of the Act.[26] This latter point is perhaps the most pertinent: if the 1949 Act had been deemed invalid it would have caused numerous difficulties in its exercise in the past twenty years and that alone was cause for the courts to be slow to question its validity.

The matter inevitably proceeded to the House of Lords[27] where their Lordships upheld the decision of the Court of Appeal by dismissing the appeal but reversed the Court of Appeal on several aspects of its judgment, most notably over whether legislation passed under the Parliament Acts is delegated legislation. Lord Bingham, who gave the leading speech in the case, stated that the 1911 Act makes clear that the legislation should be an 'Act of Parliament' and Parliament did not at that time envisage any different status.[28] This, it was submitted, is a crucial point. Constitutionally there has never been any distinction drawn between the status of Acts of Parliament as distinct from legislation in general. Acts of Parliament have always been considered to be not only primary sources of law but also primary legislation—and accordingly although the courts can interpret the provisions (see 2.3) they cannot rule them illegal.

---

24. [2005] QB 579.
25. *R (Jackson and others) v Attorney-General* [2005] QB 579 (QB) 589–93.
26. ibid, 606–7.
27. *R (Jackson and others) v Attorney-General* [2005] 3 WLR 733.
28. ibid, 744.

The submissions of the appellants would have created a situation where a distinction was drawn between Acts of Parliament, which could have undermined the supremacy of Parliament.

Lord Bingham went further and argued that the case being litigated came extremely close to disrupting the separation of powers, with his Lordship noting that the courts have consistently stated that they do not have the power to look at the validity of an Act of Parliament but must merely interpret and implement its provisions.[29] This was not a view shared by all the Law Lords sitting on the case and Lord Nicholls, for example, argued that it is not a case of looking at the validity of a properly passed Act but questioning whether the Act was properly passed.[30] This is probably an important distinction to be drawn as who else could decide this point? The balance of powers in the state does not provide Parliament with any power to adjudicate on individual cases but instead leaves that to the judiciary. Whilst Parliament can overrule a decision of the courts by legislating to overrule the principle this will ordinarily have no impact on the specific case being litigated. The only way that the validity of the Parliament Act process could be raised is through the courts and for this reason a relaxation of the traditional rules would appear appropriate.

Importantly, the decision in *Jackson* leaves open some questions on the limits of parliamentary accountability to the judiciary, with Cooke (a former Lord of Appeal in Ordinary) suggesting that some judges were prepared to hold that there are certain measures (eg the abolition of judicial review or a similar restriction of judicial access) that could not be passed under the Act.[31] However, it is quite clear from the unanimous decision of the House that legislation passed under the Parliament Acts is not delegated but has exactly the same status as legislation that is passed in the usual way. It is, of course, open to Parliament to repeal the Parliament Acts but unless the repealing Act expressly stated that it was to operate retrospectively the decision of the House of Lords in this case demonstrates that all Acts passed under those instruments are as valid as any other statute.

33

⟳ QUESTION FOR REFLECTION

Lord Cooke suggests that the *Parliament Act 1949* cannot be used to amend the *Parliament Act 1911* in such a way as to remove the safeguards against a money Bill or the extension of Parliament. Consider the case of *Jackson* (see 'Validity of the *Parliament Act 1949*'), in particular the speech of Lord Bingham. Do you think Lord Cooke is right? If so, does that mean there are no safeguards to prevent a rogue government indefinitely extending the lifetime of Parliament?

🔊 LISTEN TO THE PODCAST

For guidance on how to answer this question and a discussion of the main issues, listen to the author's podcast on the online resources:
www.oup.com/he/gillespie-weare8e

29. ibid, 746.
30. ibid, 754.
31. Lord Robin Cooke, 'A Constitutional Retreat' (2006) 122 *Law Quarterly Review* 224, 226.

2.2.2 **Content of a statute**

Having now discussed what legislation is, what does a statute look like and what are its contents? If we take, as an example, the *Constitutional Reform Act 2005* (CRA 2005), which we have already used, it can be seen that the beginning of the statute will look similar to Figure 2.4.

The relevant aspects to discuss are:

1. Short title
2. Royal Coat of Arms
3. Chapter number
4. Long title
5. Date of Royal Assent
6. Enacting formula
7. Part number and heading
8. Marginal note
9. Section

(1) Constitutional Reform Act 2005

(2) [Royal Coat of Arms]

(3) 2005 CHAPTER 4

(4) An Act to make provision for modifying the office of Lord Chancellor, and to make provision relating to the functions of that office; to establish a Supreme Court of the United Kingdom, and to abolish the appellate jurisdiction of the House of Lords; to make provision about the jurisdiction of the Judicial Committee of the Privy Council and the judicial functions of the President of the Council; to make other provision about the judiciary, their appointment and discipline; and for connected purposes.

(5) [24th March 2005]

(6) BE IT ENACTED by the Queen's most Excellent Majesty, by and with the advice and consent of the Lords Spiritual and Temporal, and Commons, in this present Parliament assembled, and by the authority of the same as follows:—

(7) **Part 1**
The Rule of Law

(8) The rule of law. 1. This Act does not adversely affect—

(9) (a) the existing constitutional principles of the rule of law; or

(b) the Lord Chancellor's existing constitutional role in relation to that principle.

Figure 2.4 An example of a statute

2.2.2.1 **Short title**

Most statutes will be referred to by their short title, ie in the example earlier the statute will normally be called the *Constitutional Reform Act 2005*. This short title is always displayed at the beginning of the Act but the authority to use a short title must be expressly provided within the statute itself and it will normally come towards the end of the statute. For this statute, s 149 CRA 2005 says: 'This Act may be cited as the Constitutional Reform Act 2005.'

Ordinarily the short title of an Act is uncontroversial but occasionally its use can be misunderstood. Perhaps a classic example of this was in 2008 during the midst of the global financial crisis. An Icelandic bank called *Landsbanki Islands hf* was in financial difficulties and after it went into liquidation the Chancellor of the Exchequer used powers given to him under the *Anti-Terrorism, Crime and Security Act 2001* to seize control of the bank's British assets. This led to the Icelandic government and many global media outlets stating that the British government had used its anti-terrorism legislation against Iceland, the inference being that Iceland was being compared to terrorists. However, the relevant provisions used by the Chancellor were not in the Anti-Terrorism parts of the Act, they were in later sections of the Act. It is easy to see how this could be misrepresented, however, given the short title of the Act. It is perhaps a warning of the political difficulties in putting too much disparate legislation in an Act of Parliament, and also of the requirement to choose short titles with care!

2.2.2.2 **Royal Coat of Arms**

An Act of Parliament is made under the authority of the Queen in Parliament because the United Kingdom is a constitutional monarchy. Accordingly, when any legislation is passed the Royal Coat of Arms is affixed to the statute to act as a seal for the legislation.

2.2.2.3 **Chapter number**

The second official way in which a statute should be cited is in respect of its chapter number. Each Act that is passed by both Houses of Parliament and which receives Royal Assent is assigned a sequential number to identify what order the legislation was passed in any parliamentary session. Modern statutes are governed by the *Parliament Numbering and Citation Act 1962* which provides that the chapter number is assigned by reference to the calendar year. The first statute to be given Royal Assent after 31 December is given the chapter number 1, and each successive piece of legislation is given a sequential number (s 1). Accordingly, in the earlier example, the *Constitutional Reform Act 2005* was the fourth Act to be given Royal Assent in the calendar year 2005.

Prior to the 1962 Act the position was significantly more complicated. Statutes were assigned a chapter number according to the regnal year in which the parliamentary session was begun. The regnal year was the year of the reign of the current monarch. The regnal year starts on the accession to the throne (eg Queen Elizabeth II acceded to the throne on 6 February 1952)[32] and continues until the day before the anniversary of accession (eg the first regnal year of Queen Elizabeth II was 6 February 1952 to

---

32. Note it is the date of the *accession* (ie assumption) of the throne and not the date of the *coronation*. A monarchy is never without a sovereign and thus as soon as a monarch dies the heir presumptive becomes monarch with this assumption being *confirmed* by coronation, but the rule starts at the time of accession. The coronation of Queen Elizabeth II was not until 1953 but she was Queen from 1952.

5 February 1953; on 6 February 1953 Her Majesty's second regnal year began). This inevitably meant that there may be an overlap between the regnal years and the parliamentary sessions which typically begin in October or November of each year with the Queen's Speech. The system was extremely confusing because of this overlap and, for example, the twenty-third Act that was passed in the parliamentary session which began in 1961 and lasted to 1962 would be referred to as *10&11 Eliz.2 c.23* which is translated to mean the 23rd Act in the 10th and 11th years of the reign of the Monarch Elizabeth II. This meant that one would need to know the year of accession for all the monarchs in order to identify what year the Act was! Even today in law libraries you will normally find a list of monarchs and their regnal years in order to facilitate paper-based searching of these Acts.[33] Thankfully the 1962 Act simplified this process and most electronic legislative search engines (eg *Westlaw, LexisNexis*) use the calendar rather than regnal year for ease of reference.

It has been argued that the only significance of the chapter number is that it allows the courts to identify in which order Parliament is deemed to have acted.[34] If, for example, in the extremely unlikely event that two pieces of legislation are given Royal Assent on the same day but appear to contradict each other, the chapter number identifies which is the later Act and would, therefore, be deemed to have implicitly repealed the earlier legislation.[35]

2.2.2.4 **Long title**

Although each Act is given a short title by which it will ordinarily be known, there is also a 'long title' to the Act which serves a description of the purposes of the Act. Bennion also notes that procedurally it is important because when a Bill is being debated in the House of Commons (see 2.2.1.1) an amendment can only be tabled to the Act if it is within the scope of the legislation and the long title broadly governs the scope of legislation.[36] Bennion also notes that it should be an aid to construction and this will be considered later (see 2.3.5.1).

2.2.2.5 **Date of Royal Assent**

It was discussed earlier that Royal Assent is the final part of the process required to enact legislation (see 2.2.1.1) and the date on which assent is given is placed on the Act and on all copies of the Act. The sovereign no longer physically signs each Act and the process is now regulated, in part, by the *Royal Assent Act 1967*, s 1(1)(b) of which permits the Speaker of the House of Commons and the Lord Speaker of the House of Lords to notify their House that Royal Assent has been granted.

2.2.2.6 **Enacting formula**

The enacting formula is just a formal wording that demonstrates that the legislation passed the relevant legislative processes. The formula identified in the earlier example is

---

33. A list can also be found on the online resources that accompanies this book.
34. Francis Bennion, *Bennion on Statute Law* (3rd edn, Longman 1990) 128.
35. For more on implicit repeal see Ian Loveland, *Constitutional Law, Administrative Law, and Human Rights: A Critical Introduction* (7th edn, OUP 2015) 31–2. The issue is not necessarily academic discussion. In *R v Richards* [2007] 1 WLR 847 the President of the Queen's Bench Division held the fact that two pieces of legislation were enacted on the same day was evidence that they did not contradict (and thus implicitly repeal) each other (at 853).
36. Francis Bennion, *Bennion on Statute Law* (3rd edn, Longman 1990) 42.

the usual one but where the Parliament Act has been invoked (see 2.2.1.2) the formula changes to:

> Be it enacted by the Queen's most Excellent Majesty, by and with the advice and consent of the Commons, in this present Parliament assembled, in accordance with the provisions of the Parliament Acts 1911 and 1949, and by the authority of the same, as follows—

Obviously it is necessary for this formula to be used as the usual one refers to the advice and consent of the Lords which, of course, did not occur if the Parliament Acts needed to be invoked.

2.2.2.7 Part number and heading

The organization of statutory material is important since, especially with long pieces of legislation, it ensures that there is a consistency of approach and permits provisions to be grouped together for interpretation. Where an Act is long it is not uncommon for the Act to be split into Parts. The *Constitutional Reform Act 2005* is divided into seven Parts each dealing with a discrete set of provisions in a broad area. Each Part is usually accompanied by a heading, or more properly referred to as a 'note' and these have the same status as marginal notes (see 2.2.2.8).

Where an Act is particularly long or complicated it is possible to further divide the Parts into chapters. For example, the *Constitutional Reform Act 2005* divides Part 4 (judicial appointments and discipline) into four chapters. In this context it is important to note that 'chapter' merely means a subdivision of a Part and is not the same as a chapter number.

2.2.2.8 Marginal note

Each section within a statute (see 2.2.2.9) is accompanied by a marginal note, which is sometimes also referred to as a side note. In effect it has the appearance of a heading and on electronic versions of statutes it appears alongside the section number with the appearance of a heading; eg s 1, as noted earlier, is presented in electronic versions as:

> (a) The Rule of Law
>
> This Act does not adversely affect—
>
> (a) the existing constitutional principle of the rule of law, or
>
> (b) the Lord Chancellor's constitutional role in relation to that principle.

However, it is referred to as a marginal note because, as was seen in Figure 2.4, in printed form the notes appear in the margins alongside text. A debate appears to exist as to whether marginal notes are part of the Act or whether they are annotations. This will be discussed in more detail later as it is relevant only to the interpretation of a statute (see 2.3.5.1).

2.2.2.9 Section

Each provision within a statute is known as a section. Each section will ordinarily deal with only one topic but it may not be possible to deal with a single topic with only one level of heading within the provision. Accordingly, it is possible to subdivide a section. Four levels are recognized and these are shown in Table 2.2.

Table 2.2 Dividing sections

Level	Name	Appearance
1	Section	1
2	Subsection	(1)
3	Paragraph	(a)
4	Subparagraph	(i)

Example *Section 9 Constitutional Reform Act 2005*

Section 9 states:

(1) The President of the Family Division is Head of Family Justice.

(2) The Lord Chief Justice may appoint a person to be Deputy Head of Family Justice.

(3) The Lord Chief Justice must not appoint a person under subsection (2) unless these conditions are met—

    (a) the Lord Chief Justice has consulted the Lord Chancellor;

    (b) the person to be appointed is an ordinary judge of the Court of Appeal.

(4) A person appointed as Deputy Head of Family Justice holds that office in accordance with the terms of his appointment.

It can be seen that s 9 is broken into four subsections each of which deals with a discrete aspect of the section's provision. Subsection (3) has to be subdivided itself in order to provide for discrete conditions and this division consists of two paragraphs. If either paragraph needed to be divided then this division would be known as subparagraphs and would be represented as (i), (ii), etc.

It is important to note that each level has a distinct appearance. If I wanted to refer to the second paragraph of subsection 3 I would do so by writing s 9(3)(b). Not using the brackets could cause confusion as s 9 3 b might be taken to mean either section 93 or a new section that follows s 93.[37]

The provisions themselves are at the heart of the statute and it is these that the courts need to interpret when adjudicating on cases brought before them.

2.3 Statutory interpretation

It has been noted that statutory law is a primary source of law. It is the statute itself that forms the law and this can cause difficulties. Statutes will invariably use technical language or may leave a degree of uncertainty as to what their meaning is. It is not possible to ask what the meaning of the term is because who would be asked? Parliament sits collectively and passes legislation collectively. It is not possible to ask each Member of Parliament what was meant when they passed the Act. Therefore whilst Parliament sets out the legislation one of the most important roles of the courts is to interpret legislation.

---

37. A further explanation of the appearance of provisions is given on the online resources accompanying this book.

Until comparatively recently it was said that there were defined rules or even 'canons' (a term that suggests something even stricter than rules) of interpretation that governed how courts will interpret legislation. However, it is now recognized that this is not what happens and that interpreting a statute is more complicated. Marshall suggests that there are two approaches to interpretation; the 'purposive approach' and the 'interpretative approach'.[38] However, the former is then immediately cross-referenced to the old 'rules' and the latter is cross-referenced to the approach arising from s 3 *Human Rights Act 1998*. This is therefore perhaps equally unhelpful because if the rules themselves are open to question then consolidating them into an approach is perhaps also unhelpful. The one issue which is undoubtedly correct is in respect of HRA 1998 introducing a new form of interpreting statutes. This will be expanded upon later in the chapter and in Chapter 5 but the approach introduced by that Act differs from the approach of the courts prior to the introduction of that Act.

It has been said that statutory interpretation is unique to common-law-based jurisdictions because in civil law systems the courts feel they have no need to construe a statute because the text is flexible and more akin to 'living instruments', with the judges having final say over what the law should mean in a particular case.[39]

The concept of statutory interpretation has become increasingly important because, at least in England, the era of 'judge-made law' is probably coming to an end and there is recognition that the legislature creates the law and the role of the courts is to apply it. That is not to say they are subservient because the courts can impact how the law comes into effect but it does mean that their role is now to interpret rather than create law.

Of course the difficulty with separating out the creation of the law and its interpretation and application is that it will undoubtedly cause tensions. Parliament may believe that it has passed a law that says x and could get frustrated if it perceives the courts as applying it as meaning y. This is perhaps particularly evident in the fields of criminal justice and asylum issues. It is perhaps not surprising that these are the areas of increased tension as they are also the most politically active areas of law with the impression that the electorate is most concerned with these matters. In the early 1990s when John Major was the prime minister and Michael Howard was the Home Secretary this tension began to become somewhat noticeable. In the early 2000s the battle recommenced when David Blunkett was appointed Home Secretary[40] and it has never eased. The current battle is over judicial review with the current government complaining that judges are frustrating the democratically elected government, but with the judges saying they are an essential check on executive misuse of power.

⚡ PARLIAMENTARY SOVEREIGNTY: 'GINGER HAIR' TEST

Earlier in this chapter the concept of parliamentary sovereignty was discussed and the ambit of Parliament was discussed in connection with the 'smoking on the streets of Paris' example (see 2.2.1). If Parliament can do what it wishes then does this mean there are no balances and that a corrupt Parliament could use its powers to act in an improper way? Those who argue

---

38. Geoffrey Marshall, 'The Lynchpin of Parliamentary Intention: Lost, Stolen or Strained' [2003] *Public Law* 236.

39. Francis Bennion, *Bennion on Statute Law* (3rd edn, Longman 1990) 83.

40. See Robert Stevens, *The English Judges: Their Role in the Changing Constitution* (Hart Publishing 2002) 129–36.

that the courts are either supreme or, at the very least, a safeguard to an overzealous legislature and executive sometimes point to the 'ginger hair' example.

The essence of this example is that Parliament passes a law that states anyone with ginger hair is to be arrested and sent to gaol. Theoretically Parliament could enact such a law but it is an unjust law and one that is a direct affront to human rights and the right to liberty. Given that the courts will be the ultimate arbitrators of this law it is argued that they could interpret the law so as to make it impossible to implement. For example, if a judge was called upon to rule whether someone had ginger hair, she could adjudicate that the person in fact had red hair or a dark copper colour hair. In this way the courts could act as a 'brake' to Parliament's desire to infringe human rights by ensuring that the law was interpreted in such a way that no injustice is done.

It was noted earlier that traditionally there were thought to be 'rules' that governed how the courts interpreted statutes. It is necessary to know what these rules are because they are discussed a lot, but it should be noted once again that these are not formulaic and are not followed rigidly, especially now. Setting aside the HRA 1998 rule the three 'rules' that are commonly referred to are:

- literal rule
- golden rule
- mischief rule.

2.3.1 **Literal rule**

The literal rule is considered to be the 'normal' rule and it complies with the traditional view of the courts that their role is not to make or subvert the law but rather to apply the law created by Parliament. The essence of the literal rule is that the courts simply look at the words and apply them as they are written with the suggestion that Parliament must have known what they meant.

≡ Example Literal rule

Parliament (hypothetically) creates a law that states:

(1) A person aged 18 must pay the sum of £150 to the government.

(2) On receipt of the £150 the government shall grant to the person a certificate.

(3) No person shall be entitled to drink an alcoholic beverage in a public house without a certificate.

There are a number of parts of this law that may need to be interpreted, including 'aged 18', 'on receipt', 'alcoholic beverage', and 'public house'. The literal approach would simply look towards the ordinary meaning of these words. Accordingly, in subsection (1) it is likely that the courts would hold that a person could not pay £150 until the eighteenth anniversary of their birth, but that they had until the day before the nineteenth anniversary of their birth to pay the £150. A literal interpretation would not suggest that the sum must be paid on the person's eighteenth birthday because it does not literally say that. A literal interpretation of subsection (2) would mean that as soon as the money has been received by the government they should issue a certificate and so, for example, an executive decision taken by the Home Secretary not to issue any certificates until two months after receipt in order to enable people to attend alcohol education programmes could be ruled illegal as it contravened a literal interpretation of the Act. A literal interpretation of subsection (3) would mean that a person could not drink any alcoholic drink in a public house regardless of whether they bought it or indeed knew whether it was alcoholic.

Where the literal interpretation can begin to come unstuck, however, is when grammar is introduced, not least because grammatical rules and styles change over the years.[41] Some have argued that grammar should be ignored but that would be a false premise as punctuation must have been used for a reason. One commentator has suggested that where there are conflicting grammatical meanings the courts must decide between them by looking at the possibilities and the section as a whole,[42] but to remember above all that the purpose of statutory interpretation is to adopt a legal meaning and not necessarily a grammatical meaning.[43]

In deciding the literal meaning of the word the judge will sometimes refer to their own interpretation of the meaning, usually arguing that it is so well known that people know what it means. Alternatively the judge will make reference to a dictionary, usually the *Oxford English Dictionary*, and suggest that this amounts to the literal meaning. The literal rule can sometimes appear harsh, with one leading commentator[44] citing the example of *Diane Blood* who was denied the right to conceive by artificial insemination using her late husband's sperm which had been harvested while he was in a coma.[45] The relevant Act (*Human Fertilisation and Embryology Act 1990*) required the consent of the donor before artificial insemination could be undertaken and this was not, of course, possible in these circumstances. Although the courts were deeply sympathetic to the predicament faced by Mrs Blood they said they were forced to rule that the literal language employed by statute was obvious and they were bound to follow the wording of the Act. This also demonstrates the limits of interpretation. Whilst there are other ways of interpreting a statute, the courts cannot interpret the legislation in such a way that contradicts the will of Parliament.

2.3.2 Golden rule

The golden rule picks up from this point. Sometimes following the literal meaning of words could actually contradict what Parliament intended. If that is the case then the courts will need to look at other interpretations and one form of this is the 'golden rule'.

Identifying precisely when the golden rule should apply is not easy. One commentator has suggested that it should be used when Parliament intended its provision to

41. Francis Bennion, *Bennion on Statute Law* (3rd edn, Longman 1990) 130.
42. ibid, 96–7.
43. ibid, 88.
44. Penny Darbyshire, *Darbyshire on the English Legal System* (11th edn, Sweet and Maxwell 2014) 29.
45. *R v Human Fertilisation and Embryology Authority, ex p Blood* [1997] 2 WLR 807.

have a wider definition and not one restricted to the literal meaning of its words.[46] This is corroborated by other commentators who note that the rule is traditionally employed when it is decided that a literal interpretation would not encompass the will of Parliament[47] but rather limit it.

However, it has also been suggested that the rule usually applies when it is thought that taking a literal meaning to the phrase in question would lead to an absurdity.[48] This is arguably wider than the suggestion put forward by Bennion in that an absurdity need not be restricted to extent but could be the result of poor drafting.

When can the court adopt the golden rule? Traditionally it has been held that the rule should only be used where the literal rule cannot be used (although this could be because there are a number of different literal interpretations). Where absurdity is the result then the rule is perhaps easier to justify since it can be legitimately argued that it is unlikely that Parliament would intend an absurd situation to arise although that, of course, raises questions as to who decides what is absurd (the answer to which can only be the courts).

The harshness of this can perhaps be illustrated by the example provided in 2.3.1 concerning the *Dianne Blood* litigation. If you read the judgment you cannot but come to the conclusion that all the courts the matter was before had sympathy with Mrs Blood who wished to conceive using her dead husband's harvested sperm. Given that the courts and indeed the parties morally supported her[49] it may be thought that the courts could simply have cast aside the literal meaning of the legislation and adopted a 'fairer' interpretation (such as 'where the person gave consent prior to dying then that consent is effective post mortem'). However, it was not able to do so because there was no uncertainty and certainly no absurdity. The requirement that a person must give active consent to the use of their frozen sperm was a plausible rule and therefore construing the legislation to require that positive consent would not be absurd. The mere fact that Parliament failed to contemplate a situation is not a reason to use the golden rule and all a court can do in these circumstances is bring the matter to the attention of Parliament and suggest that it passes new legislation.

☰ **Example** Golden rule

Section 57 *Offences Against the Person Act 1861* defines bigamy as:

> Whosoever, being married, shall marry another person during the life of the former husband or wife, whether the second marriage shall have taken place in England or Ireland or elsewhere, shall be guilty [of an offence].

It is not possible to use the literal rule here since the application of that rule would defeat the intention of Parliament. Section 57 says it is illegal to marry another person but as a matter

---

46. Francis Bennion, *Bennion on Statute Law* (3rd edn, Longman 1990) 105.
47. Colin Manchester and David Salter, *Exploring the Law: The Dynamics of Precedent and Statutory Interpretation* (4th edn, Sweet and Maxwell 2011) 47–8.
48. ibid.
49. The hospital that in effect refused to undertake the procedure did not do so because it objected in principle to the idea but rather because it believed it had no statutory right to do it and was obliged to reject the approach. This is a common feature in medical cases where there is no 'dispute' as such but doubt exists about the legality of a situation.

of civil law a second marriage under such circumstances would not be legally valid so the person has not, by law, married. Also, the statute says during the life of the 'former' husband or wife. The purpose of bigamy is to deal with situations where they are still married so 'former' would not apply. If they were the former husband or wife then it would not be bigamy.

The courts, to overcome this obstacle, have used the golden rule so as to construe bigamy as when somebody purports to marry someone else (ie go through a marriage ceremony) whilst already legally married.

🔄 QUESTION FOR REFLECTION

The online resources accompanying this book have a summary of the *Diane Blood* litigation. Read this. Do you think that the courts were unduly harsh here? Nobody doubts that the golden rule could have been used to create an exemption where a partner is dead but the question is whether the rule could be used. Instead of looking at absurdity in *the law* (ie on the face of the legislation) could the absurdity not be *in fact* (ie in this case, the fact that it was impossible to gain consent from a dead person)?

🔊 LISTEN TO THE PODCAST

For guidance on how to answer this question and a discussion of the main issues, listen to the author's podcast on the online resources.
www.oup.com/he/gillespie-weare8e

2.3.3 **Mischief rule**

The third 'rule' that is most commonly referred to is the mischief rule. This rule differs from the previous two forms of interpretation in that the importance of the words is less significant than the underlying reason of why Parliament legislated.[50] Bennion argues that the rule is historic as it dates back to the time when statutory law did not have a pre-eminent position—ie common law was the more usual and statutory law was only passed when the common law did not cover an issue[51] or, because Parliament disagreed with the common-law rule and wished to alter it (something it has been noted they have the right to do).

The rule can also be used where Parliament has acted to remedy an apparent defect in a previous statute.[52] Where there is doubt as to the meaning of a word or expression contained in the new statute the courts should start by ascertaining what defect it was that Parliament intended to rectify and construe the statute accordingly.

The mischief rule is sometimes used when a statute is in force for many years. Some statutes will remain current law for decades or even hundreds of years, and will be in continuous use. However, language will frequently move on and therefore the statute may use language that is not readily understood in the context of modern society.

---

50. Colin Manchester and David Salter, *Exploring the Law: The Dynamics of Precedent and Statutory Interpretation* (4th edn, Sweet and Maxwell 2011) 48.
51. Francis Bennion, *Bennion on Statute Law* (3rd edn, Longman 1990) 161.
52. ibid, 163.

The mischief rule permits a court to depart from the literal meaning of a word used at that time and apply the intention of Parliament—to legislate for a particular mischief—in such a way that it can be applied to modern society.

☰ **Example** Obscenity

An example of the use of the mischief rule can be seen from the case of *R v Stamford*[53] where the appellant had been convicted of sending postal packets containing indecent or obscene material. The relevant statute creating the offence, the *Post Office Act 1953*, did not provide any definition of 'indecent' or 'obscene' and this could be contrasted with the *Obscene Publications Act 1959*, which did. The Court of Appeal was called upon to consider whether it was possible to call expert evidence on what amounted to 'indecent' or 'obscene' material if someone was charged under the 1953 Act. Counsel submitted that they should be able to because expert evidence was permitted under the 1959 Act. In rejecting the submission the court looked to the mischief behind the 1953 and 1959 Acts and decided that the statutes were intended to deal with different mischiefs,[54] with the 1953 Act being intended to prevent the misuse of the postal service, and the 1959 Act being intended to regulate, inter alia, the publication of obscene material. The court argued that this meant that the test of obscenity under the 1953 Act would be purely objective as it matters not what the addressee thinks of the material, as the postal service had been misused irrespective of the intentions of both parties. This could be contrasted with the 1959 Act where it was thought that the views of the likely audience of the publication would be relevant.

The courts needed to use the mischief rule because the literal meaning of 'obscene' would not provide any clue as to the question that was being litigated, ie whether opinion evidence could be admissible. The so-called 'golden rule' would not have helped as there was no absurdity; it was simply not addressed by Parliament, and therefore the most obvious action of the courts would be to consider the mischief behind the prohibition.

2.3.4 **The Human Rights Act 1998**

Regardless of how the courts used to interpret legislation there is no doubt that the *Human Rights Act 1998* fundamentally altered this approach by introducing s 3 of the Act. As will be seen, somewhat ironically, the meaning of s 3 has itself been called into question, meaning the courts had to interpret that in order to ascertain how to depart from the customary rules of statutory interpretation.

The HRA 1998 introduces a dilemma to us here as it produces a 'chicken and egg' scenario. Do we look at s 3 HRA 1998 here—alongside the other rules of statutory interpretation—or do we leave it until Chapter 5 when the rest of the HRA 1998 is discussed? Neither solution is perfect. The first four editions of this book adopted the second solution but since the previous edition we have decided to move it to this section. However, a note of caution should be sounded. The powers of the courts under s 3 HRA 1998 exist only as a result of that provision. Therefore they can only be used in connection with cases that raise human rights issues and the powers would (probably) fall away if the HRA 1998 is repealed (which, for example, the Conservative

---

53. [1972] 2 QB 391.
54. *R v Stamford* [1972] 2 QB 391, 396–7 (Ashworth J).

government have pledged to do). Whether that remains the case is the subject of some debate because statutory interpretation is a common-law doctrine and so the courts could decide to retain the powers by introducing a new 'rule', although they could only do so if the repealing legislation did not make clear that the courts could not adopt the approach used in s 3.

The other note of caution that must be sounded is that there is a strong argument for knowing what the purpose of the HRA 1998 is before considering the powers of s 3. Certainly it would be useful to know what human rights means and so you should at least familiarize yourself with the outline of the Act before considering this rule. However, it is included here because it allows you to draw a contrast to how statutory interpretation took place before the HRA 1998 was passed.

Section 3(1) states: '[s]o far as it is possible to do so, primary legislation and sub-ordinate legislation must be read and given in a way which is compatible with the Convention rights.' This relatively innocuous statement masks its importance and provides an additional, and extremely powerful, canon to the doctrine of statutory interpretation. Section 3(2) makes it clear that reference to interpreting legislation applies to primary legislation irrespective of whenever it is enacted, meaning that it should apply both to legislation already passed and legislation that will be passed in the future.

It is ordinarily said that Parliament cannot bind its successors but this provision arguably does so, albeit to a limited extent. There is nothing to stop Parliament from repealing s 3 or indeed the whole HRA 1998 itself (discussed at 5.3), although it should presumably be done expressly. However, in the absence of a statement stating that s 3 does not apply then Parliament has decreed that any future piece of legislation can be interpreted in such a way as to make it compatible. In other words the court need not theoretically care whether it was Parliament's intention to act in a way that is incompatible with the Convention so long as it is possible to interpret legislation.

The interaction between ss 3 and 19 is interesting. Whilst s 19 requires a minister to make a statement stating either that legislation is compatible or not compatible with the Convention, nothing within s 19 disapplies the rule in s 3(1). Accordingly, where a minister states, when introducing a Bill, that he believes the provision is not compatible with the ECHR the courts could ignore this and interpret the legislation in such a way as to make it compatible (if it is possible to do so). Of course the easiest way to avoid this issue would be for Parliament to state in that Bill that the provisions of s 3(1) HRA 1998 do not apply (which it could do) but this would raise similar political issues to those discussed in respect of s 19 earlier.

2.3.4.1 **So far as it is possible**

The key words in s 3(1) are 'so far as it is possible to do so' in that this clearly indicates that Parliament expressly considered that there were limits to the ability of the courts to interpret legislation. It was never the intention of the government to allow the courts to 'strike down' legislation that is incompatible as occurs in some countries (discussed in more depth later). It will be remembered from 2.3.3 that statutory interpretation is ordinarily limited to situations where there is doubt as to the wording of the statute but the same is not true where s 3 is invoked; 'the interpretative obligations under s 3 of the 1998 Act is a strong one. It applies even if there is no ambiguity in the language in the sense of the language being capable of two different meanings.'[55] This is a significant

---

55.   *R v A* [2001] UKHL 25, [2002] 1 AC 45, 67 (Lord Steyn).

departure from the ordinary rules of statutory interpretation where, it will be remembered, the standard rule is to apply the ordinary definition of words contained in a statute. Section 3 clearly empowers a court to interpret legislation even where Parliament's intentions were clear, if not to do so would result in the provision being incompatible with the ECHR. However, this is subject to the proviso that on occasion it will not be possible to interpret the legislation in this way (as is clear from the use of the words 'so far as it is possible').

The leading case in ascertaining what s 3 means is the case of *R v A*[56] discussed below. As is evident from the wording of Lord Steyn, the House of Lords considered that it had wide discretion to construe statutes and the clear presumption was that s 3 should be used rather than, for example, declaring that the statute was incompatible (through the issuing of a declaration of incompatibility discussed later) This approach, as will be seen, has been followed by subsequent cases and certainly it is clear that the courts view their powers under s 3 as important.

▌▏ Case Box *R v A*

The case of *A* concerned the construction of s 41 *Youth Justice and Criminal Evidence Act 1999* which purported to prevent the victim of a sexual offence being questioned about previous sexual history. This provision was widely welcomed at that time and was introduced in the context of a number of cases where rape complainants had been cross-examined as to their complete sexual history, including number of partners and methods used to have sex, in great detail and in public. Parliament believed that such questioning should stop and enacted s 41 to do so.

The appellant A had been charged with the rape of a woman. He sought to question the complainant about consensual sexual intercourse that had taken place between her and the appellant in the weeks preceding the alleged rape. This was quite clearly 'sexual history' and would be excluded by virtue of s 41. However, the House of Lords argued that this evidence was vital in establishing a defence of consent and that excluding the use of what could be probative evidence would breach Article 6 of the ECHR. Their Lordships therefore unanimously invoked s 3(1) and stated that the exclusion should be subject to an overriding power of the judge to permit such questioning when a failure to do so would amount to a breach of Article 6, the right to a fair trial.

The decision of the House of Lords was unquestionably contrary to the intentions of Parliament and Kavanagh notes that it has been vociferously attacked on that basis.[57] However, Parliament had also made clear that it wished legislation to be interpreted in a way that made it compatible with the Convention and the decision of the House in *R v A* certainly made the provision compatible even though it was contrary to what Parliament had itself intended. Some argue that the House should have made a declaration of incompatibility instead[58] but this would arguably have been contrary to the intention of Parliament expressed in the 1998 Act. It was possible to interpret the legislation and the House did so.

---

56. [2001] UKHL 25, [2002] 1 AC 45.
57. Aileen Kavanagh, 'Unlocking the Human Rights Act: The "Radical" Approach to Section 3(1) Revisited' (2005) 3 *European Human Rights Law Review*, 259, 268–9.
58. ibid, 273.

It has been suggested that there are three questions that must be asked by the court when deciding whether to use their powers[59] which are:

- If the HRA 1998 did not exist what would the natural meaning of the legislation be?
- Would the natural meaning of the legislation identified earlier lead to an incompatibility with one or more articles under the ECHR?
- If the answer to the second question is 'yes' then is it possible to read the legislation in such a way as to lead to this incompatibility being resolved?

The second question may seem obvious but it is an important question that must always be answered. Section 3 should be considered as an exception to the ordinary principles of statutory interpretation and one that can only be justified when the HRA 1998 applies. Certainly Lord Woolf has made clear, in his view, that in the absence of a prima facie breach of a Convention right then s 3 can be ignored and the ordinary rules of interpretation apply.[60]

The questions identified by Elliott and Thomas are useful to the extent that they assist us in understanding how the courts approach the use of s 3. Of course what they do not tell us is how far the courts may go when deciding to use their powers. Whilst *R v A* made clear that the courts should try to construct the legislation in this way how far can they go?

In *R v Lambert*[61] the House of Lords adopted the approach of re-interpreting legislation even where Parliament had arguably been clear as to what its intention was. *Lambert* concerned a drugs offence under the *Misuse of Drugs Act 1971*. Parliament had purported to reverse the burden of proof once a person was found in possession of a controlled drug, meaning that the defendant needed to prove he was not guilty rather than the prosecution proving he was guilty. This appeared on the face of it to breach Article 6, the presumption of innocence. The House of Lords held that reverse burdens were not prima facie a breach of Article 6(1) but drew a distinction between a *legal* burden and an *evidential* burden. The House read the 1971 Act to mean that a defendant had an evidential burden (which would be compatible with the ECHR) even though Parliament almost certainly intended it to be a legal burden. Subsequent legislation has adopted this approach and it is now accepted that where a reverse burden is indicated it is an evidential and not legal burden.

⚡ LEGAL V EVIDENTIAL BURDEN

This is quite a complicated area of the *Law of Evidence* but it is possible to give a brief explanation.

The ordinary rule in criminal cases is that the prosecution must prove every element of the crime. The prosecution prove that D is guilty and it is not for D to prove he is innocent. A legal burden is where the party has to adduce sufficient evidence to satisfy the court that a matter is true. For the prosecution this means proving something beyond all reasonable doubt. Let us assume that D is charged with possessing drugs. The prosecution must prove that D was in possession (meaning custody or control) of a substance and that the substance was illegal.

An evidential burden is where a party (usually the defence) need to adduce some evidence to show *the possibility* that a fact may be true. If an evidential burden did not exist then the

---

59. Mark Elliott and Robert Thomas, *Public Law* (2nd edn, OUP 2014) 705–6.
60. *Poplar Housing and Regeneration Community Association Ltd v Donoghue* [2002] QB 48, 71–2.
61. [2001] UKHL 37, [2001] 3 All ER 577.

prosecution would have to disprove whatever the defence said even if there was no evidence to support the contention. If they could not disprove it beyond reasonable doubt then the defendant would succeed in the contention.

Let us go back to the drugs example. Ordinarily the prosecution would have to prove that the defendant knew that the substance was illegal (the *mens rea*). The *Misuse of Drugs Act 1971* states that if a person is found to have the substance in their factual possession (eg found on their person) then they have to prove that they did not know that the drug was illegal. If this was a legal burden then the defence would need to prove to their standard (preponderance of probabilities) that they did not know the substance was illegal. However, as it is an evidential burden they must simply raise some evidence that shows it is *possible* they did not know (eg it was handed to them by a stranger in a sealed envelope), and it is then for the prosecution to disprove (to the criminal standard) this is correct.

An evidential burden still places some burden on the defence—in that they cannot just say a statement, they must adduce some evidence to show it is not just a theoretical possibility— but the main emphasis is still on the prosecution. Accordingly, it does not breach Article 6.

Aside from *A* one of the cases that demonstrates how far the courts are prepared to go to find compatibility is *Ghaidan v Godin-Mendoza*.[62] This was a civil case concerning the possession of a rented flat. The defendant had been in a homosexual relationship with another man who was the protected tenant for a flat. When that man died the landlord began proceedings to evict the defendant. The *Rent Act 1977* gave protection to the spouse of a deceased person but the defendant could not legally be a spouse (this was prior to the recognition of civil partnerships and same-sex marriage). The defendant argued that the 1977 Act was incompatible with Articles 8 and 14 of the ECHR. The wording of the Act (and thus Parliament's intention) was clear, but the House of Lords believed (answering the first two questions identified by Elliott and Thomas earlier) that this would lead to an incompatibility with the ECHR. The House considered that the purpose of that part of the Act (protection of spouses) was to give protection to those in an enduring, stable relationship. That being the case, the House (with Lord Millett dissenting) argued that it was possible to re-interpret the provision of the 1977 Act, using the powers given to them under s 3, to construe it in such a way as to include same-sex partners who were living in a relationship akin to a marriage.

Ghaidan shows how far the courts are prepared to use their powers under s 3. There is no question that the decision the House of Lords reached would not have been possible if the HRA 1998 did not exist. There was no doubt over the wording of the provision of the 1977 Act and so none of the other canons of statutory interpretation could have led to the same result.

2.3.4.2 **Where it is not possible**

The previous section has identified that the courts will go to significant lengths to try and interpret legislation in such a way as to make it compatible with the ECHR, but there are limits. It will not always be possible to reach an interpretation. The first limitation is that the courts will not reach an interpretation that is against the intentions of Parliament. For example, in *Lambert*, discussed earlier, the House of Lords limited what Parliament wanted to do (by making it an evidential rather than legal burden)

---

62. [2004] UKHL 30, [2004] 2 AC 557.

but the essence of the intention remained (ie that the defence must still adduce *some* evidence and not simply sit back and say to the prosecution 'prove it'). Similarly in *Ghaidan* the House of Lords did not prevent the 1977 Act from applying to spouses, they simply extended the protection to include same-sex partners.

Where the only way to make an instrument compatible is to go against the wishes of Parliament then the courts will decline to use s 3 and will instead declare the statute incompatible. A good example of this is *R (Anderson) v Secretary of State for the Home Office*.[63] This case concerned the conditions of prisoners receiving parole. The legislation gave the Home Secretary the ultimate power to decide whether a prisoner should be released and the House of Lords accepted that this contravened Article 6 in that the Home Secretary, as a politician, was involved in what should be a judicial process. However, the House declined to use s 3 as the only way to make it compliant would be to remove reference to the Home Secretary, something that was clearly contrary to the intentions of Parliament (a good summary of the reasoning is provided by Elliott and Thomas).[64] This would not be a case of 'interpreting' legislation but rather rewriting it and so the House, quite correctly, declined to use s 3 and instead made a declaration of incompatibility.

2.3.5 Aids to interpretation

The preceding section has considered how the courts approach the issue of interpreting legislation but in order to do this they will sometimes look to other rules that guide how they should act and, in particular, what types of sources they should consider when construing an Act. The courts normally make reference to the notion of 'aids', ie those 'things' that can assist them in understanding the meaning of legislation. It is generally said that there are two types of aids; intrinsic aids and extrinsic aids, the differences of which are shown in Figure 2.5.

2.3.5.1 Intrinsic aids

Intrinsic aids are those contained within the statutory instrument itself. Quite what can be considered to be 'part of a statute' is open to debate. The contents of a statute were discussed earlier and the individual components of legislation may become relevant in deciding how to construe a statute.

A number of issues arise as to what is within the statute however. The two principal issues are the wording of the provisions and the explanatory features of the Act.

Intrinsic aids	**Extrinsic aids**
Looking at the content of the statutory material to assist in the interpretation of a provision	Looking at material outside the Act but within the contemplation of the legislature

Figure 2.5 Intrinsic and extrinsic aids

---

63. [2002] UKHL 46, [2003] 1 AC 83.
64. Mark Elliott and Robert Thomas, *Public Law* (2nd edn, OUP 2014) 707–8.

Wording of the statute

The first issue to examine is the wording of the Act. An important canon of interpretation is that the Act should be read as a whole[65] which gives rise to three examples, all of which are known by a Latin term notwithstanding the fact that we are trying to remove Latin from the legal language! The common rules are:

* *noscitur a sociis*
* *ejusdem generis*
* *expressio unius exclusio alterius.*

Noscitur a sociis

The first rule is that a statutory provision should be read in conjunction with its neighbouring provisions. Certainly this canon has been employed by the courts on a number of occasions and is a logical step. Given that even the most disparate of Acts will normally be divided into Parts, the neighbouring provisions should assist in ascertaining either the meaning of a word or the mischief behind the Act.

This rule can, in effect, be divided into two aspects. The first of these looks at similar words. A word should have the same meaning throughout an Act[66] although it should be noted that this is only a presumption and accordingly if Parliament expressly wishes to act differently it may do so. A good example of this can be found in the *Sexual Offences Act 2003* where 'sexual' is defined within s 78 but the Act expressly states that a different meaning of the word shall be employed for s 71.

The second aspect to this rule is its logical conclusion: that different words in a statute should normally bear different meanings.[67] Whilst this would appear to be obvious it is not necessarily so and indeed this construction has caused difficulties before.

⚡ COMPLICITY

The *Accessories and Abettors Act 1861* is a good illustration of how different words should have different meanings. The provision makes it clear that a person can become an accomplice to the principal offender by acting in one of four ways:

1. aiding
2. abetting
3. counselling
4. procuring.

At first sight it is unclear what the difference is between 'aiding' and 'abetting' or 'abetting' and 'counselling' or even 'counselling' and 'procuring'. Certainly common usage will frequently refer to someone as 'aiding and abetting' and the thesaurus provides 'aid' as the first alternative to 'abet'. In *Attorney-General's Reference (No 1 of 1975)*[68] the Court of Appeal held, however, that each had a different meaning because if it were otherwise then Parliament would not have listed these four separate ways of acting.

---

65. Francis Bennion, *Bennion on Statute Law* (3rd edn, Longman 1990) 187.
66. ibid, 188.
67. ibid, 189.
68. [1975] 2 All ER 684.

This canon can still be controversial, however, and there is sometimes a debate in the courts as to whether different words must necessarily mean anything. A good example of this is the words 'cause' and 'inflict' within the *Offences Against the Person Act 1861*. At first sight they seem to be two different words but they appear in two related sections of the Act (ss 18 and 20 which relate to grievous bodily harm). The difference between the words exercised the courts for many years and in *R v Ireland; R v Burstow*[69] the House of Lords held that for practical purposes there is no longer a distinction between 'cause' and 'inflict'.[70]

Ejusdem generis

This second rule is similar to the first but relates to similar words rather than identical or contrasting words. The expression can be translated into English as 'of the same kind or nature' and it demonstrates the purpose of this rule. The basic principle of the rule is that where words of general meaning are to be found in a provision following words with a specific meaning then the general words are to be read narrowly as though they were linked to the specific words.[71] In other words the general words are considered to be a continuation of any list of words preceding them.

The rule is subject to some restrictions. The first is that all the words must constitute a genus (or 'set' of words) and this genus should be narrower than the literal interpretation of the provision.[72] Bennion provides the following example:

> The *Customs Consolidation Act 1876*, s 43 reads: 'The importation of arms, ammunition, gunpowder or any other goods may be prohibited.'[73]

There is no doubt that the words 'or any other goods' are general words and their literal interpretation would encompass virtually any form of trade. However, the *ejusdem generis* rule would seek to limit the meaning of those general words to a context related to the preceding words, ie the 'any other goods' must be comparable to ammunition, eg gelignite (a high explosive) may come within this provision. Bennion continues by arguing that the 'genus' must also be restricted narrowly:

> The string specified as 'boots, shoes, stockings and other articles' would import the genus 'footwear' rather than the wider category of 'wearing apparel'.[74]

Clearly this is a useful and sensible approach to adopt and does ensure that a provision is no wider than it needs to be.

Expressio unius exclusio alterius

This final rule is related to the *ejusdem generis* rule in that it concerns lists of words but where the rules differ is that the *expressio* rule operates on the premise that in the absence of any general words a list will be exhaustive, and accordingly any term not listed within the list will be deemed not to be included within the provision. This principle can be identified from its English translation, 'to list one thing is to exclude another'.

The rule arguably goes further by limiting general words. Bennion's argument is that if a specific word is used to limit a general word (cf the *ejusdem generis* rule where a

51

69. [1998] AC 147.
70. *R v Ireland; R v Burstow* [1998] AC 147, 160 (Lord Steyn) and 164 (Lord Hope of Craighead).
71. Francis Bennion, *Bennion on Statute Law* (3rd edn, Longman 1990) 196.
72. ibid, 197.
73. ibid.
74. ibid, 197.

general word was used to *extend* or *complement* the specific words) then the specific word is taken to mean that it excludes other words that come within that general class.[75] He provides the following example:

> The *Immigration Act 1973*, s 2(3) states that for the purposes of s 2(1) of the Act the word 'parent' includes the *mother* of an illegitimate child. The class to which this extension relates is the *parents* of an illegitimate child.[76]

The logical conclusion of this rule is that the father of an illegitimate child would not be within s 2(1) because the use of the word 'mother' as an express inclusion must be to limit the meaning of the general word 'parent', and accordingly 'father' which is obviously within the general term has been implicitly excluded.

Explanatory issues

Although it will be noted later (see 2.3.5.2) that some explanatory material is outside of the Act, the statute itself will contain some provisions that explain the significance of the detailed provisions. The two most important features are marginal notes and the long title.

Marginal notes

It was noted that sections will normally be accompanied by something called a 'marginal note' or 'side note'. These are, in effect, descriptions of the section, but are they part of the statute and capable of being used as an intrinsic aid? Some commentators argue that the answer is 'no' and they do not form part of the Act and accordingly cannot be used as an intrinsic aid.[77] However, others disagree and argue that they *are* part of the statute albeit they usually provide only an indication of the provision rather than a necessarily accurate description of the provision.[78] It is submitted that there is no reason why a court could not take account of the marginal note of a provision although caution should be shown because the notes are not debated within Parliament but are placed on the Act by the draftsman.[79] Accordingly, not only is it not necessarily an accurate description of the provision it is the draftsman's deduction of the meaning of the provision.

⫼ Case Box *R v Tivnan*

In *R v Tivnan*[80] the Court of Appeal demonstrated that it does occasionally use marginal notes in order to assist in understanding the intentions of Parliament. The appellant had been convicted of drug dealing and a confiscation order had been made against his assets. He claimed that as it could not be proven his assets had been obtained through the proceeds of drug dealing the confiscation order should be quashed. The Court of Appeal considered that Parliament's intention was to deprive drug dealers of assets equal to the proceeds obtained by drug dealing, not necessarily just those assets that were purchased directly from the proceedings. The court made express reference to the marginal note in seeking the intent.[81]

---

75. ibid, 202.
76. ibid, 202.
77. Colin Manchester and David Salter, *Exploring the Law: The Dynamics of Precedent and Statutory Interpretation* (4th edn, Sweet and Maxwell 2011) 54–5.
78. Francis Bennion, *Bennion on Statute Law* (3rd edn, Longman 1990) 128.
79. ibid, 127.
80. [1999] 1 Cr App R(S) 92.
81. ibid, 97.

Long title

The long title of the Act may provide assistance in the construction of a provision. It will be remembered that the long title is part of the preamble to the Act which sets out the purpose of the Act. As the long title is part of, if not the official title for, the Act it would appear appropriate that it should be considered.

> **Example** Animal cruelty
>
> The *Protection of Animals (Amendment) Act 2000* permits a court to make an order, upon the application of a prosecutor, for the care, disposal, or slaughter of animals that have been kept cruelly. In *Cornwall County Council v Baker*[82] the Divisional Court was asked to rule on the meaning of 'animals in question'. The Council had prosecuted the respondent for cruelty to seven farm animals. It also sought an order under the 2000 Act relating to other animals at the farm which were not subject to the prosecution. The magistrates' court refused to make an order in respect of the other animals contending that the 2000 Act applied only to animals subject to proceedings under the *Protection of Animals Act 2011*. The Divisional Court upheld this ruling on appeal and referred to the long title to demonstrate its purpose.[83]

2.3.5.2 Extrinsic aids

In certain circumstances it may be possible to look outside of the Act for assistance in construing a statutory provision and this is known as using extrinsic aids. There are a number of extrinsic aids that the courts will consider but rules do sometimes exist as to when courts may look outside of the Act for assistance. Broadly speaking, the following aids will be examined:

- explanatory notes accompanying an Act
- parliamentary material
- other statutory provisions
- academic writing
- pre-parliamentary material.

Explanatory notes

Since 1999 all government Bills introduced into Parliament are accompanied by explanatory notes and upon Royal Assent these notes are amended to reflect the agreed wording of the Act.[84] The notes do not form part of the Act and are created by the government department sponsoring the Bill (see *Westminster City Council v National Asylum Support Service*)[85] so they have not been approved within Parliament because, while they may be the subject of discussion during the progress of the Bill, there is no mechanism for the notes to be amended by Parliament. Further, parliamentary draftsmen have argued that 'explanatory notes are informal in style, are there to improve

---

82. [2003] 1 WLR 1813.
83. ibid, 1819–20 (Toulson J).
84. Roderick Munday, 'Bad Character Rules and Riddles: "Explanatory Notes" and True Meanings of s 103(1) of the Criminal Justice Act 2003' [2005] *Criminal Law Review* 337, 340–1.
85. [2002] 1 WLR 2956, 2958–60 (Lord Steyn).

clarity for the reader, and to this end may be highly discursive'.[86] Clearly, it is contemplated that the reader of a piece of legislation will refer to the notes but does a 'reader' include members of the judiciary? Also, given that the notes are written by draftsmen and not members of the legislature, they arguably suffer from the same problem as marginal notes (discussed earlier).

The courts readily refer to explanatory notes,[87] but some question whether they go too far and accord them a 'quasi-legislative' status that it was never intended for them to have. To support this argument reference is made to the comments of Lord Bingham in *Attorney-General's Reference (No 5 of 2002)*,[88] where his Lordship argued that the explanatory notes 'strongly supported' his conclusion as to the meaning of the provisions. Given that they are a creature of the executive rather than the legislature it is somewhat surprising that the notes are so readily referred to, especially in light of the rule governing the use of parliamentary material (see 2.3.5.3). However, Lord Steyn in *Westminster City Council v National Asylum Support Service* argued that they were akin to pre-parliamentary material but arguably of more assistance than, for example, White or Green Papers since they reflect the initial wording of the provisions.[89] One concern is that ready use of these notes by the courts could encourage sloppy draftsmanship (on the basis that so long as the notes explain the provision it need not matter whether the provision is tightly defined).[90] The fact that the notes are created by the executive rather than the legislature also creates the possibility that recourse to the notes could give rise to a confusion as to whether a provision reflects the intentions of Parliament or the government, with the two not necessarily coinciding. Notwithstanding these points, however, the use of the notes has become an accepted part of statutory construction although more recent decisions of the Supreme Court would appear to suggest that a fundamental review of their use (akin to that undertaken in *Pepper v Hart*;[91] see 2.3.5.3) may soon occur.[92]

Parliamentary material

Parliament is a formal body and is a body of record, ie a number of documents exist governing its proceedings and one possible extrinsic aid may be to use these documents. However, this is one of the more controversial uses of an extrinsic aid and for this reason, and to demonstrate the importance of the general rule, the use of such material is considered in its own section later (see 2.3.5.3).

Other statutory provisions

Whilst some statutes will act as amending or consolidating instruments for existing legislation, a significant amount of legislation is 'new' in that it creates stand-alone laws and procedures. It may be thought therefore that there is little use in examining

---

86. Roderick Munday, 'Bad Character Rules and Riddles: "Explanatory Notes" and True Meanings of s 103(1) of the Criminal Justice Act 2003' [2005] *Criminal Law Review* 337, 341.
87. ibid, 341–2.
88. [2005] 1 AC 167.
89. [2002] 1 WLR 2956, 2960.
90. Roderick Munday, 'Bad Character Rules and Riddles: "Explanatory Notes" and True Meanings of s 103(1) of the Criminal Justice Act 2003' [2005] *Criminal Law Review* 337, 347.
91. [1993] AC 593.
92. See Roderick Munday, 'Bad Character Rules and Riddles: "Explanatory Notes" and True Meanings of s 103(1) of the Criminal Justice Act 2003' [2005] *Criminal Law Review* 337, 346–9, and 352–4, for a discussion of these issues.

other pieces of legislation but it is not unusual for similar words to be found in other statutes. Where the mischief is similar between the Acts then comparing or contrasting statutory words could prove useful in helping construct the meaning of the provision under scrutiny.

Ⅱ\ Case Box *R v Dooley*

In *R v Dooley*[93] the Court of Appeal needed to consider the meaning of the words 'with a view to' which appeared in s 1(1)(c) *Protection of Children Act 1978*. The Act did not define these words but it is a not uncommon phrase to be found within legislation and the court examined how it had been construed in other legislation, including ss 1(2), 20, and 21 *Theft Act 1968* and the *Obscene Publications Act 1964*. The court then argued that applying the same interpretation to the 1978 Act would be logical and it can be seen, therefore, that the other legislation acted as an extrinsic aid.

Perhaps the most common alternative statute to examine is the *Interpretation Act 1978* which, as its short title suggests, was designed to provide assistance in the interpretation of statutes. The 1978 Act is merely the latest reincarnation of the Interpretation Act and it is unlikely to be the last. The Act itself provides a series of common words and the presumption is that if one of these words is used in a statutory provision then it is deemed to have that meaning unless Parliament intended differently, this intention normally being evidenced expressly. Perhaps the most important interpretative presumptions in the Act are contained within s 6:

In any Act, unless the contrary intention appears—

(a) words importing the masculine gender include the feminine;

(b) words importing the feminine gender include the masculine;

(c) words in the singular include the plural and words in the plural include the singular.

The use of such presumptions is important because otherwise an Act of Parliament could become cluttered and unreadable when a simple provision refers constantly to 'he or she', 'him or her', 'that or those', etc. Where the context clearly means the masculine or feminine gender then obviously the interpretation is so construed as the 1978 Act creates presumptions rather than mandatory rules.

Academic writing

It is often said that the English courts have been somewhat sceptical about the use of academic writings, but this is not necessarily the case. Perhaps the most basic example of the use of books as an extrinsic aid is that of the dictionary; it was noted earlier that the usual rule in statutory interpretation is to use the literal meaning of the word and a dictionary is not infrequently consulted to achieve that aim. A dictionary cannot be anything other than an external aid.

---

93. [2005] EWCA Crim 3093.

The use of academic writing through texts and journals has been slowly developing but was used even in the nineteenth century. However, its use has arguably been growing not least because there is a greater respect between 'academic' and 'practising' lawyers.[94]

The appellate courts are now increasingly turning to the use of academic sources of writing and indeed a failure to do so has led to criticism about the courts taking an unduly lenient approach to construction.[95] That is not to say that academic sources will be automatically consulted and certainly where textbooks are concerned it is not unusual for only the most authoritative to be cited, but where a narrow point of law arises where there has been little case law, or what case law there is has been debated amongst eminent academics, then the citation of academic writings can be of assistance to the judges although, of course, they are not bound by them.

 ## ACADEMIC WRITING

BOOKS

In *R v Dooley*,[96] discussed in the previous case study, the Court of Appeal did not just use alternative statutes as an aid but also made reference to Smith and Hogan's *Criminal Law*, undoubtedly the leading criminal law textbook. The arguments made in the text by its editor and author, Professor David Ormerod, were cited by the court as being of assistance.[97]

ARTICLES

In *R (Purdy) v DPP*[98] the House of Lords became aware of an article by Professor Michael Hirst.[99] Not only did Lord Philips refer to it extensively in his speech but the House also required counsel to supply written submissions on whether they believed the points contained within it were correct.

Pre-parliamentary sources

Legislation does not 'just happen' especially when a Bill is introduced by the government. There will normally be a significant number of documents that were produced and published prior to the Bill being introduced. When the Bill arises out of government policy it is quite likely that a series of official 'papers' may have been published, with a *White Paper* being a statement of the policy with a broad indication as to how the government intends to legislate to tackle the mischief, and a *Green Paper* being a discussion paper issued by the government for assistance in structuring the way in which the mischief should be tackled. The government may also have asked the Law Commission

---

94. Indeed this 'glasnost' has led to a debate as to whether academics could be appointed direct to the bench (see Chapter 8). Arguably the most famous 'academic' lawyer was Professor Brenda Hoggett QC who moved from academia to the Law Commission. She was then appointed to the High Court bench as Hale J before being promoted to the Court of Appeal, becoming the first female Law Lord in 2004 and eventually becoming the President of the Supreme Court. However, this cannot be said to be a 'pure' academic appointment as she was appointed from the Law Commission rather than from academe.

95. See, for example, commentary by Professor Andrew Ashworth on the Privy Council decision of *Attorney-General for Jersey v Holley* [2005] 2 AC 580 (Andrew Ashworth, 'Commentary on A-G for *Jersey v Holley*' [2005] *Criminal Law Review* 966).

96. [2005] EWCA Crim 3093.

97. ibid, [14].

98. [2010] 1 AC 345.

99. [2010] 1 AC 345, 359.

to examine a particular issue and if so the Law Commission will almost certainly have produced a consultation paper and a report to Parliament.[100] In exceptional circumstances where issues of importance need to be examined it is possible that a Royal Commission will be established which will issue a report to Parliament.

Outside of the executive-controlled bodies Parliament itself may have created documents that are relevant to the provision. Both Houses of Parliament create *select committees* that investigate areas of interest to Parliament. Some of these committees are standing committees in that they remain in existence at all times (eg Home Affairs Select Committee, Defence Select Committee) and others will be created for a specific purpose. Committees will produce reports that are publicly available and sometimes these reports will call for legislation to be introduced which the executive may heed.

The use of such material is accepted by the courts but the degree to which it will be useful is perhaps more open to question since it may not reflect the proceedings in Parliament. That said the material will allow the provision to be placed into context and this could assist in its interpretation.

⚡ MODEL CODES

Pre-parliamentary material need not necessarily be accepted, or even debated, by Parliament for it to be used in the construction of a statute. Perhaps the best example of this is *R v G and R*[101] which is an important criminal law case where the House of Lords used its right to depart from its own decisions (see 3.4.3) to overrule *R v Caldwell*[102] which it stated was a 'mistake' even though it had been used for over ten years. Lord Bingham, who gave the leading speech in the House, used the model penal code to construe the meaning of the word 'reckless'. The model penal code was created by the Law Commission and was designed as an exercise to demonstrate how the criminal law could be codified. Parliament has not yet decided that the criminal law should be codified, and indeed the Law Commission has now dropped the proposals believing they are unlikely to ever be implemented, so the proposals have not been debated by Parliament but this did not stop Lord Bingham from using it as a source of identifying the meaning of 'reckless'.[103]

2.3.5.3 **The rule in *Pepper v Hart***

It has been seen that a basic distinction can be drawn between the legislature and judiciary in that Parliament enacts the law but the courts interpret it. How a court interprets legislation has been discussed and the ability to use extrinsic aids to assist in interpretation has also been identified as a source of help for the judiciary. A logical supposition that could be drawn is that an easy way of interpreting the law would be to examine what was said in Parliament when passing the provision. Debates and written answers in both Houses of Parliament are reported in a series known as *Hansard* and it is published daily both on the Internet and in hard copy.

100. Although the executive will refer a matter to the Law Commission the report will always be to Parliament.
101. [2004] 1 AC 1034.
102. [1982] AC 341.
103. *R v G and R* [2004] 1 AC 1034, 1046, and 1054.

Where the courts wish to analyse what Parliament's intention is then it may appear sensible to examine *Hansard* to provide clues as to the meaning of the legislation. However, the traditional rule was that it was not permissible to look at parliamentary proceedings to assist in interpretation; in part this was because it was thought that it would lead to unnecessary expense and delays,[104] but it was also because it was thought that it might be a challenge to parliamentary supremacy in that it was thought that the law was that which was passed by Parliament, not that which was discussed, ie the wording of Bills changes and it is only the final Act that is law. Looking at the proceedings may lead to the suggestion that the courts were questioning or impeaching the process of Parliament contrary to Article 9 of the *Bill of Rights 1689*.

However, in the landmark case of *Pepper v Hart*[105] the House of Lords, exercising its power to reverse previous decisions of the House (see *Practice Statement (Judicial Precedent)*[106] and see 3.4.3), decided to relax this rule and introduced rules governing when recourse to *Hansard* would be permitted for statutory interpretation. The rule permitted courts to make reference to ministerial statements or the promoter of a Bill so long as three rules were met:

1. The legislation in question was ambiguous, obscure, or led to absurdity.

2. The material relied on consisted of statements by a minister (or the promoter of a Bill).

3. The statements relied on were clear.

It was never thought that this would lead to *Hansard* being referred to frequently, in part because it could be considered an abrogation of the duty of a court to invoke the rule. The clear presumption is that the courts will interpret the law according to the words used (see 2.3.1) and accordingly only where this is not possible will it be possible to consider using the rule. Lord Browne-Wilkinson, who gave the leading speech in the case, stated: 'In many . . . cases reference to Parliamentary material will not throw any light on the matter.'[107] This is partly because many provisions of a Bill are not subject to detailed comment or consideration, and in part because where the language is obtuse it is unlikely that any ministerial statement will be particularly clear either. Kavanagh argues that restricting an analysis of *Hansard* to the comments of ministers inevitably misrepresents the position and confuses the distinction between the legislature (Parliament) and the executive (government).[108] She argues that Parliament passes legislation even if the majority of legislation is sponsored by the executive as the largest parliamentary party. It does not follow automatically that the language of the legislation will necessarily reflect the executive's desire and most Bills will be full of amendments, and it is always open to Parliament to enforce its powers and pass a Bill different from that required by the executive.

---

104.   *Beswick v Beswick* [1968] AC 58.
105.   [1993] AC 593.
106.   [1966] 1 WLR 1234.
107.   *Pepper v Hart* [1993] AC 593, 634.
108.   Aileen Kavanagh, '*Pepper v Hart* and Matters of Constitutional Principle' (2005) 121 *Law Quarterly Review* 98, 106.

Example Parliament v executive

A good example of where Parliament and the executive may depart from one another is over terrorism legislation. The executive has an interest in obtaining wider powers to deal with terrorists because of the threat that they pose to society at large. Terrorism differs from traditional crimes in the way that it is carried out and most developed countries will have special rules for dealing with terrorism. However, powers can be abused as easily as used and the legislature is therefore careful to ensure that there is a check on any increase in the power of the executive, and indeed this is its very purpose.

In 2005 the Terrorism Bill was being discussed and the government wished to extend the time a terrorist suspect could be held by the police without charge from fourteen days to ninety days. Parliament did not agree and it eventually defeated the government clause proposing this measure, accepting a reduced increase to twenty-eight days. The case for the government was put forward by the Home Secretary and he outlined the reasons why the powers were necessary. If there was any legislative uncertainty as to the meaning of cl 23 of the Bill would recourse to *Pepper v Hart* help? Probably not because the rule permits only statements by ministers to be cited and yet in this case the House of Commons rejected these arguments and put forward its own viewpoint.

The debate on powers may help clarify any uncertainty, and the comments of the backbenchers as to why they would not support ninety days would certainly help a court understand the intention of Parliament in this provision but the rule, as drafted, would be of no assistance—the courts would have to ignore parliamentary debates and reach their own conclusions.

Kavanagh, citing Corry, argues that a further difficulty with the rule is that Parliament is not a bipartisan place. A minister making a statement to either House will not be giving a fully independent rationale comment but will be making the point to support his, and the government's position.[109] Whilst it is true to state that the rules of Parliament make clear that a minister may not mislead either House[110] this is a far step from an independent comment, and Kavanagh argues this can be contrasted with a witness who gives testimony in court under oath.[111] Of course others will be sceptical as to whether a witness necessarily gives independent and unbiased evidence in court but the political nature of Parliament inevitably means that the ministers' statements will be geared towards their desire.

However, the threat to *Pepper v Hart* appears to have retreated for some time as the House of Lords (now the Supreme Court) showed no desire to widen the scope of its enquiry into parliamentary legislation. Kavanagh notes that when the Court of Appeal sought to widen the scope of the rule in *Wilson v Secretary of State for Trade and Industry*,[112] the Speaker of the House of Commons and Clerk to the Houses of Parliament sought the right to make representations to the House as to the application of the rule.[113] Their fear was that a wider treatment of parliamentary legislation could

109.   ibid, 98, 108.
110.   Malcolm Jack, *Erskine May's Treatise on the Law, Privilege, Procedures and Usage of Parliament* (24th edn, LexisNexis 2011) 429.
111.   Aileen Kavanagh, '*Pepper v Hart* and Matters of Constitutional Principle' (2005) 121 *Law Quarterly Review* 98, 108.
112.   [2003] 3 WLR 568.
113.   Aileen Kavanagh, '*Pepper v Hart* and Matters of Constitutional Principle' (2005) 121 *Law Quarterly Review* 98, 112.

lead to the courts scrutinizing the proceedings of Parliament, something that they are expressly not permitted to do (see Article 9 of the *Bill of Rights 1689*).[114] In *Wilson* the House did not simply prevent the rule in *Pepper v Hart* from being widened but it actually constrained its use by noting that the statement of a minister will not necessarily reflect the intention of Parliament as a whole. The House also stated that it was important to emphasize that any statement was not *law* but an aid to deciding *what* the law was. Accordingly, any statement permitted under the rule of *Pepper v Hart* was simply a tool to help the court decide what the law should be and not a definitive statement of the law. This latter point is to be welcomed and whilst Kavanagh argues that it is a restriction[115] some doubt must exist as to this because it is difficult to believe that Lord Browne-Wilkinson, when formulating the rule, ever intended that a ministerial statement should ever bind a court when deciding the meaning of the law.

So what is the status of *Pepper v Hart*? Kavanagh argues that it has been significantly reduced but in *Jackson v Attorney-General*[116] Lord Nicholls of Birkenhead appeared to disagree:

> In some quarters the *Pepper v Hart* principle is currently under something of a judicial cloud. In part this is due to judicial experience that references to *Hansard* seldom assist . . . It would be unfortunate if *Pepper v Hart* were now to be sidelined. The *Pepper v Hart* ruling is sound in principle, removing as it did a self-created judicial anomaly.[117]

His Lordship argues that the rule continues to be important even if his enthusiasm is tempered by the reminder that the rule is perhaps not as useful as some suggest. Yet Lord Steyn, in the same case, suggests that it may not be as important:

> If it were necessary to do so, I would be inclined to hold that the time has come to rule . . . that *Pepper v Hart* should be confined to the situation which was before the House in *Pepper v Hart*. That would leave unaffected the use of Hansard material to identify the mischief at which the legislation was directed and its objective setting. But trying to discover the intentions of the Government from ministerial statements in Parliament is unacceptable.[118]

Although the ruling in *Pepper v Hart* was about ascertaining the intentions of Parliament and not the government, the difference between what Parliament intends and what the government intends arguably goes to the heart of some of the difficulties that have been raised about this rule. Lord Walker of Gestingthorpe appears to summarize the crux of this area when his Lordship noted that there was a disagreement as to the application of the *Pepper v Hart* principle in the House, although his Lordship argued that this need not be resolved in that case[119] and this is probably true with the statements of the other Lords concerning its application being *obiter dicta*.

An interesting question raised by Holland and Webb is whether *Pepper v Hart* applies to criminal cases as strictly.[120] It may seem a strange question but it falls from

---

114.   For more on this see Lord McKay's speech in *Pepper v Hart* [1993] AC 593, 614–16 and Lord Browne-Wilkinson, 621–9, 638–40.

115.   Aileen Kavanagh, 'Pepper v Hart and Matters of Constitutional Principle' (2005) 121 *Law Quarterly Review* 98, 115.

116.   [2005] UKHL 56.

117.   ibid, [65].

118.   *Jackson v Attorney-General* [2005] UKHL 56 [97].

119.   ibid, [141].

120.   James Holland and Julian Webb, *Learning Legal Rules* (9th edn, OUP 2016) 292.

the particular nature of criminal trials where the liberty of a person (the defendant) is at stake. In *Thet v DPP*[121] Lord Philips, the then Chief Justice, said that he doubted whether the rule in *Pepper v Hart* could apply in criminal cases.[122] The basis of such an approach is that if a criminal statute is ambiguous then the benefit of the doubt should go to the defendant, which is often considered to be a standard legal approach. However, as Holland and Webb point out, the very same judge later used *Pepper v Hart* in a criminal trial irrespective of the fact that the use was to help the prosecution and not the defendant.[123] This perhaps just reinforces how complicated and controversial the rule is.

So what is the status of the rule? Whilst it may have been weakened in some respects it remains an important rule and one that you must try to understand. Courts remain reluctant to admit parliamentary material and certainly will not do so where there is no ambiguity in the statute, perhaps reinforcing the fact that statutory material can only be used where a court needs assistance in understanding what a statute says.

2.3.6 **Presumptions**

Alongside the rules governing interpretation and the aids used by the courts to identify the correct meaning of words are presumptions that operate in respect of the construction of statutory material. The key presumptions that will be discussed here are:

- against altering the common law
- Crown not bound by Act
- *mens rea* required for criminal offences
- against retrospective approach
- presumption in favour of the defendant.

2.3.6.1 **Common law**

It has already been noted that until comparatively recently the vast majority of law was judge-made rather than statutory, with Parliament initially simply amending or correcting defects within the common law (see 2.3.3). However, as one would expect, Parliament began to take control of the law and now it is often contended that judges no longer have any right to make law (although as will be seen in Chapter 3 this is contentious). Notwithstanding this, however, there remains a presumption that a statute will not alter the common law unless it was the intention of Parliament to do so. The rationale behind the presumption is that Parliament must know the law before it enacts legislation and accordingly unless it identifies a defect in that law then it is presumed not to be interfering with its course. In *Deeble v Robinson*[124] the Court of Appeal held that only plain words would suffice to interfere with common-law rights, which is taken to mean that the intention of Parliament to interfere with the common-law power should be obvious.

---

121. [2007] 1 WLR 2022.
122. *Thet v DPP* [2007] 1 WLR 2022, 2027.
123. See *R v JTB* [2009] 2 WLR 1088.
124. [1954] 1 QB 77, 81.

61

⚡ *DOLI INCAPAX*

Whilst the intention to interfere with the common law need not be express it is not uncommon for Parliament, when wishing to end a common-law rule, to use express blunt terms to do so. A good example of this can be found in the *Crime and Disorder Act 1998* (CDA 1998) where s 34 ended the common-law rule of *doli incapax* (where a child between the ages of 10 and 14 was presumed not to be capable of committing a criminal offence unless evidence was adduced to demonstrate they knew it was legally or morally wrong). Section 34 states:

> The rebuttable presumption of criminal law that a child aged 10 or over is incapable of committing an offence is hereby abolished

This would seem to leave little room for doubt, but see *R v JTB*[125] where the House of Lords had to rule on whether the presumption or the substantive doctrine had been abolished. The House ruled that despite the literal phrasing, the substantive defence, and not just its presumption, was removed by the CDA 1998.

It has been argued that the presumption is extremely controversial,[126] and given that Parliament is supreme and can legislate against any matter it does appear strange that there should continue to be a presumption that judge-made law will not normally be affected.

2.3.6.2 **Crown not bound by the statute**

As the United Kingdom is a constitutional monarchy its Head of State is actually the sovereign, currently Her Majesty The Queen Elizabeth II.[127] The term 'the Crown', however, is normally used to denote the machinery of the state through the executive (ie government). Since rules are considered to be binding principles handed down from *ruler* to *subject* the principle has always been that the Crown would not be bound by any law. Note, however, that this does not mean (with the exception of the sovereign) that anyone is personally immune from laws as it is the state rather than an individual who is not subject to laws. The presumption against the Crown not being bound by a statute arises from this doctrine with the principle being that as the Crown is the ruler (the state) it should not be bound unless it expressly says so.

An Act of Parliament will now normally state whether it is bound and it has been considered more appropriate for the Act to state expressly whether it is so bound rather than leave it implied, which ensures that the courts must construe the appropriate status.

2.3.6.3 *Mens rea*

Many of the important presumptions relate to the criminal law where certainty is to be expected since transgression of the criminal law could lead to the loss of liberty for the transgressor. One of the most important presumptions is that *mens rea* should be implied into statutes unless it was Parliament's intention for there to be none. It is not

---

125.   [2009] 1 AC 1310.
126.   Stephen Bailey, Jane Ching, Nick Taylor, and Michael Gunn, *Smith, Bailey and Gunn on the Modern English Legal System* (5th edn, Sweet and Maxwell 2007) 459.
127.   Although in Scotland she is technically the first Queen Elizabeth as the Queen Elizabeth who ruled between 1558 and 1603 was Queen of England but not Queen of Scotland.

possible in this text to provide a precise definition of *mens rea* and you should cross-reference to your set text for *Criminal Law* for a fuller definition but suffice it to say that most crimes require two elements; the *actus reus* (the 'conduct' part of a crime) and the *mens rea* (the 'mental requirement' for a crime). It will often be said that *mens rea* can be approximated to 'guilty mind'.

⚡ THEFT

Theft is defined under s 1 *Theft Act 1968* thus: '[a] person is guilty of theft if he dishonestly appropriates property belonging to another with the intention of permanently depriving the other of it.' The *actus reus* of this crime is appropriating property belonging to another. The *mens rea* of the crime is doing so dishonestly and with the intention of permanently depriving the other of the property.

Not every statute will, however, necessarily easily identify a mental requirement and it may appear therefore that only the *actus reus* is required for liability to arise.

II\ **Case Box** *Sweet v Parsley*

The leading case that discusses the absence of *mens rea* is *Sweet v Parsley*.[128] The appellant was the tenant of a farm but sublet rooms to other people. At the time of the offence the appellant did not live at the farm. The police found some cannabis resin at the farm and she was charged with the offence of, inter alia, being concerned with the management of premises used for the purpose of smoking cannabis or cannabis resin (s 5(b) *Dangerous Drugs Act 1965*). On the face of the section there was no requirement for *mens rea* and she was convicted by the court as she was concerned with the management of premises—as she was the landlady—at which drugs were found. The House of Lords quashed the conviction and stated that unless Parliament indicated otherwise, *mens rea* should be an essential requirement for any crime. They implied the requirement for knowledge into the criteria.

It is important to note that this is simply a presumption and it can, therefore, be rebutted if it was Parliament's intention to do so. In *B v DPP*[129] and *CPS v K*[130] the House of Lords examined sexual offences against children. Their Lordships argued that indecency with a child and indecent assault (both now repealed) were not crimes of strict liability but they did accept that s 5 *Sexual Offences Act 1956* (now repealed), which created the offence of unlawful sexual intercourse with a girl under 13, was intended to be a crime of strict liability. They reached this conclusion by noting that comparable offences within the same legislation did expressly consider mental requirements and accordingly its absence in s 5 must have been deliberate.[131]

---

128.   [1970] AC 132.
129.   [2000] 2 AC 428.
130.   [2002] 1 AC 462.
131.   *CPS v K* [2002] 1 AC 462, 469–71 (Lord Bingham).

2.3.6.4 **Acting retrospectively**

The law normally works prospectively—that is to say a law will only change the way we regulate conduct that arises *after* an instrument becomes law. Attempting to regulate conduct that has occurred in the past is known as acting retrospectively and there is a strong presumption that Parliament does not intend to act in this way. Bennion argues that this rule is a matter of fairness since if a person is deemed to know the law (and that well-known saying 'ignorance is no defence to the law' does have a foundation of truth within it) then they should be able to trust the law and act in accordance with their knowledge.[132] If a law were retrospective then it would mean that even if a person knew the law and acted in the way that he knew was lawful, he could later be liable under the law as a result of the retrospective law making his actions culpable.

Where the statute relates to the criminal law then the position becomes more complicated because Article 7 of the ECHR prohibits, inter alia, retrospective crimes and punishment. Accordingly, any statute that purports to do this would be subject not only to the common-law presumption but also to s 3(1) *Human Rights Act 1998* as it would prima facie breach Article 7.

That said it should be emphasized that this is a presumption and Parliament, because it is supreme, can act in a way that is retrospective. Perhaps the most obvious example of this is the *War Damage Act 1965* which was enacted specifically to overturn a decision of the House of Lords in *Burmah Oil Co Ltd v Lord Advocate*.[133] This Act did not just statutorily overrule the decision but was expressly retrospective and ensured that the appellants did not receive that which the House of Lords had held was due to them.

Parliament can expressly choose to act retrospectively and certain retrospective acts will not be considered to harm the principle, most notably purely administrative or procedural changes.[134] It is not uncommon for procedural rules to change and these can come into effect in respect of conduct that occurs prior to the change becoming effective. Non-punitive regulatory conduct can also come within this rule.

⚡ SEXUAL OFFENDING

When the *Sex Offenders Act 1997* came into force, it required sex offenders to be subject to notification requirements through the creation of the Sex Offenders Register. Under ss 1(2) and 1(3) of the Act those who had been convicted of a sexual offence *before* the commencement of the Act were still subject to the notification requirements. In *Ibbotson v UK*[135] the applicant was serving a sentence for possession of obscene and indecent material when the 1997 Act came into force. Due to the retrospective nature of the measures in the Act he was required to register with the police under the notification requirements of the Act. The applicant argued that this retrospectivity violated Article 7 of the ECHR as the requirement to register constituted

---

132. Francis Bennion, *Bennion on Statute Law* (3rd edn, Longman 1990) 151.
133. [1965] AC 75.
134. Francis Bennion, *Bennion on Statute Law* (3rd edn, Longman 1990) 152.
135. (1997) 27 EHRR CD332.

'a heavier penalty . . . than the one which was applicable at the time the criminal offence was committed'.[136] The Commission rejected this argument, holding that because the Act did not require 'more than mere registration, it [could not] be said that the measures imposed on the applicant amounted to a "penalty" within the meaning of Article 7 of the Convention'.[137] Thus the retrospective nature of the requirements under the Act were not problematic. Whilst the *Sex Offenders Act 1997* has now been repealed, its provisions regarding the registration of sex offenders have been re-enacted and updated within the *Sexual Offences Act 2003*.

2.3.6.5 Presumption in favour of the defence

In the English Legal System—like most developed legal systems—there is, in criminal matters, a presumption of innocence which means that it is not for a defendant to prove that he is innocent but rather for the state to prove that he is guilty. Where the state is not able to demonstrate guilt then the defendant is entitled to an acquittal even if the evidence demonstrates that it is more likely than not that the defendant committed the crime.

The presumption of innocence is taken further and justifies the presumption in favour of the defence. According to this presumption if there are two possible constructions of a statutory provision and one is broadly favourable to the defendant and the other is broadly favourable to the prosecution then this rule states that the construction that favours the defence should be used, unless Parliament intends the opposite.

 Summary

In this chapter we have examined the basic concept of domestic sources of law. We have identified that there are two sources of law (primary sources and secondary sources). In particular we have noted that:

- *Primary sources* are considered to be those 'authoritative' sources that are produced by the legal process itself. *Secondary sources* are sources that are produced by others and are, in essence, a commentary on the law.

- Primary sources of law include statutory material and this itself is divided into two types of material: *primary legislation* (Acts of Parliament) and *secondary legislation* (Statutory Instruments, Orders in Council, etc).

- Statutes are Acts of Parliament and are either *Public Acts* (Acts that are of general application) or *Private Acts* (which are limited to a certain body).

- An Act will normally have to pass both the House of Commons and House of Lords and then receive Royal Assent before it becomes an Act of Parliament. However, subject to limited exceptions, it is possible to use the Parliament Acts, which will allow the House of Commons to override the House of Lords and enact legislation that has passed only one House.

- A statute will ordinarily be broken down into Parts and Chapters but the most important division is in its clauses known as sections. Sections can also be broken down into subsections, paragraphs, and subparagraphs.

136. *European Convention of Human Rights*, Art 7(1).
137. *Ibbotson v UK* (1997) 27 EHRR CD332, 334.

- The courts are called upon to interpret legislation and they do this normally by using the *literal* rule where they simply look at the wording of the legislation. Where this leads to an absurdity they can look at either the *golden* or *mischief* rules which allow them to consider what Parliament intended.

- *The Human Rights Act 1998* allows greater interpretation and expressly allows courts to decide whether legislation is compatible with the *European Convention on Human Rights*.

? End-of-chapter questions

1. Should the Parliament Acts be used in politically controversial pieces of legislation? The House of Lords is the second chamber of the legislature and thus should it not have the right to block controversial legislation? By allowing the House of Commons to bypass this block does this not mean there is no protection against, for example, a state seeking to diminish human rights?

2. The Supreme Court of the United States of America is allowed to 'strike down' legislation that is incompatible with their Constitution. Should the Supreme Court of the UK be allowed to 'strike down' legislation that is incompatible with the ECHR?

3. Why has the issue of statutory interpretation become increasingly important? What impact has the *Human Rights Act 1998* had on the way that courts interpret legislation?

4. If the intention of Parliament is important in the construction of legislation why shouldn't the courts be allowed to use parliamentary material whenever they wish and in whatever form?

5. Reread the section on the use of explanatory notes ('Explanatory notes') and also read Roderick Munday 'Bad Character Rules and Riddles: Explanatory Notes and the True Meanings of s 103(1) Criminal Justice Act 2003' [2005] *Criminal Law Review* 337, 352–4 and Aileen Kavanagh '*Pepper v Hart* and Matters of Constitutional Principle' (2005) 121 *Law Quarterly Review* 98, 105–8. Is it right that the courts look to statements produced by the government rather than Parliament as a whole when examining parliamentary material? It is used to gauge Parliament's intent and this need not be the government's intent. Should the rule be relaxed?

≡ Further reading

Kavanagh A, 'Unlocking the Human Rights Act: The Radical Approach to Section 3(1) Revisited' [2005] 3 *European Human Rights Law Review* 259–75.

This is an authoritative article where it is suggested that the courts have been reluctant to make the full use of their powers of interpretation.

Marshall G, 'The Lynchpin of Parliamentary Intention: Lost, Stolen or Strained' [2003] *Public Law*, Summer, 236–48.

This is an article that examines the place of parliamentary intention in the construction of statutes.

For self-test questions, flashcards, and links to useful websites, please visit the **online resources** at: **www.oup.com/he/gillespie-weare8e**

3

Domestic Sources of Law: Case Law

By the end of this chapter you will be able to:

- Define the principles of *stare decisis*.
- Apply the doctrine of precedent to cases.
- Differentiate between binding, overruling, and distinguishing precedent.

Introduction

The previous chapter introduced the concept of domestic sources of law and it was noted that sources can be divided into primary and secondary sources. Of the primary sources, parliamentary material is supposed to be the most important, with the courts merely implementing the will of Parliament. Often this is expressed as Parliament making the law and the courts applying it but this is not strictly true. It was noted that decisions of the superior courts are a primary source of material in their own right and this is because England and Wales has a common-law-based tradition, ie decisions of the court can amount to law in the same way as statutory law does. It is not just minor matters where the common law becomes involved; quite a significant amount of constitutional law is by convention or through common law, but murder, arguably the most important criminal offence, is a common-law offence. You will not find a statutory definition of murder but it is instead left to the courts to define.

Even where Parliament has passed a law it falls to the courts to decide what this law means and how it will be applied. In the previous chapter it was noted that the courts have created a series of statutory rules to assist them in interpreting the law, but in order to ensure that there is certainty in the law the courts have themselves developed rules on how courts must act when presented with a case. These rules are known as *stare decisis* although the common term of 'precedent' has gained favour. These rules have created a hierarchy of the courts and an understanding of how courts must act when presented with a previous decision.

3.1 **Reporting of cases**

It has already been noted that the English Legal System is a common-law-based system, which means that historically much of the law was a product of the common law rather than statutes. Even now that statutes are more usual the role of the courts is to interpret the law and many of the common-law rules continue to apply.

At the heart of the common-law system is the system of *stare decisis*, or precedent as it is also known. The term *stare decisis* can be translated as 'let the decision stand' and is designed to bring certainty to the law. The basic proposition of this doctrine is that a case should normally be dealt with in the same way as previous cases were by the courts and that the law can only be changed according to the hierarchy of the courts. How this works in practice will be examined in this chapter but the first issue to consider is how we know what the law is.

One can get the impression that the system of *stare decisis* has a long and distinguished history and to an extent it does. However, until comparatively recently the system was somewhat haphazard because few cases were ever reported. How could the doctrine be applied therefore? A judge who tried a Chancery case in Preston might not be aware of a similar case that was heard in Plymouth three months earlier. If they were decided differently then it would appear that rather than having a consistent approach to law we would have the exact opposite.

The earliest known reports were known as the 'Year Books' and these date back to the thirteenth century (and can still be seen at the Squire Law Library at the University of Cambridge) but very few cases were reported. Those cases that were mentioned tended to be extremely important cases rather than matters that were considered in typical court cases. Also the reports took a considerable time to be reported which did not contribute to a careful analysis of precedent. In the sixteenth century a series of private reports started to be published. These were reports published by individual reporters and normally cited by reference to their name. A principal difficulty with these reports, however, was that there was no sense of order as to what was reported; it tended to depend on the particular idiosyncrasies of the reporters. There was also considerable doubt as to the accuracy of the reporters as there were no rules and regulations that either required a reporter to check the accuracy of reports or indeed specified what qualification the reporters needed to have, if any. That said private reports continue to be available albeit in a changed format (see 3.1.1.2).

Eventually it was decided that if reports were to be produced then it was important that they contributed to, rather than detracted from, the consistency of law. In 1865 the Inns of Court and Law Society, who regulated the legal profession (see Chapter 10), created a new body, the *Council for Law Reporting* and in 1870 it became an incorporated body taking the name, *Incorporated Council of Law Reporting for England and Wales*, the name it continues to be known by today. The patronage of the professions, particularly the Inns of Court where the Masters of the Bench (who are in charge of the Inn) were frequently members of the judiciary (see 10.2.1.2), ensured that the Council succeeded and that its reports became authoritative; indeed even today (as will be seen) reports produced by the Council should be cited in preference to any other series.

If the Year Books and private law reports marked the first age of law reporting and the creation of the *Incorporated Council* marked the second age, we are now in the third age. We now live in the era of the Internet and as you will no doubt be aware a significant number of judgments can now be obtained freely and easily from the Internet. The Law Reports, in all their various guises, never pretend to be able to report every case that occurs in the senior courts but with the Internet this is getting close to being possible. For example, let us look at the Supreme Court. The series *Appeal Cases* did not report every case heard by its predecessor, the House of Lords, but since 14 November 1996 every judgment of the House of Lords (and subsequently the Supreme Court) has appeared on the Internet. To a lesser extent this can also be seen with the Court of Appeal. Whilst not every judgment of the Court of Appeal is reported on the Internet, the majority are, particularly in the Criminal Division where it concerns an appeal against conviction, and certainly considerably more than would have ever been reported in the traditional law reports.

The courts themselves have mixed emotions about the use of ICT to report cases, as on the one hand they have facilitated their use through the provision of neutral citations (see 3.1.2) but on the other hand the courts have argued that it is sometimes possible to refer to too many cases. Perhaps the most notable criticism was given by the Lord Chief Justice in *R v Erskine*.[1] The Lord Chief Justice provided a history of law reporting[2] and emphatically restated a principle first enunciated by Viscount Falkland in 1641: 'if it is not necessary to refer to a previous decision of [the] court, it is necessary not to refer to it.'[3] This has been followed up by the Lord Judge CJ stating that electronic cases should 'not usually be cited unless it contains a relevant statement of legal principle not found in reported authority'.[4]

3.1.1 Printed series

It has been noted that a number of printed series exist. The *Incorporated Council* is responsible for many of these but a number of private reports, normally produced by recognized legal publishers, are also to be found.

3.1.1.1 Incorporated Council

Judgments reported by the *Incorporated Council* should normally be cited in preference to any other series.[5] The reports produced by the Council are fully authorized in that the judges who gave the judgment will check the draft to see whether it is accurate and can indeed change the wording of a judgment they handed down if it clarifies issues. The reports (apart from the *Weekly Law Reports*) also contain the submission of counsel which whilst not forming any part of the judgment can be of assistance when identifying the reasoning of the court.

There are three principal series operated by the *Incorporated Council* which are: the *Law Reports*, the *Weekly Law Reports*, and the *Industrial Cases Reports*, the latter of which is a specialist report. In addition, other series are now also produced (eg the *Business Law Reports* and the *Public and Third Sector Law Reports*) but these are of lesser importance. Of the three main series the *Law Reports* are considered to be the definitive reports for the reasons already set out and they are divided into four series, each of which has a different abbreviation and colour (see Table 3.1).

69

---

1. [2010] 1 WLR 183.
2. *R v Erskine* [2010] 1 WLR 183, 201.
3. ibid, 202.
4. *Practice Direction (Citation of Authorities)* [2012] 1 WLR 780.
5. See ibid.

Table 3.1 The Law Reports

Series	Abbreviation	Colour[a]
Appeal Cases	AC	Brown
Queen's[b] Bench Division	QB	Green
Family Division[c]	Fam	Blue
Chancery Division	Ch	Red

a. The reports will either be bound in this colour or will be bound all in beige with the spine including the Division framed by the relevant colour. This tends to be a less popular method of binding now.
b. When the Sovereign is a King then it is automatically the King's Bench Division and the abbreviation KOD is used.
c. Prior to 1972 this series was known as the Probate Division and carried the abbreviation P. In that year, however, the Family Division of the High Court of Justice was established and the series was retitled.

It is important to note that the titles do not necessarily reflect exactly what their contents are. One of the most common mistakes for law students to make is to think that the *Appeal Cases* series deals with the appellate courts, most notably the Court of Appeal. In fact only matters now heard in either the Supreme Court or Judicial Committee of the Privy Council are reported in that series.[6] A significant proportion, and perhaps even the majority, of cases reported in the *Queen's Bench Division* series are not heard in the Queen's Bench Division of the High Court of Justice but are decisions of the Court of Appeal (Criminal Division), certain decisions of the Court of Appeal (Civil Division), Employment Appeals Tribunal, Consistory Courts,[7] and judgments of the Court of Justice of the EU.[8] Similarly, the Family Division and Chancery Division reports encompass decisions of the Court of Appeal (Civil Division) and European Court of Justice that originated in those divisions.

The *Weekly Law Reports* are so called because they are generally published weekly but this is not for the fifty-two weeks of the year nor are they produced in the same week as the judgment was handed down (discussed later). There are traditionally three volumes of the *Weekly Law Reports* and it is intended that those reported in volumes 2 and 3 will normally be (eventually) published in the *Law Reports*. That said, it is important to note that this is only an intention and it will not necessarily always occur, in part because by the time a report is produced it may have been considered on appeal.[9] The *Weekly Law Reports* (abbreviated to WLR) are produced much more quickly than the *Law Reports*, in part because they are not checked by judges prior to being published.

---

6. It previously reported decisions of the House of Lords and the Judicial Committee of the Privy Council.

7. These are ecclesiastical courts and established by the Church of England. Each diocese has a Chancellor who presides over the consistory court. Nowadays the vast majority of cases relate to 'faculties' which are permissions to alter the material content of a church (including its building, windows, or other features that could have a permanent effect on the church).

8. It is unlikely that these cases will continue to be reported in this way since the right to petition the Court of Justice of the EU about a British case has now lapsed (see *European Union (Withdrawal) Act 2018*, s 6(1)(b)).

9. For example, *Davis v Johnson* is reported at [1978] 2 WLR 182 but it has never been reported in *Law Reports* because it was superseded by the House of Lords ruling on that case: see [1979] AC 264.

Table 3.2 Common abbreviations for Law Reports

Series	Abbreviation
All England Law Reports	All ER
Criminal Appeal Reports	Cr App R
Criminal Appeal Reports (Sentencing)	Cr App R(S)
European Human Rights Reports	EHRR
Family Court Reports	FCR
Family Law Reports	FLR
Knight's Industrial Reports	KIR
Local Government Law Reports	LGLR

Accordingly, there may be slight differences between the reports. The speed at which they are produced is also reflected by the fact that the arguments of counsel are not contained in the report either.

3.1.1.2 **Other series**

A number of other series exist all of which are private reports. In order to have status within the courts the reports must be prepared by a qualified lawyer (see 3.1.3). With the exception of the *All England Law Reports* the series tend to be specialist in terms of reporting a narrow range of cases. The primary reason for this is that it is not easy to compete with the Council, especially given the preferential treatment awarded to it by the courts. Where a practitioner wishes to access specialist material, however, it is unlikely that the general law reports will contain many of the cases as they will not be considered 'important' enough. The principal series are referred to in Table 3.2.

Not every report will necessarily be official in that the judges may not necessarily have the opportunity to review them prior to publication although the better reports do allow this. Also very few of these reports will contain the arguments of counsel, the argument for omitting these being that they do not form part of the judgment.

3.1.1.3 **Newspapers and journals**

Before leaving the printed series it is worth noting that it is not only specialist publications that report cases but that a limited number of newspaper and journals do so too. *The Times* has long been considered the leading daily newspaper for lawyers in part because it contains law reports usually on an almost daily basis. The reports are highly abridged and would normally only be referred to in court in highly exceptional circumstances (because the case would ordinarily be reported by a series in due course). In contrast to the reporting series already discussed, the words of the judge are not reported verbatim but are simply abridged. The principal advantage of these reports, however, is that the reports are normally produced within days of the judgment being handed down, something that not even the weekly reports can manage.

Legal periodicals also sometimes report cases and perhaps the two most obvious examples of this are the *Solicitors' Journal* and the *New Law Journal*. Both series suffer the same drawbacks as *The Times* in terms of their detail but the speed in which they are reported continues to make them a particularly useful resource.

3.1.1.4 A note on dates

Although all law reports contain a date where the report is carried in print rather than electronically it is likely that there will be a delay between the judgment being handed down and the report being produced. It is a convention that rather than using the date of the judgment the year will normally be taken from the report.

> ### ☰ Example *R v G and R*
>
> The judgment in the leading case of *R v G and R* was handed down by the House of Lords on 16 October 2003. However, it was reported in the *Appeal Cases* series at [2004] 1 AC 1034 and could, therefore, be abbreviated as *R v G and R* (2004).

Of course nothing is simple and some reports are produced earlier than others, most notably the *Weekly Law Reports*. This may mean that there are different years.

> ### ☰ Example More about *R v G and R*
>
> The case of *G and R*, discussed earlier, is also reported at [2003] 3 WLR 1060. However, the year can be taken from whichever series you refer to. It could also, therefore, be referred to as *R v G and R* (2003).

Printed reports do not include every case and occasionally there may be a significant delay in reporting a decision. Where a report is particularly late then it would be wiser not to adopt this convention. Perhaps the classic example of this is *Regal (Hastings) Ltd v Gulliver* where the judgment was handed down on 20 February 1942; it was reported by the *All England Law Reports* at [1942] 1 All ER 378 but the official *Law Reports* did not report the case for another twenty-five years ([1967] 2 AC 134)!

3.1.2 Internet sources

The growth in electronic reports led to an increase in the number of unreported cases that were being presented to the courts. Traditionally these were referred to by their case name or the year and 'unreported'. It was difficult for all counsel and the courts to keep track of the cases and clearly as more judgments were becoming available it was preferable for a standardized form to be introduced.

In *Practice Direction (Judgments: Form and Citation)*[10] Lord Woolf CJ issued a direction that transformed the way that judgments were presented. All judgments would now follow a standard pattern with each paragraph being numbered sequentially through the judgment. Also each case would be assigned a neutral citation number so

---

10. [2001] 1 WLR 194.

that even unreported cases could be readily indexed, identified, and retrieved. Initially, the practice was restricted solely to the Court of Appeal and Divisional Court of the Queen's Bench Division but it was later extended to the High Court.[11] The House of Lords, Privy Council, and now Supreme Court also follow the system.

The citation has three elements to it: the date, the court code, and the case number. Each number is assigned sequentially by the relevant courts in order of its appearance. The codes are as follows:

Supreme Court	UKSC
House of Lords	UKHL
Privy Council	UKPC
Court of Appeal	
Criminal Division	EWCA Crim
Civil Division	EWCA Civ
High Court of Justice	
Administrative Court[12]	EWHC Admin or EWHC (Admin)
Queen's Bench Division	EWHC (QB)
Chancery Division	EWHC (Ch)
Family Division	EWHC (Fam)
Specialist Courts	
Patents Court	EWHC (Pat)
Commercial Court	EWHC (Comm)
Admiralty Court	EWHC (Admlty)

The code EW stands for England and Wales whereas UK is used for the Supreme Court (which has jurisdiction across the United Kingdom) and the Privy Council. Whilst the Privy Council's cases will now no longer originate in the United Kingdom this convention remains. Rather confusingly there remains some uncertainty where the case number is sometimes to be found. Where the court code does not include parentheses then the number occurs immediately after the code whereas where parentheses are used then the case number is written immediately after the code but before the court code which is placed in parentheses.

≡ Example Neutral citations

The 123rd case in the Court of Appeal (Civil Division) for the year 2003 would be written as:
    [2003] EWCA Civ 123

whereas the 45th case to be heard in the Chancery Division of the High Court during the year 2003 would be written as:
    [2003] EWHC 45 (Ch).

---

11.   See *Practice Direction: Supreme Court: Judgments: Neutral Citations* [2002] 1 WLR 346.
12.   Also known as the Divisional Court of the Queen's Bench Division.

Neutral citations should usually be used at least once even in reported cases and the (printed) reports should not renumber the paragraphs but use the ones assigned in the judgment. Where a paragraph is being referred to the number is placed in square brackets.

> **Example** Neutral citations—paragraphs
>
> To refer to the 13th paragraph in the (fictional) case of *Smith v Jones*, which has the neutral citation number [2003] EWHC 45 (QB), the following format is used:
> [2003] EWHC 45 (QB) at [13].

3.1.3 Reporters

So far it has been recognized that cases are often reported but who reports them? The short answer is qualified lawyers. Traditionally cases were reported by barristers and the vast majority of reporters continue to be barristers. In part this was because of the historical divide between the professions (see 10.2.1) with barristers having the exclusive right to litigate in the superior courts. It was thought that as only a barrister could litigate in the superior courts only a barrister would fully understand the procedure and detail of the cases in sufficient detail to report the matter. However, the *Courts and Legal Services Act 1990* ended the Bar's monopoly on accessing the superior courts and s 115 of that Act provides that a law report by a solicitor or other person with a senior courts qualification shall have the same authority as one by a barrister. Accordingly, the position is now that either a solicitor or barrister can act as an official law reporter. It is important to note that the reporter, regardless of which profession he belongs to, must be fully qualified, ie have the right (even if they do not avail themselves of it) to conduct litigation in the higher courts.

3.2 Hierarchy of courts

The system of precedent depends on there being a hierarchy of courts. It is necessary to identify the structure of the courts in order to understand how precedent works. Figure 3.1 sets out a basic understanding of the English Legal System. It can be seen that the Supreme Court is at the very top of the structure and the magistrates' courts are at the bottom. The position of the European Court of Human Rights (ECtHR) is somewhat complicated and different texts will place it at different levels of the system. The ECtHR is linked by a broken line to reflect the fact that technically the ECtHR does not bind any court nor is it reached by an appeal *per se* (see Chapter 5 for an explanation of this). However, the UK has traditionally operated on the basis of following the rulings of the ECtHR, and so it must rank highly in the structure.

Before the withdrawal from the EU, the Court of Justice of the EU (CJEU) was often found alongside the Supreme Court. This was because the UK was bound by treaty to follow the judgments of the Court of Justice, and domestic law gave effect to that.[13]

---

13. *European Communities Act 1972.*

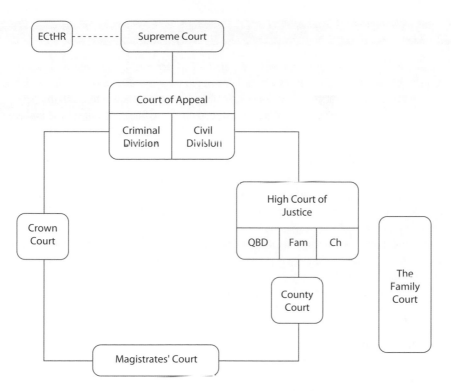

Figure 3.1 The hierarchy of the courts

However, domestic courts are no longer required to follow decisions of the Court of Justice,[14] and so it does not form part of the structure of the courts. However, it will remain a source of law due to the fact that many of the laws passed while in the EU remain in force. This will be discussed at 4.2.

The hierarchical principle means that each court will act in accordance with its place in the hierarchy and has responsibilities to those above and below it. When and how the courts can act will be discussed later although it should be noted that the lower courts (ie those below the High Court) do not play any role in *setting* rather than *following* precedent.

3.3 **Legal principles**

Not every statement of a superior court will necessarily amount to a precedent. Indeed the system of precedent applies only to a narrow part of any case—the legal decision for a case. Harris notes that this is a significant limiting factor as in the vast majority of cases, including appellate cases, there will be no dispute as to the law but rather a dispute as to the facts.[15] In those situations no precedent will arise as decisions of fact do not bind courts.

---

14. *European Union (Withdrawal) Act 2018*, s.6(1)(a).
15. Rupert Cross and JW Harris, *Precedent in English Law* (4th edn, Clarendon Press 1991) 40.

> ### :≡ **Example** Facts v law
>
> Parliament creates the (fictional) *Motor Vehicle in the Park Act 2015*, which states that a person is guilty of an offence if he drives a vehicle powered by a motor in a public park. Edith is stopped by the police after driving her electrically powered wheelchair through the park.
>
> The district judge trying the case decides that an electric wheelchair is a vehicle powered by a motor and as she drove it in the park convicts her. Edith appeals to the High Court and they decide that permitting wheelchairs to be brought within the legislation would be 'absurd' and contrary to other parliamentary statutes. Applying the 'golden rule' of statutory interpretation (see Chapter 2) they quash the conviction and hold that the purpose of the legislation was to stop motor vehicles (cars, vans, etc) driving through the park and that a wheelchair could not be considered a 'motor vehicle' because although it may be driven by a motor it was not a vehicle but a disability aid.
>
> Whether Edith was driving and whether she was in the park are decisions of fact. Whether a wheelchair amounts to a 'vehicle powered by a motor' is a matter of law as it requires the law to be interpreted. In this situation the decision of the High Court that a wheelchair is not a motor vehicle will become a precedent as it is a decision of law.

However, in a case many apparent decisions of law may be made but some of them may not be binding as they do not form part of the decision of the case. In the earlier example, the High Court held that the mischief of the Act was to stop cars and vans being driven in the park. This must be a legal rather than factual point but it does not form part of the decision of the case as Edith's case did not involve a car or van; it is an ancillary legal point.

The two types of legal statement identified previously are known as the *ratio decidendi* and *obiter dictum*. The *ratio decidendi* is the legal reasoning for the decision and forms the binding precedent, *obiter dicta* are legal opinions that did not go to the decision but are, in essence, side comments on legal issues.

3.3.1 *Ratio decidendi*

At the heart of precedent is the notion of the *ratio decidendi* as it is this which will form the binding precedent. The term is often shortened to just *ratio* and notwithstanding the fact that there is a retreat from the use of Latin in law the term remains in use.

The *ratio* is sometimes presented as being an easy principle. It is the binding element of the case and it is the reason for this case. Simple. Except it isn't. Judges do not often signpost why they have reached their decision and so there may be several reasons why they have reached their decision. Does that mean that there are multiple *ratios*? Also, who decides what the *ratio* is? Judges do not say 'the *ratio* of this case is . . . ' and it is for the later courts to try and ascertain what it is. Thus it is quite possible that what a later judge declares to be the *ratio* of a case might actually be a different proposition than what the judge giving the initial judgment intended.

Identifying the *ratio* is even more difficult where there is more than one judge pronouncing judgment. Whose judgment forms the *ratio*? It has been suggested that where there are multiple judgments it is possible that there will be no *ratio*[16] although not

---

16. James Holland and Julian Webb, *Learning Legal Rules* (9th edn, OUP 2016) 192 citing Lord Justice Jacob.

everyone agrees with this and Harris has suggested that every case must have a *ratio* but it does not follow that there must be only one *ratio*.[17] It is submitted that Harris must be correct since the term *ratio* denotes that there must be a reason for the decision, it is just that identifying precisely what that definition is can be difficult.

The difficulties caused by multiple judgments can perhaps be best illustrated by reference to cases. In *R (on behalf of R) v Durham Constabulary*[18] the issue in question was whether a juvenile offender must consent to being given a formal reprimand or final warning rather than being prosecuted. The decision of the House of Lords that no consent was required was unanimous but Lady Hale disagreed radically with Lord Bingham on the reasons for this. What is the *ratio* of this case? Arguably in this particular case it was the reasoning of Lord Bingham because a clear majority of Law Lords backed his arguments but does this necessarily follow? In this case there were two 'primary' judgments that conflicted on some aspects: what happens if the other judges all agree with the comments of the other judgments even though they say slightly different things (as arguably happened in *R v Ireland; R v Burstow*[19])?

These complications are one reason why in some jurisdictions only a single judgment is given (most notably the US Supreme Court).[20]

So how do we define the *ratio*? Unfortunately there is no easy answer and indeed nobody has suggested a foolproof method. As you read more cases you will start to understand their structure and logic better, meaning that it is likely you will identify a possible *ratio* almost subconsciously but proving that it is the *ratio* will be difficult. To an extent it is irrelevant because it is for a court to determine what the *ratio* of a case is and not you (be it now as a student or later as a solicitor or barrister) but it is important that you recognize what *could* amount to a *ratio* so that you can extrapolate how the court will rule. If you can identify a thread as the *ratio* you can then as a lawyer seek to argue that a judge is *bound* to act in a particular way (discussed later) or in an essay you can persuade your tutor the answer is *x* because you can point to the development of the law.

Despite these difficulties some have attempted to show how you can identify a precedent and the two most common theories put forward are those proposed by Wambaugh and by Goodhart.

3.3.1.1 Wambaugh's test

The first possible method of identification is to use the test formulated by Wambaugh. Harris reproduces the earlier text of Cross in considering this work.[21] The test is quite complicated in that it is presented in the negative. It also does not identify the *ratio* but allows a reader to test whether their supposition of what the *ratio* is could be correct. The test, at its most basic level, is that one identifies the supposition of law that the reader believes is a *ratio* and then reverses its meaning.[22] The reader then considers whether the outcome of the case would have been the same. If the answer is 'yes' then the proposition can only be *obiter* and not the *ratio*.

---

17.   Richard Cross and JW Harris, *Precedent in English Law* (4th edn, Clarendon Press 1991) 48.
18.   [2005] UKHL 21.
19.   [1998] AC 147.
20.   Where the court is divided then there will tend to be a single majority verdict and a separate single dissenting judgment. As a dissenting judgment will not count towards the *ratio*, this means there is no possibility that the judges contradict each other on the *ratio*.
21.   Richard Cross and JW Harris, *Precedent in English Law* (4th edn, Clarendon Press 1991) 52–7.
22.   ibid, 52.

> ☰ **Example** Edith
>
> Let us return to the earlier example of Edith. What is the *ratio* of the High Court in that case?
>
> The first possible *ratio* of the case is that only cars and vans are classed as 'motor vehicles'. We reverse the proposition (cars and vans are not classed as motor vehicles) and ask ourselves whether the same decision would have been made in respect of Edith? The answer must be 'yes' because the case did not concern either a car or van and so that proposition will not be the *ratio*.
>
> The second possible *ratio* is that wheelchairs are not motor vehicles. If we reverse our proposition (wheelchairs are motor vehicles) then we need to ask ourselves if the decision would be the same. The answer must be 'no' because the law prohibits the use of motor vehicles so they would have to acquit. Accordingly, the proposition that 'wheelchairs are not motor vehicles' may be the *ratio* of that case.

A difficulty with Wambaugh's test is, however, that it does not work particularly well where there is more than one possible *ratio*. For example, it could be decided that the *ratio* of the example earlier is that a vehicle required for the conveyance of a disabled person is exempt from the legislation. If this proposition was reversed it would not obviously lead to Edith's case being decided differently but is this the *ratio*? Arguably if it does then had Edith not had an electric wheelchair but a quad bike to allow her to move around then are we saying the court would still acquit? It would seem unlikely and yet according to Wambaugh's test is possible. Harris argues that this is a difficulty with the test: it is very good at identifying what *is not* a *ratio* but it is not particularly efficient at identifying what *is* the *ratio* unless there is only a single possible reason[23] and as has been pointed out already this is perhaps unlikely.

3.3.1.2 **Goodhart's test**

The more authoritative test is that which was put forward by the theorist Goodhart. His test is based on the premise that it is possible to identify the *ratio* by examining the material facts of the case that set the precedent. The logic behind this premise is that all decisions are necessarily based on the analysis of facts and is in line with the comments of Lord Halsbury, the then Lord Chancellor, who has stated that 'a case is only authority for what it actually decides'.[24] Harris, reproducing the work of Cross in commenting on this case, notes that his Lordship was not stating that a case has no binding power beyond its decision but rather was indicating that precedent only applies where the material facts are similar.[25] We will return to this proposition when examining how to escape precedent (3.4.2) but it does validate the premise of Goodhart that an analysis of some facts could reveal the *ratio*.

Not all the facts of a case will be relevant in the search for a *ratio*, indeed a significant proportion of them are unlikely to be critical. Goodhart, therefore, refers to the need to find 'material' facts which are those that go to the central issues of the case. Goodhart himself, however, noted that one particular difficulty with this theory is that

---

23. ibid, 56–7.
24. See *Quinn v Leathem* [1901] AC 495, 506.
25. Richard Cross and JW Harris, *Precedent in English Law* (4th edn, Clarendon Press 1991) 57–8.

it will be for the judge to decide what the material facts are and this may not necessarily be an objective approach to deciding such facts.[26] Whether something is a 'material' fact depends on whether it is essential to the decision of the case.

> ### ≡ Example Material facts
>
> The defendant, a 31-year-old female called Sheila, is accused of stabbing the victim, her husband of nine years, in the stomach following an argument. The marriage was a turbulent one with frequent allegations of domestic violence including two where the husband was formally cautioned by the police.
>
> There are a series of facts in this example but the age, name of the accused, and duration of the marriage are unlikely to be material facts in that it would not really matter whether they were present or changed. The sex of the defendant may be a material fact but on the other hand it may not.
>
> The material facts in this case would appear to be that the defendant stabbed the victim in the stomach, that the defendant and victim were in a relationship (the fact that it was a marriage is probably immaterial), and the allegations (and particularly the proven incidents) of domestic violence.
>
> The material facts are relevant to the decision in the case and therefore go to the *ratio* of the case whereas the immaterial facts are simply irrelevant.

An advantage of Goodhart's theory is that if it were correct then not only would it assist in the identification of a *ratio* but it would also primarily be of assistance in escaping precedent. It will be seen that the most useful tool for a judge or lawyer seeking to escape precedent is the concept of distinguishing (see 3.4.2) and if Goodhart is correct then a case can be distinguished if any of the material facts are not present. This would free the judge to decide the case by doing what she thought most just and not what she believes the higher courts require.

The disadvantage of this approach, however, is that not every case necessarily turns on the material facts of the case. An example of a case where the material facts are not as important is *Donoghue v Stevenson*,[27] arguably one of the most important cases in English law.[28] The material facts of this case were that a third party purchased a drink (ginger ale but the type of drink cannot be considered material) in a dark glass bottle, and the bottle contained (unbeknown to any party in the case until the material time) a decomposed snail. The judgment of the House of Lords arguably had very little to do with any of these material facts and certainly the use of the *ratio* of this case, which became the very foundations upon which the tort of negligence came to be based, have very little to do with the material facts of this case other than the fact that it was a third party that bought the article (and thus it was not a contract case). That being the case then it would suggest that Goodhart's test is not helpful either, meaning we are left with the fact that identifying the *ratio* is very difficult, at least in respect of some cases. The one advantage is that if even the leading theorists and jurists cannot agree how to identify the *ratio* then nobody can expect you to either. Anyone that tells you that they do know how to identify a *ratio* is almost certainly wrong.

26. Arthur Goodhart, *Essays in Jurisprudence and the Common Law* (CUP 1931) 11.
27. [1932] AC 567.
28. Which is somewhat ironic given that it is actually a Scottish case albeit one heard in the House of Lords!

Perhaps this demonstrates the fallacy of trying to seek the *ratio*. Bagaric and McConvill have questioned whether the Australian High Court, which operates on almost identical *stare decisis* principles, has caused itself problems by giving separate judgments rather than a single majority and minority judgment but they concluded that, in practice, it made very little difference.[29] This could lend support to the argument that we should not overly worry about what the *ratio* actually is and instead just identify the principal reasons why the judge reached his decision. Once that is understood it is possible to apply the rules of precedent to seek to persuade another judge that they are either bound, or not bound, by one or more of those reasons.

3.3.2 *Obiter dictum*

This second phrase is often shortened to *in obiter* or the *dictum* depending on the preferences of the author although the former is more usual. It is important to note at the outset that a judge will often accidentally create *obiter* statements but in other cases they will wish specifically to raise ancillary issues in this way.[30] One reason for doing this would be to indicate an opinion on how the law should move forward. Accordingly, a judge might say something like, 'whilst I have not been asked to rule on the meaning of [a particular phrase] I would, had I been asked, ruled that it bore the meaning [x]'. This can only be *obiter* because it cannot have formed the reason for the decision and so it is *in obiter*.

A difference of opinion appears to exist over whether a judge can ensure that remarks are *only* considered to be *obiter* rather than go to the *ratio* of a case. Lord Devlin in *Behrens v Bertram Mills Ltd*[31] suggested that a judge can, and the principal method of doing so would be to state that the comments are an opinion rather than a cogent statement of the law[32] whereas Megarry J has suggested that a judge has no power to prevent a decision from becoming a precedent, ie part of the *ratio*.[33]

To an extent, Megarry J is correct in that it is for subsequent courts to decide whether they are bound by a decision, but similarly when a court is trying to escape precedent (see 3.4.2) then the motivation for the statement is undoubtedly going to be a factor. One way that a judge may seek to alter a *ratio* to an *obiter* statement would be to state that the reasoning adopted is restricted to the facts of the case. Such a formula is clearly stating that the judge thinks that he foresees no general application of the principle to other cases and it should, therefore, be considered as persuasive rather than binding. But strictly speaking it remains a decision of the later court as to whether they find themselves so bound.

It is also important to note that just because comments are made *in obiter* does not mean that they are unimportant. *Obiter* comments are *persuasive* authority—ie a court should consider them even if they are not strictly bound by them. Where the statement is made by a particularly authoritative body, eg the Supreme Court or Lord Chief

---

29.   Mirko Bagaric and James McConvill, 'The High Court and the Utility of Multiple Judgments' (2005) 1 *High Court Quarterly Review* 13.
30.   Richard Cross and JW Harris, *Precedent in English Law* (4th edn, Clarendon Press 1991) 42.
31.   [1957] 2 QB 1.
32.   ibid, 25.
33.   See *In Re Showerings, Vine Products and Whiteways Ltd* [1968] 1 WLR 1381 and see Richard Cross and JW Harris, *Precedent in English Law* (4th edn, Clarendon Press 1991) 42.

Justice, then it is quite possible that the consideration that should be given to these persuasive comments is significant. Indeed it has been stated:

> *Dicta* of the highest degree of persuasiveness may often, for all practical purposes, be indistinguishable from pronouncements which must be treated as *ratio decidendi* . . . [34]

A good example of this is presented by Harris[35] when he discusses the well-known case of *Donoghue v Stevenson*.[36] The case was an appeal brought under Scottish law to the House of Lords but the House, as it not infrequently did, suggested that English and Scottish law were the same on this point. The case concerned a person who drank a bottle of ginger beer from a brown bottle and found a decomposed snail at the bottom of the glass. No contract exists between the manufacturer and the consumer (as the consumer will purchase the bottle from a shop and not the manufacturer direct) but the House permitted a duty in tort to be established to take reasonable care in the manufacture.

Donoghue v Stevenson is an important case not just for the reasoning in respect of that manufacturer but because of the comments of, in particular Lord Atkin, when he referred to his 'neighbourhood principle', where his Lordship argued that a person owed a duty to a neighbour to take reasonable care. From this statement arguably developed the law of negligence and this comment is still cited today. Yet the comments about neighbours are almost certainly *obiter* because it did not go to the decision of the case. Accordingly, it was not part of the *ratio* but these *obiter* comments have undoubtedly become more important than the *ratio* itself.

3.4 The operation of precedent

Harris argues that '[precedent] creates the expectation that, save for the intervention of the legislature, the law will remain as it is stated to be in the precedent'.[37] However, as will be seen this is not strictly true as the courts do alter precedent through its application. The earlier distinction drawn between *ratio decidendi* and *obiter dictum* is important because it goes to the heart of how precedent operates. Only the *ratio* is applied to precedent as it is this which encapsulates the law and should, according to Harris, continue to be applied. Whilst the *dictum* of a judge is important it does not set out what the law is but rather illustrates potential ways that the law could be applied or developed.

In order to examine how precedent works in practice it is necessary to identify some more of its key terms. These are all discussed in further detail later but are summarized in Table 3.3 for reference.

These terms, or more properly their actions, are the very operation of precedent as they demonstrate how a court should decide cases before it. It is important that the terms are used appropriately. One of the most common mistakes made by students is

---

34. Richard Cross and JW Harris, *Precedent in English Law* (4th edn, Clarendon Press 1991) 77.
35. ibid, 43–4.
36. [1932] AC 562 and see Richard Cross and JW Harris, *Precedent in English Law* (4th edn, Clarendon Press 1991) 43–4.
37. Bruce Harris, 'Final Appellate Courts Overruling their own "Wrong" Precedents: The Ongoing Search for Principle' (2002) 118 *Law Quarterly Review* 408, 413.

Table 3.3 The operation of precedent

Term	Meaning
Binding/bound	A court has to follow the precedent established in an earlier case
Distinguish	The court believes that the case before it is not factually the same as the precedent and accordingly is not bound by it
Not following	Where two or more conflicting precedents are presented the court chooses to follow one and not follow the remainder
Reverse	When an appeal succeeds the decision of the lower court in that case is reversed
Overrule	A higher court (or the Supreme Court) alters a precedent; the original precedent ceases to be good law

to use the term 'overrule' when this is not, in fact, what has happened. It is far more common for a precedent to be escaped by either distinguishing or not following it. In neither situation has there been a change of law—the precedent continues to exist and if another case arises then the courts should be bound by it. Where a precedent is overruled, however, then the law changes—the legal principle that was encapsulated by the precedent no longer applies and where another case arises on these issues the courts cannot follow the original precedent any more but must now follow the principle enunciated by the overruling case which becomes, therefore, the new precedent. It is also important to note that not every court has the power to overrule precedents (see 3.4.1) and an extremely common mistake is for a student to say that a court has overruled a precedent when it has no power to do so.

3.4.1 **Bound by precedent**

If the notion of *stare decisis* is that decisions continue ('let the decision stand') then that means there must be a system of ensuring that judges do not contradict the earlier decisions. This is done by saying that a court is *bound* to follow the previous decision (ie they have to). Obviously if this was strictly enforced then law would never alter and so the system of binding authorities is more complicated as it is necessary to understand which courts are bound and under what circumstances. A higher court, as is seen in Table 3.3, can overrule a lower court and therefore this becomes the new binding process. The question therefore becomes who is bound by whom?

3.4.1.1 **Supreme Court**

The simplest court to deal with is the Supreme Court. As the highest court in the English Legal System its decisions bind all the courts below it unless they are able to escape the precedent through distinguishing (see 3.4.2).

The House of Lords (which preceded the Supreme Court) decided in 1966 that it did not consider itself bound by its previous decisions.[38] More than this, it has claimed the power to overrule its earlier decisions.[39] What this means will be discussed later but, in

---

38.   *Practice Statement (HL: Judicial Precedent)* [1966] 1 WLR 1234.

39.   See, for example, *R v G and R* [2004] 1 AC 1034 where the House of Lords expressly overruled the case of *R v Caldwell* [1982] AC 341 ([2004] 1 AC 1034, 1055 (Lord Bingham)).

essence, 'overruling' means that the earlier precedent ceases to exist and the new decision forms the continuing precedent.

The justification for assuming the power to depart from its own decisions was undoubtedly to help bring clarity to the law since previously the House was either not permitted to depart from its own rulings meaning that no matter how sympathetic they were only legislation could remedy the fault or they would do so by distinguishing previous cases and accordingly leave a number of possible precedents 'active'.

The *Practice Statement* did not give the House of Lords complete freedom and they continued to view decisions as *ordinarily* binding on themselves.[40] The House did, for example, on a number of occasions note that the fact a decision was merely 'wrong' was not enough to justify the use of the statement.[41] Some commentators suggest that distinguishing should be used wherever possible.[42] Harris argues that this is needed to make the law more certain and predictable[43] but given that he expressly includes precedents that were decided *per incuriam* or are distinguishable because of social movements it is difficult to see why leaving these decisions 'live' would be preferable. It could be argued that simply distinguishing them and labelling them as *per incuriam* etc would be sufficient to inform the lower courts not to follow them. Nevertheless, whilst this may be true, certainty and predictability are not achieved by refusing to tinker with the law unless absolutely necessary, but rather by ending bad decisions. Overruling those types of precedent rather than merely not following them would ensure that no court could resurrect them and would accordingly bring about certainty in the law.

In *Austin v Southwark London Borough Council*[44] the Supreme Court stated that it had assumed the power put forward in the *Practice Statement*. Lord Hope, the Deputy President of the Supreme Court, stated that the Supreme Court had not found it necessary to reissue the statement since it formed part of the ordinary jurisprudence of the court that Parliament had transferred to the Supreme Court.[45] Accordingly, it is clear that the Supreme Court will act in the same way as the House of Lords, ie it will claim the power to depart from its own decisions (or the decisions of the House of Lords) but will do so only when necessary, taking account of the consequences that this can have for the certainty of law. This has been seen in *R v Jogee*,[46] where the Supreme Court departed from the previous decision of the House of Lords in *R v Powell (Anthony); R v English*[47] (as well as disapproving a Privy Council decision[48]) in relation to joint enterprise. In *R v Powell (Anthony); R v English*,[49] the House of Lords held that foresight of an act as a possible incident of the joint enterprise was sufficient to make the secondary party liable. However, in *R v Jogee*, the Supreme Court departed from this, holding that 'foresight was not to be equated with intent to assist' in joint enterprise cases, but rather 'the correct approach is to treat it as *evidence* of intent'.[50]

---

40. Richard Cross and JW Harris, *Precedent in English Law* (4th edn, Clarendon Press 1991) 136.
41. See, for example, *Knuller (Publishing, Printing and Promotions) Ltd v DPP* [1973] AC 435.
42. Bruce Harris, 'Final Appellate Courts Overruling their own "Wrong" Precedents: The Ongoing Search for Principle' (2002) 118 *Law Quarterly Review* 408, 422.
43. ibid, 420–1.
44. [2011] 1 AC 355.
45. ibid, 370.
46. [2016] UKSC 8.
47. [1991] 1 AC 1.
48. *Chan Wing-Siu v The Queen* [1985] AC 168.
49. [1991] 1 AC 1.
50. [2016] UKSC 8 [87] (Lord Hughes and Lord Toulson JJSC).

3.4.1.2 **Court of Appeal**

The Court of Appeal is second in precedence in the English Legal System and is the more usual appellate court (the Supreme Court hearing only a highly limited number of appeals). The simple rule for the Court of Appeal is that it is bound by the Supreme Court and it binds all courts lower than it. Where the complication arises is whether the Court of Appeal is bound by itself.

The leading authority on the matter is *Young v Bristol Aeroplane Co Ltd*[51] where the Court of Appeal stated that it was bound by its own decisions subject to the following exceptions:

1. Where there are two conflicting decisions of the Court of Appeal it may choose which to follow.

2. Where the previous decision of the Court of Appeal, even if not expressly overruled, conflicts with a Supreme Court or House of Lords decision.

3. Where the decision was made *per incuriam*.

Others argue that the second ground of *Young* must have been expanded to include the situation where the previous decision of the Court of Appeal conflicts with the European Court of Justice[52] and this is undoubtedly correct. The term *per incuriam* means 'through want of care' and covers those situations where a court neglected to consider an issue that it should have, eg a statutory provision or a binding precedent.

Davis v Johnson

The ruling in *Young v Bristol Aeroplanes* continued for some decades before it came up against Lord Denning MR, who was arguably one of the most influential judges of the past century. Lord Denning had been a Lord of Appeal in Ordinary but had accepted the Master of the Rolls position in part because he believed the Court of Appeal was more influential than the House of Lords due to the number of cases it heard. Lord Denning did not like the fact that the Court of Appeal was bound by itself whereas the House of Lords was not. This dislike culminated in the case of *Davis v Johnson*[53] where Lord Denning empanelled a full Court of Appeal, namely five judges, including Sir George Baker, the President of the Family Division. The case concerned a non-molestation order made under the *Domestic Violence and Matrimonial Proceedings Act 1976*. Previous Court of Appeal decisions, most notably *B v B*,[54] had construed this Act in a way that a majority of the court disagreed with[55] but, according to the rule in *Young v Bristol Aeroplane*, the Court of Appeal should have been bound by that decision. However, a majority of the Court of Appeal held that they could choose not to follow the precedent.[56] Lord Denning sought to argue that the Court of Appeal should have the same right to depart from its own decisions as the House of Lords reserved to itself in the *Practice Direction* of 1966. He based his argument on the fact that the House of Lords may never get an opportunity to reverse a bad law because of the cost

---

51. [1944] KB 718.
52. Colin Manchester and David Salter, *Manchester and Salter on Exploring the Law: The Dynamics of Precedent and Statutory Interpretation* (4th edn, Sweet & Maxwell 2011) 18.
53. [1978] 2 WLR 182.
54. [1978] 2 WLR 160.
55. Only one judge, Cumming-Bruce LJ, dissented from this part of the case.
56. Goff LJ joined Cumming-Bruce LJ in dissenting from this decision but he expressly stated that he did so reluctantly as he disagreed with the original precedent.

of litigation and leave requirements.[57] He also argued that where a ruling was obviously wrong this placed the lower courts in a quandary because an appeal may take a year to be heard by the House but until judgment is handed down by the House the lower courts would be obliged to rule on matters it knows are wrong.[58]

Lord Denning attempted to argue that the doctrine of precedent was not a legal principle but rather a custom of the courts.[59] This would be important because if it was mere custom then courts would have the power to alter the principle whereas, of course, if it was a legal rule then *stare decisis* would bind itself, ie only the House of Lords could rule as to whether the Court of Appeal had the authority to depart from its own judgments. He was joined in this by Sir George Baker P who thought that the decisions could be distinguished but argued that this was itself unsatisfactory because it meant a lower court could still consider them valid precedent when his Lordship believed they were wrong. Sir George Baker suggested that the new exception should be slightly narrower by arguing that a new exception should be granted where a decision is wrong and appears contrary to the intentions of Parliament.[60] The President appeared to be trying to extend the *per incuriam* rule by stating that it goes against Parliament's will but it cannot come within the rule as of right because the provision was (presumably) brought to the court's attention initially.

The matter proceeded to the House of Lords[61] and their Lordships wasted little time in stating that the Court of Appeal was wrong to believe that it was not bound by itself, with Lord Diplock even suggesting that Lord Denning MR, had 'conducted what may be described . . . as a one-man crusade with the object of freeing the Court of Appeal from the shackles . . . of *stare decisis*'.[62] His Lordship continued by stating that whilst there was a justification in a final appellate court to have a discretion to right obvious wrongs, there is less justification for this in a lesser court where certainty of law should be a primary consideration[63] before concluding:

> In my opinion, this House should take this occasion to re-affirm expressly, unequivocally [*sic*] and unanimously that the rule laid down in the *Bristol Aeroplane* case . . . as to *stare decisis* is still binding on the Court of Appeal.[64]

This invitation was taken up by every other member of the House in their speeches. Lord Salmon tackled the argument of Lord Denning that the costs of litigation and leave requirements may lead to an injustice by commenting that the Court of Appeal itself had the power to grant leave to appeal and could order that the costs are paid by the Exchequer.[65] This is an important point and recognizes the inherent powers of the court. The Court of Appeal did not believe that leave could be granted because leave had been refused in the earlier cases but this misses the point that where the court believes that its earlier decision was wrong this adds weight to that ground of appeal and introduces a public policy argument in favour of leave.

57. *Davis v Johnson* [1978] 2 WLR 182, 194–5.
58. ibid, 196.
59. ibid, 197–8.
60. ibid, 206.
61. *Davis v Johnson* [1979] AC 264.
62. ibid, 325.
63. ibid, 326.
64. ibid, 328.
65. ibid, 344.

To an extent, Lord Denning did have a point regarding the custom or law issue. When the Court of Appeal created its rules of precedent in *Young v Bristol Aeroplane* it must have done so *in obiter*. The actual dispute that led to the litigation in that case had nothing to do with precedent and the comments on precedent did not go to the heart of the reasons for the decision, meaning that it could not form part of the *ratio*. Similarly the House of Lords when rebuking the Court of Appeal in *Davis v Johnson* must also have been speaking *in obiter* as it did not go to the heart of the case. Indeed if one looks solely at the judgment of the courts, the law reports record that the House of Lords *affirmed* the decision of the Court of Appeal even though we are discussing it *reversing* the Court of Appeal in terms of precedent. It has already been noted that *obiter* is not strictly binding so to that extent Lord Denning was probably correct.

However, the House of Lords decision in *Davis v Johnson* was inevitable and would probably have arisen through an appeal in any event where the matter could have been dealt with as a *ratio*. It may have been preferable for the House of Lords to clarify this situation by issuing a Practice Direction but the alternative construction is that this is another example of Harris's comment that some *obiter* comments can be as powerful as a *ratio*. Certainly the decision of the House of Lords in *Davis v Johnson* as to the proper function of the Court of Appeal was plain and it did not lead to the Court of Appeal making such a blatant attempt at escaping precedent again.

An emerging exception?

However, some commentators argue that although the Court of Appeal has never expressly challenged the principle in the way that occurred in *Davis v Johnson* they have begun to assert an additional exception to the *Young v Bristol Aeroplane* case, that of declining to follow a case where it was 'manifestly wrong'.[66] The argument stems from the case of *Cave v Robinson Jarvis & Rolf (A Firm)*[67] where counsel argued that the Court of Appeal was not bound by a previous decision of a two-judge bench of the Court of Appeal. It had long since been recognized that the Court of Appeal was not bound to follow a decision made on an interlocutory appeal where the full court argued the case was manifestly wrong.[68] The Court of Appeal declined, in *Cave*, to rule on this proposition principally because it believed there was no longer any difference between two-, three-, and five-judge benches of the court and in part because it was not convinced that the decision was 'manifestly wrong'.

Prime and Scanlan argue, however, that the *obiter* comments made in the case demonstrate that the principle of 'manifestly wrong' is a new exception to *Young v Bristol Aeroplane* and that the court had, albeit *in obiter*, suggested that it had a wider application than merely interlocutory appeals.[69] They also suggested that support for their proposition could be gathered from the case of *Limb v Union Jack Removals Ltd*[70] where Brooke LJ stated, inter alia:

> Any departure from a previous decision of the court is in principle undesirable and should only be considered if the previous decision is manifestly wrong.[71]

66. Terence Prime and Gary Scanlan, 'Stare decisis and the Court of Appeal: Judicial Confusion and Judicial Reform' (2004) 23 *Civil Justice Quarterly* 212, 220.
67. [2002] 1 WLR 581.
68. *Boys v Chaplin* [1968] 2 QB 1.
69. Terence Prime and Gary Scanlan, 'Stare decisis and the Court of Appeal: Judicial Confusion and Judicial Reform' (2004) 23 *Civil Justice Quarterly* 212, 220–1.
70. [1998] 1 WLR 1354.
71. ibid, 1365.

The difficulty with this is that it is not certain that Brooke LJ was creating a new exception. This line follows a rehearsal of the reasons when the Court of Appeal may depart from its own decisions and was immediately preceded by this passage:

> The doctrine [of precedent] does not extend to a case where, if different arguments had been placed before the court or if different material had been placed before it, it might have reached a different conclusion.

In this context it would appear that Brooke LJ was arguably developing the *per incuriam* ground. Admittedly, the reference to alternative arguments would widen the doctrine further than it has traditionally been but reference to other material does appear to be in line with that exception. More problematic for Prime and Scanlan is that they argue that a majority in *Cave v Robinson* agreed that a new exception exists but the case does not necessarily say that. Whilst Potter LJ does appear to accept that the rule in *Boys v Chaplin* may still exist he is less than convinced that it has any practical modern use or that it may be analogous to the current 'leave' hearings; Sedley LJ, who Prime and Scanlan argue also approved of such a distinction, is less certain. The language used by Sedley LJ is not particularly transparent but his Lordship expressly states: 'the solution which this court felt able to adopt in *Boys v Chaplin* would not be adopted in similar circumstances today.'[72] Whilst this does not, of course, say that the exception is closed it does suggest that it is unlikely that it will ever be used.

The position does appear therefore to be somewhat transient although Prime and Scanlan argue that any new exception based on 'manifestly wrong' would be inappropriate.[73] Given the obtuse statements by the Court of Appeal, upon which their hypothesis is based, it would seem more likely that the Court of Appeal is bound by its own decisions subject to the exceptions identified in *Young v Bristol Aeroplanes*.

The Criminal Division

The decision in *Young v Bristol Aeroplanes* was a decision of the Court of Appeal (Civil Division) and accordingly it could be argued that it only bound that Division. However, the Criminal Division has stated that it too is *normally* bound by its own decisions subject to the exceptions set out in *Young*[74] but with an additional exception that arises as a result of the unique cases that the Court of Appeal (Criminal Division) hears. Given that invariably a person who appeals to the Court of Appeal in criminal matters is incarcerated in gaol, the court has, perhaps not unreasonably, taken the approach that where a decision is obviously wrong and would otherwise lead to the appellant remaining in gaol then *stare decisis* should be departed from as even awaiting an expedited Supreme Court ruling would lead to a situation where a person has been deprived of their liberty unnecessarily.

The 'liberty' rule has to be considered exceptional, however, because if there were any area of law where certainty would be desirable it would be the criminal law[75] and the courts appear to have recognized this with Lord Diplock saying:

> [A]lthough the Criminal Division of the Court of Appeal is not so strictly bound by its own decisions as is the Civil Division, its liberty to depart from a precedent which

87

---

72. *Cave v Robinson Jarvis and Rolf* [2002] 1 WLR 581, 595.
73. Terence Prime and Gary Scanlan, '*Stare decisis* and the Court of Appeal: Judicial Confusion and Judicial Reform' (2004) 23 *Civil Justice Quarterly* 212, 222–4.
74. See the comments of May LJ in *R v Spencer* [1985] QB 771, 779.
75. Rupert Cross and JW Harris, *Precedent in English Law* (4th edn, Clarendon Press 1991) 117

it is convinced is erroneous is restricted to cases where the departure is in favour of the accused.[76]

The latest pronouncement by the Criminal Division was contained in *R v Simpson*[77] where the Court of Appeal (Criminal Division) stated:

> We consider a degree of discretion remains in this court to decide whether a previous decision should be treated as a binding precedent in future or not when there are grounds for saying that the decision is wrong.[78]

Moreover, the court suggested that the 'constitution of the court may be relevant'[79] and Lord Woolf expressly drew attention to the fact that this was a five-judge bench of the court. This appears to contradict earlier decisions and the custom of the Civil Division where it has been held that the number of judges is irrelevant: the authority flows from the court not the numbers. This is certainly the accepted position and the remarks of Lord Woolf bear a striking similarity to the approach of Lord Denning in *Davis v Johnson*.

Arguably *Simpson* concerns the *per incuriam* rule in that it discusses whether all the relevant authority was before the earlier court. To some degree this mirrors the suggestion of Brooke LJ in *Limb v Union Jack Removals Ltd* which suggests that the Court of Appeal is beginning to push the boundaries of precedent once more. The exception of *per incuriam* has previously been restricted to those situations where the court was not referred to relevant statutory material or a binding precedent but both *Limb* and *Simpson* appear to suggest that where alternative arguments could, or rather should, have been submitted this may justify departure from the precedent. *Simpson* is also important because it appears to contradict the approach in *Merriman* in that in this case the decision to depart from precedent was not favourable to the defendant. There is no question that the ruling in *Simpson* was against the interests of defendants and yet the Court of Appeal still departed from precedent.

That said, the limits of *Simpson* should be recognized. In *R v Varma*[80] the Court of Appeal declined to follow *Simpson* when ruling on a matter relating to confiscation orders and their applicability when a defendant has been given a discharge. The facts are not important but the court found itself bound by an earlier decision in *R v Clarke*[81] although this was the only decision that referred to this point (ie there was no conflict of authorities) and the judges of that court had been referred to all the relevant authority. Whilst the Court of Appeal in *Varma* was prepared to concede that *Clarke* may be wrong, it stated that it was bound by it and that *Simpson* did not apply where there was no conflict of interest and where 'it was considered in meticulous detail, and given the closest possible attention'.[82] Whilst *Varma* was reversed in the Supreme Court,[83] it was not reversed in respect of the *Simpson* point and therefore it remains a case of interest on that point.

---

76. *R v Merriman* [1973] AC 584, 605.
77. [2004] QB 118.
78. [2004] QB 118 (QB) 131 (Woolf LCJ).
79. ibid.
80. [2010] EWCA Crim 1575.
81. [2010] 1 WLR 223.
82. [2010] EWCA Crim 1575 [31].
83. [2012] UKSC 42.

It appears therefore that, rather than attempt a full-frontal attack on precedent itself, the Court of Appeal has decided to attempt to broaden the recognized exceptions. The easiest exception to broaden is the *per incuriam* rule and both divisions of the court have sought to tackle this. More importantly the Criminal Division has decided to broaden its approach to errors and widen the meaning of injustice to include a guilty person escaping justice rather than just an innocent person wrongly imprisoned. There appears no evidence that the Supreme Court wish to be as rigid as the House of Lords were in *Davis v Johnson*, with the Supreme Court having had sufficient time to comment on this issue if they so wish. It would seem likely that their silence can be taken as affirmation of the minor change brought about by *Simpson*.

↻ QUESTION FOR REFLECTION

Read *Davis v Johnson* (1978) and also *R v Simpson* (2004). Do you think that the Court of Appeal should be allowed to depart from its own precedent where it believes it is wrong? Few cases reach the Supreme Court (the number of cases has increased in the last few years but there have never been more than seventy-five) and even fewer cases relate to the criminal law. Is it realistic to suggest that only the Supreme Court can correct mistaken precedent?

◀) LISTEN TO THE PODCAST

For guidance on how to answer this question and a discussion of the main issues, listen to the author's podcast on the online resources:
www.oup.com/he/gillespie-weare8e

89

3.4.1.3 The High Court

The High Court of Justice is next in the hierarchy. Whilst there are three principal divisions (Queen's Bench, Family, and Chancery) together with specialist courts (Commercial, Admiralty, etc)[84] the other significant court to examine is the Administrative Court, which has a supervisory jurisdiction. Of the three divisions the Family Division also requires special attention when it deals with the welfare of children for public policy reasons akin to the Criminal Division of the High Court.

Non-supervisory jurisdiction

The High Court sits below the Supreme Court and Court of Appeal in the hierarchy and is accordingly bound by their decisions. It binds all lower courts although its principal binding role is in respect of its supervisory jurisdiction (see 'Divisional Court').

When the court is not sitting in its supervisory capacity (ie it is not sitting as either an appellate court or hearing a judicial review case but is rather adjudicating on litigation brought between two parties) then its previous decisions are persuasive but are not binding on itself. That is to say that a judge will normally follow the decision for reasons of consistency but they are able to depart from the decision should they wish to and do not need to find a reason like the Court of Appeal must.[85]

---

84. Although these are technically part of the other divisions. For example, the Admiralty Court is part of the Chancery Division and the Technology Court is part of the Queen's Bench Division although they are treated for everyday purposes as separate.

85. See *Police Authority for Huddersfield v Watson* [1947] KB 842.

Where children are concerned it is sometimes suggested that the Family Division adopts a more relaxed attitude to the notion of precedent although Wilson J speaking extrajudicially has suggested this is not strictly true.[86] The latitude is said to arise from the fact that s 1(1) *Children Act 1989* states that where a matter relates to the upbringing of a child then the welfare of the child is to be the paramount consideration. In other words nothing is supposed to be more important than the welfare of the child. That does not mean that courts have the right to disregard *stare decisis*, however, something reinforced by Wilson J and evident from cases where matters in the Family Division have been litigated before the appellate courts.[87] However, the welfare principle does allow some leeway in that every case that involves the upbringing of a child will necessarily have individual facts and accordingly it is perhaps easier for the Family Division to distinguish (see 'Divisional Court') precedents than other divisions may find it. However, where a clear principle of law is enunciated by the appellate courts then the Family Division must follow it.

Divisional Court

Where the High Court is sitting in a supervisory capacity then matters become more uncertain. The supervisory capacity is ordinarily exercised in the Administrative Court where the challenge is to a public body but all divisions of the High Court exercise supervisory jurisdiction although they would ordinarily do so as a Divisional Court, ie where more than one judge is sitting. The Administrative Court always used to sit as a Divisional Court but increasingly it is sitting with only a single judge. Even then, however, it is exercising supervisory jurisdiction.

It was always thought that when the High Court is exercising its supervisory jurisdiction then the rules of precedent change and the court is treated in much the same way as the Court of Appeal. The High Court, including a Divisional Court, is quite clearly below the Court of Appeal in hierarchy so it is bound to follow decisions of that court but it was generally thought that it was bound by *its own* decisions unless the exceptions in *Young v Bristol Aeroplanes* apply.[88] However, this has not been conclusively proved and in *R v Greater Manchester Coroner, ex p Tal*[89] the Divisional Court stated that when it was acting in a supervisory role at first instance (rather than when it was acting as an appellate court in, for example, civil or certain criminal cases) it was in no different position than the (ordinary) High Court.

Accordingly, it would now seem that the general rule for the High Court is that whenever it sits as a court of first instance then no binding precedent is set, but when it sits in an appellate capacity binding precedent does apply, something confirmed, albeit probably *in obiter*, by Laws J in *C (A Minor) v DPP*.[90]

3.4.1.4 Family Court

Chapter 6 will discuss the creation of the Family Court. Prior to its creation family matters were heard either by the High Court (Family Division), county court, or Family Proceedings Court (the equivalent of the magistrates' court). However, the

---

86.   See 'The Misnomer of Family Law', The Atkin Lecture 2002 by Hon Mr Justice Wilson.
87.   Perhaps the most notable of these decisions is *Re H (Minors)(Sexual Abuse: Standard of Proof)* [1996] AC 563 where the House of Lords conclusively held that the standard of proof to be used in care proceedings where sexual abuse is alleged was the civil standard but that where a serious allegation was made more evidence would be required to meet this standard. The Family Division has followed this ruling in accordance with *stare decisis*.
88.   See *Police Authority for Huddersfield v Watson* (discussed earlier) and *Younghusband v Luftig* [1949] 2 KB 354.
89.   [1985] QB 67.
90.   [1994] 3 WLR 888, 898.

Family Court created a court that acts across all levels. So there is 'one court' albeit staffed with judges of different rank.

Section 31C(2) *Matrimonial and Family Proceedings Act 1984* (MFPA 1984) (inserted by the *Crime and Courts Act 2013*) specifically addresses the issue of hierarchy and binding precedent. It states that a decision of a certain category of judge is to be followed by an inferior judge. This can only be considered to be the creation of a binding precedent. The judges who create this precedent are:

- a puisne judge, judge of the Court of Appeal, a Head of Division (including the Lord Chief Justice and Master of the Rolls), Senior President of Tribunals, or a person sitting as a deputy judge of the High Court,
- a former judge of the Court of Appeal, or
- a former judge of the High Court.

In other words, while there is a single Family Court it would seem that the decision of a High Court judge (including a deputy judge) sitting in the Family Court creates a precedent that lower-ranked judges must follow. Interestingly s 31C(2) only talks about lesser-ranked judges and therefore presumably the decision of a puisne judge sitting in the Family Court does not bind another puisne judge sitting in the Family Court.

What s 31C does not address is the relationship between the Family Division and the Family Court. Section 31I states that proceedings can be transferred instead to the High Court which would imply that the High Court is superior to the Family Court but it is not clear that it is for the purposes of precedent. Section 31C referred to 'decisions of the Family Court', so what should a circuit judge do when sitting in the Family Court and she is referred by counsel to a decision of the High Court (Family Division)? The Family Court can exercise the powers of the High Court[91] but it is obviously not the High Court. Prudence would indicate that the circuit judge follows the precedent but it is less than clear that he is obliged to do so. It is unlikely that a puisne judge sitting in the Family Court would consider himself bound by a decision of the Family Division (save potentially where it was sitting in its supervisory capacity) but again there is no rule stating that this is the case.

3.4.1.5 Crown Court and inferior courts

It will be seen that the Crown Court is not technically an inferior court[92] but for the purposes of precedent it is de facto an inferior court. No court below the High Court sets a precedent for anyone. Similarly, decisions of each court are not binding on other divisions of that court although it has been said that decisions of a High Court judge sitting in the Crown Court are persuasive despite the fact that Ashworth argues the status of the judge should be irrelevant.[93]

The position of the Crown Court is interesting because it is unquestionably higher than the magistrates' court and indeed appeals take place from the magistrates' court to the Crown Court. However, any decision reached by that court is restricted to the facts and does not set a precedent. It is for this reason that decisions of law are more frequently taken to the Divisional Court, which does bind all magistrates' courts and Crown Courts sitting in its appellate capacity.

91. *Matrimonial and Family Proceedings Act 1984*, s 31E.
92. *Senior Courts Act 1981*, s 45(1).
93. Andrew Ashworth, 'The Binding Effect of Crown Court Decisions' [1980] *Criminal Law Review* 402, 403.

3.4.1.6 **The Privy Council**

The Privy Council is in an unusual position in terms of precedent. Its current jurisdiction does not include English law (as the *Constitutional Reform Act 2005* transferred the last remaining UK jurisdiction of the Council to the Supreme Court) and thus it technically has no place in the English Legal System. It is, however, worth noting its place within precedent, albeit briefly.

Precedent within the Council

The Privy Council has always adopted a relatively lax attitude to precedent in respect of its own decisions, considering them only to be persuasive rather than binding.[94] That said, it is also clear that the Council appreciates that certainty is desirable and will therefore seek to follow its earlier decisions where possible.[95]

Precedent within the English Legal System

Whilst not strictly speaking part of the English Legal System, the Council is in a peculiar position in that those who sit on the judicial committee are usually Justices of the Supreme Court[96] and accordingly their decisions must, at the very least, be considered highly persuasive.

It has been stated:

> It is possible to refer to cases in which a decision of the Privy Council has not been followed by an English judge of first instance, but it is also possible to point to cases in which a decision of the Privy Council has been persistently preferred to a decision of the Court of Appeal, although the decision of that court has never been overruled.[97]

In other words, Harris is arguing that the Court of Appeal has, in some cases, used a decision of the Privy Council as a method of invoking the *per incuriam* exception in *Young v Bristol Aeroplanes*. This should be relatively uncontroversial as the Privy Council, whilst not strictly part of the English Legal System, is a senior court and its decisions warrant investigation. The Court of Appeal should be able to consider whether the decision reached in that case alters the understanding of the issues they have previously adjudicated.

Where the position becomes more complicated, however, is what happens when a decision of the Privy Council conflicts with a decision of the Supreme Court or House of Lords? Theoretically since the Supreme Court is the most senior domestic court in the English Legal System the Court of Appeal should follow it as precedent but see *R v Mohammed*.[98] The partial defence of provocation[99] entertained the courts for many years prior to its repeal but *R v Smith*[100] appeared to resolve one central part of this partial defence, namely what subjective characteristics could be imputed to the reasonable man used in the test for provocation. The position seemed clear but in *Attorney-General for Jersey v Holley*[101] the Privy Council stated that it thought *Smith* was wrong.

---

94. Michael Littlewood, 'The Privy Council, the Source of Income and *stare decisis*' (2004) 2 *British Tax Review* 121, 122.
95. ibid, 123.
96. Although it is not restricted to them and certain foreign senior judges and all Lord Justices of Appeal are entitled to sit on the judicial committee.
97. Rupert Cross and JW Harris, *Precedent in English Law* (4th edn, Clarendon Press 1991) 102.
98. [2005] EWCA Crim 1880.
99. *Homicide Act 1957*, s 3. Now repealed by the *Coroners and Justice Act 2009*.
100. [2001] AC 146.
101. [2005] AC 580.

Theoretically this was merely persuasive precedent and the Court of Appeal, together with all courts in the English Legal System, would be required to follow *Smith* but the Court of Appeal in *Mohammed* refused to do so and argued that the position in English law was that put forward by the majority in *Holley*.[102] This decision has been followed by other decisions of the Court of Appeal.[103]

It is important to note that this is not a situation where the Court of Appeal has decided that its own decision is *per incuriam* but rather it is making a decision as respects a precedent that it should be bound by, namely the House of Lords decision in *Smith*. It would have been tidier for the court to send the matter to the House of Lords, and it could have done so by granting leave. It is important to note that this was not a case where the liberty of the appellant was at stake (see 3.4.1.2) as the appeal in *Mohammed* was dismissed (as it was in *Shickle*) and thus it would have been tidier to do so. If *stare decisis* is supposed to bring certainty then following the decision of a court outside of the English Legal System is contrary to that principle and if a future comparable situation arises it would be tidier to send the matter to the Supreme Court so that the normal rules of precedent apply.

In *Willers v Gubay*[104] the Supreme Court considered the role of the Privy Council in the system of precedent, and held that it is possible for the Privy Council to depart from a House of Lords or Supreme Court decision:

> There will be appeals to the JCPC where a party wishes to challenge the correctness of an earlier decision of the House of Lords or the Supreme Court, or of the Court of Appeal on a point of English law, and where the JCPC decides that the House of Lords or Supreme Court, or, as the case may be, the Court of Appeal, was wrong. It would plainly be unfortunate in practical terms if, in such circumstances, the JCPC could never effectively decide that courts of England and Wales should follow the JCPC decision rather than the earlier decision of the House of Lords or Supreme Court, or of the Court of Appeal. In my view, the way to reconcile this practical concern with the principled approach identified . . . above is to take advantage of the fact that the President of the JCPC is the same person as the President of the Supreme Court, and the fact that panels of the JCPC normally consist of Justices of the Supreme Court.[105]

Where a House of Lords or Supreme Court decision is to be challenged, an appropriate Privy Council can be convened and:

> they can, if they think it appropriate, not only decide that the earlier decision of the House of Lords or Supreme Court, or of the Court of Appeal, was wrong, but also can expressly direct that domestic courts should treat the decision of the JCPC as representing the law of England and Wales.[106]

3.4.2 **Distinguishing**

Whilst a court is bound to follow precedent it is sometimes possible to escape precedent. To an extent this was discussed earlier when it was decided that courts were able to fail to follow a precedent (ie not follow) either because it was decided *per incuriam*

---

102.   [2005] EWCA Crim 1880 [42].
103.   See, for example, *R v Shickle* [2005] EWCA Crim 1881.
104.   [2016] UKSC 44.
105.   ibid, [19] (Lord Neuberger).
106.   ibid, [21] (Lord Neuberger).

or because there were two conflicting decisions. The most usual form of escaping precedent, however, is to distinguish a case. It has already been noted that only the *ratio decidendi* binds a court and this only applies therefore where the facts of a case would lead to the same *ratio* being applied. The concept of distinguishing is where a court argues that the *material* facts of a case are different and accordingly the *ratio* will not apply but rather a different reasoning must be adopted.

Where a judge decides to distinguish a case he should normally explain why the precedent is being distinguished and this reasoning will be subject to criticism by later courts and where the decision is itself appealed it could be reversed by the appellate court.

It can be argued that the concept of distinguishing can be taken further and need not be restricted to factual differences but could also include situations where 'societal factual circumstances have changed since [the precedent] was originally decided'.[107] If this is correct then it would allow courts to develop the law in a way that reacts to society progressing and not require such developments to be constrained by the appellate system.

3.4.3 Overruling

So far the discussion on precedent has concerned situations where a court has either followed precedent or has escaped it. The final issue that needs to be examined is where a precedent ceases to exist because it is overruled. One principal justification for using the power to overrule authority is where the precedent was decided *per incuriam* or its application has left the law unworkable.[108] In both of these situations the court can safely overrule a case knowing that it will bring certainty to the law, something that is supposedly at the heart of *stare decisis*. Similarly, where a decision has created conflicting precedents then simply following one authority may not lead to certainty arising since the absence of overruling the other could mean that a court is still able to 'resurrect' the other potentially increasing uncertainty. It is for this reason that in *Young v Bristol Aeroplanes* it was said that where the Court of Appeal chooses between two conflicting earlier decisions of the court the one it does not follow is overruled.[109] Where a difficulty arises, however, is where the court does not consciously attempt to reconcile all the previous decisions as this could lead to an argument that the judgment was made *per incuriam*. It is therefore incumbent on the court to state expressly that it is choosing between conflicting decisions and stating which case is therefore overruled.

Perhaps the more usual method of overruling is when either a more senior court than that which created the precedent or the Supreme Court overturns the precedent. It is important to note the terminology here. The precedent, ie the case that created the *ratio* that was applied in the case which forms the appeal, is *overruled*. The actual case that is being litigated on appeal will be *reversed*.

The simplest situation is where a more senior court overrules a precedent of a lower court (eg Court of Appeal overruling the High Court, Supreme Court overruling the Court of Appeal). In these situations the court has the right to overrule a case and once this has been done then the case that is being litigated forms the *new* precedent with the old one ceasing to be good law although any *dicta* in the court may continue to be relevant.[110]

---

107.   Bruce Harris, 'Final Appellate Courts Overruling their own "Wrong" Precedents: The Ongoing Search for Principle' (2002) 118 *Law Quarterly Review* 408, 411.

108.   ibid, 416.

109.   [1994] KB 718, 728.

110.   Rupert Cross and JW Harris, *Precedent in English Law* (4th edn, Clarendon Press 1991) 128.

Example Overruling

The (fictional) case of *Smith v Jones* is before the Court of Appeal (Civil Division). The judge at first instance argued that he was bound by the earlier case of *Brown v Bloggs* which was heard by the Divisional Court. The Court of Appeal decides that *Brown v Bloggs* was wrong and that it should no longer be the law. It therefore overrules *Brown v Bloggs* and that case may no longer be cited.

A different judge in the High Court is hearing a case that is very similar to *Brown v Bloggs* and *Smith v Jones*. The judge is bound to follow the Court of Appeal decision in *Smith v Jones*, which is now the only precedent available.

A difficulty arises when the superior court does not state that the case is overruled but merely does not follow the lower precedent (which of course they do not need to) or distinguishes it. The higher court may, in *dicta*, cast doubt on it but without overruling it; then presumably it continues to be a precedent. It will be noted that one of the grounds in *Young v Bristol Aeroplanes* was that it was inconsistent with a House of Lords decision and thus it might be that the court could escape the doubted precedent. But this action itself would not overrule the case and it could mean that the position becomes more confused with an additional precedent being created without any being overruled. This can cause difficulty:

> A High Court judge of first instance when confronted with a decision of the Court of Appeal which has not been expressly overruled by a later House of Lords' case may cease to be bound by it because the House of Lords considered that the Court of Appeal misinterpreted the authorities . . . The judge is then not obliged to follow the Court of Appeal, but he is not bound to dissent from their conclusion. The previous decision is undermined rather than directly overruled.[111]

If the purpose of *stare decisis* is to introduce certainty into the law then it is obvious that situations such as that described above would not be helpful and yet this is a not an uncommon outcome. It is submitted that it is incumbent on the superior courts, particularly the Supreme Court, to take care when they discuss authorities and to use their power to overrule a case where they believe it is necessary—merely doubting its application but leaving it open to be used again is a recipe for confusion in law.

<> Summary

In this chapter we have examined how the courts use case law. In particular we have noted:

- The courts operate a system of precedent known as *stare decisis* ('let the decision stand').
- The type of precedent set depends on the court sitting, with the most complicated rules arguably occurring in the Court of Appeal. As a general rule of thumb, the court setting the precedent will bind every court below it.
- Only the *ratio decidendi* of a case forms the precedent. Any other aspects of the case are known as the *obiter dicta*.

111. ibid, 129–30.

- Whilst every case must have a *ratio* there need not necessarily be a single *ratio*. Also, identifying the *ratio* can be quite complicated especially where there is more than one judgment.

- Where a superior court changes the ruling of a lower court this is called 'reversing'. A decision is only 'overruled' when the court is saying that the precedent was wrong and should not be followed.

- Lower courts are able to 'escape' precedent by 'distinguishing' a case. This is where they accept the validity of the precedent but suggest that it does not apply to the case at hand because there are factual differences between the precedent and the case they are adjudicating.

❓ End-of-chapter questions

1. What do the terms 'binding', 'reversing', 'overruling', and 'distinguishing' mean in relation to precedent?

2. Read *Attorney-General for Jersey v Holley* [2005] UKPC 23, *R v James; R v Karimi* [2006] EWCA Crim 14, and *Willers v Gubay* [2016] UKSC 44. Does this now mean that the Privy Council has become part of the English Legal System for the purposes of *stare decisis*?

3. Consider the following cases and identify their *ratio*:

   (a) *R v G and R* [2003] UKHL 50

   (b) *Redmond Bates v DPP* [2000] HRLR 249

   (c) *Partridge v Crittenden* [1968] 1 WLR 431.

   The online resources accompanying this book provide clues and the answers!

4. Read Harris Rupert Cross and JW Harris, *Precedent in English Law* (4th edn, Clarendon Press 1991) 129–30 and Bruce Harris 'Final Appellate Courts Overruling their own "Wrong" Precedents: The Ongoing Search for Principle' (2002) 118 *Law Quarterly Review* 408, 420–2. Are there circumstances when leaving a precedent 'live' by either distinguishing or disapproving of it would be better than formally overruling it? Does that complicate or ease the burden of the lower courts in applying the principle of *stare decisis*?

📑 Further reading

Ashworth A, 'The Binding Effect of Crown Court Decisions' [1980] *Criminal Law Review* 402–3.

This short note discusses whether a judge in the Crown Court sets any precedent for other judges of the Crown Court or magistrates.

Harris B, 'Final Appellate Courts Overruling their own "Wrong" Precedents: The Ongoing Search for Principle' (2002) 118 *Law Quarterly Review* 408–27.

This is an interesting article that examines whether there is any rationale behind the circumstances governing final appeal courts overruling themselves.

Kavanagh A, '*Pepper v Hart* and Matters of Constitutional Principle' (2005) 121 *Law Quarterly Review* 98–122.

This is a wide-ranging but interesting article that examines the role of the courts in precedent and statutory interpretation.

For self-test questions, flashcards, and links to useful websites, please visit the **online resources** at: **www.oup.com/he/gillespie-weare8e**

4

International Sources of Law

By the end of this chapter you will be able to:

- Understand the key sources of law in international law.
- Identify the ways in which international instruments influence the law.
- Understand how EU law will continue to influence UK law post-Brexit.
- Understand the role of the Council of Europe.

Introduction

This book is about the English Legal System. Chapter 1 explained why this book should, more properly, be known as the 'Legal System of England & Wales', but law does not operate solely within territorial boundaries. The United Kingdom sits within a global arena, and its legal systems must recognise this. The United Kingdom is part of international groupings (eg the United Nations, the Council of Europe, NATO) and has bilateral agreements with several countries. This chapter considers how these international agreements influence the English Legal System.

This chapter is divided into three sections. The first relates to international law. As will be seen, this is an elusive concept, and there is not always agreement as to what international law is, or what it does. The second and third parts will consider the UK's relationship with its nearest neighbours, Europe. The UK has recently left the European Union but, as will be seen, its law will continue to influence UK law for some time. Some would suggest that EU law is a question of supranational rather than international law, but both our entry to, and exit from, the EU was a result of the basic instrument of international law, a Treaty. The final part of the book will consider the Council of Europe, which is separate from the EU, and whose *European Convention on Human Rights* is increasingly important within English law, partly as a result of the *Human Rights Act 1998*. Both the ECHR and the HRA 1998 will be considered more extensively in Chapter 5.

4.1 **International law**

The first issue to consider is international law. What is international law, and does it even exist? Unlike domestic law, it is difficult to identify what the exact framework of international law is. There are principles, but not all countries will necessarily accept the various definitions. If law is the rules that hold (domestic) society together, then international law can be said to be the rules that hold communities together. It is about how countries interact with each other, and the rules of doing so.

The reason why 'does it even exist?' was included above is that it is difficult to identify what international law is. Over 200 years ago, Carl von Clausewitz stated that war is the continuation of politics by other means. The same is probably true of law. As will be seen in this chapter, politics, law, and war probably all exist on the same plane. Arguably this is true of domestic law too. The executive and the legislature of a country is inherently political. Many would argue that the judiciary are too, indeed this concept lending itself to a seminal piece of work in legal academia in England and Wales.[1] However, in domestic legal systems it is possible to identify the institutions of a country. There is (typically) a legislature, an executive and a judiciary. We can identify who is in which, what the relationship between each are, and what the rules governing that relationship are, and where they can be found.

The same is not true of international law. There is no global legislature. There is no global executive. There is no global judiciary. So, how does law exist without these concepts? Where does international politics end and law starts? As will be seen, some argue that war is the ultimate way of enforcing international law. But not all war is lawful, although, as will be seen, some suggest that the concept of 'laws of war' is absurd.

We can identify some common principles that are at the heart of international law. There may be disagreements as to how these are defined and nuanced, but the basic structures and principles are present. Like in many legal systems, this is because time allows the concepts to emerge. Shaw, who is probably the leading scholar of international law in the UK, notes that modern international law emerged approximately 400 years ago, but many of its principles date back thousands of years.[2] Perhaps the earliest concept is that of agreement. Two states agree to trade with one another. A document (now known as a Treaty) would be produced that would set out how this relationship would work, what it would cover, and (eventually) how disputes would be resolved.

4.1.1 **Actors in international law**

In Chapter 1 it was noted that law could be divided between public law (the relationship between the state and an individual or individual body) and private law (the relationship between two or more individuals). In international law, the actors are usually the countries themselves, and not an individual.

⚡ STATES

It is usual in international law to refer to 'states'. While some countries, most famously the United States of America, have states within them, the term 'state' means the legal entity of the country. So, for example, it was noted in Chapter 1 that the United Kingdom consists of four countries, but the actual 'state' is the United Kingdom in its entirety.

---

1.   John AG Griffiths, *Politics of the Judiciary* (Fontana 1977) 764. This book's final edition was the 5th Edition (Fontana Press 1997).
2.   Malcolm Shaw, *International Law* (8th edn, Cambridge 2017) 10.

Individuals are rarely the subject of international law. Instead, the subjects of the instruments are states themselves. So, for example, an individual cannot point to a right within a particular instrument and say, 'I have been denied this' without it first forming part of domestic law. International law places burdens onto the individual states although this may, ultimately, lead to domestic law making those rights accessible.

The exception to this is international criminal law. The title of this type of law would make one believe that it concerns international instruments relating to criminal acts. That is only partly true. The majority of instruments that deal with criminal law do not exist within the field of international criminal law, but ordinary international law (known as public international law), because the instruments do not criminalize the individual. Instead, they require the state to enact domestic legislation which will, ultimately, criminalize a person.

⚡ CRIMINAL LAW IN ORDINARY INTERNATIONAL LAW INSTRUMENTS

The *United Nations Convention on the Rights of the Child* (UNCRC) is an instrument that has been signed by every country in the world, and ratified by all bar the United States of America. The UNCRC commits countries to a series of minimum rights for childhood.

Protocols (ie optional additions) exist to the UNCRC. One of which is the *Optional Protocol on the sale of children, child prostitution and child pornography*.[3] This is an instrument that commits signatory states to protecting children from commercial child sexual exploitation. Article 3 establishes a series of criminal offences relating to these forms of sexual exploitation. However, it does not establish criminal liability for individuals. Instead, it commits states to enacting domestic offences that, as a minimum, meet the standard set out in the optional protocol.

It can be seen, therefore, that the international instrument does not criminalize an individual but, instead, commits states to introduce domestic legislation that will ultimately criminalize individuals.

International criminal law is an area that deals with crimes that are so terrible that they infringe the basic standards of humanity. It is where the law recognizes that they were not just individual crimes, but that they are crimes that undermine global peace and security. They are largely restricted to war crimes and crimes against humanity (eg genocide). Perhaps the most famous example of these acts being the subject of criminal law is the Nuremburg Trials after the Second World War which, realistically, led to the establishment of international criminal law.[4]

The Nuremberg Trials were established by the victors of the Second World War, but recent tribunals have been established under the auspices of the United Nations. The *International Criminal Tribunal for the Former Yugoslavia* was established by the UN Security Council (4.1.3.2), acting under the powers of the United Nations Charter. This meant that, for example, individual countries were not obliged to consent to have their citizens tried by this tribunal.[5] A permanent International Criminal Court (ICC) has now been established to investigate and try suspects. This has proven controversial, and its actions will be considered later (4.1.5.1).

---

3. A/RES/54/263. Open for signatures 25 May 2000. Entered into force 18 January 2002.
4. Malcolm Shaw, *International Law* (8th edn, Cambridge 2017) 290.
5. ibid, 292.

4.1.1.1 **Private international law**

Before leaving this introduction to international law, the distinction between private and public international law should be noted.

Public international law is, in essence, ordinary international law and it is that which people typically refer to when talking about 'international law'. It is, as has been noted, the legal relationship between states and how they interact with each other. Private international law is different. It concerns international agreements with domestic disputes. It is sometimes referred to as 'conflict of laws' and is, in essence, the rules that govern which legal system a dispute will be litigated in when there is an international element. This will not be discussed in this book.

☰ Example Private international law

Debbie, and English citizen, marries Robert, an Australian in Dubai. They then live in Switzerland for fifteen years. Debbie discovers that Robert has been conducting an extra-marital affair and she returns to England. She seeks a divorce.

Private international law will govern in which country the divorce petition should be lodged (England, Dubai, or Switzerland).

4.1.2 **International bodies**

As will be seen, international law can apply to a bilateral agreement ('treaty') between two countries. However, it can also regulate groupings or entities of states. Perhaps the most obvious of these are the United Nations (4.1.3) but regional groupings exist too. Perhaps the most notable of these are:

- **Council of Europe.** The Council of Europe (CoE) predates the European Union, with it being established in 1948 (*Treaty of London*) in the aftermath of the Second World War. Its primary focus is on human rights and the rule of law. Its most famous instrument is the *European Convention on Human Rights* (ECHR). This will be considered in 4.3 later.

- **African Union.** The African Union (AU) was established in 1963, with the production of a Charter. Eventually it has spread to encompass fifty-five countries across the continent of Africa. In modern times, it has established a series of treaties that commit Member States to work together on a variety of issues. This includes natural resources,[6] human rights,[7] and, very recently, cyber-security.[8]

- **Organization of American States.** The Organization of American States (OAS) was established by charter in 1948. It encompasses most countries in the continents of North and South America. The overall aim of the OAS is to strengthen peace and justice. It has published a series of instruments covering subjects such as combatting the trafficking of children,[9] mutual assistance in criminal justice,[10] and the rights of women.[11]

---

6. *African Convention on the Conservation of Nature and Natural Resources* (Adopted 15 September 1968. In force 16 June 1969).
7. *African Charter on Human and Peoples' Rights* (Adopted 1 June 1981. In force 21 October 1986).
8. *African Union Convention on Cyber Security and Personal Data Protection* (Adopted 27 June 2014).
9. *Inter-American Convention on International Traffic in Minors* (B-57. Adopted 18 March 1984).
10. See, for example, *Inter-American Convention on Mutual Assistance in Criminal Matters* (A-55).
11. *Inter-American Convention on the Granting of Civil Rights to Women* (A-45).

There are many more international groupings, and it shows that a problem with international law is that there is no defined entity. Indeed, there is a question as to whether these regional groupings properly create international law, or whether it is regional law. Certainly, the instruments that bind the countries together are creatures of international law, but what of the instruments passed within those groups? It will depend, in part, on what the enforcement mechanism is (see 4.1.5).

Another issue with these international groupings is that the obligations on Member States differ dramatically between the organizations. Thus, there is no parity at global level, although it is possible to understand the relationship within each regional grouping.

4.1.3 United Nations

Perhaps the most famous international grouping is that of the United Nations (UN). It is worth pausing on the UN to outline some of its key features because the UN is undoubtedly a key influence on UK law, with the courts taking note of obligations under UN Treaties.[12] It also reinforces the fact that, unlike with domestic institutions, international bodies rarely have the ability to create or enforce law.

The United Nations was established after the Second World War, with it being the successor to the *League of Nations*, which had proven somewhat ineffective. It has become the largest international organization, with most countries having joined the UN. The principal aim of the UN is 'to maintain international peace and security'[13] and to that extent it has become a custodian of international law and a provider of peace.

The UN is not a 'world government'. Membership is premised on the basis of equal sovereignty for all Member States,[14] although, as will be seen, some states are perceived as more important than others. In essence, this recognizes geopolitical realities. The UN has no competence to interfere in the domestic activities of a Member State, unless it is to enforce measures of the Security Council to uphold peace and security.[15]

The UN has a complex structure and it is not necessary to consider all the various agencies that belong to it. It has been suggested that there are six principal organs of the UN: the General Assembly, the Security Council, the Economic and Social Council, the Trusteeship Council, the Secretariat, and the International Court of Justice.[16] Again, not all of these will be considered as they are not relevant to us, and instead reference should be made to specialist texts.

4.1.3.1 General Assembly

The General Assembly is the principal entity, and includes at least one representative, and no more than five, of each Member State.[17] Regardless of the size of the country, or the number of representatives it has, each Member State has one vote.[18] Where an issue is a 'major issue' (which includes recommendations about the maintenance of international peace and security, the composition of the Councils and the admission,

---

12. See, for example, *MS (Pakistan) v Secretary of State for the Home Department* [2020] UKSC 9 where the Supreme Court considered the UK's obligations under the *United Nations Convention on Transnational Organized Crime*.
13. *UN Charter*, Art 1(1).
14. *UN Charter*, Art 2(1).
15. *UN Charter*, Art 2(7).
16. Malcolm Shaw, *International Law* (8th edn, Cambridge 2017) 924.
17. *UN Charter*, Art 9
18. *UN Charter*, Art 18(1).

suspension or expulsion of Member States) a vote is only passed where two-thirds of states present vote in favour of the resolution.[19] All other votes, including whether something constitutes a 'major issue', is decided by a simple majority of states present.[20]

The General Assembly is, in essence, the political and legislative organ. It allows Member States to raise issues of international importance, seeking to build alliances to pass resolutions. It may make recommendations or resolutions about any issue that is not under the authority of the Security Council.[21] It also receives reports from the Security Council although it would be wrong to say that it scrutinizes its work. The General Assembly does not have direct power over the Security Council.

The General Assembly can delegate matters to assist it in discharging its obligations. So, for example, the *Human Rights Council*, was set up by the General Assembly, and it reports to it.[22] This Council is tasked to promote the development and education of human rights across the world. It does this through programmes of education, inspections, and thematic reports on issues of importance. The General Assembly has six committees that cover issues ranging from economic activity, social and humanitarian issues, cultural issues, and decolonization.

The General Assembly is based in the main headquarters of the United Nations, which is based in New York.

4.1.3.2 **Security Council**

While the UN General Assembly is technically the principal organ, the most powerful is the Security Council.

The Security Council has fifteen members (it was originally eleven). Five of these are permanent members (China, France, Russia,[23] the United Kingdom, and the United States of America). The remaining ten are elected by the General Assembly for two-year terms.[24] These permanent members reflect the geopolitical power of these countries after the conclusion of the Second World War. There have been debates about whether the same membership should continue,[25] but the reality is that it would be extremely difficult to change because it would require the acquiescence of those five powers.[26]

Votes in the Security Council are slightly complicated. For substantive motions, it requires nine votes in favour, but these must include either a vote in favour of the motion from the permanent members, or for them to abstain.[27] Where a permanent member votes against a resolution, the motion cannot pass. This is known as a 'veto' and both its use, and potential use, has seen drama and controversy over the years.[28] When applied to the civil war in the Former Yugoslavia, it led to action being taken

---

19. *UN Charter*, Art 18(2).
20. *UN Charter*, Art 18(3).
21. *UN Charter*, Arts 13–14.
22. General Assembly Resolution 60/251 of 3 April 2006.
23. Russia is considered to be the natural successor to the USSR upon its demise.
24. *UN Charter*, Art 23.
25. See, for example, Thomas G Weiss and Karen E Young, 'Compromise and Credibility: Security Council Reform?' (2005) 36 Security Dialogue 131.
26. Michael J Kelly, 'United Nations Security Council Permanent Membership and the Veto Problem' (2020) 52 Case Western Reserve Journal of International Law 101, 104.
27. *UN Charter*, Art 27.
28. Philippa Webb, 'Deadlock or Restraint? The Security Council Veto and the Use of Force in Syria' (2014) 19 *Journal of Conflict and Security Law* 471.

outside of the UN framework, something that has remained controversial for many years (see 4.1.5.2). However, as any change to the constitution of the Security Council requires a vote of the Security Council, it is unlikely that any will lose their veto particularly soon.

The principal function of the Security Council is set out in the Charter:

> In order to ensure prompt and effective action by the United Nations, its Members confer on the Security Council the primary responsibility for the maintenance of international peace and security, and agree that in carrying out its duties under this responsibility the Security Council acts on their behalf.[29]

This is a clear statement that the operational aspects of monitoring and securing international peace and security is vested in the Security Council and not the wider General Assembly that includes all countries. While the Assembly may pass resolutions relevant to peace and security, it is the Security Council who decides what action can be taken to uphold international law, peace, and security. Also, when the Security Council is acting in respect of a dispute, the General Assembly is prevented from passing resolutions on this.[30] More than this, any decision of the Security Council is binding on Member States,[31] which can be important in terms of it resolving disputes and/or imposing, for example, sanctions on a country. A failure to follow the instructions of the Security Council would be reported to the Council who could consider what action to take in order to seek compliance.

In maintaining or enforcing peace, the Security Council has a number of tools available to it. At the heart of its role is the rule of law. Where a state threatens peace and security, the Security Council will attempt diplomatic moves initially. There could also be formal warnings through the issuing of resolutions etc. Ultimately, however, if a dispute is not resolved, it is for the Security Council to resolve this. Chapters VI and VII of the UN Charter provides the authority to do so, including both peacefully and through the use of force. This is discussed later. The Security Council is also ultimately responsible for ensuring that parties adhere to rulings of the International Court of Justice (see 4.1.5.1).

The Security Council has responsibility for the military preparations of the United Nations.[32] This primarily means the deployment of peace keepers or peace-enforcers although, as will be seen later in this chapter, increasingly in modern times, some countries are acting outwith the UN banner. That said, there are approximately 70,000 soldiers from Member States acting on behalf of the UN, each wearing a 'blue' helmet or beret.[33]

An important power that exists outwith the UN Charter is the right of the Security Council to refer matters to the International Criminal Court (ICC) (considered at 4.1.5.1). As will be seen, the ICC ordinarily only has the power to investigate and prosecute individuals from states that have signed the Rome Treaty which establishes

103

---

29. *UN Charter*, Art 24(1).
30. *UN Charter*, Art 12(1).
31. *UN Charter*, Art 25.
32. *UN Charter*, Art 26.
33. See https://peacekeeping.un.org/en/military#:~:text=Global%20contribution%20for%20global%20peace &text=We%20have%20more%20than%2097%2C000,their%20determination%20to%20foster%20peace>. The blue beret or helmet is designed to be distinctive and was chosen to reflect the UN official colours. It also does not replicate the colours of any Member State, meaning that they should be distinctive in battle. Their vehicles are also traditionally coloured white, so that they are distinctive on the battlefield

the ICC. However, that Treaty provides the right of the Security Council to refer matters to it where they would not otherwise have jurisdiction.[34] The first time that such a referral occurred was in 2005, when the Security Council referred the matter of Darfur to the ICC. Sudan fell into civil war, and allegations of war crimes, including genocide and crimes against humanity, were made. After investigating them, the Security Council resolved to refer the matter to the ICC even though Sudan was not a signatory to the ICC.[35] Six suspects have been charged by the ICC, although none have been arrested as they are suspected of being shielded by allies. The second referral to the ICC was in respect of crimes alleged to have occurred in Libya.[36]

4.1.3.3 **Secretariat**

The final organ that is worth noting is the Secretariat. This is the administrative leadership of the United Nations. It is headed by the UN Secretary-General, who is chosen by the General Assembly, acting on a recommendation from the Security Council.[37] The Secretary-General is considered the head of the UN, although it is questionable how much power they hold in comparison to the permanent members of the Security Council. As the General Assembly only gets to vote on candidates cleared by the Security Council this means that the five permanent members have a veto, as the leadership of the UN is considered a major issue. In reality, the members do not need to exercise the veto since the knowledge that they will veto a candidate is sufficient to ensure the candidate is never put forward.

It is an unwritten rule that the Secretary-General will not come from one of the five permanent members,[38] although that is partly because the other members are unlikely to permit this. The same undoubtedly means that close allies of the permanent members are unlikely to succeed. It is often said that the Secertary-General is a compromise candidate, and this is undoubtedly true as it has to be someone who each of the five permanent members do not object to. This tends to mean that they are relatively unknown before succeeding to the role.

While not holding any power, the Secretary-General holds influence. Often, the Secretary-General can use personal diplomacy to either assist states in disputes, or to bring the sides closer to reconciliation. The Secretary-General is often used before a formal reference is made to the Security Council. The Secretary-General also has the power to refer any matter to the Security Council that he[39] believes may 'threaten the maintenance of international peace and security'.[40]

The Secretary-General acts as the chief administrative officer of the UN and is able to attend meetings of any of the six organs of the UN.[41] In practice, the operations of the UN are in the hands of key civil servants employed within the UN, but the

---

34. *Rome Statute of the International Criminal Court*, Art 13(b).
35. Resolution 1593 (2005).
36. Resolution 1970 (2011).
37. *UN Charter*, Art 97.
38. The exception to this was the first Secretary-General who was, more properly, only an Acting Secretary-General. Sir Gladwyn Jebb was a UK diplomat who served as Acting Secretary-General for the first three months of the UN. This is perhaps not surprising since the Second World War allies were the original sponsors of the UN.
39. There has not, so far, been a female Secretary-General of the UN.
40. *UN Charter*, Art 99.
41. *UN Charter*, Art 98.

Secretary-General has wide powers to ensure that his voice his heard in respect of the direction of the UN. Personal envoys can be created to act as 'troubleshooters' or diplomats for specific issues.

4.1.4 Sources of international law

What then are the sources of international law? If international law can influence UK law, then we need to identify where this law comes from. It should be noted that this section is not designed to provide a detailed examination of sources of international law, and it will not necessarily cover all sources. The question of what the sources of international law are is somewhat contested and occupies a significant chunk of any international law module. The purpose of this section is simply to highlight the key sources and the principles that underpin them. For a detailed examination of sources, you should consult a specialist text on international law.

4.1.4.1 Custom

While many would argue that treaties are the primary sources of international law, Shaw believes that custom is perhaps the first source.[42] He makes the very pertinent point that before we understood what law was, communities would agree on common standards and rules. These customs and practices became, in essence, the first rules. The same is true of relationships between countries. Quite often a formal document ('Treaty') was not possible because there was no shared language, or because the relationship was not that developed. The common rules began to be recognized as custom.[43]

In essence, custom simply means that a state (or states) consider that certain practices have the force of law. This means that it is not enough for a custom to exist, it must be recognized as providing a legal basis for an act, rather than, for example, the application of a law. It is, by its very nature, imprecise. While some have tried to draw an analogy to the English common law, it is an imprecise analogy, not least because there is a degree of certainty as to how the common law develops, with the hierarchy of courts. The same is not true of custom, where it is unlikely to be the decision of a tribunal that leads to the custom being established. It is, instead, a series of customs and practices that are now recognized as giving legal obligations. Greenwood suggests that an example of when customs can form part of international law would be the rules of war. To many, the concept that there are laws of war would seem absurd. But they do exist. Many are now set out in Treaty (perhaps most famously, the *Geneva Convention*[44]) but they originated in custom between the warring parties.[45]

Unlike the position in English law, where common law tends to develop very slowly, the position in international law is more varied. A 'custom' may be incorporated into international law quickly in contemporary fields such as aviation or space law, whereas in other areas (for example, the rules of the sea) the process could be much slower.[46]

---

42.   Malcolm Shaw, *International Law* (8th edn, Cambridge 2017) 54.
43.   Peter Malanczuk, *Akehurst's Modern Introduction to International Law* (7th edn, Routledge 1997) 39.
44.   Technically there are four Geneva Conventions, but most reference is to the Third Geneva Convention on, inter alia, the treatment of prisoners of war.
45.   For example, in the Napoleonic Wars it was customary for officers to be given the freedom to walk around anywhere. They gave their 'parole', a promise that they would not seek to escape. This was never written down but it was considered a gentleman would not break his word. Concepts of duty changed, and more recently, it is considered that the duty of an officer is to escape. An illuminating history can be found in Gary D Brown, 'Prisoner of War Parole: Ancient Concept, Modern Utility' (1998) 156 *Military Law Review* 200.
46.   Malcolm Shaw, *International Law* (8th edn, Cambridge 2017) 56.

Of course, an issue with international custom is that it, to some degree, codifies geopolitical forces. So, for example, Shaw notes that many of the rules of the sea arose out of British practices. Similarly, the laws of space have mainly come from the practices of the USA and the USSR/Russia.[47] To an extent, this should not be surprising. During the Napoleonic period, the United Kingdom was undoubtedly the premier sea power. 'Britannia Rules the Waves' was true. The United Kingdom had almost complete superiority over the seas, and it allowed it to carry forward its power.[48] Similarly, the original space powers were the USA and the USSR. Even today, the USA and Russia account for the vast majority of space launches. Thus, it is obvious their customs and practices would eventually constitute international law since they were the only ones who were, at the relevant time, conducting space operations. Other countries would then follow these practices, establishing them as a norm, but also restricting the opportunity of minor powers to distance themselves from it. However, as will be seen, this is hardly the only time when geopolitics and international law interact.

4.1.4.2 Conventions and treaties

While custom may have been the original source of international law, and continues to be important, the principal source in modern times is arguably the treaty. Fitzmaurice notes that a treaty 'provides a precise method of regulating relations between States'[49] and a simple analogy could be drawn to a contract. While 'Treaty' is the most common name for these instruments, there are a variety of other names that are used, including: International Agreements, General Acts, Charters, Statutes, Declarations, and Covenants.[50] It is not clear whether the different names are supposed to indicate anything, although it makes no difference in law.

Whatever they are called, a treaty is an agreement between two or more states to regularize some behaviour between them. While treaties have now surpassed custom as the principal source of new international rules, this effectiveness relies on a customary rule to be effective. It is a long-standing custom that states intend to be bound by the instruments they ratify.

The *Vienna Convention on the Law of Treaties*, which is itself a treaty, now formalizes many of the rules relating to treaties, including their definition. Article 2(2) defines them as:

> [An] international agreement concluded between States in written form and governed by international law, whether embodied in a single instrument or in two or more related instruments and whatever its particular designation.

The latter sentence is important because, as noted earlier, there is a wide variety of names for treaties. The purpose of Article 2(2) is to focus on the substance and not the name. The key point under Article 2(2) is that the parties to it have an intention for the agreement to be subject to international law.[51]

---

47. ibid, 59.
48. The most notable example of which was the Royal Navy's role in the suppression of the slave trade once the United Kingdom (eventually) denounced the practice. See, for example, Bernard Edwards, *Royal Navy Versus the Slave Traders: Enforcing Abolition at Sea, 1808–1898* (Casemate Publishers 2008).
49. Malgosia Fitzmaurice, 'The Practical Working of the Law of Treaties' in Malcolm Evans (ed), *International Law* (OUP 2003) 173.
50. Malcolm Shaw, *International Law* (8th edn, Cambridge 2017) 69.
51. A loose analogy could be drawn to English contract law where there must be an intention to create legal relations.

If it is an agreement, does this mean that a treaty is, in essence, no more than a contract? If so, how does it become a source of law? We would not point to a contract and state that it was a source of law. It is clearly a source to understand what the parties intended to agree to, but it does not set out any proper source of law. Some treaties are the same. Bilateral agreements (ie reciprocal agreements between two or more parties) are unlikely to give rise to laws. They are, more likely, to be an arrangement between those countries (perhaps the paradigm of this would be a trade treaty between two states). The treaty is likely to say how the agreement is to be enforced, but, again, this is not a source of law but, rather, pointing to those laws that deal with adjudicating disputes.

Other treaties are sometimes referred to as *law making* treaties.[52] These are instruments where there is an intention to establish laws that will govern those who join them and where, eventually, it may become a source of law for other instruments. These tend to be lateral agreements, and they are, quite often, referred to as Conventions or Charters, although the actual title is irrelevant. A good example of this is the *Vienna Convention on the Law of Treaties*, which we referred to previously. From its very title it is clear that this lateral treaty was designed to create a set of legal principles. Thus, this can properly be considered a source of international law.

> ### ☰ Example   UN Charter
>
> The UN Charter is another example of a lateral treaty where, in part, it was designed as a law-making treaty. For example, Chapter VI sets out the principle (which has become a law) that disputes should be settled peacefully initially. Chapter VII sets out the laws by which force can be used to counter acts of aggression. Arguably this is the chapter that has caused most dispute, but it undoubtedly sets out principles, which the signatories intended to be laws.

It would be easy to draw an analogy between treaties and, in the English context, Acts of Parliament. While there is some approximation, an important distinction is that a treaty does not extinguish customary law. If a treaty sets out a principle that is also a customary rule, it has been held that the custom is not extinguished and, therefore, can be pleaded even where a treaty may subtlety differ.[53]

Ratification

There are normally two stages to a state becoming bound by a treaty. The first is that they must sign it. That provides an intention to be bound by its contents, but in the vast majority of situations that does not make them bound by the provisions of the treaty. The second stage is that for most treaties, it must be ratified.[54] Ratification is where the state itself acknowledges that it is bound by the terms of the treaty. There is usually a delay between signature and ratification and this is partly to allow the state to prepare itself for the obligations that arise under a treaty.

How a treaty is ratified is a matter for domestic law rather than international law. In the United Kingdom, ratification was traditionally a matter for the Crown, with

---

52. Malcolm Shaw, *International Law* (8th edn, Cambridge 2017) 70.
53. *Nicaragua v United States of America* ICJ Reports, 1986.
54. *Vienna Convention on the Law of Treaties*, Art 14.

its consent being indicated through the use of the Great Seal. However, Parliament was increasingly asked to provide its consent, and the *Constitutional Reform and Governance Act 2010* (CRGA 2010) expressly provides for this.[55]

A Treaty should be placed before Parliament after being published in a way that the relevant minister considers appropriate. Parliament then has 21 sitting days[56] to pass a motion that the Treaty should not be ratified.[57]

If the House of Commons passes a resolution that the Treaty should not be ratified, then a Minister of the Crown must explain why the government wishes to continue to ratify the treaty. The House then has another twenty-one sitting days to pass a motion that the Treaty should not be ratified.[58] If such a motion is passed, then a minister may make another statement, leading to another twenty-one day period being created.[59]

If the House of Lords passes a resolution that the Treaty should not be ratified, but the House of Commons did not, then the treaty can be ratified so long as a minister places, in writing, a statement before both Houses explaining why he believes it is necessary to do so.[60] In other words, the House of Lords does not have a veto whereas the House of Commons does.

⚡ SUSPENDING THE REQUIREMENTS

The CRGA 2010 is an Act of Parliament and this means that its provisions can be disapplied by another Act of Parliament according to the principle of parliamentary sovereignty.

An example of this is in respect of the withdrawal agreement that was negotiated between the UK and the EU. This is undoubtedly a treaty that is enforceable under international law. However, the *European Union (Withdrawal) Act 2020* waived the requirement for this agreement to be subject to the provisions of the CRGA 2010.[61]

There are exceptions to the procedure under CRGA 2010. Perhaps the most significant of which is that s 22 states that s 20 can be disapplied where 'a Minister of the Crown is of the opinion that, exceptionally, the treaty should be ratified without the requirements' of s 20.[62] Such a resolution cannot be made once either House has objected under s 20,[63] but it otherwise gives the government broad powers to set aside s 20. If they use this power, they must lay a copy of the treaty before Parliament and explain why they considered s 20 should not apply.[64] Parliament cannot prevent ratification in such circumstances although it could, presumably, pass a motion of censure which would be politically damaging for the government. It is perhaps notable that the government chose not to use s 22 in respect of the EU withdrawal treaty and instead simply relied on disapplying the provision in statute.

The twenty-one sitting days period mentioned in s 20 can also be extended by a minister.[65] Presumably, this could be used to provide additional opportunities for the whips to discuss the concerns of MPs, and to try and reach an accommodation.

---

55. *Constitutional Reform and Governance Act 2010*, s 20.
56. Parliament does not always sit five days per week, so it must be 21 days during which Parliament is sitting.
57. *Constitutional Reform and Governance Act 2010*, s 20(1), (2).
58. *Constitutional Reform and Governance Act 2010*, s 20(4), (5).
59. *Constitutional Reform and Governance Act 2010*, s 20(6).
60. *Constitutional Reform and Governance Act 2010*, s 20(8).
61. *European Union (Withdrawal) Act 2020*, s 32.
62. *Constitutional Reform and Governance Act 2010*, s 22.
63. *Constitutional Reform and Governance Act 2010*, s 22(2).
64. *Constitutional Reform and Governance Act 2010*, s 22(3).
65. *Constitutional Reform and Governance Act 2010*, s 21.

4.1.4.3 **General principles of law**

The third primary source is the general principles of law. It may be immediately thought, 'aren't these customary rules?' but they are considered separate. General principles of law are sometimes considered to be inherent principles that exist for the operation of justice. They are, not infrequently, about the operation of the judicial system etc. Perhaps a classic example of this would be the concept that court hearings should be fair. It is not really a custom that they should be fair, it is just an accepted reality that proceedings should be fair.[66]

Perhaps unsurprisingly, it has been noted that what constitutes a general principle of law is contested.[67] The competing arguments do not need to be rehearsed here, as it is an issue that will be explored more fully should you study international law.

One of the more important principles recognized is that known as *res judicata*, which means that a judicial decision is final and binding. Part of this principle means that those who are subject to the decision cannot refuse to implement the finding against them. For example, in the *Administrative Tribunal* case,[68] the UN had sacked staff and the UN General Assembly had not provided the usual financial recompense which was expected. The Administrative Tribunal of the UN determined that they were entitled to the money, but the General Assembly refused to pay. The ICJ was asked for its advice as to whether the Secretariat was bound to follow the decisions of the Tribunal. The ICJ held that a general principle of international law was that those who had agreed to be subject to a tribunal should consider its ruling to be binding. Clearly, this is an important principle since otherwise there is little point in having judicial resolution. It could not be a custom as most tribunals were relatively new, but it is clearly an inherent principle of justice that should be properly recognized as a legal principle.

4.1.4.4 **Judicial decisions**

Disputes under international law require adjudication and this will sometimes mean that they are heard before an international court (discussed further at 4.1.5.1). This means that decisions of courts should form a source of law. However, it should be noted at the outset that judicial decisions are considered to be a secondary source of law, and not a primary source.[69] This is partly because decisions of international courts only bind the parties before it. That said, decisions of the courts are likely to give an indication of how they are likely to rule if a similar issue came before it. Thus, it does not create a law *per se*, but provides an insight into how the judicial body considers the legal principle should be interpreted. There is no formal principle of *stare decisis* in the international courts. While they may prefer to follow their previous decisions to ensure consistency, it is not a rule of law as it is within England and Wales.

It is not just decisions of the international courts that are relevant, but also decisions of other adjudicating bodies. So, for example, a considerable amount of international disputes are resolved through arbitration (see 4.1.5.1 and 19.3.1.1 for how this applies domestically), and the decisions of international arbitrators can also be relevant.[70] Decisions of national courts who are considering international obligations can also be relevant, as this provides another example of professional judiciary considering issues.

---

66. Of course, what constitutes 'fair' is often disputed in the context of disputes.
67. Malcolm Shaw, *International Law* (8th edn, Cambridge 2017) 73.
68. ICJ Reports, 1954.
69. Malcolm Shaw, *International Law* (8th edn, Cambridge 2017) 81.
70. Malcolm Shaw, *International Law* (8th edn, Cambridge 2017) 82.

While it is perhaps more common to refer to decisions of the international courts, it should be noted that there is no reason why an international court should not refer to the decisions of national courts.

4.1.5 **Adjudication and enforcement**

In the same way that disputes may arise in domestic law, the same is true of international law. In a bilateral agreement that this might be because one party believes that the other has done something contrary to its terms. In a lateral treaty, it may be that it is thought that a state has not adhered to its responsibilities. If the instruments are to be law, then there needs to be both adjudication and enforcement.

4.1.5.1 **Peaceful resolution**

The first issue to note is that the primary purpose of international law is to ensure that disputes are peacefully resolved. Before treaties and the existence of international law, disputes were frequently the cause of battles and war. International law seeks to move away from this, with this being the case even where there is no treaty or agreement between states. So, for example, Article 33 of the *UN Charter* states that any dispute that 'is likely to endanger the maintenance of international peace and security' should be solved through negotiation, mediation, conciliation, arbitration, or judicial settlement initially.

Shaw argues that peaceful resolution can be divided into two types. The first is diplomatic, and the second is adjudicative.[71]

Diplomatic

Diplomatic approaches could be as simple as ambassadors or ministers on both sides talking to each other, ensuring that each understands their respective points, and trying to reach a compromise. This negotiating stance can take the temperature out of disputes. To an extent, it replicates the creation of a treaty where negotiations are an essential part of their creation.

Occasionally, negotiation will be a requirement of the treaty itself. So, for example, the *Convention on the Law of the Sea* provides that in any dispute, the parties will initially try to resolve the matter through negotiation.[72] This could mean that a court or other adjudicator refuses to engage with the dispute until negotiations have at least been tried since that is the mechanism provided for the resolution of disputes.

Mediation and conciliation are additional forms of diplomatic solutions. They have at their heart, a negotiation but whereas a traditional negotiation involves only the parties, both mediation and conciliation use a third-party. The mechanics of such a dispute resolution will be considered more extensively in Chapter 19, when Alternative Dispute Resolutions (ADR) are examined within the context of English cases. In international law, ADR is more common than in domestic law (save for certain commercial disputes). This is, in part, because there are limits as to what international courts can do.

Mediation involves a person seeking to act as a 'middle-man' to the parties. They will chair discussions and seek to narrow differences. They will ultimately seek to reach

---

71.   Malcolm Shaw, *International Law* (8th edn, Cambridge 2017) 764.
72.   Article 283(1), see Malcolm Shaw, *International Law* (8th edn, Cambridge 2017) 768.

a position where both parties will speak to one another and reach a compromise agreement. In international disputes that concern the interests of a state, it is not unusual for the UN Security Council (see 4.1.3.2) to appoint an individual as mediator, or for the UN Secretary-General to do so himself.

Conciliation differs in that rather than the independent person leading negotiations, they will tend to investigate the dispute. They will not adjudicate on the matter but will, instead, identify the areas of common ground and dispute that can be presented to the parties. The investigation will speak to the parties and those who the parties believe can support their cases. All of these points and any evidence gathered during the investigation will be put forward to the parties to narrow the disputes. This should then allow the negotiations to move forward.

Adjudicative

Shaw's second category is adjudicative, ie someone adjudicates on the dispute rather than helping the parties resolve their dispute. There are different forms of adjudicative remedies. However, for our purposes it is necessary to consider only two; arbitration and courts.

Arbitration is another form of ADR. In Chapter 19 it will be noted that some question what the difference between arbitration and litigation is. The distinction in international law is arguably even more vague, not least because international courts tend to have limited jurisdiction, meaning that some disputes cannot come before them. Also, some treaties will require the use of arbitration rather than litigation.

A key difference between arbitration and litigation is that the parties can choose the arbitrator whereas, of course, the same is not true of litigation. This means that both parties may have confidence in the arbitrator. The parties can also decide that certain rules or principles should apply to the arbitration, even where they are not necessarily recognized international legal principles. Indeed, on occasion the states could decide that the dispute should be resolved according to a territorial jurisdiction rather than international law.

While arbitration is sometimes seen as a modern concept, Shaw notes that it has been used in international law for over 200 years.[73] Over the years, it has been both in and out of favour, but it remains popular in some contexts. It is particularly useful where there is a need for a specialist or expert to adjudicate on a technical dispute (reducing the need for expert witnesses to be brought before a generalist judge) or where there is a desire for greater speed, as many of the international courts are slow.

The second form of adjudicative resolution would be courts. Not every treaty or Convention has recourse to an international court. For example, the *United Nations Convention on the Rights of the Child* is not adjudicated in any court.[74] Some treaties will specifically create a court and confer jurisdiction upon it. So, for example, the *European Convention on Human Rights* establishes the *European Court of Human Rights*,[75] which is tasked with resolving disputes concerning the ECHR (see 4.3.2).

It is not just regional courts that exist. At global level, there is the *International Tribunal for the Law of the Sea*, which sits in Hamburg, Germany. This is the court

---

73. Malcolm Shaw, *International Law* (8th edn, Cambridge 2017) 795.
74. Instead matters are reported to a Committee on the Rights of a Child, with the various reports then being submitted to the UN General Assembly. See Trevor Buck, *International Child Law* (3rd edn, Routledge 2014).
75. *European Convention on Human Rights*, Section II.

which considers disputes that arise from the *UN Convention on the Law of the Sea*, which as its name suggests, sets out rules on how the sea is governed, including rules on the environment, transit, and the exploitation of minerals. The Tribunal has twenty-one judges assigned to it (and they elect one of their number as President), but *ad hoc* judges are appointed where the judges do not include the states litigating. This is a common feature of international law and will be explored further below in respect of the *International Court of Justice* (ICJ).

International criminal courts

International courts are not just civil in nature. It was noted earlier, that international criminal law governs crimes against humanity, including war crimes. Until comparatively recently, such courts were *ad hoc*. For example, in the field of international criminal law, the *International Criminal Tribunal for the former Yugoslavia* (ICTY), was established in 1993[76] to investigate and prosecute alleged war crimes committed in the civil war that encompassed the state that is now known as Yugoslavia. Similarly, the *International Criminal Tribunal for Rwanda* was established in 1994,[77] to investigate potential war crimes that occurred in the civil war there.

While called tribunals, it is clear that they are courts. The ICTY had over eighty judges serving it throughout its existence, coming from multiple countries. It followed its own laws and procedures, although it is closer to the continental system in that it has no jury: the decision is made by the judges by majority. Importantly, these courts had the power to not only convict a person, but to sentence them. While there were detention facilities where the courts sat, there are no international gaols. Instead, Member States of the UN agree to house prisoners convicted by the tribunals.[78]

While the success of the international tribunals has been debated,[79] it is clear that in modern times, there has been a need for crimes against humanity to be adjudicated. As early as the 1950s discussion was given as to whether there should be a single international court, although progress was undoubtedly slow, partly due to political considerations.[80] Eventually, however, in 1998 the *Rome Statute on the International Criminal Court* was signed, and by 2002, sufficient states had ratified the treaty for it to come into force, although it applies only to those who have ratified it or where the Security Council refers a matter to it. In the latter instance it is enforcement action by the Security Council and it is therefore irrelevant whether the member state whose citizen has been referred, consents.

The International Criminal Court (ICC) has not been universally welcomed. During its drafting, the then US President, Bill Clinton, signed the Rome Statute. However, as noted earlier, ratification is required for a state to be bound by a treaty. Ratification is by Congress in the USA, and no serious attempt was ever made to ratify the treaty. In 2002, the then President, George Bush, wrote to the UN Secretary-General to say that the USA was withdrawing from the treaty. The lack of ratification and subsequent withdrawal represents significant concerns by the USA over an international court having jurisdiction over individual members of the USA.[81]

---

76.   The UN Security Council established the tribunal: S/RES/808 (1993).
77.   Again, under the direction of the UN Security Council: S/RES/955 (1994).
78.   For example, Charles Taylor, the former president of the Liberia, is currently serving life imprisonment in HMP Frankland Prison in Durham after being convicted of war crimes by the UN Special Court for Sierra Leone.
79.   See, for example, Kirsten MF Keith, 'Justice at the International Criminal Tribunal for Rwanda: Are Criticisms Just' (2009) 27 *Law Context: A Socio-Legal Journal* 78.
80.   Malcolm Shaw, *International Law* (8th edn, Cambridge 2017) 298.
81.   Diane Marie Amann and Mortimer NS Sellers, 'The United States of America and the International Criminal Court' (2002) 50 *The American Journal of Comparative Law* 381.

While the USA is undoubtedly against the ICC, it has been pointed out that it would be a mistake to believe that the USA is hostile to the principle of international criminal law *per se*. It has devoted resources to the *ad hoc* tribunals and participated in peace-keeping missions (see 4.1.5.2).[82] However, it does not recognize that tribunals should have jurisdiction over its own citizens. This will be picked up as a difficulty of international law. How do you enforce international law on a global super-power? While it is easy to put pressure on a small country to cooperate, it is another matter to persuade a key power to do so, particularly one that exercises a veto on the UN Security Council.

International Court of Justice

The International Court of Justice (ICJ) is perhaps one of the more important, and notable, permanent international courts. Its genesis goes back over a century, with the establishment in 1920 of the *Permanent Court of International Justice* (PCIJ) after the First World War.[83] After the Second World War, the PCIJ was superseded by the ICJ.

Fifteen judges are elected to take office for nine-year terms by the UN General Assembly and UN Security Council to sit for nine-year terms. The exact method of election is complicated, and outside the scope of this book, but it is clear that it is a mixture of both politics and law.[84] Traditionally, the members of the UN Security Council have occupied at least one seat, but China and Russia have not always occupied a seat, and in 2017, the United Kingdom judge—Sir Christopher Greenwood—withdrew from seeking re-election when there was a deadlock between the UN General Assembly and Security Council. This perhaps reflects the gradual feeling that the General Assembly is starting to cease being overtly subservient to the Security Council.

In domestic courts it would be extraordinary for a person who had a relationship with one of the parties to sit on a matter (see 9.3.3) but in the international context the reverse is true. Where a country brings a matter to the ICJ then they are entitled to appoint an ad hoc judge to the ICJ if one of the judges is not already of that nationality. The argument for this policy at international level is that it is possible for the national judges to explain the legal implications of a particular policy in their own jurisdiction[85] but Thirlway questions the merits of such an approach by noting that whilst permanent judges of the ICJ have not infrequently voted against their own country, no ad hoc judge ever has.[86] It is perhaps understandable that this is the case given the nature of a temporary appointment (and the desire to be nominated for cases again in the future) but the judges are, theoretically, supposed to take the same oath. This perhaps adds weight to the argument that judicial independence can only be secured when tenure is certain (see 9.2.3).

The ICJ has two principal functions. The first is to adjudicate on disputes between states.[87] The second is to offer advisory opinions when an appropriate body asks for it to do so.[88] It is for the ICJ itself to decide whether to accept a case, although it is likely to do so where two states are in dispute about their respective obligations.

113

---

82. William A Schabas, 'International Criminal Court: The Secret of Its Success' (2001) 12 *Criminal Law Forum* 415, 420.
83. Malcolm Shaw, *International Law* (8th edn, Cambridge 2017) 803.
84. Malcolm Shaw, *International Law* (8th edn, Cambridge 2017) 804.
85. See David Harris et al, *Law of the European Convention on Human Rights* (Butterworths 1995) 654.
86. Hugh Thirlway, 'The International Court of Justice' in Malcolm Evans (ed), *International Law* (OUP 2003) 563.
87. *Statute of the International Court of Justice*, Art 36.
88. *Statute of the International Court of Justice*, Art 65.

III\ **Case Box** *Nuclear Weapons*

It was noted that the ICJ can give advisory opinions. In 1994, the UN General Assembly asked the ICJ for advice on the legality of using nuclear weapons. Ever since the first nuclear explosion, debate has arisen as to whether it can be lawful to use weapons that are intrinsically weapons of mass destruction.

The ICJ accepted jurisdiction and issued an opinion in 1996.[89] It has become one of the most important cases handed down by the ICJ because it does not just provide guidance on the legality of nuclear weapons, but also discusses the circumstances in which force can be used as self-defence.

Ultimately, the ICJ held that there was no international law that approved the use of nuclear weapons, but also no law that prohibited them. It held that threatening the use of such weapons could constitute a breach of law, but not always. Ultimately, and perhaps obviously, decided it could not rule on whether the use of nuclear weapons in self-defence was lawful on a theoretical basis.

Of course, that raises the question about who would be alive to adjudicate on a dispute after thermonuclear war, which was sort of the point the UN General Assembly was trying to make when it sent the reference to the ICJ in the first place.

It is important to note that, in common with most international courts, only states can bring matters before the court.[90] While less important now, when most countries belong to the UN, it was historically possible for a state that was not a member of the UN to bring matters before the ICJ so long as they accepted the provisions of the *Statute of the ICJ*, including abiding by the decisions.[91]

It is not enough that a state is a signatory to the Tribunal, the parties must also consent to the matter being heard before the ICJ. That said, the ICJ is increasingly able to infer consent, so that express consent may not be as required.[92] However, there are undoubtedly limits, and the inference principle is probably recognizing the acquiescence of a state. Where a state expressly does not give consent to the court to resolve the matter then it does not have jurisdiction. The exception to this is where a treaty provides the ICJ with jurisdiction over disputes. In such circumstances, the ratification of the treaty undoubtedly serves as consent for the ICJ to litigate.

The usual remedy from the ICJ is a declaration. The notion behind this is that states acknowledge that they are in dispute, and will comply with the ruling of the ICJ. Thus, if a state is doing something that is in breach of international law/agreement, then they will stop doing so; if they are not doing something they should, then they will start to do something. However, occasionally, the states will also ask for either reparations or compensation, something that the ICJ has, on comparatively rare occasions, awarded.[93]

Judgments of the ICJ are not enforced by it. The UN Charter requires Member States to obey the findings of the court,[94] and it will be remembered that non-members will be required to agree to do so before the court will accept jurisdiction. Where there is a

---

89. ICJ Reports, 1996.
90. *Statute of the International Court of Justice*, Art 34.
91. Malcolm Shaw, *International Law* (8th edn, Cambridge 2017) 815. While it may be thought that this would apply to 'newer' countries this is not the case. Switzerland did not join the UN until September 2002.
92. Malcolm Shaw, *International Law* (8th edn, Cambridge 2017) 817.
93. Malcolm Shaw, *International Law* (8th edn, Cambridge 2017) 838.
94. *UN Charter*, Art 94.

failure to adhere to the judgment then the matter will ultimately be referred to the UN Security Council. Of course, it was noted earlier (4.1.3.2) that the UN Security Council is intrinsically political and this may mean that a member or ally may escape censure. Otherwise, the UN Security Council can put political pressure on a country to comply and can, ultimately, use more persuasive tactics such as sanctions.

4.1.5.2 **Non-peaceful measures**

In an ideal world, international disputes would be settled by peaceful means. This would mean recourse to the rule of law, adherence to the ICJ or other appropriate tribunal and abiding by that ruling. Unfortunately, that is not always going to happen. In some instances, the matter will be resolved by conflict.

This section of the chapter is not intended to provide a comprehensive analysis of what is a very controversial issue. It does not present the rules of armed conflict etc, which is a technical discussion. It outlines the idea that force can be used for good, ie it can be used to compel a state to cease doing something that is illegal.

Perhaps the most commonly used justification is that of self-defence, which Article 51 of the UN Charter expressly retains. However, precisely what amounts to self-defence is, of course, open to debate especially in the post-September 11 era when governments, particularly those of the United States, the United Kingdom, and Australia, have considered self-defence from terrorism acts to be legitimate and used such a justification for the invasion of Afghanistan. The issue of self-defence is extremely controversial[95] and demonstrates the inevitable paradox that arises from the idea that there can be a legal war.

Outside of self-defence, the use of force is ostensibly exercised through the United Nations, although it will be seen that not everybody agrees with that as a concept. The Security Council is charged under the UN Charter to 'determine the existence of any threat to the peace, breach of the peace, or act of aggression'.[96] If the Security Council determines that such a threat exists, it is empowered to do one of two things. The first is to exercise non-military powers, including calling upon Member States of the UN to exercise diplomatic penalties, including economic sanctions.[97] The second power is to engage in military action to 'maintain or restore international peace and security' and this can include blockades or offensive action.[98]

Where action is taken under Article 42 it is usually taken under the auspices of the United Nations, as the Charter provides that Member States shall make available to the UN military forces upon request.[99] These are sometimes referred to as 'peacekeepers' and they normally wear a UN blue beret rather than domestic insignia, to indicate that they are acting under the auspices and authority of the United Nations. That said, it is not required that the action is taken under the command of the UN and perhaps the most notable example of when it was not was during the first Gulf War. A resolution of the Security Council authorized Member States to 'use all necessary measures to uphold and implement resolution 660 (1990)'[100] (which required the removal of Iraqi

---

95.   For an introduction to the arguments see Christine Gray, 'The Use of Force and International Legal Order' in Malcolm Evans (ed), *International Law* (OUP 2003) 599–605.
96.   *UN Charter*, Art 39.
97.   *UN Charter*, Art 41.
98.   *UN Charter*, Art 42.
99.   *UN Charter*, Art 43.
100.   UNSC Resolution 678 (1990).

forces from Kuwait). When Iraq refused to leave, a coalition of forces led by the United States of America launched an offensive conflict that ultimately led to Iraqi forces being removed from Kuwait. This coalition did not serve under the banner, or colours, of the UN and instead they fought as national units within the coalition.[101]

Action taken under Article 42 is relatively uncontroversial from a legal perspective. It is authorized by the UN, and thus is in compliance with international law. However, in 4.1.3.2 it was noted that the politics of the Security Council can complicate matters. This is particularly true where the five permanent members disagree. The use, or threat, of a veto means that strategic allies can sometimes be protected from action by the Security Council, fundamentally weakening its ability to uphold peace and security.

Kosovo

In the late 1990s, a civil war erupted in the province of Kosovo, which was part of the former Yugoslavia. Albanian-descent rebels sought independence, something that Serbia fiercely resisted. Religion undoubtedly played a part, with Kosovo being mainly Muslim, whereas Serbia was predominantly Orthodox Christian.

Conflict arose and there were quickly reports that Serb forces were systematically arresting, torturing, and killing Kosovans, irrespective of whether they were involved in military action. Reports of atrocities and evidence of mass graves began to emerge. Yugoslavia was in a strategically important place within the continent of Europe. The EU and Western powers began to grow alarmed that such conduct was allowed to take place within continental Europe. The UN Security Council adopted Resolution 1199 which required that both sides ended hostilities and observed a ceasefire. Importantly, however, it did not contain any reference to the use of force. Given there was, by that time, clear evidence of atrocities, why? Serbia traditionally had close ties to Russia. Therefore, there was concern that any resolution that would authorize action would be vetoed by Russia.

In the absence of a resolution under Article 42, Western powers eventually decided to use the NATO umbrella to act. Two justifications can be put forward. The first is that NATO is undoubtedly a 'regional grouping', and Article 52 of the UN Charter states that, 'nothing in the present Charter precludes the existence of regional arrangements or agencies for dealing with such matters relating to the maintenance of international peace and security as are appropriate' although it then states that such action must be 'consistent with the Purposes and Principles of the United Nations'. Proponents argue that NATO was a regional grouping that was acting under Article 53. However, it has to be noted that such an argument is not considered particularly attractive.[102]

The second basis was to argue that it was necessary to intervene for humanitarian reasons, with NATO acting because the Security Council was impotent because of the threat of veto.[103] Once action was launched, Russia, Belarus, and India (at that time all close allies) tabled a resolution before the Security Council stating that the NATO action was illegal, and demanding it ended. The resolution was rejected by twelve votes to three (without the need of either France, the United Kingdom, or the United States of America to exercise its veto). Shaw, however, notes that this does not mean that the

---

101. The coalition being led tactically by Gen. Norman Schwarzkopf of the US Army.
102. See, for example, Louis Henkin, 'Kosovo and the Law of "Humanitarian Intervention"' (1999) 93 *American Journal of International Law* 824.
103. Abraham D Sofaer, 'International Law and Kosovo' (2000) 36 *Stanford Journal of International Law* 1, 4.

Security Council was stating that NATO was acting lawfully, simply that they refused to declare that it was not justified.[104] This means that the legality of the use of force for humanitarian purposes remains uncertain. Realistically, it is a flaw with the constitution of the UN, and the political power wielded by the permanent members of the Security Council. However, that is not something that is likely to change soon.[105]

☰ Example Iraq

The (then) Attorney-General, Lord Goldsmith QC, had to consider, prior to the invasion of Iraq in 2003, whether the United Nations had authorized the use of force. Self-defence had been mentioned (which would provide authority under the UN Charter[106]), although it was widely considered that this was unrealistic given the tenuous link that existed between Iraq and terrorist activities in the United Kingdom or United States.

The Attorney-General (controversially) argued that three resolutions of the UN Security Council, taken together, did authorize the use of force (Resolutions 1441, 678, and 687). The argument was controversial because the only resolution that expressly stated that force could be used was Resolution 678, which authorized the use of force to expel Iraq from Kuwait. Resolution 687 suspended Resolution 678 but did not repeal it. The Attorney-General argued that Resolution 1441 lifted the suspension on Resolution 678 but it certainly did not do so expressly. If, however, the Attorney-General was correct then the use of force would have been legal.

It had originally been thought that a separate resolution would be required to authorize the use of force and to avoid any uncertainty but the politics of the Security Council became involved again and with the threat of a veto by other permanent members of the Security Council, the United Kingdom and the United States believed it was better to proceed under the ambiguous authority on the basis that they believed it could authorize the use of force whereas a defeated resolution might be taken as reimposing the suspension on Resolution 678 meaning force would not be authorized. The decision remains extremely controversial, with scholars generally denying the logic.[107] It shows, however, how governments will, following Kosovo, identify ways in which force can be claimed to have been approved by the UN.

4.1.6 **International law and domestic law**

Of course, the primary interest to us is to understand how international law intersects with domestic law. Unlike the position that existed with EU law until the time of our withdrawal, international law does not automatically become part of UK law (see 4.2.4). Even if we ratify a treaty, its terms do not become part of UK law unless Parliament passes a law that incorporates it into domestic law. As will be seen, the courts will sometimes take account of international law, particularly customary law, but it is the exception.

---

104. Malcolm Shaw, *International Law* (8th edn, Cambridge 2017) 882.

105. Eventually the Security Council authorised a military force to bring stability to the region. See Security Council Resolution 1244 (1999).

106. *UN Charter*, Art 51.

107. See, for example, Alex J Bellamy, 'International Law and the War with Iraq' (2003) 4 *Melbourne Journal of International Law* 497.

Perhaps the starting point is the comments of Lord Bingham in *A and others v Secretary of State for the Home Department (no 2)*[108] who stated:

> . . . a treaty, even if ratified by the United Kingdom, has no binding force in the domestic law of this country unless it is given effect by statute or expresses principles of customary international law.[109]

This powerful statement immediately draws a distinction between treaties and customary law. As noted earlier, customary law has typically (but not always) grown over the years into an accepted state of affairs. In many instances, the English courts have considered that these principles are to be found in the common law itself. The case of *A and others* is a good example of this. At the heart of the dispute was whether a court should receive evidence that may have been gathered through torture. While the House of Lords considered the position in international law, they noted that the prohibition of torture was a common-law rule that dated back until at least the fifteenth century.[110] In that way, they believed that international and common law developed together. Of course, it is easier to say that in respect of something like torture, where the general consensus is going to be to decry its use.

In *R v Secretary of State for the Home Department, ex parte Thakrar*,[111] Lord Denning MR stated that, 'the rules of international law only become part of our law in so far as they are accepted and adopted by us'.[112] In other words, there must be acceptance, be that from Parliament or from the common law. Also, if they form part of national law then they are subject to the norms of national law. This case concerned immigration and there was said to be a tension between the principle that a national of a country cannot be refused entry to their national country (even if they have never lived there), and the provisions of the *Immigration Act 1971*. The Court of Appeal questioned whether Mr Thakrar was properly a British national but noted, even if he was, that domestic law trumped international law when they were in conflict.[113]

The High Court later held that international law does not require the establishment of a common law rule.[114] In other words, while international law may be compatible with the common law, it does not require the courts to create a rule of law that has never existed within English law before. That, it was said, is a matter for Parliament and not the courts.

Where, however, the law is not in conflict, or does not establish a new rule to be created, then the courts will be more flexible:

> . . . it is already well settled that, in construing any provision in domestic legislation which is ambiguous in the sense that it is capable of a meaning which either conforms to or conflicts with [international law], the courts will presume Parliament intended to legislate in conformity with . . . , not in conflict with it.[115]

---

108.   [2005] UKHL 71.
109.   ibid, [27].
110.   ibid, [11].
111.   [1974] QB 864.
112.   ibid, 701.
113.   ibid, 708. The judgment is also notable because of the language used by Lord Denning MR where he talks of immigrants not coming 'in singles "but in battalions"' and 'this country would not have room for them' (at 702). It is difficult to conceive of the most senior civil judge in England and Wales using such language today.
114.   *Chagos Islanders v Attorney-General* [2003] EWHC 2222 (QB).
115.   *R v Secretary of State for the Home Department, ex parte Brind and Others* [1991] 1 AC 696 at 747 per Lord Bridge of Harwich.

Thus, international law becomes part of the canons of interpretation that are used when interpreting legislation.[116] Perhaps the best expression of this was provided by Lord Mance in *R (Yam) v Central Criminal Court*[117] where it was said:

> . . . a domestic decision-maker exercising a general discretion (i) is neither bound to have regard to this country's purely international obligations nor bound to give effect to them, but (ii) may have regard to the United Kingdom's international obligations, if he or she decides this to be appropriate.[118]

In other words, the court is not bound to take account of international law but may do so where it does not conflict with a rule of domestic law. The same can be seen in respect of the common law. For example, in *In the application by JR38 for Judicial Review*[119] the Supreme Court were asked to consider whether the release of a photograph of a minor committing a criminal offence was contrary to Article 8 of the ECHR. The Supreme Court held that the rights of a child did not exist in isolation:

> . . . the nature and content of a child's right under Article 8 must be informed by relevant international treaty provisions.[120]

The Supreme Court then went on to consider the *UN Convention on the Rights of the Child* and the *Beijing Rules*,[121] both of which are instruments that the United Kingdom has ratified.[122]

However, it is important to note that again this was the *interpretation* of the law and it does not contradict the salient point that international instruments do not by themselves provide rights that can be litigated within the UK. Perhaps the most useful illustration of this is *R v Jones et al.*[123]

119

II\ Case Box *R v Jones and others*

Margaret Jones illegally entered an RAF base that housed US Air Force aircraft and personnel (RAF Fairford). After securing entrance, she caused damage to fuel tankers and trailers that were present on the base.

She was charged, inter alia, with criminal damage contrary to the *Criminal Damage Act 1971* and sought to argue that she should be allowed to plea reasonable force under *Criminal Law Act 1967*, s 3. That section allows reasonable force to be used, inter alia, to prevent a crime. Jones argued that the jets at RAF Fairford were being used to further an illegal war (the action taken by the United Kingdom and United States in Iraq).

Jones' argument was that crimes of aggression were illegal under customary international law. As that formed a source of English law, it meant that crimes of aggression were illegal under domestic law, meaning reasonable force could be used to prevent that crime.

The House of Lords rejected this argument, noting that even if customary international law recognized a crime, it did not follow that the *Criminal Law Act 1967* was designed to repel such crimes, as it was aimed at preventing domestic crimes.

---

116. These canons were discussed more extensively 2.3.
117. [2016] AC 771.
118. ibid, 809.
119. [2015] UKSC 42.
120. ibid, [49].
121. More properly known as the *United Nations Standard Minimum Rules for the Administration of Juvenile Justice* (adopted by the UN General Assembly in resolution 40/33 of 1985).
122. [2015] UKSC 42 at [50]–[52].
123. [2006] UKHL 16.

The House of Lords was prepared to recognize that a crime of aggression probably existed in customary international law, noting that it was ultimately the basis behind the Nuremberg trials.[124] The House also noted that crimes recognized in customary international law may be assimilated into domestic law, but they doubted that this would follow automatically.[125] They also stated:

> In constructing a domestic statute the ordinary practice is to treat 'offence', in the absence of an express provision to the contrary, as referring to an offence committed here against a common law or statutory rule.[126]

In other words, the presumption remains that Parliament intends something to apply domestically unless the contrary is expressly stated. This would echo the approach noted earlier, that international law requires a positive step to mark its incorporation into UK law, save where it is already a feature of the common law. The House followed this by noting that the courts no longer claim to hold the power to create criminal offences, with new offences being established by Parliament.[127] Thus, even if a crime of aggression existed in international customary law, it would not apply domestically unless Parliament so directed it. Without that crime being recognized, it meant it was not possible for the appellants to argue the right to use reasonable force to prevent crime.

⟳ QUESTION FOR REFLECTION

Are the English courts too timid in their approach to international law? If the United Kingdom has signed and ratified a treaty, it has committed to being bound by its terms. Does this not mean the court should ensure that all laws are interpreted to ensure compliance?

4.1.6.1 **Do we follow international law?**

As this chapter was being rewritten in September 2020 a live issue erupted which shows the importance and political controversy over international law.

The United Kingdom's relationship with the EU is somewhat 'challenging', and this will be explored more in the next section of this chapter. The United Kingdom left the EU on 31 December 2020. In October 2019, the so-called 'withdrawal agreement' between the UK and EU was signed.[128] This agreement was between the United Kingdom and the EU so as a matter of international law is a treaty (4.1.4.2).

In October 2019 rumours circulated that the United Kingdom was going to do something that contradicted the withdrawal agreement. At the time of writing, we are negotiating any subsequent trading treaty, with the negotiations not going well.[129] There is a suggestion, therefore, that this might be a negotiating tactic. However, in the House of Commons, Brendon Lewis MP, the Secretary of State for Northern Ireland, was asked

---

124.   ibid, [19].
125.   ibid, [23].
126.   ibid, [26] per Lord Bingham.
127.   ibid, [28].
128.   The full text is available online at: https://eur-lex.europa.eu/legal-content/EN/TXT/HTML/?uri=CELEX:12019W/TXT(02)&from=EN.
129.   It is ironic that we are writing this now because, of course, by the time this book is published all these matters may have been resolved. However, this remains an important example of how the United Kingdom (currently) treats international obligations.

whether the introduction of the *United Kingdom Internal Market Bill* would breach international law. His answer was:

> I would say to my hon. Friend that yes, this does break international law in a very specific and limited way.[130]

Regardless of the politics of Brexit, this is a cabinet minister stating in the House of Commons that the United Kingdom was prepared to deliberately breach international law. It is not accidentally or inadvertently breaching international law. This answer was given two days before the draft law was published. So, it is a deliberate acceptance that the United Kingdom is prepared to breach international law.

The reaction to this statement was swift. Interestingly, it was not unlike what may happen in the United States, divided along party lines. Politicians on both sides of both Houses of Parliament were unhappy with the statement. This included those who would ordinarily be sympathetic to the Eurosceptic cause. Lord (Michael) Howard, the former leader of the Conservative Party and prominent Eurosceptic said:

> My Lords, does my noble and learned friend simply not understand the damage done to our reputation for probity and respect for the rule of law by those five words uttered by his ministerial colleague, in another place, on Tuesday—words that I never thought I would hear from a British Minister, far less a Conservative Minister? How can we reproach Russia, China or Iran when their conduct falls below internationally accepted standards, when we are showing such scant regard for our treaty obligations?[131]

This was echoed by many speeches. Can the UK breach international law? Yes. As noted above, enforcement of international law is a challenge. The government issued a formal legal statement on the Bill:

> Parliament is sovereign as a matter of domestic law and can pass legislation which is in breach of the UK's Treaty obligations. Parliament would not be acting unconstitutionally in enacting such legislation.[132]

This is true. As was noted in Chapter 2, Parliament is sovereign and can pass (almost) whichever law it wishes. It is therefore not *unconstitutional* to pass this Bill, but it may well be *unlawful*, at least under international law. It is notable that the government did not deny this, with the statement of the Secretary of State for Northern Ireland agreeing with it.

At the time of writing it is not possible to identify what will happen. If the matter proceeds before a domestic court it is inconceivable that the courts would rule anything other than Parliament has the power to pass the legislation. International law is not supreme. Therefore, the courts will have to uphold the legislation if it is passed. Whether that leads to disputes before international tribunals is more interesting. By the time you read this, you should know the answer!

121

---

130. HC Deb 8 September 2020, vol 679, col 509.
131. HL Deb 10 September 2020, vol 805, col 920.
132. See https://assets.publishing.service.gov.uk/government/uploads/system/uploads/attachment_data/file/916702/UKIM_Legal_Statement.pdf.

4.2 **European Union**

Perhaps the biggest change since the last edition of the book is in respect of EU law. The first seven editions of this book used this chapter to explain the EU, including identifying how it took precedence over UK law. Of course, the latter was always the most contentious in any debate around the EU, but it is worth noting that we always knew that EU law would take precedence. The *European Communities Act 1972* expressly stated that EU law would automatically form part of UK law, and would take precedence over statutes and cases.[133]

At the time of writing (September 2020) it is still not clear whether the United Kingdom will leave the EU with a trade deal or not. It is the intention of the current government to leave on 1 January 2021 regardless. To an extent, this does not strictly matter to our examination. We are (now) looking at the EU as a source of influence over UK laws. Any trade deal will be a treaty and will follow the rules identified in the previous part of this chapter. That deal may require us to introduce legislation to enact some of those obligations. It is highly likely to require us to match EU standards on various products (which is common in trade agreements). This, together with the fact that existing EU law will become part of UK law, means that understanding the EU remains important.

The online resources contain a copy of the fourth chapter from the 7th Edition of this book. That was the last chapter to consider in detail the way that the EU operates, and how its law is made. That is not as important to us now as a source of English law. If you study EU law (and currently it remains a professional requirement to do so), then these aspects will almost certainly be covered in that module.

This chapter can now, in the 8th Edition, change course. Its focus will be on how EU law acts as a source of UK domestic law. The detail on the making of EU law is reduced as it is not strictly relevant in terms of it being a source.

It was seen from Chapters 2 and 3 that EU law will continue to influence UK law for some time to come. All existing EU law has been incorporated into UK law by the *European Union (Withdrawal) Act 2018*.[134] While domestic courts are no longer bound to follow EU law, including decisions of the Court of Justice of the EU,[135] and can no longer refer questions to the Court of Justice for advice,[136] the courts will need to look to the law and judgments to help them interpret how the law should apply to the United Kingdom.

> **Example** GDPR/Data Protection Act 2018
>
> Perhaps the biggest change to data protection laws in recent years was brought about by the *EU General Data Protection Regulation*[137] (GDPR). The UK was required to incorporate this into UK law, and it did so by passing the *Data Protection Act 2018* (DPA 2018).

133. *European Communities Act 1972*, s 2.
134. *European Union (Withdrawal) Act 2018*, ss 2–4.
135. *European Union (Withdrawal) Act 2018*, s 6(1)(a).
136. *European Union (Withdrawal) Act 2018*, s 6(1)(b).
137. Regulation (EU) 2016/679 [2016] OJ L119/1.

The DPA 2018 is an unusual piece of legislation as it is, in essence, an enabling Act. It does not replicate the GDPR and instead states that the GDPR itself forms part of UK law. It states: 'The GDPR, the applied GDPR and this Act protect individuals . . .'.[138] In other words, the GDPR sets out the rules, and the Act sets out how these can be enforced, including through criminal offences.[139]

The *European Union (Withdrawal) Act 2018* states that all existing EU law forms part of UK law. Thus, the GDPR remains part of UK law. While subsequent amendments to it will not form part of UK law (unless the UK decides to mirror such changes), where an English court needs to rule on a matter relating to data protection, it is inevitable that this will require them to look to the GDPR to understand what the law says. It may also require them to look at how the Court of Justice of the EU has interpreted its provisions.

A working knowledge of the EU and its laws is therefore necessary to understand the law now incorporated into domestic law. It is important to note that the EU law in force at the time of withdrawal does not have the same status as international treaties. It forms a direct part of UK law, albeit it can now be amended domestically rather than through the EU.

4.2.1 **From the EEC to the EU**

While it is now known as the European Union (EU), the original grouping was the *European Economic Community* (EEC). This was formally established in 1957 although its inception would appear to have taken place in the 1950s.[140] The original grouping of states was: France, West Germany, Italy, Belgium, the Netherlands, and Luxembourg. The original intention was simply to form a community governing European steel and coal and so the *European Coal and Steel Community* (ECSC) was formed in 1952. This was then followed by EURATOM, the *European Atomic Energy Community* and then the *European Economic Community*, these being created by the *Treaties of Rome*.

⚡ TREATIES OF ROME

The status of treaties has already been discussed (4.1.4.2). It became commonplace to talk about the *Treaty of Rome*, meaning the treaty that established the EEC, but in fact there were two treaties since one created EURATOM. In essence, however, the principal treaty prior to the *Lisbon Treaty* was the EEC *Treaty of Rome* and all new members of the EEC had to sign the *Treaty of Rome*.

In 1967 these communities were, in effect, merged (see *Merger Treaty 1965*) and two institutions were created, the *European Commission* and the *Council of the European Communities*. It is essential that the latter is not confused with *the* Council of Europe since they do remain separate. Following the *Treaty of Maastricht* the Council of the

---

138. *Data Protection Act 2018*, s 2(1).
139. Contained in Part 6 of the Act.
140. John Fairhurst, *Law of the European Union* (10th edn, Pearson Education 2014) 5.

European Communities became known as the Council of Ministers or, following the *Treaty of Lisbon*, simply 'the Council'.

As the Community grew so did its mission and it moved from being a purely economic grouping to much more, with greater harmony in respect of laws and more general cooperation. Successive treaties have then been used to modify the Community and Union and it is certainly clear that the present Union is significantly different from the EEC first created.

4.2.1.1 **The road to Lisbon**

The *Treaty of Lisbon* changed the structure of the treaties and the EU. However, it is worth pausing momentarily to place this into context. Perhaps the first treaty of significance was the *Single European Act* (SEA) which should not be confused with domestic definitions of an Act as it is an international treaty. The SEA was signed in 1986 by ministers of the then Member States and the three new Member States that joined later that year. It came into force in 1987 and its primary purpose was to bring about closer cohesion within the European market. In terms of the policy changes, the SEA defined the internal market as being free from all internal constraints in respect of certain fundamental freedoms, this being enforced by the changes to the Commission etc. The Treaty also sought to harmonize certain laws in respect of health and safety etc. It also, importantly, began the trend away from pure economic considerations with the establishment of the framework for a common foreign policy whereby Member States would work together to assist in the security of the Community.

Changes were also made to the European Parliament, allegedly to make it more democratic, but, in reality, this did not happen until some time later. As will be discussed momentarily, the European Parliament poses a conundrum for Europeans. It cannot replicate domestic Parliaments, and it does not have exclusive competence over legislation (as this is shared with the Council of Ministers).

The *Treaty on the European Union*, otherwise known as the Maastricht Treaty, was perhaps the most significant instrument before Lisbon. This marked the shift from the EEC to the European Union. The EU was to have three pillars (European Communities (roughly what the EEC covered), a Common Foreign & Security Policy, and a Justice & Home Affairs pillar). These pillars were later abolished by the Lisbon Treaty, with their work being subsumed into other aspects of their work.

The Maastricht Treaty is perhaps most famous for a push towards monetary and economic union. The most notable change here, was the creation of what is now known as 'the Euro', the common currency used by many European countries.

The next treaty was the Amsterdam Treaty. Some commentators have argued that this Treaty did little other than renumber the Treaty of Rome,[141] and that in essence it was a 'smoke and mirrors' treaty that allowed certain EU countries to work together in a closer way but without the need for all Member States to be involved with ancillary matters.

Perhaps the most significant issue that the Amsterdam Treaty brought was a formal link to the *European Convention on Human Rights*, which is operated by a separate organization. The Amsterdam Treaty sought to strengthen the ECHR by allowing the Council to suspend the voting rights of a Member State if it persistently breaches

---

141.   Nigel Foster, *Foster on EU Law* (6th edn, OUP 2017) ch 1.

the ECHR.[142] It will be noted later that there is no direct enforcement action for decisions of the *European Court of Human Rights*, but this provision perhaps introduces an 'ultimate' sanction for those members of the EU who refuse to adhere to the rulings of the ECtHR.

The final treaty before Lisbon, was the *Treaty of Nice*. This was a relatively short treaty whose purpose was to prepare the EU for expansion through the introduction of new Member States (taking the total to twenty-eight). A key change introduced in the Treaty of Nice was to make it easier for the Council to suspend the voting rights of those who consistently breached the ECHR. Instead of requiring unanimity (which is always difficult due to the politics of groupings within the EU), suspension could occur where four-fifths of the Council voted in favour of the resolution.

Other parts of Nice, dealt with the wider remit of the EU, including foreign policy, common defence plans, the European Arrest Warrant, and closer cooperation between Member States.[143] These are matters that are, however, best considered in specialist modules relating to the European Union, particularly as they are no longer relevant following the departure of the UK from the EU.

4.2.1.2 The Treaty of Lisbon

The Treaty of Lisbon has become the most important treaty and yet this was not supposed to happen. The EU envisaged a single treaty document that would act as a Constitution of the EU. However, this proved extremely controversial, and voters in both France and the Netherlands rejected the proposed constitution.

EU leaders, realizing that a constitutional treaty would not pass, decided to establish a new treaty. Parts of it were undoubtedly constitutional in significance, but, formally, it was not considered to be a constitution and this meant that some countries did not feel the need to consult domestic voters.[144]

The Treaty of Lisbon (TL) did not just renumber the Treaty of Rome, but it changed its name. Instead of its formal title being the *Treaty establishing the European Community* (TEU), it becomes the *Treaty on the Functioning of the European Union* (TFEU).[145] This demonstrates that the Treaty of Rome is not just about how to join the EU, but is its rulebook. After Lisbon, the EU was considered to be 'ruled' by the TFEU and the Treaty of the EU (TEU—aka the Maastricht Treaty), both of which have equal status.[146]

The Lisbon Treaty changed many of the organizational structures of the EU, introducing, for example, the *President of the European Council*, but again these are now less relevant to a textbook on the English Legal System. Instead, they will be of relevance to specialist modules on the European Union.

125

---

142. Amsterdam Treaty, Art 7.
143. John Fairhurst, *Law of the European Union* (10th edn, Pearson Education 2014) 23.
144. Most notably this was the position in the United Kingdom. While the then PM, Tony Blair, had promised a referendum for the EU constitution, his successor, Gordon Brown, argued this was not necessary because the Treaty of Lisbon was not a constitution, and simply amended the powers. The courts ultimately held that it was a matter for Parliament and the English courts could not interfere with the proper processes of Parliament (see *R (on the application of Wheeler) v Office of the Prime Minister* [2008] EWHC 1409 (Admin)).
145. *Treaty of Lisbon*, Art 1(11).
146. TFEU, Art 1(2).

The TEU and TFEU establish a system of competences. If something is not considered a competence of the EU, then it remains a sovereign matter for the Member States.[147] 'Sovereignty' was starting to become a political issue within the EU at this time (not least in the United Kingdom), and so this statement was considered to be a demonstration that the EU only claimed jurisdiction over certain matters. It also emphasized the principle of consent. Member States choose to join the EU and part of acceding to the EU is to accept so-called joint sovereignty, ie that states recognize that there is pooled sovereignty over certain issues across the EU. As noted previously, this was ever thus, and it is clear from the *European Communities Act 1972* that Parliament understood that this was the case when it joined the (then) EEC.

The competences

The competences of the EU are divided into three:

- areas where the EU has exclusive competence[148]
- areas where there is shared competence[149]
- areas where the EU can take action to support, coordinate, or supplement action by Member States.[150]

The differences between them is set out in Article 2 TFEU. Article 2(1) states that where a matter is within the exclusive competence of the EU, 'only the Union may legislate and adopt legally binding acts, the Member States being able to do so themselves only if so empowered by the Union'. In other words, Member States surrender the power to legislate in these areas save where permitted to do so by the EU. Article 2(2) states that shared competence means that both the EU and Member States may legislate but that 'Member States shall exercise their competence to the extent that the Union has not exercised its competence'. In other words, Member States may legislate in those areas where the EU has not. Article 2(5) states that where the EU takes action to support, coordinate, or supplement action by Member States it does so 'without thereby superseding their competence in these areas'. In other words, the EU will only support the actions of Member States and their laws will not take precedence over domestic laws in these areas.

In addition to these three competences the EU has competence in respect of economic, employment, and social policy[151] and a common foreign and security policy.[152] The latter, in particular, demonstrates the fact that the pillar structure adopted by the *Treaty of Maastricht* has been superseded and that the EU now has general competence in these areas, subject to opt-outs negotiated by various countries.

It has been stated that 'the Treaty of Lisbon distinguishes between the existence of competence . . . and the use of such competence, which is determined by subsidiarity and proportionality'.[153] Subsidiarity is explained by Article 5(3) TEU which states that

---

147. TEU, Art 4.
148. TFEU, Art 3.
149. ibid, Art 4.
150. ibid, Art 6.
151. ibid, Art 2(3).
152. ibid, Art 2(4).
153. Paul Craig, 'The Treaty of Lisbon, Process, Architecture and Substance' (2008) 33 *European Law Review* 137, 149.

save where a matter is within the exclusive competence of the EU, the EU can only act where it is satisfied that 'the objectives of the proposed action cannot be sufficiently achieved by the Member States . . . [but can] be better achieved at Union level'. This is limiting the circumstances under which the EU can act outside of situations where it has exclusive jurisdiction and it is notable that the Treaty of Lisbon has given additional power to national parliaments in assessing subsidiarity (see Articles 4 and 6 of Protocol 2 to the TFEU on the application of the principles of subsidiarity and proportionality). National parliaments will be consulted on draft legislation and where, within eight weeks of receiving the draft legislation, it believes that it does not comply with the principle of subsidiarity it may notify the Presidents of the European Parliament, Council, and Commission with a reasoned opinion stating why it does not believe that it complies. Such notifications must be taken into account[154] and where at least one-third of all votes allocated to national parliaments question whether the draft legislation complies with subsidiarity then the relevant institution must formally review the instrument.

4.2.2 The institutions

Before considering the sources of EU law, it is worth pausing to note some of the institutions of the EU. Article 13 of the TEU lists the following institutions:

- the European Parliament
- the European Council
- the Council
- the European Commission
- the Court of Justice of the European Union
- the European Central Bank
- the Court of Auditors.

In common with the new approach for this chapter, a much more condensed summary of the key institutions will now be presented. A fuller discussion can be found in the 7th Edition chapter available on the online resources, but also EU textbooks.

4.2.2.1 The European Parliament

When the then EEC was created there was no European Parliament, as the initial legislative body was drawn from the representatives of national legislatures. Eventually it was believed that Parliament should be more democratic, and the Single European Act (see 4.2.1.1) attempted to do this. For the first time, the Members of the Parliament (known as MEPs) were elected by direct suffrage through European constituencies. MEPs hold office for a five year term but can be re-elected as often as voters wish.

Unlike constituencies in the Westminster Parliament which are based on population, the same is not necessarily true of the European Parliament. Each Member State is allocated a number of seats and this differs according not only to the size of the country but also its importance. The TFEU has attempted to alter this a little by adjusting the numbers slightly but there continue to be significant differences with, for example,

---

154. TFEU, Protocol 2, Art 7.

Germany having ninety-six seats, Belgium having twenty-one, and Ireland having thirteen. However, given the variances of population this can mean that the smaller countries do have proportionately better representation than the larger countries[155] but they may have less 'power' than the larger countries. Rather than sitting in national groupings the Parliament divides itself into transnational groupings that reflect the relevant political ethos of the group. Rule 30 of the *European Parliament's Rules for Procedure* dictates when a grouping is recognized. It must currently be a grouping of a minimum of twenty-five MEPs but these must be representatives from at least one-quarter of the Member States (currently six Member States). Thus if thirty MEPs from five Member States wish to form a grouping this would not be formally recognized and would not, for example, receive staffing or resources beyond that given to individual MEPs.

The European Parliament cannot be directly compared to a national Parliament since it forms only one part of the legislature (the other being the Council). Until the Treaty of Lisbon the powers of the Parliament were somewhat limited but the TL greatly increased the powers of the Parliament, with it being described as an 'institutional winner'.[156] Prior to the Treaty of Lisbon the European Parliament was to an extent inferior to the Council but they now act primarily on an equal basis. However, the European Parliament does not, unlike the Westminster Parliament, have the right to initiate legislation (this being primarily the preserve of the Commission). Article 225 TEU allows the Parliament, by a simple majority, to request the Commission to submit a proposal for legislation but the Commission need not do so, merely needing to explain to the Parliament why it has failed to do so should it decide not to bring forward any legislation.

The European Parliament has three principal roles. The first is the participation in the legislative process, the second is its scrutiny of the budget, and the third is to supervise the Commission. It also has additional political powers in that it can conduct investigations or hearings into appropriate matters. Its final power is that the Parliament must approve the admission of new Member States.[157]

The Parliament's power to scrutinize legislation is perhaps its most important power. Originally this power was simply to be consulted on legislation and its views could be disregarded. However, the TL has significantly increased the power of the Parliament and it is now involved in the passing of most legislation, including treaties entered into by the EU.

Supervision of the Executive

Perhaps one of the most important functions of the European Parliament is to assist in holding the European Commission, as the EU's executive, to account. The Commission is not part of the Parliament (and in this way can be distinguished from the Westminster Parliament where the executive is drawn from member of the legislature) but will frequently be involved in giving evidence to parliamentary committees considering evidence etc. Thus Parliament can question the Commission and consider the reasoning behind appropriate legislation and, in defined circumstances, veto the legislation.

---

155. For example, Germany has a ratio of 1 MEP per 860,000 citizens whereas Ireland has 1 MEP per 368,000.
156. Paul Craig, 'The Treaty of Lisbon, Process, Architecture and Substance' (2008) 33 *European Law Review* 137, 156.
157. TEU, Art 19.

Article 239 TFEU makes clear that the Commission has a legal responsibility to answer questions put to it by MEPs and this includes written questions. Accordingly, this creates another method by which Parliament may hold the Commission to account not least because most questions and answers will be publicly reported. An important extension of the TL was that approval of the budget is based on the ordinary legislative process[158] and therefore the Parliament now has considerable power over the proposed budget since it has a number of opportunities to reject it.[159]

The European Parliament has the right to approve the appointment of the Commission. The President of the Commission is now elected by the European Parliament[160] although this is slightly limited by Article 17(7) TEU, which states that the European Council, acting by a qualified majority (see 'Voting'), proposes to the Parliament the candidate for President. The Parliament can then approve the appointment by absolute majority and if the candidate fails then the Council must propose a new candidate. Reference to 'new candidate' in Article 17(7) would suggest that it is not open to the European Council to suggest the same person. The Parliament does not have the right to consider individual commissioners (whose appointment is a matter for the European Council: see Article 17(7) TEU) but the Commission as a whole is responsible to Parliament via the power of censure.

4.2.2.2 The European Council

Confusingly, the TEU lists two institutions that sound similar; the *European Council* and *The Council*. 'The Council' is sometimes referred to as the '*Council of the European Union*' although it is notable that Article 13 TEU does not refer to it in this way. 'The Council' will be discussed later (4.2.2.3) but is a member of the legislature and acts in conjunction with the Parliament (discussed earlier). The 'European Council' is different; it is a body that comprises the Heads of state or government of each Member State together with the President of the Council and the President of the Commission.[161] It only became a formal institution as a result of the Treaty of Lisbon; before that it had an unofficial political existence.

The European Council must meet twice every six months when convened by its President[162] and its work can be assisted by ministers or commissioners. The European Council is charged with a number of matters but perhaps two of its most important charges are quite generic. The first is: 'The European Council shall provide the Union with the necessary impetus for its development and shall define the general political directions and priorities thereof'[163] and the second is Article 222(4) TFEU which requires the European Council to 'regularly assess the threats facing the Union in order to enable the Union and its Member States to take effective action'. Clearly therefore, the European Council is an important institution not least because it represents the ultimate executive authority for each Member State. It is also clear that the European Council is principally a political body and one that is charged with taking the necessary political steps to facilitate the work. It has no legislative authority.[164]

158.　TFEU, Art 314.
159.　For a further discussion see G Love, 'Oh Brave New World! Lisbon Enters into Force' (2010) *EU Focus* 1, 8.
160.　TEU, Art 14(1).
161.　TEU, Art 15(2).
162.　ibid, Art 15(3).
163.　ibid, Art 15(1).
164.　ibid, Art 15(1).

The European Council will have certain policy matters reserved to it, for example, Article 68 TFEU states: 'The European Council shall define the strategic guidelines for legislative and operational planning within the area of freedom, security and justice.' Also numerous other aspects of the Treaties require matters of dispute to be referred to the European Council. Again, this is a pragmatic decision as it means that where there is dispute between Member States it can be resolved by the heads of government. The Council should ordinarily act by consensus[165] which must mean unanimity. However, there are a number of issues within the Treaty that require decisions to be taken by qualified majority (a system discussed later).

4.2.2.3 Council

The second of the two 'Councils' is 'The Council' which is also, following the Maastricht Treaty, referred to as either the *Consilium* or the '*Council of the European Union*'. However, in both the TEU and TFEU it is simply referred to as '*The Council*'. Whilst the European Council is a member of the executive and acts on a policy level, the Council is a member of the legislature (sharing legislative authority with the European Parliament).[166]

The Council is established by a representative of each Member State who is of ministerial level[167] and so it is a council of ministers (indeed, this is what it was previously called). However, it would be wrong to say that there is a single representative since the actual representation will depend on what is being discussed, this compromise being defined as the Council sitting in different 'configurations'. Accordingly, if, for example, the Council is discussing foreign affairs then the minister will be drawn from the foreign office for each state (which may not be the primary minister but may be a junior minister depending on the importance of the matter) and if it is discussing the agricultural policy then the minister will be drawn from the Department of Agriculture. The Presidency of the Council rotates every six months in the way that the European Council did until a permanent President was appointed.

It has been noted that the Council is there to represent the national interest,[168] unlike many of the other institutions who are there to represent the European Union. Originally, the Council was the principal legislator of the EU, but it is now co-legislator with the European Parliament. However, for most business, the European Parliament now has a veto because proposals from the Commission go to both, and if the Parliament disagrees, the legislation can no longer be passed.[169]

The voting of the Council is somewhat controversial as there are three types of vote. The first is unanimity which is self-explanatory. The second is 'simple majority' which means that there must be a mathematical majority of those present. As there are now twenty-seven Member States, this would mean that if all countries were represented, a simple majority would require fourteen votes. The final, and most controversial, is a 'qualified majority'. The qualified majority is now the most usual form of voting, and it means that each country's vote is weighted according to their population.[170] For a matter to be passed, at least fifty-five per cent of Member States must agree to the

165. ibid, Art 15(4).
166. ibid, Art 16(1).
167. ibid, Art 16(2).
168. Karen Davies, *Understanding European Union Law* (5th edn Taylor & Francis 2013) 36.
169. TFEU, Art 294.
170. Karen Davies, *Understanding European Union Law* (5th edn Taylor & Francis 2013) 37.

resolution, but these must account for at least sixty-five per cent of the EU population.[171] The effect of this is that the larger countries can obstruct legislation more easily, particularly where they work together.

4.2.2.4 **European Commission**

Perhaps the most famous of the institutions is the European Commission, and arguably it is the most powerful. Originally it was the sole executive of the EU although it now sits alongside the European Council as the executive. The size of the Commission is controversial[172] and currently amounts to one member (commissioners, President, and the High Representative for Foreign Affairs) per country.[173] This position should have ended in 2014 with the Commission then numbering the same as two-thirds of the Member States (currently twenty-seven so it would number eighteen). It was intended that the members would be adopted on 'a strictly equal rotation between the Member States, reflecting the geographical range of all the Member States'.[174] This would have meant countries would, for the first time, lose 'their' commissioner and some doubted whether politically it would ever be possible to move to this new system.[175] In order to ensure that Ireland voted in favour of the ratification of the *Lisbon Treaty* the Council agreed to ensure that representation on the Commission continued to be based on the 'one per member state' basis.[176] It is perhaps somewhat ironic that in order to ensure *Lisbon* passed the Council committed itself to ignoring one of the key changes that the Treaty itself proposed. How long this can be justified if the EU continues to expand is perhaps more questionable, not least because the number of commissioner 'briefs' must be limited.

The President of the Commission is now elected by the Council and European Parliament. The President allocates the 'portfolios' of each commissioner[177] although the President is likely to consult national governments as part of their campaign for election. The creation of a President has also transformed the way in which commissioners can be dismissed. Whilst individual commissioners are able to resign it has traditionally been difficult for them to be removed. However, the Treaty of Lisbon has altered this position to a certain extent and the President of the Commission is now able to ask an individual commissioner to resign.[178] Assuming the President does not do this then the powers of dismissal remain limited.

The principal power of dismissal is exercised by the Court of Justice of the EU. They have the power to order the compulsory retirement of a commissioner where he or she 'no longer fulfils the conditions required for the performance of his duties or if he is guilty of serious misconduct'.[179] This jurisdiction is exercised by the Court of Justice sitting *en banc* and has never happened. Otherwise, the only power of dismissal is where the European Parliament passes a vote of censure,[180] when the entire Commission must resign.

131

---

171.   See https://www.consilium.europa.eu/en/council-eu/voting-system/.
172.   Paul Craig, 'The Treaty of Lisbon, Process, Architecture and Substance' (2008) *33 European Law Review*, 137, 155.
173.   TEU, Art 17(4).
174.   ibid, Art 17(5).
175.   John Fairhurst, *Law of the European Union* (10th edn, Pearson Education 2014) 92–3.
176.   Margot Horspool and Matthew Humphreys, *European Union Law (Core Text Series)* (7th edn, OUP 2012) 48.
177.   TEU, Art 17(6).
178.   ibid.
179.   TFEU, Art 247.
180.   TFEU, Art 234 when read in conjunction with TEU, Art 17(8).

Whilst Commission members are drawn from the Member States, Article 17(3) TEU makes clear that they are independent of the Member States and must operate on behalf of the EU and not take instructions from their national government or other domestic body. Their term of office is for five years although they can be reappointed. The primary duties of the Commission are summarized in Article 17(1) TEU:

> The Commission shall promote the general interest of the Union and take appropriate initiatives to that end. It shall ensure the application of the Treaties, and of measures adopted by the institutions pursuant to them. It shall oversee the application of Union law under the control of the Court of Justice of the European Union. It shall execute the budget and manage programmes. It shall exercise coordinating, executive and management functions, as laid down in the Treaties . . .

Article 17(2) TEU expressly notes that the ability to initiate legislation is vested solely with the Commission unless the Treaties say otherwise. This is what provides authority for the Commission to be the key instigator of policy and legislative instruments. The wording of Article 17 also provides a basis for its policing function. As it is the guardian of the implementation of law, this means that it is also responsible for taking action against those who appear to breach EU law, be that private bodies of Member States.

Example Microsoft

One of the biggest examples of the Commission taking action against a private body is its action against Microsoft. The Commission considered that Microsoft had been acting in such a way as to abuse its dominant position in the market, particularly in respect of the way that it 'bundled' software on new computers.[181]

The Commission required Microsoft to cease its anti-competitive practices and when it believed that it had failed to do so it issued a fine of €280 million.

The Commission is the initiator of draft legislation and so while they are not part of the legislature, they control what legislative instruments are passed to the Parliament and Council for consideration. Once legislation is drafted it is sent to both parties where it may be subject to amendment. An important part of the Commission's role is negotiating with these bodies to enable the legislation to be passed.

4.2.2.5 Court of Justice of the European Union

The *Treaty of Lisbon* significantly altered the judicial branch of the EU. Prior to Lisbon, there were two courts; the *Court of First Instance* (CFI) and the *European Court of Justice* (ECJ). Lisbon altered this and Article 19(1) TEU creates the *Court of Justice of the European Union* (CJEU), which encompasses the *Court of Justice* (that which was the ECJ) and the *General Court* (that which was the CFI). Several *specialized courts* are created which are, in essence, specialist tribunals that deal with matters relating to the Civil Service. The courts sit in Luxembourg,[182] which is a deliberate signal that the

---

181.   For a useful history of this read Simonetta Vezzoso, 'The Incentives Balance Test in the EU Microsoft Case: A Pro-innovation "Economics-Based" Approach' (2006) 27 *European Competition Law Review* 382.

182.   TFEU, Protocol 6.

CJEU is independent of both the executive and the legislature which is based in Brussels and Strasbourg.

Each Member State must nominate one judge from their own jurisdiction,[183] and they are assisted by eight Advocates-General (A-G)(discussed shortly). Judges and Advocates-General must be qualified for appointment to 'the highest judicial offices in their respective countries'.[184] When the United Kingdom had a judge, this meant that they had to be qualified as a pusine judge (discussed in Chapter 8) if they were from England & Wales, or a Senator of the College of Justice, the equivalent in Scotland.[185]

The judges are appointed for a renewable term of six years', although their appointment is staggered so that there is a partial replacement every three years. They are required to be independent, and they elect one of their own number to be President of the Court. Of course, there are always questions over the extent to which a judge on a renewable contract can ever truly be considered independent. It has been suggested that the practice of the CJEU ordinarily issuing only a single judgment protects individual judges from a retributive national government.[186]

⚡ ADVOCATES-GENERAL

Advocates-General have no comparable counterparts within the United Kingdom, with their closest comparison being an *amicus curiae* (friend of the court, ie counsel appointed separate from the parties to put forward a neutral argument or one in the public interest). It is not unusual for the *amicus* to be the Attorney-General.

Article 252 TFEU makes clear that the role of the Advocate-General is 'to make, in open court, reasoned submissions on cases which ... require his involvement'. In other words, the Advocate-General will read the written submissions of both parties and provide an independent viewpoint to the Court of Justice on what it believes the law is.

Although the court is not bound in any way by the opinion of the Advocate-General it normally carries with it significant weight and it will, in fact, frequently be followed.[187] Thus, the opinion of the Advocate-General can often be an early clue to the parties when identifying how the court is likely to rule.

Court of Justice

The Court of Justice has the power to review decisions of the General Court[188] and, accordingly, it acts as an appellate court to the General Court although this power is exercisable only in respect of points of law.

Article 251 TFEU states that the Court of Justice will sit in chambers, a Grand Chamber or, when set out in statute, a full court. Protocol 3 TFEU provides for a 'Statute on the Court of Justice of the European Union', which, in essence, provides further details on how it shall operate. Chambers will ordinarily be divided into

---

183.   TEU, Art 19(2).
184.   TFEU, Art 253.
185.   They did not have to be puisne judges, merely qualified to be appointed as one. That said, all bar one judge was either a senior judge or was appointed a senior judge upon their return. The exception was Sir David Edward who retired after returning from Luxembourg.
186.   Karen Davies, *Understanding European Union Law* (5th edn Taylor & Francis 2013) 40.
187.   John Fairhurst, *Law of the European Union* (10th edn, Pearson Education 2014) 160.
188.   TFEU, Art 256(1).

divisions of three and five judges[189] and each chamber will elect one of their number as President. A Grand Chamber shall consist of thirteen judges[190] and is presided over by the President of the Court. A matter is heard by a Grand Chamber whenever a Member State or an EU institution so requests it. The full court is heard only when in specific circumstances or where the Court or A-G considers that it raises such a serious point that it should be heard by the full court. Confusingly, whilst the full court should mean that it sits *en banc* (ie all twenty-seven judges) Article 17 of Protocol 3 states that a full court will be quorate with only fifteen judges sitting. The same provision states that a Grand Chamber (which should consist of thirteen judges) is quorate if nine judges sit.

An important jurisdiction of the Court of Justice is to hear preliminary references. This is a procedure whereby a national court may (and in some instances must) refer a question of EU law to the Court of Justice.[191] While called a preliminary ruling it is, in fact, a final decision of the Court: it is preliminary because the domestic proceedings are suspended while the reference is heard.

In *Irish Creamery Milk Supplies v Ireland*[192] the (then) ECJ said that the preliminary reference system was 'a framework for close co-operation between the national courts and the Court of Justice based on the assignment of different functions'.[193] In essence, it is a way of ensuring that domestic courts do not deviate too far from EU law by adopting this own interpretations of EU law.

General Court

According to Article 256 TFEU the General Court has jurisdiction to determine first-instance actions or proceedings under Articles 263, 265, 268, 270, and 272 unless they are expressly reserved by Treaty to the Court of Justice. In addition it has jurisdiction to hear appeals against the decisions of the specialized courts.

Whilst the General Court does have an A-G it is notable that Article 49 of Protocol 3 TFEU states that judges of the General Court can be asked to perform the task of an A-G. The duty of an A-G is the same as with the Court of Justice, ie to provide an independent assessment on the merits of the case. Article 50 of Protocol 3 states that the General Court should sit in chambers of three and five and that each chamber shall elect its own President, but the Article also provides that in some instances it is possible that work of the Court can be exercised by a single judge.

4.2.3 Sources of EU law

The most relevant issue for us now are the sources of EU law. The precise number of sources that exist is open to debate. However, as with domestic sources, they can be divided into primary and secondary sources. The primary source are the EU Treaties. Particularly after the Treaty of Lisbon, these remain the definitive rulebook for the EU. Secondary sources include:

- secondary legislation
- case law

---

189.   ibid, Protocol 3, Art 16.
190.   ibid.
191.   TFEU, Art 267.
192.   [1981] ECR 735.
193.   [1981] ECR 735 at [5]

- general principles
- international agreements.[194]

The latter two are the equivalent of the ordinary principles of international law discussed in earlier sections.

4.2.3.1 Treaties

Post-Lisbon, the TEU and TFEU are the most important treaties, but the other treaties are consulted where necessary, particularly when it is to understand what it is that the Member States agreed. It is not just the text of the treaties themselves that are relevant, but also the protocols to the treaties which include, for example, reference to how the courts work[195] and what measures countries have opt-outs for.[196]

Charter of Fundamental Rights

The *Charter of Fundamental Rights* demonstrates how treaties can change in status. This was originally a stand-alone agreement by some Member States and was never intended to be legally binding.[197] Its status was then reviewed, and ultimately it became incorporated into EU law. Article 6(1) TEU states:

> The Union recognises the rights, freedoms and principles set out in the Charter of Fundamental Rights of the European Union . . . which shall have the same legal value of the Treaties.

The Charter was the centre of considerable dispute with the United Kingdom, who negotiated a 'clarification' of its applicability, although the extent to which this clarification was of any legal status was open to question.[198] The position is now clear as it does not form part of UK law following our departure from the EU.[199]

European Convention on Human Rights

As noted earlier, the ECHR, while technically a separate treaty, has been recognized within EU law. Article 6(3) TEU states that the ECHR shall constitute general principles of EU law. The effect of this is, presumably, that the CJEU could decide that the actions of an institution, or a piece of legislation is contrary to the ECHR, in which case, according to EU law it could strike down the relevant instrument.

4.2.3.2 Secondary legislation

Article 288 TFEU provides that there are three types of secondary legislation: regulations, directives and decisions. The effects of these are set out within the Article.

> A regulation shall have general application. It shall be binding in its entirety and directly applicable in all Member States.

135

---

194.   Karen Davies *Understanding European Union Law* (5th edn, Taylor & Francis 2013) 53.
195.   For example, TFEU, Protocol 3.
196.   For example, TFEU, Protocols 15–18 and 20–2.
197.   Karen Davies *Understanding European Union Law* (5th edn, 2013, Taylor & Francis) at 66.
198.   For a further discussion see, Paul Craig, 'The Treaty of Lisbon, Process, Architecture and Substance' (2008) 33 *European Law Review* 137, 163.
199.   *European Union (Withdrawal) Act 2018*, s 5(4).

A directive shall be binding, as to the result to be achieved, upon each Member State to which it is addressed, but shall leave to the national authorities the choice of forms and methods.

A decision shall be binding in its entirety. A decision which specifies those to whom it is addressed shall be binding only on them.

'General application' means that it automatically binds all Member States. Indeed, regulations come into force at the time published, and are enforceable irrespective of the actions of Member States. That said, Member States can choose to legislate separately so long as it is done within the appropriate timeframe. The *General Data Protection Regulation* (GDPR) was mentioned at the start of this section. While being automatically bound by it, the UK government chose to legislate to detail how it would apply and be enforced domestically (passing the *Data Protection Act 2018*).

A directive binds the Member States to the objective set out in the directive, but it allows Member States to decide how to bring about these objectives. Importantly, a directive does not come into force until it has been incorporated into national law.[200] Decisions are binding only on those to which they have been addressed, and do not establish a legal principle throughout the EU.

Article 288 also makes reference to 'recommendations' and 'opinions' but it is clear that these are not binding. However, they are considered to be persuasive, and highlight how the EU believes a matter is supposed to be implemented. There are no consequences to failing to follow a recommendation or opinion, although a domestic court may seek the ruling of the CJEU where a national measure appeared to contravene a recommendation or opinion.

How legislation is passed is no longer relevant in a book on the English Legal System, as only legislation passed prior to our departure from the EU will remain relevant to the courts of England and Wales. If you wish to understand how legislation is passed, then you should consult either a textbook on EU law or the earlier version of this chapter which is available on the online resources.

4.2.3.3 Decisions of the Court of Justice of the EU

An important source of EU law is unquestionably the decisions of the CJEU and, before it, the ECJ. While the CJEU does not formally adhere to precedent as we would understand it in England and Wales, it does try to be consistent, meaning that the decisions of the Court allow us to understand how the law is intended to apply.

Some students reading for an English law degree sometimes struggle with EU law. This is, in part, because the approach to case law is very different to that in England (a point judicially recognized by Lord Denning MR in *Bulmer v Bollinger*[201] which was one of the first cases in the appellate courts of England and Wales to look at EU law). To an extent, this should not be surprising because the EU has more in common with continental Europe, which has a civil law tradition, than the common law tradition of England and Wales.[202] The most important effect of this is that there is no inherent power of the CJEU: it's actions and activities are limited by the Treaties. More importantly, the post-Lisbon approach to competences means that anything that is not

---

200.   Karen Davies *Understanding European Union Law* (5th edn, 2013, Taylor & Francis) at 56.
201.   [1974] 3 WLR 202.
202.   The distinction between these traditions were discussed in Chapter 1.

reserved to the EU is within the competence of the Member States, meaning that neither the EU nor the CJEU can act.

Another significant difference between the courts of England and Wales and the CJEU is that the latter has more widespread powers of review. As noted in Chapter 2, the courts of England and Wales do not have the power to 'strike down' legislation, nor can they interpret a piece of legislation in such a way as to nullify it. The CJEU however, has this power. The CJEU can declare any legislation (of either the EU or a Member State) void where it is considered incompatible with EU law.[203] Thus, it is a powerful body that all EU institutions and Member States must respect.

Judgments

Although it is often said that the CJEU will ordinarily only give a single judgment, this is not necessarily correct. Where the Court is divided, at least one judge will typically give a dissenting judgment. It is also open to judges to provide a separate assenting judgment, particularly where they disagree with the extent to which the majority have so-ruled, or where they believe an ancillary point needs to be developed. Of course, this means that the 'shielding' that was suggested as a positive feature of judicial independence (4.1.5.1) is minimized. However, giving more than one judgment is an approach that is adopted in many countries, most notably the UK Supreme Court and the Supreme Court of the United States of America.

The official language of the CJEU is French, and so this is the definitive version. Judgments are invariably published in English (as this is the working second language of many countries), and where a case involves a domestic dispute, the judgment will invariably also be published in that language (eg where a Spanish court refers a matter to the CJEU, the judgment will inevitably be published in Spanish). However, where there is any dispute as to the meaning of words, it is the French version that is considered to be definitive.

Where a domestic court has asked the CJEU for a preliminary reference under Article 267 (see 4.2.2.5), the judgment is binding on the courts of that country.[204] However, it is only the legal principle that is binding. The application of that principle to the facts is for the domestic court, although the CJEU may provide 'hints' as to how it believes the matter should be resolved.

Preliminary references are not binding on the other Member States although clearly they are highly persuasive as it indicates the CJEU view of how a particular instrument should be interpreted.

4.2.4 **EU Law as source of English law**

Declaration 17 of the *Declarations annexed to the final act of the intergovernmental conference which adopted the Treaty of Lisbon* states:

> The conference recalls that, in accordance with well settled case law of the Court of Justice of the European Union, the Treaties and the law adopted by the Union on the basis of the Treaties have primacy over the law of Member States, under the conditions laid down by the said case law.

---

203.   TFEU, Art 263.
204.   In the context of English law, this meant that the courts must apply the ruling even if an Act of Parliament was inconsistent—effectively allowing the courts to 'strike down' primary legislation. See *R v Secretary of State for Transport, ex parte Factortame and others (No 2)* [1991] 1 AC 603.

In other words, for Member States, EU law is considered to take precedence over domestic law where the EU has competence. Many laws have 'direct effect' meaning that they automatically became part of the Member States' law. In England and Wales this was achieved through the *European Communities Act 1972*.[205]

The United Kingdom is no longer a member of the EU. Thus, EU law is no longer supreme. While the *European Union (Withdrawal) Act 2018* (EU(W)A 2018) has ensured that all existing EU law continues in force as though it were domestic law, it has a similar status as domestic law. Had the EU(W)A 2018 not incorporated all existing EU law into domestic law then it was questionable whether it would have continued in force. As the ECA 1972 is repealed, and that is what led to EU law being considered part of UK law, there was, at the very least, concerns that some law would cease to apply. The EU(W)A 2018 ensures that this is not the case.

A crucial difference between the position that exists now and that which existed when we were in the EU, is the primacy of Parliament. Where an Act of Parliament conflicted with EU law that had direct effect then, when we were a member of the EU, the EU law was supreme. The doctrine of implied repeal (2.1.1) did not apply. That is no longer the case. Parliament has incorporated EU law into domestic law with the intention that it will be possible to amend the law, meaning that Parliament is, once more, supreme.

≡ Example Data Retention and Investigatory Powers Act 2014

In response to organized crime and terrorist incidents, the United Kingdom, in common with other European countries, wanted to retain communications data for mobile telephones and Internet service providers (put simply, the 'who', 'how', and 'when' of communications but not the 'what').[206] The EU ultimately passed legislation permitting Member States to retain such information (Directive 2006/24/EC on the retention of data generated or processed in connection with the provision of publicly available electronic communications services or public communication networks). The Directive was struck down by the Court of Justice of the EU (*Digital Rights Ireland v Minister for Communications, Marine and Natural Resources*[207]) but the UK government continued to permit data retention, passing the *Data Retention and Investigatory Powers Act 2014* (DRIPA 2014).

In *Secretary of State for Home Department v Davis and others*[208] the Court of Appeal upheld a decision of the High Court that DRIPA 2014 was incompatible with EU law and should be 'disapplied'. Ultimately, the disapplying was suspended to allow other legislation to replace it, but it illustrates how EU law granted English courts powers it would not ordinarily hold (the power to strike down legislation).[209]

If DRIPA 2014 had been passed after the United Kingdom had left the EU, then the High Court and Court of Appeal would not have so-ruled. They may have tried to interpret the legislation in a way that made it compatible to the EU law but, in that instance, they would have failed. Left with a piece of legislation passed by Parliament that directly contradicts EU law, the courts would now uphold the UK legislation, and note that UK law in this matter has departed from its EU origins.

---

205. *European Communities Act 1972*, s 2.
206. Alisdair A Gillespie, *Cybercrime: Key Issues and Debates* (2nd edn, Routledge 2019) 336–47.
207. Case C/594/12.
208. [2015] EWCA Civ 1185.
209. Technically, of course, it was domestic law that granted the courts that power, as the *European Communities Act 1972* provided that EU law was supreme, and that domestic law could be disapplied where it conflicted with EU law.

4.2.4.1 **Continuing supremacy of EU Law**

While we have already left the EU,[210] the transition agreement meant that EU law remained in force until 31 December 2020.

Any law passed by the EU or decision of the CJEU that takes place after 1 January 2021 will no longer automatically form part of UK law.[211] However, there will continue to be internal supremacy of EU law for laws passed prior to our departure from the EU. Where there is a conflict between domestic and EU law that was passed prior to exit day, then the former EU law should be read as being supreme over the conflicting domestic law.[212]

≡ Example Data Protection

Let us assume that there is a dispute between two parties over data protection. One party is suggesting that the traditional English approach to privacy (where it is not properly recognized) applies, whereas the second party argues that the rights under the *General Data Protection Regulation* applies.

Where there is clear conflict between the two principles, the GDPR remains supreme, and so the courts should rule in such a way that gives effect to the GDPR.

However, the limits of this internal supremacy should be noted. It applies to laws that were in existence *before* exit day. Where a domestic law is passed after 1 January 2021, then the ordinary principles of legislative supremacy apply. Thus, it will be incumbent on Parliament to ensure that they carefully consider the implications of the legislation they are passing, and whether they specifically intend it to change any matter that was previously a matter of EU law.

Where there is no precedence is in respect of the *Charter of Fundamental Rights*. As was noted earlier, this was always a controversial document, and the UK was of the opinion that it was not bound by it. The *European Union (Withdrawal) Act 2018* expressly states that the Charter does not form part of domestic law.[213] Of course, some rights contained within the Charter exist independently of it. So, for example, Article 2(1) of the Charter states that 'everyone has the right to life'. That is also a right contained within the ECHR, Article 2. As the ECHR is incorporated into UK law,[214] that right exists separately from the Charter. Similarly, Article 3(1) provides the 'right to respect for his physical and mental integrity'. While not expressly mentioned in ECHR, Art 8(1), the jurisprudence of the ECtHR makes clear that Article 8 includes the right to respect for physical and mental integrity.[215] Again, this right, therefore, exists separately from the *Charter*. The EU(W)A 2018 makes clear that such rights remain in existence,[216] but it is because they are recognized elsewhere than the *Charter*.

---

210. The UK ceased to formally be a member of the EU at 11pm on the 31 January 2020 (11pm because that is midnight in Brussels timezone).
211. *European Union (Withdrawal) Act 2018*, s 5(1).
212. *European Union (Withdrawal) Act 2018*, s 5(2).
213. *European Union (Withdrawal) Act 2018*, s 5(3).
214. Discussed in Chapter 5.
215. See, most notably, *X and Y v Netherlands* (1986) 8 EHRR 235.
216. *European Union (Withdrawal) Act 2018*, s 5(4).

4.2.4.2 **Domestic courts and EU law**

As should be apparent, EU law is going to remain of interest to English law for a considerable period of time. How then do English courts approach the decisions of the Court of Justice of the EU?

Perhaps the easiest issue to note is that domestic courts are not bound 'by any principles laid down, or any decisions made, on or after exit day by the European Court'.[217] Three points arise from this. The first is the literal statement. Courts are not bound in precedent to follow the rulings of the CJEU made on or after 1 January 2021. It can be argued that this is superfluous because the courts were only bound by CJEU as a result of the ECA 1972, which has been repealed. However, it reinforces that position.

The second point follows from this. The statute says they are not *bound* by the decision but it does not say that the courts cannot have *regard* to these decisions. In other words, the courts are perfectly entitled to follow the decisions of the CJEU if they so wish. Of course, they need to sure that the ruling of the CJEU is compatible with English law, but there is nothing stopping the courts from considering, or indeed following, the ruling.

The third point that follows is that, by implication, the courts must be bound by decisions of the CJEU made *before* exit day.[218] This is perhaps not as controversial as it may seem at first sight because, of course, the rulings of the CJEU form part of EU law and, therefore, form part of domestic law as a result of its incorporation via the EU(W)A 2018.

Of course, there must be some way of allowing UK law to diverge from EU law, particularly where later domestic developments call historic law into account. Thus, the Supreme Court (and the Court of Session in Scotland when it sits as the final court of appeal), are granted the right to depart from CJEU rulings where appropriate.[219] The test that they should use for departing from EU law is the same that they use to depart from their own decisions.[220]

The decision to restrict divergence to the final court of appeal was controversial, and when Boris Johnson became Prime Minister, Parliament amended the EU(W)A 2018 to allow the government to introduce regulations to permit other courts to depart from EU precedent.[221] Before introducing legislation, the government must consult on the proposed regulations, with the proposal being sent to the most senior judges of the United Kingdom.[222]

The government did issue a consultation paper,[223] where they argued that allowing more courts to depart from EU law was necessary to allow the UK to be more flexible in shifting away from the EU. The concern is that if only the Supreme Court has the ability to depart from previous decisions, then it creates a delay. It can take some time for a case to reach the Supreme Court, and they only hear a relatively small number of cases per year. The counter-argument, of course, is that if you let lower courts depart from

---

217.   *European Union (Withdrawal) Act 2018*, s 6(1).
218.   This is also reinforced by the *European Union (Withdrawal) Act 2018*, s 6(3).
219.   *European Union (Withdrawal) Act 2018*, s 6(4).
220.   *European Union (Withdrawal) Act 2018*, s 6(5). For the Supreme Court this is the Practice Note first issued by the House of Lords (*Practice Statement (HL: Judicial Precedent)* [1966] 1 WLR 1234 discussed at 3.4.1.1).
221.   *European Union (Withdrawal Agreement) Act 2020*, s 26.
222.   *European Union (Withdrawal) Act 2018*, s 6(5C).
223.   *Retained EU Case Law: Consultation on the departure from retained EU case law by UK courts and tribunals* (2020, Ministry of Justice).

the law, the danger of losing precedent and the clarity of law increases. This potentially places additional pressure on the Supreme Court (who would need to resolve conflicting precedent), potentially meaning that they could not hear other cases of note.

The government did not reach any decision other than suggesting that the Supreme Court should not be the only court that has the power to depart. They suggest two alternatives. The first is to allow the Court of Appeal (and its equivalent in Scotland and Northern Ireland) to depart, and the second is for the High Court (and its equivalent) to depart from the law. The latter would be significantly more radical as the High Court is a court of first instance and deals with thousands of cases per year.

At the time of writing no decision has been made, but it is inevitable that it will not just be the Supreme Court that will be allowed to depart from EU precedent, meaning that UK and EU laws may begin to depart more quickly than initially thought. That said, it must be remembered that the EU(W)A 2018 just provides the *ability* to depart from EU law. It does not *require* them to do so, not least because that is a matter of judicial independence. If the courts ultimately choose not to depart, it is likely that the tension between the judiciary and government will continue to increase.

4.3 European Convention on Human Rights

One of the most important treaties that the UK has signed, is the *European Convention on Human Rights* (ECHR). As noted already, this is not, contrary to what the media sometimes imply, an instrument of the EU but is, instead, a creature of a much older institution, the Council of Europe. The ECHR is just one of several treaties that the UK has signed with the Council of Europe, and it has ratified 122 other treaties established under the auspices of the Council.[224]

The ECHR has had increased significance since the passing of the *Human Rights Act 1998* and its importance will be considered in Chapter 5, along with a more detailed analysis of the rights contained within the ECHR. This section will consider how, despite the implementation of the HRA 1998, the ECHR remains an important source of English law. It will also detail, albeit briefly, the institutions that surround the ECHR, most notably the European Court of Human Rights (ECtHR).

4.3.1 Background to the Convention

The ECHR was created in the aftermath of the Second World War and was designed to ensure that some of the atrocities that preceded and occurred during the war could not happen again. That said, it is important to realize that the Convention is not a treaty governing war but rather the treatment of citizens in general. A significant number of the lawyers who drafted the Convention were British and the United Kingdom was the first country to sign the Treaty in 1950.[225] Although the Treaty came into force in 1953 and some countries directly incorporated it into their domestic law, the United Kingdom did not do anything that would lead to it being used by the individual citizen, believing that this was unnecessary as the Treaty simply gave effect to freedoms already secured by the common law. However, in 1966 the United Kingdom accepted the right

---

224.   See https://www.coe.int/en/web/conventions/search-on-states/-/conventions/chartStats/UK.
225.   Lord Bingham, *The Business of Judging: Selected Essays and Speeches* (OUP 2000) 134.

of individual petition. This allowed UK citizens (and from 1981 citizens of its territories (excluding Hong Kong[226] and the Isle of Man)) to petition the European Commission on Human Rights (ECmHR) alleging a breach of the Convention. Since that time a significant number of cases have been brought and Bingham argued that the high number of cases was one reason to incorporate the Convention into a domestic setting.[227]

The Convention itself consists of sixty-six Articles but of these the most important are Articles 2–18 which create the human rights and fundamental freedoms that citizens of the Council of Europe have as protection. The remaining Articles create the machinery by which the rights and freedoms will be protected. Existing alongside the Convention itself are a number of protocols. The protocols can be divided into two classes. The first are those protocols that amend the Treaty (eg Protocols 3, 5, 8, and 11) and the second are those that create additional rights and freedoms (eg Protocols 1, 4, 6, 7, and 12). Where the protocols create additional rights then Member States are not obliged to safeguard these rights and freedoms unless they agree to be bound by the protocol or some parts of the protocol.

⚡ PROTOCOLS

Article 1 of Protocol 6 abolishes the death penalty subject to a reservation under Article 2 of the Protocol permitting the penalty to continue in time of war for certain offences. The Protocol was created on 28 June 1983 but the United Kingdom did not ratify this protocol until 1 June 1999 (see s 1(1)(c) HRA 1998 and associated delegated legislation). Protocols 4, 7, and 12 have not been ratified by the United Kingdom and accordingly the additional rights set out in those protocols are not afforded to citizens of the United Kingdom or its territories.

4.3.2 **The European Court of Human Rights**

Perhaps as important as the convention itself is the ECtHR, which adjudicates disputes regarding matters concerning the ECHR. Despite domestic courts now adjudicating on the ECHR (via the HRA 1998), the ECtHR continues to be an important source of domestic law, including adjudicating whether the domestic courts got it right.

As an international court, the ECtHR has jurisdiction over disputes between states concerning matters under the Convention.[228] This will sometimes be because it is believed that actions of a state directly affect another state,[229] and in other instances it is because it is believed that state actions have adversely treated its citizens.[230] However, unlike most international courts (see, for example, the discussion at 4.1.5.1), the ECtHR recognizes the right of individual petition,[231] meaning that a citizen of any of the signatory countries can petition the court.

---

226. This was, of course, prior to Hong Kong being returned to Chinese rule in 1997.
227. Lord Bingham, *The Business of Judging: Selected Essays and Speeches* (OUP 2000) 135–6.
228. ECHR, Art 33.
229. Perhaps the most notably example of this is when Georgia petitioned the ECtHR to hear its case against Russia following its conflict.
230. Perhaps a classic example being *Ireland v United Kingdom* (1979–80) 2 EHRR 25 where Ireland accused the United Kingdom of torture in respect of the way it treated suspected members of the IRA (who were Irish citizens).
231. ECHR, Art 34.

4.3.2.1 **Structure of the court**

The current ECtHR is an amalgamation of two different bodies; the old ECtHR and the European Commission on Human Rights (ECmHR). The ECmHR acted as a 'filter' for the ECtHR, in that it would hear all cases first and provide a (non-binding) opinion (in a way not dissimilar to the role of the Advocate-General of the Court of Justice of the EU (see 4.2.2.5)). However, having a case heard twice undoubtedly delayed matters and it was eventually decided to do away with the ECmHR, with the Court itself deciding on admissibility issues and being the sole arbitrator of the law.

The number of judges equals the number of contracting states,[232] meaning that there are currently forty-seven judges. A judge must be of 'high moral character' and must usually meet the criteria for high judicial office or be experts in the law.[233] Those judges from the United Kingdom meet the criteria for a senior judicial appointment, meaning that, for England and Wales, they would ordinarily meet the criteria to be a puisne judge.

Unlike the position for the Court of Justice of the EU, the state does not select the judge. Instead, they put forward three potential names for election to the ECtHR.[234] The Parliamentary Assembly of the Council of Europe then elects the judges, although they can choose to reject the nominations. The Parliamentary Assembly is the legislative branch of the Council of Europe but unlike Members of the European Parliament, they are not elected by direct suffrage, but are, instead, members of the legislatures of the nations of the Council of Europe. The United Kingdom has eighteen delegates, and they are members of either House of Parliament. They are appointed by patronage of the Prime Minister, although their membership historically reflects the balance of the House of Commons (meaning that the UK members come from all parties). It is the Parliamentary Assembly as a whole (and not just those from the relevant Member State) that chooses the judges.

Judges are appointed for a single, non-renewable term of nine-years,[235] with the vacancies staggered to ensure that there remains consistency. As the term is non-renewable, this reduces any suggestion that the judge is acting on behalf of the state as there is no chance that they can be 'rewarded' for their service by reappointment. Judges are told that they sit in a personal capacity and not a representative of their Member State.[236]

As with other international courts, a judge of the relevant national state must be present when hearing a case.[237] This is not to 'represent' the state, but to ensure that the court has an independent source of advice on the state of domestic law. Where a judge has to recuse him or herself, then the Member State is allowed to send an *ad hoc* judge to take his or her place.[238]

While some matters, usually those that are wholly misconceived, can be dealt with by a single judge,[239] most decisions are taken by chambers. There are five chambers which consist of seven judges. The chamber will decide on admissibility and, save where

232.   ECHR, Art 20.
233.   ECHR, Art 21(1). Experts in the law could be an academic and some countries have appointed academics to the ECtHR.
234.   David Harris et al, *Harris, O'Boyle and Warbrick Law of the European Convention on Human Rights* (4th edn, OUP 2018) 111.
235.   ECHR, Art 23(1).
236.   ECHR, Art 21(2).
237.   ECHR, Art 28.
238.   David Harris et al, *Harris, O'Boyle and Warbrick Law of the European Convention on Human Rights* (4th edn, OUP 2018) 115.
239.   ibid, 126.

it is thought to be sufficiently important enough to be heard by a Grand Chamber, will normally decide upon the merits of the case too.

A Grand Chamber is a judge of seventeen judges. They sit as first-instance on the most important and controversial cases,[240] but it also sits after a chamber judgment where one of the two parties requests a referral to it.[241] A chamber of five judges will decide whether to accept that referral, but, if it does, then the matter is heard by the whole court. It is important to note that this process is not an appeal *per se*. It is a re-hearing, so the issues are re-litigated, but before the grand chamber.

The Grand Chamber will also hear a case where, before giving judgment, a Chamber decides that either the matter is so serious it should be heard by the Grand Chamber, or where they wish to depart from previous decisions.[242] Again, in such matters, the hearing is *ab anitio*, with the matters being rehearsed before the seventeen judges.

4.3.2.2 Admissibility of a decision

While there is a general right of petition to the ECtHR, it does not follow that a case is admissible. The principal rule is that the ECtHR will only deal with a matter once all domestic remedies have been exhausted, and only when it is brought within six months of that decision.[243] In the context of England and Wales, this means that all appeals must have been exhausted. This does not mean that the Supreme Court has ruled on the matter, it would suffice that the appellate courts refuse permission. Accordingly, although it would be quite rare to do so, it is possible that a matter could proceed direct from the High Court where, for example, both the High Court and Court of Appeal refuse permission to appeal. As Article 35 states the six months runs from the date of the final decision, the time period would run not from the date of judgment but from the date at which permission to appeal was refused.

Under Article 35(2), an individual applicant cannot be anonymous: they must prove their identity to the court, although it has been noted that the rules of the court allow for the applicant to be publicly anonymized, ie not referred to by name in either the proceedings or the judgment of the court.[244]

A matter should not be a matter that is substantially the same as a matter previously decided by the ECtHR.[245] Taken literally, that would mean that the court would only hear original applications, and it would also mean that the court's jurisprudence could not move forward. However, it does not mean this, and it, in effect, means that a person cannot relitigate an issue before the ECtHR unless there are significant changes to the material facts.[246]

Where an application is by an individual, the court has the right to declare it manifestly ill-founded.[247] This is normally done when the matter is first received, to decide whether there is an arguable case that there has been an infringement of the ECHR.[248]

---

240. ibid, 129.
241. ECHR, Art 43.
242. ECHR, Art 30.
243. ECHR, Art 35(1).
244. David Harris et al, *Harris, O'Boyle and Warbrick Law of the European Convention on Human Rights* (4th edn, OUP 2018) 69.
245. ECHR, Art 35(2)(b).
246. David Harris et al, *Harris, O'Boyle and Warbrick Law of the European Convention on Human Rights* (4th edn, OUP 2018) 70.
247. ECHR, Art 35(3).
248. David Harris et al *Harris, O'Boyle and Warbrick Law of the European Convention on Human Rights* (4th edn, OUP 2018) 75.

However, sometimes the decision is taken later on in the proceedings, indeed after legal arguments have even been heard. Where this happens, the judgment is brief.

While an individual can petition the ECtHR, the dispute must be against a contracting state and not a private citizen or body. However, it is clear that the ECtHR will not allow a state to evade its scrutiny through subcontracting its obligations to private bodies.[249] There will also be occasions when the inactions of the state will lead to a dispute. Some rights place positive obligations onto the state (see 5.4.1.2), meaning that the state must take steps to protect the individual's rights.

States and individuals are not alone in being able to petition the ECtHR, non-governmental organizations and groups of individuals may also bring an action,[250] but they, along with individuals, must show that they are 'victims'. The term 'victim' has an autonomous meaning within the ECHR and so even if domestic law does not recognize a person or body as a victim, the ECtHR may.[251] In many instances it will be obvious that a person is a victim, as the actions or inactions of the state, directly affect them. In other instances, it is perhaps more abstract, but the central question is the extent to which a person is likely to be affected by the actions of the state.

☰ **Example** Victim

In *Open Door and Dublin Well Woman v Ireland*[252] the ECtHR allowed two not-for-profit organizations and four individuals to bring a challenge against a ban on advertising services that offered abortions abroad. The Irish government argued that the four individuals were not victims unless they were pregnant, and seeking the services of the organizations. The ECtHR disagreed and noted that they belonged to 'a class of women of child-bearing age which may be adversely affected by the restrictions imposed by the injunction . . . they can thus be claimed to be "victims" . . .'[253]

4.3.2.3 **Proceedings before the court**

In common with other international courts, advocates appear before the court in their appropriate national dress. Accordingly, a barrister of England and Wales will wear the wig and gown of either a QC or junior counsel. The judges themselves all wear the same plain gown, emphasizing that they sit as judges of the court and not the contracting state.

Only those with appropriate domestic rights of audience can appear before the ECtHR. So, for example, in England and Wales this means either a barrister or solicitor holding rights of audience to the senior courts (see 10.3.2.2). Counsel must ordinarily be approved to litigate in the respective state so, for example, it would not be usual for a French advocate to present a case on behalf of an English citizen in a case against the United Kingdom.

---

249.   ibid, 84.
250.   ECHR, Art 34.
251.   David Harris et al, *Harris, O'Boyle and Warbrick Law of the European Convention on Human Rights* (4th edn, OUP 2018) 87.
252.   (1992) 15 EHRR 44.
253.   ibid, at [44].

Many of the issues and submissions of counsel are set out in the papers. However, oral argument can also be given, and this is particularly common before the Chambers and Grand Chambers. Before the submissions are heard, the ECtHR will normally submit a list of points or questions that they wish the advocates to concentrate on.[254]

4.3.2.4 **Just satisfaction**

Where a complaint is upheld, the ECtHR shall provide 'just satisfaction'.[255] This means that it should consider how to compensate the individual. This is perhaps one of the most controversial, and yet misunderstood, aspects. Media stories will refer to hardened criminals being 'rewarded' by the ECtHR, but such awards will often include costs, not necessarily the actual costs claimed.

The typical remedies that the ECtHR imposes are costs, pecuniary and non-pecuniary damages. Of course, as the ECHR is binding—and this includes respecting the judgments of the ECtHR—the actual judgment itself is considered to be the principal remedy.

Where a party succeeds before the ECtHR they are entitled to their costs. However, it is clear that the court will only award the costs that go towards the violation found.[256] This means that where a person, for example, alleges that there has been a breach of two rights, but ultimately the court finds a breach on only one, it is likely to apportion the costs, meaning that the defendant will not receive full costs. The ECtHR does not necessarily pay incurred, or contracted, costs. It will not infrequently reduce costs where it is thought that they are too broad. Indeed, often the ECtHR will simply provide a lump sum to cover what it believes is appropriate. This means that sometimes a successful party can be out of pocket.

Example Costs in the ECtHR

In *PG and JH v United Kingdom*[257] the two applicants had been suspected of being involved in an armed robbery. They were arrested and detained in adjoining cells. Unknown to them (at the time), the police had installed a covert listening device, allowing them to hear the applicants conversation.

PG and JH argued that there was a breach of Article 8 of the ECHR. At the time, there was no statutory basis upon which such devices were installed,[258] and so it could not be said that the surveillance was 'in accordance with the law'. The breach was, therefore, admitted.

The applicants claimed £16,510.51 in costs[259] but the UK government argued that this was too high, and suggested it should be no more than £9,000. The ECtHR decided to award £12,000 as 'an assessment on an equitable basis', ie they came up with the figure themselves.

If the applicants' costs were, indeed, £16,510 then the applicants would be liable to pay just over £4,500 themselves even though they won their claim.

---

254.   David Harris et al, *Harris, O'Boyle and Warbrick Law of the European Convention on Human Rights* (4th edn, OUP 2018) 147.
255.   ECHR, Art 41.
256.   David Harris et al, *Harris, O'Boyle and Warbrick Law of the European Convention on Human Rights* (4th edn, OUP 2018) 166.
257.   Application 44,787/98.
258.   This basis was later provided by the *Regulation of Investigatory Powers Act 2000*.
259.   Application 44,787/98 at [93]. It shows how precise some costs claims are—no rounding of pence!

Damages are perhaps the more controversial subject, not least because the press tend to combine both costs and damages together, assuming that the court has awarded compensation when, quite often, they do not. There are two types of damages that can be awarded; pecuniary damages and non-pecuniary damages. The former relates to tangible losses. So, for example, where a person can show that they suffered loss of employment as a result of the breach, then they could quantify that loss. Similarly, if a breach led to the reduction in worth of an asset, that could be quantified, and claimed as pecuniary damages.

Non-pecuniary damages is that which is not quantifiable as a loss. It primarily concerns compensation for pain, anguish, distress, or anxiety etc. The court is more likely to simply assign a sum to this.[260] Often they may be relatively trivial sums. For example, in *PG and JH v United Kingdom*,[261] discussed earlier, the court awarded £1,000 as non-pecuniary damages. Of course, given they were both convicted of serious criminal offences, it could perhaps be questioned whether they deserved compensation for the state discovering something that proved their guilt.

The larger sums tend to be in Article 5 cases where the ECtHR argue that a person should never have been incarcerated. Even then, it is very difficult to quantify how much compensation should be given for being detained without lawful excuse. How does one put a figure on this, and should it include consideration of whether there was a reason for the detention (albeit one that was wrong) or the conditions of the detention?[262]

To try and bring consistency across the various chambers of the ECtHR, and the numerous claims that are brought, the Registry of the Court has established a table of compensation. This describes the typical sums that are awarded in such cases, meaning that there should become a standard tariff that allows for comparability across cases. Of course, given the wide socio-economic differences that exist across the signatory states, it is questionable to what extent this provides consistency.

4.3.3 Sources of law

The ECtHR has developed rules about what its sources of law are.

4.3.3.1 The Convention

The most obvious source is the Convention itself. The detail of the rights within the Convention will be considered in the next chapter. However, it is important to note the Court's approach to the Convention. Unlike the position in the United States where, for example, some Supreme Court justices are clear that the document should be interpreted as it was written,[263] the ECtHR is clear that the Convention changes with society:

> That the Convention is a living instrument which must be interpreted in the light of present-day conditions is firmly rooted in the Court's case law . . . It follows that these provisions cannot be interpreted solely in accordance with the intention of their authors as expressed more than 40 year ago.[264]

---

260. David Harris et al, *Harris, O'Boyle and Warbrick Law of the European Convention on Human Rights* (4th edn, OUP 2018) 168.
261. Application 44,787/98.
262. David Harris et al, *Harris, O'Boyle and Warbrick Law of the European Convention on Human Rights* (4th edn, OUP 2018) 169.
263. This is known as the originalist construction. Justice Scalia was a key proponent of this. At the time of writing, Judge Amy Coney Barrett, who has been nominated by President Trump to the Supreme Court of the USA, also considers herself to be an originalist. Hilary Clinton, the former Presidential nominee, noted the irony of a female judge holding originalist views when women could not even vote when the Constitution was drafted.
264. *Loizdou v Turkey* (1995) 20 EHRR 99, 133.

147

This makes sense. The Convention is considered to be an instrument that sets out the minimum standards for human rights and dignity. As society develops, so will its expectations of how we are to be treated. The court's approach to interpreting the Convention in this way ensures that the treaty does not need to continually be redrafted.

> ### ☰ **Example** Transsexuals
>
> One of the most obvious examples of the Convention acting as a living instrument can be seen from the treatment of transsexuals. In *Rees v United Kingdom*[265] the European Commission on Human Rights[266] rejected the suggestion that a ban on transsexuals marrying was an infringement of Article 12 (the right to marry), with the ECtHR later confirming this in *Cossey v United Kingdom*.[267] However, in *Goodwin v United Kingdom*[268] the ECtHR reversed that stance, and held that the bar was a breach of Article 12. In its judgment, the court notes that society had moved on and that it recognized the fairness in providing greater rights and protection. It, therefore, held that an absolute bar on marriage was unfair.

However, the limits of this must be recognized. The court will not create a right that does not exist, even if society may have moved towards this. Thus, Article 12 (right to marry) cannot be read to include a right to divorce, as that is distinct from the right set out in the text.[269] Similarly, Article 2 (right to life) does not provide a right to death through recognizing assisted dying.[270]

European or domestic context?

There are forty-seven countries that have ratified the ECHR. Each has its own culture and tradition. A question that arises is whether the ECtHR should take account of domestic conditions, or should they try to reach a standard that applies across all signatory states?

The answer is not particularly clear as the ECtHR will adopt both approaches. To an extent, it depends on what is being interpreted. Where it is a domestic instrument then it is unlikely that the court will seek to change that definition. Where it is the Convention itself, then the court will often try to reach a decision that can be applied across all signatory states. Of course, it is rarely that simple as it will often be both instruments that need to be interpreted. Perhaps the classic example of the approach of the ECtHR to this is the wording 'criminal charge' in Article 6.

The ECtHR has held that what constitutes a *criminal* charge must be autonomous of domestic law. Were that not to be the case, individual states could circumvent the protection of Article 6 by deciding that a matter was one of civil law rather than criminal law. In *Engel v Netherlands*[271] the ECtHR noted that the possible sanctions of breach is a key indicator of whether something is criminal. Where custody is possible, it is highly likely that the ECtHR will consider this to be a criminal matter irrespective of what domestic law says.

---

265. A 106 (1986).
266. See 4.3.2.1 for a brief note on what the European Commission on Human Rights was.
267. A 184 (1990).
268. [2002] IRLR 664.
269. *Johnston v Ireland* (1986) 9 EHRR 203.
270. *Pretty v United Kingdom* (2002) 35 EHRR 1.
271. (1976) 1 EHRR 647.

In deciding whether to adopt a pan-European approach, the court will sometimes take account of consensus. For example, where signatory states have begun to shift in the same direction, it is more likely that the court will recognize this shift and rule against states that have not done so. Harris et al provide the example of the rights of a child who is born outside of marriage. They note that the majority of states were providing such children with many of the rights that those within a marriage would have, and they were unsympathetic to countries that did not do so for traditional reasons.[272]

Margin of appreciation

A key issue in interpreting the Convention is the margin of appreciation. This is recognition by the court that it is not best placed to decide local political and sociological factors. Sometimes, therefore, it will accept that the domestic courts are best placed to decide how something should be applied, and will not interfere with domestic decisions that are based on such factors. Arguably the first use of the doctrine was in *Handyside v United Kingdom*,[273] which concerned an obscenity trial. The ECtHR noted that Article 10(2) allows for restrictions on the right to freedom of expression (Article 10), *inter alia*, for the protection of morals. The ECtHR accepted that moral standards would differ between countries, and that signatory states were probably in the better position to understand this and to assess the extent of the proposed measures.

It should be noted, however, that the discretion is not absolute, and the ECtHR is clear that the margin is subject to its supervision. Where, therefore, it is thought that a domestic institution is being overly restrictive, it reserves the right to set its own standard. The court is more likely to be restrictive where the matter relates to a particularly important part of an individual's autonomy, or where it relates to the protection of the rule of law.

149

4.3.3.2 Other international instruments

As an international court, it accepts that neither the Convention nor the Council of Europe exists within a vacuum. The ECtHR will take account of other international instruments, including international treaties and soft-law. For example, in *S and Marper v United Kingdom*[274] the ECtHR was asked to rule on the retention of DNA and fingerprints. The applicant S had been arrested as a juvenile, and the ECtHR considered carefully the UN Convention on the Rights of the Child when making its decision. In *Molla Sali v Greece*,[275] an unusual case that concerned whether Sharia law could be used to solve a property dispute, the ECtHR made reference to the Treaty of Lausanne, a peace treaty between, *inter alia*, Greece and Turkey, in which Greece undertook to protect the rights of the minority Muslim population in Greece.

4.3.3.3 Judgments of the ECtHR

The third source of law is undoubtedly the judgments of the court. The court's judgments act not only as a record of the resolution of the dispute, but also a source of law. So, for example, it is the ECtHR that decided that certain Articles (most notably

---

272. David Harris et al, *Harris, O'Boyle and Warbrick Law of the European Convention on Human Rights* (4th edn, OUP 2018) 9.
273. (1979) 1 EHRR 737.
274. (2009) 48 EHRR 50.
275. Application 20,452/14.

Articles 2, 3, and 8) have positive obligations, meaning that it is not enough that the state does not actively interfere with the rights, it is necessary for them to uphold the rights. So, for example, Articles 3 and 8 require the state to use the criminal law to protect the autonomy of an individual from sexual attacks.[276]

Article 45 of the Convention states that the ECtHR must give reasons for its decisions, meaning that its judgments are set out in writing. All of the judgments are freely available on HUDOC,[277] and they are published in multiple languages. Ordinarily, the ECtHR will write only a single judgment, although where there are dissenting opinions, there will be one or more dissenting judgments. It is also possible for some judges to write a concurring opinion. This is where, for example, they wish to either expand on a point that the other judges did not, or where they agree with the decision but not the reasoning that led to it.

The judgments can provide an insight into how the court will rule, particularly in those situations where it edges towards a decision because it starts to recognize the shifting changes in European society. When it rules against an application it will sometimes state that it can foresee a time when a different decision may be made.

There is not formal precedent, but in *Goodwin v United Kingdom*[278] the following was said:

> While the Court is not formally bound to follow its previous judgments, it is in the interests of legal certainty, foreseeability and equality of the law that it should not depart, without good reason, from precedents laid down in previous cases . . . [279]

In other words, it will usually follow its own cases although it reserves the right not to do so. This is significantly weaker than the position that, for example, the UK Supreme Court adopts, where the *de facto* position is that it will not overturn its own previous decisions (see 3.4.1.1). Of course, if it was slow to depart from its own decisions it would be difficult to reconcile this with the concept of the 'living instrument'. It will also be recalled from earlier, that one reason for a Chamber transferring a matter to the Grand Chamber is because it wishes to go against a previous decision (4.3.2.1). This indicates that it treats its decisions seriously.

4.3.4 **Enforcing the judgment**

While the ECtHR passes judgment, like most international courts it cannot enforce its own judgments. If a person refuses to follow an order of an English court, then this could either be treated as contempt or the fine or compensation could be passed to a bailiff. However, this is not true of international courts. In international courts, enforcement is by political means and the same is true of the ECtHR.

The Council of Ministers of the Council of Europe are charged with enforcing the judgments of the ECtHR.[280] The Council is made up of ministers from each signatory state, and they meet for three-day sessions, quarterly. Where a matter is relatively uncontroversial (including, for example, because the state has done all that the court told it to do) then the matters are dealt with by papers.

---

276. *MC v Bulgaria* (2005) 40 EHRR 20; *X and Y v Netherlands* (1986) 8 EHRR 235.
277. See https://www.echr.coe.int/Pages/home.aspx?p=caselaw/HUDOC&c=.
278. [2002] IRLR 664.
279. ibid, at [74].
280. ECHR, Art 46.

The Council considers three issues:

1. whether the 'just satisfaction' has been paid. This is normally the least controversial

2. whether there were any specific legal remedy that would be implicit within that case (so, for example, if there was a finding of a violation of Article 5, is the person still in custody),

3. what measures are being taken by the signatory state to ensure that there will not be a further breach.

The third of these is often the most complicated and can also be controversial, particularly where the state does not agree with the decision.

The reality, however, is that unlike with EU law, there is no direct enforcement mechanism. The Council of Europe relies on it being politically difficult to ignore a decision of the ECtHR. However, ultimately, some states may just decide that they are content to live with those political consequences. Ultimately, expulsion would seem the obvious solution to a country refusing to implement judgments of the ECtHR. However, the fact that both Turkey and Russia both remain within the Council of Europe, despite repeatedly breaching the most fundamental rights within the ECHR shows that it is not a power that the Council wishes to implement, and it is *de facto* recognition that the judgments of the court are not enforceable. To be fair, however, most judgments are followed as countries take their responsibilities seriously.

 ## Summary

In this chapter we have examined the sources of international law that may have an impact on the English Legal System. In particular we have noted:

- International law ordinarily governs states not individuals.

- The primary source of international law is now the Treaty, although these have lots of different names. A Treaty is an agreement between two or more countries where they agree to abide by the terms contained within it.

- International law also relies significantly on custom. These are rules that have existed as customary practice and are now recognised as appropriate international standards that should have the force of law.

- International courts exist but they are primarily for the resolution of disputes between countries.

- Individuals are only subject to international law in exceptional circumstances. A good example would be International Criminal Law, but this only deals with the most serious crimes that can be said to infringe international standards. These can usually be summarized as 'war crimes' or 'crimes against humanity'.

- Enforcing international law obligations can be very difficult, particularly where the transgressor is either a major power or a close ally to a major power. It is for this reason that sometimes countries or blocks of countries have sometimes acted independently of, for example, the United Nations.

- The United Kingdom joined the (then) EEC in 1972. As part of the conditions for joining, the United Kingdom agreed that EEC (now EU) law would automatically form part of domestic law.

- The United Kingdom left the EU on 31 December 2019, left the transition period on 31 December 2020. The United Kingdom will no longer be automatically bound by EU law from that date.

- If the EU and United Kingdom agree any further Treaties, these will be governed under international law and it may, for example, require the United Kingdom to follow EU laws but it will only do so by agreement.

- EU law in existence at the time of withdrawal automatically forms part of UK domestic law. It will be a considerable time before this will all be amended, meaning EU law will remain an important source of UK law for some time.

- The principal instruments of EU law are the *Treaty on the European Union* and the *Treaty on the Functioning of the European Union*. Disputes about EU law are adjudicated by the *Court of Justice of the EU*. This court has the power to enforce its judgments, including through fining Member States for non-compliance.

- UK courts will no longer be *bound* by the Court of Justice of the EU, but they can continue to take account of their decisions. It will be comparatively rare for them to ignore rulings save where the law has changed.

- The EU has its own Executive, which is divided between two bodies. The *European Commission* is the larger of the two and is in day-to-day control of the EU. The *European Council* is made up of the heads of government (or state) of the Member States.

- The *Council* and the *European Parliament* make up the legislature of the EU. The powers of the Parliament have been strengthened by the *Treaty of Lisbon*.

- Only the *European Commission* can instigate legislation, but both the *Council* and *European Parliament* can suggest legislation to the Commission. Legislation is only passed if both the *Council* and the *European Parliament* agree.

- The *European Convention on Human Rights* was written in the aftermath of the Second World War.

- The ECHR is the principal treaty of the *Council of Europe*. This is separate from the EU, and is a much older body, but membership of the Council of Europe is a pre-requisite for membership of the EU.

- The ECHR is considered to be a 'living instrument', meaning that its interpretation moves with societal trends.

- Individuals are allowed to petition the European Court of Human Rights (ECtHR) but only where they allege that a signatory state has breached a right, or has failed to protect their rights.

- The ECtHR will consider not only the ECHR but other international instruments. Some matters (eg what 'criminal' means) will be given an autonomous meaning, ie it is a meaning that applies across the signatory states irrespective of how domestic countries define an issue.

- Most judgments of the ECtHR are complied with. However, there is no power to enforce its judgments, with political pressure being the only way to persuade countries to follow the rules.

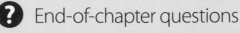 End-of-chapter questions

1. Is there such a thing as international law? If the USA acted against international law could anything realistically happen? How can law exist without an enforcement mechanism?

2. Can it truly be said that international law acts as a source of law? If domestic action is required to implement an international treaty then it is the domestic law that is a source, surely?

3. Can it truly be said that Brexit has happened? The *European Union (Withdrawal) Act 2018* allows the courts to continue to follow EU law. They are bound to do so. That being the case, how have we become independent in terms of law?

4. Why should we comply with the rulings of the European Court of Human Rights if we allow states like Russia and Turkey ignore rulings that relate to Articles 2 and 3? There is obviously no enforcement mechanism to the ECtHR, so why follow rulings?

Further reading

Read the text of the Attorney-General's advice on the legality of the invasion of Iraq. A copy can be found at (2004) 54 *International and Comparative Law Quarterly* 767–78.

The Attorney-General considers many aspects of the applicability of international law to English Law and also potential remedies that may be used against the government if it had been proven to be illegal.

Giannoulopoulos, D, 'What has the European Convention on Human Rights ever done for the UK?' [2019] *European Human Rights Law Review* 1–10.

This is an interesting article that considers the impact of the ECHR on UK law and suggests that the benefits are worth the political controversy. It also considers the calls by some to withdrawal from the ECHR.

Grogan, J, 'Rights and remedies at risk: implications of the Brexit process on the future of rights in the UK' [2019] *Public Law*, Oct, 683–702.

This reflects on whether Brexit will pose a risk to rights, including the Charter of Fundamental Rights.

Klabbers, J, 'The Cheshire cat that is international law' (2020) 31 *European Journal of International Law* 269–83.

This is an interesting article that suggests that too often legal scholars ignore the political realities surrounding international law.

153

For self-test questions, flashcards, and links to useful websites, please visit the **online resources** at: **www.oup.com/he/gillespie-weare8e**

5

Human Rights Act 1998

By the end of this chapter you will be able to:

- Identify the principal Articles of the ECHR.
- Discuss which bodies are bound by the HRA 1998.
- Assess how the HRA 1998 has been used in domestic contexts.
- Understand the HRA 1998's impact on the domestic legal system.

Introduction

In 1997 a Labour government was elected to power in the United Kingdom under the leadership of Tony Blair. One of the manifesto commitments of that administration was to incorporate the *European Convention on Human Rights* (ECHR) into domestic (UK) law. It was seen in the previous chapter that the Convention had been drafted in the aftermath of the Second World War but that the United Kingdom had traditionally decided that there was no need to incorporate it into domestic law arguing that its protections were all to be found in the common law.

By the 1990s there was a growing recognition that this was not true and Labour, who traditionally had been against incorporation, decided that the Convention should be given domestic force. The *Human Rights Act 1998* (HRA 1998) is one of the most important pieces of legislation to have been passed in recent years but its impact was arguably overstated at the time.

This chapter will examine the HRA 1998 and discuss some of the important issues that arise from its use. An overview of the relevant Convention Articles will also be given.

The HRA 1998 itself is a short piece of legislation containing only twenty-two sections but this disguises its importance. In Chapter 2 the changes the Act has made to statutory interpretation were considered and it has been seen that there was a definite change of mindset when human rights issues were involved. However, it is important that we recall that the HRA 1998 does not completely rewrite statutory interpretation and that it only applies where the normal rules of interpretation would lead to a conflict with the ECHR (see 2.3.4).

5.1 **The decision to incorporate**

Bingham, speaking extrajudicially at the time he was Master of the Rolls, stated:

> I would suggest that the ability of English judges to protect human rights in this country
> and reconcile conflicting rights . . . is inhibited by the failure of successive governments
> over many years to incorporate into United Kingdom law the European Convention on
> Human Rights and Fundamental Freedoms.[1]

This was not a universally popular opinion but by the time the speech was given a significant debate had arisen as to the need to incorporate the ECHR into domestic law.
There had been three attempts to incorporate the Convention into domestic law; once
in 1987 by Sir Edward Gardiner QC, a conservative MP, and twice in 1994 and 1996
by Lord Lester of Herne Hill QC, a Liberal Democrat peer.[2] The attempts had been
resisted because it was thought that the rights were to be found already in domestic
law through the common law. Since 1966 UK citizens had the right to petition the
European Court of Human Rights (ECtHR) where they believed the state had breached
their rights[3] but the decision of the Court was theoretically unenforceable although
successive governments had voluntarily acceded to judgments even when they disagreed
with them.[4] By the 1990s there was 'an ever-lengthening list of occasions . . . [when] the
Commission or the Court have found the United Kingdom to be in breach of its obligations',[5] which appeared to contradict the traditional opinion that the domestic courts
were equally able to give force to the Convention rights.

A matter is only admissible before the ECtHR where domestic remedies have been
exhausted (Article 35(1)) so where the ECtHR had ruled against the United Kingdom
these matters had already been adjudicated on domestically without any such finding. This caused difficulties as the ECtHR is swamped with work, meaning the delay
between petition and hearing can be significant.

The new Labour government argued that it would be more appropriate to allow
the Convention to be litigated domestically and issued a White Paper (*Rights Brought
Home*) setting out its proposals. The long title of the Act is: 'an Act to give further effect
to rights and freedoms guaranteed under the European Convention on Human Rights'
and it does not therefore make reference to either incorporation or domestic authority.
The Lord Chancellor argued that this phraseology was correct because the Convention
was already being complied with and the Bill (now Act) was simply extending this
compliance,[6] and another commentator argues that the true position of the HRA can
be described thus:

> The Human Rights Act 1998 maintains the dualist distinction between the United
> Kingdom's obligations in international law and the provisions of domestic law. The
> United Kingdom's international obligations under the European Convention are not

---

1. Lord Bingham of Cornhill, *The Business of Judging: Selected Essays and Speeches* (OUP 2000) 131.
2. Rights Brought Home: The Human Rights Bill, October 1997 (Cmnd 3782) para 1.5.
3. Bingham (2000) notes that the decision to grant a right of petition to the ECtHR was extremely controversial at the time (p 134).
4. Rights Brought Home: The Human Rights Bill, October 1997 (Cmnd 3782) para 1.10.
5. Lord Bingham of Cornhill, *The Business of Judging: Selected Essays and Speeches* (OUP 2000) 135.
6. Jonathan Cooper, 'Parliamentary Debates on the Human Rights Bill' [1998] *European Human Rights Law Review* 1–4 at 4.

directly applicable in domestic law. Instead, the Human Rights Act 1998, s 1 and s 2, makes a list of 'Convention rights' . . . available as rights before the domestic courts.[7]

It is for this reason that the term 'incorporation' would be inappropriate not least because the Convention has not become a full part of the English Legal System. The HRA 1998, as will be seen, only directly applies in respect of actions against the state and not against private disputes although it may exist through 'horizontal effect'[8] because courts are classed as public bodies.[9] Dwyer argues that the HRA 1998 is designed to establish this domestic framework and not to minimize the international obligations of the United Kingdom which can only be regulated by treaty. Fredman suggests that its summary could be:

> [The Act] simply   empower[s] United Kingdom judges to adjudicate in an area that was formerly the exclusive preserve of the European Court of Human Rights.[10]

Other commentators agree, noting that nothing in the HRA 1998 stops someone from petitioning the ECtHR save that, since the Court itself requires domestic options to have been exhausted, petitioners will have to try domestic proceedings first.[11] It is quite possible that this could have a beneficial impact on the Court itself and Bingham, when arguing for a scheme similar to that created by the HRA 1998, suggested that a full reasoned examination at domestic level could help influence law at the ECtHR.[12]

5.2 **The basic framework**

It has been remarked that the HRA 1998 is quite a short Act and its key parts are in a small number of sections. Perhaps the most important is that of s 6 which places an obligation on public authorities to act in a way compatible with the ECHR, s 7 which proscribes how it can be used to obtain a remedy in the courts, and ss 2–4 which detail how the Act is to be applied and how legislation can be construed before the courts.

5.2.1 **Duty to act compatibly**

Arguably the cornerstone of the Act is s 6(1) of the Act which states:

> It is unlawful for a public authority to act in a way which is incompatible with a Convention right.

This recognizes the issue about vertical effect discussed earlier, that at its heart the HRA 1998 is concerned with the relationship between the citizen and the state. It is for that reason that the Act (subject to the discussion on horizontal effect set out later) applies only to public authorities.

---

7. Deirdre M Dwyer, 'Rights Brought Home?' (2005) 121 *Law Quarterly Review* 359–64, 362–3.
8. Horizontal effect in this context means the adjudication between two private parties as distinct from the 'vertical effect' of adjudicating between the state and private citizen.
9. For a summary of the arguments surrounding 'horizontal effect' see William Wade 'Human Rights and the Judiciary' [1998] 5 *European Human Rights Law Review* 524–5 and Deryck Beyleveld and Shaun Pattinson, 'Horizontal Applicability and Horizontal Effect' (2002) 118 *Law Quarterly Review* 623–46.
10. Sandra Fredman, 'Bringing Rights Home' (1998) 114 *Law Quarterly Review* 538–43, 538.
11. David Feldman, 'Remedies for Violations of Convention Rights under the Human Rights Act' [1998] 6 *European Human Rights Law Review* 691–711, 709–11.
12. Lord Bingham of Cornhill, *The Business of Judging: Selected Essays and Speeches* (OUP 2000) 137, 140.

Of course this immediately begs the question who is a 'public authority' and the HRA 1998 itself is only partially helpful in this regard. Section 6(3) states:

'public authority' includes—

(a) a court or tribunal, and

(b) any person certain whose functions are functions of a public nature,

but does not include either House of Parliament or a person exercising functions in connection with proceedings in Parliament.

Thus it is clear that courts and tribunals are expressly public authorities and that Parliament is exempt. Prior to 2009, when the Supreme Court was established, the highest court in the land was the House of Lords but s 6 expressly dealt with this apparent contradiction by stating that when it sat in its judicial capacity the House of Lords was a public authority.[13]

Why is Parliament exempt? The government and Parliament were obviously concerned that the HRA 1998 could be used to allow the courts to interfere with the parliamentary process. Traditionally it is said that the *Bill of Rights* ensures that the proceedings of Parliament are exempt from judicial scrutiny (the limits of this were discussed in *R v Chaytor*[14] which concerned the criminal prosecution of Members of Parliament who fraudulently claimed expenses). If Parliament was considered to be a public authority then the courts would be able to hold Parliament to account for why it did something and, perhaps more importantly, why it did not do something, which would undermine the principle that Parliament is supreme within the United Kingdom. Whilst it will be seen that there is some question whether the courts are able to interfere with parliamentary supremacy through the interpretation clauses within ss 2–3 of the Act, classifying Parliament as a public body bound to act in a way compatible with the Convention would be an express limitation on parliamentary supremacy.

Interestingly the Act does introduce an element of parliamentary adherence to human rights in that s 19 HRA 1998 states that a minister, when introducing an Act to Parliament, must make a statement that it is compatible with the ECHR. Section 19(1)(b) expressly reserves the right of the government to make clear that it does not believe the legislative instrument is compatible with the ECHR but nevertheless wishes to continue with the legislation. Quite when such a statement would be made is open to question since it would arguably be electoral suicide to state that the government was introducing legislation that it believed was incompatible with its human rights obligations (as distinct from merely stating that it believes that the current interpretations are wrong) and it would be difficult to see how, for example, such legislation could be defended before the European Court of Human Rights.

Section 19 is, to an extent, largely cursory since there is no real enforcement mechanism. Since Parliament is exempt from being a public body as a result of s 6 there is little that a person can do if they believe that the minister is wrong when they make the claim under s 19, indeed the courts have noted that they would be unable to entertain any challenge without infringing the *Bill of Rights*.[15]

---

13. HRA 1998, s 6(4).
14. [2010] UKSC 52.
15. The submissions of counsel in *R (Huitson) v Revenue and Customs Commissioners* [2011] QB 174 clarifies this point (see p 176).

5.2.1.1 **Who is a public authority?**

It will be remembered that s 6 provides only a partial definition. Whilst it expressly includes the courts and expressly excludes Parliament it leaves the status of other bodies vague. It will be remembered that the wording is that it must be a 'person certain' (which simply means a legal entity) 'whose functions are functions of a public nature'; but what does this mean? Section 6(5) adds to the uncertainty by stating that a legal entity is not a public authority if 'the nature of the Act is private'.

At the time of the passage of the Bill there was a belief that this language created two tiers of public bodies; those that are obviously public and those which are *capable* of being a public body but which would require further analysis. In *Aston Cantlow and Wilmcote with Billesley Parochial Church Council v Wallbank*[16] the House of Lords accepted that this duality of public bodies was correct and noted that their constitutional significance was less significant than what their functions are. A Parochial Church Council is a legal entity of a parish of the Church of England—an established (ie state) church—and yet the House of Lords held that it was not necessarily a public body for the purposes of the HRA 1998.

The first group of public bodies, which have now been labelled 'core public authorities', are the least problematic and are those that will be inherently a public authority. Classic examples of this would be the police, Fire and Rescue Service, and government departments (it will be remembered that whilst Parliament is exempt, the government is separate from Parliament and government departments are inherently public).

The second group, sometimes known as hybrid public authorities, are arguably the more complicated because they are only bound by the HRA 1998 when they exercise public functions and not when they exercise private functions. There are a wide range of bodies that could be considered to be a hybrid body. Perhaps the classic example would be that of a private company who runs a prison. Clearly private security firms are not ordinarily public bodies but when they are running a prison they are exercising a public function since the detention of prisoners lawfully sentenced to imprisonment (or a suspect remanded in custody) by a court is certainly a public function.

In *Aston Cantlow* the test of a 'public function' was to assess the status of what the entity was trying to do and, for example, to consider factors such as whether it was 'in possession of special powers, democratic accountability, public funding in whole or in part, an obligation to act only in the public interest, and [has] a statutory constitution'.[17] In the context of that case the Parochial Church Council (PCC) was trying to exercise a 'rectorial property' charge on the lands of the respondent. This is a special type of property interest that could have meant that the owners of a farm were liable for the full cost of repairing the chancel of the local parish church (something that was commonplace centuries ago). The court considered that the essence of what the PCC was trying to do was to enforce a civil debt and therefore this was not a public matter and so in this instance the PCC was not acting as a public body and was therefore not bound by the HRA 1998 (which could have been relevant since arguably the enforcement of the civil charge may have been incompatible with Article 1 of the First Protocol to the ECHR which concerns property rights).

This test was refined by the House of Lords in *YL v Birmingham City Council*.[18] The matter at dispute here was the costs and provision of residential care for the elderly.

---

16. [2004] 1 AC 546.
17. ibid, 554.
18. [2008] 1 AC 95.

This was a statutory duty (*National Assistance Act 1948*) and the Council met this, in part, by contracting out some services to private providers. YL was an 84-year-old woman who suffered from Alzheimer's disease. The relatives of YL were, it was alleged, disruptive to the private provider of the residential care and the provider sought to cancel the contract, meaning that YL would be evicted. YL (suing by means of representatives) sought to argue that this would be a breach of the ECHR (Article 8). The question was whether the care home, when cancelling the contract, was acting as a public body.

Applying *Aston Cantlow* it may seem that the answer was 'yes' because although termination of a contract is private, the essence of what they were trying to do was to no longer provide residential care for YL and, as this was a statutory responsibility, it would seem to be of a public nature. However, by a majority of 3:2 the House of Lords held that they were not a public authority. The reasoning of the majority was quite technical, with them drawing a distinction between the provision of a service and the statutory duty to make arrangements to provide accommodation. Thus the House believed that whilst the council was under a duty the care home provider was not exercising a public function—that function being making arrangements—but was instead exercising a private function through the provision of a contractual relationship. In terms of the narrow reading of this decision the government enacted legislation to statutorily overrule the decision in respect of making the provision of accommodation a public function[19] but the reasoning of the case remains. The consequences of this are quite significant in that it is not unusual for public authorities to contract out some of the provision of services and the implications of *YL* are that this may mean that the person delivering the service is not a public body even if the provision of the service is a public function. That said, it will depend on the nature of the contract and what the relevant duties are.[20]

The narrow approach adopted by the House of Lords has not been welcomed and it is noticeable that the Parliamentary Joint Committee on Human Rights has questioned whether such a narrow approach is appropriate.[21] That said, it would be difficult to reverse *YL* without amending the HRA 1998 itself, something that would be politically problematic particularly during the current Conservative government where the very existence of the HRA 1998 itself is subject to debate (see 5.3). It is more likely that the courts will consider the need to soften the approach of *YL* and consider the inherent nature of the contractual arrangement (something that appears evident from *London and Quadrant Housing*).

That said, the courts remain wedded to the principles of both *Aston Cantlow* and *YL*. In *TH v Chapter of Worcester Cathedral and the Bishop of Worcester and Worcestershire County Council*[22] the High Court applied these decisions to a case involving a bell ringer of Worcester Cathedral. Safeguarding concerns had been raised involving TH and the Chapter[23] decided to withdraw permission to ring the bells of the Cathedral. TH sought to challenge this, inter alia, on the grounds that it interfered with his rights under Article 8 ECHR.[24] Coulson J held that neither the Chapter nor

19.   See Health and Social Care Act 2008, s 145.
20.   For an illustration of this see *R (Weaver) v London and Quadrant Housing Trust* [2009] EWCA Civ 587.
21.   See the report of the Committee on the Health and Social Care Bill (HC 46 HL 303 2007–08).
22.   [2016] EWHC 1117 (Admin).
23.   The chapter consists of a group of clerics (the Cathedral Dean and residentiary Canons) and certain laypersons. They are charged with the administration of the Cathedral on behalf of the Bishop.
24.   Right to respect for private and family life, home, and correspondence (see 5.4.7).

the Bishop sitting in his corporate capacity[25] was a hybrid public authority. He notes that neither act on behalf of the public, exercised any governmental function, have any statutory power in respect of safeguarding, or were subsidized by public funds. Neither were democratically accountable[26] nor is the United Kingdom accountable to the ECtHR for their actions.[27]

The decision is a useful read for students wishing a summary on how the courts should approach what is, or is not, a public authority for the purposes of the HRA 1998.

An interesting distinction between core and hybrid public authorities is whether they themselves can use the HRA 1998. According to Lord Nicholls in *Aston Cantlow* core public authorities will not be able to use the HRA 1998[28] whereas hybrid public authorities may be able to do so.[29] The logic behind this distinction refers back to the vertical nature of the protection of human rights within the ECHR and the HRA 1998. It will be remembered that the purpose of the HRA 1998 is to facilitate the actions of a citizen calling the state to account for breaches of their human rights. As a core public authority is, in essence, an instrument of the state then it cannot, in essence, sue itself for breaches of human rights. A hybrid public authority, when acting in its private capacity, could bring an action because when it is acting in its private rather than public role it is not an instrument of the state but is instead a private legal entity that may seek to hold the state to account for its human rights obligations.

5.2.1.2 **Horizontal effect**

It has been seen that the HRA 1998 theoretically only applies to public bodies but on occasion there will be circumstances when the Act may be said to have horizontal effect, ie it would seem to apply even in circumstances where it involves no obvious public authority.

> **≡ Example** Horizontal effect
>
> Amy is suing Mandy, her neighbour, for playing her music too loud and is asking the court to restrict the ability of Mandy to play loud noise. This would seem to be a classic private dispute, neither Amy nor Mandy are public bodies. The right to freely enjoy one's private life is contained within Article 8 and being subject to unreasonable loud music would certainly constitute interference. The court is expressly a public body by virtue of s 6(3) and so Amy could argue that because Article 8 includes positive obligations the court must protect her Article 8 rights. Thus even though the dispute is between two private citizens, the HRA 1998 and ECHR can become engaged because the court should act in a compatible way.

Horizontal effect can be quite controversial since, in essence, it rests on the basis that the courts, as a public authority, could bring Convention rights into any matter. Elliott

---

25. Diocesan bishops of the Church of England hold both a spiritual office (the bishopric) and a secular office, the latter is designed to allow for diocesan property and businesses to be held by the corporate body of the Bishop's office rather than the bishop in a personal capacity.

26. Bishops are appointed by the Queen as Head of the Church of England and chapter members are appointed by the Church of England.

27. [2016] EWHC 1117 (Admin) [67].

28. [2004] 1 AC 546, 554.

29. ibid, 555.

and Thomas note that the concept of horizontal effect, if it exists, is open to significant doubt as to its impact ranging from denying its very existence (vertical effect only) through to providing full horizontal effect through requiring *all* cases to be decided compatibly even if this means that the courts have to adopt a new cause of action because of a gap in domestic law.[30]

Phillipson makes an important point in this regard. He notes that some rights within the ECHR have no obvious impact on disputes between private parties (eg Article 6) but that others will be of more importance (eg Article 8). He argues that although all rights are probably *capable* of horizontal effect they do not *in fact* all have this effect.[31] This is partly because the HRA 1998 was not intended to incorporate the ECHR but rather to give it 'greater effect' by permitting their use in the domestic courts. Whilst some matters will require the courts to act in a compatible way on other occasions it will not be necessary because domestic law suffices or human rights are not engaged. That said, this should only be done in a way that will not usurp the rights of Parliament who remain supreme. This could mean implementing horizontal effect where it is possible to do so either by interpreting legislation or developing the common law but not by inventing new laws or processes.

The leading case on the development of horizontal effect is *Campbell v Mirror Group Newspapers Ltd.*[32] This case involved a report in the *Daily Mirror* newspaper which had reported that Naomi Campbell, a well-known supermodel, was attending meetings of Narcotics Anonymous. The story included details of when the meetings were, what was said, and photographs of her leaving the meetings. Traditionally English law did not recognize a tort of privacy but Article 8 of the ECHR recognized the protection of, inter alia, respect for private life and so the question arose as to what the courts should do. The newspaper publishers could not be said to be a public body, either core or hybrid, and thus it became clear that this would be one of the more important tests of whether the HRA 1998 had horizontal effect. If the HRA 1998 did apply then the circumstances of the case would be interesting as there was a direct clash between fundamental human rights; private life on the one hand (Campbell) and the freedom of expression (newspaper) on the other.

In the event the House of Lords arguably sidestepped the issue by deciding that it was not necessary to expressly consider the applicability of the HRA 1998 due to the fact that an alternative cause of action, confidence, was recognized by English law. That said, the tort of confidence that was applied would, prior to *Campbell*, not have covered the circumstances of that case and so there was a development of that law. Why did the law develop? The House, particularly Lord Hoffman, believed that the HRA 1998 empowers the courts to develop the underlying common law in such a way as to include the values of human rights and thus whilst the *ratio* of *Campbell* does not tell us how the courts will interpret horizontal effect the reality of the case is that it is recognition that the courts will take account of human rights principles even in private cases where the rights arguments are important and real. To this extent it is perhaps notable that Article 8 is commonly considered to have a positive element to it—the state must not only ensure that it does not interfere with the right but also should seek to protect it—and this may make it easier for horizontal effect to be developed.

---

30. Mark Elliott and Robert Thomas, *Public Law* (3rd edition, OUP 2017) 800–4.
31. Gavin Phillipson, 'The Human Rights Act 1998, "Horizontal Effect" and the Common Law: A Bang or a Whimper?' (1999) 62 *Modern Law Review* 824–9, 837.
32. [2004] 2 AC 457.

5.2.1.3 **Acting in a way incompatible**

Section 6(1) talks about 'acting' incompatibly but s 6(6) makes clear that a failure to act is also actionable unless the failure is in respect of parliamentary material (s 6(6)(a)–(b)). The latter provision was required because although s 6(3) exempts Parliament from the provisions of the Act, without s 6(6)(a)–(b) it would have been possible to bring an action against the relevant government minister alleging that he *should* have brought legislation before Parliament or exercised authority delegated to him by Parliament.

The inclusion of omissions is important because, as will be seen, a number of Articles in the ECHR include positive obligations—ie a duty is imposed on the state to secure the Convention by not merely refraining from interfering with the right itself but also to provide assistance to ensure that the right is not interfered with by others.

The requirement in s 6(1) is that the public body must not act (or fail to act) in a way that is incompatible with the Convention. This simply means that it must act in accordance with the Convention and ensure, where relevant, that it respects a person's rights and freedoms including facilitating this where a positive duty is imposed. The courts must decide whether an action is incompatible and it will be seen later that the HRA 1998 empowers the courts in the way that it interprets legislation and ECHR jurisprudence.

5.2.2 **Litigating the Act**

It has been noted that public authorities must act in a way compatible with the ECHR but how is the Act used before the courts? To answer this question it is necessary to consider who is allowed to bring an action and how this action is brought or defended.

5.2.2.1 **Victim**

In order for a person to bring an action under the HRA 1998 they must be considered a 'victim' (s 7(1) HRA 1998). Victim is then defined by s 7(7) as a person who is considered a victim for the purposes of Article 34 of the ECHR. Article 34, however, does not provide much more clarity, simply stating: '[t]he court may receive applications from any person, non-governmental organisation or group of individuals claiming to be the victim of a violation'. It is interesting that the HRA 1998 should link to Article 34 since it has been said that Article 34 itself is an autonomous concept that the ECtHR considers independently of any domestic law considerations.

The key consideration under Article 34 is that a person must be directly or indirectly affected by the issue they are complaining of. This can potentially be quite wide. For example, in *Open Door and Dublin Well Women v Ireland*,[33] a case that concerned the provision of advice in respect of abortions, the ECtHR appeared to accept that any woman of child-bearing age was potentially a victim.[34] However, what is clear is that there must be some tangible link to the issue and where there is the mere potential that the applicant could be a victim then there is a requirement to produce reasonable and convincing evidence of the potential harm, with mere conjecture being unacceptable.[35] This makes the position of campaign groups more

---

33. (1992) 15 EHRR 44.
34. David Harris et al, *Law of the European Convention on Human Rights* (3rd edn, OUP 2014) 791.
35. ibid, 792.

difficult since it has been noted that 'organisations will not be able to claim to be a victim of measures which affect the rights of their members'[36] although of course this restriction can be circumvented by having one of their members bring the action.

It is clear that the HRA 1998 test is more restrictive than the test of standing that ordinarily applies to, for example, judicial review which is not based on being a victim but only being 'sufficiently interested'.[37] Potentially this can cause difficulties where an action is alleging either breach of domestic law or human rights although it is likely that careful drafting can ensure that the issues are appropriately apportioned, even if it is through relying on the development of common law rather than human rights itself.

It is not clear why the government sought to link the status of victims with Article 34 as no clear rationale was put forward. Some believe, however, that the issue is really something of a distraction since if a victim cannot be found then it probably suggests that the issue is completely hypothetical and the courts should not be troubled by it.[38] Certainly this suggestion may account for why the rule was introduced since at the time of its introduction there was concern in some quarters that the courts would be 'clogged up' with challenges under the HRA 1998, including vexatious ones. In fact, this did not materialize, a point that was made by Lord Irvine, the then Lord Chancellor.[39]

||\ Case Box *R (Al-Skeini) v Ministry of Defence*

It may seem that a victim for the purposes of the HRA 1998 would be a UK citizen or resident but in *R (Al-Skeini) v Ministry of Defence*[40] the House of Lords held that this was not the case. This was a case that arose as a result of military action in Iraq. Several relatives of those who were killed by UK troops petitioned the English courts under the HRA 1998. The House of Lords held that whilst ordinarily the actions of soldiers in places of conflict would be outside of the jurisdiction of the English courts, this was not always the case. One death occurred while the person was within the custody and control of UK forces on a British Army base. The House of Lords held that in these circumstances it could be said that the HRA 1998 should be applied because the prisoner was within the jurisdiction of a UK public body (the military). The decision was extremely controversial, and somewhat misunderstood, because there was a belief by some that human rights have no place on a battlefield. However, this perhaps misses the point that the House of Lords ruled on that point and declared many of the applications inadmissible. What made this case justiciable was the fact that the claimant was brought onto a sovereign base, into the care and custody of British troops. It does show that a 'victim' of a public authority can, in certain circumstances, be someone who resides abroad.

5.2.2.2 **Sword**

Assuming that a person can be considered to be a victim then they can litigate the Act. Section 7 permits action to be used in two ways; as a sword,[41] ie by using the Act to

---

36. ibid, 795.
37. See Senior Courts Act 1981, s 31.
38. Jonathan Cooper, 'Parliamentary Debates on the Human Rights Bill' [1998] *European Human Rights Law Review* 1–4 at 2.
39. Lord Irvine of Lairg, 'The Impact of the Human Rights Act: Parliament, the Courts and the Executive' [2003] *Public Law* 308–25, 312–13.
40. [2006] UKHL 26.
41. HRA 1998, s 7(1)(a).

initiate civil proceedings against a public body, or as a shield,[42] ie by using the Act to defend action brought against it by the state (be that civil or criminal).

Of the two forms of litigation the use of the sword is perhaps more usual, not least because it includes the possibility of bringing action in anticipation of a breach (s 7(1) expressly makes reference to the fact that a public authority proposes to act in an unlawful way).

> ### ☰ **Example** Anticipated action
>
> Robert is organizing a protest march against capitalism. The police do not wish the route of the march to proceed through the city centre. They plan to use their powers to order the route to be re-routed through outlying areas.
>
> Prima facie this is a breach of Articles 10 (freedom of expression) and 11 (freedom of assembly) and Robert, as a direct victim, could bring an action against the police before the march takes place alleging the actions of the police, a public authority, will interfere with his rights.

The HRA 1998 does not itself create any new form of litigation but instead states it can be used as a basis of action under existing procedures. The HRA 1998 expressly refers to judicial review[43] and it is likely that this will be one of the more usual forms of litigating the Act. The issue of judicial review is discussed in Chapter 17 but it could also be for other forms of action, most notably tort.

Ordinarily actions under the HRA 1998 must be instigated within one year of the alleged breach occurring[44] although the courts have discretion to vary this where they believe it is fair to do so.

5.2.2.3 **Shield**

The second way that the HRA 1998 can be litigated is as a shield, ie by raising human rights issues as a defence to an action brought against an individual. This could cover a variety of different types of situations. For example, in the civil sphere this may relate to a person raising human rights issues where a local authority seeks to bring an action for breach of planning rules. There is no limitation on the use of s 7 as a shield and it could also be used in criminal trials where a person may wish to suggest that a prosecution amounts to a breach of his human rights. The most likely argument in such circumstances would be to raise procedural issues and allege that they have breached Article 6 (right to fair trial) but may also include arguments that some laws are too vague and thus amount to a breach of Article 7[45] or that a sentence imposed on him is greater than that which was prescribed at the time he committed an offence.[46]

---

42.   ibid, s 7(1)(b).
43.   ibid, s 7(3)(4).
44.   ibid, s 7(5).
45.   David Harris et al, *Law of the European Convention on Human Rights* (3rd edn, OUP 2014) 334–5 who discuss the extent to which the ECtHR are prepared to become involved in such arguments.
46.   ibid, 337 although it should be noted that this applies only to penalties and thus where an ancillary matter is attached that is not punitive then Article 7 will not apply; see, most notably, *Adamson v UK* (1999) 28 EHRR CD 209.

5.2.3 Interpreting legislation and the Convention

The HRA 1998 places the compatibility of UK laws with the ECHR at the heart of the legislation. It provides specific powers to the courts in how it construes English laws and also how it considers the ECHR when considering the compatibility or otherwise of domestic law. Arguably these are the most important provisions within the Act since, as will be seen, it provides the courts with the ability to go beyond that which ordinary principles of statutory interpretation may require of them.

There are two sections that deal with interpretation in the HRA 1998. Section 2 relates to how the domestic courts should interpret the ECHR itself and s 3 relates to how the courts should interpret domestic legislation so as to make it compliant with the ECHR. There is an obvious interaction between the two sections but of the two s 3 has proven to be the more important.

5.2.3.1 Interpreting legislation

Section 3 of the HRA 1998, it will be remembered from Chapter 2, allows the courts to interpret legislation in a way that is compatible with the ECHR (see 2.3.4). It will be remembered that there are limits to what the courts can do and it does not provide any power to 'strike down' legislation but it certainly allows the courts to go much further than they could under the traditional rules of statutory interpretation.

5.2.3.2 Interpreting the Convention

It has been seen that at the heart of the power under s 3 is the fact that the domestic courts must consider whether they believe legislation is compatible with the ECHR. The HRA 1998 prescribes how the courts should do this in terms of them considering not only the ECHR itself but also the jurisprudence of the ECtHR. This is necessary because, as it will be remembered from Chapter 4, international law does not easily divide into 'primary' and 'secondary' sources and so the decisions of the ECtHR are extremely important in ascertaining what the Convention means, not least because the ECHR has been described as a 'living instrument', ie subject to evolution.[47]

Section 2(1) of the HRA 1998 states that a court 'must take account of', inter alia, a judgment of the ECtHR or the European Commission on Human Rights. The wording is interesting because although it is mandatory ('must') the decision is not to bind the courts but merely to 'take account of' the decisions. It has been noted that the effect of this is that the statute does not instruct courts on how the authorities should be treated by the courts, nor what weight should be given to them.[48]

The general approach by the courts has been to operate on the basis that whilst they are not bound by the ECtHR the courts will mirror the decisions of the ECtHR (ie follow them) if there is clear and consistent authority.[49] The justification for this approach differs but in *R (Anderson) v Secretary of State for the Home Department*[50] Lord Bingham stated that 'the House will not without good reason depart from the principles laid down in a carefully considered judgment of the court sitting as a Grand

47. See *Marckx v Belgium* (1979–80) 2 EHRR 330.
48. Philip Sales, 'Strasbourg Jurisprudence and the Human Rights Act: A Response to Lord Irvine' [2012] *Public Law* 253–67, 257.
49. ibid, 255–7.
50. [2002] UKHL 46.

Chamber'.[51] This perhaps recognizes that the ECtHR has had the best opportunity of considering the issues before the Court, including the fact that some aspects of the ECHR are considered to have an autonomous meaning, ie one that is considered purely in the context of the ECHR and not by reference to national definitions.[52] However, some have been critical of this rule as it arguably means that decisions of the ECtHR are treated in the same way the Supreme Court treats its own decisions, ie they will ordinarily follow them but exceptionally may depart from them.[53] Certainly this would be beyond that which was ever contemplated by Parliament when the Bill was being passed (where, for example, the government specifically rejected an amendment that would have made the UK courts bound by the ECtHR[54]) but perhaps this is reading too much into what the mirror principle means and it is difficult to understand what else the courts can do in the face of clear rulings from the ECtHR, as to do otherwise would arguably mean the UK breaches international law.

Whilst the courts will ordinarily follow Strasbourg they do reserve the right not to do so and one particular exception is where they believe that the ECtHR has not fully understood the subtleties of domestic law. The most notable example of this was *R v Horncastle*.[55] This was an evidence case before the Supreme Court. The appellant had been convicted of causing grievous bodily harm with intent[56] and whilst the victim had given a statement to the police, the victim had (for unconnected reasons) died before the matter came to trial. The statement was read out in court and, whilst there was other evidence, the Court of Appeal (Criminal Division) had ruled that it was 'to a decisive degree' the basis upon which the appellant had been convicted.

The appellant sought to argue that the admission of the statement breached Article 6 of the ECHR as he was unable to cross-examine the victim: the jury therefore only heard one side of the story. Reliance was placed on *Al-Khawaja and Tahery v United Kingdom*[57] where the ECtHR had held that where a statement of a person not able to be cross-examined was 'the sole, or at least, the decisive basis' for a conviction then Article 6 was breached.

The Supreme Court refused to follow the decision of *Al-Khawaja*, in part because Article 43 of the ECHR allows a party to a decision to petition that the matter is heard by the Grand Chamber of the ECtHR (discussed in Chapter 4). This had happened in this case although the matter had not, at that time, been heard. The Supreme Court held that whilst s 2(1) meant that ordinarily a decision would be followed, the Supreme Court reserved the right to rule that certain decisions of the ECtHR did not sufficiently appreciate or accommodate particular aspects of the UK domestic process. In such circumstances it could refuse to follow the Strasbourg court.

Some scholars place emphasis on the fact that because it is possible to disagree with the ECtHR this means that a 'dialogue' exists between the domestic courts and Strasbourg.[58] The genesis of this idea can be traced back to the consultation paper proposing the HRA 1998 with it expressly stating that 'judges will be able to contribute

---

51.   ibid, [26].
52.   David Harris et al, *Law of the European Convention on Human Rights* (3rd edn, OUP 2014) 16.
53.   Aileen Kavanagh, *Constitutional Review under the UK Human Rights Act* (CUP 2009) 148.
54.   Francesca Klug, 'Follow or Lead? The Human Rights Act and the European Court of Human Rights' [2010] 6 *European Human Rights Law Review* 621–30, 623.
55.   [2010] 2 WLR 47.
56.   Contrary to *Offences Against the Person Act 1861*, s 18.
57.   (2009) 49 EHRR 1.
58.   See, for example, Philip Sales, 'Strasbourg Jurisprudence and the Human Rights Act: A Response to Lord Irvine' [2012] *Public Law* 253–67, 264–6

to this dynamic and evolving interpretation of the Convention'. However, the logic of this contribution is somewhat dubious, not least because there is not a formal system of reviewing cases to the court (cf the position with the Court of Justice of the EU). Where the individual loses before the domestic courts he can petition the ECtHR which, if it takes the case, can review the logic of the domestic courts' approach to the Convention, but where the individual succeeds and it is the public body that disagrees with the view of the court then there is no recourse to the ECtHR. Given the inherent delays of the Court (discussed in Chapter 4) it must also be questioned whether there is any true discussion since by the time the matter is re-litigated it is quite possible the position has moved on in both domestic and international law.

Some commentators have noted that a difficulty of not generally following the rulings of Strasbourg would be that it could make the law less certain. The rationale behind such a suggestion is that not only would lawyers, advising their clients, have to understand how the ECtHR interprets particular sections of the Convention they would also have to identify the separate domestic interpretation and attempt to reconcile the two.[59] If true, this would certainly seem to be contrary to the general purpose of the law in England and Wales. It will be remembered from Chapter 3 that *stare decisis* was initiated, in part, because there was a belief that certainty of the law was desirable. It would be regrettable if an interpretation of s 2 was to make the law uncertain.

⚡ PRECEDENT V SECTION 2

It has been noted that s 2 requires the courts to take account of ECHR issues and there has been some discussion as to what this means in terms of precedent. How has this resolved itself in practice? In *Kay v Lambeth London Borough Council*[60] the House of Lords stated that the rules of precedent should be followed and that where a binding precedent is incompatible with a decision of the ECtHR the matter should be sent to appeal, even invoking the 'leap-frog' procedure that allows decisions of the High Court to be appealed to the Supreme Court where a matter is of public importance.

An example of this in practice can be found in *R (on behalf of Purdy) v DPP*[61] where the Divisional Court was asked to rule on an assisted suicide issue. The claimant suggested that the DPP should have to publish a specific policy in respect of when he would prosecute people for assisted suicide. This raised a similar (but sufficiently distinct) point from the 'Diane Pretty' litigation. An issue arose as to whether Article 8(1) was engaged. The House of Lords had held in the *Pretty* case that it was not[62] but Diane Pretty had then taken the matter to the ECtHR who held that it had invoked Article 8 (although deciding it was a justifiable interference).[63]

The Divisional Court had to decide whether it was bound by the House of Lords decision in *Pretty* or whether it could follow the ECtHR (which s 2 would seem to imply). They held that the ruling in *Kay* was clear and that they were bound by the House of Lords and that only the House (now Supreme Court) could alter this precedent.[64] The decision in *R v Horncastle*[65]

---

59. ibid, 260.
60. [2006] 2 AC 465.
61. [2008] EWHC 2565.
62. *R (on behalf of Pretty) v DPP* [2002] 1 AC 800.
63. *Pretty v United Kingdom* (2002) 35 EHRR 1.
64. [2008] EWHC 2565 [46].
65. [2010] 2 WLR 47.

would lend support to this argument as the Supreme Court was, in that case, expressly stating that it had the right to depart from Strasbourg and that other courts must follow the ruling of the Supreme Court.

Margin of appreciation

Whilst the ECtHR will sometimes seek to find a uniform approach to the ECHR it will sometimes recognize that it is not best placed to decide how some matters should be applied and will leave this adjudication to the signatory state. When the ECtHR decides that the state is best placed to decide how to implement a particular issue this is known as the doctrine of the margin of appreciation.[66] The doctrine applies because the essence of the Convention is that the signatory states are responsible for the protection of human rights and the Court has a supervisory role, meaning that it checks that states are adhering to their obligations, taking account of the individual circumstances of countries.[67]

The doctrine was first identified in *Handyside v United Kingdom*[68] which concerned an obscenity trial. The ECtHR held that deciding how to protect morals was primarily a matter for signatory states as each state has different moral standards reflecting the different make-up of society and liberal tendencies. That said, the Court was also clear that any margin of appreciation was subject to its scrutiny, ie it reserves the right to consider whether a state has exercised its discretion in an improper way.

Does the doctrine apply to the HRA 1998? Lord Hope in *R v DPP, ex p Kebilene*[69] thought it did not as it was a matter of international law whereby an international court showed deference to a state in terms of its individual society[70] but Lord Irvine, the then Lord Chancellor, has argued that the courts have adopted their own version of this test.[71] He argues that this version is where the courts defer to Parliament and the executive over some issues surrounding society on the basis that certain areas are political rather than purely legal.[72] It has been said that this deference began with judicial review[73] and has become an established part of HRA 1998 actions with the concept being that the courts will defer to the executive where there is a 'fair balance' between the interests of society as a whole and the individual's human rights.[74] However, Leigh argues that it should be restricted solely to qualified rights (ie Articles 8–11) and not to absolute rights, for example Articles 2 and 3.

Others disagree with this proposition and suggest that there is no reason why deference should not occur in absolute rights too.[75] This argument is based on the premise that there is no such thing as a 'qualified' right and that Articles 8–11 are erroneously so

---

66. David Harris et al, *Law of the European Convention on Human Rights* (3rd edn, OUP 2014) 11.
67. ibid, 13.
68. (1979) 1 EHRR 737.
69. [2000] 2 AC 326.
70. ibid, 380.
71. Lord Irvine of Lairg, 'The Impact of the Human Rights Act: Parliament, the Courts and the Executive' [2003] *Public Law* 308–25, 315.
72. ibid.
73. Ian Leigh, 'Taking Rights Proportionately: Judicial Review, the Human Rights Act and Strasbourg' [2002] *Public Law* 265–87, 266.
74. ibid, 276.
75. Simon Atrill, 'Keeping the Executive in the Picture: A Reply to Professor Leigh' [2003] *Public Law* 41–51, 44.

called because, in essence, the first part of each Article provides only a prima facie right or freedom and it is only when the derogation (the second paragraph of each Article) is applied that it can be decided whether the right applies or not. Accordingly, Atrill argues that all rights are unqualified and that there is no difference between the Articles themselves. Certainly it is true to say that the rights and freedoms traditionally labelled as qualified are not subservient to the absolute rights, with the ECtHR itself arguing that Article 10 (freedom of expression) is an essential foundation for democracy[76] which suggests that it recognizes this as one of the more important rights. However, this would also be slightly misleading in that the ECtHR itself has adopted a strict interpretation to Articles 2 and 3 with any margin of appreciation being highly restricted. That said, it is clear that the ECtHR has applied the margin to Articles 5 and 6, which whilst not absolute are not ordinarily classified as qualified,[77] and so there is no reason why any domestic application should be restricted to Articles 8–11.

Atrill argues that the domestic equivalent to a margin of appreciation—judicial deference—is required for all rights and that not doing so would restrict the development of rights.[78] Lord Irvine appears to believe the correct approach is somewhere between these two polarized opinions. He recognizes that there is a need for the courts to hold the executive and legislature to account and that proportionality (see 'Necessity and proportionality') is a powerful tool in checking the validity and extent of any deference[79] but he also argues that there are some situations where the courts need to defer to the executive and legislature, as bodies with democratic authority.

Necessity and proportionality

Central to many of the Convention rights, but in particular the qualified rights under Articles 8–11, are the concepts of necessity and proportionality. Arguably this is a little simplistic as proportionality is referred to in many Convention Articles, particularly Article 6 (right to a fair trial), and necessity is also a flexible concept. Some argue that necessity is part of proportionality as at its simplest it can be argued that necessity means that just because a public body has the right to do something does not mean that it should. A public authority should only interfere with someone's rights when it has to, not just when it wants to: in other words it is when it *has* to—not when it would be *merely convenient* to do so.

In *Soering v United Kingdom*[80] the ECtHR explained the principle of proportionality:

[I]nherent in the whole of the Convention is a search for a fair balance between the demands of the general public interest of the community and the requirements of the protection of the individual's fundamental rights.[81]

Thus proportionality is remembering that although a person has a right, this right must be kept in the context of society's rights and should not create a position whereby it causes undue problems for society. In respect of the qualified rights (see 5.4.1.1) proportionality will often mean that the extent of a right should be limited so as to ensure that the public are not unduly constrained. Arguably proportionality

169

---

76. See, for example, *Hertel v Switzerland* (1999) 28 EHRR 534.
77. David Harris et al, *Law of the European Convention on Human Rights* (3rd edn, OUP 2014) 12.
78. Simon Atrill, 'Keeping the Executive in the Picture: A Reply to Professor Leigh' [2003] *Public Law* 41–51, 51.
79. Lord Irvine of Lairg, 'The Impact of the Human Rights Act: Parliament, the Courts and the Executive' [2003] *Public Law* 308–25, 316.
80. (1989) 11 EHRR 439.
81. ibid, 469.

has two dimensions to it. The first is whether a right should be interfered with (and this will incorporate the idea of necessity) and the second is how far the interference should go. It is, in particular, this latter dimension that is particularly relevant to the qualified rights.

☰ Example Proportionality

In Northern Ireland there is a 'Parades Commission' that seeks to adjudicate on disputes aris-ing from marches that occur each year in the Province. The marches are normally undertaken by Protestant organizations (eg the Orange Order) and commemorate historic battles. The battles were part of a series of campaigns between Protestant and Catholic monarchs that sought control of Europe, the United Kingdom, and Ireland. Many marches throughout the island of Ireland take place peacefully but the march in Belfast has often been controversial and has, on a number of occasions, led to violence between Republican and Loyalist factions hiding under the cloak of Protestant and Catholic allegiances.

Articles 10 and 11 provide the right to freedom of expression and freedom of assembly and, taken together, could provide a right to march. However, both are qualified rights and the state (through the Parades Commission in this instance) can interfere with the rights so long as it is for a legitimate aim and proportionate.

In recent years the Parades Commission has banned the march from passing through Catholic areas of Belfast City and instead re-routed it through Protestant areas. Although this is highly controversial to the Orange Order (who claim the right to walk down the Queen's Highway) the decision is arguably proportionate as it seeks a balance between the right of people to march (and indeed the parades and marches do occur) but also between the wider members of certain sections of society who consider the marches offensive. Finding the bal-ance is not easy and it is this tension which the ECtHR was considering (albeit in a different context) in *Soering* and its later pronouncements on proportionality.

When considering whether a public body acted appropriately, the concept of pro-portionality was alien to the English courts. The traditional view taken was that the courts would only interfere when a decision was illegal, procedurally improper, or irrational (see, for example, *Associated Provincial Picture Houses Ltd v Wednesbury Corporation*[82]). However, proportionality arguably differs considerably from these tra-ditional grounds as the latter examined whether a decision was wrong and yet pro-portionality is suggesting that there are competing rights. In *R (on behalf of Daly) v Secretary of State for the Home Department*[83] Lord Steyn summarized what he believed were three differences:

> First, the doctrine of proportionality may require the reviewing court to assess the bal-ance which the decision maker has struck, not merely whether it is within the range of rational or reasonable decisions. Secondly, the proportionality test may go further than the traditional grounds of review inasmuch as it may require attention to be directed to the relative weight accorded to interests and considerations. Thirdly, even the heightened scrutiny test . . . is not necessarily appropriate to the protection of human rights.[84]

82. [1948] 1 KB 223.
83. [2001] 2 AC 532.
84. ibid, 547.

His Lordship certainly believed that the intensity of the review of a decision-making process under proportionality is greater than in traditional reviews presumably because of the balance required: ie the courts must look at the rights of both the claimant and society in deciding where the balance is to be struck and not just at whether the decision was wrong. However, it should be remembered that this only applied where a Convention right is in issue; if the matter is purely one of domestic law then the traditional grounds of review continue to be used.

5.2.4 Remedies

It will be remembered that s 7 allows a person to use the HRA 1998 as either a 'sword' or a 'shield' in terms of litigation. Assuming that the courts, when interpreting legislation, conclude that the victim has had their rights infringed (or, if it is anticipatory action, will have their rights infringed) what remedies are available?

To some degree the simple answer is the reference within s 8(1) which states:

> [A court] may grant such relief or remedy, or make such order, within its powers as it considers just and appropriate.

However, this disguises some of the intricacies involved in the discussion of remedies and a number of issues need to be discussed.

5.2.4.1 Article 13: The missing Article

Article 13 of the Convention provides that everyone whose rights are breached under the Convention has the right to an effective remedy. However, Article 13 has, controversially, not been included within the HRA 1998. In part, this is because the government argued that the HRA 1998 itself was the realization of Article 13 and that, whereas before a remedy could only be obtained by petitioning the ECtHR itself, the HRA 1998 allows for domestic remedies. Given that the HRA 1998 does not create any new procedures it was also thought that a remedy will always be granted but this misses the point that damages and relief are often discretionary.

Where the omission of Article 13 may have some relevance is in respect of delayed trials. It will be seen that Article 6 provides, inter alia, that a person will be brought to trial quickly. The ECtHR has held that remedying a breach for Article 6 in these circumstances through the provision of compensation is unlikely to suffice by itself and that it would be more appropriate to provide a solution, ie expediting the trial. Whilst the criminal justice system has suffered considerable delays in recent years it is perhaps questionable whether the delays will be sufficient to lead to a breach of Article 6, as longer periods than are usual in the United Kingdom have been upheld by the ECtHR. That said, if such a breach were to be found then in the absence of Article 13 it could be questioned whether the court has sufficient powers to act. It is submitted that the generic wording of s 8 means that a remedy could be granted since the *Criminal Procedure Rules* provide for sanctions to quicken trials and also, where appropriate, the ability to stay proceedings for lack of care. Thus the absence of Article 13 is unlikely to prove too problematic.

5.2.4.2 Declarations of incompatibility

Some courts, most notably the Supreme Court of the United States of America, have the power to 'strike down' legislation, ie declare that it is no longer in force. As noted already the courts in England and Wales do not have this power and the government was very careful, when introducing the HRA 1998, to ensure that this power was not given to the courts.

The previous section identified that the courts have express power to interpret legislation, so far as is possible, in such a way as to ensure compatibility. However, it was also seen that there are limits to the power of the courts under s 3 and sometimes a court will face the conclusion that legislation is incompatible and cannot be interpreted in such a way as to make it compatible. In those circumstances the court is able to make a declaration of incompatibility under s 4 HRA 1998.

One of the first points to note about declarations of incompatibility is that it is discretionary. The wording of s 4(2) is very clear that the court *may* make a declaration and thus even if it believes that legislation is incompatible with the ECHR it could decide that it is not necessary to make a declaration and could instead simply make a ruling that the legislation is incompatible and not, for example, trigger some of the ancillary issues related to a s 4 declaration. It will be seen that the effects of a s 4 declaration can be quite significant and it is for this reason that only certain powers have the right to make a declaration of incompatibility under s 4. Whilst any court can exercise the interpretation clause within s 3, of the English courts only the Supreme Court, Court of Appeal, and High Court can make a declaration.[85] The exception to this is the Court of Protection, which is a relatively new statutory court, but this court may only make a declaration where it is being presided over by the President of the Family Division (who is also the President of the Court of Protection), Chancellor of the High Court (who is its Vice-President), or a puisne judge.[86]

A declaration of incompatibility is an unusual remedy in that it does not have any impact on the matter before the court. This is clear from s 4(6) which states:

A declaration of [incompatibility]—

(a) does not affect the validity, continuing operation or enforcement of the provision in respect of which it is given, and

(b) is not binding on the parties to the proceedings in which it is made.

The effect of this section is twofold. The first is that when deciding the matter in front of it, the court has to ignore the fact that the law is incompatible and proceed on the basis that the law is valid. It is for this reason that the courts have sometimes suggested that a declaration of incompatibility should be a remedy of last resort, with strong preference being given to the use of their interpretative powers under s 3.[87] This would be preferred because, where interpretation is permissible, it would at least mean that the courts could solve the issue that led to the breach of human rights. The second effect of course is that subsequent cases must also be dealt with by applying the law *as is* and not take account of the fact that there is a recognized breach of human rights.

Of course where the court is recognizing a breach of human rights but is not providing a remedy this would appear to be a breach of Article 13 and this is perhaps an additional reason why the government wished to exclude Article 13 from the HRA 1998. It does, however, leave the government in a difficult position since if the claimant takes the matter to the ECtHR then it is highly likely that it would also find a breach

---

85. HRA 1998, s 4(5).
86. ibid, s 4(5)(f).
87. See *Ghaidan v Godin-Mendoza* [2004] UKHL 30, [2004] 2 AC 557, 576.

(although they are not bound to follow the domestic court) and, having ruled that there is a breach, could award damages as a remedy.

What is the point of a s 4 declaration if it does not affect the issue that is being litigated? The answer lies in the fact that it empowers the government, if it so wishes, to rectify the breach without the need to introduce primary legislation. Section 10 empowers, but does not require, the government to amend primary legislation to make it compatible with the ECHR through the use of secondary legislation, a so-called 'Henry VIII' order. The power can only be exercised if a court has made a declaration under s 4 and there has been no appeal, the time for an appeal has lapsed, or all parties to the dispute state in writing they will not appeal.[88] If the test is met and the minister believes that there are 'compelling reasons' for amending the legislation then the amendment may be by order. The principal advantage of this is speed. It will be remembered from Chapter 2 that primary legislation can take a considerable period of time to progress through Parliament, especially where it is controversial or where there are pressures on parliamentary time. A statutory instrument takes considerably less time and thus the legislation and, presumably the incompatibility, can be undertaken quickly. Whilst legislation is not ordinarily retrospective it does mean that any future challenges would be dealt with under (what would be hoped to be compatible) legislation rather than the text that has been ruled incompatible.

⚡ REMEDIAL CORRECTIONS

In *R (on the application of H) v Mental Health Review Tribunal (North and East London Region)*[89] the Court of Appeal made the first declaration of incompatibility when it held that s 73 *Mental Health Act 1983* was incompatible with Article 5 (right to liberty) of the ECHR. Section 73 stated that where a person had been detained under the Mental Health Act then the burden of showing that the detention was no longer justified was on the patient rather than on the health authority. The government sought to use its powers under s 8 and the *Mental Health Act 1983 (Remedial) Order 2001*[90] was made which amended s 73 to place the burden on the authority.

Of course whilst secondary legislation is quicker it does mean that there is less parliamentary scrutiny which potentially means the government could alter primary legislation without the full consent of the Houses of Parliament (although from Chapter 3 it will be remembered that there are ways of objecting to secondary legislation). It appears that remedial orders are relatively unusual and that it is more common for Parliament to pass primary legislation to amend the offending legislation, presumably in part because of the transparency concerns noted earlier.

5.2.4.3 **Remedies against judicial acts**

Where the allegation is that a court (which is expressly a public authority by virtue of s 6(3)(a)) has acted contrary to the Convention then the only remedy that lies is a right of appeal or judicial review.[91] This is to ensure that people do not re-litigate

---

88.   HRA 1998, s 10(1)(a).
89.   [2002] QB 1.
90.   SI 2001/3712.
91.   HRA 1998, s 9.

their disputes by suing individual judges when they believe that the judgment of the court has infringed their Convention rights. This is a necessary step and has led to little dispute.

Judicial immunity (see 9.2.4) is also expressly contained in the Act when it states that damages may not be awarded when a judicial act has been undertaken in good faith.[92] The only exception to this rule is in respect of Article 5 of the ECHR (right to liberty). Article 5(5) expressly states that where a person has been detained unlawfully by the state they have an automatic right to compensation. Section 9(3) HRA 1998 makes clear, therefore, that the rule against damages does not extend to breaches of Article 5 although the government (via the appropriate minister) must be made a party to the proceedings when any court believes that it will be necessary to award damages under that section.[93]

5.2.4.4 Civil remedies

Assuming that a declaration of incompatibility is not required, what remedies are available when a court adjudicates? Section 8 does not limit the type of remedies available in civil matters and accordingly the full range of remedies are available to the court (discussed more extensively in Chapter 18). The actual remedy will depend on what action was being brought. Where, for example, it was anticipatory action then it is likely that the remedy sought will be an injunction preventing the breach from occurring. Where the action is because there is a belief that human rights already have been breached then it is likely that damages may be sought. That said, it is likely that in some instances a simple declaration would suffice—ie a statement by the judge that rights have been, or will be, infringed. Let us return to our earlier example of Robert (see 'Sword'). It will be remembered that the police wished to re-route his march. It is quite possible that Robert may seek an order quashing the decision of the police to re-route the march but it is also possible that a simple declaration by the judge that the actions would be illegal would suffice, with the police agreeing to respect the ruling.

Damages are perhaps the best-known form of civil remedy and the HRA 1998 does place some limitations on how these operate. The first rule is that only a court or tribunal that has the power to order damages may do so.[94] That may seem obvious, but not every court has the right to make damages, the most notable one being the Crown Court. The effect of s 8(2) would be to prevent the Crown Court, when making a finding that a person's human rights were infringed, ordering compensation (although the defendant could then initiate action in the civil courts which may be difficult to rebut).

The second issue in respect of damages is that the court can only award them if, after considering the other relief that it may order, it is satisfied that it is 'necessary to provide just satisfaction' in the case.[95] When deciding whether to award damages and, if so their quantum, the court must 'take into account the principles applied by the [ECtHR] in relation to the award of compensation under Article 41'.[96] This is an important principle as the ECtHR has adopted particular approaches to the granting of damages, including the fact that sometimes it will decline to provide any compensation beyond legal costs. This is because it sometimes believes, particularly in procedural

---

92. ibid, s 9(3).
93. ibid, s 9(4).
94. ibid, s 8(2).
95. ibid, s 8(3).
96. ibid, s 8(4).

matters, that the mere finding that a person's rights have been infringed will amount to 'just satisfaction'. The ECtHR has also, on occasion, refused to grant compensation on the grounds of public policy although it does so only rarely, but this is something that the domestic courts should take into account.

> **☰ Example** Denying compensation
>
> A significant case where the ECtHR refused to order compensation was *McCann v United Kingdom*.[97] This was one of the most controversial cases before the ECtHR. Three terrorists were shot dead in Gibraltar by members of the Special Air Service. The soldiers believed that the suspects were carrying a remote detonator that would allow them to set off a large explosive device. In fact, there was neither a detonator nor a bomb, as the suspects were on a reconnaissance exercise. In a controversial judgment the ECtHR held that the actual shootings did not breach Article 2 but the circumstances leading up to it did breach Article 2. The Court (in a 10:9 majority decision) believed that there was insufficient planning to identify whether it was possible to arrest the suspects, ie in essence suggesting the plan was always to shoot dead the suspects. Whilst the ECtHR found a breach of Article 2 it refused to award compensation to the relatives of the dead, in part because it was acknowledged that the three were intending to plant a bomb that was likely to cause death, injury, and significant damage.

Where damages are linked to financial loss the ECtHR will require proof that 'there is a causal link between the violation and any financial loss alleged'[98] and mere speculation will not suffice. As an example of circumstances when they will not find this link, it has been noted that loss of earnings from being imprisoned will not be compensated where a person succeeds in showing a breach of Article 6, the right to a fair trial.[99] Presumably the logic behind this is that it is not the unfair trial that caused the person to be imprisoned, it was the conduct that led to him being charged with an offence in the first place that was the cause (on that basis, where a person is imprisoned for a retrospective law that contravenes Article 7 of the ECHR it is possible that compensation would be awarded).

5.2.4.5 Remedies in criminal cases

It was noted earlier (5.2.2.3) that it is possible to use the HRA 1998 in criminal proceedings. Where a person is charged with a criminal offence what is the remedy for a breach of a Convention right? The HRA 1998 makes clear that it is possible to rely on the Convention as a defence and accordingly it may be possible, in extreme situations, to argue that a defendant should not be convicted as a result of the breach of the Convention but these will be relatively rare examples. More likely is that a serious breach of the Convention could lead to a successful argument that prosecuting the defendant would amount to an abuse of process and, accordingly, the prosecution should be halted. The House of Lords accepted that this could be the case, albeit *in obiter* and *per curiam* in the conjoined cases of *Attorney-General's Reference (No 3*

---

97. (2005) 42 EHRR 849.
98. David Harris et al, *Law of the European Convention on Human Rights* (3rd edn, OUP 2014) 859.
99. ibid.

of 2000); R v Looseley[100] where they accepted that the abuse-of-process doctrine was compatible with the ECHR. However, in a later decision the House stated quite clearly that it would be exceptional for breaches to halt criminal proceedings.

In *Attorney-General's Reference (No 2 of 2001)*[101] the House of Lords was called upon to consider the appropriate remedy in situations where there had been excessive delay in prosecuting defendants and bringing them before the courts for trial. Article 6(1) states a defendant has the right to a trial 'within a reasonable time' and the judge at first instance had stayed the trial arguing this was the appropriate remedy. The Attorney-General referred the matter to the appellate courts[102] and it eventually reached the House of Lords.

The House agreed that undue delay could breach Article 6(1) and argued that the 'clock' will normally start when a person is charged or summonsed before the court although this was not always the case as excessive delay between a formal interview and a charge may also be relevant. However, the House was dismissive of the idea that the only 'effective remedy' for undue delay is a stay of proceedings. Lord Bingham argued that remedies such as an acceleration of the timetable, the granting of bail, or even financial compensation might suffice.[103] His Lordship suggested that a stay should only be granted if the delay was so long that it would no longer be possible to guarantee a fair trial. The rationale behind this is that of proportionality: society has the right to expect protection from those who commit crimes and that where it is possible to do so fairly then a trial should continue. Lord Nicholls went further and argued that a stay would not be an effective remedy because it was against the wrong breach. His Lordship argued that normally the breach is not holding a trial after an excessive delay but rather not holding a trial in sufficient time. If, as the House believed, it is the latter then the trial is not unfair even if there has been a breach of Article 6. If the trial is not unfair then it cannot be an effective remedy to stay the trial. The House was leaving open the possibility that there could be circumstances in which holding a trial after excessive delay would be unfair (but that it is likely to be as a result of other factors, eg witness availability) and in those circumstances the effective remedy *may* be the stay of a trial.

It would seem therefore that the opportunities to use the HRA 1998 as a defence in criminal trials are now somewhat restricted although it has been suggested that this is not yet settled law and that the ECtHR itself has been taking a stricter line on procedural defects in trials, especially improper delay.[104] Ashworth appears to be arguing, therefore, that the ECtHR may suggest that delay may by itself lead to an unfair trial which would, following Lord Nicholls' argument, lead to the only effective remedy being a stay. It is notable that in the *Attorney-General's Reference* Lord Hope gave a strong dissenting judgment where he argued that it is not possible to detach the timing of the trial from the fairness of its execution[105] and that any delay that takes place after undue delay is necessarily a breach of the right to a fair trial. Lord Hope was alone in his views but if

100.   [2001] 1 WLR 2060.

101.   [2004] 2 AC 72.

102.   An Attorney-General's Reference in this context is a hypothetical appeal whereby the appellate courts are asked a point of law that arises from an acquittal. It proceeds as though it were an appeal but the decision of the appellate courts does not alter the acquittal, it simply forms a precedent for future cases (see 16.4.1).

103.   [2004] 2 AC 72, 89.

104.   Andrew Ashworth, 'Delay in Criminal Proceedings: Unreasonable Delay (AG Ref (No 2 of 2001))' [2004] *Criminal Law Review* 574–6, 576.

105.   [2004] 2 AC 72, 110.

Ashworth is correct his analysis may find favour in the ECtHR. Given that Article 13 is not within the HRA 1998 it is conceivable to see that a person convicted after undue delay but within Lord Bingham's reasoning could petition the ECtHR alleging a breach of Article 6 *and* a breach of Article 13. The ECtHR has no power to quash convictions but it could, presumably, state whether it thought that financial compensation or the granting of bail is an 'effective remedy' for the purposes of Article 6. Whether a domestic court would then follow that decision is perhaps more moot.

↻ QUESTION FOR REFLECTION

What do you think the remedy should be where a person on trial claims that his human rights have been breached? Does it matter what right is claimed to be breached (eg substantive (such as a complaint that he was beaten in custody) or procedural (eg that he has been subject to unfair questioning))? A difficulty with human rights arguments is that just because a person's rights have been infringed does not mean that he did not commit the crime. Can it ever be justified to quash a conviction, or order a person's acquittal, because a suspect's human rights have been infringed?

5.3 The future of the Human Rights Act 1998

The HRA 1998 came into full force in 2000 and thus has been in effect for over two decades. Yet since the decision to introduce the legislation was first announced in 1997 it has been one of the most controversial pieces of legislation. The Conservative party have been very clear in their dislike of the legislation and much of the media, particularly those that are considered to be to the right of the political spectrum, share the desire to repeal the Act.

The dislike of the Act is nothing new and, speaking sometime after the commencement of the Act, Lord Irvine of Lairg, the then Lord Chancellor, stated:

> One commentator asked recently why the Human Rights Act is still disliked. It is a good question.[106]

If anything, the Act has become more controversial since that statement was made. The press, particularly the right-wing press, have a dislike of the Act which, in some publications, borders on hatred. Like health and safety legislation the press gleefully report stories of 'human rights violations' which generally are false, misinformation, or the product of a non-lawyer suggesting something that the legislation never contemplated. Health and Safety has been the bogeyman for several years (with (erroneous) stories of, for example, banning conker matches at school being prevalent) but human rights is catching up fast in terms of implausible stories.

The Conservative party, which did not vote against the HRA 1998 when introduced into Parliament, has picked up on this zeal and has latterly called for its repeal. In the 2005 general election campaign Michael Howard, the then leader, called for its repeal and this call was repeated in 2010 with the forming of the coalition government.

---

106. Lord Irvine of Lairg, 'The Impact of the Human Rights Act: Parliament, the Courts and the Executive' [2003] *Public Law* 308–25, 324.

The presence of the Liberal Democrats in the coalition prevented the Conservative party from repealing the Act but it is clear that both the Conservative front and back benches desire change and the 2015 election saw the Conservative party again promise to replace the Act. It is an interesting change from the position in 1998 where there was some ambivalence and even in 2005 the whole of the front bench was not signed up to repeal, with Dominic Grieve MP, the then shadow Attorney-General (and who subsequently became Attorney-General in the coalition government) stating:

> The Human Rights Act has many benefits which it has conferred . . . I don't think the . . .
> Act has anything to do with fuelling a compensation culture at all.[107]

The suggestion that the HRA 1998 has fuelled the so-called compensation culture is one of the most prominent attacks against the Act although the reality is that claims-management firms (that are frequently managed by non-lawyers) are more likely to be responsible. Certainly by the time of the next general election Grieve had had a change of heart (or was more politically on message) and campaigned for the repeal of the Act and the introduction, in its place, of a British Bill of Rights. Grieve, without any apparent irony, argued that the British courts were going further than Strasbourg and [showed] 'a marked deference to Strasbourg'. A principal source of irritation to Grieve was apparently the way that the courts had approached s 2 and he proposed rewording it to allow for UK-specific traditions whilst 'acknowledging the relevance of Strasbourg Court decisions'.[108] That said, it is notable that after each election this threat to change the HRA 1998 has never been carried out.

Much of the criticism appears to be piggybacked onto the general Euroscepticism. The media, and indeed many MPs, fail to distinguish between the UK and the EU and thus the ECHR and the HRA 1998 are caught up in the ideology of reacting against 'Europe telling us what to do'. The fact that the ECHR is significantly older than the EU passes many by. A more interesting criticism is that the ECtHR is interfering in issues that were never contemplated at the time the Convention was written. This is arguably a stronger line of attack. There is no question that the ECHR, when drafted, was written to encapsulate a series of minimum standards of *fundamental* human rights. The ECtHR has undoubtedly broadened the scope of this instrument beyond that which the drafters would have contemplated, particularly in respect of social justice where issues such as same-sex rights and immigration matters have become increasingly important. That said, the ECtHR has been clear for some time that the Convention, unlike for example the US Constitution, is considered to be a 'living instrument'. US Constitutional interpretation is frequently based on ascertaining what the 'founding fathers' intended. The ECHR is not and arguably was never intended to be. There is no doubt that rights under the ECHR have shifted dramatically since the 1950s, most notably in respect of same-sex relationships. In earlier decisions of the ECtHR the court adopted a highly sceptical approach yet recently it has adopted an extremely liberal approach. The answer would seem to lie in the fact that society has progressed significantly. In the twenty-first century society expects that people are treated differently and this is particularly true of issues of sexuality where the expectation is now that gay,

---

107. *The Times*, 30 March 2005, news (p 28).
108. Francesca Klug, 'Follow or Lead? The Human Rights Act and the European Court of Human Rights' [2010] 6 *European Human Rights Law Review* 621–30, 627.

lesbian, and bisexual persons should enjoy the same rights as heterosexuals. This is an example of a seismic shift and when coupled with other social changes, most notably in the way that states deal with, for example, immigration, surveillance, or pre-trial detention, undoubtedly causes tension.

A popular attack on the HRA 1998 is that it has politicized judges. The issue of judicial independence will be considered elsewhere in this book (see Chapter 9) but it is clear that there is an argument that relations between the judiciary and government have suffered in recent years, under both Conservative and Labour administrations. Interestingly, there were fewer attacks during the coalition period, perhaps because the Liberal Democrats tempered some of the anger that was traditionally found in the Conservative party.

It will be seen in Chapter 9 that it is difficult for the judges to defend themselves against public, political attacks made against them. This is perhaps one reason why they are made. They are stories that the press like as they can be portrayed by the 'liberal elite'. Such criticism peaked shortly after the decision of the Supreme Court that the prorogation of Parliament was illegal.[109] This led to complaints that judges were interfering in inherently political grounds, and the HRA 1998 was quickly blamed. That is somewhat ironic as the HRA 1998 was not mentioned at all in the *Miller* decision.

The 2019 Conservative Party manifesto raised the issue of judicial activism again:

> We will update the Human Rights Act and administrative law to ensure that there is a proper balance between the rights of individuals, our vital national security and effective government. We will ensure that judicial review is available to protect the rights of the individuals against an overbearing state, while ensuring that it is not abused to conduct politics by another means. . .[110]

A commission on judicial review was created,[111] but it is clear that this is only the first step, with the Secretary of State for Justice indicating that an 'independent review of the Human Rights Act' will be announced later.[112] Of course, how independent an 'independent' review is can become a serious issue. The government chooses the commission so it is not truly independent. For example, the judicial review commission is chaired by Lord Faulks QC, a Conservative peer who criticized the decision in *Miller*. It has led some to wonder whether the commission has been created with the answer already given. That said, Lord Faulks has noted that he is a supporter of judicial independence, and this included resigning a government position when he believed that a potential Lord Chancellor would not uphold her oath.[113]

The reality is that, as will be seen in the discussion on judicial independence, 'independent' can mean very different things. However, it is certainly clear that the government is, for the first time, more serious about seeking to curb the use of the HRA 1998. It is unlikely, however, that the commission would seriously consider repealing the HRA 1998 and withdrawing from the ECHR, as some would wish.

Of course, even if the HRA 1998 was repealed, it is less than clear that it would make a difference. Is it likely that the genie could be placed back in the bottle? Arguably judges have become more active in recent years although there is a debate as to what extent this

179

109.   *R (on the application of Miller) v The Prime Minister* [2019] UKSC 41.
110.   *Get Brexit Done: Unleash Britain's Potential. The Conservative and Unionist Party Manifesto 2019* (London, 2019) at 48.
111.   'Government launches independent panel to look at judicial review' Ministry of Justice Press Release, 31 July 2020.
112.   M Fouzder 'Government to Review Human Rights Act' (2020) *Law Society Gazette*, 7 October.
113.   F Gibb 'Lord Faulks interview: "Has judicial review gone too far?"' (2020) *The Times*, September 10.

is the fault of the HRA 1998 and not, for example, the common-law development of judicial review (although it must be conceded that the HRA 1998 has probably encouraged judges to become more active in the field of judicial review). If the HRA 1998 was abolished is it likely that the courts would simply stop holding the government to account or believe that the government has the right to act in a way that is incompatible with human rights? It is difficult to believe that this would ever be the case. Whilst the HRA 1998 can, of course, be repealed it is not clear that the judges would not just rely on the common law to fill the gap, at least in terms of fundamental rights.

Some have suggested that we withdraw from the European Convention on Human Rights. While Theresa May MP, the then Prime Minister, was thought to be in favour of doing so, it is thought that relatively few MPs are in favour of doing so. Given the Convention is, in essence, a document that sets out minimum rights, it would be a brave government to withdraw from the Convention when other countries, with poorer records of human rights, remain. More likely is the use of derogations to limit the scope of certain Articles, but a full withdrawal is unlikely to be politically appealing.

5.4 The Convention Articles

In this section a very brief examination will be made of the key Convention rights. Not all rights will be discussed here but rather the ones you are most likely to read about. This section is designed to help you understand the basic principle of the Convention rights and how it may be used in practice.

5.4.1 General issues

Before considering the principal Convention rights there are two issues that must be briefly considered. The first relates to the difference between 'absolute' and 'qualified' rights and the other relates to 'positive' and 'negative' obligations.

5.4.1.1 Absolute and qualified rights

It is sometimes said that Articles can be divided into absolute and qualified rights, the latter being Articles that can be interfered with under certain circumstances. The ECtHR itself uses this language when referring to Articles 8–11, each of which is in two parts. The first part sets out what the right or freedom is, and the second part sets out the circumstances under which the state can interfere with this right.

However, some have suggested that this is too basic an analysis[114] and that all rights are subject to some qualifications. Certainly, as will be seen, there is an argument that this may be true. Article 2, the right to life, is often referred to as an 'absolute' right and yet on the face of the Article it states there are circumstances under which the state can kill and not infringe this right. Is this not a qualification? Similarly, other Articles do not appear to contain any qualification, eg Article 6 (right to fair trial), and yet the ECtHR has stated that this is not an absolute right.[115] That said, this is perhaps merely a recognition that there is no 'binary divide' between absolute and qualified rights but that each exists alongside other laws.

---

114.   See, for example, Simon Atrill, 'Keeping the Executive in the Picture: A Reply to Professor Leigh' [2003] *Public Law* 41–51, 44.

115.   See, for example, *Condron v United Kingdom* (2001) 31 EHRR 1.

The term 'qualified right' will continue to be used in this text especially in relation to Articles 8–11 as this is the wording used by the Strasbourg authorities. This will be discussed further later.

5.4.1.2 Positive and negative obligations

Article 1 of the ECHR requires states to 'secure to everyone in their jurisdiction the rights and freedoms [of the Convention]' and this has been construed to mean that some Articles will have a positive obligation on the state to secure the right. A negative obligation is quite standard and merely means that the state (in our case the United Kingdom) must not infringe the rights under the Convention. For example, therefore, this means that the state must not use torture on someone. However, certain Articles (most notably Articles 2, 3, and 8) also place a positive obligation on the state to *protect* a citizen from receiving such treatment.[116] Thus a state will not only be liable for actually infringing a right but also for allowing a private citizen to be harmed by another. That said, the positive obligation is not absolute and merely requires the state to take reasonable action and this includes, for example, ensuring that there are effective laws protecting an individual.[117] To this extent it can be said that there is a limited 'horizontal effect' to the ECHR and, therefore, the HRA 1998.

5.4.2 Article 2: The right to life

The first substantive right to consider is Article 2, which states:

1. Everyone's right to life shall be protected by law. No one shall be deprived of his life intentionally save in the execution of a sentence of a court following his conviction for a crime for which this penalty is provided by law.

2. Deprivation of life shall not be regarded as inflicted in contravention of this article when it results from the use of force which is no more than absolutely necessary:

   (a) in defence of any person from unlawful violence;

   (b) in order to effect a lawful arrest or to prevent escape of a person lawfully detained;

   (c) in action lawfully taken for the purpose of quelling a riot or insurrection.

In England and Wales Article 2(1) could, in fact, be shortened by the deletion of the second sentence (beginning 'No one shall . . . ') because the United Kingdom has also signed the Sixth Protocol to the Convention which abolishes the death penalty[118] although theoretically it may be introduced to a limited extent in time of war.[119] Whether this means anything in practice is perhaps open to question since the last time the United Kingdom formally declared war was in the Second World War (all other military actions since then have been 'conflicts' not 'war', the latter bearing a particular definition in international law).

5.4.2.1 Positive obligation

Article 2 is a classic example of where a positive obligation arises. Not only does Article 2 prevent the state from killing someone, it has been held that 'everyone's right to life shall be protected by law' means that there is a positive obligation on the state to

---

116. See, for example, *Osman v United Kingdom* (2000) 29 EHRR 245.
117. See, for example, *X and Y v Netherlands* (1986) 8 EHRR 235.
118. Art 1 of the Sixth Protocol.
119. Art 2 of the Sixth Protocol.

safeguard those who live within their jurisdiction.[120] This has been explained as putting in place a legal framework that deters the commission of homicides but also a law enforcement mechanism to investigate and prosecute homicides.

The obligation to protect life does not mean that euthanasia must be criminalized[121] and this would seem to apply to both active and passive forms of euthanasia[122] and certainly some signatory states, most notably Switzerland, famously have euthanasia laws. What is clear, however, is that there is no right to die implicit within Article 2. Thus where a state does not permit euthanasia, Article 2 cannot be pleaded in an attempt to force the state to permit the ending of a life.

Perhaps the issue that has developed most significantly in recent years relates to the prevention of death. It was noted above that Article 2 includes a positive obligation and this has extended to situations where the state knows, or should know, that a danger exists.[123] The ECtHR has indicated, in particular, that this duty exists where a person is in the detention of the state.[124] The duty has also been considered to apply not only to homicides but also to suicides[125] and thus where the state is aware that a prisoner may commit suicide then they should take preventative measures. One of the more controversial aspects of this positive duty is that it also applies to the level of planning that can be expected from law enforcement operations, in particular there should be careful consideration of the circumstances when lethal force may arise (which, of course, is expressly contemplated by Article 2(2)) and a plan formulated that minimizes those circumstances.[126]

There is also a procedural aspect to Article 2 and it has been held that there should be an independent and effective investigation into any death that has been inflicted by the state or, where the state has breached the duty discussed earlier.[127] This procedural requirement has become increasingly important in recent years with cases discussing whether investigations into shootings by police officers conducted by the Independent Police Complaints Commission satisfy the requirements of Article 2.[128]

5.4.2.2 **Use of lethal force**

In terms of the circumstances under which lethal force can be contemplated, ie those set out in Article 2(2), it is unlikely that this will cause too many difficulties in the domestic context and it is very similar to domestic law under s 3 *Criminal Law Act 1967* although there is a subtle difference of wording between s 3 and Article 2(2)(a).

5.4.3 **Article 3: Prohibition of torture**

Article 3 is the shortest of all the Convention articles:

No one shall be subjected to torture or inhuman or degrading treatment or punishment.

This is another absolute right and one that contains a positive obligation on states, ie not only must it not subject somebody to torture, inhuman, or degrading treatment,

---

120. *LCB v United Kingdom* (1999) 27 EHRR 212.
121. *Widmer v Switzerland* App No 20527/92 (1993).
122. See the discussion in *Pretty v United Kingdom* (2002) 35 EHRR 1.
123. See, most notably, *Osman v United Kingdom* (2000) 29 EHRR 245.
124. See, for example, *Edwards v UK* (2002) 35 EHRR 487 where a prisoner was killed by another prisoner in circumstances where an attack was possible.
125. *Keenan v United Kingdom* (2001) 33 EHRR 38.
126. *McCann v United Kingdom* (1996) 21 EHRR 97.
127. See, for example, *Jordan v United Kingdom* (2003) 37 EHRR 2.
128. See, for example, *Saunders and another v IPCC and others* [2008] EWHC 2372 (Admin) which raised questions about the practice of allowing police officers to confer before making their statements.

it must protect the person suffering this from others. Some uncertainty arose as to what the difference in wording was but in *Ireland v United Kingdom*[129] the ECtHR defined the terms. The case followed accusations of mistreatment by the security force in Northern Ireland of suspected terrorists. The Court found that whilst no suspect had been tortured, they had suffered inhuman and degrading treatment, the Court believing that torture involved 'deliberate inhuman treatment causing very serious and cruel suffering' (p 80).

In order for a treatment or punishment to amount to either degrading or inhuman treatment it must pass a minimum threshold of severity[130] since not every type of shameful treatment will amount to a breach of Article 3. That said, this is not to say that it is not actionable since it is possible action could be brought under the right to personal integrity under Article 8 (see 5.4.7). One of the principal battlegrounds in relation to Article 3 is the concept of corporal punishment, with the European Court reaching different conclusions as to its compatibility with Article 3.[131]

Outside of corporal punishment it has been suggested that a respective imbalance in power may lead to the threshold being passed, and accordingly abuse that takes place by law enforcement agencies while a suspect is within their custody is likely to constitute a breach of Article 3.[132]

Sexual assault will almost certainly pass the threshold for Article 3, not least because of the psychological issues that arise in respect of any sexual assault. This is most relevant in the context of the positive obligation placed on states and means that they must have appropriate and effective laws in place to criminalize sexual assaults and ensure they are appropriately investigated.[133] In the (hopefully exceptional) circumstances where a prisoner is sexually assaulted by a state agent this will almost automatically lead to a breach of Article 3.[134]

5.4.4 Article 5: Right to liberty

Article 5 is an important Article within the ECHR as it governs protection from, inter alia, arbitrary arrest. Its form is as follows:

1. Everyone has the right to liberty and security of person. No one shall be deprived of his liberty save in the following cases and in accordance with a procedure prescribed by law:

   (a) the lawful detention of a person after conviction by a competent court;

   (b) the lawful arrest or detention of a person for non-compliance with the lawful order of a court or in order to secure the fulfilment of any obligation prescribed by law;

   (c) the lawful arrest or detention of a person effected for the purpose of bringing him before the competent legal authority on reasonable suspicion of having committed an offence or when it is reasonably considered necessary to prevent his committing an offence or fleeing after having done so;

---

129. (1979–80) 2 EHRR 25.
130. See *Costello-Roberts v United Kingdom* (1995) 19 EHRR 112.
131. See ibid; cf *A v United Kingdom* (1999) 27 EHRR 611.
132. See, for example, *Selmouni v France* (2000) 29 EHRR 403.
133. See *X and Y v Netherlands* (1986) 8 EHRR 235.
134. *Aydin v Turkey* (1998) 25 EHRR 251.

(d) the detention of a minor by lawful order for the purpose of educational supervision or his lawful detention for the purpose of bringing him before the competent legal authority;

(e) the lawful detention of persons for the prevention of the spreading of infectious diseases, of persons of unsound mind, alcoholics or drug addicts or vagrants;

(f) the lawful arrest or detention of a person to prevent his effecting an unauthorised entry into the country or of a person against whom action is being taken with a view to deportation or extradition.

2. Everyone who is arrested shall be informed promptly, in a language which he understands, of the reasons for his arrest and of any charge against him.

3. Everyone arrested or detained in accordance with the provisions of paragraph 1.c of this article shall be brought promptly before a judge or other officer authorised by law to exercise judicial power and shall be entitled to trial within a reasonable time or to release pending trial. Release may be conditioned by guarantees to appear for trial.

4. Everyone who is deprived of his liberty by arrest or detention shall be entitled to take proceedings by which the lawfulness of his detention shall be decided speedily by a court and his release ordered if the detention is not lawful.

5. Everyone who has been the victim of arrest or detention in contravention of the provisions of this article shall have an enforceable right to compensation.

It can be seen that this is a very long Article and accordingly only certain parts of the Article will be considered. If you study *Civil Liberties, Human Rights*, or some *Public Law* modules then you are likely to spend considerable time examining this Article because it is a crucial feature of the relationship between the state and the citizen in terms of restricting liberty.

Article 5 provides the circumstances in which a person can be deprived of liberty. It is sometimes said that it provides protection from arbitrary arrest but this is not necessarily true since Article 5 will be engaged only if the arrest leads to a person's liberty being removed, although this could include being prevented from leaving the scene of arrest. Also, Article 5 does not necessarily provide administrative safeguards after arrest as certain aspects (eg police interviews) are to be found in other Convention Articles (eg Article 6).

That said, arrest is arguably the most important frequently used part of Article 5, and Article 5(1)(c) provides that this may be lawful but only where a person is brought before 'the competent legal authority'. It is not immediately clear from the face of Article 5 what this means but in England and Wales the first person a suspect will face is a custody sergeant, a police officer, who will decide whether to authorize his detention.[135] An inspector will then decide whether to continue detention after nine hours[136] and finally a superintendent can take the decision to extend the time, for certain offences, to thirty-six hours in exceptional circumstances.[137] After this time has elapsed the police have two options open to them. They either release the offender or they bring the offender before a magistrate. It is clear that this is the competent authority to whom

135. *Police and Criminal Evidence Act 1984*, s 37.
136. ibid, s 40.
137. ibid, s 42.

Article 5(1)(c) refers. Article 5(2) and 5(3) then provide additional safeguards such as knowing why a person has been arrested and that he should be brought before a judge, which would appear to be an overlap with Article 5(1)(c) but it is clear that the primary purpose of Article 5(3) is dealing with securing liberty rather than the purpose of the arrest. Article 5(3) therefore provides that a person should either be brought before a court or granted bail. It is important to note, however, that it is possible for bail to be subject to conditions. In the early days of the HRA 1998 this had caused some difficulties with some lawyers suggesting that conditional bail was an infringement of human rights but this was quite clearly a misreading of the legal position.[138]

An important aspect of Article 5 is to provide a mechanism for securing liberty. This is to be found in Article 5(4)–(5). This provides that everyone shall have the right to petition a court to question the appropriateness of any detention and that where any detention is found to be unlawful there should be an automatic right to compensation. To an extent this may be thought comparable to the procedure known as *habeas corpus* but it is an important safeguard.

5.4.5 Article 6: Right to a fair trial

One of the most important rights in the Convention and certainly one of the most quoted is Article 6 of the ECHR. This provides:

1. In the determination of his civil rights and obligations or of any criminal charge against him, everyone is entitled to a fair and public hearing within a reasonable time by an independent and impartial tribunal established by law. Judgment shall be pronounced publicly but the press and public may be excluded from all or part of the trial in the interests of morals, public order or national security in a democratic society, where the interests of juveniles or the protection of the private life of the parties so require, or to the extent strictly necessary in the opinion of the court in special circumstances where publicity would prejudice the interests of justice.

2. Everyone charged with a criminal offence shall be presumed innocent until proved guilty according to law.

3. Everyone charged with a criminal offence has the following minimum rights:

    (a) to be informed promptly, in a language which he understands and in detail, of the nature and cause of the accusation against him;

    (b) to have adequate time and facilities for the preparation of his defence;

    (c) to defend himself in person or through legal assistance of his own choosing or, if he has not sufficient means to pay for legal assistance, to be given it free when the interests of justice so require;

    (d) to examine or have examined witnesses against him and to obtain the attendance and examination of witnesses on his behalf under the same conditions as witnesses against him;

    (e) to have the free assistance of an interpreter if he cannot understand or speak the language used in court.

185

---

138. Alisdair Gillespie, 'Curfew and Bail' (2001) 151 *New Law Journal* 465–6.

Entire books have been produced on Article 6 and this discussion will be brief and only consider some of the core elements of the Article. However, this is an issue that you will return to throughout your legal studies as the concept of a fair trial goes to the very heart of due process in the law.

The key words of the Article are actually its marginal note, and the ECtHR will frequently consider everything holistically and balance matters against the 'right to a fair trial' rather than focus on the individual rights. It should be noted that Article 6 applies to both civil and criminal matters although from the wording it is clear that most guarantees exist in respect of criminal trials. It is also important to note that 'in the determination of his civil rights and obligations' does not mean every civil matter will come within Article 6 and issues such as the treatment of state employees have been considered to be outside the scope of Article 6.[139]

In terms of its application to criminal law it can probably be said that the most important aspects of the Article are the 'independent and impartial tribunal',[140] the presumption of innocence,[141] the ability to defend oneself in court,[142] and an implicit doctrine known as the 'equality of arms'.

5.4.5.1 Independent and impartial tribunal

It may be thought that in a system of justice this would not be overly problematic but Article 6 has had a significant impact on how decisions relating to individuals are adjudicated. However, this has been an area of fruitful litigation for some time. Article 6 has had significant impact on how judges are appointed, particularly part-time judges, something most notable in the decision *McGonnell v United Kingdom*.[143] In Scotland the judicial system was placed under severe pressure when it was decided that part-time judges were not independent or impartial because of the manner in which they were appointed,[144] something that although not directly applicable to England led to the Lord Chancellor deciding that he would alter the way in which Recorders were appointed (see Chapter 9).

The same argument led to fundamental changes in the way that courts martial (ie judicial tribunals set up to adjudicate the law relating to serving members of HM Forces) were administered. The ECtHR has long had difficulties with the system of courts martial, not least because the judge and jury used to be all members of the armed services.[145] Eventually civilian judges were introduced to solve this problem[146] but it eventually culminated in new legislation being required to administer service justice.[147]

The most controversial application of this doctrine was, however, undoubtedly in relation to how those convicted of murder were sentenced. There is only one sentence that can be imposed for the crime of murder; that of life imprisonment (adult defendant) or detention for life (young offender). However, the Home Secretary decided how long a person should stay in prison by having the final say over the tariff.

---

139. See, for example, *Lombardo v Italy* (1996) 21 EHRR 188.
140. ECHR, Art 6(1).
141. ibid, Art 6(2).
142. ibid, Art 6(3)(b)–(d).
143. (2000) 30 EHRR 289.
144. *Davidson v Scottish Ministers* (No 2) [2004] UKHL 34.
145. *Morris v United Kingdom* (2002) 34 EHRR 52.
146. *Cooper v United Kingdom* (2004) 39 EHRR 8.
147. *Armed Forces Act 2006.*

> ⚡ **TARIFF**
>
> Although a person is sentenced to life imprisonment it is extremely rare for a person to spend the rest of their life in prison. There is a system of early release which allows prisoners to be released 'on licence' (ie to be on good behaviour). Where a life sentence has been imposed then the minimum period before which a person can be considered for release is known as the tariff. After this period has expired the Parole Board will decide whether a person should be released or not.

The first case to call into question the appropriateness of a politician having this power was that of *T v United Kingdom; V v United Kingdom*.[148] This was the case concerning the killers of Jamie Bulger. 'T' and 'V' were boys aged 10 years when they abducted and killed Jamie Bulger, a 2-year-old boy. The crime was controversial for a whole series of reasons but one important aspect of the case was that the ECtHR held that it was wrong for a politician to decide how long the boys should spend in prison, suggesting that this should be a judicial and not political function. This eventually culminated in *R (on the application of Anderson) v Secretary of State for the Home Office*[149] in which the House of Lords held that the Home Secretary should not have any say in the setting of *any* tariff, including those for adult offenders. The decision was hugely controversial with the then current and previous Home Secretaries arguing that it should not be a purely judicial factor as society (through the political process) should also have the right to a say in how long its worst prisoners spend in gaol. However, ultimately the rule of law prevailed and the *Criminal Justice Act 2003* gave ultimate responsibility for the setting of tariffs to the judiciary.

5.4.5.2 **Presumption of innocence**

The presumption of innocence has always featured as an inherent part of the English Legal System but Article 6(2) expressly makes reference to this. However, the ECtHR is prepared to go much further than this and have held that the presumption of innocence applies even where Article 6(2) does not. Article 6(2) relates to a 'criminal charge' and thus where a person is no longer charged (because, for example, he has been convicted of the offence) then Article 6(2) would not apply. This was relevant in *Philips v United Kingdom*[150] which concerned a confiscation order made after a person had been convicted of trafficking drugs. Article 6(2) could not apply because he was no longer the subject of a criminal charge but the ECtHR held that the 'right to a fair trial' within Article 6(1) also included the presumption of innocence.

The main source of conflict in relation to Article 6(2) in the UK context has been in respect of the privilege against self-incrimination and the so-called 'right to silence'. At one point, suspects who were interviewed by the police were able to remain silent when questioned and nothing could be drawn from that silence. However, the *Criminal Justice and Public Order Act 1994* introduced the system of adverse inferences, meaning that where a person remains silent but then testifies at court with a statement that seeks to indicate why they did not commit the offence, the jury can take into account the fact that the person remained silent at the time of questioning. In *Murray v United*

---

148. (2000) 30 EHRR 121.
149. [2003] 1 AC 837.
150. [2001] Crim LR 817.

Kingdom[151] and *Condron v United Kingdom*[152] the ECtHR held that this did not amount to an infringement of the presumption of innocence under either Article 6(1) or Article 6(2).

Another source of controversy is domestic laws that seek to reverse the burden of proof. This was discussed earlier in the context of drugs[153] but deserves brief attention here. One of the most prominent cases dealing with this point is *Salabiaku v France*[154] which concerned French legislation about the smuggling of prohibited drugs. The legislation stated that someone who was in actual possession of goods while entering the country was presumed to be smuggling them unless they could prove to the contrary. This was challenged but the ECtHR held that it did not infringe Article 6(2) because the prosecution still had to prove key elements (most notably, possession of the goods, that the goods were illegal, and that the person brought them into the country) and thus the majority of the offence still needs to be proved, it was simply a presumption that could be rebutted by adducing evidence.

5.4.5.3 **The right to defend oneself**

Article 6(3) provides a series of steps that are designed to allow a person to defend himself when accused of committing a crime. However, in certain offences, most notably sex offences, a tension exists between allowing a person to present a rigorous defence and also ensuring that the victim of a crime is not put through unnecessary distress. This tension has already been examined earlier in this book in the context of statutory interpretation[155] and it will also be examined in later chapters when we look at the course of a criminal trial where this specific issue has been discussed extensively by the courts.

The right to defend oneself is either in person or through the provision of a lawyer. A person should usually be allowed to attend proceedings against him but it is clear that legal representation should ordinarily be permitted. In *Campbell and Fell v United Kingdom*[156] the ECtHR declared there was a breach of Article 6(3) when prisoners, who refused to attend a prison disciplinary panel, were also not permitted to send lawyers in their place. Article 6(3)(c) also encapsulates a right to legal aid, although only where a person lacks 'sufficient means' (which is not defined). The second qualification to this is that it must 'be in the interests of justice to do so' which implies that not all cases will require legally aided representation, and certainly it has been held that where the maximum sentence for an offence was a modest fine legal aid was not necessary.[157] In *Granger v United Kingdom*[158] the ECtHR found a breach where an appeal was more complicated than was initially thought. Presumably the complexity meant that it was unreasonable to expect a layperson (the appellant) to be capable of arguing the appeal without expert legal assistance.

151.   (1996) 22 EHRR 29.
152.   (2001) 31 EHRR 1.
153.   *R v Lambert* [2001] UKHL 37.
154.   (1991) 13 EHRR 379.
155.   See *R v A (No 2)* [2002] 1 AC 45 and see 2.3.4.
156.   (1985) 7 EHRR 165.
157.   *Gutfreund v France* (2006) 42 EHRR 48.
158.   (1990) 12 EHRR 469.

5.4.5.4 **Equality of arms**

One of the central features of Article 6(1) is that the ECtHR has held that there must be an 'equality of arms'[159] (and this applies to both civil and criminal cases). Put simply it means that the parties should be given reasonable opportunity to present their case in circumstances that do not put them at an obvious disadvantage to their opponent. The principal effect of this is to ensure, so far as possible, the neutrality of procedural issues and the opportunities of sides to adduce expert evidence, particularly in rebuttal.

5.4.6 **Article 7: No punishment without law**

Article 7 of the ECHR is particularly important within the criminal context. It provides:

1. No one shall be held guilty of any criminal offence on account of any act or omission which did not constitute a criminal offence under national or international law at the time when it was committed. Nor shall a heavier penalty be imposed than the one that was applicable at the time the criminal offence was committed.
2. This article shall not prejudice the trial and punishment of any person for any act or omission which, at the time when it was committed, was criminal according to the general principles of law recognised by civilised nations.

Whilst there are many issues enveloped within Article 7, the most important is that criminal offences should not be retrospective. It has already been noted that whilst Parliament is competent to legislate as it sees fit, there is a convention that it will not create retrospective criminal offences (see 2.3.6.4). This rule undoubtedly pre-dates Article 7 but following the introduction of the HRA 1998 it continues to be an extremely important principle by which Parliament must be guided.

Although Article 7 prevents retrospective punishment it is important to note that the Article does not prevent the interpretation of the law evolving through time. Perhaps the most important example of this is in respect of marital rape.

> **Example** Marital rape
>
> Historically the law had taken the approach that a man could not be guilty of raping his wife. This approach was based on the fact that the contract of marriage included the right to conjugal relations. The rule was widely condemned and eventually in *R v R*[160] the House of Lords held that the rule no longer had any role in modern society.
>
> This ruling led to the appellant's conviction for rape being upheld along with his custodial sentence. He petitioned the ECtHR arguing that this ruling contravened Article 7. His argument was that at the time of the rape the law had recognized a marital exemption and that the House of Lords decision had therefore turned a lawful act into an unlawful act retrospectively. In *SW v United Kingdom*[161] the ECtHR dismissed this argument suggesting that all the House of Lords had done was evolve the law and make it applicable to contemporary society. They also held that this evolution was predictable and thus was not retrospective.

---

159. See, most notably, *Neumeister v Austria* (1979–80) 1 EHRR 91.
160. [1992] 1 AC 599.
161. (1996) 21 EHRR 363.

An important restriction of Article 7 is that it applies only to criminal penalties. This has caused some debate where governments seek to introduce preventative measures on certain offenders. Perhaps the classic example of this in the context of the United Kingdom was the introduction of sex offender notification requirements (aka 'sex offender register'). In 1997 the UK government introduced a system whereby those who were cautioned or convicted of certain offences were required to notify their name and address to the police and also to notify any changes, including being away from their house for a specified period of time.[162] The Act applied to all those cautioned and convicted on the date it came into force but it also applied to those who had been convicted prior to the date it came into force and had not yet been released. In *Ibbotson v United Kingdom*[163] the ECmHR (which was still in existence at the time) declared the application inadmissible holding that the scheme was not a punishment within the meaning of Article 7.[164]

A second use of Article 7 tends to focus on the 'quality of the law'. It has been held that a law is required to be accessible to allow a person to appreciate that they are transgressing the law. Article 7 is taken to mean that a law should be defined with such precision that a person can identify whether they are committing a criminal act.[165] Some crimes in England and Wales remain creatures of the common law, ie they are not set out anywhere in statute and only exist through the definitions established by the courts. It has been argued before that such crimes may fall foul of Article 7 although the courts remain sceptical of this argument and rarely entertain such applications.[166]

5.4.7 Article 8: Right to respect for private life

Alongside Article 6, Article 8 is one of the more popular rights that is litigated under the Convention. It provides:

1. Everyone has the right to respect for his private and family life, his home and his correspondence.
2. There shall be no interference by a public authority with the exercise of this right except such as is in accordance with the law and is necessary in a democratic society in the interests of national security, public safety or the economic well-being of the country, for the prevention of disorder or crime, for the protection of health or morals, or for the protection of the rights and freedoms of others.

This is the first of the 'qualified rights' and it can be seen immediately that the qualification is contained in Article 8(2). Article 8(1) sets out the right, and Article 8(2) states the circumstances under which the right can be infringed.

As with Article 6, entire books have been produced just on the meaning of Article 8 and this is another right that you will come across throughout your legal studies, including in modules such as *Land Law*, *Equity and Trusts*, and *Medical Law*.

---

162. *Sex Offenders Act 1997* now contained within *Sexual Offences Act 2003*, Pt 2.
163. (1999) 27 EHRR CD 332.
164. Something confirmed by the ECtHR in *Adamson v United Kingdom* (1999) 28 EHRR CD 209.
165. See, for example, *R v Rimmington* [2005] UKHL 63 (relating to the offence of public nuisance).
166. An interesting example of this can be seen in *R v Norman* [2016] EWCA Crim 1564 [47]–[49].

5.4.7.1 **Not just private life**

Article 8 is often referred to as the right to respect for private life yet Article 8(1) makes clear that a person has the right to respect for:

- private life
- family life
- home
- correspondence.

Not infrequently these will be subsumed within the concept of 'private life' but it is important to note that this need not be the case and, for example, correspondence can be a significant issue for prisoners. The ECtHR has held that it is not appropriate for prisoners' correspondence to be routinely intercepted[167] although it does accept that where there is a pressing need to do so, this can be justified (ie it will allow Article 8(2) to apply) although the limits of such interference will be strictly considered.[168]

The ECtHR has consistently stated that the purpose of Article 8 is to protect an individual from arbitrary interference with a person's rights by the state[169] and this takes on a series of forms. Perhaps one of the most significant in recent years has been in regulating surveillance. The United Kingdom traditionally operated on the basis that because the law did not state that public authorities could not put somebody under surveillance, they were free to do so[170] whereas the ECtHR argues the opposite is true under the Convention. Accordingly a legal basis must exist under which Article 8 can be interfered with[171] and this law must be readily accessible with appropriate legal (rather than administrative) safeguards against abuse of authorities.[172] Within the context of surveillance this led to the enactment of the *Regulation of Investigatory Powers Act 2000*.

There are limits to what the courts will consider an arbitrary interference. Perhaps one of the more entertaining cases in recent times concerning Article 8 is *Pile v Chief Constable of Merseyside Police*.[173] Here, Turner J summarized the case thus:

> Cheryl Pile brings this appeal to establish the liberty of inebriated English subjects to be allowed to lie undisturbed overnight in their own vomit soaked clothing.[174]

Perhaps unsurprisingly, the learned judge did not find such a right arose. The case is worth reading, however, not least as an excellent example of how sarcastic a judge can be when dismissing an unmeritorious application.

5.4.7.2 **Positive obligation**

Article 8, like Articles 2 and 3, contains both a positive and a negative obligation. This means that the state should not only ensure that they do not infringe Article 8 themselves but also ensure that they protect individuals from having their Article 8 rights infringed by others. A good example of this can be seen from *Moreno Gomez v Spain*[175] where the

---

167. *Valasinas v Lithuania* App No 44558/98.
168. *Foxley v United Kingdom* (2001) 31 EHRR 25.
169. See, for example, *Glaser v United Kingdom* (2001) 33 EHRR 1 [63].
170. See, for example, *Malone v Commissioner of Police for the Metropolis (No 2)* [1979] Ch 44.
171. *Malone v United Kingdom* (1985) 7 EHRR 14.
172. *Govell v United Kingdom* (1997) 23 EHRR CD101.
173. [2020] EWHC 2472 (QB).
174. [2020] EWHC 2472 (QB) at [1].
175. (2005) 41 EHRR 40.

ECtHR considered that the positive obligation meant that the impact of noise and smells must be considered when deciding whether to grant a licence to a night club within a residential area.

More significantly, the positive obligation also gives rise to the right to physical integrity and accordingly treatment that is below the minimum threshold for Article 3 (see 5.2.3.2) may come within Article 8.[176] In *Pretty v United Kingdom*[177] the ECtHR confirmed that 'private life' is a broad concept that cannot be precisely defined but that it covered, in essence, the respect for human dignity. The ECtHR conceded that whilst no right to suicide could be included within Article 2, it may be possible to infer a limited right under Article 8 but it also held that a blanket ban on assisted suicide could be justified under Article 8(2).

5.4.8 Article 10: Freedom of expression

Although Article 10 is a qualified right it has been said that freedom of expression is the bedrock upon which a democracy is built[178] and it is accordingly one of the most important Convention Articles. It provides:

1. Everyone has the right to freedom of expression. This right shall include freedom to hold opinions and to receive and impart information and ideas without interference by public authority and regardless of frontiers. This article shall not prevent States from requiring the licensing of broadcasting, television or cinema enterprises.

2. The exercise of these freedoms, since it carries with it duties and responsibilities, may be subject to such formalities, conditions, restrictions or penalties as are prescribed by law and are necessary in a democratic society, in the interests of national security, territorial integrity or public safety, for the prevention of disorder or crime, for the protection of health or morals, for the protection of the reputation or rights of others, for preventing the disclosure of information received in confidence, or for maintaining the authority and impartiality of the judiciary.

Article 10 is, in essence, the Convention equivalent of the right to free speech although it has a much wider remit than this. Together with Article 11 (see 5.4.9) it is the primary right to allow protests. This is another Article that you will encounter throughout your legal study and particularly in modules such as *Public Law*, *Constitutional Law*, or *Civil Liberties*.

The classic case examining Article 10 was *Sunday Times v United Kingdom*[179] which was also known as the 'Spycatcher case'. The ECtHR made clear that Article 10 should be interfered with only when strictly necessary to do so and that where the press were concerned the proportionality was raised further because the press acts as the 'public's watchdog'.[180] This is undoubtedly recognition of the fact that totalitarian states will frequently control the press and that one of the easiest ways of controlling the public is to place restrictions on the press.

---

176.   See *X and Y v Netherlands* (1986) 8 EHRR 235.
177.   (2002) 35 EHRR 1.
178.   *Bowman v United Kingdom* (1998) 26 EHRR 1.
179.   (1992) 14 EHRR 229.
180.   ibid, [50].

> ### ≣ **Example** Spycatcher
>
> In 1985 a former member of MI5 (now the Security Services) sought to publish a memoir of his time within MI5. This was unprecedented as it provided operational details of his work within what was, at that time, still a secret service (indeed MI5 was not officially recognized until the enactment of the Security Service Act 1989). This included allegations that MI5 had bugged embassies, and also allegations that it and its sister service MI6 (now the Secret Intelligence Service) planned assassinations.
>
> The book was immediately banned in the United Kingdom although ultimately certain newspapers, most notably *The Sunday Times*, tried to serialize the book. Injunctions were taken out restraining publication and when these were breached contempt of court proceedings were initiated. *The Sunday Times*, and others, alleged that this was a breach of Article 10 of the ECHR, something that the ECtHR ultimately agreed with.
>
> The book received official clearance in 1988 when it was accepted that it had been serialized and published so widely around the world that it was illogical to ban sale in the United Kingdom especially since many copies had legitimately been imported from abroad.

However, Article 10 should not be considered merely a tool of the press and it is extremely important within the context of personal protests. Perhaps one of the most important statements came in the case of *Redmond-Bate v DPP*[181] in which Sedley LJ said:

> Free speech includes not only the inoffensive but the irritating, the contentious and the eccentric, the heretical, the unwelcome and the provocative provided it does not tend to provoke violence. Freedom only to speak inoffensively is not worth having.[182]

This is an important point and one undoubtedly within the spirit of Article 10. That said, however, it is also important to note that Article 10 is not absolute. Sedley LJ expressly considered that speech that tended to provoke violence would fall outside of his scope and Article 10(2) expressly considers qualifications in other situations. Perhaps the most controversial is 'morals' since this can be used to disguise a multitude of possibilities.

The leading case on the use of 'morals' as a qualification is *Handyside v United Kingdom*[183] where the ECtHR stated that it was not possible to identify a single moral basis across all contracting states.[184] Accordingly the Court would extend a 'margin of appreciation' to the individual states meaning that they would enjoy discretion to decide the moral standpoint of their society. However, the Court was also clear that the ECtHR had a supervisory role in ensuring that the application of this margin together with any restrictions placed on expression by the contracting states were strictly necessary. In the context of morals this must also take into account that society evolves and that something which may infringe society's standards at one point in time may not do so later.

193

181.　[2000] HRLR 249.
182.　ibid, 260.
183.　(1979–80) 1 EHRR 737.
184.　ibid, [18].

5.4.9 **Article 11: Freedom of assembly**

Article 11 is another key provision within the Convention and can be considered a fundamental principle of democracy. Alongside Article 10 it governs the right to protest but it also has a wider remit. The provisions of Article 11 are:

1. Everyone has the right to freedom of peaceful assembly and to freedom of association with others, including the right to form and to join trade unions for the protection of his interests.
2. No restrictions shall be placed on the exercise of these rights other than such as are prescribed by law and are necessary in a democratic society in the interests of national security or public safety, for the prevention of disorder or crime, for the protection of health or morals or for the protection of the rights and freedoms of others. This article shall not prevent the imposition of lawful restrictions on the exercise of these rights by members of the armed forces, of the police or of the administration of the State.

It can be seen that Article 11 is concerned with the right to be associated with others, either by assembly (eg a demonstration) or to join organizations and unions. However, it is important to note that this is a qualified right and that the right to join is not universal. The final sentence makes clear that Article 11 may not extend to agents of the executive, particularly in respect of the police and armed forces. Given the nature of these agencies it is understandable that restrictions may need to be put in place to ensure the smooth operation of these important bodies. In the United Kingdom this exception has been used with the police and members of HM Forces being denied the right to join a union. As regards the police there are other bodies that fulfil some of the responsibilities of unions (the Police Federation for officers up to and including the rank of chief inspector, the Superintendents' Association for officers of the rank of superintendent and chief superintendent, and the Association of Chief Police Officers for those of chief officer rank) but their responsibilities are curtailed and the police are not allowed to strike. This rule has also been used to justify restrictions on political activity for certain posts within local authorities.[185]

However, perhaps the more usual manner of engaging Article 11 is in respect of peaceful assembly. It can be seen from the very wording of Article 11(1) that the right only exists to peaceful protest and it follows therefore that where violence is likely then interferences may be possible. That said, issues of proportionality and necessity arise and, if at all possible, the state should try to minimize disruption rather than prevent assembly as a whole.

> **Example** Parades Commission
>
> We have already discussed the issue of the Parades Commission in Northern Ireland (see 'Necessity and proportionality') but this is also a classic example of the balance to be drawn under Article 11. The parades undertaken by Loyalist members of the Northern Ireland community are extremely controversial especially when routed through or near to Nationalist areas of the Province. There has been a long history of violence breaking out on such parades. However, the Parades Commission does not find it necessary to ban such assemblies but rather it exercises its powers to re-route the parades in order to minimize violence.[186]

---

185. See *Ahmed and others v United Kingdom* (2000) 29 EHRR 1.
186. See *Re Tweed's Application for Judicial Review* [2001] NI 165.

5.4.10 **Article 17**

An important but often neglected Article within the Convention is Article 17 which prohibits abuse of the Convention itself. Article 17 is not an independent Article, in that it cannot be the sole subject of litigation but is instead used in combination with other Articles. It is particularly of importance to Articles 10 and 11. Article 17 provides:

> Nothing in this Convention may be interpreted as implying for any State, group or person any right to engage in any activity or perform any act aimed at the destruction of any of the rights and freedoms set forth herein or at their limitation to a greater extent than is provided for in the Convention.

The essence of this right is that one cannot rely on the Convention in order to undermine the rights of others. The classic example of this would be in respect of Articles 10 and 11 where someone may wish to join a racist organization that has as its purpose the undermining of the rights of others due solely to their colour. The Convention will not allow such matters because the right claimed is an affront to the rights and freedoms contained within the Convention.

||\\ Case Box *Glimmerveen and Hagenback v Netherlands*

In *Glimmerveen and Hagenback v Netherlands*[187] the applicants had been convicted under Dutch law of distributing leaflets that were racist in character and called for the creation of a white state. The European Commission on Human Rights said: 'the general purpose of Article 17 is to prevent totalitarian groups from exploiting in their own interests the principles enunciated by the Convention.'[188] It dismissed the applicants' contention that Article 10 protected their right to distribute the leaflets on the basis that they were seeking to use Article 10 in such a way as to undermine the rights and freedoms of others and thus Article 17 applied.

It is right that the ECHR contains such a provision although it is important that those who interpret the Convention do not abuse the power given to them under Article 17 since the rights under Articles 10–11 do include the right to be unpopular and offensive. However, where the rights claimed seek to undermine the rights of others it is quite clear that this should be stopped.

A recent application of Article 17 is to be found in decision of the Supreme Court in *Sutherland v HM Advocate*.[189] The appellant had been charged with sexual offences after being detected by a so-called 'paedophile hunter' group. The appellant sought a stay of the prosecution alleging that their activities breached his rights under Article 8 of the ECHR. The reasons for this are quite complicated and outside the scope of this book, but the nature of the argument was that the use of the information gathered by the paedophile hunters would breach Article 8.

---

187.   (1982) 4 EHRR 260.
188.   (1982) 4 EHRR 260, 267.
189,   [2020] UKSC 32.

The Supreme Court rejected this argument. In part, this was because they held that sexualized communications between an adult and someone they thought to be a child were not worthy of protection under Article 8. In reaching this decision, the justices noted that Article 17 prevented the applicant from using Article 8 to claim protection for acts that would have breached the Convention for others (in this instance, the sexual abuse of a child,[190] something within Articles 3 and 8).

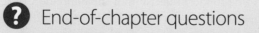 ## Summary

The *Human Rights Act 1998* is an extremely important instrument and it is one that you will encounter throughout your law studies and your career. In this chapter we have noted:

- Public bodies have a duty to act compatibly with the Convention. This is a *civil* and not *criminal* duty.

- Defining a public authority is not easy although all courts and tribunals are automatically covered.

- Public authorities tend to be divided into 'pure' public bodies (eg the police, prison service, local authorities) and 'hybrid' public authorities (eg universities).

- The courts are given a wide discretion in interpreting the legislation to ensure that it is compliant with the Convention and they may also interpret the legislation itself.

- The definition of a victim in the *Human Rights Act 1998* is more restricted than, for example, judicial review procedures but this is in line with the ECHR itself.

- Article 13 (right to an effective remedy) is not contained within the HRA 1998. There are competing arguments as to whether the HRA 1998 is itself a response to Article 13 or whether this means rights in the UK are not as protected.

- Certain rights contain a *positive obligation* on the state. This means that not only must the state ensure that it does not breach the right, it must also ensure that it can protect its citizens from others infringing their right. The most obvious example of this is Article 2 where a state must protect its citizens where there is a known risk of harm.

End-of-chapter questions

1. To what extent do you think it is possible to repeal the *Human Rights Act 1998*?

2. Should the *Human Rights Act 1998* be fully incorporated, ie apply both vertically and horizontally? What do you think the implications of extending the Act horizontally would be?

---

190. While no child was involved, the reasoning is that if the defendant carried out the actions according to his intentions then he would have sexually abused a child.

3. Read the box at 5.2.3.2 concerning precedent and s 2. Is the decision in *Kay* not in direct contravention of s 2 HRA 1998? Was it not Parliament's intention that the courts follow decisions of the ECtHR and does this not mean that a court of first instance, when faced with such a precedent, will be acting incompatibly with the ECHR, thus breaching it?

4. Read Chapter 16 on criminal appeals. If a court, including the ECtHR, considers that a trial is unfair should the conviction be quashed? Read *R v Rowe, Davis and Johnson (No 3)* [2001] 1 Cr App R 8.

Further reading

Dwyer DM, 'Rights Brought Home' (2005) 121 *Law Quarterly Review* 359–64.

This is a useful article which looks at how the HRA 1998 has been implemented.

Klug F and Starmer K, 'Standing Back from the Human Rights Act: How Effective is it Five Years on?' [2005] *Public Law* 716–28.

This is a very good article, co-authored by the former Director of Public Prosecutions, which examines how the Act has been used in practice.

Fredman S, 'From Deference to Democracy: The Role of Equality under the Human Rights Act 1998' (2006) 122 *Law Quarterly Review* 53–81.

This is a good article which includes a useful examination of the margin of appreciation.

Sales P, 'Strasbourg Jurisprudence and the Human Rights Act: A Response to Lord Irvine' [2012] *Public Law* 253–67.

This is an excellent article that dissects the approach adopted to s 2 HRA 1998.

197

For self-test questions, flashcards, and links to useful websites, please visit the **online resources** at: **www.oup.com/he/gillespie-weare8e**

PART II

THE COURTS AND THE PRACTITIONERS

6

The Structure of
the Courts

By the end of this chapter you will be able to:

- Identify how the courts in England and Wales are organized and funded.
- Identify the principal courts in England and Wales.
- Discuss the types of cases heard in each court.
- Understand what the other courts do.

Introduction

Of all the institutions within the English Legal System, the courts are perhaps the most recognizable. Most people are aware of what a court is but they perhaps do not know that there are several different types of courts, nor fully understand what each does.

This chapter will consider how the modern court structure is organized and what each court does. It will not consider the historical development of the courts, but those wishing to understand the evolution of the courts should consult the further reading identified at the end of the chapter.

The tribunals are not dealt with in this chapter (instead being discussed in the next chapter) for ease of understanding. However, it is important to note at the outset that there are increasing links between the courts and tribunals. Indeed, there are perhaps more similarities than differences in their roles, how they are run, and certainly in how they are staffed (discussed in Chapter 8).

6.1 Context

Before exploring the organization and roles of the courts it is worth providing some context on the current situation of courts within England and Wales. Since 2010 the courts estate has changed significantly as part of reforms to the justice system aiming to make it more fit for purpose. These changes have increased more rapidly since 2016, when HM Courts and Tribunals Service (HMCTS) announced a programme of modernization for the courts and tribunals system. Part of these reforms have included the closure (and sale) of court buildings, and thus the relocation of services to buildings elsewhere within the estate. Between 2010 and 2019:

- 50% of magistrates' courts have closed (162 out of 323)
- Over a third (37.5%) of county courts have closed (90 out of 240)
- Nearly 10% of family courts have closed (17 out of 185)
- 8.7% of Crown Courts have closed (8 out of 92).[1]

By 2025/26 the government plans to close 77 more courts.[2]

The Lord Chancellor has promised that savings from these closures and profits from the sales of court buildings will be reinvested into the justice system. However, these significant changes to the courts estate have raised questions about the ability of people to access justice, especially if they are geographically and economically more isolated from court buildings as a result of these closures (see Chapter 20 for a more detailed discussion on the reforms).

6.2 The organization of the courts

The first issue to examine is how courts are organized. As will be seen later, there are many different types of court and this raises questions as to how they can be classified and how their day-to-day business is organized.

6.2.1 Classifying the courts

The first issue to examine is how courts are classified. The variety of courts have led some to question whether the courts can be grouped together but, as will be seen, this is not necessarily the easiest thing to do.

6.2.1.1 Civil/criminal

It may be thought that the easiest way of classifying the courts would be to designate whether they are civil or criminal. In principle this would seem appropriate since it is recognized that there is a civil justice system and a criminal justice system.

The difficulty is that whilst it is easy to designate the Crown Court as a criminal court and the Family Court as a civil court it is less easy to categorize any other court. The magistrates' court (see 6.3.1), for example, deals with the vast majority of criminal cases, but it also has a civil jurisdiction and so it cannot be said to be a purely criminal court. The High Court of Justice (see 6.3.5) is predominantly a civil court but it also has a limited criminal jurisdiction. The Court of Appeal (see 6.3.6) is divided into two divisions, the civil division and the criminal division, so that is relatively easy, but the Supreme Court (see 6.3.7) has jurisdiction over both civil and criminal matters.

It can be seen therefore that classifying courts as either civil or criminal courts is impracticable.

---

1. Georgina Sturge, *Court statistics for England and Wales, Briefing Paper Number CBP 8372* (House of Commons Library, 2019) https://researchbriefings.files.parliament.uk/documents/CBP-8372/CBP-8372.pdf 16.

2. National Audit Office, *Transforming courts and tribunals—a progress update* (National Audit Office, 2019) https://www.nao.org.uk/wp-content/uploads/2019/09/Transforming-Courts-and-Tribunals.pdf 7.

6.2.1.2 **Original or appellate jurisdiction**

Another potential classification system is to examine whether courts have original jurisdiction, ie they hear matters of first instance (eg trials), or whether they hear appeals from other courts.

As an abstract idea, this, as with the civil/criminal distinction, seems logical but the existing court structure immediately poses challenges. For example, whilst the magistrates' court and county court only possess original jurisdiction, the Crown Court exercises both an original and appellate jurisdiction. The same is true of the Family Court and the High Court, and this is without even considering whether judicial review is original or appellate jurisdiction (something complicated by the fact that certain courts and tribunals may be subject to judicial review).

Accordingly, it can be seen that this categorization does not assist either.

6.2.1.3 **Superior and inferior courts**

One of the most traditional forms of classifying the courts is to examine whether they are superior or inferior courts.

Ascertaining what the superior courts are is not always easy. The starting point is that those labelled a superior court within s 1 *Senior Courts Act 1981* (SCA 1981) are. The courts listed are the *Crown Court*, *High Court of Justice*, and *Court of Appeal*.

However, other courts are known to be superior courts. For example, the Employment Appeals Tribunal which, as its name suggests, is technically a tribunal is, in fact, a superior court. It is so designated by statute.[3] The Courts-Martial Appeal Court is considered to be a superior court,[4] so could it be argued that the superior courts are only those that are so designated by statute? Certainly now the Supreme Court is in being then this may be true (as s 40(1) *Constitutional Reform Act 2005* (CRA 2005) states that the Supreme Court is a superior court of record), but it was certainly not true historically since the House of Lords was a superior court and yet this arose not through statute but through the fact that it was an intrinsic part of Parliament.

What of inferior courts? Statute rarely states that they are inferior so perhaps the solution is that where a statute does not state that a court is superior then it should be treated as inferior. Unfortunately this does not appear to be a safe proposition as historically some courts were treated as being superior in the absence of statute (eg, the Central Criminal Court prior to the establishment of the Crown Court).

In *R v Cripps, ex parte Muldoon and others*[5] it was said:

> It is necessary to look at the relevant functions of the tribunal in question including its constitution, jurisdiction and powers and its relationship with the High Court in order to decide whether the tribunal should properly be regarded as inferior . . .[6]

The meaning of its relationship with the High Court is taken to be that where the High Court is able to act in a reviewing capacity over the tribunal, ie it is subject to judicial review, then the court is an inferior court. However, this does not always work since, for example, the Crown Court may sometimes be subject to judicial review (where the

---

3. *Employment Tribunals Act 1996*, s 20(3).
4. *Courts-Martial (Appeals) Act 1968*, s 1(2).
5. [1983] 3 WLR 465.
6. ibid, 87 (Robert Goff LJ).

matter does not concern its jurisdiction over indictable offences) and yet it has been seen that, by statute, it is a superior court.

6.2.1.4 A need for classification?

It can be seen that it is not easy to identify a classification for the courts. In practice it is rarely necessary to clarify the courts and instead a distinction is drawn between the types of justice. Some would argue that there are three types of justice systems; criminal, civil, and family, but in reality the distinction is between two: civil and criminal. Accordingly, it can be said that the need for classification, at least in practice, is perhaps questionable.

6.2.2 HM Courts and Tribunal Service

Setting aside the classification of the courts, how are they organized in practice? The main courts of England and Wales (ie the magistrates' court, county court, Family Court, Crown Court, High Court, and Court of Appeal) are operated by Her Majesty's Court and Tribunals Service (HMCTS), an executive agency of the Ministry of Justice. The Supreme Court is not operated by HMCTS but is responsible for its own administration (through its chief executive). This status reflects the fact that it is a court of the United Kingdom and not just of England and Wales, and also because historically the House of Lords (its predecessor) was administered separately.

Prior to 2011 the courts were administered by HM Court Service (HMCS), a body created in 2005 when the previous Court Service was combined with the administration of the magistrates' courts (which had previously been a complicated administration based on localities). In 2011 it was decided to merge HMCS with the Tribunal Service which administered the tribunals, in part to save costs. However, it should be noted that some tribunals are devolved (ie are specific to either Scotland or Northern Ireland) and they remain administered locally. The Lord Chancellor, as Minister of Justice, is politically responsible for the functioning of the service although it is headed by a chief executive, a senior civil servant. HMCTS is also overseen by an executive board which includes four executive members (ie senior members of HMCTS including the chief executive), three judicial members (ordinarily a member of the senior judiciary, a senior tribunal judge, and a district judge representing magistrates' courts), three non-executive members (usually including a lawyer), and a Ministry of Justice representative member. The board is overseen by an independent chairman. The *Courts Act 2003* (CA 2003) provides that the Lord Chancellor has responsibility for appointing court officers and staff responsible for serving the courts, and HMCTS exercises this power on his behalf.

Historically, (the then) HMCS was organized into forty-two areas corresponding to the previous geographical areas used by the criminal justice areas, but this ultimately changed and it is now organized into eight regional areas (seven geographical and one specifically dedicated to the Royal Courts of Justice). Each area has its own director who is responsible to the chief executive and the executive board. HMCTS itself employs the staff that service the courts, including the administrative staff, the clerks to the courts (or legal advisers), ushers etc. It does not employ members of the judiciary as they are office holders who, depending on their rank, are appointed either by the Lord Chancellor himself or by the Queen (discussed in Chapter 8).

6.2.2.1 Judicial administration

Whilst HMCTS have responsibility for the administration of the courts they do so alongside the judiciary.

The courts in England and Wales are divided into six circuits and each is assigned at least two presiding judges[7] (the South-Eastern circuit, which is one of the busiest, currently has four). The presiding judges are puisne judges (meaning judges of the High Court: see 8.1.2.2) and while presiders they have responsibility for the administration of justice on the circuit, a Lord Justice of Appeal (Court of Appeal judge: see 8.1.2.1) is appointed as the senior presiding judge[8] who coordinates the work of the presiding judges (currently the post is held by Lady Justice Thirlwall).

Having at least two presiding judges for each circuit means that ordinarily one judge will always be on circuit (at least during the legal year). This means that they are in a better position to oversee matters. In the early days it was said:

> In broad principle the Presiding judges were responsible for the judicial or operational side of the circuit, while the circuit administrator was responsible for the administrative support. But in practice the two overlapped . . . [9]

This overlap continued and by 2008 it was being suggested that their administrative responsibilities were becoming almost overwhelming. The principal responsibility of the presiding judge is to assign judges to the relevant cases. It will be seen in Chapter 8 that only certain judges are entitled to sit on certain cases. However, even where a judge is entitled to sit on a case, the presiding judge has to identify who is the most appropriate.

6.2.3 The Supreme Court

It was noted earlier that HMCTS does not administer the Supreme Court.

Section 48 CRA 2005 states that the Supreme Court will have a chief executive. They are appointed by the President of the Court.[10] Section 49 permits the President of the Supreme Court to appoint staff to service the court, although the chief executive will decide the number and type of staff. Presumably the President will also be involved in such discussions although it is notable that s 49 does not require this. The Supreme Court would seem to have a larger staff than when it was the House of Lords although this is, in part, because much of the administration of the judicial committees was subsumed within the wider House of Lords administration.

6.2.4 Funding

It will be remembered that HMCTS is an executive agency of the Ministry of Justice. Accordingly, the funding for the courts—except for the salary of the judiciary—comes from the departmental budget of the Ministry of Justice. Prior to the creation of the Ministry, in 2007, the money came from the Lord Chancellor's Department.

---

7. *Courts and Legal Services Act 1990*, s 72(1).
8. ibid, s 72(2).
9. Robin Dunn, *Sword and Wig: Memoirs of a Lord Justice* (Quiller Press 1993) 217.
10. *Constitutional Reform Act 2005*, s 48(2).

The creation of the Ministry of Justice led to considerable tension between the judiciary and executive. It will be seen in Chapter 8 that changes to the office of the Lord Chancellor also led to concerns, and it would have been thought that the government would have attempted to resolve these issues by being careful to keep the judiciary informed of planned changes to the organization of the courts. However, following a series of political difficulties for the Home Office it was decided to separate some parts of the functions of the Home Office and to combine them with the powers of the Lord Chancellor's Department to create the Ministry of Justice. In an extrajudicial speech, the then Lord Chief Justice Lord Philips of Worth Matravers commented:

> The first I or the then Lord Chancellor, Lord Falconer, learnt of the creation of the Ministry of Justice was when we were reading our Sunday Telegraphs on the 21 of January 2007 Once again the government had not consulted on a key constitutional change ... No guarantees of the protection of the independence of the judiciary were given. There was no promise to protect the administration of justice within the new Department.[11]

The concern of the judiciary was focused on a number of issues but one of the most important was whether the budgets of the court were separate.

One department was to uphold the rule of law and the independence of the judiciary and yet the same department would also have responsibility for criminal justice. That department would have one pot of money from which to fund the court system and the prisons. The judiciary was concerned that the department would rob Peter to pay Paul—Peter being the judges and Paul being the prisons. Would the department be able to prioritize the administration of justice while dealing with criminal justice policy?

Since the administration of government is a matter of prerogative not statute, no legislative measure was required to establish the Ministry of Justice. This, in turn, meant there were few opportunities to address concerns. The judiciary wished the budget of HMCTS to be 'ring-fenced', ie it could only be used for the administration of the courts and not used when other aspects of the Ministry's budget were under strain. The government refused this request and the dispute between the judiciary and executive became public.

Eventually a pragmatic solution was created. This was twofold. The first was the establishment of an executive council (now the Board of HMCTS: see 6.2.2) which includes representatives of the judiciary. The second was the establishment of a formal *Framework Document* which was published by the Ministry of Justice in April 2008. This document was designed to recognize that the administration of justice requires cooperation between the executive and the judiciary and, in particular, a commitment to the independence of the judiciary. In 2011 this document was revised to take into account the inclusion of the Tribunal Service into the new agency. Most recently it was updated in 2014 to take into account additions to the executive board (discussed at 6.2.2), introduced to secure additional expertise and experience.

A key part of the *Framework Document* is that all staff 'have joint responsibility to the Lord Chancellor and the Lord Chief Justice for the effective, efficient and speedy operation of the courts and tribunals',[12] which reinforces the fact that HMCTS is truly a partnership between the executive and the judiciary.

11. Lord Philips of Worth Matravers, 'The Supreme Court and other constitutional changes in the UK' Address to Members of the Royal Court, the Jersey Law Society, and the members of the States of Jersey, May 2008.
12. Her Majesty's Court and Tribunals Service, *Framework Document* (HMCTS, 2014) 5.

It was stated earlier that the budget for HMCTS is not formally 'ring-fenced' but the document sets out how the judiciary is involved in the setting of the budget. The Lord Chancellor will hold discussions with the Treasury in the same way that any departmental Secretary of State will. The Lord Chancellor must inform the Lord Chief Justice about these discussions[13] and the Lord Chief Justice shall have the right to write to the Lord Chancellor setting out the views of the judiciary and, if he does so, this will be forwarded to the Chief Secretary to the Treasury.[14] This is an interesting provision as it would, of course, provide the Lord Chancellor with detailed support since the document would invariably form part of the public record and thus a government would be careful to take note of the contents.

Once the Lord Chancellor has been given his allocation by the Treasury he will then set the budget for HMCTS and in doing so will have regard to his statutory and other duties to ensure the efficient and effective support of the courts. Where the Lord Chief Justice has concerns about what the budget is then he has the right to make representations to the Lord Chancellor and, if he so wishes, to Parliament. This is, in effect, a 'nuclear option' in that it would demonstrate a breakdown in the trust between the government and judiciary and it would be likely to create a political storm. Whilst this is not as effective as a ring-fence it does act as an effective tool of pressure as both the government and judiciary would wish to avoid such public disagreement and the inevitable political consequences that would arise from that.

🔄 QUESTION FOR REFLECTION

Were the judges right to be concerned that the budgets for the courts are not 'ring-fenced'? If the prison population continues to rise then pressures on the budget will increase. It is theoretically possible that pressure could then be placed on the judges to sentence offenders in a particular way, potentially compromising their judicial independence.

Do you think a framework document is sufficient or should there be a statutory rule stating that the budget for HMCTS should be set annually and kept 'ring-fenced'?

6.3 **Key courts**

So far this chapter has discussed how courts are classified, organized, and funded, but what are the courts in the English Legal System? A number of courts exist and so if a detailed discussion of all these were to take place then this chapter would be extremely long! Instead a summary will be given of the key courts that feature commonly within the English Legal System and later (6.5) a brief outline of some other common courts will be made.

The courts that will be considered in this part are:

- magistrates' court
- county court

---

13. ibid, 11.
14. ibid. Note that the Chief Secretary to the Treasury is the second-highest political minister in the Treasury (the Chancellor of the Exchequer being the first). The Chief Secretary is of cabinet rank and it is his job to lead the budgetary negotiations with each government department.

- Crown Court
- Family Court
- High Court of Justice
- Court of Appeal
- Supreme Court.

Figure 6.1 shows the approximate structure of the English Legal System. It will be seen that the precise placing of the courts is a matter of debate and also alters depending on the type of work that the court is undertaking.

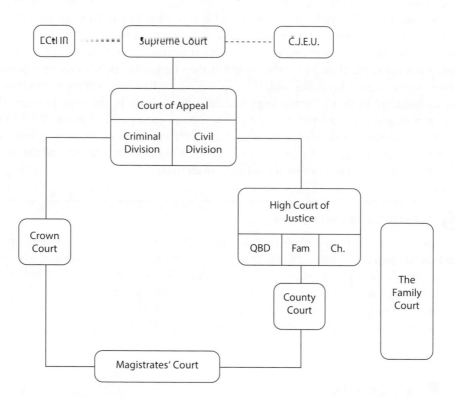

Figure 6.1 The hierarchy of the courts

6.3.1 **Magistrates' court**

The first court to note is the magistrates' court. This is the lowest of the courts that we are concerned with. Magistrates' courts are local courts, however as noted at the beginning of this chapter, the number of magistrates' courts has decreased by over 50% since 2010.[15] Before the implementation of the CA 2003, the courts were divided into local petty sessional areas and run by local *Magistrates' Courts Committees*. Now, however, they are subsumed within HMCTS and whilst they continue to sit in local locations, their organization and management is undertaken by the local area and regional offices of the Court Service.

---

15.   Georgina Sturge, *Court statistics for England and Wales, Briefing Paper Number CBP 8372* (House of Commons Library, 2019) https://researchbriefings.files.parliament.uk/documents/CBP-8372/CBP-8372.pdf 16.

Magistrates' courts primarily have a criminal jurisdiction and indeed the vast majority of criminal cases heard in England and Wales take place in the magistrates' court. It will be seen later in this book that criminal matters can be divided into summary matters, indictable matters, and those that can be tried either summarily or on indictment (see 13.3.1). Summary trials take place in the magistrates' court before either a district judge (magistrates' court) (see 8.8.2) or a bench of lay magistrates (see 8.8.1). The punishment an offender can receive in the magistrates' court is currently limited to six months' imprisonment for a single offence although, at a time yet to be announced, their powers will be increased to imposing twelve months' custody.

A separate criminal jurisdiction that exists in the magistrates' court is in respect of adolescent crime. Here the court is known as the 'youth court' and whilst they are frequently located in the same building, matters are heard in specific courtrooms that are laid out in a less formal manner and a separate entrance from the adult magistrates' court must be maintained. The youth court has jurisdiction over all but the most serious of adolescent crime, even where an offence is theoretically triable only on indictment for adult offenders. Separate punishments also exist for youth crime, with the overall aim to be preventing reoffending rather than punishing transgressions of the law.

The magistrates' court also has a limited civil jurisdiction. Its largest role was historically in relation to family law matters, however, with the introduction of the Family Court (see 6.3.4) the magistrates' court no longer deals with such cases. The majority of the courts' civil jurisdiction relates to the recovery of certain debts (including, for example, the supply of services such as gas and electricity) and the licensing of gambling institutions.

6.3.2 County court

The second court to examine is the county court. Like the magistrates' court, this is an inferior court (see 6.2.1.3). The county court is a purely civil court and its jurisdiction is set out in statute. The original jurisdiction was set out in the *County Courts Act 1846*, but such courts had a very limited jurisdiction and the modern version of the courts was established by the *County Courts Act 1984*.

As an inferior court created by statute, the county courts have limited jurisdiction. If a statutory provision does not grant it jurisdiction to deal with the matter, then a judge of the county court has no right to adjudicate on the matter. In April 2014, with the introduction of the *Crime and Courts Act 2013*, the 173 county courts were replaced by one single county court.[16] The court may sit anywhere in England and Wales, and will, despite the seemingly radical change, largely continue to sit in the current county court buildings, which have been rebranded as 'county court hearing centres'. These court buildings are distributed across the country, however as noted at the beginning of the chapter their number has decreased by over a third since 2010.[17]

As noted earlier, the county court has an exclusively civil jurisdiction. Many of the matters relate to types of actions that could also be heard in the High Court but which are considered less serious because either the nature of the claim or the amount of compensation sought is reduced. In terms of general civil jurisdiction the county court

16. *Crime and Courts Act 2013*, s 17(1).
17. Georgina Sturge, *Court statistics for England and Wales, Briefing Paper Number CBP 8372* (House of Commons Library, 2019) https://researchbriefings.files.parliament.uk/documents/CBP-8372/CBP-8372.pdf 16.

deals with matters such as breach of contract, claims in tort (negligence, nuisance etc), personal injury, certain disputes as to land, and even some admiralty claims.

Historically, the county court also had a family jurisdiction, with the vast majority of divorce cases being dealt with by the county court. However, with the introduction of the Family Court (see 6.3.4), any claims or proceedings in relation to family matters must now be heard there. The county court has exclusive jurisdiction over small claims. It is common to hear of the 'small claims court', a title that has quasi-recognition within HMCTS. In fact it is an informal part of the county court and proceedings are instituted within the county court.

The county court originally had its own procedural rules (known as the *County Court Rules* printed in a green volume so colloquially known as 'the Green book') but following a series of reviews it was decided that a single set of procedural rules should exist for the county court, High Court, and Court of Appeal (Civil Division). These rules, known as the *Civil Procedure Rules*, were introduced by the *Civil Procedure Act 1997* and the rules continue to be updated.

6.3.3 The Crown Court

The Crown Court is the first superior court that is to be considered (see 6.2.1.3). It is a court of both original and appellate jurisdictions; in other words, some trials at first instance take place but it also hears certain appeals. It is often said that it has an exclusively criminal jurisdiction but that is not quite true in that it has a limited civil jurisdiction in its appellate capacity.

The Crown Court is a relatively modern invention although it is a development from the system of assize courts (which were presided over by puisne judges sent on circuit) and quarter sessions which were locally based criminal courts. The fusion retains some elements of the assize system in that today puisne judges will preside in the Crown Court while sitting on the circuit they are assigned to. The Crown Court came into being through the *Courts Act 1971* although its jurisdiction is now based on the SCA 1981.

6.3.3.1 Trials of first instance

The principal work of the Crown Court is to deal with trials that take place on indictment, ie involving a jury. The work of the Crown Court in this capacity is discussed in Part 3 of the book. The Crown Court can currently sit at seventy-seven Crown Court centres across England and Wales although the most famous remains the *Central Criminal Court*, also known as the 'Old Bailey'. Theoretically each Crown Court centre has the same jurisdiction but, in practice, the Crown Court is divided into different types of court centre. The allocation is by tier and there are three tiers:

Tier One: These are courts where High Court judges will regularly visit and preside and at which circuit judges and recorders will also sit for the full range of Crown Court business. These are also courts where High Court judges will preside over civil High Court business.

Tier Two: Tier-two courts are, in effect, the same as tier-one courts except there is no civil work undertaken.

Tier Three: These are courts where a High Court judge would not normally preside and where cases are heard by circuit judges and recorders.

Circuit judges and recorders deal with Crown Court criminal business in all three of the tiers.

A contested trial will take place before a judge and jury. The process of the trial is discussed in Chapter 15.

6.3.3.2 Appeals

The Crown Court also has an appellate jurisdiction. It may hear appeals from the magistrates' court. This type of appeal is discussed at 16.2.1. Whilst the appeal will ordinarily be for criminal matters, the Crown Court does have a limited civil appeal over some civil orders such as the *Anti-Social Behaviour Order*, *Sexual Offences Prevention Order*, and *Foreign Travel Order*. These are imposed by the magistrates' court sitting in their civil capacity but they are quasi-criminal orders in that they prohibit an offender from doing something contained in the order, and breach of an order amounts to a criminal offence.

6.3.4 The Family Court

The Family Court came into existence on 22 April 2014 by s 17(3) *Crime and Courts Act 2013* as a result of the recommendations made by *The Family Justice Review* report. With the introduction of the Family Court, the separate family divisions in the magistrates' and county courts ceased to exist, and instead applications for family proceedings are now made directly to the Family Court. The Family Court has jurisdiction over all family proceedings, with the exceptions of cases involving jurisdiction in wardship (this is a type of court order giving custody of a minor to the court), and international jurisdiction cases, where the case will be heard exclusively in the Family Division of the High Court. It should be noted that the jurisdiction of the Family Division of the High Court (see 6.3.5.3) remains largely unaffected by the creation of the Family Court.

The Family Court deals with any family matters which arise and are in dispute. These can include the more commonly known matters of adoption, marriage and divorce, and domestic violence. The court can also hear cases specifically involving children. These types of cases fall into two categories; public law and private law. Public law cases are brought by local authorities and may involve proceedings concerning supervision orders, which place the child concerned under the supervision of their local authority. Private law cases are brought by individuals, usually the child's parents or relatives, and may concern issues such as parental responsibility agreements and child arrangement orders.

The Family Court is a national court and therefore can technically sit in any court building in England and Wales. However, in practice hearings tend to be held in county or magistrates' court buildings. The Family Court comprises judges from all levels of the family judiciary, including lay magistrates. Including different levels of the judiciary within the court allows for cases to be allocated by 'gate-keepers' to the appropriate judge depending on the type of proceedings and their complexity.[18] The 'gate-keeping and allocation team' for the local Family Court consists of a justice's clerk and a district judge. Allocating appropriate cases to specific judges aims to ensure that the same judge deals with the case throughout proceedings in the court, therefore streamlining the court process for those involved.

---

18. See *The Family Court (Composition and Distribution of Business) (Amendment) Rules 2014*, SI 2014/3297, sch 1 'Allocation'.

Alongside the creation of the Family Court, numerous Family Justice System reforms were also introduced in April 2014 in the *Children and Families Act 2014*, with the aim of improving the overall functioning of the family courts system. For example, under s 14 of the Act, a time limit of twenty-six weeks has been introduced for completing care and supervision cases to ensure speedier outcomes in finding permanent placements for vulnerable children. Moreover, under s 10 *Children and Families Act 2014*, there is now a legal requirement for separating couples to attend 'family mediation information and assessment meetings' to consider the alternatives to initiating court proceedings when trying to resolve issues associated with finances and their children. There are exceptions to this requirement, for example in cases involving domestic violence or where the court needs to make an urgent order. However, in the majority of cases a 'mediation information and assessment meeting' is required.

6.3.4.1 Appeals

Appeals can be heard within the Family Court. As noted previously, the court includes judges from all levels of the family judiciary, and cases will be allocated to judges depending upon the type of proceedings and the cases' complexity. Appeals can therefore be made from a case heard by a 'lower-level' judge to a more senior member of the family judiciary within the Family Court. Practice Direction 30A (which supplements the Family Practice Directions Part 30) sets out the available routes of appeal. For example, a case decided by a bench of two or three lay magistrates can be appealed to a judge of circuit level sitting within the Family Court. Appeals can also be made outside of the Family Court to the Family Division of the High Court and to the Court of Appeal.

6.3.5 High Court of Justice

The High Court of Justice (or High Court as it is invariably known) is probably the most important court in the English Legal System. It has unlimited jurisdiction in civil matters which means that in the absence of a statutory or common-law rule prohibiting a judge sitting on such a case, the High Court has jurisdiction over the dispute. Whilst it is primarily a court of civil jurisdiction, it does have an important appellate and reviewing jurisdiction in respect of criminal matters.

The High Court is based in the Royal Courts of Justice in the Strand although it also sits in first-tier Crown Court centres (see 6.3.3.1) outside of London. Each circuit has at least one court exercising High Court jurisdiction.

The High Court is divided into three divisions, into which all business of the court will be assigned. The three divisions are the Queen's Bench Division (King's Bench Division when the monarch is a King), Chancery Division, and the Family Division.[19] In 1988 the judiciary suggested that the divisions should be abolished and in the mid-1990s a further proposal was brought forward to reformulate the divisions by, for example, merging the Chancery and Queen's Bench Divisions. In his interim report on *Access to Justice*, Lord Woolf rejected this argument[20] believing that the specialist jurisdiction of the Chancery Division would be lost in a merger and he noted that, for example, there are only a small number of Chancery puisne judges (at the time of

---

19. *Senior Courts Act 1981*, s 5.
20. Lord Woolf, *Access to Justice: Interim Report to the Lord Chancellor* (HMSO 1995) ch 12, para 17.

writing there are only fourteen judges (including the Chancellor) out of a total of 106 puisne judges) and they work closely together as a team. Lord Woolf, in his final report, did not recommend any changes to the divisional structure and so it continues to consist of three divisions.

6.3.5.1 Queen's Bench Division

The largest of the three divisions is the Queen's Bench Division (it currently being staffed by 73 out of 106 puisne judges and with Lord Justices of Appeal sitting in the Administrative Court where required). The principal work of the division can be divided into three distinct areas although, as will be seen, other specialist work also occurs within the division.

General work

The Queen's Bench Division deals with much of the high-value civil work assigned to the High Court. All civil work that falls outside of the Chancery Division or Family Division is heard in the Queen's Bench Division and this includes, for example, most claims from contract, personal injury claims, and libel actions. As will be seen from Chapter 17, much of the classes of work this division hears could also be heard in the county court but the High Court is selected where a matter is particularly complicated or where the amount of compensation sought is high.

Appellate work

The Queen's Bench Division has an appellate jurisdiction. Under the procedure for civil appeals (see Chapter 18) an appeal is ordinarily to the next level of judge. So where a person wishes to appeal against a procedural matter in the county court this will ordinarily be heard by a High Court judge and it will normally be a judge of this division.

The Queen's Bench Division also has a criminal appellate jurisdiction. It is possible to appeal against a finding of magistrates by way of case stated (see 16.2.2). Such an appeal is brought before this division.

Supervisory jurisdiction

The High Court has always had an important supervisory jurisdiction. This is where it exercises the power of review over inferior courts, tribunals, and some public bodies. It is now commonly referred to as 'judicial review' and it is a jurisdiction that has developed extensively over the past few decades yet can be extremely controversial, especially when it involves the court overturning decisions of ministers. This jurisdiction is discussed at 17.3.

The supervisory jurisdiction is exercised by the 'Administrative Court'. Unlike certain 'courts' within the Queen's Bench Division, this is an administrative title that has no statutory force. It is, therefore, technically just a panel of the Queen's Bench Division although the Civil Procedure Rules set out a separate body of rules for this work.[21]

The Administrative Court is headed by a 'lead judge' (currently Sir Jonathan Mark Swift) who works with the appropriate administrative staff to administer the working of the court. Other judges of the High Court are designated by the Lord Chief Justice to hear matters in the Administrative Court. Where the judges are not already

---

21. *Civil Procedure Rules*, pt 54.

assigned to the Queen's Bench Division they are considered to be additional temporary judges of that division when hearing the matter.

Specialist jurisdictions

The Admiralty Court and Commercial Court both exist within the Queen's Bench Division. These are statutory courts[22] and deal with specific types of jurisdiction. The Admiralty Court, as its name suggests, exercises particular claims in relation to maritime law, for example, claims relating to salvage or disputes as to the carriage of goods. The Commercial Court is a very specialist jurisdiction and relates to international business law and banking law. The court also has a role in arbitration (a concept discussed in Chapter 19).

The final specialist court is the Technology and Construction Court. Like the Administrative Court, this is not a statutory court but rather an administrative title. The work of the court is set out in Part 60 of the *Civil Procedure Rules* and its work will cover, for example, disputes as to the supply and installation of computer systems, or disputes in relation to construction or engineering projects. Its work requires specialist judges and outside of London it is not unusual for specially trained circuit judges to sit temporarily as acting judges of the High Court.

6.3.5.2 Chancery Division

The Chancery Division is a specialist division of the High Court and considers work relating to, for example, trusts, wills, companies, certain land claims, and certain claims relating to tax. Its work is technical and the judges of this division are supplemented by masters of the Chancery Division. Masters hold a judicial office similar to that of the district judge (see 8.1.3.3) but exercise jurisdiction in the High Court. Whilst the masters cannot hear full trials, they dispose of much of the procedural matters and frequently their involvement will lead to the case being settled before the matter proceeds to trial.

Within the Chancery Division exist three specialist courts. The first is the Patents Court.[23] This court deals with disputes relating to copyright, patents, and intellectual property disputes. The work is very specialist and the judges who sit on these matters are normally given specific training and it is not uncommon for circuit judges to act as an additional judge of the High Court when hearing these matters.

The second court is the Bankruptcy and Companies Court. As with the Administrative Court within the Queen's Bench Division, this is an administrative title for convenience. The court, as its name suggests, deals with disputes relating to bankruptcy and insolvency.

The third and final court is the Intellectual Property Enterprise Court (IPEC) which became a specialist court within the Chancery division in October 2013. The court, as its name suggests, deals with disputes relating to intellectual property between small and medium-sized enterprises, typically in relation to patents, copyright, and trade-marks.

6.3.5.3 Family Division

The Family Division is the newest of the three divisions. Prior to 1971 the third division was the Probate, Divorce, and Admiralty Division. The probate function was transferred

---

22. *Senior Courts Act 1981*, s 6.
23. ibid.

to the Chancery Division and the admiralty work was assigned to the Queen's Bench Division. Wardship—the state's care of children who cannot care for themselves—was exercised by the Queen's Bench Division but this was transferred to the new Family Division.

The Family Division, as its name suggests, deals with most matters relating to divorce, family disputes, and children. Complicated public childcare matters are heard in this division as well as complicated or high-value matters relating to private disputes.

There are currently twenty judges of the division (including its president) but their work is supplemented by specialist district judges who will be responsible for a considerable amount of the work of the division, including some contested trials. In addition, outside of London it is not unusual for a specialist circuit judge to sit as an acting judge of the Family Division, especially where matters are urgent.

Whilst all divisions will have a judge 'on call' the work of this division often means that the court will 'sit' at unusual times. There is always at least one judge who can be contacted at any time, day or night, and hearings can be heard over the telephone. This may occur, for example, where there is a dispute as to whether a child should have urgent medical treatment, or where somebody is seeking to remove a child from the jurisdiction.

6.3.5.4 Divisional Courts

A Divisional Court is when two or more judges sit in the High Court together to hear the same case.[24] This will ordinarily happen in their appellate or reviewing capacity. Whilst a Divisional Court can be created in any of the three divisions of the High Court, most Divisional Courts have been of the Queen's Bench Division, especially when it is exercising its powers of judicial review. However, since the establishment of the Administrative Court it is more common for judges to sit individually to hear some matters. Where this happens, it is not technically a Divisional Court but simply a hearing of the Queen's Bench Division (within the courtesy-titled 'Administrative Court').

6.3.6 The Court of Appeal

The modern Court of Appeal came into existence in 1966, fusing the previously separate Court of Appeal and Court of Criminal Appeal into a single court consisting of two divisions: the Criminal Division and the Civil Division. The Criminal Division is presided over by the Lord Chief Justice and the Civil Division is presided over by the Master of the Rolls. The Lord Chief Justice, as head of the judiciary, can (and has) appointed judges of the Court of Appeal as vice-president of either or both divisions.[25] The judges of the Court of Appeal can sit in either division and in both divisions (but most frequently in the Criminal Division). Puisne and even certain circuit judges can sit in the court as additional judges.

The Court of Appeal can sit in panels and in both divisions it is common for a single judge (in the Criminal Division this will normally be a puisne judge) to consider whether leave to appeal should be given and within the Criminal Division to hear applications for bail. The Criminal Division ordinarily sits in panels of three, and it must sit in an uneven number of no less than three judges when determining appeals

---

24. ibid, s 66.
25. ibid, s 3.

against conviction[26] and certain other appellate decisions. When it sits in panels of two judges (eg for sentences against appeal) if the judges are divided then it must relist the matter for a hearing before three judges.[27] The Civil Division can theoretically dispose of an appeal by a single judge[28] but ordinarily it will sit with at least two judges. As with the Criminal Division, if an even number of judges sit and they are divided as to the outcome, the case should be relisted before a panel of the court consisting of an uneven number of judges.[29]

The Court of Appeal ordinarily sits in the Royal Courts of Justice in London and any number of courts can sit at the same time so long as they are properly constituted. In recent years the Court of Appeal has sat in locations outside of London. This originated with the Civil Division but it has included the Criminal Division and the court has sat in a number of locations, including Cardiff, Manchester, and Newcastle-upon-Tyne. Recently the Criminal Division has also begun using live video-links to allow an appellant to see (and participate) in an appeal hearing whilst saving the costs of transporting the prisoner to London.

6.3.7 The Supreme Court

The Supreme Court is the newest court within the English Legal System although, as noted already, it is a UK court as its jurisdiction is not restricted to English cases. The Court was established by Part 3 CRA 2005 and it came into being in October 2009 (at the start of the legal year). Its jurisdiction, broadly speaking, includes that which the House of Lords exercised but it also assumed responsibility for devolution issues that were previously within the jurisdiction of the Judicial Committee of the Privy Council (6.5.1).

The Supreme Court was created as part of wider constitutional changes, and an attempt to lead to the separation of powers in respect of the legislature and judiciary. As part of this process, the Lord Chancellor had his judicial functions removed (see Chapter 9) and it was decided to remove the judiciary from the legislature. Members of the judiciary have been debarred from being a member of the House of Commons for some time, but a number of judges, most notably the Lords of Appeal in Ordinary, were entitled to sit in the House of Lords and participate both in its judicial and legislative capacity. The *Constitutional Reform Act 2005* (CRA 2005) altered this by stating that peers who serve as a judge may not sit in the House of Lords during their employment,[30] although they will be free to sit when they have retired.

Whilst the government was clear that the primary reason for the establishment of the Supreme Court was the separation of powers,[31] it was suggested that an additional reason was the fact that the work of the Law Lords could not be adequately supported because of the lack of space available in Westminster.[32] This was perhaps a slightly unconvincing reason since there is no reason why a separate annexe could not have been created to provide additional support and space. For example, MPs have been given an annexe across from the Palace of Westminster (known as Portcullis House) and a similar arrangement could have been established.

---

26. ibid, s 55.
27. ibid, s 55(5).
28. ibid, s 54(2).
29. ibid, s 54(5).
30. CRA 2005, s 137.
31. Department for Constitutional Affairs, *Constitutional Reform: A Supreme Court for the United Kingdom* (HMSO 2003) 10.
32. ibid, 12.

Although the separation of the legislature and judiciary was generally welcomed, the Law Lords themselves were divided as to whether the changes were needed or desirable, with some arguing that their presence in the House of Lords was 'of benefit to the Law Lords, to the House and to others including litigants'.[33] That said, the argument that the Law Lords could intervene in debates to ensure that errors of law were corrected during the parliamentary process was arguably overstated, since in 2000 the Law Lords committed themselves to being bound by two principles:

1. that the Law Lords were supposed to be impartial and accordingly in matters of party-political controversy they would not normally speak;

2. participating in parliamentary proceedings may debar them from sitting as judge when a matter relating to the legislation appears before the Appellate Committee.[34]

However, it was only a convention and there were some interventions. For example, Lord Woolf (the then Lord Chief Justice) and Lord Steyn (a then Law Lord) both criticized elements of the (then) *Asylum and Immigration Bill* as it was passing through Parliament, and at the time this was one of the most politically sensitive and partisan pieces of legislation.[35]

The Law Lords made other contributions to the House. It was reported that twelve places on House of Lords scrutiny committees were taken by serving Law Lords and that one Law Lord had served as the chairman on nine committees.[36] Whilst there may therefore have been a benefit in using the Law Lords for the purpose of scrutinizing legislation it could be questioned whether this was an appropriate use of the most senior judges' time. There are others with legal qualifications in the House, including retired Law Lords, and surely they were just as able to identify potential flaws.

The Supreme Court hears only a small number of appeals. In 2018/19 the court received 201 permissions to appeal (it refused 133) and it heard 91 appeals.[37] This can be contrasted with the Court of Appeal. During 2018/19 in the Criminal Division alone a total of 4,434 applications were made and approximately 736 appeals were allowed.[38] For a matter to be heard by the Supreme Court it must involve a point of public importance and the court is slow to allow leave, so as to ensure that it is not overwhelmed by cases. The Court of Appeal (and, to a lesser extent, the High Court) are also now very slow to grant leave to the Supreme Court, arguing that it is for that court to decide which cases it will hear.

The Supreme Court, like its predecessor the House of Lords, does not (unlike the Supreme Court of the USA) usually sit *en banc*, ie together. Instead panels of the court are established, with each panel being a minimum of three justices.[39] Ordinarily leave

217

---

33. Law Lords, *Law Lords' Response to the Government Consultation on a Supreme Court* (House of Lords 2003) para 2.

34. Hansard, HL Deb, vol 614, col 419, 22 June 2000.

35. David Windlesham, 'The Constitutional Reform Act 2005: The Politics of Constitutional Reform: Part 2' [2006] *Public Law* 35, 40–1.

36. David Windlesham, 'The Constitutional Reform Act 2005: Ministers, Judges and Constitutional Change: Part 1' [2005] *Public Law* 806, 813.

37. The Supreme Court, *Annual Report and Accounts 2018–2019* (Supreme Court, 2019) https://www.supreme-court.uk/docs/annual-report-2018–19.pdf 39.

38. Court of Appeal, *In the Court of Appeal (Criminal Division) 2018–19,* (Court of Appeal, 2020) https://www.judiciary.uk/wp-content/uploads/2020/02/LCJ-18-to-19-FINAL-PDF-1.pdf Annex F.

39. CRA 2005, s 42(1)(h)

is dealt with by a panel of three justices and ordinarily this will be dealt with on paper without an oral hearing,[40] although the justices could refer the matter for an oral hearing,[41] again usually heard by a panel of three justices. Substantive appeals are usually heard by five justices although it can sit in larger panels (so long as there is an odd number of justices)[42] and it has done so on a number of occasions, including constitutions of seven[43] and nine.[44] Criteria used when deciding whether to sit in panels of more than five have now been published on the Supreme Court website and are put forward as:

- if the court is being asked to depart, or may decide to depart from, a previous decision
- a case of high constitutional importance
- a case of great public importance
- a case where a conflict arises between decisions in the House of Lords, Judicial Committee of the Privy Council, and/or the Supreme Court has to be reconciled
- a case raising an important point in relation to the *European Convention on Human Rights*.

In *R (on the application of Miller) v Secretary of State for Exiting the European Union*,[45] which was the so-called 'Brexit' case, the Supreme Court did, for the first-time, sit *en banc* with all eleven justices sitting together.[46] They did this because of the constitutional importance of the case. Whether it was wise to do so, however, is perhaps open to question. The *Pinochet* case[47] set the precedent that decisions of the House of Lords/Supreme Court can be challenged. The rehearing of *Pinochet* was by judges who were not involved in the original decision. If the Supreme Court sits *en banc*, how would this occur? Whilst there is provision for acting justices[48] it would seem slightly odd if a Supreme Court case could be re-heard before judges who had never formed part of the court.

6.3.7.1 **The House of Lords**

Prior to the establishment of the Supreme Court the highest court was the House of Lords. Traditionally judicial matters were heard in the chamber of the House and any peer could participate, but during the nineteenth century it became clear that a more professional approach should be taken and life barons were created as Lords of Appeal in Ordinary, commonly known as the 'Law Lords'.

The modern House of Lords organized itself into an appellate committee to determine substantive appeals.[49] The appellate committee had to be distinguished from the appeals committee, which was a committee of three Law Lords that decided on applications for leave.

---

40. *Supreme Court Rules 2009*, SI 2009/1603, r 16(1).
41. ibid, r 16(2)(c).
42. CRA 2005, s 42(1)(a).
43. *Re S-B (Children)* [2009] UKSC 17.
44. *Norris v Government of United States of America* [2010] UKSC 9.
45. [2017] UKSC 5.
46. Whilst there should have been twelve justices, no replacement had yet been appointed for Lord Toulson who retired in July 2016.
47. *R v Bow Street Metropolitan Stipendiary Magistrate, ex p Pinochet Ugarte (No 2)* [2000] 1 AC 119.
48. *Constitutional Reform Act 2005*, ss 38 and 39.
49. *Appellate Jurisdiction Act 1876*, s 5.

6.4 The 'European Courts'

The structure diagram (Figure 6.1) shows that next to the Supreme Court are two European Courts; the European Court of Justice (which has jurisdiction over matters relating to the European Union) and the European Court of Human Rights (whose primary function is to rule on matters relating to the *European Convention on Human Rights*). Both of these are important courts in their own rights and whilst one will often hear people refer to 'appealing to Europe' this is not technically correct since neither court operates as an appellate court as such.

The detail of these courts and their interrelationship with the English Legal System was discussed earlier in the book (see Chapter 4) and rather than duplicate material, readers should cross-refer to these sections for a discussion of these institutions.

6.5 Other courts

Section 6.3 discussed the key common courts within the English Legal System. Among the other courts three deserve a brief discussion, those are the:

- Judicial Committee of the Privy Council
- Court of Protection
- Coroners' Courts.

The discussion of these courts will be much briefer but will allow the reader to understand the broad jurisdiction of each court.

6.5.1 Judicial Committee of the Privy Council

The Judicial Committee of the Privy Council was established by the *Judicial Committee Act 1833* (JCA 1833), although the Privy Council itself is an ancient advisory body to the monarch. Prior to 1833 the Privy Council heard appellate matters and legal petitions from the colonies, but it was Privy Councillors rather than judges who resolved the matter. By 1833 this was considered inappropriate and the Act of that year stated that judicial matters were to be heard by the Judicial Committee which would consist of senior judicial officers of the United Kingdom and Commonwealth countries (colonies at that time).

Whilst Court of Appeal judges are appointed to the Privy Council upon appointment (see 8.1.2.1) the modern Privy Council ordinarily takes the form of five Justices of the Supreme Court sitting, thus continuing the traditional staffing that saw it having the reputation as being the House of Lords in all but name. That was never quite true since, for example, other judicial officers sit, including a number of Commonwealth judges, but it is more common for the Justices of the Supreme Court to sit.

The current jurisdiction of the Judicial Committee can be summarized as follows:

- *Appeals to the Queen in Council.* A number of Commonwealth countries and British overseas territories continue to have the Privy Council as their head. Under this jurisdiction the Judicial Committee is technically tendering advice to the monarch and their judgment is then given legal standing by an Order in Council.

- *Appeals to the Head of State.* The Kingdom of Brunei allows an appeal against civil matters to proceed to the Privy Council. By agreement between the UK monarch and the sultan of Brunei the Privy Council tenders advice to the Sultan rather than the Queen.

- *Appeals to the Judicial Committee.* Certain republics within the Commonwealth continue to allow appeals to the Privy Council even though the Queen is no longer Head of State. Under this jurisdiction the judgment of the Privy Council is final rather than it being merely advice to the monarch.

- *Domestic jurisdiction.* Appeals from the Channel Islands are heard by the Privy Council as are appeals from certain disciplinary bodies and ecclesiastical courts. Where the High Court sits as a 'prize court' an appeal lies to the Privy Council rather than through domestic avenues of appeal. Prior to the establishment of the Supreme Court, devolution issues (discussed in Chapter 1) were also heard by the Privy Council but they are now heard by the Supreme Court.[50]

In addition, the Queen can refer any matter of law to the Privy Council for its advice.[51]

Regardless of which jurisdiction is being exercised, only a single judgment is given (in contrast to, for example, the Supreme Court, Court of Appeal, and Divisional Courts where additional assenting and dissenting judgments are presented).

6.5.2 **Court of Protection**

The *Mental Capacity Act 2005* (MCA 2005) created the Court of Protection as a superior court (see 6.2.1.3) in its own right.[52] Prior to this, issues concerning those adults who were considered to be unable to act for themselves were dealt with either by the High Court of Justice, usually the Chancery Division or the Family Division. The statute expressly states:

> The court may sit at any place in England and Wales, on any day and at any time.[53]

The implications of this are that the court can sit outside of a formal courtroom and can deal with urgent matters. It will be seen in Chapter 8 that a High Court judge has an inherent power to sit anywhere at any time (see 8.1.2) but this provision is ensuring that there is no doubt that a judge, of whatever rank, has this power when sitting in the Court of Protection.

The court must have a president and vice-president[54] and the President of the Family Division is the president of that court and the Chancellor of the High Court (head of the Chancery Division) is the vice-president. Judges of the High Court, circuit court, and district judges can be designated by either the Lord Chief Justice or the president of the court (if the Lord Chief Justice so delegates) to sit in the Court of Protection. A circuit judge or district judge must be nominated by the Lord Chief Justice (in consultation with the Lord Chancellor) to be the senior judge of the Court of Protection[55] who is, in essence, in day-to-day administrative charge of the court.

The jurisdiction of the court concerns the mental capacity of adults and the court can determine whether a person has appropriate mental capacity and, if not, make

---

50. CRA 2005, sch 9, pt 2.
51. *Judicial Committee Act 1833*, s 4.
52. MCA 2005, s 45.
53. ibid, s 45(3).
54. ibid, s 46(3).
55. ibid, s 46(4).

declarations as to their finances or welfare, along with adjudicating on disputes relating to lasting or enduring powers of attorney, including their discharge. Powers of attorney are where a competent adult is assigned to make decisions as to the welfare of the person lacking capacity.[56]

6.5.3 **Coroners' courts**

Coroners' courts are one of the most ancient forms of court within England and Wales, with the office of coroner dating back to medieval times. The modern coronial system investigates unnatural and violent deaths or those who die in custody, together with a specialist jurisdiction relating to treasure trove (a rather complicated provision but, at its simplest, it is gold, silver, or coins from the same find, that are over 300 years old discovered buried). The coronial system was subject to major changes with the introduction of Part 1 *Coroners and Justice Act 2009* (CJA) on 25 July 2013. This section of the chapter will consider the new system.

As with other aspects of the English Legal System (most notably the system of tribunals, discussed in Chapter 7), the changes to the coronial system were designed, in part, to strengthen their accountability and to reform the offices. Traditionally a coroner did not need to be a lawyer and could instead be a medical practitioner (although under s 2(1) *Coroners Act 1988* such persons needed to obtain a specific legal qualification). However, with the introduction of the CJA 2009, coroners must now be judicial appointments (and satisfy the judicial eligibility condition on a five-year period).[57]

Coroners have traditionally been employed by local authorities and this link survives the CJA 2009 reforms. England and Wales has been divided into coronial areas, each of which equates either to a local authority or a combination of local authority borders.[58] Each coronial area has a senior coroner who is the principal coroner and who is assisted by area and assistant coroners.[59] Coroners will have the equivalent status to an inferior judge in that they hold office for good behaviour, but can be removed administratively by the Lord Chancellor with the consent of the Lord Chief Justice.[60]

Coroners' courts differ from the rest of the English Legal System in one very important respect; they are inquisitorial rather than adversarial (see 1.3.2). Accordingly, there are no 'sides' to a coroners' court and this can mean that there is difficulty in a family of the bereaved securing legal aid for representation before the coroners' courts. This matter was litigated in *R (on the application of Main) v Minister for Legal Aid*.[61] The applicant lost her mother and sister after a railway accident. She claimed for legal aid to provide representation at the inquest and whilst the Legal Services Commission recommended that representation be given, the Lord Chancellor (as minister responsible for legal aid) refused to allow representation. The Court of Appeal, upholding this decision, stated that the coroner was able to identify the issues without representation from the family and placed strength on the fact that the coronial system was inquisitorial rather than adversarial.

---

56.   ibid, pt 1.
57.   CJA 2009, sch 3, para 3.
58.   ibid, sch 2.
59.   ibid, sch 3.
60.   ibid, sch 3, pt 4.
61.   [2007] EWCA Civ 1147.

Coroners' courts are inferior courts and are thus susceptible to judicial review, something that has been exercised a number of times.[62] The jurisdiction of a coronial court is now set out clearly in statute. In respect of deaths, a coroner must investigate where:

- the deceased died a violent or unnatural death
- the cause of death is unknown, or
- the deceased died while in custody or otherwise in state detention.[63]

The purpose of the investigation is:

- to ascertain who the deceased was
- how, when, and where the deceased came by his death
- the particulars (if any) required to be registered concerning the death.[64]

Interestingly s 5(2) continues by stating that the second element will also require ascertaining in what circumstances the deceased came by his death where this is necessary to prevent a breach of the *Human Rights Act 1998*. This, it is submitted, is a reference to the jurisprudence that has been established under Article 2 (discussed in Chapter 5 where it was seen that there are positive obligations in respect of the investigation of any death).

The issue of when a jury should be established has long proven controversial (and was one of the principal reasons for litigation in the inquest relating to Diana, Princess of Wales: see *R (on the application of Paul) v Deputy Coroner of the Queen's Household and Assistant Deputy Coroner for Surrey*[65] (note the office of the Coroner of the Queen's Household was abolished by s 46 CJA 2009)). Statute has now clarified this and stated that a jury should not normally hear an inquest,[66] save where the coroner has reason to suspect:

- the deceased died while in the custody of the state and the death was violent, unnatural, or unknown
- the death resulted from an act or omission by a police officer or a member of the armed services police in the purported execution of their duty
- the death was caused by a notifiable accident, poisoning, or disease, or
- the senior coroner believes that there is sufficient reason for doing so.[67]

Where a jury is empanelled then it is a jury of seven to eleven persons,[68] the exact number being a decision for the senior coroner. A decision of the jury need not be unanimous, but only where only one or two jurors disagree and the jury has had sufficient time to attempt to reach a verdict.[69] The CJA 2009 has also strengthened the rules relating to jury service, including providing for criminal penalties for those who act inappropriately in respect of being summoned to attend as a juror.[70]

---

62. See, most notably, *R (on the application of Paul) v Deputy Coroner of the Queen's Household and Assistant Deputy Coroner for Surrey* [2007] 2 All ER 509 and *R (on the application of Al-Fayed) v Assistant Deputy Coroner of Inner West London* [2008] EWHC 713 (Admin).
63. CJA 2009, s 1(2).
64. ibid, s 5(1).
65. [2007] 2 All ER 509.
66. CJA 2009, s 7(1).
67. ibid, s 7(2)–(3).
68. ibid, s 8(1).
69. ibid, s 9.
70. ibid, sch 6.

The coronial system, whilst locally based, will be under the administration of a Chief Coroner and Deputy Chief Coroner. The Chief Coroner is appointed by the Lord Chief Justice and must either be a puisne or circuit judge.[71] The current Chief Coroner, HHJ Mark Lucraft QC, was appointed in October 2016. The Lord Chief Justice may also appoint as many persons as he deems appropriate to be a Deputy Chief Coroner and these persons must be puisne or circuit judges or a senior coroner.[72]

QUESTION FOR REFLECTION

The decision in *R (on the application of Main) v Minister for Legal Aid*[73] was that the Lord Chancellor could not be compelled to grant legal aid for representation in an inquest. Had the family been able to fund counsel privately then representation would have been permitted. Does this not show a flaw in the coronial system? Does it mean that justice can be 'bought'?

Why do you think the family wanted their own representative? Was the Court of Appeal right to think that a coroner can identify matters without representation from the family?

LISTEN TO THE PODCAST

For guidance on how to answer this question and a discussion of the main issues, listen to the author's podcast on the online resources: **www.oup.com/he/gillespie-weare8e**

Summary

In this chapter we have noted:

- Classifying the courts is not a simple process since many of the courts have both a civil and a criminal jurisdiction.
- The courts in England and Wales (ie excluding the Supreme Court which is a UK court) are now administered by a single agency, HMCTS.
- The courts of original jurisdiction (ie which hear trials of first instance) are the magistrates' court, county court, Crown Court, and High Court.
- The Crown Court and High Court have both an original and appellate jurisdiction.
- All family-related matters are now heard in the Family Court.
- The High Court is divided into three divisions (Queen's Bench Division, Chancery Division, and Family Division) and when two or more judges sit together in the High Court it is known as a Divisional Court.

---

71. ibid, sch 8, para 1.
72. ibid.
73. [2007] EWCA Civ 1147.

❓ End-of-chapter questions

1. Given that the county court and High Court have similar jurisdiction is there any point in keeping them as separate courts? Would it not be appropriate for there to be just one court—a civil court—which could be staffed by different judges? Are there any advantages or disadvantages to this approach?

2. A single Family Court has now been established. What are the advantages of this new court? Are there any disadvantages?

3. At the beginning of the chapter it was noted that the courts estate in England and Wales has changed substantially since 2010, with the closure and sale of many court buildings. What problems could arise by closing courts and reducing the number of courts across the country? Are there any advantages?

☰ Further reading

Lord Mance, 'Constitutional Reform, the Supreme Court and the Law Lords' (2006) 25 *Civil Justice Quarterly* 155–65.

This is an interesting article written by a Lord of Appeal in Ordinary discussing the work of the House of Lords and considering the changes that a Supreme Court may (or may not) bring.

Robins J, 'Strength in Unity' (2005) 102 *Law Society Gazette* 18–19.

Discusses the possible advantages of creating a single family court.

Samuels A, 'A Unified Civil Court' (2006) 25 *Civil Justice Quarterly* 250–60.

This article discusses whether it would be appropriate to introduce a unified civil court to streamline civil proceedings.

The House of Commons Library has recently published an online dashboard where you can see magistrates' court closures by constituency. Visit <https://commonslibrary.parliament.uk/local-data/constituency-data-magistrates-court-closures/> to find out about court closures in your area.

You may also find it interesting to read the annual reports of the Court of Appeal (each Division produces a separate report and they are housed on the judiciary website). A link to the publications can be found in the online resources at: www.oup.com/he/gillespie-weare8e

For self-test questions, flashcards, and links to useful websites, please visit the **online resources** at: **www.oup.com/he/gillespie-weare8e**

7

The Structure of the Tribunals

By the end of this chapter you will be able to:

- Identify the type of disputes that are heard by tribunals.
- Discuss the accountability of tribunals.
- Understand how a matter is heard by the Employment Tribunal.
- Understand how a matter is heard by the Investigatory Powers Tribunal.
- Understand the relationship between the courts and tribunals.

Introduction

Not every dispute will necessarily be dealt with before a court; some disputes will be settled before they reach court. Other cases will never proceed before a court but will instead be heard by a different body. This chapter will look at the tribunal system, which sits 'parallel' to the courts (see Figure 7.1). The system of tribunals has been created to deal with specific statutory issues. They are administrative rather than purely legal bodies and the rules will often vary between tribunals. The reforms to the court estate, noted at the outset of the previous chapter, have also impacted the tribunals, with over 20% of dedicated tribunal buildings being closed (18 out of 83) between 2010 and 2019.[1]

7.1 The tribunal system

The then Senior President of Tribunals, Carnwath LJ, has commented:

> There is no doubt . . . that tribunals represent one of the most important pillars of the system of justice in this country . . . It is fair to say that more people bring a case before a tribunal than go to any other part of the justice system.[2]

---

1. Georgina Sturge, *Court statistics for England and Wales, Briefing Paper Number CBP 8372* (House of Commons Library, 2019) https://researchbriefings.files.parliament.uk/documents/CBP-8372/CBP-8372.pdf 16.
2. Trevor Buck, 'Precedent in Tribunals and the Development of Principles' (2006) 25 *Civil Justice Quarterly* 458, 459.

This is a worthy point and demonstrates the importance of a 'parallel' system of justice that exists alongside the courts. Tribunals are administrative bodies that are created by statute to resolve certain disputes. Historically dozens of tribunals have been created by statute although in recent years this has been reduced to a core number of tribunals that undoubtedly regularly exercise judicial authority. The use of tribunals became quite widespread in the latter half of the twentieth century where it was considered that their use would be preferable to allowing courts to settle administrative disputes. In part, this response was also to minimize pressure on the judicial process by diverting these disputes from the courts.

Whilst tribunals are not strictly courts, they must adhere to the general principles of due process (and a failure to do so will be corrected readily by review either by judicial review or appeal). A key finding of the *Franks Report*, the report of a committee that was set up to examine how tribunals worked, was:

> In the field of tribunals openness appears to us to require the publicity of proceedings and knowledge of the essential reasoning underlying the decisions; fairness to require the adoption of a clear procedure which enables parties to know their rights, to present their case fully and to know the case which they have to meet . . . [3]

This is probably the distillation of the minimum requirements of due process but is probably not directly comparable to the judicial system. Since the *Franks Report* the number of tribunals has increased and their importance within the English Legal System has grown. After the *Woolf Report* into civil litigation it was thought that a review of tribunal justice would also be needed, in part to identify whether a separate system of dispute resolution was required alongside a reformed court system. Assuming that such a system was necessary (and the abolition of tribunals was never seriously on the agenda), then their status and effectiveness needed to be discussed in a way similar to the *Woolf* reforms. Together with the *Auld Report* into the criminal justice system this meant that there were, in effect, three reports that covered the entire justice system.

The task of examining the tribunals was given to Sir Andrew Leggatt, a former Lord Justice of Appeal, and he reported in 2001. Leggatt argued that tribunal justice carries with it two advantages: the first is that it consists of a mixture of legal and expert assistance, and the second is that their preparation and hearings should be simpler and more informal than courts.[4] However, he also found that the development of tribunals was ad hoc rather than systematic and that this had created a situation where there was no consistent application of justice within the tribunal system.[5] He recommended that this should change and, as will be seen, it has. The tribunal system is undoubtedly now a parallel system of justice that sits alongside the courts. Recent administrative changes have brought the two systems closer together but they remain distinct, at least in title.

7.2 Structure of tribunals

The *Tribunals, Courts and Enforcement Act 2007* (TCEA 2007) transformed the structure of the tribunals. The Act created a new unified structure, creating two tribunals, known as the 'First-Tier Tribunal' and the 'Upper Tribunal'.

---

3. Oliver Franks, *Report of the Committee on Administrative Tribunals and Enquiries* (Cmnd 218, HMSO, 1957) 10.
4. Andrew Leggatt, *Tribunals for Users: One System, One Service* (HMSO 2001) para 1.2.
5. ibid, para 1.3.

7.2.1 **First-Tier Tribunal**

The First-Tier Tribunal consists of seven chambers, known as:

- Social Entitlement Chamber
- Health, Education and Social Care Chamber
- Taxation Chamber
- General Regulatory Chamber
- Immigration and Asylum Chamber
- War Pensions and Armed Forces Compensation Chamber
- Property Chamber.

Each of these chambers comprises specific jurisdictions and involves multiple tribunals and panels. For example, the jurisdictions of the *Health, Education and Social Care Chamber* include mental health, special educational needs and disability, care standard, and primary health lists.

Individual tribunals have varying jurisdiction, for example the *Immigration and Asylum Tribunal* has UK-wide jurisdiction, whereas the *Environment Tribunal* is confined to England and Wales only. The First-Tier Tribunal is, in essence, the equivalent of a first-instance jurisdiction even though this jurisdiction may include an appeal from an administrative judgment (eg Criminal Injuries Compensation).

7.2.2 **Upper Tribunal**

The Upper Tribunal consists of four chambers: the *Administrative Appeals Chamber*, *Tax and Chancery Chamber*, *Lands Chamber*, and *Immigration and Asylum Chamber*. The Upper Tribunal largely deals with appeals from the First-Tier Tribunal. As shown in Figure 7.1 the First-Tier Tribunals have a specific appeal route they follow to the Upper Tribunal. For example, the *War Pensions and Armed Forces Compensation Chamber*, the *Social Entitlement Chamber*, the *Health, Education and Social Care Chamber*, and the *General Regulatory Chamber* all appeal to the *Administrative Appeals Chamber*. This ensures that there is one clear system of appeal for the First-Tier Tribunals.

Some complicated first-instance matters on, for example, tax and land can also form part of the work of the Upper Tribunal. Like the High Court, the Upper Tribunal is a superior court of record.

7.2.3 **Appeals**

As noted in 7.2.2, appeals from the First-Tier Tribunals proceed to the Upper Tribunal.[6] Further appeals from the Upper Tribunal proceed to the Court of Appeal (Civil Division).[7] A further appeal is only permitted on matters of law and only with leave to appeal from either the Upper Tribunal or the Court of Appeal (Civil Division).[8]

---

6. TCEA 2007, s 11.
7. ibid, s 13.
8. ibid, s 13(3).

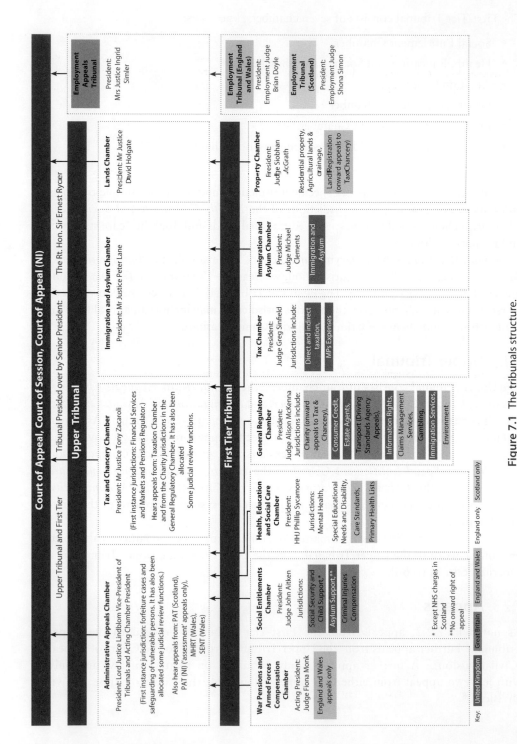

Figure 7.1 The tribunals structure.

Reproduced with permission from HM Courts and Judiciary Tribunal website (https://www.judiciary.uk/wp-content/uploads/2020/08/tribunals-chart-updated-May-2020.pdf) and acknowledged as subject to Crown copyright.

7.2.3.1 **Judicial review of tribunals**

The TCEA 2007 left unanswered an interesting question over the judicial review of tribunals. Before the reforms of the TCEA 2007, most tribunals were ordinarily considered to be inferior bodies and thus subject to the judicial review of the High Court. However, with the revised tribunal structure (ie the creation of the first tier and upper tier), the First-Tier Tribunal remains an inferior body but the TCEA 2007 purports to transfer the judicial review jurisdiction over this tribunal from the High Court to the Upper Tribunal.[9] Therefore the High Court should decline jurisdiction and instead leave this to the Upper Tribunal (in part based on the rule that judicial review by the High Court should only be permitted where no alternative remedy exists).

What of the Upper Tribunal? It is clear that the Upper Tribunal is a superior court of record[10] but this is not conclusive by itself since, of course, the Crown Court is also a superior court and it is reviewable for matters other than trials on indictment. The answer to the question is to be found in the decision of the Court of Appeal (Civil Division) in *R (on the application of C) v Upper Tribunal*.[11] The Court of Appeal held that the Upper Tribunal is subject to judicial review because it does not have the same status as the High Court, not least because its jurisdiction is based on statute rather than the inherent jurisdiction to resolve matters. The Court of Appeal also noted that the belief that a superior court of record could not be reviewed has never been clarified by the English courts and is not recognized by the Scottish courts (which may be relevant as the First-Tier and Upper Tribunals are UK bodies, not simply bodies of England and Wales). The court preferred to reason that as Parliament is aware of the High Court's power to judicially review, it would have used express words to divest the Upper Tribunal from this power had it so intended, and in the absence of such language, the tribunal is theoretically at least reviewable.

However, the court noted that the fact that it can be reviewed as a matter of law does not mean that it will be in practice or identify what it may be reviewed for. The court noted that judicial review related to various grounds, some of which were controlled by discretion, but that it would be a dereliction of the High Court's duty to let a court or tribunal act in excess of its authority or where it had denied a party a fair hearing.[12] However, in terms of other matters of judicial review (eg procedural impropriety) the court noted that Parliament had created the tribunal system to be an independent and self-sufficient system that should correct its own errors of adjudication.

Accordingly, the Court of Appeal held that the Upper Tribunal is amenable to judicial review by the High Court where it purports to exercise jurisdiction it has not been given by Parliament or where it denies the right to a fair trial through, for example, allowing someone to sit as judge who should not. At one level this decision could be considered to be a reasonable compromise in that such challenges will be rarely brought: and the Court of Appeal is stating that where the judicial review is in respect of their adjudication then a review will not be heard and the ordinary appellate rules should apply. On another level, however, this can be said to be a fudge. A right of appeal exists from the Upper Tribunal to the Court of Appeal (Civil Division) on matters of law.[13] The jurisdiction of the tribunal and the right to a fair trial are both matters of law

---

9. ibid, s 15.
10. ibid, s 3(5).
11. [2010] EWCA Civ 859.
12. ibid, [26].
13. TCEA 2007, s 13.

and so it must be questioned whether it is truly necessary for the High Court to claim the right to judicially review the tribunal rather than, for example, allowing the Court of Appeal to correct such an error. It may have perhaps been simpler to do this but the courts are slow to limit their own jurisdiction.

7.3 Other tribunals

The First-Tier Tribunal and Upper Tribunal are not the only tribunals in existence. Other tribunals also exist outside the system, most notably the *Employment (and Employment Appeal) Tribunals*. These tribunals are within the *Tribunal Service* but do not feature in the revised 'First Tier–Upper Tier' structure. The Employment (and Appeal) Tribunals are more difficult to locate within the structure, not least because the EAT is considered to be a superior court of record (discussed in more detail below and at 7.5.2). The *Investigatory Powers Tribunal* also sits outside the system. Both of the tribunals are considered in more detail below.

7.3.1 Employment Tribunals

The Employment Tribunals are one of the more well-known tribunals. Their jurisdiction is set out, inter alia, in the *Employment Tribunals Act 1996*, and covers over seventy different types of dispute between employers and employees in relation to employment rights. These include, for example, unfair dismissal and discrimination claims.

In the same way that both civil and criminal courts have rules governing their procedure, so does the Employment Tribunal, these being contained within Sch 1 of the *Employment Tribunals (Constitution and Rules of Procedure) Regulations 2013*.[14] Reference must be made to these rules in order to progress a case, although the tribunal does produce a series of guides to progressing a case.

Once a claim to the employment tribunal has been made, but before the tribunal hearing itself takes place, there will be a preliminary hearing[15] which will ordinarily decide whether there is a prima facie case. This will involve a person demonstrating that they have, for example, suffered unfair treatment or discrimination. Types of evidence that could be adduced at this stage include witnesses, witness statements, and documentary evidence, such as contracts of employment or pay slips. This will be a hearing that usually takes place in private. If the judge decides there is a prima facie case then a date and time is normally set for the final hearing.

The final hearing usually takes place in public.[16] The tribunal is not bound by rules of evidence[17] which theoretically means that any evidence that is relevant can be heard. This can be contrasted with the traditional position in the courts where the probity of evidence was considered to be a relevant factor. Traditionally, hearsay (which for our purposes can be summarized as second-hand evidence) was not permitted by the courts, although in recent years this has changed.[18]

---

14. SI 2013/1237.
15. *Employment Tribunals (Constitution and Rules of Procedure) Regulations 2013*, SI 2013/1237, sch 1, paras 53–6.
16. Subject to the exclusions noted in the *Employment Tribunals (Constitution and Rules of Procedure) Regulations 2013*, SI 2013/1237, sch 1, para 59.
17. *Employment Tribunals (Constitution and Rules of Procedure) Regulations 2013*, SI 2013/1237, sch 1, para 41.
18. See *Civil Evidence Act 1995* and *Criminal Justice Act 2003*.

As will be discussed in 8.1.3.4, similarly to other tribunals, the Employment Tribunal panel constitutes a judge and lay members. Those who sit as lay members of the Employment Tribunals represents employers and employees, and one from each should normally sit.[19]

Once a judgment has been handed down by the tribunal a party can apply to the tribunal, within fourteen days of the original decision being sent to them, to reconsider the judgment.[20] An explanation for why the party wants the decision to be reconsidered must be provided, detailing reasons to justify the reconsideration, for example, the emergence of new evidence. The tribunal can also reconsider cases on its own initiative and this may happen where, for example, a request has come from the Employment Appeal Tribunal.[21] If the tribunal reconsiders its own decision it will either be confirmed, varied, or revoked.[22]

If a party believes that a *legal* mistake was made in their case then they can apply to the *Employment Appeal Tribunal* (EAT). Indeed, the role of the EAT is to rule on the lawfulness of decisions made by the Employment Tribunals.[23] Any party wishing to appeal a point of law in their case must do so within forty-two days of the date that the written reasons for the tribunal panel's decision was sent out to them.[24] If a case is heard by the EAT then, unlike many other appeal tribunals which consist of a judge sitting alone (as the matter under consideration is one of law), lay members continue to sit alongside the presiding judge.

7.3.2 **Investigatory Powers Tribunal**

Unlike the Employment Tribunals, and indeed many other tribunals, the Investigatory Powers Tribunal (IPT) is not open to the public. Indeed, it is perhaps one of the most restrictive tribunals due to the nature of the work it deals with. The IPT was created by Part IV *Regulation of Investigatory Powers Act (RIPA) 2000*, a statute which (as its name suggests) regulates the use of covert investigation powers by the state. The tribunal has been described as:

> being different from all others in that its concern is with security. For this reason it must remain separate from the rest and ought not to have any relationship with other tribunals.[25]

Although Leggatt is correct to argue that its work relates to security it is less clear as to what this means exactly. There are currently over forty bodies that are authorized to use some or all of the powers within RIPA 2000 (see, eg, the *Regulation of Investigatory Powers (Directed Surveillance and Covert Human Intelligence Sources) Order 2003* (SI 2010/521)), and whilst some undoubtedly deal with security matters (eg GCHQ, the Security Services (MI5), and the Secret Intelligence Service (MI6)) others may appear less important (eg the Food Standards Agency or the Gaming Board for Great Britain).

231

19. *Employment Tribunals (Constitution and Rules of Procedure) Regulations 2013*, SI 2013/1237, reg 8.
20. ibid, sch 1, para 71.
21. ibid, sch 1, para 70.
22. ibid, sch 1, para 70.
23. See, for example, *Jafri v Lincoln College* [2014] EWCA Civ 449.
24. *Employment Appeal Tribunal Rules 1993*, r 3.
25. Andrew Leggatt, *Tribunals for Users: One System, One Service* (HMSO 2001) para 3.11.

The powers that are available to these bodies are extremely sensitive and are outside the scope of this book and their use of the powers can be very controversial. The detailed use of the powers will frequently be kept secret, even during a criminal trial, through a process known as *public interest immunity* (PII).[26] The *Investigatory Powers Act 2016* provides for the regulation of these powers by the *Investigatory Powers Commissioner's Office* (which replaced the *Office of the Surveillance Commissioners)*, which focuses on whether the powers are, in general, being used appropriately; they do not examine individual complaints. However, the use of covert surveillance against a person is a prima facie breach of Article 8 ECHR in that it is an interference with a person's private life (see, eg, *Malone v United Kingdom*[27]). If used appropriately this will not matter as it is justified under Article 8(2), but how can this be tested?

It has been noted already that courts, both civil and criminal, are prima facie public bodies and should sit in public and provide for a public pronouncement of the decision. The powers available under RIPA 2000 are so sensitive that the government would not wish them to be discussed in public because it could assist those that they could be used against (ie criminals could use the knowledge to develop anti-surveillance techniques). The HRA 1998 requires that someone who believes the powers are being used against them inappropriately should have the right to take action against authorities[28] and the IPT is this action. Section 65(2) RIPA 2000 states that an action can *only* be brought in the IPT. In *R (on the application of A) v B*[29] the Supreme Court upheld this provision of RIPA 2000 and rejected an argument that the HRA 1998 required that there should be access to the ordinary courts. The Supreme Court held that the IPT had been given exclusive jurisdiction by Parliament and that the courts had no jurisdiction to hear matters within s 65 RIPA even where they did not relate to the regulation of investigatory powers.

The rules of the tribunal are loosely set out in secondary legislation (*Investigatory Powers Tribunal Rules 2018*)[30] but RIPA 2000 itself states that the tribunal shall decide its own procedure in respect of complaints.[31] It is taken to mean that the tribunal can, therefore, issue its own rules but also that it may alter them depending on the circumstances. This rule is subject to the rules set out in the statutory instrument but the tribunal, as the sole arbitrator of claims under HRA 1998, has used its authority to strike down at least one section of the rules (that which requires it to sit in secrecy; see later in this section). Accordingly, the position appears to be that where the rules are incompatible with the ECHR the tribunal reserves the right to be the ultimate arbitrator of its own procedure, in part because of the fact that decisions of the tribunal are not ordinarily the subject of an appeal.

Unlike a traditional matter, the adjudication of a matter raised in the IPT could lead to an investigation. Members of the tribunal are empowered to require the Intelligence or Security Services Commissioners to assist them,[32] or to require any public authority to disclose to it such documents and information as it requires.[33] It can be seen, therefore, that the adjudication appears to take the form of an inquisitorial hearing rather

---

26. Andrew Ashworth and Mike Redmayne, *The Criminal Process* (4th edn, OUP 2010).
27. (1985) 7 EHRR 14.
28. *Human Rights Act 1998*, s 7.
29. [2009] UKSC 12.
30. SI 2018/1334.
31. RIPA 2000, s 68(1).
32. *Investigatory Powers Tribunal Rules 2018*, SI 2018/1334, r 6(b).
33. ibid, r 6(b) and (c).

than a simple adjudication. This is taken further by the fact that there is no disclosure of documents; indeed the statutory rules make it clear that the general rule is that the claimant will *not* be given any details of information provided by the state bodies.[34]

The IPT does not, unlike most other tribunals, have to hold a hearing, the rules making clear that any hearings are purely discretionary,[35] although there may be concerns as to whether this is necessarily compatible with the ECHR since Article 6 is generally taken to mean that there is a right to access a court (or tribunal) where a civil right or obligation is in dispute. As has been noted, covert surveillance is a prima facie breach of Article 8 and thus it is a matter of civil rights or obligation. Accordingly, a person should ordinarily have a right to judicial adjudication, although it is less clear whether this right requires an actual hearing or whether it is merely a judicial determination of the issues which could, for example, mean the matter being disposed of by an examination of the relevant papers.

Even if hearings do take place, however, they are unlikely to take the format of the traditional adversarial approach with both sides being in the same room hearing and challenging all the evidence. Rule 10(3) states that it is possible to hold separate hearings for the different sides and at least one commentator has suggested that this will be the normal position.[36] Again this must raise questions over its compatibility with Article 6 ECHR since this places significant restrictions on the ability of a person to conduct their case.

Assuming that hearings are held, the statutory rules are quite clear about their nature:

A hearing . . . may be held wholly or partly in private.[37]

In other words the majority of matters relating to the tribunal are held in secret with members of the public and press excluded. Again this raises questions about compliance with basic freedoms under both domestic and ECHR jurisprudence where the traditional rule is that hearings are in public. There has always been the opportunity for courts to sit in camera (meaning in secret) where it is necessary to protect information in the interests of security or other public interest matters, but this has always been the exception to the rule.

It can be seen, therefore, that the IPT operates in a significantly different way from both ordinary tribunals and the courts. Certainly it makes a clear contrast from courts where there are more rigid and formalistic approaches to the adjudication of matters and where the adversarial model of justice remains important. This distinction continues when it relates to evidence. Like the Employment Tribunal the IPT has wide powers over evidence but its rule is formulated slightly differently:

The Tribunal may receive evidence in any form, and may receive evidence that would not be admissible in a court of law.[38]

Arguably this is very similar to the form of words adopted for the Employment Tribunals but it is expressed in a stronger way, making clear that there is no doubt that the IPT

233

34. ibid, r 7 and RIPA 2000, s 69(6).
35. *Investigatory Powers Tribunal Rules 2018*, SI 2018/1334, r 10(1).
36. Helen Fenwick, 'Covert Surveillance under the Regulation of Investigatory Powers Act 2000, Part II' (2001) 65 *Journal of Criminal Law* 521.
37. *Investigatory Powers Tribunal Rules 2018*, SI 2018/1334, r 10(2).
38. ibid, r 13(1).

can receive inadmissible evidence. This can be contrasted immediately with both civil and criminal courts where certain evidence, particularly in respect of covert surveillance, would ordinarily not be admissible in evidence. This would appear to support the earlier argument that the IPT adopts an inquisitorial rather than adversarial system when deciding whether a person's rights have been infringed.

The secrecy of the IPT invariably leads to questions being raised as to whether it is a fair system, especially since it rejects many of the adversarial principles that are so coveted in other aspects of the judicial system. The fact that a person is not necessarily able to be involved with the full case nor able to see the evidence on which the state relies must certainly raise questions as to fairness even if these are unproven. These questions are perhaps given more weight when an analysis is made of the statistics.

During 2016 (the most recent year for which data is available) there were 209 complaints made to the IPT of which only 15 (7%) were upheld; 120 (52%) were ruled as 'frivolous or vexatious'.[39] Complaints can be heard in open court, however, once again due to the nature of the IPT's work, the vast majority of cases are heard behind closed doors. Only four complaints were heard in open court in 2016.[40]

7.4 Administration of tribunals

The vast majority of tribunals are administered by HM Courts and Tribunals Service (discussed at 6.2.2) including the Employment Tribunal and EAT. However, there are certain tribunals that are administered differently. For example, School Exclusion Panels are administered by local authorities.

The TCEA 2007 created the Tribunal Procedure Committee,[41] which produces and keeps under review the *Tribunal Procedure Rules*. These Rules are, in essence, the equivalent of the *Civil Procedure Rules* and the *Criminal Procedure Rules* used in the court system. As with the *Civil Procedure Rules*, *Criminal Procedure Rules*, and *Family Procedure Rules* they are based in statutory instruments but are updated frequently. The Tribunal Procedure Committee includes nominees of the Senior President of the Tribunals, the Lord Chancellor, and the Lord Chief Justice.[42]

7.4.1 Judicial administration

The role of Senior President of the Tribunals was created under the *Tribunals, Courts and Enforcement Act 2007*.[43] Sir Keith Lindblom is the current holder of the post. The responsibilities of the Senior President include coordinating the work of the tribunals and, in particular, representing the views of the tribunal judiciary.[44] In order to discharge this duty the Senior President has the statutory power to lay written representations before Parliament,[45] and he does not need the permission of, for example, the Lord Chief Justice to do so.

---

39. The Investigatory Powers Tribunal, *Statistical Report* (IPT, 2016) https://www.ipt-uk.com/docs/IPT%20 Statistical%20Report%202016.pdf 5.
40. ibid.
41. TCEA 2007, sch 5, pt 2.
42. ibid, sch 5, pt 2, para 20.
43. ibid, s 2.
44. ibid, sch 1, pt 4.
45. ibid.

7.5 Court or tribunals or courts and tribunals?

Having considered both courts (in Chapter 6) and tribunals, the key question in this area that needs to be answered is what, if anything, is the difference between a court and a tribunal. The answer is not easy, and is arguably getting harder each year. The judiciary—in this context meaning both the courts judiciary and the tribunals judiciary—are determined to bring the two systems of justice closer together. The *Senior President* and the *Lord Chief Justice* are committed to having a single judiciary, capable of sitting in either courts or tribunals. This process has begun with the introduction of the *Courts and Tribunals (Judiciary and Functions of Staff) Act 2018* which increases the flexibility of the judiciary, allowing judges to be deployed where they are most needed. For example, Deputy High Court Judges can be deployed to any court or tribunal where they are able to sit, and recorders can sit in cases in the Upper Tribunal (as well as the First-Tier Tribunal where they can already sit).[46]

Despite the closeness between the courts and tribunals (something which is set to continue in development), there are areas within which some have argued there are differences between the courts and tribunals. We will consider three of these areas next, namely, jurisdiction, precedent, and representation.

7.5.1 Jurisdiction

Some argue that the difference between the courts and tribunals is as regards their jurisdiction. There are two parts to this argument. The first is that a court will ordinarily have general rather than specific jurisdiction, ie its work will not be limited to one small aspect of the law, whereas tribunals are created by statute to examine certain specific areas (eg the *Employment Tribunal* which examines employment issues, the *Special Educational Needs and Disability Tribunal* (now within the *Health, Education & Social Care Chamber of the First-Tier Tribunal*) which allows parents and children to ensure that their educational needs are appropriately resourced by the appropriate authorities). As a rule of thumb this can be quite a useful test but it is often said that it is flawed because specialist courts do exist, most notably the Bankruptcy Court (which deals with bankruptcies), the Commercial Court (which deals with high-value commercial transactions between companies, often relating to trade marks), and the Admiralty Court (which deals with disputes relating to shipping). However, it could be argued that this does not contradict the point which is made because technically these 'courts' are not individual courts but rather groupings within the Queen's Bench Division of the High Court of Justice (see 6.3.5.1). Accordingly, the overarching body—the High Court—does still have general jurisdiction.

The second aspect to the argument about jurisdiction concerns not just the area of law but also the type of decision reached. It is sometimes said that tribunals are there to ensure that administrative actions have been taken correctly. Whilst this is undoubtedly true for some tribunals (eg the *Land Tribunal* (subsumed within the Upper Tribunal) which examines questions about compensation arising from the compulsory acquisition of land by government), it becomes less clear for other tribunals (eg the *Employment Tribunals*). Also, it cannot be determinative since the High Court has

---

46. *Courts and Tribunals (Judiciary and Functions of Staff) Act 2018*, s 1.

a reviewing jurisdiction through the doctrine of judicial review and one of the three grounds for invoking this procedure is procedural impropriety, ie not following the correct administration.[47]

It can be seen therefore that it is not simple to identify what the difference between a court and tribunal is. At one point it was thought that perceptions may be the difference: ie the executive views tribunals as administrative bodies although the judiciary views them as judicial or quasi-judicial bodies.[48] Leggatt suggested that there were three tests to decide whether a matter should be heard by a tribunal or court:

1. **Participation**. Tribunals are considered to be inclusive and are designed, so far as possible, to be dealt with without the need for a lawyer.

2. **Special expertise**. Where a matter is outside the knowledge of the tribunal of fact a court will ordinarily permit the parties to adduce expert evidence by calling witnesses. Tribunals, however, will ordinarily consist of a legally qualified chair with experts sitting alongside them.

3. **Specialist administrative expertise**. Tribunals specialize in dealing with the combination of law and administration that relates to administrative or regulatory bodies. The absence of this would ordinarily leave judicial review as the only option.[49]

However, it is not clear that this necessarily helps because many of these factors can be applied to both. For example, the absence of representation (which is discussed later at 7.5.3) is also a feature of the small claims court although this is perhaps not as significant since the small claims court is perhaps not representative of a 'court' and indeed the scheme is often considered closer to arbitration than litigation. However, Leggatt was not necessarily suggesting that these factors will only be found in a court but that it makes it more likely that a matter will be heard in a tribunal.

To an extent it can be argued that the distinction between tribunals and courts is not particularly relevant. Modern tribunals are bound by the HRA 1998 in the same way as courts[50] and the disputes heard by tribunals will almost certainly be considered a 'right or obligation' within the meaning of Article 6(1) ECHR. On that basis it could be legitimately questioned whether there is any significant disadvantage that arises from a matter being heard by a tribunal rather than a court. Two further issues that tend to give rise to concern are issues of precedent and representation.

7.5.2 Precedent

The importance of precedent to the English Legal System has been noted already (see, most notably, Chapter 3) but what is the position with tribunals setting precedent? It has been suggested that this can be a way in which they differ from the courts:

[A] tribunal is . . . in a radically different position from a court of law. Its duty is to reach the right decision in the circumstances of the moment, any discretion must be genuinely exercised, and there must be no blind following of its previous decisions.[51]

47. See *Council of Civil Service Unions v Minister for the Civil Service* [1985] AC 374.
48. Oliver Franks, *Report of the Committee on Administrative Tribunals and Enquiries* (Cmnd 218, HMSO, 1957) 9.
49. Andrew Leggatt, *Tribunals for Users: One System, One Service* (HMSO 2001) paras 1.11–11.13.
50. *Human Rights Act 1998*, s 6(3)(a) states that a 'public authority' includes a 'court or tribunal'.
51. William Wade and Christopher Forsyth, *Administrative Law* (11th edn, OUP 2014) 778.

Before examining what this means it is necessary to pause to consider whether this is 'radically different' from courts of law. Decisions of the county court do not set precedent nor, it will be remembered, do decisions of the High Court when it is sitting as a court of first instance (see 3.2). However, it is clear that the courts need to follow the precedent of higher courts and also will normally be slow to depart from their own decisions even when technically not bound by them.

However, the point made by Wade and Forsyth is that a tribunal is (supposedly) concentrating on the individual facts of the case at hand rather than adopting a consistent approach to principles. However, is this necessarily either correct or appropriate? It has been suggested that whilst this was true historically the modern role of tribunals requires them to interpret legislation in a similar way to the courts.[52] Accordingly, it can be questioned whether it would not be more appropriate for their interpretations to be consistent? It will be remembered from Chapter 3 that the principle of *stare decisis* is considered to be a fundamental principle of English justice and so the abandonment of this policy at tribunal level could be construed as a lowering of fairness.

In fact it would be naive to suggest that there is no precedent within the tribunal system. Certain tribunals publish their decisions and allow them to be cited (the most obvious example being the EAT). Also, most tribunals are inferior bodies (the principal exceptions being the EAT, IPT, and the Immigration Tribunal) and may (unless prohibited by statute) be the subject of judicial review. If they are subject to judicial review then they are required to follow the rulings of the High Court (now Upper Tribunal in some cases—see 7.2.3.1) and thus a rudimentary form of *stare decisis* is created.

Even where a tribunal is not subject to judicial review it is possible that rudimentary precedent will be created. It had been customary to differentiate between First- and Second-Tier Tribunals and it has been suggested that precedent replicates the appellate structure and the relationship between the tribunals,[53] and this has now been formalized by the TCEA 2007 reforms.

237

⚡ FIRST- AND SECOND-TIER TRIBUNALS

It is customary to refer to 'first-tier' and 'second-tier' tribunals. In essence first-tier tribunals are those tribunals that exercise original jurisdiction, ie they make findings of fact and provide an appropriate relief or declaration. Examples of this would include the Employment Tribunal and now the First-Tier Tribunal itself.

Second-tier tribunals are appellate tribunals and are more concerned with ensuring that a person who believes a decision made by a first-tier tribunal has been wrongly made has a means of redress. Perhaps the classic example of this is the EAT. Leggatt proposed a single second-tier tribunal be created to hear appeals from most first-tier tribunals[54] but he did accept that a small number of tribunals would be excepted from this regime and appeals would proceed directly to the courts,[55] and that as a consequence alternative appeals, including judicial review, should no longer be permitted.[56] As noted earlier, this is the position that has now largely been created (see 7.2.3) although certain first- and second-tier tribunals exist outside of this structure.

---

52. Trevor Buck, 'Precedent in Tribunals and the Development of Principles' (2006) 25 *Civil Justice Quarterly* 458, 465.
53. ibid, 466.
54. Andrew Leggatt, *Tribunals for Users: One System, One Service* (HMSO 2001) para 6.10.
55. ibid, para 6.14.
56. ibid, para 6.30.

Leggatt considered how precedent should work following his reforms. He suggested that first-tier tribunals should not set precedent,[57] ie a first-tier tribunal would not be bound by the previous decision of a first-tier tribunal. This would appear somewhat logical and comparable to first-instance decisions of courts. However, Leggatt also ruled out decisions of second-tier tribunals automatically creating precedent[58] because he believed that it would be a barrier to access, since users of tribunals would be required to be familiar with decisions of the second-tier tribunal. However, others suggest that precedent in tribunals could actually assist tribunal users, not least by efficiently clarifying and developing the law[59] and ensuring that someone seeking advice is able properly to predict the law. The compromise suggested by Leggatt is that some decisions will set a precedent but others will not.[60] The tribunal itself would select which decisions would become precedents and these would be published.

This suggestion can be immediately contrasted with the position in the courts where it has been held that it is *not* for a judge passing judgment to decide what does, or does not, create precedent (see 3.3.2). Also, it is not immediately clear how this system will assist users of tribunals as they must become familiar with certain precedents. Presumably, however, since there will be a small number of binding precedents, these could be accompanied by summaries prepared and publicized on, for example, tribunal websites.

⟳ QUESTION FOR REFLECTION

If tribunals adjudicate on questions of law (including the application of a statutory provision) rather than just examine whether an administrative process has been followed, should the system of *stare decisis* not apply in the same way as it does in the court system? One of the reasons why it does not appear to be followed literally is the informal nature of tribunals[61] but is this a valid excuse? Should a person seeking justice before a tribunal not expect a consistent approach to be taken as to the law?

◀)) LISTEN TO THE PODCAST

For guidance on how to answer this question and a discussion of the main issues, listen to the author's podcast on the online resources: **www.oup.com/he/gillespie-weare8e**

7.5.3 **Representation**

It has been seen that in both the civil and criminal justice system it is not strictly necessary to employ a lawyer to represent oneself in court. However, with the exception of certain proceedings in the magistrates' court (eg guilty pleas to driving offences) or small claims court, it is probably more desirable if lawyers are engaged, but what is the position with tribunals?

---

57. ibid, para 6.19.
58. ibid, para 6.24.
59. Trevor Buck, 'Precedent in Tribunals and the Development of Principles' (2006) 25 *Civil Justice Quarterly* 458, 465.
60. Andrew Leggatt, *Tribunals for Users: One System, One Service* (HMSO 2001) para 6.26.
61. ibid, para 6.24.

A principal advantage of the tribunal system is said to be that they are informal and user-friendly.[62] All of the tribunals try to make themselves accessible to those that need to access them. This includes the provision of step-by-step instructions on how to access the service.[63]

An example of accessibility is the fact that there are extremely wide rights of audience in most tribunals. Not only can the applicant act as a litigant in person during a tribunal but he has the choice to engage a lawyer (unless specifically prohibited by statute) or take any other person as representative.[64] A difficulty with engaging a lawyer is the fact that legal aid is not generally available for tribunals, and where a tribunal does not specifically permit a lawyer to be engaged it is unlikely that the rules of the tribunal will permit the fees to be reclaimed by the successful party. Where legal aid has failed many bodies have stepped in. Those who belong to a trade union will normally be given representation, with most unions employing workers who specialize in tribunal litigation. The Citizens Advice Bureau (CAB), an independent charity, has also begun to adopt a representation service for those areas of work within its expertise (usually employment, rent, and social welfare). Even universities have entered this sector with some undergraduate law programmes including a 'law clinic' whereby undergraduates, under the supervision of staff (who frequently hold professional practice certificates), undertake legal work in the community, including providing representation before tribunals.

If representation is permitted by others then this does raise the question whether tribunals are litigant-friendly. It is one thing suggesting that a lawyer does not need to be engaged, but if a representative (eg a union official or CAB worker) is useful then does this not mean that legal representation would be useful? There is evidence to suggest that representation is beneficial to those using tribunals,[65] and yet despite this there is strong resistance to the use of representation in tribunals. Some argue that engaging a lawyer would simply add to costs, delay, and complexity.[66] Why is it that the lack of legal representation is considered to be an advantage? Is it truly an advantage or is this a justification that is used to disguise the fact that it would be expensive for lawyers to be used in all tribunals?

It is difficult to argue against the suggestion that representation is helpful because the representative is almost certainly familiar with the tribunal process and will therefore be able to structure the submissions in an effective way that demonstrates the claim made. A litigant in person is unlikely to have legal training and yet is being asked to put forward an argument based, in part at least, on law, something they are unlikely to know anything about. It has been noted that the right to representation, including legal representation, has not traditionally been considered a principle of natural justice,[67] but the decision of the European Court of Human Rights in *Steel and Morris v United Kingdom*,[68] which suggested that Article 6 could require legal assistance to be provided where lack of it would lead to an inequality of arms, does take a further step towards identifying a right to legal representation. Whilst it may be thought that an inequality of arms may not exist within a tribunal system of justice it is conceivable to identify

62. Mark Elliott and Robert Thomas, *Public Law* (3rd edn, OUP 2017) 687.
63. The online resources that accompany this book provide links to the principal tribunal websites which will allow you to access the materials available and understand how to initiate proceedings.
64. *Employment Tribunals Act 1996*, s 6.
65. Andrew Leggatt, *Tribunals for Users: One System, One Service* (HMSO 2001) para 4.21.
66. ibid, para 4.21.
67. William Wade and Christopher Forsyth, *Administrative Law* (11th edn, OUP 2014) 782.
68. (2005) 41 EHRR 22.

circumstances. A spin on the facts of *Steel and Morris* is possible whereby a private individual is seeking to refer a large multinational corporation to an employment tribunal. Other examples may include situations where it is a private individual against the state where one party (the state) can afford to engage leading counsel whereas the individual litigant may not. However, the counter-argument is that the decision in *Steel and Morris* was based, in part, on the fact that High Court proceedings are inherently formal and technical. Since tribunal proceedings are not then it could be argued that the same level of representation is not required.

In this era of restricted public legal funding (discussed in Chapter 11) it is perhaps unrealistic to expect an absolute right to legal representation. The current system relies on specialized laypersons stepping into the breach but is this appropriate? In a now rather dated report, Bell noted that there was a perception that tribunal justice did not consider that lawyers needed to be engaged but thought that tribunals should be more inclusive.[69] To some degree this has been taken on board by the tribunals through the provision of guidance to bringing a case, but can a litigant in person ever be considered comparable to a professional representative? It has been suggested that a fundamental principle of tribunal justice is that tribunals are adversarial,[70] but it is not clear why this is the case. It is suggested that deviating from the adversarial process means that favouritism could be shown but this does not automatically follow. An inquisitor can remain independent and it has been noted elsewhere that there is a tendency in the civil litigation system to move away from strict adversarial approaches.

Is the solution therefore not to adopt a more inquisitorial system? In that way the emphasis is placed on the tribunals and not the litigants, but this may not necessarily be welcome as it could lead to more focus on the constitution of the tribunal, including a consideration as to whether all members (including lay members) should be better rewarded as they will need to alter their approach to a case. The conundrum as to rights of audience looks as though it will continue for some time yet.

⟳ QUESTION FOR REFLECTION

Tribunals are, potentially, dealing with extremely important issues, including the integrity of litigants (in, eg, employment disputes or disputes before the *Care Standards Tribunal* (now *Health, Education and Social Care* Chamber of the First-Tier Tribunal) which decides, inter alia, upon the suitability of teachers to work with vulnerable members of society), and certain disputes will concern significant sums of money. Is it right, therefore, that the engagement of a lawyer should be exceptional in such cases?

What advantages and disadvantages are there to the routine appointment of lawyers (including state-funded lawyers where appropriate)?

🔊 LISTEN TO THE PODCAST

For guidance on how to answer this question and a discussion of the main issues, listen to the author's podcast on the online resources: **www.oup.com/he/gillespie-weare8e**

---

69. Kathleen Bell, *Research Study on Supplementary Benefit Appeal Tribunals* (HMSO 1975) 19.
70. William Wade and Christopher Forsyth, *Administrative Law* (11th edn, OUP 2014) 775.

Summary

This chapter has examined the jurisdiction of tribunals and noted their increasing role within the justice system. In particular it has:

- Noted that tribunals have existed for many years but traditionally operated as an oversight system for administrative issues.

- Identified the fact that in recent years the number of tribunals has increased and their work has included questions of law and not just administrative propriety.

- Considered the work specifically of the *Employment Tribunals* and the *Investigatory Powers Tribunal*.

- Discussed whether tribunals are separate from the judicial system or whether there is an argument that they should be recognized as courts.

- Identified that tribunals see themselves as being more informal adjudicating bodies where traditional rules of evidence do not necessarily apply.

- Considered whether litigants in a tribunal should be represented.

 End-of-chapter questions

1. Read Chapter 4 of the *Leggatt Report* (available online). Do you think tribunals are truly accessible to ordinary members of the public or do you still require the services of someone who knows the law and procedure? Is there any way of making them truly accessible and would this be desirable?

2. Read *Ewing v Security Service*[71] where the High Court decided that the IPT bore many of the characteristics of a court. Also read Helen Fenwick, 'Covert Surveillance under the Regulation of Investigatory Powers Act 2000, Part II' (2001) 65 *Journal of Criminal Law* 521. Is the IPT really a tribunal or is it a court? What, if any, are the differences and do you believe that the tribunal can properly be said to safeguard a citizen's human rights?

3. Given that the exact distinction between tribunals and courts is unclear, what are the main advantages of tribunals when compared to courts? What about the disadvantages?

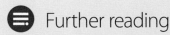 Further reading

Bradley A, 'The Tribunals Maze' [2002] *Public Law* 200–2.

This short article considers the proposals in the *Leggatt Report* to consolidate the tribunals into one service with a smaller number of tribunals.

Buck T, 'Precedent in Tribunals and the Development of Principles' (2006) 25 *Civil Justice Quarterly* 458–84.

This is an interesting piece that considers whether precedent exists within tribunals, whether precedent should exist in tribunals, and, if so, how it would operate.

---

71. [2003] EWHC 2051 (QB).

241

Carnwath LJ, 'Tribunal Justice: A New Start' [2009] *Public Law* 48–69.

This article was written by the then Senior President of Tribunals and set out the major changes brought about by the TCEA 2007 and discussed how tribunal justice would operate.

David S, 'Employment Tribunals: Room for Improvement?' (2019) 7859 *New Law Journal* 8

This piece provides insights into challenges faced in the employment tribunals due to increasing numbers of claims and limited resources.

For self-test questions, flashcards, and links to useful websites, please visit the **online resources** at: **www.oup.com/he/gillespie-weare8e**

8

The Judiciary and their Appointment

By the end of this chapter you will be able to:

- Identify the key judicial offices, their ranks, and styles.
- Understand how judges are appointed and assess the recent changes.
- Understand the staffing of the tribunal system.
- Assess the differences and similarities between the court judiciary and the tribunal judiciary.
- Understand the quasi-judicial role of magistrates.

Introduction

At the heart of the English Legal System is the judiciary, a body of persons often caricatured in the media as doddery old men who are bordering on senile. The truth, however, is that both the full-time and part-time judiciary in England and Wales are extremely professional persons who have come from the very best of the Bar and solicitors. That is not to say that controversy does not surround the judiciary and, in particular, the way that they operate and are appointed to their office. Whilst the courts judiciary is well known, the tribunals judiciary is perhaps less so, and therefore both will be considered in this chapter. Whilst not part of the judiciary, magistrates will also be considered at the end of this chapter due to the 'quasi-judicial' role that they occupy within the English Legal System.

8.1 The judicial office

As will be seen, there are different types of judges within the English Legal System and these differences are echoed in how they are styled and referred to, something that will be explored in what follows.

The position of a judge is not one that is taken by employment but it is, rather, an office that the holder possesses during his tenure. It is not the place of this chapter to discuss the differences between an office holder and an employee save to say that it normally means an office holder cannot use employment legislation as regards the performance and termination of their office, and the manner in which a person is accountable for disciplinary issues would also differ.

The style, number, and type of judges have differed over the centuries but the modern English Legal System now has a relatively fixed hierarchy of judicial appointments, both full- and part-time. It should be noted at the outset however that recruiting to the judiciary is becoming increasingly challenging, with many vacancies being left unfilled in recent appointment rounds. For example, there are currently vacancies in the High Court, the Family Court, and on the Circuit Bench, and problems are also beginning to emerge at District Bench level.[1] The primary reason for the increasing number of unfilled vacancies is that potential judges from the senior ranks of the legal professions are not applying in sufficient numbers because the judicial role is being viewed as increasingly unattractive. Whilst judicial salaries may appear high (see 8.6), they are significantly lower than top solicitors or QCs can earn in practice. Moreover, changes to tax and pensions that were introduced in 2015 have reduced the total net remuneration for judges by between 21 and 36 per cent compared to a decade ago (this equates to £80,000 less for a new High Court Judge).[2] Other issues are also at play, including 'inadequate administrative and IT support for judges in the courts, a significant increase in workload, inflexible working patterns, inadequate rewards for judges taking on leadership roles, and a large-scale breakdown in trust in the government.'[3] Whilst the government has attempted to mitigate the recruitment crisis by introducing a temporary recruitment and retention allowance for High Court, Circuit, and Upper Tribunal judges,[4] this is unlikely to fix the unprecedented recruitment challenges in the long-term. The challenge in judicial recruitment is significant and complex, and it is in this context that you should read this chapter.

The modern judiciary has been divided into six pay grades (although there is some subdivision) and this illustrates their relevant place within the hierarchy. Table 8.1 lists the key judicial appointments in each grade. It also, out of simplicity, states where each judge will ordinarily sit and how they are referred to in court. This grading of judges looks quite complicated but, as will be seen in this chapter, it is key to the way that the judiciary are now deployed. As has been noted already, the court judiciary and tribunal judiciary are being brought closer together and some of the particularities of this will be discussed later in this chapter.

Broadly speaking, the judiciary can be divided into three categories:

1. **Senior judiciary.** These are the most senior roles, carrying with them judicial leadership functions.

2. **Superior judiciary.** These are judges who sit, as of right, in the higher courts (High Court of Justice and above).

3. **Inferior judiciary.** This is all other judges.

---

1. Ministry of Justice, 'Government acts urgently to protect judicial recruitment' (June 2019) <https://www.gov.uk/government/news/government-acts-urgently-to-protect-judicial-recruitment>.

2. Review Body on Senior Salaries, *Supplement to the Fortieth Annual Report on Senior Salaries 2018 (Report No 90)—Major Review of the Judicial Salary Structure* (SSRB 2018) <https://assets.publishing.service.gov.uk/government/uploads/system/uploads/attachment_data/file/750331/supplement-fortieth-annual-report-senior-salaries-2018.pdf> 1.

3. ibid.

4. Ministry of Justice, 'Government acts urgently to protect judicial recruitment' (June 2019) <https://www.gov.uk/government/news/government-acts-urgently-to-protect-judicial-recruitment>.

Table 8.1 Judicial appointments

Grade	Judicial Title	Ordinarily sit in . . .	Referred to in court as . . .
1	Lord Chief Justice	Court of Appeal; High Court of Justice	My Lord/My Lady
1.1	Master of the Rolls	Court of Appeal	My Lord/My Lady
	President of the Supreme Court	Supreme Court	My Lord/My Lady
2	Chancellor of the High Court	High Court of Justice; Court of Appeal	My Lord/My Lady
	President of the Family Division	High Court of Justice; Court of Appeal	My Lord/My Lady
	President of the Queen's Bench Division	High Court of Justice; Court of Appeal	My Lord/My Lady
	Senior President of Tribunals	Court of Appeal; High Court; Upper Tribunal	My Lord (in courts); Sir (in Tribunals)
	Justices of the Supreme Court	Supreme Court	My Lord/My Lady
3	Lords (or Ladies) Justice of Appeal	Court of Appeal	My Lord/My Lady
4	Puisne judge	High Court of Justice	My Lord/My Lady
5	Circuit judges at the Old Bailey	Crown Court	My Lord/My Lady[5]
	Vice-President of the Upper Tribunal	Upper Tribunal	Sir or Madam
	Presidents of the First-Instance Tribunal Chambers	First-instance tribunal	Sir or Madam
	Senior Circuit judges	Crown Court; county court	Your Honour
	Senior district judge (chief magistrate)	Magistrates' court	Sir or Madam
6.1	Circuit judges	Crown Court; county court	Your Honour
	Deputy Chamber Presidents of the First-Tier Tribunal	First-Tier Tribunal	Your Honour
	Upper Tribunal judges	Upper Tribunal	Sir or Madam
6.2	Deputy senior district judge (magistrates' court)	Magistrates' court	Sir or Madam
	Immigration judges	Upper Tribunal; First-Tier Tribunal	Sir or Madam
7	District judges	County court; High Court of Justice	Sir or Madam
	District judges (magistrates' court)	Magistrates' court	Sir or Madam
	First-Tier Tribunal judges.	First-Tier Tribunal.	Sir or Madam

8.1.1 **Senior judiciary**

The senior judiciary are those that are listed as 'senior judges' in statute.[6] However, to this the Senior President of Tribunals should also be added (although his office has not yet been added to the statutory list). It is clear from Table 8.1 that the Senior President

---

5. *Constitutional Reform Act 2005*, s 60.
6. Whilst circuit judges are ordinarily referred to as 'Your Honour', all circuit judges in the Old Bailey are, for historical reasons, called 'My Lord' or 'My Lady'.

now ranks with the Heads of Division (see later) and indeed, under statute, the Senior President technically ranks alongside the Lord Chief Justice in terms of judicial leadership[7] (the Lord Chief Justice being responsible for the court judiciary and the Senior President being responsible for the tribunal judiciary).

The senior judiciary for our purposes[8] are therefore:

- Lord Chief Justice of England and Wales (who is also *President of the Courts of England & Wales*)
- Master of the Rolls (who is also the *Head of Civil Justice*)
- President of the Supreme Court
- Supreme Court Justices
- President of the Family Division (who is also the Head of Family Justice)
- Chancellor of the High Court
- President of the Queen's Bench Division
- Senior President of Tribunals.

8.1.1.1 **Lord Chief Justice**

The Lord Chief Justice has always been the most senior professional judge but, following the changes to the role of the Lord Chancellor, he became the head of the judiciary with the title *President of the Courts of England and Wales*.[9] As President of the courts, he can sit in any of the courts as of right, although traditionally he restricts himself to the Court of Appeal, High Court of Justice, and Crown Courts. The Supreme Court is not one of 'his' courts because it is a UK court, but the Lord Chief Justice is entitled to sit in the Supreme Court as an additional member if requested by the President of the Supreme Court.[10] However, this has happened relatively rarely since the Supreme Court has come into existence.

The Lord Chief Justice was, by tradition, given a peerage upon appointment. However, following the constitutional reforms to the House of Lords and the removal of professional judges from the House of Lords it was thought unlikely that this position would continue, in part because by statute, the title remains 'Lord Chief Justice' regardless of whether the holder was a peer or not.[11] However, the practice of peerages upon appointment has continued despite the reforms, with the exception of the current Lord Chief Justice, Lord Burnett of Maldon. He was the first Lord Chief Justice since the nineteenth century not to be given a peerage upon appointment when he was sworn in on 1 October 2017, with his peerage being delayed (without explanation) until 30 October 2017.

The Lord Chief Justice was traditionally the head of criminal justice and the CRA 2005 makes him titular *Head of Criminal Justice*.[12] The Act does, however, provide for a deputy head in order to allow the Lord Chief Justice to delegate some of the administrative authority and this person will be someone who is a Lord or Lady Justice of Appeal.[13] Currently it is Dame Victoria Sharp DBE, who is also President of the Queen's Bench Division.

---

7. *Tribunals, Courts and Enforcement Act 2007*, s 2 and sch 1.
8. The senior judiciary in Scotland and Northern Ireland have not been included in the list.
9. *Constitutional Reform Act 2005*, s 7(1).
10. ibid, s 38(1).
11. A comparison could perhaps be drawn to Northern Ireland where the Lord Chief Justice is so called but is actually a knight (the current holder being Sir Declan Morgan). It is also notable that the title remains Lord Chief Justice even if a female holds it, so it would become 'Lady X, Lord Chief Justice of England & Wales'.
12. *Constitutional Reform Act 2005*, s 8.
13. ibid, s 8(4)(h).

8.1.1.2 **Master of the Rolls**

The Master of the Rolls, along with the President of the Supreme Court, ranks joint second to the Lord Chief Justice in precedence and is traditionally the head of the Court of Appeal (Civil Division) and, following the *Courts Act 2003* (CA 2003), was created the *Head of Civil Justice*.[14] The current Master of the Rolls is Sir Terence Etherton. The 'Rolls' in his title reflects the fact that historically the Master of the Rolls was the clerk responsible for maintaining the rolls and records of the Chancery Court. This responsibility was later transferred to the Public Records Office under ministerial responsibility but the ancient title remains.

The CA 2003 permits a Deputy Head of Civil Justice to be created in order to assist the Master of the Rolls in his work (currently it is Lord Justice Coulson).

8.1.1.3 **President of the Supreme Court**

Historically the House of Lords, the predecessor to the Supreme Court, did not have a dedicated president: the judge who had served the longest was considered the 'senior' and thus administratively responsible for the allocation of judges to individual cases.

This changed on 6 June 2000 when Lord Bingham was 'promoted' to the House of Lords to become Senior Law Lord (the promotion carrying with it a pay cut). It was said at the time that creating a Senior Law Lord would bring a more professional management approach to the judicial committee with someone being designated as its head. This was important in the preparatory work for its transformation into the Supreme Court.

The CRA 2005 formalized this approach and created a *President of the Supreme Court*[15] (currently Lord Reed) and a deputy (currently Lord Hodge). The President and Deputy President have administrative responsibilities over, for example, the judicial operation of the Supreme Court, and the President superintends the Chief Executive for the administrative operation of the Supreme Court.[16] The President also has the power to issue rules and practice directions[17] and these regulate the proceedings of the Supreme Court. The President and Deputy President are responsible for allocating the justices to each case but there is no requirement that either of them preside over every case, and indeed there are a number of occasions when they do not sit, even where the court constitutes a bench of seven (eg *R v Rollins*).[18]

When Lady Hale was appointed President of the Supreme Court in September 2017 (succeeding Lord Neuberger), she was the first woman in this role. This continued her succession of firsts, following her appointment as the first—and only—female Lord of Appeal in Ordinary (the previous judicial title for Justices of the Supreme Court when they sat as the Appellate Committee in the House of Lords) in 2004, the first woman appointed to the newly established Supreme Court in 2009, and the first female Deputy President of the Supreme Court in 2013.[19] Lady Hale retired from the Supreme Court in January 2020.

It should be noted that the President of the Supreme Court, together with the Justices of the Supreme Court, are not judges of England and Wales, as the Supreme Court has UK jurisdiction. However, they are included here for completeness.

---

14. CA 2003, s 62(1).
15. *Constitutional Reform Act 2005*, s 23(5).
16. ibid, s 48.
17. ibid, s 45.
18. [2010] UKSC 39.
19. Erika Rackley, 'First Woman President of the UK Supreme Court, Brenda Hale, 2017' in Erika Rackley and Rosemary Auchmuty (eds), *Women's Legal Landmarks: Celebrating the History of Women and Law in the UK and Ireland* (Hart Publishing 2018) 645–50.

8.1.1.4 Justices of the Supreme Court

The ordinary judges of the Supreme Court are referred to as the *Justices of the Supreme Court*[20] and their number is currently fixed at twelve[21] which was the same number as the Law Lords. That said, the *Crime and Courts Act 2013* altered this to a reference for the equivalent of twelve full-time judges. This was part of a wider process of permitting part-time judicial appointments, including potentially by job-share (discussed at 8.4.2.2).

The first justices of the Supreme Court were the existing Law Lords at the time of its creation.[22] At the time the Court was created Lord Scott was due to retire and Lord Clarke, the then Master of the Rolls, became the first Justice of the Supreme Court to be appointed direct to the Supreme Court. Law Lords were peers and thus upon their appointment they became Lord or Lady [n]. Lord Clarke had been given a peerage prior to his appointment and thus all the original justices were peers. The first appointment not to be appointed a peer was Sir John Dyson, and for a few months he sat as Sir John Dyson JSC. This was the subject of some criticism, the argument being that differentiating between titles could lead to a perception that the non-ennobled justice was somehow less worthy than the others.[23] Eventually the Queen gave her consent to adopt the procedure traditionally used in Scotland for their senior judges, where they were given the honorific title 'Lord' or 'Lady' but without formally being made a peer. Sir John Dyson promptly became Lord Dyson and the same procedure has been adopted for each of the new justices.

Additional judges

The fact that there are only twelve justices can cause difficulties in terms of the work-load of the court, especially where there are vacancies. For much of the year 2011/12 the Supreme Court operated with only ten justices due to the vacancy caused by the retirement of Lord Collins not being filled for several months until Lord Sumption assumed office, and also because of the illness and death of Lord Rodger. The CRA allows for the President to ask for 'additional judges' to work in the Supreme Court, of which there are two classes:[24]

- a person who holds 'office as a senior territorial judge' (which is defined as a judge of the Court of Appeal in England (which, of course, will include the Heads of Division and the Lord Chief Justice)) or the equivalent in Scotland and Northern Ireland;[25] and

- a member of the supplementary panel under s 39 (ie a former justice of the Supreme Court (or senior territorial judge)) who has retired but is not yet 75 but only if he is appointed to the Panel by the President.[26]

Lords of Appeal in Ordinary

Whilst they no longer exist, it is of historical interest to note that the judges of the House of Lords were known as the Lords of Appeal in Ordinary, although they are often referred to as the Law Lords. The 'in ordinary' meant they were remunerated for their work. Each judge was granted a life peerage upon appointment, becoming *Baron*

---

20. *Constitutional Reform Act 2005*, s 23(6).
21. ibid, s 23(2).
22. ibid, s 24.
23. Phillip Morgan, 'Don't Let Politicians Dangle Baubles in Front of Judges' *The Times* (24 June 2010).
24. *Constitutional Reform Act 2005*, s 38(1).
25. ibid, s 38(8).
26. ibid, s 38(4).

or *Baroness X*. Technically any judge who held, or had held, a high judicial office within the meaning of the *Appellate Jurisdiction Act 1876* and who was also a peer could sit in the House of Lords. This included retired Law Lords, the current and retired Lord Chief Justices, and certain Masters of the Rolls.

8.1.1.5 Heads of Division

In Chapter 6 it was noted that the High Court is divided into three divisions (Queen's Bench, Family, and Chancery). Each division has a Head of Division, although prior to the CRA 2005 only the *President of the Family Division* was a Head of Division as of right. The President of the Family Division is now also the Head of Family Justice. A deputy (who must be a Lord Justice of Appeal) can also be created.

The CRA 2005 created the new offices of the *President of the Queen's Bench Division* and the *Chancellor of the High Court*. Prior to the 2005 Act the Lord Chief Justice was President of the Queen's Bench Division, but this new office recognizes the fact that, now the Lord Chief Justice is the head of the judiciary, a new Head of Division is required to oversee the work. Judge LJ (as he then was), who previously held the honorific title of *Deputy Chief Justice* (which was neither a statutory office nor remunerated differently to a Lord Justice) became the first holder of this post (in 2008 he was subsequently promoted to be Lord Chief Justice). The Lord Chancellor was also the president of the Chancery Division but there existed a *Vice-Chancellor* who was a de facto Head of Division. The 2005 Act has renamed this office the *Chancellor of the High Court* to reflect the fact that the Lord Chancellor no longer has any judicial responsibilities.

8.1.1.6 Senior President of Tribunals

A Senior President of Tribunals is created by s 2 *Tribunals, Courts and Enforcement Act 2007* (TCEA 2007). Originally the Senior President was to be appointed by the Lord Chief Justice but the statute now requires that appointment is made by the Queen on advice of the Lord Chancellor.[27] The CRA 2005 has now been amended and the Senior President is a post that the *Judicial Appointments Commission* should now fill.[28] The fact that the Senior President is a UK post is reflected by the fact that the Commission must consult the Lord Chief Justice of England and Wales, Lord President of the Court of Session (Scotland), and the Lord Chief Justice of Northern Ireland.[29]

The first Senior President was (the then) Carnwath LJ who had been the Senior President (designate) for several years while the legislation was being drafted, ie he existed in 'shadow' form in that he had no formal statutory role but assumed a de facto role that was extremely important in the transition of tribunal justice to a parallel system of court justice. The expertise that he brought and the ability to undertake this complex role (even in times when there was no statutory role) was rewarded by his being appointed to the Supreme Court.

When Lord Carnwath was appointed to the Supreme Court there was a delay in appointing his successor and there was some talk about whether the role would be filled or subsumed within, as for example, the role of the Lord Chief Justice. However, ultimately Sullivan LJ was appointed to the post, although following his appointment he

27. *Tribunals, Courts and Enforcement Act 2007*, s 2(1).
28. *Constitutional Reform Act 2005*, s 75B.
29. ibid, s 75B(3).

styled himself as Sir Jeremy Sullivan, Senior President of Tribunals, presumably partly because he had responsibility for the tribunals in devolved countries and so the style 'Lord Justice' would be inappropriate. The same approach has been adopted by successive Senior Presidents of the Tribunals. For example, the current President Sir Keith Lindblom, who is also a Lord Justice of Appeal. When sitting in the Court of Appeal, he is known as Lord Justice Lindblom, but when sitting in the tribunals he is known as Sir Keith Lindblom.

The responsibilities of the Senior President include coordinating the work of tribunals and, in particular, representing the views of the tribunal judiciary.[30] In order to discharge this duty the Senior President has the statutory power to lay written representations before Parliament[31] and he does not need the permission of, for example, the Lord Chief Justice to do so. This gives the Senior President proper power as President in his own right and not as a delegate of the Lord Chief Justice.

It is no accident that all of the Senior Presidents have been Lord Justices of Appeal given that the head of the EAT and *Asylum and Immigration Tribunal* are both puisne judges. Whilst the Presidents continue to have leadership within their own tribunals the post of Senior President is obviously central to their coordination and the unification of tribunal justice (and its integration into the wider judiciary).

8.1.2 **Superior judiciary**

Those judges who are considered to be superior judges are:

- Justices of the Supreme Court (discussed at 8.1.1.4 as they are also members of the Senior Judiciary)
- Lord Justices of Appeal
- puisne judges.

These are judges who sit, as of right, in the higher courts—the High Court and above. Superior judges have unlimited jurisdiction in that their jurisdiction is not limited specifically by statute. In practice this means that they can use something called the *inherent jurisdiction*, ie the common-law powers, and unless a rule of law or statute limits the jurisdiction of the courts in a particular way the judges have the right to act as they deem fit.

≔ Example Unlimited authority

A simple, but perhaps illustrative, example of the difference in authority can be seen by where a judge sits. An inferior judge can only sit in a designated court—ie one that has been approved by the Ministry of Justice as a court. However, in *St Edmundsbury & Ipswich Board of Finance v Clark*[32] Megarry J decided that he had an inherent power to sit anywhere.[33] The use of the inherent power was permitted because the judicial authority for a superior judge arises from his office, whereas the judicial authority for an inferior judge arises from the court. The judge therefore sat in Iken village hall to hear the evidence of a witness. The judge also,

---

30. *Tribunals, Courts and Enforcement Act 2007*, sch 1, pt 4.
31. ibid.
32. [1973] Ch 323.
33. ibid, 327.

as a safeguard, asked the Lord Chancellor to designate the town as a place where the High Court could sit,[34] but Megarry J was adamant that this was merely a 'fail-safe' procedure and through the use of the inherent jurisdiction he could sit anywhere.

8.1.2.1 Lord Justices of Appeal

The ordinary judges of the Court of Appeal are known as Lords or Lady Justices of Appeal.[35] Prior to the CA 2003 the statutory title for a judge of the Court of Appeal was Lord Justice of Appeal.[36] This meant that when Dame Elizabeth Butler-Sloss became the first female member of the Court of Appeal she was officially known as Her Ladyship, Lord Justice Butler-Sloss LJ. Sometime after her appointment, the Lord Chancellor and Lord Chief Justice issued a practice direction[37] which stated that for informal purposes she was to be known as Lady Justice Butler-Sloss, but it took until 2003 before the feminine alternative was formally permitted.

Upon appointment to the Court of Appeal a person is sworn in as a member of the Privy Council and is thus entitled to the prefix 'Rt Hon' but in court is styled *Lord/Lady Justice X*.

8.1.2.2 Puisne judges

Puisne judges (pronounced 'puny') is the formal name given to the ordinary judges of the High Court although in practice they tend to be referred to as 'High Court judges'. The term 'puisne' means lower rank and means that they are the lowest rank of the superior court judges. That said, all puisne judges rank above the inferior judges.

Puisne judges are given the honorific title 'Honourable' while they hold that rank and are referred to as Mr or Mrs Justice X—the full title, therefore, being the *Honourable Mr(s) Justice X*. Upon appointment they are also knighted or made Dames, something that happens in a private audience with the Queen rather than at a traditional investiture.[38]

8.1.3 Inferior judiciary

The inferior judges are so called because they do not exercise unlimited jurisdiction but instead their powers are defined by statute. Accordingly, if the statute does not prescribe any authority then they may not exercise any jurisdiction. For our purposes, the inferior judges that we will consider are:

- Circuit judges
- Recorders
- District judges and district judge (magistrates' court)
- Tribunal judiciary.

Of these, most attention in this chapter will be focused on circuit judges since, as will be seen, these are the most directly comparable to puisne judges. Circuit and puisne judges are the two grades of judge who primarily undertake first-instance trials in the court. Their status is, however, markedly different.

---

34. ibid, 328.
35. *Courts Act 2003*, s 63.
36. *Supreme Court Act 1981*, s 2(3).
37. *Practice Note (Mode of Address: Lord Justice Butler-Sloss)* [1994] 1 FLR 866.
38. Robin Dunn, *Sword and Wig: Memoirs of a Lord Justice* (Quiller Press 1993) 184. As there is no female equivalent to a Knight Bachelor, female puisne judges are awarded the DBE (Dame of the British Empire), meaning that they 'rank' their male counterparts in terms of etiquette.

8.1.3.1 **Circuit judges**

The office of circuit judge is relatively modern, being created by s 16 *Courts Act 1971*, although prior to this other judicial appointments did exist, including the county court judge although this was a civil judge. The office of circuit judge now spans both civil and criminal work and a judge can expect to sit on both types of work. When a judge is appointed he is assigned to one of the six circuits and he will, especially when quite junior, spend time sitting at the various courts within the circuit. As a judge becomes more senior it is more likely that he will sit primarily in one or two courts although they can, at any time, be asked to sit in other courts within the circuit where it is necessary to do so.

Each court centre has a resident judge, who is in administrative control of the criminal list and that judge will normally be the senior judge of that centre. Some resident judges (in the largest court centres) are paid extra for this role and are designated as senior circuit judges: the other resident judges are not paid extra and the role tends to rotate according to seniority. The resident judge has recently been joined by the designated judges who have similar responsibility for the civil work. There are two types of designated judge: the designated family and designated civil judges. Along with the administrative responsibilities, the designated judges will frequently hear High Court-level work. As with resident judges, at the major court centres the designated judges will be paid as senior circuit judges.

Some circuit judges also bear the title *recorder*. This can be a source of confusion for law students as a recorder can be either one of the most junior judicial roles or the title given to the most senior circuit judges, and it is best not to confuse the two! Where it is the senior circuit judge, the term is honorary recorder and it is an office that has existed for many years although traditionally only three full-time posts existed: those of London, Manchester, and Liverpool. These recorderships are substantive posts (ie the posts are specifically advertised as such) and they are automatically senior circuit judges.[39] In the passing of the CA 1971, Parliament had specifically retained the power of local authorities to grant an honorary recordership of the borough.[40] Theoretically this power was vested in the local authority (because the holder of the office becomes a borough dignity, second only in precedence to the lord mayor) but in practice it is made in consultation with the senior presiding judge. No increase in pay is given to the (local) honorary recorders but those appointed have all tended to be the senior judge in the larger court centres (eg Middlesbrough, Bristol, Plymouth) and so were all paid as senior resident judges in any event. The local honorary recorder is not, however, a substantive post and it lapses upon the retirement of the resident judge, when the judge moves to another circuit, or if it was for a determinate period of time. It is for the local authority to decide if, and when, it should be granted again. In recent years the Lord Chief Justice has encouraged the appointment of honorary recorders and their numbers do seem to have expanded.

All circuit judges are styled *His (or Her) Honour Judge X* and upon retirement are entitled to the honorific His or Her Honour. Honorary recorders who are also senior circuit judges wear a different robe (it is red) and are referred to as 'My Lord' or 'My Lady' in court (although ordinarily only when in the town they are recorder of). Upon retirement they keep only the honorific His or Her Honour as with all circuit judges.

---

39.   Historically the recorders of London, Liverpool, and Manchester were knighted on appointment although this appears to have lapsed as neither the recorder of Liverpool nor Manchester are currently knights.

40.   *Courts Act 1971*, s 54.

8.1.3.2 **Recorders**

The second type of recorder is more common and is a part-time judicial role held by practising lawyers. The office, like the circuit judge, is relatively modern and was created by s 21 CA 1971 although part-time roles previously existed,[41] including those bearing the title recorder and assistant recorder. A recorder can be appointed to hear either civil or criminal cases but they are restricted to circuit-bench work. Thus, their jurisdiction is broadly similar to that of circuit judges, however, they will usually handle the less complex cases that come before the court.

A recorder is styled as *Mr or Mrs Recorder X* when in court but is given no style or title when they are not sitting as recorders. They are referred to in court as 'Your Honour' since they are sitting as de facto circuit judges. They may continue in private practice. Recorders are expected to sit for thirty days a year.

8.1.3.3 **District judges**

The most junior judicial rank in the courts is that of the district judge. It is important at the outset to distinguish the district judge from the district judges (magistrates' court) with the former acting solely as a civil judge. Part-time district judges are also permitted and are known as deputy district judges.

The district judge deals with the majority of cases in the county court so will normally hear procedural and interlocutory matters but they also hear nearly all of the claims heard in the small claims court and some divorce matters. The role of the district judge (magistrates' court) is considered in more detail later in this chapter alongside the quasi-judicial role of lay magistrates (at 8.8.2).

District judges are styled *District Judge X* for the duration of their appointment and are not given any honorific title. They are referred to as 'Sir' or 'Madam' in court.

8.1.3.4 **The tribunal judiciary**

There are arguably three levels of judiciary in the tribunals:

- Chamber Presidents
- Upper Tribunal judges
- First-Tier Tribunal judges.

Upper Tribunal and First-Tier tribunal judges are relatively straightforward in terms of where they sit. Technically there is no difference between them in terms of their status as inferior judges. Whilst there is a (not insignificant) pay differential, an analogy could be drawn between a circuit judge and a district judge. Both are inferior judges, it is just the type of work that they do that will differ. The same is true of these judges.

One issue to note is that some tribunals, unlike courts, will sit as a mixed bench, that is to say a mixture of judicial and lay (non-judicial) staff. The latter are ordinarily experts in their respective fields (eg accountants, medical practitioners, surveyors, or those who have specialist knowledge of disability, discrimination, or the military). The legally qualified member will preside and they are the only members of the panel

---

41. These tended to be criminal-only appointments and were deputy judges of the assizes or Deputy Chairman of the Quarter Sessions.

who are given the honorific 'Judge'.[42] The other members of the tribunals are known as 'members' and are not technically part of the judiciary.

How the tribunals operate and what they do is considered in Chapter 7.

8.2 **Judicial dress**

One of the more distinctive elements of the English court system is the dress worn in courts. The dress of lawyers is discussed elsewhere (Chapter 10) but what of the judiciary? Traditionally the court judiciary, particularly puisne judges, had a wide range of judicial robes to wear but now the system of robes has been simplified.

Leaving aside the formal state robes a judge possesses (which are really only used for the ceremony at the start of each legal year) what is the working dress of the judiciary? The simplest of them all are the Justices of the Supreme Court. The justices do not sit in robes although they do have ceremonial robes that were newly created for the court. The robes are only worn at the opening of the court and at other ceremonial occasions. The Justices of the Supreme Court are following the tradition set by the House of Lords where no robes were worn, in part because the appellate and appeals committees were, in essence, comparable to other committees where no robes are worn.

Judges of the Court of Appeal used to sit in the Court of Appeal wearing a black silk robe (similar to that worn by Queen's Counsel) and a judicial wig. Following the *Practice Direction (Court Dress) (No 5) and Amendment No 20 to the Consolidated Criminal Practice Direction (Court Dress)*[43] judges in the Civil Division of the Court of Appeal will now wear a civil gown (with gold tabs at the neck) (discussed later) and no wig. The practice direction states that there is no change in the Criminal Division[44] so wigs and the black silk gown are worn.

Puisne judges' dress now differs according to their work. In civil matters, the civil gown (with red tabs at the neck) will be worn, but the President of the Family Division and President of the Court of Protection (the same person) has stated that no gown should ordinarily be worn in those proceedings save when they are in open court, something that rarely happens.[45] Puisne judges in criminal matters wear the 'winter' robe, which consists of a red robe, black scarf girdle, and a scarlet casting-hood or tippet (sash) worn with a judicial wig.

Circuit judges have a violet robe. Even for civil cases they will not wear the civil robe because during the consultation they indicated a preference to retain their robe. Quite why this was permitted is open to question since it would have made more sense for a single civil robe to be used rather than accede to the sartorial preferences of the circuit bench. However, wigs and collars will no longer be worn and, as noted earlier, no robe is to be worn in family matters. When sitting on criminal business, a circuit judge wears the lilac robe, a judicial wig, and a red tippet over their left shoulder.

District judges will ordinarily not sit in robes but when they sit in open court in the civil courts they will wear the civil robe (with blue tabs at the neck) and no wig. District judges (magistrates' court) will not wear a robe while in the magistrates' court but if they sit in the Crown Court they will wear a black silk gown and judicial wig.

42. As with district judges they gain no additional styling (cf His or Her Honour for circuit judges and the honorific 'Honourable' and knight/damehood for puisne judges). Thus when they retire they return to Mr or Mrs X.
43. [2008] 1 WLR 1700.
44. ibid, [5].
45. *Practice Note (Family Proceedings: Court Dress)* [2008] 1 WLR 1701.

For completeness it should be noted that recorders, as part-time members of the judiciary, wear the practitioner's robe of a barrister (silk if they are Queen's Counsel otherwise a stuff gown) and a practitioner's wig (when sitting in criminal matters) or no wig (when sitting on civil matters). They wear these robes even when the recorder is a solicitor.[46]

Tribunal judiciary do not wear any robes when they sit in tribunals. Where they sit in court, then they will wear their judicial robe if they hold a substantive judicial appointment[47] or, if they do not, then they would wear the same robes as a recorder.

8.2.1 Civil robe

The civil robe was introduced on 1 October 2008 and is a simple black robe that is worn without wig, band, wing collar, or a collarette. The 'rank' of the judge is set out on colour tabs worn at the neck of the gown as follows:

- Court of Appeal (inc Heads of Division)—gold
- High Court—red
- District judges—blue.

Members of the High Court Masters Group (which are analogous to district judges but for High Court civil work) wear pink tabs.

8.3 Judicial appointments

The process of choosing judges has been the source of some debate for many years and has recently changed to reflect the constitutional changes of the late 1990s and early 2000s. Traditionally judicial appointments, particular of superior judges, were clouded in mystery and secrecy with 'secret soundings' being normal. Lord Elwyn-Jones, the former Lord Chancellor, explained the process:

> When a vacancy had to be filled, the heads of the Divisions . . . were invited into my office to consider likely names. Usually we agreed as to the one most meriting appointment. Occasionally two names were equally supported. Then the choice was left to me.[48]

When the Lord Chancellor had decided on the appropriate person he would invite them in for a chat and ask whether they would accept a seat on the bench. It was comparatively rare for a person to refuse an appointment[49] although some did, either because they did not wish to cease to be an advocate or because they did not want the inevitable drop in pay.

The traditional system of appointing judges was increasingly said to be untenable, not least because of concerns that the 'old boys' network' was creating a non-diverse and non-representative judiciary. This resulted in two significant changes to the system of appointments. The first was the introduction of advertising for inferior judges, this being extended in 1998 to include the first advertisement for a High Court judge[50] and ultimately now for all posts. Whilst a useful first step, this was, at least initially, used only to create a 'long list' of suitable people from whom the Lord Chancellor could select a judge. Additionally, the Lord Chancellor retained the right to invite someone

255

---

46. It will be seen in Chapter 10 that it is discretionary for a solicitor to wear a wig.
47. Some chamber presidents are circuit judges and therefore they would wear the appropriate robe.
48. Frederick Elwyn-Jones, *In My Times: An Autobiography* (Weidenfeld & Nicolson 1983) 265.
49. David Pannick, *Judges* (OUP 1987) 9.
50. The advertisement was placed on 24 February.

who had not applied to take up a judgeship. The second important step towards accountability was the appointment of the Commissioners for Judicial Appointments who had the responsibility for auditing the appointment process. The Commissioners were independent of the government and published annual reports on the appointment process, the most critical of which was probably their first annual report,[51] although the 2003 review of the High Court competition was also critical and specifically stated that the idea of having a mix of invitations and advertisements was unfair.

Eventually the government published a consultation paper on the appointment of the judiciary, something that one commentator described as both 'logical and disappointing'.[52] Stevens argued that it was logical because the pressure for the reform of the judiciary had been building for a considerable time, and disappointing because, in his opinion, it led to a fudge whereby the integrity of the system is not as guaranteed as in other states, most notably through a lack of majority of laypersons. The CRA 2005 placed judicial appointments onto a statutory basis. Two schemes apply for constitutional reasons. The first applies to members of the Supreme Court and the second applies to all other judicial appointments.[53] The systems are actually comparable but the principal distinction is that the former is an ad hoc commission that is constituted when a member needs to be nominated whereas the latter is a permanent body.

What follows applies equally to the court and tribunal judiciary. As already noted, the tribunal judiciary (other than the Senior President of Tribunals) are inferior judges[54] and therefore they are appointed in the same way as other inferior judges. Lay members of tribunals are not considered here as they are not members of the judiciary.

8.3.1 Judicial Appointments Commission

Focusing on the appointments in England and Wales, the CRA 2005 created the *Judicial Appointments Commission* (JAC) which, unlike the first commission, has a role in the appointing of persons instead of just auditing the process. The *Crime and Courts Act 2013* (CCA 2013) made significant changes to the CRA 2005, principally removing all the procedural detail from statute into statutory instruments, where it is easier to change. Three regulations have been made under the 2013 Act:

- *Judicial Appointments Commission Regulations 2013*,[55] which set out the details of the Commission and how they work

- *Judicial Appointments Regulations 2013*,[56] which set out how judicial appointments will operate in practice

- *Supreme Court (Judicial Appointments) Regulations 2013*,[57] which, as their name suggests, govern how justices of the Supreme Court are selected.

---

51.   Commission for Judicial Appointments, *Annual Report 2003* (JAC 2003).
52.   Robert Stevens, 'Reform in Haste and Repent at Leisure: Iolanthe, the Lord High Executioner and Brave New World' (2004) 24 *Legal Studies* 1, 22.
53.   For clarity this does not include appointments to the magistracy since these are not technically a judicial appointment. Magistrates are discussed later in the chapter at 8.8.
54.   It has been mooted that there is no reason why judges of the Employment Appeal Tribunal should principally be court judges, and they could be appointed tribunal judges in their own right. As EAT judges include puisne judges, there is no reason why a superior (tribunal) judge could not be appointed as a tribunal judge.
55.   SI 2013/2191.
56.   SI 2013/2192.
57.   SI 2013/2193.

The JAC itself consists of fifteen members, including the chair.[58] The remaining fourteen members are allocated accordingly:

- seven judicial members
- five lay members
- two practising or employed lawyers.[59]

There are quite detailed rules on how these posts are to be filled, particularly the judicial members. Table 8.2 sets out who the members are. The chair must always be non-legally qualified[60] and thus there is a majority of non-judicial members within the JAC, although not a majority of lay members.[61] The JAC's independence is also shown by the fact that the Commissioners may not be civil servants,[62] this being considered an important feature of judicial independence.

Commissioners are recommended by the Lord Chancellor after an appointment process,[63] although that does not apply to the Lord Justice of Appeal, puisne judge Commissioners, and the senior tribunal Commissioner. For the former, the Judges' Council appoints these,[64] and for the latter the Tribunal Judges' Council chooses.[65]

Table 8.2 Judicial Appointments Commission members

Commissioner Type	Description
Judicial Commissioners	1 Lord Justice of Appeal
	1 puisne judge
	1 senior tribunal office-holder[66]
	1 circuit judge
	1 district judge of a county court, district judge (magistrates' court), or Master of the High Court of Justice
	1 first-instance tribunal judge[67]
	1 non-legally qualified judicial member
Lawyer Commissioners	2 lawyers, meaning a barrister, solicitor, or fellow of CILEx, but they may not hold the same qualification[68]
Lay members	5 who have never held judicial office, never been an employment tribunal member, or have never practised or been employed as a lawyer

58. *Judicial Appointments Commission Regulations 2013*, reg 3.
59. ibid, reg 4.
60. *Constitutional Reform Act 2005*, sch 12.
61. There will be six lay (non-legal) members compared to nine judicial or lawyer appointments.
62. *Constitutional Reform Act 2005*, sch 12.
63. *Judicial Appointments Commission Regulations 2013*, reg 9.
64. ibid, reg 10. The 'Judges' Council' is not a statutory body and instead is a body that is constituted by the Lord Chief Justice. It consists of the senior judges and those selected to represent certain constituencies. The current list of members is available on the online resources.
65. ibid, reg 11. The Tribunal Judges' Council is, as its name suggests, the equivalent for the tribunal judiciary and it is empanelled under the authority of the Senior President of Tribunals.
66. This means a judge of the Upper Tribunal, a chamber president of the first-instance or Upper Tribunal, or president of the Employment Tribunals in either England or Scotland *Judicial Appointments Commission Regulations 2013*, reg 5.
67. This means a judge of the First-Tier Tribunal, regional employment judge, or an employment judge (*Judicial Appointments Commission Regulations 2013*, reg 4(3)).
68. *Judicial Appointments Commission Regulations 2013*, reg 4(4)(5). Thus there could be a solicitor and barrister, or solicitor and CILEx, or barrister and CILEx etc but not two barristers or two solicitors.

Commissioners are to be appointed for not more than five years at a time and may not serve as a Commissioner for a period of ten years or more, consecutively or otherwise.[69] Those Commissioners who do not hold judicial office are remunerated, the others are not.

The principal work of the JAC is, of course, the appointment of the judiciary and the mechanisms by which this should occur. The *Judicial Appointments Regulations 2013*[70] set out five different forms of selection procedures:

- Selection of the Lord Chief Justice
- Selection of the Heads of Division
- Selection of the Senior President of Tribunals
- Selection of Lord Justices of Appeal
- Selection of puisne judges and all other judicial appointments.

The subsequent sections of this chapter will consider the manner of appointment, albeit briefly.

8.3.2 Selection of the Lord Chief Justice

The first selection process is to select the Lord Chief Justice (LCJ). A panel to appoint the LCJ must consist of five members,[71] who shall be:

1. The chair of the Commission[72]
2. The most senior England and Wales Supreme Court judge (or their nominee)[73]
3. A lay member of the Commission selected by the chair
4. A member of the Commission selected by the chair after consultation with the Lord Chief Justice
5. An England and Wales Supreme Court, Head of Division, or Lord Justice of Appeal chosen by the Lord Chief Justice.

Where there is no Lord Chief Justice (the appointments panel should begin before an LCJ retires, so realistically this means where the LCJ has died or is incapacitated), then the Supreme Court judge mentioned in #2 exercises those functions for the establishment of the panel.

The language of the fourth person is interesting. It does not say that it must be a judicial member of the Commission, merely a member. However, by saying that the Lord Chief Justice must be consulted (although it does not say that the LCJ has any sort of veto), it is perhaps suggesting it should be a judicial appointee.

When choosing any of the members, the person making the choice must have regard to the 'desirability' of the panel to include 'both women and men' and 'members drawn

---

69. ibid, reg 17.
70. SI 2013/2192.
71. *Judicial Appointments Regulations 2013*, reg 5(1).
72. Where the chair is vacant or the post-holder is incapacitated or unavailable the chair will be selected by the five lay members.
73. *Judicial Appointments Regulations 2013*, reg 5(5). This is the most senior justice (by appointment) of the Supreme Court who, before appointment, was a member of the English judiciary.

from a range of different racial groups'.[74] It may seem extraordinary to consider this only 'desirable' but it is perhaps a reflection of the judiciary. As at least two, and probably three, members will be from the senior judiciary, it may not be possible to always choose a female or someone who is black or from a minority ethnic background. That said, this makes the initial appointment of the Commissioners even more important.

Where any of the members would otherwise apply for the position of Lord Chief Justice (and it is quite possible that a Supreme Court judge, Head of Division, or Lord Justice of Appeal may choose to do so) then they must obviously stand down, although it is likely that, save for the Supreme Court judge, they would be chosen in the first place as they would have discussed this with the current Lord Chief Justice informally.

The selection panel shall determine how the process will take place,[75] meaning that they will decide whether the post is advertised, for how long, what sort of exercise will be required etc. They will then select a single preferred candidate and forward this to the Lord Chancellor.[76] There are then three stages:

Stage One. Where a person has been selected for appointment as Lord Chief Justice

Stage Two. Where a person has been selected following a rejection or reconsideration

Stage Three. Where a person has been selected following a rejection or reconsideration at stage two.[77]

At stage one, the Lord Chancellor has three options:

1. Accept the selection
2. Reject the selection
3. Require the selection panel to reconsider its decision.[78]

A rejection is an outright refusal to accept that person. The Lord Chancellor may only do this where he believes 'the person selected is not suitable for the office concerned'.[79] Written reasons must be provided to the panel for doing this.[80] It does not say whether the applicant will be told the reason for that rejection and it does raise an interesting question about whether the decision is challengeable. It would certainly be (politically) difficult to judicially review the decision, but it is probably susceptible to review even if it is highly unlikely a candidate will do so.

The power to order the panel to reconsider can only be given if 'there is not enough evidence that the person is suitable for the Office of Lord Chief Justice', or 'there is evidence that the person is not the best candidate on merit'.[81] Again, this would seem to be more of a fig-leaf then anything else, because who would determine whether the Lord Chancellor is right or wrong? Would a prospective candidate for the office of Lord Chief Justice really pursue legal action to establish their right to become the President of the Court? Could such a person be tenable as LCJ?

At stage two, the Lord Chancellor has the same three options, but they can only reject the selection if it was made following a reconsideration at stage one, and they can

74. *Judicial Appointments Regulations 2013*, reg 5(16).
75. *Constitutional Reform Act 2005*, s 70(2).
76. *Judicial Appointments Regulations 2013*, reg 7.
77. ibid, reg 8(1).
78. ibid, reg 8(2).
79. ibid, reg 9(1).
80. ibid, reg 9(3).
81. ibid, reg 2(2).

only ask the panel to reconsider if the candidate was rejected at stage one.[82] This is a slightly convoluted way of saying the following:

> If at stage one, the panel were asked to reconsider, then the Lord Chancellor can either only accept the new recommendation or reject it. He cannot ask the panel to reconsider.

At stage three the Lord Chancellor must accept the recommendation, unless he decides to appoint a person who was previously selected but not put forward again, following reconsideration.[83] This would be extremely rare but an example would be:

> Somebody LJ and Anybody LJ apply to become Lord Chief Justice. The selection panel prefer Somebody LJ and they nominate him at stage one. The Lord Chancellor asks them to reconsider. They do so, but decide that they will still nominate Somebody LJ.
>
> At stage two, the Lord Chancellor again asks them to reconsider. This time, they decide that Anybody LJ is to be preferred.
>
> At stage three, the Lord Chancellor decides that actually Somebody LJ was better and appoints him.

It would be extremely inglorious for this to happen and it would be interesting to know what the Judicial Appointments Commission would make of it. Nothing requires the procedure to be secret and it is likely therefore that if the JAC were annoyed that the Lord Chancellor had rejected their selection, they could presumably say so publicly. Whilst, to the best of our knowledge, no senior judge has been rejected by the Lord Chancellor, in 2010 it was reported that the then Lord Chancellor (Rt Hon Jack Straw MP) asked the JAC to reconsider their proposal in respect of a Head of Division. They nominated the same person again, and he decided not to reject them.

8.3.3 Selection of a Head of Division

The selection of a Head of Division operates on a very similar basis, but the selection panel differs. It again consists of five persons but this time it is:[84]

1. The Lord Chief Justice or his nominee
2. The most senior England and Wales Supreme Court judge or their nominee
3. Chairman of the JAC, or their nominee (who must be a lay commissioner)[85]
4. A lay member of the JAC designated by the person appointed as #3
5. A person designated by the Lord Chief Justice, in consultation with the Chair of the Commission, who must be a judicial Commissioner.[86]

Where it is a nominee for #1 or #2, the nominee must be an England and Wales Supreme Court judge, Head of Division, or Lord Justice of Appeal.[87] This time, it is the Lord Chief Justice who will preside over the panel,[88] which does leave open the question as to why there is a chair of the JAC if they will not actually chair appointment panels.

When the panel reports, the Lord Chancellor has the same three options as he did under the Lord Chief Justice appointment.[89]

---

82. ibid, reg 8(2).
83. ibid, reg 8(5).
84. ibid, reg 11.
85. ibid, reg 11(11).
86. ibid, reg 11(12).
87. ibid, reg 11(10).
88. ibid, reg 11(14).
89. ibid, reg 14.

8.3.4 **Senior President of Tribunals**

The appointment of the Senior President of Tribunals is very similar to the previous one, but the panel this time is as follows:[90]

1. The Lord Chief Justice or the Lord Chief Justice's nominee
2. A person designated by the Lord Chief Justice
3. Chairman of the JAC
4. A lay member of the JAC designated by the Chair of the JAC
5. A judicial member of the JAC[91] appointed by the Lord Chief Justice.

The rules for who is the person appointed as #2 are somewhat more complicated. They must be:

(a) a person who has held but does not currently hold the office of Senior President of Tribunals

(b) a person who holds, or who has held, office as Chamber President of a chamber of the First-Tier or Upper Tribunal

(c) a person who has been a judge of the Employment Appeals Tribunal

(d) a person who has been the President of Employment Tribunals in either England or Scotland

(e) a person who holds, who has held, 'an office that, in the opinion of the Lord Chief Justice, is such that a holder of it would acquire knowledge or experience of tribunals broadly similar to those above'.[92]

This is interesting because the Senior President of Tribunals is a UK office and yet the members of the panel will generally come from the English jurisdiction. By statute, the Senior President of Tribunals does not need to be an English judge,[93] although all three Senior Presidents to-date have been Lord Justices of Appeal. The Lord Chief Justice is required to consult the Lord President of the Court of Session and the Lord Chief Justice of Northern Ireland[94] (who are his equivalents), but there is nothing that provides them with a veto.

The same three options are open to the Lord Chancellor,[95] and it is notable that nothing appears to require the Lord Chancellor to consult his equivalents in Scotland or Northern Ireland, even though the judiciary is a devolved matter.

8.3.5 **Lord Justice of Appeal**

The same process is adopted, with the panel being:[96]

1. The Lord Chief Justice or nominee
2. A person designated by the Lord Chief Justice

---

90. ibid, reg 17.
91. Or its equivalent in Scotland or Northern Ireland: see ibid, reg 17(11).
92. ibid, reg 17(8).
93. *Tribunals, Courts and Enforcement Act 2007*, sch 1, pt 1(2)(b).
94. *Judicial Appointments Regulations 2013*, reg 17(9).
95. ibid, reg 20.
96. ibid, reg 23.

3. The Chairman of the JAC or a lay member of the JAC

4. A lay member of the JAC chosen by the Chair of the JAC

5. A person nominated by the Lord Chief Justice, in consultation with the Chair of the JAC.

The person chosen as #2 must be a Head of Division or Lord Justice of Appeal.[97] The following can be a person under #5:

(a) England and Wales Supreme Court judge

(b) Head of Division

(c) Senior President of Tribunals

(d) puisne judge of the High Court

(e) a judge holding an office under Sch 14, *Constitutional Reform Act 2005* (the principal court judiciary ranks)

(f) a member of the Commission who is not a Lord Justice of Appeal.[98]

Technically (f) means that it could be a lay member of the Commission but the preceding provisions make it more likely that it will be a judge. It is not clear why it does not have to be a judicial or lay commissioner of the JAC rather than more broad membership.

Once again, the Lord Chancellor has all three options.[99]

8.3.6 **All other judicial appointments**

The CRA 2005, as amended by the CCA 2013, creates a single scheme for all judicial appointments for or below the grade of puisne judges (although this does not change the distinction between superior and inferior judges). The process differs in that there is no statutory panel but, rather, it is for the JAC to decide how it will fill the vacancies and, presumably, constitute panels from the members within the JAC. The JAC reports back to the Lord Chief Justice who can accept or reject their selection or require the JAC to reconsider the selection.[100] An additional option also arises where the JAC decide that none of the applicants was suitable for appointment and decline to make a recommendation.[101] When this happens the Lord Chief Justice can ask the JAC to reconsider that decision.[102] In the Annual Report for 2015/16 the JAC reported that during that year the JAC recommended an individual for judicial office (they do not say what level) but the Lord Chancellor rejected the individual due to lack of particular experience required for the office.[103] This demonstrates that although the JAC is independent of the government it cannot be said that all judicial appointments are, since the Lord Chancellor, who is a senior government minister, has the power to reject the recommendation.

It is worth noting that the JAC must now establish a pool of persons who can be designated as deputy High Court judges or who are circuit judges asked to sit as High

---

97. ibid, reg 23(8).
98. ibid, reg 23(10).
99. ibid, reg 26.
100. ibid, reg 32.
101. ibid, reg 35(1).
102. ibid, reg 35(2).
103. Judicial Appointments Commission, *Annual Report and Accounts 2015–16* (JAC 2016) 14.

Court judges.[104] Traditionally the Lord Chief Justice could simply appoint someone as a 'section 9 judge' but now they must have been approved by the JAC to form a pool of judges who may be so authorized.[105]

8.3.7 **Appointment to the Supreme Court**

Appointments to the Supreme Court have to be kept separate because it is a court of the United Kingdom and not England and Wales, and the Acts of Union creating the United Kingdom guaranteed that the legal systems of Scotland and Northern Ireland would be preserved as sovereign systems in their own right. Therefore as a United Kingdom court, the Supreme Court cannot be under the direction of English procedures. As appointments are rare—there being only twelve justices in total—there is not a permanent commission but instead the Lord Chancellor must convene an ad hoc commission whenever he is notified that there will soon be a vacancy.[106]

The criteria for appointment to the Supreme Court mirror that of the House of Lords and is either holding high judicial office for a period of at least two years or having higher rights of audience for fifteen years.[107] Whilst the criteria expressly contemplate someone other than a judge being appointed (by reference to the rights of audience), this had not happened in the House of Lords in over sixty years[108] and many thought that only judges of the Court of Appeal (and their equivalent in Scotland and Northern Ireland) would be appointed. However, in recent years this has been proved not to be true. In 2011, Jonathan Sumption QC (as he then was) successfully applied to become a Justice of the Supreme Court. Whilst he had sat as both a recorder and a deputy High Court judge he had never sat in a full-time judicial role. In 2012 he was sworn in as a Justice of the Supreme Court having been appointed direct from the Bar and assumed the honorific title Lord Sumption.[109] Most recently in June 2020, Professor Andrew Burrows QC became the first Justice to be appointed direct from academia, having previously been a Professor of the Law of England at the University of Oxford. Like Lord Sumption, he had sat as both a recorder and a deputy High Court judge, but had never sat in a full-time judicial role prior to becoming a Justice of the Supreme Court.[110]

By convention two members of the Supreme Court are from Scotland and one from Northern Ireland. The CRA 2005 does not enshrine this convention into the statute although s 27(8) hints at it by stating:

> In making the selections for the appointment of judges of the Court the commission must ensure that between them the judges will have knowledge of, and experience in, the law of each part of the United Kingdom.

It is regrettable that this language should be employed as it would have been better to use precise language requiring a judge from each of the legal systems within the United Kingdom, but perhaps this phrase is sufficient to ensure the convention remains.

---

104. *Senior Courts Act 1981*, s 9.
105. *Judicial Appointments Regulations 2013*, pt 8.
106. *Constitutional Reform Act 2005*, s 26(5).
107. ibid, s 25(1).
108. Lords Reid and Radcliffe were appointed Lords of Appeal in Ordinary direct from the Bar in 1948 and 1949 respectively (Lord Reid from the Scottish Bar).
109. Lord Sumption retired in December 2018.
110. Supreme Court, 'Biographies of the Justices'<https://www.supremecourt.uk/about/biographies-of-the-justices.html> Lord Burrows.

The position in relation to having a member of the Supreme Court from Wales is less certain. Indeed, it will be remembered from Chapter 1 that traditionally Wales was part of the English Legal System but it is now starting to diverge in small areas. This is perhaps reflected in the fact that upon his appointment in 2017, Lord Lloyd-Jones became the first Justice of the Supreme Court to come from Wales.

The Prime Minister recommends to the Queen who will be appointed to the Supreme Court,[111] but the Lord Chancellor will provide only one name to the Prime Minister for recommendation and they may not decline the name.[112] This is significantly different from the previous position where Prime Ministers had the ultimate patronage. Lord Hailsham, Conservative Lord Chancellor between 1970 and 1974 and again between 1979 and 1987, makes clear in his autobiography that Mrs Thatcher, the then Prime Minister, ensured she was involved in the discussions and that a list of possible names was submitted, although he is careful to note that she did not appoint anyone that was not on the list.[113]

The CRA 2005 expressly states that the ad hoc commission must determine the selection process to be applied[114] and this must include, for example, whether it is necessary in order to comply with the convention noted earlier that the competition is restricted to judges from a particular jurisdiction. So far, the selection process has included advertising the positions and this is true of the most recent selection exercises in which vacancies were advertised for three Supreme Court Justices, to replace Lady Hale, Lord Carnwath, and Lord Wilson. Their replacement appointments were Lord Hamblen, Lord Leggatt, and Professor Burrows. Lord Reed (already an existing Supreme Court Justice) was appointed to the role of President of the Supreme Court, the role previously held by Lady Hale. Whatever process is adopted the statute makes clear that as part of any process, the Lord Chancellor must consult with the following:

- the First Minister in Scotland
- the Lord President of the Court of Session
- the Lord Chief Justice of Northern Ireland
- the First Minister for Wales
- the Lord Chief Justice of England and Wales
- the Northern Ireland Judicial Appointments Commission.[115]

A panel, similar to that used for senior judicial appointments in England and Wales, is created, the members being:

- at least one judge of the Supreme Court (normally the President of the Court)
- a senior judge from anywhere in the United Kingdom who is not a Justice of the Supreme Court (nominated by the President of the Supreme Court)
- one member of each of the JAC for England and Wales, Scotland, and Northern Ireland (at least two of whom must be non-legally qualified).[116]

---

111. *Constitutional Reform Act 2005*, s 26(2).
112. ibid, s 26(3).
113. Lord Hailsham, *A Sparrow's Flight* (Collins 1990) 427.
114. *Constitutional Reform Act 2005*, s 27(1).
115. ibid, s 27A(3). It is not known why, in Northern Ireland, the discussion should not be devolved to the First Minister in the same way it is with Scotland.
116. *Supreme Court (Judicial Appointments) Regulations 2013*, reg 11.

Under changes introduced by the CCA 2013, where the post of President is vacant then the outgoing President cannot be a member of the panel.[117] Similarly, if the post of Deputy President is vacant, then the outgoing Deputy President cannot sit on the panel.[118] The panel is chaired by the most senior judge on the panel, normally the President.

Although there is a requirement that the JAC for each jurisdiction within the United Kingdom is represented the statute does not state, at least expressly, that it must be their lay chair, rather it specifies that two of the three representatives from the JACs must be non-legally qualified.

When the ad hoc commission has nominated a person then the Lord Chancellor has the same three options open to him as exist for judicial appointments in England and Wales and eventually, therefore, a nominee will be recommended to the Queen for appointment to the Supreme Court via the Prime Minister.

The President and Deputy President of the Court are selected by the same process and this would appear to suggest therefore that the tradition of seniority by appointment, ended by the appointment of Lord Bingham, is unlikely to return, as the JAC could decide to appoint someone from outside the Supreme Court to either position.

8.3.8 Judicial appointments? The solution?

The JAC is certainly a marked contrast to the way in which judges have traditionally been appointed but is this the way forward and will it lead to perceived improvements? Not everyone was supportive of the idea of a commission, including those senior judges who believed that the wider constitutional reform process (including the creation of the Supreme Court) was correct. It has been noted that both Lord Bingham and Lord Woolf have argued that one person is better placed to decide on the suitability of a candidate than a committee which, Lord Woolf argues, could lead to a system of 'Buggins' turn next'.[119]

An independent appointments commission should, at least, remove the potential for bias or partisan politics to play a role. Even in more recent times there have been allegations that judicial appointments have been made not on the basis of merit but on connections to the government.

Example President of the Family Division

When Lord Falconer, the then Lord Chancellor, appointed Potter LJ to the position of President of the Family Division in 2005 the media instantly referred to him as a 'crony' because he was the pupil-master to both Lord Falconer and Lord Goldsmith, the Attorney-General. Did that mean the appointment was wrong? The professionals working in the Family Division (ie solicitors and barristers) were surprised as custom appeared to indicate the President would come from within the division, whereas Potter LJ was a Chancery Division judge,[120] but others believed that it was a welcome appointment as it was thought that the Family Division was becoming a little too inward-looking and needed an outside manager to ensure efficiency and a fresh look at the issues.[121]

---

117. *Constitutional Reform Act 2005*, s 27(1C).
118. ibid, s 27(1D).
119. Robert Stevens, 'Reform in Haste and Repent at Leisure: Iolanthe, the Lord High Executioner and Brave New World' (2004) 24 *Legal Studies* 1, 23.
120. See, for example, Grania Langdon-Down, 'A Fair Hearing' (2003) 100 *Law Society Gazette* 21, 22.
121. Philip Hoult, 'Press Round-up: "Crony" Controversy as Potter Becomes Family President' (2005) 102 *Law Society Gazette* 10.

However, others would suggest that Lord Chancellors have proven themselves to be extremely robust when making appointments that may appear controversial. Perhaps the classic example of Lord Chancellors ignoring political issues occurred in 1979 when Lord Hailsham decided to recommend to the Queen that Elizabeth Butler-Sloss, then a registrar of the Principal Registry of the Family Division (which is comparable to, but slightly higher than, a district judge), be elevated to the High Court bench. Civil servants were concerned because she was the sister of the Attorney-General,[122] but such concerns were brushed aside as it would be 'wrong in principle to discriminate against her'.[123] Butler-Sloss became one of the most popular and respected judges on the bench, including being made the first Lady Justice of Appeal and first female Head of Division (she became the President of the Family Division).

In his article, 'Rethinking the Lord Chancellor's role in judicial appointments',[124] Gee argues that the Lord Chancellor should be more involved in the individual appointment of senior members of the judiciary, for example, puisne judges, Court of Appeal judges and those holding leadership positions, such as the Lord Chief Justice. He makes four key arguments to support his position. First, he argues that the Lord Chancellor has a legitimate interest in the selection of individual judges because as part of his role he must account to Parliament for the appointments process. Secondly, he notes that involving the Lord Chancellor in individual appointment decisions 'ensures that the executive has a genuine stake in and responsibility for the selections regime . . . [and] senior judges can partly ground their authority on the executive's participation in their selection.'[125] Thirdly, he suggests that political pressure and leadership may be useful in supporting the diversity of the judiciary. Finally, Gee argue that judicial independence can be protected with an increased role for the Lord Chancellor by ensuring that the executive are informed and engaged and have a 'firm grasp of [their] responsibility to ensure that independent judges are able to discharge their constitutional function.'[126] To enhance the Lord Chancellor's involvement in the recruitment of individual judges within the senior judiciary, Gee makes a case for the introduction of shortlists. Rather than receiving one recommendation for a senior vacancy, as is the case under the current system, Gee argues that the Lord Chancellor should be presented with a shortlist of between three and five judges per vacancy, and be allowed to pick his preference for the post from the shortlist. Gee notes that such an approach would maintain the JAC's involvement, whilst 'sensibly' expanding the Lord Chancellor's involvement.[127]

The Lord Chancellor has not, of course, been removed from the decision-making process, as he still has the power to accept, reject, or ask for reconsideration of recommendations for judicial appointments and, unlike Gee, some may have concerns as to whether this level of involvement undermines the integrity of the appointment system. It has been noted already that a Lord Chancellor chose to exercise that right to question the selection of an individual and some may see this as undermining the judicial appointments process. It was unclear how this accountability would arise but in 2010, when the then Lord Chancellor asked the JAC to reconsider the appointment of Wall LJ as President of the Family Division, it was stated that if he had rejected the nomination

122.   Geoffrey Lewis, *Lord Hailsham: A Life* (Pimlico 1997) 268.
123.   ibid, 269.
124.   Graham Gee 'Rethinking the Lord Chancellor's role in judicial appointments' (2017) 20(1) *Legal Ethics* 4–20.
125.   ibid, 15.
126.   ibid, 16.
127.   ibid, 18.

he would have had to publicly state the reasons why. This has been clarified with the introduction of the Judicial Appointments Regulations 2013, which make clear that 'the Lord Chancellor must give the selection panel reasons in writing for rejecting or requiring reconsideration of a selection'.[128]

The constitution of the JAC has also led to some concern. The Commission for Judicial Appointments strongly argued that lay members should constitute a majority of people appointed to the JAC.[129] This is now reflected in the amendments made to the CRA 2005 by the CCA 2013 which states in Sch 12 (para 3A): 'the number of commissioners who are holders of judicial office must be less than the number of Commissioners (including the chairman) who are not holders of judicial office.'

⟳ QUESTION FOR REFLECTION

Read CJA (2004) para 3.4 where it is argued that lay members should form a majority of the panel and contrast this with Thomas Legg, 'Brave New World: The New Supreme Court and Judicial Appointments' (2004) 24 *Legal Studies* 45, 53, who suggests the opposite and is of the opinion that a judge should be a chair. Why do you think there need to be lay members on a panel that is deciding whether to appoint (or promote) members of the judiciary? Will lay members understand the subtleties of the judicial office? Who should chair the panels?

8.4 Diversity

Perhaps one of the key areas of controversy of the judiciary is their diversity. A long-held criticism of the judiciary is that they are all from the same mould: white, male, middle-class, privately educated Oxbridge graduates. This position is perhaps exemplified by the current senior judiciary. The five most senior judges (the Lord Chief Justice and the four Heads of Division) list their educational backgrounds. Three of the five were educated at either the University of Oxford or the University of Cambridge (Dame Victoria Sharp, President of the Queen's Bench Division, was educated at the University of Bristol, and Sir Andrew Macfarlane, President of the Family Division, studied Law at Durham University). All were privately educated. All are white, and four are male. When Dame Victoria Sharp became President of the Queen's Bench Division in June 2019, she became the first woman to hold this position, and only the second to hold the post of Head of Division. It is also noteworthy that the second most senior judge in the country—the Master of the Rolls—is gay. Not that long ago it would have been thought unlikely that this could be the case.

Speaking in 1992, Lord Taylor the then Lord Chief Justice said:

The present imbalance between male and female, white and black in the judiciary is obvious . . . I have no doubt that the balance will be redressed in the next few years . . . Within five years I would expect to see a substantial number of appointments from both these groups. This is not just a pious hope. It will be monitored.[130]

---

128. *Judicial Appointments Regulations 2013*, regs 9(3), 15(3), and 27(3).
129. Commission for Judicial Appointments, *Annual Report 2004* (CJA 2004) para 3.4.
130. Lord Taylor, 'The Judiciary in the Nineties' (Richard Dimbleby Lecture 1992).

Twenty years later, Lord Judge LCJ stated:

> I am extremely concerned and unhappy about the proportion of women and people from different minorities who are not represented on the Bench, and, as I repeat, I spend a lot of my time as Lord Chief Justice trying to address that problem.[131]

This could only be an acknowledgment that little had changed in the twenty years between Chief Justice speeches. It is eight years since Lord Judge gave his comments—and twenty-eight years since the comments of Lord Taylor, Whilst recent years have seen some improvements, in many ways little has changed.

8.4.1 Current statistical position

What is the position as regards diversity at the time of writing?

8.4.1.1 Gender

The number of female students entering university to read law has been increasing since 1970 and since 1988 there have actually been more female entrants than male. Since 1992 there have been marginally more newly qualified female solicitors than male solicitors.[132] The last census reported that there was a population in England and Wales of just over 52 million people, of which approximately 26.7 million (51 per cent) are female and approximately 25.3 million (49 per cent) are male. It can be seen, therefore, that in society in general, in law schools, and among newly qualified lawyers there are slightly more females than males.

However, if the judicial statistics are examined it can be seen that the position in terms of gender is mixed at best, and that there are particular issues within the more senior ranks of the judiciary. There is (as at 1 April 2020) one female Head of Division, Dame Victoria Sharp who is President of the Queen's Bench Division. She is the first woman to hold this position and prior to her appointment there had only been one other female Head of Division, Lady Justice Butler-Sloss who was President of the Family Division between 1995 and 2005. Of the twelve Justices of the Supreme Court in July 2020 only two (25 per cent) are female.[133] This represents a decrease from a record number of three female Justices between 2018 and 2020, and follows the retirement of Lady Hale in January 2020. Lady Hale was appointed a Lord of Appeal in Ordinary in 2005 and prior to that there had been no female Law Lords. She was the first, and only, female President of the Supreme Court. There are (as at 1 April 2020) eight (21 per cent) Lady Justices of Appeal.[134] There are twenty-eight (28 per cent) female puisne judges,[135] an increase on previous years.

Of the more junior ranks of the judiciary the position is marginally better. There are 221 (33 per cent) female circuit judges, and 234 (41 per cent) district judges and district

---

131.   Lord Judge LCJ, *Lord Chief Justice's Press Conference* (HMCTS 2012) <http://www.judiciary.gov.uk/announcements/lcj-press-conference-2012/ 10.

132.   Ericka Rackley, 'Representations of the (Woman) Judge: Hercules, the Little Mermaid and the Vain and Naked Emperor' (2002) 22 *Legal Studies* 602, 605.

133.   The Supreme Court, 'Biography of the Justices' (July 2020) <https://www.supremecourt.uk/about/biographies-of-the-justices.html>.

134.   Ministry of Justice, 'Diversity of the judiciary: Legal professions, new appointments and current post-holders – 2020 Statistics' (2020, MoJ) <https://assets.publishing.service.gov.uk/government/uploads/system/uploads/attachment_data/file/918529/diversity-of-the-judiciary-2020-statistics-web.pdf> 18.

135.   ibid.

judges (magistrates' court) (the most junior branch of the full-time court judiciary).[136] Of the part-time judiciary, there are 191 (22 per cent) recorders (ie part-time judges of the circuit bench), and 300 (37 per cent) deputy district judges and deputy district judges (magistrates' court) (ie part-time district judges).[137]

Overall this means that only 32 per cent of the courts judiciary are female.[138] Admittedly there has been an increase in recent years but it is still half of the representation of women in society. Why is this? The usual reason was that put forward by Lord MacKay, the then Lord Chancellor:

As more women progress through the profession, it is to be expected that the numbers of women within the judiciary will increase.[139]

However, this misses the point that as of 2020 women have legally been able to become members of the profession for over 100 years (the centenary was in 2019), yet still make up less than a third of judiciary. It has been noted that historically the judiciary have been recruited from the Bar and females have, despite their representation more generally, suffered, in the words of one commentator, 'institutional discrimination' at the Bar.[140] The latest figures from 2019 show that women account for 38 per cent of barristers currently in practice (an increase of just 0.6 percent since 2018),[141] the traditional route for members of the judiciary.

There therefore does not appear to be much evidence for the idea that the numbers will eventually increase (in line with the optimism of Lords Taylor and MacKay). There is an expectation that full-time members of the judiciary will be drawn from part-time members of the judiciary, yet it was seen that the representation of women in the part-time judiciary is still below that which can be legitimately expected.

Lord Judge, the former Lord Chief Justice, whilst acknowledging the problem, attempted to argue that this is a problem that is not restricted to the law:

[W]e are turning a tanker around, and it takes time, 11 per cent of the Queen's Counsel in this country are women. That means 89 per cent are men. Solicitors who are partners in solicitors' firms, who are women, amount to 25 per cent—that is 75 per cent men. It would be surprising if you had a Bench which was not inevitably affected by those sort of statistics when you are choosing lawyers to become judges . . . What is our society like in relation to the opportunities given to women and the appointments given to women? . . . how many editors of national newspapers are female? . . . how many directors of large companies are female? In that sense the judicial system . . . is . . . reflective of society.[142]

This is an argument that was reiterated more recently by Lord Sumption:

One has to look at the totality of these problems and not simply at one of them. The lack of diversity is a significant problem, but it isn't the only one. It takes time. You've got to be patient. The change in the status and achievements of women in our society, not just

136. ibid.
137. ibid.
138. ibid.
139. Clare McGlynn, 'Women, Representation and the Legal Academy' (1999) 19 *Legal Studies* 68, 89.
140. ibid, 89.
141. Bar Standards Board, 'Diversity at the Bar 2019: A Summary of the latest available diversity data for the Bar' (BSB January 2020) <https://www.barstandardsboard.org.uk/uploads/assets/912f7278-48fc-46df-893503eb729598b8/Diversity-at-the-Bar-2019.pdf> 3.
142. Lord Judge LCJ, *Lord Chief Justice's Press Conference* (HMCTS 2012) <http://www.judiciary.gov.uk/announcements/lcj-press-conference-2012/> 9.

in the law but generally, is an enormous cultural change that has happened over the last 50 years or so. It has to happen naturally. It will happen naturally. But in the history of a society like ours, 50 years is a very short time.[143]

As has been seen this is a common argument that is employed to justify the absence of females in the judiciary. Whilst there may be something to be said for the 'tanker' argument, there have been high numbers of very good barristers over the past several decades and it seems incredible that of the top 152 judges in the country (ie the senior and superior judiciary) only thirty-five females were found to be good enough to be a member. These figures suggest it is much more than the turning around of a tanker. This is something recognized by the current Lord Chief Justice, Lord Burnett of Maldon:

> Our aim is for a judiciary that is more representative of society in general and to achieve this sooner rather than later. Change does not happen overnight nor, as the progress made in recent years shows, need it take many decades. It requires the nature of a problem to be identified and acknowledged. It calls for thought to understand what can be done to tackle the problem and to put in place effective measures to achieve that end.[144]

To that end, the judiciary have introduced a series of measures to promote diversity and increase the speed at which change is occurring. This is discussed in more detail later in the chapter at 8.4.2.

8.4.1.2 **Ethnicity**

The position in respect of ethnic representation is even worse. The last census suggests that approximately 7.9 per cent of the population consider themselves to be a member of the ethnic minorities. However, the latest judicial statistics demonstrate that only one Head of Division[145] and no Justices of the Supreme Court are from a black or minority ethnic background. There is one (3 per cent) Lord Justice of Appeal who belong to an ethnic minority and four (4 per cent) puisne judges.[146] This means that of the senior judiciary as a whole only four per cent of judges are from a black or ethnic minority background.[147]

Of the junior judicial ranks, there are twenty-seven (4 per cent) circuit judges who belong to an ethnic minority. There are fifty (9.5 per cent) district judges and district judges (magistrates' court). Of the part-time judiciary, there are sixty-six (9 per cent) recorders and fifty-five (6.5 per cent) deputy district and deputy district (magistrates' courts) judges.[148] Whilst there have been improvements in the number of judges from a black and ethnic minority background over recent years, as a whole, only 8 per cent of the judiciary would consider themselves as belonging to a member of the ethnic minorities,[149] an increase from 5.9 per cent in the previous edition of this book. It is

---

143. Peter Walker, 'Don't Rush Gender Equality in UK Judiciary, Says Supreme Court Judge' (*The Guardian*, 2015) <https://www.theguardian.com/law/2015/sep/22/gender-equality-warning-uk-legal-profession-supreme-court-judge-jonathan-sumption>.

144. Lord Chief Justice of England and Wales, The Right Hon. The Lord Burnett of Maldon, 'A Changing Judiciary in a Modern Age – Treasurer's Lecture 2019' (18 February 2019) <https://www.judiciary.uk/wp-content/uploads/2019/02/mt-treasurers-lecture-final-for-publishing.pdf> para 14.

145. Ministry of Justice, 'Diversity of the judiciary: Legal professions, new appointments and current post-holders – 2020 Statistics' (2020, MoJ) <https://assets.publishing.service.gov.uk/government/uploads/system/uploads/attachment_data/file/918529/diversity-of-the-judiciary-2020-statistics-web.pdf> 26.

146. ibid.

147. ibid.

148. ibid.

149. ibid.

clear that despite the increase in overall numbers the stereotype of a middle-class, white, male judge still exists and the latest statistics suggest that this stereotype has a factual basis behind it.

8.4.1.3 **Diversity in the tribunals**

What of the tribunal judiciary? Can it be said that these are more diverse? Historically the answer appeared to be 'no' but what of modern times? The position appears to compare favourably to the court judiciary. According to the latest statistics, 47 per cent of tribunal judges were female.[150] The statistics suggest that 12 per cent of tribunal judiciary are from a black or minority ethnic background.[151]

It would also appear that the Bar does not have the same grip on the tribunal judiciary. Sixty-three per cent of the tribunal judiciary come from professions outside the Bar, and whilst they note that the proportion reduces towards the senior grades, it remains in excess of 45 per cent for the higher levels of the tribunal judiciary,[152] which compares favourably with the court judiciary. Indeed, in the court judiciary, only 32 per cent of the judiciary come from professions outside the Bar, with this number reducing to single digit percentages when looking at the senior judiciary.[153]

Happily, the data that accompanies the statistical bulletin allows us to delve deeper into the issue of gender and ethnicity. It will be remembered from Table 8.1, presented at the very beginning of the chapter, that the judiciary are broken down into grades. This allows us to compare their equivalences more easily. Table 8.3 summarizes the equivalences between tribunal and court judiciary.

Tables 8.4 and 8.5 then present a comparison between the courts and tribunal judiciary.[154]

Table 8.3 Equivalences between tribunal and court judiciary

Salary Scale	Tribunal Judge	Court equivalent
5	Chamber Presidents	Senior circuit judge
6.1	Upper Tribunal judge	Circuit judge
7	First-Tier Tribunal judge	District judge
7	Employment judge	District judge

Table 8.4 Gender in the court and tribunal judiciary

	Courts			Tribunals		
Grade	Total number	Female	Male	Total number	Female	Male
Circuit judge	669	2221	4446	61	25	36
District judge[155]	419	184	235	1387	666	721

Adapted from Ministry of Justice, 'Diversity of the judiciary: legal professions, judicial appointments and judicial office holders 2020 statistics' (2020 MoJ) https://assets.publishing.service.gov.uk/government/uploads/system/uploads/attachment_data/file/918530/diversity-of-the-judiciary-2020-data-tables.ods Table 3.1

150. ibid, 18.
151. ibid, 26.
152. ibid, Table 3.1.
153. ibid.
154. The total number of judges differs between Tables 8.4 and 8.5 because it depends on the information that is contained within the statistics.
155. This only includes district judges (county courts).

Table 8.5 Ethnicity in the court and tribunal judiciary

Grade	Courts				Tribunals			
	Total number	White	BME	Not Known[156]	Total number	White	BME	Not known
Circuit judge	669	5588	27	54	61	448	110	3
District judge[157]	419	3356	40	23	1387	11,139	1155	93

Adapted from Ministry of Justice, 'Diversity of the judiciary: legal professions, judicial appointments and judicial office holders 2020 statistics' (2020 MoJ) https://assets.publishing.service.gov.uk/government/uploads/system/uploads/attachment_data/file/918530/diversity-of-the-judiciary-2020-data-tables.ods Table 3.1.

Thus, if we compare gender, it can be seen that 33 per cent of circuit judges are female, compared to 41 per cent of the tribunal judiciary.[158] At district-judge level, 44 per cent of the court judiciary are female compared to 48 per cent of first tier tribunal judges.[159] Whether this is reflected in the type of role, or the fact that there is a broader range of professions feeding into the tribunals judiciary (including those who come from CILEx) is perhaps more open to question.

If we look at ethnicity, of those who have declared an ethnicity, 4 per cent of circuit judges are of black or minority ethnicity, compared to 17 per cent of the equivalent role of upper tribunal judge in the tribunal judiciary.[160] Of district-judge's, the position is that 10 per cent of the court judiciary are black or minority ethnic, compared to 12 per cent of the tribunal judiciary.[161]

It can be seen that the tribunal judiciary do appear more representative than the court judiciary. Of course, knowing this and knowing *why* this is, are two very different issues. However, it does suggest that there is something to work with here. If the idea of an integrated judiciary (discussed in Chapter 20) is to progress, then this means judicial promotion within the bands. If the tribunal judiciary could be promoted, then it could have a positive effect on judicial diversity.

8.4.2 **Extending diversity**

Despite these figures it can be seen that the professions and senior members of the judiciary are trying to make the judiciary more diverse. The question is perhaps whether these are mere words or whether there is a true move towards the diversification of the judiciary.

Perhaps the first point of note is that whilst recent statutory reforms have allowed feminine judicial titles to be used (eg Lady Justice of Appeal instead of Lord Justice of Appeal and even provision for a Lady Chief Justice)[162] the title of the Law Lords was not changed and thus Lady Hale states that when she was introduced to the House of

---

156.   Not known, ie the judge has not declared their ethnicity.
157.   This only includes district judge (county courts).
158.   Ministry of Justice, 'Diversity of the judiciary: legal professions, judicial appointments and judicial office holders 2020 statistics' (2020 MoJ) <https://assets.publishing.service.gov.uk/government/uploads/system/uploads/attachment_data/file/918530/diversity-of-the-judiciary-2020-data-tables.ods> Table 3.1.
159.   ibid.
160.   ibid.
161.   ibid.
162.   See *Courts Act 2003*, s 64(2).

Lords by letters patent she was introduced as a Lord of Appeal in Ordinary.[163] At a simplistic level this can be dismissed as irrelevant, with everyone knowing that Lady Hale is female, but it does demonstrate what could be perceived as an inherent male bias within the judiciary and prior to appointment she noted that such matters were 'trivial but . . . annoying manifestations of the assumption that this is a male profession which women are allowed to join provided that they pretend to be men'.[164]

When thinking about this whole area, one commentator asks quite a pertinent question: '*Why* [*sic*] should we want a more representative judiciary? Is it simply that there *ought* to be more women judges?'[165] Presumably this could be extended further, ie to ask why we should want more members of the ethnic minorities. It could be argued that we expect our judiciary to be representative of society but is that really what is desired? It is unlikely that in terms of socio-economic factors there would be a desire or expectation for representation and surely the public would wish the best members of the legal profession to become its judges—so why diversity? It has to be something more than just 'to make up the numbers'[166] but Hale, speaking extrajudicially, argues that it is about 'individuals and their rights',[167] ie the right to progress within a profession and not to be discriminated against.

⟳ QUESTION FOR REFLECTION

Do you think the judiciary should be diverse? What about representative? What does judicial representation actually mean? Think about *why* you want a more representative judiciary; what are the advantages that this would bring to the justice system?

It could be suggested that it is a matter of public confidence. How can a white male bastion inspire confidence in the justice system? Whilst one should be wary of looking to the media where attacks are often intemperate, inappropriate, and frequently completely wrong, it is not difficult to think that the judiciary currently make themselves difficult to defend against accusations that they do not know the 'real world'. If they do not represent a multicultural society how can they possibly adjudicate on such matters?

8.4.2.1 **Appointment on merit**

One commentator notes that the current system of diversity and appointment has been summarized accurately by Lord Lloyd of Berwick, a Lord of Appeal in Ordinary:

> I would like, obviously, the judiciary to be as diverse as we can get it. But that must not interfere with the fundamental principle that we have got to choose the best man for the job.[168]

One cannot help but focus on the last words of this quote. Although, as has been noted, the convention within law is to refer to the masculine and indeed this book follows the

---

163. Baroness Hale of Richmond, 'The House of Lords and Women's Rights or Am I Really a Law Lord' (2005) 25 *Legal Studies* 72 and see *Appellate Jurisdiction Act 1876*, s 6.

164. Brenda Hale, 'Equality and the Judiciary: Why Should We Want More Women Judges?' [2001] *Public Law* 489, 497.

165. Ericka Rackley, 'Representations of the (Woman) Judge: Hercules, the Little Mermaid and the Vain and Naked Emperor' (2002) 22 *Legal Studies* 602, 609.

166. ibid.

167. Brenda Hale, 'Equality and the Judiciary: Why Should We Want More Women Judges?' [2001] *Public Law* 489.

168. Kate Malleson, 'Rethinking the Merit Principle in Judicial Selection' (2006) 33 *Journal of Law and Society* 126.

convention because to use 'he or she' or the even worse '(s)he' is awkward prose, one cannot help but think that there are times when the inclusion of the words 'or woman' or the substitution of 'person' would be appropriate. Arguably the quote from Lord Lloyd is such an example.

The justification for the slow progress of diversity is that only the best are appointed to be judges and that any move towards positive assistance would be contrary to this rule and could even dilute the quality of judges. Deciding who the 'best' candidate is can always be difficult because if one gets the best schooling and education it can be easy to be the 'best' especially if those choosing you meet the same profile, but what does that mean here?

In a review of the appointments system, it was noted that whilst there is almost unanimity in accepting that judges should be appointed on merit, interestingly there was no clear consensus on what 'merit' actually means.[169] However, the report differentiated between two types of merit, namely 'maximal merit' where only one candidate is judged suitable for appointment as he is the best person available,[170] or 'minimal merit' where the selected panel identifies a number of people who are qualified for the appointment and then a person is chosen from that pool on the basis of policy decisions.[171] The implication of this argument is that the latter approach is an inferior way of appointing members of the judiciary even though it can be justified on policy grounds, not least the fact that a more diverse judiciary may assist in securing public confidence.

However, is it this simple? Part of the difficulty of locating the maximal best candidate is the advantages that arise from the status quo. There has, for several years now, been considerable debate as to whether those educated in the public schools were being over-represented at the very best universities, particularly Oxbridge. Those who qualified at Oxbridge were certainly well represented in the major law firms and at the Bar. Did it mean that those who were educated at public schools were more intelligent than those at state schools, or could it reflect the fact that public schools, because of their teaching patterns and staff/student ratios, are better able to devote more time and attention to their students, thus allowing students to demonstrate their full potential? If it is the latter, as many believe, then simply selecting the maximal merit candidate each time will mean that the cycle could become self-sustaining, with those who had the best opportunities becoming the best candidates. The minimal merit scheme (although we dislike the term) has the advantage of setting out the competencies of the judges, allowing a broad analysis to be made of their qualities, and then deciding how someone fits into the wider considerations. This is not the same as positive discrimination and is no different to many companies who will state that they 'particularly welcome applicants from the ethnic minorities'. This is not watering down quality but ensuring that all applicants have the same opportunities.

Malleson, probably the most authoritative commentator on the area, argues that there need not be a binary system where it is either the maximal or minimal system but rather that the maximal system could be altered through the provision of a 'tie-breaker' system.[172] The basis of this argument is that there will not necessarily be 'one' candidate

---

169.   Thomas Legg, 'Brave New World: The New Supreme Court and Judicial Appointments' (2004) 24 *Legal Studies* 45, 49.

170.   ibid, 50.

171.   ibid, 51.

172.   Kate Malleson, 'Rethinking the Merit Principle in Judicial Selection' (2006) 33 *Journal of Law and Society* 126, 129.

that appears best but there may be a number of applicants who are equally qualified. In those circumstances it is suggested that there should be a 'tie-break' feature whereby those who come from an under-represented group should be given the position.[173] This is arguably distinct from the 'minimal' system in that the minimal system looks solely at the criteria and ranks the person thereafter, whereas the 'tie-break' system is a derivative of the maximal system because it looks at persons, but where there is difficulty in deciding between two or more persons, the 'tie-break' is under-representation.

The CCA 2013 introduced provisions in relation to increasing diversity in the judiciary which are somewhat reflective of Malleson's tie-break principle. Schedule 13, Part Two of the Act has amended the previous provisions found in the CRA 2005 on judicial appointments being solely on merit. Instead it allows that where two persons being considered for judicial appointment are of equal merit, the commission can prefer one over the other in order to increase diversity within the judiciary. Moreover, the Act makes specific reference to the fact that the Lord Chancellor and Lord Chief Justice '[m]ust take such steps as that office-holder considers appropriate for the purpose of encouraging judicial diversity'.[174]

⟳ QUESTION FOR REFLECTION

What do you think of the reforms introduced by the CCA 2013? Are they a sufficient compromise between the need to appoint judges on merit but also to create a 'level playing field' upon which under-represented groups of society can compete for judicial appointments?

8.4.2.2 Family-friendly policies

With the introduction of the CCA 2013, there has been an additional focus on introducing family-friendly policies within the judiciary. It will be seen that it is unusual for a circuit judge to be promoted to the High Court bench or beyond (9.2.3) and therefore if women are to become members of the senior judiciary they will ordinarily begin their full-time career as a puisne judge. The difficulty with the role of a puisne judge is that judges in the Queen's Bench and Family Divisions (and to a lesser extent the Chancery Division) will spend a considerable time 'on circuit', ie sitting away from their home. Life on circuit is not, as the media sometimes presents it, a luxurious exercise since QBD judges will normally act as the 'single judge' during that time and thus work on papers. High Court judges also hold an important social rank and thus there is a considerable amount of entertaining that must also be done in the evening.

Until recently a judge 'on circuit' was *required* to stay in judge's lodgings even if his home was within commutable distance. Other circuits will (not infrequently) be a significant distance away from their home so that the judge will spent four to six weeks away from home, three and possibly four, times a year.[175] This can hardly be described as 'family friendly' and is undoubtedly a disincentive to both male and female judges but, arguably, a greater disincentive to female judges who do not wish to be away from what might be young members of a family.[176] McGlynn, citing Sandra O'Connor—the

275

---

173.   ibid, 129.
174.   *Constitutional Reform Act 2005*, s 137A.
175.   Rt Hon Lord Justice Auld, *A Review of the Criminal Courts of England and Wales* (HMSO 2001) 238.
176.   Kate Malleson, 'Rethinking the Merit Principle in Judicial Selection' (2006) 33 *Journal of Law and Society* 126, 131.

first woman to be appointed to the US Supreme Court—noted that a significant issue may be that a woman may wish to have a child and that the judicial structure should be able to take this into account.[177] This should not just be in respect of a 'pregnant judge' but should also take account of the fact that if a female lawyer takes time out to raise a family this should not prejudice an application for a judgeship later.

In an attempt to combat some of these issues the CCA 2013 has introduced flexible working for judges sitting in the High Court or above, as well as extending the opportunity to work part time to those judges working in both the High Court and the Court of Appeal. Opportunities to work flexibly will be made clear during each JAC selection process. Finally, the Act has introduced a system of 'deployment of the judiciary',[178] whereby judges can move more easily and flexibly between working in courts of equal or lower status. It is hoped that this will help with career development.

Family-friendly policies are increasingly commonplace in many workplaces and it is clear that such policies are beginning to be adopted within the judicial system. This is as big an issue as the diversity of the profession since a more diverse application system will only be achieved if people apply for judicial appointments. If they believe the conditions of the post are not suited to their lifestyle they will simply not apply for them regardless of how open the system becomes.

⟳ QUESTION FOR REFLECTION

What do you think of the introduction of 'family-friendly' policies within the judiciary? Do these policies go far enough, or is more needed to allow judges, particularly puisne judges, to provide for 'family time' around their judicial commitments?

8.4.2.3 Judicial Diversity Forum

The Judicial Diversity Forum replaced the Judicial Diversity Taskforce in 2015 as the body responsible for coordinating efforts to encourage judicial diversity. The following organizations are members of the Forum:

- Ministry of Justice
- the judiciary
- the Judicial Appointments Commission
- the Bar Council
- the Law Society
- the Chartered Institute of Legal Executives
- the Legal Services Board.

The forum meets twice a year, with the organizations working together in partnership to identify ways of improving judicial diversity. For example, exploring the best ways to address barriers to appointment for underrepresented groups, considering reasons for differences in progression within the legal professions and judiciary, and gathering and analyzing data.

---

177.   Clare McGlynn, 'Judging Women Differently: Gender, the Judiciary and Reform' in Susan Millns and Noel Whitty (eds), *Feminist Perspectives on Public Law* (Cavendish Publishing 1990) 97–9.
178.   CCA 2013, sch 14.

The Forum also runs joint initiatives, the first of which was launched in April 2019; the Pre-Application Judicial Education Programme. The aim of the programme is to provide additional support to lawyers eligible for judicial appointment who are from underrepresented groups within the judiciary, eg black and minority ethnic lawyers, women lawyers, solicitors and chartered legal executives, and lawyers with disabilities. Support is provided through online learning resources and discussion group courses which allow participants to explore the realities of a judicial career. It is hoped that the programme will support participants to feel more confident about working in the judiciary and so encourage them to apply for future judicial roles.

8.4.3 The Bar's grip

A particular difficulty in diversification is the fact that there is an undisputed link between the Bar and the Bench and arguably this creates a situation whereby significant numbers of persons are not considered. The reforms of the *Courts and Legal Services Act 1990* (CSLA 1990)[179] altered the Bar's exclusive privilege of putting forward candidates for the senior judiciary but doubts continue to exist as to whether the gap has truly narrowed. The first solicitor to be appointed to the High Court bench was Sachs J, although he was appointed via the circuit bench (to which solicitors had been appointed for some time). Appointment for solicitors via other judicial roles is a trend that seems to have continued with more recent appointments, with for example, Sarah Falk, who was appointed to the High Court having previously been a fee-paid deputy judge of the Upper Tribunal (Tax and Chancery Chamber).[180] Few solicitors have been directly appointed from practice. The first of these was Lawrence (now Lord) Collins who went on to become the first ever solicitor-appointee of the Court of Appeal (2007) and House of Lords (2009), and then subsequently a Justice of the Supreme Court on its creation.

One reason why the grip has not yet been broken is that the primary criterion for a judgeship was 'visibility' meaning appearing or at least interacting with senior members of the judiciary frequently.[181] The Bar, as will be seen in Chapter 10, traditionally had exclusive rights of audience in the higher courts and even today barristers continue to undertake the bulk of the work there. In addition to this, the Inns of Court are vital and again this lends assistance to the Bar. The Inns are governed by Masters of the Bench who are ordinarily either senior members of the judiciary or Queen's Counsel. A prospective puisne judge who is also a barrister will almost certainly be trying to ingratiate himself with his Inn by undertaking extra work etc which brings him to the attention of the senior members of the profession, an advantage that solicitors simply do not have.

In order to increase diversity and recruit more solicitors into the judiciary, in 2018 the JAC ran for the first time a deputy High Court judge selection exercise that was open to practitioners without judicial or litigation experience. A support programme was introduced alongside the selection exercise for those from under-represented groups who were interested in applying. It is questionable whether the exercise was a successful one, at least in relation to increasing the number of solicitors within the more senior ranks of the judiciary, with only four of the thirty-two deputy High Court appointments

179. See s 71.
180. Max Walters, 'Magic circle solicitor gets High Court nod' *Law Society Gazette* (2018) <https://www.lawgazette.co.uk/law/magic-circle-solicitor-gets-high-court-nod/5067752.article>.
181. Brenda Hale, 'Equality and the Judiciary: Why Should We Want More Women Judges?' [2001] *Public Law* 489, 492.

being solicitors. However, whilst the majority of appointments still came from the Bar, it appears that they came from more diverse backgrounds than in previous selection exercises, suggesting some positive outcomes from this new approach to appointments. Despite the small number of solicitors being appointed to the judiciary, and in particular in more senior positions, it is difficult to believe that there are no solicitors who deserve appointment to the High Court bench. The relative rarity of promotion from circuit to puisne bench does seem to ensure that the Bar continues to dominate judicial appointments especially when, as it will be remembered, most Court of Appeal and Supreme Court appointments come from the High Court and Court of Appeal respectively.

The lack of solicitor judges is increasingly being recognized as an issue. As well as running the open selection exercise for the most recent round of deputy High Court judge appointments, the JAC has a dedicated solicitor member and are working closely with the Law Society to increase applications. The Law Society and the JAC have identified several factors which appear to be deterring solicitors from pursuing a career in the judiciary. The 'attitude of law firms' has been identified as one such reason, as once solicitors are experienced enough to apply for a judicial position they are likely to be at the height of their earning power, and thus firms do not want these solicitors moving their ambitions elsewhere.[182] Moreover, the fact that many applicants have to apply for a judicial position multiple times before being successful deters many solicitors who are not used to such processes involving repeated rejections. A further issue is that of geography, especially if applicants are not told which court they will be based at. This can be particularly challenging and off-putting for those who have partners who also work, or those who have a family with children at school and who may need to move to take up their judicial position.[183]

8.4.3.1 **Other professions**

The then Labour government suggested that restricting the judiciary to the two principal professions was not appropriate and in 2005 proposed that legal executives should be eligible to become members of the judiciary,[184] albeit in the more junior positions, eg deputy or full district judges. However, such a system would potentially provide access to other benches since appointment as a district judge can (eventually) act as a 'threshold' for appointment for the Circuit Bench.

The judiciary were not happy with the proposal but Fennell, a legal correspondent for *The Times*, argued the concerns were misplaced, stating: 'I imagine that the proposal to allow legal executives to become judges should do a lot to enhance the quality of common sense on the bench',[185] although his point then becomes confused as the basis of his premise is that the Chartered Institute of Legal Executives (CILEx) provides the opportunity to become qualified as a solicitor. This, as we shall see, is perfectly true (see 10.4.3) but theoretically such persons are not disqualified from judicial appointments since when they are made solicitors they will have a general qualification (and thus the most junior positions will be available after a number of years), and if the higher advocacy examinations were taken then all appointments would be open.

---

182.   Monidipa Fouzdar, 'Law firm attitudes "deterring solicitors from becoming judges"' (*Law Society Gazette*, 1 March 2017) <https://www.lawgazette.co.uk/law/law-firm-attitudes-deterring-solicitors-from-becoming-judges/5060037.article>.

183.   ibid.

184.   'Judges to Come from Wider Pool of Applicants' DCA Press Release 181/05.

185.   'Wider Bench', *The Times*, 19 July 2005, Law Supplement.

The government argued that allowing CILEx members to access judicial appointments would bring more diversity to the bench but there are significant numbers of solicitors and barristers who are from diverse social, ethnic, and sexual backgrounds and it is difficult to see why the judicial members could not be drawn from these ranks. Further, is the quest for diversity or representation? The Law Society and Bar Council have both argued that judicial appointments should reflect society rather than represent it; by this they mean that class, gender, ethnicity, religion, and sexual orientation should not be a bar to any appointment and that a diverse bench would enhance merit and the judiciary, but that appointments should not be made on a quota basis.[186]

The government progressed with the proposals and in 2010 the very first CILEx appointment was made.[187] Ian Ashley-Smith, a CILEx Fellow, was appointed to the position of Deputy District Judge (Civil) and sits in Kent.[188] Despite several more CILEx Fellows being appointed to the judiciary since then, the current number in post only sits at two, both of whom are deputy district judges.[189] If one looks to tribunals, as of 1 April 2020, there were no CILEx Fellows in post as judges.[190] Thus, whilst there is increasing recognition of CILEx as the 'third profession' (discussed further at 10.4), it is clear that CILEx Fellows have not made significant inroads into the judiciary, in much the same way as solicitors before them.

8.5 Judicial training

When judges are appointed should they be trained? It may seem a peculiar question to ask yet traditionally training was not offered and a lack of experience was certainly no barrier to appointment. Lord Devlin recalled that when he was appointed to the High Court in 1948: 'I had never exercised any criminal jurisdiction and not since my early days at the Bar had I appeared in a criminal court . . . Two days after I had been sworn in, I was trying crime at Newcastle Assizes.'[191]

Dunn notes that when he was appointed it was a case of speaking to other members of the judiciary to understand the principles of giving judgment and discovering the usual awards for compensation etc.[192] The Lord Chief Justice began to operate 'sentencing conferences' for members of the circuit judiciary and this was eventually extended by the President of the Family Division to include training on family work.

The ad hoc approach of judicial training needed reform, however, and in 1979 the *Judicial Studies Board* (JSB) was created to have an oversight of judicial training. It has been suggested that it 'discharge[d] an ever more important function' and as it was operated by the judges (as its successor the *Judicial College* is) it contributed to judicial independence.[193] The JSB was originally restricted to criminal law but its successor now applies to all types of law and all levels of the judiciary.

186. Catherine Baksi, 'World at their Feet' (2005) 102 *Law Society Gazette* 26.
187. Judicial Appointments Commission, *Annual Report 2010–11* (JAC 2011) 16.
188. ibid, 29.
189. Ministry of Justice, 'Diversity of the judiciary: legal professions, judicial appointments and judicial office holders 2020 statistics' (2020 MoJ) <https://assets.publishing.service.gov.uk/government/uploads/system/uploads/attachment_data/file/918530/diversity-of-the-judiciary-2020-data-tables.ods> Table 3.1.
190. ibid.
191. David Pannick, *Judges* (OUP 1987) 69.
192. Robin Dunn, *Sword and Wig: Memoirs of a Lord Justice* (Quiller Press 1993) 181–3.
193. Thomas Bingham, *The Business of Judging: Selected Essays and Speeches* (OUP 2000) 67.

On 1 April 2011 the JSB ceased to exist and the Judicial College took over. This is not a physical college but rather a virtual one—whilst it will be seen that lectures and seminars do take place it is not in a central location but rather occurs in multiple locations and, increasingly, online. The Judicial College also assumed responsibility for the training of the tribunal judiciary and also for legal advisers within the courts.

The Judicial College is governed by a Board whose president is a Court of Appeal judge, currently Lady Justice King. Its other members are:

- a member of the courts judiciary
- a member of the tribunal judiciary
- a representative with responsibility for magistrates and legal advisers
- the Director of Training for the courts judiciary
- the Director of Training for the tribunal judiciary
- the Executive Director of the Judicial College.

In addition to the Board the Judicial College has a series of committees, these being:

- Tribunals Committee—as its name suggests it has responsibility for the training programmes specifically tailored towards the tribunal judiciary
- Courts Committee—which sets out plans for the training for all levels of the courts judiciary
- Diversity & Development Committee
- Wales Training Committee—a recently established committee that is tasked to consider whether specialist training is required as a result of devolution in Wales
- International Committee—the Judicial College is asked to participate in a number of international events, including hosting visiting judges, and this committee considers these issues.

The actual training is more complicated and broken down into a series of different types of training, the principal groups being:

- civil
- criminal
- cross jurisdictional (this is primarily skills-based training and seeks to tackle those aspects of judging that are common to all jurisdictions)
- family
- magistrates
- tribunals
- senior judiciary (this now includes puisne and Court of Appeal judges although this is still at their own discretion whereas for the inferior judiciary it remains mandatory)
- international (for judges who work internationally).

The actual training that is undertaken by judges will differ depending on level and appointment. Upon initial appointment there is often a requirement that a judge attends a residential induction programme of training that will cover many of the basics of the judicial role. The Judicial College produces a 'prospectus' that lists all the training that is available to judges and allows them to pick the courses that they feel are most relevant to them. The 2020/21 prospectus lists seminars across all areas of work.[194] The actual training requirement is relatively minimal. All court judges (with a few exceptions) are required to attend a two-day continuation seminar each year.[195] One such exception is where a judge holds five or more authorizations, they can attend a one-day plus a two-day seminar, or two two-day seminars.[196] Moreover, any judge who has authorization to try murder, serious sexual offences, or public family law cases, or who holds a specialist civil authorization must attend seminars associated with that authorization at least once every three years.[197] Within the Judicial College's prospectus it is explained that members of the Senior Judiciary and Supreme Court Justices are welcome to attend any seminars that are of interest to them.[198] For puisne judges it is noted that attendance should 'accord with the protocol governing their training, details of which are available from Heads of Division.'[199]

It should be noted here that the Judicial College's use of the term 'seminar' does not equate to what a university student would understand it to be, as it may include a series of modules within the seminar, often requiring a residential stay (see, eg, the 'Civil Law Seminar' which is constituted of sixteen distinct modules of which the judge must choose four as part of their programme).[200] Alongside the national seminars is further training. Some of this will be at a more local level. Each circuit will usually organize a series of training events for the judiciary.

Judicial training has progressed considerably since the times discussed at the start of this section. The Director of Studies of the College, writing in the final annual report of the Judicial Studies Board, notes that the JSB was called 'studies' not 'training' because there was a belief that judges would reject the suggestion that they required training,[201] and yet the modern Judicial College is based on the premise that there is an acceptance that training is an essential part of the life of a judge. Some of the training courses—for example the serious sexual offences seminar—is an essential part of authorizing a judge to sit on certain cases. It is this which allows a judge to be 'ticketed' to hear rape and serious sexual offences cases. There are other examples, including the fact that a seminar has been created specifically for those puisne judges who have been appointed to hear matters in the Administrative Court.

However, there remains some concern that there is perhaps more to do. At the very beginning of the section it was stated that Lord Devlin was just thrown in at the deep end when he was a newly appointed judge. It may be thought this is no longer true but even in modern times it can still happen as noted in the comments of a senior judge presented by Darbyshire:

> I gave a party at my old chambers to say goodbye and I asked some friends who came from outside of the law. One said . . . 'Well I imagine you go off now for three months' training?' I said, 'As a matter of fact you don't'. He said, 'When do you start sitting?' I said 'Tomorrow morning at half past ten'. He said, 'Well I imagine then that they are

---

194.   Judicial College, 'Prospectus April 2020 -March 2021 Judicial College' (Judicial College, 2019) <https://www.judiciary.uk/wp-content/uploads/2020/04/Judicial-College-Prospectus-2020-2021.pdf>.
195.   ibid, 12.
196.   ibid, 12.
197.   ibid, 14.
198.   ibid, 14.
199.   ibid, 14.
200.   ibid, 21.
201.   Judicial Studies Board, *Annual Report 2010/11* (JSB 2011) 11.

giving you a case of the kind you used to do at the Bar because you know all about them'. I muttered that they don't and that I was doing an asylum case . . . He said 'How many of those have you done before?' I said 'None'.[202]

Darbyshire does not state how old that story is, although in the context of the book it seems relatively recent. Full-time judges will, of course, initially sit as part-time judges, but there is still the problem that their appointment and training will rarely coincide on the basis that judges do not retire, nor are they appointed, at specific points in the year. They are appointed throughout the year and it would not be very efficient to have individual training programmes for each judge. Perhaps surprisingly there is no requirement for the induction to have occurred before the judge starts sitting and this means situations like Darbyshire's can still occur.

Some have suggested that judges should attend a 'judicial college' for a period of up to two months, with lectures and seminars being supplemented with mock trials.[203] Pannick rejects the idea that because a judge comes from practice there is an inherent ability to cope with the work of a judge, pointing out that the differences between practice and the bench are significant. The cost of doing so would be high and in addition the scheduling of appointments would also have to be centralized so that there was a 'start date' for judicial appointments to allow this to occur. Realistically it is difficult to see how this would happen.

The Judicial College is part of the judiciary of England and Wales and therefore it does not formally have a role for Justices of the Supreme Court, however as noted earlier Supreme Court Justices are welcome to attend seminars run by the College. The Supreme Court website does not include any formal reference to training for the justices and yet presumably there is recognition that specific training is valuable for them too. It would be sensible for the court to consider disclosing what training is offered to, and undertaken by, the Justices so that there can be full confidence in the work that they undertake.

🔄 QUESTION FOR REFLECTION

Pannick has suggested that those wishing to be judges should be 'trained' before becoming full members of the judiciary. Do you think this is now unnecessary since full-time judicial appointments will ordinarily come from the part-time judiciary?

8.6 Judicial salaries

Judicial salaries will be considered in the next chapter in the context of judicial independence (9.2.2), as the paying of salaries raises an interesting constitutional question regarding how independent the judiciary are from the state. However, in this section the more mundane aspect of the amount judges are paid will be discussed.

It will be remembered that the judiciary are separated into grades (Table 8.1) and this is reflected in their pay (see Table 8.6).

---

202. Penny Darbyshire, *Sitting in Judgment: The Working Lives of Judges* (Hart Publishing 2011) 111–12.
203. David Pannick, *Judges* (OUP 1987) 71.

It will be remembered that many judicial jobs are also part-time. This most notably includes recorders and deputy district judges, but can also include counsel acting as a deputy High Court judge, and retired judges who continue to act until they are unable to do so for statutory reasons.[204] A fixed daily fee is given for these, as set out in Table 8.7.

In October 2016, the then Lord Chancellor commissioned the Review Body on Senior Salaries (SSRB) to carry out a major review of the judicial salary structure. The Board's report was published in October 2018 and recommended increasing judicial

Table 8.6 The current salary grades of the judiciary (as at 1 April 2020)

Judicial Grade	£
1	267,509
1.1	238,868
2	230,717
3	219,396
4	192,679
5+	163,585
5	154,527
5.1	148.820
5.2	143,095
6	134,717
7	114,793
8	91,217

Table 8.7 Daily fees for part-time judiciary

Description	£
Retired Supreme Court judge	1048.72
Retired Lord Justice of Appeal[205]	997.26
Retired High Court judges	917.52
Deputy High Court judge[206]	917.52
Recorder[207]	681.40
Deputy circuit judge[208]	681.40
Deputy district judge, including district judge (magistrates' court)	533.92

204. A judge who has retired may continue to sit until the age of 75, see, for example, *Constitutional Reform Act 2005*, s 39(2)(c).
205. When sitting in the Court of Appeal. When sitting in the High Court, they receive the retired High Court fee.
206. This is a practitioner sitting as a High Court judge.
207. A practitioner sitting at circuit level.
208. A retired judge sitting at circuit level.

pay between 2.5 and 32 per cent, depending on judicial grade and which of the two pension schemes a judge is in.[209] Media reporting on the proposal was overwhelmingly negative, with headlines such as 'Where is the justice! Judges set for thumping £60,000 pay rises while hardworking Britons are forced to watch every penny.'[210] It is perhaps as a result of the backlash against the proposals that it was a 2 per cent pay rise that was actually announced by the Lord Chancellor in October 2018. However, in June 2019 the government announced the introduction of a 'recruitment and retention allowance' in an attempt to address the ongoing recruitment crisis within the judiciary (discussed earlier at 8.1). Puisne judges received an allowance worth twenty-five per cent of their basic salary, and a fifteen per cent allowance was granted to Crown Court and Upper Tribunal judges. The government also committed to long-term pension scheme change. In July 2020, an additional 2 per cent pay rise was announced for the judiciary.

Whilst at first sight judicial salaries look high when compared to 'ordinary' salaries, it must be remembered that these are the brightest and most senior people in their profession. A comparison can be drawn to 'flag rank'[211] in the military who receive comparable pay. However, if one were to compare them to the salaries of the chief executives of FTSE100 companies it would look extremely modest.[212] The same could be true of commerce, where high salaries are paid. If we look to the professions, it has already been noted that high salaries can be commanded by the very best practitioners. It is those that we should target to become judges, meaning that for many a significant pay cut is taken to become a judge. In their review of judicial salaries, the SSRB noted that the judicial role needed to be made more attractive in order to recruit more high quality legal professionals as judges in the context of unprecedented difficulties with filling judicial vacancies (as noted at the beginning of this chapter). The role of salaries in this are significant when considered in the context of tax and pensions changes which have reduced (by up to £80,000 in some cases) the total net remuneration for new judges, and a significant increase in workload, amongst other factors.[213]

8.7 Sharing the judiciary

Traditionally, apart from the *Employment Appeals Tribunal*, where puisne and circuit judges would regularly sit, there was no overlap between the court judiciary and tribunal judiciary. They were considered to be distinct personnel and there was no crossover. Indeed, tribunal judges were not given the title 'judge' and were considered more akin to civil servants than judges.

However, the *Tribunals, Courts and Enforcement Act 2007* brought about changes and the belief that the tribunal judiciary were part of the judicial system. Along with

209. Review Body on Senior Salaries, *Supplement to the Fortieth Annual Report on Senior Salaries 2018 (Report No 90)—Major Review of the Judicial Salary Structure* (SSRB 2018) <https://assets.publishing.service.gov.uk/government/uploads/system/uploads/attachment_data/file/750331/supplement-fortieth-annual-report-senior-salaries-2018.pdf> 2.
210. Simon Walters, 'Where is the justice! Judges set for thumping £60,000 pay rises while hardworking Britons are forced to watch every penny' (*Daily Mail*, 2018) <https://www.dailymail.co.uk/news/article-6266937/Judges-set-thumping-60K-pay-rises-hardworking-Britons-forced-watch-penny.html>.
211. ie Rear Admiral/Major General/Air Vice-Marshal and above.
212. Where an average salary of around £5m per annum can be expected.
213. Review Body on Senior Salaries, *Supplement to the Fortieth Annual Report on Senior Salaries 2018 (Report No 90)—Major Review of the Judicial Salary Structure* (SSRB 2018) <https://assets.publishing.service.gov.uk/government/uploads/system/uploads/attachment_data/file/750331/supplement-fortieth-annual-report-senior-salaries-2018.pdf> 1.

creating the Senior President of Tribunals as a judicial post, the Act permitted an English judge[214] to sit in a tribunal, with the agreement of the Lord Chief Justice and Senior President of Tribunals.[215] This meant that some of the more complicated tribunal work began to be heard by judges, bringing greater certainty to the process.

There was then a desire for the tribunal judiciary to be able to sit in the courts too. There was recognition that the tribunal judiciary have extensive judicial experience and would be suitable for sitting on cases within the courts too. Given that there is chronic delay in both the civil and criminal justice systems, permitting judges to sit in tribunals and tribunal judiciary to sit in the courts would mean that resources could be deployed more easily. Ultimately this has happened, with the *Crime and Courts Act 2013* stating:

> The Lord Chief Justice's deployment responsibility includes (so far as it would not otherwise do so, and subject to having regard to the responsibilities of the Senior President of Tribunals) responsibility for the maintenance of appropriate arrangements for—
>
> (a) the deployment to tribunals of judiciary deployable to tribunals, and
> (b) the deployment to courts in England and Wales of judiciary deployable to such courts.[216]

This has been followed by further statutory amendments that allow chamber presidents, judges of the Upper Tribunal, and presidents of the employment tribunals to act as High Court judges when required.[217] Similarly, judges of the First-Tier and Upper Tribunals have the right to sit in the Crown and County Courts when requested by the Lord Chief Justice with the consent of the Senior President of Tribunals. This has the potential to increase the number of judges who can sit in those courts, something that could be important in the county court where there is concern at the number of circuit judges dealing with civil matters.[218]

The *Courts and Tribunals (Judiciary and Functions of Staff) Act 2018* has further increased the mobility of the judiciary by allowing for the deployment of judges between the courts and tribunals, as long as they have met the statutory eligibility for their appointment.[219] So, for example, recorders are able to sit as judges in the Upper Tribunal, senior employment judges can sit in both the First-tier and Upper Tribunals, and temporarily appointed deputy High Court judges can sit in any court or tribunal to which a deputy High Court judge is usually deployed (ie the Crown Court or High Court).

An advantage of the courts and tribunal judiciary being able to sit in either jurisdiction is that it is even possible for them to sit concurrently. This is something that the Senior President of Tribunals has flagged as a potential solution to inefficiencies within the justice system.[220] Certain property disputes require adjudication between two different locations. Certain issues are matters reserved to the county court and yet others are reserved to the tribunals. Issues being resolved in one hearing would save

285

---

214. ie Lord Justice of Appeal or below.
215. *Tribunals, Courts and Enforcement Act 2007*, s 6.
216. CCA 2013, s 21.
217. *Senior Courts Act 1981*, s 9(1) as amended. Note that the judges, including tribunal judges, must have been approved by the JAC to sit as s 9 judges.
218. See Rt Hon Lord Justice Briggs, *Civil Courts Structure Review: Final Report* (HM Judiciary: London 2016) 87–90. This is partly because the circuit judges are needed to sit in the Crown Court and the Family Court, meaning that civil work is often left to other judges.
219. *Courts and Tribunals (Judiciary and Functions of Staff) Act 2018*, s 1.
220. See Sir Ernest Ryder 'The Context of Change' Speech to Lancaster University Law School, 4 November 2016. Available at: <https://www.lancaster.ac.uk/law/blogs/research/lord-justice-ryder-law-school-lecture/>.

considerable costs and is of greater benefit to the parties who only need to attend once. There are a number of areas where allowing business to be dealt with by a judge sitting as both a tribunal and court would make sense.

8.8 Magistrates

So far this chapter has explored judicial posts. This section will explore the role of magistrates. Whilst they are not members of the judiciary in the way that the posts discussed so far are, they do exercise a 'quasi-judicial' function hearing and ruling on summary trials (ie those that take place in the magistrates' court). The office of magistrate is an ancient one that dates back to their use by the Sovereign to keep order. It is now a quasi-judicial role although, as will be seen, not usually a full-time role.

For the purposes of this section it is necessary to distinguish between lay magistrates and district judges (magistrates' court), the latter of whom, as has been mentioned briefly earlier in the chapter (at 8.1.3.3), are members of the judiciary. This section will detail both discuss the merits of each, and then consider whether either should be preferred.

8.8.1 Lay magistrates

The first type of magistrate to discuss is the lay magistrate, also known as a Justice of the Peace (JP), an ancient office that indicated a person was assigned the role of the keeping the King's Peace over a defined area. The office has changed significantly over the years and now, rather than being directly responsible for the arrest of persons and the investigation of crime, modern magistrates keep the peace by sitting in judgment on those who are brought before them.

Lay magistrates are the biggest of the 'judicial' groupings. On 1 April 2020 there were 13,177 magistrates,[221] a number which has been in decline since 2012. Indeed, since the previous edition of this book, the number has declined by over 1,800, from 15,003 in 2018. The reduction is partly because there has, in common with other branches of the court service, been a reduction in the number of magistrates' courts and, therefore, magistrates. There has also been a reduction in recruitment, combined with the resignation or retirement of approximately 2,000 magistrates a year. The shortage of magistrates looks set to continue, with over 50 per cent set to reach the age of retirement within the next decade.[222]

Apart from certain preliminary matters, lay magistrates do not sit alone and they are therefore assigned to a local justice area which is often known as a 'bench'. Each year they elect a lay magistrate as the Chairman of the bench[223] who is responsible for keeping the magistrates on their bench up to date with criminal justice reforms and dealing with pastoral issues. This is an unpaid administrative role that involves the person being the leader and representative of the bench. It also involves the chair (and nominated deputies) convening the training and ensuring that, in conjunction with the courts' legal advisers (see 14.6) the operation of the bench runs smoothly.

---

221.   Ministry of Justice, 'Diversity of the judiciary: legal professions, judicial appointments and judicial office holders 2020 statistics' <https://assets.publishing.service.gov.uk/government/uploads/system/uploads/attachment_data/file/918530/diversity-of-the-judiciary-2020-data-tables.ods> Table 3.5.
222.   Judiciary of England and Wales, *A Strategy for the Magistracy 2019–2022* (Judicial Office, 2019) 9.
223.   *Courts Act 2003*, s 17.

The organization of magistrates' courts used to be rather complicated with benches being accountable to Magistrates' Courts Committees (MCCs), but from April 2005 the system was simplified when magistrates' courts were brought into (the now) HM Courts and Tribunal Service.

8.8.1.1 Appointment

As might be imagined from the term, lay magistrates are not legally qualified although, interestingly, neither is legal qualification a barrier to appointment and there have, in the past, been lawyers and legal academics who have sat as lay magistrates. However, the vast majority of lay magistrates have no legal knowledge other than that gained through their training. Lay magistrates are also so styled because, unlike their professional brethren (discussed later), they are unpaid. Lay magistrates are volunteers but they are eligible for expenses[224] to cover loss of wages (although this amount is 'capped', meaning some justices will actually sit at a loss), travelling expenses, etc.

To be appointed a lay magistrate, a person must either reside in the petty sessional area that they wish to sit in, or live within fifteen miles of this area. This is, in part, because it has always been thought that a significant advantage of the magistracy is that they know the local area. That said, whilst magistrates were traditionally not allowed to sit outside of their petty sessional area, this is no longer true and there is now a mechanism that permits magistrates to sit in other areas.[225] This change was recommended as it was believed it could be useful for justices to assist neighbouring benches to tackle any delay that might accrue because of a reduction (temporary or otherwise) in the number of justices sitting in that area.[226] To an extent it can be argued that this is not dissimilar to the way that circuit judges can be moved around a circuit, although on a much smaller scale. That said, it does appear to conflict with the idea of the magistracy bringing local representation.

The maximum age for appointment to a magistrate is 65 on the basis that they must retire at the age of 70 and accordingly the Lord Chancellor will not appoint someone over 65 since by the time the training programme has been completed effectively there will be little time left for the justice to sit. The minimum age for appointment is 18 although the Lord Chancellor used to state that it would be exceptional for a person to be appointed under the age of 27. However, the Lord Chancellor has withdrawn this comment and there has been a concerted effort by the government to appoint younger magistrates. The rule was effectively relaxed in 2003.[227] In 2015 Alex Hyne became the youngest person to be appointed to the magistracy at age 18.

⟳ QUESTION FOR REFLECTION

Is it realistic to suggest that a magistrate can be appointed at the age of 18? Would they command the required respect of defendants, lawyers, and fellow magistrates?

---

224. ibid, s 15.
225. ibid, s 10.
226. Lord Justice Auld, *A Review of the Criminal Courts of England and Wales* (HMSO 2001) 100.
227. 'Younger Magistrates Wanted', DCA Press Release, 27 October 2003.

🔊 LISTEN TO THE PODCAST

For guidance on how to answer this question and a discussion of the main issues, listen to the author's podcast on the online resources: **www.oup.com/he/gillespie-weare8e**

Certain persons are automatically disqualified from being a magistrate, the most notable being those listed in Table 8.8.

There is also, of course, the proviso that individuals may not be suitable depending on their own circumstances. The Ministry of Justice has listed the qualities of a magistrate:

- good character
- maturity and sound temperament
- understanding and communication
- sound judgement
- social awareness
- commitment and reliability.

Table 8.8 Automatic disqualification

Serving or recently retired police officers (including Special Constables)	Bailiffs
Traffic wardens/officers or civilian employees of police forces	An undischarged bankrupt
Prison Service employee (and spouses/partners)	Anyone who has, or whose partner has, been convicted of a serious offence or number of minor offences
Spouses, partners, or close family relative of the above if they work in same local justice area.	Store detective
Those whose work on community activities that make being appointed a magistrate inappropriate (CPS, Probation Service, Police and Crime Commissioner, etc)	National Crime Agency employee

As noted at the beginning of this section, there is a shortage of magistrates. To increase recruitment, the judiciary have set out a series of objectives within the *Magistracy Strategy 2019–2022* to increase the number of applicants. These include:

- asking magistrates to share ideas on how to attract people to the role
- conducting exit interviews with those who leave the magistracy to try and understand whether aspects of the role may be impacting retention and recruitment rates
- the establishment of a national steering group to promote the profile of the magistracy across England and Wales.[228]

It remains to be seen how effective these strategies are going to be. However, it is clear that sustainable recruitment is needed within the magistracy, however it is secured.

228. Judiciary of England and Wales, *A Strategy for the Magistracy 2019 2022* (Judicial Office, 2019) 9.

8.8.1.2 Diversity

Successive governments have attempted to broaden the magistracy because there continues to be a perception that the magistracy, like most of the judiciary, is a bastion of white, middle-class men. Actually, as will be seen, this is no longer true and lay magistrates are amongst the more representative 'members' of the judiciary. Traditionally perceptions persisted because of media caricatures but it is now possible to rebut some of these perceptions through the use of published statistics.

As of 1 April 2020 there were more female lay magistrates (7,399) than male magistrates (5,776),[229] something that has been the case since 2008.

What of ethnicity? The latest judicial statistics suggest that the magistracy are more representative than other sectors of the judiciary. Thirteen per cent of the lay magistracy consider themselves to be a member of an ethnic minority,[230] which roughly equates to the percentage of people who identify themselves as a member of an ethnic minority in the general population. This is significantly better than any other group within the judiciary (discussed earlier in the chapter) although it does not, of course, mean that recruitment campaigns to increase ethnic minority representations can end, since it should not just be a question about getting fair representation, but ensuring that members of the ethnic minorities are an accepted part of the judicial system.

Whilst sex and race appear to contradict the traditional stereotypes of the magistracy other data are perhaps less helpful. Age is particularly relevant. The latest judicial statistics show that over 80 per cent of the magistracy are above the age of 50, with just over 1 per cent below the age of 30.[231] This is perhaps one of the greater challenges and arguably should be less problematic than with members of the judiciary. Whilst judges will be somewhat older by the time they are appointed because they have had to prove themselves as a member of the legal professions first (discussed earlier in the chapter) the same is not necessarily true of lay magistrates. It will be recalled from earlier that the Lord Chancellor has previously appointed teenagers to the magistracy. Whilst there may be some eyebrows raised by such appointments it is clear that a magistracy where over 80 per cent are above the age of 50 does not assist in rebutting the criticism that magistrates are all old.

289

⟳ QUESTION FOR REFLECTION

Were you surprised by the figures on representation in the judiciary given earlier? Before reading this page what were your perceptions on how diverse the magistracy were? Do you think it matters whether the magistracy are diverse or not?

Apart from ethnicity and race the other factor that is often a talking point is their socio-economic backgrounds. Certainly Auld accepted, without adducing any modern evidence to support this, that magistrates were not necessarily representative but that this did not prevent them from discharging their duties.[232] Identifying the socio-economic background of the magistracy is not easy since the government does not apparently

---

229. Ministry of Justice, 'Diversity of the judiciary: legal professions, judicial appointments and judicial office holders 2020 statistics' <https://assets.publishing.service.gov.uk/government/uploads/system/uploads/attachment_data/file/918530/diversity-of-the-judiciary-2020-data-tables.ods> Table 3.5.
230. ibid.
231. ibid.
232. Lord Justice Auld, *A Review of the Criminal Courts of England and Wales* (HMSO 2001) 98.

collate such information.[233] However, in a recent report published by *Transform Justice* it was suggested that 'magistrates are still disproportionately middle class, with over half in manager, senior official or in professional occupations . . . and only 1.5 per cent in sales or customer services . . . '.[234] Collating more detailed data in this area is certainly a way of tackling diversity (including correcting misperceptions), as seen in the context of ethnic minority diversity, and it may be advisable for the same to occur in relation to socio-economic backgrounds.

Another possible reason for lack of diversity in the socio-economic background of magistrates is that they tend to be appointed from professional backgrounds,[235] in part because of the sitting requirements. Unlike with jury service there is no obligation to let an employee have time off to sit as a magistrate although there are benefits in doing so. Public bodies will consider it a civil obligation and will normally therefore give the time off without a requirement for leave. The same could be true of medium-to large-scale professional firms but how easy would it be for a builder or decorator to take a day off?

8.8.1.3 **Training**

One of the significant changes in recent years has been the training that lay magistrates undertake. As noted earlier, they are not normally legally qualified but, although they are assisted by a legal adviser, they do form the tribunal of both fact and law in summary trials, ie they do decide on legal points. Also, criminal justice policy is one of the faster-moving areas of political controversy and most governments will introduce changes to criminal process or sentencing regularly. Lay justices need to understand their powers and duties, along with having a basic familiarity over some of what they hear.

Training is now overseen by the Judicial College (discussed earlier in the chapter at 8.5) although much of it is undertaken locally. According to the Magistrates Association, the main associative body for lay magistrates, training is split into initial training (undertaken during the first year) and continuing training (which, as its name suggests, continues while a magistrate continues to sit).

The initial training consists of five phases:

1. **Initial basic training.** This takes place before a new magistrate will sit in court. This will involve the basic training about the role of a magistrate, conduct of trials, etc.

2. **Mentoring.** Each new magistrate will be assigned an experienced magistrate who will act as their mentor and guide them through the training process. The new magistrate will undertake six formal mentored sittings during the first year or so where the mentor will discuss issues that arise.

3. **Core training.** To ensure that magistrates are aware of all aspects of the criminal justice system they will visit penal establishments, police stations, etc. They will also be given an individualized work plan that will discuss the training that they are required to undertake.

---

233. Hansard, HC WA, vol 434, col 638W (9 June 2005).
234. Transform Justice, *Magistrates: Representatives of the People?* (Transform Justice 2014) 11.
235. Penny Darbyshire, 'Magistrates' in Mike McConville and Geoffrey Wilson (eds), *The Handbook of the Criminal Justice Process* (OUP 2002) 296.

4. **Consolidation training**. This takes place at the end of the first year and builds upon the sittings that the magistrate has undertaken and also the various training courses that the magistrate has attended.

5. **First appraisal**. The new magistrate will, sometime after the first year, be given a formal appraisal where a more experienced (and specially trained) magistrate will sit in court and observe how the magistrate acts, follows procedures, etc.

Continuing training is required for all magistrates. Every three years a magistrate will be given a formal appraisal which is designed to ensure that the magistrate continues to meet the competencies required of their role. If a magistrate does not meet this then remedial training may be given. As legislation is passed or key decisions made then they will be given update training. Increasingly this may be by e-learning or will take place in small groups led, for example, by the justices' clerk or a senior legal adviser.

Specific training is also required to do more than the 'basic' work. Thus, for example, if a magistrate wishes to sit in the youth court they will need to undertake specialist training and appraisals. Similarly, a person who wishes to sit as chair of a panel will also need further training and assessment.

8.8.1.4 Duties

Magistrates must sit for a minimum of twenty-six sessions each year, each session normally lasting a half-day, although it is not uncommon for magistrates to combine their sittings into a full day. Where the magistrates sit in the family proceedings court or youth court then there is normally an expectation that they will sit more often. The Magistrates Association states that the average magistrate sits for thirty-five sittings per year (seventeen and a half days) and the ordinary maximum is seventy sessions (although some believe that this is occasionally broken).[236] The average of thirty-five is a reduction from research published in 2000 where it was found that the average was forty-one sittings.[237] No reason has been given for this reduction but, even with the overall reduction in numbers of magistrates, it does not appear that the reduction in sittings is perhaps a result of less demand.

Lay magistrates will ordinarily sit in panels of three, and will always do so during trials. However, a single lay justice does also have some powers. Broadly speaking these are pre-trial matters, including the issuing of a summons or arrest warrant, certain matters relating to bail, including extending bail, the power to dismiss information where no evidence has been offered, the power to seek reports relating to sentencing, the granting of legal aid and some case-management rulings, including setting a timetable, and the service of documents and even ascertaining how the offender wishes to plead. Moreover, with the introduction of the *Criminal Justice and Courts Act 2015* (CJCA 2015), single magistrates can now conduct proceedings 'on the papers' against adults.[238] They are only able to try a written charge in relation to an adult who has been charged with a summary offence that is not punishable with imprisonment. The term 'trial by single justice on the papers' essentially refers to cases where everything is conducted in writing and there is no attendance of a prosecution or defence and thus

---

236. Penny Darbyshire, *Sitting in Judgment: The Working Lives of Judges* (Hart Publishing 2011) 411.
237. Rod Morgan and Neil Russell, *The Judiciary in the Magistrates' Courts* (Home Office 2000) 13, 18.
238. *Magistrates' Courts Act 1980*, s 16A as amended by CJCA 2015, s 48.

the case does not need to be heard in a courtroom. The types of cases that would be tried in this way include driving without insurance and TV licence evasion, with the aim of dealing with such cases, where uncontested and straightforward, in a more timely and proportionate manner.

8.8.2 District judge (magistrates' court)

The second type of magistrate is a very different creature. Now known as a district judge (magistrates' court) (DJMC) they used to be known as a 'stipendiary magistrate'. As their old name suggests, DJMCs are paid a salary (unlike lay magistrates), and, also unlike lay magistrates, they are members of the judiciary (noted at 8.1.3.3) and have similar terms of service to the other members of judiciary.

According to the most recent statistics there are 131 DJMCs and 86 deputy DJMCs (a part-time appointment akin to a recorder in the Crown Court).[239] Under s 23 CA 2003 there is provision to create the senior district judge (chief magistrate) and a deputy. The Act is silent as to what responsibility the holders of these offices have but the website of HM Courts and Tribunals Service states that the chief magistrate will hear the most sensitive cases in the magistrates' court, provide pastoral support for other DJMCs, and liaise with the senior judiciary on matters relating to DJMCs. The current senior district judge (chief magistrate) is District Judge Emma Arbuthnot and she is based in Marylebone magistrates' court.

8.8.2.1 Appointment

As noted earlier, the DJMC is a judicial post and in order to be appointed as either a DJMC or deputy DJMC a person must 'satisfy the judicial appointment eligibility condition on a five-year basis'.[240] This, in effect, means a solicitor (with rights of audience) or a barrister who has been qualified for five years. Realistically, however, a person would have to be qualified for a longer period than this to be appointed.

The actual appointment of DJMCs and deputy DJMCs is handled by the Judicial Appointments Commission (discussed earlier at 8.3.1) and the same process that is discussed for circuit judges and recorders applies equally to DJMCs. Before being appointed a DJMC it is expected that a person will have served as a deputy DJMC first. The expectation for deputies is that they will sit for a minimum of fifteen days per year although it is possible that they will sit for more. A deputy will be superintended by a full DJMC but it is quite possible that they will be sitting in different petty sessional areas and thus the deputy may be the senior judge in a petty sessional area. A DJMC is currently paid £114,793.[241] Deputy DJMCs are paid a daily rate which is currently £533.92.

Unlike circuit judges and above, a DJMC is not accorded any honorific title and so they remain simply Mr, Mrs, or Ms [n]. This is true of even the senior district judge (chief magistrate) who is given no special styling. DJMCs do not normally wear robes in court. They will be referred to as 'Sir' or 'Madam'.

---

239. Ministry of Justice, 'Diversity of the judiciary: legal professions, judicial appointments and judicial office holders 2020 statistics' <https://assets.publishing.service.gov.uk/government/uploads/system/uploads/attachment_data/file/918530/diversity-of-the-judiciary-2020-data-tables.ods> Table 3.5.

240. *Courts Act 2003*, s 22.

241. And is classified as a group 7 appointment. The deputy senior district judge (magistrates' court) is a group 5.2 appointment and is paid £140,289 and the senior district judge (magistrates' court) is a group 5 appointment and paid £154,527.

8.8.2.2 **Diversity**

It was noted earlier that the lay magistracy is diverse, at least in terms of sex and race, and certainly more diverse than the judiciary. What is the position of DJMCs? A key difference, of course, is that DJMCs are drawn from lawyers and, as has been noted already, lawyers are not necessarily representative of society as a whole.

The latest statistics show that there are fifty (38 per cent) female DJMCs and twenty-nine (34 per cent) female deputy DJMCs.[242] Certainly this is not as representative as the lay magistracy where, as was seen earlier, there are actually more female magistrates than male, but it compares favourably with the mainstream judiciary (discussed earlier in the chapter at 8.4.1.1). In terms of ethnicity, only nine per cent (ten) of DJMCs declare themselves as being from a black or ethnic minority background.[243] In terms of deputy DJMCs the position is similar, with four per cent (three) declaring themselves as being from a black or ethnic minority background.[244]

It would seem therefore that DJMCs (including deputies) are not representative of society as a whole but how do they compare with other members of the judiciary? It will be remembered from earlier in the chapter that the latest statistics suggest that, of the full-time circuit bench, only 4 per cent declare themselves as coming from an ethnic minority, with an even lower proportion being found in the senior judiciary. Accordingly, it can be argued that DJMCs are slightly more representative than the mainstream judiciary.

The latest figures also show the professional backgrounds of DJMCs and deputy DJMCs. Unlike in the mainstream judiciary, there are more former solicitors who are DJMCs (seventy-eight or 60 per cent) and deputy DJMCs (fifty-one or 60 per cent) than barristers.[245] It is not clear why this should be the case although it could partly be the belief of barristers that they stand a higher chance than solicitors of gaining a circuit-bench appointment. It may also be about perceptions of status. It has been noted that DJMCs believe that they are the 'forgotten judiciary'[246] and that they have little to do with the ordinary judiciary.

8.8.2.3 **Duties**

Unlike lay magistrates, DJMCs will ordinarily sit alone and when they do so they have the same powers as the bench of three lay magistrates. If they do sit with lay magistrates (which is rare) then they would automatically become the chair and the lay magistrates would sit as wingers. That said, they would each have only one vote and it would be perfectly possible for the lay magistrates to outvote the DJMC.

DJMCs and deputy DJMCs have, since 2000, been able to sit nationally and, unlike lay magistrates, they tend to sit outside their 'base' court more frequently. This is particularly important because district judges will frequently sit on complicated or lengthy trials, in part because they can sit alone.[247] One of the difficulties traditionally with lay magistrate trials is that the justices will only sit in a half-day block which means they

---

242. Ministry of Justice, 'Diversity of the judiciary: legal professions, judicial appointments and judicial officeholders 2020 statistics' <https://assets.publishing.service.gov.uk/government/uploads/system/uploads/attachment_data/file/918530/diversity-of-the-judiciary-2020-data-tables.ods> Table 3.1.
243. ibid.
244. ibid.
245. ibid.
246. Penny Darbyshire, *Sitting in Judgment: The Working Lives of Judges* (Hart Publishing 2011) 168.
247. *Courts Act 2003*, s 26.

can only conduct short cases. Where a trial is likely to take longer than this then a district judge can hear the case as he will sit either permanently or, where he is a deputy, in a block of time. This type of case may not arise in one single petty sessional area so a national jurisdiction allows the district judges to try matters in other areas in a way analogous to how circuit judges move around the circuit.

There has undoubtedly been tension between lay magistrates and DJMCs and stories abound about how DJMCs have been shunned by members of the lay magistracy.[248] Auld, who identified a similar trend, believed that there was a belief in the lay magistracy that there was somehow a national policy to replace lay magistrates with DJMCs,[249] although he rejected this belief. Certainly given the number of lay magistrates that exist it would seem highly unlikely that such a policy could ever succeed, not least because of the cost. Increasingly the DJMCs have tried to 'build bridges' with the lay magistrates and this has included, for example, inviting lay justices to talk with them and to observe them in court.[250]

8.8.3 **Lay magistrates or DJMCs?**

It has already been noted that there is tension between lay magistrates and DJMCs but which should be used and why? It has also been noted that lay magistrates do not appear to always trust DJMCs and believe that they are trying to replace them which seems somewhat unrealistic. Perhaps the greater fear, however, is that some lay magistrates are concerned that if DJMCs are appointed to their courts they will lose the 'interesting' work.[251] Certainly if 'interesting' is classified as the more serious crimes then it is quite likely that this will be true. It has been noted that DJMCs can sit for longer periods of time, including consecutive days, and thus the more serious trials, which are probably lengthier, will take place before DJMCs.

8.8.3.1 **Representative**

It is clear from the preceding analysis that DJMCs are less representative than lay magistrates but does this matter? Certainly there is some evidence that people believe it can matter. Research has showed that '[m]agistrates were perceived to come from a wider cross section of society than DJs'[252] and that they were perceived to be more 'in touch' and 'down to earth' which could have an impact on the confidence that people have in the magistracy.

What do we mean by representative though? It will be remembered that whilst statistics clearly demonstrate that they are representative in terms of sex and race, it is less clear that they are representative in other ways, particularly social demographics. Arguably this is even more true of those who sit in family and youth matters where the minimum number of sittings is greater, meaning that unless an employer gives them the time off as a public duty (which tends to occur only in the public sector and professional backgrounds) there is less likelihood of people wishing to undertake these duties as it would require them using their annual leave allowance.[253] There is also concern

---

248. *See Penny Darbyshire, Sitting in Judgment: The Working Lives of Judges* (Hart Publishing 2011) 166, who presents some examples.
249. Lord Justice Auld, *A Review of the Criminal Courts of England and Wales* (HMSO 2001) 98.
250. Penny Darbyshire, *Sitting in Judgment: The Working Lives of Judges* (Hart Publishing 2011) 166.
251. ibid.
252. Ipsos Mori, *The Strengths and Skills of the Judiciary in the Magistrates' Courts* (Ministry of Justice 2011) 18.
253. ibid, 19.

about age. Whilst it was noted earlier that some very young magistrates have been appointed (which potentially raises issues as to their life experience) the majority of lay justices are over 50 and just over 1 per cent are younger than 30.

The idea of magistrates being local officers of justice has always been considered an important factor and certainly there is some evidence that this means they can represent local issues.[254] The same research suggested that the link to localities was welcomed by many respondents. However, is this necessarily true or important anymore? Robson, herself a magistrate, has argued that the concept of locality is being eroded. 'Even before the [court closures], courts have been serving wider areas so that although the personnel may seem more representative of the population at large it may no longer have many local ties.'[255] Certainly over recent years there has been a push towards closing small, local courts and merging them into larger courts that cover a wider regional area. Whilst the magistrates are still appointed through a link to their community, at these larger courts they will sit on cases from all over the area, not just the cases from their own locality. Accordingly, can it be said that they are representative of the locality and, in any event, is that always a good thing? Whilst there have been some community justice initiatives it must be questioned whether we want local variances when it relates to crimes actually being dealt with at court.

8.8.3.2 Efficiency

The manner in which DJMCs hear cases will often differ dramatically from how lay magistrates hear cases. As practitioners of law they are familiar with many of the aspects and arguments that are likely to be raised, including legal issues. Whereas a lay bench would have to confer about decisions and also receive advice from their legal adviser on any legal issues that were raised, including any submission of no case to answer, a DJMC is able to just deal with the matter alone.

An effect of this is that trials are conducted considerably faster than in a trial presided over by lay magistrates.[256] It may be thought that the trials take place more quickly because they are more prepared to accept the arguments of the prosecution, but when Darbyshire undertook shadowing of a DJMC she found that it was often the prosecution who were at the wrong end of judicial wrath for inappropriate preparation[257] and that this was, in part, to demonstrate their independence.

An interesting comment that arose out of the research of Darbyshire was that some DJMCs considered their role to be inquisitorial rather than adversarial.[258] It will be remembered from Chapter 1 that the English Legal System tends to operate on the basis of the adversarial principle save for very few exceptions. The criminal justice system is supposed to be the paradigm of the adversarial system and it is perhaps surprising therefore that such comments are made. However, DJMCs do appear to be more interventionist than lay magistrates are or indeed what a circuit judge would be (for fear of prejudicing a jury).

---

254.   ibid, 17.
255.   Glenna Robson, 'No Further Forward?' (2012) 176 *Criminal Law & Justice Weekly* 39, 40.
256.   Penny Darbyshire, *Sitting in Judgment: The Working Lives of Judges* (Hart Publishing 2011) 162, and Rod Morgan and Neil Russell, *The Judiciary in the Magistrates' Courts* (Home Office 2000).
257.   Penny Darbyshire, *Sitting in Judgment: The Working Lives of Judges* (Hart Publishing 2011) 163.
258.   ibid.

The judicial skills research showed that DJMCs will ordinarily deal with matters in a proactive way: 'A number of professional users and court staff also noted that district judges were more proficient case managers as they got to the heart of the issue and moved cases on more efficiently than magistrates.'[259] This can be an important point and links to the 'inquisitorial' point made earlier. As a legally qualified professional, with the powers of both the tribunal of fact and law, it is likely that a DJMC can identify what the key issues are that will lead to him deciding guilt or innocence and direct attention to these points, removing some of the superfluous statements or evidence that will not greatly assist (eg, opening speeches). Careful and rigorous case management is now a requirement of the *Criminal Procedure Rules*[260] and where cases are longer and more complex then this may be a significant reason for allowing a DJMC to deal with the matter.

8.8.3.3 Case-hardened?

Padfield argues that district judges are more likely to become 'case-hardened' (meaning they become less convinced by arguments since they see the same excuses being used in each case) and 'judicially burnt out' than lay magistrates,[261] although no conclusive evidence is shown for this. There has always been some concern as to whether magistrates become 'case-hardened' and thus less inclined to acquit a suspect. Certainly it was found that district judges were more likely to remand a person into custody rather than provide bail[262] and significantly more likely to impose a harsher punishment.[263] However, this by itself does not necessarily mean that district judges are more 'case-hardened' because these judges tend to get the more serious and complicated cases and this may explain the distinction. Morgan and Russell were unable to compare a trial by a lay bench with a trial by a district judge because the number of trials observed was so low that any comparison would be meaningless.[264]

Darbyshire, in her impressive anthropological study on judges, sat with three DJMCs and whilst it would be unwise to draw empirical conclusions from this study, it was clear that she did not necessarily find evidence of case-hardening. It is particularly noticeable that one of the DJMCs—Portia—sitting in the youth court was prepared to give the prosecution a hard time and was regularly exasperated by their preparation and presentation.[265] That said, it was also clear that matters were dealt with very briskly. On the first day that Darbyshire sat with Portia in the youth court she dealt with three cases in under fifteen minutes,[266] although it would seem that they were guilty pleas. However, it was also clear that she was concerned that defendants were given an opportunity. Darbyshire recounts a story of a 15-year-old boy who was charged, inter alia, with driving with excess alcohol and who 'wanted to get it over with'. The DJMC persuaded the mother not to allow him to make a plea straight away but instead to talk to the duty solicitor first as 'these cases can be complex and I don't know how a 15-year-old can be confident he can understand the technicalities'.[267] A case-hardened judge may not have done so since a 15-year-old cannot legally drive in any event.

---

259.   Ipsos Mori, *The Strengths and Skills of the Judiciary in the Magistrates' Courts* (Ministry of Justice 2011) 21.
260.   The Criminal Procedure Rules 2020, SI 2020/759 r 3.2.
261.   Nicola Padfield and Jonathan Reed, *Text and Materials on the Criminal Justice Process* (5th edn, LexisNexis 2016) 277.
262.   Rod Morgan and Neil Russell, *The Judiciary in the Magistrates' Courts* (Home Office 2000) 50.
263.   ibid, 52.
264.   ibid, 52.
265.   Penny Darbyshire, *Sitting in Judgment: The Working Lives of Judges* (Hart Publishing 2011) 161.
266.   ibid, 155–6.
267.   ibid, 156.

The speed at which DJMCs handle cases and the fact that they are significantly more interventionist than lay magistrates may lead to the appearance that DJMCs are case-hardened, but without being able to properly account for the differences in conviction rates (including the possibility that lay magistrates may improperly acquit) it is difficult to know whether case-hardening does, in fact, exist.

8.8.3.1 Tinkers, tailors, and judges?

One interesting issue of note is that there is suspicion of the lay magistracy by the judiciary, including (but not restricted to) DJMCs. Darbyshire notes that the DJMCs are contemptuous of lay magistrates[268] and that the feeling was shared by many judges who considered them to be 'biased towards authority—the police and social workers'.[269] Of course it is difficult to prove such assertions, not least because there are so many reasons why the conviction and acquittal rates may be different. Certainly, however, it is clear that DJMCs convict a higher proportion of defendants, but lay magistrates convict a higher proportion of defendants than juries (discussed later). Whether that tells us anything is another question though since it is impossible to know how many convicted people are innocent or guilty people acquitted. However, research does appear to suggest that some lay justices do appear to set the criminal standard of proof too low[270] and that this is one reason why there are concerns within the professional judiciary about the quality of the lay magistracy.

It was noted earlier that some people believe that DJMCs may get case-hardened and the speed at which they deliberate on cases may raise questions as to whether justice is too summary. Some have suggested that the ideal solution would be to merge the current position, ie make the magistrates' court a 'mini Crown Court' with a DJMC presiding over the court alongside two lay justices.[271] Under such an approach the tribunal of law would be the DJMC and the lay justices would have to take the law from him but the tribunal of fact would be the three judges collectively (this model currently occurs in appeals from the magistrates' court to the Crown Court, see 16.2.1). Some wonder whether, however, such an approach could lead to the DJMC dominating the court, and the lay justices feeling that they must follow the lead of the DJMC.

Liberty suggested an alternative whereby the tribunal would be a DJMC and three lay justices, the DJMC being the tribunal of law and the lay justices being the tribunal of fact.[272] This would, in effect, create a true 'mini Crown Court' albeit with justices of the peace rather than jurors. The immediate difficulty with this is that lay magistrates sit for half-days and thus complicated or longer trials would not be able to cope with this system. The solution that Liberty proposes is that lay magistrates sit in blocks of time[273] but this itself carries with it disadvantages, not least the fact that it may put off more employers from releasing their staff, thus potentially increasing the reliance on magistrates drawn from the public sector.

268. ibid, 166, 172.
269. ibid, 411.
270. Penny Darbyshire, 'An Essay on the Importance and Neglect of the Magistracy' [1997] *Criminal Law Review* 627.
271. See Liberty, *Magistrates' Courts and Public Confidence* (The Civil Liberties Trust 2002) who believed strongly that a mixed bench could bring much-needed certainty to the bench.
272. ibid, 10–13.
273. ibid, 12.

Nothing came of the suggestion of a hybrid court and DJMCs continue to primarily sit alone. Auld argued that this was the preference of both the lay magistracy and the district judges,[274] with the former liking the ability to chair their own courts,[275] and the latter not seeing any real purpose in using lay magistrates. An issue that has never been truly resolved is that there is no clear guidance as to when a district judge should be used and when a case should be heard by a lay bench. It has been noted that the suggestion has always been that a district judge should be used for the more serious and complicated cases, but lay magistrates may well be unhappy with this as it creates a de facto second class of summary trials, ie those presided over by magistrates.

The use of district judges is likely to continue, not least because of their efficiency as discussed earlier. This can only be taken so far though. Morgan and Russell argue that one district judge could replace thirty lay magistrates,[276] but the expense of that would be enormous (24,000 lay justices, on that formula, would be replaced by 800 DJMCs, each on over £100,000 per year) and so it is simply not realistic. The judicial skills research suggested that it was more complicated than Morgan and Russell suggested it was and that efficiency of a DJMC did not always compensate for the extra expense,[277] although it was true when they were dealing with the more complex 'either-way' offences.

However, irrespective of the costs, successive governments have reaffirmed their commitment to the lay magistracy, as have senior members of the judiciary, and it is likely that district judges will, therefore, continue to act alongside, rather than replace, lay justices.

◀▶ Summary

This chapter has introduced the judiciary and the concept of the judicial office. In particular it has:

- Identified that there are different levels of judges, with the senior judiciary comprising the Lord Chief Justice, Master of the Rolls, and the Heads of Division.

- Noted that the Lord Chief Justice is the head of the court judiciary but that the Senior President of Tribunals heads the tribunal judiciary.

- Identified how the tribunal judiciary are beginning to be integrated into the court judiciary and how judges can now sit interchangeably in the courts or tribunals.

- Identified that superior judges (puisne judges and above) have unlimited authority whereas the inferior judiciary are limited to the jurisdiction provided by statute.

- Considered how appointments to the judiciary are made and discussed how to make the judiciary more diverse.

- Explored the quasi-judicial role of magistrates, their appointment, and what the difference is between a lay magistrate and a district judge (magistrates' court).

---

274. Lord Justice Auld, *A Review of the Criminal Courts of England and Wales* (HMSO 2001) 102.
275. Obtainable from the Judicial Communications Office.
276. Rod Morgan and Neil Russell, *The Judiciary in the Magistrates' Courts* (Home Office 2000) 85.
277. Ipsos Mori, *The Strengths and Skills of the Judiciary in the Magistrates' Courts* (Ministry of Justice 2011) 48.

End-of-chapter questions

1. How can we boost the number of women and judges from black and other minority ethnicities? Has the JAC actually made any difference in terms of progressing this? How much longer should we wait?

2. Should the Lord Chancellor be able to veto the appointment of a judge? Why have a judicial appointments commission if their decisions can be set aside on a ministerial whim?

3. Have a look at the current judicial vacancies that need to be filled (https://www. judicialappointments.gov.uk/vacancies). What problems could be caused by vacancies not being filled in appointment rounds?

4. Read Liberty, *Magistrates' Courts and Public Confidence* (The Civil Liberties Trust 2002) and Penny Darbyshire, 'Magistrates' in Mike McConville and Geoffrey Wilson (eds), *The Handbook of the Criminal Justice Process* (OUP 2002) 292–4. Why do you think we continue with the idea of lay benches? Would it not be advisable for at least one justice to be a district judge (magistrates' court)? Can a trial before lay justices properly be called fair?

Further reading

Lord Burnett of Maldon LCJ, 'A Changing Judiciary in a Modern Age' Treasurer's Lecture 2019 (Ministry of Justice 2019), available at <https://www.judiciary.uk/wp-content/uploads/2019/02/mt-treasurers-lecture-final-for-publishing.pdf>.

This is the Lord Chief Justice's Treasurer's Lecture from 2019 in which he discusses judicial appointments and judicial diversity.

Darbyshire P, *Sitting in Judgment: The Working Lives of Judges* (Hart Publishing 2011) ch 8.

This presents the working lives of district judges (magistrates' court) in a very informative and user-friendly way.

Grove T, *A Magistrate's Tale* (Bloomsbury 2002).

Ordinarlly we would be loath to recommend an entire book but this is a fascinating insight of the author's selection to be a member of the magistracy and his initial period of sitting.

Hale B, 'Equality and the Judiciary: Why Should We Want More Women Judges?' [2001] *Public Law* 489.

This remains one of the most important pieces on why greater diversity is required. It is written by Lady Hale, the first female Supreme Court Justice and current President of the Supreme Court.

Lord Chancellor, Lord Chief Justice, and Senior President of Tribunals, *Transforming our Justice System* (Ministry of Justice 2016).

A policy statement by the Lord Chief Justice and Senior President of Tribunals that discusses how the justice system must transform to stay relevant. Within this plan there is considerable attention paid to ensuring the right judge hears the right case, and discusses ways in which the judiciary may change.

For self-test questions, flashcards, and links to useful websites, please visit the **online resources** at: **www.oup.com/he/gillespie-weare8e**

9

Judicial Independence

By the end of this chapter you will be able to:

- Assess the independence of the judiciary.
- Understand how independence of the judiciary is secured.
- Understand issues around judicial ethics.
- Consider restrictions on practice.

Introduction

Judicial independence is an important concept that is often discussed and yet there is very little literature that attempts to provide a definition.[1] It is frequently suggested that the classic definition is that judges should be independent from the executive but this is not possible in the most literal sense:

> Judges sit in courts provided by the state, they have offices provided, heated and lighted by the state, they have clerks paid by the state, they use books and computers mostly provided by the state, they are themselves paid by the state.[2]

This is an astute point and demonstrates that full independence is neither practicable nor particularly desirable but what does independence mean and why should judges be independent?

Before considering these questions and others in detail, it is important to recognize that when discussing judicial independence, what is being referred to is the independence of *both* the courts and tribunal judiciary. Indeed, s 1 of the *Tribunals, Courts and Enforcement Act 2007* amended the *Constitutional Reform Act 2005*, to ensure that the guarantee of judicial independence contained therein also applies to the tribunal judiciary.

---

1. Robert Stevens, *The Independence of the Judiciary: View from the Lord Chancellor's Office* (Clarendon Press 2003) 3.
2. Thomas Bingham, *The Business of Judging: Selected Essays and Speeches* (OUP 2000) 57–8.

9.1 Independent from whom?

The first issue to examine is who judges should be independent from. The law dictionary defines judicial independence as:

> The practice in the UK whereby judges are freed from outside pressures . . . .[3]

The notion of 'outside pressure' is significantly wider than simple independence from the executive although the definition continues by stating:

> [It is] secured by, eg the charging of judges' salaries on the Consolidated Fund, separation of judiciary from Parliament, security of tenure of office, judicial immunity.

This demonstrates that independence will ordinarily mean independence from the other arms of the state (executive and legislature) but that it need not be restricted to this, and the opening sentence of the definition—'outside pressures'—does suggest that it could be wider than this.

9.1.1 Independence from the state

It was noted earlier that complete independence from the state would be extremely difficult because the operation of the judiciary is a state responsibility, hence the reason it is considered to be one of the three arms.

9.1.1.1 Legislature

The *Constitutional Reform Act 2005* (CRA 2005) made a number of significant changes to the judiciary and one of these changes was to remove all full-time members of the judiciary from the legislature. Under s 137 CRA 2005 a full-time member of the judiciary may not sit in either House of Parliament. This is a direct contrast to the old system whereby the Law Lords, Lord Chief Justice, and (quite frequently) the Master of the Rolls were members of the House of Lords. Certainly the rule demonstrates independence from the legislature in so far as they are no longer members of both the judiciary and Parliament.

Judicial independence from the legislature is also provided for in parliamentary rules. A good example of this is *Erskine May* (which sets out the rules and protocols of Parliament), which states that a Member of Parliament should not criticize a judge by name in Parliament.[4] Interestingly, of course, this does not stop a Member from criticizing a judge *outside* Parliament and it will be seen that this has happened on a number of occasions. However, if it is outside Parliament then it could be suggested that this was not the *legislature* but merely someone who is a member of the legislature criticizing a judge.

9.1.1.2 Executive

The principal challenge for judicial independence is normally its relationship with the executive. Lord Bingham has already noted that pragmatically there will always be a degree of interrelationship between the executive and the judiciary but the nature of the interaction is crucial to independence. Until 2005 the principal link between the executive and the judiciary was through the Lord Chancellor.

---

3.   Leslie Curzon and Paul Richards, *The Longman Dictionary of Law* (7th edn, Pearson 2007) 327.
4.   UK Parliament, *Erskine May Online* (25th edn, 2019) <https://erskinemay.parliament.uk/> pt 3, ch 21, para 21.23.

Lord Chancellor

The Lord Chancellor (more formally the Lord High Chancellor of Great Britain) was historically an extremely important person. It is a historic office whose primary role was as Keeper of the Great Seal (the stamp by which formal documents were sealed by the monarch), but who was often the key counsellor to the monarch. Even in its more modern guise the office was important, and in social precedence is outranked only by members of the Royal Family and the Archbishop of Canterbury. Until 2005 the Lord Chancellor was also paid more than the Prime Minister although the last holder of the office prior to the 2005 reforms—Lord Falconer QC—voluntarily relinquished some of that pay.

The Lord Chancellor was anathema to the separation of powers. This was the doctrine first put forward by Montesquieu, an eighteenth-century jurist, who stated that man could only be free where the three elements of the state (executive, judiciary, and legislature) were separate. In its modern guise (but before the 2005 reforms) the Lord Chancellor was primarily a member of the executive. He ran his own department (what was known as the *Lord Chancellor's Department* but which then subsequently became the *Department for Constitutional Affairs* and then the *Ministry of Justice*) and was a member of the Cabinet. The Lord Chancellor was a political appointee and he had to resign when required to do so by the Prime Minister (including during reshuffles) or when the results of a General Election led to a new government being formed.

The Lord Chancellor, like all members of the UK executive, was a member of the legislature but he held a key role in that he presided over the deliberations of the House of Lords. Arguably this was less important than, for example, the Speaker of the House of Commons since the Lords traditionally regulates itself, but he was at least in name the presiding member. Finally, the Lord Chancellor was also a member of the judiciary since he was titular head of the judiciary and, as a member of the House of Lords, could sit (and would preside) in the appellate committee of the House of Lords.[5]

Although there was no doubt about the individual integrity of any modern Lord Chancellor[6] the fact that the Lord Chancellor was both a member of the government and a judge was considered inappropriate by many. The Labour government sought to amend this initially by abolishing the office of Lord Chancellor. The initial attempts were sloppy and created a political and constitutional storm when the Prime Minister did not apparently tell either the Queen or the Lord Chief Justice that he was going to abolish this most historic of offices. In the end it was decided abolishment was too difficult because of the thousands of references that were made to the office in legislation. Instead the office was reformed.

Section 7 CRA 2005 appoints the Lord Chief Justice as the head of the judiciary and, with the removal of the judges from the legislature, this meant that the Lord Chancellor was no longer a judge. Schedule 6 CRA 2005, as amended by the CCA 2013, also makes provision for the House of Lords to elect a 'Lords Speaker' and so he ceased to be the presiding officer of the Lords.

Under the CRA reforms the post of Lord Chancellor remains but it no longer needs to be a peer; as with all other members of the Cabinet he can be a member of either House and simply bears the honorific title 'Lord Chancellor'. In fact after Lord Falconer

---

5. Lord Falconer was the only modern Lord Chancellor not to sit on cases but this was because, by the time he was appointed, it had been decided to reform the office of Lord Chancellor.

6. Thomas Bingham, *The Business of Judging: Selected Essays and Speeches* (OUP 2000) 229.

the subsequent Lord Chancellors[7] have belonged to the Commons. Indeed there is no requirement for the Lord Chancellor to be a lawyer[8] and in the 2012 government reshuffle the first non-lawyer, Rt Hon Chris Grayling MP, was appointed to the office. There was some controversy over the appointment because the CRA 2005 requires that the Lord Chancellor be 'experienced' and Downing Street refused to divulge how this statutory criterion was met, although the statute does permit experience to be gathered not only through the legal professions but also through being a minister, member of either House of Parliament, or 'any other experience the prime minister considers relevant'. The three subsequent holders of the Lord Chancellor position were also non-lawyers. However at the time of writing, the current post-holder, Rt Hon Robert Buckland QC MP, is a lawyer, having been called to the Bar in 1991.

Whilst the office of Lord Chancellor has therefore been significantly reformed, he still does have (political) responsibility for the judiciary through being the Secretary of State for Justice. The Lord Chancellor also has particular responsibility for securing judicial independence, as evidenced by the oath that he must take:

> I [*name*] do solemnly swear that in the office of Lord High Chancellor of Great Britain I will respect the rule of law, defend the independence of the judiciary and discharge my duty to ensure the provision of resources for the efficient and effective support of the courts for which I am responsible.[9]

The oath reinforces the fact that the Lord Chancellor should remain the voice in government that upholds the independence of the judiciary (this is discussed in more detail at 9.2.1).

Some have commented that the old system may have meant that the judges had a stronger voice since the Lord Chancellor was a key figure in that he had no 'political ambition'[10] and yet was a political heavyweight that commanded respect around the cabinet table. At that time the Lord Chancellor was not responsible for penal policy (it was the responsibility of the Home Secretary), but as Secretary of State for Justice that is no longer true and there may be concerns that the statements of the Lord Chancellor are seen to be less the cautions of one of the most senior office holders in the land and more, nowadays, the complaints of a cabinet minister who fears colleagues are treading on his territory, ie the ordinary political turf-war of cabinet government. So far, however, there has been no indication that the independence of the judiciary is under threat and the reforms do make the office look more suitable for the twenty-first century as it removes, at the very least, the appearance of executive control. That said, the appointment of the first 'lay' Lord Chancellor did lead some to suggest that the judicial functions should be transferred to the President of the Supreme Court, leaving the Secretary of State for Justice as a pure politician.

Securing independence from the executive

Independence from the executive will include reference to their work. Lord MacKay, a former Lord Chancellor, noted that judges required administrative freedom and control,

---

7. At the time of writing those being the Rt Hon Jack Straw, the Rt Hon Kenneth Clarke, the Rt Hon Chris Grayling, the Rt Hon Michael Gove, the Rt Hon Elizabeth Truss, the Rt Hon David Lidington, and the Rt Hon David Gauke.
8. CRA 2005, s 2.
9. *Promissory Oaths Act 1868*, s 6A.
10. Robert Stevens, 'Reform in Haste and Repent at Leisure: Iolanthe, the Lord High Executioner and Brave New World' (2004) 24 *Legal Studies* 1, 9.

most notably in the selection of cases and listing of matters.[11] In essence this protects against the 'Judge Deed' type situation where there is a perception that the government 'picks' the judge that will sit on a case. Although much of the listing is dealt with by court administrative staff, who are employed by HM Courts and Tribunal Service (part of the executive), they may only do so in conjunction with the judiciary since the resident judge and presiding judge provide guidance on how cases are assigned to judges. It will also be remembered from the previous chapter that court staff owe a joint duty to the Lord Chancellor (representing the executive) and the Lord Chief Justice (representing the judiciary). Were there to be anything untoward there is also the ultimate sanction in that a judge (usually the resident or presiding judge as senior judge in a particular court) can transfer a matter from one list to another or reserve the case for himself. In this way it would suggest that it is possible to demonstrate independence over cases.

Political attacks

What of attacks from the executive? It was noted earlier that Members of Parliament may not criticize a judge by name in Parliament, and in the United Kingdom ministers are drawn from members of either House. The executive should not ordinarily criticize the personal decisions of a judge and yet this has happened on a few occasions. One judge has argued that the relationship between the executive and the judiciary was 'fraught and imbalanced'[12] although the then Lord Chief Justice, Lord Woolf, argued that the relationship was 'based on a satisfactory working relationship . . . probably, it is much better than ever before'.[13] That is not to say there have not been tensions, however, in part demonstrated by the fact that Lord Woolf had postponed his retirement because he believed there was a danger that judicial independence might be undermined.

Occasionally highly personalized attacks are made in contravention of the principles enshrined earlier. Perhaps the most notable of these in more recent years was the campaign by David Blunkett when he was Home Secretary. In interviews he suggested 'it was time for judges to learn their place'.[14] This comment followed the judgment of Collins J in respect of the treatment of asylum seekers,[15] which the Home Secretary saw as undermining his campaign to regulate illegal immigration. In an interview with the BBC he named Collins J as being responsible for undermining Parliament and suggested that he would continue to do so.[16] In fact, despite the highly personalized comments and briefings by the government against the judge, the Court of Appeal largely upheld the ruling[17] and yet this latter ruling did not meet with any criticism.[18]

Did the criticisms of the Home Secretary undermine judicial independence? It could be argued that they did in that they could be viewed as an attempt to put pressure on the judiciary to rule a particular way. However, the counter-argument is that the Home Secretary was a litigant and was, in effect, suggesting unease at a particular decision, albeit in intemperate terms. When the appellate courts ruled (in effect terminating further legal resolution) the government accepted the matter.

11. Thomas Bingham, *The Business of Judging: Selected Essays and Speeches* (2000 OUP) 56.
12. Harold Wilson, 'The County Court Judge in Limbo' (1994) 144 *New Law Journal* 1453, 1454.
13. Lord Woolf, *The Needs of a 21st Century Judge* (Judicial Studies Board 2001) 5.
14. Anthony Bradley, 'Judicial Independence under Attack' [2003] *Public Law* 397, 402.
15. *R (on behalf of Q) v Secretary of State for the Home Department* [2003] EWHC 195 (Admin).
16. Anthony Bradley, 'Judicial Independence under Attack' [2003] *Public Law* 397, 400.
17. *R (on behalf of Q) v Secretary of State for the Home Department* [2003] EWCA Civ 364.
18. Anthony Bradley, 'Judicial Independence under Attack' [2003] *Public Law* 397, 405.

In recent years the personalized attacks on the judiciary appeared to have been reduced somewhat. However, this changed in 2016 following the UK's decision to leave the EU (discussed in more detail in 'A note on Brexit'), when Lady Hale came under attack from several MPs for commenting on the Brexit process during a speech to students in Kuala Lumpur. Jacob Rees-Mogg MP commented: 'Lady Hale's speculation on a comprehensive replacement for the 1972 European Communities Act is a remarkable one for someone who is about to judge the case. It is not an idea that was mentioned in the High Court judgement so it is surprising for a Supreme Court judge to freelance in this way'.[19] Iain Duncan Smith MP accused Lady Hale of 'always [having] been opposed to Britain leaving the EU'.[20] Such criticism was particularly controversial due to her being one of the justices due to hear the government's appeal in the Supreme Court.

There were further attacks on the judiciary both before and after the hearing of the 'prorogation case' in the Supreme Court in September 2019,[21] another case associated with Brexit. There was huge political and public interest in the case which was to decide whether Boris Johnson's prorogation of parliament the previous month had been lawful. Prior to the Supreme Court hearing, judicial review cases regarding the prorogation were heard in the Scottish Courts, and the High Court.[22] For the duration of the cases being heard in the courts, and following the decision in the Supreme Court, the impartiality of the judiciary in particular was attacked. The Rt Hon Kwasi Kwarteng MP, Minister for Business, Energy and Clean Growth suggested the judiciary were politicized:

> Many people are saying the judges are biased, the judges are getting involved in politics . . . I think they are impartial but I'm saying that many people, many leave voters . . . are beginning to question the partiality of judges . . . The extent to which lawyers and judges are interfering in politics is something that concerns many people.[23]

305

Following the Supreme Court judgment it was reported 'senior allies' of Boris Johnson within number 10 were briefing against the judiciary, saying:

> The effect of this is to pose the question, who runs the country? Are the courts saying they want to run the country now? It will be very interesting to see what the public makes of that.[24]

Jacob Rees-Mogg MP, at that time Leader of the House of Commons, was reported as having accused the judges of mounting a 'constitutional coup'.[25] It should be noted however that the government did issue a statement accepting the decision of the Supreme Court, and the Lord Chancellor, the Rt Hon Robert Buckland QC MP, publicly defended the independence of the judiciary (see 9.2.1). Further attacks were nevertheless levelled at the judiciary from the media (see 9.1.2 next).

19. Jonathan Brady, 'Labour Defends Supreme Court Judge After Tory MPs Attack Her Over Possible Brexit Delay' *The Huffington Post* (2016) <http://www.huffingtonpost.co.uk/entry/supreme-court-lady-hale-brexit-article-50-comprehensive-legislation_uk_582c2d33e4b0311a3da243e1>.

20. ibid.

21. *R (Miller) v Prime Minister; Cherry v Advocate General* [2019] UKSC 41.

22. *R (Gina Miller) v The Prime Minister* [2019] EWHC 2381 (QB).

23. BBC News, 'Kwasi Kwarteng criticized for "biased judges" comment' BBC News (2019) <https://www.bbc.co.uk/news/uk-politics-49670901>.

24. Jason Groves, '"Who runs this country?": Boris Johnson's allies blast 'constitutional coup' after judges rule PM broke the law by suspending Parliament and he's forced to fly back from New York TODAY to face a furious resumed Commons' *Daily Mail* (2019) <https://www.dailymail.co.uk/news/article-7500691/Boris-blasts-runs-Britain-PM-Johnsons-allies-declare-war-judiciary.html>.

25. ibid.

⟳ **QUESTION FOR REFLECTION**

Should the government be able to criticize members of the judiciary? Does it matter which member of the government it is? For example, if the Lord Chancellor or Prime Minister were to criticize a judge *by name* would that be more serious than a Secretary of State doing so?

◀⟩ LISTEN TO THE PODCAST

For guidance on how to answer this question and a discussion of the main issues, listen to the author's podcast on the online resources:
www.oup.com/he/gillespie-weare8e

9.1.2 **Independence from the media**

Judicial independence need not necessarily be restricted to the state and it has been noted that:

> One of the most dramatic changes that has taken place over the past thirty years or so has been the increasing freedom felt by newspapers, in particular, to attack judges with a vigour . . . that was formerly quite unknown.[26]

In the years since the article that this statement is taken from was written, the position has arguably become even more vociferous especially by the tabloids. For example, *The Sun*, supposedly the most popular newspaper in the country, consistently referred to Lord Woolf, the then Lord Chief Justice, in derogatory terms and in September 2004 asked readers to sign a petition requiring him to be sacked,[27] even sending 'removal men' to the Royal Courts of Justice and his private residence.[28] This was followed in 2006 with a campaign to 'out' judges that *The Sun* believed had imposed unduly lenient sentences. The names of the judges were given together with derogatory comments made about the sentences that they had passed.

It is not just the criminal justice system that has incurred the wrath of the media. Perhaps the most notable attack by the media in recent times has been in relation to the judiciary's involvement following the UK's decision to leave the EU (commonly referred to as Brexit). Following the High Court's judgment that Parliament needed to be consulted before Article 50 could be triggered and that this was not something that could be done through the Prime Minister's exercise of prerogative powers, many branches of the media launched serious attacks on the judiciary. Newspaper headlines included: 'Enemies of the people' (*Daily Mail*); 'The judges versus the people' (*Daily Telegraph*); and 'Who do EU think you are?' (*The Sun*). In particular, the three High Court judges who ruled on the Article 50 case came in for individual criticism. The *Daily Mail* published an article on its website singling each of the judges out: 'The judges who blocked Brexit: One founded a EUROPEAN law group, another charged the taxpayer millions for advice and the third is an openly gay ex-Olympic fencer.' Such an attack was unprecedented, and the *Daily Mail* eventually had to change their headline due to the widespread criticism they received.

---

26. Derek Oulton, 'Independence of the Judiciary: A Review' (1994) 21 *Journal of Law and Society* 567, 569.
27. 'The Sun Calls on Lord Chief Justice to Quit' *The Sun* (22 September 2004).
28. *The Sun* (23 September 2004).

The response of the legal professions was swift, with many taking to Twitter and other social media platforms to criticize the media's response, demonstrate their support for the judiciary, and highlight the importance of judicial independence. Public statements were also made from numerous high-ranking QCs, with chairwoman of the Bar Council Chantal-Aimée Doerries QC saying: 'Publicly criticising individual members of the judiciary over a particular judgment or suggesting that they are motivated by their individual views, political or otherwise, is wrong, and serves only to undermine their vital role in the administration of justice. It also does no favours to our global reputation.'[29] It is certainly arguable that the extremely vocal response from the professions and legal experts was not only due to the media's attacks, but also due to the perceived failures of the then Lord Chancellor, Liz Truss, to adequately deal with the issue in a timely and appropriate manner (discussed in more detail at 9.2.1).

The scale of the media attack was such that it was not just the legal profession who responded, but also politicians from all parties, well-known public figures, and many members of the public. What was perhaps most interesting, however, was the lack of immediate response from many key members of the executive including the Prime Minister and the Lord Chancellor (discussed at 9.2.1).

As for the response from members of the judiciary themselves, this was muted, particularly from the senior judiciary. This was perhaps unsurprising given the fact that leave to appeal to the Supreme Court was granted and the government immediately declared their intention to do so. Indeed, in the Lord Chief Justice's Annual Press Conference in November 2016 following the backlash, but before the hearing of the case in the Supreme Court, he declined to be drawn on the issue in any significant detail. He simply said:

> I think that our independence is paramount. We are an attractive jurisdiction because everyone knows, not only are the judges the best or amongst the best in the world but that we are totally uninfluenced by external events. If and insofar as we need to do things to strengthen that, this is something to which I would like to discuss but it is very difficult for me to discuss that now in the present context, ie anything I say in relation to that will be interpreted by one person or by another as some comment on the existing case in relation to Article 50 and what people have said about it and I take the very firm view that it is better to wait until this is over.[30]

Most recently, the judiciary found themselves under attack following the Supreme Court decision in *R (Miller) v Prime Minister; Cherry v Advocate General*,[31] when the Justices ruled unanimously that Boris Johnson's decision as Prime Minister to prorogue Parliament from 9 September to 24 October 2019 was unlawful. The prorogation had been politically controversial due to fears that reduced time for parliamentary debate would have increased the chances of the United Kingdom leaving the EU without an agreed withdrawal agreement. Therefore, when the Supreme Court decision was announced the reaction was polarized, with Brexit supporters voicing concerns that the judgment would make Boris Johnson's plans for leaving the EU more difficult.

---

29.   Will Worley, 'Liz Truss Breaks her Silence but Fails to Condemn Backlash over Brexit Ruling' *The Independent* (2016) <https://www.independent.co.uk/news/uk/home-news/bar-council-liz-truss-brexit-ruling-decision-serious-unjustified-attacks-judiciary-judges-high-court-a7399356.html>.

30.   Judicial Press Office, 'Press Conference held by The Lord Chief Justice of England and Wales' (Judicial Press Office 2016) <https://www.judiciary.uk/wp-content/uploads/2016/11/lcj-annual-press-conference-2016-transcript-1.pdfpdf-1.pdf> 1–2.

31.   [2019] UKSC 41.

Lady Hale came under personal attack within the media, with *The Sun* publishing a comment piece that referred to her as 'the beady-eyed old nanny goat who read yesterday's verdict in the court. Brenda Hale has long been seen as a quintessential liberal blue-stocking. If she's a leaver, I'm a Martian.'[32] Her independence, and those of the other Supreme Court Justices was directly questioned: 'What's sauce for Boris is sauce for Brenda Hale. Her Supreme Court questioned Boris's motives in proroguing Parliament. The British people can now question her motives in reaching that verdict.'[33]

The limited response from the judiciary to the media attacks raise ongoing questions about what the response should be to such events. Some judges have, when the media comment has been particularly unpleasant, resorted to the laws relating to defamation and some judges have even suggested that derogatory press comments could amount to contempt of court.[34] This argument would only work with superior courts but even then it would be a complete overreaction and Lord Bingham has stated that the contempt laws should ordinarily have no place in such battles.[35] Indeed His Lordship suggests that judges should be 'thick-skinned' enough to ignore press comments. Pannick questioned who should respond to attacks. He suggested that it should not be for the Lord Chancellor[36] since although he is protected with upholding judicial independence, this is primarily in respect of attacks by the executive and indeed it could compromise independence if the executive responds on behalf of the judiciary. The answer is perhaps not easy and Lord Bingham's suggestion to leave well alone appears to be the default position.

⟳ QUESTION FOR REFLECTION

Do you believe that judges should have a remedy against the media if they make unjustified personal attacks? Should the press not have the right to comment on the administration of justice? Read Article 10 of the ECHR (see 5.4.8). Does this have any impact on your answer?

9.1.3 **Independence from each other**

Perhaps one of the most unusual examples of judicial independence relates to the judges themselves. The courts in England and Wales adopt a hierarchical structure and it has been noted already that there are different ranks within the judiciary (discussed in Chapter 8). This means that, potentially, there may be situations where a judge tries to interfere with another. The Courts and Tribunals Judiciary, when discussing judicial independence, notes this possibility:

> It is vitally important in a democracy that individual judges and the judiciary as a whole are impartial and independent of all external pressures and of each other . . .[37]

Obviously judicial independence from each other does not extend to ignoring the principles of *stare decisis* as this would cause confusion and end certainty within the English

32.   Quentin Letts, 'Judges blew their hallowed status with the Supreme Court ruling and will now be fair game for public scrutiny' *The Sun* (2019) <https://www.thesun.co.uk/news/9998887/judges-supreme-court-public-scrutiny/>.
33.   ibid.
34.   Robin Dunn, *Sword and Wig: Memoirs of a Lord Justice* (Quiller Press 1993) 182.
35.   Thomas Bingham, *The Business of Judging: Selected Essays and Speeches* (OUP 2000) 61.
36.   David Pannick, 'Should Judges Respond to Criticism?' *The Times* (27 November 2008).
37.   Courts and Tribunals Judiciary, 'Independence' (HMCTS) <https://www.judiciary.gov.uk/about-the-judiciary/the-judiciary-the-government-and-the-constitution/jud acc ind/independence/>.

Legal System. It will also be seen that the hierarchical structure has led to quasi-disciplinary measures being adopted by the higher courts, but the principle is just as important. Traditionally this approach has led to judges adopting an extremely independent system whereby they act in isolation and rarely look at each other's work (although they may discuss cases during lunch or after sitting with other judges as any visitor to the judge's dining room can attest). Lord Woolf, the then Lord Chief Justice, suggested that perhaps judges should look at each other's performance on the bench,[38] although he rejects the idea of it becoming even a peer-review appraisal system[39] and expressly states the principle of annual reflections would not compromise the independence of the judiciary.[40] So far this scheme has been resisted by the court judiciary, although appraisals do occur in the Tribunal Service. It will be interesting to note whether the court judiciary will follow suit in due course.

9.2 Securing independence

If judicial independence exists how is it secured? The CRA 2005 attempts to encapsulate the protection in statute but other factors are equally important. Some forms have already been discussed but the key issues of securing independence would include salary, tenure (including promotion and discipline), and immunity.

9.2.1 Statutory independence

It has been noted that the judiciary were keen to ensure that with the abolition of the Lord Chancellor there would be provision to guarantee the independence of the judiciary. It was seen earlier that one of the principal responsibilities of the Lord Chancellor was to act as a 'buffer' between the executive and the judiciary.[41] Arguably the Lord Chancellor may still have this responsibility since his oath says, inter alia: 'I will . . . defend the independence of the judiciary'. In addition to this the CRA 2005 places a statutory duty on the government:

> The Lord Chancellor, other ministers of the Crown and all with responsibility for matters relating to the judiciary or otherwise to the administration of justice must uphold the continued independence of the judiciary.[42]

This includes:

(a) the need to defend that independence;

(b) the need for the judiciary to have support necessary to enable them to exercise their functions;

(c) the need for the public interest in regard to matters relating to the judiciary or otherwise to the administration of justice to be properly represented in decisions affecting those matters.[43]

These duties are imposed primarily on the Lord Chancellor. Yet how will this be achieved?

309

---

38. Lord Woolf, *The Needs of a 21st Century Judge* (Judicial Studies Board 2001) 7.
39. ibid, 8.
40. ibid, 7.
41. See 9.1.1.2 and see Lord Elwyn-Jones, *In My Times: An Autobiography* (Weidenfeld & Nicolson 1983) 267.
42. CRA 2005, s 3(1).
43. ibid, s 3(6).

Liz Truss, Lord Chancellor in 2016/17, was accused of failing to uphold the independence of the judiciary following her response, or lack thereof, to the unprecedented media attacks on the judiciary (discussed in more detail at 9.1.2) following the 'Brexit' High Court decision in relation to triggering Article 50. Truss initially stayed silent in the wake of the attacks and was urged by the Bar Council to speak out 'as a matter of urgency', with them noting that they regretted 'the lack of public statement by the Lord Chancellor condemning these attacks'.[44] On Twitter the hashtag #wheresliztruss was extensively used by legal commentators. When she did issue a statement, however, she was widely criticized for merely affirming the independence of the judiciary and failing to specifically address the attacks that were made. She said:

> The independence of the judiciary is the foundation upon which our rule of law is built and our judiciary is rightly respected the world over for its independence and impartiality.

It is worth noting here that whilst upholding judicial independence is primarily the job of the Lord Chancellor, it is also the responsibility of 'other ministers of the Crown', including the Prime Minister. Despite this, Theresa May's response to the media attacks on the judiciary was similarly limited. She commented: 'I believe in and value the independence of our judiciary. I also value the freedom of our press. I think these both underpin our democracy and they are important.' By highlighting the importance of press freedom when discussing judicial independence, it is certainly questionable whether, similarly to Liz Truss, Theresa May fulfilled her duty.

Following the most recent high-profile media attacks after the prorogation decision by the Supreme Court in 2019, the Lord Chancellor Robert Buckland was much quicker to defend the judiciary. The day after the judgment he tweeted:

> We must all remember that our world-class judiciary always acts free from political motivation or influence and that the rule of law is the basis of our democracy, for all seasons. Personal attacks on judges from any quarters are completely unacceptable.

As Lord Chancellor, Robert Buckland has been outspoken in his support of judicial independence, especially when compared to the approach taken by Liz Truss, noted earlier. For example, at a fringe event during the Conservative Party Conference in September 2019 not long after the prorogation judgment, he reiterated:

> We have an independent judiciary. We have respect for the rule of law. And that is what your Lord Chancellor will do, time and time again without worrying about the politics of it, without worrying about what No.10 might say.[45]

There are other examples of where the Lord Chancellor has effectively interceded in media attacks, some of which have been particularly effective. In 2006 there was considerable controversy over the sentence imposed in relation to Craig Sweeney, a convicted paedophile who abducted and sexually abused a very young girl. The media were very critical of what they saw as an extremely lenient sentence and John Reid, the Home Secretary, also criticized the sentence, making comments that were probably comparable to those of David Blunkett.[46] The Lord Chancellor, Lord Falconer,

---

44.   Bar Council, 'Bar Council Calls on Lord Chancellor to Condemn Attacks on Judiciary' (The Bar Council 2016) <http://www.barcouncil.org.uk/media-centre/news-and-press-releases/2016/november/bar-council-calls-on-lord-chancellor-to-condemn-attacks-on-judiciary/>.

45.   Steerpike, 'Robert Buckland hits out at "unaccountable" critics of judiciary' *The Spectator* (2019) <https://www.spectator.co.uk/article/robert-buckland-hits-out-at-unaccountable-critics-of-judiciary>.

46.   Alisdair Gillespie, 'Sentencing: The Spider's Web' (2006) 156 *New Law Journal* 1153.

publicly stated that it was not the fault of the judge that the sentence was wrong but the legal framework. However, Vera Baird QC, a junior minister in the Department for Constitutional Affairs, criticized the judge by name on BBC Radio 4 suggesting that the judge had personally got the matter wrong.[47] Interestingly, there was then a public exchange of letters between the Lord Chancellor and the junior minister whereby Vera Baird formally withdrew her remarks. This was followed by further public confirmation by the Lord Chancellor that the judge had not erred, even though this implicitly criticized the Home Secretary for making his comments. The media were very much against this sentence and thus the easy political decision would have been either to stay silent or to support the Home Secretary, but Lord Falconer did not do this and, in effect, met his statutory obligations.

When appointed, some questioned whether the first 'lay' Lord Chancellor (ie the first non-lawyer to be appointed Lord Chancellor), Chris Grayling MP, necessarily appreciated this part of the role. Certainly, without a legal background it is perhaps easier to concentrate on the role of Secretary of State for Justice, a purely political post, rather than being the Lord Chancellor and many of the apolitical aspects that this brings. When he was appointed much was written about him coming from the 'right' of the Tory party (although many believed that this was an oversimplification) and that he would bring a 'tougher' stance to punishment than his predecessor, the perceived liberal conservative, Kenneth Clarke. The reality of course is that in times of financial constraints the punishment of offenders is as much dictated by the Treasury (through the funding of the Prison Service) as it is by the Secretary of State for Justice. However, this does set up the interesting question of whether the Secretary of State for Justice would wish to attack judges for 'soft' sentencing since, when wearing his other 'hat' as Lord Chancellor, he must protect the judiciary from inappropriate political attacks.

When Chris Grayling was first appointed there was a belief that the roles of Secretary of State for Justice and Lord Chancellor should be separated once more, with the title Lord Chancellor being given to a judge (probably the President of the Supreme Court). Whilst this may be attractive in some respects, it does have some disadvantages. The first is that the role of Lord Chancellor has always been political, though the political extent of the post has differed with holders of the office, and the second is that it would almost certainly mean that there would no longer be a senior member of the government who would be responsible for defending the judiciary. Whilst the CRA 2005 could be amended to ensure the Secretary of State for Justice was responsible for securing the independence of the judiciary it is open to question whether a purely political Secretary of State would consider this a primary function of his office.

⟳ QUESTION FOR REFLECTION

It was noted earlier (9.1.1.2) that the Lord Chancellor need not, following the CRA 2005, be legally qualified. Could someone without a background in the law safeguard the independence of the judiciary?

---

47. ibid, 1154.

9.2.2 **Salary**

At first sight judges would appear to be very well paid, with the Lord Chief Justice receiving £267,509 and a circuit judge receiving £143,095 (as of April 2020), but this should be placed into context when many practitioners will earn several times this.[48] Yet salary is important, as has been noted by Lord Bingham:

> There is of course, a close connection between judicial salaries and judicial independence . . . if a judge's salary is dependent on the whim of the government, the judge will not have the independence we desire in our judiciary.[49]

In recognition of this, in England and Wales where there has been concern about the salary levels of the judiciary, the Ministry of Justice have generally responded positively. Following the 2018 report from the *Review Board on Senior Salaries* (SSRB) (which makes recommendations as to the salaries for Senior Civil Servants, the judiciary, and senior public figures), the Ministry of Justice gave a 2 per cent pay rise across the judiciary. Whilst being hailed as the 'biggest pay rise for judges in nearly 10 years', this was not in line with the proposals put forward by the Review Board, which suggested increases in pay of between 2.5 and 32 per cent, depending on judicial grade and which of the two pension schemes a judge is in.[50] One reason for this is likely to be the negative backlash from the press following publication of the report (discussed in more detail at 8.6).

A further pay rise for the judiciary was announced in June 2019, with the introduction of a 'recruitment and retention allowance' in an attempt to address the ongoing recruitment crisis within the judiciary. Puisne judges received an allowance worth 25 per cent of their basic salary, and a 15 per cent allowance was granted to Crown Court and Upper Tribunal judges. In July 2020, the government announced an additional 2 per cent pay rise in response to the frontline work conducted by the judiciary during the COVID-19 pandemic.

The current position as regards judicial salaries is that they are undoubtedly less than an applicant for a judgeship earns in practice,[51] but that there are alternative benefits. The judges are paid out of the consolidated fund[52] which means that there is no parliamentary debate on their salaries. The government continue, however, to influence the salary levels because although the SSRB, an independent body, recommends the salary levels, it is for the government of the day to decide whether they will accept the recommendations or not. The decision as to whether to accept the recommendation is reported to Parliament who are entitled to question the relevant ministers as to the reasons for this. In 2005 the SSRB published a consultation paper on whether the judicial salaries bands were correct and how they should be 'pegged' to comparable posts.[53]

---

48.   For an interesting analysis on this see Hazel Genn, *The Attractiveness of Senior Judicial Appointments to Highly Qualified Practitioners* (UCL 2009) and also see Penny Darbyshire, *Sitting in Judgment: The Working Lives of Judges* (Hart Publishing 2011), who recounts that a puisne judge initially turned down the appointment because he decided that he could not afford it.

49.   Thomas Bingham, *The Business of Judging: Selected Essays and Speeches* (2000 OUP) 65.

50.   Review Body on Senior Salaries, *Supplement to the Fortieth Annual Report on Senior Salaries 2018 (Report No 90)—Major Review of the Judicial Salary Structure* (SSRB 2018) <https://assets.publishing.service.gov.uk/government/uploads/system/uploads/attachment_data/file/751903/Supp_to_the_SSRB_Fortieth_Annual_Report_2018_Major_Review_of_the_Judicial_Salary_Structure.pdf> 2.

51.   For an analysis see Hazel Genn, *The Attractiveness of Senior Judicial Appointments to Highly Qualified Practitioners* (UCL 2009).

52.   *Senior Courts Act 1981*, s 12.

53.   Review Body on Senior Salaries, *Annual Report 2005* (HMSO 2005).

Ultimately they decided not to 'peg' salaries but they did undertake a comprehensive review of judicial salaries, partly because of the changes of duties and responsibilities brought about by the *Constitutional Reform Act 2005* (CRA 2005).[54] A revised system was recommended, including shifting some categories of judges into a high pay-band, and this was accepted and implemented by the government.[55] It is important to note that not all recommendations made by the SSRB are accepted and implemented by the government. This has especially been the case in recent years where recommendations to significantly increase pay have been made but rejected in favour of smaller pay rises.

9.2.3 Tenure, promotion, and discipline

Three directly related issues that could conceivably interfere with judicial independence are the tenure of judges, any promotion they receive, and how they are disciplined. In order to discuss these issues it is necessary to distinguish once again between superior judges and inferior judges as the manner in which they are treated is significantly different. The position of judges of the Supreme Court, although obviously superior judges, will also be considered separately because of the changes introduced by the CRA 2005.

9.2.3.1 Superior judges

Superior judges enjoy significantly stronger protections than members of the inferior judiciary. Puisne judges and Lord Justices of Appeal hold office until retirement age (currently 70)[56] 'during good behaviour, subject to a power of removal by Her Majesty on an address presented to her by both Houses of Parliament'.[57] In other words, subject to an additional power of removal through disability, a superior judge may only be removed if both Houses of Parliament pass a resolution requiring them to go. Only one judge has ever been removed in this way, in 1830,[58] and it would be extremely rare for anyone to achieve this 'distinction', not least because most judges would probably prefer to resign rather than be subjected to such an approach.

Where a superior judge is incapacitated by illness or disability then the SCA 1981 provides that the Lord Chancellor may remove him.[59] To ensure that this power cannot be abused, subsection (9) requires judicial consent to this procedure. Where the incapacitated judge is a Head of Division then at least two other Heads of Division must agree; where it is a Lord Justice of Appeal the Master of the Rolls must agree; and where it is a puisne judge the appropriate Head of Division must agree. Given that all of the judges who must agree with this are superior judges holding similar security of tenure, it should ensure that the measure can never be used by a Lord Chancellor in an inappropriate manner.

The CRA 2005 has, however, provided additional disciplinary procedures that may be exercised by the Lord Chief Justice, as head of the judiciary. These powers apply to all levels of judges and are considered in further detail later.

Promotion for the superior judge is a controversial area. Lord Denning once wrote that a judge when appointed had nothing to gain from promotion and did not seek it,[60]

---

54. Review Body on Senior Salaries, *Annual Report 2006* (HMSO 2006).
55. Review Body on Senior Salaries, *Annual Report 2007* (HMSO 2007).
56. *Senior Courts Act 1981*, s 11(2).
57. ibid, s 11(3).
58. David Pannick, *Judges* (OUP 1987) 90.
59. *Senior Courts Act 1981*, s 11(8).
60. Lord Denning, *The Road to Justice* (Stevens & Sons 1995) 17.

and at the time this was probably true because there were so few posts in the Court of Appeal. However, this may no longer necessarily be true and Bingham concedes that there may have been a concern that some judges would tailor their judgments in such a way as to gain judicial advancement although he states that he cannot think of any examples of this and it would amount to a violation of the judicial oath.[61] It is certainly not possible to identify any candidates where it might be thought that their decisions had denied advancement, although some may argue that it is possible to identify the opposite, where judges who may have appeared controversial have gained advancement. The changes made by the CRA 2005 have essentially meant that such tailoring would not bring any advantages since appointment to the High Court, Court of Appeal, and Supreme Court will be made by independent appointment commissions. The appointment of Sir Nicholas Wall as the President of the Family Division (discussed at 8.3.8) perhaps illustrates this. There were some who argued that the Lord Chancellor did not want Wall LJ appointed because of his pronouncements but the independent appointments commission led to this issue being resolved in a fair and transparent way.

9.2.3.2 **Inferior judges**

The security of tenure for a circuit judge is significantly different from that of a superior judge. Circuit judges must retire at the age of 70 but they are also subject to removal by the Lord Chancellor 'on the ground of incapacity or misbehaviour' and with the agreement of the Lord Chief Justice.[62] The CRA 2005 states that where this is to be undertaken then 'prescribed procedures'[63] must be followed which suggests that there will now be a statutory scheme that will lead to dismissal.

In recent times only one circuit judge has been removed by the Lord Chancellor, and Hailsham, the Lord Chancellor who was responsible for the dismissal,[64] makes it clear in his autobiography that he would have preferred the judge to resign but, at that time, a pension would not be payable to someone who resigns whereas a part pension would be paid to someone who was dismissed.[65] That said, there have been two occasions when dismissal could have occurred. One case arose under the 'old' system and one under the 'new' system of judicial discipline. The difference between the cases is perhaps instructive.

The first of these cases was when senior judges asked the then Lord Chancellor to remove a judge.[66] Lord Hailsham does not mention the judge by name but Judge James Pickles names himself in his own autobiography.[67] Judge Pickles was perhaps one of the most controversial judges in modern times and, by his own admission, was something of a maverick. Hailsham describes him as:

[an] obscure and absurd judge whose only real claim to fame was the number of times when his behaviour had been criticized and his judgements [*sic*] reversed by the Court of Appeal . . .[68]

---

61. Thomas Bingham, *The Business of Judging: Selected Essays and Speeches* (OUP 2000) 60.
62. *Courts Act 1971*, s 17(4).
63. CRA 2005, s 108(1).
64. More junior judges have been dismissed. For example, in 2015 it was reported that two district judges, a deputy district judge, and a recorder were dismissed as a result of viewing pornography on judicial computers. The district judges were full-time appointees and were dismissed under the same procedure. These have not been discussed, however, because this section is comparing the position of the two principal first-instance judges, ie the circuit judge and puisne judge.
65. Lord Hailsham, *A Sparrow's Flight* (Collins 1990) 429.
66. ibid, 430.
67. James Pickles, *Judge for Yourself* (Coronet 1992) 175–96.
68. Lord Hailsham, *A Sparrow's Flight* (Collins 1990) 430.

Part of the controversy of Pickles was his unconventional views of sex crimes, something that led to him being denied the right to sit on such cases. In his own autobiography he discusses the dress of women and says:

> If [a woman] seems to want sex but does not, a man who tries to grab it from her cannot be excused but she must share the blame.[69]

Sadly such pronouncements were also uttered on the bench and he appeared to ignore sentencing precedents, passing sentences that were frequently anomalous and led to him being criticized in the Court of Appeal, most notably in *R v Scott*.[70] Judge Pickles reacted to these developments by discussing matters with the press and, rather famously, provided an interview on television where he referred to the Lord Chief Justice as 'an ancient dinosaur living in the wrong age'.[71] Lord Hailsham declined to dismiss him because he felt it was unfair that he acted as prosecutor, judge, jury, and executioner.[72] Later when Lord MacKay informed Judge Pickles that he was contemplating dismissing him, Pickles used this argument as a defence to the charges.[73] In the end, the position led to a public letter of rebuke by the Lord Chancellor and Pickles eventually retired.

The second case was more recent. His Honour Judge Gerald Price QC was a circuit judge assigned to the Welsh circuit. He was the subject of a tabloid investigation where he was accused of having an affair with a male sex worker. His conduct was investigated by the *Office of Judicial Complaints* and the Lord Chancellor and Lord Chief Justice had decided that he should be removed from office, although he resigned before the disciplinary process could be completed.

The cases of Judges Pickles and Price demonstrate a difference between the way in which inferior and superior judges can be dismissed. For example, it would be extremely difficult to administratively control the type of cases a puisne judge can sit on (as there is no requirement of 'ticketing') although the Lord Chief Justice could re-assign the judge to a different division of the High Court. A puisne judge accused of the same conduct as Judge Price would have required an address of both Houses of Parliament to dismiss. One circuit judge has publicly suggested that it is inappropriate for the distinction to remain, not least because circuit judges spend a not inconsiderable period of their time doing High Court work.[74] The reception to the call has not been unanimous with Lord Bingham suggesting that the risk of inappropriate dismissal is theoretical and with little practical consequence.[75]

⟳ QUESTION FOR REFLECTION

It has been suggested by Wilson that judges of all ranks should receive the same security of tenure. Is there any justification for allowing more junior judges to be dismissed by the executive, even where it is supported by the senior judiciary? If not, how does one deal with a problem like Judge Pickles or Judge Price? Had either judge been a puisne judge could either the judiciary or executive have done anything about him?

---

69.   James Pickles, *Judge for Yourself* (Coronet 1992) 138.
70.   [1990] Crim LR 440.
71.   James Pickles, *Judge for Yourself* (Coronet 1992) 180.
72.   Lord Hailsham, *A Sparrow's Flight* (Collins 1990) 430.
73.   James Pickles, *Judge for Yourself* (Coronet 1992) 185–95.
74.   Harold Wilson, 'The County Court Judge in Limbo' (1994) 144 *New Law Journal* 1454. Note that some work can be released to a circuit judge and in other cases a circuit judge can sit as a High Court judge (s 9 SCA 1981) and while doing so he has all the powers of a puisne judge.
75.   Thomas Bingham, *The Business of Judging: Selected Essays and Speeches* (OUP 2000) 59.

🔊 LISTEN TO THE PODCAST

For guidance on how to answer this question and a discussion of the main issues, listen to the author's podcast on the online resources:

www.oup.com/he/gillespie-weare8e

Promotion for the circuit bench has traditionally been extremely limited. It has already been noted that some may be eligible to become a senior circuit judge through the assumption of administrative responsibility for which they are remunerated, but access to the senior judiciary is normally denied to them. Some circuit judges are appointed to the High Court bench but as has been noted already this is quite rare. Given that the statutory qualification for a puisne judge is appointment as a circuit judge[76] it may have been thought that this would lead to an increase in appointments, but this does not appear to have been reflected. Darbyshire, in her book on the lives of judges, recognizes this issue and states that a problem is that few circuit judges wish promotion beyond the circuit bench.[77] This is partly because some do not believe they are 'clever' enough to be a High Court judge (which seems unlikely in many instances), but also because many perceive their job to be better since they are not required to stay away from home or sit regularly in the Court of Appeal. They believe, quite rightly according to the research conducted by Darbyshire, that High Court judges frequently work longer hours and many circuit judges prefer the life that they have.

It would seem therefore that whilst denying inferior judges promotion would appear unfair in theory, the reality is that the majority do not seem interested in pursuing that option. It should be noted that of those few circuit judges who have been promoted to the High Court bench only a few have progressed to becoming a Lord Justice of Appeal and so any promotion would seem to be rather limited.

9.2.3.3 Extending disciplinary measures

Judge Pickles, in his autobiography, states:

It is absurd that the Lord Chancellor has no effective control except the power to remove circuit (not High Court) judges for 'misbehaviour' . . . [78]

This, of course, misses the point that the presiding judge and Lord Chief Justice had the power to make directions restricting the types of cases a judge could hear (used against Pickles) but there is some truth to this point, that the only disciplinary measure was dismissal. The CRA 2005 provides a solution to this although the power now rests with the Lord Chief Justice as head of the judiciary. The provisions do not differentiate between inferior and superior judges and empower the Lord Chief Justice, after following due process, to issue 'formal advice, or a formal warning or reprimand'.[79] It is not clear what the effects of such measures are but, presumably, they could be used in conjunction with directions to ensure that judges are limited to the types of work that they carry out if this is appropriate. A recent example of these powers being used involved Judge Karen Holt, who accessed confidential files in a case where her daughter was a witness. She was 'accused of accessing a wide range of materials, including witness

---

76. *Senior Courts Act 1981*, s 10(3)(c).
77. Penny Darbyshire, *Sitting in Judgment: The Working Lives of Judges* (Hart Publishing 2011) 415–17.
78. James Pickles, *Judge for Yourself* (Coronet 1992) 196.
79. CRA 2005, s 108(3).

statements made by her daughter and transcripts of interviews. She also sent an email to police which "risked being seen as an attempt to influence" the case.'[80] Whilst she was cleared of criminal charges, her actions were found to have amounted to serious misconduct and she was reprimanded.

> **Example** Lord Justice Thorpe
>
> Judges are, of course, expected to uphold the law and the new powers available to the Lord Chief Justice have been used when a judge has transgressed the law. A notable example was when the Lord Chief Justice issued Thorpe LJ with a reprimand after he received a driving ban after accruing twelve penalty points for driving offences. An interesting nugget that arose from the case is that Thorpe LJ also runs a farm complete with an eighty-strong herd of cattle!

The Act also gives the Lord Chief Justice the power to suspend someone from being a judge where a judge is subject to criminal proceedings, serving a sentence, or where the action that led to the criminal proceedings taking place is being used to begin dismissal proceedings.[81] The Lord Chief Justice may also suspend someone who has been convicted of an offence, but where it has been decided not to dismiss the person, if the Lord Chief Justice believes it is necessary to do so in order to maintain the confidence of the judiciary[82] or where a judge is being investigated for misbehaviour other than a criminal offence.[83]

Whilst sometimes the reprimands can be as a result of extrajudicial behaviour it is clear that the power of reprimand exists where a judge, in exercising his judicial functions, does something notably wrong. Perhaps the most striking example is that of Peter Smith J, a puisne judge of the Chancery Division. The judge acted in an unprofessional way towards a barrister who had suggested he should recuse himself from a case concerning a legal firm where the judge had attempted to seek employment.[84] The Court of Appeal, in determining the appeal, issued an informal rebuke, but Peter Smith J then issued a somewhat bizarre and argumentative public statement challenging many of the issues. The matter was referred to the Office of Judicial Complaints (as it was called then, now the Judicial Conduct Investigations Office) who decided that his behaviour did amount to misconduct and he was formally reprimanded by the Lord Chief Justice.

The annual report for the Judicial Conduct Investigations Office (JCIO) 2018–19 notes that fifty-five disciplinary sanctions were issued for judicial office holders (ie magistrates, courts judiciary, tribunals, coroners). Of these, six members of the courts judiciary were provided with formal advice and less than five were removed from office. In contrast twelve magistrates received formal advice, and thirteen were removed from post.[85]

80. 'Judge disciplined for viewing files in case involving daughter' *The Times* (30 August 2018).
81. CRA 2005, s 108(4).
82. ibid, s 108(5).
83. ibid, s 108(6), (7).
84. The full details are set out by the Court of Appeal in *Howell and others v Millais and others* [2007] EWCA Civ 720.
85. Judicial Conduct Investigations Office, *Annual Report 2018–19* (JCIO 2019) <https://www.complaints.judicialconduct.gov.uk/reportsandpublications/> 15.

9.2.4 **Judicial immunity**

In Chapter 10 it will be noted that advocates have lost their immunity for negligence but the judiciary have traditionally been immune from actions arising out of their judicial actions. Immunity apparently dates back to the seventeenth century and acts as a privilege to any words that a judge utters within a case.[86] However, there continues to be a distinction between inferior and superior judges in that the latter have immunity from all actions even when acting outside their jurisdiction so long as the words or actions were done in good faith, whereas an inferior judge's immunity is restricted to actions within their jurisdiction.

The argument advanced for judicial immunity is that it protects judges from vexatious litigants and an attempt to try and re-litigate each matter, and it has been suggested that in order for the immunity system to work properly the privilege must be absolute: including acts where a judge acts negligently or inappropriately.[87] The same reasons were advanced in support of the immunity of advocates (see 10.5.3) and yet this has been ended so why should judges continue to have absolute immunity? At least one commentator believes they should not and that it would not contravene the independence of the judiciary to allow judges to be sued for misconduct in their office.[88] However, it seems unlikely that the judges themselves would ever end their own immunity (through the appellate courts so ruling), nor is it likely that Parliament would do so either; indeed s 9 *Human Rights Act 1998* expressly preserves judicial immunity.

9.3 **Judicial ethics**

Sir Thomas Bingham (as he then was) wrote extrajudicially:

> Judicial ethics . . . appears to have been largely neglected in this country in recent years.[89]

This is a fair comment but indeed the position is arguably replicated by the whole legal profession, which barely touches upon ethics from education through to practice.[90] Yet ethics are an essential part of the administration of justice and, although a significant amount of attention is placed on the ethics of the legal profession, this applies equally to judges.

The ethics of judicial office are arguably based on the principle which requires the judge to try cases 'without fear or favour, affection or ill-will'. Certain aspects of this will be discussed elsewhere in this book, most notably in relation to the conduct of judges within a trial, but the issue that should be discussed here is the idea implicit within the oath, that a judge should not be biased or compromised.

9.3.1 **Financial issues**

If judges are to try cases 'without fear or favour' then their financial interests may well become relevant. It has been noted earlier that their salary tends to be less than that

---

86. David Pannick, *Judges* (OUP 1987) 95.
87. ibid, 98.
88. ibid, 99.
89. Thomas Bingham, 'Judicial Ethics' in Ross Cranston (ed), *Legal Ethics and Professional Responsibility* (Clarendon Press 1995) 35.
90. See, for example, Andrew Boon, *The Ethics and Conduct of Lawyers in England and Wales* (3rd edn, Hart Publishing 2014) 171.

which they received in practice and accordingly it is likely that they may be in possession of various investments. It is clear, however, that judges must ensure that their investments do not conflict with their role as a judge. It has been suggested that whilst a judge could, theoretically, be a 'name' for Lloyds of London,[91] if they sat in the Commercial Court (which principally deals with high-value commercial transactions such as insurance claims) then they would ordinarily relinquish this[92] to save an appearance of bias (see 9.3.3). Many Lord Justices of Appeal will similarly relinquish their status since the Court of Appeal (Civil Division) will not infrequently deal with such matters.

Judges, especially members of the senior judiciary, are frequently asked to undertake extrajudicial work. What should the position be in terms of remunerating such work? If, for example, a judge is asked to provide an after-dinner speech, can he ask for money?

The rules are not set down but it is implicit within the judicial oath and office that a judge will not bring the office of judge into disrepute. Commanding significant fees for outside work would almost certainly do so. It has been suggested:

> [I]t would [not] be generally regarded as improper for a judge to accept a modest honorarium for a lecture or address which he had given, although most would perhaps decline or ask that the sum be paid to charity: a gift of wine or a book a judge might, properly in my view, accept, but the identity of the donor and the value of the gift would plainly affect his decision.[93]

Most members of the judiciary would probably agree with this statement and from the occasions when we have organized for judges to speak at functions this does appear to be the rule, with judges simply accepting the offer of a dinner and specifically rejecting any suggestion of an honorarium.

9.3.2 **Politics**

By convention judges must be apolitical, and the Lords of Appeal in Ordinary and other senior members of the judiciary when they were entitled to sit in the House of Lords sat on the cross-benches of the House of Lords, ie they were 'independent' members. Whilst there were a number of judges who were appointed from the ranks of Members of Parliament[94] this 'tradition' appeared to have happily faded out in recent years, but in 2007 (Sir) Ross Cranston, a former Labour party MP and former Solicitor-General, was appointed a puisne judge. That said, his appointment was not the source of any political controversy. The establishment of the independent JAC should prevent any future appearance of political bias. A judge should not become involved in any party political issue once appointed and should ordinarily resign from any political party they may belong to. In July 2008 Cranston J recused himself from a case in the High Court because it raised issues about hunting and he had, while an MP, made comments about hunting when the *Hunting Act 2004* was proceeding through Parliament. His Lordship (correctly) considered that it would be inappropriate for him to preside (in part, because it was thought there was a risk of the appearance of bias, see 9.3.3).

319

---

91. Lloyds of London is one of the principal insurance markets in the world. It is not an insurance company but rather facilitates its members (known as 'names') to underwrite insurance policies. If nothing happens then the 'names' can achieve significant gains; if there are many disasters they can lose a lot of money. In the early 1990s there was considerable controversy when a number of 'names' faced bankruptcy as a result of many natural disasters.

92. Thomas Bingham, 'Judicial Ethics' in Ross Cranston (ed), *Legal Ethics and Professional Responsibility* (Clarendon Press 1995) 41.

93. ibid.

94. John Griffith, *Politics of the Judiciary* (5th edn, Harper Collins 1997) 16.

⚡ RETIRED JUDGES

Whilst there is no rule to suggest that retired judges cannot become political it appears customary for retired Law Lords to sit on the cross-benches, whereas retired Lord Chancellors (as political appointees) will ordinarily continue to sit with their party. It appears the same rule applies to retired judges who succeed to peerages. A good example of this is Baroness Butler-Sloss who was elevated to a life peerage in 2006 after retiring in 2005 from her position as President of the Family Division. Baroness Butler-Sloss sits on the cross-benches.

9.3.3 Appearance of bias

Perhaps the most important aspect of judicial ethics is in respect of bias or, perhaps more correctly, the appearance of bias (as it is difficult to know whether a judge has truly been biased).[95] The issue of bias is undoubtedly central to the judicial oath and it is also one of the areas where there has, in recent years, been considerable debate.

It has been suggested that disqualification for bias can be divided into two forms: automatic disqualification and disqualification for apprehended bias.[96] Automatic disqualification will normally follow when a judge has an interest in the case that creates a situation where the judge appears to be sitting in his own cause. Apprehended bias exists where there is some other reason to believe that there is a 'real danger' that the judge will not consider the matter independently.

9.3.3.1 Automatic disqualification

A judge should never judge his own cause, in other words if the judge has an interest in a case then he should not sit as judge. In *Locabail* it was held that a *de minimis* principle existed within this rule meaning that minor or inconsequential interests could be ignored.[97]

> ☰ **Example** Rental income
>
> The case of *Locabail* was actually a series of conjoined appeals and one of the appeals was known as *R v Bristol Betting and Gaming Licensing Committee, ex p O'Callaghan*. The facts of this case are not strictly relevant and can be summarized by stating that the appellant had attempted to judicially review the Committee's decision to grant an extended gaming licence to a branch of Corals, a national bookmakers' firm. The judge in the case was the then Dyson J. It transpired that the family of Dyson J owned a property investment company and that some of their property was rented to branches of Corals. The actual amount disputed was calculated at £5,000 and the Court of Appeal dismissed the suggestion that if a national company the size of Corals was ordered to pay £5,000 it might jeopardize its ability to pay rent on one of its shops—in effect the only interest that Dyson J could have had. This was clearly within the *de minimis* principle and the appeal was dismissed.[98]

95.   See *Locabail (UK) Ltd v Bayfield Properties Ltd* [2000] QB 451, 472.
96.   Abimbola Olowofoyeku, 'The nemo judex Rule: The Case against Automatic Disqualification' [2000] *Public Law* 456.
97.   *Locabail (UK) Ltd v Bayfield Properties Ltd* [2000] QB 451, 473.
98.   ibid, 498–500.

Precisely what is significant would depend on each individual case but the benchmark is ensuring that the law is not brought into disrepute. *De minimis*, when translated, means 'minimal things' and thus it is not 'small' or 'reasonable' but 'minimal', meaning, in effect, that anything not trivial would lead to automatic disqualification.

The concept of 'cause' had been restricted in effect to pecuniary or proprietary interests[99] but this was to change in the most dramatic way.

Pinochet

In the late 1990s significant controversy existed over the case of Senator Pinochet, the former dictator of Chile. Senator Pinochet had been visiting the United Kingdom for years for medical treatment, but he was considered a 'war criminal' by many and a Spanish judge had issued an extradition warrant for his arrest. As a result of bilateral EU extradition treaties, extradition had to be contemplated and a stipendiary magistrate issued two provisional arrest warrants, both of which were executed.

Senator Pinochet claimed diplomatic immunity and sought to judicially review the decisions claiming both warrants should be quashed. The Divisional Court held that both warrants should be quashed but stayed this until an appeal was heard by the House of Lords (the quashing order needed to be stayed otherwise Senator Pinochet could have left the country which would have rendered any appeal moot). Before the matter reached the House of Lords the campaigning group *Amnesty International* sought, and received, leave to intervene in the proceedings (meaning they could make representations as an 'interested party'). The House of Lords ruled by a majority of 3:2 that the appeal should be granted[100] and thus the arrest warrant was upheld.

However, shortly after the hearing, Senator Pinochet's solicitors were contacted with the allegation that Lord Hoffmann, one of the Law Lords who heard the case and who had voted with the majority, was a director of the charitable arm of *Amnesty International*. The legal team for Senator Pinochet petitioned the House of Lords to overturn the decision arguing that it was procedurally flawed since Lord Hoffmann was party to the proceedings and therefore was automatically excluded from the case.

The House of Lords had never been asked to overturn one of its previous decisions in this way before, but held unanimously that it did have jurisdiction to do so.[101] Further, the House held that the decision did have to be set aside because Lord Hoffmann was automatically disqualified from sitting in judgment on the case because one of the parties to the case (albeit simply as an intervener) was *Amnesty International*. There was no suggestion that there was any financial or proprietary interest in this case; Lord Hoffmann was not paid for his role as director and chair of the charity but it was stated that he did have an interest. The organization *Amnesty International* is unincorporated but the activities of its headquarters are divided into two companies; the first is an ordinary limited company which deals with the non-charitable aims of the organization, and the second was the charitable company that Lord Hoffmann chaired.

The charitable arm of *Amnesty International* had provided funding for a report into the activities of the Chilean government which had concluded that breaches of human rights had occurred and that nobody had ever been held to account for these. Whilst it was *Amnesty International* that intervened (and Lord Hoffmann was not a member of *Amnesty International*) the House of Lords held that though it was not possible to say

---

99. Timothy Jones, 'Judicial Bias and Disqualification in the Pinochet Case' [1999] *Public Law* 391, 395.
100. *R v Bow Street Metropolitan Stipendiary Magistrate, ex p Pinochet (No 1)* [2000] 1 AC 61.
101. *R v Bow Street Metropolitan Stipendiary Magistrate and others, ex p Pinochet (No 2)* [2000] 1 AC 119.

that Lord Hoffmann was a party to the proceedings—in that *Amnesty International* and the charitable organization were theoretically separate entities—the charitable arm did have an interest in the outcome because its founding documents stated it was, inter alia, incorporated to 'procure the abolition of torture'.[102] Given that it had an interest in the proceedings it then followed that Lord Hoffmann, as one of its directors, also had an interest in the matter and so should have been automatically disqualified.

The decision was unanimous and there were some concerns as to its effect. Lord Hutton had said that the links between Lord Hoffmann and *Amnesty International* were 'so strong that public confidence in the integrity of the administration of justice would be shaken if his decision was allowed to stand'[103] which is a damning indictment of the position. Lord Irvine, the then Lord Chancellor, reportedly argued that it had undermined justice[104] and it was reported that some members of the judiciary believed Lord Hoffmann should have resigned.

The decision of the House of Lords was largely welcomed but at least one commentator has noted that the decision has led to a 'growth industry' of lawyers attempting to find interests that debar a judge from sitting.[105] The vast majority of these challenges are doomed to fail, however, since the House of Lords was quite clear as to why Lord Hoffmann should have disclosed his interest. The facts of that case were unusual in that *Amnesty International* had intervened in the case: had the charity not intervened then the issue would not have arisen.

9.3.3.2 **Apprehended bias**

The other significant manner in which a judge can be asked to stand down is in respect of apprehended bias. This remains an ethical issue not least because it is apprehended bias—ie there is some factor that makes people believe that there could be the appearance of bias rather than the fact that the judge is *actually* biased.

Precisely what would meet this criterion will differ according to different sets of facts but in *Locabail* the Court of Appeal was quite clear about what would *not* ordinarily give the appearance of bias, including 'religion, ethnic or national origin, gender, age, class, means or sexual orientation'[106] and this has to be right. Perhaps more controversially they stated: 'the judge's social or educational or service or employment background or history . . . membership of sporting or charitable bodies'[107] would not lead to the appearance of bias. This may, at first sight, appear to be surprising because it would be relatively easy to think of situations when these factors could lead to the suggestion of bias.

The House of Lords considered similar issues in *Helow v Secretary of State for the Home Department*.[108] This was a Scottish case where the appellant, a Palestinian, had sought leave to remain in the United Kingdom but her application was rejected, and subsequent appeals had been denied and she was to be deported. She complained that Lady Cosgrove, a member of the Court of Session (in this context this is roughly the equivalent of the High Court) who had adjudicated on the final appeal was a member of

---

102. ibid, 135.
103. ibid, 146.
104. Timothy Jones, 'Judicial Bias and Disqualification in the Pinochet Case' [1999] *Public Law* 391, 398.
105. Fred Phillips, *Ethics of the Legal Profession* (Cavendish Publishing 2004) 113.
106. *Locabail (UK) Ltd v Bayfield Properties Ltd* [2000] QB 451, 480.
107. ibid.
108. [2008] UKHL 62.

the *International Association of Jewish Lawyers and Jurists*, and had been the founder member of the Scottish branch of this organization.

The appellant sought to argue that the association had a strong commitment to causes and beliefs at odds with the appellant, and she specifically contended that the organization was anti-Palestinian. To support this she adduced speeches by the president of the Association.

The House of Lords rejected her appeal stating that mere membership of the organization was insufficient to show the appearance of bias, and that some stronger connection would need to be shown, for example a link between the president and the judge. This is certainly consistent with *Locabail* but this decision, and the comments from *Locabail* identified earlier, need to be put into context, in that on the vast majority of occasions where they would be relevant it would not be through the appearance of bias but because of an automatic disqualification. This would apply equally to the employment context. If a judge had worked for a considerable period of time in a firm that was party to the proceedings, then it is likely that this would be covered by automatic disqualification and not appearance of bias.

The test for disqualification for appearance of bias is whether there is a 'real danger of bias'[109] and this should be considered through the eyes of a 'fair-minded and informed observer'. In essence this means questioning whether a reasonable person would perceive the risk of bias. If they do then the judge should step down.

▐▌ Case Box *AWG Group Ltd v Morrison*

A good example of this test can be seen from the case of *AWG Group Ltd v Morrison*.[110] The judge assigned to the case was looking through the papers when he saw that he recognized one of the directors to be called as a witness. This was someone well known to him and the judge would not have wanted to preside over a case which necessitated him deciding whether the witness was telling the truth or not. The response of the respondents to this dilemma was to remove the director from the list of witnesses and replace him with another director.

The Court of Appeal held that this was not an appropriate response. If there was the appearance of bias then the judge was disqualified from trying the case; a discretionary case-management decision could not remedy this appearance of bias. The director the judge knew was involved in the case even if he was not (now) giving evidence and a reasonable person would perceive a real risk of bias in such a situation.

Solicitors

Where life becomes slightly more interesting is in respect of part-time judges. The rule as to automatic disqualification applies to all judges. Barristers are, as will be seen, technically self-employed and thus are, or should be, aware of those for whom they are currently acting. It is irrelevant whether another barrister within a particular set of chambers is appearing before the judge because as self-employed persons they are not in partnership so the judge is not acting as one of the parties. In *Locabail* it was noted that

---

109. *Helow v Secretary of State for the Home Department* [2008] UKHL 62 [14].
110. [2006] EWCA Civ 6.

the position for solicitors is different. A partner in a solicitor's firm is legally responsible for the professional acts of all other partners and employees.[111] Accordingly it would, in the opinion of the Court of Appeal, be inappropriate for a part-time judge to sit on a case where his firm has an interest. This will be relatively easy when the representative of one of the parties is the judge's firm but what about the position whereby the firm used to act for a party? The solution, according to the Court of Appeal, is that the solicitor who is sitting part-time as a member of the judiciary should, when invited to sit on a case, undertake a careful conflict check to ensure that the firm has never acted for either party in the past.[112]

⟳ QUESTION FOR REFLECTION

The House of Lords were undoubtedly correct to state that apparent bias can undermine the integrity of the justice system but is it realistic to expect a solicitor to check all clients in order to decide whether they can sit on a case? To take an example, Allen & Overy are one of the largest law firms to be based in the United Kingdom. They operate worldwide and have over 5,500 staff including 550 partners. How easy would it be for a solicitor to check that no work had been undertaken? Or should firms who allow their staff to sit as judges have sufficient systems in place to ensure that there can be no conflict of interest?

9.4 Restrictions on practice

Where a person is elevated to a full-time judicial position then they must cease to practise,[113] something that is quite reasonable as it ensures that there is no conflict of interest. Is the decision to become a judge irrevocable, however? Those who are elevated to the bench will normally consider it to be their last employment with the intention of serving until retirement. However, this need not be the case and in 1970 a puisne judge, Mr Justice Fisher, decided to resign from the bench and work in the city instead. This decision was greeted with outrage[114] as the expectation of the public was that judges would accept a judgeship and sit for the duration of their appointment.

Fisher J did not return to practice but is it possible? It had always been assumed that it was not possible[115] but this assumption was challenged by the resignation of a puisne judge (Laddie J) and the retirement of a circuit judge (HHJ Cook).[116] Both indicated that they wished to be involved with practice, with HHJ Cook joining a solicitors' firm as a partner and Laddie J joining a solicitors' firm as a senior consultant. HHJ Cook was reported to have commented that whilst the Bar traditionally refused to allow a former judge to return to practice, the Law Society had no such ethic[117] which demonstrates an interesting division between the professions.

---

111. *Locabail (UK) Ltd v Bayfield Properties Ltd* [2000] QB 451, 478.
112. ibid, 479.
113. *Courts and Legal Services Act 1990*, s 75.
114. David Pannick, *Judges* (OUP 1987) 7.
115. ibid.
116. *The Times* (28 June 2005) Law Supplement.
117. 'Lord Chancellor Reviews Ban on Judges Returning to Practice Law' *The Times* (23 June 2005).

Should judges be permitted to return to practice? It is widely reported that the senior judiciary do not believe that it should be possible, with the suggestion that it undermines the appearance of judicial impartiality and, potentially, their independence. However, one argument is that the previous rules have never been more than conventions[118] and questions whether some practitioners may be more ready to join the bench if they believe it is possible eventually to return, but this misses the point that they could accept a part-time judicial appointment such as recorder or deputy High Court judge.

 Summary

This chapter has discussed the independence of the judiciary. In particular it has:

- Noted that a fundamental constitutional principle is that judges are independent.
- Explored the difficulties around securing the independence of the judiciary, in particular, the role of salaries, tenure, promotion, and discipline.
- Acknowledged the differences between the security of tenure for superior and inferior judges.
- Considered the role of judicial ethics in relation to being a judge as well as the part that ethics play in securing judicial independence.
- Noted that where a person is elevated to a full-time judicial position, then they must cease to practise.

End-of-chapter questions

1. Why is securing the independence of the judiciary so important?

2. Who are the judiciary independent from?

3. How is judicial independence secured? Do you think that this is sufficient?

4. Read David Pannick, 'Judges Must be Able to Take up any Position Once They're off the Bench' *The Times* 12 July 2005, and compare and contrast Thomas Bingham, 'Judicial Ethics' in Ross Cranston (ed), *Legal Ethics and Professional Responsibility* (Clarendon Press 1995) 50–1. Given the importance of judicial independence is there not a danger that by allowing judges to move between practice and the bench a judge may be influenced by an advocate appearing before him to whom he may wish later to apply for a job?

---

118. David Pannick, 'Judges Must be Able to Take up any Position Once They're off the Bench' *The Times* (12 July 2005).

☰ Further reading

Bingham T, 'Judicial Independence' in *The Business of Judging* (OUP 2000).

This is an essay written by Lord Bingham who discusses the concept of judicial independence and places it in the context of the modern judiciary.

Lord Hodge, 'Preserving judicial independence in an age of populism' available at <https://www.supremecourt.uk/docs/speech-181123.pdf>.

Lord Hodge, Justice of the Supreme Court, gave a speech on judicial independence at the North Strathclyde Sheriffdom Conference in November 2018.

Lord Thomas LCJ, 'Judicial Independence in a Changing Constitutional Landscape' available at <https://www.judiciary.gov.uk/wp-content/uploads/2015/09/speech-lcj-judicial-independence-in-a changing constitutional-landscape2.pdf>.

Lord Thomas LCJ gave a speech to the Commonwealth Magistrates' and Judges' Association on the subject of judicial independence and the position of the judiciary in the United Kingdom.

For self-test questions, flashcards, and links to useful websites, please visit the **online resources** at: **www.oup.com/he/gillespie-weare8e**

10

The Legal Professions

By the end of this chapter you will be able to:

- Identify the various branches of the legal profession.
- Understand the differences between the three principal professions.
- Understand how a person qualifies as a member of the professions.
- Identify ethical issues relating to the practice of law.

Introduction

Many of you will start your studies in law with the intention of becoming a lawyer, although by the end of their studies only approximately 50 per cent of law students actually seek a position as a member of the legal professions. In this chapter we will discuss what the legal professions are, what they do, and how it is possible for someone to qualify as a member of the professions. The chapter will also examine the rules governing practice as a member of the professions and, in particular, the issue of ethical behaviour.

10.1 Defining the professions

The term 'lawyer' has become an almost standard term that is heard in daily use and the *Oxford English Dictionary* defines it as 'a member of the legal profession'. However, this masks the point that there is no single legal profession but instead there are three principal professions and some secondary ones. It is for this reason that most law dictionaries will not define 'lawyer' because it is a colloquialism that is used as shorthand but does not describe anyone in particular, as nobody in the United Kingdom is a 'lawyer' *per se* but has a more specific title.

It is often said that England and Wales is one of three countries to continue to have separate legal professions[1] with the vast majority of countries having a single profession. However, this is not necessarily correct in that a distinction must be drawn between qualified members of the legal profession and non-qualified members of the profession. In England and Wales there are commonly thought to be three branches of

---

1. The others being Scotland and the Republic of Ireland, both of which obviously have strong links to the English Legal System.

the qualified legal profession: barristers, solicitors, and legal executives. In other countries, for example the United States of America, there is one, commonly known as an attorney. However, other people will consider themselves to be a 'lawyer' and in other jurisdictions, and increasingly within England and Wales, they are an important part of a functioning legal system. In England and Wales the three principal professions are joined by other types of 'lawyer', for example 'paralegals' (who may also be known by other terms, for example, fee-earners), a type of lawyer that has been largely imported from America.

The main focus of this chapter will be on solicitors, barristers, and legal executives as these remain the principal branches of the profession and the ones most people are familiar with. However, other roles will also be considered.

10.2 Barristers

The first group to be examined are barristers, who are also referred to as 'counsel' and are frequently thought to be the specialist advocates although, as will be seen, this is not necessarily accurate.

⚡ 'COUNSEL'

Barristers, especially those who practise as advocates, are often referred to as 'counsel' and may sometimes style themselves as 'of counsel', eg Martin Squires of counsel. When a solicitor instructs a barrister, he will usually summarize the case and the action requested by preparing a document known as 'instructions to counsel' which is also called a 'brief to counsel'. Precisely why barristers are also called counsel is lost in the mists of time but it is important to recognize their dual title.

10.2.1 History of the Bar

Barristers collectively are known as 'the Bar' for reasons that will become clear later. The profession is the oldest branch, with the term barrister existing as far back as the thirteenth century and until relatively recently they had the sole rights of audience in the higher courts. Whilst there is in existence the Bar Council (more properly known as the General Council of the Bar for England and Wales) which acts as the 'trade body' of barristers, their responsibility is to their Inns of Court, to which all members must belong.

⚡ RIGHTS OF AUDIENCE

'Rights of audience' is a specific legal term. A person does not automatically have the right to appear in the courts and perform advocacy, the rules on when a person may do so differ depending on the profession, the court, and the type of case. The ability to act as an advocate in a court is known as 'rights of audience' and so if one is said to have rights of audience in the High Court, it means that the person can appear in the High Court as an advocate and represent his or her client.

10.2.1.1 **Inns of Court**

There are now four Inns of Court, all of which are honourable and learned societies, which is why barristers are referred to as *learned* whereas solicitors and legal executives are not. The Inns are Middle Temple, Inner Temple, Gray's Inn, and Lincoln's Inn. Traditionally each Inn was slightly different and the choice of Inn to some degree was a conscious choice for a barrister's career. Lincoln's Inn was primarily considered to be a Chancery based Inn, ie its members would specialize in Chancery matters and to an extent this has remained, although its members are certainly more general practitioners now. Gray's Inn traditionally had a provincial focus, again something that has been retained to an extent with many members of the North-Eastern Circuit belonging to this Inn. However, realistically the modern Inns no longer act as specialists and the choice of an Inn is now one of pure personal preference rather than any career choice.

Traditionally the Inns of Court were responsible for the training of barristers and all education took place within their own Inn. From the mid-nineteenth century, however, the four Inns decided that it would be best to cooperate in the education of barristers and they established the Council of Legal Education and the Inns of Court School of Law which took over the education of student members of the Inns. However, the importance of the Inns to education remains and even today a student member of an Inn is (theoretically) restricted to his own Inn and may only use its facilities until he has become a barrister, at which point the facilities of all four Inns become available. The *Bar Standards Board* (BSB) has taken over as the main body with the day-to-day responsibility of regulating barristers but the Inns of Court continue to have the sole right to call members to the Bar and they execute any punishment arising out of disciplinary hearings, including the ultimate sanction of removing a barrister.

In recent years there has been some discussion as to the purpose of the Inns with one eminent QC describing them as 'self-perpetuating geriatric oligarchies',[2] and another describing them as a glorified private club (something that Dunn, a former Court of Appeal judge, agrees with[3]). However, others disagree and Robins reports the words of a junior barrister who joined the Inn during his vocational training year and says, '[my time] made me feel included in the inn [*sic*] and the workings of the inn, and it gave me a sense of professional history'.[4]

10.2.1.2 **Masters of the Bench**

The Inns of Court are presided over by a series of senior members of the Inns known collectively as the 'Masters of the Bench' and colloquially referred to as 'benchers'. Most benchers are elected by members of the Inn, although some are, by tradition, ex officio benchers, most notably the senior judiciary. All High Court judges are automatically made a bencher if they have not already been elected (and Rothwell notes that this applies to High Court judges who used to be solicitors).[5] Clementi has questioned whether it is correct for members of the judiciary to take an active role in the running

329

---

2. Jon Robins, 'Inn a Time Warp?' (2005) 102 *Law Society Gazette* 19.
3. Robin Dunn, *Sword and Wig: Memoirs of a Lord Justice* (Quiller Press 1993) 186.
4. Jon Robins, 'Inn a Time Warp?' (2005) 102 *Law Society Gazette* 19, 21.
5. Rachel Rothwell, 'The Inn Crowd' (2005) 102 *Law Society Gazette* 22, 23.

of the Inns,[6] although he did not take his questioning to the extent of recommending any substantive change. Any change would undoubtedly be resisted by the judiciary, who consider their membership of the Inns as advantageous, particularly to student members who will come into contact with them at an early stage of their careers and in a friendly place.

⚡ MASTERS OF THE BENCH

Regardless of what title a Master of the Bench holds (a judicial office such as Lord Justice of Appeal, Mr Justice, etc) when they are performing their role as a Master of the Bench they are referred to as 'Master [n]' and referred to simply as 'master' (even if they are female). This can cause some confusion to junior members who, for example, see one of their Masters sitting in the Supreme Court (where he will be referred to as 'My Lord') and in the evening be calling him 'Master'. The purpose of the rule is to ensure that all realize that they are all members of the same Inn and, therefore, part of the same community.

The head of the Inn is the Master Treasurer and he is appointed for a one-year term. Whilst it is not a full-time position, it is not far from it and the person appointed will normally undertake less professional work (even judicial work if they are a judge when appointed) during their year of office. The person who is in day-to-day control of the Inns is the Under Treasurer (sometimes called Sub-Treasurer), who is not usually legally qualified but is experienced in senior management and will lead the team of employees of the Inns. A crude, but somewhat accurate, analogy to explain the relationship between the Master Treasurer and Under Treasurer is that between the chairman (Master Treasurer) and chief executive or director of operations (Under Treasurer) of a company, thus reinforcing that the post of Master Treasurer is not a ceremonial one, but one that carries with it executive responsibilities.[7]

10.2.1.3 **The 'Bar'**

When a person becomes a barrister he is said to have been called to the Bar. This term is another that has historical significance. Before the Inns of Court School of Law was established, the training of barristers took place in the Inn and by members of the Inn. The students and instructors (senior members of the Inn) would sit in the centre of the room set out like a courtroom. The students would sit in the middle of the court, within the bar, and when they were called to 'the utter bar' which means 'outer' they left the middle of the court and took their places outside the bar signifying they were no longer students. When a barrister is called they become a junior barrister and they remain a junior for the rest of their careers unless they opt to 'take silk' and become a Queen's Counsel (QC). This process is discussed later but is mentioned here because when a member of the Inn is appointed a QC they are called 'into' the Bar (as distinct from 'to the Bar').

---

6. David Clementi, *Review of the Regulatory Framework for Legal Services in England and Wales* (HMSO 2004) 31.
7. Robin Dunn, *Sword and Wig: Memoirs of a Lord Justice* (Quiller Press 1993) 186–8.

⚡ SITTING IN COURT

In many of the old courts the status of a barrister will be reflected in where they sit. In the older and more important courts the first row of the advocates' benches will be separated from the rest by a gate or bar. Only those who have been called into the bar, ie QCs, may sit in that row of benches, with junior barristers having to sit in the row behind. In more modern courts where no gate exists barristers will sit in any row except when a junior barrister is being 'led' by a QC in which case the junior will ordinarily sit behind the QC.

10.2.2 Education and training

The way that barristers were historically trained has been discussed but how are they trained now? The training of barristers has recently been reformed, with the BSB announcing in March 2017 a 'Future Bar Training' programme. Historically, training prior to full qualification was divided into three parts:

- academic stage (gaining knowledge of the law itself)
- vocational stage (acquiring barristers' core skills)
- pupillage (learning 'on the job').

The reforms proposed by the BSB were approved by the Legal Services Board (see 10.5.1) in March 2019. The completion of the three stages above will still be required, but new rules will be introduced which are designed to make the training more flexible, accessible, and affordable. A key aspect of the new approach is that the three stages of training can be delivered under four approved pathways:

1. A three-step pathway: academic, followed by vocational, followed by pupillage/work-based component (this is the same as the previous pathway)

2. A four-step pathway: academic component, followed by vocational component in two parts, followed by pupillage or work-based component

3. Integrated academic and vocational pathway: combined academic and vocational components followed by pupillage or work-based component

4. Apprenticeship pathway: combined academic, vocational and pupillage or work-based components.

Three of the four new pathways (1–3 above) have been running since September 2020. The three step and four step pathway are most well established and therefore it is those that will be discussed in this chapter. The apprenticeship pathway is not yet available, although discussions are ongoing about the introduction of barrister apprenticeships.

Before looking at each stage in the training process, it is important to note that the reforms introduced by the BSB are underpinned by the publishing of their Professional Statement.[8] The Statement describes the knowledge, skills, and competences that all barristers are expected to have from 'day one' of their practice, helping prospective barristers to understand the standards to which they must aspire, and underpinning the

---

8. Bar Standards Board, 'Professional Statement for Barristers' (BSB 2016) <https://www.barstandardsboard.org.uk/media/1787559/bsb_professional_statement_and_competences_2016.pdf>.

training that must be taken. Interestingly, prior to the publication of the Professional Statement, there was no single source that could be referred to that set out the threshold standard and competences expected of barristers.

10.2.2.1 Academic stage

The academic stage for those who wish to become solicitors or barristers under the three-step or four-step pathway is the same as it was prior to the reforms. Currently, the length of time it takes depends on the educational background of the candidates. There is no requirement for graduates to complete a law degree. If, however, the candidate is not a law graduate then they can undertake a conversion course known as the Graduate Diploma in Law (GDL). Some universities also allow graduate entry to a law degree which is a 'fast track' law degree on the basis that it is not necessary to develop undergraduate learning techniques as the entrant is already a graduate, which means that the programmes can focus purely on the law. Typically these programmes will last two, rather than three, years.

During the academic stage, regardless of which route is taken, the candidate must, as a minimum, receive education in the following:[9]

- Constitutional Law
- Contract Law
- Criminal Law
- Equity
- Law of the EU
- Land Law
- Law of Tort.

It is also expected that students will receive a good understanding of how to research law and acquire the general skills required to study law. The GDL programme will normally focus solely on these exemption subjects, whereas a law degree will generally allow the student to undertake a series of optional subjects which provide a slightly wider grounding in law.

The minimum requirement for acceptance onto the vocational stage for the Bar is a lower-second-class honours degree.

The BSB reforms have made minimal changes to the academic stage of training. However, they note that they will be 'encouraging innovation by academic institutions in the ways in which subjects are taught: through their provision, for example of opportunities for students to gain work based experience or undertake clinical legal education.'[10] Many institutions already offer students such opportunities, for example through law clinics and work placements.

10.2.2.2 Vocational stage

Since September 2020 the vocational stage of training has changed. Prior to this it involved completing the Bar Professional Training Course (BPTC). The primary focus

---

9. Note that some of the names may change between institutions.
10. Bar Standards Board, 'BSB Policy Statement on Bar Training' (BSB 2017) <https://www.barstandardsboard.org.uk/media/1825162/032317_fbt_-_policy_statement_version_for_publication.pdf> 2.

of the BPTC was the application of legal knowledge to situations and a number of practical training exercises were used to take the form of 'mock' briefs where the student was expected to undertake work likely to occur in the early years of practice. The BPTC concentrated largely on advocacy, drafting legal documents, and legal research. The importance of ethics was also highlighted on the course.

From the 2020/21 academic year the BPTC no longer exists. In its place are a variety of Bar training courses run by different 'Authorised Education and Training Organisations' (AETOs). All courses must fulfil the BSB requirements of flexibility, accessibility, affordability, and high standards. Whilst there are differences between the old BPTC and the new Bar training, for example more variety of teaching approaches within AETOs, there have not been substantive changes to much of what is required in terms of the syllabus. All Bar training courses will include the following modules:

- Advocacy
- Civil Litigation and Alternative Dispute Resolution
- Criminal Litigation, Evidence, and Sentencing
- Conference skills
- Drafting
- Opinion Writing and Legal Research
- Professional Ethics

Before being able to enrol on the BPTC, candidates needed to pass the Bar Course Aptitude Test (BCAT) and that is still the case for the new Bar training courses. The BCAT was introduced in November 2013 in response to recommendations made by the *Bar Vocational Course Review Group* and aims to ensure that those embarking on Bar training have the aptitude to successfully complete this stage of their training.

The vocational stage can now be delivered in two parts (under the four-step pathway). Under this approach 'part one' can be completed by self-study, with students not paying fees for 'part two' until they have successfully completed the first stage. Students can also take a break after completing 'part one' and come back to complete 'part two' at a later date. This provides increased flexibility for students completing the vocational stage, especially for those who may have work or caring responsibilities. The two-part option also eliminates some of the financial risk associated with pursuing a career at the Bar which is highly competitive (see 10.2.2.3). Part-time study options are available on both the three-step and four-step pathways.

10.2.2.3 **Pupillage**

Regardless of the pathway followed, a work-based component or pupillage must be completed. Pupillage was also required under the previous qualification requirements, and is perhaps the most important part of the training for becoming a barrister. It is perhaps the most difficult to secure as Mason notes that there are over three times the number of would-be pupils as there are pupillages.[11] Indeed the most recent detailed statistics released by the BSB show that in 2018/19, 1,753 students enrolled on the BPTC[12] (the vocational element prior to the 2020 reforms), yet in the same year only

11.   D Mason, 'A Ticking Time Bomb?' (2004) 154 *New Law Journal* 1601.
12.   Bar Standards Board, 'Statistics on BPTC students' (BSB) <https://www.barstandardsboard.org.uk/news-publications/research-and-statistics/statistics-about-the-bar/bptc.html>.

333

525 BPTC graduates commenced first-six pupillages.[13] Although the pupil will have been called to the Bar, during pupillage he will refer to himself as a 'pupil barrister'. Pupillage will normally last for twelve months but exceptionally it is possible that it could last up to eighteen months. Pupillage is broken into six-month blocks referred to as the first six and second six (and exceptionally a third six) and although some chambers will offer twelve-month pupillages these are, in fact, two separate six-month arrangements.

The BSB refers to pupillage as:

> work-based training in legal work under supervision . . . Pupillage is an essential component of training for the Bar.[14]

A barrister of at least ten years' experience can apply to become a pupil-master, ie someone who is entitled to train pupils. Accordingly it can be seen that it is very much practitioner-led. Not every barrister of at least ten years' call can act as a pupil-master and sets of chambers must first register with the BSB as a 'Pupillage Training Organisation' (PTO). Once appointed a PTO chambers will have to adhere to rules on pupillage (including funding, discussed later) set out by the BSB.

In the first six months the pupil barrister is restricted as to what he can do, and realistically this work amounts to a 'shadowing' operation in which the pupil will observe the work of the master. Although a first-six pupil will not be allowed to perform advocacy or meet with a client alone, he will begin to work on paperwork relating to legal cases, including claim forms, defences, and particulars of claim. All of this documentary work will, of course, be under the supervision of, and probably corrected by, the pupil-master but these are the first steps into practice.

In the second six months a pupil barrister gains limited rights of audience and the ability to undertake legal work, albeit under the (loose) supervision of his master. A pupil in the second six months may well begin to undertake advocacy work, probably in the magistrates' court (crime) and county courts (civil) and is entitled to meet clients in the same way as fully qualified barristers will. It should be emphasized, of course, that the pupil is not yet fully qualified and he can anticipate a lot of questioning from his master as to how he intends to undertake the advocacy etc.

Traditionally pupils were never paid and indeed in historical times (until the early to mid-twentieth century) it was expected that pupils would pay barristers for acting as their masters. However, currently pupils must be paid no less than £15,728 per annum as well as having travel expenses and training costs covered.

Under the 2020 BSB reforms, there is now greater flexibility in how pupillage is completed with pupillages also known as 'periods of work-based learning'. This 'work-based learning' can be offered, for example, by employers offering training to future members of the employed Bar. The normal duration of pupillage (and other forms of work-based learning) will continue to be twelve months. However, the new rules allow it be up to twenty-four months with authorization from the BSB. During pupillage a number of compulsory courses must be completed including an advocacy course and a new negotiation skills course.

---

13. Bar Standards Board, 'Pupillage Statistics' (BSB) <https://www.barstandardsboard.org.uk/news-publications/research-and-statistics/statistics-about-the-bar/pupillage.html>.

14. Bar Standards Board, 'C1 Overview and Structure of Pupillage' (BSB) <https://www.barstandardsboard.org.uk/training-qualification/bar-qualification-manual/part-2-for-students-pupils--transferring-lawyers/c1-overview-and-structure-of-pupillage.html>.

10.2.3 **Practice**

Once a barrister has fully qualified how do they practise? The rules differ between those who serve as employed barristers and those who act in private practice.

10.2.3.1 **Private practice**

Perhaps the recognizable type of barrister is that in independent (private) practice.

Chambers

After pupillage it is necessary for a person to find a place from where he can practise, known as a tenancy. Barristers are all self-employed and until 2010 they were not allowed to establish a legal partnership with each other but instead they joined together in loose associations known as chambers (also known as 'sets') in order to pool resources (something that continues to be the norm). Each barrister (known as a tenant within chambers) will pay rent and a proportion of their income to cover the expenses of chambers. Chambers itself will employ some staff; some will include administrative assistants, but the most important of the employees are the clerks. The clerk to a barrister is an unusual position and has often been likened to the 'pimp' of a barrister. It is not possible for individual barristers to tout for business and, accordingly, the clerk is responsible, in part, for bringing work into the set. Many briefs will be for specific barristers but some will be chambers briefs where a firm of solicitors is happy to deal with anyone within the set and it will then be for the clerk to decide who gets the brief. Where a trial overruns and this prevents a barrister from starting another case the clerk will also redistribute the work. Traditionally a clerk was given a percentage of the brief fee but in modern times it is now more likely that clerks will be on a salary with bonuses paid depending on performance. The attraction this brings is that clerks will concentrate on all barristers whereby when it was a percentage system there was always the risk that the clerk would concentrate on the more experienced practitioners for whom he could attract a higher fee. Chambers normally has a team of clerks, with one being the senior clerk who has ultimate responsibility for supervising the rest and the general operation of clerking. Increasingly in modern times the senior clerk is being called the 'practice manager' or even 'chambers manager'. Good clerks are extremely useful to chambers and there is a strong market in poaching the best. The very best senior clerks can expect high six-figure salaries and the vast majority of senior clerks will earn significant salaries, quite frequently more than what many of the barristers within their chambers will earn.

Once a person is of at least three years' call he is entitled to work without being a member of chambers, ie from home if he so wishes, or he can establish chambers himself.[15] There does appear to be an increase in the number of sole practitioners and some clever clerks have created schemes whereby they will perform an agency-type clerking service for these persons. Acting as a sole practitioner does bring the advantages of more control over work and is undoubtedly cheaper (no chambers expenses, rent, etc) but there is the difficulty that if a sole practitioner's source of work is not strong it is unlikely that they would pick up briefs from others within a set when they become available because of overrunning trials etc.

---

15. Bar Standards Board, *The BSB Handbook* (Version 4.4, BSB 2020) rS20.

Court work

The stereotypical view of a barrister is that they spend most of their time in court, in part because once they are qualified a barrister has rights of audience in every court. However, this general impression is not strictly accurate. Whilst it is true to say that barristers specialize in litigation and advocacy it does not mean that all their time will be spent in court, indeed this depends on their area of practice. Whilst criminal and family practitioners will spend the majority of their time in court, other practitioners will not and for those with a primarily civil practice, especially Chancery matters, court is the measure of last resort and they will feel that they have almost failed if it gets to court (because of the costs of litigation) in that most matters can be settled before trial.

It is, however, true to say that advocacy is the most important tool of a barrister but it need not be restricted to oral advocacy and a considerable amount of written documentation will be prepared by barristers. One of the most important aspects of the work of a barrister is the provision of counsel's opinion. This normally takes place at the beginning of litigation and it is the time when a barrister will assess the likely success of any litigation and identify the key evidential difficulties. The preparation of counsel's opinion will normally require the barrister to undertake research on a specialist area and then to present this advice to the solicitor and those instructing them. If, after considering the advice of counsel, it is decided to proceed with litigation it is likely that the barrister will also be involved in the drafting of the various documents that are needed for litigation, including the claim form, particulars of claim, defences, and questions between all the parties. All of these are specialist skills and training developed during the vocational stage of qualification.

When a barrister does appear in open court he appears in the full rig that the public know so well. Except for tribunals and the magistrates' courts where no robes are worn, all barristers will ordinarily wear a gown, wig, and bands. The robes of QCs will be discussed later, but junior barristers wear a stuff gown, bands (which are the white tails that are worn around the neck—ladies have a wrap-around version which includes a collar whereas male barristers' shirts have detachable collars and they replace the normal collar with a winged one), and the infamous wig. There has been a debate for many years as to whether this costume should remain and in 2003 the government issued a consultation paper which suggested a number of options, the simplest of these being that advocates (of all grades) should only wear a gown.

Despite the fact that civil judges have now abandoned their wigs (see 8.2) proceedings in open court will ordinarily see the barrister fully wigged and gowned although where a judge sits without robes counsel will ordinarily not wear robes either. The Supreme Court has also recently decided that counsel need not robe although all parties must be in agreement.[16]

The retention of wigs and gowns was considered an important matter for the Bar when consulted, although this was perhaps more relevant in criminal matters where it has been suggested that they provide a degree of authority and anonymity (Megarry J in *St Edmundsbury & Ipswich Board of Finance v Clark* made *obiter* comments that discussed the merits of judicial and advocates robes[17]). The degree of safety this brings is perhaps slightly questionable. In any event it must be seriously questioned whether advocates will continue to wear wigs in civil matters now that judges do not.

---

16. The Supreme Court of the UK, *Practice Direction 6* (UKSC) <https://www.supremecourt.uk/procedures/practice-direction-06.html> 6.6.8.

17. [1973] Ch 323, 333.

It would seem inevitable that a practice direction will ultimately follow that counsel follow the lead of the judiciary and abandon wigs, at least for civil matters.

The 'cab rank rule'

Solicitors, to an extent, have the right to pick and choose their clients (although it will be seen later that they tend not to exercise this right). Barristers in independent practice, on the other hand, are bound by their Code of Conduct to adopt something which is called the 'cab rank rule' which is described as:

If you receive instructions from a professional client, and you are:

- a self-employed barrister; or
- an authorized individual working within a BSB entity; or
- a BSB entity and the instructions seek the services of a named authorized individual working for you,

and the *instructions* are appropriate taking into account the experience, seniority and/or field of practice of yourself or (as appropriate) of the named *authorized individual* you must . . . accept the *instructions* addressed specifically to you, irrespective of:

- the identity of the client;
- the nature of the case to which the instructions relate;
- whether the client is paying privately or is publicly funded; and
- any belief or opinion which you may have formed as to the character, reputation, cause, conduct, guilt or innocence of the client.[18]

Pannick quotes Lord Irvine QC (later a Lord Chancellor) who describes the rule as:

. . . the duty to appear for the Yorkshire Ripper or any other defendant against whom there may be a hostile climate of public opinion. In civil cases, it is also his duty to appear not only for a particular interest group with which he might prefer to identify but for every interest group . . . [19]

In other words personal preference cannot decide what case a barrister takes. A criminal practitioner cannot, for example, decide that he will only defend cases and will never accept a prosecution brief as this would breach the cab rank rule. Similarly, a barrister could not decide that he will refuse to take briefs from companies that trade with a particular country because such personal ethics infringe the rule.

> ### ⊟ Example Cab rank rule
>
> Arthur Hoskins has been charged with two counts of robbery. The Crown Prosecution Service approaches the clerk to Rhiannon Holloway, a barrister who practises in criminal law. The cab rank rule states that if it is possible for Rhiannon to do this case (ie there is no conflict of interest and she is available during the likely time that this will come to court) then she must accept the brief. Rhiannon could not reject the brief in the knowledge that the defence solicitors, who regularly instruct her and other members of the set, may well approach her and she could get more money acting as the defence. The prosecution came first and therefore that brief has to be taken.

---

18.   Bar Standards Board, *The BSB Handbook* (Version 4.4, BSB 2020) rC29.
19.   David Pannick, *Advocates* (OUP 1992) 136.

The rule is not universally approved of. Some have argued that it is a restriction on freedom and that it cannot be justified, but Pannick states: 'any lawyer who does not understand [the purpose of the rule] really has no business being an advocate'.[20] The basis for this statement is Pannick's belief that to remove the rule would be to prejudice the impartiality of the advocate and would cause people no longer to understand that an advocate's arguments are not necessarily his own beliefs but rather the instructions of his lay client.[21] Whether society fully understands this distinction is perhaps somewhat questionable but the essence of the point is almost certainly true, and it undoubtedly makes it easier for an advocate to perform his duty without needing to like or approve of his client.

↻ QUESTION FOR REFLECTION

It is arguable that the cab rank rule is archaic; do you agree? If yes, how would people who are suspected of the most serious crimes (eg child abuse or murder) ever be represented? Read 10.6.2.1 which discusses how a lawyer should deal with defending someone they believe guilty. Is there not a danger that by abandoning the cab rank rule the jury will become superfluous with defence counsel deciding whether someone suspected of committing a serious crime is guilty or not? (On this point see *Ridehalgh v Horsefield and another*.)[22]

◀) LISTEN TO THE PODCAST

For guidance on how to answer this question and a discussion of the main issues, listen to the author's podcast on the online resources:
www.oup.com/he/gillespie-weare8e

Is the rule enforced? The BSB does attempt to uphold it and breach of this rule is considered to be a serious disciplinary offence but Pannick noted that, even in the early 1990s, there was concern that the rule was being avoided through, for example, instructing the barrister's clerk to pretend that the barrister is already committed and a suggestion that a barrister would only act for certain parties (eg trades unions) or would never defend a rapist.[23] Clementi, when discussing the merits of the rule, notes that one submission by a barrister stated:

> [A]ny reasonably successful barrister will be able credibly to assert that his current professional and private commitments preclude him or her taking on a case that is unattractive to him or her—until the next interesting case comes along which they would rather do.[24]

It would appear that the rule can be obscured but whether this should justify the end of the rule is perhaps more questionable. Whilst some believe it is a restriction on practice, to others it is an inherent protection to the vulnerable that no matter how unpopular

---

20. ibid, 145.
21. ibid, 140.
22. [1994] Ch 205, 234.
23. ibid, 144.
24. David Clementi, *Review of the Regulatory Framework for Legal Services in England and Wales* (HMSO 2004) 131.

they are, or how abhorrent an allegation against them is, they can ensure that they are provided with access to the law.

The barrister's client

Using the earlier example, let us assume that the Crown Prosecution Service (CPS) did not brief Miss Holloway first; the solicitors for Mr Hoskins offered the brief to Miss Holloway first and this was accepted. Who is the client of the barrister? It may be thought that given Mr Hoskins is the person who has been charged with the crime and who will ultimately appear in court it will be him but this would be wrong. In fact the client of the barrister is ordinarily the solicitor, and the relationship that exists in respect of this case is between solicitor and barrister not between Mr Hoskins and Miss Holloway. The ultimate client, Mr Hoskins, will be referred to as the 'lay client'.

This 'third party' approach historically caused difficulty in terms of payment. Historically a barrister was not able to sue a solicitor for fees because it was considered that the relationship between solicitor and barrister was not a contractual one[25] and this led to a position whereby barristers incurred a significant amount of 'aged debt', ie debt where a solicitor refused to pay for the barrister's service or held on to the money for a longer period of time (thus recouping the interest). There were undoubtedly tensions that existed between the professions on the subject of late or delayed paying,[26] with solicitors frequently (and perhaps from their point of view somewhat understandably) using a finite amount of money to pay their expenses first and then paying the remainder to the barrister even if this was less than the agreed fee. However, in 2004 the Bar Council changed its position from presuming that the relationship between solicitor and barrister was *not* contractual to presuming it *was* contractual and accordingly the position is now that a barrister can sue a solicitor for reduced or non-payment of fees.

Direct access

The other historical feature of the third-party rule was that a lay client could *only* access the services of a barrister via a solicitor, and indeed at one point a barrister was never allowed to meet with the lay client without the solicitor being present. Increasingly this rule has been reduced, partly in response to solicitors increasingly exercising rights of audience, but also because there is recognition that requiring two lawyers is unnecessary. The initial approach was through BarDirect which allowed a limited category of persons to approach a barrister but this has now been significantly changed and its latest guise, *Public Access*, widens the range of persons who are able to instruct a barrister direct although it does not apply in respect of some forms of work, most notably criminal trials.

Not all barristers will accept work through *Public Access* and those who do wish to do so will need to have received appropriate training on conducting such work. *Public Access* does not take away the duties under the *Code of Conduct* and, in particular, the fact that a barrister should not accept work that could lead to him being professionally embarrassed because, for example, he has no knowledge of that area.[27] A barrister who

339

25. See, for example, *Kennedy v Broun* (1863) 143 ER 268.
26. See Lord Hailsham, *A Sparrow's Flight* (Collins 1990) 440–1.
27. Bar Standards Board, *The BSB Handbook* (Version 4.4, BSB 2020) rC21.

decides that it is in the interests of justice for his lay client to have a solicitor must not act and instead advise his client of that conclusion.

Whilst there are undoubtedly challenges with *Public Access* it is clear that many of the skills of a barrister, particularly in respect of negotiation, arbitration, and the provision of detailed advice, are likely to be welcome by many and it is this type of work that will primarily be undertaken through *Public Access*.

One of the significant changes that arises with *Public Access* is that the cab rank rule is suspended;[28] a barrister is not required to accept instructions from a member of the public and can, in essence, pick and choose which cases they are prepared to accept direct instructions for. This is perhaps partly because the barrister will have to consider how he will maintain a relationship with the client and may therefore prefer to accept instructions from only certain types of individuals (eg law centres, professional firms (architects, surveyors etc)) rather than everyone.

Public Access does not broaden the type of work that a barrister can do. There remain general restrictions on the type of work that a barrister can conduct and it is important to note that public access is simply a different way of gaining access to a barrister rather than widening the range of activities.[29]

10.2.3.2 **Employed practice**

Whilst the majority of barristers will remain in independent practice a significant number of barristers are now employed. The numbers have increased in recent years because of a change in the rights of audience such barristers have. Traditionally only barristers in independent practice had unlimited rights of audience, and a barrister who became employed lost their rights of audience in the higher courts and was restricted to those courts that solicitors could appear in. Until comparatively recently this caused problems for agencies such as the CPS where even the Director of Public Prosecutions (DPP), usually a senior barrister, would lose his rights of audience upon taking up his employment. It also meant that those agencies who did seek barristers, eg the CPS, Government Legal Service, could not attract the best barristers because the loss of the rights of audience meant their opportunities were somewhat reduced.

The CLSA 1990 reforms, together with the Bar Council relaxing its Code of Conduct does, however, now mean that the opportunities for barristers in employed practice are quite good. Access to the higher courts is now possible and this means that some companies are creating in-house legal services sections that include barristers. The employed Bar can be quite attractive to barristers, especially newly qualified barristers, because there are not the problems that arise out of self-employment in that an employed barrister will get paid leave, capped working hours, and a regular salary.

Historically the limitations and prohibitions of practising barristers forming partnerships applied to the employed Bar too, and thus barristers working in-house could not own shares in the practice (effectively barring them from being a partner). The *Legal Services Act 2007* (LSA 2007) reforms have relaxed this and as from 2010 it has been possible for barristers to own shares in *Legal Disciplinary Practices*, meaning for example they could be an equity partner in a solicitor-led legal practice.

---

28. ibid, rC123.
29. Bar Standards Board, *Public Access Guidance for Barristers* (BSB 2019) <https://www.barstandardsboard.org.uk/uploads/assets/6cc15510-8da5-4620-ae99720af7be9464/Public-Access-Guidance-for-Barristers.pdf> paras 5 and 6.

10.2.4 **Queen's Counsel**

The highest branch of advocates in England and Wales are called Queen's Counsel (QC).[30] Both barristers and solicitors are entitled to become QCs (although before 1996 it was restricted solely to barristers). However, the vast majority of applicants and appointees continue to be barristers. Indeed, in the 2018 competition only nine applications were from solicitors, with four being appointed.[31] The dominance of the Bar within QC competitions means that we have chosen to place the discussion on QC's within this section on barristers, although it applies equally to solicitors. The process of becoming a QC is known as 'taking silk', the name coming from the fact that the court dress of a QC is a silk rather than stuff robe, worn over a court coat (a long, formal frock coat that is worn instead of a suit jacket). The robe and process has also led to QCs being called 'silks'.

10.2.4.1 **Appointment**

The appointment process for QCs has proven to be very controversial and it was suspended from 2003 until 2005 while a new process was established. Before the new system, the Lord Chancellor (as chief legal adviser and representative of the Queen) had absolute control over who was allowed to take silk and this undoubtedly led to a number of silks being created for political reasons.[32] A junior barrister would apply to the Lord Chancellor for silk and would nominate two friendly judges for their application, and the Lord Chancellor would then confidentially ask senior judges and barristers what they thought of the candidate (this being later extended to include major law firms). The Lord Chancellor could also take into account any other issues he believed were relevant[33] and thus the process was far from transparent. Unsurprisingly, in 2002 Sir Colin Campbell, the Commissioner for Judicial Appointments, suggested that the system was deficient and this led to the suspension of the scheme.

The current scheme begins with an application form which includes the provision of a 'self-assessment' scheme where a person is asked to evaluate themselves against a series of competencies. An application can be made by either a barrister or a solicitor–advocate and the same system applies to both. The application forms are then sifted and those who pass the sift stage are sent to the senior judiciary to assess whether there are any issues of integrity. On the application form the candidate must list twelve important cases involving a matter of substance (ie a trial rather than preliminary matter) that they have dealt with in the past two years. The candidate identifies one judge from that list who would provide a reference and the selection committee chooses three others from the list provided. All four judges are approached to provide a commentary on the competence of the applicant. In addition to this, six practitioners (normally already QCs) must be listed. Those who are considered suitable after this stage will be interviewed by a panel nine strong. The panel will be chaired by a distinguished lay (ie non-lawyer) person; the remaining eight will consist of:

- three lay members
- one senior retired judge

---

30. When the Sovereign is a King then an order of the Privy Council translates all QCs into KCs (King's Counsel).

31 Queen's Council Appointments, 'Queen's Council statistics from 1995 to present' (QC 2019) <https://qcappointments.org/2019-competition/>.

32. Lord Hailsham, *A Sparrow's Flight* (Collins 1990) 386.

33. See, for example, the description of the process put forward by Dame Elizabeth Lane, *Hear the Other Side* (Butterworths 1985) 100–1.

- two senior barristers
- two senior solicitors.

The names of those candidates who are selected by the panel are then passed to the Lord Chancellor and then to the Queen where the letters patent appointing the person a QC will be made.

This new process bears little resemblance to the old system and is certainly more transparent. Indeed it could actually be argued that it is too transparent and that the Bar Council and Law Society may have created a beast that is too burdensome. In 2003 (the final year operated under the old scheme) 394 applicants applied for silk,[34] and by 2019 there were 258 applicants (an increase of 18 on 2018),[35] although this continues to be a significant number. Each applicant must nominate at least eighteen assessors ('referees'), comprising at least eight judicial, six practitioner, and four client assessors. This is a considerable burden on the judiciary when, as it has been seen, judges are already subject to significant administrative burdens. The Judicial Appointments Commissioners were already concerned at the bureaucracy involved in the old system and whether this could lead to references being missed or mislaid[36] and this new scheme does not appear to resolve these issues. The cost of the process must also be of concern. Previously the Department for Constitutional Affairs (DCA) administered the process but it is accepted that this was wrong and it is now administered by an independent body created by the professions. The current fee that applicants must pay is £2,160 (£1,800 plus VAT) with an additional fee of £3,600 (£3,000 plus VAT) being payable for successful applicants. In 2019 of the 258 applicants, 114 were successful (44 per cent).

Practice

A person who is appointed QC will see a dramatic shift in their practice with the real possibility that their fees will rise because silks are paid more than juniors. However, it is a gamble because a silk should only undertake work that is suitable for them, and thus it is possible that someone may have a thriving junior practice but a less stable practice as a silk actually earning less money.[37]

A silk is sometimes also known as a 'leader' because in many cases the QC will appear with other counsel to conduct the litigation, and the QC, as the senior advocate, would normally lead this team (although there is no longer a rule that states a QC must appear with a junior barrister). Unlike in America where huge teams of lawyers are engaged, it is more normal in England and Wales for a team to involve two, and sometimes three, advocates led by one silk. The junior barristers on the team will normally have been involved in the case before the silk is appointed and will conduct much of the preliminary work. However, the junior barristers will also usually be involved in the litigation, not only in reading the papers and deciding on tactics but also normally conducting the examination of more junior witnesses.

---

34. Commission for Judicial Appointments, *Commissioners for Judicial Appointments Audit Report 2003* (HMSO 2003).

35. Queen's Council Appointments, 'Queen's Council statistics from 1995 to present' (QC 2019) <https://qcappointments.org/2019-competition/>.

36. Commission for Judicial Appointments, *Commissioners for Judicial Appointments Audit Report 2003* (HMSO 2003) Annex c, para 3.7.

37. See the cautions of Elwyn-Jones on this matter; Lord Elwyn-Jones, *In My Times: An Autobiography* (Weidenfeld & Nicolson 1983) 153.

When a QC appears in court, he should wear a silk robe over a court jacket (a long formal buttoned jacket that is worn instead of a suit jacket) and a wig. A solicitor who is appointed QC was entitled to wear a wig even before the changes made to the court working dress for solicitor–advocates. Upon being appointed a silk, the QC will purchase a full-bottomed wig (similar to the ones judges possess) but these are never worn in court.

An interesting issue arose during the Lord Chief Justice's annual press conference in 2012 which impacts on the practice of QCs. The Lord Chief Justice was asked a question about the deployment of QCs in cases and, in particular, about a perceived criticism he made about the CPS not engaging leading counsel in a complicated loss of control case (although the official transcript of the case merely records the Lord Chief Justice stating that the trial judge 'did not have the advantage of the careful and detailed submissions made to us by leading counsel').[38] The Lord Chief Justice in the press conference said:

> In our adversarial system high quality advocacy on both sides is more likely to produce a just result . . . [W]here there is a new bit of law which is difficult . . . it is sensible for a top-flight lawyer to be appointed to deal with the case. Now, it may be . . . when the law has settled down and we all know what Parliament actually meant by the statute, that it is not necessary. But where you have new criminal justice provisions which do change the law, or appear to change the law, generally speaking you get a better answer if you have a good quality advice.[39]

This is an interesting comment as it shows that the Lord Chief Justice believes that QCs are important in the development of the law. Judges do not know all the law, they are guided by advocates who put their views on the law. The judge will then read the appropriate authorities and make a ruling. The Lord Chief Justice is clearly stating that where legislation is complicated it is important that the best advocates, QCs, are used even if this may appear to bring additional expense to a trial or in cases where a silk would not ordinarily be used (such as a voluntary manslaughter trial where senior junior counsel may be commonly used).

10.2.5 Complaints and discipline

Discipline is, strictly speaking, a matter for the Inn of Court that a barrister belongs to but all four Inns have established common procedures to ensure that complaints and action are dealt with appropriately. Until comparatively recently, the Bar Council dealt with matters of discipline through its *Professional Conduct and Complaints Committee* but recently this was replaced by the BSB.

The BSB is an arm's-length organization of the Bar. Whilst it is funded by the Bar Council and half of the board is from the Bar (although its chair and seven other members are lay members), it is considered to be independent from the Bar Council and no member of the BSB is part of the Bar Council.

In October 2010 the *Legal Ombudsman* (see 10.5.2) came into effect and now lay complaints (ie those from a lay client) will be made to that organization which includes

---

38. *R v Clinton* [2012] EWCA Crim 2, [2012] 3 WLR 515, 536.

39. Judge, *Lord Chief Justice's Press Conference* (MOJ 2012) http://www.judiciary.gov.uk/announcements/lcj-press-conference-2012/ 6–17.

the right to order compensation. The *Legal Ombudsman* does not have jurisdiction to consider allegations of professional misconduct and such matters continue to be within the jurisdiction of the BSB. If the BSB believes that a barrister has breached the Code of Conduct then the matter is sent to the Investigations and Enforcement Team. After an initial investigation the matter may, if it is not dealt with administratively, be passed to the Independent Decision-making Body. This is made up of both barristers and lay members. They have the following options open to them:

- dismiss the complaint
- dismiss the complaint but advise the barrister as to his future conduct
- direct that a formal written warning or financial penalty be imposed
- impose conditions on the barrister's licence or authorization to practice
- order the barrister to completed continuing professional development.

This is called 'Determination by Consent' because the barrister must agree to the Independent Decision-making Body making a decision in their case. The consent procedure is a less formal way of resolving complaints. It is the equivalent of a 'summary procedure' and should apply where there is no substantial dispute of facts and where it is unlikely that any sanction would include suspension from practice or disbarment.

If the matter is more serious or the barrister disputes what has happened the case is heard by the Disciplinary Tribunal. A tribunal will consist of either three or five persons with the former not being able to suspend a barrister for more than three months or disbar a barrister. If, when hearing a matter, a three-person tribunal decides that its powers are not sufficient then it can require the matter to proceed to a five-person panel.

A three-person panel will ordinarily consist of a QC as chair, a lay member, and a barrister. Where the person subject to action is himself a QC then a judge may be appointed to chair the tribunal. A five-person panel will ordinarily consist of a judge, two barristers (who could include a QC), and two lay members.

The panels usually proceed as though it is a criminal trial (ie the 'prosecution' go first, evidence is tendered and resisted etc). The proceedings take place in open and any findings are listed on the website of the BSB.

10.2.6 **Diversity at the Bar**

The legal profession is considered to be quite conservative, and suffers from a stereotypical view of its members. This is particularly the case in relation to the Bar, with many believing that barristers are white, middle-class men, and that success and progression within the profession is based upon 'who you know', rather than aptitude. So, what is the current position in relation to diversity?

In relation to gender, according to the latest report published by the BSB, as of December 2019, women constituted 38 per cent of the Bar, an increase of 0.6 per cent from 2018. On the face of it these figures may not seem too bad, however they should be read in the context that there is a greater proportion of female pupils in comparison to male pupils (54.8 per cent v 45.2 per cent). Moreover, when you look at the proportion of female QCs (a role discussed in more detail at 10.2.4), this stands at 16.2 per cent.[40]

---

40. Bar Standards Board, 'Diversity at the Bar 2018' (BSB 2020) <https://www.barstandardsboard.org.uk/uploads/assets/912f7278-48fc-46df-893503eb729598b8/Diversity-at-the-Bar-2019.pdf> 10.

From this it is possible to surmise that whilst the number of women at the Bar has increased, it is still a male-dominated profession, particularly in the higher-echelons, ie QC. At current rates of change, it will take approximately fifty years for women to comprise half of all QCs. The data above highlights that the problem does not seem to be attracting women to the Bar (they make up over half the number of pupils), but rather the issues seems to exist around retention and promotion. Women leave the Bar for a number of reasons, but many disclose issues around taking maternity leave and career breaks and a lack of flexible working practices, which presents challenges around balancing their careers and meeting caring responsibilities (which often continue to fall disproportionately on women).

In terms of ethnicity, in December 2019 13.6 per cent of barristers were from Black, Asian, and Minority Ethnic (BAME) backgrounds. This is an increase of 0.6 per cent from the year before. The percentage of QCs from BAME backgrounds stands at 8.1 per cent (an increase of 0.3 per cent on year).[41] Similarly to the position in relation to gender, it can be seen here that there is a disparity between the overall percentage of BAME barristers across the profession and the number of QCs.

The existing data available in relation to the socio-economic background of barristers is not particularly reliable. This is partly because 'accurately measuring socio-economic background can be challenging, and there is no universal proxy for gathering such data,'[42] and thus gathering data in relation to the type of school attended and whether they were the first generation in their family to attend university are useful barometers. This approach is taken by the BSB, and in their most recent report, they note that a disproportionate number of the Bar attended a UK independent school (17 per cent, compared to for example an average 7 per cent of children in England).[43] In relation to being the first generation of their family to go to university, 46.8 per cent of respondents were and 52.5 per cent were not.[44] It should be noted here that the response rates to these questions were low and thus it is difficult to provide a reliable barometer in this area. Nevertheless these findings are interesting and provide some evidence to support the belief that those at the Bar are from wealthier socio-economic backgrounds.

10.3 Solicitors

The second branch of the legal profession is solicitors, who are regulated by the *Law Society for England and Wales*, often referred to as the *Law Society*. Solicitors are, compared to barristers, relatively modern creatures. Until the mid-nineteenth century, non-barristers were split into different types of lawyers, including attorneys, proctors, and solicitors, the latter being principally Chancery specialists. In 1831 an amalgamating body was granted its Royal Charter under the name of the *Society of Attorneys, Solicitors, Proctors and others not being Barristers, practising in the Courts of Law and Equity of the United Kingdom*, a name which hardly trips off the tongue! In 1903 the name was (thankfully) changed to the *Law Society* and at around that time the term

---

41. ibid, 13.
42. ibid, 23.
43. ibid, 24.
44. ibid, 25.

'solicitor' replaced the other forms of address as the accepted title for this branch of the profession.

The Law Society is governed by an elected president, vice-president, and Council. The day-to-day operation of the Law Society is the responsibility of the chief executive who is a non-legally qualified person responsible for the general operations of the organization. The chief executive is, as one might expect, assisted by a number of non-legally qualified staff who undertake administrative responsibility for the work of the society.

When contrasting solicitors and the Bar, people are often tempted to make the analogy that solicitors are the equivalent of GPs, with barristers being akin to consultants. The nature of this analogy is supposed to demonstrate that barristers are more likely to specialize than solicitors but it contains two critical flaws. The first is that consultants tend to be considered a promoted post whereas a would-be lawyer makes the decision as to which branch to enter before commencing training. The second flaw is that it is not actually true to suggest that solicitors do not specialize. Whilst those within a small high-street firm may undertake a variety of work there is still the ability to undertake a degree of specialism, with one solicitor perhaps focusing on crime and another on family etc. Within large firms there is arguably even more scope to specialize with many firms being dedicated to one form of work, most usually company or commercial law, and specialisms existing within that field. More than this, however, solicitors are entitled to be employed by other firms and most medium-sized companies will have a legal department, and this allows specialisms through, for example, employment law. Solicitors are also employed by the Crown and this allows for specialist areas to be created; can it be said that a solicitor employed by the CPS is any less specialist in crime than a barrister in a set of chambers dedicated to criminal work?

10.3.1 Education and training

In the same way as reforms have been introduced to the training required to become a barrister (see 10.2.2), reforms have also been announced to the process of qualifying to become a solicitor. However, these are much more far-reaching and significant than those proposed for barristers. As such, rather than discussing them alongside the current approach, as was done in relation to barristers' training, this section will first explore the current approach, before moving on to consider the reforms.

At the time of writing (until September 2021), there are four stages to qualifying as a solicitor:

- academic stage
- vocational stage
- training contract
- Professional Skills Course.

The academic stage is exactly the same as for those wishing to join the Bar.

10.3.1.1 Vocational training

Everyone who wishes to qualify as a solicitor must currently undertake a vocational training course known as the Legal Practice Course (LPC). There are currently thirty institutions at which the LPC can be studied, and given that that the 'University of Law' and BPP have a number of sites, this leads to over forty locations where the course can be completed.

The modern LPC has many similarities to the BPTC in that there are a lot of practical exercises involved in the scheme, and whilst there is a core of subjects that must be studied by all students, including conveyancing, accountancy, etc there is also the opportunity to study a series of electives, helping to demonstrate to potential employers the type of work the applicant is interested in. A considerable period of time is spent on preparing the student for the type of work and forms that they are likely to encounter in their early years of practice and thus the preparation of court forms and instructions to counsel follow, together with advocacy skills since it is a myth to say that solicitors do not perform advocacy—many do although it tends to be restricted to the more junior courts (albeit those where the bulk of the work is heard, eg magistrates' courts).

10.3.1.2 Training contract

The third stage of qualification is the training contract. The training contract is similar to the pupillage stage for barristers in that it is 'hands-on' and is the first opportunity where pure practitioners are involved in the training rather than those who are also academics. The training contract lasts two years and could involve working in more than one body as some firms do form loose partnerships that give a wider experience to the trainees. It is also worth noting that whilst competition for training contracts is intense, especially in the larger city firms, it is not quite as competitive as that for pupillage.

Unlike the position that currently exists for barristers, a person is not entitled to call themselves a 'solicitor' until they have signed the Roll of Solicitors and this will only take place where all the requisite stages have been completed. A person undertaking a training contract will be referred to as a 'trainee solicitor' but they must not hold themselves out as a full solicitor.

The training contract must involve the trainee experiencing at least three types of law (personal injury, family law, crime, etc), although some firms will provide a broader base and others will provide different experiences between a particular broad specialism (litigation, company formations, etc). The trainee must be quite closely supervised, and unlike at the Bar where there is normally a single person for each part of the pupillage (eg first six months, second six months), a trainee solicitor may, and probably will, be under the supervision of a team.

Trainee solicitors are paid throughout their training contract. The minimum starting salary of a trainee solicitor is set by the Law Society. Historically it was set at £18,590 pa for those employed within Greater London and £16,650 pa for those outside London. In 2012, however, the SRA voted to abolish the minimum training salary and instead from 1 August 2014, trainees could be paid the national minimum wage (currently £7.38 an hour for those aged between 21 and 24 years old, and £7.83 for those aged 25 and over). However, the Law Society recommends, as a matter of good practice, that trainee solicitors are paid £22,541 in London and £19,992 elsewhere. The argument behind relaxing the minimum salary is that in tough economic climates firms are unable to provide the salary. It has to be questioned how realistic this is. The difference in wage between the national minimum wage and the old Law Society minimum wage is approximately £4,000. The majority of the costs of a training contract are almost certainly in the training provision rather than the salary. The *Young Lawyers Division*, an association for junior lawyers, notes that the new scheme is based on an hourly rate but it is highly unlikely that a trainee will work only thirty-five hours a week. Is it realistic that a firm will pay the hourly rate or, as they do now, pay a salary and expect employees to work such hours as are necessary? If the latter, then the change is arguably more exploitative. The counter-argument of course is that even the national minimum wage (which, based on a thirty-five-hour week will be over £12,000 pa) compares favourably with what pupil barristers are currently paid.

Throughout the training contract a trainee solicitor will be completing a portfolio-type document that demonstrates the skills and experiences of their practice. Those responsible for supervising the trainee solicitors must ensure that this is kept up to date and is an accurate record of what happens.

10.3.1.3 Professional Skills Course

The final, and most recently introduced, part of the training to become qualified as a solicitor is completing the Professional Skills Course. This course must be completed by all would-be solicitors regardless of what route they take to qualification. The course is the equivalent of twelve full-time days, although it can be done either in a block or part-time, and takes place at the same time as the training contract and it is the employer, not the trainee, who pays for the costs of the course. There are three core modules on the course:

- advocacy and communication skills
- financial and business skills
- client care and professional standards.

Other modules designed to examine specific areas of law or practice can also be undertaken. The course is designed to allow a trainee solicitor to receive further vocational training (akin to the LPC), while at the same time being linked to the practice that they are experiencing through the training contract.

10.3.1.4 Admission to the Rolls

A person formally becomes a solicitor when they are admitted to the Rolls. A practising certificate must be obtained from the Law Society, for which a fee must be paid (currently £338). The admission can take place either in the person's absence or at a ceremony that takes place twice a month. This used to be before the Master of the Rolls, who was responsible for admission to the Rolls, but the *Solicitors Regulation Authority* (SRA) has now assumed this responsibility.

10.3.1.5 Reforms to training

As noted at the beginning of this section, the SRA has announced plans to significantly reform the training required to qualify as a solicitor. In October 2020, these proposals were formally approved by the Legal Services Board (LSB), the independent body responsible for overseeing the regulation of lawyers in England and Wales. The reforms will be introduced in September 2021. It is noteworthy that anyone who started a law degree, LPC, or GDL before the introduction of the reforms will not have to follow this new pathway. Therefore there is likely to be a long lead-in period, with the both the 'old' and 'new' qualification systems running concurrently.

So, what is changing? The academic stage of training will remain similar, ie the need to have an undergraduate degree in any subject. However, the qualifying law degree will have no special meaning in the process, meaning that non-law graduates will not need to take the GDL as they do now (although having a law degree is likely to be advantageous for completing the new Solicitors Qualifying Exam). The SRA are keen that solicitors come from a variety of backgrounds to improve diversity and inclusivity within the profession, and the move away from requiring a law degree/the GDL aims to go some way towards supporting this. The Legal Practice Course (LPC) will be abolished. Instead, prospective solicitors will need to complete Stage 1 and Stage 2 of the new Solicitors Qualifying Exam (SQE). It should be noted here that the SQE is not a course of study like the LPC; it is a set of exams with the focus being on prospective solicitors meeting a standard of knowledge and competence. Students will be able to take courses to help them to prepare for the SQE. SQE Stage 1 will assess legal knowledge through the use of multiple-choice questions, and this must be completed and passed before moving on to Stage 2. Stage 1 tests a combination of substantive legal knowledge (akin to that currently studied on a qualifying law degree), ie property law, criminal law, etc, and more vocational content (also known a functioning legal knowledge) similar to that previously studied on the LPC. SQE Stage 2 will use practical exams and assessments to assess five key legal skills; client interviewing, advocacy, analysis (of cases and matters), legal research and written advice, and legal drafting.

In another departure from the current system, both SQE stages can be completed before, alongside, or after the qualifying work experience component (which is replacing the training contract, at least in name). This can be compared with the current system where the LPC must be passed before beginning a training contract. The SQE will be aligned with the SRA's Statement of Legal Knowledge, which sets out the knowledge that all solicitors must demonstrate at the point of qualification. Finally, what was the training contract stage will be known as the qualifying work experience stage. This remains two years in length, however it can be completed by working for up to four different employers, and pro bono work and placements gained through university will be able to count towards the total, for example working in a law clinic.

10.3.2 Practice

Some aspects of the solicitors' practice have already been discussed and it has been noted that they have a more flexible practice than barristers, there being those who practise in a law firm and those who are employed in a non-law firm to undertake legal services. Like at the Bar, it is not possible for a newly qualified solicitor to set up immediately as a sole practitioner; this is a protection on the basis that newly qualified solicitors still require an element of training and development. It would be naive to suggest that a person at the end of their training contract is fully able to undertake all aspects of legal work.

Before starting a practice (be that as a sole practitioner or in a partnership) there must be at least one person who is entitled to supervise others, and the Law Society define this as being someone who has held a practising certificate for at least three of the last ten years, and who has completed management Continuing Professional Development (CPD).

Promotion for a solicitor can arise in a number of ways. Because solicitors have always been able to form partnerships (and indeed frequently do so) the promotion path normally involves someone progressing to a partnership, even though in major firms the partnership may still involve a salary rather than equity share (and so is arguably not a true legal form of partnership).

10.3.2.1 **Rights of audience**

When a solicitor first qualifies he has very limited rights of audience, generally restricted to the junior courts and tribunals. A solicitor's rights of audience encompass all matters in the magistrates' court and county court. Within the Crown Court a solicitor may only appear for preliminary matters following a transfer for trial (see 13.3.2) or for appeals against the decisions of magistrates where their firm was involved at first instance. In the High Court a solicitor has no automatic rights of audience in open court but can be heard in chambers although this would normally be for preliminary matters.

A solicitor can, however, gain higher rights of audience by taking additional training.

10.3.2.2 **Solicitor–advocates**

Historically the Bar had exclusive rights to the higher courts (defined as the Crown Court, High Court (in open session), the Divisional Courts, Court of Appeal, and House of Lords), but this caused considerable disquiet from solicitors and certain governmental bodies. It was argued that denying higher rights of audience to solicitors raised costs for a litigant because he needed to brief both a solicitor and a barrister even if the matter was relatively simple.

The then government decided in the late 1980s that it was necessary to break the traditional monopolies held by the professions and the *Courts and Legal Services Act 1990* permitted, for the first time, solicitors to appear in the higher courts. However, the statutory authority was only the first step and it was necessary, before any solicitor–advocates were created, for the Law Society and senior members of the judiciary to agree on a system of authorizing such advocates. It took until 1994 for the agreement to be reached and the first solicitor–advocates to be appointed.

Qualifying

Until 2011 it was necessary for a person seeking to qualify as a solicitor–advocate to have been in practice for at least three years, but the *SRA Higher Rights of Audience Regulations 2011* have abolished this requirement and a person can seek to qualify with higher rights as soon as they qualify as a solicitor. There also used to be a requirement that a practitioner could show that he had undertaken *actual* advocacy in the courts (eg, magistrates' court or county court), but this has now also been removed and a person must simply take a specific course offered by the SRA.

There are now two types of licence that can be sought:

- civil proceedings (ie a solicitor–advocate would be able to appear in the higher courts for civil matters but not the Crown Court)
- criminal proceedings (ie a solicitor–advocate could appear in the Crown Court and higher courts for criminal matters but not for civil matters with the exception of the Crown Court where all business is licensed).

It may seem strange to have different types of licence but it makes sense given the type of practice that solicitors may have. A solicitor who is employed by the CPS will not appear in civil matters so why should they need to learn the civil litigation rules etc? Similarly, a solicitor who works for a commercial law firm will never undertake criminal work so why should they learn the specific rules of evidence and court rules governing criminal trials? A person can, of course, seek to hold both licences, in which case he will be able to exercise higher rights of audience in respect of both civil and criminal matters. It used to be possible to seek a combined licence but a person must now ask for both licences and undertake the relevant assessments for each.

A solicitor who does qualify to exercise higher rights of audience must undertake additional CPD for the first five years of holding the rights. This CPD must relate specifically to the exercise of higher rights.

Court work and dress

Once the higher rights of audience have been granted a solicitor–advocate is entitled to serve in all higher courts relevant to their licence, including the Supreme Court. A solicitor–advocate is entitled to appear in all matters that counsel can and may appear as though counsel. A solicitor–advocate remains subject to the Law Society's regulations, including further regulations on the conduct of litigation, and does not become subject to the Bar Council's regulations. The regulator remains the SRA which has developed particular competences for higher-rights work.

Traditionally a solicitor–advocate was not able to wear the wig and simply wore the gown and bands but eventually the judiciary brought about equality and in *Practice Direction (Court Dress)(No 4)*[45] it was stated that solicitor–advocates may (which implies that, unlike counsel they do not have to) wear wigs.

Perceptions of solicitor–advocates

The exercise of higher rights of audience by solicitors is still relatively recent and there continues to be something of a problem in perception of the quality of advocacy. This is in part because the Bar, and therefore by extension the judiciary (who, it will be recalled, are inevitably drawn from the Bar), are always sceptical about those who exercise advocacy and are not in independent practice. The quality of advocacy, for example, by the Crown Prosecution Service has been questioned for years and the same appears true of solicitor–advocates. Darbyshire, in her study on the working lives of judges, shows that some judges do not appear to believe the quality of advocacy is the same.[46] Moreover, research conducted by the BSB in 2012 found that over three-quarters of responding practitioners felt that the standards of criminal advocacy had declined over the past five years, partly due to the increased involvement of solicitor–advocates.[47]

To an extent this can be seen to be 'double-counting' since, for example, in the criminal courts the CPS has encouraged its own solicitors to seek higher rights. Whilst it is clear that the criticism is levelled it is perhaps more difficult to know whether it is fair. There is no transparent system of fairly assessing the competencies of advocates and whilst it is undoubtedly true that some solicitor–advocates will be poor the same is true of barristers; there are a number of barristers who are not any good either. It is not something that will be easily resolved but it is clear that solicitor–advocates are here to stay and the relaxation of, for example, the three-year qualification suggests the Law Society are keen to increase the number of solicitor–advocates.

---

45.   [2008] 1 WLR 357.
46.   Penny Darbyshire, *Sitting in Judgment: The Working Lives of Judges* (Hart Publishing 2011) 206.
47.   Bar Standards Board, *Perceptions of Criminal Advocacy* (BSB 2012) <https://www.barstandardsboard.org.uk/media/1402386/orc_international_-_perceptions_of_advocacy_report.pdf> 3.

10.3.3 **Complaints and discipline**

Solicitors are bound by a separate code of conduct to barristers. It is the Law Society who traditionally regulates the activities of all solicitors, including solicitor–advocates, although solicitors are technically officers of the senior courts (something that barristers are not), and so the court theoretically has the power to regulate solicitors' conduct too although it would be rare for it to do this except through, for example, wasted costs orders (which can also be imposed against barristers).

The Law Society, like the Bar Council, has created an arm's-length organization for its regulation, the SRA. Where there has been professional misconduct by a solicitor then this is a matter for the SRA, and this will include matters relating to, for example, CPD or the misappropriation of client funds.

Adjudicating on disciplinary matters relating to solicitors is the responsibility of the *Solicitors Disciplinary Tribunal* (SDT). This is a statutory tribunal established under s 46 *Solicitors' Act 1974*. The members of the tribunal are appointed by the Master of the Rolls[48] and include solicitors and laypersons (who may not be barristers or solicitors). One of the solicitor members shall be elected by the members of the tribunal to be President and will serve as President for three years, although this is renewable once. Two vice-presidents (one lay member and one solicitor member) shall also be elected, again for a single renewable term of three years.[49]

The tribunal sits in divisions of three; two solicitors (one of which will chair) and one lay member. The tribunal is formal and takes the format of a court trial. Ordinarily the SRA will 'prosecute' the matter and it is empowered, in very serious matters, to instruct counsel where appropriate. The tribunal has significant sanctions including:

- striking a solicitor from the Roll
- suspending a solicitor from practising
- reprimanding a solicitor
- fining a solicitor[50]
- excluding a person from legal aid work
- banning the person from working as a solicitor.

The tribunal will also consider requests from solicitors suspended (or struck) from the Roll to resume practice.

An appeal from decisions of the tribunal exists to the High Court[51] although certain administrative matters can be dealt with by the Master of the Rolls. Where the High Court hears the matter it may 'make such order on an appeal . . . as it may think fit'.[52]

10.3.4 **Diversity**

We have already noted the position regarding diversity at the Bar, but what is the position in relation to solicitors? The most recent data available was collected in Summer

---

48. It has been noted already that the Master of the Rolls traditionally had responsibility for the management of the Rolls of Solicitors and whilst this obligation has been transferred to the SRA the Master of the Rolls continues to exercise certain administrative regulatory functions.
49. *Solicitors (Disciplinary Proceedings) Rules 2007*, SI 2007/3588, r 3.
50. Any fine is payable to HM Treasury not to the Law Society.
51. *Solicitors Act 1974*, s 49.
52. ibid, s 49(4).

2019 by the SRA and covers 96 per cent of law firms who reported their data. In terms of gender, women make up 59 per cent of solicitors across all firms. Lawyers from a BAME background total 21 per cent (no change since 2017, but an increase from years before this), demonstrating that progress is being made in this area as well. On the whole, diversity in relation to gender and ethnicity within the solicitors' profession is much higher when compared to the Bar. However, in the same way that diversity reduces at the Bar in the context of seniority, ie QCs, this also happens for solicitors when the senior levels are looked at, ie partners. This is particularly the case in relation to gender, where only 34 per cent of partners are women. This is favourable when compared to the position at the Bar, with women only making up 16.2 per cent of QCs, however it is clear there is still work to do here. In the context of BAME lawyers, there is little difference by seniority, with 22 per cent of partners being from BAME backgrounds (compared with 21 per cent of total lawyers).[53]

As noted in relation to the Bar, it is difficult to capture data in relation to the socio-economic backgrounds of solicitors. The SRA have taken a similar approach to the BSB by using attendance at a fee-paying school and whether someone was the first to attend university to capture this data. Of those surveyed 21 per cent attended fee paying schools, compared with 7 per cent in the general population. Similarly to the Bar, this shows that law continues to attract those from wealthier socio-economic backgrounds. When looking at partners, 23 per cent attended a fee-paying school, however it should be noted that this has decreased from 43 per cent in 2014. Interestingly, in relation to being the first person in their family to attend university, 50 per cent of solicitors and 48 per cent of partners fell into this category.[54] This perhaps highlights that whilst there is still some progress that needs to be made around the issue of diversity, at least in relation to socio-economic backgrounds, becoming a solicitor is more frequently being pursued as a career by those from a range of socio-economic backgrounds, something that was historically not the case.

QUESTION FOR REFLECTION

Do you think that the size of a law firm and the type of work being undertaken by those firms and the solicitors working within them makes a difference to diversity in relation to gender, ethnicity, and socio-economic background? If so, in what way?

10.4 Chartered Legal Executives

The third branch of the legal profession are Chartered Legal Executives. The professional association for the 20,000 Chartered Legal Executives within England and Wales is the *Chartered Institute of Legal Executives* (CILEx). They are regulated by *CILEx Regulation*.

Chartered Legal Executives are the most recently recognized branch of the legal professions. They emerged from the role of 'solicitors managing clerks' after the Second

---

53. Solicitors Regulation Authority, 'How diverse is the legal profession?' (SRA, 2019) https://www.sra.org.uk/sra/equality-diversity/key-findings/diverse-legal-profession/.
54. ibid.

World War when, due to a lack of training of solicitors during the war, there was a hiatus in the legal profession. Consequently, as there was a lack of individuals with the required experience and training to enter the professions, a decision was made to create a 'new form' of lawyer to help resolve the problem. The Institute of Legal Executives (as it was originally known) was created on 1 January 1963. Whilst the role has existed since this time, the beginning of the change of status to the third branch of the legal profession was arguably the reforms introduced by the *Courts and Legal Services Act 1990* (CLSA 1990), which provided legal executives with limited rights of audience and allowed them to undertake some litigation work in their own right. Since these reforms the role of legal executives has received increased recognition and respect, with CILEx becoming a chartered body in 2012.

What is the difference between a legal executive and a solicitor or a barrister? The main differences relate to the training process and the type of practice undertaken. This will be discussed further in the following sections. It will also be noted that whilst legal executives constitute a profession in their own right, they are also able to train to become solicitors (discussed in more detail at 10.4.3).

10.4.1 **Training**

The structure and form of training to become a Chartered Legal Executive is different to that required to become a barrister or a solicitor. There are three stages to the training:

- academic stage
- qualifying employment
- work-based learning outcomes.

10.4.1.1 **Academic stage**

Unlike solicitors and barristers, legal executives need not be graduates when they commence their training and indeed the minimum academic qualifications are GCSEs. However more recently, a graduate entry scheme has begun and, as with the other principal branches, where a person is a graduate in law an exemption from the academic stage can be granted. It is fair to say, however, that the vast majority of entrants to CILEx continue to be non-law graduates. An attraction of becoming a legal executive is that, unlike for solicitors and barristers, all the training can take place alongside work. Accordingly, instead of accruing debts by attending university, a prospective legal executive will be paid from the moment that they start with a firm.

To become a qualified Chartered Legal Executive (for those who have not completed a law degree or the GDL), two diplomas must be completed and passed, firstly a level 3 *Professional Diploma in Law and Practice* and then secondly a level 6 *Higher Diploma in Law and Practice*. The level 3 diploma will ordinarily take two years and the level 6 diploma a further two years (both of which can take place part-time while working). One advantage of following this CILEx route to qualification is the significantly reduced cost to do so. CILEx note that in 2019/20 the typical cost to complete all of the above academic stages of qualification totalled just over £10,000.[55] This is almost

---

55.   Chartered Institute of Legal Executives, 'Indicative cost of qualifying as a Chartered Legal Executive' (CILEx 2019) <https://www.cilex.org.uk/study/lawyer_qualifications/typical_costs>.

equivalent to the cost of one year's study on a Law degree at university (with tuition fees currently set at £9,000 per year), with a university student having a further two years to fund, as well as postgraduate study, for example the Bar training course. This, combined with the ability to work alongside completing the academic stage, makes it an attractive alternative for many interested in a career in law who may be concerned about finances.

For Law and GDL graduates, CILEx offer a Fast-Track Graduate Diploma which focuses on the development of legal practice and professional skills, rather than academic legal knowledge (as this will already have been gained during the degree). CILEx indicate that the Graduate Diploma equates to approximately 125 hours of study and it can be studied full-time, part-time, or on a distance learning basis.

10.4.1.2 Qualifying employment

Qualifying employment is described as being work that is 'wholly of a legal nature' for at least twenty hours per work, and involves 'the application of the law, legal practice or procedure'.[56] During this time, the applicant must be supervised by a lawyer. Those wishing to qualify as Chartered Legal Executives must have completed three years' qualifying employment, of which:

- one year must be served as a graduate member of CILEx
- the two years immediately before applying to become a fellow must be served consecutively.[57]

Where a person proceeds through the diploma route this will mean that they have only a further year of work (as they will usually have completed two while studying), whereas a graduate may not have any (unless they have worked, for example, as a paralegal). This does mean that a graduate is arguably worse off than a non-graduate wishing to qualify as a Chartered Legal Executive in that they will qualify more slowly since the full three years is required.

10.4.1.3 Work-based learning

In order to apply for Fellowship of CILEx and qualify as a Chartered Legal Executive, by the end of their qualifying employment applicants must be able to demonstrate that they meet eight competencies. This is done through the completion of a learning portfolio. The eight competencies are:

- practical application of the law and legal practice
- communication skills
- client relations
- management of workload
- business awareness
- professional conduct

56. Chartered Institute of Legal Executives, 'Fellowship Work Based Learning Handbook' (CILEx) <https://www.CILEx.org.uk/~/media/pdf_documents/main_CILEx/membership/membership/qe_and_wbl/wbl_handbook_CILEx_regulation_final__260718.pdf?la=en> 4.

57. ibid 5.

- self-awareness and development
- working with others.

Each competency has associated learning outcomes that must be evidenced.[58]

10.4.2 **Practice**

Whilst both barristers and solicitors will frequently specialize, they need not and a number remain as general practitioners who will undertake a variety of work. Legal executives, on the other hand, will tend to specialize in an area and remain in that area of work. Legal executives will tend to practise only in civil law although there is no reason why they could not, for example, also qualify as accredited police-station representatives, but their practice will tend to be civil-orientated. Legal executives will choose their specialism while training and in order to get the qualifying employment experience required to become a Fellow, they will focus on that area. That said, although they tend to specialize, it can be in a reasonably broad way and could encompass subject headings (family law, company law, etc).

A significant part of their work will be assisting a solicitor, and it is worth noting that legal executives do not have independent practising rights; that is to say, they must be supervised by solicitors and cannot create a firm that exists solely of legal executives, although following the reforms of the LSA 2007 it is now possible for a legal executive to own shares in a practice (and indeed this has been one of the main reasons why some firms have begun *Legal Disciplinary Practices*). Much of the work of a legal executive will be quite similar to the provision of legal advice by solicitors and will frequently involve dealing with clients direct. Following the reforms of the CLSA 1990 legal executives are now entitled to have limited rights of audience,[59] which are generally procedural matters not heard in open court in the magistrates' and county courts.

10.4.2.1 **Chartered Legal Executive Advocates**

In a similar way that solicitors can apply to become solicitor–advocates, Chartered Legal Executives can also seek to become advocates. However, it should be noted that whilst the rights of audience that Chartered Legal Executive Advocates can achieve are comparable to the rights of audience a solicitor has upon qualification, they are not comparable to the higher rights that solicitors can accrue by becoming a solicitor–advocate.

In order to apply for advocacy rights, an applicant must be a fully qualified CILEx Fellow, apply for a Certificate of Eligibility, and complete and pass a six-day advocacy skills course. Fellows apply for advocacy rights in the area in which they practice, either civil litigation, criminal litigation, or family litigation. The civil proceedings certificate provides advocates with rights of audience in open court in the county court (except in family proceedings) and magistrates' court, as well as in tribunals or coroners' courts. The criminal proceedings certificate provides rights of audience within the magistrates' court (including the youth court), the Crown Court for an appeal against a decision of the magistrates' court, and rights to appear in chambers in the Crown Court or High Court for bail, as well as in coroners' courts. Finally, the family proceedings certificate provides rights of audience in all family matters in the county court and the family proceedings court (magistrates' court), or in coroners' courts.

---

58. ibid, 7.
59. The rights of audience available to legal executives are set out in *Legal Services Act 2007*, sch 3, para 1(7).

10.4.3 **Qualifying as a solicitor**

Although Charted Legal Executives represent a profession in their own right, a significant incentive for those who join CILEx is that it is also a path to becoming a solicitor. As noted earlier, the current normal route for qualifying as a solicitor is to study law at undergraduate or graduate level, then undertake a vocational training course and finally undertake a training contract. However, the Law Society will also allow CILEx Fellows to qualify as a solicitor once they have the requisite experience and have passed the Legal Practice Course. Once qualified, a CILEx Fellow normally does not need to undertake a training contract because of the qualifying employment component of three years' experience that is undertaken to become a Fellow, which acts as the equivalent of a training contract.

The advantages of a CILEx Fellow converting include less restriction on their practice, the ability to become sole practitioners or to set up their own practices, and also to study for wider rights of audience in the higher courts. It is not known precisely how many CILEx Fellows convert to solicitors, and there are some anecdotal comments about how well their future careers compare to traditionally qualified solicitors, but within a small to medium-sized firm it would be an attractive method of qualifying, not least because of the fact that from the very earliest stage the legal executive will have been earning money.

10.4.4 **Complaints and discipline**

Chartered Legal Executives are regulated by a different body to barristers and solicitors; CILEx Regulation (formally known as ILEx Professional Standards), who follow the Investigatory, Disciplinary and Appeals Rules (IDAR) when investigating complaints. CILEx Fellows are governed by the CILEx Code of Conduct and CILEx Regulation Rules and it is where a breach of the code or rules is alleged that a disciplinary investigation begins. Once the investigation has been completed the matter is normally referred to the Professional Conduct Panel (PCP) for consideration. The PCP consists of one professional CILEx member and two independent lay members. After they have reviewed the case they can either:

- reject the complaint because they have decided that it cannot be upheld
- refer the case to the Disciplinary Tribunal (discussed below)
- reprimand the individual involved if they admit their misconduct. This may involve for example requiring undertakings to be given in relation to the individual's future conduct.[60]

Not all cases will be sent to the PCP. The two main exceptions to this are: where the misconduct has been admitted by the individual(s) involved and they have accepted a penalty or if the case is very serious, when it will be referred directly to the Disciplinary Tribunal. The Tribunal is constituted in the same way as the PCP, that is with two independent lay members and one professional CILEx member. The Tribunal has the power to impose more serious punishments if the allegations are proven. The most significant of these include being able to remove CILEx membership (and thus bar individuals from the profession) and impose fines (of up to £100,000 for CILEx members).[61]

---

60. CILEx Regulation, 'Complaints and Disciplinary Procedures' (CILEx Regulation, 2015) <https://cilexregulation. org.uk/wp-content/uploads/2018/12/Complaints-and-Disciplinary-Procedures.pdf>.

61. ibid.

The individual who has been disciplined has the ability to appeal the decision of the PCP or the Disciplinary Tribunal to an Appeals Panel.

10.4.5 Diversity

How does this third arm of the professions match up in terms of diversity? The most recent data provided by CILEx on their members shows that 78.1 per cent of them were women in 2019.[62] This is a significantly higher proportion of women than in the other legal professions. In terms of ethnicity, 10.9 per cent of members were from a BAME background.[63] Nevertheless, the proportion of BAME CILEx members is lower than that found in the other arms of the legal professions, with a greater proportion of solicitors and barristers identifying as being from a BAME background. This suggests that in relation to ethnicity, there is more work to do to increase the diversity of CILEx membership.

Compared to both solicitors and barristers, the socio-economic backgrounds of CILEx members are more diverse. This is something that CILEx are proud of, as they note that: 'The House of Lords recognised that the CILEx route already draws from a wider social background than other parts of the legal profession'.[64] This is reflected in membership data which shows that 81.5 per cent of members do not have parents who attended university, a much higher proportion than the other legal professions. Moreover, only 2 per cent of CILEx members have a parent who is a lawyer.[65] This is perhaps to be expected because CILEx is the only route to legal qualification that does not require a degree and thus university attendance. Moreover, the substantially reduced costs associated with CILEx qualification makes this pathway to qualification much more accessible to those from a range of socio-economic backgrounds.

10.5 Independent oversight of the professions

As noted in relation to each arm of the professions, there are respective regulators associated with discipline and complaints. Despite this, there has long been concern about the regulation of lawyers. In 2003, the Lord Chancellor created a review of the regulation of the legal professions and chose Sir David Clementi as its Chair. He delivered his report in 2004. Whilst Clementi was broadly sympathetic to some parts of the regulatory systems he did believe it was necessary to increase the accountability of the professional bodies, especially in connection with complaints procedures. The government responded to the report in the LSA 2007 by transforming the oversight of the professions with the establishment of a system of independent oversight of the professions. This occurred through the establishment of the *Legal Services Board* (LSB)[66] and an *Office for Legal Complaints* (OLC).[67]

---

62. CILEx, 'Diversity Report 2019 (CILEx 2019) <https://cilexregulation.org.uk/wp-content/uploads/2020/06/Diversity-Report-2019-final-PSC-1.pdf> 2.

63. ibid.

64. CILEx, 'CILEx and Social Mobility' (CILEx) <https://www.cilex.org.uk/about_cilex/who_we_are/equality_and_diversity/cilex-and-social-mobility>.

65. ibid.

66. LSA 2007, s 2.

67. ibid, 114.

10.5.1 **Legal Services Board**

The LSB has a statutory responsibility, inter alia, to ensure standards of regulation, training, and education. Whilst the LSB does not replace the BSB, the SRA, or CILEx Regulation it holds these bodies to account on matters such as educational require-ments (including both the academic and vocational stages), continuing professional development, and the regulation of lawyers. A body can only act as a regulator for legal services if it is approved by the LSB. Along with approving the regulators the LSB has considerable control over how the regulatory bodies discharge their functions. Under the LSA 2007 the regulators must consult the LSB before they change any of their rules of professional conduct, and the LSB must give consent to any regulatory changes. This ensures that the bodies are accountable for all aspects of the regulatory process, ensur-ing that the process is fair, transparent, and accountable to both the professions and service users.

The LSB board is chaired by a layperson and consists of the chair, the chief execu-tive, and between seven and ten persons appointed by the Lord Chancellor (there are currently seven members excluding the chair) although this is now also done in con-sultation with the Lord Chief Justice. A majority of the LSB must be lay[68] meaning not qualified as lawyers.

The LSB must create a 'consumer panel'[69] which includes representation from those who seek the work of lawyers. The panel cannot include a member of the LSB (other than the person appointed to chair the panel, who will be a member of the LSB); a member of the OLC; a lawyer; or member of a regulator of lawyers. The panel will provide advice to the LSB as to the functioning of the provision of legal advice and, presumably, issues such as whether regulation is working.

10.5.2 **Office for Legal Complaints and the Legal Ombudsman**

The LSB is responsible for the creation of the *Office for Legal Complaints* (OLC). The primary responsibility of OLC is to create the *Legal Ombudsman*.[70] Whilst the term appears in the singular the reality is that there is more than one ombudsman, the most senior being known as the *Chief Ombudsman*. The Ombudsman has assumed responsi-bility for all complaints from service users about the work of lawyers. The Ombudsman is designed to be fully independent from the professions in order to provide reassurance to the public that any complaint will be treated fairly.

Once a complaint has been registered it will be considered and an analysis made of whether, for example, it meets the criteria of the scheme.[71] One of the more important aspects of the scheme is that the initial complaints should be directed to the lawyer first. With barristers it is likely that this is simply registering a complaint with the barrister himself but with solicitors and Chartered Legal Executives the SRA and CILEx requires each firm to have a complaints procedure and this must be complied with.

One of the more controversial aspects (at least from the perspective of the lawyers) is that each complaint leads to a 'case fee' which is paid not by the complainant but by the lawyer. That said, the fee is not charged where the complaint is not upheld *and* the

---

68.   ibid, sch 1, para 2.
69.   ibid, s 8.
70.   ibid, s 115.
71.   The website of the Legal Ombudsman produces guidance to the rules of complaints. A link to these can be found on the online resources.

Ombudsman accepts that the lawyer took all reasonable steps to resolve the complaint under their own procedure. The fee is currently charged as a 'flat rate' and is £400 per case. The complainant does not pay any fee for making a complaint and so it could be thought that they are free to dispute any degree of service, including fees, just to be a nuisance but the protection that the lawyer has, of course, is that so long as the guidance is complied with then the complaint will be dismissed and no fee paid.

The Ombudsman states that they do not 'take sides' and their initial approach is to deal with the matter informally at first (which would not attract a case fee). If this is not possible then they will proceed to conduct an investigation. Their approach is to consider all the evidence submitted by both the complainant and lawyer and decide whether the standard of service has been appropriate, and whether a legal wrong has been committed, for example, a breach of confidence.

The principal powers of the Ombudsman are to require a lawyer to tender an apology, pay compensation, or rectify a mistake that has been made. Where they believe that action by a court is required to resolve a complaint then the Ombudsman has the power to refer a matter to a relevant court. This may be required, for example, where an improper charge has been placed on property. Where the Ombudsman orders an apology or compensation to be paid then the lawyer is under a professional obligation to comply with the order of the Ombudsman and failure to do so will amount to professional misconduct.

It is quite possible that during the investigation the Ombudsman considers that the complaint raises issues of professional misconduct. Whilst the Ombudsman cannot deal with such matters it can pass the case to the regulators to action on their behalf. Where the matter raises issues of both misconduct and inappropriate service then both matters can proceed independently.

10.5.3 Immunity

Those of you who are also studying the *Law of Tort* at the same time as the module you are currently on will be familiar with the idea of negligence. For those of you who are not currently studying Tort, the law recognizes that where someone holds themselves out as a professional in an area of service, they should be accountable if they fail to meet a basic standard of care in the discharge of their duties, known as being negligent.[72] Should an advocate be liable in law for the negligent handling of cases?

Traditionally the answer was 'no'—a lay client could not sue an advocate on the basis that they lost a case because of their advocate's negligence,[73] but eventually this immunity began to become restricted solely to negligence in court or litigation papers,[74] and where a lawyer gave advice negligently an action could arise. There were a number of reasons why this was so, perhaps the most commonly cited being that it could lead to re-litigation. If a person charged with a crime is convicted then the way to challenge this decision is by way of an appeal. If, the argument went, an advocate could be sued for negligence then when the appeals were exhausted a person would have nothing to lose by suing his advocate for negligence. If he won this action then would this grant him the right to another appeal?

72. See, for example, *Hedley Byrne & Co v Heller & Partners* [1964] AC 465.
73. See, for example, *Rondel v Worsley* [1969] 1 AC 191.
74. *Saif Ali v Sydney Smith Mitchell & Co* [1980] AC 198 comprehensively discussed the immunity.

In *Hall v Simons*[75] the House of Lords was called to re-examine whether there was a justification for advocates to have an absolute exemption from negligence and they decided there was not. The House carefully considered every possible reason why the immunity should remain and decided each was unconvincing and that it was against public policy to exempt one profession from litigation when others, arguably with a higher stake for public policy exemptions (eg doctors), have no exemption. The House did not believe that their decision would 'open the floodgates' as they pointed out that the rules of civil litigation permit a judge to strike out vexatious proceedings at an early stage.[76] The House also argued that criminal practitioners would have an additional protection in that using civil negligence laws to challenge convictions would almost certainly be viewed as an abuse of process by the courts and the action quickly stayed.[77]

The decision in *Hall v Simons* was eminently sensible: it is difficult to justify granting immunity to one profession when real harm could be caused by the negligent actions of an advocate. There is not one standard of negligence and since the case there have been few cases alleging negligence perhaps demonstrating that the fears of the profession were unfounded.

10.6 Legal ethics

A central part of a lawyer's conduct can be summed up as ethics and yet it is comparatively rare for students to be introduced to legal ethics during an undergraduate course.[78] However, it is important that you are able to understand some of the ethical issues that lawyers encounter.

10.6.1 Responsibility to clients

Some of the more significant ethical issues relate to what a lawyer can, and cannot, do in respect of their clients (normally meaning their 'lay client' when it is a barrister). Complete books have been written about the issue of ethics but in this section some of the main ethical duties that arise will be discussed.

10.6.1.1 Providing advice not seeking control

Lawyers provide advice but one of the questions that arises is how far they may go in terms of encouraging people to act on that advice. In the criminal context this will ordinarily take place in relation to a 'plea bargain'. However, the concept is wider than this and needs to be outlined here.

A lawyer is supposed to serve his client's best interests but also allow the client to act autonomously so that they are making decisions on the basis of advice. However, concern has been raised as to whether the actions of lawyers seek to push this envelope and actually control or manipulate the decisions of the clients.[79] Perhaps one of the classic examples of this is where a lawyer 'misleads clients in personal injury matters

---

75. [2002] 1 AC 615.
76. *Hall v Simons* [2002] 1 AC 615, 681–3 (Lord Steyn).
77. ibid, 679–81.
78. Andrew Boon, *The Ethics and Conduct of Lawyers in England and Wales* (3rd edn, Hart Publishing 2014) 178.
79. Donald Nicolson and Julian Webb, *Professional Legal Ethics* (OUP 1999) 123.

by playing down expectations as to likely compensation so as to encourage earlier settlement'.[80] It has been remarked that the advantage of this is that there can be a high turnover of work through the processing of more cases.[81] However, it could equally work in reverse whereby for a high-value claim it may be in the interests of a lawyer to raise expectations so that early settlement offers are rejected, thus prolonging the litigation and increasing the costs.

It is essential that lawyers simply set out the legal position and put forward options to the client, but ultimately it must be for the client to decide which option to take. The possible tactics are for the lawyer to explain but it is important that a client is not 'bounced' into accepting something that he does not wish to do. This is particularly true in respect of plea bargains where there is evidence to suggest that some people will feel pressurized by the lawyer to plead guilty even though they believe they are innocent.[82] This simply cannot be justified and it is a particular duty of a judge to ensure that any guilty plea is being tendered correctly and not simply for the sake of convenience.[83]

10.6.1.2 Client confidentiality

One of the most important ethical issues is that of client confidentiality. Yet interestingly it is a duty that could involve a lawyer in other ethical difficulties, for example when a client plans to commit a crime.[84] The justification for the rule is that a person must be entitled to engage a lawyer to seek advice without worrying whether he will inadvertently disclose something that would undermine his own case.[85]

Some have, however, criticized the rule in that whilst it does protect both the individual and lawyer, it does nothing to assist third parties or society who may be affected by that individual's actions.[86] Indeed the rule could even cause significant harm to society or an individual since client confidentiality will not be waived even where to do so would protect an innocent person from going to prison.[87]

> **Example** Client confidentiality
>
> Wendy has been accused of the murder of Vanessa. Trevor has been accused of theft but when talking to his counsel, John, he indicates that he was the person who actually killed Vanessa not Wendy. John is bound by client confidentiality and cannot tell anyone what Trevor has said even though Wendy may be sentenced to life imprisonment as a result of this.

The only exceptions to this rule are where someone is at risk of serious harm or where a lawyer is being used to facilitate a crime,[88] but the circumstances surrounding these exceptions are somewhat confused, not least because the suggestion is that it is only against *serious* harm, so what happens where less serious harm is to be inflicted? Also, what does

---

80. ibid, 137.
81. Andrew Boon, *The Ethics and Conduct of Lawyers in England and Wales* (3rd edn, Hart Publishing 2014) 376.
82. Fred Phillips, *Ethics of the Legal Profession* (Cavendish Publishing 2004) 145–6.
83. Phillip Otton, 'The Role of the Judge in Criminal Cases' in Mike McConville and Geoffrey Wilson (eds), *The Handbook of the Criminal Justice Process* (OUP 2002) 326.
84. Donald Nicolson and Julian Webb, *Professional Legal Ethics* (OUP 1999) 248.
85. ibid, 249.
86. ibid, 253.
87. ibid, 254.
88. Andrew Boon, *The Ethics and Conduct of Lawyers in England and Wales* (3rd edn, Hart Publishing 2014) ch 10.

facilitate a crime mean? It appears to include crimes in the future[89] so that, at least, a person cannot go to a lawyer and ask for advice on how to commit 'the perfect murder'.

Money laundering

In recent years some of the most controversial aspects of the rule governing client confidentiality are in respect of money laundering which is described as:

> the process by which 'dirty money'—the proceeds of crime—is changed so that the money appears 'to originate from a legitimate source'.

Solicitors and legal executives are arguably most likely to be a target for such behaviour since they hold money for clients and can make transactions on behalf of their clients (including investments and property deals). In recent years the government has attempted to ensure that the proceeds of crime are recovered and this culminated in the *Proceeds of Crime Act 2002* (PoCA 2002) which has led to a statutory exception to the rule of confidentiality.

The Act creates a positive duty on persons to report money laundering, including 'reasonable suspicions'[90] and the fact that it was given in confidential situations is no defence. Further offences are created to deal with situations where, for example, a solicitor tips off his client that money recovery procedures have begun,[91] or where a person becomes involved in a transaction that he knows, or suspects, to involve money laundering.[92] It has been suggested that all solicitors must be fully familiar with the money laundering regulations.[93] However, recent decisions have cast doubt on this, with the suggestion that legal professional privilege may 'trump' PoCA 2002.

Legal professional privilege is something that you will study in more depth during a course on *Evidence* but is an offshoot of the confidentiality regime. In essence, anything said to a lawyer in contemplation of, or during, judicial proceedings is privileged—ie it may not be disclosed and is not admissible in court.

363

II\ Case Box *Bowman v Fels*

The principal decision in this area is *Bowman v Fels*.[94] This was a family case. The solicitors acting for one party received documents that made them believe that repairs to the matrimonial property had been included (illegally) in the business accounts of that party. This could amount to money laundering (although not exactly the typical scenario) and the solicitors believed that they needed to make a disclosure to comply with PoCA 2002 and prevent them from committing an offence.

The Court of Appeal decided that if something arose in the course of ordinary proceedings then there would be no duty to disclose this to the authorities as it would be privileged information. The Court suggested that privilege would override PoCA 2002 except when the solicitor was deliberately trying to act dishonestly, ie by facilitating money laundering with the knowledge that he was so doing.

---

89. ibid.
90. PoCA 2002, s 330.
91. ibid, s 333A.
92. ibid, s 328.
93. Fred Phillips, *Ethics of the Legal Profession* (Cavendish Publishing 2004) 79.
94. [2005] EWCA Civ 226.

It is easy to overestimate the importance of *Bowman v Fels*. Although it is an important case[95] it does not state that lawyers are exempt from PoCA 2002 but only decides that if they become suspicious of activity *during the course* of litigation then they do not need to report the matter. Accordingly, if the suspicions arise outside of litigation or if it is more than suspicion—ie direct knowledge—then presumably the matter must be reported.

10.6.1.3 Conflicts of interest

Another significant ethical issue that arises in respect of lawyers is that there must not be a conflict of interest when representing a party. To an extent this has been discussed already in respect of part-time judges who sit on cases where a client of the firm is a party to the proceedings (see 9.3.3). A similar position arises in respect of representing clients, ie a firm should not represent more than one person in the same or similar proceedings. However, there are a multitude of different guises to this head of ethics including, perhaps most notably, where the proposed transaction or litigation has an impact on the lawyer's personal interests.[96]

⚡ PERSONAL CONFLICTS

There are numerous examples of when there may be a personal conflict with the solicitor. Perhaps the classic example is where a client wishes to make a will but wishes to leave a substantial amount of money to the solicitor. It would not be appropriate in those circumstances for the solicitor to act unless the client took further independent legal advice. Arguably this could also apply where, for example, the interest is personal but slightly detached. For example, if the solicitor is the treasurer of a local charity and the client wished to leave a substantial amount of money to that charity, there would still almost certainly be a personal conflict of interest.

Perhaps the most common (potential) conflict of interest is that which arises between clients. The rule appears quite clear here: if a dispute arises between two people who are clients of the lawyer then he must not act for either.[97] This rule is not a personal one and so it does not just apply to the individual solicitor dealing with the matter but the whole firm. Accordingly, this does mean that where a firm is engaged by a party they must undertake a careful check of existing clients to ensure that they will not create a conflict of interest.

🔄 QUESTION FOR REFLECTION

Is it realistic to suggest that a large firm will have no conflicts of interest? For example, if a firm has offices across the United Kingdom is it a conflict of interest if their Birmingham office takes a client who is in conflict with a client serviced by the Exeter office? However, is geography a sufficient 'wall' in the era of the Internet and global communication systems?

---

95. See Michael Pace, 'Litigation and Money Laundering after *Bowman v Fels*' (2005) 4 *Journal of Personal Injury Law* 345.
96. Fred Phillips, *Ethics of the Legal Profession* (Cavendish Publishing 2004) 294 provides a useful summary of possible conflicts of interest.
97. Andrew Boon, *The Ethics and Conduct of Lawyers in England and Wales* (3rd edn, Hart Publishing 2014) 379.

There is an exception to the rule[98] and this is where a lawyer does not have any 'confidential information' in respect of the other party. In those circumstances it is possible to act although it may be unwise to do so. However, some argue that this is not sufficient protection and that the mere fact that they used to be a client should prevent the law firm acting for the new client.[99] This is justified on the basis that although there may be no confidential information in existence, the lawyer may have knowledge of their anxiety or how they react to stress etc which could provide a tactical advantage. Similar issues were raised in *Re Z*.[100] A husband and wife were involved in high-value divorce proceedings that had taken over a decade because of reconciliations. The wife was being represented by Mr A from F & Co, the senior partner of which was Mrs F, who used to represent the husband when she worked with the firm G & Co. The husband sought an injunction preventing F & Co from representing the wife. The High Court applied the ruling of the House of Lords in *Prince Jefri Bolkiah v KPMG*[101] which had said that an injunction can be granted where the claimant can show a real risk that confidential information could be disclosed, however slight that risk is, unless the respondent solicitors can show that they have taken steps to remove the risk. The High Court in *Halewood International Limited v Addleshaw Booth & Co*[102] ruled that confidential information may continue in memories and that whilst a person may not recollect something, this may alter as circumstances change and memories are prompted.

Brodey J ruled in *Re Z* that because Mrs F had acted for the husband for over a year it is likely that she would continue to be aware of some of the circumstances and possibly also the manner in which he conducted himself and business, which could be relevant. Whilst F & Co had undertaken to ensure Mrs F was not involved in the case, the fact that she was the 'hands-on' senior partner of a small firm meant that there was a real risk that confidentiality could be breached. This case perhaps demonstrates how seriously the courts take potential breaches of confidentiality.

10.6.2 **Practical ethical issues**

Alongside the particular relationship with a client, other ethical issues arise in respect of those who seek to practise law. Two of the more commonly raised ethical issues will be discussed in this area: defending the guilty (which is inevitably linked to the 'cab rank rule' for barristers) and whether those who have been convicted of crimes should be allowed to become lawyers.

10.6.2.1 **Defending the guilty**

If you qualify as a lawyer then when you attend dinner parties and other social functions you will probably stop telling people that you are a lawyer and start to make up another profession because one question is asked above all others: 'How can you represent somebody you know is guilty?'

Suspected guilt

The answer to this question depends on whether a lawyer suspects that the client is guilty or whether he has been told by the client that he is guilty. Initially let us concentrate on

---

98. ibid.
99. ibid.
100. [2009] EWHC 3621 (Fam).
101. [1988] 2 AC 222.
102. [2000] Lloyds LR 298.

the first possibility. The answer to the question in this case is quite complicated and an entire book could be produced discussing the answer. The brief answer, however, is part practical and part philosophical.

The philosophical answer can be simplified to asking the question, who says a person is guilty? The law provides for three mechanisms by which a person is to be found guilty (depending on the court):

- the client pleads guilty
- at summary level, either a majority decision of three justices of the peace or a single district judge (magistrates' court) must declare guilt
- at Crown Court level, at least ten members of the public sitting as jurors must declare guilt.

If for the moment we leave aside the first method and assume the client is saying that he is not guilty but the lawyer believes that he is, then in either situation is it open to a single lawyer to decide guilt or innocence? The state has set down the rules by which a person is to be tried and someone who agrees to work in the legal system must adhere to this principle. If it were to be otherwise then why have a trial? If the lawyer is to decide guilt or innocence then we could save a lot of taxpayers' money by having all cases brought before lawyers who could dispense summary justice on their beliefs. The system would break down and thus it must remain with the duly constituted tribunals of fact. This simple philosophical argument can be easy when one is discussing the theft of a bar of chocolate or a basic assault case but what about cases of child abuse, rape, or murder? Arguably the rule applies even more to these cases as due process is most important in the worst cases. A barrister does not have to like his client but by entering criminal practice he is saying that he is prepared to conduct criminal litigation, and unless he withdraws from private practice then this means both prosecuting and defending cases. If someone does not believe that they can defend a rapist then they should not work in independent practice.

Client confirms guilt

What happens in the alternative scenario, where a person tells his lawyer that he is guilty? The Code of Conduct for barristers states that one of the most important principles for a barrister is the duty not to mislead the court,[103] and this means that a barrister may not suggest in court that his client is not guilty if he has been *told* by his client that he is guilty. Does this mean that a guilty person cannot be represented? It cannot mean this since where a person intends to plead guilty he still has the right to make representations to the court, and he is able to engage a lawyer to do this on his behalf. Can a guilty person ever legitimately plead 'not guilty'? The answer, perhaps surprisingly, is 'yes' and *Written Standards of Work* exist for this.

In England and Wales the law states that a person is to be found guilty by the courts only where the prosecution can prove beyond all reasonable doubt that the accused committed the crime. Accordingly, it has been decided that it is possible for a barrister to 'test' the prosecution evidence of a guilty client to see whether this threshold has been passed.

The position is normally, therefore, that a lawyer can act for the defendant up until the point of the close of the prosecution case but cannot put forward a defence

---

103.   Bar Standards Board, *The BSB Handbook* (Version 4.4, BSB, 2020) rC3.

case as this would tend to suggest that a person is not guilty which would be misleading the court.[104]

10.6.2.2 Criminals as lawyers

Whilst it may seem a strange issue to discuss, can a person who has been convicted of a crime become a member of the professions? The answer is yes although they have additional hurdles to overcome.

In order to gain entrance to the Law Society, Inns of Court, or CILEx a student must demonstrate that they are of good character. The professions define this in a subjective way, ie they will look at individual applicants rather than create an overarching rule that would apply regardless of the specifics of a case. It is important to note that it is not only criminal convictions that could affect the ability of a person to join the professions but also disciplinary and other matters. For example, findings of plagiarism and examination irregularities at undergraduate level are considered to be extremely serious and have stopped people from joining the professions.

For applicants who are not of good standing, the professions have special procedures. For the Law Society this involves calling them in front of a special committee which is likely to include a member of the Council and members of the profession. For the Bar it is the Inn that the applicant is applying to that will hear the matter, and it is likely that the committee will include the Masters of the Bench of the Inn. For CILEx, the applicant is referred to CILEx Regulation, where some prior conduct can be resolved by way of a delegated decision, but where this is not possible applicants are put before the Professional Conduct Panel. Regardless of the approach taken by the individual professions, the circumstances of the reasons for the bad character will be discussed together with any relevant information on rehabilitation etc. The decision whether to admit will be based purely on whether the panel believes that it would cause professional embarrassment to the profession if such a person is admitted.

367

Example Louise Woodward

Perhaps the most infamous example of this rule is that of Louise Woodward who was convicted in America of the manslaughter of a child while acting as an au pair after her A-levels. Upon returning to the United Kingdom she read for a law degree and, upon its completion, applied to the Law Society for permission to join them as a student lawyer and begin studying the LPC. Her application was considered by a special panel of lawyers and they allowed her to commence studies and a firm of solicitors in Manchester (who did not undertake criminal work) provided her with a training contract. Many people felt uncomfortable about this decision, not least because there was doubt as to whether other people convicted of homicide would be allowed in. The Law Society itself said that it was a unique case and at the time of the trial there was a perception in the United Kingdom that she had been treated unfairly in America (although little authority was adduced for this) and this may have swayed its decision.

---

104.   It should be noted that solicitors have to follow similar rules—see the SRA Code of Conduct for Solicitors.

⟳ QUESTION FOR REFLECTION

Do you think there are any crimes that should lead to a person not being fit to practise as a lawyer? How do you think the general public would react to a lawyer who has a history of fraudulent or violent offending? Do you think that Louise Woodward should have been able to practise as a lawyer? Imagine that the crime had taken place in this country: would the parents of the child believe that the law was being brought into disrepute?

🔊 LISTEN TO THE PODCAST

For guidance on how to answer this question and a discussion of the main issues, listen to the author's podcast on the online resources:
www.oup.com/he/gillespie-weare8e

10.7 Other legal professionals

The main focus of this chapter has been the three arms of the legal profession. However there are other legal professionals who have significant roles to play. The most notable of these is the 'paralegal'. Paralegal work is increasingly becoming the norm for law graduates as a step before securing a training contract or pupillage.

10.7.1 Paralegals

'Paralegal' was originally an American term, but has become an established part of the English legal framework. Traditionally the paralegal was a euphemism for someone who would photocopy documents and prepare extremely basic documentation, but over recent years there has been an expansion in the number of non-legally qualified people who assist in the execution of legal work. Within the United States a paralegal is a separate profession in its own right (although it bears some similarity to our legal executives) but in the United Kingdom this has not yet taken place.

The more usual type of paralegal within England and Wales is someone who does have a legal background. A person in this group will normally become a paralegal at one of two points in their life. The first is after the completion of their law honours degree and before going on to do postgraduate study, eg the Bar training course, and the second point is after completing postgraduate study but where they have not secured a training contract or pupillage. For those in this group, it is likely that the post of paralegal will be viewed as a temporary one, with the intention of using it as a stepping stone to a position as a solicitor or barrister. The logic behind this is sound in that as a paralegal one will be meeting members of the profession every day, and where the post sought is in a firm of solicitors it is quite possible that the company that hires the person as a paralegal may, when they recruit a trainee solicitor, look favourably upon someone who has proven themselves already.

Since there is no single definition of a paralegal it is not really possible to say what their duties would be; they will inevitably differ between the firms and organizations that use them. The common theme is that in private practice they will normally act as 'fee earners', that is to say they will conduct a limited caseload for which the company will be able to bill the client. Precisely what work is undertaken will depend on the qualifications and experience of the paralegal but it is likely to include document preparation (witness statements, claim forms, defences, etc) and may even include limited advocacy work in tribunals and non-contested issues.

Paralegals are not restricted to the private sector, although they may not be known by this title within the public sector. However, if one were to consider the work of caseworkers within, for example, the CPS and the *Criminal Cases Review Commission* it could be argued that these are undertaking comparable work. Caseworkers will undertake much administrative and quasi-legal work on a live case and will often help instruct counsel, attend court, and provide summaries of evidence etc. The work is vital to the smooth operation of these organizations and can provide an interesting career for those who have not sought to become professionally qualified or who have not been able to access the relevant training elements to qualify.

 ## Summary

This chapter has examined the legal profession and identified who is entitled to practise law in England and Wales. In particular it has noted:

- There are three principal branches to the legal profession in England and Wales: barristers, solicitors, and Chartered Legal Executives.

- The stages for qualification vary slightly depending on which branch of the profession is being considered. However, all three professions involve some form of academic stage and a work-based training stage. There have been recent reforms to the qualification process to become both a solicitor and a barrister.

- Each of the professions is regulated by a different body which is responsible for complaints and discipline. For barristers the regulator is the Bar Standards Board, for solicitors it is the Solicitors Regulation Authority, and for Chartered Legal Executives it is CILEx Regulation.

- Concern continues to exist over the diversity of the legal professions. The various professions face different challenges when it comes to diversity. For example, CILEx members are from much more diverse socio-economic backgrounds than found in the other professions. Diversity is improving but more work needs to be done across the professions.

- A number of ethical challenges exist to the work of the professions and the traditional regulatory role of the professions is being challenged. In recent years, independent oversight of the regulatory process has been introduced to create public confidence in the system.

 ## End-of-chapter questions

1. David Pannick, *Advocates* (OUP 1992) states: 'any lawyer who does not understand [the purpose of the cab rank rule] really has no business being an advocate' (p 145) yet others disagree and David Clementi, *Review of the Regulatory Framework for Legal Services in England and Wales* (HMSO 2004) appears to question whether the rule has any modern application (pp 130–2). Should the cab rank rule be abolished?

2. Read A Myers and L Flannery, 'Wannabe Barristers?' (2004) 154 *New Law Journal* 1698 (at pp 1698–9) where two solicitor–advocates are interviewed about their job. One suggestion put to them is that they should become barristers. Is this not the crux of the matter? Why should solicitors be given higher rights of audience when they are not constrained by the regulations governing barristers (prohibition of partnerships, cab rank rule etc)? If we are going to allow solicitors to have higher rights of audience then should the distinction in dress and mode of address be removed?

3. Stephen Irwin QC, the chair of the Bar Council during 2004, argued that Clementi was wrong to suggest that a central regulatory system was required saying: 'the Bar regulates itself very successfully and very cheaply because we have high degree of commitment from barristers who are pretty tough on their own colleagues.' Why should lawyers be investigated or regulated by outside bodies rather than their own internal systems?

4. Why is diversity within the legal professions important? What more could be done to increase diversity?

☰ Further reading

Sommerlad, H, Webley, L, Duff, L, Muzio, D, and Tomlinson, J, 'Diversity in the Legal Profession in England and Wales: A Qualitative Study of Barriers and Individual Choices' (2010) University of Westminster

Findings from a research project exploring diversity in the legal profession funded by the Legal Services Board.

Robins J, 'Inn a Time Warp?' (2005) 102 *Law Society Gazette* 19–20.

This article questions the relevancy of the Inns of Court in the modern legal practice and questions whether they hold the profession back as 'gentlemen's clubs'.

Webb J, 'Legal Disciplinary Practices: An Ethical Problem in the Making?' (2005) 8 *Legal Ethics* 185–94.

This article considers whether the disciplinary changes proposed by the Clementi report will in fact raise greater ethical dilemmas.

For self-test questions, flashcards, and links to useful websites, please visit the **online resources** at: **www.oup.com/he/gillespie-weare8e**

11

Funding Access to Justice

By the end of this chapter you will be able to:

- Understand how legal aid was developed, and how it has subsequently been severely restricted in recent years.
- Identify sources of funding civil and criminal litigation.
- Understand some of the difficulties that are caused when a person cannot afford to litigate without assistance.
- Identify how cuts in legal aid has meant that universities and the legal profession are increasingly trying to fill the gap through providing free legal advice.
- Begin to understand that some people will now invariably have to litigate without assistance (known as Litigants in Person).

Introduction

Perhaps the most controversial aspect about the legal profession and litigation is how it is funded. As was noted by the 'Secret Barrister' in their latest book, the media puts forward a particular narrative, whereby we spend the most expensive legal-aid bill in the world, which allows 'fat-cat' lawyers to line their pockets.[1] The reality, as will be seen, is that this is far from true. While a small number of privately-funded silks specializing in commercial law may earn a considerable amount of money, the position for high street solicitors or the junior bar is very different, as was noted in Chapter 10. This is because of changes to the way that litigation, both civil and criminal, is funded. In essence, this chapter is a story about the move away from legal aid.

---

1. Secret Barrister, *Fake Law: The Truth About Justice in an Age of Lies* (Picador 2020) 2.

11.1 **Background to legal aid**

Legal aid is a comparatively modern concept within the English Legal System and in effect traces its history to the Second World War. But it has expanded to the point where it is considered to be an everyday feature of the legal process. Since the 1980s, however, it has become an incredibly political 'hot potato' with Conservative, Labour, and coalition governments suggesting that 'fat cat' lawyers have abused the system although at least one commentator argues that the latest attacks are arguably just more noticeable since legal aid has always had a troubled existence.[2] It has been suggested that the principal justification for legal aid is that failing to assist the poorest in society accessing the law is a 'significant denial of justice'.[3] This is a particularly strong argument since it is frequently the very poor who are most in need of the law's protection as they can be readily exploited by those who know they are unable to take action. Within the sphere of employment law this was one of the reasons why unions became important since they would assist with legal proceedings to enforce conditions of employment. A similar rationale lies behind the national minimum wage (see the *National Minimum Wage Act 1999*) and here the state, through HM Revenue and Customs, acts on behalf of the low-waged to ensure that they are given an appropriate wage.

It has been suggested that there have been three stages of legal aid in this country[4] although since 2013 a fourth must now probably be added. The first stage was when it was funded directly by the state and administered by the Law Society. This period lasted forty years (1949–1989). The second stage was when the Legal Aid Board (LAB) took over the administration of the scheme from the Law Society, in part because there were concerns at solicitors being responsible for their own payment. This also marked the beginning of the principal political controversy surrounding this area. This second phase is said to have lasted from 1989 to 1999 but realistically it was not until 2000 when the third phase began. The third phase was the creation of the *Legal Services Commission* (LSC) created by the *Access to Justice Act 1999* with a remit to revolutionize the legal aid scheme. The fourth, and current phase, has been introduced by the *Legal Aid, Sentencing and Punishment of Offenders Act 2012* (LASPOA) which has abolished the LSC and brought legal aid back under the direct control of the Ministry of Justice.

A common aspect within all the phases of the legal aid scheme has been the concept of means-testing. Since legal aid is considered to be a solution for those who cannot access lawyers it was considered appropriate that it should be restricted to those who could prove they were of low income. This was particularly true in respect of representation at court but was also supposed to happen at the pre-trial hearings. However, there has, for many years, been suspicion about how high-profile figures have managed to obtain legal aid, including key businessmen who lived in houses worth millions. Some have suspected that it is possible to 'hide' money by ensuring that income and assets are held elsewhere.

Linked to the concept of means was the recovery of legal aid. As will be seen later in this book, the general rule in civil litigation is that the 'loser pays' all costs.

---

2.   John Flood and Avis Whyte, 'What's Wrong with Legal Aid? Lessons from outside the UK' (2006) 25 *Civil Justice Quarterly* 80.

3.   Michael Zander, *Cases and Materials on the English Legal System* (10th edn, OUP 2007) 585.

4.   Michael Zander, *Cases and Materials on the English Legal System* (10th edn, OUP 2007) 586.

Accordingly, if a person who is legally aided wins then the costs of the litigation should be claimed against the opposing side, meaning that the legal aid budget does not suffer. There are several exceptions to the 'loser pays' principle (see 17.1.5), and the legal aid provisions did allow for legal fees to be recovered from any awards that were made to the claimant.

Perhaps the biggest change from the initial legal aid scheme and the current one is that of budgets. Theoretically, throughout all stages of legal aid there has been a budget set but until the most recent set of reforms there was no upper limit on the expenditure set, ie it did not matter if the budget was overspent, often by significant amounts. This led to enormous pressures on the system and transformed the way the practices operated. One commentator noted that the greatest growth was in the period 1975–1984 where the Bar's legal aid earnings rose threefold and accounted for half of the Bar's income.[5] The rise for solicitors was even more pronounced, rising from £40 million in 1975 to £280 million in 1984, a sevenfold increase.[6]

The then Conservative government was determined to cut back on legal aid and commented that although it was an important feature of the legal system it 'could not be a blank cheque from the taxpayer'.[7] One of the strongest criticisms was that it encouraged cases to be dragged out since lawyers were paid by the hour. However, the profession's response to this was that this was also true with private cases but they were a professional body and accordingly would not prolong matters that were not justified. Academics agreed that the legal aid system potentially encouraged lawyers to pursue cases even when there was little prospect of success.[8] This meant that the legal aid budget became one of the biggest in the world.[9]

The Conservative government argued that it was necessary to centralize the legal aid system, in part to recognize that it was not just private law firms that provide advice but that other bodies (eg Citizens Advice Bureaux, Law Centres, etc) also provided assistance and were supported by the state. The government wished to rationalize this system[10] but also ensure that there was a control mechanism on spending. It proposed the creation of the LSC and suggested that it would be operationally independent although funded by the government. The LSC would have the power to decide what areas of law to fund and there was an intention that not every area of law would continue to be funded.

Ultimately the Conservative reforms were left unfinished and the incoming Labour government had to decide what to do. In opposition, the Labour party had been strongly opposed to many of the Conservative measures, arguing that limiting legal aid could be considered a barrier to access,[11] but this position altered dramatically after it was elected and at least one commentator has suggested that the Labour government

5. Richard Abel, *English Lawyers between Market and State* (OUP 2003) 241.
6. ibid, 241.
7. ibid, 244.
8. Natalie Byrom, 'Cuts to Civil Legal Aid and the Identity Crisis in Lawyering: Lessons from the Experience of England and Wales' in Asher Flynn and Jacqueline Hodgson (eds), *Access to Justice & Legal Aid: Comparative Perspectives on Unmet Legal Need* (Hart Publishing 2017) 230.
9. Although the Secret Barrister notes that comparing legal aid budgets is difficult because of the differences between the inquisitorial and adversarial systems mean that some of the costs of lawyers in England may be classed as judicial costs in other countries. The Secret Barrister suggests that the only true measure is comparing the costs paid by the state for the operation of the judicial system: Secret Barrister, *Fake Law: The Truth About Justice in an Age of Lies* (Picador 2020) 180–1.
10. Michael Zander, *Cases and Materials on the English Legal System* (10th edn, OUP 2007) 586.
11. Richard Abel, *English Lawyers between Market and State* (OUP 2003) 293.

effectively ended 'legal aid as we know it'[12] which, whilst dramatic, is undoubtedly correct.

The reality of the system was that legal aid continued to place increased pressure on the government's budget and that it was unsustainable for this to increase whilst the government sought to limit funding on other aspects of the state. The professions reacted badly to the proposals of the government and it culminated in a heated debate between the professions and the government. Perhaps the most notable aspect of the debate was when the government produced a list of the top earners from legal aid which was condemned by the professions as an attempt at humiliating them.[13] However, the government argument was that it demonstrated a problem with the legal aid scheme, that a judge would receive a salary of only £100,000 per year but some lawyers earned £1 million per year from legal aid. However, at the junior end of the profession the position was significantly different with small rewards being given.[14] Nonetheless, the media debate inevitably focused on the 'high end' of the profession since it was easy to portray lawyers as 'fat cats'. This ultimately turned the tide of the discussion and led to the government winning the battle for legal aid.

In the end the budget continued to grow and controversy existed over the types of persons and cases that provided for legal aid. Ironically, given they were responsible for the creation of the LSC, the Conservative-led coalition government abolished it and decided to centralize legal aid within the Ministry. This gives the Lord Chancellor more direct control over the budget and how it is to be spent.

11.1.1 Reviews of legal aid

Continued pressure on the legal aid budget led to a major review of legal aid conducted by Lord Carter in 2005. A further review (the Magee Review) was held in 2009 and this was read in conjunction with the report of Jackson LJ on costs in civil litigation. Many of the recommendations of these reviews have been brought forward in LASPOA.

Carter believed that a more market-orientated approach to legal aid should be developed and certainly this was something that quickly took hold. The primary response was to ensure that a smaller number of firms held a larger proportion of the work, these contracts being awarded through a competitive bid process whereby (generally) the lowest bid won the contract (subject to certain quality thresholds and performance indicators). The reforms were extremely controversial since it meant that many firms did not hold a contract for legal aid work meaning that a person could not necessarily have their lawyer of choice.

Another key change was the manner in which legal aid was paid to lawyers. Traditionally legal aid was similar to ordinary payments of fees, ie a lawyer was paid depending on how much work he undertook. Carter recommended a move away from negotiated fees to standardized graduated fees.[15] This means that a lawyer would be given a set fee for a set classification of work. It was designed to promote efficiency but, of course, some critics noted that no two law cases are the same and this may mean that lawyers would have less time to spend on complex matters. A safeguard against lawyers cutting corners was the introduction of a peer-review scheme to assess the quality of service provided by firms.

---

12. ibid, 293 and ch 8.
13. ibid, 304, 310.
14. ibid, 304.
15. Lord Carter, *Legal Aid: A Market-based Approach to Reform* (Department for Constitutional Affairs 2006) 4.

A unique problem within criminal law is that known as Very High Costs Cases (VHCC) which were the small number of complex criminal cases that would cost the most in terms of legal aid (murder, fraud etc). Carter believed that this accounted for a disproportionately high part of the legal aid budget[16] and that tendering could be used to try and reduce costs. The initial approach by the *Legal Services Commission* was to attempt to limit the pay of counsel conducting VHCC work. The rates of the Bar would have been cut dramatically but the response was one of intransigence, with many silks and senior juniors refusing to undertake legal aid work. They could do this without breaching the 'cab rank rule' because the process of tendering meant that lawyers, including advocates, would have to 'sign up' to the scheme in order to receive work. Thus by not signing up to the scheme they were never put in the position of refusing a case since it could not have been offered to them in the first place.

The stand-off led to some heated words and potential injustices. In the autumn of 2008 it was reported that the trial of the persons accused of the murder of the schoolboy Rhys Jones might have had to be postponed because there was no agreement as to fees. In the event the LSC backed down and provided an exemption from the scheme. A compromise was reached in 2010 when a panel-based system was rejected for individual contracts but with fixed fees being paid for much of the work. The fees were also a reduction in what had previously been paid but not to the extent that was first proved. That said, VHCC continues to be extremely controversial and it is likely to prove so under the new scheme.

Civil legal aid was similarly problematic and there was thought to be a case for reducing the type of cases that would be funded by civil legal aid. Carter appeared to believe that, subject to certain exemptions, the civil legal aid budget should not be fixed but would rather be whatever was left of the overall budget after criminal legal aid had been paid. There was concern that the tendering process adopted for legal aid work could lead to communities being without any legal representation services and he suggested that firms could form alliances with community organizations to overcome this.[17]

The Magee review differed in some respects from Carter, most notably in recommending that there should be separate budgets for civil and legal aid[18] which would have, in effect, led to more protection for civil legal aid than was envisaged by Carter. One of the principal recommendations made by Magee was acted upon quickly when the administration of legal aid was removed from the LSC, a non-departmental public body, and brought back within the Ministry of Justice. Magee suggested that social welfare law could be removed from legal aid funding and replaced by providing additional assistance to community organizations, including the Citizens Advice Bureaux (CABs), to permit social advice to be provided in a more efficient manner. Whether this has happened is more questionable. Whilst there has undoubtedly been a greater expectation that social welfare advice should be provided by the CAB there was a question of whether the budget was similarly carried over. Many CABs had legal aid contracts but the ending of legal aid for certain types of advice (discussed later) meant that they lost a substantial amount of income. Ultimately the government had to step in because they realized that CABs are essential to the functioning of advice and large grants were ultimately made to individual bureaux.

---

16. ibid.
17. ibid.
18. Ian Magee, *Review of Legal Aid Delivery and Governance* (HMSO 2009) 72.

11.1.2 **Legal aid today**

Legal aid, for both criminal and civil litigation, is now set out in the *Legal Aid, Sentencing and Punishment of Offenders Act 2012* (LASPOA).

11.1.2.1 **Legal Aid Agency**

One of the key reforms of LASPOA was to return legal aid to executive control. Previously, legal aid was administered by the *Legal Services Commission*,[19] which was a non-departmental body, meaning that it was quasi-autonomous. The *Legal Aid Agency* now has responsibility for the administration of justice and it is formed as an executive agency of the Ministry of Justice.[20] The Lord Chancellor (who is also the Secretary of State of Justice) is charged with 'securing' legal aid,[21] although that is then subject to the qualification that the duty applies only to those proceedings within Part I of LASPOA. Thus, the statutory duty to an extent masks the fact that the primary purpose of LASPOA was to reduce the availability of legal aid.

The day-to-day running of the LAA is left in the hands of a senior civil servant who acts as chief executive and Director of Legal Aid Casework.[22] As will be seen the Director has responsibility for making decisions in respect of individual cases. In order to protect the independence of the legal process the Act specifically provides that whilst, as would be expected, the Director can be directed as to how to carry out his functions[23] which, in essence, means detailing how the legal aid scheme will be carried out, the Lord Chancellor is expressly prevented from making directions in respect of an individual case,[24] and 'must ensure that the Director acts independently of the Lord Chancellor' when making such decisions. The latter phrasing is quite interesting because it is potentially wider than not making directions. It is difficult to believe that when the Secretary of State for Justice, a senior governmental minister, makes his views known, a civil servant may not be influenced by that, but the phrasing of s 4(4)(b)—to ensure that independence is maintained—would arguably cover such situations meaning the Lord Chancellor may have to be extremely careful about making comments in respect of an individual case.

The Lord Chancellor is empowered to set quality standards for those who wish to provide legal aid services,[25] including by creating a system of accreditation.[26] This carries on an initiative that had existed under the LSC, where under the *Access to Justice Act 1999* (AJA 1999) the LSC only granted legal aid contracts to those who achieved a 'quality mark' and a failure to adhere to that mark, meant that the contract could be removed. The idea behind such an approach is that the state guarantees that its money is providing a service of a particular standard, but it does create the theoretical possibility that the government can influence which firms have contracts.

The Director of Legal Aid Casework must ensure that an annual report on legal aid is produced[27] and the Lord Chancellor must ensure that this is laid before

---

19. *Administration of Justice Act 1999*, s 1.
20. LASPOA, s 38.
21. ibid, s 1(1).
22. ibid, s 4.
23. ibid, s 4(3).
24. ibid, s 4(4).
25. ibid, s 3(1).
26. ibid, s 3(2).
27. ibid, s 7.

Parliament and published. Whilst this is statutory recognition of the need to be transparent about the legal aid budget and how it has been administered, it does not differ dramatically from what happened under the LSC as the LSC and its daughter agencies (the *Community Legal Service* and *Criminal Defence Service*) all provided annual reports.

11.2 Criminal legal aid

The first issue to consider is that of criminal legal aid. It will be seen in Chapter 12 that legal aid exists as of right for certain aspects of the criminal justice system. Perhaps the most notable example of this is the 'duty solicitor' scheme whereby a person who is arrested can receive free legal advice (although it will be seen that it is now no longer the case that it will necessarily be either in-person or by a qualified solicitor—see 12.3.2.2). What of the position where someone is brought before the courts?

Historically, legal aid in criminal trials was relatively easy to obtain. Through the years, changes were introduced to try and restrict costs, perhaps most notably when legal aid changed from a per-hour to a per-case payment,[28] something that remains true even today. There are different views as to whether this change has had an impact. One study showed a majority of lawyers questioned thought that a fixed-fee was acceptable because there tended to be an averaging between complicated and straight-forward cases.[29] However, Thornton found that some lawyers believed that they were more likely to encourage a client to plead guilty because the fee was so low.[30] Of course, what that study could not know is the strength of the cases in which a person was convinced to plead guilty. It could well be that it is in their client's best interests for a guilty plea to be advanced (discussed in 10.6.2.1). However, it does raise the suspicion that clients are put under pressure to plead guilty when they may not otherwise wished to have done so.

LASPOA introduced radical changes, including the use of means testing. This means that some people are not eligible for legal aid due to their income, meaning they either must defend themselves, or pay a solicitor or barrister privately. As will be seen, the thresholds for payment are low, raising questions about whether ordinary people can receive legal aid to defend themselves.

Setting aside the issue of pre-charge advice, the rules for representation are set out within LASPOA. Section 14 defines 'criminal proceedings and this is given a broad definition so as to include, amongst others, trials, sentencing hearings, and appeals. The Lord Chancellor is to provide, by regulations, the provision of advice and assistance in connection with legal proceedings.[31] This is then taken further by s 16 which provides the right to representation in criminal proceedings.

---

28. Lucy Welsh, 'The Effects of Changes to Legal Aid on Lawyers' Professional Identity and Behaviour in Summary Criminal Cases: A Case Study' (2017) 44 *Journal of Law and Society* 559, 562.

29. ibid, 573.

30. James Thornton, 'The Way in Which Fee Reductions Influence Legal Aid Criminal Defence Lawyer Work: Insights from a Qualitative Study' (2019) 46 *Journal of Law and Society* 559, 576.

31. LASPOA, s 15.

The test for representation is set out in s 17. The basic test is that a person must satisfy the financial eligibility ('means-testing') and that representation is 'in the interests of justice'.[32] The latter requires the following to be considered:

(a) whether the individual would be likely to lose his liberty or livelihood or suffer serious damage to his reputation if he were to lose

(b) whether the proceedings involve consideration of a substantial question of law

(c) whether the individual may be unable to understand the proceedings or to state his or her own case

(d) whether the proceedings may involve the tracing, interviewing or expert cross-examination of witnesses on behalf of the individuals

(e) whether it is in the interests of another person that the individual be represented.[33]

▤ Example Substantial question of law

Factor (b) is quite important because it will sometimes be the case that what appears to be a simple case is actually more complicated because of issues that have not been raised before. A good example of this is in respect of the parliamentary expenses claim. In *R v Chaytor*[34] three former Members of Parliament sought to argue that they could not be tried for fraud in respect of their parliamentary expenses because to do so would have breached the *Bill of Rights* which excludes court action from the proceedings of Parliament. This was an important issue that had not been raised before and eventually reached the Supreme Court. The Supreme Court accepted that it was an important point but ultimately ruled that privilege did not apply. Leaving aside privilege the facts of the cases were relatively simple but it was in the interests of justice for this matter to be considered by the courts, including the Supreme Court, before being tried.

The decision to grant legal aid is one for either the Director of Legal Aid or a court. Previously, it was the courts that ultimately made the decision, but now it is a shared responsibility and it is comparatively rare for the courts to order legal aid funding, believing that it is properly the role of the *Legal Aid Agency* to decide such matters.

11.2.1 **Means testing**

The more controversial aspect is the means testing that is now required. The result of this test will decide whether someone is either funded, partially-funded (ie a person will need to contribute to their costs), or not funded.

Two elements are required to calculate a person's means. The first is the adjusted gross income. This is the person's salary (or other income) before tax, national insurance, pension contributions, or other expenses are paid. However, it is subject to adjustment where a person has a family.

---

32. ibid, s 17(1).
33. ibid, s 17(2).
34. [2010] UKSC 52, [2011] 2 AC 684.

A partner has a factor of 0.64 and a child's multiplier depends on the age of the child.

Age	Multiplier
0–1	0.15
2–4	0.30
5–7	0.34
8–10	0.38
11–12	0.41
13–15	0.44
16–18	0.59

Example Adjusted gross income

Adrian has an annual salary of £34,000. His wife has a salary of £18,000. They have 2 children; a girl aged 2 and a boy aged 5.

Adrian and his wife have a factor of 1.64 (1 for him and 0.64 for his wife), and the children have a factor of 0.64. This provides a total factor of 2.28.

Their gross income is £52,000. Dividing this by the adjustment, means that they have an adjusted gross income of £22,807.

The second part of the means test is to calculate the 'disposable income'. While it may be thought that this means the income after all expenses etc have been settled, it only relates to certain outgoings. These include:

- tax and national insurance
- council tax
- annual rent or mortgage payments
- childcare
- maintenance payments (where the person is divorced or paying child support) and
- living costs.[35]

'Living costs' are set at £5,676 per annum,[36] but this is multiplied by the same factor as before.

Example Disposable income

Adrian has an annual salary of £34,000. His wife has a salary of £18,000. They have 2 children; a girl aged 2 and a boy aged 5. They rent a house and this comes to £675 per month, and their council tax is £120 per month. They pay childcare of £160 month.

---

35. *Criminal Legal Aid (Contribution Orders) Regulations* 2013, SI 2013/483, reg 11(3).
36. ibid, reg 21(3)(g).

Adrian will be liable to pay £7,238 in tax and national insurance, and his wife will be liable to pay £2,118 for tax and national insurance.

As before, Adrian and his wife have a factor of 1.64 (1 for him and 0.64 for his wife), and the children have a factor of 0.64. This provides a total factor of 2.28 for the living costs.

Adrian's disposable income will be:

Household income	52,000
Tax & NI	9,356
Rent	8,100
Council Tax	1,440
Child care	1,920
Living costs	12,941
Total expense	(33,757)
Disposable income	**18,243**

As you can see, working out a person's income is not straight forward!

While the 'living costs' factor means that the costs rise with a family, it is still not by very much. So, for example, in the example of Adrian we have just used, the living costs are £12,941. This is £1,078 per month. That might seem a lot but, remember, the only other expenses that have been deducted (other than tax and national insurance) are rent, council tax and childcare. So that £1,078 has to cover food, travel expenses, clothes, debt repayments etc. A small car will cost approximately £250 a month to buy, £80–100 per month for insurance, and perhaps £100 per month of fuel. Thus, they now have just over £500 per month for food, clothes and everything else. Is that realistic?

11.2.1.1 Magistrates' courts

It will be seen in Chapter 14 that c.95% of criminal cases are dealt with in the magistrates' court. What are the rules for the means test there?

(a) the individual's gross annual income does not exceed £12,475; or

(b) the individual's gross annual income is more than £12,475 and less than £22,325, they are eligible if the annual disposable income does not exceed £3,398.[37]

Where the gross annual income is above £22,325, then they are not eligible for representation within the magistrates' court. The first point to note is that these sums are not very high. Of course, it does not take account of the adjustments above, but it is still a low threshold.

The example of Adrian was given earlier. We noted his adjusted gross income was £22,807. Therefore, if Adrian was charged with an offence before the magistrates' court then he would not be eligible for representation. Let us take another example.

---

37. ibid, reg 18(1).

☰ **Example** Minimum Wage

Carla works in a factory for 37.5 hours per week at minimum wage (currently £8.72 per hour). She is 26 and has a four-year old child. She pays £525 in rent, £96 in council tax and childcare of £110.

Carla's gross income will be £17,004. Her 4-year-old child attracts an adjustment of 0.3, so her adjusted income is £13,080. This is above the £12,475 that permits automatic granting of legal aid, so we must look at the disposable income.

Carla's disposable income is:

Salary	17,004
Tax and NI	1,802
Council Tax	1,152
Rent	6,300
Childcare	1,320
Living expenses	7,378
Total expenses	(17,952)
Disposable income	**(948)**

Here, Carla will be eligible because her disposable income is more than what her actual income is, and so it is less than £3,398 required under the second rule. Had Carla received the average UK wage (c.£26,000) then she would not have been eligible, as her disposable income would have been £8,048.

⟳ QUESTION FOR REFLECTION

Are you surprised at the threshold at which representation in the magistrates' court will work? Let us take the example of Carla earning the average wage. Her disposable income would be £8,048, or £670 per month. That would need to cover all of her food, travel, clothes, work expenses, loans, credit card bills, toys for her child etc. How realistic is it that someone who has £670 per month could afford to pay privately for a solicitor? If the average expenses of a car was included, that would leave her with c.£300 month. Is that a rich person?

Assuming a person is eligible for legal aid, the process of obtaining legal aid can be quite time consuming. This is problematic because, at least in the magistrates' courts, there has been a push to reduce delays. This means that solicitors are finding that there is a need to contemplate representing their client at a time when they do not know whether they are going to be paid for their work.[38] If this happens too often then it is likely that increasing numbers of solicitors will refuse to engage in criminal legal aid work.

---

38. Lucy Welsh, 'The Effects of Changes to Legal Aid on Lawyers' Professional Identity and Behaviour in Summary Criminal Cases: A Case Study' (2017) 44 *Journal of Law and Society* 559, 581.

Thornton presents an interesting quote from a solicitor which can show the issue with merits and means.

> [Y]our ideal shoplifting client is somebody who's in receipt of incomes support [*easy to prove means test*] [SIC], on a suspended sentence, in custody [*easy to pass merits test*] [SIC].[39]

This is interesting because of what would happen if the variable changed. As noted earlier, that would be an ideal person for a solicitor. What about a person who earns £16,000 per year? This is someone who will earn significantly less than the average income, but this person will not be eligible for legal aid. They are unlikely to be able to pay for a private solicitor with such an income, and thus the risk for this second defendant is that he could receive a custodial sentence, whereas the person on income support may not.

11.2.1.2 **Crown Court**

As will be seen in Chapter 15, the Crown Court hears the most serious offences. It may be thought that someone charged with a serious offence before the Crown Court would receive legal aid, but they are also subject to both the merit and the means test, although the merits test is usually more easily satisfied.

The same means test calculation is used to identify Crown Court means, but the thresholds are increased. The basic means test-rule is as follows:

(a) has a gross income that does not exceed £12,475, or

(b) has a gross income that exceeds £12,475 but whose disposable income is less than £37,500, or

(c) is a child, or

(d) is in receipt of a relevant benefit.[40]

The difference between (a) and (b) is that in (b), a defendant is likely to be required to make a contribution to her defence costs. This contribution is set at six payments of 90 per cent of one-twelfth of the annual disposable income.[41] In other words, 90 per cent of the monthly disposable income is paid for a period of six months. Given the limitation of 'disposable income' above, this potentially means that there could be real hardship.

Where a person has a disposable income of over £37,500 then they are not eligible for legal aid, and must pay for any representation privately.

Let us consider two examples.

Esther is accused of false accounting from a local charity. Her salary is £36,000 but she also receives dividend income of £2,000 from shares.	Paresh is accused of actual bodily harm, but it was committed while serving a suspended prison sentence.
She has two children, aged 3 and 7. Her mortgage is £650 per month. Her council tax is £110 per month and childcare is £125 per month.	Paresh has a salary of £16,000, but he is given £1,500 per month from his parents. His rent is £800, and his council tax is £125. He has no children.

---

39. James Thornton, 'The Way in Which Fee Reductions Influence Legal Aid Criminal Defence Lawyer Work: Insights from a Qualitative Study' (2019) 46 *Journal of Law and Society* 559, 578.

40. *Criminal Legal Aid (Financial Resources) Regulations* 2013 (SI 2013/471), reg 31.

41. *Criminal Legal Aid (Contribution Orders) Regulations* 2013 (SI 2013/4483), reg 12(2)(a).

Paresh's gross income is £34,000 which is over the £12,475 initial threshold. Thus, his disposable income will need to be considered. Esther's income is £38,000, but this must take into account her children. Using the factor presented earlier, the income must be divided by 1.64 (1.0 for her, 0.3 for one child, and 0.34 for the second child). This produces an income of £23,170. Thus, Esther comes within the second category. Again, we must work out her disposable income.

Esther	Paresh
Income 38,000	Income 34,000
Tax & NI 8,518	Tax & NI 1,478
Mortgage 7,800	Rent 9,600
Council Tax 1,320	Council Tax 1,500
Childcare 1,500	Living Costs 5,676
Living Costs 9,308	Total Expenses (18,254)
Total Expenses (28,446)	Adjusted income **15,746**
Adjusted income **9,554**	

It can be seen here that Esther's adjusted income is less than £12,475 and, accordingly, she will be given legal aid without the requirement to contribute anything. However, Paresh's income is £15,746. This means that he earns more than £12,475 but less than £37,500. He is, therefore, entitled to legal aid, but he needs to make a contribution. The contribution is set at one-twelfth of the adjusted income (£1,312), and he must make six payments (£7,872).

It will be remembered from the earlier section (11.2.1) that the living costs of £5,676 is to cover all expenses, including shopping, travel and clothes etc. This works out as £473 per month. If Paresh has a car, bank loans or credit card debts, it is highly likely that Paresh will be out of pocket during the six months he must pay the legal aid contributions.

Civil legal aid is controversial but, in some instances, it can be seen why the state refuses to pay for the litigation. In many instances, a person chooses whether to litigate and this may include where, for example, they feel that an offer of compensation is not sufficient. As it is a private matter between two parties, the state could say 'not our problem' requiring private funding mechanisms (discussed later at 11.5). Criminal litigation is different. Nobody chooses to be the subject of the criminal justice system. It is the state, through the police and the Crown Prosecution Service, that decides to bring a prosecution against someone. The individual has no choice.

One of the foremost principles of the criminal justice system in England and Wales is that a person is innocent until proven guilty. In other words, unless a person admits their guilt, then at the time of the trial they are not guilty of a crime. Why is it that an innocent person should be told to contribute to their costs (either partly or in full) when it is the state that is deciding to prosecute them? A person who is either told to pay contributions, or is not eligible for legal aid, can suffer real financial hardship in defending themselves in the Crown Court.

> **≡ Example** Nigel Evans MP
>
> Nigel Evans MP is the Member of Parliament for the Ribble Valley. In 2013 he was arrested on suspicion of sexual assault, something he denied rigorously. The CPS decided to prosecute him, and in 2014 he was tried in the Crown Court and acquitted.
>
> Evans had voted for LASPOA but indicated he had not understood the implications of it, and subsequently said the changes it made were wrong.
>
> As an MP, his disposable income was such that he was not eligible for legal aid. He spent over £130,000 defending himself against allegations that were not proven. Evans admitted that LASPOA was wrong and that if it were to be voted on now, he would vote against it.[42]
>
> Evans had to sell his grandfather's business and remortgage his house, but even then he used up his life savings. He also discovered that his costs were not fully recoverable even after acquittal (see 11.2.2.2).

The problem of criminal legal aid is not in it being given, it is in the fact that it is not recovered from a convicted defendant. While a defendant can be ordered to repay the legal aid costs, it comes lower down the 'pecking order' than fines or compensation. If recovery was considered differently, then the acquitted could be given legal aid, while those who are ultimately convicted would be required to pay. That arguably strikes a better balance than the state forcing financial disadvantage on a person by its own actions.

A consequence of the current legal aid funding is that people are starting to defend themselves in criminal proceedings, both in the magistrates' court and the Crown Court. The Home Affairs Select Committee has noted that there are a number of difficulties with unrepresented defendants, including the fact that they rarely understand the proceedings, slow proceedings down, and lead to a reduction in guilty pleas.[43]

There is also the perception of fairness. The prosecution will be represented. For serious cases in the Crown Court, this could include representation by Queen's Counsel, one of the best and most experienced advocates. How realistic is it that a defendant in person is able to respond to issues as well as a trained lawyer? If you study *Law of Evidence*, you will see that many of the laws on what is, or is not, admissible within a criminal trial are extremely complicated. Is it realistic or, indeed, fair to expect an unrepresented defendant to be able to understand these rules? That must put them at a disadvantage, particularly in the Crown Court where a jury may understandably wonder why the defendant is not represented and may, for example, believe that it is because no barrister or solicitor would take their case, implying that it is weak.

⟳ QUESTION FOR REFLECTION

The Unrepresented Defendant Do you think a jury would find it odd that a defendant is not represented? The only thing most people know of courts is what they see on television, where everyone is represented by a bewigged barrister. Is there a chance that a jury will think that a lawyer was not prepared to represent the client? If so, will that prejudice the jury against the defendant?

---

42.   See, for example, Amelia Hill and Owen Bowcott 'Its Completely Wrong: Falsely Accused Tory MP Attacks Legal Aid Cuts' *The Guardian* (27 December 2018).

43.   Justice Committee, *Criminal Legal Aid* (2017–2019, HC 1069) at [83].

11.2.2 **(Criminal) legal aid payments**

The second issue of concern around criminal legal aid is the payments that are given to lawyers representing the defence. A linked issue relates to the amount that an acquitted defendant can reclaim in fees if they are acquitted.

11.2.2.1 **Fixed fees**

As noted earlier, one of the first changes to criminal legal aid was the introduction of fixed fees. Instead of a lawyer submitting what their usual fee is per hour, and the number of hours that have been worked on, the Legal Aid Agency now decides what fee a matter is worth. In some matters, this is a per-case fee where the same is paid irrespective of how much time a person works on the matter (discussed briefly at 11.2).

The same is true for trials. There are two schemes: the *Advocates Graduated Fee Scheme* (AGFS), which pays the costs of the advocate representing the defendant. The second scheme is the *Litigators Graduated Fee Scheme* (LGFS). The latter pays for the non-advocacy aspects of the trial (eg legal advice, instructing counsel, taking notes for counsel, preparing witness statements etc). For simplicity, we will focus on the AGFS, as this is perhaps the most illustrative in a court scenario.

The AGFS separates crimes into seventeen bands, although some have sub-bands within them. Murder and manslaughter are considered to be 'band 1', rape is 'band 5', burglary is 'band 11', and there is a catch-all 'band 17' which includes all offences that are not otherwise categorized within a band.[44] Each band attracts a particular fee. There are two fees; a 'basic fee' and a 'daily fee', which is then provided for the second and subsequent days of trial. The payment also depends on the status of the advocate, with there being three categories:

- junior counsel acting alone, or being led
- junior counsel leading another junior counsel
- Queen's Counsel.

For band 5 (rape), the basic fee would be £1,800 for a junior acting alone, rising to £3,600 for a QC.[45] The daily fee is £525 for a junior acting alone, rising to £1,050 for a QC. This money is subject to VAT, tax, chambers expenses, and person expenses (eg travel and sustenance). Additional payments are given for each page of evidence (usually £0.98 per page for a junior, rising to £1.63 per page for a QC), and for each witness called (£4.90 per witness for a junior acting alone, rising to £6.53 per witness). The latter perhaps shows one of the more remarkable aspects of the fees. While the case preparation will invariably consider the evidence before them, it seems somewhat paltry to suggest that all the preparatory work that goes into either an examination-in-chief or cross-examination of a witness is remunerated at approximately £5.

In addition to the fees, the LAA also limits the amount of personal expenses that can be received. So, for example, the LAA states the limits for payment of overnight accommodation. If a lawyer needs to stay in London, Birmingham, Manchester, Leeds, or Newcastle upon Tyne, then they will receive up to £85.25 per night and £55.25 for anywhere else. However, how realistic is this? You would be hard-pressed to get a hotel

385

---

44. Ministry of Justice 'Banding of the offences in the Advocates' Graduated Fee Scheme' (2018). Available at <https://www.gov.uk/government/publications/banding-of-offences-in-the-advocates-graduated-fee-scheme>.
45. *The Criminal Legal Aid (Remuneration) Regulations 2013*, SI 2013/435 (as amended), sch I.

in London or Birmingham for £85 and certainly hard-pressed to get a hotel in most towns with a Crown Court for £55 per night. This invariably means that the lawyer will have to pay the difference between the cost and allowance themselves.

Fewer barristers were engaging with legally aided cases and in March 2018 it culminated in barristers performing an unprecedented strike.[46] This led to cases being delayed or, in many instances, defendants having to represent themselves. While the government referred to a small number of leading QCs who make six or even seven figure sums from legal aid (although, it should be noted, that the fees paid in a single year might actually reflect fees from multiple years, particularly in respect of complex cases that span several years), the reality of life at the Bar is very different. The 'Secret Barrister' notes that a 'typical' barrister doing legal aid work will have an income of around £27,000.[47] This is approximately the UK average wage. This is subject to tax in the usual way. Is it the amount that you would expect a barrister of several years' call to earn? If you are living in London, will that give you a decent standard of living? Particularly after you remember that the professional stage of qualification (see Chapter 10) is not covered by a student loan, and, therefore, you are likely to have significant personal debt after qualification. There is a danger that the junior criminal bar is now only for those with independent wealth, which is far from ideal in terms of diversity.

The strike was eventually settled with the government promising an additional £15 million in funding.[48] However, this was also supposed to lead to a review of the scheme but there remains repeated concerns about how the legal aid scheme was working, and threats continue to be made that barristers might strike once more.

11.2.2.2 Recouping defence costs

Let us start with an example.

> **Example** The Acquitted defendant
>
> Stephen was charged with two counts of sexual assault. A band manager earning £60,000 per annum and with two grown-up children, he was not eligible for legal aid. Instead, he instructs a solicitor and barrister to represent him. Immediately after the conclusion of the prosecution evidence, the judge accepts that there is no case to answer (see 15.2). Stephen is acquitted. The judge, discharging him from the dock, states 'you leave without a strain on your character'.
>
> Stephen has paid £23,000 in defence costs.

In this example Stephen has been acquitted. Not only has he been acquitted, but he has been acquitted at the earliest possible opportunity. The prosecution could not even establish their case, and it was unnecessary for him to put forward his case for the defence. Surely, Stephen will have his costs repaid, since the state has failed to show that he committed an offence?

---

46. 'Barristers go on Strike in Protest at "Collapsing" Criminal Justice System' *Daily Telegraph* (30 March 2018) News.
47. Secret Barrister, *Stories of the Law and How It's Broken* (MacMillan 2018) 210.
48. 'Barristers in England and Wales Call off Industrial Action' *The Guardian* (12 June 2018) News.

The answer is 'yes. . .ish'. It is true that he will get some defence costs returned to him, but the second sting in the tail of criminal legal aid is that you do not receive the costs back that you paid. Rather, you receive a contribution based on what would have been paid had you been eligible for legal aid. The difficulty here is that, as noted previously, legal aid rates are low, and the expense regime is restrictive. Private legal advice is going to be more expensive as counsel are going to charge a rate that reflects their true market value. This means that a person accused of a crime has effectively no 'good' option. They can pay for the best counsel, but lose money despite them being acquitted, or they can choose to go with counsel who will only charge private clients legal aid rates, in which case they may not be particularly good.

The Secret Barrister refers to the fact that you do not get your full costs back as the 'innocent tax'.[49] By this, (s)he[50] means that a person who is found to be innocent is, in essence, taxed by the state for being acquitted. It is this innocence tax that cost Nigel Evans MP so dearly, and which he considered so unfair.

⟳ QUESTION FOR REFLECTION

The Secret Barrister expresses the dilemma thus:

> We have a system which focuses a wrongly accused person from a middle-class family to choose between financial destitution and the fool's gamble of self-representing in criminal proceedings.[51]

It is probably right that the state should not pick up the expenses of a party irrespective of what they are. To do so, would allow private counsel to charge exorbitant fees in cases where there is a reasonable chance of acquittal. This would game the system and mean that prosecution decisions could be based on how expensive the defence lawyers are.

However, it cannot be right for defendants to be tends of thousands of pounds out of pocket in order to defend their name. The old rules allowed for reasonable costs to be paid, and the courts decided whether claims too high. Does that not strike the right balance?

11.3 Civil legal aid

Civil legal aid has seen even more dramatic changes than the criminal system. This section will explore some of the more contentious aspects, including noting how few are now covered by legal aid.

11.3.1 Matters covered by legal aid

Until LASPOA, legal aid operated under an exclusionary model. That is to say, all forms of litigation were eligible for legal aid unless a rule said to the contrary. LASPOA reversed this by creating an inclusionary rule. That is to say, legal aid is now only

---

49. Secret Barrister, *The Secret Barrister: Stories of the Law and How It's Broken* (Picador 2018) 212.
50. We do not know the gender of the Secret Barrister.
51. Secret Barrister, *The Secret Barrister: Stories of the Law and How It's Broken* (Picador 2018) 218.

permissible if the Act says it is.[52] The detail of what is permitted is set out in sch 1 LASPOA. Part II of sch I excludes specific types of actions even if they appear to fall within Part I. Broadly speaking, sch I limits funding to issues relating to:

- public childcare proceedings (ie where a child is sought to be placed under the supervision or care of a local authority)
- special educational needs of a child
- abuse of a child or vulnerable adult
- challenging decisions relating to being banned from working with children or vulnerable adults
- mental health or mental capacity
- clinical negligence and severely disabled infants
- community care funding
- facilities for those with a disability
- welfare appeals
- housing where there is a risk of homelessness
- child abduction
- domestic violence
- forced marriage
- judicial review where a breach of fundamental rights is being alleged
- *habeas corpus* (ie an order of the court to release a person from unlawful detention)
- applications for asylum
- victims of trafficking.

A range of work that used to be covered by legal aid is now no longer eligible. Actions for personal injury are generally not eligible for legal aid, and neither are private family law disputes (eg divorce or residence of a child). The government argued that private family law disputes do not require legal aid as it will generally not be in the child's best interests to go to court. For that reason, they provide legal aid for mediation (a form of Alternative Dispute Resolution discussed in 19.3.2.1).

The government actively seeks to portray family litigation as a failure, and that it is a 'battle' that does not acknowledge the interests of the child.[53] There is undoubtedly an element of truth behind this, but this does not acknowledge the potential imbalance of power that exists. The government appears to base its logic on the fact that neither party will be represented, when it is not clear that this is the case. It is eminently possible that one party can afford (private) representation and the other cannot. In those instances, mediation is unlikely to assist. The party who can afford litigation may well believe that they have a better chance in court than a negotiated agreement. They have little to lose, as the courts are not going to prevent a parent seeing their child to mark their disapproval, and thus litigation is inevitable. During that litigation, the represented

---

52. LASPOA, s 9(1).
53. Rosemary Hunter and others, 'Access to What? LASPO and Mediation' in Asher Flynn and Jacqueline Hodgson (eds), *Access to Justice & Legal Aid: Comparative Perspectives on Unmet Legal Aid* (Hart Publishing 2017) 245.

party has all the advantages that legal representation brings, and yet the party denied legal aid does not. Where, for example, the party is nervous, shy, or is culturally unused to speaking in public, they are going to be disadvantaged. It is difficult to see how this accords with the best interests of the child.

QUESTION FOR REFLECTION

Edith and Fred marry in 2013 and have two children (aged 4 and 2). Fred has an affair with someone he works with and Edith takes the children to her parents. Fred moves his mistress into the house and says he wants to divorce Edith.

Edith does not work because Fred has a good job and it was decided that Edith would bring up the children.

Fred says he is going to seek residence of the children, 'because they're better off with me'. Edith only has the money that she is given from Fred. Even if she sought interim maintenance as a separated spouse (for which she would probably need legal assistance), this is not going to be enough to pay for a lawyer to resist the residence application. Fred, on the other hand, can afford to pay for a solicitor and barrister.

Who is going to be better prepared in any court proceedings? Surely Fred, with his legal team, is going to be able to put forward rational, supported arguments in a way that draws upon their experience. Edith will not. Where is the justice here? Edith is at a disadvantage, and yet the state will not assist. Is that fair?

11.3.1.1 Exceptional cases

Where an issue is not within Schedule 1 then it is not ordinarily eligible for legal aid. That said, LASPOA 2012, s 10 provides the Director of Legal Aid Coursework with discretion to provide legal aid for matters outside of the schedule in exceptional cases.

The extent to which exceptional cases have been accepted has been the subject of some controversy. In *R (on the application of Gudanaviciene and others) v Director of Legal Aid Coursework and the Lord Chancellor*[54] the Court of Appeal held that guidance issued on how s 10 should operate was incompatible with the ECHR because it was overly restrictive. The guidance suggested s 10 should only be used where a failure to offer legal aid would make 'the claim practically impossible or lead to an obvious unfairness in proceedings'. It was held that this was too high a threshold, and that other factors should also be taken into account so as not to limit exceptional circumstances to those cases where Article 6 was potentially breached.

Following this case the guidance was revised, but it remains controversial. An issue of particular concern is the fact that the form required to apply for exceptional circumstances under s 10 is extremely complex. The guidance under s 10 also suggested that it should only be used where a claim would be impossible or unfair without legal aid. In *Director of Legal Aid Casework and the Lord Chancellor v IS*[55] the criteria was, once again, challenged as being unfair. The Court of Appeal this time rejected the challenge, albeit unenthusiastically. A key point was that the form under s 10 was so complex that,

---

54. [2014] EWCA Civ 1622.
55. [2016] EWCA Civ 464.

realistically, it required the assistance of a lawyer to complete, and yet legal aid would not be available to do this. The Court of Appeal criticized the form, its complexity, and how literally the form was read by the LAA, but ultimately concluded that complexity was not, by itself, sufficiently unfair to render it unlawful.[56]

Following criticism, the form has been altered again.[57] However, it remains eleven pages long, and uses internal jargon. For example, the very first question (after personal details) is this:

Type of case

Complete this section if either:

1. You are applying for Controlled Work services.

2. You have not completed type of case details on page 5 of CIVAPP1 or page 3 of CIVAPP3.

3. The type of category is not listed on CIVAPP1 or CIVAPP3.

While there is accompanying guidance, it is far from user-friendly. How likely is that a person without any legal knowledge or background would be able to complete this question? Legal aid is not available to make an application under s 10 (although costs can be backdated where it is successful), meaning that a litigant in person would need to write this or a solicitor firm needs to operate *pro bono* while they assist someone to make that application.

11.3.1.2 Inquests

In recent years one of the more controversial examples of legal aid restrictions has been inquests, particularly in high-profile cases.

An inquest is a formal hearing that takes place in a coroner's court to ascertain the identity of a deceased and how their death arose. An inquest is normally required where the death was violent or unnatural, sudden or of unknown cause, or when the person who died was a prisoner of the state. Coroner's courts were mentioned briefly in Chapter 6, and differ from most of the courts of England and Wales in that they are inquisitorial in nature.

In recent years, a coroners' inquiry has sometimes been replaced, or superseded, by a judicial inquiry. This is the case where there are multiple deaths, and it is thought that circumstances beyond that which an inquest could investigate is necessary. A good example of this is the inquiry that is ongoing into the Manchester Arena attack at the time of writing.[58]

> **Example** Manchester Arena
>
> On 22 May 2017, Salman Abedi committed a suicide attack on the Manchester Arena, that was hosting a pop concert. In addition to the attacker, twenty-two people lost their lives, including children.

56. ibid, at [55].
57. It is available here: <https://assets.publishing.service.gov.uk/government/uploads/system/uploads/attachment_data/file/879163/CIVECF1_form_fillable.pdf>.
58. See <https://manchesterarenainquiry.org.uk/>.

An inquest was initially opened but it was thought that its powers would be limited. An inquest is primarily there to ascertain who the deceased were, the time of the death, the cause of death (sadly, obvious in most instances here), and the circumstances of their death.

The assistant coroner who was appointed for this inquest (Sir John Saunders, a former High Court judge), decided that the rules of an inquest would not allow for an investigation into why the attack happened, and whether opportunities were missed. He stated that Article 2 of the ECHR required a fuller investigation, and recommended a judicial inquiry instead. The Home Secretary agreed, and the Manchester Arena Inquiry now has fuller powers to investigate the attack.

Inquiries, as with inquests, are inquisitorial rather than adversarial. This causes a difficulty because the government and Legal Aid Agency then question whether families of the bereaved, or those who were injured in attacks, require legal representation. The argument is that the coroner or presiding judge (for an inquiry) should be able to ensure that the proceedings are understandable to those who are not represented. While that may be true, there can be little doubt that having legal representation can be useful, not least as it can help focus the questions being asked, and suggest new avenues to be examined, and better questions to be asked of witnesses. Indeed, that is why many parties to an inquest come legally represented, and it is this which causes the problem.

At several inquests or inquiries, the relevant public bodies will be represented by counsel, often Queen's Counsel. These are state bodies, and thus the state is ultimately paying for them to be represented at the inquest or inquiry. At the same time, however, the state refuses to give public money (in the form of legal aid) to family members. This has the appearance of both a conflict of interest and unfairness. The state will pay for the best legal representation to save itself from the questions of the family while, at the same time, not providing legal assistance to those same families.

Article 2 of the ECHR protects the right to life (see 5.4.2). This is both a substantive right ('the state will not kill') but also a procedural right, ie that Article 2 provides the right to an effective investigation as to the circumstances in which a person was killed. This is generally where there is an allegation that the state has failed to protect a person and is particularly relevant to deaths in custody, but can also apply to the suicide of people who should be under its care.[59] There is not an automatic right, but the extent to which an individual could properly participate in an inquest without legal assistance is a matter that must be taken into account.[60]

Example Molly Russell

Molly Russell was aged 14 when she committed suicide after looking at self-harm websites. Considerable disquiet arose form the case, and it was used as an example of how social media can be negatively impacting children.

---

59. The principle is discussed in *R (on the application of Letts) v Lord Chancellor* [2015] EWHC 402 (Admin).
60. *R (on the application of Khan) v Secretary of State for Health* [2003] EWCA Civ 1129.

A coroners inquest was to be held, and this was going to look at how social media firms protected children from inappropriate content. Not unsurprisingly, it became clear that the large social media firms would be represented at the inquest by senior counsel, potentially including QCs.

Molly's family asked for legal aid to be represented at the inquest. They were initially turned down because of the usual rule that families did not need legal representation. Article 2 is not engaged against the state either. The decision led to considerable disquiet. They appealed and this time the LAA provided assistance.

There is no doubt that Molly's family would have been at a disadvantage if they had not received legal assistance. The case also demonstrates a fallacy in the argument. How can grief-stricken parents be expected to act dispassionately in a court of law?

An official review of legal aid at inquests rejected the suggestion that there should be automatic legal aid even when the state is represented by a lawyer.[61] The Ministry of Justice argued that providing legal aid 'could have the unintended consequence of undermining the inquisitorial nature of the inquest system'.[62] It is difficult to accept that point. Surely it would not be legal aid that has the potential to undermine the inquisitorial system. It would, on that logic, be legal representation that undermines the inquisitorial approach. There has, however, been no serious suggestion that legal representation should be withdrawn from coroner's courts.

11.3.2 Eligibility

The mere fact that a case comes within Schedule 1 does not mean that it will receive legal aid. Before granting legal aid, the LAA will need to consider both means-testing and the merits of the case. As will be seen, these tests are very strict and it has been estimated that 62 per cent of people who were eligible for legal aid prior to LASPOA are no longer eligible.[63]

11.3.2.1 Means test

As with criminal legal aid, the principal limitation on funding is a person's means. The eligibility requirements are set out in a statutory instrument,[64] and are somewhat complicated. Indeed, the guides that are produced to explain the eligibility *to solicitors* is forty pages long for family matters and 141 pages long for general work.[65]

Where a person is in receipt of certain benefits, there is no requirement to means-test their income, although their capital needs to be assessed.[66] This is because the income

---

61. Ministry of Justice, *Review of Legal Aid for Inquests* (TSO 2019) 10–11.
62. ibid, 11.
63. Asher Flynn and Jacqueline Hodgson, 'Access to Justice and Legal Aid Cuts: A Mismatch of Concepts in the Contemporary Australian and British Legal Landscapes' in Asher Flynn and Jacqueline Hodgson (eds), *Access to Justice & Legal Aid: Comparative Perspectives on Unmet Legal Need* (Hart Publishing 2017) 1.
64. *Legal Aid (Financial Resources and Payment for Services) Regulations 2013*, SI 2013/480. The regulations have been amended a number of times.
65. Both guides are available at <https://www.gov.uk/guidance/civil-legal-aid-means-testing>.
66. SI 2013/480, reg 6(2).

threshold to receive these benefits are sufficiently low to automatically meet the legal aid means-test. The benefits include:

- income support
- income-based job seekers allowance
- income-related employment and support allowance
- universal credit

For all others, both their income and capital need to be assessed. Where a person has a partner, their income and capital must be assessed and treated as though it is accessible by the applicant.[67] 'Partner' has a wide definition:

(a) an individual's spouse or civil partner, from whom the individual is not separated due to a breakdown in the relationship which is likely to be permanent

(b) a person with whom the individual lives as a couple

(c) a person with whom the individual ordinarily lives as a couple, from whom they are not separated due to a breakdown in the relationship which is likely to be permanent.[68]

Technically, there is no legal obligation for unmarried couples to support each other, but the rule is obviously designed to ensure that people do not escape liability by simply residing with each other and not marrying. What constitutes 'living together' or a temporary breakdown in the relationship is not defined in the regulations, and is, presumably, for the LAA to determine.

Where the applicant (including their partner) have a *gross* income above £2,657 per month then they are ineligible. Gross income is before any deductions for tax, national insurance, etc. This equates to a salary of £31,884. This is higher than the average UK salary for women (approximately £22,000) but less than the average UK salary for men (approximately £32,000). Where the income is less than this then tax and national insurance etc are deducted. Deductions for legal aid contributions (eg from criminal proceedings) are also deducted, presumably because otherwise there is a risk that the LAA would not recover money owed to it.

The regulations recognize that where a person is paying maintenance for a former partner or a child (or, presumably, both) then a 'reasonable deduction' should be made.[69] It is notable that they do not state that the maintenance payments will be deducted, only that a reasonable deduction will be made. Where a court has ordered these maintenance payments (including, presumably, in a consent order) it would presumably be difficult for the LAA to decide that such rates were 'not reasonable' but there is nothing in the regulations to say this.

After this, housing costs are deducted. This is the net rent or mortgage payment. Where someone is not formally renting or paying a mortgage, the maximum housing costs are £545 per month. This could include, for example, an adult who is still living in the parental home. It is unlikely that such an adult would pay formal rent, but they may be paying a sum to the parent to take account of the fact that they continue to reside at home.

---

67. ibid, reg 16.
68. ibid, reg 1.
69. ibid, reg 26.

Set payments are then deducted as follows:

Description	Amount per month (£)
Employment-related expenses.[70]	45
Partner	181.41
Child aged 15 or under	290.70
Child aged 16 or over[71]	290.70

Note that this 'disposable income' does not take account of any outstanding loans or finance (eg car finance), nor does it include shopping or clothes etc. The latter are considered to come out of the fixed 'allowances' given for the partner and children. Similarly, travel costs are not considered. While £45 is given for 'employment-related expenses', that is just over £10 per week. Most travel to work is likely to be in excess of this.

☰ Example Means-testing

Sheila is applying for legal aid in respect of a dispute. Sheila lives with her wife, Alison. Sheila has a 10-year-old son and a 12-year-old daughter from her previous marriage. Sheila has an income of £28,000 per year, and Alison has an income of £9,000 per year. Sheila pays £250 to her former husband as spousal maintenance. Sheila and Alison own a house and pay £680 per month in mortgage payments.

Sheila's income will be £22,578 after tax and NI, meaning £1,881 per month. Alison's income will be £8,956 or £746 per month. Thus, their monthly income is £2,627. They are therefore *just* under the £2,657 limit.

Sheila's expenses are the mortgage (£680), plus the £45 per month as 'employment-related' expenses. An allowance of £181.41 is given for Alison and £581.40 for the two children. The maintenance payment of £250 to her former wife will also be included. Thus, her expenditure totals £1,737.81.

Her disposable income is considered to be £889.19.

Where a person's disposable income exceeds £733 per month, as in Sheila's case, then funding must be refused as it fails to meet the means test. This is a very low cap. £733 per month equates to approximately £170 per week. Given how few expenses are discounted when considering the cap (including finance costs, clothes, costs of running a car etc.) then it seems unrealistic. It undoubtedly means that the average person will be ineligible for legal aid.

Where they meet the income threshold, there is then a capital threshold. All capital held by an individual, including capital that is achieved through loans, must be counted.[72] Where the capital is not cash then it must be valued by what it could be

---

70. Where a person is an employee, this should be deducted to take account of incidental expenses that will be incurred in respect of employment: ibid, reg 27.
71. Although 'child' means someone under the age of 18.
72. SI 2013/480, reg 30.

realized for.[73] Presumably in respect of, for example, cars and houses this would not be what the advertised sale price would be, but would instead be what realistic sum could be achieved through disposal.[74] Furniture within a house, personal clothing, and the tools of trade are not to be considered disposable income, save where they are exceptionally valuable. So, for example, while ordinary furniture would not count, the fact that someone had an antique clock worth £50,000 may be considered relevant (of course, where this is a family heirloom, it is likely to be of concern to the applicant that they may be forced to sell it).

There are a number of relatively complicated rules surrounding property, land, and businesses, but for our purposes we do not need to worry about what these are, save to understand that these are valued and would constitute capital. However, this is subject to allowances. So, for example, if there is a mortgage on the property then an allowance of the mortgage or £100,000 is allowed, whichever is the smaller. The first £100,000 of the remaining capital is also offset. It does mean, however, that someone with a house worth over c. £250,000 is likely to be considered to have capital irrespective of how much mortgage is actually held against the house.

Where a person has disposable capital exceeding £8,000 then they will not meet the means test irrespective of whether they meet the income threshold. Where someone does not own a house, this could mean that somebody with either modest savings or a reasonable car (that is no longer financed) will be denied legal aid.

11.3.2.2 Merits of the case

If a person does 'pass' the means test, it is then necessary to consider the merits of the proposed case. Again, the test is set out in statutory instrument.[75] Some proceedings are not subject to the merits test, most notably public childcare proceedings and abduction proceedings.[76]

The merits of a case are referenced as the 'prospects of success', which means 'the likelihood that an individual who has made an application for civil legal services will obtain a successful outcome at a trial or other final hearing . . .'.[77] In other words, how likely it is that the party will 'win'. In determining this, prospects are categorized accordingly as set out in Table 11.1.[78]

Table 11.1 Prospects of success

Category	Likelihood (%)
Very good	80+
Good	60–79
Moderate	50–59
Borderline	Unclear or c 50.
Marginal	45–50
Poor	<45

73. ibid, reg 31.
74. ibid, reg 34.
75. *The Civil Legal Aid (Merits Criteria) Regulations 2013*, SI 2013/104 as amended.
76. ibid, reg 11(9).
77. ibid, reg 4(1).
78   ibid, reg 5(1).

The merits test will only be satisfied if the prospects of success are at least moderate, ie that it is more likely than not that the case will succeed. Perhaps that would seem logical: why would the law provide assistance when it is likely that a person will lose, but it has been noted that one difficulty with a merits test is that it almost automatically rules out any challenge to existing law.[79] As noted in Chapter 3 courts are bound by precedent. Therefore, if a case seeks to challenge a decision of the Court of Appeal then the initial litigation in the High Court will have no prospects for success as the High Court is bound by the Court of Appeal. This could be important where a precedent does not consider the nuances of a particular situation. Chapter 13 provides a good example of this. In that chapter, the issue of assisted dying will be discussed, in particular whether someone should be prosecuted for helping a spouse die (see 13.1.1.4). When the first judicial review was brought, the law was clear: assisted suicide is a criminal offence, and so the merits were negligible. Yet, as will be seen, the litigators won, and the position is now more nuanced.

Even where the probability test is satisfied, there is public-interest criteria that must be satisfied in respect of different types of litigation. This is to ensure that there is a real need to litigate and that it could not be dealt with differently. The complexity of the criteria is beyond the scope of this book.

11.4 Legal aid as a human right

This chapter is entitled funding access to justice, and it is deliberately called this. The legal system is supposed to allow a litigator the right to justice in resolving a dispute. While there will sometimes be trivial matters litigated, the Secret Barrister notes:

> The circumstances in which you might need legal assistance are often those you would rather not contemplate. A sobering rule of thumb is that, if you are seeking legal help or representation, something in your life has most likely not gone to plan.[80]

This is undoubtedly true. While businesses may litigate for commercial reasons, the reality is that most ordinary people only see the inside of a courtroom when things have gone wrong, something particularly true when it is a criminal court.

Where someone cannot afford a lawyer during one of those bad points in life, it raises questions about whether a person is denied access to justice in these circumstances. Access to justice is considered a fundamental part of the legal system. While the Magna Carta is invariably misquoted, particularly around trial by jury (something discussed in Chapter 14, it prized the concept of access to justice, and it is now considered to be a fundamental part of the rule of law.[81]

Of course, it would be difficult to argue that legal aid is part of the rule of law. As noted earlier in this chapter, legal aid in England and Wales has only existed for less than 100 years, and it has gone through many different changes during that time.

---

79. Natalie Byrom, 'Cuts to Civil Legal Aid and the Identity Crisis in Lawyering: Lessons from the Experience of England and Wales' in Asher Flynn and Jacqueline Hodgson (eds), *Access to Justice & Legal Aid: Comparative Perspectives on Unmet Legal Need* (Hart Publishing 2017) 223.

80. Secret Barrister, *Fake Law: The Truth About Justice in an Age of Lies* (Picador 2020) 166.

81. A powerful discussion is put forward by Lord Bingham, who held the three top judicial posts. See Tom Bingham, *The Rule of Law* (Penguin UK 2011).

However, it has begun to be questioned whether legal aid should be considered a fundamental human right. To an extent, we have already discussed one aspect of this when it was noted that Article 2 requires some families to now be given legal aid for inquests (see 11.3.1.2). However, could a wider right to legal aid be framed?

11.4.1 **Criminal trials**

It may be thought that it would be easier to establish a right to legal aid in respect of criminal trials. The consequences of a conviction can be significant. There are reputational and economic consequences, and, depending on the crime, the defendant's liberty is at risk. Any argument would need to be based on the fact that a lack of legal representation infringes Article 6. While Article 6(1) guarantees a fair trial, Article 6(3) provides specific rights for defendants, including:

> to defend himself in person or through legal assistance of his own choosing or, if he has not sufficient means to pay for legal assistance, to be given it free when the interests of justice so require.[82]

Thus, there is an express reference to legal assistance being given free. However, it is not an absolute right because it is qualified by the statement, 'when the interests of justice so require'. Note, it refers to free legal advice, and not partial contributions, although the government would no doubt argue that the interests of justice should take account of means, and also point towards the statement that the right applies only where 'he has not sufficient means'.

The right exists from the moment of arrest,[83] and it will be seen in Chapter 12 that this happens in England and Wales where, ironically, it is easier to get free legal advice upon arrest than it is to get it for representation at trial. The ECtHR has not ruled on what 'has not sufficient means' is to mean, and most of its jurisprudence has been relating to the interests of justice. Again, access to justice is at the heart of such decisions. The rule of law is considered to require accessibility, and this is a concept that is seen when then ECtHR rules over whether crimes are certain.[84] Where a matter is so complex that a lay person is unlikely to understand the process, or be able to defend themselves, then the interests of justice require legal aid to be provided.[85]

Perhaps unsurprisingly, the type of sentence that can be imposed is widely considered to be a key factor in identifying the interests of justice. For example, a likely custodial sentence will invariably be sufficient to require legal assistance.[86] Again, this is perhaps unsurprising because the deprivation of liberty is one of the most serious punishments that the state can inflict on a person. Again, it should be noted that a possible custodial sentence is one of the factors used by the Legal Aid Agency in the criminal merits test.

While some may argue that LASPOA 2012 infringes human rights, there is little appetite from the courts to rule accordingly. The terms of Article 6(3)(c) appear to map onto LASPOA 2012, particularly in the absence of an understanding of what insufficient means are. The English courts have never ruled the rules are a breach of

---

82. ECHR, Art 6(3)(c).
83. David Harris et al, *Harris, O'Boyle and Warbrick Law of the European Convention on Human Rights* (4th edn, OUP 2018) 473.
84. ECHR, Art 7. See 5.4.6.
85. *Granger v United Kingdom* (1990) 12 EHRR 469.
86. *Quaranta v Switzerland* A 205 (1991).

human rights. While they clearly dislike the cuts in many instances,[87] they have not held that it infringes the rule of law. Indeed, the High Court has ruled that the rule which prohibits defendants recovering the full costs of their defence (discussed at 11.2.2.2) is not a breach of human rights.[88]

A final, but important, point was made by the Divisional Court in *R (on the application of Ames) v Lord Chancellor*[89] which concerned a dispute between counsel and the legal aid agency at the rate at which they should be remunerated for a very high costs case. While the Divisional Court held against the Lord Chancellor on some points, the judges stated:

> Article 6 does not give an accused person an unqualified right to select the advocates of his choice . . . there is no evidence on which the court could find that no competent advocates would be willing to take the case at the fees offered by the LAA.[90]

Article 6(3)(c) states that a defendant has the right to counsel of his choice, but that precedes the sentence on legal aid. In other words, a defendant has the right to choose to pay privately whichever counsel he wishes, but when the state is providing legal aid, that right does not exist.

11.4.2 **Civil trials**

What is the position in civil trials? This is an area where the judiciary have perhaps been even more vocal, suggesting that the cuts are harming the operation of the courts.[91] However, that is very different from suggesting that there is a right to legal aid. Civil trials are not covered by Article 6(3)(c), ECHR, and the only basis of argument would be that civil legal aid comes within Article 6(1), which provides the overarching right to a fair trial.

The first case of note before the ECtHR to discuss civil legal aid was *Airey v Ireland*.[92] This was a case where a woman sought judicial separation from her husband, who had been physically abusive towards her. She had no means to pay for court proceedings or a solicitor to represent her in court. She claimed that the state should pay for such matters. The ECtHR accepted that Article 6 could require state aid in certain circumstances. They noted that if there was no access to court then the rights an individual possesses become almost illusionary. The ECtHR, having regard to the complexity of the law and practice of the High Court at that time, ruled that a litigant in person would not be able to present their case effectively, and that this breached Article 6.

Airey thus set an important precedent, but it did not mean that legal aid had to be provided in all circumstances. One approach to the judgment would be to make proceedings accessible. It was the complexity of proceedings that led the ECtHR to conclude that Article 6 had been breached. Where proceedings can be more readily explained then Article 6 may not be triggered. Also, the fact that these were proceedings to protect an individual from violence was almost certainly a factor.[93]

87. See, for example, the Judge's Council response to the consultation that led to LASPOA at <https://www.judiciary.uk/wp-content/uploads/JCO/Documents/Consultations/response-judges-council-legal-aid-reform-consultation.pdf>.

88. *R (on the application of Henderson) v Secretary of State for Justice* [2015] EWHC 130 (Admin).

89. [2018] EWHC 2250 (Admin).

90. [2018] EWHC 2250 (Admin) at [80].

91. See, for example, 'Legal aid: UK's top judge says cuts caused "serious difficulty"' (BBC News, 27 December 2019).

92. (1979) 2 EHRR 305.

93. Something reinforced by the fact that the ECtHR also found a violation of Article 8 (right to respect of private and family life).

The limits of Article 6 are perhaps best illustrated by the case of *Steel and Morris v United Kingdom*,[94] which again related to whether the complexity of proceedings could constitute a breach of human rights.

III\ Case Box Steel and Morris v United Kingdom: The 'McLibel' case

Steel and Morris v United Kingdom marked the end of one of the most interesting legal campaigns to have been fought in recent times. Steel and Morris were two environmental campaigners who handed out leaflets outside a McDonalds restaurant which made various claims about the nutrition of McDonalds burgers and the way in which the company performed its operations.

McDonalds decided to sue Steel and Morris for libel. They were represented by a high-profile legal team led by Richard Rampton QC whereas Steel and Morris could not afford representation. Legal aid was not available for defamation actions (either as a defendant or claimant) and thus they had to represent themselves. The trial judge (Bell J) assisted them in some of the technical rules relating to the litigation but they were otherwise responsible for their own litigation. By popular assent it was considered that Steel and Morris performed extremely well in court and possibly even better than some lawyers!

However, the absence of funding did cause significant problems. The cost of transcribing each day's proceedings was £750 which they could not afford. Initially McDonalds provided the transcripts to the respondents without charge but this was withdrawn because Steel and Morris refused to provide an undertaking that they would only use it for the purposes of court proceedings and not for publicity etc. There were over 20,000 documents produced and many of the factual and legal issues were extremely complicated. It was suggested that without proper assistance they could not adequately prepare their defence.

The litigation undertaken before the domestic courts was extremely complicated and indeed at the time this was one of the longest cases that had taken place before the courts (although this may in part be as a result of only one side having legal representation) but the quantity of written materials produced together with the number of ancillary proceedings and witnesses examined meant that realistically both Steel and Morris were at a disadvantage compared to McDonalds in the exercise of the litigation. The ECtHR stated that a fundamental part of Article 6(1) is the right to equality of arms; in other words in order for both sides to receive a fair trial they should ordinarily be in roughly the same position in terms of access to the law. The ECtHR stated that during this litigation, because legal aid was not permitted, there was an inequality of arms and that this was caused, at least in part, by the state, thus creating a breach of Article 6.[95]

399

Steel and Morris is simply a further extension of *Airey*. There is no doubt that libel proceedings in the High Court are extremely complicated, and the representation afforded by McDonalds meant there was an imbalance of power. However, the limits of the decision should again be noted. The ECtHR did not say that Steel and Morris should have been given legal aid. They ruled that the blanket refusal to provide legal aid to defend legal proceedings was a breach of Article 6.

---

94.   (2005) 41 EHRR 22.
95.   That said, it has been noted that this decision was a departure from the usual jurisprudence of the ECtHR, and that this may have been due to the 'strong and sympathetic facts': David Harris et al, *Harris, O'Boyle and Warbrick Law of the European Convention on Human Rights* (4th edn, OUP 2018) 402.

The decision is one reason for the existence of s 10 LASPOA 2012 (which provides that cases not falling within sch 1 can still receive legal aid). Section 10 arguably meets the test for Article 6 by providing the ability to request legal aid in exceptional circumstances. Despite the belief of many that access to justice has been undermined by LASPOA, it would seem unlikely that a credible case can be made that there is a definitive and enforceable right to legal aid, at least in respect of civil litigation. There is a stronger argument that can be made in criminal proceedings,[96] but that is partly due to the fact that Article 6 is stronger in respect of criminal trials.

11.5 Alternative funding arrangements

The reduction in legal aid has meant that, at least in civil cases, alternative means of funding litigation must be found. This chapter does not pretend to put forward a comprehensive analysis of all the ways that civil litigation can be funded, but there are three of note:

- conditional fee arrangements (sometimes known as 'no win, no fee')
- before the event insurance (where insurance is taken out to cover the cost of future litigation)
- third-party funding (where a third-party provides the finance, with that party taking some of the damages).

Of course, the government and, increasingly, the courts would note that litigation is not inevitable and that prior to litigating, claimants should seek to use Alternative Dispute Resolutions (see Chapter 19). The reality, however, is that a considerable amount will continue to be the subject of litigation.

11.5.1 Conditional fee arrangements

Perhaps the most common form of alternative funding arrangement is that which is popularly known as 'no-win, no-fee', but which is more properly known as a 'conditional fee arrangement' (CFA).

CFAs came into existence because of reforms put forward in the *Courts and Legal Services Act 1990*, but it was the *Access to Justice Act 1999* (AJA 1999) that led to their increased use because they became attractive to lawyers and litigants. Put briefly, a conditional fee arrangement is an agreement whereby a solicitor will not seek payment if they lose the case, but if they win a case, they will expect to receive more than they would usually charge for a case of that kind. The AJA 1999 allowed this additional fee to be recoverable from the other party (as in civil proceedings, the loser normally pays all costs). Thus, litigants were offered the opportunity to litigate without risk of costs, and still receive full compensation. As will be seen, this has now changed, but CFAs remain a popular form of litigation because they arguably carry with them less risk than private litigation, where there is a risk of costs when losing.

---

96. Article 6(3)(c) expressly refers to the ability to 'defend himself in person or through legal assistance of his own choosing or, if he has not sufficient means to pay for legal assistance, to be given it free when the interests of justice so require . . .'. That does not mean that there is an absolute right to legal aid, but certainly the closing words suggest that there will be occasions when a person should be given legal aid to defend themselves from serious crime.

⚡ **NO WIN, NO (OR SOME) FEE**

A sues B for negligence on a contingency fee basis. A loses. B is allowed to claim the costs of defending the action from A. While A's lawyers will not charge A for his fees, A is still liable for the fees of B. Most CFAs will require A to take out an insurance policy that will pay out if A loses. Some solicitors will waive the cost of the premium (paying it themselves), but others will not, meaning that A will be responsible for the premium of that insurance policy.

CFAs were/are attractive to lawyers because although there is a risk that they may lose a case, if they choose cases wisely this should be a managed risk. Providing 'free' legal services mean that more people are likely to litigate, as those who could not otherwise afford it will do so. As a solicitor can charge more than the fees than they would otherwise charge, they are 'rewarded' when they win the case.

However, CFAs were also controversial because the 'success fee' (ie the additional costs that are levied) were entitled to be up to 100 per cent of the costs. This meant that the losing side of litigation could be unfairly penalized, even in circumstances where they were not challenging liability.

📋 **Example** Contingency fees

Vanessa sues Lowprices Ltd, her local supermarket, because she slipped on a spill that they negligently failed to clean up. Vanessa suffers a broken arm and collarbone.

Vanessa approaches Sue, Grabbit & Run, a local firm of solicitors, who agree to take the matter on a contingency fee basis. Vanessa paid £20 per month insurance (for the twenty months the matter lasts for) to protect her from costs in the event of 'losing'. The success fee was set at 100 per cent.

Lowprices Ltd admitted liability although questioned the value of the claim. Vanessa was awarded £12,000 in damages.

Lowprices Ltd were liable to pay the following:

Compensation	£12,000
Vanessa's Legal Fees	£4,300
Vanessa's Insurance Premiums	£400
Success Fee	£4,300
Their Legal Fees	£5,200
Total	£26,200

If Vanessa had paid privately, they would only be liable to pay £21,500.

Inevitably challenges were made to CFAs, arguing that they were inappropriate. One of the first legal challenges was *King v Telegraph Group Ltd*[97] where the Court of Appeal was asked to declare that a 100 per cent success fee was unfair, and, in the context of

---

97. [2005] 1 WLR 2282.

a defamation action constituted a breach of Article 10 ECHR. The court rejected these arguments but noted that there was the potential for unfairness. However, they ruled that Parliament had provided for these schemes and the court must acquiesce to their use when mandated by Parliament. That said, in *Campbell v Mirror Group Newspapers (Costs)*[98] the House of Lords warned that the use of CFAs can have a chilling effect on litigation, recognizing that it meant litigation could become a weapon to frighten a defendant into settling inappropriately.[99]

The courts did have the power to mitigate the potential unfairness primarily through the use of a costs cap. This is a rule whereby the costs payable by the losing side are limited to a prescribed sum, in essence limiting the amount of 'success fee'. In *Henry v BBC (Costs Capping)*[100] the Court of Appeal recognized that CFAs could create a situation where the matters were so unequal between the parties that it would be unreasonable to allow the uplift and thus a cap could be imposed (although in that case no cap was imposed because any cap must be prospective and not retrospective). However, the courts were slow to exercise this power, in part because Parliament was clear that CFAs, including a 100 per cent success fee (the level having been set by Parliament), could be used.

There was particular disquiet on how CFAs impacted public authorities. In late 2010 the Metropolitan Police Commissioner wrote to the Home Secretary to complain about the manner in which compensation is awarded for police misconduct. The reaction to this was extremely negative, with it being presented that the police were seeking to avoid responsibility for their errors, but their argument was partly true. The costs of claims against the police were inflated as a result of CFAs. Where, therefore, the police decide to defend a claim or refuse to pay the compensation sought by the claimant, there was a risk that the police ended up paying the costs of defending the litigation, plus the costs incurred and an additional uplift. As they have a finite pot of money, those costs would invariably mean that less could be spent on policing.

While it is true that it could have an adverse impact on public-sector bodies (the NHS was similarly impacted because the costs of clinical negligence cases can amount to hundreds of thousands of pounds, so a 100 per cent success fee could be crippling), it does not alter the basic premise of the CFA. That is, the lawyer has taken the risk of not being paid if the litigation is not successful. To justify the reduction in legal aid, the CFA was seen as an incentive to provide access to justice. Treating the public and private sector differently would be inappropriate. However, as in the example of Lowprices Ltd given earlier, it is clear that a CFA leads to the defendant having to pay potentially twice the fees of a claimant, not as a result of a fault on their side, but because the claimant used a CFA.

11.5.1.1 Variable CFAs

An interesting variation on CFAs arose in *Gloucestershire County Council v Evans*.[101] Although the standard CFA is premised on the basis that you do not pay anything if you lose, the AJA 1999 does not state that this is the premise of a CFA. In the *Evans* case, the county council reached an agreement with solicitors about the cost of litigation. The basic hourly charge was £145 per hour, and a success fee of 100 per cent would be

---

98. [2005] UKHL 61.
99. ibid, at [31].
100. [2006] 1 All ER 154.
101. [2008] EWCA Civ 21.

payable if the council won. However, if the council lost, then the solicitors would only charge the council £95 per hour. In other words, this CFA was not a 'no-win, no-fee' but a 'no-win, lesser fee' arrangement.

When the council won, the losing party appealed against the order of the costs judge that they were liable for the success fee. Their principal argument was that the correct figure was £95 per hour, and, therefore, if a 100 per cent success rate was levied then they should be liable to pay £190 per hour and not the £290 per hour that was being claimed.

The Court of Appeal rejected this contention and noted that the legislation was clear. A success fee was payable on the costs incurred by the winning party. The agreement clearly stated that these fees would be £145 and thus a 100 per cent uplift was permitted. If the solicitors were prepared to accept a lesser amount when they lost (but not the 'no fee' that ordinarily would be given) then this was a matter for them. To an extent this may seem a surprising decision since it would appear to alter the risk/benefit ratio at the heart of CFAs. The solicitors were taking the risk that they would recover a lower fee than their standard charge but this is arguably a lower risk than not being paid at all.

A criticism of CFAs was that solicitors sometimes only allowed them to be used in cases where there was a high probability of success (since otherwise they risk not receiving their fees). Variable fees arguably make cases with a lower probability of success more attractive, as a lawyer will still recoup some of the costs that are expended on litigating.

11.5.1.2 CFAs and LASPOA 2012

Jackson LJ was asked to prepare a report on the costs of litigation and one of the issues that he was asked to look at was the CFA scheme and whether it leads to injustices. The Labour government had previously attempted to reduce the 'success fee' from 100 per cent to 10 per cent but had dropped the proposal after concerns that it would lead to lawyers simply refusing to take cases.

Jackson LJ's report led to the suggestion that there should be a marked shift in the CFA scheme.[102] He agreed that the CFA scheme could be problematic and he recommended that allowing for the insurance premiums and success fee to be claimed from the loser is inappropriate. He preferred the system whereby the costs are recovered from the compensation awarded although he recommended that this should be subject to a cap of 25 per cent.

These plans were taken forward by LASPOA 2012 and, in effect, merge CFAs with damages-based agreements, something that was previously only permitted in employment law. Section 44 continues to authorize CFAs but only if they are made in such a way that complies with conditions, some of which are contained in the statute and others in regulations to be made under the Act. The most significant condition is that any success fee must be expressed as a percentage of damages and will be subject to a limit set by regulations.[103] For personal injury cases this cap has been set at 25 per cent[104] but for other litigation it remains at 100 per cent.[105]

---

102. Lord Justice Jackson, *Review of Civil Litigation Costs: Final Report* (HMSO 2010).
103. *Courts and Legal Services Act 1990*, s 58(4B).
104. *The Conditional Fee Agreements Order 2013*, SI 2013/689, reg 5(1)(a).
105. ibid, reg 3.

LASPOA then carried forward Jackson LJs recommendations by transforming the way that the success fee is paid. Section 58A(6), *Courts and Legal Services Act 1990* states:

> A costs order made in proceedings may not include provision requiring the payment by one party of all or part of a success fee payable by another party under a conditional fee arrangement.

In other words, the losing party now no longer pays the success fee. Any success fee comes from the damages. Section 58C then states that the insurance premiums for the insurance usually required by CFAs are not normally recoverable, although it remains recoverable for certain clinical negligence cases, partly due to the high costs that are incurred in such litigation.

What are the implications of this? Let us return to the Lowprices Ltd example given at 11.5.1.

Example Lowprices Ltd rerun

It will be remembered that Vanessa slipped on a spillage within the shop. The store was found liable. The relevant sums were:

Compensation	£12,000
Vanessa's Legal Fees	£4,300
Vanessa's Insurance Premiums	£400
Success Fee	£4,300
Their Legal Fees	£5,200

Under the old rules, Vanessa would receive all of the £12,000 compensation and the £400 for insurance premiums. Her solicitor would receive £8,600 in fees (£4,300 plus the success fee £4,300).

Let us assume that Vanessa arranges a CFA. The solicitors agree to charge a 75% success fee. As it is a personal injury claim, the fee cannot exceed 25% of damages. The fees charged by Vanessa's solicitors are £4,300 and so the 75% success fee would be £3,325. However, 25% of the damages is £3,000 so the cap will apply.

Vanessa will receive:

Compensation	£12,000
Less	
Insurance premiums	£400
Success Fee	£3,000
Amount receivable	£8,600

Her solicitors will receive £7,300 (her fees and the success fee). LowPrices Ltd will pay a total of £21,500 (compensation, Vanessa's fees plus their fees).

Thus, Vanessa receives £3,800 less than she would have under the old regime. Lowprices Ltd pay the same amount of money regardless of whether Vanessa is privately funded or not. That would seem fairer to Lowprices Ltd but is it fair for Vanessa? If Margaret also fell on the same spillage and suffered the same injuries, but she could afford to pay privately, she would receive £3,000 more compensation than Vanessa. Yet the injuries were the same. The argument is that Vanessa is not carrying any risk. The solicitors are. That could mean that the success fee should vary depending on the strength of the claim, but there is no evidence that this is happening particularly frequently, with 'standard' success fees being used by many claim firms.

It has been suggested that 'it was not intended that claimant's recoverable damages should be reduced'[106] and the courts have slightly increased compensation awards, but not by enough to offset the fees. Certainly, it has been suggested that (after the event insurance, unrecovered costs (not all CFAs will cover all costs)) then some claimants are receiving only 60% of the damages that they would have recovered.[107]

QUESTION FOR REFLECTION

Are CFAs now fairer post-LASPOA 2012? Have we not now created a situation whereby someone without means is punished for not having the means to pay privately for litigation? Legal aid has been heavily restricted, meaning CFAs are often the only recourse. Why is it fair that someone who has the means to pay privately will receive more money than someone who does not?

The counter argument, of course, is why should the defendant be liable to pay more to someone who cannot afford to pay privately (which was the position pre-LASPOA)?

11.5.2 Third-party funding

A relatively recent form of funding is third-party funding (TPF). This is not dissimilar to CFAs in that it is an exchange of fees for a percentage of damages, but it is not the solicitor who takes the risk here, it is the third-party. They are normally used in high-value litigation, and are, in essence, a speculative investment.

Example Third party funding

Garion Enterprises Ltd has a patent on a particular device. SeqTearan plc are alleged to have infringed this patent when producing their most popular electronic device. Garion Enterprises Ltd is owned by two individuals and the turnover is currently less than £50,000 per year. It is estimated the patent infringement could be worth £80m.

Garion Enterprises Ltd approaches an investment fund. They offer to pay up to £3m in legal costs in return for 20 per cent of any damages received. Garion Enterprises Ltd uses a specialist broker to find insurance to cover the fees of SeqTearan plc if they lose.

---

106. Paul Fenn, David Marshall and Neil Rickman, 'The Impact of Legislation on the Outcomes of Civil Litigation: An Empircal Analysis of the Lega Aid, Sentencing and Punishment of Offenders Act 2012' [2019] *Journal of Personal Injury Law* 285, 296.
107. ibid.

In the example above, it is highly unlikely that any legal firm would offer a traditional CFA. The costs could easily be in the millions for both sides. Losing the case could bankrupt a firm so a traditional CFA is not an option, although as will be seen, variable CFAs sometimes play a role.

Let us assume the chance of success for Garion Enterprises Ltd is estimated at 75 per cent. For the venture capital firm, they are, in essence, betting £3 million against a 3-in-4 chance of receiving £19 million (the £3 million investment (i.e. the fees[108]) plus their share of the damages). Few investment opportunities would offer that level of return with that level of risk. It can, therefore, be extremely attractive, and it has been noted that this is now a 'thriving and lucrative' industry.[109]

TPF is often used in conjunction with variable CFAs whereby the solicitors engaged by the TPF offer to discount their 'standard' rate if they lose, but take a success fee if they win.[110] As was noted earlier, that is permissible under the law. While the success fee will now, post LASPOA 2012, come from the damages, in these sort of cases the amount of damages will be so vast that there would still be sufficient money to go around.

There are, of course, risks. One issue is that the litigant has to be sure that the TPF will pay. It is the litigant who incurs the fees, and therefore unless the TPF pays in advance then it is the litigant that will be ultimately responsible for the costs. While an action would arise to sue the funder, this may not help if the litigant is now devoid of resources to do so. Similarly, it is crucial that there is a binding contract between the litigant and the TPF to ensure that there is legal certainty that the TPF is attached to proceedings. This is important because s 51(1) *Senior Courts Act 1981* is wide enough to allow a court to direct costs against the TPF direct rather than the litigant where that would be more appropriate (ie where there is more chance that the costs would be paid as they have the means to do so!).

Another risk is that the litigant may lose control of the action. So, for example, the contract that provides the funding could decide that where a party offers a certain amount of money this should be accepted even if it is thought that at trial a greater sum could be offered. This is perhaps understandable as the funders are risking their money and will control what level of risk they are comfortable with. This may include a requirement, for example, for any offer to be considered by the funders.

☰ Example TPF and Part 36

In Chapter 17, Part 36 offers will be discussed. This is where a formal offer to settle is made, and it can have serious implications for costs. Let us take the Garion Enterprises Ltd example given earlier.

Garion Enterprises have been told that they have a 75 per cent chance of obtaining £80 million in damages if the matter goes to court. The agreement they have with the TPF is that a Part 36 offer has to be discussed with them and if it is 'reasonable' it must be accepted.

SeqTearan plc offer to settle the matter for £50 million. By this point, legal fees have reached £1.2 million. The TPF believe that £10 million (20% of the settlement) is a good return for their £1.2 million stake. The estimate of fees is now £3.7m. While there is insurance to cover

---

108. The fees would be paid by the losing side, so these payments would then be returned to the investment fund, meaning that they reclaim their original 'stake'.

109. I Benson, 'Liabilities of Litigation Funders' (2017) 33 *Professional Negligence* 72–85, 81.

110. ibid, 82.

the other side's fees, the TPT is risking £2.5m (the difference between the fees now and the estimated total). Given that the TPF will only receive £6m more if the claim succeeds,[111] they may decide that the 25% chance of losing is now too great a risk for those rewards.

Garion Enterprises Ltd will almost certainly have to go along with that because they will not be able to afford the litigation without the TPF. So they potentially lose £24 million in damages. However, they have not had to risk any money.

The final risk is that of satellite litigation. If the TPF believes that the litigant has not litigated properly, or believes their money has been used improperly, then they may choose to recover any losses from the litigant. Of course, defining what is reasonable etc. is always going to be open to dispute. Here, however, the TPF is likely to have power. The litigant went to a TPF because they did not have the financial means to litigate. How likely is it, therefore, that they would have the means to defend litigation brought by the TPF?

11.5.3 Before the event insurance

A popular form of funding is 'before the event insurance' (BTEI). Many of you will already have this insurance. When you insure your car or your house, have you been asked whether you want to add 'legal protection'? If so, and you selected 'yes', then, congratulations, you have BTEI.

BTEI can be contrasted with the insurance required for CFAs (known as 'after the event insurance'). BTEI is a more traditional form of insurance: you pay premiums in case you ever need it. While you may think that your car or home contents insurance is linked to driving or damage, the policies are usually wide and cover issues such as employment law, personal injury, and consumer disputes. Some disputes are excluded from the policies, the most notable usually being family law disputes. That said, it is possible to buy insurance policies that will cater for specific types of litigation. Landlords can buy insurance that will help them with eviction or pursuing rent arrears, and businesses can buy insurance policies that safeguard against litigation.

While it may be thought that BTEI is a relatively recent phenomenon, it has been noted that the first product dates back to 1905,[112] although it was the 1970s before it reached the United Kingdom.[113] A key advantage of BTEI is that it is cheap. Premiums are typically around £10 per month. When purchasing other insurance, this seems like a relatively cheap 'add-on'. Of course, it is an interesting question whether there is value for money. For example, a £10 per month policy equates to £120 per year. If no litigation is brought within ten years (and very few people do actually need to litigate), then potentially £1,200 has been spent. However, the reality is that for all rather than the simplest of matters, £1,200 will constitute a fraction of the fees that are likely to be incurred. Unlike CFA, someone with BTEI will get 100 per cent of the damages awarded.

407

---

111. 20% of £50m is £10m, 20% of £80m is £16m, a difference of £6m.

112. Matthias Kilian, 'Alternatives to Public Provision: The Role of Legal Expenses Insurance in Broadening Access to Justice: The German Experience' (2003) 30 *Journal of Law & Society* 31–48, 32.

113. RichardLewis, 'Litigation Costs and Before-the-Event Insurance: The Key to Access to Justice?' (2011) 74 *Modern Law Review* 272–86.

While there has almost certainly been an expanding market within the United Kingdom, BTEI has a larger market share in Germany. This is in part because of how restricted legal aid is in Germany (which puts into context the argument about a 'right' to legal aid), and BTEI is one of the key funding mechanisms there.[114] There is no doubt that in the UK it is growing, although it has to be questioned how many people remember they have the insurance and, therefore, use it when they need to seek legal advice or to litigate.

It has been suggested that the growth in BTEI means that people are more likely to litigate, including for weaker cases.[115] A greater preparedness to sue when one has one's costs covered is perhaps somewhat obvious. However, it is not known whether this is a result of BTEI or because society is arguably becoming more litigious due to alternative sources of litigation. Also, greater litigation is not necessarily a bad thing. Where a person is wronged, they should have the opportunity to access justice, particularly where legal aid is being cut back.

A difficulty with BTEI is, as with CFAs and TPF, the fact that funding is contingent on a probability. BTEI will only allow litigation where it meets a merits test.[116] What threshold that test is set at will depend on the insurer and the type of work. However, the threshold could, as with CFA, be set relatively high. The difficulty that this brings was explained in relation to legal aid: if you are challenging the *status quo* then, by its very nature, a merits test will not be met, potentially denying that person access to justice.

Concern has also been raised about the control that a person has over litigation when funded by BTEI. Similar to the position with TPF, there is concern that litigators are put under pressure to settle earlier than they might do if they were privately funded. Certainly, for similar reasons to those described in the section above, there will be a loss of control. Those who fund the litigation are able to exercise control through costs control. That said, it should be remembered that all solicitors are regulated by the SRA and therefore they cannot recommend a client accepts an offer that would be unreasonable.

Who is the lawyer? BTEI rarely allow you to choose your lawyer. Normally the insurance company will require you to use a lawyer on their list.[117] Again, this appears to mirror the position under legal aid. The argument is that insurers can command better prices because they will use their financial power and workload to drive a bargain with solicitors. Whether that means they get the best solicitors or the cheapest solicitors is more open to question (although some would argue that price is not an indication of quality).

Does the absence of choice mean anything? How many people know a solicitor? Very few people have contact with a solicitor particularly regularly. Most people probably select a solicitor these days on the basis of an advert or a ratings service. This is not necessarily a poor way of selecting a solicitor, but it might suggest that the fact that a choice is made for them is not necessarily detrimental.

One potential concern in respect of BTEI is a conflict of interest. There are only so many underwriters. Therefore it is eminently possible that the underwriter of a BTEI

---

114. Matthias Kilian, 'Alternatives to Public Provision: The Role of Legal Expenses Insurance in Broadening Access to Justice: The German Experience' (2003) 30 *Journal of Law & Society* 31–48, 43.
115. ibid and Lewis, n 116 at 278.
116. Richard Lewis, 'Litigation Costs and Before-the-Event Insurance: The Key to Access to Justice?' (2011) 74 *Modern Law Review* 272, 280–6.
117. ibid, 281.

will also be the defendant to any claim in a motor accident.[118] This risk is escalated because, while there are many insurance companies, they are normally underwritten by a smaller number of firms. Let us take an example to show the potential issue:

≡ Example A conflict of interest?

Zurich Insurance are one of the leading insurance providers. Danny was driving his car when he claimed to be blinded by the sun. This meant that he did not see Tom crossing the road on a zebra crossing. Tom was hit by the car and suffered a broken leg and lacerations.

Zurich provided the BTEI that Tom held, but also underwrote the car insurance that Danny holds.

Potentially this means that Zurich will be funding solicitors to sue itself.

While true, it should be noted that this is not unique. It is eminently possible that in a car accident involving two cars, both cars could be insured by the same company. Again, one must consider the regulation of lawyers. They are under a professional duty to represent their client, so ultimately there may not be a conflict of interest although it must be acknowledged that there is a *perceived* conflict of interest.

11.5.4 **Free legal advice**

While in some of the examples given earlier a person may not have to pay for the costs of litigation, they are not free in the truest sense of the word. They have involved someone else who is paying for the costs (the state (legal aid), the lawyer, TPF, or insurers). The reduction in legal aid has meant that there is an increase in those seeking initial free legal advice, particularly where they don't have insurance etc.

11.5.4.1 **Citizens Advice**

Perhaps the best-known example of free legal advice comes from Citizens Advice (previously known as the 'Citizens Advice Bureaux' (CABs)). This is a network of local charitable organizations that exist to provide advice and support on a number of matters. Each bureau is managed locally, but they are affiliated with the national organization and are provided with their case management and advice systems.

Prior to LASPOA 2012, many CABs bid for legal aid contracts meaning that, along with general advice, they could provide specific advice for those who met the legal-aid tests. LASPOA 2012 has withdrawn legal aid from most of the areas that the CABs operate,[119] although there are a few areas where they can still operate. Citizens Advice was mentioned by the government as an example of why the cuts in legal aid would not cause any undue difficulty to those who cannot afford legal advice. This showed a lack of understanding that many CABs were funded through legal aid. Eventually, the government had to step in and provide some funding to Citizens Advice, although considerably less than what they received through legal aid.

The time of austerity has led to further challenges. A considerable amount of their funding is provided by local authorities, but in recent years, councils have had their

---

118.   ibid, 282.
119.   Debra Morris and Warren Barr, 'The Impact of Cuts in Legal Aid Funding on Charities.' (2013) 35 *Journal of Social Welfare and Family Law* 79.

budgets cut considerably. This has led to cuts in funding to Citizens Advice, and individual bureaux have closed down or merged as a result of a lack of funding. However, others have diversified their funding models and there is little doubt that the service continues to play an important part in first-contact legal advice.

11.5.4.2 **Law clinics**

Those of you who are at a university reading law may find yourselves being given the opportunity to provide free legal advice. Universities have, in recent years, been establishing law clinics. While the format differs between each university (ranging from something akin to Citizens Advice to a legal disciplinary practice that can offer a full range of services[120]), the basic format is that students provide free legal advice to members of the public.

Students are given training before they begin clinical work, and they are supervised by qualified lawyers either employed by the university or from the local community. There are strong pedagogic benefits to the student,[121] not least from learning how law is applied in the real-world context. Often this helps students understand that law is not a series of boxes that mirror the modules studied (ie a problem is either a 'contract' problem, or a 'tort' problem) and that it will involve strands from across modules. It also provides valuable work experience for those who work in clinics. This can be particularly important if the proposed Solicitors Qualifying Exam (SQE) is introduced (see 10.3.1.5), as it is suggested that time in clinic may count as 'qualifying' time for the purposes of SQE 2.

The benefit to the community of law clinics is that they provide free legal advice, although often in limited fields. In some parts of the country this might be the only free legal advice that can be accessed. Most law clinics do not offer a 'full service' and, therefore, their work is often limited to the provision of initial legal advice. Where there is a case, they can refer a person to a firm that offers, for example, CFAs or legal aid where the client is eligible.

Not every law clinic only provides advice, some provide assistance in litigation through, for example, representation. The *Free Representation Unit* (FRU) was one of the earliest examples of this. It was established by the Bar Council and Inns of Court to provide free legal advice to those appearing in courts or tribunals. FRU was originally staffed exclusively by those studying for the Bar, but increasingly it also works with qualified barristers too. Some other universities have adopted a similar approach, and provide representation in tribunals, although it remains relatively unusual, not least because court and tribunal hearings rarely map onto university term dates.

11.5.4.3 **Pro bono**

The final form of free legal advice is provided by lawyers themselves. There has been a long history of lawyers acting *pro bono* (which means without a fee). Sometimes this is in an organized way. For example, local solicitors or barristers assisting a law clinic or creating their own equivalent. The Bar has long operated a Bar Pro Bono

---

120. See <https://www.lawgazette.co.uk/university-claims-legal-first-with-student-law-firm/5069331.article>. Sheffield Hallam University claims to be the first university to have LDP status.

121. See, for example, Richard J. Wilson, 'Training for Justice: The Global Reach of Clinical Legal Education' (2004) 22 *Pennsylvania State International Law Review* 421–32.

Unit (now known as Advocate[122]) which encourages barristers to provide free legal advice and representation in a range of cases. There is a solicitor equivalent called LawWorks,[123] which involves a range of firms ranging from sole practitioners to leading magic-circle firms, all providing free legal assistance.

Of course, the number of cases that can be taken on for free is often limited, but the demand is increasing. In 2019, LawWorks reported that they provided assistance to nearly 78,000 people.[124] Perhaps unsurprisingly, the biggest need for advice was in family law which, it will be remembered, is one of the areas where legal aid has been cut.

Why do lawyers undertake *pro bono* work? There is a long tradition of both barristers and solicitors occasionally waiving their fees or providing free advice. Many see it as a fundamental part of access to justice and the rule of law. Others recognize that not everyone can afford to pay fees, and, therefore, for reasons of social responsibility they provide assistance to those who cannot otherwise pay. It is clear that lawyers find providing *pro bono* work rewarding in many instances, but there needs to be a sense of reality as to how many people can be helped. Barristers, in particular, receive their earnings from cases. If they are spending several days assisting someone for free, they are not earning money. It was seen from Chapter 10 that the earnings of many barristers are not as glamorous as some may think. Therefore, the opportunity for *pro bono* work is limited.

11.5.4.4 DIY law

The reduction in legal aid and unavailability of CFAs and BTEI for all forms of litigation mean that unfortunately for many there is no legal advice or assistance. Individuals must litigate themselves (known as 'Litigants in Person' (LiP) or sometimes 'Defendant in Person' when in the criminal courts).

The Internet has revolutionized knowledge. Information that was the preserve of all but a few knowledgeable individuals is now available to all. However, there is no guarantee that the information on the Internet is correct. The context of information is often lacking, meaning that technical information is misunderstood. It has been hypothesized that the Internet has led to an increase in the 'DIY lawyer', ie someone who uses the Internet to find their legal rights instead of consulting a lawyer.[125]

Law on the Internet is arguably simply an extension of existing initiatives that seek to educate people about their rights. For example, many universities offer *Street Law* or the equivalent, where students explain legal issues (often revolving around things like employment law or consumer rights) to community groups. Pre-action protocols also place emphasis on negotiation prior to litigation (discussed further in Chapter 19), and this often requires people to have an understanding of their rights before attempting this. Indeed, some forms of ADR provide participants with an overview of their legal status to ensure that they speak at the same level, and try to engage on resolving the dispute rather than assessing who is 'right'.

411

122. <https://weareadvocate.org.uk/>.
123. <https://www.lawworks.org.uk/>.
124. <https://www.lawworks.org.uk/sites/default/files/LawWorks-Clinics-Report-2019-web.pdf>.
125. Kathy Laster and Ryan Kornhauser, 'The Rise of "DIY" Law: Implications for Legal Aid' in Asher Flynn and Jacqueline Hodgson (eds), *Access to Justice & Legal Aid: Comparative Perspectives on Unmet Legal Need* (Hart Publishing 2017) 123.

However, the counter-argument is that unlike these initiatives, the Internet does not guarantee that advice is correct. People will examine issues in discussion pages or boards but they are rarely by qualified lawyers and, in some instances, they are simply a presentation of what somebody thinks their rights are. This is particularly obvious in family law disputes where even the simplest of Google searches on residence or contact will find threads where people complain about their situation, and are encouraged by others to litigate without a knowledge of what the law is.

Of course, in other instances the advice can be correct. Citizens Advice (11.5.4.1) operate a website that provides people with key information about their rights on a variety of topics. The government provided funding to Citizens Advice to take over consumer advice, providing guidance on faulty purchases, consumer credit, etc. The *Coram Children's Legal Centre*[126] operates a series of websites that help provide basic advice on issues relating to children, but also signpost people who are entitled to legal aid to them. These are but two examples, but a difficulty with the Internet is identifying what information can be trusted and what cannot.

Later chapters in this book will consider the impact that the growth of LiPs has had. A difficulty with the DIY lawyer is that there is nobody to tell you the strength of your case. Few people who think they have been wronged are prepared to admit that they might not have been, or that there were others to blame. Private family law disputes, such as contact following a divorce are rarely conducted in calm, rational ways. Without a qualified lawyer to say, 'this is not worth it' or 'this case is weak', unnecessary litigation is begun, and this has a key impact on the courts. Litigation involving a LiP tends to be much longer (as they will not understand the court processes or which points to concentrate on), and there are fears, therefore, that the cutback in legal aid is a false economy, ie, that the money saved on advising people is simply spent on longer court cases.

Summary

In this chapter we have noted:

- State assistance (known as legal aid) began in the aftermath of the Second World War.

- Legal aid quickly grew and in the 1980s and 1990s there was a time when legal aid was almost freely available.

- The legal aid budget quickly became one of the most expensive in the world, and there was pressure to begin to cut back. Means-testing became more restrictive.

- LASPOA 2012 led to wholescale changes to legal aid. It has led to significant restrictions to criminal legal aid, particularly through the means test which excludes many middle-class families.

- Civil legal aid adopted an inclusionary, rather than exclusionary, approach. This means that only certain types of civil litigation would be eligible for legal aid. At the same time, the means and merits tests were tightened, meaning very few people are now eligible.

126. <https://www.childrenslegalcentre.com/>.

- Alternative sources of funding began to replace legal aid. A popular form of funding is known as a 'conditional fee arrangement' (CFA). A CFA is often referred to as 'no-win, no-fee' although that is only one variant. Sometimes there is a fee (albeit reduced), or sometimes there are still costs involved (eg insurance premiums).

- CFAs allow a solicitor to charge a 'success fee'. Originally this was up to 100 per cent of the legal costs, and was payable by the losing party. Following LASPOA 2012, the success fee is expressed as a percentage of damages, and is capped at 25 per cent for personal injury. The success fee comes from the damages awarded to the litigant and not paid by the losing side.

- For large-value claims, venture capitalists are starting to offer third-party funding (TPF). This is where someone unconnected with the claim offers to pay the costs of the proceedings (and sometimes the cost of losing), but in return for a percentage of the damages to be recovered. A difficulty with TPF is that the litigant can lose control of the action, as the TPF effectively can terminate proceedings by not providing further funds.

- Before the event insurance (BTEI) is becoming increasingly popular and is seen by some as a solution to funding litigation. An individual pays an insurance premium and the insurance company will fund the cost of certain litigation in the event that this is necessary. Disadvantages include the fact that policies rarely cover all forms of litigation and insurance companies will normally only authorize litigation if it has a particular likelihood of success.

- The cuts in legal aid has meant that free legal advice is now being offered primarily by the not-for-profit sector. This has increasingly included universities who have opened 'law clinics'. These provide opportunities for students to experience what life is like advising real clients. However, they generally only offer initial legal advice, and they are not a direct replacement for legal aid.

❓ End-of-chapter questions

1. Why should the state pay for legal aid for anyone? Would a better solution not be to ensure that the court processes are sufficiently easy to allow anyone to appear in them alone?

2. The Secret Barrister states:

> [W]here anyone falling under the jurisdiction of English and Wales law does not have the means to pay, assistance should be provided and the cost shared among all of us. Justice only for those able to pay for it is not justice at all.[127]

   In essence, this is an argument for universal legal aid. Nobody should be denied a lawyer and general taxation should be used to pay for it. How realistic is this? Does that not mean the state has to pay for spurious litigation, or litigation that is doomed to fail? If we do not do this though, then how do we ensure that there justice is accessible by all?

3. Should we mandate before the event insurance? If people had to take out insurance for issues such as family disputes, personal injury, and property disputes then we would not need to worry about either legal aid or CFAs. Is that not a fairer approach?

4. Are law clinics a good idea? If you have a legal dispute then surely you want a properly qualified lawyer to advise you, not a student pretending to be a lawyer?

---

127. Secret Barrister, *Fake Law: The Truth About Justice in an Age of Lies* (Picador 2020), 168.

≣ Further reading

Benson, I, 'Liabilities of litigation funders' (2017) 33 *Professional Negligence* 72–85.

This is an interesting article that considers the different ways that litigation can be funded but, importantly, what the liability of those who do fund litigation are.

Fenn P, Marshall D, and Rickman N, 'The Impact of Legislation on the Outcomes of Civil Litigation: An Empirical Analysis of the Legal Aid, Sentencing and Punishment of Offenders Act 2012' [2019] 4 *Journal of Personal Injury Law* 285.

This is an interesting article that considers the effects of LASPOA 2012 on the issue of personal injury.

Flynn A and Hodgson J (eds), *Access to Justice & Legal Aid: Comparative Perspectives on Unmet Legal Need* (Hart Publishing 2007).

This is a collection of essays that compares the English and Australian systems for legal aid. The individual essays track the development of legal aid, and how cuts have affected litigation.

Shipman S, 'Steel and Morris v United Kingdom: Legal aid in the European Court of Human Rights' (2006) 25 *Civil Justice Quarterly* 5–19.

This is an interesting article that critiques the case of Steel and Morris v United Kingdom and suggests that the ECtHR has raised many questions that it has so far failed to answer.

Wilson R, 'Training for Justice: The Global Reach of Clinical Legal Education' (2004) 22 *Pennsylvania State International Law Review* 421–32.

This is a good piece that summarizes what is important about clinical legal education, what the benefits are to students, teachers, and the community.

For self-test questions, flashcards, and links to useful websites, please visit the **online resources** at: **www.oup.com/he/gillespie-weare8e/**

PART III

THE CRIMINAL JUSTICE SYSTEM

12

The Investigation of Crime

By the end of this chapter you will be able to:

- Identify how law enforcement is organized in England and Wales.
- Understand the structure of the police and how they are accountable for their performance.
- Identify the 'base' power for stop and search, and understand why this power is so controversial to sections of society.
- Identify the powers of the police to arrest and detain someone who is believed to be about to commit, is committing, or has committed a crime.
- Understand how the rights of suspects are protected by the law when they are in police detention.

Introduction

This chapter considers how crime is investigated. This is the entry-point to the criminal justice system which exists to assess whether a person is guilty of a crime they are accused of. It is important at the outset to be clear about that. The purpose of the courts is not to assess whether they are guilty or not guilty, as everyone is presumed to be innocent until the contrary is shown. In other words, until the magistrates' or jury decide that a person is guilty, then they remain not guilty.

The police are the most well-known law enforcement agency, but they are not the only agency that exists to investigate crime. In the next chapter, it will be seen that the police (who investigate crime) and the Crown Prosecution Service (who prosecute crime) are independent of each other, albeit cooperating closely. Law enforcement agencies are given considerable powers to investigate crime including the power to stop and search someone, the right to arrest someone and, ultimately, the right to detain someone while an investigation takes place. Such powers should be used carefully, and rights are given to those subject to these powers to ensure that they are used appropriately. The extent to which this happens is one of the key issues to be discussed in this chapter.

12.1 **The police and their independence**

In terms of general crime there is, in England and Wales, a separation between those who investigate crime (law enforcement) and those who prosecute crime (the prosecutors). As will be seen, this distinction does not apply to all types of crime: fraud is a good example where there is a joint approach. However, for the vast majority of crime, the investigation and prosecution are dealt with separately. This differs from a number of other countries, including Scotland where the procurator fiscal is responsible not only for the prosecution of certain offences, but also their investigation.[1] Similarly, in the USA the Assistant District Attorney is both a prosecutor and a member of law enforcement.

Historically there was no organized police presence in England and Wales. Policing was a private initiative by the wealthy. Eventually, there began to be more formalized structures. Public policing in the UK arguably began in Glasgow in the late 1770s,[2] but perhaps the most famous establishment came with Sir Robert Peel's founding of the Metropolitan Police, the first force that was full-time and organized by rank.[3]

12.1.1 **Law enforcement in England and Wales**

Whilst we traditionally think of 'the police' as being law enforcement in England and Wales, they are simply one (although the largest) branch of law enforcement. Other agencies also exist to uphold the law. Some examples are:

- **National Crime Agency.** This is discussed briefly in the next section.
- **HM Revenue & Customs.** This is an agency that combines the old Inland Revenue and HM Customs & Excise. The agency has responsibility for the collection of tax and the prevention of smuggling.
- **Serious Fraud Office.** This is an organization that both investigates and prosecutes serious and complex crime. It is discussed further at 12.1.1.2.
- **Border Force.** This is an agency operated from within the Home Office. It took over from the UK Border Agency (and previous iterations) and has responsibility for immigration and customs.

There are other national policing bodies that are akin to territorial forces (see 12.1.2). These are forces whose jurisdiction are not constrained by local geography. Good examples include the *British Transport Police*,[4] who have jurisdiction over incidents on railways and railway stations etc,[5] and the *Ministry of Defence Police*,[6] who have jurisdiction over the various military infrastructures of UK Armed Forces whilst in the UK.[7]

---

1. Crown Office and Procurator Fiscal Service, 'About us' <https://www.copfs.gov.uk/about-us/about-us>.
2. David G Barrie, 'Patrick Colquhoun, the Scottish Enlightenment and Police Reform in Glasgow in the Late Eighteenth Century' (2008) 12 *Crime, Histoire & Sociétés/Crime, History & Societies* 59.
3. *Metropolitan Police Act 1829.*
4. *Railways and Transport Safety Act 2003*, s 20.
5. ibid, s 31. This includes the railways in Scotland, making it a truly national police force (s 31A).
6. *Ministry of Defence Police Act 1987*, s 1.
7. ibid, s 2. When deployed overseas operationally, the *Royal Navy Police, Royal Air Force Police*, or *Royal Military Police* have jurisdiction.

12.1.1.1 **National Crime Agency**

The closest national agency to traditional policing is the *National Crime Agency* (NCA). This is the latest guise of a national law enforcement agency that seeks to tackle serious and organized crime.[8] Each variation has inevitably been accompanied by newspaper reports that announce that it is the UK's equivalent of the FBI. Such comparisons miss the point that the UK is not a Federal jurisdiction. It also misses the point that the NCA is not truly national, in that its jurisdiction does not extend to Scotland.[9]

The NCA took over from two agencies; the *Serious and Organised Crime Agency* (SOCA) and the *Child Exploitation and Online Protection Centre* (CEOP). The decision to merge these two organizations was controversial and led to the resignation of the chief executive of CEOP.[10]

⚡ CEOP

CEOP was established in 2006 at about the time there was increasing attention being paid to online child sexual exploitation. Whilst CEOP was a law-enforcement organization, it had a much broader remit and it included work with victims and an educational focus. From the very beginning, CEOP was designed to be multi-agency and although police officers were seconded to it, social workers, psychologists, and private industry was also involved. Commercial partners such as Microsoft, AOL, and Vodafone also worked with CEOP, particularly in the development of technologies that could identify or disrupt child sexual exploitation.

CEOP coordinated the response to international instruments, working closely with Europol, Interpol, and the *Virtual Global Taskforce*, an organization that saw law enforcement agencies from several countries pool their resources to combat this area of work.

While the multi-agency approach undoubtedly had benefits, there was concern that the separate 'back-office functions' that are inherent within any organization meant that valuable resources were being wasted. During times of austerity, the government incorporated CEOP into the new NCA, meaning that the costs of back-office functions such as finance, HR, and administration were pooled. CEOP now features as a 'Command' within the NCA. In this way, it has its own head (now known as a Director) who reports to the Director-General of the NCA via the Deputy Director-General.

SOCA was itself an amalgamation of two previous agencies that had a national remit; the *National Crime Squad* (NCS) and the *National Criminal Intelligence Service* (NCIS).[11] Previously, these two agencies meant there was a differential between operations and intelligence and yet in modern policing, particularly in respect of organized crime, the two were integrated. While SOCA was a national unit, it played a supportive role. In other words, the local police were responsible for the final aspects of the operations and they could decide to prioritize other issues.

---

8. *Crime and Courts Act 2013*, s 1.
9. Serious and organized crime in Scotland largely remains the responsibility of Police Scotland.
10. Terry Thomas, 'Police Investigation of Reports: The National Level', *Policing Sexual Offences and Sex Offenders* (Springer 2016).
11. Glen M Segell, 'Reform and Transformation: The UK's Serious Organized Crime Agency' (2007) 20 *International Journal of Intelligence and CounterIntelligence* 217.

A Home Office consultation paper heralded the arrival of the NCA as a beefed-up national unit.[12] The new organization would be headed by a senior chief constable and it would have greater powers to control and task operations.[13] This has largely been carried forward. The NCA has two principal statutory functions:

1. Crime-reduction function. This is securing efficient and effective activities to combat organized crime and serious crime.

2. Criminal-intelligence function. This relates to the acquisition, processing, and dissemination of intelligence to combat organized crime, serious crime, and to disrupt the proceeds of crime.[14]

It must discharge these duties either itself or through cooperation with other forces.[15] Ordinarily cooperation would be achieved through mutual requests in much the same way that police forces cooperate on everyday tasks. However, in a significant shift away from previous models, the Director-General of the NCA ultimately has the power to require a chief constable to perform a task to assist its work.[16] If required to do so, the chief constable must comply with that request.[17] While no sanction is imposed on the face of the statute, it would presumably be a disciplinary matter not to comply. It has not been necessary to issue such requirements because ultimately the National Police Chief's Council has fostered appropriate cooperation. That cooperation may have been facilitated by the knowledge that ultimately chief constables can be ordered to assist, although that is tempered by the fact that (a) it relates only to serious and organized crime, and (b) the political consequences of such a requirement would be significant.

As a law enforcement agency, the NCA is inspected by HM Inspectorate of Constabularies and the Fire and Rescue Services.[18] However, much of the work that the NCA does is sensitive and therefore the reports tend to be brief or not published at all.[19] Whether this meets the test for transparency that the inspecting regime was supposed to bring is perhaps open to question. The public should have the right to know that agencies, including the NCA, are operating appropriately and effectively.

One slight oddity over national policing remains the issue of terrorism. Traditionally the Metropolitan Police Commissioner has national responsibility for terrorism, although in practice it is delegated to a deputy who is known as the 'Senior National Co-ordinator'. The Metropolitan Police were given national responsibility partly because it was thought prudent for terrorism to be dealt with in a coordinated manner, and the Metropolitan Police are the largest constabulary. That is not to say that the Metropolitan Police take over all terrorism cases, merely that they have lead responsibility. However, some have questioned whether it would not be more appropriate for the NCA to assume this function, not least because terrorism is both organized and serious. Despite it being mooted[20] the government has never undertaken the transfer. The failure to do so does arguably downplay the 'first amongst equals' strategy of the NCA.

---

12. Home Office, 'Policing in the 21st Century: Reconnecting Police and the People' (Home Office 2010) Consultation Paper Cm 7925.
13. ibid, 29.
14. *Crime and Courts Act 2013*, s 1(4), (5).
15. ibid, s 1(7)–(9).
16. ibid, s 5(5).
17. ibid, s 5(7).
18. ibid, s.11.
19. HMCIFRS, 'National Crime Agency inspections' <https://www.justiceinspectorates.gov.uk/hmicfrs/our-work/article/the-national-crime-agency/>.
20. Vikram Dodd, 'National Crime Agency Could Replace Police in Leading Fight against Terrorism' *The Guardian* (1 January 2016) <https://www.theguardian.com/uk-news/2016/jan/01/national-agency-could-replace-police-in-leading-fight-against-terrorism>.

Are there not certain issues that should be under the control of a national authority? For example, terrorism. Would it not make more sense for a single agency to have powers over these functions, to ensure that a consistent and coordinated response occurs?

12.1.1.2 Serious Fraud Office

The Serious Fraud Office (SFO) should be briefly considered because it is structured differently from other law enforcement agencies and also because it remains somewhat controversial. The SFO was established in 1987[21] as a specialist organization designed to tackle serious fraud. Uniquely in the structures that we look at in this book, it has a role both as an investigator and a prosecutor (unless like the other agencies mentioned in this chapter, all of whom pass files over to the Crown Prosecution Service for prosecution, something discussed in Chapter 13). The logic is that serious fraud is so complicated that it requires investigators and prosecutors to work together.[22] However, the same argument could be made about certain other types of crime, and, as will be seen, not everyone is convinced that the current arrangement works.

The policing of fraud in the UK has long been controversial,[23] in part because it is largely ignored by mainstream police forces. Indeed, the expansion of cybercrime means that the police are overwhelmed by fraud and only a tiny proportion of frauds are ever actioned.[24] However, serious fraud represents a risk to the economic security of the country as it has the potential to undermine confidence in banks and big businesses, or carries the risk of mass redundancies in the event of a large business becoming bankrupt. For that reason, serious fraud should be tackled appropriately.

The SFO is headed by a Director who has the express power both to investigate and prosecute.[25] While the SFO does employ a number of investigators, it also works closely with the police, and statute expressly caters for joint investigations with the police.[26] Working with the police means that there are greater pooled resources, but it also means that the investigators can rely on the powers of uniformed constables. While the Director is nominally in charge, the day-to-day responsibilities are delegated to others. Teams are established within the SFO, each headed by a lawyer who can exercise all the powers of the Director.[27] The teams will also include investigators, accountants, analysts, and specialists in tracing money.

The SFO can only investigate a limited number of cases and in deciding whether to investigate, it will consider the need for its specialist capabilities and the harm that is occurring, or could occur, to the public, the reputation, or integrity of the UK's financial status, or the economic prosperity of the UK.[28] Writing more than twenty-five

---

21. *Criminal Justice Act 1987*, s 1.
22. John Wood, 'The Serious Fraud Office' [1989] *Criminal Law Review* 175–84.
23. Graham B Rooks and Mark Button, 'The Police and Fraud Investigation and the Case for a Nationalised Solution in the United Kingdom' (2011) 84 *The Police Journal* 305.
24. Alisdair A Gillespie, *Cybercrime: Key Issues and Debates* (2nd edn, Routledge 2019) 315.
25. *Criminal Justice Act 1987*, s 1(3), (5).
26. ibid, s 1(4).
27. ibid, s 1(7), (8).
28. Serious Fraud Office, 'Guidance, policy and protocols' (SFO 2020) <https://www.sfo.gov.uk/publications/guidance-policy-and-protocols/>.

years ago, the then Director of the SFO noted that they would ordinarily not become involved in a crime worth less than £5 million,[29] but the reality is that modern cases are likely to involve hundreds of millions of pounds or more.

The SFO has, over the years, been subjected to harsh criticism, particularly when it fails to secure convictions.[30] Of course, it is not always clear whether acquittals demonstrate a failure on behalf of investigators and prosecutors, a failure of the system, or because the defendants were, in fact, not guilty. Serious fraud is extraordinarily complicated. It was noted that the SFO was established as a joint unit because of this complexity. Regardless of how complex the cases are, however, a case is ultimately heard by a jury of twelve lay persons. As will be seen in Chapter 14, questions have been raised as to whether this should change. There have also been questions raised as to whether the law is overly complicated, even though the *Fraud Act 2006* was designed to simplify it.[31]

In recent years, a particularly controversial issue that has arisen is the use of so-called 'plea deals' with the SFO. Formally, these are 'deferred prosecution agreements'[32] and allow corporations (but not individuals) to reach agreement on how a case will be disposed. Typically, it will involve the payment of a fine but avoid the costs and publicity of a trial. This is something that will be considered more fully at 13.1.6.

12.1.2 **Territorial police forces**

The term 'the police' is used colloquially to refer to the police service in general. However, as has been noted already, policing is largely regionally based in a series of constabularies (although many no longer use that term).[33] In the United Kingdom there are forty-five separate police constabularies. Forty-three of these are based in England and Wales (roughly mapping onto the old county boundaries, but with London having two forces: the Metropolitan Police and the City of London Police). Scotland used to have eight local constabularies but since 2013 these were amalgamated into a single constabulary known as 'Police Scotland'.[34] Northern Ireland has traditionally only had one force. This was historically known as the 'Royal Ulster Constabulary' (RUC) but as part of the peace settlement that brought about the end of hostilities in the province, the force was renamed the 'Police Service of Northern Ireland' (PSNI) in 2001.[35]

12.1.2.1 **Operational independence**

Apart from the two London forces, each constabulary is headed by a 'chief constable'.[36] The two London forces are headed by a 'commissioner'.[37] Each chief constable/commissioner is responsible for what is happening in their force area, save for those

---

29. George Staple, 'Serious and Complex Fraud: A New Perspective' (1993) 56 *Modern Law Review* 127, 129.

30. Michael Chan, 'Serious Fraud Office Report' (1997) 4 *Journal of Financial Crime* 232.

31. Carol Withey, 'The Fraud Act 2006 – Some Early Observations and Comparisons with the Former Law' (2007) 71 *Journal of Criminal Law* 220–37.

32. *Crime and Courts Act 2013*, s 45 and sch 17.

33. For example, Cleveland no longer uses the term 'Cleveland Constabulary' and instead refer to themselves as 'Cleveland Police'. The Metropolitan Police now refer to themselves as the 'Metropolitan Police Service'. However, others remain with the old nomenclature. For example, Lancashire remains Lancashire Constabulary.

34. *Police and Fire Reform (Scotland) Act 2011*. Technically the name of the force is 'The Police Service of Scotland' (s 6) but 'Police Scotland' is used as a working title.

35. *Police (Northern Ireland) Act 2000*, s 1.

36. *Police Reform and Social Responsibility Act 2011*, s 2(1).

37. ibid, s 4.

situations relating to serious and organized crime. In other words, there is no 'Head of the Police' in the UK or indeed England and Wales. Whilst the Commissioner of the Metropolitan Police, as the largest force, has some national responsibilities (primarily Royal and Diplomatic Protection and anti-terrorism), generally speaking the individual chief constable is responsible for what happens within their force area.[38]

Police officers are appointed to each police force but may be seconded to national or regional units as required. Previously the authority of a police officer was restricted to the force area that they were a member of but that is no longer the case, with the powers of a constable being employed throughout England and Wales.[39]

In order to provide certainty and consistency of justice, the police seek to cooperate on issues so far as possible. For a number of years an organization known as ACPO (Association of Chief Police Officers) would formulate policy on behalf of the police. ACPO was controversial as it was, technically speaking, a private limited company. Income was derived from some of their activities and there were concerns that, in effect, a private company was deciding how law would be applied. A National Police Chief's Council (NPCC) was established as a successor organization, but with more transparent links to policing. The NPCC continues to develop national policies and strategies, but with more input from outside of the organization. Ultimately, however, it has no power to require chief constables to adhere to the rules set forward, and chief constables remain operationally independent.

12.1.2.2 **Political oversight**

Whilst chief constables are operationally independent, ie nobody can tell them to do a particular action, they are subject to political oversight. It is perhaps a surprise to many that the Home Secretary does not have direct power over chief constables. Instead, local control outside of London is through the Police and Crime Commissioners (PCCs).[40] A PCC is an elected office,[41] with their term of office lasting four years.[42] That said, the Home Secretary has the right to establish national police priorities[43] and chief officers 'have regard' to these priorities.[44] However, that remains political accountability and not operational. The Home Secretary cannot tell either a chief constable to undertake, or not to undertake, a particular operational task.

A PCC has two principal purposes in respect of policing.[45] Broadly speaking these can be considered to be the maintenance of a police force and then holding the chief constable to account. In respect of the first function, the PCC is responsible for securing the maintenance of a police force and ensuring that it is efficient and effective.[46] For the second function, the PCC is charged with holding the chief constable to account for the exercises of his functions and any functions under the direction and control of the chief constable.[47]

---

38. ibid, s 2(3).
39. *Police Act 1996*, s 30(1).
40. *Police Reform and Social Responsibility Act 2011*, s 1.
41. ibid, s 1(4).
42. ibid, s 50(1).
43. ibid, s 77.
44. ibid, s 77(2).
45. PCCs can now also exercise responsibility for the local Fire and Rescue Service (*Policing and Crime Act 2017*, s 6) although few PCCs have chosen to do this.
46. *Police Reform and Social Responsibility Act 2011*, s 1(6).
47. ibid, s 1(7).

This is administrative control and relates to matters such as the policing plan, strategic policing requirements, local consultation, and the discharge of funding.[48] It does not include operational oversight of any matter, which remains under the sole control of the chief constable.[49]

The PCC is also responsible for the appointment of the chief constable and has the power to suspend the chief constable or to require them to resign or retire.[50] They must also be consulted in the appointment of a deputy or assistant chief constable.[51] Whilst this would seem a broad power that could provide the PCC with the ability to interfere operationally (because they could threaten to dismiss a chief constable who did not agree with their operational requirement), the statute is alert to that and requires dismissal to follow a 'scrutiny process'.[52] This process requires them to explain to the chief constable why they are considering removal, permitting them to make written submissions to rebut those grounds, and also to refer the matter to the police and crime panel.[53] Ultimately, the PCC can decide to reject the recommendation of the panel (which could, for example, decide that dismissal is not required),[54] but clearly the intention is that politically it would be damaging to do so.

The power to dismiss a chief constable has been rarely exercised, perhaps reflecting how difficult it is to do so. The chief constable of Cheshire Constabulary, Simon Byrne, was suspended amidst allegations of gross misconduct but although he faced a disciplinary hearing, his contract expired before dismissal. The best-known example is when the PCC of South Yorkshire sacked David Crompton, the chief constable. This is also important because the decision was challenged in court and therefore provides an insight into how these powers should be exercised.

South Yorkshire police was responsible for the policing of Hillsborough, which was the scene of one of the worst disasters in sport, when ninety-six people died in a crush at a semi-final played between Liverpool and Nottingham Forest. From the outset, fans were blamed for the deaths but, as eventually became apparent, it was actually the fault of systematic failings by the police, ambulance service, and local authorities. Compton, who was not the chief constable at the time of the Hillsborough disaster, put out a press statement that was widely reported as potentially blaming the fans even though the inquest had suggested the converse. In fact, the purpose of the statement was to state that the police were not wholly to blame (however wise such a statement was). Internal emails had also suggested that he was questioning the account of the families.

Following intense public disquiet, the PCC for South Yorkshire suggested that the chief constable should resign and gave him one hour to consider his position. When the chief constable refused, the PCC suspended the chief constable. The process identified earlier was then followed, which included referring the matter to HM Inspectorate of Police (at that time) who indicated that he did not believe that there were grounds to dismiss the chief constable. Ultimately, the PCC required the chief constable to resign and he did so later that day. Compton then issued legal proceedings against the PCC.

48. A comprehensive list is provided in the *Police Reform and Social Responsibility Act 2011*, s 1(8).
49. ibid, s 2(3).
50. ibid, s 38.
51. ibid, ss 39–40.
52. ibid, s 11.
53. ibid, sch 8, paras 8–15.
54. ibid, sch 8, para 16.

In *R (on the application of Compton) v Police and Crime Commissioner for South Yorkshire*[55] the High Court ruled on the propriety of Compton's dismissal. The chief constable argued that the decision to require him to resign was irrational, disproportionate, and a breach of Article 8.[56] It was clear from the 'scrutiny process' identified earlier, that HM Inspector of Constabulary believed there was no grounds to dismiss the chief constable but the (local) police and crime panel believed that there was. The High Court confirmed that the PCC is obliged to hold the chief constable to account for all of his actions, and those actions that are conducted in his name.[57] However, it also confirmed that the PCC is not entitled to interfere with the operational decisions of the chief constable.[58] The High Court held that in deciding whether the actions of a chief constable were improper, they should apply the ordinary principles of public law and decide whether the action was not one that would be reasonable for a chief constable to undertake.[59]

When the statement that was ultimately put out by the chief constable was being drafted, the PCC decided that it was not his responsibility to help draft it. The High Court were deeply unimpressed with that argument, saying that 'we regard that approach as surprising in the extreme',[60] which is language that is not often found in the judgments of the courts. They noted that the PCC and chief constable are supposed to work together to discharge many functions relating to the public face of policing. The High Court also believed that there was nothing to suggest that the public in general were against the statement put out,[61] although it must be questioned whether that was true. Technically the High Court could be right, in that it is difficult to identify sources that attack *that statement*. However, there was undoubtedly anger about the way that South Yorkshire Police approached the inquest, matters that were unquestionably within the responsibility of the chief constable.

Ultimately the High Court decided that the decision to both suspend the chief constable and to dismiss him was irrational. This is a landmark decision because the decision to dismiss him was unquestionably (politically) popular. It is perhaps notable that the PCC was re-elected despite the decisions that he took. The decision attracted positive news coverage and therefore was almost certainly politically popular. Legally it was wrong. However, it is notable that the courts did not order that the chief constable was reinstated. The chief constable's contract expired and so that difficult decision was not faced. It is interesting to wonder what would have happened if the chief constable was at the beginning of his contract. The decision in *Compton* is clear that the law will restrict the broad powers of the PCC, but it is not clear that this aligns to the political realities of oversight.

12.2 Stop and search

Identifying where one should start in an examination of the investigation of crime is not easy. A logical approach would be arrest and detention but arguably this misses a crucial power that will sometimes precede an arrest. That power is the right of the

425

---

55. [2017] EWHC 1349 (Admin).
56. ibid, at [6].
57. ibid, at [76].
58. ibid, at [77].
59. ibid, at [94].
60. ibid, at [120].
61. ibid, at [140].

police to stop and search a person. Of all the powers available to the police, this is one of the most controversial, partly because some believe it is used in a discriminatory way by police against members of the public who come from minority ethnic backgrounds. It is therefore worthy of study here.

12.2.1 **Background to the power**

While there was no historic power to detain a person without their consent, there were a multitude of statutory powers that allowed a constable to do so.[62] It was thought appropriate to consolidate these various powers into a single national power, which was the object of the *Police and Criminal Evidence Act 1984* (PACE 1984). That said, some powers were not incorporated, perhaps most notably the power to stop and search a person who is believed to be carrying a firearm in public.[63] Despite the intention to consolidate the various powers, there has been a significant increase in new powers introduced after PACE 1984. Indeed, it has been noted that there are now so many different powers that it would be almost impossible to list and analyse them in a single piece of academic writing.[64] That is certainly true for this book, and this chapter will concentrate on the 'simple' power.

A brief overview of the usual powers would include the power to stop and search for the purposes of detecting prohibited articles.[65] This is the 'ordinary' power. The firearms power has also been noted. The *Misuse of Drugs Act 1971* provides a power to stop and search when a constable has reasonable grounds to believe that a person is in possession of illegal drugs.[66] Not every power requires reasonable suspicion. The *Terrorism Act 2000* allowed an assistant chief constable to designate an area or place as a location whereby a constable could stop a person or vehicle and search that person or anyone within the car.[67] The search was to find articles useful to terrorism,[68] and specifically applied 'whether or not the constable has grounds for suspecting the presence of [such articles]'.[69] In other words, the power could be used by the constable at any time. While the power was upheld by the courts in England and Wales,[70] the European Court of Human Rights considered it to be so wide as to be arbitrary and, therefore, not in accordance with the law.[71]

Section 44 was replaced by s 47A. This also provides the right for a constable to stop and search anyone for the purposes of identifying whether they are carrying anything useful for terrorism.[72] As with s 44, it does not require the constable to have reasonable suspicion in order to exercise the power,[73] but the senior officer who designates the area must have reasonable suspicion that an act of terrorism will take place, and that he reasonably believes that the designation is necessary, and that it will be in place for no longer than necessary.[74]

---

62. Helen Fenwick, *Fenwick on Civil Liberties and Human Rights* (5th edn, Routledge 2017) 842.
63. *Firearms Act 1968*, s 47.
64. Ben Bowling and Coretta Phillips, 'Disproportionate and Discriminatory: Reviewing the Evidence on Police Stop and Search' (2007) 70 *Modern Law Review* 936, 937.
65. PACE 1984, s 1.
66. *Misuse of Drugs Act 1971*, s 23.
67. *Terrorism Act 2000*, s 44.
68. ibid, 45(1)(a).
69. ibid, 45(1)(b).
70. *R (on the application of Gillan) v Commissioner of the Police for the Metropolis* [2006] UKHL 11.
71. *Gillan v UK* (2010) 50 EHRR 45.
72. *Terrorism Act 2000*, ss 47A(2)–(4).
73. ibid, 47A(5).
74. ibid, 47A(1).

The *Criminal Justice and Public Order Act 1994* creates a similar rule in relation to serious violence. An officer of at least the rank of Inspector can designate an area where he reasonably believes that incidents of serious violence may take place, have taken place (and which requires a weapon to be recovered), or that persons are carrying weapons.[75] This is a time-limited power, and requires an officer of at least the rank of a superintendent to extend the authority.[76] Again, the particular constable who makes the stop does not need to have reasonable grounds to suspect the individual is acting illegally.[77]

Whilst the powers under the *Terrorism Act 2000* and the *Criminal Justice and Public Order Act 1994* appear to authorize indiscriminate searches by individual constables, they are constrained by the fact that the overarching authorization must be justified. It has been remarked that this is recognition that in order to combat terrorism or violence, it is sometimes necessary to act quickly and unpredictably.[78] Of course, the difficulty is that where the authorized areas are home to sections of society who believe that they are being victimized by the police through disproportionate stop and search (discussed later), these powers might exacerbate such tensions. This is particularly true where a person is stopped and, upon asking why they have been stopped, are not given any reason that relates to them. In such circumstances the individual may well take this as evidence that they are being victimized through profiling.

A final concern is whether the police rely on the ignorance of procedural rules to circumvent the rules. Whilst PACE 1984 governs situations where the police can require a person to stop and be searched, there was a belief that in some instances the police are doing this by guile. If a police officer stops a person in a car and says: 'I'm going to look around this, can you open the boot please?' how many people will know that she only has that power if the provisions of PACE 1984 are satisfied? Similarly, if a police officer stops a person in the street and says, 'show me what is in your pockets', would they know that they were not obliged to do so unless the statutory power exists? In both examples, if the person stopped permitted the search, this would be recorded as a 'voluntary search'. Yet, many would question to what extent this is truly voluntary.[79] Eventually Code A of PACE 1984, which governs stop and search powers, was amended. The latest version of Code A states:

> An officer must not search a person, even with his or her consent, where no power to search is applicable. Even where a person is prepared to submit to a search voluntarily, the person must not be searched unless the necessary legal power exists, and the search must be in accordance with the relevant power and the provisions of this Code.[80]

As will be seen, there continues to be concern that the power is being used inappropriately, thus continuing its controversial life.

---

75. *Criminal Justice and Public Order Act 1994*, s 60(1).
76. ibid, s 60(3).
77. ibid, s 60(5).
78. Helen Fenwick, *Fenwick on Civil Liberties and Human Rights* (5th edn, Routledge 2017) 852–3.
79. For a useful discussion see ibid, 853.
80. Home Office, *Code of Practice (Code A)* (Stationery Office 2015) para 1.5.

Does the change in Code A mean anything? If people did not know the powers of the police before, why do we believe that they know their powers now? Is it not more likely that a member of the public would acquiesce to the search, erroneously believing that the police officer was permitted to do so? If the police officer does not then record that search, how would anyone find out that the officer is breaching the law?

12.2.2 'Ordinary' stop and search

As has been noted, stop and search now encompasses a number of different powers that are exercisable by the police. However, the ordinary power of stop and search remains arguably the most prolific and most controversial of them all.

The Police and Criminal Evidence Act 1984 provides:

(1) A constable may exercise any power conferred by this section—

    (a) in any place to which at the time when he proposes to exercise the power the public or any section of the public has access, on payment or otherwise, as of right by virtue of express or implied permission; or

    (b) in any other place to which people have ready access at the time when he proposes to exercise the power but which is not a dwelling.

(2) Subject to subsection (3) to (5) below, a constable—

    (a) may search—

        (i) any person or vehicle;

        (ii) anything which is in or on a vehicle, for stolen or prohibited articles . . . ; and

    (b) may detain a person or vehicle for the purpose of such a search.

(3) This section does not give a constable power to search a person or vehicle or anything in or on a vehicle unless he has reasonable grounds for suspecting that he will find stolen or prohibited articles . . .

A prohibited article means an offensive weapon, an article made or adapted for the use of theft, burglary or robbery, or a firework.[81]

12.2.2.1 Location

The first thing to note is where the power of stop and search may be exercised. A person must be in a public space, which is given a wide definition. However, it cannot take place in a dwelling (ie house). Where a person is in a garden or yard attached to a dwelling, then the powers cannot be exercised unless the officer has reasonable grounds to believe that the person does not live in that dwelling, or that they do not have permission to be in that yard or garden.[82]

The formulation of in public or to which the public has access is designed to cover situations where, for example, an event takes place on private land. So, for example, the power would exist in a field that was being used for a music festival as a section of

81. PACE 1984, ss 1(7), (8), (8B).
82. ibid, s 1(4).

the public has access (including by payment). It would also cover a railway platform. Again, that is private land, but the public have an express invitation to enter the platform area.

Where it is wholly private, however, then the power does not exist.

> **Example**
>
> Arnold and Beth are sitting in a small woodland they own close to where they live. A fence encloses the woodland. There are notices saying 'Private Woodland, Keep Out'. Constable Jones suspects Arnold is carrying an offensive weapon.

In this example, Constable Jones could not exercise the power of stop and search as Arnold is not in a space to which the public have ready access to the property. If there was no fence then it is possible that the power might exist under s 1(1)(b) because the public would have ready access.

12.2.2.2 **Reasonable suspicion**

In essence, both the power to stop people and stop vehicles require a constable to have reasonable suspicion that the person, or a person within the vehicle, is in possession of stolen goods or prohibited articles (which primarily relates to offensive weapons). The power is exercisable in public, or where 'people have ready access to it' although it does not apply to dwellings.

Code A explains that 'reasonable suspicion' is a two-part test:

> Firstly, an officer must have formed a genuine suspicion in their own mind that they will find the object for which the search power being exercised allows them to search . . . , and
>
> Secondly, the suspicion that the object will be found must be reasonable. This means that there must be an objective basis for that suspicion based on facts, information and/ or intelligence . . . [83]

The Code is clear that, save in circumstances where information or intelligence has provided a description of a person sought, then the physical characteristics of a person, including age, gender, disability, race, or religion cannot be taken into account when determining whether there is reasonable suspicion.

> **Examples**
>
> Constable Jones sees a person walking down the street. She has a hunch that he is carrying an offensive weapon. Colleagues have often noted that she has a 'sixth sense' in identifying 'the baddies'.
>
> Constable Smith is walking down the street. She sees a man walking towards her. The man stops when he sees Constable Smith and then looks around as if to see if there is an

429

83. Home Office, *Code of Practice (Code A)* (Stationery Office 2015) para 2.2.

alternative route. He puts his head down and appears nervous. From the way that he has positioned his arms, it is clear that he is carrying something underneath his coat.

Constable Richards is walking down the street. She sees someone wearing Rastafarian dress walking down the street. He has some home-made cigarettes in his hand and Constable Richards thinks it's worth stopping as the cigarettes are bound to contain marijuana.

In two of the examples above there are clearly no reasonable grounds for the purposes of a stop and search. In one, it is possible that reasonable suspicion may exist. Constable Jones has just gone on 'a hunch'. It will be remembered that the first criterion is that there must be a 'genuine suspicion' that a person is carrying a prohibited article. It would be very difficult to argue that a hunch constitutes genuine suspicion.

Constable Richards has used personal characteristics and prejudices to reach the conclusion that she is entitled to stop and search the gentleman. She is basing her reasoning purely on the basis that the man appears to be of Rastafarian descent and a prejudicial belief that all Rastafarians use marijuana. Accordingly, no reasonable suspicion can apply here.

Constable Smith is more likely to have grounds to stop and search the man she has seen. She could reasonably have a genuine belief that he is holding something that he should not. His evasion and nervousness and overall actions may mean that her suspicion is reasonable in the circumstances. This means that the stop and search would be lawful even if it turns out that he is not holding anything illegal. The results do not justify the search; it is the initial belief that justifies the search.

A further difficulty with reasonable suspicion is that it is extremely difficult to challenge. In the examples above, we could identify the justification of the stop and search if the police officer explained their reasoning in the way set out above. However, what if they do not? Bradford has noted that reasonable suspicion simply requires a police officer to say: 'I thought I saw him holding drugs' and it is very difficult to contest that.[84] The police should give further details (discussed in more detail later), but it is perhaps easier to justify the reasoning after the fact.

It was noted that there is a prohibition on using personal characteristics to justify reasonable suspicion. How far does that go? For example, if there are known characteristics that are relevant to particular crime, can the police base their decision on that? Let us take an example:

Example

Detective Sergeant Keene has briefed all of the officers in a particular location that a number of gang members are known to be carrying knives. The members of the gang are black and have a distinctive tattoo on their hands, and will all wear at least one item of purple clothing.

Constable Tearley sees two black men walking toward her. They both have the distinctive tattoo and are wearing purple hoodies.

---

84. Ben Bradford, *Stop and Search and Police Legitimacy* (Routledge 2017) 21.

In the example above, can Constable Tearley exercise her powers under PACE 1984 to stop and search these individuals? It might be thought that the answer would be 'no' because the suspicion is based on their race, their clothing, and their tattoos. However, PACE 1984 recognizes that it would be illogical to ignore known intelligence that supports a logical deduction. Code A, therefore, provides that reasonable suspicion can be founded on distinctive features where they are based on reliable information or intelligence.[85]

12.2.2.3 Procedural requirements

Where an officer does conduct a stop and search, there are a number of subsequent procedural steps that must be taken. The officer must state his name, the name of the police station that he is attached, the purpose of the search, the grounds upon which the decision has been reached, and how the search is to be conducted.[86]

A search may not require a person to remove any clothing other than an outer coat, jacket, or gloves in public.[87] Should it be necessary to do this, then the search must take place out of site of the public, which is considered to be within a police van (where practicable) or at a nearby police station.[88] Where this happens, the search should be conducted by a person of the same sex and should not take place in the sight of an officer of the opposite sex[89] unless the person specifically requests otherwise. Searches of the intimate parts of the body (not defined but presumably including the breast or genital areas of a person) may not be conducted in a police van and should ordinarily be conducted at a nearby police station.[90]

Where a stop and search power is exercised, there is an obligation to make a record of the search unless it is impracticable to do so.[91] This record shall include:

- details of the officer who conducted the search
- the object of the search
- the grounds for making it
- the date and time when it was made
- the place where it was made
- save where it is a search of an unattended vehicle, the ethnic origins of the person searched or the person in charge of the vehicle.[92]

It has been noted that when ethnicity was first recorded it was determined by the police officer which was almost certainly flawed.[93] The ethnicity is now recorded according to the determination of the person being searched and that must be more appropriate, as it means that there is less opportunity to evade the monitoring of ethnicity.

431

---

85. PACE 1984, s 2(2), (3).
86. PACE 1984, s 2(2), (3).
87. ibid, s 2(9)(a).
88. Home Office, *Code of Practice (Code A)* (Stationery Office 2015) para 3.6.
89. The Code of Practice continues to refer to 'male' and 'female' although good practice would suggest that the police should ordinarily consider a person's gender to be that which they identify and are presenting themselves as. Thus, for example, if a person is identifying and presenting themselves as female then they should be considered female even if they have not yet legally altered their gender.
90. Home Office, *Code of Practice (Code A)* (Stationery Office 2015) para 3.7.
91. PACE 1984, s 3(1).
92. ibid, s 3(6).
93. Ben Bradford, *Stop and Search and Police Legitimacy* (Routledge 2017) 22.

One of the reasons for the record to be provided is that it allows a person to challenge the legality of the search. The police officer must justify the search through, for example, setting out the reasoning behind it. This means that a court or others can decide whether there were reasonable grounds for the search. That said, it has been noted that Article 5 (right to liberty and security of the person) does not normally apply to stop and search, and the principal remedy is an action in tort for trespass to the person.[94]

The requirement that a search is conducted properly means that it remains relevant even if the officer was correct and that the individual was in possession of an illegal item. The courts have consistently deprecated breaches of PACE[95] and where evidence is gathered through an illegal stop and search, the courts can exclude this evidence as being prejudicial.[96] Potentially this could be a more valuable sanction. An individual police officer may be less concerned about his or her force being sued under trespass than they may be that an offender could be acquitted because of failings in an investigation.

12.2.2.4 Failing to comply

What is the position where a person refuses to accede to a stop and search? A police officer is entitled to use reasonable force in order to carry out the stop and search,[97] although it is perhaps more likely that the officer would execute an arrest. The grounds that gave rise to the reasonable suspicion, plus the failure to cooperate, is likely to meet the threshold for arrest (discussed at 12.2.3). A failure to cooperate could also potentially constitute the offence of obstructing a police officer in the execution of his duty.[98]

12.2.3 A racist power?

The principal controversy is over whether the power is being used in a racially discriminatory way. Stop and search provokes considerable debate amongst commentators, with many arguing that it is the only way that crime involving weapons or drugs can be curtailed. Supporters of stop and search would argue that if there is any discrepancy in their use, it is because there is discrepancy within crime. So, for example, some will argue that gang killings in London are often perpetrated by black males against other black males.[99] Accordingly, they would argue that it is logical that stop and search would be used against more black males. The counter-argument is that the power is used to victimize and label black members of society. The police, they argue, do not see black males as anything other than potential subjects. Therefore, if they see a black male in, for example, an expensive car they will think 'drug dealer', or if they see them wearing a sports top they will think 'gang member'.

This is not a new discussion, whether stop and search was being used in a racially discriminatory way featured in both the official reports following the aftermath of the Brixton riots and the murder of Stephen Lawrence.[100] Thus, for over forty years,

---

94. Helen Fenwick, *Fenwick on Civil Liberties and Human Rights* (5th edn, Routledge 2017) 855–9.
95. ibid, 860–1.
96. PACE 1984, s 78.
97. ibid, s 117.
98. *Police Act 1996*, s 89(2). This is a summary-only offence, albeit one that carries with it a maximum sentence of imprisonment.
99. Hayley Dixon, 'Police Fighting Knife Crime Should Be Exempt from Race Discrimination Laws, Trevor Phillips Says' *The Telegraph* (11 November 2018) <https://www.telegraph.co.uk/news/2018/11/11/policefighting-knife-violence-should-exempt-race-discrimination/>.
100. Ben Bowling and Coretta Phillips, 'Disproportionate and Discriminatory: Reviewing the Evidence on Police Stop and Search' (2007) 70 *Modern Law Review* 936.

a question has arisen over whether the power is being used appropriately. Incidents where high-profile black members of society such as Bishop John Sentamu (previously Archbishop of York) and Neville Lawrence (the father of Stephen Lawrence) have been subjected to stop and search does not help dispel the concerns of the black community, who use such cases as evidence that the police profile black people in a misleading way.

The temperature of the debate is often inflamed, partly because of a misunderstanding of what is being said. When Sir William MacPherson labelled the Metropolitan Police 'institutionally racist',[101] the press enjoyed reporting how individual officers were outraged that they were being labelled racist. Yet that was not what the term meant. Sir William was saying that the institutional procedures of the Metropolitan Police (and, realistically, the police service in general) were racist. That did not mean that each individual was racist, it was saying that race had not been considered appropriately when the policy and practices of the police (which individual officers were obliged to follow) were established. Similarly, there is a danger when talking about the possible discriminatory use of stop and search that one can inadvertently label all police officers racist. That is not what the debate is about. It is not suggesting that all uses of stop and search is discriminatory, but, instead, arguing whether the systematic use of stop and search by some officers has led to it being used in a discriminatory way.

There appears considerable evidence that black people are proportionately more likely to be stopped than white people.[102] However, it has been noted that identifying what 'disproportionate' means in this context is difficult to assess.[103] Statistics only show one aspect of the problem. It is also how the community perceives the use of the power. If the community perceives that the power is being used in a discriminatory way, then saying 'but it's not' will not assist. Perceptions can be drawn from different sources, but one issue is that there is evidence that the police do not always follow the procedural steps that are identified in 12.2.2.3. In particular, it has been noted that in 91 per cent of stops of white people a reason was given for the stop. When black people were stopped, this dropped to 86 per cent.[104] If no reason is given, then it is perhaps not surprising that a person may decide that the stop would be for improper purposes. More than this, however, only 61 per cent of black people thought that the reason given was legitimate. Where a person believes the stop has been illegitimate then, even if it was, this will lead to distrust. It will be remembered from earlier that there is concern that justifying a stop is too easy, perhaps explaining why so few believe stops are legitimate.

There is an inherent difficulty between theory and practice. Fenwick notes that the powers originally existed 'to maintain a fair balance between the interests of individuals and society'.[105] Thus, there was an acceptance that in order to combat crime it would sometimes be necessary to inconvenience a (law abiding) member of the public to do so. PACE 1984 required that there was a threshold for the use of such powers, thus providing protection from arbitrary interference, but as will be seen, not everybody agrees that these safeguards work.

101.   William MacPherson of Cluny, 'The Stephen Lawrence Inquiry: Report of an Inquiry' (1999) Cm 4262-I.
102.   Amongst others see Ben Bradford, *Stop and Search and Police Legitimacy* (Routledge 2017) 21; Ben Bowling and Coretta Phillips, 'Disproportionate and Discriminatory: Reviewing the Evidence on Police Stop and Search' (2007) 70 *Modern Law Review* 936.
103.   Ben Bowling and Coretta Phillips, 'Disproportionate and Discriminatory: Reviewing the Evidence on Police Stop and Search' (2007) 70 *Modern Law Review* 936 et seq.
104.   ibid, 944.
105.   Helen Fenwick, *Fenwick on Civil Liberties and Human Rights* (5th edn, Routledge 2017) 840.

Other authors suggest that at least some police believe that stop and search is for different reasons than that which the law contemplates. PACE 1984 (and other instruments) consider the power to be an investigative power. In other words, it is used to try to detect or prevent the commission of an offence. However, it has been suggested that the police consider it to be an intelligence tool too. In other words, they use it to gain intelligence on members of the public and sections of society.[106] While not contradictory (in that intelligence-led policing is considered a key part of modern law enforcement), they do approach an issue from different ends of the spectrum. Certainly, some intelligence stops will not be based on the reasonable suspicion that *the individual* is committing an offence by, for example, carrying an offensive weapon.

Perhaps the biggest issue in terms of perception is a lack of understanding about what effect a stop may have on the individual. A police officer who finds nothing may be reassured by the fact that they acted 'properly' because the grounds were genuine. However, what the officer may not think about is what the effect of that stop is on the person. For example, Delsol and Shiner note a common comment, which is that the individual searched feels humiliated by the actions of the police.[107] This may be particularly true in public settings where the individual is likely to feel that they are being judged by members of the community walking past them. Where the power is used repeatedly—and many studies show that individuals tend to be subjected to repeated exercise of the power—then the humiliation grows and society begins to view the power negatively.

Whether the powers are being used in a discriminatory manner is not an issue that is going to go away. At the time of writing, the question of racial discrimination has been raised again, with the Black Lives Matter movement returning to headlines around the world following the death of George Floyd in the United States at the hands of police officers. There have also been several high profile stop and searches in the UK which have gained media attention. In Summer 2020, Labour MP Dawn Butler said that the Metropolitan Police force remained 'institutionally racist' after officers stopped her and a friend when they were driving through Hackney. Great Britain sprinter Bianca Williams also accused the Metropolitan Police of racial profiling after her and her partner were stopped and searched when driving through west London.

The most recent data on stop and search, published in March 2020, shows that black people are disproportionately subjected to stop and search. The data shows that there were thirty-eight stop and searches for every 1,000 black people, compared to four for every 1,000 white people in 2018/19. Whilst the rate has decreased since 2009/10 (when there were 117 stop and searches for every 1,000 black people), the 2018/19 rate represents the highest rate since 2013/14.[108] According to Bradford, in London, approximately one in five stop and searches will lead to an arrest, although in some rural areas it can be as low as one in a hundred.[109]

Of course, as will be seen, an arrest does not necessarily lead to a criminal justice resolution (caution (or equivalent) or conviction). Thus, the exercise of the power could mean that it leads to the detection of very few criminals. Supporters of the policy will argue that even detecting a small number of people carrying offensive weapons is an important

106. Ben Bowling and Coretta Phillips, 'Disproportionate and Discriminatory: Reviewing the Evidence on Police Stop and Search' (2007) 70 *Modern Law Review* 936, 938.
107. Rebekah Delsol and Michael Shiner, 'Regulating Stop and Search: A Challenge for Police and Community Relations in England and Wales' (2006) 14 *Critical Criminology* 241, 245.
108. Gov.uk, 'Stop and search' (2020) <https://www.ethnicity-facts-figures.service.gov.uk/crime-justice-and-the-law/policing/stop-and-search/latest#by-ethnicity>.
109. Ben Bradford, *Stop and Search and Police Legitimacy* (Routledge 2017) 29.

way of combating knife crime. Detractors will argue, however, that the damage caused to community relations in utilizing what appears to be a relatively ineffective power is too great. It is often said that policing is on the basis of consent[110] but the same is arguably true of the whole criminal justice system. If society fails to believe that the criminal justice system is fair, then the system is in difficulty. Stop and search arguably contributes to that belief and expansive use of the power will only aggravate that.

12.3 Arrest and detention

Perhaps the most notable police power is the right to arrest a suspect on suspicion of committing a crime. It may come as something as a surprise that 'arrest' is not defined in statute, and it remains a creature of the common law. This is partly because the police are, in terms of the law, a relatively modern creature.[111] Even today, an arrest need not be conducted by the police. You may have heard the term 'citizen's arrest'. Whilst that is not strictly true as a term, it remains the law that any citizen can make an arrest if a person is carrying out an indictable offence, or any person that he has reasonable grounds to suspect may be committing an indictable offence.[112] However, it is a risky venture as wrongful arrest and unlawful detention constitute torts of trespass, rendering the wrongful arrester liable for compensation. A chief constable is liable in tort for the actions of his constables,[113] but a private citizen would be personally liable.

What then is an arrest? Put simply, it is the power to take a person suspected of an offence into lawful custody. The touching of a person with a view to restraining them amounts to an arrest.[114] Save where there is another power to do so (eg stop and search as discussed earlier), exercising the power of arrest is the only way that restraining or detaining a person can be considered lawful and if the police do not exercise that power then they commit a battery.

‖\ Case Box *R v Iqbal*

In *R v Iqbal*[115] the appellant had been detained by the police and placed in handcuffs because the officers thought that he was wanted for a crime. He was told that he would be arrested, but it would be by other officers. Indeed, the relevant officer expressly stated that he was not arrested.[116] The appellant escaped and was charged and convicted of attempting to escape from lawful custody.[117] The Court of Appeal quashed his conviction holding that while it was illegal to escape once arrested, it was not illegal to do so when merely detained but not arrested. The Court of Appeal noted that without a power of arrest, a person has the right to leave 'at will'.[118]

435

110. Robert Reiner, 'Policing a Postmodern Society' (1992) 55 *Modern Law Review* 761.
111. Organized policing arguably began in the nineteenth century (initially in Glasgow) and it was not until Sir Robert Peel passed the *Metropolitan Police Act 1829* that a full-time force was established.
112. PACE 1984, s 24A.
113. *Police Act 1996*, s 88.
114. *Wood v DPP* [2008] EWHC 1056 (Admin).
115. [2011] EWCA Crim 273.
116. ibid, at [3].
117. A common law offence.
118. PACE 1984, s 29 and see [2011] EWCA Crim 273 at [14].

An arrest is not necessary for a suspect to be interviewed (discussed at 12.3), but it is necessary to stop a person leaving. Thus, a person could be interviewed, including under caution, voluntarily and without being arrested. However, if that person wished to terminate the interview and leave, they would have that absolute right unless, at that point, they were arrested. An arrest provides additional powers to the police, including the potential to search the property of the person arrested.[119] However, the belief that a person would not consent to a search being carried out does not justify a decision to arrest someone who has attended the station to voluntarily answer questions, because the police could seek a search warrant.[120]

12.3.1 Arrest with or without warrant

There are two principal forms of arrest under English law. An arrest with a warrant and an arrest without a warrant. A warrant is the order of a court (usually a magistrates' court or Crown Court but it could include the civil courts) that empowers the police to arrest the person named on it and requiring them to be brought before them. A warrant may be 'backed by bail', meaning that the suspect can be bailed on condition that he attends court at the given time. More commonly, however, an arrest warrant will require the production of the person before the court, meaning that they remain in police custody until the court decides whether to grant bail.

The more common power is an arrest without a warrant. This is the power of the police (or others) to arrest a person who has commissioned, or is suspected of commissioning, a crime. While other powers exist, we will concentrate on the 'ordinary' power of arrest without a warrant which is now governed by PACE 1984.[121] Under PACE, a constable may arrest without a warrant:

- anyone who is about to commit an offence
- anyone who is in the act of committing an offence
- anyone whom he has reasonable grounds for suspecting to be about to commit an offence
- anyone whom he has reasonable grounds for suspecting to be committing an offence
- where a constable has reasonable grounds to believe a crime has been committed, anyone who he has reasonable grounds to have committed it
- where an offence has been committed, anyone who is guilty of the offence or anyone who he has reasonable grounds for suspecting him to be guilty of it.[122]

In other words an officer can arrest someone he thinks is about to commit an offence, is committing an offence, or has committed an offence (or someone he has reasonable grounds to suspect of the above). This is a very broad power, although logical in terms of the duties of the police. They have a duty to prevent crime (about to commit an offence), detect crime (committing an offence), and investigate crime (has committed the offence).

---

119.   PACE 1984, s 18.
120.   *R (on the application of TL) v Chief Constable of Surrey Police* [2017] EWHC 129 (Admin).
121.   PACE 1984, s 24.
122.   ibid, ss 24(1)–(3).

In order to justify the arrest, the officer must have reasonable grounds to believe it is necessary for one or more of the following purposes:

- to enable the name of the person to be ascertained
- to enable the address of the person to be ascertained
- to prevent the person in question
  - causing physical injury to himself or any other person
  - suffering physical injury
  - causing loss or damage to property
  - committing an offence against public decency or
  - causing an unlawful obstruction of the highway
- to protect a child or other vulnerable person
- to allow the prompt and effective investigation of the offence or the conduct of the person
- to prevent any prosecution for the offence from being hindered by the disappearance of the person.[123]

The length of this list may be surprising, as it could be thought that the most obvious reason would be the 'prompt and effective investigation of the offence'. While this is likely to be the most common reason for most offences, other reasons could be given. Let us take two examples:

Example Speeding

A man has been stopped by the police whilst driving a car. The car was recorded as driving 53mph in a 40mph zone. The driver refuses to provide his name.

Example Protests

Five people have formed a 'human chain' to block the road in and out of an army base to draw attention to the fact that, in their opinion, the army are causing harm and misery to people around the world.

In neither of these examples would an arrest be necessary to investigate an offence. In the first example, the crime has already been detected and the appropriate evidence gathered. All that is required is to prove that D was responsible for driving the car, and that the car was driving at excess speed.[124] The police would ordinarily deal with such matters by issuing a fixed penalty notice (although they could summon him to court). However, if they do not know who he is then the chances of him paying the fine or

---

123. ibid, ss 24(4), (5).
124. *Road Traffic Regulation Act 1984*, s 89.

attending court is minimal. Thus, the constable could decide to arrest him in order to ascertain his name. This could be done through, for example, searching him,[125] or by asking him questions to ascertain his identity.

In the second example, the crime of obstructing the public highway has been committed.[126] There will be little need to investigate the crime as it is obvious who has done it. Here, the constable may decide to arrest in order to prevent the (continuing) unlawful obstruction of the highway. Interestingly, this is also an example of when an arrest may not lead to a prosecution. In this example, the police may decide that preventing the obstruction is sufficient. While a person arrested outside of a police station should ordinarily be conveyed there as soon as practicable,[127] this is subject to the power of the police to release a person before conveying the person to the police station.[128] This is sometimes known as being 'de-arrested'. Thus, the police in this example may decide to arrest the protesters, move them away from the army base and then de-arrest them, releasing them without any further action. This would be a perfectly lawful arrest (subject to any debate concerning an interference with Article 10 ECHR, but it is not necessary to discuss that here).

12.3.1.1 Reasonable suspicion

As was the case with stop and search, the key threshold for arrest is 'reasonable suspicion'. Much of what was said in respect of stop and search applies here. This includes, for example, the fact that it can sometimes be difficult to challenge a perception. So, for example, if a police officer says: 'I had reasonable grounds to believe that you were going to punch x' it can be difficult to challenge that as it, in essence, relates to the belief of the arresting officer.

In *Hayes v Chief Constable of Merseyside Police*[129] Hughes LJ accepted that there are two steps to ascertaining reasonable grounds:

1. a police officer must honestly believe that arrest is necessary, for one or more identified s 24(5) reasons; and
2. his decision must be one which, objectively reviewed afterwards according to the information known to him the time, is held to have been made on reasonable grounds.[130]

The wording of stage 2 is interesting. The question of objective reasonableness must be judged on the information known to the officer at that time. Thus, if there was other information that was not known (including, presumably, information that should have been known), then this will not be taken into account.

12.3.1.2 Information upon arrest

Where a person is arrested, then certain information must be provided. This includes the fact that he is under arrest.[131] This is not a formality and it applies even where it would seem obvious that a person is under arrest.[132] It will be remembered from

---

125. PACE 1984, s 32.
126. *Highways Act 1980*, s 137.
127. PACE 1984, s 30(1A).
128. ibid, s 30A when read in conjunction with s 30(1B).
129. [2011] EWCA Civ 911.
130. ibid, at [40] and [42].
131. PACE 1984, s 28(1).
132. ibid, s 28(2).

R v Iqbal[133] that the courts consider this an important function of the arrest process, and they will render an offence unlawful if it is not done. The grounds for the arrest must also be provided, including if they are obvious.[134]

The rule that a person must be notified that he is under arrest and the reasons for it is one that predates PACE 1984 and in *Christie v Leachinsky*[135] it was held that it was a long-standing rule, that owed its existence to the fact that the arrest is the beginning of the process by which a person would be held to account for his actions. For a person to account for his actions, he must be aware of what he is being asked to account for.

While not expressly mentioned in statute, Code G makes clear that a police officer must caution an offender upon arrest if they are to be asked questions.[136] The wording of the caution is considered at 12.4. Custom and practice is that a person arrested will be immediately cautioned. Strictly speaking this is not required but it ensures that anything an offender says upon arrest can be considered as evidence.

12.3.1.3 **Necessity**

Section 24 makes clear in a number of instances that it must be *necessary* to make an arrest. As has been noted before, PACE is accompanied by Codes of Practice. Code G governs the execution of arrests.[137] The Code of Practice makes clear that arrest is, in essence, a measure of last resort,[138] but it has been suggested that the police will ordinarily resort to arrest routinely.[139]

Code G does give one example where an arrest may not be necessary.

> **Example** Ascertaining identity from fingerprints
>
> In an example given earlier, it was suggested that where a driver of a speeding car refuses to provide his name, it was possible that this could justify an arrest under s 24. Code G, however, notes that if the police officer has a portable fingerprint device then an alternative would be to use the power under PACE to require fingerprints to be taken by an officer.[140] An arrest is probably more draconian than requiring fingerprints and therefore that probably does mean that fingerprints should be tried first. Of course, if the suspect's fingerprints are not on file and no match is produced then it may be necessary to arrest but it is easier to show necessity when alternatives have been tried.

439

The courts are becoming increasingly prepared to entertain challenges to the necessity of an arrest. In *Hayes v Chief Constable of Merseyside Police*[141] the Court of Appeal noted that the requirement to justify the necessity of the arrest is an important safeguard under Article 5 ECHR.[142] In *Richardson v Chief Constable of West Midlands Police*[143] the High

---

133. [2011] EWCA Crim 273.
134. PACE 1984, s 28(3),(4).
135. [1947] AC 573 at 586.
136. Home Office, *Code of Practice (Code G)* (Stationery Office 2012) para 3.1.
137. ibid.
138. ibid, para 2.4.
139. Helen Fenwick, *Fenwick on Civil Liberties and Human Rights* (5th edn, Routledge 2017) 878.
140. PACE 1984, s 61(6A).
141. [2011] EWCA Civ 911.
142. ibid, at [15].
143. [2011] EWHC 773 (QB).

Court reiterated that where a person is prepared to be interviewed voluntarily, then the police must properly articulate the reason why it is then necessary to arrest the offender, rather than ask the questions voluntarily. Evidentially there is no difference between questions asked when arrested or voluntarily, the only difference is that the suspect can leave at will if not arrested. However, the police always have the right to arrest at that point of time if they reasonably believe that this would impede their investigation.

In *Lord Hanningfield of Chelmsford v Chief Constable of Essex*[144] the High Court noted that when considering the necessity of an arrest, it was important that alternatives were not treated as a 'box-ticking exercise' but, rather, that the arresting officer carefully considers alternatives and be able to justify why they were not chosen.[145] Of course, that is more likely in the context of a planned operation (as was the case in *Hanningfield*). Where an incident is occurring live, particularly a violent offence, then it is more likely that the immediate reaction of a police officer will be supported.

12.3.1.4 Record of the arrest

A police officer is obliged to record, either in his pocket book or other equivalent record, the following matters:

- the nature and circumstances of the offence leading to the arrest
- the reason or reasons why arrest was necessary
- the giving of the caution
- anything said by the person at the time of the arrest.[146]

This record should be made at the time of the arrest or, alternatively, as soon as possible thereafter.[147] This phrasing is somewhat odd because it is highly unlikely the record will be made as soon as the arrest is made, as there are other aspects that must occur at that time. The key point is that it should be made contemporaneously. If done so, it can be adduced as evidence where the lawfulness of the arrest is being challenged.[148]

12.3.1.5 Transfer to a police station

While some arrests will be made at a police station, it is more likely that the arrest will take place elsewhere. The prisoner should be conveyed to a police station as soon as possible after arrest.[149] This is subject to the point noted earlier, that there is the right to release an offender before they reach the police station.

Ordinarily the prisoner must be transferred to a 'designated police station',[150] although exceptions are made where it is intended that the prisoner will be detained for less than six hours,[151] or where a constable acting alone has arrested the prisoner and he believes it will not be possible to take him to a designated police station without

144. [2013] EWHC 243 (QB).
145. ibid, at [22].
146. Home Office, *Code of Practice (Code G)* (Stationery Office 2012) para 4.1.
147. ibid, para 4.2.
148. The Law of Evidence is outside the scope of this book, but the record would undoubtedly constitute documentary evidence that would be admissible in a criminal trial.
149. PACE 1984, s 30.
150. ibid, s 30(2).
151. ibid, s 30(3).

assistance and where there is a fear the prisoner will injure himself, the constable, or any other person.[152]

While many police stations used to be designated, increasingly only a small number of police stations within a police force are now designated.[153] This creates larger prisoner-handling capacity in a smaller number of places. The idea behind this is that it is more resource effective (not least because each designated police station must have an officer of at least the rank of sergeant who is appointed as a 'custody officer'[154]). However, there are concerns that in rural areas this can mean that people who are arrested are taken tens of miles away from where they reside.

🔄 QUESTION FOR REFLECTION

The police have no legal obligation to return someone to the place they are arrested. In rural areas (eg, the police area of Dyfed Powys Police) it could take several hours by public transport to get back home after release (if public transport even serves such locations). Is this fair? While the police are under pressure for policing, is it right that someone potentially innocent may incur considerable cost and inconvenience if they are arrested?

12.3.2 **Detention**

When a person is arrested and brought to a police station, it is necessary to decide whether they can be detained against their will. Separate procedures exist in respect of the detention of those suspected of terrorism[155] but in this section we will consider those who are detained for 'ordinary' crimes.

Along with the statute, Code of Practice C governs the detention, treatment, and questioning of suspects. As with the other codes, this is where much of the detail is included.

There is, in essence, a presumption against continued detention at a police station. PACE 1984 states that, save where it appears a person was unlawfully at large,[156] a custody sergeant must order the release of a detained person if he becomes aware that the grounds for detention have ceased to apply, unless justified by other grounds.[157]

In the example below, the original reason for detention (reasonable grounds to suspect Tim of burglary and the need to ascertain his identity) no longer applies. However, the arrest warrant provides other lawful grounds to detain him and so he will not be released.

☰ **Example** Justified by other grounds

Tim was arrested by PC Dobson when she thought that he was going to break into a shop at night. He refused to give his name and he was detained, in part, to ascertain his identity.[158] His identity is confirmed, and he provides convincing reasons why he was by

---

152. ibid, s 30(5).
153. Chief constables can designate police stations as suitable for detaining prisoners (PACE 1984, s 35).
154. ibid, s 36(1),(3).
155. These rights are set out in Code H. In essence, this replaces Code C for the purposes of those who are arrested under the *Terrorism Act 2000*.
156. For example, an escaped prisoner.
157. PACE 1984, s 34(2), (4).
158. ibid, s 24(5)(a)

the shop. However, Tim failed to attend a previous court hearing and an arrest warrant was issued by the Crown Court at Lancaster, ordering him to be brought before the relevant judge.

12.3.2.1 **Initial decision**

When a person is first brought to the police station upon arrest, the custody officer shall decide whether there is sufficient evidence to charge the person with a crime.[159] The answer to this will invariably be 'no' and so the suspect should be released on bail or otherwise unless the custody officer has reasonable grounds to believe that continued detention is required to secure or preserve evidence or to obtain evidence by questioning him.[160] The person detained should be informed of the reasons for the detention and a written record of the reasons and the details of his detention should be created.[161]

The written record should contain:

- the reason for the arrest
- the reasons why the custody sergeant has concluded that it is lawful to detain him
- details of whether the defendant avails himself of his rights (see 12.3.2.2), and, if not, that it has been made clear to him that he has those rights
- details of all reviews taken of the right to detain him.

The suspect and his legal advisers have the right to view the whole of the custody record.[162] This is, in part, because they have the right to challenge the appropriateness of a decision to detain an individual following arrest. Without knowing the official reasons for the detention, it would become impossible to challenge the decision of the custody sergeant.

The suspect should be informed of his rights, and written confirmation of those rights and how they are exercised should also be provided.[163] The suspect should be told to sign the written record to indicate that he has been provided with this information or, if he refuses to do so, a note should be contained on the record to that effect.[164]

If the offender says anything when he is brought into the police station and presented for the initial question on detention, this should be noted on the custody record. Similarly, any comment made in response to being told that he is to be detained for a relevant purpose should also be recorded in the written record.[165]

Each chief constable must ensure that there is a process in place by which detained persons can be risk-assessed. The custody sergeant should conduct that risk assessment

---

159.   ibid, s 37(1).
160.   ibid, s 37(3).
161.   ibid, s 37(4), (5). Where a person is incapable of understanding what is being said, is violent (or likely to become violent), or in need of urgent medical attention, then they do not need to be told immediately of the reasons (s 37(6)).
162.   Home Office, *Code of Practice (Code C)* (Stationery Office 2018) para 2.4.
163.   ibid, paras 3.1–3.2.
164.   ibid, para 3.2A.
165.   ibid, para 3.4.

and ensure that a copy of that risk assessment, its conclusion, and any plan arising from this, is included within the custody record. This could include, for example, the requirement that a person sees a medical practitioner or is watched frequently because they are at risk of self-harm.

12.3.2.2 Rights of those detained

A person who is detained in police custody after arrest has a number of rights available to them, namely:

- the right to consult privately with a solicitor[166]
- the right to have someone informed of their arrest[167]
- the right to consult the Codes of Practice
- the right to an interpreter or translator (where necessary)
- the right to understand why they have been arrested and why they have been detained.[168]

Not to be incommunicado

The wording of these rights may cause some surprise since television dramas often suggest that a person has the right to make a 'telephone call'. The right is primarily the ability to have someone informed of the fact that the suspect has been arrested. However, other rights flow from this, including:

- the police responding truthfully if a relative or someone interested in the welfare of the detainee asks whether the detainee has been arrested (unless the detainee says otherwise)[169]
- the right to have friends, family, or those interested in his welfare, visit him in custody, but only at the discretion of the custody officer[170]
- be given writing materials and allowed to telephone one person for a reasonable time, the cost of which can be borne at public expense.[171]

So the television is correct, there is a right to a telephone call. Save where that call is to a solicitor, it can be listened to and anything said on the telephone can be adduced in evidence at court.[172]

Legal advice

Perhaps the most important right when detained is the right to a solicitor.[173] As soon as a person is brought to the police station, he should be asked by the custody officer if he wishes to avail himself of this right.[174] Regardless of what his answer is, this should

443

---

166. PACE 1984, s 58.
167. ibid, s 56.
168. Home Office, *Code of Practice (Code C)* (London, TSO 2018) para 3.1.
169. ibid, para 5.5.
170. ibid, para 5.4. These will be comparatively rare in most instances.
171. ibid, para 5.6.
172. ibid, para 5.7. Presumably the latter is conditional on the fact that the suspect has been cautioned.
173. PACE 1984, s 58.
174. Home Office, *Code of Practice (Code C)* (London, TSO 2018) para 3.2A.

be put in the custody record and the detainee asked to sign the record to indicate that response. Where the detainee chooses not to sign the register, that fact should be included in the record.[175]

Traditionally a solicitor would attend the police station to provide advice but in modern times this is comparatively rare, save when paid privately or when the matter is particularly serious. Where the defendant wishes to avail himself of free legal advice, then the initial contact is now by telephone. There are two types of telephone contact: CDS Direct and the Duty Solicitor Scheme. CDS Direct is a telephone hotline that is maintained by the Legal Aid Agency and provides advice on the following matters:

- detained for a non-imprisonable offence
- arrested on a bench warrant and being held for production at court
- arrested for drink driving
- detained in relation to breach of police or court bail.[176]

CDS Direct is the only way that free legal advice can be obtained for the above cases unless the police wish to interview the suspect, they need an appropriate adult, they cannot communicate by telephone, or they allege serious misconduct by the police. In any of those situations, the matter should be referred to a duty solicitor.

One issue with CDS Direct is that it has been reported that the advisers are generally not solicitors and can include paralegals and former police officers.[177] Of course, the advisers are still bound by a code of conduct and therefore the mere fact that a person used to be a former police officer is not, by itself, problematic, not least because a number of police officers will subsequently qualify as a solicitor or barrister. However, the fact that all advisers are not legally qualified could be more problematic. While these may appear technical crimes, it is not always possible to identify all the relevant circumstances, including whether the arrest was itself lawful. The safeguard is that if they are to be questioned then it will be passed to a duty solicitor but, as will be seen, that does not necessarily mean that a solicitor will be despatched.

The second way that telephone advice may be given is through the duty solicitor. The police now contact the 'Defence Solicitors Call Centre' (DSCC) who maintain the rota of duty solicitors for a particular area. These are solicitor practices that have a contract with the *Legal Aid Agency* to provide a service to that police station. The DSCC will contact the solicitor next on rota and ordinarily the initial advice will be by telephone.[178] This is partly out of expediency. In some areas, particularly rural areas, the geographical reach of duty solicitors can be considerable. It may take time for the solicitor to attend the station. Therefore, an initial telephone conversation where, for example, the solicitor can identify whether the arrest took place properly, what issues are likely to arise, and provide immediate advice (eg 'do not attend an identification parade or answer questions without me') can be provided. Ordinarily, a visit would then follow this initial consultation.

---

175. ibid, para 3.2A.
176. ibid, para 6B.
177. Rosemary Pattenden and Layla Skinns, 'Choice, Privacy and Publicly Funded Legal Advice at Police Stations' (2010) 73 *Modern Law Review* 349, 352.
178 ibid

Where a person wishes to use their own solicitor (at private expense) then the details are provide to the DSCC and they will make contact. If they cannot make contact with them, the person will be offered the services of the duty solicitor telephone service while awaiting their solicitor to get in contact.

While the statute refers to 'a solicitor',[179] Code C makes it clear that it need not be a solicitor, but could include an accredited station representative.[180] The *Legal Aid Agency* operates this scheme, and it gives paralegals, law graduates, and others the opportunity to attend to provide legal assistance during interviews. Does this satisfy PACE? Pattenden and Skinns argue that it does, because PACE 1984 does not state that a person is entitled to access to a solicitor for free.[181] That is correct. All s 58 states is that a person has the right to legal advice if he requests it. A person has that right, but the solicitor can levy a charge. Code C and the Legal Aid Agency goes further than PACE 1984 by providing free legal assistance but it does not state that this legal assistance has to be provided by a solicitor.

Concern has previously been raised about whether legal consultations are private,[182] but more recent studies have suggested that the police have improved their approach to privacy.[183] The difference may be explained by the fact that the police have, as noted earlier, been centralizing custody operations, creating newer, larger facilities that have been designed with private communication in mind.

Deferring notification or legal advice

Whilst the right to have someone informed of the arrest and the right to legal advice should ordinarily take place as soon as requested, PACE 1984 does allow them to be deferred for a period of time in limited circumstances.

Where a person has been arrested for an indictable offence,[184] the right to notify someone that they have been arrested can be deferred by up to thirty-six hours by an officer who is at least the rank of an inspector.[185] The deferral can only be where there is reasonable cause to believe that telling someone the name of the arrested person:

- will lead to interference with or harm to evidence or persons
- will lead to other suspects not yet identified being alerted
- will hinder the recovery of property obtained by the offence or
- the person arrested has benefited from the conduct, and the recovery of the benefit would be hindered by informing someone of the arrest.[186]

While the delay can be for up to thirty-six hours, it should only be for so long as the grounds remain relevant.

445

---

179.   PACE 1984, s 58(1).
180.   Home Office, *Code of Practice (Code C)* (London, TSO 2018) para 6.12.
181.   Rosemary Pattenden and Layla Skinns, 'Choice, Privacy and Publicly Funded Legal Advice at Police Stations' (2010) 73 *Modern Law Review* 349, 353.
182.   ibid, 358.
183.   Layla Skinns, Andrew Wooff, and Amy Sprawson, 'Preliminary Findings on Police Custody Delivery in the Twenty-First Century: Is It "good" Enough?' (2017) 27 *Policing and Society* 358, 364.
184.   Indictable means an indictable-only offence or either-way offence: see 13.3.
185.   PACE 1984, s 56(2), (3).
186.   ibid, s 56(5),(5A).

> ☰ **Example** Delaying notification
>
> Arthur has been arrested on suspicion of burglary. Arthur and one other person was seen coming out of a house. When presented at custody, an inspector refuses to allow Arthur to notify anyone he has been arrested because they are trying to find the other suspect. Three hours later, Paul is arrested and admits, upon arrest, that he was in the house with Arthur.
>
> The grounds for not permitting someone to be notified of arrest now no longer apply, and thus Arthur should now have the right to tell someone that he has been detained.

The more controversial power is that which relates to delaying legal advice. An officer of at least the rank of superintendent can authorize a delay where a person is arrested for an indictable offence for no longer than thirty-six hours.[187] The grounds for the deferral are the same as those described earlier in respect of not notifying a person of arrest.[188] However, it is obviously more serious to delay legal advice.

In *R v Samuel*[189] the Court of Appeal was clear on the importance of s 58. The Court notes that the Act requires that a superintendent has reasonable cause to believe that a solicitor *will* lead to interference in the investigation. That is not the same as *may* and the police should take into account the fact that if a solicitor were to do any of the acts identified in PACE, they would commit a criminal offence.[190] The court noted that as solicitors are officers of the court, it would be comparatively rare for the grounds to be satisfied, and it would almost certainly need to relate to a particular solicitor and not solicitors in general.[191] In other words, they must have reasonable grounds to believe that solicitor *x* will hinder the investigation, not that *any* solicitor will do so. The threshold for denying access is high and the police should be slow to deny access.

The exception to this position relates to breath sample analysis. In *Kennedy v CPS*[192] the defendant was accused of drink-driving. When he was arrested and taken to the police station he was required to provide two samples of breath.[193] He refused, stating that he wished to speak to his solicitor first. While the custody sergeant had placed a telephone call to the duty solicitors, he refused to delay the process for obtaining a sample. The defendant refused to cooperate, and he was convicted of refusing to provide a sample.[194] He claimed that Article 6 ECHR and the provisions of PACE 1984 meant that he was entitled to consult his solicitor. The High Court rejected this argument. The court noted that Article 6 does not prescribe a particular point in time at which legal representation should be given.[195] The court noted that the public interest was served in the breath samples being identified as soon as practicable (so that the reading is proximate to the driving).

---

187.   ibid, s 58(5), (6).
188.   ibid, s 58(8), (8A).
189.   [1988] 2 WLR 920.
190.   ibid, at 626. The conduct would undoubtedly constitute, at the very least, perverting the course of justice.
191.   ibid, at 626.
192.   [2002] EWHC Admin 2297.
193.   *Road Traffic Act 1988*, s 7.
194.   ibid, 7(6). This is punished in the same way as driving with excess alcohol.
195.   [2002] EWHC Admin 2297 at [31].

It should also be noted that, of course, the breath sample is only one aspect of the investigation. A person would ordinarily be interviewed following the provision of a positive sample. There is no reason why that interview could not be delayed until a solicitor arrives, and that would seem to strike the correct balance between legal representation and gathering perishable evidence.

12.3.2.3 **Duration of detention**

There are strict limits as to how long a person can be detained before charge when arrested. The ordinary rule is that a person cannot be detained for longer than twenty-four hours without charge.[196] Ordinarily, the 'clock' starts ticking from the moment of his arrest[197] although alternative rules exist where the person was arrested abroad or outside the force area of the force seeking his arrest.[198]

Where a person has been arrested for an indictable offence, an officer of at least the rank of a superintendent can authorize detention for a period not exceeding thirty-six hours (ie a maximum of twelve hours' extension) if he has reasonable grounds to believe:

- the continued detention is necessary to secure or preserve evidence relating to the offence he is under arrest for, or to obtain such evidence by questioning
- the investigation is being conducted diligently and expeditiously.[199]

The decision to extend detention to thirty-six hours must take place before the expiry of the ordinary twenty-four hour period.[200] This is presumably to ensure that the decision is taken seriously and without pressure of time. Where the decision was taken to hold the offender incommunicado or to defer legal advice, or the suspect has chosen not to exercise this right, then the superintendent should remind the suspect of that right or, when it has been deferred, decide whether the right should now be allowed to be exercised.[201]

If, after thirty-six hours, the police wishes to hold the suspect for longer they must seek the permission of a court. The police must seek the permission of the magistrates' court.[202] The person should ordinarily be brought before the court when such an application is made and must be given a copy of the application.[203] A suspect is entitled to legal representation and the hearing shall be adjourned to facilitate this.[204] As they have not been charged, the suspect is still entitled to free legal representation by the duty solicitor. If, however, they engage their own solicitor then they will be required to pay for this.

The police will detail the charges that the suspect is being investigated for and provide a summary of the evidence against him and information about how the investigation has proceeded so far.[205] The grounds for continued detention are the same as must be addressed by the superintendent,[206] but obviously this time it is a judicial matter and the magistrates are expected to scrutinize the evidence.

196. PACE 1984, s 41(1).
197. ibid, s 41(2)(a), (c).
198. ibid, s 41(2)(b) and s 41(3).
199. ibid, s 42(1).
200. ibid, s 24(4).
201. ibid, s 42(9).
202. ibid, s 43(1).
203. ibid, s 43(2).
204. ibid, s 43(3).
205. ibid, s 43(14).
206. ibid, s 43(4).

The police must ensure that they bring the matter to the court before thirty-six hours after arrest (ie the time that the police can authorize detention),[207] and if they do not then the magistrates are required to decide whether it would have been reasonably possible to apply before the expiry of thirty-six hours. If they believe it was then the application should be dismissed,[208] meaning the suspect is released.

The maximum period that the court can extend the detention for is thirty-six hours,[209] but it should be noted that this is the maximum period and the court could prescribe a lesser period. The thirty-six hours is added to the thirty-six hours that the police can authorize, meaning that the maximum duration is seventy-two hours. The 'clock' does not stop if the suspect is released before seventy-two hours (but later questioned) because the time is from, inter alia, the time of arrest.[210]

If the investigation is still not complete then the police can re-apply to the magistrates' court for a final extension.[211] Such an extension cannot be for longer than thirty-six hours and it cannot take the total period of extension beyond ninety-six hours.[212] The grounds are the same as before but the court is expected to scrutinize this even more intensely.

Reviews of detention

While the maximum period of detention is as discussed, there is a requirement to periodically review the detention of the individual.[213] The purpose of the review is to ascertain whether the criteria for detention is satisfied. If it is not, then, as noted above, the person should be released. The suspect or his legal representative is entitled to make representations to the review officer[214] unless he is unfit to do so, either by reason of condition or behaviour.[215] That said, it is important to note that it is comparatively rare for a review to reach such a decision.

The first review must take place no more than six hours after the suspect has been brought to the police station.[216] The second review should take place no more than nine hours after the first review, and subsequent reviews should take place no longer than nine hours from the previous one.[217] It should be noted that the second and subsequent reviews refer to the previous review and not when the person is brought in. There is no reason why a review cannot take place before six or nine hours and this may happen where, for example, a person was intoxicated and is becoming sober enough to communicate clearly.

☰ Example Reviews

Emma is arrested and brought into a police station at 10:00. Her detention must be reviewed no later than 16:00 but the review takes place at 15:00. Her second review must take place no later than midnight (nine hours after 15:00).

---

207.   ibid, s 43(5).
208.   ibid, s 43(7) and see *R v Slough Justices, ex parte Stirling* (1987) 151 JP 603.
209.   PACE 1984, s 43(12).
210.   *R (on the application of Chief Constable of Manchester) v Salford Magistrates' Court* [2011] EWHC 157 Admin.
211.   PACE 1984, s 44.
212.   ibid, s 44(3).
213.   ibid, s 40.
214.   ibid, s 40(13).
215.   ibid, s 40(14).
216.   ibid, s 40(3)(a).
217.   ibid, s 40(3)(b), (c).

The review of persons who have not yet been charged should take place by an officer of at least the rank of an inspector and may not be someone directly involved in the investigation.[218] While, in many instances, the review will take place in person, it is recognized that in some police forces (particularly rural ones) this may not be possible as the duty inspector may be based at a different police station. In such circumstances there is the right to conduct the review by telephone,[219] and the person continues to have the right to make representations etc either by telephone or in writing.[220]

Reviews can be postponed if it is not practicable to carry out the review at the time it is due.[221] Ordinarily, this would be because the person is being interviewed (and it is, in the opinion of the review officer not appropriate to interrupt that interview) or because the review officer is unavailable.[222] Where it is postponed, the reasons must be recorded in the custody record and the review should take place as soon as possible thereafter. If the suspect is asleep, the review can still take place and the person does not need to be woken up to make representations, not least because there is a constant duty on the custody officer to consider whether to release a person and therefore any representations could be taken into account when the person wakes up.

It should be noted that the reviews take place every nine hours irrespective of whether a court has extended the maximum period of duration. The court is not second-guessing whether there is sufficient evidence to charge, they are simply saying that the grounds exist to justify the further detention of the suspect. The police must decide, at each review, whether those grounds remain live or whether the offender should be released or charged.

12.4 Interviewing the suspect

The final issue to consider, albeit briefly, is the rules on how to interview a suspect who has been arrested and detained within the police station. Many of these rules will be covered in other modules, most notably the Law of Evidence, but it is an important part of the investigation of crime and therefore they deserve to be summarized here.

Along with PACE 1984 itself, Code C remains the key document that governs the rules on interviewing a suspect. Before being interviewed, the suspect should be reminded of the caution.[223] The terms of the caution are:

> You do not have to say anything. But it may harm your defence if you do not mention when questioned something which you later rely on in Court. Anything you do say may be given in evidence.[224]

12.4.1 Right to silence

The caution identified above was introduced in 1994 and was, and arguably remains, controversial because it is seen as potentially contradicting the right to silence. The change was to incorporate amendments to the right to silence introduced by

---

218. ibid, s 40(1)(b).
219. ibid, s 40A.
220. ibid, s 40A(4).
221. ibid, s 40(4)(a).
222. ibid, s 40(4)(b).
223. Home Office, *Code of Practice (Code C)* (London, TSO 2018) para 11.1A.
224. ibid, para 10.5.

the *Criminal Justice and Public Order Act 1994*.[225] Prior to the changes, there was an absolute right to silence when interviewed. A suspect could remain silent and a jury would be told that they could not take the silence into account. The logic of this is that it is for the state to prove that a suspect is guilty and therefore there is no requirement on the defendant to assist. The emphasis on 'tough on crime' in the 1990s led to the new system of adverse inferences.

While there is still a right to remain silent—indeed, the opening words of the caution indicate this—there are now restrictions. For the purposes of the *investigative interview*, there are three instances when adverse inferences may be relevant:

- When a person fails to mention something during the interview that they later rely on as evidence in their trial.[226] This tends to be an exculpatory statement, for example, an alibi or comments about what clothing was being worn (where distinctive clothing may have been mentioned by a witness).

- When a person fails to account for objects, substances, or marks found on him.[227] For example, if a person is suspected of burglary and, when arrested, he is found in possession of skeleton keys that allow locks to be picked.

- When a person fails to account for presence at a particular place.[228] For example, a person is arrested on suspicion of robbery and he is found in a street next to where the robbery is alleged to have happened late at night, when he lives in a different town.

Realistically the latter two can be thought of as true interferences with the right to silence. They will allow adverse inferences to be drawn when they do not answer a question asked of them in respect of physical evidence (property or presence). The first is only an interference in that if the person makes an exculpatory statement during his trial, an adverse inference can be drawn. But, for example, if he does not (eg he only denies matters) then no adverse inference can be drawn.

Adverse inferences cannot be used as the sole evidence to convict a person[229] but they can be used to 'top-up' a finding of guilt. This remains extremely controversial because, to many, it breaches the presumption of innocence that requires the state to prove all matters independently of the defendant. However, the courts have consistently ruled that the rules are compatible with the right to a fair trial.[230]

☰ Example 'Topping up guilt'

Ron has been accused of the robbery of Gail. Gail said that someone matching Ron's description grabbed her, pushed her against a wall, and grabbed her mobile telephone. When Ron is arrested he is found in possession of Gail's telephone. When asked how he came to have that telephone in his possession, he refuses to say anything. At trial, he testifies that he found

---

225. *Criminal Justice and Public Order Act 1994*, ss 34–9.
226. ibid, s 34.
227. ibid, s 36.
228. ibid, s 37.
229. *Condron v United Kingdom* (2001) 31 EHRR 1.
230. See, for example, *R v Cowan* [1996] QB 373.

the mobile telephone in the street and was on his way to the police station to hand it into the police.

The jury have heard lots of evidence, including some contradictory evidence from witnesses as to whether they saw Ron actually taking the telephone from Gail. They cannot be certain that he is guilty of robbery. However, they find it very strange that he has not mentioned the story about finding the telephone before now.

The jury could take into account the fact that Ron had plenty of time to explain how he came into possession of the telephone in deciding how realistic it was that he found the telephone. They could consider why if, on his evidence, he innocently came into possession of the telephone he did not mention that to the police. If they believe that his silence is significant in that regard, they can draw an adverse inference from this and therefore decide that the evidence is now strong enough to make them sure that he is guilty of robbery.

Perhaps the most controversial aspect of the adverse inferences regime is its relationship to legal advice. Where a person is at a police station and is being interviewed, no adverse inference can be drawn if the suspect has not been allowed an opportunity to consult a solicitor.[231] It is important to be clear about what this means. It does not mean that adverse inferences can only be drawn when a person has received legal advice. The statute is clear that the defendant must have the *right* to consult a solicitor. If they decline to consult a solicitor, then adverse inferences can be drawn.

What of the situation where the suspect does speak to a solicitor and he is advised to remain silent. Can relying on legal advice prevent an adverse inference from being drawn? The answer, as ever in law, would appear to be, 'it depends'. In *R v Beckles*[232] the Court of Appeal was asked to re-examine a case after the European Court of Human Rights had held that there had been a breach of Article 6 in respect of adverse inferences.[233] The defendant claimed that, while he had initially made a comment, he later replied 'no comment' to all questions on the basis of legal advice. He was prepared to waive legal professional privilege and to testify on what basis that advice was given. This offer was not taken up by the prosecution and the judge at first instance had told the jury that there was no independent evidence of what was said by the solicitor. While that was true, it was only true because the prosecution had failed to ask questions about the matter.

The Court of Appeal recognized that the essential question was whether the defendant remained silent because of the legal advice or whether it was because they had no, or no satisfactory explanation, to the questions asked.[234] In other words, the jury can still take account of whether the facts that are now being mentioned could *reasonably* have been said at the time of the questioning. If the answer is 'yes' and, in essence, the legal advice is 'you shouldn't say anything, because you can't actually answer any of these questions' then that is the type of circumstance adverse inferences was prepared for.

---

231. *Criminal Justice and Immigration Act 1994*, s 34(2A).
232. [2004] EWCA Crim 2766.
233. *Beckles v United Kingdom* (2002) 36 EHRR 162.
234. *R v Beckles* [2004] EWCA Crim 2766 at [46].

However, if the legal advice is different; for example, the solicitor believes that the questions would require him to reveal privileged information or because there was a belief that an error of law had been committed, then it may be reasonable to rely on that advice.

12.4.2 Interview locations

The general rule is that a person arrested must only be interviewed at a designated police station unless the delay in doing so would lead to interference or harm to evidence connected to the offence, a person, or serious loss or damage to property.[235] This rule exists because there have been too many instances over the years where doubts as to the integrity of interviews has led to miscarriages of justice.

12.4.3 Recording interviews

Over the years there was concern that police officers were 'verballing' suspects, that is to say, they were alleging that a suspect said something, usually a confession, and their written notes were then tendered against them in evidence. While the suspect could deny saying such things, the reality is that juries often preferred the evidence of police officers who would be seen to be trustworthy.

One of the significant changes introduced by PACE 1984 was the requirement that interviews should ordinarily be recorded in some way. There are now two ways that this can occur. The first is through audio recording[236] and the second is through video recording (ie visual and audio combined).[237] PACE 1984 requires that a Code of Practice is developed for each and these are known as Code E (audio recording) and Code F (video recording). Whilst technically separate, they are now published together,[238] partly because it is recognized that many of the rules are common.

No rule states which form of recording should be taken, although Code F notes that visual recording would be particularly suited where a suspect is especially vulnerable or uses visual communication (eg sign language).[239] It is often simply a case of what equipment the relevant police station has. There is no right to decline to be video recorded, although Code F does state that where a suspect objects to it they should state their objections on camera and the relevant officer shall decide whether to proceed with the video-recorded interview or whether to record audio only.[240]

Where removable media is used then at least one copy should be sealed in the presence of the suspect so that he is aware that there is a 'master' copy that cannot be corrupted.[241] The master copy cannot be opened only by the police. If, for whatever reason, the master version needs to be opened then it must be done in the presence of a member of the Crown Prosecution Service and after the suspect, or the suspect's legal representative, has been invited to attend too.[242] The latter is to ensure that there is transparency over how the master tape has been dealt with.

235. Home Office, *Code of Practice (Code C)* (Stationery Office 2018) para 11.1.
236. PACE 1984, s 60.
237. ibid, s 60A.
238. Home Office, *Code of Practice (Codes E and F)* (Stationery Office 2018).
239. ibid, para F2.2.
240. ibid, para F2.8.
241. ibid, para E3.19.
242. ibid, para E3.25.

Where the recording has been made using a digital recording device without removable storage, the file must be stored locally until such time that it can be uploaded to the master storage device.[243] The files must be stored as read-only files and held securely on a digital network. While it may appear that there is less security in respect of digital-only recordings (in that there is no physical 'master'), the reality is that it is probably more secure because (a) it is stored in a location that will show how, and who, has accessed the media, and (b) digital forensic technologies will allow someone to identify if any part of a recording has been modified. It can be more difficult to do that with traditional recordings.

12.4.4 Conduct of the interviews

At the commencement of the interview the following should occur:

- the suspect should be told that the interview is to be recorded, what type of recording is to take place, and how that will occur
- the investigators in the room should identify themselves to the suspect
- the suspect, appropriate adult, legal representative, or interpreter should all identify themselves
- the date, time, and start time of the interview should be provided
- an explanation should be provided as to how a copy of the interview will be given to the suspect.[244]

It is normally good practice to remind the suspect that they are being interviewed under caution and that they have the right to legal advice if they have not availed themselves of this already.[245]

Where a person enters a room after the interview has begun, they should identify themselves. Similarly, if anyone leaves the room during the interview, the person who has left should be identified and the time at which they left mentioned, so that it is on the recording. If a break is taken during the interview then this should be recorded audibly, including when the interview stops, was restarted, and why the break was called.

Where it is alleged that a person has said something, or did not say anything, either at the time of arrest or at the time they were detained, this should be put to them at the very beginning of the interview so that they can respond. Code C notes that no question can be elicited through oppression,[246] but this is not simply a matter for the Code of Practice. PACE 1984 requires a court to exclude any confession that is obtained by oppression or inappropriate conduct.[247] The meaning of these terms are discussed later.

It is, in essence, at the discretion of the interviewing officer how long an interview lasts, but this is subject to a number of caveats. The suspect, or his legal adviser, can ask for a break. Within a twenty-four-hour period, a person should also have an eight-hour period free from interview and travel that allows them to sleep.[248] Meals should also be provided to the prisoner.[249] The reality is that an interview that takes too long is not

---

243. ibid, para E4.15.
244. ibid, para E3.4.
245. Home Office, *Code of Practice (Code C)* (London, TSO 2018) para 11.2.
246. ibid, para 11.5.
247. PACE 1984, s 76.
248. Home Office, *Code of Practice (Code C)* (Stationery Office 2018) para 12.2.
249. ibid, para 8.6.

going to be productive and Code C suggests that breaks should be taken at least every two hours.[250] An interview cannot take place simply for the sake of an interview. Where an investigator is satisfied that they have asked all the questions they need to, including giving the suspect an opportunity to provide their version of events, then the interview should be terminated.[251]

At the end of the interview the interrogator should summarize what has been said and where any statement has been taken, this should be read back to the suspect whilst the interview is being recorded.[252] The suspect should be asked if there is anything else he wishes to add and, if not, the interview should be terminated.

The key issue that is raised within interviews is the extent to which defendants are pressurized into making inculpatory statements when questioned. While this is ordinarily best left to modules such as the *Law of Evidence*, a brief summary can be provided here. PACE 1984 governs the admissions of confessions. A confession is considered to include: 'any statement wholly or partly adverse to the person who made it, whether made to a person in authority or not and whether made in words of otherwise'.[253] This is a broad definition and goes far beyond what one might ordinarily think of as a confession, which tends to be thought of as a complete confession. However, the wording of PACE makes clear that partly adverse statements are included as confessions.

Example Partly adverse statements

Arnold is accused of committing a burglary alongside two other people. He denies any involvement with the burglary and says he was nowhere near the area. He says that he was 'driving around with Kev all night'. Unknown to Arnold, 'Kev' has admitted that he did commit the burglary.

In this example, Arnold has not confessed in the true sense of the word. Indeed, he has denied committing the burglary. However, admitting that he was with 'Kev' all night is undoubtedly an adverse statement if Kev has admitted to committing the burglary.

Confessions are admissible as evidence of what was said unless they are excluded by any rule of evidence.[254] The two principal ways of excluding the confession are because it was obtained improperly (s 76(2)) or because it was obtained unfairly (s. 78). Improperly obtained evidence is divided into two categories.

If, in any proceedings where the prosecution proposes to give in evidence a confession made by an accused person, it is represented to the court that the confession was or may have been obtained—

(a) by oppression of the person who made it; or

(b) in consequence of anything said or done which was likely, in the circumstances existing at the time, to render unreliable any confession which might be made by him in consequence thereof,

250. ibid, para 12.8.
251. Home Office, *Code of Practice (Codes E and F)* (Stationery Office 2018) para 11.6.
252. ibid, E3.18.
253. PACE 1984, s 82(1).
254. ibid, s 76(1).

the court shall not allow the confession to be given in evidence against him except in so far as the prosecution proves to the court beyond reasonable doubt that the confession (notwithstanding that it may be true) was not obtained aforesaid.[255]

The two categories are 'oppression' or 'things said or done . . . to render [it] unreliable'. These are not mutually exclusive, and both can be alleged. The closing words of the section should be noted. It is for the prosecution to prove beyond all reasonable doubt that the confession was not gathered in this way. The defence do not need to prove it was so gathered. It is also notable that the statute expressly notes that it does not matter that the confession was true. If it was gathered inappropriately then it must be excluded. This is one reason for ensuring that interviews are recorded as it provides clear evidence of the circumstances in which the confession was obtained.

'Oppression' is defined as including: 'torture, inhuman or degrading treatment, and the use or threat of violence'.[256] This is the same wording as is used in Article 3 ECHR and thus the threshold for this is extremely high. The Court of Appeal has noted that, in essence, it required 'unjust or cruel treatment' and that 'oppression' was one of 'detestable wickedness'.[257]

The more usual attack is 'things said or done'. As it refers to 'things said' and 'things done', this means that conduct that does not meet the definition of oppression can be considered in this context. Where it does, it would almost certainly be considered to make it unreliable, as a confession made in fear of violence etc would not be credible. However, the phrase also means that it must be something external. So, for example, in *R v Goldenberg*[258] the defendant was a heroin addict. He made a confession but it was the contention of the defence that he did so in order to be granted bail so that he could then procure more drugs. The Court of Appeal held that this was outside the remit of s 76(2)(b) because it was not something said or done. If the police, knowing that he was a drug addict, had said, 'tell us what happened and we'll let you out on bail' then that would almost certainly have breached s 76(2)(b).

It should be remembered that s 76 applies to confessions made to other people and not just to police officers. In *R v Roberts*[259] a shop manager told a suspect that if he admitted shoplifting, the police would not be called. He did admit it, and the police were called. Even though he did not retract his statement, the Court of Appeal held that it should not have been admitted in evidence because of the promise that had been made.

The second way that a confession can be ruled inadmissible is because it is unfair. Technically, this exclusionary power applies to all prosecution evidence, and a confession is simply one form of prosecution evidence. In respect of confessions, the power is most commonly used where there has been a significant breach of the PACE Codes of Practice.[260] As the Codes of Practice set out how a person should be treated and questioned in police custody, it makes sense that tangible breaches of this should be reflected by the courts as potentially rendering the evidence unfair. That said, it is not automatic exclusion (as is the case with s 76(2)(b)), and the judge must take into account all of the

---

255.   ibid, s 76(2).
256.   ibid, s 76(8).
257.   *R v Fulling* [1987] 2 All ER 65.
258.   (1989) 88 Cr App R 285.
259.   [2011] EWCA Crim 2974.
260.   Adrian Keane and Paul McKeown *The Modern Law of Evidence* (12th edn, OUP 2007) 430.

circumstances. In *R v Dunford*[261] a suspect was improperly denied access to a solicitor. However he had several previous convictions and 'knew the score'. There was nothing within the interview where legal advice may have made a difference and thus the judge declined to exclude the evidence. However it is more doubtful that this would be the case if it happened now. The courts, quite rightly, now treat access to a solicitor as a fundamental right and so would almost certainly exclude the evidence.

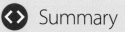 ## Summary

In this chapter we have examined some of the issues relating to investigating crime. In particular, we have noted that:

- The police are only one branch of law enforcement. There are a variety of agencies that hold law enforcement powers, some of which are national agencies.

- There are forty-three territorial police forces in England and Wales. London has two (the Metropolitan Police and the City of London Police). Apart from the London constabularies, each is headed by a chief constable.

- Chief constables are operationally independent of each other and, while subject to local police oversight, decisions relating to police matters remain solely for them.

- The head of the National Crime Agency, a national law enforcement power, does now have the power to 'request' that a chief constable assists him, and the chief constable has to comply. However, this only applies to serious and organized crime.

- The police have a number of powers open to them. One of the most controversial is known as 'stop and search'.

- While the police must have reasonable suspicion to believe that a person is in possession of prohibited article, there is an argument that 'reasonable suspicion' is easily informed and difficult to question. The police cannot take account of personal characteristics when formulating reasonable suspicion.

- A higher proportion of the black population are subject to stop and search procedures. There is considerable suspicion that the tactic is not being used to detect crime but is instead being used to gather intelligence. Certain sections of the community have suspicions that it is being used in a racist way, to harass them.

- The most famous power that the police have is the power of arrest. This is a power that also requires reasonable suspicion, and, again, there are concerns about whether that test is helpful in determining whether a police officer had the right to detain a person. That said, it is difficult to see what alternative test could be formulated.

- Where a person is arrested, they should ordinarily be taken to a designated police station, but there is a residual power that allows for a person to be de-arrested and this might be useful where the arrest was, for example, to prevent something happening at a particular time or at a particular location.

- A person who is arrested has a series of rights and these are the responsibility of the custody sergeant. The sergeant's first responsibility is to ensure that there are grounds to support detention

261.　(1990) 91 Cr App R 150.

after arrest. Thereafter, the sergeant should ask whether the suspect wishes legal advice and whether they wish someone to be made aware of the arrest. Both of these rights can be deferred but only when the appropriate procedure is called.

- A formal police interview with a detained person must follow particular rules. The interview must be recorded, either audio only or video recorded. The integrity of the recorded interview is guarded by procedural rules that ensure that there is always an uncorrupted copy of the interview so that any disputes about what was said can be resolved.

End-of-chapter questions

1. Is it not time that England and Wales followed Scotland and Northern Ireland in reducing the number of constabularies there are? Forty-three separate constabularies, each varying in size dramatically, means that there is no consistency in police practice. Is it not more appropriate to have a more structured approach where local variations will no longer exist?

2. If the police's job is to prevent and detect crime then they should be able to stop whoever they wish and ask them questions about what they are doing. If a person is innocent then they will have nothing to hide and should not be afraid to ask a few questions. Do you agree with this statement?

3. Is it appropriate that a person who has been arrested should be advised by someone who has not yet qualified as a solicitor? How can this protect a vulnerable person's rights? Is it not more appropriate for everyone to see (rather than telephone) a fully qualified lawyer so that they are given the most appropriate advice relevant to their case?

4. Can delaying a person's right to contact a solicitor ever be justified? Solicitors are regulated by the *Solicitors Regulation Authority* and, therefore, there should be no argument that they would compromise a live investigation. Is it not more likely that the police seek to delay a person's access to a solicitor to ensure that they can ask questions without them having the benefit of legal advice?

457

Further reading

Bradford B, *Stop and Search and Police Legitimacy* (Routledge 2017).

This is an excellent study of the issues surrounding the practice of stop and search. Bradford sets out the competing arguments and uses empirical data to show the extent of the problem.

Pattenden R and Skinns L, 'Choice, Privacy and Publicly Funded Legal Advice at Police Stations' (2010) 73 *Modern Law Review* 349.

While now slightly dated, this remains an important source of information about how those arrested by the police gain access to legal advice, and whether the process is appropriate in the modern age.

Police and Criminal Evidence Act 1984 Codes of Practice.

The Codes of Practice are essential reading if you are to understand the rights that a person has when dealing with the police and also the procedure that must be adopted by the police. It is notable that although they try to make the Codes of Practice accessible, there remains a lot of technical language within them and therefore it can be questioned whether they provide the average person with the information required.

Skinns L, Wooff A, and Sprawson A, 'Preliminary Findings on Police Custody Delivery in the Twenty-First Century: Is it 'good' Enough? (2017) 27 *Policing and Society* 358.

This is an important piece that reports on empirical research being conducted on the custody process. It charts how technology and centralization has changed the way that police custody is now managed and questions whether more still needs to be done to meet the needs of the police and safeguard the rights of suspects.

For self-test questions, flashcards, and links to useful websites, please visit the **online resources** at: **www.oup.com/he/gillespie-weare8e/**

13

Pre-Trial Matters

By the end of this chapter, you will be able to:

- Understand how a person is charged, and what criteria is applied.
- Identify what the Crown Prosecution Service is and understand its relationship with the police.
- Identify the steps taken when deciding whether to prosecute a suspect.
- Understand how a decision to prosecute, or not to prosecute, can be challenged.
- Identify how crimes are classified and allocated to a court.
- Understand the process by which a case is transferred to the appropriate court.

Introduction

The last chapter ended with the interview of a suspect. The next 'gateway' decision is to decide whether to charge a suspect with a crime. After that, a decision must be taken whether to prosecute him. Who makes these decisions and what process do they adopt? These are questions that will be asked in this chapter.

The decision whether to prosecute someone is perhaps the most important decision in the criminal justice system. If the decision is to prosecute then the defendant will have uncertainty hanging over him for some months, and, potentially, it will mark the beginning of an expensive period of time where legal advice is sought and paid for. If the decision is not to prosecute, then where does that leave the alleged victim? Can it be said that their rights have been upheld if someone is not prosecuted?

Finally, the chapter will consider how the matter arrives at the correct court. There are two courts that hear criminal matters; the magistrates' court and the Crown Court. Who decides in which court the matter is tried? How do they reach that decision?

13.1 **Charging and prosecuting**

Before any trial takes place, there are two key 'gateway' decisions that need to be taken. Subsequent decisions (on matters such as bail and the allocation of court) will flow from these decisions. The two decisions are:

1. **Whether to charge the suspect.** After the police investigation has completed they must decide whether there is sufficient evidence to charge the suspect with an offence. As will be seen, this is a decision that the police no longer normally take by themselves. A person charged is formally on notice that proceedings are to commence.

2. **Whether to prosecute the suspect.** The mere fact that a person has been charged does not mean that he will be prosecuted for the crime. As will be seen, a different set of tests apply. Once the decision has been made, court proceedings will follow.

13.1.1 **Crown Prosecution Service (CPS)**

In Chapter 12 a number of law enforcement agencies were discussed, including the *Serious Fraud Office* (SFO), who acts as both investigator and prosecutor. It is more normal for the functions to be separated. In this chapter we will focus solely on one public prosecutor, the *Crown Prosecution Service* (CPS), as they are responsible for the vast majority of prosecutions that take place in England and Wales.

13.1.1.1 **History of the CPS**

The CPS is a modern creature established in 1985[1] and going 'live' in 1986. Its professional head is the *Director of Public Prosecutions* (DPP) and this is an ancient office.[2]

Until the formation of the CPS the responsibility for prosecuting offences was largely in the hands of the police. Sometimes this was quite literally, and until the establishment of the CPS, it was not unusual to see serving officers (usually of the rank of Inspector), standing in the magistrates' court acting as prosecutor,[3] although it was more customary to employ a solicitor to prosecute. For other crimes, and certainly trials in the Crown Court, the police would engage barristers to prosecute the case. The most serious cases were referred to the DPP and he would decide whether to 'take it over'. If he[4] did, then he would either personally prosecute the case or, more usually, he would appoint Treasury Counsel to do so.

⚡ TREASURY COUNSEL

Treasury Counsel are barristers (and, lately, solicitor–advocates) who are appointed by the Attorney-General to represent the state. They act in only the most serious and complex cases. Treasury Counsel (Criminal) are a team of seventeen advocates headed by the First Senior Treasury Counsel.

1. *Prosecution of Offences Act 1985*, s 1.
2. David Calvert-Smith and Stephen O'Doherty, 'Legislative Technique and Human Rights: A Response' [2003] *Criminal Law Review* 384.
3. Joshua Rozenberg, *The Case for the Crown: The Inside Story of the Director of Public Prosecutions* (Equation 1987) 80.
4. At the time, all the DPPs were male. The first female DPP was Barbara Mills QC, who was appointed in 1992. The CPS had been formed by then and so she was DPP and Head of the CPS.

The fact that there was a localized structure meant that there was very patchy performance across the country. A particular problem was that there was no independent review of the evidence. Local solicitors would not wish to lose their most important client (the police constabulary) by continually advising not to prosecute a case. Where 'in-house' solicitors were employed, the problem was arguably worse because they would be seen to be working against their employer's interests.[5] While there has long been a duty on a solicitor not to mislead a court, bringing an action when there is only a minimal chance of success would not meet that criterion.

A Royal Commission—the 'Phillips Commission'—noted that hopelessly weak cases were being prosecuted. Indeed, it was estimated that nearly 50 per cent of cases led to an acquittal, the majority being terminated before the conclusion of the trial.[6] Ultimately they recommended that there should be a separation of the investigators (police) and prosecutors. They recommended that a national organization of state-employed prosecutors should be established under the leadership of the DPP. This became the Crown Prosecution Service.

The CPS was mandated to review all cases that were referred to them for prosecution, something that continues to this day. Originally, the CPS was organized into thirty-one areas, which mapped onto the police constabulary boundaries, with some covering two force areas.[7] The CPS struggled from the beginning because there was a perception that they did not recruit the best staff. Partly this was because the pay was not thought to be particularly attractive and partly because it was thought that there was little prospect of career progression.[8] This could be contrasted with private practice where progression, including to full equity partner, was possible.

Problems persisted during its initial years of operation, and it was thought to be overly bureaucratic. Eventually a formal review of the CPS was undertaken, chaired by Sir Ian Glidewell, a former Lord Justice of Appeal. His report was highly critical of the CPS. He found that it had not achieved many of the goals set out upon its creation. He thought the CPS was too centralized and focused on administration. He believed that there was a failure of leadership and, ultimately, the then DPP, Dame Barbara Mills QC, resigned.

461

13.1.1.2 The CPS today

Today, the CPS is organized as follows:

1. **'Local' CPS areas.** While the CPS is a national organization, it is divided into fourteen regional areas.

2. **'Out of hours' area.** CPS Direct is a nationally run unit that offers advice when the local CPS areas are not working.

3. **Specialist divisions.** There are three national, specialist divisions. These are:

   (a) **International Justice and Organised Crime Division.** As its name suggests, this is a specialist division that deals with the most complicated serious and organized crime or that which relates to international crime.

5. Joshua Rozenberg, *The Case for the Crown: The Inside Story of the Director of Public Prosecutions* (Equation 1987) 80.

6. ibid, 82.

7. For example, Durham and Northumbria shared a CPS area although they had separate constabularies. The same was true of Gloucestershire and Wiltshire.

8. Joshua Rozenberg, *The Case for the Crown: The Inside Story of the Director of Public Prosecutions* (Equation 1987) 100.

(b) **Special Crime and Counter Terror Division.** The bulk of this division's work relates to terrorism offences, but it also deals with complex cases such as assisted suicide, deaths in custody, corporate crime, and election offences.

(c) **Specialist Fraud Division.** As its name suggests, this tackles serious and complex fraud. Not all fraud is assigned to the division as smaller-scale fraud will be dealt with locally as an 'ordinary' crime.

4. **Proceeds of Crime Division.** This division does not relate directly to prosecutions, but will instead lead work relating to recovering the proceeds of crime, including seeking confiscation orders where appropriate.

Each of these areas and divisions is led by a senior prosecutor. For the local CPS areas and CPS Direct this person is known as the Chief Crown Prosecutor (CCP), a statutory role.[9] The four divisions are led by a 'Head of Division' who is treated as though he were a CCP. Heads of Division are not a statutory role, but the DPP can organize the staff as he chooses. Previous DPPs have noted that CCPs are, in essence, 'mini-DPPs'. They superintend the work of their area, ensure that the work is delegated to the appropriate person, and that prosecution policies are adhered to.

The structure underneath the CCP will depend on the area or division, but along with Deputy Chief Crown Prosecutors there will be a series of units that look after the work. If, for example, we take the North-West area (that covers the policing areas of Cumbria, Lancashire, and Greater Manchester), the area is divided into four units:

1. **Magistrates' Court Unit.** This is the unit that deals with matters heard in the magistrates' court.

2. **Crown Court Unit.** This is the unit that deals with the more serious offences that are dealt with in the Crown Court.

3. **Complex Crime Unit.** The Complex Crime Unit deals with the more complicated work that remains within the areas. This can include organized crime, or crime that takes has a cross-border element to it.

4. **RASSO Unit.** This is the 'Rape and Serious Sexual Offences' Unit. They deal with rapes and serious sexual offences, including those that relate to the sexual abuse of children. While some lower-level sexual offences may be dealt with by the magistrates' court or the Crown Court unit, the majority will be dealt with the RASSO Unit. The RASSO Unit has specialist training in sexual offences.

While there is logic in such a structure, there remain doubts as to whether this actually reflects what happens in practice. So, for example, HM Inspectorate of the CPS has questioned whether RASSO Units are properly resourced and staffed by experts in the area.[10] Yet that was the very purpose they were set up.

In most areas there will be a number of CPS offices and management structures are put in place to assist the CCP in discharging his duties. For example, District Crown Prosecutors have responsibility for a geographical area within the larger CPS area. Alongside the formal offices, CPS are now also to be found alongside the police, with the intent that this allows for easier cooperation, particularly in respect of charging.[11]

---

9. *Prosecution of Offences Act 1985*, s 1(4).
10. HMCPSI, *Thematic Review of the CPS Rape and Serious Sexual Offences Unit* (HMCPSI 2016) 4.
11. See, for example, HMCPSI, *Area Assurance Inspection of CPS North West* (HMCPSI 2018) 13.

The CPS has been subject to considerable cuts in both budget and resources, with it being estimated that budgets have fallen by almost one-third.[12] Such cuts must necessarily have an impact on performance. HM Inspectorate of the CPS notes, for example, that CPS North West (the example we used earlier), has seen a significant reduction in staffing and there is a perception by the staff that they are under-resourced.[13] The government rejects the assertion that funding cuts have caused problems within the criminal justice system, but has acknowledged that the room for further cuts is limited.

13.1.1.3 CPS staff

It may be thought that the CPS will primarily be staffed by lawyers but this is not the case. The CPS website itself notes that approximately only 50 per cent of its staff are lawyers, with the rest doing other roles. Perhaps more surprising is the fact that it is not just the lawyers who will make decisions or conduct proceedings in court.

Those that are qualified as a solicitor or barrister can be designated a 'Crown Prosecutor'.[14] Crown Prosecutors have 'all the powers of the [DPP] as to the institution and conduct of proceedings but shall exercise those powers under the direction of the Director'.[15] This phrase means two things. The first is that Crown Prosecutors have the same powers and authority as the DPP in terms of prosecutions. Thus they make the decision whether to charge, prosecute, or terminate proceedings against individuals. However, the second thing it means is that they can only do this under the direction of the DPP. Obviously the DPP does not personally direct such matters, but it does mean that he could decide that only Crown Prosecutors of a certain grade can deal with certain matters, or direct how the offences should be reviewed etc.

The right to exercise the powers of the DPP also extends to providing consent. There are a small number of statutory offences that require the consent of the DPP before a prosecution can commence. The power of delegation includes this too, meaning that a Crown Prosecutor can give DPP authority to proceed.[16] However, it is important to note that this is a distinct step and therefore a conscious decision must be given to consent to the prosecution, and although that need not be documented in writing, it is preferable to do so and ordinarily would be.[17]

> **≔ Example** DPP Consent
>
> An example of a crime that requires the consent of the DPP is the possession of a prohibited image of a child.[18] In these circumstances, the CPS must decide that the tests for prosecution are met *but also* decide that they will provide the consent of the DPP to proceed. In essence, this is simply requiring the CPS to consider carefully the need for a prosecution.

---

12. John Hyde, 'CPS Can Take No More Cuts – Attorney General' (2019) *Law Society Gazette* 23.
13. HMCPSI, *Area Assurance Inspection of CPS North West* (HMCPSI 2018) 3.
14. *Prosecution of Offences Act 1985*, s 1(3).
15. ibid, s 1(6).
16. ibid, s 1(7).
17. *R v Jackson* [1997] Crim LR 293.
18. *Coroners and Justice Act 2009*, s 62(9)(b).

Whilst the DPP could decide that certain matters require his personal attention (in that it will be remembered that the delegated powers of a Crown Prosecutor are under his direction), there are very rare examples of situations where Parliament require the DPP to give his personal attention to the matter. This requirement applies only to the most serious or complicated offences, and is designed as a safeguard to ensure that the need for a prosecution is considered carefully.

> **≔ Example** DPP personal consent
>
> The *Bribery Act 2010* sets out a series of offences that are designed to tackle corruption. The offences under the Act require the consent of the DPP and the statute makes clear that it requires the *personal consent* of the DPP.[19] Thus, a Crown Prosecutor cannot give DPP permission for this offence.

The *Crime and Disorder Act 1998* provided a new power to the DPP. This was the ability to designate non-legally qualified staff to act in certain legal proceedings.[20] The CPS refers to such persons as 'Associate Prosecutors' although statute does not provide them with any legal powers. The CPS now require associate prosecutors to undertake training by CILEx,[21] and thus it would be wrong to say that they no longer have any legal qualifications, but they do not have the same qualifications as Crown Prosecutors. The work of an associate prosecutor is limited,[22] and does not include deciding whether to instigate prosecutions, nor does it involve contested proceedings.[23]

While the CPS will prosecute most cases themselves, they have historically also drawn upon barristers in independent practice to act as ad hoc prosecutors in court. The power to do this arises in statute,[24] although the statute is silent as to how many cases should be handled in this way. When the CPS was first established all cases in the Crown Court were dealt with by independent counsel because employed barristers could not exercise their higher rights of audience.[25] When the rules were relaxed the CPS began to employ more barristers but also encouraged solicitors to seek their higher rights.

13.1.1.4 **Code for Crown Prosecutors**

The DPP is obliged to publish guidance to be known as the 'Code for Crown Prosecutors' that sets out the general principles to be applied to them when deciding whether to institute proceedings, what charges to bring, and decisions relating to the mode of trial to be sought.[26] The code is always available online and the current version is dated October 2018.

The Code notes that the function of the CPS is not to decide whether someone is guilty of an offence (as that is the role of the trial) but it is to decide whether it is

---

19. *Bribery Act 2010*, s 10(1), (4).
20. *Crime and Disorder Act 1998*, s 53.
21. For further discussion see 10.4.
22. *Prosecution of Offences Act 1985*, s 7A.
23. Their role is discussed further in Chapter 14.
24. *Prosecution of Offences Act 1985*, s 5.
25. Rights of audience are discussed in Chapter 10.
26. *Prosecution of Offences Act 1985*, s 10(1).

appropriate to present the matter before the court by prosecuting the suspect.[27] The Code also notes that prosecutors 'must always act in the interests of justice and not solely for the purpose of obtaining a conviction'.[28] This can be contrasted with the position in some other countries who see their role as obtaining convictions. In this country, however, we are used to dispassionate prosecutors who identify which cases are appropriate for prosecution. The Code continues in this vein by noting that it has never been the rule in England and Wales that a prosecution will take place when there exists sufficient evidence to show that the suspect committed the crime.[29] That said, Sanders has argued that the CPS maintains a 'pro-prosecution' stance[30] and notes that regulatory prosecutors initiate cases in far fewer cases. Sanders believes that the CPS should identify reasons *why* to prosecute someone, rather than identify reasons *why not* to do so. That said, given the tendency in recent years for politicians to appear increasingly 'tough' on crime, it is unlikely such a change will be forthcoming. While the CPS are, in practice, independent, the DPP is appointed by the Attorney-General[31] and discharges his duties under the 'superintendence of the Attorney-General'.[32]

The primary purpose of the Code is to put forward the two tests. The first is the 'Full Code Test', and a prosecution may only be commenced or continued by reference to this code.[33] There are two tests within the 'full code test', which are the evidential test and the public interest test. These will be considered more fully later (13.1.2.1). The second test set out in the Code is the 'threshold test'. This is used when deciding whether to charge an offender.[34] If the decision is to charge the offender then the full test must be satisfied before the prosecution can commence. The threshold test is also considered later (13.1.2.1).

Specific advice

As has been noted, the Code for Crown Prosecutors is quite general. There has, since the creation of the CPS, been guidance issued to prosecutors that suggests how factors should be balanced in favour of, or against, a prosecution.[35] Gradually this advice has been published, but its legal status was unclear. The Code was the only document that Crown Prosecutors were formally bound by. In recent years, questions were asked whether the Code was sufficiently detailed for some crimes. It was argued that for more complex crimes, a person should be aware of the factors that make a prosecution more, or less likely, to take place.

This has primarily been an issue in respect of the law pertaining to assisted dying. There have been numerous cases in recent years where applicants have sought to argue that assisting someone to die should not lead to culpability for homicide. Perhaps the most notable case in this field was *R (Pretty) v Director of Public Prosecutions*.[36] Diane Pretty suffered from advanced Motor Neurone Disease (MND) and wanted to die on her own terms. However, her MND had reached the point where she would not be

465

27. Crown Prosecution Service, *The Code for Crown Prosecutors* (CPS 2018) para 2.2.
28. ibid, para 2.7.
29. ibid, para 4.10. See the discussion later on the public-interest test.
30. Andrew Sanders, 'The CPS – 30 Years On' [2016] *Criminal Law Review* 82, 98.
31. *Prosecution of Offences Act 1985*, s 2(1).
32. ibid, s 3(1).
33. Crime Prosecution Service, *The Code for Crown Prosecutors* (CPS 2018) para 4.1.
34. ibid, para 5.1.
35. Joshua Rozenberg, *The Case for the Crown: The Inside Story of the Director of Public Prosecutions* (Equation 1987) 159.
36. [2002] 1 AC 800.

able to administer a lethal dose of pills by herself. Whilst suicide is now decriminalized,[37] assisting someone to commit suicide is not.[38] However, the offence can only be instigated with the permission of the DPP[39] and thus Diane Pretty asked the DPP for assurance that if her husband helped her to administer a lethal overdose he would not be prosecuted. The DPP refused to give such an assurance.

Diane Pretty sought judicial review of the matter and the proceedings eventually ended up in the House of Lords. The majority of the decision considered whether the ECHR included a right to die. The House concluded that it did not, something that the European Court of Human Rights implicitly upheld when it declined Diane Pretty's application.[40] However it also considered whether the DPP was right not to provide an assurance that Mrs Pretty's husband would not be prosecuted. Lord Bingham, providing the key speech in the case, noted that, in essence, what was being asked was an assurance of immunity, something that the DPP has no power to give.[41] However, Lord Bingham also suggested that while there was no power to require the DPP to give precise instructions on how he would prosecute such offences, there was no reason why he could not give those instructions either.[42]

This nuance was picked up on in *R (on behalf of Purdy) v Director of Public Prosecutions*,[43] the final case to be heard in the House of Lords before its powers were transferred to the Supreme Court. Debbie Purdy suffered from progressive multiple sclerosis, from which there was no cure. She foresaw a time when she believed that she would no longer wish to live and would seek to go to a country where euthanasia was lawful. However, by that time, she would be unable to travel by herself. If her husband were to assist her in his travels, then he could be considered to be assisting her to commit suicide and would thus be potentially liable under the *Suicide Act 1961*, s 2.

Relying on Lord Bingham's *dicta* she asked the DPP for a list of factors that he would take into account when deciding whether to prosecute someone under that offence and, in particular, related to when his consent to a prosecution would be given. The DPP refused to provide the details. The House of Lords this time went further than Lord Bingham. While they upheld the principle of *Pretty* they noted that Purdy was not trying to argue for immunity, she simply wanted clarity as to what her husband could or could not do. The House held that Article 8(1)[44] was engaged in the case, and that for an interference under Article 8(2) to be supported, it needed to be 'in accordance with the law'. The House believed that requiring DPP consent meant that Parliament did not intend all those to have assisted in a suicide to be prosecuted (for why else would the consent be required), and that Article 8(2) required that the law is accessible and foreseeable.[45] The House required that the DPP provide specific guidance that set out how he would judge these very individual cases so that people would be aware as to when they were taking steps that would transgress the law.[46]

37. *Suicide Act 1961*, s 1. At one point attempted suicide was a capital offence. Therefore, you could be tried and then hung for trying to kill yourself!
38. *Suicide Act 1961*, s 2.
39. ibid, s 2(4).
40. *Pretty v United Kingdom* (2002) 35 EHRR 1.
41. [2002] 1 AC 800 at [39].
42. ibid, at [39].
43. [2010] 1 AC 345.
44. Right to respect, inter alia, for private life.
45. [2010] 1 AC 345 at [53] (Lord Hope).
46. Sadly for Debbie Purdy her health deteriorated quicker than thought and she could not travel to a country to commit suicide. She died in November 2014 in a hospice.

Purdy was a landmark case that demonstrated that the Code for Crown Prosecutors is not always sufficient guidance for prosecutorial discretion. While it will be comparatively rare for cases to require specific guidance, the decision does demonstrate that for certain offences it is necessary to provide greater certainty as to what will lead to a prosecution. Such guidance must be published and it can, for example, be found on the CPS website.[47]

The guidance issued following *Purdy* is also interesting as it demonstrates how delegation to Crown Prosecutors works under direction from the DPP. The guidance does not require the DPP to personally consider such cases, although he may be consulted, but it does require that the matter is considered by the Special Crime Division of CPS HQ.[48] Thus, a Crown Prosecutor outside of that division cannot act on behalf of the DPP or give his consent to a prosecution, because to do so would not be 'under the direction of the Director'. A decision outside of that division would accordingly be *ultra vires*.

13.1.2 **Charging an offender**

Historically the police were solely responsible for deciding whether to charge an offender, but it was suggested that this led to inconsistent practices with suspects being charged or released irrespective of the strength of evidence against them.[49] To assist this, the CPS began to deploy staff within police stations to try and encourage early discussion with prosecutors. Unfortunately, the experiment was not particularly successful, with few offences being discussed before charge.[50] In his review of the criminal justice system, Lord Justice Auld was concerned that the disparity between charging and review was stark, leading to a waste of resources in reviewing inappropriate cases.[51] He recommended that the CPS and police should agree from an early stage what the charge should be, something that quickly followed.

By statute, the custody sergeant is responsible for deciding when there is sufficient evidence to charge a suspect[52] but, as noted, Auld recommended that this now took place in conjunction with the CPS. For a relatively short period of time, the CPS was responsible for the vast majority of charging decisions, but in 2010 the police began to receive more responsibility for charging decisions, with the CPS being responsible for only the most serious. This suggests a retreat from what Auld proposed, but it is perhaps the more serious offences that require specialist assistance. In the more routine matters (common assault, shoplifting, drink-driving, etc) there is perhaps little reason to consult.

When the custody sergeant considers that there is sufficient evidence, he has four options:

1. release the suspect without charge and on bail, or keep him in police detention, for the purposes of consulting the DPP as to whether to charge or caution the person

2. release the suspect without charge and on bail, but not for that purpose

---

47. For the specific guidance see <https://www.cps.gov.uk/legal-guidance/suicide-policy-prosecutors-respect-cases-encouraging-or-assisting-suicide>.

48. ibid, para 49.

49. Andrew Sanders, 'Prosecution Systems' in Mike McConville and Geoffrey Wilson (eds), *The Handbook of the Criminal Justice System* (OUP 2002) 154.

50. Andrew Ashworth, 'Developments in the Public Prosecutor's Office in England and Wales' (2000) 8 *European Journal of Crime, Criminal Law and Criminal Justice* 257, 272.

51. Rt Hon Lord Justice Auld, *A Review of the Criminal Courts of England and Wales* (HMSO 2001) 399.

52. *Police and Criminal Evidence Act 1984*, s 37.

3. release the suspect without charge and without bail, or

4. charge the suspect.[53]

The DPP is obliged to publish guidance to assist the police in understanding how to charge and when to refer a case to the CPS.[54] These are publicly available and are currently in their fifth edition.[55] The guidance provides that the following can be charged by the police without reference to the CPS:

1. any summary-only offence (including criminal damage where the value of the loss or damage is less than £5,000) irrespective of the likely plea

2. any offence of retail theft (shoplifting) or attempted retail theft irrespective of plea provided it is suitable for sentence in the magistrates' court and

3. any either-way offence anticipated as a guilty plea and suitable for sentence in a magistrates' court.

However these rules do not apply where:

- the offence requires the consent of the DPP or Attorney-General
- a case involves death
- it is connected to terrorist activity or official secrets
- it is classified as hate crime or domestic violence under CPS Policies
- an offence of violent disorder or affray
- an offence of causing grievous bodily harm or wounding, or actual bodily harm (ABH)
- a sexual offence committed by or upon a person under 18 or
- an offence under the Licensing Act 2003.[56]

Some of these might be surprising. For example, ABH is a relatively minor offence, but its inclusion could be to ensure that it is properly reserved for the more serious matters, with common assault usually being preferred even when bodily harm occurs.[57] Similarly, reserving potential hate crime and domestic violence cases can ensure that such cases are dealt with appropriately. There has long been concern about how the police tackle such crimes,[58] although it is argued that they are improving. However, there are aggravated crimes that relate to hate crime and domestic violence[59] and referring matters to the CPS ensures that these crimes are considered carefully.

---

53. *Police and Criminal Evidence Act 1984*, s 37(7).
54. ibid, s 37A.
55. Director of Public Prosecutions, 'Charging (The Director's Guidance) 2013 - fifth edition, May 2013 (revised arrangements)' (DPP 2013) <https://www.cps.gov.uk/legal-guidance/charging-directors-guidance-2013-fifth-edition-may-2013-revised-arrangements>.
56. ibid, para 15.
57. David Ormerod and Karl Laird, *Smith, Hogan, and Ormerod's Criminal Law* (15th edn, OUP 2018) 659.
58. For a historical approach see A Sanders, 'Personal Violence and Public Order: The Prosecution of Domestic Violence in England and Wales' (1988) 16 *International Journal of the Sociology of Law* 359.
59. See, for example, *Crime and Disorder Act 1998*, s 29 ('racially or religiously aggravated assaults') and *Serious Crime Act 2015*, s 76 ('controlling or coercive behaviour in an intimate or family relationship').

13.1.2.1 **Test for charging**

The clear presumption is that the full code test will be applied when deciding whether to charge an offender.[60] This is the same test as is used for the decision to prosecute. However, it is recognized that sometimes this will not always be possible in which case the 'threshold test' can be used. The test is usually only permitted when a person is in custody and where a charge under the threshold test would allow more time to find the evidence required for the full test.

Threshold test

The threshold test is set out in the *Code for Crown Prosecutors*.[61] There are five elements to the test, each of which must be 'rigorously' examined.[62] The elements, called conditions, are as follows:

1. There are reasonable grounds to suspect that the person to be charged has committed the offence.

2. Further evidence can be obtained to provide a realistic prospect of conviction.

3. The seriousness or the circumstances of the case justifies the making of an immediate charging decision.

4. There are continuing substantial grounds to object to bail in accordance with the *Bail Act 1976* and in all the circumstances of the case it is proper to do so.

5. It is in the public interest to charge the suspect.

Conditions 3 and 4 perhaps best explain why there is a separate test. It is to be used where releasing a suspect on bail while further investigations take place, or while a decision is made by the CPS, would not be appropriate. Condition 2 is important because charging someone is not supposed to be speculative, it is designed to ensure that there is a realistic opportunity to gather enough evidence to justify a prosecution.

While Condition 1 may appear superfluous as it is the same test as both arrest and detention, it should be remembered that these tests are supposed to be continuous. Therefore, the threshold test is prompting the police (or prosecutor, where relevant) that they must identify whether there remains the right to hold the suspect. This decision will not just be the original 'gatekeeper' decision but will take into account all of the other information that has become available during the detention.

The final condition, the public-interest test, requires the police and prosecutors to consider one of the tests in the full code, the public-interest test. As will be seen, this requires a consideration not only of whether a suspect did something, but whether they deserve to be prosecuted for it. That said, it should be remembered that this is also the test that Sanders criticizes as still being pro-prosecution.[63]

Full code test

There are two elements to the full code. The first is known as the 'evidential stage' and the second as the 'public-interest stage'. Even when the threshold test is used, police or

---

60.   Director of Public Prosecutions, 'Charging (The Director's Guidance) 2013 - fifth edition, May 2013 (revised arrangements)' (DPP 2013) <https://www.cps.gov.uk/legal-guidance/charging-directors-guidance-2013-fifth-edition-may-2013-revised-arrangements> para 11.

61.   Crime Prosecution Service, *The Code for Crown Prosecutors* (CPS 2018) pt 5.

62.   ibid, para 5.2.

63.   Andrew Sanders, 'The CPS - 30 Years On' [2016] *Criminal Law Review* 82, 98.

prosecutors will need to have recourse to the full test. The *Code for Crown Prosecutors* is clear that the evidential test should be considered first,[64] which reinforces the fact that if there is no evidence against the suspect then it is irrelevant what the public interest is and there should be no prosecution.

A summary of the evidential stage is that the prosecutor must be satisfied that 'there is sufficient evidence to provide a realistic prospect of conviction against each suspect on each charge'.[65] A realistic prospect means that the prosecution need to consider the strength of the evidence, potential defences, etc. In other words, the prosecutors should not simply operate on the assumption that everything they have been told is correct.

The Code makes clear that the test is whether 'it is more likely than not' that an impartial court would convict the defendant.[66] The Code notes that this is a different test to what the courts themselves will apply. That is true, but it is not as simple as the test appears to contemplate. The evidential test is not whether it is more likely than not that the defendant is guilty but whether it is more likely than not that the defendant will be *convicted*. That is a very different test as prosecutors will be aware that not every guilty person is convicted. The prosecutor will need to consider how certain evidence is treated by juries or magistrates, whether there are likely to be witnesses that would not come up to proof, etc.

If the evidential test is satisfied, then the second test, the public-interest test, is then considered. This requires prosecutors to consider a series of questions:

1. How serious is the offence committed?
2. What is the level of culpability of the suspect?
3. What are the circumstances of, and harm caused to, the victim?
4. What was the suspect's age and maturity at the time of the offence?
5. What it the impact on the community?
6. Is prosecution a proportionate response?
7. Do sources of information require protecting?[67]

The first three factors effectively relate to the seriousness of the crime. The first factor notes that the more serious a crime, the more likely it is in the public interest for it to be prosecuted. The second question operates on the basis that the more culpable an offender is, the greater the likelihood that a prosecution should take place. Culpability requires consideration on the role that the suspect played, whether it was predetermined, the motivation behind the crime, whether it is likely to be repeated, etc.[68] Again, this is relatively uncontroversial as one would expect those who deliberately commit crime to be considered more seriously than where an incident took place without planning. The third factor looks at the impact the crime has had on the victim. Whilst prosecutors do not represent the victim, clearly one purpose of a prosecution is to ensure that victims feel that they have received justice.[69] As will be seen further later, there is greater emphasis on the role of victims than has traditionally occurred.

---

64. Crime Prosecution Service, *The Code for Crown Prosecutors* (CPS 2018) para 4.2.
65. ibid, para 4.6.
66. ibid, para 4.7.
67. ibid, para 4.14.
68. ibid, 9.
69. Jonathan Doak, 'Victims' Rights in Criminal Trials: Prospects for Participation' (2005) *32 Journal of Law and Society* 294.

Related to the issue of victims is the impact on the community (question 5). There will be certain crimes that have an impact beyond the individual victim. Hate crime is a good example of this. Where a community is affected by the crime then this might make it more serious, not least because it could lead to others in the community fearing that they may be a victim next.

> **Example** Hate crime
>
> Veronica is a member of the Jewish community in Anytown. Richard painted a swastika on her garage wall and included the words, 'Jews out'. This would constitute a hate crime.[70] While the impact on Veronica herself may be not insignificant, it is likely that this particular crime would have an impact on the Jewish community as a whole. It is more likely, therefore, that Richard would be prosecuted as the victim of his crime is not just Veronica but the community more broadly. A prosecution may also reassure the community and send a signal to others not to engage in such behaviour.

Not all of the factors are necessarily focused towards a prosecution. Question 4 refers to the fact that where a person is particularly immature, eg a child, then it may be more appropriate for a less formal response.

The final question is interesting. The use of confidential sources (sometimes known as informants) has a long history in the criminal justice system.[71] It is generally necessary for the identities of sources not to be released because of risks to their personal safety, and because other people will not give information if they believe their identity will be released. The courts developed a series of rules referred to as 'public interest immunity' which govern how matters, including the identities of sources, can be kept confidential.[72] However, the right to keep matters confidential must be balanced against the right of a suspect to a fair trial. Occasionally this will mean that a prosecution can only go ahead if the identity of the source or technique is revealed.[73] The CPS will need to decide which is more important, prosecution or keeping the source confidential. It will not always be a simple decision (because, for example, the source might be offered protection through witness protection programmes[74]) but, in consultation with the police, it may be necessary to decide to halt a prosecution so that the identity of the source is not compromised.

13.1.2.2 Selecting the charges

Assuming that it is appropriate to charge an offender then how are the charges selected? Where the CPS has been asked to provide advice on whether to charge the offender then they select the charges and the police must follow that instruction.[75] Where the police have the power to charge an offender then the custody sergeant ultimately decides what charge to lay.

---

70.   *Crime and Disorder Act 1998*, s 30 ('racially or religiously aggravated criminal damage').

71.   Colin Dunnighan and Clive Norris, 'A Risky Business: The Recruitment and Running of Informers by English Police Officers' (1996) 19 *Police Studies* 1.

72.   Adrian AS Zuckerman, 'Public Interest Immunity—A Matter of Prime Judicial Responsibility' (1994) 57 *Modern Law Review* 703.

73.   Some sophisticated surveillance techniques are not widely known and revealing them in a public trial could lead to their use being compromised in future operations. This raises the same issues as the identity of a source.

74.   Nicholas R Fyfe, *Protecting Intimidated Witnesses* (Ashgate 2001).

75.   *Police and Criminal Evidence Act 1984*, s 37B(6).

The Code states that the charges should:

- reflect the seriousness and extent of the offending
- give the court adequate powers to sentence and impose appropriate post-conviction orders
- allow a confiscation order to be made in appropriate cases, where a defendant has benefitted from criminal conduct
- enable the case to be presented in a clear and simple way.[76]

The Code also notes that this means it will not necessarily be the most serious charge that will be prosecuted, and nor should more charges than necessary be selected in the hope of persuading an offender to plead guilty to some.[77]

The CPS publish 'prosecution guidance'[78] which incorporates factors that should be taken account. Where there are multiple crimes that could be charged, this allows prosecutors to understand what charge they should incorporate. Prosecutors should also have reference to the various sentencing guidelines that are produced by the *Sentencing Council*[79] as this can assist them in understanding the likely sentence for a particular crime, allowing them to decide whether that is appropriate to the gravity of the offence.

Example Wounding

Let us take an example:

Jordan was holding some paper when David came over and ripped it from his grasp. This action caused a paper cut to Jordan's finger. It stopped bleeding after approximately thirty seconds.

When studying Criminal Law, you will identify that, as a matter of law, any cut that penetrates all the layers of a skin, causing even a single drop of blood, constitutes a wound.[80]

Wounding is a serious matter. There are two offences, s 18[81] and s 20.[82] There is no intention to cause grievous bodily harm, so s 18 will not apply. But, David has, at the very least, recklessly inflicted a wound. This is an offence ordinarily tried in the Crown Court and punishable by a maximum of five years' imprisonment.

Regardless of what the law technically says a wound is, charging s 20 would be a gross overreaction. Indeed, it is not clear that any criminal response would be required. However, assuming that one was, the offence of common assault, which is a summary-only matter, would be more representative of the actions of David. Thus, this should be the charge selected.

---

76. Crime Prosecution Service, *The Code for Crown Prosecutors* (CPS 2018) para 6.1.
77. ibid, para 6.4.
78. CPS, 'Prosecution Guidance' <https://www.cps.gov.uk/prosecution-guidance>.
79. Sentencing Council, 'Sentencing Council' <https://www.sentencingcouncil.org.uk/>.
80. *Moriarty v Brookes* (1834) 6 C & P 684.
81. *Offences Against the Person Act 1861*, s 18.
82. ibid, s 20.

13.1.3 **Decision to prosecute**

Not every prosecution requires a person to be charged,[83] but the majority of crimes do arise in this way and, for our purposes, we will assume that a person has been charged. The next decision to be made is whether they are to be prosecuted. Even when the CPS are involved in the decision to charge, there will be a later decision as to whether to prosecute the offender.

The decision to prosecute is kept under review.[84] This means taking account of any issues that arise during the pre-trial process. Thus, if the defence provide further information about what their argument will be at trial,[85] then the prosecutor must decide whether this affects either the evidential or public-interest test. If the tests are no longer satisfied then the prosecution should be discontinued.

While there is adherence to the Codes it has been noted that prosecutors must be free to 'take a chance' occasionally. For example, Sanders notes that the landmark decision in *R*,[86] which held that a man could lawfully rape his own wife, would have failed the Codes test as there was no reasonable prospect of success.[87] This is because the law, until that point, had been very clear. Therefore, prosecutors must reserve the right to prosecute cases where they believe that a rule of law needs to be challenged. It is difficult to articulate that as a test.

13.1.4 **Challenging a decision**

Not everyone will agree with whatever decision is made. The two most likely people are the defendant themselves and the victim of a crime.

13.1.4.1 **Defendant**

The first person who may wish to challenge a prosecutorial decision is the defendant. The most likely issue is that he will seek to challenge a decision *to* prosecute him. However, is that possible? Where a defendant believes that it was wrong to prosecute him then the most obvious mechanism to challenge this would be to plead 'not guilty'. However, there may be circumstances where, for example, the defendant does not challenge the fact that, in law, he could be considered guilty of an offence but he believes that a prosecution is inappropriate.

In *R v DPP, ex parte Kebilene*[88] the House of Lords was asked to consider the justiciability of challenging a consent to prosecution. *Kebilene* was charged under the *Prevention of Terrorism (Temporary Provisions) Act 1989*, s 16A. This requires the consent of the DPP before an offence can be prosecuted. It was argued that this offence was incompatible with Article 6(2) ECHR. As the DPP is unquestionably a public authority, it was argued that continuing to consent to such prosecutions was unlawful and thus amenable to judicial review. Lord Steyn, with whom all the other Law Lords agreed, stated that, 'absent dishonesty or mala fides or an exceptional circumstance, the decision of the

---

83. For example, speeding would not be dealt with by arrest, detention, and charge. It would be dealt with by laying information before the magistrates' court.

84. Crime Prosecution Service, *The Code for Crown Prosecutors* (CPS 2018) para 3.6.

85. Something that should happen through disclosure: see *Criminal Procedure and Investigations Act 1996*, ss 5–6E.

86. *R v R* [1992] 1 AC 599.

87. Andrew Sanders, 'The CPS - 30 Years On' [2016] *Criminal Law Review* 82, 98.

88. [2000] 2 AC 326.

Director to consent to the prosecution ... is not amenable to judicial review'.[89] Lord Hope noted that judicial review could not require a DPP to either prosecute or not prosecute, all it could do is to ask him to think again, as it is a matter wholly for discretion.[90]

Kebilene concerned DPP consent but what about substantive decisions? In *R (on the application of Pepushi) v Crown Prosecution Service*[91] the applicant sought to challenge the decision to prosecute him for an immigration offence, citing an incompatibility between the domestic crime and an international treaty. The challenge was after the magistrates' court had transferred the matter to the Crown Court and the Divisional Court was clear that judicial review was not appropriate. The court held that it wanted to make it clear that 'save in wholly exceptional circumstances, applications in respect of pending prosecutions that seek to challenge the decision to prosecute should not be made to this court'.[92] The court noted that the correct route to challenge is to the Crown Court and, if necessary, to the Court of Appeal (Criminal Division). In *R (on the application of O) v DPP*[93] the Divisional Court reiterated this point when rejecting an argument that the CPS had previously indicated that an out of court disposal would suffice. Again, the court noted that this was not an administrative matter but one for the trial court.

It is not just a case of pleading not guilty. There may be circumstances where, in fact, a person would appear to have committed a crime but where it would be inappropriate for the prosecution to take place. However, the criminal courts have the ability to act in such cases. The most obvious solution would be to stay the prosecution as an abuse of process.[94] The doctrine of abuse of process allows the courts to stop prosecutions that it would be unfair to proceed with. Thus there is no need for a prosecution to be challenged administratively, because it can be challenged in court.

☰ Example Entrapment

Edith has been accused of supplying an illegal drug to Rachita.[95] Rachita is an undercover police officer and Edith argues that Rachita tricked her into supplying the drug, and she felt that she had no choice but to do so. As a matter of fact, Edith has probably satisfied the *actus reus* and *mens rea* for s 4. However, the trickery could render the prosecution unfair. Instead of challenging the decision to prosecute, Edith should ask the Crown Court to stay the prosecution as an abuse of process. If they fail to do so and she is convicted (or, more likely, pleads guilty under such circumstances) then she can then take the matter to the Court of Appeal (Criminal Division).

What about the position where a suspect wishes to challenge a decision *not* to prosecute him? The problem with the investigation and charging processes is that when information leaks, it can sometimes allow people to prejudge the outcome. Where the CPS decide not to prosecute because, for example, it is not in the public interest to do so, can they challenge this? In essence, demanding that they have their 'day in court' so that they can prove their innocence. It is highly unlikely that a court would entertain

---

89. ibid, at 371.
90. ibid, at 376.
91. [2004] EWHC 798 (Admin).
92. ibid, at [49] (Silber J).
93. [2010] EWHC 804 (Admin).
94. Andrew LT Choo, *Abuse of Process and Judicial Stays of Criminal Proceedings* (2nd edn, OUP 2008)
95. Contrary to *Misuse of Drugs Act 1971*, s 4(3).

such a challenge, pointing out that they are innocent because everyone is innocent until proven guilty. Where people believe that he is guilty, then the remedy would presumably be in the tort of defamation, although that would be expensive to litigate. The courts are unlikely to require the CPS to prosecute in circumstances when they do not wish to (save where it involves the victim's right of review), and thus no challenge will be permissible.

13.1.4.2 Victim

The second person who is likely to want to challenge a prosecutorial decision is the victim. This is an area that has been through significant changes in recent years.

The most likely challenge would be where a victim disagrees with a decision not to prosecute an offender. Traditionally the courts have been slow to accede to such applications, but they are more willing to do so than when the defendant seeks to challenge a decision. This is primarily because a victim has, in essence, no other alternative. Technically the latter is not true because, as will be seen, it is possible for a victim to privately prosecute a perpetrator, but the courts have been slightly dismissive of this:

> . . . only the most sardonic could regard the launching of a private prosecution (a process which, incidentally, is becoming regarded with increasing disfavour in this country) as being equally convenient, beneficial and appropriate as [judicial review].[96]

Thus, in the absence of a real alternative, the courts are prepared to entertain a challenge, something that was expressly noted by the House of Lords in *Kebilene*.[97] The leading authority on this was *R v DPP, ex parte C*,[98] a case that concerned a decision not to prosecute a husband for alleged non-consensual buggery on his wife. The Divisional Court held that it had the power to review a decision not to prosecute, but that it should be used sparingly.[99] There was evidence in this case that the Crown Prosecutor who had reviewed the case had not properly followed the *Code for Crown Prosecutors* and, in particular, had conflated two separate offences (consensual buggery and non-consensual buggery). On that basis, the court quashed the decision, but they reverted it back to the DPP to decide.[100] This is an important point. There remains prosecutorial discretion: it is clear that not every crime has to be prosecuted and therefore the court cannot tell the CPS to prosecute, it can simply tell it that it did not consider the matter appropriately and to think again.

Judicial review remained the only way that the decision could be challenged until 2013 when a new internal system was created known as the *Victims' Right to Review*. The background to this was EU legislation which required Member States to provide the right to review a decision not to prosecute but leaving the decision how such a scheme operates to domestic law.[101] The requirement for a right to review was incorporated into the *Code of Practice for Victims of Crime*,[102] which must have Parliamentary approval.[103] The mechanics of how it applies are set out in prosecution guidance.[104]

---

96. *R v Police Commissioner of the Metropolis, ex parte Blackburn* [1968] 1 All ER 764, 777 (Edmund Davies LJ).

97. *R v DPP, ex part Kebilene* [2000] 2 AC 326 at 369.

98. [1995] 1 Cr App R 136.

99. ibid, at 140.

100. ibid, at 144.

101. Directive 2012/29/EU of the European Parliament and of the Council of 25 October 2012 on establishing minimum standards on the rights, support and the protection of victims of crime [2012] OJ L 315/57.

102. *Domestic Violence, Crime and Victims Act 2004*, s 32.

103. ibid, s 33.

104. Crown Prosecution Service, 'Victims' Right to Review Scheme' (CPS 2020) <https://www.cps.gov.uk/legal-guidance/victims-right-review-scheme>.

A victim is defined not only as the person who suffered harm, but also the bereaved relatives or partners of a homicide victim, the parents of a victim aged under 18, and those who look after someone who is unable to communicate appropriately due to a physical or mental disability. The CPS states that it prefers reviews to take place within five days of a decision not to prosecute being communicated, although that would seem unrealistic. They will, however, consider applications within three months of the date, something that would seem more realistic.

The review takes place by asking a Crown Prosecutor previously unconnected with the case to consider whether the original decision was correct. There are three potential outcomes:

1. The review concludes that the decision was wrong and, where it is possible to do so, proceedings will be recommenced.

2. The review concludes that the decision was correct but that insufficient information was provided to the victim about the reasoning behind the decision. In which case, further information will be provided.

3. The review concludes that the decision was correct and sufficient information was provided.

If the victim continues to disagree with the decision then they can ask for an external review. This could be a reviewing prosecutor at CPS HQ (rather than a Crown Prosecutor within the region or division that first handled the case) or it could, in the more serious offences, involve the matter being sent to an independent barrister. The latter is more likely where the dispute concerns the admissibility or sufficiency of evidence or the meaning of the offence in question. It is less likely to be used where the issue is the public interest, as that is a matter that the CPS arguably have more experience of.

The right to review scheme is not absolute, however. There are a number of circumstances where it does not apply. The most notable are:

- where the police decide not to investigate the case, or not to investigate the case further[105]

- where a decision is to proceed against some, but not all, suspects

- where a single charge is brought instead of multiple charges, including where the prosecution accept a plea in respect of one charge but not others

- where charges are altered

- where some charges are left 'on file'

- where proceedings are dealt with by out of court disposals.

The legality of these restrictions have been tested but have been upheld by the courts. In *R (on the application of AC) v DPP*[106] the Court of Appeal noted that the right to review is not absolute either under domestic law or under the EU Directive.[107] This was a case where proceedings had not been brought against all those involved in the alleged crime. The Court of Appeal accepted that requiring the CPS to consider all possible suspects was disproportionate.

---

105. Although the police service have a similar review process and a decision not to investigate is itself amenable to judicial review where it is unreasonable, although the threshold is extremely high.

106. [2018] EWCA Civ 2092.

107. ibid, at [37].

> **:= Examples** No right to review
>
> Arnold attacks Victoria causing significant injuries. Arnold is charged under the *Offences Against the Person Act 1861*, s 20 but prosecutors later change this to s 47 (ABH). There is no right to review this decision.
>
> Tom, Richard, and David are accused of burglary. Amy accuses them of stealing her laptop and jewellery. The CPS decide only to prosecute Tom and David. There is no right to review the decision not to prosecute Richard.

The fact that the right to review does not apply does not mean that there is no remedy when the decision was wrong. In essence, the position reverts to the old rules. Thus, for example, a decision to caution an offender instead of prosecuting him (something that is not within the right to review process as a caution is an out-of-court disposal), can be challenged by way of judicial review.[108]

Another restriction to the right to review relates to its consequences. The review applies in four situations:

1. the CPS decide not to charge the suspect
2. proceedings against the suspect are discontinued (or withdrawn in a magistrates' court case), thereby ending those proceedings
3. no evidence is offered in those proceedings
4. the charges are left to 'lie on file', marked 'not to be proceeded with without the leave of the Crown Court or the Court of Appeal'.[109]

Where a decision is made in situation 1, 2, or 4, it is technically possible to recommence proceedings. This will be subject to the defendant seeking to argue the recommencement is an abuse of process, although that is unlikely to succeed.[110] However, the position in situation 3 is different. Where no evidence is offered in either the magistrates' court or Crown Court, then the defendant is formally acquitted.[111] Therefore it is not possible to recommence proceedings as to do so would lead to the defence of *autrefois acquit*. In *R (on the application of Hayes) v CPS*[112] the applicant sought to argue that proceedings should be adjourned pending any review, so that an acquittal did not occur. The Divisional Court rejected this, once again noting that the review was not absolute. Why allow a review when no evidence is admitted? The court noted that recommencing a prosecution is not the only remedy and that the review could lead to an apology which may be an appropriate disposal.[113]

13.1.5 Private prosecution

While the vast majority of prosecutions take place by the CPS, there is nothing in law that requires this. Indeed, when the CPS was created, its founding legislation expressly

---

108. *R (on behalf of Guest) v DPP* [2009] EWHC 594 (Admin).
109. Peter Hungerford-Welch, 'Victim's Right to Review Scheme: *R (on the Application of Hayes) v CPS*' [2018] *Criminal Law Review* 500, 502.
110. *R v Killick* [2011] EWCA Crim 1608.
111. *Criminal Justice Act 1967*, s 17 and *Magistrates' Courts Act 1980*, s 27.
112. [2018] EWHC 327 (Admin).
113. ibid, at [51]. For a useful summary of these issues see Peter Hungerford-Welch, 'Victim's Right to Review Scheme: *R (on the Application of Hayes) v CPS*' [2018] *Criminal Law Review* 500, 503.

reserved the right of a person to initiate a private prosecution.[114] Notwithstanding this, the CPS does have an important power to stop inappropriate private prosecutions.

In *Gouriet v Union of Post Office Workers*[115] Lord Diplock stated that the private prosecution was an important constitutional safeguard 'against capricious, corrupt, or biased failure or refusal of those authorities to prosecute offenders'.[116] However it can be questioned whether this remains true. As was noted in the previous section, the CPS is now subject to judicial review of its decisions and therefore it could be argued that this constitutional safeguard is protected in other ways.

In *Jones v Whalley*[117] Lord Bingham described the continuing retention of the private prosecution as 'anomalous' and suggested 'it cannot outweigh an extant decision of a responsible official on what will best serve the public interest'.[118] Lord Bingham was questioning the continuing purpose of private prosecutions and laying down a marker that they cannot be used to circumvent a rational decision not to prosecute. In this case Whalley was accused of assaulting Jones. The police were informed and they dealt with the matter by way of a caution. The notice of caution included a statement that by accepting a caution, no court action would take place.

Whalley decided to initiate a private prosecution, but the magistrates' ruled that to do so was an abuse of process. This was overturned by the Divisional Court, who ruled that the right to instigate a private prosecution should not be impugned, but the House of Lords reversed this decision. Lord Bingham, giving the key speech, noted that the assurance meant that Whalley legitimately believed that he would not be prosecuted and therefore a prosecution would be inappropriate under those circumstances.[119] Lord Bingham accepted that Jones could use judicial review to quash the conviction (leaving him free to prosecute), but this would only be possible where it was irrational to have cautioned Whalley, something that seems unlikely on the facts. The House did indicate that the police should not have used the form of words that they did[120] but by doing so it precluded a private prosecution.

III\ Case Box *R (on the application of Lowden) v Gateshead Magistrates' Court* [2016] EWHC 3536 (Admin)

If the ruling in *Jones v Whalley* was intended to limit private prosecutions, it did not. In *R (on the application of Lowden) v Gateshead Magistrates' Court*[121] the victim was assaulted by a man. The police decided to caution him. The form of wording used by the police was still wrong (in that it still did not refer to the possibility of private prosecutions) but it did not indicate that the offender would never be prosecuted. The Gateshead Magistrates' Court refused to issue a summons when asked to do so by the victim, and the Divisional Court quashed that decision, requiring the summons to be issued. This shows that *Jones v Whalley* concerns the promises made rather than the fact that a person receives an out of court disposal.

---

114. *Prosecution of Offences Act 1985*, s 6.
115. [1978] AC 435.
116. ibid, at 477.
117. [2006] UKHL 41.
118. ibid, at [15].
119. ibid, at [13].
120. See, for example, [2006] UKHL 41 at [44] (Lord Mance).
121. [2016] EWHC 3536 (Admin).

While the term 'private prosecution' may inevitably lead one to think of a private citizen conducting a prosecution, it need not mean that. In *R v Rollins*[122] the Supreme Court were asked to rule upon whether a corporate body has the power to prosecute. By law, companies are considered to be a 'corporate person'[123] and as the *Prosecution of Offences Act 1985* does not exclude corporate persons from s 6, it follows that it is possible for a corporate body to begin a private prosecution.[124] Over the years a number of corporate bodies have launched private prosecutions, the most obvious being the RSPCA (in respect of animal cruelty cases) and the NSPCC (in respect of child cruelty cases).

▍ Case Box *R v Rollins* [2010] UKSC 39

The *Financial Services Authority* (FSA) is a body corporate that is established by statute. It has powers to prosecute for offences under the *Financial Services and Markets Act 2000* (FSMA 2000), which broadly relate to the financial regulation of the financial services industry. The FSA wished to prosecute Rollins and another for offences under the *Proceeds of Crime Act 1985*, including insider dealing and money laundering.

Rollins sought to challenge this, arguing that the FSA was restricted to the powers it was given, meaning it could only prosecute for offences under the FSMA 2000. The Supreme Court rejected this and noted that nothing in the statute, nor the Articles of Association of the FSA restricted their activities in this way. As the *Prosecution of Offenders Act 1985* (PoOA 1985) expressly preserved private prosecutions then there was nothing stopping the FSA from prosecuting offences under it.

The ruling in *Rollins* potentially widens the remit of organizations who are tasked to investigate impropriety. Indeed, it has been suggested that the Electoral Commission, the body who investigate impropriety in elections, could prosecute cases in its own right rather than pass the matter onto the police for investigation. That said, some are opposed to these moves and fear that it is more appropriate for an independent prosecutor to be involved.[125]

13.1.5.1 **Taking over a prosecution**

While there is nothing to stop someone from beginning a private prosecution, the PoOA 1985 does provide that the DPP may take over the conduct of any criminal proceedings.[126] There are two reasons for taking over proceedings. The first is where it is thought that they should continue, but at public expense. The second is where the DPP believes that the proceedings should be taken over and terminated. It is the latter which has proven most controversial.

In *R v Bow Street Stipendiary Magistrate, ex parte South Coast Shipping Co*[127] the Court of Appeal noted the broad discretion that the DPP has in such circumstances:

[The DPP] may discontinue [proceedings] . . . if the evidence is insufficient, or if the proceedings would be contrary to the public interest, or to avoid duplication, or for any other good reason.[128]

---

122. [2010] UKSC 39.
123. *Companies Act 2006*, s 1173(1).
124. *R v Rollins* [2010] UKSC 39 at [9].
125. Edward Malnick, 'Tory Fury as Election Watchdog Seeks Police Powers amid Fears of Bias' *Daily Telegraph* (26 January 2019).
126. *Prosecution of Offences Act 1985*, s 6(2).
127. [1993] QB 645.
128. ibid, at 650 (Lloyd LJ).

Where proceedings have already reached court, the DPP may still take over the proceedings, and simply decline to offer any evidence, which would lead to the acquittal of the defendant.

It is notable that the quote above refers both to the sufficiency of evidence and the public interest. It reinforces the fact that criminal proceedings are not the same as civil proceedings. They are not conducted for the benefit of an individual; a prosecution should only be brought to enforce society's condemnation of illegal activities. Where a private prosecution is not in the public interest, then the state (through the DPP) will step in and halt proceedings.

What about the sufficiency of evidence? Private prosecutors are not bound by the *Code for Crown Prosecutors* since it is not a Crown Prosecutor who is commencing the proceedings. How then does the CPS decide the sufficiency of evidence? Until comparatively recently, the DPP considered whether there was sufficient evidence that could be left to the tribunal of fact. This replicates the test used by the courts at the conclusion of the prosecution case (see 15.2).[129] However, since 2009, the test has been whether it is more likely than not that the defendant will be convicted, in essence, replicating the test for public prosecutions. In *R (Gujra) v CPS*[130] the Supreme Court was asked whether this approach was lawful. In a majority decision, they ruled it was. Lord Wilson JSC who gave the leading speech was dismissive of the belief that the lower standard (left to the tribunal of fact) should be used. Lord Wilson noted that the most pertinent question was the likelihood that a conviction could be sustained.[131] This must be correct because a person should not be put through the cost and difficulty of defending proceedings save where there is a realistic prospect that a conviction can be sustained.

⟳ QUESTION FOR REFLECTION

If Parliament expressly retained the right of a private citizen to bring a prosecution, why should the state then interfere with that decision? Should the prosecution not be allowed to continue irrespective, but with the proviso that the prosecutor is liable for all costs if the prosecution fails?

13.1.6 **Deferred prosecutions**

A relatively new phenomenon in the English Legal System are deferred prosecution agreements (DPA). These relate to corporate fraud, and they were introduced in response to the difficulty of prosecuting corporate crime.[132] In some countries a plea agreement can be made whereby the prosecutors and defence agree what penalty the court should impose, but the courts in England have been very clear that this is inappropriate.[133]

DPAs were introduced by the *Crime and Courts Act 2012*. They apply only to corporate bodies and not to individuals.[134] Where a director of a company is accused of personal misconduct, along with facilitating corporate misconduct, the DPA can lead

---

129.   R v Galbaith [1981] 1 WLR 1039.
130.   [2012] UKSC 52.
131.   ibid, at [35].
132.   Michael Bisgrove and Mark Weekes, 'Deferred Prosecution Agreements: A Practical Consideration' 6 *Criminal Law Review* 416, 417.
133.   ibid, 418.
134.   *Crime and Courts Act 2013*, sch 17, para 4.

to a deferral for the corporate misconduct but the individual director continues to be subject to personal prosecution. Only the DPP or the Director of the SFO can settle a DPA, and, unusually, it requires their personal attention.[135] This reinforces the importance of the DPA and is a clear presumption that they should be exercised cautiously.

A DPA must contain the following:

- a statement of facts relating to the alleged facts, which may include admissions by the corporate body
- an expiry date for the DPA by which time it will expire if it does not expire through breach
- requirements placed on the corporate body, which can include:
  - a financial penalty
  - to compensate victims of the alleged offence
  - to donate money to a charity or third-party
  - to disgorge any profits made through the offence
  - to implement a compliance programme
  - to cooperate in any investigation related to the alleged offence
  - to pay any reasonable costs
- a statement setting out the consequences of breach.[136]

The level of financial penalty should be broadly comparable to a fine that a court would impose on the body corporate following a guilty plea.[137] That said, the prosecutor can then discount this fine to take into account the level of cooperation that has been offered.

A DPA must be approved by a court through two hearings. The first hearing takes place once negotiations have started but before the terms are settled. The prosecutor must apply to the Crown Court for a declaration that entering into the DPA is likely to be in the public interest and that the proposed terms are fair and proportionate.[138] Given that the terms are still being negotiated, it appears somewhat odd to ask the second question. However it is perhaps ensuring that the courts would find the proposed terms acceptable so that detailed negotiations do not take place before the courts reject it. That said, the fact that the broad terms have to be known must mean the application will be relatively late-on. The second, and more substantive, hearing takes place after the terms are agreed. Again, the court must rule on whether the DPA is in the public interest and whether the terms are fair, reasonable, and proportionate.[139] The court must give its reasons,[140] and this has so far taken the form of the judge handing down a judgment setting out the factual circumstances of the case, the terms of the DPA, and indicating his approval. Once approved by the court, the DPA and the judgment must be published, unless to do so would compromise other proceedings (most notably, prosecutions against individuals).[141]

135.   ibid, para 3(2).
136.   ibid, para 5.
137.   ibid, para 5(4).
138.   ibid, para 7(1).
139.   ibid, para 8(1).
140.   ibid, para 8(4).
141.   ibid, para 8(7) when read in conjunction with para 12.

Where a DPA is to be used then proceedings must formally be initiated by preferring an indictment in the Crown Court.[142] This means that an indictment setting out the charges is drawn up and lodged with the Crown Court. This is the equivalent procedure to 'charging' an individual and means that the person (or, in this case, the company) is formally to be prosecuted for the failure. However, as soon as the indictment is lodged the proceedings are suspended and can only be lifted by breach.[143] Importantly, the statute provides that *nobody* may prosecute the corporate body while the DPA is in effect.[144] This means that a private prosecution against the corporation for the same offence would not be permitted. If the DPA lapses without breach then the proceedings are formally terminated.[145]

The first DPA was authorized by the courts in 2016 and Padfield notes that the case demonstrated that judges will not consider themselves to be 'rubber stamps' and instead will carefully scrutinize the appropriateness of both (a) the DPA and (b) the sanctions imposed.[146] The policy of the SFO is currently to only use them where a company self-refers potential criminal liability and also cooperates fully with the investigation.[147] In this way, the SFO argues that it is encouraging companies to report matters that would be otherwise difficult to detect. However some argue that DPAs simply distract attention from the fact that corporate crime by individuals is still not prosecuted sufficiently. Certainly, there have been high-profile acquittals of individuals even in circumstances where a corporate DPA has been settled.[148] Whether that is a failure of DPAs or a failure of the law of fraud is more open to question.

║\ Case Box Tesco's DPA

Tesco was accused of fraudulent activity by false accounting. In order to safeguard the share price of the company, Tesco brought forward income from future accounting periods and encouraged illegal practices to meet accounting targets, including overestimating its trading performance.

When senior managers of Tesco discovered the irregularities, it asked internal and external auditors to assess the position. They then reported the irregularities to the SFO and cooperated with them during the investigation.

As part of the DPA, Tesco agreed to the following:

- a fine of £129 million
- a contribution of £3 million to the costs of investigating the matter
- an ongoing compliance programme.

Sir Brian Leveson, the President of the Queen's Bench Division, approved the DPA on 10 April 2017.[149] He fully scrutinized the terms and the public interest in authorizing the DPA, reinforcing the importance of judicial scrutiny.

---

142.   ibid, para 2(1).
143.   ibid, para 2(2), (3) when read in conjunction with para 9.
144.   ibid, para 2(4).
145.   ibid, para 11.
146.   Nicola Padfield, 'Deferred Prosecution Agreements' [2016] *Criminal Law Review* 449.
147.   Alistair Graham and Chris Roberts, 'SFO Director Makes Case for Deferrred Prosecution Agreements' *The Times* (22 March 2018).
148.   Emma Simpson, 'Tesco Trial Collapse Heaps Pressure on SFO' (6 December 2018) <https://www.bbc.co.uk/news/business-46468228>.
149.   *Serious Fraud Office v Tesco Stores Limited* (2017) <https://www.judiciary.uk/wp-content/uploads/2019/01/sfo-v-tesco-stores-ltd-2017-approved-final.pdf>.

13.1.7 **Immunity**

Throughout the history of criminal justice, questions have been raised about what should happen to those who commit a crime but who cooperate with the state to secure the conviction of others. An offender in such circumstances can expect a discount to his own sentence[150] but there has always been doubt as to whether *de facto* immunity was granted through, for example, not prosecuting the individual or selecting a lesser charge. Arguably such an approach could be justified under the public-interest test: it is in the public interest for crimes, in particular, serious crimes to be prosecuted. If the only way to successfully prosecute someone is to allow someone with lesser involvement to go free then that might be justified.

Relying purely on prosecutorial discretion meant that there was a lack of transparency. While immunity should only have been given with the consent of the Attorney-General,[151] there was no guarantee that this happened. A statutory power was introduced by the *Serious Organised Crime and Police Act 2005*.[152] This provides:

1. If a specified prosecutor thinks that for the purposes of the investigation or prosecution of an indictable offence or an offence triable either-way it is appropriate to offer any person immunity from prosecution for any offence he may give the person a written notice under this subsection (an 'immunity notice').

2. If a person is given an immunity notice, no proceedings for an offence of a description specified in the notice may be brought against that person in England and Wales or Northern Ireland except in the circumstances specified in the notice.

It can be seen that the requirement is that there is a written basis for the immunity and a notice is given to this effect. This is important because it will be remembered from earlier in this chapter, that where a person has been told that they will not be prosecuted it would constitute an abuse of process to proceed with a prosecution. That said, it is notable that s 71(2) provides that there can be exceptions to the immunity. Presumably this allows prosecutors to indicate that the immunity will be void if they do not cooperate in the manner which has been prescribed. It may also include conditions on, for example, future conduct.

Section 71 is a practical and transparent system. However nothing in s 71 overturns the common-law position. Thus, prosecutorial discretion continues. It has been suggested that prosecutors are not using s 71 and are instead preferring to use their discretion because it is thought to be easier.[153] That might be correct but it does nothing to answer the criticism that such deals lack transparency. It would be more appropriate for s.71 to be the only way that immunity can be given in return for cooperation.

---

150. See, for example, *R v A (Informer: Reduction in Sentence)* [1999] 1 Cr App R (S) 52.
151. David Corker, Gemma Tombs, and Tamara Chisholm, 'Sections 71 and 72 of Serious Organised Crime and Police Act 2005: Wither the Common Law?' [2009] Criminal Law Review 261, 261.
152. Serious Organised Crime and Police Act 2005, s 71.
153. David Corker, Gemma Tombs, and Tamara Chisholm, 'Sections 71 and 72 of Serious Organised Crime and Police Act 2005: Wither the Common Law?' [2009] Criminal Law Review 261, 268.

QUESTION FOR REFLECTION

While the CPS and other prosecutors have general discretion as to whether to prosecute some-one, surely a decision to provide immunity to someone should be carefully spelt out? A written agreement should be produced that sets out what cooperation is to be expected, what will happen to the defendant if he does cooperate, and how that decision can be reconsidered if he fails to do so.

What do you think about that as a proposition? Are you comfortable with people having immunity where the public interest and evidence tests would be otherwise satisfied? Should immunity be granted for all crimes or only some? Who should decide?

13.2 Out of court disposals

It was noted previously that when the evidential test is met the police or CPS may decide to proceed by way of an out of court disposal. This is a mechanism by which an offender admits responsibility for their actions but is not prosecuted and is, instead, dealt with administratively.

13.2.1 Types of disposals

There are five key types of out of court disposals that can apply to adults and adolescents:

1. simple caution
2. conditional caution
3. reprimand (for juveniles)
4. community resolutions
5. fixed penalty notices.

It is not necessary to consider all in depth but is useful to outline the key features of the various schemes.

13.2.1.1 Simple caution

The simple caution (previously referred to as 'a caution') is the oldest form of out of court disposal. Joshua Rozenberg, the long-standing BBC law editor, reports that tech-nically there are two types of simple caution: the formal and the informal. He provides an example of the latter:

> I was once stopped for speeding on an empty motorway by a police officer who told me 'at twenty to five in the morning, sir, take a bollocking'.[154]

These days this would not be classed as a caution (it would just probably be classed as 'advice') but the point is well made in that it demonstrates that out of court disposals have occurred probably ever since the police were formed. It is another example of the

---

154. Joshua Rozenberg, *The Case for the Crown: The Inside Story of the Director of Public Prosecutions* (Equation 1987) 15.

fact that just because there is sufficient evidence to show a crime took place does not mean a prosecution is inevitable. Sometimes it will be dealt with informally by the police (as with Mr Rozenberg's speeding) but other times it will be dealt with more formally.

The least formal of all disposals is the simple caution. A simple caution does not exist as a creature of statute but is instead either a creature of common law or, more realistically, an administrative creation. The rules relating to simple cautions are set out in guidance notes published by the Ministry of Justice,[155] whereas previously it was through 'Home Office Circulars' which had similarly little authority. The courts have held that the guidance should be followed[156] but it remains a matter largely of discretion as to when a simple caution is administered.

A simple caution is, in essence, a warning. An offender is told that he has acted inappropriately but no action will be taken against him. That said, cautions form part of a person's criminal record and the guidance makes clear that the offender should understand this.[157] For this reason, it is also important that a caution is only given to someone who accepts that they have committed an offence, and is prepared to accept a caution.[158] This can pose a dilemma because there is no guarantee that someone who refused to accept a caution will be prosecuted: for trivial matters it is quite possible that the CPS decides it is not in the public interest to bring the offender to court. However, the risk a person takes in turning down a simple caution is that they might, and a court will impose some form of punishment, costs, and a victim surcharge. That said, it is also important that the admission is made freely, and it has been noted that the promise of a caution cannot be made to incentivize a confession.[159]

Save in those situations where a person must be referred to the CPS for consultation over charging, the police have the right to administer a caution without the permission of the CPS. That said, the CPS will also sometimes refer the matter back to the police with the suggestion that a case is suitable for a simple caution. This is more likely to be done where it is a trivial offence and it is not thought that the public interest is met in prosecuting.

While simple cautions are not set out in statute, the *Criminal Justice and Courts Act 2015* has put limits on their use. The initial limitation is that a simple caution can only be administered for an indictable-only offence in exceptional circumstances and with the consent of the DPP.[160] Indictable-only offences are those that can only be tried in the Crown Court (see 13.3.1 later) and they constitute the most serious offences. To that extent, it could be suggested that this is not a particularly controversial limitation and indeed the converse is true. Perhaps it is more surprising that a simple caution could be administered for serious sexual offences such as rape.

Either-way offences (the next level of seriousness down) are broken down into two lists. Those that are prescribed by the Home Secretary, and those that are not. Where an offence is prescribed[161] then the police may not administer a simple caution unless exceptional circumstances arise in respect of the person or offence.[162] The offences prescribed

---

155. Ministry of Justice, *Simple Cautions for Adult Offenders* (TSO 2016).
156. See, for example, *R (on the application of Omar) v Chief Constable of Bedfordshire* [2002] EWHC 3060 (Admin).
157. Ministry of Justice, *Simple Cautions for Adult Offenders* (TSO 2016) para 13.
158. ibid, para 9.
159. *R v Commissioner of the Metropolis, ex parte Thompson* [1997] 1 WLR 1519.
160. *Criminal Justice and Courts Act 2015*, s 17(2).
161. *Criminal Justice and Courts Act 2015 (Simple Cautions) (Specification of Either-Way Offences) Order 2015* (SI 2015/790).
162. *Criminal Justice and Courts Act 2015*, s 17(3).

largely relate to offences against children (particularly sexual offences), firearms, and drugs offences. Note that the consequence of this limitation is not necessarily that a prosecution will take place, because other forms of out of court disposal are possible.

The final limitation is that where a person has received a caution for another offence within the past two years, then a simple caution should not ordinarily be administered.[163] Again, this is perhaps not a surprising limitation. At least one purpose of a caution is to allow an offender a 'second chance'. Giving repeated second chances would suggest that the offender is not getting the message.

13.2.1.2 **Conditional caution**

While the simple caution has no statutory basis, the second form of out of court disposal does. The *Criminal Justice Act 2003* (CJA 2003) introduced a new form of caution known as a 'conditional caution'. A conditional caution is defined as, 'a caution which is given in respect of an offence committed by the offender and which has conditions attached to it with which the offender must comply'.[164] In other words, it is an administrative sanction that carries with it requirements to do something. Conditions can only be imposed if they have the purpose of:

- facilitating the rehabilitation of the offender
- ensuring that the offender makes reparation for the offence
- punishing the offender.[165]

It is notable that punishment is expressly mentioned since, of course, it will be remembered that the evidence that allegedly shows a criminal transgression has not been tested. It remains a pre-trial disposal. Before a conditional caution can be imposed, the following conditions need to be satisfied:

1. Evidence exists that shows that the offender has committed the offence.
2. The CPS must consider that the evidence satisfies the evidential test (within the CCP) and that the case is suitable to be dealt with by way of conditional caution.
3. The suspect admits that he committed the offence.
4. The police must explain the consequences of accepting a conditional caution.
5. The offender signs a document that sets out:

    - the details of the offence
    - an admission by him that he committed the offence
    - his consent to being given a conditional caution and
    - the conditions of the caution.[166]

As with the simple caution, therefore, a conditional caution can only be given where the suspect both admits the offence and consents to being dealt in this way. That would, at face value, perhaps deal with the matter that the evidence has not been tested, but

---

163. ibid, s 17(4).
164. CJA 2003, s 22(2).
165. ibid, s 22(3).
166. ibid, s 23.

there is concern that people are too prepared to accept cautions, including conditional cautions, and therefore cautions are being administered in circumstances when a person may not be guilty in law.[167]

Along with the conditions that can be imposed on a conditional caution, perhaps the biggest difference between it and the simple caution is the fact that it is, in essence, a deferred prosecution. If a person fails to adhere to the conditions that were imposed on the condition then he may be prosecuted for the initial criminal offence.[168] The document signed by the offender mentioned earlier can be adduced as evidence and, given that it requires a clear admission of guilt, means that, in essence, the court will be asked to sentence the offender as guilt is unlikely to be an issue.

Both cautions and conditional cautions have proven controversial with the belief that they are sometimes being used for inappropriate cases because it is an easy disposition.[169] If this is still occurring—and the pressures of funding cuts means that there must be a real risk that it is—then this would be deeply unfortunate because it is important that both forms of cautions are used where appropriate. The more serious an offence (including in its circumstances) the less likely it would be appropriate.

> **≔ Examples** Same offence, different seriousness
>
> Rebecca and Eve are playing netball in opposing teams. The game is getting heated and Rebecca deliberately throws the ball into Eve's face causing severe bruising.
>
> Susan and her partner Tamzin have been arguing. Tamzin stands up and punches Susan several times in the head. It causes severe bruising to her cheek and eye.
>
> Both of these offences could be dealt with as assault, occasioning actual bodily harm.[170] It is possible that Rebecca's case may be suitable for a caution if she has not done anything like this before. It is less likely that Tamzin's case should be dealt with by way of a caution because it is an incident of domestic violence, undoubtedly making it more serious.

13.2.1.3 Youth cautions

A separate system has always existed for out of court disposals for youths under 18. Until comparatively recently this was through the issue of 'final warnings' or 'reprimands' but these have now been replaced by the 'youth caution'[171] and 'youth conditional caution'.[172]

The distinction between the caution and conditional caution is the same as with adults but there are extra procedural hurdles that need to be fulfilled before a caution can be administered to someone under the age of 18. As with an adult, there must be a confession to the crime, and the officer must be satisfied that there is sufficient evidence to charge the youth with an offence, but decide that a prosecution or conditional caution is not appropriate in the circumstances.[173]

---

167. Paul Hynes and Matthew Elkins, 'Suggestions for Reform to the Police Cautioning Procedure' [2013] *Criminal Law Review* 966.

168. *Criminal Justice Act 2003*, s 24.

169. See the discussion in Nicola Padfield, 'Out-of-Court (out of Sight) Disposals' (2010) 69 *Cambridge Law Journal* 6.

170. *Offences Against the Person Act 1861*, s 47.

171. *Legal Aid, Sentencing and Punishment of Offenders Act 2012*, s 135.

172. *Criminal Justice and Immigration Act 2008*, s 48.

173. *Crime and Disorder Act 1998*, s 66ZA(1).

A caution must be administered by a police officer who has been suitably trained for these purposes[174] and the child must be accompanied by an appropriate adult.[175] An appropriate adult means the child's parent, a local authority representative where that child is the subject of care proceedings, a social worker, or any person aged 18 or over who is neither a police officer nor employed by the police.[176] The latter should only be used where the other appropriate adult is not available. The requirement for an appropriate adult to be present is to ensure that the child understands what is happening.

When the caution is administered, the child must be told in plain language that this is a formal criminal justice disposal and what the implications of that are. This includes, for example, explaining that while a caution is normally instantly 'spent' for the purposes of the *Rehabilitation of Offenders Act 1974*, for certain types of offences it must always be disclosed. The child should also be told that if they commit another offence within two years then a court will ordinarily not be permitted to impose a conditional discharge on them.[177]

While there is a requirement that a child consents to the imposition of a conditional caution,[178] there is no such requirement for the imposition of a simple caution. This was true of the previous system of reprimands and final warnings and the House of Lords expressly rejected a submission that fairness required consent to be obtained first.[179] The decision can be criticized for denying due process to a juvenile[180] but it is notable that the European Court of Human Rights rejected an application by *R*, indicating that as the police were expressly not prosecuting him there was no determination of a criminal charge within the meaning of Article 6.[181] The fact that a conditional caution potentially only defers a prosecution may be one reason why the position is different for them. Also, the 'conditions' are highly likely to be considered punishments, therefore perhaps also bringing the matter further within Article 6. However, it undoubtedly remains unsatisfactory and a child should consent to a simple caution in the same way as an adult does. This should only be done in the presence of an appropriate adult to ensure that the child understands the implications of his or her decision.

Where a youth caution is administered the police must refer the child to the Youth Offending Team (YOT).[182] The YOT must assess the child and consider arranging the child to participate in a rehabilitation programme.[183] Where it is a second caution, then there is a presumption that the child will participate in rehabilitation unless it is considered inappropriate to do so.[184] The rehabilitation programmes are generally based on restorative justice principles,[185] meaning that youths would be encouraged to work with victims or community groups to understand the impact on their offending.

---

174. Ministry of Justice, *Youth Cautions: Guidance for Police and Youth Offending Teams* (HMSO 2013) 20.
175. *Crime and Disorder Act 1998*, s 66ZA(2).
176. ibid, s 66ZA(7).
177. Ministry of Justice, *Youth Cautions: Guidance for Police and Youth Offending Teams* (HMSO 2013) 21.
178. *Crime and Disorder Act 1998*, s 66B(6)(c).
179. *R v Durham Constabulary and another, ex part R* [2005] 1 WLR 1184.
180. Alisdair Gillespie, 'Reprimanding Juveniles and the Right to Due Process' (2005) 68 *Modern Law Review* 1006.
181. *R v United Kingdom* App No 33506/6.
182. *Crime and Disorder Act 1998*, s 66ZB(1).
183. ibid, s 66ZB(3).
184. ibid, s 66ZB(2).
185. Ministry of Justice, *Youth Cautions: Guidance for Police and Youth Offending Teams* (HMSO 2013) 24.

13.2.1.4 **Fixed penalty notices**

One of the biggest changes in recent years has been the increase in fixed penalty notices (FPN). Traditionally, these were used for regulatory matters such as parking infringements. A notice indicating what transgression had taken place is issued and a financial penalty imposed. There is usually a right of appeal against an FPN, but it is not always to a court, it is sometimes to an adjudicator. Speeding tickets are sometimes thought of as FPNs, but that is not strictly true because the speeding ticket is, in essence, an opportunity to settle the matter before it proceeds to trial. If it is not settled, the matter is treated as a crime and prosecuted accordingly. The same is not true of all FPNs.

A wide range of agencies use FPNs but the number issued has increased significantly in recent years, partly because they have become an out of court disposal in their own right. They apply to a wide range of offences. The *Criminal Justice and Police Act 2001* introduced the power to issue FPNs in respect of 'disorderly behaviour'. The definition of 'disorderly behaviour' encapsulates twenty-two separate offences[186] ranging from the throwing of a firework,[187] through to theft (to cover shoplifting), and even the use of a 'public electronic communications network in order to cause annoyance, inconvenience or needless anxiety'.[188] This demonstrates that it is not simply trivial matters such as loud or obnoxious behaviour, but a variety of criminal acts.

It has been noted that FPNs are 'visible justice' in that not only can the offender see that they are being dealt with, but society can see that actions have consequences.[189] They are, however, also a speedy form of justice. The issuing of an FPN can (but does not have to) take place at the scene and this means that the police officer remains 'on the streets', whereas if they were to arrest a suspect then they could spend several hours in the police station.[190] While it may seem that FPNs are ideal for, for example, being drunk and disorderly, and indeed this is one of the specified offences,[191] it can be questioned as to whether it can properly be used, because guidance requires that FPNs are only given where a person is able to understand what is being given to them and why.[192]

Unlike with a caution, there is no requirement that a person admits that their conduct amounts to an offence,[193] and the constable must have reason to believe that the relevant person has committed an offence. That is a significantly lower standard than would be expected when deciding whether someone should be prosecuted. The argument in favour of this approach is that there is the right to challenge the issuing of an FPN so where a person believes that they did not commit an offence they can reject the penalty. However, doing so could lead them being brought before the Magistrates' Court.

Technically there is no way that an FPN can be challenged.[194] Instead, the defendant asks to be tried for the offence he is alleged to have committed.[195] The police and

---

186. *Criminal Justice and Police Act 2001*, s 1(1).
187. *Explosives Act 1875*, s 80.
188. *Communications Act 2003*, s 127(2).
189. Samantha Coates, Paula Kautt, and Katrin Muller-Johnson, 'Penalty Notices for Disorder: Influences on Police Decision Making' (2009) 5 *Journal of Experimental Criminology* 399, 402.
190. ibid. This will because of the detention and interview procedure documented in Chapter 12, but also the need to update the pocket book etc.
191. *Criminal Justice and Police Act 2001*, s 1(1) when read in conjunction with *Licensing Act 1872*, s 12.
192. Ministry of Justice, *Penalty Notices for Disorder* (HMSO 2014) 12.
193. ibid, 7.
194. Judicial review is presumably possible as it is an administrative matter but because there is a procedure whereby the notice can be rejected, that would presumably be considered the appropriate avenue and judicial review would not be possible at all.
195. *Criminal Justice and Police Act 2001*, s 4(2).

CPS will then need to decide whether to prosecute him for that offence. This will, of course, mean that the full prosecution codes will need to be applied, which imposes a higher evidential test than that required for an FPN. Where a person believes that the FPN has been given without full consideration of the evidence then they may wish to challenge this, knowing that a prosecution is not automatic, and placing their faith in prosecutorial review.

However, there are two risks of doing so. The first is financial and the second is reputational. FPNs for disorder carry either a £60 or £90 fine.[196] Were a person to be prosecuted and attend the magistrates' court then the costs would be significantly more than this. In all likelihood they would receive a fine greater than this. Even if they are given a discharge they would still have to pay the costs of the prosecution and, if they chose to engage a lawyer, their own fees (subject to legal aid—discussed in Chapter 11). In addition, they will be required to pay a victim surcharge of £20. Thus, the total cost of defending the proceedings in the magistrates' court could be several times more than the FPN fine.

The second risk is reputational. A person is prosecuted in the magistrates' court. An FPN is not considered to be a criminal conviction. However, where a person is prosecuted and they are found to have contravened the law, then they will receive a sentence and will have a criminal conviction. While it is likely to become spent quickly in most instances, it will not alter the fact that the defendant has a criminal conviction that might be disclosed under such circumstances.

The consequences of these two risks are that few will choose to challenge an FPN. This means that there is the risk that FPNs are being given without due consideration of the evidence, including whether there is sufficient proof to show that the suspect committed a crime.

Where an FPN is issued and a person does not request prosecution instead but refuses to pay it, the sum is increased to a sum 1.5 times the fine (ie £60 becomes £90; £90 becomes £135).[197] Further non-payment is considered a debt and is enforced as a debt rather than a breach of criminal law.[198]

13.3 Mode of trial

Assuming a prosecution does take place, then it is necessary to identify in which court the proceedings will be heard. As noted in Chapter 6, there are two courts of first instance that hear criminal matters; the magistrates' court and the Crown Court. Determining which court hears which matters is known as 'mode of trial'.

13.3.1 Classifying offences

Offences are divided into one of three categories:

1. summary-only offences
2. offences triable only on indictment
3. either-way offences.

---

196.   Ministry of Justice, *Penalty Notices for Disorder* (HMSO 2014) 25–7.
197.   *Criminal Justice and Police Act 2001*, s 4(5).
198.   *Criminal Justice and Police Act 2001*, s 10.

Summary matters are dealt with in the magistrates' court and cases heard on an indictment take place in the Crown Court. Thus, summary-only offences can ordinarily only be heard in the magistrates' court and offences triable only on indictment take place in the Crown Court. Those offences that are classed as 'either-way' can, as their name suggests, be heard in either the magistrates' court or the Crown Court.

How do you ascertain what an offence is? The usual answer is to look at how the offence is created. Crimes of common law are triable only on indictment unless the contrary is stated. The vast majority of offences are now created by statute and that will explain the mode of trial.

Example Common-law offences

The offence of murder is a common-law offence. Accordingly, murder can only be tried in the Crown Court.

The offences of assault and battery are common-law offences. However, *Criminal Justice Act 1988*, s 39 states that they should be tried summarily. Thus, although common-law offences will normally be heard in the Crown Court, assault and battery are heard in the magistrates' court.

Occasionally the statute will set out expressly when an offence should adhere to a particular mode of trial. Usually, however, the statute will imply mode of trial when identifying sentence.

CLASSIFICATION OF OFFENCES

The following are examples of how to discover the classification of offences from statute.

SUMMARY-ONLY OFFENCES

(4) A person guilty of an offence under this section is liable on summary conviction to a fine.

TRIABLE ONLY ON INDICTMENT

(4) A person guilty of an offence under this section is liable on conviction on indictment, to imprisonment for a term not exceeding 10 years.

TRIABLE EITHER WAY

(4) A person guilty of an offence under this section is liable-

(a) on summary conviction, to imprisonment for a term not exceeding 12 months or to a fine, or both;

(b) on conviction on indictment, to imprisonment for a term not exceeding 5 years.

As can be seen, therefore, the key is to identify whether the terms 'summary' or 'indictment' are used. However, this does not always work with historic statutes. For example, *Theft Act 1968*, s 7 states:

A person guilty of theft shall on conviction on indictment be liable to imprisonment for a term not exceeding seven years.

This would suggest that theft is triable only on indictment. However, it's not. It is an either-way offence. Why? The *Criminal Law Act 1977* reformed the law by downgrading several offences to either summary or either-way offences. Schedule 1 to the *Magistrates Courts Act 1980* provides a consolidated list of either-way offences so, if in doubt, this Schedule can be consulted, but the easiest way of checking is to consult one of the practitioner texts such as *Blackstone's Criminal Practice*.

Theft has proven to be one of the most controversial either-way offences. The *Theft Act 1968* defines theft as dishonestly appropriating property belonging to another with the intention of permanently depriving that other of it.[199] 'Property' is defined expansively, and could include extremely low-level goods. While we colloquially talk of 'shoplifting', a person is actually charged with theft, in the same way that someone stealing £100,000 is.

While figures are not published, it is estimated that a Crown Court case can cost between five and eight times more than a summary trial, partly because of the increased number of individuals involved in the trial (see Chapter 6) and partly because Crown Court trials take so much longer. In 2009, a man was charged with stealing a banana worth 25p. He exercised his right to be tried in the Crown Court (see 13.3.2.2).[200] The prosecution costs were in excess of £20,000 and the total costs for the trial would be considerably more when salaries, buildings, fees, and expenses are taken into account. A trial in the magistrates' court would cost approximately one-tenth of this.

While it may appear inappropriate that a trial over such a trivial amount could take place in the Crown Court, it must be recognized that the consequences of a conviction can be significant. Let us take two examples:

Example Theft with consequences

Arnold and Edwina are accused separately of each stealing a Mars bar worth 60p each.
Arnold is a barrister practising in private practice.
Edwina is a curate in the Church of England.

Any punishment is likely to be trivial, possibly including an absolute discharge, but the consequences for their personal life could be very serious. A barrister is obliged to report themselves to the Bar Standards Board if they are convicted of a crime. Theft is considered a crime of dishonesty and therefore it could lead to sanctions being imposed on Arnold. The same is equally true of Edwina. It is unlikely the Church of England would welcome a priest being convicted of theft and it could have implications for her living.

Does that justify a Crown Court hearing? The only argument in favour of doing so must be premised on the basis that somehow trial by jury is fairer than trial by magistrates. It would be difficult to hold that line as to do so would call into question the trials for summary-only offences, many of which could also have repercussions for careers (eg a police officer who was convicted of assault or battery while off-duty). Senior judges have called for the right to elect jury trial for such matters to be removed[201] but

---

199. *Theft Act 1968*, s 1.
200. Jo Adetunji, '£20,000 Trial for Stealing Banana Ends in Acquittal' *The Guardian* (8 August 2009).
201. See, for example, the speech given by Lady Justice Hallett, Trial by Jury—Past and Present (2017) <https://www.judiciary.uk/wp-content/uploads/2017/05/hallett-lj-blackstone-lecture-20170522-1.pdf>.

the government has never gone that far. Low-level shoplifting (meaning under the value of £200[202]) was reclassified as summary-only, but even then it is subject to the right of a defendant to seek trial by jury.[203] Thus, the amendment merely prevents magistrates declining jurisdiction to hear low-level shoplifting cases, but still permitting a defendant to choose to be tried in the Crown Court.

⟳ QUESTION FOR REFLECTION

Is it right that a person who is charged with theft of a trivial amount of money can require the matter to be heard in the Crown Court? Think about the examples of Arnold and Edwina given earlier. Does that make you change your mind? If it does, why is theft any different to violent offences? For example, if Arnold or Edwina was charged with battery would the consequences not be the same? Yet they would have no right to a jury trial in those circumstances.

13.3.2 Transferring to the court

Now that we understand the classification of offences, how does a case arrive at the correct court? The real distinction is between offences triable either-way and those that are not.

13.3.2.1 Non either-way offences

Where an offence is not triable either-way then transfer to the appropriate court is usually administrative. The term 'indictable' is used because the accused will be tried on an 'indictment', that is to say, a formal document that sets out the statement of offence and briefly summarizes the alleged circumstances of the offence. The equivalent for summary offences is known as the 'information'.

Where a person has been charged with a summary offence by the police then the charge sheet will be given to the local magistrates' court and the information is prepared from that. Not every summary offence arises from arrest. A good example would be speeding. Where a person has not been arrested then the details of the offence are sent to the CPS who prepare the information. This is then laid before the court and a summons issued, which informs the defendant when he should present himself to court.

For summary-only matters, the information must be laid within six months of the crime being committed.[204] If this deadline is missed then ordinarily no further action can be taken. It should be stressed that this six month deadline applies only to those offences that are summary only and not those that are either-way. Presumably it will include low-value shoplifting because although the defendant has the right to elect trial by jury, the statute makes clear that low-value shoplifting cases are to be considered summary-only offences.[205]

For indictable-only offences the matter is now comparatively simple. Traditionally, the position was somewhat convoluted with committal hearings being necessary. Initially, a committal hearing was almost a 'mini-trial', which involved prosecution witnesses giving

---

202. *Magistrates' Courts Act 1980*, s 22A(3).
203. ibid, s 22A(1), (2).
204. ibid, s 127.
205. ibid, s 22A(1).

evidence before magistrates. While the defence had the right to adduce evidence, they rarely did so, as that would just 'give away' their defence before the trial itself. Eventually, committal proceedings became paper-based whereby proof of evidence was adduced, but there was still an element of trial whereby magistrates had to decide whether there was a case to answer. While this was useful in terms of an outside body considering the evidence, it was not really doing anything other than confirming the decision to prosecute. Statistics suggested that only 0.2 per cent of cases were dismissed at committal stage,[206] suggesting that there was an element of 'rubber stamp' in the process.

The *Crime and Disorder Act 1998* introduced a new 'fast track' approach to transferring to the Crown Court. Section 51 of the Act ensures that where an offender is charged with an indictable-only offence this matter is sent directly to the Crown Court and there is no requirement, or indeed power, for magistrates to review the case save for the issue of bail. Where the offender has been charged with an either-way offence at the same time as the indictable-only offence, then so long as the charges are related (meaning 'it arises out of circumstances which are the same or connected with those giving rise to the indictable only offence'[207]) then that offence also automatically proceeds to the Crown Court.

Where a person believes that there is insufficient evidence to justify standing trial then he may petition the Crown Court for the matter to be dismissed for lack of evidence.[208] If, after reviewing the evidence, the judge does not believe that there is sufficient evidence that a jury, properly directed, would be able to convict the offender, then the matter should be dismissed.[209] It is extremely rare for this to happen.

13.3.2.2 Either-way offences

The more controversial situation relates to either-way offences. As noted already, these are offences that can be heard in either the Crown Court or the magistrates' court. Which court they should be heard in, and who chooses, is a matter of continuing controversy. During the period from 1998 to 2000 there was a concerted effort by the newly elected Labour government to abolish the defendant's de facto veto. It is important, when considering this debate, to ensure that the language is correct. Whilst many will talk about the right of a defendant to elect his or her trial venue, this is not strictly true. A defendant can elect trial on indictment and veto a summary trial but cannot demand a matter to be tried summarily. If the magistrates disagree with his request and think that a trial on indictment would be more suitable then the defendant has no veto.

The debate was long and became quite intemperate at times but ended with the government conceding that the defendant's veto should not be removed. Why did this debate arise? In 1999, the Home Office argued that during 1998 some 18,500 cases were sent to the Crown Court and that 75 per cent of offenders pleaded guilty at Crown Court. The implication was, therefore, that this was wasting Crown Court time since if defendants were to plead guilty then they could have done at magistrates' court level. However, it has been suggested that these figures were slightly misrepresentative in that the 75 per cent included those who were sent to the Crown Court on matters that were triable only on indictment and where the magistrates had decided that the case was too serious for the offence to be heard as a summary matter.[210] The then Attorney-General

---

206. Crime Prosecution Service, *Annual Report and Accounts 2014–15* (CPS 2015) 68.
207. *Crime and Disorder Act 1998*, s 51(2).
208. ibid, sch 3, para 2.
209. ibid, sch 3, para 2(1).
210. Satnam Choongh, 'Defendant's Right to Elect Jury Trial Under Threat – Again' [1998] *Justice of the Peace* 936.

appeared to recognize this when, in the House of Lords debate, he argued that 60 per cent of those who elect trial in the Crown Court pleaded guilty,[211] although those figures were controversial as not everyone accepted them.

The principal justification for attempting change was undoubtedly costs. There is a significant difference between the costs of a summary trial and a trial on indictment, in part because there are a greater number of lawyers and a professional judge together with a jury. Whilst members of a jury are not paid, they do receive expenses, but it appears that they add to the length of the trial, with jury trials taking significantly longer than those in magistrates' courts. The government estimated in 1999 that the changes to mode of trial would have saved it approximately £100 million per year.[212]

Despite these perceived advantages, the attempts were rejected after two separate government Bills were introduced to bring about this change. In part it can be explained by comments of the then Lord Chief Justice, Lord Taylor, who stated: 'in our culture and perception trial by jury is a fundamental right.'[213] Whilst this may be true it is slightly less obvious than it may seem. Many at the time argued that trial by jury was a historic right, even tracing it back to the Magna Carta; this is simply not true. The Magna Carta did provide for trial by one's peers—it meant just that a peer (Lord) could be tried by other peers (Lords) and it did not apply to the ordinary citizens. However, Lord Taylor was almost certainly correct when he argued that in recent times the choice has taken on the mantle of a right.

495

QUESTION FOR REFLECTION

Why should the right to a jury trial be considered a fundamental right? If anything other than a jury trial is 'not as fair' then why do we allow those courts to hear criminal matters that could lead an individual being sent to gaol?

Plea before venue

The *Criminal Justice and Public Order Act 1994* (CJPOA 1994) heavily altered the mode-of-trial position but left the right of veto intact. The principal changes were to allow for a smoother transfer to the Crown Court where both parties wished the matter to proceed there, and also for the defendant to provide an early indication as to how he was likely to plead before the decision as to mode of trial was taken. This is known as 'plea before venue'.

In essence, 'plea before venue' requires that the charge is put to the defendant in words of ordinary language and he is asked to indicate how, if the matter proceeds to trial, he is likely to plead.[214] If he indicates that he would plead guilty, then the court should treat the matter as a summary trial, and that the defendant has pleaded guilty to the matter.[215] However, that does not mean that the case will remain in the magistrates' court because the magistrates have the right to commit a defendant to the Crown Court where they believe that their sentencing powers are not sufficient.[216] This will be picked up on again later.

211.   HL Deb, 20 January 2000, vol 608, col 1292. Lord Williams of Mostyn.
212.   Explanatory Notes to the Mode of Trial Bill 1999, para 15.
213.   Andrew Ashworth, 'Plea, Venue and Discontinuance' [1993] *Criminal Law Review* 830, 832.
214.   *Magistrates' Act 1980*, s 17A.
215.   ibid, s 17A(6).
216.   *Powers of Criminal Courts (Sentencing) Act 2000*, s 3.

Where the suspect indicates that he intends to plead not guilty (or refuses to indicate a plea) then the court must determine mode of trial. Initially the court must decide whether the matter is more suited to summary trial or trial on indictment.[217] In doing so they must listen to submissions from both the prosecution and the defence. They should also be told about any relevant previous convictions that an offender has.[218] This may appear surprising as it could, in essence, be thought of as prejudging the defendant, but it concerns their powers of sentencing. The court must consider their sentencing powers, but also the guidelines produced for the allocation of proceedings by the Sentencing Council.[219] As a previous conviction will invariably affect sentence then the court is now told of the conviction in advance.

If the court believes that a trial on indictment is more suitable then the court shall indicate that to the defendant and then transfer the matter to the Crown Court without any committal proceedings.[220] This reinforces the point earlier that a defendant cannot choose which court to be tried in. If the defendant wishes to be tried summarily but the justices believe that the case is more suited to the Crown Court then the matter proceeds there irrespective of the defendant's wishes.

If the court believes that a summary trial would be more suitable then the court should in plain language inform him:

- that this the view of the court
- that he has the right to consent to this, or to elect trial in the Crown Court
- that if the magistrates retain jurisdiction, he can still be committed to the Crown Court for sentence.[221]

To assist the defendant in deciding whether to accept summary trial, it is now possible to ask the court for an indication of sentence.[222] This does not give a precise sentence, but is, instead, a request to know whether a custodial or non-custodial sentence is more likely. The court does not need to provide an indication, but has the power to do so.[223] Given the importance of sentencing guidelines, it is perhaps questionable how relevant this request now remains as most lawyers should be able to tell, from reading the guidelines, how likely it is that a custodial sentence would be imposed.

If the court does indicate a likely sentence, the court will ask whether the defendant wishes to reconsider his indication of plea.[224] This is to provide another opportunity for an offender to plead guilty, although he does not need to, and if he declines to revisit his plea but accepts a summary trial then the matter proceeds to a summary hearing. If he declines to be tried summarily then the matter proceeds to the Crown Court for a trial on indictment.[225]

Committal for sentence

In two places, reference has now been made to committal for sentence. This is a power that exists under the *Powers of Criminal Courts (Sentencing) Act 2000*. It applies irrespective of whether a person pleads guilty or is convicted after summary trial. The court

217. *Magistrates' Courts Act 1980*, s 19(1).
218. ibid, s 19(2).
219. ibid, s 19(3).
220. ibid, s 21 when read in conjunction with *Crime and Disorder Act 1998*, s 51(2)(b).
221. *Magistrates' Courts Act 1980*, s 20(2).
222. ibid, s 20(3).
223. ibid, s 20(4).
224. ibid, s 20(6).
225. ibid, s 20(9)(b).

must decide whether the offending is 'so serious that the Crown Court should . . . have the power to deal with the offender in any way it could deal with him if he had been convicted on indictment'.[226] If so, it can send the case to the Crown Court for sentencing.

Why should this be permitted? It would seem to undermine the premise of the mode of trial decision. It seems unfair to suggest that a defendant should not have any of the advantages of a Crown Court trial but then be subject to all the disadvantages (the full range of sentences). Before the CJA 2003 amended the *Magistrates' Courts Act 1980* by allowing justices to be told the previous convictions of the defendant, it was perhaps more understandable. Now that they are told about previous convictions the position is more difficult to accept. It has been suggested, very reasonably, that people will elect summary proceedings over a trial on indictment because of the capped powers.[227] If they are at risk of receiving a harsher sentence in any event then why not go to the Crown Court and take one's chances, particularly when the acquittal rate in the Crown Court is usually significantly higher than in the magistrates' court?

↻ QUESTION FOR REFLECTION

Is it not appropriate to abolish committal for sentence? The CPS should be told to prepare a summary that puts the case fairly. The magistrates should decide whether they could accept jurisdiction if they accept the prosecution case is correct (as, theoretically, the defence case should simply lessen the seriousness of the offence rather than increase it). They should, as now, be told about convictions but if they decide to retain jurisdiction then the defendant should get the benefit of capped powers.

Do you think that this is the fairest approach? If not, what is the justification for allowing someone to be sentenced in the Crown Court even if they were not tried there?

13.3.2.3 **Powers of a single justice**

As will be seen from Chapter 15, magistrates will normally sit in panels of three, although low numbers of magistrates will sometimes force them to sit in panels of two. Increasingly, certain work can be undertaken by a single justice of the peace. While district judge (magistrates' court) sit alone (see 8.8.2), lay justices ordinarily would not.

The *Criminal Justice Act 2003* amended the *Magistrates' Courts Act 1980* to permit a single justice of the peace to conduct mode of trial decisions.[228] The argument is presumably based on the premise that a person is not either convicted or sentenced during mode of trial. Where the defendant indicates that he will plead guilty, the matter would then be adjourned and listed before an appropriately constituted bench. The same would be true where the defendant elects to be tried summarily: the matter would be adjourned to be listed for trial.

However, it does mean that important decisions such as indications of sentence and a decision on whether to accept or reject jurisdiction is being made by a single person who is not legally qualified. While that person should have access to legal advice, they do not need to seek advice, and sitting as a bench of three was always supposed to ensure that there was collective wisdom.

---

226. *Powers of Criminal Courts (Sentencing) Act 2000*, ss 3(2), 4(2).
227. Anthony Edwards, 'The Other Leveson Report - the Review of Efficiency in Criminal Proceedings' [2015] *Criminal Law Review* 399, 402.
228. *Magistrates' Courts Act 1980*, s 17E.

‹·› Summary

In this chapter we have identified how a person is charged with an offence, and how a decision is taken to prosecute an offender. We have also seen how crimes are broken into three categories, and tried in one of two courts. In particular, we have identified that:

- The police must decide whether sufficient evidence has been gathered to charge an offender. For the most serious offences, they must ask the Crown Prosecution Service for advice on whether there is sufficient evidence and, if so, what they should be charged with.

- The Crown Prosecution Service was established in 1986 and became the first national prosecution service in England and Wales. It is headed by the Director of Public Prosecution, and is broken into regional units (each headed by a Chief Crown Prosecutor) and central divisions

- When deciding whether to prosecute someone, they must apply two tests. The 'evidential test' which requires a realistic prospect for conviction, and the 'public-interest-test' which examines a number of factors to ascertain whether a prosecution is more, or less, likely.

- If a person is not prosecuted, there are a range of out of court disposals, including cautions, conditional cautions, and fixed penalty notices.

- Where a corporation commits serious fraud, it is possible that they can avoid prosecution by agreeing to a 'Deferred Prosecution Agreement'. A DPA will require them to cooperate with the *Serious Fraud Office* and to pay a financial penalty.

- Crimes are divided into one of three classifications: summary offences (triable only in the magistrates' court); indictment-only offences (triable only in the Crown Court); and either-way offences (triable in either the magistrates' court or the Crown Court).

- The process of deciding where an either-way offence is tried is known as mode of trial. It is an extremely controversial subject, but the default position continues to be that for an either-way offence, a defendant can require his case to be heard in the Crown Court. He cannot, however, require that it is heard in the magistrates' court.

❓ End-of-chapter questions

1. Is it correct that the police should decide whether to charge a suspect or not? Surely the decision to charge someone means that an independent assessment of the evidence is required.

2. Was the House of Lords correct to require that the DPP provide specific guidance on when someone who assists a person to commit suicide abroad will be subject to a prosecution? We do not do this with all other offences, and so is this not an example of the courts creating a hurdle to deal with a law they do not like?

3. If prosecutions are not brought on behalf of victims, then why should victims be given the right to a review of a decision not to prosecute a suspect? If the CPS conclude that it is not in the public interest to prosecute an individual, then should that not be the end of matter?

4. How can it possibly be correct to allow a defendant to choose trial by jury for trivial matters? A person has no choice for summary-only offences and the consequences of a conviction for those offences may be significant (eg a conviction for common assault could lead to someone working with the vulnerable losing their jobs). The historic 'right to choose jury trial' is absurd

and is based on a misunderstanding of the ancient principles. At the same time, sentencing guidelines[229] now indicate the likely level of a sentence. Would it not be more appropriate to say that anything that is likely to attract a sentence of sixteen weeks' imprisonment or less should be tried in the magistrates' court and any case where the sentence could be more than that should be tried in the Crown Court?

Further reading

Ashworth A and Strange M, 'Criminal Law and Human Rights' (2004) 2 *European Human Rights Law Review* 121–40.

This is a comprehensive article that examines many of the key issues relating to how human rights legislation has impacted upon the criminal justice system, requiring it to adopt different approaches.

Cammiss S, 'I Will in a Moment Give you the Full History' [2006] *Criminal Law Review* 38–51.

This is a fascinating study that uses empirical research to assess how mode of trial decisions are conducted. Whilst dated, it is one of the few insights into the area, and remains invaluable.

Crime Prosecution Service, *The Code for Crown Prosecutors* (CPS 2018).

There is no substitute to reading the Codes themselves. As is evident from this chapter, it is essential that you understand how the CPS reaches a decision to prosecute, not least because any challenge will be based on a failure to follow the Code.

Sanders A, 'The CPS - 30 Years On' [2016] *Criminal Law Review* 82.

This is an informative, and yet very readable, article. It reflects on the highs and lows of the CPS after thirty years of operation. It highlights how certain practices may need tweaking and challenges the current policy, suggesting it is not yet radical enough.

499

For self-test questions, flashcards, and links to useful websites, please visit the **online resources** at: **www.oup.com/he/gillespie-weare8e/**

229. Issued by the Sentencing Guidelines Council (<https://www.sentencingcouncil.org.uk/>).

14

Those in Court

By the end of this chapter you will be able to:

- Identify who sits in each type of trial.
- Identify who presides in each trial.
- Understand the role of the principal actors in the trials.
- Understand why each person is required and whether there are circumstances when someone (eg lawyers or the defendant) does not need to be present.

Introduction

Chapter 13 left at the point where a trial was about to start, either in the magistrates' court or the Crown Court. Before examining the trial process (which will occur in Chapter 15) it is first necessary to consider who will be present during the trial. This chapter will not explore each of the people involved in the trial process (eg witnesses, probation officers etc), but rather it will look at the principal actors in the court process. Presenting these people will allow you to understand what role each has during the trial and will allow you to more readily understand how the trial process takes place. The roles of these people will be considered in the context of both summary trials in the magistrates' court, and trials on indictment in the Crown Court.

14.1 The 'Judge'

14.1.1 Summary trials in the magistrates' court

A summary trial is one that takes place within the magistrates' court (or youth court when the defendant is under the age of 18: see 15.7) and so the most obvious starting point is the magistrates. It will be remembered from Chapter 8 that there are two types of magistrate that may sit in the magistrates' court; lay justices of the peace (who are not legally qualified and will ordinarily sit in panels of three) and district judges (magistrates' court) who used to be known as 'stipendiary magistrates' and who will ordinarily sit alone. It will be remembered that a district judge (magistrates' court) is technically a member of the judiciary and is therefore legally qualified.

The appointment of both lay justices and district judges (magistrates' court) was considered previously in Chapter 8. How does one decide whether lay magistrates or a district judge will preside? The answer is not necessarily easy. Some courts have a tradition of using stipendiary magistrates (now district judges (magistrates' court)), particularly in inner London, and so a trial that is held there will ordinarily be heard by a district judge. The lay magistracy remains the more common panel and these will be found in the vast majority of courts. As lay magistrates are often employed they can ordinarily only sit for a finite period of time. Indeed it will be remembered from Chapter 8 that the minimum requirement is twenty-six half-days. Whilst many will sit for a full day, not all will. Therefore, where a trial will take longer than one day it is quite possible that the court may decide that it is more appropriate for the matter to be heard by a district judge.

District judges will ordinarily also be used where the case is likely to raise significant points of law. Some quite technical laws are triable only summarily, particularly certain environmental offences, where the powers of the magistrates' court are beyond that which they can ordinarily impose. Some of these technical offences will raise issues of law that are better decided by a district judge. Similarly, in an ordinary trial it is possible that some of the evidence will be the subject of legal challenge (because, for example, it raises issues such as hearsay or has been illegally obtained). Even though lay magistrates are not legally qualified they are not prevented from making decisions of law, indeed they do so routinely, and are advised on the law by legal advisers within the court (see 14.6), but where it is particularly complex it may be advisable to use a district judge, who is legally qualified and able to make the decision without advice.

Chapter 8 rehearsed the competing arguments for the use of lay magistrates or district judges and this will not be repeated here. The magistrates are in charge of the court and are ordinarily accorded the respect that would be due to a judge. They hear the evidence, rule on submissions, decide guilt or innocence, and impose sentence. Where a panel of three lay justices sits it is ordinarily only the chairman (who will sit in the middle of the panel) who will speak; the other lay justices will present their questions through the chair. That said, it should be remembered that the magistrates are in charge of proceedings and local courts do sometimes differ: do not be surprised if you go into a court and see one of the other magistrates speaking.

⚡ CHAIR AND WINGERS

It will be remembered from Chapter 8 that one lay magistrate holds the office of 'chairman of the bench' which carries with it certain administrative responsibilities. Every time the court sits, however, there must be a chair of that court. Chairs are experienced magistrates who have sat for a number of years and who have received additional training. The remaining justices are known as 'wingers' because they sit on either 'wing' of the chair. Ordinarily they will not speak in a public court but instead pass their questions via the chair. However, they remain an important part of the panel and they have an equal vote when making rulings on submissions and deciding issues of law.

14.1.2 Trial on indictment in the Crown Court

Perhaps the key difference between a summary trial and trial on indictment is the presence of a judge and jury. The judge has ultimate responsibility for the proceedings and has sole responsibility for the law. The judge is always a legally qualified paid person and the following judges are entitled to sit in the Crown Court:

- any judge of the High Court
- any circuit judge (including deputy circuit judges)[1]
- a recorder
- a district judge (magistrates' court).[2]

In addition to these judges the Lord Chief Justice, as the President of the Courts of England and Wales, has the inherent right to sit in the Crown Court.[3] Recent Lord Chief Justices have tended to exercise this right albeit only occasionally, and even then they have tended to sit on sentencing matters rather than trials. In the past the Lord Chief Justice would invariably sit on the most serious trials but this has not occurred for many years. Other members of the judiciary are permitted to sit in the Crown Court but only if invited to do so by the Lord Chief Justice,[4] and if they are not so invited then they have no jurisdiction to act in the Crown Court regardless of the seniority of their office.[5]

14.1.2.1 **Allocation of the judge**

In the review of the criminal justice system it was said:

One of the greatest ills of the system is its lack of flexibility in the matching of judges, courts and cases.[6]

The decision as to how a judge is appointed to a particular case is relatively complicated and arguably a matter of chance in the majority of cases, but with some there is a defined procedure that must be followed. Not every judge is permitted to hear every case and, for example, in cases of murder and sexual offences a judge below the rank of puisne judge must receive additional training before he can hear such cases. This system is known as 'ticketing' and is designed to ensure that only experienced judges hear sensitive cases.[7] It had been suggested that the system of ticketing should be removed,[8] but as yet this does not appear to have been acted upon, not least because there is a danger that removing the ticketing system could undermine the confidence of the public in the judicial system.

> **Example** His Honour Judge Pickles QC
>
> One of the most controversial judges in modern times was HHJ Pickles QC who was a circuit judge who attracted significant controversy, particularly in respect of sex crimes (see 9.2.3). Following a series of incidents, including a rebuke in *R v Scott*,[9] Pickles was informed that he would no longer be sitting on further sex offence cases. In effect his 'ticket' was removed.

1. These are persons who retired as a Lord Justice of Appeal, puisne judge, or circuit judge but who are still under the age of 75 (s 24 *Courts Act 1971*).
2. District judges (magistrates' court) sit as recorders when in the Crown Court (s 65 *Courts Act 1971*).
3. *Constitutional Reform Act 2005*, s 7.
4. *Senior Courts Act 1981*, s 9(1).
5. *R v Lord Chancellor, ex parte Maxwell* [1997] 1 WLR 104.
6. Lord Justice Auld, *A Review of the Criminal Courts of England and Wales* (HMSO 2001) 226.
7. Ministry of Justice, *Criminal Practice Directions* (Ministry of Justice 2018) CPD XIII. D.1–D.3.
8. Lord Justice Auld, *A Review of the Criminal Courts of England and Wales* (HMSO 2001) 237.
9. [1990] Crim LR 440.

Criminal matters on indictment are divided into three classes (see Table 14.1) and the *Criminal Practice Directions* then sets out which type of judge can hear what type of case (see Table 14.2).

It should be noted that the release in class 1 is specific—ie the presiding judge (unless he designates this responsibility to a senior circuit judge) shall examine each case and state that it can be released to a particular judge. The release in class 2 is more general and is a statement that particular crimes could be released to particular types of judges (eg senior circuit judges, resident judges, deputy circuit judges, recorders). The role of the presiding judge is, therefore, an important one but also a time-consuming one. It is an onerous job and perhaps this is why it is held only for a short time.

Table 14.1 Classification of offences

Class 1	(A)	Murder, attempted murder, manslaughter, infanticide, child destruction, abortion, assisting a suicide
	(B)	Genocide, torture, and offences under the *War Crimes Act 1991*, terrorism offences, piracy, treason, an offence under the *Official Secrets Acts*
	(C)	Prison mutiny, riot in the course of serious civil disturbance, serious gang related crime, complex sexual offences cases, cases involving people trafficking
	(D)	Causing death by dangerous, careless, disqualified, or uninsured driving, cases resulting in a fatality or permanent serious disability
Class 2	(A)	Arson with intent to endanger life, cases involving explosives or firearms, kidnapping or false imprisonment, cases in which the defendant is a police officer, member of the legal profession or public figure, cases where the complainant or an important witness is a public figure, child cruelty
	(B)	Any sexual offence (other than those in class 1C), some kidnapping or false imprisonment cases
	(C)	Serious and complex fraud, money laundering, bribery, corruption cases, complex cases in which the defendant is a corporation, where the defendant is a corporation with a turnover in excess of £1bn
Class 3		All other offences not listed in classes 1 or 2

Table 14.2 Allocation of judiciary

Class 1	(1)	a High Court judge, or
	(2)	a circuit judge ... provided (a) that in all cases save attempted murder, such judge is authorized by the Lord Chief Justice to try murder cases, and (b) the presiding judge has released the case for trial by such a judge
Class 2	(1)	a High Court judge, or
	(2)	a circuit judge ... or recorder, provided that in all cases the judge is authorized to try class 2 cases by the Lord Chief Justice and the case has been assigned to the judge by or under the direction of either the presiding judge or resident judge in accordance with guidance given by the presiding judges
Class 3		Cases in class 3 may be tried by a High Court judge, or in accordance with guidance given by the presiding judges, a circuit judge ... or a recorder. A case in class 3 shall not be listed for trial by a High Court judge except with the consent of a presiding judge

503

QUESTION FOR REFLECTION

Why should there be such a complex way of allocating judges to cases? If a person is appointable as a judge then why should he not be able to sit on any crime? If a judge has particular expertise in a particular area in practice should he not be able to sit on those trials without added experience? Are there any safeguards in allocating trials in this way?

Whilst a different judge may be responsible for the pre-trial arrangements, once a judge has begun to hear a case then it is not possible to change the judge and if, for some reason, the judge must retire from the case (eg sickness) then the trial ends and it must begin again.

14.1.2.2 **Responsibilities of the judge**

It was seen earlier that magistrates have responsibility for both fact and law. It is often said that in the Crown Court this responsibility is divided between judge and jury, but in fact that is an oversimplistic distinction because there are numerous situations when a judge will have to make findings of fact.[10] Examples of where decisions of fact will need to be made include preliminary matters, admissibility decisions, and where a guilty plea is tendered the judge may actually become the sole tribunal of fact (in a procedure known as a *Newton* hearing; see 14.5.1).

Although a civil case, the leading statement of what the responsibilities of a judge in an adversarial trial are was set out by Lord Denning MR:

> [He] is to hearken the evidence, only himself asking questions of witnesses when it is necessary to clear up any point that has been overlooked or left obscure, to see that the advocates behave themselves seemly and keep to the rules laid down by law.[11]

And his Lordship warns that the principal danger for a judge is dropping 'the mantles of a judge and assum[ing] the robes of an advocate'; in other words the judge has to rise above the cut and thrust of advocacy and assure that the rules are followed. The role of a judge is often given a sporting analogy:

> The judge is not an advocate. Under the English and Welsh system of criminal trials he is much more like the umpire at a cricket match. He is certainly not the bowler, whose business it is to get the batsman out.[12]

Perhaps the most important duty of a judge is to control proceedings. The judge has ultimate responsibility for proceedings including the order of witnesses and evidence that may be adduced.[13] The *Criminal Procedure and Investigations Act 1996* (CPIA 1996) marked a significant change in the way judges controlled proceedings through the provision of formalized pre-trial hearings.[14] These hearings are known as Plea and Directions Hearings (PDH).

10.   Sean Doran, 'The Necessarily Expanding Role of the Criminal Trial Judge' in Sean Doran and John Jackson (eds), *The Judicial Role in Criminal Proceedings* (Hart Publishing 2000) 5.

11.   *Jones v National Coal Board* [1957] 2 QB 55, 65.

12.   *R v Gunning* [1994] 98 Cr App R 303, 306 (Cumming-Bruce LJ).

13.   Philip Otton, 'The Role of the Judge in Criminal Cases' in Mike McConville and Geoffrey Wilson (eds), *The Handbook of the Criminal Justice Process* (OUP 2002).

14.   Jenny McEwan, 'Co-operative Justice and the Adversarial Criminal Trial: Lessons from the Woolf Report' in Sean Doran and John Jackson (eds), *The Judicial Role in Criminal Proceedings* (Hart Publishing 2000) 172.

If controlling the proceedings is the most important duty, perhaps the least well-known duty of a judge is to halt a case where it is no longer appropriate for it to continue. Although the Crown Court is often thought to be a 'jury court', only about 1 per cent of defendants dealt with through the criminal justice system will actually be placed in the hands of a jury.[15] This may seem surprising but it is indicative of the system: 97 per cent of defendants are dealt with summarily. Of the 3 per cent who will go to Crown Court, a significant number will plead guilty and others will be acquitted without the jury deliberating. Up to two-thirds of those ultimately acquitted in the Crown Court are actually acquitted on the direction of the judge,[16] meaning that the jury have no option but to acquit and do not retire to consider their verdict.

Why should a judge intervene? If a defendant pleads not guilty then is it not for the jury to decide guilt or innocence? The answer lies in the fact that a conviction is both a matter of law and fact. In its most understandable guise it is a matter of fact: the jury decide that a person has in fact done the crime that he was accused of. It is also a matter of law, however, in that a person can only be convicted if there is proof beyond all reasonable doubt that he committed the offence. Whilst it will normally be for the jury to decide whether that proof exists, there may be circumstances when a judge concludes that there is insufficient evidence to go before a jury and that it is simply not possible for them to convict. In those circumstances there is no point in asking the jury to deliberate because, as a matter of law, their decision can only be not guilty. Under those circumstances the judge would step in and direct a jury to acquit. The mechanics of this are that the judge will choose a person as the foreperson (usually it is the person in the front row of the jury box sitting closest to the judge) and tell the foreperson that as a matter of law they can only acquit the person. He will then require the foreperson to say that the jury find them 'not guilty'. It could be argued that this last bit is an unnecessary piece of stage management: if the jury cannot convict then the judge should be able to acquit the defendant but the law requires that in the Crown Court a jury must deliver the verdict once a trial has begun so this unnecessary farce is played out.

14.2 Lawyers

14.2.1 Summary trial in a magistrates' court

To some it may appear obvious that lawyers would be involved in a summary trial but this is not necessarily the case and some trials could theoretically take place without a lawyer being present.

14.2.1.1 Rights of audience

The magistrates' court is the lowest court in the English Legal System and the rights of audience are wide. The general rule is that all solicitors and barristers have rights of audience for summary trials as of right and this was the position prior to the extension of rights under the *Access to Justice Act 1999*.

---

15. Andrew Sanders and Richard Young, *Criminal Justice* (4th edn, Butterworths 2010).
16 ibid

14.2.1.2 **Lay prosecutors**

Section 53 of the *Crime and Disorder Act 1998* inserted a provision within the *Prosecution of Offences Act 1985* (PoOA 1985)[17] to permit non-legal staff to be designated as 'associate prosecutors' (formerly they were called 'designated caseworkers' but have since been renamed 'associate prosecutors'). Those so designated were able to exercise the powers of a crown prosecutor for matters relating to, inter alia, bail and the conduct of criminal proceedings in magistrates' courts other than trials, including sentencing matters following a guilty plea.[18]

The use of lay prosecutors is undoubtedly controversial but it could be argued that it is beneficial to allow lawyers to concentrate on those matters where liability is to be contested or where difficult issues of law arise. Given the CPS will only employ a finite number of lawyers there may be some logic to this argument but the concern must be that instead of using associate prosecutors to plug any gap caused by a shortage of lawyers they are being used to reduce the number of lawyers required, ie it is justice on the cheap. Associate prosecutors are given additional training (undertaken by CILEx) but this is not the same as being legally qualified and there is no requirement, for example, for them to qualify as legal executives. It is perhaps regrettable that the CPS has introduced a fourth category of lawyers without considering whether it would have been better for associate prosecutors to become legal executives. Indeed, arguably that is one of the reasons why legal executives exist and this procedure should have been used.

There is no doubt that associate prosecutors undertake a significant part of the work of the CPS. In 2003/4 there were 254 designated caseworkers (the title used prior to them being (administratively) labelled 'associate prosecutors') but by 2012 this number had risen to 434.[19] In 2004 a review was launched into their use[20] (CPS) and this led to further changes to the PoOA 1985 by the *Criminal Justice and Immigration Act 2008* (CJIA 2008) which widened the scope of their use. The revised s 7A states that those designated by the DPP may act in the following matters:

- applications for, or relating to, bail in criminal proceedings
- the conduct of trial in the magistrates' courts other than trials of offences triable either-way or offences which are punishable with imprisonment in the case of persons aged 21 or over
- the conduct of applications or other proceedings relating to preventative civil orders
- the conduct of proceedings (other than criminal proceedings) assigned to the DPP.

When associate prosecutors were first authorized there was a restriction on them dealing with matters that were triable only on indictment, ie the most serious offences, but the CJIA 2008 reforms abolished this[21] meaning that theoretically an associate prosecutor could deal, for example, with bail matters relating to the most serious offences, including murder.

---

17. PoOA 1985, s 7A.
18. ibid, 7A(2).
19. Freedom of Information Request, June 2012.
20. Crown Prosecution Service, *Annual Report and Accounts 2003–04* (CPS 2004) 22.
21. CJIA 2008, s 55(4).

The extension of these powers is significant. Perhaps the most notable change is that associate prosecutors can now undertake trials so long as they are not an either-way offence or imprisonable. There are a number of offences that are non-imprisonable including many common offences, for example speeding and careless or inconsiderate driving. As legal aid may now not cover non-imprisonable matters (see Chapter 11) extending rights of audience to associate prosecutors in these cases means that potentially neither side will be represented by a legally qualified individual and the magistrates will be reliant on their legal adviser to ensure that the law is adhered to. It is submitted that there is a danger in this approach. Even a matter as simple as a speeding offence can raise issues of law, including the admissibility of evidence and the appropriateness of defences.

It must be seriously questioned whether it is right for the state to prosecute matters without a lawyer being present to ensure that all legal aspects have been followed. There was a danger under the old regime that a person could plead guilty to a crime not known to law (because, for example, the particular factual circumstances of the case mean that they cannot, in law, be guilty) but at least there was the protection that it was likely the case had been reviewed by a lawyer. By extending associate prosecutors' rights of audience to trials the danger of a miscarriage of justice is increased. The guilt or innocence of a person is not something that should be treated as a trivial matter even where there is no risk of liberty being deprived. A conviction can have social consequences, including the loss of employment, and a contested trial should, it is submitted, only occur where the prosecution are represented by a legally qualified individual. To do otherwise is trivializing justice.

14.2.2 Trial on indictment in a Crown Court

Unlike in the magistrates' court, matters dealt with in the Crown Court are normally dealt with by professional lawyers. The use of associate prosecutors, permitted in summary matters (see 14.2.1.2), is not permitted in the Crown Court; the prosecution must *always* be represented by a professional lawyer. No such rule applies to the defendant, but because of the seriousness of the charges normally heard in the Crown Court it is most common for the defendant to be represented.

The Crown Court is part of the Senior Courts of England and Wales and, accordingly, the rights of audience differ from those in the magistrates' court and county court. Solicitors do not have any automatic right to appear in the Crown Court, but barristers do. The distinction in the rights of audience is discussed elsewhere (Chapter 10) but historically the Bar had the exclusive rights to advocating in the higher courts. The *Courts and Legal Services Act 1990*, as is well known, extended the rights of audience in the higher courts to solicitors on completion of an additional course. Accordingly, solicitor–advocates can appear in the Crown Court although solicitors by themselves cannot.

14.2.2.1 Prosecuting counsel

Counsel for the prosecution has a specific role in these cases. Whilst they do represent the Crown in order to try and achieve a conviction, the overarching position is contained in an often cited statement that prosecutors are 'to regard [themselves] as ministers of justice'.[22] This means that prosecuting counsel is not to consider his duty

22   See *R v Paddick* (1865).

as having the responsibility of securing a prosecution at all costs but of presenting an impartial view of the prosecution case. This, it has been argued, extends to how counsel should present his argument:

> It is important that a prosecution advocate avoids the use of emotive language or any words which will inflame an already tense situation.[23]

Viewing prosecution counsel in this way can be contrasted with other jurisdictions, most notably America, where prosecutors frequently deal with the victim on a one-to-one basis and can be seen in front of the media holding hands with the victim or, in homicide cases, the victim's family. This is, in part, because, it will be remembered from Chapter 13, that in England and Wales prosecutions are not brought on behalf of the victim but of society as a whole.

An important part of the 'ministers of justice' role is that prosecuting counsel has a particular duty to the court. It has previously been noted that all advocates have a duty not to mislead a court (see 10.6), but prosecuting counsel has a duty actively to assist the court in the application of the law, even when this may mean a ruling prejudicial to the prosecution case. The other implication of this role is to be found in the duties of disclosure, including potentially any adverse issues in respect of the witnesses they are calling (eg any previous convictions of their witnesses).

14.2.2.2 Defence counsel

Counsel for the defence does not operate any function equivalent to that of the 'ministers of justice' expected of prosecuting counsel. However, it is important to note that they are bound, like all advocates, by the general rules of conduct and, in particular, the duty not to mislead the court. Bearing that in mind, however, defence counsel does have a much wider scope to advocate the matter and this may mean not always bringing legal technicalities harmful to their case to the attention of the court, unless not to do so would mislead the court.[24] The Court of Appeal has, subsequently, decided that counsel do have a duty to bring obvious errors to the attention of the judge at trial and not reserve them for a decision to terminate the case or even as a ground of appeal after conviction.[25] The scope of the freedom is even more obvious when one looks at errors of law where, as Blake and Ashworth note, there is no duty to bring factual errors to the attention of the court even though the corresponding duty exists for prosecutors.[26]

14.3 The defendant

14.3.1 Summary trial in the magistrates' court

It may seem obvious that the defendant will be in court but this is not necessarily true in a summary trial.

---

23. Stephen Solley, 'The Role of the Advocate' in Mike McConville and Geoffrey Wilson (eds), *The Handbook of the Criminal Justice Process* (OUP 2002) 317.
24. Meredith Blake and Andrew Ashworth, 'Some Ethical Issues in Prosecuting and Defending Criminal Cases' [1998] *Criminal Law Review* 16, 23–4.
25. *R v Gleeson* [2003] EWCA Crim 3357.
26. Meredith Blake and Andrew Ashworth, 'Some Ethical Issues in Prosecuting and Defending Criminal Cases' [1998] *Criminal Law Review* 16, 24–5.

14.3.1.1 **Pleading guilty by post**

Section 308 of the *Criminal Justice Act 2003* (CJA 2003) permits a defendant to plead guilty by post to any summary-only offence irrespective of what penalty can be imposed on them. It is important to note that the provision applies only to summary-only offences and not, for example, either-way offences. When a summons issued in a summary-only offence is posted the defendant is given a brief summary of the prosecution facts and details of the postal procedure.[27]

If the defendant chooses to plead guilty then the prosecution are not allowed to expand on the facts given in the statement,[28] this being a protection to ensure that the prosecution do not seek to allege a more serious version of events (potentially leading to a greater sanction) than that which the defendant has accepted. The defendant has the right to put forward written representations in reply to the accusation and this will be considered to be his plea of mitigation (ie the reasons he wishes the court to take into account when deciding sentence).

QUESTION FOR REFLECTION

Why should a person be permitted to plead guilty by post? If a person is summoned to court should they not attend? What reasons might there be for permitting a person to plead guilty by post?

A person cannot be sentenced to prison in his absence under this procedure, and accordingly if the magistrates are minded to impose a custodial sentence they must adjourn the matter and summon the defendant to court. In reality the system tends to be used only for minor offences and therefore this issue rarely arises (where there is a risk of imprisonment it is likely that the defendant would wish to be legally represented in any event).

14.3.1.2 **Defendant in person**

The defendant may wish to represent himself in court, and in common with other trials this is to be permitted. There is no rule in the magistrates' court that requires an offender to be represented legally, and the court cannot order representation in the absence of a request by the defendant. A defendant can be accompanied by someone who is not legally qualified. These have, in the past, been referred to as a 'McKenzie friend',[29] although the Court of Appeal has disapproved of this term as it suggests a special class of person when, in fact, any person has the right to lay assistance and it does not matter what their qualifications are.[30] Ordinarily such a person cannot act on behalf of the defendant (that is to say, speak) but rather assists in the preparation of the case and makes suggestions as to the questioning of witnesses etc.[31]

---

27. *Magistrates' Court Act 1980*, s 12.
28. ibid, s 12(8).
29. *McKenzie v McKenzie* [1970] 3 WLR 472.
30. *R v Leicester City Justices, ex parte Barrow* [1991] 3 WLR 368 and see Philip Thomas, 'From McKenzie's Friend to Leicester Assistant: The Impact of the Poll Tax' [1992] *Public Law* 208, for a critique of the case.
31. It should be noted that in February 2016 the Lord Chief Justice issued a consultation on reforming the courts' approach to McKenzie friends. No further action has been taken as of yet following the consultation.

QUESTION FOR REFLECTION

If the prosecution are allowed to be represented by non-legally qualified persons in contested trials (see the discussion of 'associate prosecutors' at 14.2.1.2) why should the defendant be restricted in who can present on his behalf? With legal aid being restricted does this mean that a shy, nervous defendant may be at a disadvantage? If so, does that make the trial unfair? What are the dangers in allowing anyone to appear for a defendant, however?

14.3.1.3 The missing defendant

What happens where a defendant is summoned to appear but does not attend (or does not use the plea by post scheme)? Traditionally the magistrates had discretion to decide how to proceed in such matters but amendments contained within the CJIA 2008 have fettered this. The first step was to adjourn the proceedings and attempt to secure the attendance of the defendant at the next hearing. The usual method of securing attendance would be to issue a warrant of arrest for the offender. If the offender was already on bail then this would be by way of an arrest warrant,[32] but if he was not then the arrest warrant could only be issued if the justices are satisfied that the summons was served appropriately, or that the non-appearance arises from a previous adjournment where the accused was present.[33]

Before the CJIA 2008 the magistrates had discretion to try an offender in his absence[34] although they had to be sure that the summons and/or the date of any adjourned hearing had been properly served on the defendant. The CJIA 2008 amended s 11 of the *Magistrates' Court Act 1980* to state that, when dealing with an adult, the court 'shall proceed in his absence unless it appears to the court to be contrary to the interests of justice to do so'.[35] Section 11(2A) states that where the court believes that there is an acceptable reason for the defendant not appearing then it should not proceed in his absence.

Even under the new system the magistrates will ordinarily adjourn the hearing once, usually also issuing a warrant of arrest. A new date will be decided and if the defendant fails to turn up again (and it is quite possible that he will not as it is unlikely that in many summary-only matters the defendant would be remanded in custody prior to the trial) then they may consider a trial in his absence.

If the magistrates do decide to proceed with a trial in his absence then a not guilty verdict is formally recorded and the prosecution case then proceeds as set out in 15.1. This is not a mere formality: the prosecution are required to satisfy the burden of proof and if, at the conclusion of the prosecution case, the court is not satisfied to the appropriate standard that the prosecution have shown guilt then the bench must acquit the defendant.

Where a person is sentenced to prison in his absence then he must first be brought before the court.[36] Presumably this is to provide an opportunity for him to explain himself and, as importantly, for the court to explain to the offender why they viewed the matter as one requiring him to be imprisoned. The court will also explain the duration of any sentence, including arrangements for release on licence.

---

32. *Bail Act 1976*, s 7.
33. ibid, s 13.
34. *Magistrates' Court Act 1980*, s 11.
35. ibid, s 11(1)(b) as amended.
36. ibid, s 11(3).

🔄 **QUESTION FOR REFLECTION**

In *Lala v Netherlands*[37] the European Court of Human Rights held that it was 'of utmost importance' that a defendant should be present at his trial. Do you think it can ever be fair to try a defendant in his absence? (You may find it useful to read *R v Jones*.[38])

14.3.2 Trial on indictment in the Crown Court

Unlike the position in a summary trial (discussed earlier), it is not possible to plead guilty by post during a trial on indictment. The defendant is summoned to appear and he must appear in person. If a defendant fails to attend then the judge will almost certainly issue a warrant for his arrest, requiring the police to identify the offender and bring him before the courts.

Unlike the position in the magistrates' court where it will be remembered there is now a statutory presumption that a trial in the absence of the defendant will occur, the same is not true on a trial on indictment. In *R v Jones*[39] the House of Lords held that a judge does have the discretion to try an offender in his absence but that this discretion should be exercised sparingly. That said, their Lordships noted that where a defendant voluntarily absented himself, particularly after the trial had started, then it is quite possible that it would be appropriate to continue the trial. This is an obvious protection and is designed to prevent, for example, a trial being adjourned because a defendant refused to attend court or appear in court.[40] 'Voluntary' has been taken to include situations where a person takes intoxicating substances rendering them incapable of following or attending the trial.[41]

511

📋 **Example** Jack Shepherd

The issue of offenders being tried in their absence was highlighted most recently in the case involving Jack Shepherd, who was found guilty of the manslaughter by gross negligence of Charlotte Brown in his absence. He had been on a date with Charlotte and taken her on a speedboat on the River Thames which subsequently crashed and threw them both overboard, resulting in Charlotte's death. Days before his trial was due to begin he fled the country (eventually being arrested in Georgia). The trial continued and he was convicted in his absence and sentenced to six years' imprisonment. The high-profile nature of the case was increased when it was announced that the Court of Appeal had granted him leave to appeal his conviction whilst still on the run, with widespread reporting of the case in the media.

14.4 The jury

The discussions in this section only apply to trials on indictment in the Crown Court, because this is the court in which trial by jury occurs. The jury undoubtedly has an important status within the criminal justice system with Lord Devlin, a one-time Lord

---

37. (1994) 18 EHRR 586.
38. [2002] UKHL 5.
39. [2003] 1 AC 1.
40. See generally, *R v O'Hare* [2006] EWCA Crim 471.
41. See, for example, *R v Simms* [2016] EWCA Crim 9 and *R v Ehi-Palmer* [2016] EWCA Crim 1844.

of Appeal in Ordinary, commenting that it is 'the lamp that shows freedom lives.'[42] This statement was approved of by Lord Taylor, a previous Lord Chief Justice, who said: 'in our culture and perception trial by jury is a fundamental right'.[43] Both are therefore of the opinion that juries demonstrate democracy in action, something that the House of Lords affirmed:

> The institution of jury trial, with all its imperfections, is still trusted by the public as a method of determining the guilt of persons charged with criminal offences.[44]

What is interesting from this quotation is that there is recognition that trial by jury is arguably not a perfect way of dealing with trials, indeed it can be argued that it is quite flawed. If you ever speak to a lawyer or judge who specializes in criminal law you will always find that they have at least one story to tell about a jury who managed to reach the wrong verdict or who approached their task in an unprofessional manner etc. Yet these same practitioners will almost certainly state that the jury system retains their confidence.[45]

Juries are often quoted as being a historic guarantee of the rights of the common man to sit in judgement on his fellow citizen; however, this is not strictly true and until 1972 property was a primary factor in the eligibility of people to serve on a jury, meaning that juries tended to be men of a certain economic status.[46] However, the use of lay members is often cited as being an important part of the democratization of the justice system[47] and the fact that a jury consists of twelve members is often cited as being reason to ensure that the decision is fair, as the prejudices or lack of interest shown by an individual juror can be counterbalanced by the others. However, this point is somewhat weakened when one examines the rules as to majority verdicts (see 15.6.2.6) and does not take account of the strength of character of some individuals.

14.4.1 Eligibility for jury service

Those who are prima facie eligible for jury service are:

- registered on the electoral roll and between the ages of 18 and 75
- ordinarily resident in the United Kingdom, Channel Islands, or Isle of Man for the last five years
- not disqualified from jury service.[48]

These criteria mask a more significant change which is that previously a wider range of persons were either able to ask for excusal or were disqualified from sitting as a juror. Those who were eligible for excusal (and thus it was a matter for them as to whether to seek an excusal) included those between the ages of 65 and 70, Members of Parliament, members of the medical profession, and members of HM Forces.[49] However, the new scheme removes this excusal system other than for members of HM Forces where their commanding officer certifies that it would be 'prejudicial to the efficiency of the service'

---

42. Patrick Devlin, *Trial by Jury* (Stevens & Sons, 1956) 164.
43. Andrew Ashworth and Mike Redmayne, *The Criminal Process* (4th edn, OUP 2010).
44. *R v Smith (No 2)* [2005] UKHL 12, [7] (Lord Carswell).
45. Lord Justice Auld, *A Review of the Criminal Courts of England and Wales* (HMSO 2001) 135.
46. Michael Zander, *Cases and Materials on the English Legal System* (10th edn, OUP 2007) 486.
47. See, in particular, Patrick Devlin, *Trial by Jury* (Stevens & Sons, 1956).
48. *Juries Act 1974*, s 1.
49. ibid, s 9(1) and sch 1, pt III, as originally enacted.

for them to serve, although even then normally a deferral rather than full excusal should be permitted.[50]

What the *Juries Act* 1974 (JA 1974) does not do, of course, is to tackle the issue of under-representation identified by Auld. It is accepted that the turnout for elections is very low, especially amongst the younger members of society and the ethnic minorities. Given their apathy towards voting it is not unreasonable to assume that they have neglected to register themselves with the appropriate authorities. The suggestion of Auld to use alternative methods of identifying those eligible to serve was worthy of more consideration and its rejection should be reviewed by Parliament.

⟳ QUESTION FOR REFLECTION

Do you agree that alternative databases should be used to widen the jury pool? What databases do you think should be used? How important is it that the potential pool contains representatives of as many sections of society as possible?

◀)) LISTEN TO THE PODCAST

For guidance on how to answer this question and a discussion of the main issues, listen to the author's podcast on the online resources:

    www.oup.com/he/gillespie-weare8e/

14.4.1.1 Disqualification

Alongside the changes to the excusal from jury service, the range of those who are disqualified from serving was dramatically altered by the *Criminal Justice Act 2003* (CJA 2003). Previously those whose occupation, or whose spouse's occupation, was allied to the criminal justice system (judiciary, lawyers, police, etc) were disqualified from sitting on a jury, as were members of the clergy. Auld had argued that this was a historical irrelevancy and he spent a considerable time noting that in the United States of America it was not uncommon for members of the legal profession, including members of the judiciary, to be called to serve.[51] This proposal caused much controversy but it was accepted by the government and the list of people who are disqualified (ie may not sit on a jury regardless of whether they wish to or not) is now restricted to those who are subject to certain provisions within the *Mental Health Act 1983* or *Mental Capacity Act 2005* and those convicted of a crime and may be summarized as shown in Table 14.3.

Nobody is now automatically excused as a result of their occupation and since the CJA 2003 has come into force two Lord Justices of Appeal, Dyson LJ (as he then was) and Tuckey LJ, have served on a jury along with numerous other judges and lawyers. Whether this is correct remains a topic of heated debate. Auld clearly wished to widen the pool of available juries but the use of judges, particularly senior judges, does appear slightly at odds with the overriding principle of the review which was to quicken up the criminal justice system. Jury trials are longer than summary trials and although a juror will often sit for only a two-week period, that is two weeks when a court, including the

---

50.   ibid, ss 9(2) and 9A.
51.   Lord Justice Auld, *A Review of the Criminal Courts of England and Wales* (HMSO 2001) 140–1, 146–9.

Table 14.3 Disqualification from jury service

Subject to provisions within the Mental Health Act 1983 and Mental Capacity Act 2005	Disqualified for duration of being subject to provisions
Life imprisonment (or equivalent)	Disqualified for life
Imprisonment for public protection	Disqualified for life
Imprisonment for a term of five years or more	Disqualified for life
Any term of imprisonment (including suspended)	Disqualification for ten years
Community sentence	Disqualification for ten years

Court of Appeal (which suffers from delays), will be without a judge; is this necessarily in the best interests of the criminal justice system?

More serious, however, is the issue of bias. It was noted in Chapter 9 that the issue of perceived bias is something that needs to be guarded against (9.3.3) and this must be true of juries too. Whilst it may be unproblematic if a judge—who is supposed to be impartial—sits, what signal does it send if a police officer or prosecutor sits on a jury? The matter inevitably led to litigation. The first, and most important, case is *R v Abdroikov*.[52] Abdroikov and two other appellants (from different trials) appealed to the House of Lords complaining about the composition of the juries hearing their trials. In *Abdroikov*, the foreperson of the jury was a serving police officer, and in another appellant's case a member of the jury was employed by the CPS although the juror did not know anyone connected to the case.

The House of Lords noted that the law had changed and it was quite clear that the range of people entitled to sit on the case had been widened but Baroness Hale makes the pertinent point that just because a person can be summoned for jury service does not mean that they should sit on the case they have been summoned for.[53] Her Ladyship noted that whether they can sit depends on whether it would render the trial unsafe.

In respect of the police officer sitting, the House noted that there was no real dispute between the evidence of the police and defendant and there was no link between the station in which the police officer was based and the police witnesses in the trial. The House concluded there was no risk of prejudice. However, it reached a different conclusion in respect of the CPS employee. Lord Bingham noted that it was doubtful it was ever intended for a crown prosecutor to sit on a jury brought by their agency since that would appear to have the appearance of bias because a juror is employed by the prosecutor.

This ruling was explained by the Court of Appeal in *R v Khan*[54] which concerned similar issues. The court in that case indicated that the mere fact that a police officer works in the same locality as a witness does not provide evidence of bias, nor does the fact that he works on similar types of cases. The court also noted that the limitation on CPS employees sitting on juries was limited to those trials where the CPS was the prosecutor. Where an alternative prosecuting agency brought the prosecution (in this case the Department of Trade and Industry) then being the employee of a prosecution service would not show bias.

---

52. [2007] 1 WLR 2679.
53. ibid, 2696–7.
54. [2008] 2 Cr App R 13.

QUESTION FOR REFLECTION

Do you think the House of Lords and Court of Appeal were right to say there is no appearance of bias where a police officer on a jury is in the same police force as a police witness? Is there realistically any difference between this and the CPS employee? Should police officers only be permitted to sit on jury cases which involve police witnesses from outside their police area (eg a Warwickshire police officer could sit on a case involving Leicestershire police but not Warwickshire police)? Could that cause any practical difficulties?

LISTEN TO THE PODCAST

For guidance on how to answer this question and a discussion of the main issues, listen to the author's podcast on the online resources:

www.oup.com/he/gillespie-weare8e/

Bias is not restricted to those who come within the criminal justice system. What happens where someone has made public statements in respect of law and justice issues? Does this raise the possibility of bias? In *R v Cornwall*[55] a juror was a well-known columnist for the *Sun* who had made a series of pronouncements about knife crime, drugs, and immigration. The appellant was a drug dealer who was accused of stabbing a person to death. The Court of Appeal rejected an argument that the juror was biased and noted that there was no evidence that he had not tried the case in accordance with his oath. The court noted that a jury may well have people with strong views on the criminal justice system but that will be one person amongst twelve. The court accepted that public pronouncements could lead to an allegation of bias but they would need to relate specifically to issues before the jury, and in this particular case they did not and there was no risk that an independent observer would consider the juror to be biased.

14.4.1.2 Disability

Section 9B JA 1974 states that there is a clear presumption in favour of disabled jurors being able to sit but that where a judge is of the opinion that the person could not, as a result of his disability, act 'effectively' as a juror he should be stood down. In *Re Osman*[56] His Honour Judge Verney, the Recorder of London, stood down a juror who was profoundly deaf and who could only follow the proceedings if a sign-language interpreter was used. The principal reason for this ruling was that the interpreter would have to attend the jury room and would, therefore, become a thirteenth person when only twelve are permitted.[57] The fact that the interpreter would not be expressing personal opinions was not considered sufficient safeguard. This case was followed in 1999 when a Mr McWhinney was called to the jury. Mr McWhinney was also profoundly deaf and required the services of an interpreter and he was similarly stood down.[58]

These cases were controversial and there was a commitment to review the matter[59] but no change in the law has yet occurred. Indeed, in 2000 the then Lord Chancellor, Lord Irvine, argued that he saw no reason why a deaf person should not

---

55. [2009] EWCA Crim 2458.
56. [1996] 1 Cr App R 126.
57. *Re Osman* [1996] 1 Cr App R 126, 128.
58. Amir Majid, 'Jury Still out on Deaf Jurors' (2004) 154 *New Law Journal* 278.
59. ibid, 279, and Lord Justice Auld, *A Review of the Criminal Courts of England and Wales* (HMSO 2001) 153.

serve on a jury[60] but he left open the argument as to the effect of a thirteenth person being in the jury room.

Where a third person is not needed then there is no significant objection and it is notable that, for example, there have been cases where a blind juror has sat, although there may be objections if evidence at a trial is particularly focused on visual evidence. Where it is not (and a significant proportion of trials will not require visual evidence to be shown, as distinct from it merely assisting a jury) then there is no reason why a blind person should not sit. Indeed, it is submitted that it is a matter of disgrace that the de facto presumption against deaf jurors still appears to be in existence. There is no reason why a qualified interpreter could not be appointed by the judge and such interpreters be given training as to the limits of their duties (ie not to enter into personal discussions within a jury room). There are currently approximately 11 million people in the UK who are deaf or hard of hearing although only approximately 900,000 of them are severely or profoundly deaf. However, in an era where we are trying to expand jury service it is nonsensical not to permit deaf people to sit on a jury.

☺ QUESTION FOR REFLECTION

Do you agree that deaf and blind jurors should be able to sit on juries? Are there any reasons why they should not be permitted? Are these reasons that would stop a juror sitting in a particular case or such that it justifies a blanket ban?

14.4.1.3 **Enforcing jury service**

Jury service is a civic responsibility and accordingly when a potential juror is summoned to court he is expected to attend. However, Auld noted that 15 per cent of jurors refused to answer the jury summons. It is a criminal offence to fail to answer a jury summons, theoretically as contempt of court but more frequently as a summary-only offence punishable by a fine.[61] However, Auld noted that it was comparatively rare for courts actually to pursue those who neglect a jury summons, and accordingly this had created a position whereby significant numbers failed to meet their civic duty. Arguably the position may be somewhat better now since a central jury-summoning bureau has been established, so instead of individual courts being responsible for deciding the eligibility or otherwise of jurors a central bureau does this. Accordingly, if courts make the appropriate returns to this system they could be charged with pursuing those who neglect their service.

However, some disagree with this policy, and Auld himself noted that the difficulty with enforcement is that it could clog up courts with a relatively trivial matter. Auld suggested the imposition of a fixed penalty notice,[62] although that does raise the question why it is that Auld believes that someone who fails to respond to a jury summons would respond to a fixed penalty notice; presumably a significant proportion would fail to pay the ticket necessitating enforcement proceedings at this stage. However, Auld

---

60.   Lord Justice Auld, *A Review of the Criminal Courts of England and Wales* (HMSO 2001) 153.
61.   JA 1974, s 20.
62.   Lord Justice Auld, *A Review of the Criminal Courts of England and Wales* (HMSO 2001) 145.

is undoubtedly correct in deciding that something has to be done since the jury system is based upon the premise that citizens will do their part and accordingly those who neglect this duty should be held to account.

14.4.2 Diversity

Juries should ordinarily be randomly selected[63] and so it may seem unusual to talk about diversity but there have been, for some years, questions about how diverse juries are. The two principal questions that arise in respect of diversity are in respect of race and also in terms of the professional background of juries.

14.4.2.1 Race

A particular concern over the years has been whether juries are diverse in terms of racial composition. There has, to an extent, been a belief that juries are predominantly white and do not reflect the diversity of the United Kingdom. A leading study published in 2007 noted, however, that there was no evidence of this, and they also noted that apart from two courts (out of eighty-four) there were no statistical anomalies between the jurors summoned and the ethnic minority population of the relevant catchment area,[64] and that indeed in some courts ethnic minority jurors were over-represented. The survey also found that there was no mass avoidance of jury service by members of the public, directly disputing myths that suggest that minority ethnic jurors in particular were more likely to seek to avoid jury duty.[65]

Being called to jury service does not necessarily mean that there will be appropriate representation on each jury since jurors are brought within a 'pool' of jurors from which the trial jury are selected. Cheryl Thomas' research demonstrated that there was more sporadic diversity in respect of each individual jury,[66] and this echoes concerns that have been raised previously about whether juries should be empanelled in respect of a particular racial composition. One interesting finding was that, at least anecdotal evidence suggested that one reason for this is that the final 'draw' is made in open court and that clerks may 'avoid cards where a juror's name is difficult to pronounce'.[67] It was difficult to confirm this finding[68] although it certainly was not disproved. If this is true, it is certainly an issue that should not occur. The most obvious solution is to 'number' the jury-in-waiting rather than 'name' them so that the position becomes less subject to decisions being made on the ease of pronunciation.

The issue of whether there should be a particular racial bias has been discussed on a number of occasions. The first was *R v Danvers*[69] where the Court of Appeal found that a court had no power to order the empanelment of a jury in a way that provided specific representation on the basis of ethnicity. This rule was challenged under human rights legislation in *R v Smith*[70] where the defendant was one of three men convicted in

---

63. JA 1974, s 11.
64. Cheryl Thomas, *Diversity and Fairness in the Jury System* (Ministry of Justice 2007) 57.
65. ibid, ii.
66. ibid, 147.
67. ibid, 151.
68. ibid, 152.
69. [1982] Crim LR 680.
70. [2003] 1 WLR 2229.

respect of charges relating to, inter alia, grievous bodily harm with intent (contrary to s 18 *Offences Against the Person Act 1861*). Much of the evidence in the case related to witness testimony and the appellant sought to argue that there were racial dimensions to the case, including the fact that all the jury were white.[71] Whilst the defendant had not asked for a multiracial jury at the time of trial he sought to argue that his being tried by an all-white jury in a case that contained racial elements and where the defendant felt he had been racially abused breached Article 6 ECHR.[72] The Court of Appeal specifically rejected this argument, stating that they were not convinced that there was any residual unfairness in being tried by a randomly called all-white jury[73] and that a properly directed jury would be able to try the offender in a fair manner.

Interestingly, whilst they said that nothing in their judgment should be taken as meaning that alternative methods should be required, they did specifically say of this case that '[i]t was not a case where a consideration of the evidence required knowledge of the traditions or social circumstances of a particular racial group',[74] which does beg the question whether if that was required a different result would have been achieved. Whether, if such circumstances exist, this is a requirement for a jury of a particular ethnic mix or a requirement for expert evidence on cultural factors is perhaps another question.

The courts place great emphasis on the random nature of a jury and where this randomness is missing then they will intervene.[75] However, others have disputed the idea of randomness in all respects and have suggested that there should be racial profiling, at least in part.

Perhaps the most notable recent call to alter the empanelment of a jury was made by Auld who recommended that a jury should, where race is a factor, be empanelled on a random basis but if, after nine persons have been empanelled, the jury is all-white then the remaining three spaces should be filled by members of an ethnic minority.[76] Part of the justification for this was that Auld LJ believed that research indicated that 'white juries are, or are perceived to be, less fair to black than to white people'.[77] However, in Thomas' 2010 study involving case simulation and jurors, she found that 'all-White juries did not discriminate against BME defendants [with] no tendency for all-White juries to convict a Black or Asian defendant more than a White defendant'.[78] Of course Auld referred not only to actual unfairness but perceptions of unfairness too although it is difficult to see how this perception will be solved by requiring a minimum number of ethnic minorities to be included within a jury because it could be argued that this shows white jurors cannot be trusted by themselves to pass a fair judgment.

There were practical problems with Auld's recommendation (including how one identifies that a correct number of people are summoned for the jury pool—it is not a case of having three members of the ethnic minority per jury since the randomness could, for example, lead to a jury with many more members) but also the point about whether this assists. Auld's report treats all ethnic minorities the same—they are just

71. *R v Smith* [2003] 1 WLR 2229, 2233.
72. ibid, 2234.
73. ibid, 2239.
74. ibid, 2239.
75. See, for example, the Privy Council case of *Rojas v Berllaque* [2004] 1 WLR 201 where the fact that juries were inevitably all male because of the nature of how juries were called was considered to be inappropriate.
76. Lord Justice Auld, *A Review of the Criminal Courts of England and Wales* (HMSO 2001) 159.
77. ibid, 158.
78. Cheryl Thomas, *Are Juries Fair?* (Ministry of Justice 2010) ii.

'not white'. There is no indication or evidence that a person belonging to a particular ethnic minority is going to be more (or indeed less) reassured by the presence of other members of ethnic minorities of ethnicities different from his own. It may well be that this is not true and it will inevitably lead to questions about whether juries must belong to particular ethnicities, and whether certain ethnicities should not sit on juries because of perceived biases against each other's ethnicities.

⟳ QUESTION FOR REFLECTION

Should juries be empanelled in such a way that each panel is representative of the diversity in the particular catchment area of a court? If a defendant is a member of an ethnic minority should a jury always include a member with an ethnic minority background and, if so, should it be of the same ethnicity as the defendant?

14.4.2.2 Social demographics

The second area of concern about diversity has always traditionally been the perception that 'intelligent' or professional jurors escape jury service and that juries 'are made up of the unemployed and retired'.[79] Interestingly the research conducted by Thomas did not show this and indeed suggested that the opposite may even be true. Thomas found that employed jurors were, if anything, over-represented on juries,[80] and that when occupation was taken into account the largest group of employed persons were professionals.[81] It would seem therefore that the perceived concern is simply not true.

An interesting question, however, is how pleased we should be about this and whether jury service can actually cause the public difficulties. It will be remembered that the CJA 2003 reforms widened eligibility and were coupled with a stricter approach to granting exemptions from jury service. Some have questioned the desirability of this, with Parliament and the media being quite exercised by health practitioners and, to a lesser extent, the judiciary. For example, reference has been made to the fact that a senior consultant had to cancel 300 patient appointments to undertake jury service and a sole-practitioner GP had to close her surgery for weeks to accommodate jury service.[82] When judges have been called to serve on juries, questions have been raised about whether that has meant further delays in the court system because the judge (who could preside on trials) is serving on a jury.

It is relatively easy to see the logic in arguing that some people may be exempted. The doctor would seem to be a classic example but then who else? Presumably the same can be said of dentists, but what of nurses and other medical practitioners? What of the emergency services? Leaving aside the police (who have been discussed already) there is the Fire and Rescue Service, paramedics, and even the RNLI. Each of these may be impacted if a member has to take a significant period of time off work. The difficulty with exemptions is that it is possible to identify a category of persons who will always be able to claim that they will be materially affected by jury service or that it will have

79. Cheryl Thomas, *Diversity and Fairness in the Jury System* (Ministry of Justice 2007) 134.
80. ibid, 134.
81. ibid, 137.
82. S Broadridge, 'Recent Developments Concerning Juries' House of Commons Library Paper, 2009 SN/HA/2867, 3–4.

an impact on others. If exemptions are given then it could quickly develop to the situation before where there were real doubts about how diverse the juries were in terms of socio-economic disparity.

14.5 Summary trials or trials on indictment?

Perhaps the key question that arises in respect of lay justice is whether a defendant should be tried summarily (at the magistrates' court) or on indictment (at the Crown Court). It has been seen that a summary trial will not necessarily involve lay justice since it may be conducted by a district judge (magistrates' court) but in the majority of situations this decision will be between what role laypersons play in the trial: as the tribunal of both fact and law (summary trial) or simply the tribunal of fact (trial on indictment).

The process of sending a case to the correct court was discussed in the previous chapter, but it is worth remembering that the decision as to whether matters should be dealt with at summary level or in the Crown Court is one of the most contested and controversial issues of the criminal justice system. This is partly because there is a belief that the right to jury trial can be traced back to the Magna Carta although that claim is slightly disingenuous in that the Magna Carta was not designed for the common man but for nobles, and trial by peers was arguably as much about trial by combat or for the nobility to be tried by themselves as anything else. However, irrespective of its origins it is clear that the right to jury trial as we now understand it has existed for several centuries and, as noted earlier, it is considered by many the ultimate safeguard.

Yet the reality is that juries are rarely used in the context of overall crime. It has already been noted that 95 per cent of cases are tried in the magistrates' court where no jury sits. Of those matters that do reach the Crown Court, juries are used in about 1.5 per cent of cases. Of course these bare statistics mask the fact that juries are used in the most serious of cases (such as homicide and serious sexual offences) but it shows that the place of juries in the criminal justice system is not necessarily as it is perceived by the public at large although, of course, the place of lay justice is significant.

Jury trials are expensive and they are usually slower than a trial in the magistrates' court, especially one conducted by a DJMC. The costs are higher because of the greater number of people involved in a case (discussed at 13.3.2.2) and the fact that many of those are paid. Whilst jurors are not paid, they can receive expenses and (a capped) contribution to financial loss. In 1999 the government argued that they could save some £100 million per year if they restricted the number of cases that proceeded to the Crown Court.[83]

The debate surrounding the decision as to which court a matter should be tried in has rarely been about whether jury trials should be abolished, or even whether further offences should be listed as triable only in the magistrates' courts, but rather who should decide what court an offender is tried in. There are three categories of offences; those triable only summarily (which are heard in the magistrates' court), those triable only on indictment (which are tried in the Crown Court), and those triable either-way (which can be tried in either the magistrates' court or Crown Court). The mechanics of this decision were considered in Chapter 13 but it will be remembered that the

83. Explanatory notes to the *Mode of Trial (No 1) Bill 1999*, para 15.

defendant, charged with an either-way offence, has a veto over being tried in the magistrates' court. He cannot demand to be tried in the magistrates' court (although he can request this the magistrates do not need to accede to this submission) but he can demand to be tried in the Crown Court.

Successive governments have attempted to keep more cases within the magistrates' court[84] and the usual rationale has always been considerations of cost and delay rather than any reasoned discussion about justice requirements. Three of the most important reviews into the criminal justice system (the Royal Commission on Criminal Justice (1993), Narey Report on Delays (1997), and Auld Report (2001)) have all recommended that the right of a defendant to veto a summary trial should be altered by allowing the court, rather than the defendant, to decide where the trial will take place.

Perhaps the most significant attempt to introduce this change took place around the turn of the millennium when the New Labour government sought to introduce legislation to remove the veto. The Bills led to an outcry with the (inevitable) suggestion that the government was seeking to remove jury trial which was not strictly true, although it would have led to the removal of the right to demand a jury trial in respect of either-way matters. Whilst made before these attempts, the comments of the then Lord Chief Justice, Lord Taylor, summarize the approach of the judiciary: 'in our culture and perception trial by jury is a fundamental right.'[85] Of course this is simply not true since summary justice has existed for centuries but the perception of the right exists and public pressure, together with a rebellious House of Lords, meant that two separate Bills failed.

It can be argued whether this was more about posturing than any identifiable problem. Whilst a defendant can veto a summary trial it has been shown that defendants are increasingly less likely to be responsible for the trial venue.[86] In 2003/4 73 per cent of relevant cases arrived at the Crown Court because the magistrates declined jurisdiction;[87] in 2012 this statistic reached 88 per cent.[88] However, the latest 2018/19 data shows this has decreased substantially to 56.2 per cent.[89] This suggests that abolishing the veto would not make a significant difference.

More interesting is to know why the magistrates send matters to the Crown Court. The usual reason given is that their powers would be insufficient to deal with an offender. Magistrates are currently only able to sentence an offender to a maximum of six months' imprisonment (whilst the *Criminal Justice Act 2003* provided for the power to allow this to be raised to twelve months' imprisonment this has never come into force), and so if they feel that a higher sentence is likely to be required then they should pass the matter to the Crown Court. That said, there is clear evidence that a substantial number of defendants then receive a sentence that is well within the powers of a magistrate,[90] and perhaps this means that more training needs to be provided on likely sentences. Of course the discrepancy in sentences could be as a result of evidence that is only adduced during the trial but, when deciding the mode of trial, the magistrates

---

84. Steven Cammiss, 'I Will in a Moment Give you the Full History' [2006] *Criminal Law Review* 38, 39.
85. Andrew Ashworth, 'Plea, Venue and Discontinuance' [1993] *Criminal Law Review* 830, 832.
86. Steven Cammiss, 'I Will in a Moment Give you the Full History' [2006] *Criminal Law Review* 38, 40.
87. ibid.
88. Crown Prosecution Service, *Annual Report and Accounts 2011–12* (CPS 2012).
89. Crown Prosecution Service, CPS Source of Committals For Trial 2015–19 (CPS 2019) <https://www.cps.gov.uk/underlying-data/cps-annual-report-and-accounts-data-2018–2019>.
90. Steven Cammiss, 'I Will in a Moment Give you the Full History' [2006] *Criminal Law Review* 38, 41.

should consider whether, if the prosecution evidence is all accepted, the sentence is outside of their powers. If it is not then perhaps the presumption should be that magistrates should accept jurisdiction unless other reasons can be advanced.

14.5.1 Trial by judge alone

Although it may seem that the jury is synonymous with the Crown Court it is possible for a judge to hear a trial alone and without a jury. In this situation the judge is both the tribunal of fact and law and the position is perhaps somewhat analogous to that of a district judge (magistrates' court) sitting on a summary trial.

In England and Wales such trials are extremely controversial and rare but in other jurisdictions within the United Kingdom it is not that unusual. During the period when Northern Ireland was subject to what is commonly referred to as 'the Troubles' there was a real risk of jury tampering and thus the 'Diplock courts' were born in Northern Ireland. The courts were so named after Lord Diplock, the former Law Lord, who had recommended that trial by jury was suspended for certain terrorist-related trials. In Scotland there has long been a tradition of a Sheriff (the equivalent of a circuit judge) sitting by himself to try a number of offences, including those punishable by imprisonment.

The CJA 2003 allowed for the possibility of trial by judge alone. It should be noted that in this context a trial means the hearing that leads to a decision on the guilt or innocence of the defendant. There are other occasions when a judge may sit alone, most notably when ruling on the admissibility of evidence (which could lead to a *voir dire* (a so-called 'trial within a trial')) or a *Newton* hearing (where the judge decides the factual basis upon which a person should be sentenced). The power is set out in s 44 CJA 2003 and applies where the judge concludes that there 'is a real and present danger that jury tampering [will] take place' and that despite alternative arrangements being put in place (including the possibility of police protection for jurors) it is in the interests of justice to hold a trial by judge alone. The first approval for a trial to take place by judge alone was given in *R v T*,[91] which concerned the trial of a number of defendants for an alleged large-scale robbery that took place at Heathrow Airport. After several previous cases collapsed, the Court of Appeal agreed that there was a real risk of jury tampering and that those risks could not be adequately minimized by the police. The trial began in January 2010 and led to the conviction of four men. The trial was extremely controversial with many lawyers arguing that trial by jury was an inherent human right (but see *R v Twomey*[92] where one of the four defendants appealed on the basis that it was a breach of human rights but where the court dismissed the appeal).

It had been thought that *T* would lead to a number of judge-alone trials but the Court of Appeal has shown that it is willing to approve such trials only where a trial by jury is unfeasible. In *R v J*[93] the Court of Appeal quashed the decision of a judge to order trial by judge alone where it believed that preventative measures could be taken. The court emphasized that trial by judge alone was a last resort and the strong presumption is that a jury should hear a matter. The court noted that a trial could take place and if jury tampering occurred then the judge could always discharge the jury and

---

91. [2009] EWCA Crim 1035.
92. [2011] EWCA Crim 8.
93. [2010] EWCA Crim 1755.

hear the remainder of the matter alone,[94] although such a course of action is likely to be extremely controversial, not least because counsel will have prepared the case on a very different basis.

14.5.2 Empanelling the jury

Jurors are rarely summoned for a single trial but instead form part of a general jury pool that attends court on a specific date. The actual process is that the court service, on behalf of the court, issues a jury summons, ie a legal summons addressed to an individual requiring them to attend court. Jury service is considered a civil responsibility and thus the expectation is that jurors should attend when summoned.

14.5.2.1 Employers

Some jurors may wish to attend jury service but are prevented by their employers, or are reluctant to attend jury service fearing how it may impact their jobs. An employer is legally obliged to release an employee for jury service and a refusal to do so amounts to contempt of court for which the employer could be fined or even imprisoned. An employee has the right not to be subjected to any detrimental treatment as a result of being on a jury[95] and a person who is dismissed for serving as a juror will be considered to have been dismissed unfairly.[96]

An employer does not need to pay an employee who is serving as a juror. This potentially can cause financial hardship (which may be considered a reason for excusal) since whilst a juror is paid expenses, they are subject to fixed limits. Financial loss (which includes loss of earnings, child-minding fees, etc) is limited to £64.95 per day for the first ten days of a jury trial, so long as at least four hours per day have been spent on jury service (otherwise it is one-half the rate), and then it is raised to £129.91 per day for trials that last over ten days, and up to 200 days and then £228.06 per day for trials that last over 201 days. The ordinary payment of £64.95 equates to just over £320 per week, leading to a 'salary' of £16,887. Many employees will receive significantly more than this as salary and it should be remembered that this allowance includes payment for childcare, something that is likely to take up most, if not all, of this allowance. Where an employer does not pay an employee for undertaking jury service this, in effect, means that a person could lose quite significant sums of money for serving on a jury and it is perhaps not surprising therefore that some seek to avoid service.

14.5.2.2 Vetting

Earlier in the chapter it was noted that some jurors are disqualified, either temporarily or permanently, if they have been convicted of a criminal offence. It is perhaps not surprising that potential jurors are now routinely matched against the Police National Computer (PNC) to ensure that the members called are not so disqualified.[97] This is uncontroversial and indeed sensible but it may be a surprise to know that certain trials involve a more detailed vetting, including consulting police intelligence and sometimes the Security Services.[98]

---

94. CJA 2003, s 46.
95. *Employment Rights Act 1996*, s 43M.
96. ibid, s 98B.
97. See CPS, Jury Vetting (Crown Prosecution Service 2018) <https://www.cps.gov.uk/legal-guidance/jury-vetting> which sets out the current policy.
98. See *Practice Note (Juries: Right to Stand By: Jury Checks)* (1989) 88 Cr App R 123, discussed in Sean Doran, 'Trial by Jury' in Mike McConville and Geoffrey Wilson (eds), *The Handbook of the Criminal Justice Process* (OUP 2002) 389.

This practice has a long history although the first identifiable case of jury vetting took place in relation to a trial under the Official Secrets Act where the prosecution had vetted 'for loyalty' the jury pool but had not removed three potential jurors, two of whom had signed the Act in question and one of whom (who became the foreperson of the jury) was a former member of the Special Air Service (SAS).[99] The result of this disclosure was significant criticism and the Attorney-General agreed to produce guidelines that would limit when any vetting could occur.[100]

The guidelines make clear that vetting should only occur where the trial concerns a matter of public interest or in a terrorist case. The vetting takes place only with the authorization of the Attorney-General[101] and is designed to allow the prosecution to exercise their power of 'stand by' (see 'Challenging a juror'), the reason presumably being something in the juror's background that is a cause for concern.

A particular difficulty with this whole exercise is that although the guidelines are published they are not particularly clear and are open to interpretation in a way that would allow the state to 'rig' a jury if they so wished. It has been noted that the guidelines do not place an obligation on the prosecution to 'stand by' a juror who would be biased against the defendant and yet the defendant would have no real way of knowing that they were.[102] It also goes against the rule that a jury should be drawn randomly and that the specific characteristics of jurors should not ordinarily be taken into account.[103]

Article 6 ECHR is commonly said to have an 'equality of arms' dimension to it, that is to say that both parties should be operating at roughly the same strength. Whilst it is never possible to obtain absolute parity (in either direction) the rule is based on the fact that one side should not be able to abuse its own position to the detriment of the opposing party. The system of jury vetting would appear to be a classic example of an inequality-of-arms position since the defence do not have the resources or contacts to be able to vet potential jurors. The complete absence of independence and the inevitable security that accompanies the vetting system also lead to the conclusion that there is no transparency within the process. It is difficult to see how this would not amount to a breach of Article 6 but perhaps its limited scope may save it. The European Court of Human Rights (ECtHR) has stated before that Article 6 is not an absolute right and that issues of national security may mean that some aspects of a fair trial may need to be balanced against important state interests.

For the moment the position of vetting appears settled but this is, in part, because the defence will not always know when jury vetting has taken place. Challenges for cause can be made at any stage and could theoretically be made to the judge without the defence knowing (on the basis that their objection might lead to the jurors never being included in the 'jury in waiting'). This makes the possibility of challenging the regime somewhat difficult.

---

99.   Andrew Sanders and Richard Young, *Criminal Justice* (4th edn, Butterworths 2010) 558.
100.   The guidelines are to be found at (1989) 88 Cr App R 123. Before this, the guidelines were not public and were instead dealt with by virtue of a Home Office Circular and communicated to chief constables and certain other officials (see *R v Mason* [1981] QB 881, 885).
101.   It is not possible to delegate this power (other than to the Solicitor-General) and thus one of HM Law Officers must personally authorize the vetting.
102.   Andrew Sanders and Richard Young, *Criminal Justice* (4th edn, Butterworths 2010) 558.
103.   Sean Doran, 'Trial by Jury' in Mike McConville and Geoffrey Wilson (eds), *The Handbook of the Criminal Justice Process* (OUP 2002) 390.

14.5.2.3 **The trial jury**

As noted earlier, jurors are summoned into a general pool from which the usher will bring twenty into a court and they become known as the 'jury in waiting'. The potential jurors will normally be told the name of the defendant and asked if they know him. If they do then they will leave the court and return to the jury pool to be used by an alternative court. The names of the individual potential jurors are on cards and handed to the clerk. The clerk of the court then shuffles the cards and calls twelve names out. In *R v Comerford*[104] the Court of Appeal upheld a policy adopted by the judge of assigning numbers to jurors instead of calling their names out. However, in that case there was a real risk of jury intimidation and accordingly it was accepted as an exception to the general rule.

Where a trial is going to be lengthy or complicated the *Criminal Procedure Rules* state that judges should ask the jury whether they have any personal commitments that may affect their service.[105] This is purely discretionary and the judge can decide not to waive the summons. In certain traumatic cases jurors have been excused because it may have been difficult for them to concentrate on the case, but this is again highly exceptional because arguably the more traumatic a case is, the more important an independent jury is.

Challenging a juror

In the United States empanelling a jury can take a considerable period of time because both parties have the right to object to a juror. In Northern Ireland the right to per-emptorily challenge a juror (ie to object to a juror without having to give any reason) still exists, but in England and Wales this right was abolished in 1988.[106] That is not to say that there is no opportunity to challenge a juror but the defence can now only challenge for cause although the prosecution have the additional ground of asking a juror to 'stand by'.

Challenges for cause exist for both parties and the challenge is made by counsel (or the defendant himself if unrepresented) who says 'Challenge' immediately before the juror takes the oath. The party who makes the challenge has the burden of proving, on the balance of probabilities, the unsuitability of the juror. The normal reason is bias but there must be proof of the appearance of bias, something that is not easy when, as Doran notes, it is not possible to ask questions of jurors in the way that is common in America.[107] It is relatively uncommon for challenges to be made.

The other possible method of objecting to a jury is when the prosecution use their power of asking a juror to stand by. Theoretically this just means that the person does not automatically become a member of the jury and returns to the jury in waiting. If enough potential jurors were unable to be sworn in then this could mean that the person stood by could be sworn in but this would be highly unlikely and, in fact, it would mean that the person is not used. Indeed it has been stated that:

> The guidelines [of the Attorney-General] restrict the exercise of the right of stand by to two situations; first, where a juror is clearly unsuitable and the defence agrees that the juror should be excluded, for example where it becomes apparent that a juror selected

---

104. [1998] 1 Cr App R 235.
105. *Criminal Procedure Rules 2020*, r 26.4
106. CJA 2003, s 118.
107. Sean Doran, 'Trial by Jury' in Mike McConville and Geoffrey Wilson (eds), *The Handbook of the Criminal Justice Process* (OUP 2002) 388.

to try a complex case is in fact illiterate; secondly, where jury checks reveal information justifying the exercise of the right to stand by.[108]

The first ground is relatively uncontroversial but the second undoubtedly remains controversial. That said, the concept of jury vetting (see 14.5.2.2) appears to be something that is here to stay.

The judge also has an inherent power to stand down a juror and the usual reason for this would be when the judge realizes that the person is not sufficiently literate to serve on the jury[109] or where disability or infirmity may make the person unsuitable to sit as a juror (see earlier discussion at 14.4.1.2).

14.5.2.4 **Taking the oath**

A juror in waiting becomes a juror when he is selected and takes the oath. The *Criminal Practice Directions* state that jurors can either swear an oath or make an affirmation. Where the person chooses to swear an oath they are given 'the opportunity to indicate to the court the Holy Book on which [they] wish to swear. The precise wording will depend on [their] faith as indicated to the court.'[110]

Where the person does not wish to swear an oath then they may affirm instead, the wording being:

> I do solemnly, sincerely and truly declare and affirm that I will faithfully try the defendant and give a true verdict according to the evidence.[111]

At this point the person is a juror and he will take his seat in the jury box. When all twelve jurors have been sworn in then the jury is complete.

14.5.2.5 **Judicial direction on behaviour**

The *Criminal Practice Directions* state that a judge must then direct the jury about their behaviour and expectations, providing clear guidance on:

- the prohibition on internet searches on any matters or individuals relating to the trial
- the importance of not discussing the case with anyone outside of the jury group
- the importance of ignoring media reporting on the case
- bringing concerns to the judge (including about the conduct of other jurors) as soon as possible.[112]

The reason for this is that there have been a number of situations when jurors have acted in a way that could prejudice the trial and/or the rights of the defendant. Indeed, under ss 20E–20G JA 1974 it is not an offence to disclose information about jury deliberations where jury impropriety is suspected or occurs during the trial. This may include, for example, racist comments being made in the jury room or ignoring the judge's direction not to discuss the case outside of the courtroom or bringing external material into court.

---

108.   Sean Doran, 'Trial by Jury' in Mike McConville and Geoffrey Wilson (eds), *The Handbook of the Criminal Justice Process* (OUP 2002) 388.

109.   John Sprack, *A Practical Approach to Criminal Procedure* (15th edn, OUP 2015) 258, 18.35.

110.   *Criminal Practice Directions 2015*, as amended 2019, CPD VI 26E.2.

111.   ibid, CPD VI 26E.3.

112.   ibid, CPD VI 26G.3.

In recent years there have been a number of issues of misbehaviour by a jury. This will be discussed in the next chapter (15.6.2 on jury deliberations and delivery of the verdict) but it is worth noting that the Internet has caused new opportunities for jurors to act improperly and judges must now warn jurors specifically about the use of the Internet.[113] Depending on the misconduct of the juror it may lead to their discharge or it could lead to criminal proceedings being taken against them.

▤ Example Joanne Fraill

One of the more unusual examples of juror misconduct relates to Joanna Fraill. She was a juror who heard a complicated trial involving eight defendants. After deliberating the jury brought in partial verdicts in relation to some defendants, including acquitting one female defendant of all counts.

That evening Fraill sought out the female defendant on Facebook and began to have conversations with her about the trial, including information concerning how the jury were voting. This was capable of amounting to contempt of court (s 8 *Contempt of Court Act 1981*)[114] but was also completely against directions the judge had given about the use of the Internet in a trial.

The judge ultimately discovered the contact because the female defendant, worried that she was in more trouble, informed her solicitor and barrister who, in turn, told the judge.

Fraill was separated from the other jurors and then discharged. However, the judge decided that her conduct was so serious that he had to discharge the whole jury. The Attorney-General sought to commit Fraill for contempt of court and the Divisional Court convicted her, sentencing her to eight months' imprisonment.[115]

527

14.5.2.6 **Discharging a juror**

The final aspect to discuss concerning the empanelment of a jury is that of their discharge. Of course this is unlikely to take place immediately after their empanelment but it is discussed here for convenience. This section will examine the discharge of the entire jury (which if it takes place before the jury retire to consider their verdict would normally be as a result of an irregularity in the trial) or the discharge of an individual juror.

In respect of discharging the entire jury, it is always a matter for the trial judge to decide when this is necessary, although he should discuss this with counsel and not infrequently the decision will be made after a submission from (defence) counsel to invite the discharge of the jury. The normal reason for this is if significant inadmissible evidence is given to the jury but it could also be as a result of an external factor and, in the past, cases have arisen where the jury has been discharged because of media comments. Where the latter occurs it has normally resulted in contempt proceedings being instigated.

113.　See *R v Thompson* [2010] EWCA Crim 1623, [2011] 1 WLR 200, 205 (Lord Judge LCJ).
114.　This offence has now been repealed and replaced with offences in the *Juries Act 1974*, ss 20A–20D.
115.　*Attorney-General v Fraill* [2011] 2 Cr App R 21.

R v McCann[116] is an interesting example of this. This case concerned a terrorist case and in the middle of the trial the Home Secretary announced the end of the automatic right to silence, something widely reported. Commentators in the media noted that this could have a particular impact on terrorism cases. The Court of Appeal ruled that the jury should have been discharged when it was apparent that the suspects would not be testifying. This is an example of an innocent external factor that still necessitated the discharge of a jury in order to ensure that the defendant received a fair trial.

It is not always necessary to discharge the whole jury but it is sometimes necessary to discharge a single juror. This is permissible under s 16 JA 1974 and the provision states that when this occurs it need not lead to the discharge of the whole jury, although this is something that a judge will have to take into account. The discharge need not arise as a result of misconduct and could, for example, be as a result of personal circumstances (eg illness) but misconduct is certainly a significant factor in discharges.

The key test in all of this is whether the juror is biased. What does bias mean, however? Traditionally it was thought that it meant bias from a subjective point of view, ie was the juror biased, but in *Sanders v United Kingdom*[117] the ECtHR said that bias had to be looked at objectively not just subjectively, that is to say whether a reasonable person would believe that the juror is biased. Arguably this is a wider test and could lead to more jurors being discharged. This test also has a wider implication in that it may lead to the discharge of the entire jury. If there is a risk that the bias of one juror has contaminated the others in the jury then the whole jury should be discharged. Ultimately it is for the judge to decide whether this has happened, although his ruling would almost certainly provide a ground of appeal.

Where the entire jury is discharged for whatever reason then the defendant is not acquitted and is liable to a retrial. Two possible impediments stand in the way of a retrial. First, the prosecution must choose to bring a retrial. The circumstances that led to the original discharge will be considered as this could affect the evidential or public-interest test, which could mean that the decision to prosecute will change and the prosecution could decide not to progress a retrial. The second possible impediment is the judge. It is possible that the judge may decide that it is not possible to have a fair retrial and he has an inherent power to order that proceedings are stayed. In *R v Taylor*[118] the Court of Appeal adopted this discretion after they quashed the conviction of two teenage sisters accused of murder, in part because of pre-trial publicity. The court stated that the publicity was so prejudicial that a retrial would not be possible.

14.6 **Legal advisers**

Prior to the introduction of the *Courts and Tribunals (Judiciary and Functions of Staff) Act 2018* (CTA 2018), one of the most important positions in the magistrates' court was that of the justices' clerk. Justices' clerks were legally appointed and had two principal

---

116. (1991) 92 Cr App R 239.
117. (2001) 31 EHRR 44.
118. (1994) 98 Cr App R 361.

functions; the provision of advice to the magistracy and exercising judicial functions. When advising the magistracy, justices' clerks were meant to set out the legal framework and state the principles of law that magistrates should apply. However, as magistrates are responsible for matters of both law and fact, advice from a justices' clerk was just that, advice, and the ultimate decision rested with the magistrates. Indeed, where a justices' clerk went beyond this and suggested to magistrates how the law should be applied, or what the obvious conclusion to their advice was, then this was seen as encroaching on the judicial function of the magistrates and should have been ignored.

Alongside their advisory role, justices' clerks also carried out a number of functions that would ordinarily have been considered clearly judicial, including the issuing of an arrest warrant[119] and the discharging of an accused where the prosecution offers no evidence.[120] They also had functions relating to costs, bail, and the transfer for trial of an accused. Permitting justices' clerks to exercise these functions was somewhat controversial since, unlike lay magistrates and district judges (magistrates' court) they have not been appointed to a judicial role, their primary function is administrative and advisory. That said, they were legally qualified and so it was suggested that it may be more efficient to use them to undertake certain pre-trial matters, allowing magistrates to concentrate on their core function, that of hearing cases.

With the introduction of the CTA 2018, the specific role of the justices' clerk has been abolished. However the functions associated with the role, ie the exercise of judicial functions and the provision of legal advice are to be kept and broadened. Indeed, under the CTA 2018 legally qualified staff will be deployed as legal advisers much more widely across the courts and tribunals (not just in the magistrates' courts as was the case with justices' clerks). Under the CTA 2018 'authorised persons' or 'authorised' staff who work for HMCTS are able to exercise specific judicial functions under the authority of the Lord Chief Justice or his nominee. These judicial functions can be exercised across any courts and tribunals, not simply the magistrates' court. Thus, in the Crown Court which deals with the most serious criminal cases, legal advisers can carry out a range of judicial functions.

The judicial functions authorized to be exercised by legal advisers vary depending on the court or tribunal they are working in.[121] However, rule 2.4 of the Criminal Procedure Rules 2020 sets out what legal advisers are *not* authorized to do, regardless of the criminal court they are working in. For example, legal advisors cannot:

- authorize a person's committal to prison
- authorize a person's arrest (but that exclusion does not apply to the issue of a warrant of arrest)
- determine the admissibility of evidence
- make findings of fact for the purpose of sentence, defer or pass sentence, impose a penalty or commit a defendant to the Crown Court for sentence
- make an order for a party or other person to pay costs, unless that party or person agrees.

Similar rules exist in relation to the family and civil courts.

---

119. *Justices' Clerks Rules 2005*, SI 2005/545, sch 1, para 3.
120. ibid, sch 1, para 5.
121. See the *Criminal Procedure Rules 2020* rr 2.5–2.9.

In a policy statement released prior to the passing of the CTA 2018, the justification for the expansion of legal advisers who are authorized to carry out judicial functions was:

> to improve efficiency within the courts service by diverting judges' time from routine tasks to allow them to focus their time and expertise on more complex matters before them.[122]

Certainly the issue of delay has long been a cause of concern to the criminal justice system and authorizing legal advisers to exercise some judicial functions may help to minimize this delay by allowing them to quickly deal with more administrative matters and allowing judges to spend their time hearing trials. Nevertheless, the judicial functions which they are able to exercise are extensive, and therefore caution should be exercised given they are not members of the judiciary and have not got the experience nor undertaken the training that judges have as the only ones historically able to exercise these functions.

14.7 Other roles in the Crown Court

14.7.1 Court clerk

Each Crown Court centre has a court clerk but their role is one of administration rather than legal advice since judges are professionally legally qualified. The clerk has no statutory qualification and assists the resident (or senior resident) judge and the senior administrative grade in the smooth operation of the courts.

14.7.2 Stenographer

The Crown Court, as a superior court of record, has all its proceedings recorded. Historically this was completed by a stenographer who used to type out the proceedings using a shorthand-enabled typewriter but in more modern times they have been recorded using either tape recorders or solid-state recording equipment. The stenographer need not now appear in court at all times but, rather, is responsible for ensuring that the recording equipment is working. In many Crown Court trials the stenographer is absent except at the beginning and end of each session.

14.7.3 Usher

The usher is a visible symbol of the Crown Court and yet has no statutory or formal authority except when a jury retires; however, he is present throughout the trial. The usher assists the clerk in the smooth running of a trial and normally identifies which witnesses are within the court building. The primary purpose of the usher is to assist the jury (see 15.6.2.2).

---

122. Ministry of Justice 'Courts and Tribunals (Judiciary and Functions of Staff) Bill Policy Statement (MoJ, 2018) available at <https://assets.publishing.service.gov.uk/government/uploads/system/uploads/attachment_data/file/723835/courts-and-tribunals-judiciary-and-functions-of-staff-bill-policy-statement.pdf>1.

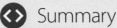

Summary

This chapter has introduced the people that will be involved in a trial. In particular it has:

- Shown that whilst many of the same people appear in the magistrates' court and Crown Court they may fulfil different functions.

- Identified that there is considerable difference in the role of a judge and magistrate. In the magistrates' court the magistrates are the tribunal of both fact and law whereas a judge in the Crown Court is only the tribunal of law and the tribunal of fact is the jury.

- Noted that it is possible to hold a hearing in the magistrates' court without any lawyer appearing either for the prosecution or defence.

- Explored the role of the jury, including the eligibility for jury service and disqualification.

- Demonstrated that jurors must serve and employers must release employees to serve. If they do not then they commit a criminal offence.

End-of-chapter questions

1. Do you think it is right that in summary trials the magistrates are both the tribunal of law and fact? Is there any danger in trusting magistrates to ignore evidence that they have already heard? Is it possible to put out of mind something that has been heard?

2. Have a look at the provisions in Part 3 of the *Criminal Justice and Courts Act 2015*. Do you think that the introduction of 'trial by single justices on paper' is a good idea? Why or why not?

3. Do you think that there should there be restrictions on who can serve on a jury? Why? Do you agree with the current restrictions and disqualification criteria?

4. Is it right that juries can be vetted by the police and Security Services? Does this not lead to the situation whereby it looks as though the prosecution are 'picking' the jury to hear a particular case? Would it be better to ask jurors questions in the way that they do in the US so that we can identify anyone who has pre-judged the matter or who has particular prejudices (both pro- or anti-prosecution)? Is that feasible?

Further reading

Darbyshire P, *Sitting in Judgment: The Working Lives of Judges* (Hart Publishing 2011) ch 9.

This shows how judges are perceived in their role during a trial.

Doran S, 'Trial by Jury' in Mike McConville and Geoffrey Wilson (eds), *The Handbook of the Criminal Justice Process* (OUP 2002).

This is an intelligent essay that highlights some of the controversies of a trial on indictment, including issues relating to the jury.

Grove T, *A Juryman's Tale* (Bloomsbury 2000).

This is an excellent read on the experiences of the author sitting as a jury. It provides useful information on how people in court are perceived.

Solley S, 'The Role of the Advocate' in Mike McConville and Geoffrey Wilson (eds), *The Handbook of The Criminal Justice Process* (OUP 2002) 311–22.

An interesting chapter that examines what the role of the advocate is during a Crown Court trial.

For self-test questions, flashcards, and links to useful websites, please visit the **online resources** at: **www.oup.com/he/gillespie-weare8e/**

15

The Trials

By the end of this chapter you will be able to:

- Understand how a summary trial and trial on indictment progress.
- Identify the differences between a summary trial and trial on indictment.
- Understand how the prosecution proves its case.
- Identify the order that witnesses provide testimony.
- Understand how a verdict is reached.

Introduction

Chapter 13 presented the pre-trial procedures for both summary trials (those trials that take place in the magistrates' courts) and trials on indictment (those trials that take place in the Crown Court), including presenting how the decision is taken as to which trial mode will be chosen.

Previous chapters also presented the difference between a judge, jury, and lay magistrates. It will be remembered that magistrates have the power to hear two types of cases; summary-only matters and matters that are triable either-way. Similarly the Crown Court may hear two types of cases; either-way offences and those that are triable only on indictment. In both types of case the matter is heard by a judge and jury.

This chapter will present the course of a trial to you. Both the summary trial and trial on indictment will be presented which will allow you to compare the differences between them.

15.1 The prosecution case

The prosecution will always go first. This is because of the presumption of innocence. Probably the most important rule in the criminal justice process within England and Wales is the presumption of innocence, ie a person is innocent until found guilty. This rule means that it is not for a person to prove his innocence, it is for the prosecution to prove his guilt. Accordingly, the prosecution must establish a case to answer, ie they adduce sufficient evidence to show, to the required standard, that the defendant could be guilty. If they establish this then the defence must adduce their evidence to convince the tribunal of fact that he is not guilty.

15.1.1 **The opening speech**

The prosecution always have the right to make an opening speech and this is true of both summary trials and trials on indictment. In a summary trial the speech will be made to the justices and it will ordinarily be brief because the magistrates are familiar with the type of cases that they deal with. It is likely that the speech will simply refer to the alleged facts and how the prosecution intend to prove the matter. In the Crown Court the position is slightly different. Here, the speech is to the jury—as the tribunal of fact—and not to the judge. The speech is likely to be longer and will ordinarily include a reference to the burden of proof and a summary of the legal issues that will ordinarily be raised.[1] The prosecution will then outline how they intend to prove their case, ie giving a summary of the prosecution case. By convention the prosecution does not talk about contested evidence in the prosecution case (ie evidence that the defence do not agree with), but this is often not possible, for example, in respect of a confession. The position is often easier in modern trials because most of the issues relating to the admissibility of evidence (see 15.1.2) will be dealt with at the plea and case management hearing(s) and so the prosecution should know what evidence they will be allowed to adduce. Where, however, the matter has not yet been decided (because sometimes a judge will adjourn an issue of admissibility until other consequential evidence has been heard) then the prosecution should never mention this to the jury.

15.1.1.1 **Defence opening speech**

Where the defence intend to call a witness other than the defendant himself then they too have the right to make an opening speech. Sometimes this will take place at the opening of their case (15.3) but in longer or more complicated cases it is not unusual for the judge to ask for the speeches to be heard at the same time.

15.1.2 **Calling the evidence**

This book does not address the issue of evidence and reference should be made to other texts that cover this topic or to the substantive module *Law of Evidence* that many universities provide as an optional subject. However, it is necessary to understand that there are different types of evidence that can be adduced to help prove a case.

If someone was to ask 'what type of evidence is adduced in a criminal trial?' the first answer would probably be 'witnesses' and certainly this is perhaps the form of evidence that will be used in almost every case. That said, it is recognized that witness testimony is sometimes flawed[2] and that will be discussed if you study evidence. Despite this they remain an important form of evidence and are discussed later.

There is lots of other evidence that can be adduced. 'Real' evidence is often used to describe physical evidence so as to distinguish it from witness testimony. This could include, for example, objects found at a crime scene or photographs of a scene or incident, including CCTV evidence.[3] This can be very important evidence, not least because

---

1. Iain Morley, *The Devil's Advocate* (3rd edn, Sweet & Maxwell 2015) 110.
2. Andrew Choo, *Evidence* (3rd edn, OUP 2012) 360.
3. See, for example, *Attorney-General's Reference (No 2 of 2002)* [2002] EWCA Crim 2373 discussed in Andrew Choo, *Evidence* (3rd edn, OUP 2012) 10.

it is something that the tribunal of fact (be that a jury or magistrates) can touch, look at, and reach their own conclusions on. Sometimes real evidence will be accompanied by witness testimony and this is particularly true where, for example, the real evidence is scientific evidence where the tribunal of fact requires assistance to understand the evidence being put forward.

A branch of real evidence is documentary evidence. In many trials there can be a variety of documents that would help a jury in understanding whether a defendant committed a crime. Documentary evidence has proven to be one of the more controversial types of evidence, with the rules governing its admissibility having changed over the years.[4] At one point documents had to be the 'best available' or the original which sometimes caused difficulties but s 133 *Criminal Justice Act 2003* (CJA 2003) provides that a document can be proved either by adducing the original or a certified copy.

15.1.2.1 **Witnesses**

Perhaps the type of evidence that people are most familiar with are witnesses. This is where a person provides testimony in court by being asked a series of questions on what they have seen or done. Nearly every case will involve at least one witness although sometimes there may only be one (for example where a person contests a speeding offence it is likely that the only evidence will be the police officer who operated the device that measured the speed), and complex cases may have multiple witnesses of various descriptions.

Again, for our purposes it is not necessary to consider all the evidential rules that relate to witnesses but instead we should focus on key aspects. The evidence of witnesses in England and Wales is taken usually by means of questioning, with each type of question being referred to by a specific name and it alternating between sides. In a prosecution the order of witnesses is given in Table 15.1.

Where there is more than one defendant then each defendant is allowed to cross-examine the witness for the prosecution although there is no obligation to do so, and in long trials it is not unusual for minor witnesses to be asked questions on behalf of only one defendant, and for the other lawyers to 'adopt' those answers in support of their own case.

The order does not change between trials in the magistrates' court or Crown Court. Where it does differ is in respect of questions from the bench. In the magistrates' court it will be remembered that the magistrates are the tribunal of both fact and law and so they can ask whatever questions they wish. Questions are fed through the chair of

Table 15.1 Order of witness testimony

Examination-in-chief	Prosecution lawyer asks the questions
Cross-examination	Defence lawyer asks the questions
Re-examination	Prosecution ask questions but only to clarify points already adduced from the witness
Questions from the bench	Judge or magistrates ask questions

---

4. Andrew Choo, *Evidence* (3rd edn, OUP 2012) 8.

the bench, the wingers putting their questions through the chair. It will be remembered from Chapter 8 that district judges (magistrates' court) (DJMCs) will sit by themselves and are also the tribunal of fact and law. There is some evidence to suggest that district judges are more likely to be proactive in a trial and ask questions of witnesses.[5] It is believed that this is because district judges are better able to understand the legal and evidential issues arising from the case and will therefore seek direct answers to questions that relate to those issues.

The position in the Crown Court is more complicated. The judge is the tribunal of law and the jury are the tribunal of fact. A judge can ask questions of the witnesses although he will ordinarily only do this where he thinks it is necessary to assist the jury in clarifying some of the issues. Judges will ordinarily be slow to ask questions because it can be seen as interfering in the role of the lawyers and could lead to an appeal where, for example, there is an appearance of bias.

Theoretically the jury can also ask questions although it is a cumbersome procedure. The juror who wishes to ask a question passes a note to the judge. The judge then reads the note and decides whether the question can be put to the witness. If the answer to that is 'yes' then the judge will put the question direct to the witness. It has been noted that the courts try so far as possible to deter notes being passed[6] and this creates, in the words of one observer, the rather strange position whereby the tribunal of fact takes a 'very passive role in the course of the trial'[7] which, of course, can be contrasted with the position in the magistrates' court where they may take a more active part. Of course it is difficult to see how an alternative arrangement could exist. There are twelve persons on a jury and if each were permitted to ask questions then it could become extremely complicated very quickly.

Witnesses not present

Sometimes a witness will exist but not attend court. There may be any number of reasons why this is the case, including the fact that the defence may not contest the evidence given of a minor witness. In those circumstances it is usual for the witness statement to be read out aloud to either the magistrates or jury and they treat this as though it was (uncontested) evidence from the person himself.

There are other reasons why a witness may not turn up, including fear or unavailability. Rules do exist for whether the statement of the witness can be read in court.[8] It is not necessary to discuss these in depth here but it is worth noting that allowing the evidence of an unavailable witness to be given where it is contested is extremely controversial. Article 6(3)(d) ECHR provides that everyone has the right to examine witnesses, ie that they should be able to test the truthfulness of the witness or put alternative questions to that witness. Where the witness is not present then this is not possible and so it could be said that a breach of Article 6 may be found. In practice the right to examine witnesses is not absolute, in part because of the fact that there may be legitimate reasons why a witness is not available to testify. Again, it is not necessary to summarize these rules here as they are best left to a study on the law of evidence.

---

5.   Rod Morgan and Neil Russell, *The Judiciary in the Magistrates' Courts* (Home Office 2000) 46.
6.   Sean Doran, 'Trial by Jury' in Mike McConville and Geoffrey Wilson (eds), *The Handbook of The Criminal Justice Process* (OUP 2002) 395.
7.   ibid, 394.
8.   See, for example, *Criminal Justice Act 2003*, s 116.

The unrepresented defendant

There is no obligation for a defendant to be represented although in contested matters funding will ordinarily be available for a lawyer, particularly in the Crown Court (Chapter 11 discusses the funding of legal services in criminal cases).

In summary trials the clerk to the court (or the justices' legal adviser) will ordinarily assist the defendant by asking questions of witnesses where it is helpful to do so, although the defendant may demand the right to ask questions himself. In trials on indictment the judge does not act as a surrogate lawyer for the defendant although he does have an obligation to ensure a fair trial, and this will sometimes require him to ask certain questions of witnesses so that the jury are aware of the theory of the defence but he must not put forward the case for the defence, that is a matter for the defendant.

Where matters become complicated is where the defendant wishes to personally examine vulnerable witnesses. Historically, sexual offence cases and those committed against children were considered to be the same as any other case, and therefore a defendant could personally cross-examine the complainant regardless of what effect this could have on the victim.

Example Ralston Edwards

Ralston Edwards had been charged with the rape of Julia Mason (Julia bravely waived her right to anonymity to highlight her case) and he represented himself. His defence was not clear but he made her describe the attack and his genitalia in detail. He also went through her entire sexual history, ie asking questions about every sexual partner she had ever had. The cross-examination lasted for six days and Ms Mason said it felt as if she had been raped again. The judge felt unable to end the ordeal although this is perhaps highly questionable since controlling cross-examination and the protection of witnesses is undoubtedly a role of the judge.[9]

537

The criticism of Ms Mason's treatment was immense and the government eventually acted by restricting the right of a defendant in person to conduct cross-examination of a victim when charged with a sexual offence.[10] Where a person is restrained from personally cross-examining a witness, how will the defendant's case be put to him? There had been a ban on the cross-examination of child witnesses that pre-dated the 1999 Act and under those circumstances the judge would cross-examine the child[11] but this was unsatisfactory, not least because it is the classic example of a judge assuming the 'robes of an advocate', to borrow Lord Denning's phrase (see 14.1.2.2). The 1999 Act created a more acceptable system when it decided that the court, when denying the opportunity to a defendant to cross-examine, could appoint counsel to conduct the cross-examination even if the defendant did not request one.[12]

This provision is undoubtedly controversial for a number of reasons. First, it can be argued that it could place the defendant at a disadvantage since, in effect, any counsel will be appointed late in the day and the person appointed will not necessarily

---

9. Philip Otton, 'The Role of the Judge in Criminal Cases' in Mike McConville and Geoffrey Wilson (eds), *The Handbook of The Criminal Justice Process* (OUP 2002) 327.

10. *Youth Justice and Criminal Evidence Act 1999*, s 34.

11. Jenny McEwan, 'Special Measures for Witnesses and Victims' in Mike McConville and Geoffrey Wilson (eds), *The Handbook of The Criminal Justice Process* (OUP 2002) 247.

12. *Youth Justice and Criminal Evidence Act 1999*, s 38.

be counsel for the defence, meaning that issues arise as to cooperation and indeed privilege.[13] Second, it could be argued it is contrary to Article 6 ECHR. Article 6(3)(c) states that everyone has the right to:

> defend himself in person or through legal assistance of his own choosing or, if he has not sufficient means to pay for legal assistance, to be given it free when the interests of justice so require.

It could be argued that preventing personal cross-examination is not allowing the defendant to defend himself in person but the syntax of Article 6(3)(c) does not appear to require that absolutely and does provide for the right of assistance. Admittedly it does appear to suggest that ordinarily the defendant should be able to choose his own counsel but this is then qualified by the final sentence which implies that it may be possible to provide alternative counsel. Similarly, any challenge under Article 6(3)(d), which provides the right to examine or have witnesses examined, would fail since the court-appointed lawyer can examine witnesses. It should also be noted that the ECtHR has on occasions said that Article 6 is not an absolute right and it needs to be placed into context. In this situation, other Convention rights are in play because the victim almost certainly has rights under either Article 3 (prohibition of, inter alia, degrading treatment) or Article 8 (right to respect for private life).

15.2 No case to answer

It will be remembered from the beginning of the previous section that the burden of proof is on the prosecution to prove their case. At the conclusion of the prosecution case the defence may seek to argue that the prosecution have not discharged that burden, ie they have not proven to the required standard that the evidence shows the defendant is guilty. This is known as a submission of no case to answer although it is colloquially known as a 'half-time submission'.

Whilst the test is the same for both summary trials and trials on indictment the process of making the submission differs. As the tribunal of fact and law are the same in the magistrates' court then the submission is made to either the lay justices or the DJMC, whereas in the Crown Court it is made only to the judge and the jury are not present when the judge makes the decision. The principal reason the jury are not present is so that they are not prejudiced by hearing the judge rule that a defendant is prima facie guilty and so they may feel less persuaded to acquit the defendant after hearing his evidence. That said, it does raise an interesting issue in respect of summary trials where, of course, the magistrates or district judge will continue to hear all the evidence and must somehow put out of their mind the legal ruling they have made that the defendant has a case to answer.

The principle behind the submission was set out by the Court of Appeal in *R v Galbraith*.[14] The essence of the test is:

> [I]f the judge comes to the conclusion that the prosecution evidence, if taken at its highest, is such that a jury properly directed could not properly convict upon it, it is his duty . . . to stop the case.[15]

---

13. Jenny McEwan, 'Special Measures for Witnesses and Victims' in Mike McConville and Geoffrey Wilson (eds), *The Handbook of The Criminal Justice Process* (OUP 2002) 248.
14. (1981) 73 Cr App R 124.
15. *R v Galbraith* (1981) 73 Cr App R 124, 127.

The test is the same in a summary trial save that it is formulated that the justices must consider whether any reasonable tribunal could convict the defendant on the evidence heard.[16] The difference in the tribunal of fact between summary trials and trials on indictment does raise an issue in terms of what can be taken into account when deciding the submission. The judge in the Crown Court should not usurp the role of the jury and the Court of Appeal in *Galbraith* continued by noting that where the decision involves making an assessment of the reliability or credibility of the witness then the case should ordinarily continue, as the judge should not try to become the arbitrator of facts. That said, where a witness has obviously no credibility then this must be something the judge will take into account. In summary trials, however, the magistrates or district judge are also the tribunal of fact and therefore they can take into account their findings on the credibility or reliability of a witness as it is their job to make these findings. This potentially means that the same trial could lead to two different decisions depending on where the submission was made.

Where the trial takes place in the Crown Court then it is important to note that this is not an 'all or nothing' submission. Whilst a judge may reject an initial submission of no case to answer he must continually have the test in his mind and if, following evidence from the defence, he concludes that the *Galbraith* test is satisfied then he must stop the case.

At both summary trials and trials on indictment it is perfectly possible for a judge or the magistrates to decide that a submission succeeds in part. In other words they may conclude that the evidence adduced does not show a case to be answered by the defendant in respect of some charges. In those situations the correct decision is to direct an acquittal in respect of those charges where the defendant has no case to answer but to allow the trials to proceed in respect of the others. Whilst the submission is an important part of the trial process, it leads to very few cases being stopped.

15.3 Defence case

If a submission of no case to answer is not made, or if it is rejected, then the trial proceeds on to the case for the defence. In the Crown Court it will be remembered that so long as a witness other than the defendant himself will be called to give evidence then the defence are entitled to make an opening speech. Traditionally this will take place at the opening of the defence case but increasingly it is taking place immediately after the prosecution opening speech.

The order of testimony for defence witnesses is the same as for prosecution witnesses but obviously the nature of the questioning changes, as presented in Table 15.2.

Table 15.2 Order of witness testimony

Examination-in-chief	Defence lawyer asks the questions
Cross-examination	Prosecution lawyer asks the questions
Re-examination	Defence ask questions but only to clarify points already adduced from the witness
Questions from the bench	Judge or magistrates ask questions

16. *Practice Note* [1962] 1 All ER 448.

Where there is more than one defendant then each defendant can ask questions to the witness in cross-examination. Note that their questions are classed as cross-examination rather than examination-in-chief because the witness was not called on their behalf.

15.3.1 **Defendant testifying**

The defendant himself is competent to give evidence (ie he may be legally heard) but he is not compellable (ie he cannot be forced to testify). While this continues to be true, if a defendant does not give evidence in court, the justices or jury can draw an adverse inference against the defendant.[17] In both summary trials and trials on indictment the lawyer for the defence will ordinarily be asked whether he has warned the defendant about the consequences of not testifying, this question taking place in open court.[18] Precisely what constitutes an adverse inference is a matter of some debate,[19] but it is clear that an inference by itself cannot be the sole or main reason for a conviction.[20]

If the defendant does intend to testify then ordinarily he should give evidence first, although the judge (trial on indictment) or justices (summary trial) do have discretion to allow other witnesses to be heard first;[21] however, it is likely that this discretion would be exercised only in exceptional circumstances. The reason for the defendant going first is that, unlike all the other witnesses, he will be present in court throughout the whole trial. By going first there is no danger that he tries to 'adapt' his answers so as to be compatible with the comments of other witnesses, potentially making the answers seem more credible.

15.4 **Closing speeches**

After the evidence is complete there is an opportunity for closing speeches.

15.4.1 **Summary trials**

The defence always have the right to make a closing speech and they will ordinarily take the opportunity to highlight evidence that they believe supports their case theory. Where the trial is heard by a district judge the speech is likely to be shorter because it is unlikely that the district judge would welcome being told the law or the implications of various factual findings. Where the case is heard by lay justices then it is likely the speech will be longer and it could involve inviting the justices to consider certain legal proceedings and also inviting them to make findings in respect of the credibility of witnesses etc.

Traditionally the prosecution did not have the right to give a closing speech although the latest version of the *Criminal Procedure Rules* now make clear that the prosecution can give a statement in two instances: where the defendant is represented by a lawyer and irrespective of whether the defendant is represented, if he introduced witnesses other than himself.[22] It is not immediately clear why the fact that a lawyer represents

---

17. *Criminal Justice and Public Order Act 1994*, s 35.
18. See *R v Cowan* [1996] QB 373.
19. Andrew Choo, *Evidence* (3rd edn, OUP 2012) 127–42.
20. *Criminal Justice and Public Order Act 1994*, s 35(3) and see *Murray v United Kingdom* (1996) 22 EHRR 29.
21. *Police and Criminal Evidence Act 1984*, s 79.
22. *Criminal Procedure Rules 2020* r 24.3(3)(h).

the defendant should be a ground for the prosecution making a closing speech, it would seem more sensible to limit it to situations where more than one defence witness gave evidence. At least in that situation there is an argument for the prosecution reminding the justices, as the tribunal of fact, of their evidence whereas where only the defendant testifies it is likely that this evidence will remain.

15.4.2 Trials on indictment

The general rule is that both the prosecution and defence have the right to make a closing speech. Of course just because a person has the right to make a speech does not mean that they always will and in some simple trials it is possible that at least one counsel may decide not to give a closing speech.

Assuming that both sides do intend to make a closing speech then the prosecution goes first. The principle of counsel for the prosecution acting as a 'minister of justice' still applies and accordingly counsel should give a fair speech. It is likely that the prosecution will remind the jury of the standard and burden of proof and then highlight key issues that the jury have heard. The defence go last and they will ordinarily remind the jury of issues that they believe help support their case.

An important restriction on closing speeches is that counsel can only comment on evidence that has been seen or heard and this includes questions put to witnesses. Therefore if counsel did not put a point to a witness then they are not able to adduce it during the closing speech; they must only remind the jury of what they have seen or heard. This can be problematic where counsel forgot to put a point to a witness during cross-examination but it is an important rule: counsel are not supposed to speculate about what a witness may have said and must restrict themselves to what they did say.

Even if the defendant is not legally represented he is entitled to make a closing speech to the jury.

15.5 Judicial summing up

In other jurisdictions the closing speech of counsel for the defence is the last word in a trial but in trials on indictment in England and Wales the judge speaks last, his speech being known as the 'summing up'. There are two primary functions of the summing up; first to direct the jury as to the law; and second to remind the jury of the facts and evidence of the case.

Guidance on summing up and directing juries is provided in the new *Crown Court Compendium*,[23] which has replaced all previous guidance issued by the Judicial College. The Compendium provides checklists of points that may need to be covered by judges when summing up particular cases, as well as example directions. The aim is to 'provide guidance on directing the jury in Crown Court trials', but it is explicitly noted that judges must tailor the guidance given in relation to each particular case.[24] Valuable guidance on what a summing up should contain was also provided by Lord Justice Simon in the case of *R v Reynolds*.

541

23. Judicial College, *The Crown Court Compendium. Part I: Jury and Trial Management and Summing Up* (Judicial College 2020) <https://www.judiciary.uk/wp-content/uploads/2020/07/Crown-Court-Compendium-Part-I-July-2020-1.pdf>.
24. ibid, 1–9.

Some question why a judge should sum up, given that, in essence, the summing up not infrequently leads to a ground of appeal.[25] However, others believe that reminding the jury of the evidence they have heard and possible links between the issues is helpful. They do not, however, explain why it is that Scotland, for example, manages to do well without a full summing up (the judge merely provides legal directions to a jury) and so does America where, in effect, they do not allow the judge to sum up.[26]

Another problem with the English summing up is that it is often far too long and it has been suggested that it could either be summarized or even handed to the jury in written form.[27] While this has not yet been accepted in practice, the Court of Appeal in *R v Sanghera*[28] stated that a short summing up was possible and that it was not necessary to go through each evidential point but merely to provide a summary of the points for and against the defence, although it is imperative that important points favourable to the defence are included. This was reinforced and further guidance provided by Lord Justice Simon in the case of *R v Reynolds*,[29] where it was noted that a succinct summing up was particularly important in longer and complex cases, and that the focus should be on reminding the jury about what really matters in the case.

15.6 Reaching the verdict

The final stage of the trial (ie the proceedings that lead to a determination of whether a person is guilty or innocent) is the verdict. The procedure for reaching the verdict differs between summary trials and trials on indictment.

15.6.1 Summary trials

Where lay justices preside it is likely that they will retire, ie leave the courtroom, to consider their verdict. It is not unusual for a district judge to give judgment straight away.

15.6.1.2 Pronouncement

The verdict of the court will always be given in open court. The justices are allowed to decide by majority but in open court there will never be an indication as to how justices voted—the decision is a collective one and ordinarily a magistrate should not state that he disagreed with the others. Only the chairman will speak and he will state the verdict in respect of all the charges. Where there were alternative charges a verdict on the lesser charge will not be returned if the more serious charge was proven.

In the magistrates' court the usual way of pronouncing guilt or innocence is to say whether the case has been 'proved' (ie guilty) or 'not proved' (ie not guilty). The justices must follow the same rules as a jury in the Crown Court, ie if there is any doubt as to the guilt of an offender they must acquit.

If the defendant is acquitted then he is free to go. If he is convicted then the court will proceed to the sentencing stage.

---

25. Philip Otton, 'The Role of the Judge in Criminal Cases' in Mike McConville and Geoffrey Wilson (eds), *The Handbook of the Criminal Justice Process* (OUP 2002) 328.
26. Andrew Sanders, Richard Young, and Mandy Burton, *Criminal Justice* (4th edn, OUP 2010).
27. Lord Justice Auld, *A Review of the Criminal Courts of England and Wales* (HMSO 2001) 534–5.
28. [2005] EWCA Crim 1248.
29. [2019] EWCA Crim 2145.

15.6.2 **Trials on indictment**

In the Crown Court the verdict on guilt or innocence is in the hands of the jury and there are a number of procedural steps that arise in how this verdict is ascertained and reported to the court.

15.6.2.1 **Immediate steps**

The first step is that the judge directs the jury that they should elect a foreperson of the jury. The person who is elected becomes, in effect, the chair of the jury and will help structure their deliberations. The foreperson is the only member of the jury who will speak in court.

The second step is that the jury are told to ignore anything that they have heard about majority verdicts. A judge will explain that at least initially a unanimous verdict must be reached, this being to comply with the requirements of s 17 *Juries Act 1974* (JA 1974). The judge will explain when a majority verdict is appropriate (see 15.6.2.6).

15.6.2.2 **Jury bailiff**

The jury is placed in the charge of a jury bailiff who is an usher and who swears an oath to keep the jury in their charge, not to discuss the case with them, or to allow anyone to talk to the jury. The oath is not mere words and the bailiff is the only person who can speak to the jury outside of the courtroom while they are considering their verdict. This means that he should be in a position to stop anyone speaking to the jury, ie he should stay outside and guard the jury room.

The bailiff is, in essence, the conduit between the jury and the judge and if questions arise (see 15.6.2.3) it is the bailiff who alerts the judge and carries the question from the jury to the judge. In *R v Anderson and Mason*[30] the Court of Appeal stated that the jury bailiff must pass on all communications to the judge and not screen them, a point that was restated in *R v Finlayson*.[31] Interestingly in *Finlayson* the court held that if a single juror asked to write a note to the judge then the jury bailiff could direct that should not happen (as notes should come from the jury as a whole) but it implied, albeit *in obiter*, that if the note was actually passed to the bailiff then it would need to be passed on.

Whilst the bailiff is not entitled to be inside the room, he does have responsibility for ensuring that the deliberations occur at the correct time. In *R v Hastings*[32] a juror was always late to court after retirement. The Court of Appeal stated that the bailiff should have reminded the jury not to deliberate until all twelve members were present although they also noted that the ultimate responsibility for this lay with the judge.

15.6.2.3 **Questions**

The jury are not cut off from all contact and they have the right to ask questions if they wish clarification of either the law or evidence, or if they want to be reminded of evidence. The jury (normally the foreperson) will write the question and hand it to the bailiff. The bailiff will then pass the note to the judge who will normally convene the court and ask both counsel for their opinion on how to answer the question although the decision on how to answer is ultimately one for the judge. The jury will then be

---

30. 1990, unreported.
31. See [2012] EWCA Crim 1139.
32. [2003] EWCA Crim 3730.

brought into court and the answer given to them. No discourse is entered into and if this does not answer their question then the process is repeated.

15.6.2.4 **Improper considerations**

A problem that has become increasingly prominent in recent years is what to do where there is the suspicion that the jury have considered something improperly. It should be understood that the jury does not necessarily hear all the evidence in a case. The judge may rule that some facts are not admissible and cannot be put before the jury. Perhaps one of the most common facts withheld is whether the defendant has previous convictions. In these modern times it is increasingly easy to find out information that has not been presented to the jury.

A difficulty where there are allegations of improper deliberations is the secrecy of jury deliberations. This area was previously governed by the *Contempt of Court Act 1981*, but new offences were introduced in 2014. Section 74 *Criminal Justice and Courts Act 2015* amended the *Juries Act 1974* to create the offence of disclosing jury deliberations, thus making it a criminal offence to solicit, obtain, or disclose information about the deliberations of the jury.[33] This will be considered in more detail in Chapter 16. The general rule is that a court can inquire about potential improper deliberations before the verdict has been reached,[34] although it is conceded that it will be comparatively rare for the court to discover this before the verdicts are returned and the majority of reported situations have been considered on appeal.

It is also an offence for jurors to research the case or information relevant to the case during the trial period[35] and for jurors to share research with other members of the jury.[36] The consequences of failing to follow the judicial direction on behaviour and to introduce improper material can be serious. In *Attorney-General v Dallas*[37] the Attorney-General sought to commit the defendant, a juror, for contempt of court[38] as she had introduced inappropriate material into the jury deliberations. The defendant had been empanelled as a member of a jury who were called upon to try a person for grievous bodily harm with intent contrary to s 18 *Offences Against the Person Act 1861*. During the trial the defendant looked at the Internet, ostensibly because she did not understand the meaning of the word 'grievous' and then to conduct research on dangerous crime in Luton.[39] After the jury were sent out one of the jurors approached the jury usher and complained that the defendant had sought to tell them about the information she found on the Internet.[40] The defendant was kept separate and the foreperson of the jury was asked about the incident in open court and confirmed it. The jury were then discharged. The Divisional Court found that contempt of court was proven and the Lord Chief Justice, presiding, stated: 'misuse of the Internet by a juror is always a most serious irregularity and an effective custodial sentence is virtually

---

33. JA 1974, s 20D.
34. See *R v Mirza* [2004] 1 AC 1118 and JA 1974, s 20E. This remains the case even after the introduction of the 2015 reforms.
35. JA 1974, s 20A.
36. ibid, s 20B.
37. [2012] 1 WLR 991.
38. This was an offence under the *Contempt of Court Act 1981* before the Act was repealed by the *Criminal Justice and Courts Act 2015* and new offences introduced under the JA 1974, s 20.
39. *Attorney-General v Dallas* [2012] 1 WLR 991, 996.
40. ibid, 997.

inevitable. The objective of such a sentence is to ensure that the integrity of the process of trial by jury is sustained.'[41] The court sentenced the defendant to six months' imprisonment.[42]

⟳ QUESTION FOR REFLECTION

Is it realistic to expect members of the jury not to use the Internet and related resources to consider issues relating to the case? Given that witnesses give their name out in court, is there a danger that the jury could try to look up the witnesses and defendant on the Internet or social networking sites (eg Facebook)? Can this be avoided? Do you agree with the Lord Chief Justice that looking at the Internet undermines the 'integrity of the process of trial by jury'?

The Internet has led the courts to reconsider the warnings they issue to the jury. There is now a specific jury direction that must be given to the jury about attempting to conduct research on the Internet.[43] This has been reinforced by the fact that courts will now include notices specifically informing jurors that they are not to conduct their own research in the jury rooms, including the deliberation room.[44]

Continuing issues of juror misconduct have meant that judges now have the power to order that electronic communication devices are surrendered at court,[45] as well as being able to order court staff to search jurors in order to find electronic devices.[46] These powers were introduced under the *Criminal Justice and Courts Act 2015*, following recommendations made by the Law Commission on dealing with juror misconduct.[47]

It can be seen therefore that improper deliberations by a jury are considered serious by the criminal justice system and it will be interesting to see whether the offences and procedures outlined above mean that fewer jurors try to break the rules.

15.6.2.5 Deliberating for more than a day

Until 1994 a jury, once sent out to begin its deliberation, had to be kept together until they reached their verdict. In cases where the jury could not arrive at a decision on the first day they would be sequestered and taken to a hotel overnight. Section 43 *Criminal Justice and Public Order Act 1994* (CJPOA 1994) abolished the automatic application of this rule although it is important to note that a judge still has the discretion to order a jury to stay in a hotel overnight. Where the jury are permitted to disperse and go home for the night, the judge must warn them not to talk to anyone about the case.

One point to note about this direction is the swearing of the jury bailiff. The bailiff must be sworn each day because in order to permit the jury to be dispersed then the usher must be released from his oath, and accordingly each new day involves the usher being sworn in as jury bailiff in open court.

---

41. ibid, 1001.
42. Dallas complained to the European Court of Human Rights, alleging that her rights under Article 7 had been breached in relation to her conviction for contempt of court. Her complaint was dismissed by the Court (*Dallas v United Kingdom* (2016) 63 EHRR 13).
43. Discussed in *R v Thompson* [2011] 1 WLR 200, 205.
44. *Attorney-General v Dallas* [2012] 1 WLR 991, 995.
45. JA 1974, s 15A.
46. *Courts Act 2003*, s 54A.
47. Law Commission, *Law Commission Report No 340: Contempt of Court (1): Juror Misconduct and Internet Publications* (HMSO 2013).

Reconsider the earlier issue about the use of the Internet. If juries are now allowed to go home does this make it more or less likely that they could access the Internet for issues relating to the case? Also, is there a danger that the jury could talk about the case on, for example, Facebook or instant-messenger services?

15.6.2.6 Returning the verdict

The verdict will ultimately be for the jury to decide. Whilst it has been noted that a judge has the right to order the acquittal of a person the converse is not true and it is never permissible for a judge to direct a jury to convict.[48]

Unanimous verdict

Ideally the jury will return with a unanimous verdict. If they do then the clerk of the court asks the foreperson to stand and asks them whether they have reached a verdict upon which they all agree. Assuming that the answer is 'yes' then the clerk reads each count aloud and asks whether the jury finds the defendant guilty or not guilty. The verdict is then recorded.

Majority verdict

It was noted earlier that when a jury is first asked to retire to consider their verdict they are told that only a unanimous verdict will be permitted. However, it is also known that this is not always true and s 17 JA 1974 permits a majority verdict to be reached. Majority verdicts are controversial because some argue that it contradicts the burden of proof—if some of the jury cannot agree the guilt of the defendant then surely there must be some doubt and yet the standard of proof is 'beyond all reasonable doubt'.[49] The counter-argument, however, is that it is an insurance policy against intransigent jurors or 'nobbling' a jury by bribing a single juror.[50]

It is for the judge to decide when a majority verdict should be permitted but s 17 states that the minimum period of deliberation is two hours since they originally retired. The current *Criminal Practice Directions* repeat previous practice directions, which add ten minutes to this time to ensure there is no doubt as to compliance with the statute.[51] The argument is that the deliberation does not start until they reach the jury room and not as soon as they leave the court; the extra ten minutes is supposed to account for the time it will take to walk to and from the courtroom etc. However, it is important to note that this is merely a *minimum* time and in complicated cases this period of time may not be sufficient and in very serious cases judges have been known to continue with the requirement of a unanimous verdict for two or three days. Indeed nothing in the statute requires a judge to permit majority verdicts and the judge could, theoretically, decide that a case was not suited to one.

Section 17 JA 1974 states that the permissible majority depends on the size of the jury (bearing in mind that jurors can be discharged). The rules are set out in Table 15.3.

48. *R v Wang* [2005] UKHL 9.
49. Sean Doran, 'Trial by Jury' in Mike McConville and Geoffrey Wilson (eds), *The Handbook of the Criminal Justice Process* (OUP 2002) 396.
50. ibid.
51. *Criminal Practice Directions 2015* as amended May 2020 CPD VI 26Q.2.

Table 15.3 Permissible majority

Twelve jurors	11–1; 10–2
Eleven jurors	10–1
Ten jurors	9–1
Nine jurors	Must be unanimous

Receiving a majority verdict is quite complicated and it is set out in the *Criminal Practice Directions*.[52] The process can be summarized as follows. If the jury return before two hours and 10 minutes have elapsed:

- the foreperson stands
- the clerk of the court asks, 'Have you reached a verdict upon which you are all agreed? Please answer "Yes" or "No"'
- if the answer is 'No' then the judge sends them out again (or considers discharging them) for them to consider a majority verdict if they cannot arrive at a unanimous one.[53]

When the jury finally return:

- the foreperson stands
- the clerk of the court asks, 'Have at least ten (or nine if appropriate) of you agreed on a verdict?'
- if the answer is 'Yes' then the clerk says: 'What is your verdict?' Where there is more than one count on the indictment this process is repeated for each count
- if the foreperson says 'Not guilty' then the verdict is so recorded
- if the foreperson says 'Guilty' then the clerk asks: 'Is that a verdict of you all or by a majority?'
- the foreperson will (presumably) reply 'Majority'
- the clerk then asks: 'How many of you agreed to the verdict and how many dissented?'
- the foreperson provides the numbers but not the names.[54]

This convoluted process is designed to ensure that if an acquittal is reached nobody knows whether it was a majority verdict or not, whereas if it is a guilty verdict a check is built in to ensure that it is a valid majority verdict (and not, for example 7–5). The importance of this was reiterated by the Court of Appeal in *R v Turner*[55] where the clerk to the court asked the judge whether the acquittal was by majority, something the Court of Appeal said should not have happened.

52. ibid, CPD VI 26Q.
53. ibid, CPD VI 26Q.2–26Q.3.
54. ibid, CPD VI 26Q.4.
55. [2011] EWCA Crim 604.

547

⟳ QUESTION FOR REFLECTION

Not every jurisdiction permits a majority verdict, perhaps the most obvious example being America. Is it right to allow for a majority verdict? The argument against such a verdict is that the prosecution must prove guilt beyond all reasonable doubt. If one or two jurors do not believe that he is guilty how can it be said that there is no reasonable doubt since at least two members of the jury obviously doubted the evidence?

Are there any consequences to only allowing a unanimous verdict?

15.6.2.7 Failure to reach a verdict

It is quite possible that a jury will not be able to reach a verdict no matter how long they are given. The judge should give them as much time as possible to reach a decision but eventually there may come a time when the judge needs to ask whether, even if more time was given to the jury, they would be capable of reaching a verdict. At this time the judge will give what is known as a *Watson direction*,[56] which states that part of the jury oath is that if they are not able to reach a verdict they should say so. If the foreperson of the jury states that the jury is deadlocked then the jury can be discharged and a retrial is considered.

15.6.2.8 Perverse verdicts

It has been noted that each juror must swear 'to faithfully try the defendant and give a true verdict according to the evidence'. In the review of the criminal justice system, Auld LJ believed this did not always happen and that jurors would return what he categorized as 'perverse verdicts'.[57]

Auld admits that:

. . . there are many, in particular the Bar, who fervently support what they regard as the right of the jury to ignore their duty to return a verdict according to the evidence and to acquit when they disapprove of the law or the prosecution in seeking to enforce it . . . [58]

This is an interesting dimension of a jury trial. Nobody can order a jury to convict[59] and thus a jury could, if they so wished, decide to ignore the law and bring in a verdict for whatever reason they wish. Indeed the fact that juries do not have to give reasons for their verdict (something Auld noted was in itself extremely controversial),[60] means that it is sometimes impossible to decide why a jury reached a particular verdict. When the defendant is convicted this is something that can be corrected on appeal, especially where the verdict is inconsistent or clearly against the evidence (see Chapter 16 for further details on this), but what troubled Auld more was where the perverse verdict was an acquittal.

Auld noted that 'although juries may have the ability to dispense with or nullify the law, they have no right to do so',[61] and suggested that it was 'an affront to the legal

---

56. *R v Watson* [1988] QB 690.
57. Lord Justice Auld, *A Review of the Criminal Courts of England and Wales* (HMSO 2001) 173ff.
58. ibid, 173.
59. A principle forcibly restated in *R v Wang* [2005] UKHL 9.
60. Lord Justice Auld, *A Review of the Criminal Courts of England and Wales* (HMSO 2001) 168–73.
61. ibid, 174.

process'.[62] One reason for this statement was that since only 1 per cent of crime was heard by a jury, why should it be entitled to disapply the law when those subject to summary trial will not receive such favour?[63] On the other hand, this ability of the jury has long been considered a notable feature of the system and has attracted the label 'jury equity'.[64]

⚡ CLIVE PONTING

Perhaps one of the most famous examples of 'jury equity' is the case of Clive Ponting who was charged with breaching the *Official Secrets Act 1911*. Ponting was a senior civil servant in the Ministry of Defence and came across material that related to the sinking of the *General Belgrano*, an Argentine cruiser which was sunk during the 'Falklands War'.[a] The official version of events was that the *Belgrano* was a threat to the Royal Navy Task Force and was sunk near an exclusion zone. The documents that Ponting identified demonstrated that it had been sighted a day earlier and was steaming away from the Task Force.[b] Ponting passed these papers to a Labour MP who had been critical of the execution of the campaign.

As a matter of law this was a simple breach of the *Official Secrets Act 1911* yet the jury acquitted him. The defence was, in essence, that it was in the public interest and yet this would not afford any defence in law. However, this did not stop a jury from acquitting him.

a   The campaign colloquially known as the 'Falklands War' took place in 1982 when Argentinian military forces invaded the disputed Falkland Islands, a British colony. In fact although known as the 'Falklands War' this is not strictly accurate since war was not declared by either the United Kingdom or Argentina. Instead the military action took place under the auspices of the United Nations Convention.

b   Not that this would mean that it could not be counted as a threat to the Task Force. Whilst the sinking of the *Belgrano* remains controversial most military observers believe it was a legitimate military tactic but politically the sinking was handled badly.[65]

The difficulty with this 'jury equity' power is that in effect it means that the law laid down by Parliament is circumvented and observers have even suggested it 'sabotages crime control'[66] and others agree that it does have serious implications for the administration of justice.[67] Alternatively it can be argued that this is society deciding whether it wishes its laws (for laws are made on behalf of society) to be enforced in circumstances where they believe the 'greater good' should prevail. Mischievously a comparison to the public interest prosecution test (see 13.1.2.1) could be drawn. At the pre-trial procedure the prosecution may halt some crimes stating it is not 'in the public interest' for them to be prosecuted. One way of looking at 'jury equity' is to suggest that it is the jury saying that it is not 'in the public interest' for a person to be convicted. If the prosecution can

---

62.   ibid, 175.
63.   ibid, 174.
64.   Andrew Ashworth and Mike Redmayne, *The Criminal Process* (4th edn, OUP 2010) 301.
65.   The definitive statement of the sinking is given in Lawrence Freedman, *The Official History of the Falklands Campaign: Volume 2* (Routledge 2005).
66.   Andrew Sanders, Richard Young, and Mandy Burton, *Criminal Justice* (4th edn, OUP 2010).
67.   Sean Doran, 'Trial by Jury' in Mike McConville and Geoffrey Wilson (eds), *The Handbook of The Criminal Justice Process* (OUP 2002) 399.

decide it is not in the public's interest not to prosecute, why can't the public decide that it is not in the public interest to convict?

It should be noted, finally, that the government did not act upon Auld's recommendation and thus the principle of 'jury equity' is alive and well, although its controversiality remains untouched.

15.7 **Youth trials**

What has been discussed so far in this chapter is how trials take place for adults. However, a different system exists for youths (ie those who have not yet reached their 18th birthday) and it is necessary to briefly summarize this.

15.7.1 **The need for a separate system**

Why is it that youths should be treated differently from adults? This is not a particularly new concept, with youth courts first being created as a separate branch of the court system in 1908 (originally this was for those under the age of 16 but this was later extended to include those under 18). From the very beginning the youth courts sat at different times, and in different locations from the magistrates' court[68] in an attempt to ensure that young defendants did not mix with adult offenders.

Whilst youth courts are undoubtedly criminal in nature s 44 *Children and Young Persons Act 1933* states that the courts must 'have regard to the welfare of the child or young person'.[69] This is in line with the (later) requirements under the UN Convention on the Rights of the Child (see, for example, Article 40), but there is some doubt as to the extent to which this influences youth justice policy in reality.[70] This is perhaps particularly true in respect of the age of criminal responsibility which is set at 10 in England and Wales, an age that many find unreasonably low.[71]

The 1980s and 1990s led to a system whereby the serious and persistent offenders were treated more seriously but the so-called 'nuisance' offenders were dealt with in a less serious way.[72] The election of the New Labour government in 1997 led to significant changes to youth justice and, in particular, a more formalized approach. Whilst the welfare principle included within the 1933 Act was never repealed, the *Crime and Disorder Act 1998* stated that the 'principal aim' of the youth justice system should be to prevent offending by children and young persons.[73] It was suggested that this perhaps meant a more punitive approach should be adopted. This was combined with more formalized approaches to non-court disposals. Instead of police cautioning there was a defined system that incrementally responded to actions, with an informal warning only being permitted once, before more formal responses and ultimately the matter having to be referred to a court.[74]

---

68. Nicola Padfield and Jonathan Bild, *Text and Materials on the Criminal Justice Process* (4th edn, Routledge 2008) 404.
69. *Children and Young Persons Act 1933*, s 44(1).
70. Jane Fortin, *Children's Rights and the Developing Law* (3rd edn, OUP 2009) 710.
71. The competing issues in respect of this are discussed in Jane Fortin, *Children's Rights and the Developing Law* (3rd edn, OUP 2009) 684–93.
72. Nicola Padfield and Jonathan Bild, *Text and Materials on the Criminal Justice Process* (4th edn, Routledge 2008) 405.
73. *Crime and Disorder Act 1998*, s 37.
74. Jane Fortin, *Children's Rights and the Developing Law* (3rd edn, OUP 2009) 707.

Although the process has become more formalized, what has not changed is the belief that the systems should be separated and, as will be seen, the actual trial should not be as formalistic as an adult trial. The judgment of the ECtHR in *T and V v United Kingdom*,[75] which will be discussed later, has arguably strengthened this distinction and the clear presumption is that those under 18 should ordinarily be tried in the youth court.

15.7.2 **The youth court**

The 'default' court for dealing with youth crime is the youth court. This is a branch of the magistrates' court but, as will be seen, it has much greater powers. It also differs in a number of crucial ways from the traditional magistrates' court.

The key difference between the youth court and the magistrates' court is its informality. Whilst it is a formal trial, the courtroom is usually set out differently and the procedure will ordinarily involve more explanation so that the defendant can follow proceedings. The first point to note is that a youth court must have its own separate entrance. Whilst the youth court will, more often than not, be located inside an ordinary magistrates' court building, there should be a separate entrance that can be used to access the building together with separate waiting areas.[76] The idea behind this is to ensure that children are not forced to wait with adult offenders.[77]

The youth court is not a public court and so ordinary members of the public cannot attend (unlike the magistrates' court and the Crown Court). That said, the parents (or persons with responsibility for the child) will be permitted to attend and indeed where the defendant is under the age of 16 the parent must be present.[78] Whilst the media are able to attend proceedings of the youth court[79] they may not report the names and address of any offender without leave of the court,[80] and leave may only be given once an offender has been convicted; even then it will be only given rarely.

The layout of the youth court will often be more informal than a traditional court. The youth defendant will not appear in a dock but rather the offender will sit with his lawyer and, where appropriate, his parents or other supporters. This allows the young offender to follow proceedings more closely and is also supposed to ensure that the child is not objectified by sitting in a dock. It is usual in youth courts for everyone to sit on the same level, ie there is no raised dais upon which the bench would sit. The furniture is usually less formal too.

As with the magistrates' court, a youth court will ordinarily be presided over by three lay magistrates (known as a panel in the youth court rather than a bench) or by a single DJMC. Where the matter is presided over by lay magistrates the panel must contain at least one male magistrate and at least one female magistrate. Lay magistrates are given special training before they are permitted to sit on youth courts and they will normally be experienced magistrates before sitting. It is not uncommon for DJMCs to now sit and again these will ordinarily be specially trained. It is the responsibility of the judge or panel to ensure that the young defendant is able to follow the proceedings and this will include avoiding using legal language where possible and explaining the relevant terms and procedure.

---

75. (2000) 30 EHRR 121.
76. *Children and Young Persons Act 1933*, s 31.
77. *R (on the application of T) v Secretary of State for Justice* [2013] EWHC 1119 (Admin).
78. *Children and Young Persons Act 1933*, s 34A(1).
79. ibid, s 47.
80. ibid, s 49.

15.7.2.1 Jurisdiction

It will be remembered from Chapter 8 that the magistrates' court may only hear cases that are classified either as summary only or triable either-way (with the consent of the defendant). The youth court, however, has much wider jurisdiction and can hear matters that include indictable-only offences[81] although it has no jurisdiction where a juvenile is charged with homicide, in which case the matter must be heard in the Crown Court.

Where a child is charged alone or with another juvenile then the clear presumption is that they should be tried in a youth court and may only be sent to the Crown Court where it involves homicide or certain firearms offences.[82] The senior courts have been very clear that it should be rare for a trial not to proceed in the youth court. In *R (On the application of W) v Southampton Youth Court*[83] Lord Woolf CJ stated:

> There is no doubt that the general policy of the legislature is that young offenders should where possible be tried by a youth court. That is a policy which the courts should promote. It is obviously desirable that, where appropriate, young offenders should not be tried before the Crown Court unless this is clearly necessary.[84]

Lord Woolf continued by noting that where a child is particularly young then it may be more appropriate for the trial to proceed in the youth court irrespective of sentencing powers because of human rights considerations, particularly whether it will be possible to achieve a fair trial.[85]

15.7.2.2 Procedure

The procedure in the youth court is the same as that would occur in a summary trial and thus the steps presented in this chapter continue to be followed. That said, there are a couple of relatively crucial differences. The charges are still read to the defendant but they must be explained in language that the child understands. Similarly, the nature of the proceedings and what the process is going to be should also be explained to the defendant even when he is represented by a lawyer. This is to ensure that the court is satisfied that the child understands what is happening.

Where the young defendant is under the age of 14 then, if they testify, they will not testify under oath.[86] Even though the evidence is unsworn this does not prevent a person who lies while giving unsworn testimony from being charged with perjury although it would be somewhat rare for this to ever happen to a juvenile defendant.

The final subtle change between a trial in the magistrates' court and trial in the youth court is in respect of the decision. By statute, the term 'conviction' is not permitted[87] and instead the term 'guilty' is used, presumably because it is thought that children will understand what that means. Of course, in the adult magistrates' court it is more common to say the case is 'proved' or 'not proved', but in the youth court clarity and understanding is paramount and therefore guilty and not guilty should be used.

---

81. *Magistrates' Courts Act 1980*, s 24(1).
82. ibid, s 24(1B).
83. [2002] EWCA Civ 1640.
84. *R (on the application of W) v Southampton Youth Court* [2002] EWCA Civ 1640 [11].
85. ibid, [16].
86. *Youth Justice and Criminal Evidence Act 1999*, s 55.
87. *Children and Young Persons Act 1933*, s 59.

15.7.3 **The Crown Court**

As identified earlier, exceptionally youths can be sent to the Crown Court for trial. Unlike the youth court, where special processes and procedures are in place, there tend to be far less amendments to the Crown Court process, although following the ruling in *T and V v United Kingdom*[88] there are more adaptions than there were before.

‖ Case Box *T and V v United Kingdom*

One of the most important and controversial cases in this area was the decision of the ECtHR in *T and V v United Kingdom*.[89] This was a case that concerned Robert Thompson and Jon Venables, two 10-year-old boys who abducted and murdered a 2-year-old boy, Jamie Bulger.

The case provoked uproar in the general population and they were put on trial in the Crown Court at Preston. The ordinary rules of the Crown Court were followed in that it took place in open court and the defendants sat in a dock. The dock had been specially raised—so that the defendants could follow the proceedings—but this had the effect of making the defendants more visible and able to see the (hostile) public watching the trial.

The judge did make some concessions in an attempt to minimize the effect on the children. The trial followed school-day times (which the children would be familiar with) and a ten-minute break was taken every hour to allow a rest from the proceedings.

The ECtHR rejected the argument that it would always be unfair to subject 10-year-olds to a trial but they did state that Article 6(1) means that 'a child charged with an offence is dealt with in a manner which takes full account of his age, level of maturity, and intellectual and emotional capacities, and that steps are taken to promote his ability to understand and participate in the proceedings'.

The court continued: 'in respect of a young child charged with a grave offence attracting high levels of media and public interest, it would be necessary to conduct the hearing in such a way as to reduce as far as possible his or her feelings of intimidation and inhibition'.[90]

The court found that the raised dock, whilst done for the right reason, almost certainly raised the fears of the defendant and many of the arcane proceedings of the Crown Court would look strange and mean it was unlikely that 11 year olds (the age the defendants were when the trial started) could follow the trial. Accordingly, they held that there had been a breach of Article 6.

Whilst the ruling of the ECtHR provoked a political and popular storm of criticism, the courts took on board many of the comments and the then Lord Chief Justice, Lord Bingham, issued a practice direction specifically targeted at such trials.[91]

The Practice Direction includes a number of statements that demonstrate the willingness of the English courts to react to the decision in *T and V*:

> The trial process should not itself expose the young defendant to avoidable intimidation, humiliation or distress. All possible steps should be taken to assist the young defendant to understand and participate in the proceedings. The ordinary trial process should so far as necessary be adapted to meet those ends.[92]

---

88.   (2000) 30 EHRR 121.
89.   ibid.
90.   ibid, [87].
91.   *Practice Direction (Crown Court: Young Defendants)* [2000] 1 WLR 659.
92.   ibid, [31].

553

The Direction then lists a number of factors that should ordinarily occur, including the fact that pre-trial visits should occur so that the child is aware of the court, the police should attempt to bring the child to court in such a way as to minimize potential disruption, the trial should take place in a courtroom where everyone is on the same, or almost the same, level (as occurs in the youth court), the child should ordinarily not be in the dock, and the proceedings should be explained in a language that the child is used to. Robes and wigs should ordinarily not be used unless the young defendant wishes them (which mirrors the position that occurs with child witnesses), and the court should consider limiting the number and types of people allowed into the public gallery.

To an extent these would seem obvious steps but they were a major shift from how Crown Court proceedings ordinarily proceeded. That said, whilst it is clear that the Practice Direction sets out a number of steps that should ordinarily be followed, breaches of this will not necessarily be fatal to a case unless the reviewing court believes that the omissions are such that it causes the fairness of the trial to be brought into question.[93]

Auld LJ, in his report, had recommended that young defendants should no longer find themselves in the Crown Court. Auld believed that it would be preferable for a specially created youth court to be empanelled, it being presided over by a judge and specially trained magistrates.[94] This was rejected, in part because the three-tier court structure proposed by Auld was also rejected, but it must be questioned whether a distinction could have been drawn for young defendants. It has already been noted that the youth court has jurisdiction to hear matters that ordinarily would be heard by a jury. It is only a small step to state that any crime committed by a young defendant should be heard in the absence of a jury and, if there are concerns about the training of those in the youth court to deal with grave crimes, the solution, as Auld proposed, would be to introduce a senior judge into the process. Sadly there appears little likelihood of such proposals being introduced but it must be seriously questioned whether subjecting young defendants to a Crown Court trial, even when it is adapted along the lines of the Practice Direction, would be considered fair.[95]

⟳ QUESTION FOR REFLECTION

Auld LJ reported that in 2000 some 4,718 young defendants were sent to the Crown Court. Are you surprised that so many young people found themselves in the Crown Court? What is the justification for allowing offenders to appear in the Crown Court rather than a specially formed youth court?

15.7.4 Young defendants in the adult courts

For completeness it should also be noted that some young defendants will be tried in the adult courts. Of course technically the Crown Court, even when specially adapted, is an adult court but this part of the book addresses the fact that a child can find themselves in an ordinary adult court.

The youth court has jurisdiction to deal with youths. It therefore has no jurisdiction to deal with adults (although where it proceeds on the basis that D is a youth but later

---

93. See, for example, *R v H* [2006] EWCA Crim 853.
94. Lord Justice Auld, *A Review of the Criminal Courts of England and Wales* (HMSO 2001) 214.
95. See, for example, *SC v United Kingdom* (2005) 40 EHRR 10.

discovers that he is an adult they can decide to continue hearing the matter).[96] What is the position where a child is charged with a person who is obviously an adult?

☰ Example

Michael, aged 13, is charged with Alfred, aged 32, of theft. The particulars are that Michael caused a diversion in a supermarket, allowing Alfred to place a bottle of whisky in his coat.

In this example both Robert and Alfred would appear prima facie to be guilty of an offence under the *Theft Act 1968*. As Alfred is an adult he cannot be tried in the youth court. Theft is an either-way offence and assuming that both plead not guilty then it would seem likely that both Michael and Alfred will appear in either the (adult) magistrates' court (if both elect this) or the Crown Court.[97] If Michael pleaded guilty and Alfred not guilty (or vice versa for that matter) then the trials may be separated and Michael's could be heard in the youth court but where they both plead not guilty then they will appear together.

There is discretion where the defendants are not charged together but are charged as a result of the same circumstances.

☰ Example

Rebecca, aged 14, is charged with causing criminal damage. Sarah and Tina, both aged 32, are charged with being drunk and disorderly, affray, and assault occasioning Actual Bodily Harm. The particulars are that Rebecca meets up with Sarah and Tina, who she knows, and who have been drinking. Sarah and Tina start a fight with another girl and as they are being arrested Rebecca, who dislikes police officers, thinks it would be funny to throw a brick through the police car's window.

555

In this example Rebecca's liability is not dependent on the liability of Sarah and Tina. Whilst it all arguably comes from the same incident, it is possible to separate the liability of Rebecca, and statute provides the court with discretion to either hear the matter in the (adult) court (alongside the adult defendants) or to send the young defendant to the youth court for trial.[98]

↻ QUESTION FOR REFLECTION

Is it not unfair for a young defendant to be tried in an adult court in circumstances where, if they committed the crime alone, they would be tried in a youth court? What reasons do you think there are for not having two trials (one in the adult court and one in the youth court)?

---

96. *Children and Young Persons Act 1933*, s 48.
97. ibid, s 46.
98. ibid, s 18.

‹› Summary

In this chapter we have examined the trial process and identified the differences between summary trials and trials on indictment. In particular we have noted that:

- In the magistrates' court the tribunal of fact and law are the same—either the lay justices or the DJMC—whereas in the Crown Court the tribunal of law is the judge and the tribunal of fact is the jury.

- The prosecution always tenders its evidence first as this is an important part of the presumption of innocence. The defendant should only be required to call evidence when the prosecution have proved that there is a case to answer.

- Each witness that is called by a party will then be asked questions by the opposing side(s). This is known as cross-examination. There then follows a short period of re-examination by the side calling the witness but that is subject to rules restricting what can be asked.

- In a trial on indictment the jury will sum up the evidence to the jury, ie produce a summary of the evidence and direct them as to the type of questions they should ask. There is no equivalent in a summary trial.

- In a Crown Court trial the jury will retire, ie leave the court, to consider their verdict. In a summary trial it is likely that lay justices will retire but a DJMC is likely to give an immediate answer.

- It is not always necessary to reach a unanimous decision. In the magistrates' court the decision can be by majority (although no one will know) and in the Crown Court a majority verdict is also permitted but not when the jury first starts to deliberate.

❓ End-of-chapter questions

1. It has been seen that the primary role of the judge is to ensure that there is a fair trial and that the judge should not adopt the mantle of an advocate. However, an important aspect of that role is to allow advocates to put forward their case. Read *R v Lashley*[99] which is an extraordinary case where a judge becomes hostile to counsel. What do you think the jury and defendant would have made of this? Is it possible for it to be a fair trial in such instances?

2. Read Sean Doran, 'Trial by Jury' in Mike McConville and Geoffrey Wilson (eds), *The Handbook of The Criminal Justice Process* (OUP 2002) 398–9. Do you think it is right that a jury should be able to disapply the law, or is Auld LJ correct to say that it is 'an affront to justice'?

3. Is it realistic to expect jurors not to check the Internet when deciding a case? How will removing telephones etc from the jurors combat jurors looking at inappropriate material?

4. Read Jane Fortin, *Children's Rights and the Developing Law* (3rd edn, OUP 2009) 709–14. Can it ever be justified to try children in the adult Crown Court?

---

99. [2005] EWCA Crim 2016.

☰ Further reading

Darbyshire P, *Sitting in Judgment: The Working Lives of Judges* (Hart Publishing 2011) ch 8.

This considers the experiences of district judges (magistrates' court) while hearing matters in both the adult magistrates' court and also the youth court.

Doran S, 'Trial by Jury' in Mike McConville and Geoffrey Wilson, *The Handbook of The Criminal Justice Process* (OUP 2002).

This is an intelligent essay that highlights some of the controversial aspects of a trial on indictment.

Fortin J, *Children's Rights and the Developing Law* (3rd edn, OUP 2009) ch 18.

This chapter considers the treatment of young offenders and, in particular, how their rights under the UN Convention on the Rights of the Child are upheld (or not).

Thornton P, 'Trial by Jury: 50 Years of Change' [2004] *Criminal Law Review* 683–701.

This is an interesting piece that demonstrates how far trial by jury has altered in fifty years, particularly in respect of those who are entitled to sit on a jury.

For self-test questions, flashcards, and links to useful websites, please visit the **online resources** at: **www.oup.com/he/gillespie-weare8e/**

16

Criminal Appeals

By the end of this chapter you will be able to:

- Identify where appeals following summary trials and trials on indictment are heard.
- Distinguish between interlocutory and final appeals.
- Discuss the circumstances in which the prosecution may make an appeal.
- Explain how appeals are heard.
- Identify the powers an appellate court has.

Introduction

The previous chapters have identified how criminal trials take place. We have noted that there are two forms of trial: the summary trial which takes place in the magistrates' court and the trial on indictment which takes place in the Crown Court. However, the trial does not necessarily end the matter since in certain circumstances it is possible for either the defendant or prosecution to appeal against rulings of the judge.

This chapter will examine under what circumstances someone is entitled to appeal and how that appeal is heard. It completes our examination of criminal trials and will help place the duties and responsibilities of the appellate courts into context.

16.1 Summary trials or trials on indictment

It has been seen from the previous chapters that the law differentiates between summary trials and trials on indictment and this distinction continues with appeals. It will be seen that there are completely separate ways of dealing with appeals depending on the mode of trial, this distinction including even whether it is possible to appeal against matters of fact.

Figure 16.1 demonstrates the different paths that can be taken depending on the type of trial and these will be explored in the remainder of this chapter. The dotted line demonstrates the path an appeal from a summary trial takes and the solid line demonstrates the path an appeal following a trial on indictment takes. It can be seen that although some courts share jurisdiction the processes are quite distinct and accordingly will be discussed separately.

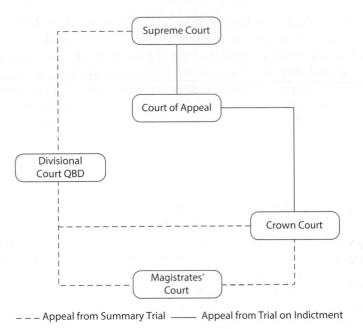

Figure 16.1 Appellate structure of the Criminal Justice System

16.2 **Appeals from a summary trial**

Figure 16.1 presents the appellate structure for summary trials and it can be seen that there are two possible avenues for an appeal from the magistrates' court: either to the Crown Court or to the Divisional Court. A third possibility also exists, that of judicial review (since the magistrates' court is an inferior body), but the courts prefer the matter to proceed on the basis of appeal by way of case stated as they argue that this is the more appropriate avenue.[1] That said, it remains an important method of appeal and the decision over which method to adopt is not always easy.[2]

16.2.1 **Appeal to the Crown Court**

The first appeal route is an appeal to the Crown Court. This is an opportunity that is restricted to the convicted defendant and is unique within the appellate system in that its form is not that of a legal argument but rather a complete rehearing. The appeal can be against sentence or conviction.

The appeal is permitted under s 108 *Magistrates' Courts Act 1980* (MCA 1980) and does not require leave (permission) to be granted; the appeal exists as a matter of right. The composition of the court when hearing the appeal is that a Crown Court judge (normally a circuit judge or recorder but theoretically a puisne judge could sit) presides with usually two lay justices. The judge is the tribunal of law and accordingly the lay

---

1. *R (on behalf of Stace) v Milton Keynes Magistrates' Court* [2006] EWHC 1049 (Admin) [13].
2. ibid, [15].

justices must take the law as directed by the judge. However, the judge has no veto in respect of decisions of fact where only a simple majority is required.

As noted earlier, the appeal takes the form of a complete rehearing, with all evidence being reheard (including the witnesses) and the decision made at the end of the trial. Theoretically the Crown Court could decide to remit the matter back to the magistrates' court for another hearing or for disposal regarding sentence, but usually the matter is dealt with by the Crown Court with the proviso that the powers of the Crown Court are the same as in the magistrates' court. However, that does not mean that a sentence cannot be increased: since it is a rehearing a person challenging his conviction could find that his appeal is dismissed and his sentence is actually increased. Ashworth and Redmayne argue that the ability to increase the sentence is unfair,[3] and certainly it is not comparable to the position that exists in respect of appeals from trials on indictment where the Court of Appeal has no such power (discussed later). Sprack argues that the provision is probably a tool by which appeals are discouraged,[4] but it is submitted that this is an inappropriate way of doing it: a person should not feel unable to challenge a conviction because they are afraid their sentence could be increased. A better approach would be to impose a leave requirement (16.3.1) whereby someone must convince a judicial officer that there is merit in an appeal.

Auld disagreed with this right of appeal to the Crown Court. He argued that it historically arose because there was suspicion about the competency of the magistracy[5] but he argued that this was no longer true, although it was seen in Chapter 8 that the position is arguably not so straightforward. A further argument advanced is that ordinarily the magistrates will provide reasons for their decision, and thus if there is a perception that they have acted in a way contrary to the law then an appeal by way of case stated could be brought.[6] This last point does have some weight to it. The existence of the right to a complete rehearing, purely on the basis that the defendant disagrees with the decision of the magistrates, is not replicated in respect of any other type of appeal which is based purely on an issue of law. It does have the appearance of being anomalous and can only be based on the premise of a lack of trust in the decision of magistrates. However, this is perhaps undermined by the fact that the right of appeal applies to any summary trial and thus includes trials conducted by a district judge (magistrates' court).

Auld suggested restricting appeals to matters of law and before a single judge.[7] This would have been controversial and somewhat unprecedented; appeals normally take place in front of at least two judges and this should (except for issues of leave) be retained for confidence. In any event the government rejected this proposal, or at the very least did not act upon it, and thus the current position is that the appeal to the Crown Court continues in the way that it always has. It is also undoubtedly the most popular method of appeal. In 2019, 7,831 appellants were dealt with in the Crown Court when appealing against decisions of magistrates' courts.[8]

3. Andrew Ashworth and Mike Redmayne, *The Criminal Process* (4th edn, OUP 2010) 340.
4. John Sprack, *A Practical Approach to Criminal Procedure* (15th edn, OUP 2015) 457, 27.13.
5. Lord Justice Auld, *A Review of the Criminal Courts of England and Wales* (HMSO 2001) 617.
6. ibid, 620.
7. ibid, 621–2.
8. National Statistics, 'Criminal court statistics (quarterly): January to March 2020 (tables)' <https://www.gov.uk/government/statistics/criminal-court-statistics-quarterly-january-to-march-2020> Table C8.

16.2.1.1 Subsequent appeals

For sake of completeness it should be noted that for matters of fact there is no appeal from the Crown Court when sitting in its appellate capacity, but where either the prosecution or defence wish to argue that it has made an error of law when determining the appeal then they can currently appeal by way of case stated.[9] The matter would be heard in the same way as though it was being stated by the magistrates' court, discussed later.

The Law Commission has argued that the right to appeal by way of case stated from the Crown Court should be removed.[10] The Law Commission argued that removing this appeal would simplify criminal procedure although they noted that it is relatively rare for such appeals to be made. They also noted that even if it were abolished then judicial review of the decision of the court (when acting in its appellate capacity) would still exist. The government has never accepted this proposal, presumably in part because it is used so rarely. That said it must be questioned whether there is a need for this 'additional bite of the cherry', and it would be preferable for offenders wishing to appeal against a decision of the magistrates to decide at the outset whether they wished the appeal to be premised on law (appeal by way of case stated), or fact (appeal to the Crown Court).

16.2.2 Appeal by way of case stated

The second form of appeal is to appeal to the High Court by way of case stated. This, as it will be seen, is a different species of appeal from appeal to the Crown Court and has more in common with other appeals. The first point to note is that both the prosecution and the defence can appeal by way of case stated,[11] and accordingly an acquitted person can find himself the subject of an appeal. This is an important distinction and it can be contrasted with appeals following a trial on indictment, where even with recent changes set out in the *Criminal Justice Act 2003* (CJA 2003) (see 16.4), it remains relatively rare for an acquittal to be reversed.

An appeal by way of case stated is where either party is arguing that the magistrates have made an error of law, and requires the magistrates to identify the case upon which they based their decision, ie the reasons for their finding. It is for this reason that it is known as 'case stated'. Along with this, they will identify a series of questions that they want the High Court to answer. Since the appeal arises out of a matter of law it is unusual for an appeal to relate to a sentence passed, as it would be rare for a court to pass an illegal sentence, but in exceptional cases such appeals have been brought, most notably in driving cases where the prosecution have sought to overturn a decision not to disqualify a driver.[12]

Any appeal must be lodged within twenty-one days of the determination by the magistrates and should initially be made by requesting the justices to state a case.[13] The magistrates can refuse to state a case although they should only do so where they believe

---

9. *Senior Courts Act 1981*, s 28.
10. Law Commission, *The High Court's Jurisdiction in Relation to Criminal Proceedings* (Law Comm Report No 324, 2010).
11. *Magistrates' Courts Act 1980*, s 111(1).
12. See, for example, *Haime v Walkett* (1983) 5 Cr App R(S) 165.
13. *Magistrates' Courts Act 1980*, s 111(2).

it to be frivolous.[14] In *R (on behalf of Miller) v Redbridge Justices*[15] the Divisional Court held that frivolous meant 'futile, misconceived, hopeless or academic'.[16] Where the justices do refuse to state a case, a right of appeal exists from this refusal, again to the High Court.[17] Technically that appeal is a judicial review,[18] not least because the remedy of the appeal is a compelling order, which is a traditional administrative law remedy (discussed more fully in Chapter 18).

Where a case is prepared it will initially be done in draft and this draft sent to both the appellant and respondent[19] for comment and, ideally, an agreement as to the nature of the case (ie what questions of law are raised) is made and then this case proceeds to the High Court for hearing.[20] The hearing is heard in the Administrative Court and normally takes place before at least two judges, making it a Divisional Court.[21] It is usual for at least one judge to be a Lord Justice of Appeal but it has become increasingly common for two puisne judges to sit and there does not appear to be any requirement for a Lord Justice to sit. It is not unusual in these cases for the judgment to be handed down immediately after the hearing although the court does have discretion to give judgment later. There are three options open to the court:

- dismiss the appeal
- allow the appeal and direct that the magistrates should convict or acquit the defendant[22]
- allow the appeal and remit it back to the magistrates' court for a rehearing before either the same or a new bench.[23]

A peculiar difficulty with an appeal by way of case stated is that as the constitution is ordinarily a Divisional Court of two members it is quite possible that the judges could be divided. Technically in these circumstances the rule is that the appeal fails.[24] There are circumstances when this could be considered unduly harsh, and in *Associated Lead Mills Ltd* Kennedy LJ stated that they considered relisting the matter for the consideration of a three-judge panel but decided not to do so in that particular case as they thought the point in principle was not sufficiently serious.[25] In 2012, however, the Divisional Court did just that. The Divisional Court was hearing an appeal by way of case stated by Paul Chambers who had been convicted under s 127 *Communications Act 2003* for sending a message that was grossly offensive, indecent, obscene, or of a menacing character by a public telecommunications network. Chambers had used Twitter to tweet a 'joke threat' to blow the airport up as he was upset that it had closed

---

14. ibid, s 111(5).
15. [2002] EWHC Admin 1579.
16. ibid, [14].
17. *Magistrates' Courts Act 1980*, s 111(6).
18. See *R (on behalf of Miller) v Redbridge Justices* [2002] EWHC 1579 (Admin).
19. The term 'respondent' continues to be used to indicate the party in the original proceedings (eg where the prosecution are appealing the defendant and vice versa) whereas technically, of course, it is the justices themselves who are responding to the appeal. However, the term probably continues out of ease of use and certainly both the original parties are represented at court whereas the justices ordinarily are not.
20. See, Ministry of Justice, *Criminal Procedure Rules* (Ministry of Justice 2018) r 35.3.
21. Technically, following the *Access to Justice Act 1999* any appeal by way of case stated does not have to go to a Divisional Court because the statute simply refers the matter to the High Court. However, as a matter of custom it will normally proceed before a Divisional Court and thus be heard by more than one judge.
22. This can be a partial appeal, ie the court could decide to vary the order of the magistrates.
23. See *Griffith v Jenkins* [1992] 2 AC 76.
24. *Cambridgeshire County Council v Associated Lead Mills Ltd* [2005] EWHC Admin 1627 [14].
25. ibid.

due to snow. His appeal to the Crown Court was rejected and he appealed by way of case stated, but it was reported that the two judges hearing the matter were divided and Gross LJ had ordered the matter to be relisted before three judges. The three-judge court ultimately decided that the conviction should be quashed.[26]

A further right of appeal exists from a decision of the High Court by way of case stated but only to the Supreme Court and only when it involves a point of public importance.[27] It is extremely rare for such appeals to be brought and in essence therefore the appeal by way of case stated will usually be the last stage of any appeal.

Unfortunately the courts no longer publish detailed statistics of the number of appeals by way of case stated, but the *Judicial and Court Statistics 2011* state that there were seventy-nine appeals by way of case stated, seventy-three of which were from the magistrates' court (the remaining six would be from the Crown Court). Of those appeals that were dealt with only 37 per cent were successful. It demonstrates that the number of appeals by way of case stated is small in comparison with the number of appeals brought before the Crown Court.

16.2.3 Judicial review

The third appellate route from the magistrates' court is to petition the High Court for a judicial review of the decision of the justices. This route arises because magistrates' courts are inferior bodies and thus subject to the supervisory function of the High Court[28] although, as will be seen, the courts prefer the matter to be heard by one of the other routes. This was perhaps set out most notably in *R (on the application of Clark-Darby) v Highbury Magistrates' Court*[29] where the court held that unless the matter was one where an allegation of natural justice was raised (eg a magistrate was biased and should have excused himself), then the normal recourse should be to appeal by way of case stated since that allowed the full reasoning of the magistrates to be set out before the appellate court for examination.

16.3 Appeal from a trial on indictment

Perhaps the appeals that are more readily visible are those that arise from a trial on indictment as these invariably concern the more serious offences. Apart from matters that do not relate to a trial on indictment, which will be discussed later, all appeals from the Crown Court proceed to the Court of Appeal (Criminal Division). This was created in 1966 and is a creature of statute[30] although it recognizes a progression from the original Court of Criminal Appeals.

The Lord Chief Justice is the President of the Criminal Division and this has remained true even after the reorganization of the judiciary.[31] In 1997 an honorary title of Vice-President of the Criminal Division was created, with Rose LJ being the first appointee. The *Courts Act 2003* (CA 2003) formalized this arrangement, albeit implicitly, by

26. *Chambers v DPP* [2012] EWHC 2157 (Admin).
27. *Administration of Justice Act 1960*, s 1.
28. See, for example, *R (on behalf of Stace) v Milton Keynes Magistrates' Court* [2006] EWHC 1049.
29. [2001] EWHC Admin 959.
30. *Senior Courts Act 1981*, ss 2 and 3.
31. *Constitutional Reform Act 2005*, s 7.

recognizing the term 'Vice-President' of either Division[32] but it remains, in effect, an honorary title and the holder is still formally styled a Lord (or Lady) Justice of Appeal[33] and does not receive any additional pay for the duties he discharges, nor is he classed as a 'Head of Division' (see 8.1.1.5). The current Vice-President is Lord Justice Fulford. That said, the Vice-President has important delegated authority given to him and is in de facto day-to-day charge of the Court of Appeal (Criminal Division). Apart from the Lord Chief Justice and Vice-President, the court is staffed by Lords Justices of Appeal and puisne judges asked by the Lord Chief Justice to sit (normally these will be judges of the Queen's Bench Division but they need not be and where the matter raises welfare issues it is possible a Family Division judge will be appointed). Since 1995 certain circuit judges have also been eligible to sit in the Criminal Division.[34] Previously they were restricted to sitting on appeals that were not heard at first instance by a puisne judge but this was abolished by the CA 2003. Also in any bench of the Court of Appeal only one circuit judge may sit,[35] although there is no restriction on the number of puisne judges who may sit.[36]

The Court of Appeal will normally sit in panels of three but they can sit in panels of five (known as a 'full court') for significant matters (normally reserved for the issuing of practice directions or where they seek to depart from precedent—see *R v Simpson*[37]). They may also sit in panels of two, although not where this involves the determination of an appeal against, inter alia, a conviction or unduly lenient sentence.[38] Auld argued that extending the power of a panel of two judges to include the determination of appeals against convictions could lead to greater efficiency in the court,[39] but this was rejected in part because of the dangers of a two-judge panel being divided. Whilst, as a matter of statutory law, such a split decision would lead to the rehearing before a three-judge court[40] this would lead to problems of delay, costs, and indeed added stress to a convicted appellant, especially where he is held in gaol.

16.3.1 **Leave**

There is no automatic right to an appeal to the Court of Appeal, one must get permission first. Two routes exist for the granting of leave to a convicted defendant who wishes to appeal against his conviction. The first is to seek permission from the trial judge and the second is to seek permission from the Court of Appeal itself.[41] It must be noted at the outset that the first course of action is extremely unusual, and indeed the Court of Appeal itself has stated that it should only be in the most exceptional circumstances that a judge certifies a case as fit for appeal, arguing that it should normally be for the judges of the Court of Appeal to grant leave.[42]

---

32. CA 2003, s 64.
33. CA 2003, s 63.
34. *Senior Courts Act 1981*, s 9 and *Criminal Justice and Public Order Act 1994*, s 52.
35. *Senior Courts Act 1981*, s 55(6).
36. In other words, theoretically at least a Division of the Court of Appeal could be constituted solely with puisne judges.
37. [2004] QB 118.
38. *Senior Courts Act 1981*, s 55(4).
39. Lord Justice Auld, *A Review of the Criminal Courts of England and Wales* (HMSO 2001) 646–7.
40. *Senior Courts Act 1981*, s 55(5).
41. *Criminal Appeal Act 1968*, s 1.
42. See, for example, *R v Bansal* [1999] Crim LR 484.

The most usual route is to ask the Court of Appeal for permission. The first stage in this process is deciding whether it is possible to appeal. Section 1 Criminal Appeal Act 1968 (CAA 1968) makes clear that a right exists against a conviction and this has led to the question over in what circumstances, if any, an appeal may be brought when a person has pleaded guilty, and thus has not been *convicted per se*. The Court of Appeal has adopted the approach of permitting an appeal to be brought where the plea of guilty was equivocal, ie where the defendant thought there was no other option but to plead guilty. This can arise from two principal reasons; the first is where the plea was made under duress,[43] and the second is where a judge has made a ruling in law which leaves the defendant with no other option but to plead guilty.[44]

Petitioning the Court of Appeal will normally lead to a 'single judge' considering whether to give leave. The single judge is a puisne judge and ordinarily each judge of the Queen's Bench Division will serve. All of the applications are on paper without any hearing. Auld noted that whilst some applications may be easy to dispose of, others will take a considerable period of reflection,[45] and yet no time is specifically allocated to the judges to undertake this task, with the vast majority of the applications being undertaken in the evenings or at weekends, particularly when the judge is sitting on circuit.[46] This has led some to question the consistency of single-judge decisions with the implication that pressure could lead to a cursory inspection.[47] That said, however, a right of appeal does exist from the refusal by the single judge and this is to the Court of Appeal itself although only a minority of applications will be accepted.[48] In 2018/19 there was a total of 1,078 applications for leave to appeal against conviction,[49] with 195 conviction appeals being heard.[50] Of those appeals against conviction that were heard, 32.8 per cent (sixty-four) of appeals against conviction were successful.[51]

16.3.2 **The hearing**

Assuming that leave is granted then the matter will proceed to a full hearing (although in some cases the leave and substantive issues will be rolled into a single hearing). Before arriving at the court a lot of procedural issues will have occurred, most notably counsel will be required to prepare 'skeleton arguments'. Despite their name, skeleton arguments are comprehensive documents that set out the arguments of both the appellant and respondents. The appellant will prepare their skeleton argument first and this will be served upon the respondents who will then have the opportunity to comment on it. This therefore forms the basis of the arguments, although Auld found that it was not unusual for skeleton arguments to be sent in late or amended,[52] and there is some evidence to suggest this continues today.[53] Counsel are able to depart from their skeleton argument and indeed may do so at the request of the judges.

---

43. *R v Turner* [1970] 2 QB 321.
44. *R v Clarke* [1972] 1 All ER 219.
45. Lord Justice Auld, *A Review of the Criminal Courts of England and Wales* (HMSO 2001) 639.
46. Penny Darbyshire, *Sitting in Judgment: The Working Lives of Judges* (Hart Publishing 2011) 294.
47. Andrew Ashworth and Mike Redmayne, *The Criminal Process* (4th edn, OUP 2010) 342–3.
48. ibid, 343.
49. Court of Appeal, In the Court of Appeal (Criminal Division) 2018–19 (Court of Appeal 2020) <https://www.judiciary.uk/wp-content/uploads/2020/02/LCJ-18-to-19-FINAL-PDF-1-1.pdf> Annex C.
50. ibid, Annex D.
51. ibid, Annex D.
52. Lord Justice Auld, *A Review of the Criminal Courts of England and Wales* (HMSO 2001) 643.
53. Penny Darbyshire, *Sitting in Judgment: The Working Lives of Judges* (Hart Publishing 2011) 332–3.

It is often said that the basis of an appeal remains the oral argument but even this has changed. Dunn, himself a former Lord Justice, commented that the traditional practice propagated by a senior Court of Appeal judge was:

> I like to come with an open mind to each case. So I never read anything about it, except glance at the judgment and the notice of appeal, before I go into court.[54]

The modern court will not adopt this approach. The judges will have read the papers in advance and one judge will ordinarily be tasked to write the judgment of the court. Interestingly Darbyshire sheds some light on how this decision is reached. Where the trial judge was a puisne judge then the Lord Justice will ordinarily give judgment; otherwise the Criminal Appeals Office proposes who gives it.[55] The judge who is to give judgment will take the lead on the questioning of counsel. The amount of work is increased where the judgment of the court is reserved (ie, instead of judgment being handed down immediately at the end of the case the judges adjourn for a period of weeks to allow them to conduct research and produce a written judgment that is then handed down).

Unlike an appeal by way of case stated, which is purely an argument as to law, the Court of Appeal has discretion to hear evidence although it is rarely exercised.[56] The principal reason why evidence is rarely heard is that the role of the Court of Appeal is not to conduct a trial but rather to review the trial at first instance, and this should not require them to hear much evidence. Indeed their power to hear evidence is effectively restricted to 'fresh evidence' which is defined as evidence that could not have been adduced at the original trial.[57] Where evidence is heard then the courts have to be careful as to what the purpose of the evidence is; it is not to assist the court in determining whether the appellant is guilty or not but rather whether his conviction is safe. It will be seen later that it does not necessarily follow that someone whose conviction is quashed did not necessarily commit the crime for that is a matter that only a trial at first instance, usually through the provision of a jury, can decide. Instead the purpose of the appellate court is to decide whether the conviction is safe or whether there is any doubt as to the guilt of a person; this will usually be found where the court finds that some evidential or legal rule would have affected the jury's deliberations, as at that point it cannot be predicted what the jury may have done.

⚡ WITNESS TESTIMONY

One interesting issue of distinction in the Court of Appeal is that where it decides to hear witness testimony it is quite possible that the court rather than any party will call the witness. In this case a member of the court will examine the witness (although this will not adhere to the principles of examination-in-chief) and then the person will be tendered for cross-examination. If the court decides that it does not want to call the witness but permits a party to adduce the evidence then the traditional pattern arises (see Tables 15.1 and 15.2).

---

54. Robin Dunn, *Sword and Wig: Memoirs of a Lord Justice* (Quiller Press 1993) 234.
55. Penny Darbyshire, *Sitting in Judgment: The Working Lives of Judges* (Hart Publishing, 2011) 336.
56. Andrew Ashworth and Mike Redmayne, *The Criminal Process* (4th edn, OUP 2010) 347.
57. *Criminal Appeal Act 1968*, s 23.

16.3.2.1 Improper deliberations by the jury

It will be remembered from Chapter 15 that there has been concern that some jurors use inappropriate material in their deliberations (15.6.2.4). This is a good example of when the Court of Appeal may need to receive evidence. Where the potential evidence of improper deliberation arises after the verdict has been given then it will be for the Court of Appeal to decide what, if anything, can be done. Sometimes it will be possible to ascertain whether there has been improper deliberation without looking at the deliberations of the jury. This could be because the deliberation took place where it should not have (perhaps the most notable example of this being *R v Young*[58]), or because the material shows a real risk of prejudice without needing to enquire into the deliberations of the jury. An example of this is *R v Karakaya*[59] where after the jury had returned a verdict in a rape trial, the jury usher found material that had been printed off the Internet and which must have been brought in by a juror. The material included inaccurate and controversial statements about how rape was treated within the legal system, and thus the Court of Appeal ruled that it was not necessary to consider how the material had been used, its very presence in the jury room showed that there was a real risk of prejudice which raised an issue as to the safety of the conviction.

> ### II\ Case Box *R v Young*
>
> *R v Young*[60] was one of the more unusual examples of improper deliberations. In the days when a jury was sent to a hotel overnight, the Court of Appeal accepted evidence that certain members of the jury had used a Ouija board to 'contact' one of the murder victims. The Court of Appeal quashed the conviction on the basis that the jury should not have been deliberating outside of the jury room.

The leading decision on whether a court can consider suspected improper deliberations is that of the House of Lords in *R v Mirza*.[61] *Mirza* was heard at the same time as another case—*Rollock*—and both related to letters received from jurors. Mirza did not speak English and instead relied on an interpreter. Despite being warned not to take this into account a juror complained that a number of jurors had convicted the defendant on racist grounds. In *Rollock* a juror complained that the majority had considered him and a co-defendant at the same time, and not, as instructed, separately. Again, a letter was written to that effect.

The House of Lords had the thorny issue of considering how these appeals should be disposed of without prejudicing the secrecy of jury deliberations. The House held there remained a rule that the courts will not receive evidence as to the deliberations of the jury, fearing that to do so would undermine the principle that a verdict ought to be final, but also as to do otherwise could interfere with the full and frank discussions that are essential in a jury trial. In both instances the House held that there was no evidence

58. [1995] QB 324.
59. [2005] EWCA Crim 346.
60. [1995] QB 324.
61. [2004] 1 AC 1118.

to show a lack of impartiality on behalf of the jury and so they dismissed the appeal, stating that the letters from the individual jurors were no more than an explanation of how the verdicts were reached and accordingly inadmissible.

Potentially this seems harsh, at least in *Mirza*'s case where, if the juror was correct, there was real bias on behalf of the jury and this would seem to be an abrogation of the jury oath to try matters fairly. This was picked up by the Court of Appeal in *R v Adams*[62] where they ordered an inquiry—and indeed then received witness evidence from the jury—in circumstances where there were allegations of bias. The Court of Appeal was clear *Mirza* did not prevent them from doing so,[63] partly because bias is a breach of the jury oath. This decision is to be welcomed and perhaps the better way of looking at the decision in *Mirza* was that the House of Lords was not convinced that there was sufficient evidence to show potential bias.

The House in *Mirza* acknowledged that there are exceptions to the exclusionary rule but that these are premised on the basis that the jurors acted on extraneous influences.[64] The question is how would this be proven? Obviously in the examples presented earlier—*Young* and *Karakaya*—there was clear evidence that external influences were applied and so this could be admitted without it breaching the exclusionary rule relating to jury deliberations. This will not always be possible, however. The other crucial point arising from *Mirza* was that the court itself does not breach s 8 by inquiring into the circumstances of how a jury deliberates. Thus the court can hear evidence, including from jurors themselves, if they believe that there are reasons to do so. In most cases this is impractical and where it is thought that there does need to be an investigation into the circumstances of the jury verdict—not what was said but how it was reached, ie whether there were any external influences—then the Court of Appeal relies on the *Criminal Cases Review Commission* (CCRC) to undertake this role.

Section 15 *Criminal Appeal Act 1995* authorizes the Court of Appeal to require the CCRC to make an investigation into any matter directed to it by the court. It is ordinarily an offence to disclose jury deliberations,[65] however under s 20F *Juries Act 1974* (as amended by the *Criminal Justice and Courts Act 2015*), it is not an offence to disclose information to the CCRC relating to juror deliberations where the offence of contempt of court may have been committed by a juror, or the conduct of a juror is such that it may provide grounds for appeal against conviction or sentence. The advantage of the CCRC conducting such investigations is that they are a statutory, independent body and are thus completely impartial from the case. It is obviously a sensitive matter to make these enquiries and the Court of Appeal is slow to direct the CCRC to do so. Indeed, in 2019/20 two such requests were made of the CCRC.[66]

In considering potential improper deliberations, the courts place considerable faith in the collective responsibility of jurors. In *R v Thompson*[67] the Lord Chief Justice stated

62. [2007] 1 Cr App R 34.
63. *R v Adams* [2007] 1 Cr App R 34, 460.
64. See, most notably, the opinion of Lord Hope in *R v Mirza* [2004] 1 AC 1118 at 1158.
65. JA 1974, s 20D.
66. Criminal Cases Review Commission, *Annual Report and Accounts 2019–20* (CCRC 2020) <https://s3-eu-west-2.amazonaws.com/ccrc-prod-storage-1jdn5d1f6iq1l/uploads/2020/07/CCRC-2329571-v1-CCRC_Annual_Report_and_Accounts_2019-20_Final_for_web.pdf> 30.
67. [2011] 1 WLR 200.

that where a juror did something outside of his oath—for example, stated expressly that he was going to decide the case on the basis of racial bias—then the other jurors should report that matter to the judge according to the directions given to them.[68] It can be questioned whether this is necessarily appropriate. The jury experience can be unusual and indeed unsettling for people, especially the formality of proceedings. Relying on jurors to go against one of their own and make a formal report to a judge may be placing too much reliance on the individual resilience of jurors. That said, it is difficult to see an alternative. In *Mirza* the House of Lords was concerned that investigating each allegation of impropriety could be unduly complicated, expensive, and potentially undermine the integrity of the jury. Certainly to do so would place considerable power in the hands of a single juror who could, for whatever reason, cast doubt on a conviction after a trial simply by writing a letter.

⟳ QUESTION FOR REFLECTION

How should the courts react when a juror suggests that the verdict may have been reached by improper processes? Are there dangers in investigating whenever a single juror does allege misbehaviour? If allegations are not examined, however, is there a danger that an injustice has happened but that the courts will allow it to pass in order to protect the 'greater good' of the jury trial?

16.3.3 Decision

It has been noted already that the purpose of the appellate court is *not* to decide the guilt or innocence of the appellant, although that is how it may be interpreted by some. The basis upon which the court should exercise its powers is to be found in s 2 CAA 1968 which states that the court shall:

> allow an appeal against conviction if they think the conviction is unsafe . . . and shall dismiss such appeal in any other case.

This simplified test was introduced in 1995 to replace a previous test that permitted a conviction to be quashed when the conviction was unsafe, unsatisfactory, based on an error of law, or where there was a material irregularity. Whether the change in test means anything substantively different, or whether it was simply codifying the original tests into one overarching test, has been the subject of debate since it was introduced. At the heart of the discussion is whether the Court of Appeal is able to act as suitable guarantor to prevent miscarriages of justice. In the 1970s to 1990s it would appear the answer was 'no' and some argue that the court was too ready to accept police evidence and too slow to accept allegations of corruption,[69] something that other authors have previously commented upon.[70]

---

68. *R v Thompson* [2011] 1 WLR 200, 203.
69. Andrew Ashworth and Mike Redmayne, *The Criminal Process* (4th edn, OUP 2010) 353.
70. For an illuminating potted history of how the miscarriages of justice in the 1980s led to a 'crisis' for the criminal justice system, read Richard Nobles and David Schiff, *Understanding Miscarriages of Justice: Law, Media and the Inevitability of a Crisis* (OUP 2000) 117–49, esp 124–8.

569

At its most basic, the new test shares with the old test the notion of the safety of the conviction and the Court of Appeal in *R v Graham*[71] stated:

> [The test] is plainly intended to concentrate attention on one question: whether, in light of any arguments raised or evidence adduced on appeal, the Court of Appeal considers a conviction unsafe. If the Court is satisfied that, despite any misdirection of law or irregularity in the conduct of the trial or any fresh evidence, that the conviction is safe, the Court will dismiss the appeal.[72]

Notwithstanding this, it is apparent that the conduct of the trial will be a central feature in any appeal and in *R v Togher*[73] the Court of Appeal decided that the new test effectively encapsulated the old tests, and that where there was a material irregularity this may lead to the safety of the conviction being undermined and requiring the appeal to be allowed. This case was distinguished in *R v Llewellyn*[74] although only to the extent that it was said that if the procedural error forming the basis of the appeal was known at the time of trial but not the subject of any objection then it should not normally form the basis of an appeal. To an extent this is an application of the usual rule that the Court of Appeal will not revisit issues that *should* have been addressed at first instance, but it can be argued that this is slightly harsh as there may be tactical reasons why counsel does not raise an objection at first instance.

In 2006 the government consulted on changing s 2 to prevent it quashing a conviction where the evidence suggested that the defendant was guilty despite any errors of law that had been made by judges.[75] The proposals were not welcomed but the government sought to introduce the change in the (then) *Criminal Justice and Immigration Bill*. The proposed clauses would have prevented the Court of Appeal from quashing a conviction where there was no reasonable doubt as to guilt. The clauses were not, however, supported in Parliament and they were withdrawn before the Act received Royal Assent.

16.3.3.1 **European Convention on Human Rights**

In Chapter 5 it was noted that the courts are expressly considered public authorities within the meaning of s 6 *Human Rights Act 1998* (HRA 1998) and accordingly this means they must give effect to the convention rights of an individual. Article 6 *European Convention on Human Rights* (ECHR) provides that everyone has the right to a fair trial. Whilst it was noted that Article 34 does not expressly form part of the 1998 Act[76] this is, in part, because HRA 1998 is considered to be the practical application of Article 34 and s 8 states that a court may provide 'such relief or remedy . . . within its powers as it considers just and reasonable' for a breach of the Convention. What should the remedy be for someone who has suffered an unfair trial? Should it quash the conviction even if the court considers that the person was, in fact, guilty? In other words, should a finding of a contravention of Article 6 automatically lead to a finding that a person's conviction is unsafe?

---

71. [1997] 1 Cr App R 302, 308 (Lord Bingham CJ).
72. [1997] 1 Cr App R 302.
73. [2001] 1 Cr App R 33.
74. [2001] EWCA Crim 1555.
75. Home Office, *Quashing Convictions—Report of a review by the Home Secretary, Lord Chancellor and Attorney-General: A Consultation Paper* (Home Office 2006).
76. Jason Coppel and Michael Supperstone, 'Judicial Review after the Human Rights Act 1998' [1999] 3 *European Human Rights Law Review* 301, 307.

The answer appears to be a qualified 'yes'. In *Togher* the Court of Appeal considered the impact of HRA 1998 and were clear that unfairness could undermine the safety of a conviction, something that the court had earlier stated in *R v Rowe, Davis and Johnson,*[77] which was an appeal that considered the safety of a conviction after the European Court of Human Rights (ECtHR) had considered that their Article 6 rights had been infringed.[78] However, Ashworth and Redmayne note that the position cannot be that simple and cite the example of Robert Thompson and Jon Venables, two schoolboys who were convicted for the murder of a toddler known as Jamie Bulger.[79] They note that the ECtHR had held that there had been a breach of Article 6 in respect of their trial,[80] but that it had never been seriously argued that they were *not* the killers or that the breach of Article 6 cast doubt on the safety of their conviction. They argue, therefore, that quashing a conviction need not be the appropriate remedy[81] and the courts have accepted this logic. In *R v Williams*[82] the Court of Appeal held that a breach of Article 6(2), breach of the presumption of innocence, would not automatically undermine the safety of a conviction. The submission of Ashworth and Redmayne together with the decisions of the Court of Appeal must be correct and are probably compatible with s 8 HRA 1998 which states that a court must provide the most effective remedy. Not every breach of Article 6 may necessarily require a conviction to be quashed in that this may not be the effective remedy where the safety of the conviction is not compromised; alternative remedies (eg financial compensation or a declaration that a person's rights have been infringed) may be more appropriate and in line with s 8. However, a finding of a breach of Article 6 (the right to a fair trial) must at least lead to the investigation of whether an appeal should be allowed given that the procedural process would appear relevant to the safety of any conviction.

16.3.3.2 'Lurking doubt'

It would be thought that s 2 CAA 1968 was quite specific and that given that the Court of Appeal is a statutory body it should not be able to go beyond the remit of its statutory jurisdiction. However, recently the court has begun to accept that it does have residual power and brought into effect a remedy previously used by the court for Criminal Appeals, that of quashing a conviction as a result of a 'lurking doubt'. In *R v B*[83] the court explained it thus:

> [T]here remains in this Court a residual discretion to set aside a conviction if we feel that it is unsafe or unfair to allow it to stand. This is so even when the trial process itself cannot be faulted.[84]

Thus the court is stating that even though statute sets out its jurisdiction it can continue to access the inherent jurisdictions of the court, in part because of its role as a senior court. This was not always the view it took and in *R v F*[85] a different constitution of the court held that the concept of 'lurking doubt' was no longer applicable following

---

77. [2001] 1 Cr App R 115.
78. See *Rowe and Davis v United Kingdom* (2000) 30 EHRR 1.
79. Andrew Ashworth and Mike Redmayne, *The Criminal Process* (4th edn, OUP 2010) 356.
80. See *T v UK; V v UK* (2000) 30 EHRR 121.
81. Andrew Ashworth and Mike Redmayne, *The Criminal Process* (4th edn, OUP 2010) 356–7.
82. [2001] EWCA Crim 932.
83. [2003] 2 Cr App R 13.
84. ibid, 204 (Lord Woolf CJ).
85. *The Times*, 20 October 1999.

the change to the single test for appeals. Smith, in an insightful commentary, questioned the decision in *F*, arguing that the single appellate test was simply codifying existing legislation and accordingly the 'lurking doubt' concept remained.[86] Certainly there is no reason why the single test should have abolished the 'lurking doubt' concept as the argument is that if the court have a doubt as to whether a person is guilty then his conviction cannot be safe. In *R v B*[87] and the Court Martial Appeals Court[88] it was stated:

> There can be no doubt that the lurking doubt notion . . . continues to be a tool available to this Court. It is plainly an application of the test of unsafety of a conviction, as it is now expressed in splendid isolation in section 2 of the Criminal Appeal Act 1968 as amended.[89]

This is the most accurate position and accordingly a court, even when faced with no apparent procedural impropriety, can set aside a conviction where it believes that it is in the interests of justice to do so.

16.3.4 **Frivolous appeals**

It was noted earlier that at Crown Court a person who appeals against either his conviction or sentence can have his original sentence increased (see 16.2.1). The Court of Appeal does not have this power as the ability to increase a sentence was abolished in 1966 with the formation of the Court of Appeal (Criminal Division). However, the court can order that time spent in gaol pending an appeal can be disregarded for the purposes of early release, in other words ensuring that a sentence is de facto increased as a result of appealing. This process is known as the 'loss of time' provisions.[90]

Zander notes that these provisions were used in the 1970s by the Lord Chief Justice to ensure that frivolous appeals were not brought.[91] There was an impression that the appellate rules were so relaxed that nothing was to be lost by appealing against a conviction, especially where the defendant had been imprisoned. If the gamble paid off the person would be released, whereas if it did not the person continued his or her sentence in prison. The use of the 'loss of time' provisions ensured that those in prison were more careful in bringing hopeless appeals as their sentence was, in effect, frozen during the appellate process even though they continued to be incarcerated. In the immediate years following the *Practice Note* the number of appeals almost halved,[92] but some question whether it is appropriate to use this power. Ashworth and Redmayne argue that the provisions serve as a de facto deterrent to an individual exercising their legal right[93] although the court would almost certainly contest this allegation noting that, in effect, no loss of time would be ordered where an appeal was brought on the advice of counsel,[94] the argument being that such appeals are not frivolous.

---

86.   John Smith, 'Commentary on *R v F*' [1999] *Criminal Law Review* 306, 307.
87.   [2005] EWCA Crim 63.
88.   In effect the Court of Appeal sitting under another name: the Court Martial Appeals Court hears appeals from courts martial, ie courts that try members of HM Forces for breaching laws while in service.
89.   [2005] EWCA Crim 63 [19] (Auld LJ).
90.   *Criminal Appeal Act 1968*, s 29.
91.   Michael Zander, *Cases and Materials on the English Legal System* (10th edn, OUP 2007).
92.   ibid.
93.   Andrew Ashworth and Mike Redmayne, *The Criminal Process* (4th edn, OUP 2010) 341.
94.   See *Practice Direction (Crime: Sentence: Loss of Time)* [1980] 1 WLR 270.

In recent times it has been suggested that the courts were reluctant to order loss of time. In *R v K*[95] the Court of Appeal noted, however, that the provisions are actually rarely invoked, with only four orders being made in 1998, two in 1999, none in 2000, and two in 2001.[96] It was not known why so few orders were given, whether it was the judges simply not using their power or whether it was concerns that the provisions could cause prisoners to be reluctant to risk an appeal.[97]

The Court of Appeal appears to have had a change of heart, however, and in 2014 quite publicly and forcefully stated that it would use its powers. In *R v Gray and others*[98] the Court of Appeal, presided over by the Vice-President, Hallett LJ, decided to remind everyone that the loss of time provisions applied. Hallett LJ stated: 'unmeritorious renewal applications take up a wholly disproportionate amount of staff and judicial resources in preparation and hearing time. They also waste significant sums of public money.'[99] Her Ladyship noted that whilst the court had the power to make an order for costs this was usually not effective[100] and that the more appropriate remedy is to order the loss of time served.

Hallett LJ was clear that 'in every case where the court is presented with an unmeritorious application, consideration should be given to exercising these powers'[101] and promptly did so in the series of cases that were presented. It is obviously an example of the courts losing their patience with offenders who simply try their luck with appeals.

It will be remembered that Ashworth and Redmayne disapprove of the loss of time rules and believe it is inappropriate but it is worth noting that the ECtHR has held that the 'loss of time' provisions do not breach either Articles 5 or 6,[102] although it should also be noted that the ECtHR accepted that Article 6 was engaged and, accordingly, representation as to the loss of time should be permitted. Ashworth and Redmayne disapprove of this decision,[103] but the decision appears to be a common-sense approach to the issue and recognizes that the courts should have the right to impose a 'sanction' on those who try to abuse the provisions.

16.3.5 The judgment

One point of note about judgments of the Court of Appeal is that, unlike civil appeals or civil or criminal appeals in the Supreme Court, only a single judgment is ordinarily given in the Criminal Division, particularly where the conviction is to be quashed. It has been reported that the reason for this is that the public should not be left in doubt as to whether the defendant is, in fact, guilty which may arise if it were a majority decision and the public were aware of the number of judges who believed the offender remained guilty.[104] It is also notable that most judgments are given *ex tempore* (that is to say orally immediately after the hearing rather than it being reserved) and this appears to be a deliberate policy so as to avoid further delays.[105]

---

95. [2005] EWCA Crim 955.
96. ibid, [18].
97. See Andrew Ashworth and Mike Redmayne, *The Criminal Process* (4th edn, OUP 2010).
98. [2014] EWCA Crim 2372.
99. ibid, [2].
100. ibid, [7].
101. ibid, [10].
102. *Monell v United Kingdom* (1988) 10 EHRR 205.
103. Andrew Ashworth and Mike Redmayne, *The Criminal Process* (4th edn, OUP 2010) 342.
104. Penny Darbyshire, *Sitting in Judgment: The Working Lives of Judges* (Hart Publishing 2011) 339.
105. ibid.

16.4 **Appeal following an acquittal**

Until recently the prosecution had extremely limited options open to them when faced with an acquittal at the Crown Court. To an extent it was thought that this was less problematic because of the usual rule of criminal justice that it is better for a guilty man to be acquitted than for an innocent man to be convicted and gaoled. There was also the additional issue that the vast majority of acquittals arise not from any error of law but as a result of a jury acquitting the defendant and it was thought that the jury had the right to acquit even when they thought, in law, a person was guilty because society has the right to decide when acts should be punished.

However, some trials will lead to an acquittal not because the jury have acquitted the defendant but because the trial judge has made a ruling of law that has the effect of terminating the case. It will be seen that there are two types of rulings: first, when a judge decides that the trial should be halted (eg upon a submission of no case to answer: see 15.2) and the second when a ruling by the judge as to the admissibility of evidence is such that the prosecution decides that it is no longer able to continue with the prosecution (and the prosecution are under a legal duty to continue to review the decision to prosecute during the course of the trial). It will be remembered that although the Crown Court does not create precedent, where a High Court judge sits his rulings of law can form persuasive precedent (see 3.4.1.5), and clearly there is a danger that if such a judge does make an error of law and this is cited to other Crown Court judges then a series of acquittals will arise with little opportunity for the appellate courts to correct this error of law.

Eventually, therefore, it was decided that there should exist a system of referring matters to the Court of Appeal and in 1972 the system of Attorney-General's References was created.[106] However, pressure grew for the system to be extended and the *MacPherson Report* into the tragic death and subsequent investigation of the murder of Stephen Lawrence recommended that consideration should be given to whether prosecutions should be permitted after appeal. The report identified two distinct areas: the first is the notion of 'double jeopardy' which prohibits a defendant from being retried for the offence he is acquitted of even if fresh evidence of his guilt comes to light. The second, and for our immediate purpose more relevant, was the notion of an appeal which could take place immediately after the acquittal in the same way as with appeals from conviction, a successful application for which would lead to an immediate retrial. The government asked the Law Commission to consider this and in a report[107] they recommended there should be a partial relaxation of both rules. Auld LJ, in his report, followed this up by suggesting that the rules should be relaxed but he went further since here the Law Commission thought the rule should be restricted to murder alone. Auld argued for a more widespread relaxation.[108]

Eventually the government legislated to introduce a (limited) right of appeal through the CJA 2003. However, the right of appeal has not interfered with the right of the Attorney-General to bring a reference to the Court of Appeal and thus both will be considered.

---

106.   CJA 1972, s 36.
107.   Law Commission, *Law Commission Report No 267: Double Jeopardy and Prosecution Appeals* (HMSO 2001).
108.   Lord Justice Auld, *A Review of the Criminal Courts of England and Wales* (HMSO 2001) 633–4.

16.4.1 **Reference to the Court of Appeal**

As noted earlier, the Attorney-General has had the right to refer a matter to the Court of Appeal since 1972. This type of reference differs quite radically from the sentencing reference in that although both require a specified offence and the personal approval of a Law Officer, the reference following acquittal takes the form of a de facto hypothetical appeal.

The outcome of the reference will make no difference to the acquittal of the defendant; even if the Court of Appeal agrees that the judge made an error of law and that he should never have been acquitted, the person will remain acquitted and protected from any subsequent trial for the same offence. Although the statute does not expressly say so, it is submitted that where the prosecution refers a matter to the court, rather than use its new powers under the CJA 1988, it would be unjust to allow the prosecution subsequently to use its powers to apply for the removal of the restriction of double jeopardy (see 16.4.3) unless new issues are raised that could not have been considered at the time of trial. To do so would be unjust since the prosecution could have appealed instead of referring the matter to the court.

What is the point of a referral to the Court of Appeal if it does not lead to any change in the status of the acquittal? The simple answer is one of precedent: whilst the ruling of a High Court judge may be persuasive for other judges, a ruling of the Court of Appeal is binding on the trial courts and it can thus ensure that any error of law can be corrected. This is, therefore, an important way of correcting the law following a dubious decision of first instance. It is important to note that the problem must be real, ie arising from a case, and it has been held that there is no power for the Attorney-General to refer a purely hypothetical point of law.[109]

Auld believed that even the extension of prosecution rights of appeal would not remove the justification for Attorney-General's References[110] and this must be correct. There will be any number of reasons why an appeal from an acquittal may not be possible, not least the safeguards built into the system (see 16.4.3) and the impact it could have on an *individual* defendant and the Attorney-General's Reference system continues to be the most appropriate system for dealing with such matters.

16.4.2 **Prosecution rights of appeal**

Granting prosecution rights of appeal has been somewhat controversial even though it has long been accepted for those tried summarily. One objection to the granting of such a right is because of the distress that could be caused to a person acquitted to then have the possibility of a conviction held over him, but this is to an extent a false argument. Notwithstanding the point about magistrates' courts it completely ignores the reality of the pre-CJA 2003 appellate system. If a person had been convicted at the end of his trial and imprisoned but successfully appealed to the Court of Appeal he would have his conviction quashed and be released from prison. If, however, the prosecution appealed to the (then) House of Lords (something they were entitled to do; they were simply not permitted to appeal to the Court of Appeal), and the House overturned the acquittal, then the defendant was obliged to surrender himself to custody and serve his sentence.

109. *Attorney-General's Reference (No 4 of 1979)* (1980) 71 Cr App R 341.
110. Lord Justice Auld, *A Review of the Criminal Courts of England and Wales* (HMSO 2001) 637.

For completeness it should be noted that this remains the case today—the prosecution are able to appeal to the Supreme Court where they believe that the Court of Appeal has erred in law when quashing a conviction.

The scheme contained within Part 9 CJA 2003 marks a radical departure from the historical position although not as radical as had been suggested. Auld was concerned with the issue of 'perverse acquittals' which he took to mean those where a defendant was acquitted in circumstances that were clearly contrary to the evidence presented.[111] However, this was denounced by many groups, not least because juries represent society and have the right to decide whether people deserve punishment,[112] and the government rejected this proposal. Part 9 contains two distinct appeals: appeals against terminal rulings and appeals against evidential rulings. The Act also expressly states that no appeal can be brought against a decision of the judge to discharge a jury or against any ruling where a right of appeal exercisable by the prosecution already exists.[113]

16.4.2.1 Terminal rulings

The first, and perhaps most controversial, change is that the prosecution can appeal against certain terminal rulings. Dennis notes that the term 'terminal ruling' has always been used when describing this provision even though CJA 2003 does not itself use this specific term.[114] However, it is a good summary of what the position is as s 58 permits an appeal to be brought against a decision to accept a submission of no case to answer, or a ruling that would inevitably lead to the acquittal of a person. That it will lead to an acquittal is implicit within s 58(8)–(9), which states that if leave to appeal is refused or the appeal is abandoned or unsuccessful then the defendant will be formally acquitted. The essence of this condition (discussed later) is that the prosecution would only appeal a ruling that leaves them in the position of offering no evidence against the defendant (which will lead to his acquittal), as to do otherwise risks the offender being acquitted in any event.

The prosecution must at the time of the ruling they believe will be terminal, either indicate that they are going to appeal or request an adjournment so as to consider an appeal.[115] In *CPS v C*[116] the Court of Appeal held that the requirements under s 58 were mandatory, and thus if the prosecution are denied an adjournment to consider their options they must *immediately* indicate to the judge that they intend to appeal, *and* must provide the assurance under s 58(8) that they agree that if the appeal is unsuccessful then the defendants are to be acquitted. If either of these steps does not occur then there is no jurisdiction to hear the appeal.[117] In *R v M*[118] the necessity of strictly adhering to these steps was reinforced by the Court of Appeal. In this case a judge acceded to a submission of no case to answer. Counsel for the prosecution asked whether the judge had borne in mind a particular statutory provision and the judge replied 'yes' and then immediately indicated to the defendant that he was to be discharged. There then

---

111. ibid, 636.
112. Liberty, Liberty's Briefing on the Criminal Justice Bill for the House of Lords (Liberty 2003) 94.
113. CJA 2003, s 57.
114. Ian Dennis, 'Prosecution Appeals and Retrial for Serious Offences' [2004] *Criminal Law Review* 619, 624.
115. CJA 2003, s 58(4).
116. [2009] EWCA Crim 2614.
117. See also *R v LSA* [2009] EWCA Crim 1034.
118. [2012] EWCA Crim 792.

followed an adjournment of ten minutes after which the prosecution stated they wished to appeal against the terminatory ruling. The Court of Appeal held that the procedure within s 58 had not been satisfied and that immediately meant just that: counsel for the prosecution should have immediately asked for an adjournment to consider the possibility of an appeal or instantly complied with the requirements of s 58, the ten minutes that elapsed were fatal to any possible appeal.[119] One possible reason for this decision is that the judge had adjourned adjudicating on the submission of no case to answer overnight and so counsel for the prosecution could have anticipated losing the submission and potentially on what grounds.[120] M reinforces the decision of C that prosecuting counsel must be aware of the need for speed in deciding whether they can appeal and that the procedural requirements must be complied with precisely.

If an appeal is to be brought then it is possible that the appeal could be expedited.[121] The Act suggests that only when an appeal is not to be expedited can a jury be discharged,[122] but it is submitted that this must be read in the context of the general powers of trial judges which include the dismissal of a jury when it is not possible for a person to gain a fair trial. The purpose behind this is no doubt to ensure that lengthy trials are not started again if the prosecution appeal succeeds (if the appeal fails then, of course, no jury will be required as the defendant is acquitted), but it must be seriously questioned whether a jury could continue. Whilst they cannot, presumably, be told that an appeal has been lodged (as that would appear to be highly prejudicial) the Act does not make clear what an 'expedited' appeal is. If the expedited appeal takes longer than a few days then it is submitted that a jury will inevitably speculate as to why the trial has been adjourned for a period of several days or weeks. It has been speculated that one reason for this power is that the ruling may be in relation to only certain counts on the indictment and, therefore, the trial could take place on counts not related to the appeal.[123] This would only partially solve the problem as there would no doubt be speculation, but judges are used to telling juries that a count has been withdrawn from them. The difficulty is, however, that this would ordinarily lead to a formal acquittal and thus a knowledgeable jury would be able to identify why a count has been withdrawn rather than the defendant being formally acquitted of it. It would seem more straightforward to discharge the jury pending any appeal and this would be the more likely scenario.

The Court of Appeal has three options open to it when determining an appeal:[124]

- **Uphold the ruling**. This will lead to the acquittal of the defendant on those counts that are affected by the ruling.

- **Reverse the ruling**. If the court does this then it may order that the trial is resumed or started afresh with a new jury.

- **Vary the ruling**. It may be that the prosecution are only partially successful. When this happens the Court of Appeal has the right to decide whether to acquit the defendant or to order the trial to continue/begin again.

577

---

119. ibid, [28].
120. ibid, [29].
121. CJA 2003, s 59.
122. ibid, s 59(3).
123. Richard Taylor, Martin Wasik, and Roger Leng, *Blackstone's Guide to the Criminal Justice Act 2003* (OUP 2004) 88.
124. CJA 2003, s 61.

Unlike in respect of appeals by defendants, the Court of Appeal has a much more limited discretion in deciding whether to overturn a ruling; it may only do so when it is wrong in law, involved an error of law, or was irrational[125] (this draws an immediate comparison to judicial review[126]). These requirements certainly restrict the use of the power because irrational is a high threshold; merely disagreeing with the decision or preferring an alternative decision will not suffice.

The Court of Appeal was only permitted to order the resumption of a trial or order a fresh trial when it considered that it was in the interests of justice to do so. The *Criminal Justice and Immigration Act 2008* (CJIA 2008) amended this provision and now requires the Court of Appeal to only acquit the defendant when it is satisfied that an offender could not receive a fair trial if the matter was resumed or a new trial resumed.[127] However, the Court of Appeal, albeit *in dicta*, has suggested that the interests of justice remain valid. In *R v A*[128] the Court ruled that whilst Parliament has altered s 61(5), it is notable that the Court of Appeal must grant leave (permission) before an appeal may be brought. The court suggested that the wider interests of justice must be considered when deciding whether to permit leave to be granted.[129] Their Lordships suggest that if it would never be in the interests of justice for a new trial to take place then leave will simply not be granted. On a semantic level the decision is correct in that leave is required and this is frequently granted or denied after a full hearing, but it would also seem that this is an attempt by the Court of Appeal to circumvent the intentions of Parliament. Such an approach could not be taken if, as with most defence cases, the issue of leave was dealt with separately to the determination of the appeal.

Perhaps surprisingly no statistics are published on the use of the power under s 58, and so it is not possible to state how many applications for leave are made and how many applications are successful. It would obviously be of interest to those within the justice system if such statistics were published and there would seem no reason why the CPS or the *Court Statistics (Quarterly)* could not make this available.

16.4.2.2 **Evidentiary rulings**

The second type of appeal is that which relates to evidentiary rulings. It should be noted here that the sections relevant to evidentiary rulings in the Criminal Justice Act 2003 are not yet in force, however, we will still consider these provisions. This type of appeal owes its background more to Auld as the Law Commission had rejected the idea of an appeal against anything other than a terminatory ruling.[130] However, s 62 permits evidentiary rulings to be appealed in certain circumstances. There are a number of differences between s 58 and s 62 appeals. The first is that the range of offences is more limited. Section 58 appeals can be brought in any case tried on indictment whereas s 62 appeals can only be brought in those cases that have been prescribed.[131] The second is that the appeal can only be brought in respect of a ruling that takes place before the opening of the defence case[132] and this, in effect, limits the matter to rulings on

---

125. ibid, s 67.
126. Ian Dennis, 'Prosecution Appeals and Retrial for Serious Offences' [2004] *Criminal Law Review* 619, 624.
127. CJA 2003, s 61(5).
128. [2008] EWCA Crim 2186.
129. ibid, [9].
130. Ian Dennis, 'Prosecution Appeals and Retrial for Serious Offences' [2004] *Criminal Law Review* 619, 624–5.
131. CJA 2003, sch 4.
132. ibid, s 62(2).

prosecution applications, although the vast majority are likely to be dealt with at the Plea and Directions Hearing stage. The third, and perhaps most significant, is that there is no requirement that the evidential ruling would be a terminal ruling: indeed if the result of the evidential ruling was to cause the acquittal of the person then it is more likely that s 62 would be the more appropriate appeal. That said, an appeal is only possible where it significantly weakens the prosecution case[133] although quite what this means in practice is open to interpretation.[134]

The final difference between the sections is that an unsuccessful appeal will not automatically lead to the acquittal of the defendant. The Court of Appeal has the right to uphold, vary, or reverse the ruling made by the trial judge, and can decide whether to allow the trial to continue or start again.[135] It may only acquit the defendant where the prosecution state that they do not wish the prosecution to continue,[136] presumably in circumstances where the Court of Appeal either upholds or varies the ruling.

Areas of similarity between ss 58 and 62 are that appeals may be expedited[137] and the grounds upon which the Court of Appeal can determine the appeal remain the same.[138]

It has been suggested that the case for the prosecution rights of appeal is strong[139] and, since they are restricted solely to decisions of the law by the judge, this is probably true. Trial judges are not immune from mistakes and if, as has been suggested, the purpose of the criminal justice system is to enforce the criminal law,[140] then the public have the right to expect that mistakes that occur before the final determination of an appeal can be put right. The prosecution are sometimes thwarted by perverse or incorrect rulings and until now had no avenue available to them: the defendant would be acquitted. It was difficult to identify how that necessarily served the best interests of the criminal justice system.

16.4.3 Double jeopardy

At the time of plea, a person can enter two special pleas known as *autrefois convict* and *autrefois acquit*, that being the person has previously been tried and either convicted or acquitted. Traditionally this was a barrier to any subsequent proceedings, but CJA 2003 has altered this position and it is now possible for a person who has previously been acquitted to be retried for the offence. This differs from a prosecution appeal in two ways. The first is that it is not an immediate remedy in the way that an appeal is. Where the prosecution believe that a judge has erred in law and that this resulted in the termination of proceedings prior to the jury retiring, then the more appropriate response will be to use the powers under Part 9 CJA 2003 (see 16.4.2). The second is that a person can be retried even if it was the decision of a jury to acquit the defendant whereas an appeal is only possible from decisions by the judge.

---

133. ibid, s 63(2).
134. Ian Dennis, 'Prosecution Appeals and Retrial for Serious Offences' [2004] *Criminal Law Review* 619, 622.
135. CJA 2003, s 66.
136. ibid, s 66(2)(c).
137. ibid, s 64.
138. ibid, s 67.
139. Ian Dennis, 'Prosecution Appeals and Retrial for Serious Offences' [2004] *Criminal Law Review* 619, 626.
140. Ian Dennis, 'Rethinking Double Jeopardy: Justice and Finality in Criminal Process' [2000] *Criminal Law Review* 933, 945.

It has to be recognized that the proposals to modify double jeopardy were, and are, extremely controversial as it was considered to be a long-standing freedom,[141] although, interestingly, it is not an absolute right in terms of either the ECHR or the EU *Charter of Fundamental Rights*.[142] The pressure for reform of the rule appears to stem from the *Macpherson Report* into the death of Stephen Lawrence.[143] Stephen Lawrence was a black teenager who was murdered in an unprovoked racist killing. The subsequent investigation by the police was flawed and led to the acquittal of those who were accused of his murder. The Macpherson Inquiry examined all issues surrounding the case, including allegations that the police themselves were racist in the handling of the investigation, and also the conduct of the prosecution. Recommendation 38 of the *Macpherson Report* suggested that the protection of double jeopardy should be removed. This was followed by a Law Commission report which held that there was an arguable case for the restriction of the right of double jeopardy but only to murder. This, in turn, was examined by Auld in his review of the criminal justice system and he ultimately questioned why the power should be restricted to murder and argued for a wider restriction.[144] Ultimately this led to the introduction of the power contained in Part 10 CJA 2003.

It is important to note that the double jeopardy rule is not totally abrogated as it applies only to specified offences (although the number of offences is extremely wide and can be added to without the need for primary legislation).[145] Also, it is not just for the prosecuting authorities to decide to bring a new prosecution; they must first seek permission to do so and for the acquittal to be, in effect, quashed.[146] The application must be brought with the personal consent of the DPP[147] and is heard by the Court of Appeal (Criminal Division).

The language of the statute appears to suggest that the Court of Appeal has little say in whether the acquittal should be quashed, with s 77(1)(a) stating that if the conditions are met, then the court 'must make the order applied for'. However, it is not necessarily so straightforward since the second of the two conditions is that it is in the interests of justice for the acquittal to be quashed.[148] This quite clearly provides the court with discretion as they can take almost any matter into consideration when deciding what is in the interests of justice. In tandem with this is the first condition which is that an acquittal can be quashed only where there is 'new and compelling' evidence to suggest that the acquittal should be set aside.[149]

It has been suggested that the need for compelling new evidence is directly linked to the justification for permitting an exception to the double jeopardy rule in that new evidence may cast doubt on the efficiency of the criminal justice system.[150] In other words,

---

141.   See, for example, Liberty, *Liberty's Briefing on the Criminal Justice Bill for the House of Lords* (Liberty 2003) 15–16, and Ian Dennis, 'Prosecution Appeals and Retrial for Serious Offences' [2004] *Criminal Law Review* 619, 619.

142.   Ian Dennis, 'Prosecution Appeals and Retrial for Serious Offences' [2004] *Criminal Law Review* 619, 636–7.

143.   Richard Taylor, Martin Wasik, and Roger Leng, *Blackstone's Guide to the Criminal Justice Act 2003* (OUP 2004) 96–7.

144.   Lord Justice Auld, *A Review of the Criminal Courts of England and Wales* (HMSO 2001) 631–4.

145.   Richard Taylor, Martin Wasik, and Roger Leng, *Blackstone's Guide to the Criminal Justice Act 2003* (OUP 2004) 100–2.

146.   CJA 2003, s 76.

147.   Ian Dennis, 'Prosecution Appeals and Retrial for Serious Offences' [2004] *Criminal Law Review* 619, 626.

148.   CJA 2003, s 79.

149.   ibid, s 78.

150.   Ian Dennis, 'Rethinking Double Jeopardy: Justice and Finality in Criminal Process' [2000] *Criminal Law Review* 933, 945, and Ian Dennis, 'Prosecution Appeals and Retrial for Serious Offences' [2004] *Criminal Law Review* 619, 631.

new evidence (eg, DNA evidence which was perhaps unavailable at the time of the trial)[151] may demonstrate that the criminal justice system has failed a victim and society, and that if the purpose of the criminal justice system is to enforce the criminal law then perhaps such a tainted acquittal should be quashed in the same way that a tainted conviction is.[152] Setting aside the objections to any interference with double jeopardy this point is well made. Whilst there are many reasons why the quashing of a conviction will be preferable to the quashing of an acquittal, it cannot be doubted that there have been some acquittals that, for any number of reasons, are extremely dubious, especially where the criminal justice system appears to be as faulty as it did at the height of the miscarriages of justice era. The more salient question, however, is whether this justification can permit a draconian change to a fundamental right to the finality of a trial.

It is clear from the wording of the statute that the procedure is considered to be exceptional, and the fact that there are so many stages to any retrial perhaps demonstrates this. In terms of new evidence, it has been noted that although this takes the form of evidence that was not *used* at trial, the suggestion is that the mere oversight or negligence of a prosecutor in not using the evidence at the trial would not be sufficient to justify quashing an appeal.[153] The Act does not, however, require the court to consider whether this would have an impact on the acquittal,[154] and to this extent it may be contrasted with, for example, appeals against conviction by a convicted person where the court must consider the safety of the conviction. However, it is submitted that the court will undoubtedly consider this issue when considering the 'interests of justice' as the potential impact of the evidence must, it is submitted, be a factor.

A criticism of the proposal to relax the rule of double jeopardy was that it could undermine the finality of decisions, leaving those acquitted with the constant nagging worry that they would never be left in peace by the authorities.[155] However, the Act includes two quite significant safeguards (independent of those discussed earlier) against repeated investigations. The first is that the timing of any application to quash an acquittal is crucial since, by statute, the prosecution may only make an application against an acquittal once.[156] It is important to note that the statute expressly states only one *application* and not one order quashing the conviction. Accordingly, if the application is rejected then that is the end of the matter even if, in future years, further compelling evidence is adduced. Similarly, if the retrial ends in a further acquittal (other than in circumstances whereby a prosecution appeal under Part 9 of the Act can be brought) then no further applications can be brought. The second is that investigations into the acquitted persons are constrained by the Act.[157] The Act restricts the power of arrest, search, and seizure in connection with an acquitted person, permitting it only with the written application of the DPP. Further, the application can only be made by someone of chief-officer rank,[158] which ensures that only the most significant cases are likely ever to be the subject of any application.

151. Richard Taylor, Martin Wasik, and Roger Leng, *Blackstone's Guide to the Criminal Justice Act 2003* (OUP 2004) 105.
152. Ian Dennis, 'Rethinking Double Jeopardy: Justice and Finality in Criminal Process' [2000] *Criminal Law Review* 933, 945.
153. Ian Dennis, 'Prosecution Appeals and Retrial for Serious Offences' [2004] *Criminal Law Review* 619, 633.
154. ibid, 634.
155. Liberty, *Liberty's Briefing on the Criminal Justice Bill for the House of Lords* (Liberty 2003) 15.
156. CJA 2003, s 76(5).
157. ibid, s 85.
158. ibid, s 85(4).

> ### ▌▌ Case Box William Dunlop
>
> The first application under Part 10 CJA 2003 was made in November 2005 when the DPP gave personal consent to apply to the Court of Appeal for an order quashing the acquittal of William Dunlop for the murder of Julie Hogg.[159] The murder of Julie Hogg had been a cause célèbre in the North-East of England and, to an extent, the wider United Kingdom for many years. Dunlop had been accused of the murder and had stood trial twice, testifying each time (denying the allegation), but the juries could not reach a conclusion and he was formally acquitted.
>
> In 2000 he was charged, and convicted, of perjury following a confession he made to a prisoner that he did, in fact, kill Hogg. In 2005 the DPP applied to the Court of Appeal presumably, in part, on the basis that the 'confession' was new and compelling evidence (it has been suggested that admissions by defendants are likely to be fruitful forms of new evidence).[160]
>
> The application was granted and in 2006 Dunlop pleaded guilty to murder and became the first person to be convicted of an offence having previously been acquitted. In October 2006 he was sentenced to life imprisonment.

One issue that will need to be raised in any subsequent trial will be, what will the jury be told? In simple (immediate) retrials it is not uncommon for the jury not to be told anything about the original trial. Where there has been a significant gap (eg the Court of Appeal has quashed a conviction and ordered a retrial) then it is often the case that juries are directed as to the fact that there was an original trial but not to take this into account. What will the position be here? Berlins argues that a difficulty here is that if the jury are aware of the test for quashing an acquittal (new and compelling evidence) then they may question how they could ignore this evidence and not consider it so compelling as to convict, but does that not turn the jury into a rubber-stamp?[161] It could be argued that the jury will not know that this is the test, but given that juries may now include members of the criminal justice system in their ranks this cannot be guaranteed, so how should a jury be directed? As yet there is no guidance on this point. In reality, however, it may well be that it is academic because the quashing of an acquittal will lead to a guilty plea on the basis that the defence will realize that it has no answer to the 'compelling' evidence.

16.4.3.1 **Retrospectivity**

It has been noted that the first case to be referred to the Court of Appeal seeking the quashing of an acquittal related to a murder committed in 1989 and this demonstrates an important aspect of the provisions, that being that they are retrospective. To an extent it is easy to see why this is the case: the very nature of the pressure leading to the interference with double jeopardy would imply retrospectivity, but this is a significant departure from the usual rule that criminal laws cannot be retrospective.

---

159. CPS, *DPP Refers William Dunlop Case to Court of Appeal as First under Double Jeopardy Law, CPS Press Release*, 10 November 2005.
160. Ian Dennis, 'Prosecution Appeals and Retrial for Serious Offences' [2004] *Criminal Law Review* 619, 633.
161. Marcel Berlins, 'Clarify Jury's Role Under Double Jeopardy Law' *The Guardian* (2005) <https://www.theguardian.com/society/2005/nov/14/penal.law>.

It has been noted that the argument against retrospectivity is, in effect, the same as the arguments against the provision itself,[162] and that the approach is likely to be compliant with the ECHR because the issue is whether the person knew *at the time of the conduct* that it was illegal,[163] which they would. Part 10 CJA 2003 does not render conduct that was lawful in the past unlawful under new laws but rather applies only when a person was acquitted of committing a crime then. On that basis it can be argued not to be an interference with Article 7 ECHR. Any conviction will be based upon the substantive law then (although evidential changes since the trial will be implemented), and any punishment will be based on the maximum sentence at the time the offence was committed and not based on any changes that have been brought about since the acquittal.

The powers under Part 10 CJA 2003 have been rarely exercised. Care is taken in choosing the cases, which perhaps explains why in a clear majority of cases the application has been granted. Their rarity demonstrates that the courts and the CPS are reluctant to step beyond double jeopardy and that an acquittal will ordinarily be the end of the matter, save where there are strong public interest considerations that the acquittal amounts in itself to a miscarriage of justice.

16.5 Appeal against sentence

It is not just a conviction that will give rise to an appeal: the sentence imposed by a court can also be the subject of review. Sentencing is perhaps one of the most crucial aspects of a criminal trial as it is gives rise to emotions surrounding the proper disposition of a convicted person. Sentencing has usually marked one of the principal battlegrounds between politicians and the judiciary and is certainly an area where the legislature has increasingly become involved. This was perhaps best demonstrated in mid-2006 when a furore erupted over the sentencing of sex offenders (see, for example, the case of 'Sweeney'[164] and *Attorney-General's Reference (Nos 14 and 15 of 2006)*).[165] Over the past decade there has been an increase in 'mandatory' sentences where Parliament has sought to limit the discretion of judges, although these have been robustly contested by the courts who have normally found reasons justifying an exception where they believe the interests of justice so require.[166] Against this background it is not surprising that sentences give rise to appeals and it is also notable that since 1988 the prosecution has a limited right to appeal against sentences, this being perhaps indicative of the political reality of sentencing.

16.5.1 Appeal by convicted person

The more usual appeal is that which is brought by the defendant. The defendant, when considering an appeal, is perfectly entitled to bring an appeal against both conviction *and* sentence even though this is the equivalent of saying: 'I did not do it, but if I did do it, I was sentenced too harshly!' Leave is required to appeal against sentence

---

162. Richard Taylor, Martin Wasik, and Roger Leng, *Blackstone's Guide to the Criminal Justice Act 2003* (OUP 2004) 105.
163. ibid, 106.
164. Alisdair Gillespie, 'Reviewing Unduly Lenient Sentences' (2005) 10 *Archbold News* 5.
165. [2006] EWCA Crim 1335.
166. See, for example, *R v Blackall* [2005] EWCA Crim 1128.

in the same way as with an appeal against conviction. In 2018/19 3,356 applications for leave to appeal against sentence were received, of which 672 (20 per cent) were allowed.[167]

Whereas appeals against conviction will normally be dealt with by a panel of three judges, the same is not true of appeals against sentence and indeed it is more common for an appeal to be heard by two judges. This increases the number of potential panels of the Court of Appeal (Criminal Division) that can sit on these matters.

In the same way that an appeal against conviction is not an exercise of the appellate court deciding whether they would have reached a different conclusion, an appeal against sentence is not examining whether a sentence was imposed correctly. Sentencing is perhaps more difficult in that in connection to a conviction it is possible to decide factors that may undermine the safety of a conviction, whereas a sentence must reflect the individual characteristics of an offender. Sentencing is often said to be more of an art rather than a science,[168] meaning that it is not possible to produce a mathematical formula to decide what an appropriate sentence must be. Accordingly, unless the sentence is illegal or procedurally flawed then the court must decide whether the judge could properly have reached his decision.

The two particular areas that the court concentrates on are the factual basis upon which a sentence was imposed and whether it is manifestly excessive.

16.5.1.1 **Factual basis**

A particular problem with convictions in the Crown Court is that it is not always clear what the factual basis is upon which a person is convicted. The reason for this is that sometimes a person will, as a matter of law, have committed an offence but the manner in which a person has committed the offence will make a significant difference to the sentence.

Example Grievous bodily harm

Causing grievous bodily harm is an offence contrary to ss 18 or 20 of the *Offences Against the Person Act 1861* (depending on the *mens rea*) and is committed by the infliction of grievous (meaning 'really serious') bodily harm.

Let us take an example. Derek is accused of causing grievous bodily harm to Paul after they had been fighting. The prosecution case is that Derek attacked Paul in an unprovoked manner and stamped on Paul's head. Derek denies this and says that he attacked Paul after he had called him names, and that he had hit and kicked him.

Derek cannot deny that he is guilty of grievous bodily harm but, since stamping is an aggravating factor[169] and provocation may be a mitigating factor, if he were to be sentenced on the basis of the prosecution case he could expect a more severe penalty than if he were sentenced on the basis of the facts put forward by the defence.

167. Court of Appeal, *In the Court of Appeal (Criminal Division) 2018–2019* (Court of Appeal, 2020) Annex F.
168. See, for example, *Attorney-General's Reference (No 77 of 1999)* [2000] 2 Cr App R(S) 250, 252 (Rose LJ).
169. See *Attorney-General's Reference (No 59 of 1996)* [1997] 2 Cr App R (S) 250.

How should a court resolve the matter? It was seen earlier that where the matter is by plea then the court has a number of options open to it. The most appropriate is that a written basis of plea is tendered (if the prosecution disagree with this basis then they could seek to try the defendant) and this, therefore, sets the factual background upon which a judge should sentence.[170] The other alternative is that where a jury returns a verdict of guilty the judge can, after hearing all the evidence, decide what the likely facts accepted by the jury are.[171] This is the more complicated scenario, however, and the judge must make clear that not only is his assessment consistent with the jury's verdict, but also that he expressly states the factual basis of the sentence.[172]

In these situations the Court of Appeal will simply examine whether the judge was entitled to assume the factual basis upon which he acted and whether the sentence was accurate in light of those facts.

16.5.1.2 Manifestly excessive

The most usual ground cited by appellants is that the sentence imposed by the judge is 'manifestly excessive' and should be reduced on appeal. 'Manifestly excessive' is not contained within statute but has been the traditional approach by the Court of Appeal to reviewing sentences on appeal and continues, in part, because of the doctrine of precedent. It is also a useful mechanism by which to ensure that too many appeals are not sent to the court and reinforces the point that sentencing is an art not a science.

The general basis upon which the court will act is to decide upon a range of sentences for which a person convicted of a crime is subject to, and normally to interfere only when the matter is outside of this range. A classic example of this can be provided by the *dicta* of Ackner LJ (as he then was) in *R v Waddingham*[173] when he differentiates between an excessive sentence and a severe sentence,[174] the point being that a tough sentence within the range of discretion by the sentencing judge cannot be interfered with. In *R v Bibi*[175] the Court of Appeal argued that they tried to achieve a consistency of approach rather than of precise mathematical comparisons, and that accordingly the starting point is to identify the range and then to examine the aggravating and mitigating features.

Mitigation is the usual way in which the Court of Appeal will alter a sentence, usually arguing that a judge has not given sufficient credit for a particular factor. However, the Court of Appeal is entitled to take account of information that the sentencing judge did not have available to him, and it is not unusual for it to refer to how the person has behaved in prison pending his appeal (although this was strongly disapproved of in *Waddingham*[176]).

16.5.2 Unduly lenient sentence

Prior to the system of prosecution appeals the only substantive appeal the prosecution had was in connection with unduly lenient sentences. The right of the senior appellate courts to increase sentences upon appeal was removed in 1966 with the establishment of the Court of Appeal (Criminal Division) (now incorporated in s 11(3) CAA 1968), but this was

170.   *R v Kesler* [2001] 2 Cr App R(S) 126.
171.   *R v Solomon and Triumph* [1984] 6 Cr App R(S) 120.
172.   See, for example, *R v Ibrahima* [2005] EWCA Crim 1436.
173.   (1983) 5 Cr App R(S) 66.
174.   ibid, 69.
175.   [1980] 2 Cr App R(S) 177.
176.   (1983) 5 Cr App R(S) 66, 69.

soon regretted and in 1972 Dr David Thomas, perhaps the leading authority in the field of sentencing, called for a power to review lenient sentences.[177] During the 1980s there was increased concern over the consistency of sentencing.[178] In fact the issue of sentencing has perhaps been the most controversial topic, in part because it demonstrates the tension that will invariably exist between the elected politicians and the judiciary, especially when media attention focuses on individual cases. Eventually the pressure led to the government introducing a scheme whereby the prosecution could refer certain offences to the Court of Appeal for re-sentencing where it was thought that the sentence was 'unduly lenient'.

The statutory power for this provision is contained within ss 35 and 36 of the *Criminal Justice Act 1988* and it provides a power for the Attorney-General to refer an unduly lenient sentence to the Court of Appeal, but only if it is a qualifying sentence, meaning an offence that is triable only on indictment or is prescribed by statutory instrument for this purpose.[179] The latter has proved quite controversial in part because the list of prescribed offences has not kept pace with statutory reform; for example none of the either-way offences contained in the *Sexual Offences Act 2003* was prescribed until two years after the Act came into force.[180]

The Attorney-General or his deputy, the Solicitor-General, must examine each complaint personally,[181] even though members of their legal secretariat (qualified lawyers) will have reviewed the cases and provided a summary. It must be seriously doubted whether this is actually necessary. Given that the DPP has been given the authority to seek the leave of the Court of Appeal to appeal against an acquittal (see 16.4) it seems an absurd waste of time to demand that the law officers give personal consent and the jurisdiction could easily be exercised by the Crown Prosecution Service.

⚡ THE LAW OFFICERS

The Attorney-General (A-G) and his deputy, the Solicitor-General (S-G), are known as the 'Law Officers'. The S-G is by virtue of s 1 *Law Officers Act 1997* the formal deputy of the A-G and can perform any of his functions.

The A-G and S-G are political appointments and are members of one of the Houses of Parliament. The current A-G and S-G are members of the House of Commons (Rt Hon Suella Braverman QC and Rt Hon Michael Ellis QC MP respectively) but in the last Labour government, Lord Goldsmith was A-G while also being a member of the House of Lords.

Traditionally if the A-G or S-G are not already Queen's Counsel upon appointment this distinction will be given to them. Although the term Solicitor-General implies otherwise, the first solicitor to hold the post of S-G was the Rt Hon Harriet Harman QC who was appointed in 2001 (and was appointed QC at the same time). Prior to that time all holders of the post were barristers.

As political appointees the Law Officers must resign when asked by the Prime Minister to do so and/or when the government falls. Neither is of cabinet rank although the A-G will attend cabinet when required. Although political, the primary role of the A-G and S-G is to be the principal legal advisers of the government and they act apolitically when performing their legal functions.

---

177.   DA Thomas, 'Increasing Sentences on Appeal: A Re-examination' [1972] *Criminal Law Review* 288.
178.   Stephen Shute, 'Prosecution Appeals against Sentence: The First Five Years' (1994) 54 *Modern Law Review* 745, 746.
179.   CJA 1988, s 35(3).
180.   See *Criminal Justice Act 1988 (Reviews of Sentencing) Order 2006*, SI 2006/1115.
181.   Hansard, HL Deb, vol 653, col 882 (14 October 2003) (Lord Goldsmith).

It is important to note that even if the matter is a qualifying offence it is not certain that an offence will be altered; the sentence must be 'unduly lenient'. Theoretically leave is required from the Court of Appeal to bring such an appeal, but in *Attorney-General's Reference (No 24 of 1991)*[182] the Court of Appeal indicated that it was administratively preferable for the substance of the matter and the leave to be heard at the same time.[183] This, however, confuses the substantive challenge and the requirement for leave and undoubtedly causes delay and wasted court time.[184]

An illustration of the meaning of 'unduly lenient' can be found in *Attorney-General's Reference (No 4 of 1989)*,[185] where the Court of Appeal stated that they would not interfere with a sentence merely because they would have imposed a different penalty, saying:

> A sentence is unduly lenient . . . where it falls outside the range of sentences which the judge, applying his mind to all the relevant factors, could reasonably consider appropriate.[186]

The requirement to have regard to the range of sentences undoubtedly sets the threshold reasonably high: the sentence must be outside the normal range of sentences. This can be contrasted with the appeal against sentence by the defendant where the court is prepared to interfere at a much lower range. Even if the court does decide that a sentence is unduly lenient any alteration of the sentence is discretionary.[187] Accordingly the Court of Appeal could decide that it is not going to interfere with a sentence irrespective of the fact that it is unduly lenient.[188]

Controversially, the Court of Appeal argued that there was an element of 'double jeopardy' involved in a prosecutorial appeal in that a prisoner faces the trauma of being re-sentenced. This invariably led to a discount being awarded and the courts stated that this was especially relevant where a person is to be imprisoned after initially having been handed a non-custodial sentence. It is possible to see the justification for a discount under these circumstances, but it is less easy to justify the discretion when an offender is already incarcerated, where all that is being discussed is the length of incarceration and not the possibility of being deprived of liberty once again.[189] Persons subject to an unduly lenient sentence have been convicted of a specified offence and the sentence imposed was one that was outside the usual range of sentences, ie almost certainly less than that which the person had expected to receive. Is any trauma caused in such circumstances?

The government believed that giving a discount for 'double jeopardy' was wrong, especially in the most serious offences. The CJIA 2008 amended the law so as to preclude a discount for 'double jeopardy' being given where the sentence imposed is a discretionary life sentence (mandatory life sentences were already exempt from this principle by the CJA 2003) or certain other sentences, most notably imprisonment for public protection. Where a determinate sentence is being reviewed, however, the principle still exists and the court continues to give a discount.[190]

---

182. (1992) 13 Cr App R(S) 724.
183. ibid, 725–6.
184. Alisdair Gillespie, 'Reviewing Unduly Lenient Sentences' (2005) 10 *Archbold News* 5, 8.
185. (1990) 90 Cr App R 366.
186. ibid, 371 (Lord Lane CJ).
187. Alisdair Gillespie, 'Reviewing Unduly Lenient Sentences' (2005) 10 *Archbold News* 5, 9.
188. See, for example, *Attorney-General's Reference (No 1 of 2003)* [2003] EWCA Crim 1051.
189. Alisdair Gillespie, 'Reviewing Unduly Lenient Sentences' (2005) 10 *Archbold News* 5, 9.
190. See, for example, *Attorney-General's Reference (No 105 of 2011)* [2012] EWCA Crim 257 [14].

16.6 Appeals to the Supreme Court

It is possible to appeal a decision from the Court of Appeal to the Supreme Court.[191] Either party can appeal the matter irrespective of who brought the matter to the Court of Appeal (ie if the defendant appealed against conviction to the Court of Appeal the prosecution can appeal to the Supreme Court). For the matter to be heard by the Supreme Court it is necessary for the Court of Appeal to certify a point of general public importance is raised in the case,[192] and leave must be sought either from the Court of Appeal or the Supreme Court directly. An interesting issue arose in *R v Dunn*[193] where the Court of Appeal refused to certify a point of public importance. The appellant sought to argue that this was a breach of Article 6 ECHR because the Court of Appeal was, in essence, sitting in judgment on its own decision and was biased. The appellant sought to argue that since the Court of Appeal would not wish to be reversed by the Supreme Court it could, by declining to certify a point, prevent a case from reaching the Supreme Court. Perhaps unsurprisingly the Court of Appeal ruled against the submission noting that the certification point was separate from the merits, and that an impartial observer would not consider themselves to be biased when making the decision. The requirement for points of law to be certified exists in both the civil and criminal jurisdictions and is seen by the courts as a method of ensuring that only the most important cases appear before the Supreme Court. As was seen in Chapter 6 the Supreme Court has the capacity to only hear a limited number of cases and the certification process is a part of the filter mechanism.

16.7 Miscarriages of justice: The Criminal Cases Review Commission

It has been noted already that there was, during the 1970s and 1980s, a series of miscarriages of justice that began to undermine public confidence in the criminal justice system. Part of the difficulty with the miscarriages was that they centred on terrorism trials and the person with responsibility for deciding whether to refer a matter back to the Court of Appeal, following an unsuccessful appeal after trial, was the Home Secretary and there was at the very least the appearance of bias in terms of whether to refer a matter to the court, particularly as Home Secretaries became increasingly combative with the judiciary. Whilst a politician was responsible for decisions to refer matters to the Court of Appeal, ie considering whether the criminal justice system had made a terrible mistake, there was concern that politics might interfere.

The *Criminal Appeal Act 1995* (CAA 1995) removed the political aspect of the decision from the Home Secretary through the establishment of the *Criminal Cases Review Commission* (CCRC), which from 1997 replaced the Home Secretary as the referring body for fresh appeals.[194] There are two principal methods by which the Commission can become involved. The first (and more usual) is that a convicted person will make an application to the Commission for a matter to be referred. There were early fears that

---

191. *Criminal Appeal Act 1968*, s 33.
192. ibid, s 33(2).
193. [2010] EWCA Crim 1823.
194. *Criminal Appeal Act 1995*, s 9.

the Commission would be overwhelmed by applications[195] and whilst there have been backlogs at times, most of the time they have managed to cope.[196]

The second way that the Commission may become involved is that the Court of Appeal can direct that the Commission investigate a matter and report to it.[197] This power is traditionally rarely exercised,[198] and where it is it often relates to issues around possible jury misconduct (discussed earlier). The power is undoubtedly useful and the Court of Appeal has vocally supported the CCRC in conducting its role.[199]

Although the Commission is undoubtedly independent, it is interesting to note that not everyone necessarily believes that this is preferable. Some suggest that a difficulty with the Commission is that it is not directly accountable to Parliament in the way that the Home Office, through the Home Secretary, was.[200] That is not to say, however, that there is no accountability and the Commission must issue an annual report to the Justice Secretary[201] and they can be, and indeed have in the past been, called before Parliamentary Select Committees to discuss their work. Aside from accountability, others argue that there is less freedom to refer matters since political pressure could sometimes have persuaded the Home Secretary to refer cases where there was little prospect of success, whereas the Commission can only refer where there is a 'real possibility' of success.[202] The issue of 'real possibility', however, can cause problems with some suggestions that this means that the 'lurking doubt' cases will never be referred since the Commission needs to identify some tangible ground.[203] It has been suggested that as an abstract term it is relatively meaningless[204] and that this means that the Commission must take notice of the working practice of the Court of Appeal[205] and that, in essence, this means that something 'new' (not necessarily evidence) is required before a matter could be referred. Where the 'new' matter is evidence there would appear to be an additional hurdle because not only should the Commission ask itself whether this would affect the safety of the conviction, it must also consider whether the evidence would, in fact, be admissible within the Court of Appeal.[206] Where the matter is one of due process it is perhaps easier to deal with since the court has identified that human rights requirements will usually mean that the safety of such convictions will be questioned, and accordingly the discovery of due process arguments may assist the Commission but only where they were not known at the time of the trial.

The CJIA 2008 has also resolved one question about 'old' appeals. The CCRC had begun to send cases to the Court of Appeal where the sole ground of appeal was that

---

195.   Michael Zander, *Cases and Materials on the English Legal System* (10th edn, OUP 2007).
196.   Criminal Cases Review Commission, *Annual Report and Accounts 2007–18* (CCRC 2018) <https://s3-eu-west-2.amazonaws.com/ccrc-prod-storage-1jdn5d1f6iq1l/uploads/2018/07/CCRC-Annual-Report-2017-18_Web-Accessible.pdf> 9, and Kevin Kerrigan, 'Miscarriages of Justice in the Magistrates' Court: The Forgotten Power of the Criminal Cases Review Commission' [2006] *Criminal Law Review* 124, 126–7.
197.   *Criminal Appeal Act 1995*, s 15.
198.   Criminal Cases Review Commission, *Annual Report and Accounts 2007–18* (CCRC 2018) <https://s3-eu-west-2.amazonaws.com/ccrc-prod-storage-1jdn5d1f6iq1l/uploads/2018/07/CCRC Annual-Report-2017-18_Web-Accessible.pdf> 14–15.
199.   *R v Spicer* [2011] EWCA Crim 3247.
200.   Richard Nobles and David Schiff, *Understanding Miscarriages of Justice: Law, Media and the Inevitability of a Crisis* (OUP 2000) 224.
201.   *Criminal Appeal Act 1995*, sch 1.
202.   Richard Nobles and David Schiff, *Understanding Miscarriages of Justice: Law, Media and the Inevitability of a Crisis* (OUP 2000) 224.
203.   ibid, 221.
204.   Kevin Kerrigan, 'Miscarriages of Justice in the Magistrates' Court: The Forgotten Power of the Criminal Cases Review Commission' [2006] *Criminal Law Review* 124, 133.
205.   Andrew Ashworth and Mike Redmayne, *The Criminal Process* (4th edn, OUP 2010) 359.
206.   ibid, 359.

statutory law had overridden the previous common-law rules under which the person had been convicted, ie the law had changed. The Court of Appeal itself would ordinarily refuse to allow leave to appeal to defendants in such cases but this was not possible when the matter was referred by the CCRC since leave is not required. The CJIA 2008 amendment allows for the Court of Appeal to dismiss the appeal where the only ground for the appeal is that there has been a new development in the law and where, had the appellant himself petitioned the court, leave would not have been granted.[207]

Whether the CCRC refers enough cases has long been controversial. Ashworth and Redmayne argue that the Commission largely get the balance right,[208] although they concede that it can be difficult to identify what is the appropriate rate. Other commentators have been less charitable, however. It has been noted that some miscarriage of justice campaigners believe the CCRC is too cautious.[209] Over a period of nineteen years 626 cases were referred and Cooper argues that this low number shows that 'something is not working'.[210] This is supported by others who believe that the fact that their success rate is around 70 per cent shows that there is an 'in-built conservatism'.[211] Zellick, a former chairman of the Commission, disagrees and believes that the rate is 'about right',[212] arguing that the CCRC should not be trying to clog up the Court of Appeal, a court that already suffers from chronic delays. In September 2020 the CCRC referred its 750th case for appeal.

The resources of the Commission must, however, have an impact on the work of the body. In the 2014/15 annual report, it was noted that 'the main source of risk and uncertainty faced by the Commission . . . relates to the level of funding it receives . . . The continuing need for budgetary savings to be made across government is particularly difficult for the Commission as the majority of its expenditure relates to staff costs. This makes it difficult to plan ahead with any confidence.'[213] Whilst the CCRC has not had cuts made to their most recent budgets, their funding has not been increased, which, when combined with a high workload, has proved challenging.[214] Prior to 2013–14 there was also concern about the number of Commissioners. The *Criminal Appeal Act 1995* states that the Commission must have no fewer than eleven Commissioners[215] and yet during 2011/12 there were only nine,[216] and in March 2020 there were only ten.[217] The statute makes clear that the fact that it is 'below strength' does not affect the validity of its activities,[218] but it is more likely that it was intended to cover short-term vacancies and not a determined plan to be under-strength. The CCRC make clear that the Ministry of Justice deliberately intended the number to fall below eleven[219] even though this is clearly breaching the statute. The position as of March 2020 was that there were ten Commissioners in post,[220] with additional positions expected to be appointed to.

---

207.   CJIA 2008, s 43.
208.   Andrew Ashworth and Mike Redmayne, *The Criminal Process* (4th edn, OUP 2010) 360.
209.   Jon Robins, 'The Case for the Defence' *Law Society Gazette* (9 October 2008) 12.
210.   John Cooper, 'CCRC and Court of Appeal' (2011) 175 *Criminal Law & Justice Weekly* 298.
211.   Jon Robins, 'Wrongly Accused' (2011) 175 *Criminal Law & Justice Weekly* 675.
212.   ibid, 675.
213.   Criminal Cases Review Commission, *Annual Report and Accounts 2014–15* (CCRC 2015) 29.
214.   Criminal Cases Review Commission, *Annual Report and Accounts 2007–18* (CCRC 2018) <https://s3-eu-west-2.amazonaws.com/ccrc-prod-storage-1jdn5d1f6iq1l/uploads/2018/07/CCRC-Annual-Report-2017-18_Web-Accessible.pdf> 10.
215.   *Criminal Appeal Act 1995*, s 8(3).
216.   Criminal Cases Review Commission, *Annual Report and Accounts 2011–12* (CCRC 2012) 9.
217.   Criminal Cases Review Commission, *Annual Report and Accounts 2019–20* (CCRC 2020) 47.
218.   *Criminal Appeal Act 1995*, sch 1, para 6(4).
219.   Criminal Cases Review Commission, *Annual Report and Accounts 2011–12* (CCRC 2012) 9.
220.   Criminal Cases Review Commission, *Annual Report and Accounts 2019–20* (CCRC 2020) 47.

Summary

This chapter has examined how an appeal from a decision of a first instance criminal court is dealt with. In particular, it has shown that:

- The paths of appeals differ depending on the mode of trial of the original criminal hearing.
- There are two potential criminal appeal avenues from a summary trial: either to the Divisional Court (by way of case stated or (exceptionally) judicial review) or to the Crown Court.
- Appeal from the Crown Court is to the Court of Appeal (Criminal Division).
- An appeal ordinarily requires leave (permission) but appealing to the Crown Court from the magistrates' court does not require leave.

End-of-chapter questions

1. In *R v Hanratty*[221] the Lord Chief Justice said: 'We do however emphasise that there have to be exceptional circumstances to justify incurring the expenditure of resources . . . including those of this Court, on a case of this age.' This was in connection with a murder case that took place in 1962 and for which the offender was executed later that year. The judgment in this case alone consisted of 215 paragraphs spread over eighteen pages in the law reports. In *R v Nicholson*[222] the Court of Appeal quashed a conviction for theft that dated back to 1957. The court stated that it did not condone the referral of historic cases but accepted that an error had been made in this case. Should the Commission refer historic cases or do you think that its time and money would be better spent in referring cases where the applicant is still in, or has been recently released from, prison?

2. Kevin Kerrigan ('Miscarriages of Justice in the Magistrates' Court: The Forgotten Power of the Criminal Cases Review Commission' [2006] *Criminal Law Review* 124) argues that the CCRC is not using its powers correctly in referring miscarriages of justice that occur in summary trials. Should the CCRC deal with summary matters or is it designed to protect public confidence through examining only serious cases that are heard in the Crown Court?

3. Read pp 364–9 of Andrew Ashworth and Mike Redmayne, *The Criminal Process* (4th edn, OUP 2010). Was it right to abolish the rule of double jeopardy? Can the powers be abused by the police or are there sufficient safeguards built into the legislation?

591

Further reading

Kerrigan K, 'Miscarriages of Justice in the Magistrates' Court: The Forgotten Power of the Criminal Cases Review Commission' [2006] *Criminal Law Review* 124–9.

> **This is a fascinating article that considers the power of the CCRC to appeal decisions within a summary trial. It raises important issues about the status of convictions (ie whether a summary conviction is as important as a conviction by the Crown Court).**

221.   [2002] 3 All ER 534.
222.   [2004] EWCA Crim 2840.

Leigh LH, 'Lurking Doubt and the Safety of Convictions' [2006] *Criminal Law Review* 809–15.

This is an interesting article which examines how appeals are determined by the Court of Appeal, including where there is no flaw in the trial process.

Roberts S and Malleson K, 'Streamlining and Clarifying the Appellate Process' [2002] *Criminal Law Review* 272–82.

This is an interesting critique of the Auld proposals in respect of criminal appeals, particularly the prosecution right of appeal.

Spencer JR, 'Does Our Present Criminal Appeal System Make Sense?' [2006] *Criminal Law Review* 677–94.

This is a comprehensive article which examines the history of criminal appeals and discusses, in particular, the absurdity of two appeal mechanisms from a summary trial.

Criminal Cases Review Commision, *Annual Account and Reports 2019/20* (CCRC 2020) available at <https://s3-eu-west-2.amazonaws.com/ccrc-prod-storage-1jdn5d1f6iq1l/uploads/2020/07/CCRC-2329571-v1-CCRC_Annual_Report_and_Accounts_2019-20_Final_for_web.pdf> section 1.

Section 1 of the most recent annual report by the CCRC provides an overview of their work in the financial year 2019/20.

For self-test questions, flashcards, and links to useful websites, please visit the **online resources** at: **www.oup.com/he/gillespie-weare8e/**

PART IV

THE CIVIL JUSTICE SYSTEM

17

Civil Litigation

By the end of this chapter you will be able to:

- Understand the basic elements of civil litigation.
- Identify the key principles adopted by the civil courts.
- Understand how three different types of civil litigation progress through the courts.

Introduction

Although the criminal justice system is probably responsible for the majority of the headlines and stories within the media, the civil justice system is used more frequently. The civil system straddles numerous different types of cases from public child-law cases (where the courts have to decide whether a child should be removed from its parents) through divorces to high-value litigation (eg the dispute over the building of the Wembley stadium where the parties sued for a combined total of £660,000,000) and then through to public remedies such as judicial review.

This chapter will take a slightly different approach to the issue of litigation. Whilst the initial section will discuss certain common concepts of civil litigation, the main part of the chapter will look at three examples of civil litigation. Each type of litigation will involve the presentation of a case study and the section will then identify how this matter will be litigated. This will allow you to understand how some forms of civil litigation occur in real life.

17.1 Civil litigation

The civil justice system partners the criminal justice system in providing a forum through which disputes of law can be resolved. The disputes, however, can be quite varied. It is often said that the English Legal System does not operate a separate court system for 'public law' in that there are no separate courts that deal with matters relating to the resolution of disputes between the state and the citizen. However, this is not strictly true since, as you will see from related modules, there is now a distinct body of law known either as *Administrative Law* or *Public Law* which details how citizens can hold the government to account for their actions. Indeed, arguably, there is now a de facto separate court in that there is now a court known as the Administrative Court where such matters are heard. However, technically this is just part of the High Court of Justice and so the convention may still hold.

Setting aside public-law matters the civil justice system predominantly concerns disputes between citizens. This chapter discusses some of the ways that these disputes are resolved and the next chapter will then discuss what remedies can be sought from the civil courts and how an appeal is made against a decision. Chapter 19 details methods of resolving civil disputes without recourse to formal litigation, a topic known as 'Alternative Dispute Resolution' (ADR). Given the reduction in legal aid (discussed in Chapter 11) it is likely that ADR will become increasingly common.

17.1.1 Procedural rules

As with criminal litigation, the courts have developed a series of rules that govern the way in which litigation takes place. There are two sets of rules; the *Civil Procedure Rules*, which govern the rules in most civil litigation, and the *Family Procedure Rules* which govern litigation in the Family Court. The CPR was the first set of rules to be established and they were introduced in response to the Woolf Reforms. They are publicly available[1] and are updated as and when necessary by the *Civil Procedure Rules Committee*.[2]

⚡ CIVIL PROCEDURE RULES COMMITTEE

This is a non-departmental body (ie it is independent of government) although it is sponsored, and paid for, by the Ministry of Justice. It consists of:

- Master of the Rolls (as Head of Civil Justice)
- Deputy Head of Civil Justice
- Two puisne judges
- A circuit judge
- A Master of the High Court
- Two district judges
- Three barrister members
- Three solicitor members
- Two lay members.

The *Civil Procedure Rules* (CPR) and *Family Procedure Rules* (FPR) apply on a jurisdictional rather than a court-based basis. In other words, the CPR applies to all civil litigation other than family proceedings[3] and it does not matter whether the proceedings are in the county court or the High Court. Prior to the establishment of the CPR, the rules differed between courts. Lord Woolf, in his review of civil justice, recommended that the rules were the same across jurisdictions and this led to the establishment of the CPR as it simplifies the procedure.

---

1. Justice.gov.uk, *CPR—Rules and Directions* (October 2020) available at <https://www.justice.gov.uk/courts/procedure-rules/civil>.
2. Established by *Civil Procedure Act 1997*, s 2.
3. The Court of Protection also has its own rules but these are set by Statutory Instrument: see *Court of Protection Rules 2007*, SI 2007/1744.

⚡ **REFERRING TO THE CPR**

In order to refer to the CPR and accompanying practice direction in an understandable way, we will be referring to them in the following manner:

- **Rules.** The CPR consists of 89 parts, each with individual rules. The convention CPR Part. Rule will be adopted: CPR 31.2 means rule number 2 in Part 31 of the CPR.

- **Sub-rules.** These will follow the usual convention of brackets, eg 31.2(1).

- **Practice directions.** Whilst it is technically one practice direction, in essence each Part has its own practice direction relating to it. The convention PD Part.paragraph will be adopted: PD 31.7.6 means the practice direction relating to Part 31, paragraph 7.6.

The same approach will also be made in respect of the FPR.

17.1.1.1 Overriding objective

The first rule is known as the 'overriding objective' and is, in essence, a statement of intent as to how civil litigation should be conducted. Rule 1 states:

(1) These rules are a new procedural code with the overriding objective of enabling the court to deal with cases justly and at proportionate cost.

(2) Dealing with a case justly includes, so far as is practicable–

    (a) ensuring that the parties are on an equal footing;

    (b) saving expense;

    (c) dealing with the case in ways which are proportionate

        (i) to the amount of money involved;

        (ii) to the importance of the case;

        (iii) to the complexity of the issues; and

        (iv) to the financial position of each party;

    (d) ensuring that it is dealt with expeditiously and fairly; and

    (e) allotting it an appropriate share of the court's resources, while taking into account the need to allot resources to other cases.

    (f) enforcing compliance with rules, practice directions and orders.

The overriding objective could be criticized as being more of a mission statement than a plan on how this will happen but, as will be seen, the courts take the overriding objective very seriously. The rest of the CPR sets out requirements but also provides powers to the court. The court considers the exercise of their discretionary powers in such a way as to ensure the overriding objective is met. This can include, for example, refusing adjournments where it is thought that a case is taking too long, refusing evidence where it would lead to disproportionate cost, and ensuring the right type of judge hears the appropriate case.

Rule 1.1(2)(f) was inserted comparatively recently (2013) and was designed as a culture shift: to send a signal that the courts will be proactive in terms of managing litigation and holding parties to account for their actions. It may seem a strange thing to say, because should courts not ordinarily be in charge of litigation? Traditionally, however, they were not. The nature of the adversarial system and the neutrality of the 'umpire' meant that the courts were somewhat reticent to intervene in a case, lest it generate an appeal.[4] Those days are now long gone and, as will be seen, the courts are very willing to intervene where necessary.

17.1.1.2 **Case management**

Case management is more than just ensuring that the proceedings in the courtroom are running smoothly and that relevant issues are being discussed. Case management means that judges are at the heart of many of the procedural issues that occur in a case. This means not leaving matters to the parties, but questioning and deciding matters. Common issues of case management would include:

- Deciding which court should hear the matter. Whilst the parties may apply to a particular court, it does not follow that the courts will consider themselves bound by this, and they could transfer it to another court.

- Allocate the appropriate judge to hear the case. Civil litigation is heard by a variety of judges and the case management process will ensure that the right judge is allocated for the type of case, and its seriousness.

- The court will allocate a case to a particular track (see 17.2.3). This ensures that there is greatest control and also flexibility in those situations where litigation is likely to be complicated or lengthy. Conversely, it also ensures that minor cases are dealt with swiftly.

- The courts will ensure that Alternative Dispute Resolution (ADR) is at least actively considered (discussed in Chapter 19).

- The court will usually decide the evidence it wants to hear. Unlike in criminal cases where, if it is relevant, the judge will usually be required to let the tribunal of fact (the jury) hear it, a judge in civil proceedings has much more discretion. A judge can decide that he will only listen to certain evidence. The judge could decide that certain evidence need only be provided in writing or limit the number of issues that are to be litigated.

- The court will ensure its orders and directions are dealt with. As will be seen, a failure to comply with the directions of the court can be financially significant.

17.1.2 **Actions before litigating**

The courts are now clear that litigation should only be commenced as a final resort and to ensure this they have established a series of pre-trial protocols. The *Practice Direction on Pre-action Conduct and Protocols*[5] states that the protocols have the force of the CPR, being appended to them.[6] There are a number of pre-action protocols that cover different types of litigation that can be heard by the courts but if no protocol exists then the Practice Direction must be followed.

---

4. Stuart Sime, *A Practical Approach to Civil Procedure* (19th edn, OUP 2016).
5. Justice.gov.uk, *Practice Direction—Pre-Action Conduct and Protocols* (2020) available at <https://www.justice.gov.uk/courts/procedure-rules/civil/rules/pd_pre-action_conduct>.
6. PD, para 1.

Perhaps the most important rule is that contained within paragraph 3:

Before commencing proceedings, the court will expect the parties to have exchanged sufficient information to—

(a) understand each other's position;

(b) make decisions about how to proceed;

(c) try to settle the issues without proceedings;

(d) consider a form of ADR to assist with the settlement;

(e) support the efficient management of these proceedings, and

(f) reduce the costs of resolving the dispute.

This applies to even the most minor litigation and therefore someone who hopes to use the small claims track (see 17.2) would still be expected to have tried to settle this dispute. The usual means of doing so is to send a letter to the would-be respondent stating what the dispute is about, what remedy is sought, and indicating that if they do not respond then the matter will be referred to the courts.

Realistically the pre-action procedure cannot be said to be onerous. It is designed to do four key things:

1. Test whether it is really necessary to go to court (including, by considering whether ADR is possible).

2. Identify what the issues in dispute are.

3. Identify what remedy the claimant is seeking.

4. Minimize costs by focusing only on what is in dispute.

17.1.3 Issuing proceedings

Assuming that the pre-trial approach did not work, then the beginning of the process is the issuing of proceedings.

For most forms of litigation, the general form is used. See Figure 17.1 which is a copy of form N1. The key features of this are:

Court. At the top right, the words 'In the' and a blank box appears. This is because N1 is used by most courts and therefore the claimant will indicate which court (High Court (including Division), county court (stating where it is sitting)) etc.

Personal details. The addresses for the claimant and defendant are included.

Brief details of the claim. Whilst this looks to be a relatively lengthy space to write in, it is traditionally used to provide only the most basic of details. A very concise summary of the key information is provided and a description of the remedy sought. The online resources that accompany this book has examples of N1 forms completed for the examples that are contained in this chapter.

Value. Assuming that the claim is for money, the value of the claim is placed here. There are rules on how the claim is calculated, including claiming for interest, and this will be discussed later. It is important to note, however, that if those details are not included on form N1 then the claimant will not be entitled to them. Given that litigation is extremely lengthy, omitting a claim for interest could be exceptionally costly.

Human Rights Act 1998 statement. This is a simple yes/no question but it is designed to help the courts identify those cases where there is a potential action under the *Human Rights Act 1998*. This is important because in those cases the court will normally ensure that a professional judge sits (as distinct from an acting judge) and where the matter relates to a potential declaration of incompatibility, this will normally mean that a puisne judge will be assigned.[7]

Particulars of claim. These can either be set out here or they can be attached as a separate, and more formal, document. Where they are set out on form N1 itself then it is more common for them to be slightly more informally set out. That said, it is important that the key facts and issues in dispute are set out here, so that the defendant can respond.[8]

One of the peculiarities of the English Legal System is that alternatives are permitted even though they may contradict each other. So, for example, it is perfectly reasonable to say, 'I had a contract with X, but if I did not have a contract with him, I allege that he was negligent in his actions towards me.' This seems to contain two contradictory pleadings—that there was a contract or there was not a contract—but it does not matter so long as the claimant believes that they are valid claims. That said, it should be noted that a party cannot contradict facts because they could not otherwise attest to the truth of the claim (below).[9] An alternative claim above would not fall foul of this rule because a contract may not exist because of a legal, rather than factual, dispute.

Statement of Truth. Proceedings before the courts are formal and the claimant must attest that it is true to the best of their knowledge. A deliberate lie can be construed as a criminal offence.

17.1.3.1 **Money claims online**

HMCTS has established a system whereby disputes under £100,000 not relating to a child or protected party can begin online. Indeed to facilitate this, the fee for issuing service (see later) is discounted.

Exactly the same information is completed online but in a more intuitive way. You are provided with a series of text boxes and these are then completed and the form is created automatically. When the form is submitted (with the relevant fee) it passes to the central registry (based in Northampton) who issue the proceedings. A paper copy of the claim form is sent to the claimant who can either respond online or on paper. If the proceedings go ahead to trial, the matter is transferred to the nearest relevant court to the claimant. If, however, the proceedings do not continue because, for example, the defendant admits liability or refuses to acknowledge service, the matter can be dealt with online.

17.1.3.2 **Identifying the correct court**

It was noted earlier that form N1 applies to all civil courts, so how does one identify the appropriate court to bring the action in? The rules governing where litigation starts are

---

7. PD 2B, para 7A.
8. Stuart Sime, *A Practical Approach to Civil Procedure* (19th edn, OUP 2016) 148.
9. ibid, 150 and see *Clarke v Marlborough Fine Art (London) Ltd* [2002] 1 WLR 1731.

Claim Form

You may be able to issue your claim online which may save time and money. Go to www.moneyclaim.gov.uk to find out more.

In the	
Fee Account no.	
Help with Fees - **Ref no.** (if applicable)	H W F – ☐ ☐ ☐ – ☐ ☐ ☐

For court use only	
Claim no.	
Issue date	

Claimant(s) name(s) and address(es) including postcode

SEAL

Defendant(s) name and address(es) including postcode

Brief details of claim

Value

You must indicate your preferred County Court Hearing Centre for hearings here *(see notes for guidance)*

Defendant's name and address for service including postcode			£
		Amount claimed	
		Court fee	
		Legal representative's costs	
		Total amount	

For further details of the courts www.gov.uk/find-court-tribunal.
When corresponding with the Court, please address forms or letters to the Manager and always quote the claim number.

N1 Claim form (CPR Part 7) (10.20)   © Crown Copyright 2020

Figure 17.1 Form N1: the form used for most types of civil litigation

Claim No.	

Does, or will, your claim include any issues under the Human Rights Act 1998? ☐ Yes   ☐ No

Particulars of Claim (attached)(to follow)

Figure 17.1 (Continued)

Statement of Truth

I understand that proceedings for contempt of court may be brought against anyone who makes, or causes to be made, a false statement in a document verified by a statement of truth without an honest belief in its truth.

☐ **I believe** that the facts stated in this particulars of claim are true.

☐ **The Claimant** believes that the facts stated this particulars of claim are true. **I am authorised** by the claimant to sign this statement.

Signature

☐ Claimant
☐ Litigation friend (where judgment creditor is a child or a patient)
☐ Claimant's legal representative (as defined by CPR 2.3(1))

Date

Day	Month	Year

Full name

Name of claimant's legal representative's firm

If signing on behalf of firm or company give position or office held

603

Figure 17.1 (Continued)

Claimant's or claimant's legal representative's address to which documents should be sent.

Building and street

Second line of address

Town or city

County (optional)

Postcode

If applicable

Phone number

Fax phone number

DX number

Your Ref.

Email

Figure 17.1 (Continued)

set out in *The High Court and County Court Jurisdictions Order*[10] and are also subject to Practice Direction 7A which states:

2.1 Proceedings (whether for damages or for a specified sum) may not be started in the High Court unless the value of the claim is more than £100,000.

2.2 Proceedings which include a claim for damages in respect of personal injuries must not be started in the High Court unless the value of the claim is £50,000 or more (paragraph 9 of the High Court and County Courts Jurisdiction Order 1991 (S.I. 1991/724 as amended) describes how the value of a claim is to be determined).

2.3 A claim must be issued in the High Court or the County Court if an enactment so requires.

2.4 Subject to paragraphs 2.1 and 2.2 above, a claim should be started in the High Court if by reason of:

(1) the financial value of the claim and the amount in dispute, and/or

(2) the complexity of the facts, legal issues, remedies or procedures involved, and/or

(3) the importance of the outcome of the claim to the public in general, the claimant believes that the claim ought to be dealt with by a High Court judge.

Some types of dispute have to begin in the High Court, most notably claims for judicial review. However, for the vast majority of business, the county court has jurisdiction. The jurisdiction of the county court has grown in recent years, partly to encourage more work to be dealt with in the county court. Given that, outside of London, most High Court business is dealt with by circuit judges acting as High Court judges, there is little point in starting in the High Court unnecessarily.

What happens when a case is begun at the wrong level? Theoretically where the claim has been lodged for an inappropriate reason the matter could be struck out as an abuse of process[11] but this will be comparatively rare. The more likely sanction is that the matter will be moved to the correct court and the claimant will bear the costs involved in the transfer irrespective of whether they succeed in the ultimate claim. Where the error was to begin in the High Court when the matter should have been brought in the county court the judge has power not only to order that the costs of the transfer are paid but also could reduce the overall costs bill by up to 25 per cent.[12] Where it was a bona fide mistake to start the proceedings in the wrong court then it is unlikely that a sanction would be imposed although it would seem inevitable that the party will be liable for the costs of the transfer.

17.1.4 Allocating a track

Assuming that a defendant announces that he is going to contest the action—explored later—then the next principal decision that has to be taken is to allocate the matter to a relevant track. The CPR ushered in a new system of trying to manage civil litigation and it introduced three 'tracks' which govern how cases will proceed.

The initial decision is taken by an administrative officer of HMCTS[13] but this will be notified to the parties who will have the right to make representations. At the same time,

---

10. SI 1991/724.
11. *Restick v Crickmore* [1994] 2 All ER 112.
12. *Senior Courts Act 1981*, s 51(8).
13. CPR, r 26.3(1).

a questionnaire will be sent to both parties which seeks to encourage settlement (including through ADR), identify the key issues of the case, including whether expert testimony is to be required, and which witnesses and documents they are seeking to rely upon.[14]

Once the questionnaires are received, a judge will then allocate the case to an appropriate track. The three tracks are:

Small claims track. This encompasses what was, and indeed still is, colloquially known as the 'small claims court' although it was never a separate court (it is part of the county court) and it is not necessarily that small a claim any more.

The general rule is that claims under £10,000 will ordinarily be considered suitable for the small claims track, save that the following cases will not ordinarily be so assigned:

(a) Personal injury cases, where the value of the claim for pain, suffering, and loss of amenity exceeds £1,000.

(b) Claims by tenants of residential premises seeking orders that their landlords should carry out repairs or other works to the premises where the value of the claim exceeds £1,000.

(c) Claims by residential tenants seeking damages against their landlords for harassment or unlawful eviction.

(d) Claims involving a disputed allegation of dishonesty.[15]

It should be noted that the £10,000 is not an absolute ceiling. There may be reasons why a larger sum could be considered suitable for the small claims court. As will be seen, one advantage of the small claims track is its costs regime and its informality. It is rare for lawyers to be involved in cases in the small claims track and so litigants in person may prefer larger claims to be heard under this track.

> **Example**
>
> Bernard asked Wreckers Ltd to install a swimming pool in his house. He claims that the pool is not fit for purpose as it leaks, meaning the water level is unsafe. It cost £21,000 to install and Bernard has been told it will cost £11,000 to repair.
>
> Realistically Bernard's claim will be for £11,000 (the cost of the repair) but this is over £10,000. However, if both Bernard and Wreckers Ltd agree that the issue is relatively simple then they may both seek to keep the matter in the small claims track as it will limit the potential for costs.

Fast track. The fast track is designed to be the 'normal' track for cases with a value of between £10,000 and £25,000.[16] They will also ordinarily include those cases above that were deemed not suitable for the small claims track even though the value was under £10,000. However, the financial threshold is subject to one important exception. Cases in the fast track should normally be capable of being heard within one day and will not involve more than two expert witnesses.[17]

14. Stuart Sime, *A Practical Approach to Civil Procedure* (19th edn, OUP 2016) 164ff.
15. CPR, r 26.
16. Stuart Sime, *A Practical Approach to Civil Procedure* (19th edn, OUP 2016) 175.
17. CPR, r 26.6(5).

Whilst the CPR does not require longer cases to be heard in the multi-track, as it states 'normally', it has been noted that the default position is normally that they will be sent to the multi-track.[18]

As will be seen, it is in the parties' best interests to try and ensure that the dispute is limited to issues that could be dealt with in under one day, because the costs implications between the fast track and multi-track can be significant.

Multi-track The multi-track is, in essence, the track that is to be used for cases that do not fall within either the small claims track or fast track. It is perhaps the widest track and it demonstrates that the other two tracks are really filters to try and deal with less complicated cases quickly.

17.1.5 Costs of litigation

Litigation is expensive. There can be no denial of that fact and it is one of the reasons why the courts have been so keen to try and ensure that litigants consider alternative forms of dispute resolution. In some instances the costs can far exceed what the claim is about, meaning that litigation can be potentially ruinous.

Example Warring couples and costs

In September 2012 it was reported that a judge had criticized two solicitors who squandered £1.7 million in litigation costs while fighting various issues in respect of their (own) divorce. The media reported that the litigants were left with joint assets of just over £90,000 after years of litigation. This perhaps demonstrates the challenges of the overriding objective and the fact that sometimes litigation is pursued when it is arguably unreasonable to do so.

607

Costs have become an extremely complicated area of law and realistically we cannot do justice to the topic in a book like this. It is too complex and complicated and probably far outside the scope of what you will need for a course such as *English Legal System*. Reference on specific points of costs management should be made to key texts in the field.[19]

In this section, what will be considered are the different costs regimes between the tracks and then how the courts use costs to control litigant behaviour.

17.1.5.1 Costs: The general rule

The general rule in civil litigation is that the loser pays the costs.[20] Whilst a court has general discretion as to costs, a judge departing from this general rule must give clear reasons for doing so.[21] Of course, what is meant by 'the losing side' is open to question since in some forms of litigation, deciding who wins and who loses is not always easy. There are also rules that relate to how costs will be apportioned where a party seeks to settle a case, and this is one of the things that will be discussed later. But this, again, remains an exemption from the general rule which is that the losing side pays the costs of both parties.

---

18. Stuart Sime, *A Practical Approach to Civil Procedure* (19th edn, OUP 2016) 176.
19. See, for example, ibid (which is arguably the pre-eminent academic text on civil litigation) and also the *White Book*.
20. CPR, r 44.2.
21. *Aspin v Metric Group Ltd* (2007) LTL 25/9/07; and see Stuart Sime, *A Practical Approach to Civil Procedure* (19th edn, OUP 2016) 517.

17.1.5.2 **Costs for each track**

One of the reasons for differentiating between the tracks is that the costs regime is different across them all. This section will provide a summary of the costs regime, which will help illustrate the importance of a case being assigned to the appropriate track.

Small claims track

Cases in the small claims track are the most restrictive when it comes to costs. This is considered a key advantage of the small claims track and means that, in many instances, litigation is affordable and proportionate. As will be seen (at 17.2.3), the small claims track is designed to be used by litigants in person and therefore legal fees will not ordinarily be permitted.

The CPR sets out the position as regards costs:

The court shall not order a party to pay a sum to another party in respect of that other party's costs, fees and expenses, including those relating to an appeal, except—

(a) The fixed costs attributable to issuing the claim which—

   i.   Are payable under Part 45, or

   ii. Would be payable under Part 45 if that Part applied to the claim;

(b) In proceedings which included a claim for an injunction or an order for specific performance a sum not exceeding £260[22] for legal advice and assistance relating to that claim;

(c) Any court fees paid by that party;

(d) Expenses which a party or witness has reasonably incurred travelling to and from a hearing or in staying away from home for the purposes of attending the hearing;

(e) A sum not exceeding £95[23] for any loss of earnings or loss of leave by a party or witness due to a hearing.

(f) A sum not exceeding £750[24] for an expert's fees;

(g) [Certain costs relating to personal injury claims].

This is restrictive and there are a number of points to note here. The first is that legal advice is only permitted as a cost if the remedy sought is for an injunction or an order of specific performance. In all other types of cases, it is not possible to claim for legal advice, including the initial advice that may have said that a person has a legitimate legal claim and that they should use the small claims track. Even in cases with injunctions, the cost is for legal advice and not representation. Whilst there is a right to bring a lawyer to a small claims track case, the costs of doing so are not recoverable, even if a party wins.

An additional point of interest is the amount of expenses that can be claimed for loss of earnings. Assuming that most people would need to take a day's leave to attend the court hearing, as either a party or witness, the costs do seem remarkably scant. The maximum amount payable is £95 per day. To put that into context, that would equate to a salary of £24,700 per annum. Many people are on significantly more than this. If a person is self-employed, it is more likely that it would equate to £22,800.[25] This means that a person who

---

22. PD 27, para 7.2.
23. ibid, para 7.3.
24. ibid.
25. Five days a week for forty-eight weeks per year (allowing four weeks' holiday).

needs to attend court, and take a day's holiday, is likely to lose money. Whilst it could be argued this is not unreasonable for the claimant, who has decided to initiate the litigation, it would seem less appropriate for a (successful) defendant or a witness, neither of whom will necessarily have chosen to appear. To incur a loss on behalf of someone else seems somewhat harsh. Of course there is nothing to stop the relevant party paying more money to the witness but this is the maximum that could be reclaimed from the losing party.

The fee for an expert would seem high—£750—but it will be comparatively rare for experts to be used in the small claims track, particularly where there is a dispute between experts. Such disputes are likely to be too lengthy and complicated for a hearing in the small claims track and is more likely to see a dispute shifting to the fast or multi-track. That said, it is quite possible that there may be some disputes that call for a (shared) expert opinion. Whether a maximum of £750 is appropriate for all experts is perhaps another matter though: many will charge much more, meaning that the party commissioning the expert will need to pick up the extra.

> **Example** Experts in the small claims track
>
> Deborah buys a second-hand car from 'Dodgy Dave Motors Ltd' for £21,500. It was described as having one owner who looked after it immaculately, with a full service history. The car starts to develop faults and Dodgy Dave Motors Ltd say that it is just bad luck and the fact that the car is three years old. Deborah commissions a mechanic, who reports that the engine does not look original and it looks as though other parts of the car have not been maintained properly. He quotes the costs of repair at £7,500.
>
> Deborah may wish to rely upon this report to justify her claim against Dodgy Dave Motors.

Costs on the fast track

It will be remembered that the second track is the fast track and one of the perceived advantages of this track (over the multi-track) is that costs are, to a large extent, fixed. This means that a litigant will know approximately what level of costs they may be eligible for.

The cost regime is now contained within the *Civil Procedure Rules*[26] and is somewhat complicated, so an example only will be provided here. Let us take the following example:

> **Example** Experts in the small claims track
>
> Saanvi was out running one day. At a pelican crossing, she started to cross when the 'green man' came on but Aanya, who was distracted, did not stop her car in time, causing a glancing collision with Saanvi. Whilst there were only bruises, Saanvi could not work for four days and suffered pain and discomfort for a number of weeks. She required treatment for grazes and some physiotherapy to minimize the discomfort in her leg.
>
> Saanvi is suing Aanya for personal injury damages. It is estimated that these damages will be less than £25,000 and the case is relatively simple and so has been allocated to the fast track.

Protocols exist for personal injury cases now, and these would apply to Saanvi's case. What costs would the losing party be liable for? (See Tables 17.1, 17.2, 17.3, and 17.4.)

26. CPR, pt 45.

Table 17.1 Parties agree damages before proceedings are issued

Agreed damages	At least £1,000 but not more than £5,000	More than £5,000 but not more than £10,000	More than £10,000 but not more than £25,000
Fixed costs	The greater of– £550, or the total of– £100; and 20% of the damages	The total of– £1,100 and 15% of damages over £5,000	The total of– £1,930; and 10% of damages over £10,000

Table 17.2 Parties agree a settlement after the issuing of proceedings but before trial

Stage at which it is settled	On or after the date of issue, but prior to allocation of track	On or after the date of allocation of track, but prior to the date of listing	On or after the date of listing, but prior to the date of trial
Fixed costs	The total of– £1,160, and 20% of the damages	The total of– £1,880 and 20% of damages over £5,000	The total of– £2,655; and 20% of damages over £10,000

Table 17.3 The claim is disposed of at trial

Fixed costs.	The total of– £2,655, and 20% of the damages; and the relevant trial advocacy fee

Table 17.4 The relevant advocacy fee, depends on the award

Agreed or awarded damages	Not more than £3,000	More than £3,000 but not more than £10,000	More than £10,000 but not more than £15,000	More than £15,000
Advocacy Fee	£500	£710	£1,070	£1,705

Let us return to our example of Saanvi, and let us take three possible ways that the action is resolved. What would be the total costs recoverable? (See Table 17.5.)

Table 17.5 The total recoverable costs

Disposition	Costs
Agree damages of £8,000 after issuing a claim but before the allocation of track	£1,550[27]
Agree damages of £12,000 the day before the case is due to be listed	£3,055[28]
After a (contested) trial, the judge awards damages of £14,000	£6,525[29]

27. £1,100 plus 15 per cent of £3,000 (ie the damages above £5,000).
28. £2,655 plus 20 per cent of £2,000 (ie the damages above £10,000).
29. £2,655 plus 20 per cent of £14,000 plus advocacy fee of £1,070.

In addition to this, the following additional costs can be claimed:

- the cost of obtaining medical records and expert medical reports as permitted under the Protocol
- the cost of any non-medical expert reports as permitted under the Protocol
- court fees
- the cost of any expert's fee for attendance where the court granted permission for the expert to attend
- expenses which any party or witness has reasonably incurred in travelling to or from the hearing
- a sum not exceeding £90 (where the damages are less than £10,000) or £135 (where the damages are for £10,000 or more) for the loss of earnings for a party or witness.

Of course, the costs are, in effect, doubled since both sides will have similar costs incurred amongst them. Even without this, however, it can be seen that the costs of a fast-track case are not unreasonable for relatively low amounts. It also demonstrates one of the challenges for legal professionals, however, since these are the maximum costs that can be claimed for.

Multi-track

The costs for multi-track cases are too complicated for a book of this nature. Even though it is worth noting that costs are becoming increasingly fixed for some forms of work,[30] the costs of multi-track cases can be enormous. Multi-track cases have far fewer limitations on them, and whilst the courts will use their case-management powers to try and keep costs proportionate, the reality is that some multi-track cases can incur costs of several million pounds. Indeed, costs can be so significant that it is not unusual for there to be satellite litigation after the final disposition of the hearing, with this litigation concerning who should pay what, and for how much.

17.1.5.3 Using costs to control litigation

It has been noted on a number of occasions now that the courts see their role as managing cases, and ensuring that time and resources are not wasted. Whilst the CPR states that costs will normally follow the decision, (ie 'loser pays')[31] the broad discretion the courts have in respect of costs means that they can use costs decisions to control how parties litigate. Under the rules, this specifically includes:

(a) a proportion of the other party's costs
(b) a stated amount in respect of another party's costs
(c) costs from or until a certain day only
(d) costs incurred before proceedings have begun
(e) costs relating to particular steps taken in proceedings
(f) costs relating only to distinct parts of the proceedings
(g) interest on costs from or until a certain date, including a date before judgment.[32]

---

30. Discussed in chapter 45 of Stuart Sime, *A Practical Approach to Civil Procedure* (19th edn, OUP 2016).
31. CPR, r 44.2.
32. CPR, r 44.2(6).

611

As will be seen, the courts will use some of these powers when they formally try to encourage settlement, but they can also use them informally. For example, a judge may make clear that he sees no reason why a particular issue should be gone into, or advise that they concentrate on only points *x*, *y*, and *z*. If a party chooses to also look at points *a*, *b*, and *c*, it is quite possible that the judge will consider that those costs should not be paid for by the losing party.

Where a party breaches the orders of a court, a practice direction within the CPR, or the CPR themselves, it is highly likely that discretionary costs will be incurred. For example, if party X was told to submit some documents by a particular date so that they could be considered at a hearing, but they were instead submitted at, or the day before, the hearing requiring an adjournment, then it is quite likely that the party who failed to submit the paperwork in time would bear the costs for that wasted hearing, even if they deserved the costs of litigation for winning.

17.1.5.4 Wasted costs order

Perhaps one of the most significant powers a court has at its disposal is the wasted costs order. This is an order that is used to signal extreme judicial displeasure at a course of action, and is notable because it is a position whereby a lawyer can be ordered to be personally liable for the costs of the action.[33]

The wasted costs order is a creature of statute:

> In any proceedings . . . the court may disallow, or (as the case may be) order the legal or other representative concerned to meet, the whole of any wasted costs or such part of them as may be determined in accordance with rules of court.[34]

It is used to mark judicial disapproval of the conduct of litigation or advocacy where it has led to costs (including the costs of the court) being wasted. In respect of advocates, this can include not only their work in court but also their preparation of advice, drafting, or applications.[35] It can also be used against lawyers for action before the trial takes place.

Wasted costs orders are draconian, and indeed are designed to be, and so there is a relatively high threshold for an order to be made.

'Wasted costs' means any costs incurred by a party—

(a) As a result of any improper, unreasonable or negligent act or omission on the part of any legal or other representative or an employee of such a representative; or

(b) Which, in the light of any such act or omission occurring after they were incurred, the court considers it unreasonable to expect that party to pay.[36]

The test is extremely high—improper, unreasonable, or negligent—and where a court imposes a wasted costs order on a lawyer, they must now inform the relevant regulator[37] that they have done so. The regulator will then consider whether their actions amount to unprofessional conduct and the lawyer may therefore face further sanction.

---

33. Theoretically, a third party could also be personally liable for costs if they did something that warranted it, but it is more common for lawyers to be the subject of such an order.
34. *Senior Courts Act 1981*, s 51(6).
35. *Brown v Bennett* (Wasted Costs Order) [2002] 1 WLR 713.
36. *Senior Courts Act 1981*, s 51(7).
37. eg Solicitors Regulation Authority, Bar Standards Board, and CILEx.

Case Box Wasted Costs *Thompson v Go North East Ltd*

The claimant had pursued a claim of damages in respect of a bus accident. After issuing the proceedings, he discontinued them. The respondents, the bus company, sought damages from the claimant but also from the solicitors as it became evident that the whole claim was fraudulent. The CCTV footage had been viewed by the solicitors and it was clear from the footage that the claimant's case was inconsistent with what the evidence showed. Nonetheless they issued proceedings and began the pre-trial protocols.

The judge held that wasted costs were appropriate in this case. Whilst solicitors had to act on the basis of instructions, once they had viewed the CCTV evidence they should have realized that the case was flawed and it was inconsistent with their instructions.

17.1.6 Allocating the judge

It has already been noted that a case will be allocated to a specific track, but how is the judge allocated to the case? Civil law arguably has the widest range of judges employed to adjudicate matters, ranging from a deputy district judge to a Lord Justice of Appeal sitting on a judicial review. How is a judge allocated?

The general rule is that unless a practice direction or other rule says otherwise, any judge, deputy judge, or Master shall have the right to conduct the business of the court.[38] The principal practice direction that seeks to limit jurisdiction is the one that deals with the allocation of the judiciary.[39] Reference should be made to full details of this list, with this section merely providing an overview.

17.1.6.1 High Court

The principal rules of the High Court state when proceedings cannot be heard by someone other than a judge (including a circuit judge or deputy judge acting as a High Court judge[40]). The following proceedings cannot be heard by a Master or district judge:

- search orders, freezing orders, and an ancillary order under rule 25
- orders, including interim remedies, relating to the liberty of the public, relating to criminal proceedings, claims for judicial review, appeals from Masters or district judges, appeals against costs, vexatious litigants, and certain mental health problems.[41]

Where a claim under the *Human Rights Act 1998* raises either a claim in respect of a judicial act or is a claim for a declaration of incompatibility, then a deputy judge, Master, or district judge may not try this case.[42] A circuit judge sitting as a High Court judge is not classed as a 'deputy judge' and so would be entitled to sit on such cases, although it is more common for a puisne judge or Lord Justice of Appeal to sit on these matters.

Additional rules apply to Chancery business and the specialist courts, but there is no need to rehearse these here.

---

38. CPR, r 2.4.
39. PD 2B—Allocation of Cases to Levels of Judiciary.
40. *Senior Courts Act 1981*, s 9(1).
41. PD 2B, paras 2 and 3.
42. ibid, para 7A.

17.1.6.2 **County court**

The county court is slightly easier. Small claims track cases will usually be heard by a district judge rather than a circuit judge, although the latter is able to do so.[43] Realistically it will always be a district (or deputy) district judge that sits on such matters as the pressure for judicial time is so great, particularly as many circuit judges will be undertaking High Court business on circuit.

District judges will ordinarily also deal with fast-track cases,[44] partly because these are considered to be relatively straightforward cases (as they must be capable of being heard within a day). Most preliminary matters will also be listed before a district judge[45] and this demonstrates that district judges are the mainstay of the county court. This is partly because circuit judges will primarily sit on criminal matters (in the Crown Court) and therefore when they do sit on civil cases, they tend to be the more complicated cases. Ordinarily cases in the multi-track above £25,000 will be heard by a circuit judge (including a recorder) as will certain hearings for technical matters.[46] Applications relating to liberty, including the committal of a person to prison, must be made to a circuit judge.

17.1.7 **Juries in the civil courts**

Unlike in the Crown Court, the tribunal of fact in the court is usually the judge alone. It is extremely rare for juries to be used in civil cases, partly as a response to the demands of costs and timeliness of trials.

One of the few remaining classes of action where a jury could be used was defamation. However, the *Defamation Act 2013* created a statutory presumption against the use of a jury.[47] Notably, the Act does not say under what circumstances the court should allow a jury to be used but it is clear that it is designed to be exceptional. In *Yeo v Times Newspaper Ltd*[48] the High Court implied that it would only be cases where there is a need to counter any allegations of involuntary bias on the part of a judge that would warrant trial by jury.[49] Warby J gave the example of a judge suing someone. In such instances, it would be difficult for a judge alone to be trusted to make this decision because there may be the perception that a judge has ruled a particular way to advantage their brethren. However, such examples demonstrate the fact that the courts believe that it should be truly exceptional.

In *Elliott v Rufus*[50] Sharp LJ made an interesting point about how the 2013 Act may have a tangential but important role. Prior to the 2013 Act, a judge could not make a preliminary judgment about what a potentially defamatory statement meant as to do so could pre-empt what a jury (if it were to be empanelled) would decide. This has serious implications for costs where the meaning of the statement is the only issue that the parties dispute, because it would necessitate a full trial. However, since juries will not normally be empanelled, it is now possible for a judge to make a preliminary ruling as to meaning, particularly if that means one side would settle if they believed that the statement had a particular meaning.[51]

---

43. PD 27, para 1.
44. PD 2B, para 11.1.
45. ibid.
46. ibid, para 12.
47. *Defamation Act 2013*, s 11.
48. [2014] EWHC 2853 (QB).
49. ibid, [80].
50. [2015] EWCA Civ 121.
51. ibid, [28]. Indeed this happened in *Hiranandani-Vandrevala v Times Newspapers Ltd* [2016] EWHC 250 (QB).

So when will a jury be used? In the High Court, the rule is:

Where . . . the court is satisfied that there is in issue—

(a) A charge of fraud against that party; or

(b) A claim in respect of malicious prosecution or false imprisonment; or

(c) Any question or issue of a kind prescribed for the purposes of this issue.

The action shall be tried with a jury, unless the court is of opinion that the trial requires prolonged examination of documents or accounts or any scientific or local investigation which cannot conveniently be made with a jury.[52]

Matters in the Patent Court, Admiralty Court, and Commercial Court are not permitted to be heard by a jury.[53]

If a jury is to be sought, the party seeking the use of the jury must make an application to the court within twenty-eight days of the service of the defence.[54] This ensures that the issue can be decided early on and that all the parties understand how the case is to be prepared.

The same wording is found within the *County Courts Act 1984*,[55] meaning that trials by jury are similarly restricted in the county court. The 1984 Act includes additional proceedings that may not be heard by a jury[56] but these are not mentioned here as the clear presumption against jury trial remains.

If a jury trial does take place, then a jury of eight is empanelled in the county court but a jury of twelve in the High Court. As with criminal cases, verdicts should usually be unanimous, but in the county court, a verdict of 7–1 is permissible, and in the High Court, verdicts of 11–1, 10–2, 10–1, and 9–1 are permissible.[57]

17.1.8 Encouraging settlement

The courts now see it as their duty to encourage cases to settle. Indeed, the *Civil Procedure Rules* require the court to help the parties 'settle the whole or part of the case'.[58] Chapter 19 will discuss how the courts are prepared to assist the parties to use Alternative Dispute Resolution (ADR) to settle their differences. However, the courts will also facilitate settlement and the costs regime is designed to do this.

Perhaps the most notable process for encouraging settlement is known as Part 36 offers. This is a system, now contained within the *Civil Procedure Rules* (in Part 36, hence its name!), that allows either party to make an offer to settle the litigation, with significant cost implications if a side does not do so.

17.1.8.1 *Calderbank* offers

Prior to Part 36 offers, the usual approach was one of *Calderbank* offers. This is named after the landmark case of *Calderbank v Calderbank*.[59] This was a divorce case where there was a dispute as to the financial settlement. The wife offered the husband property

---

52. *Senior Courts Act 1981*, s 69(1).
53. ibid, when read in conjunction with s 6.
54. CPR, r 26.11.
55. *County Courts Act 1984*, s 66(3).
56. ibid, s 66(1).
57. Stuart Sime, *A Practical Approach to Civil Procedure* (19th edn, OUP 2016) 448.
58. CPR, r 1.4(2)(f).
59. [1976] Fam 93.

worth a certain amount of money in a letter entitled 'without prejudice'. She then followed this up with an affidavit, undertaking to transfer the property. The husband rejected this, believing it was not sufficient. The judge at trial ordered the transfer of less money than the wife offered, but ordered that each party bear their own costs.[60] The wife appealed, suggesting the husband should pay more costs because she attempted to settle the case.

The Court of Appeal allowed the appeal. They stated that whilst she could not rely on the letter (for reasons set out shortly), she could rely on the affidavit. The husband should have accepted this (generous) offer and because he did not, he was liable for the costs of both parties from the time he should have accepted this.

Out of this case came the general rules for *Calderbank* offers. The first is that an offer must be made in writing and state on it, 'without prejudice save for costs'. This wording has two implications:

1. 'Without prejudice' means that it cannot be used in court to show, for example, a party is admitting liability or is prepared to pay x in damages etc.

2. 'Save for costs' means that the letter *is* relevant and admissible after the final disposition of the case, as it should be taken into account when deciding costs.

The offer must be clear as to the circumstances, the period by which the offer will be paid, and also the length of time the other party has to settle the dispute. Either side may make a *Calderbank* offer (ie 'I will give you x' or 'I will accept x'). If the opposing side does not accept the offer then no mention is made of it during proceedings. At the end of proceedings, a decision is made whether the order of the court is at least as good as the offer made. If it is, then the opposing side will (usually) be required to pay the costs of both sides from the date that the offer expired. That said, the courts retain discretion as to costs and so they can depart from this general rule if they so wish.

Calderbank offers still exist although using Part 36 is more common. This is partly because Part 36 is governed by a set of rules and therefore there is greater certainty as to what the outcome of the process will be in terms of costs. However, some of the flexibility that arises in *Calderbank* is lost, because Part 36 is very clear as to how the settlement will be executed etc.

17.1.8.2 **Making a Part 36 offer**

Part 36 was developed from the *Calderbank* principles. In other words, many of its features are the same. According to rule 36.5 of the *Civil Procedure Rules*, the following must be complied with to make a Part 36 offer; it must:

(a) be made in writing. Although it is not mandatory to use it, a form has been designed to facilitate this.[61]

(b) make clear that the offer is being made pursuant to Part 36.

(c) specify a period of not less than twenty-one days, during which the offeror will be responsible for the costs.

(d) state whether it applies to the whole, or part, of a claim.

(e) state whether it takes account of counterclaims.

---

60. In family proceedings it is more common for each party to pay their own costs of litigation rather than apply the 'loser pays' principle of civil litigation (see FPR, r 28.3).

61. Form N242A and see PD 36.

The period of twenty-one days mentioned in (c) is the time which a person has to accept the offer. In other words, during those twenty-one days, the usual rule as to costs applies. At the end of that twenty-one-day period, this will be considered the time at which a person could have accepted the offer. The offer can be made at any time in proceedings, but where it is made less than twenty-one days before the hearing, the twenty-one-day rule does not apply and it must be accepted before the end of the trial.

Where the offer is to pay money, it must be paid in a single lump sum and an offer to pay more than fourteen days after the date of acceptance will not be considered a Part 36 offer unless the other party accepts the offer.[62] This latter sentence means that the costs advantage that would ordinarily come with a Part 36 offer will not apply unless the claimant accepts it. The rule about a single payment within fourteen days is one reason why *Calderbank* offers remain live. There is no such restriction with a *Calderbank* offer.

> **≡ Example** *Calderbank* vs Part 36
>
> Susan is suing Edward for £45,000, which she claims she is entitled to due to Edward selling an asset without permission. Edward believes the loss is more like £30,000. He is prepared to settle for that amount but wishes to pay the sum in three tranches of £10,000 due to his cash-flow situation.
>
> In this situation, Edward could not use Part 36 because the settlement is not to be paid in a lump sum and (some of) it will be paid more than fourteen days after the offer has been accepted. Edward could, however, use a *Calderbank* offer.

617

17.1.8.3 Withdrawing an offer

It is possible to withdraw a Part 36 offer but only in certain circumstances. The first, and perhaps most important, is that it cannot be withdrawn after the other party has accepted it. If the party accepts the offer then it becomes a binding agreement.[63] However, if the other side has not yet accepted the offer, then it can be withdrawn if notice is given to the other side to that effect, but it requires the permission of the court to do so if the applicant purports to accept the offer before the expiry of the period.[64]

A Part 36 offer does not automatically lapse[65] and therefore if the offeror wishes to withdraw the offer then they must do so expressly, even after the twenty-one-day period has elapsed.

17.1.8.4 Accepting an offer

There is no prescribed manner in which an offer is accepted, but it must be done in writing and a party must inform the court that they have done so.[66]

The general rule is that where a party accepts the offer, the defendant will pay the costs of both parties up to the point at which the offer was accepted.[67] There is no

---

62. CPR, r 36.6.
63. ibid, r 36.9(1).
64. ibid, r 36.9 when read in conjunction with r 36.10.
65. See *C v D* [2011] EWCA Civ 646.
66. CPR, r 36.11.
67. ibid, r 36.13.

discretion to award partial costs, and so the position is somewhat simpler as regards the costs regime, in that certainty is shown.

It was noted that a party could accept the offer after the expiry of the twenty-one-day period. If they do so, however, then the costs position shifts. The general rule is:

- The defendant pays the costs of the claimant up until the date of the expiry period.
- The claimant pays the costs from the date of the expiry date until the date of acceptance.[68]

The parties could choose to include costs within the Part 36 offer, although that would be somewhat unusual. The slightly more complicated rule as to costs for late acceptance is to mark the court's disapproval of not accepting the offer when it should have been accepted, ie the end of the expiry period.

17.1.8.5 **Failing to better an offer**

As with *Calderbank* offers, the main issue of relevance to Part 36 offers is what happens if a person does not 'match' an offer. The principal issue is one of costs.

Offers made by defendants

Where a claimant does not obtain a judgment more advantageous than a Part 36 offer, the costs position is as follows:

1. The defendant will be liable for the costs of the claimant up until the date of expiry of the Part 36 offer. This is, in essence, an application of the usual rule that 'costs follow the event', ie because judgment was still entered against the defendant, they will be liable for the costs.

2. The claimant will be required to pay the costs of the defendant from the date of the expiry of the Part 36 offer until the date of judgment.

3. The claimant will be required to pay interest on the costs of the defendant.[69]

Thus it is in the interests of a defendant who believes that he is likely to be held liable, to make an early offer to settle. Of course, the offer needs to be sensible because it must take into account the likely judgment that is to be awarded at trial, but if he does so, he could be protected from significant costs if the judge does not better the offer.

> **Example** Defendant making an offer
>
> An accident involving Tom's water storage caused considerable damage to Amelia's property. It is estimated that the damage will cost £30,000–£40,000 to put right but Amelia is claiming £75,000.
>
> After acknowledging the service, Tom makes a Part 36 offer to settle the dispute for £42,000, giving twenty-one days to accept the offer. Amelia does not accept the offer.
>
> At trial, the judge awards damages of £37,000 to Amelia. Amelia's costs until the date the offer expired came to £2,100. Her remaining costs were £8,000. Tom's costs were £500 until the date of the expiry of the Part 36 offer and £7,500 from that date.

---

68. ibid, r 36.13(4).
69. ibid, r 36.17(3).

As Amelia has not bettered the offer, she will be awarded the £37,000 by the judge, but will only receive £2,100 in costs. She will then have to pay £7,500 of Tom's costs, plus her own costs of £8,000. She will also need to pay interest on the £7,500 costs from the date the offer expired.

Had she accepted Tom's offer, she would have received £42,000 plus £2,100 in costs.

Offers made by claimants

Where the offer was made by a claimant, then so long as the judge makes an award that is *at least as advantageous* as the one the claimant made, then the following will be the position in respect of costs:

1. Interest on the judgment at a rate not exceeding 10 per cent above base rate, for some or all of the period since the expiry of the offer period.

2. The defendant to pay the claimant's costs after the relevant expiry period on the indemnity basis.

3. Interest on those indemnity costs at a rate not exceeding 10 per cent above base rate.

4. An additional amount, as calculated below.

⚡ INDEMNITY COSTS

There are two ways of calculating costs. The first is the 'standard basis' and the second is the 'indemnity basis'. The difference is really in whose favour doubt is resolved. On the standard basis, where there is doubt as to whether the costs are recoverable or reasonable, the benefit goes to the person paying. On the indemnity basis, it is the reverse. So, where there is any doubt as to whether the costs are payable or reasonable, the benefit goes to the person receiving the money. This potentially means costs could be significantly higher on the indemnity basis than the standard basis.

The additional amount referred to in #4 was introduced as a result of the *Legal Aid, Sentencing and Punishment of Offenders Act 2012* which sought to introduce some of the changes brought about by the *Jackson Review* into the costs of litigation.[70] The 2012 Act permits the Lord Chancellor to make regulations concerning the settlement of cases[71] and this has occurred.[72] The effect of these rules is to introduce the new 'additional amount' that is to be paid where a defendant rejects an offer from a claimant, and then subsequently does not achieve a more favourable result from court.

Where the claim is for money, the additional amount is calculated as shown in Table 17.6.[73]

---

70. Lord Justice Jackson, *Review of Civil Litigation Costs* (Judiciary of England and Wales, London 2010).
71. *Legal Aid, Sentencing and Punishment of Offenders Act 2012*, s 55.
72. *Offers to Settle in Civil Proceedings Order 2013*, SI 2013/93.
73. ibid, art 2.

Where the claim involves a non-monetary claim, the additional amount is 10 per cent of awarded costs up to the value of £500,000 and for costs awarded up to £1,000,000 the additional amount is 10 per cent of the first £500,000 and 5 per cent of any costs above that figure.[74] Where costs are above £1,000,000 the award would not be increased because the order makes clear that the maximum amount *for such claims* is to be £75,000,[75] which is the amount that would be paid for £1,000,000 worth of costs.

Table 17.6 Additional amount calculation

Award	Additional Amount
Up to £500,000	10% of the amount awarded
Above £500,000 but less than £1,000,000	10% of the first £500,000 and 5% of the amount awarded above that figure
Above £1,000,000	7.5% of the first £1,000,000 and 0.001% of the amount awarded over that figure

Where a claim involves both monetary and non-monetary value, then the maximum award should be calculated for both monetary and non-monetary claims using the 10 per cent/5 per cent methodology above,[76] again with a maximum payment of £75,000.

> **Example** Claimant making an offer
>
> Charles is suing Esther for negligence in respect of some investments she was managing for him. His statement of claim states the damages sought are £750,000. However, shortly after receiving the defence statement, Charles enters a Part 36 offer whereby he agrees to settle for £700,000 payable immediately. Esther rejects this offer. It goes to trial eight months later and the judge awards £725,000 to Charles.
>
> Charles' costs were £13,000 up until the point the Part 36 offer expired and £700,000 from that point, although Esther's lawyers believe that a more reasonable figure would be £625,000. Esther's costs are £800,000.
>
> Esther will be liable for:
>
> - £725,000 damages awarded by the court
> - £13,000 costs for the period up to the expiry of the Part 36 offer
> - interest on the £650,000 damages at a rate no more than 10 per cent above base rate for the eight months since the Part 36 offer (the interest continuing until the amount is paid)
> - £700,000[77] plus interest on this in the same way as above
> - an additional amount of £61,250 calculated as above
> - her costs of £800,000.

The implications for a defendant when a claimant makes an offer are therefore significant. The new regime is designed to ensure that defendants think very carefully about refusing offers to settle, particularly where they believe that they are, or could be, held liable. In the example above, had Esther accepted the offer, she would be in a very different position.

---

74. ibid, art 3(4)(b).
75. ibid, art 3(5).
76. ibid, art 3(4)(a).
77. As it is on the indemnity basis, where there is doubt as to whether the reasonable figure is £700,000 or £625,000, the benefit will be given to Charles.

If we assume her costs were similar to Charles' at the time the Part 36 offer was made, then she would have had to pay a total of £751,000. Instead she would be looking at paying a sum in excess of £2,000,000 assuming an interest rate of 8 per cent.

The consequences of Part 36 mean that lawyers have to be very clear with clients when advising them whether to accept a Part 36 offer or not. This is particularly true when the litigation is being funded in alternative ways. Insurance companies and solicitors employing contingency fee arrangements are likely to be highly cautious about rejecting a Part 36 offer. However, even private clients would need to think extremely carefully given the potential differences.

17.1.8.6 Judge not to be told

The last point to note on Part 36 is the fact that a judge should not be told that a Part 36 offer has been made until either (a) it is accepted, or (b) the court has made its determination as to the award. The reason for this is to ensure that there is no possibility that the judge is influenced by knowledge of the Part 36 offer. Let us return to our earlier example of Charles and Esther. If the judge realized an offer had been made for £700,000 and he was minded to award £710,000, could he be influenced by that if he knew that the consequences of that additional £10,000 were that Esther could pay hundreds of thousands of pounds more? Similarly, if he had been minded to award £690,000, would he be influenced knowing that by not awarding £700,000 the consequences would be that the fees would almost certainly dwarf the award, meaning Charles would actually lose money rather than gain any?

Where a judge believes that no prejudice would be caused by his continuing to sit with the knowledge, then the case can proceed.[78] At least one commentator has stated that judges should not be too quick to stand down[79] although where either party objects, it is quite likely that it would be difficult to continue (save where the difference in costs is likely to be relatively modest) because the appearance that a determination has been influenced must be relatively strong.

17.2 Case study: The small claims track

The remainder of this chapter will look at three hypothetical case studies. The point of these is to try and show you how litigation can work and the steps that are taken during proceedings.

The first form of litigation to consider is that of the small claims track. This was presented earlier, but this section will provide a walk-through of how a case would be heard.

Example A faulty television

Amy Daventry is a resident of Northampton. She buys a television costing £250 from Screens 'R' Us Ltd a national company with a branch in Northampton (their head office is in Carlisle). After six weeks Amy's television blows up. She contacts Screens 'R' Us who say that 'it is nothing to do with us, that is what they do'. They offer to put her in contact with a repair service who will fix it for £150. She declines the offer.

---

78. *Garratt v Saxby* [2004] 1 WLR 2152.
79. Stuart Sime, *A Practical Approach to Civil Procedure* (19th edn, OUP 2016) 417.

If you consult your *Contract Law* textbook you will see that this scenario is a very simple contract matter. Since this is a private transaction between a shop and a consumer, the *Consumer Rights Act 2015* covers this purchase. Section 9 of that Act states that goods must be of satisfactory quality, and s 10 requires goods to be fit for a particular purpose. A television blowing up for no reason within six weeks of purchase would not meet either test. The 2015 Act provides a short-term right to reject goods[80] but this only lasts thirty days. However, a longer period of rejection is also contained within the Act and, for a faulty television set, this would be within six months of purchase.[81] How does Amy secure her right to a refund?

17.2.1 Pre-action procedure

The first thing that Amy must do is to complain to the shop. She has done this verbally, but it would be prudent for her to write to them, explaining she wishes a refund. Assuming she does not do this, then her next port of call could either be litigation or the *Consumer Ombudsman*.

The *Consumer Ombudsman* is a form of Alternative Dispute Resolution that was created under secondary legislation.[82] It provides a 'single point of contact' for consumers who believe that their rights have been breached. It is free to use for consumers (it is funded by charging a fee for organizations that sign up to it). However, as with other forms of ADR (discussed in Chapter 19), it is reliant on the organization cooperating with the dispute.

Let us assume that Amy did contact the *Consumer Ombudsman* but the shop refuses to cooperate with the Ombudsman, saying 'it's not our problem'. The only solution left is to litigate. As noted earlier, an attempt at resolving the dispute must be made before commencing litigation. Clearly this has happened. If, however, Amy had not gone to the Ombudsman then she would have needed to write a letter saying why she was rejecting the goods and wishes a refund.

The first action is to complete the claim form (N1), presented earlier in this chapter. The online resources include a completed form N1 in respect of Amy's claim so that you can see what needs to be included. Reference should be made to 17.1.3 for an explanation of what to complete in respect of this claim. It will be remembered that the claim can begin online. If this option is chosen then Amy need only complete the details there. If she chooses to lodge the case at court, then she will need to photocopy the form twice so that there are three copies (one for her, one for the defendant, and one for the court). All three copies are lodged with the court.[83]

A fee is payable when the form is served. The fee depends on the sum of the claim and whether it is started online or at court. The current fees are set out in Table 17.7.

17.2.2 Defendant's response

The defendant will receive a copy of the N1 claim form and the appropriate notes for completion. A 'response pack' will also be sent. A copy of the forms and response pack

---

80. *Consumer Rights Act 2015*, s 20.
81. ibid, s 24.
82. See *Alternative Dispute Resolution for Consumer Disputes (Competent Authorities and Information) Regulations 2015*, SI 2015/542.
83. For online claims, the system prints out three copies automatically.

Table 17.7 Fees payable when the N1 form is served

Amount claim(£)	Paper Fee(£)	Online Fee(£)
Up to 300	35	25
300.01–500	50	35
500.01–1,000	70	60
1,000.01–1,500	80	70
1,500.01–3,000	115	105
3,000.01–5,000	205	185
5,000.01–10,000	455	410

is included online—it is not replicated here as it can be a lengthy form. However, in essence, the defendant has four options open to him:

- admit the whole of the claim
- admit *some* of the claim but deny the rest
- deny the whole of the claim
- counterclaim.

In fact the options are slightly increased since a counterclaim can be combined with an admission and partial admission of the claim. A counterclaim is where the defendant argues that the claimant owes money. It is not necessary to discuss in detail the process of counterclaiming but in essence the defendant becomes the 'claimant' for that part of the claim and the claimant becomes the 'defendant'. To avoid doubt and ensure consistency, however, the claimant and defendant continue to be so labelled for the duration of the proceedings. We will not cover counterclaims in this section as to do so could only confuse matters and this 'walkthrough' is simply an illustration of how civil litigation can occur and is not designed to be a comprehensive analysis of all aspects of the civil litigation system.

17.2.2.1 Admission of the claim

The most straightforward situation is that the defendant admits the claim and decides to settle. No money is paid to the court but instead the defendant tells the court he admits the claim and will pay the money to the claimant. When the claimant receives the money he will notify the court that the matter is settled. An advantage of the small claims track is that this can occur relatively quickly, especially where a major business is the defendant. The consequences for a business of losing a judgment can be significant as it will be entered onto a register to which credit agencies have access. Whilst a prompt settlement will lead to the entry being withdrawn the initial damage occurs. Also, where there is an arguable case many businesses will simply pay the money owed in a small claims case as it would cost more for them to fight it (as no legal costs can be paid the 'costs' of their in-house or contracted legal department who would inevitably deal with such matters would probably be more than the amount claimed).

It is for this reason that the small claims track is particularly useful for consumers. As there is no liability for costs, the 'threat' of a court summons (which, as seen from the costs stated earlier, will not cost much money to issue) can often settle customer-relations disputes. It has been questioned whether this was an appropriate use of the court's time, and whether a better approach for consumer disputes would be by way of ADR. As noted previously, the *Ombudsman Scheme* is now operational but it is not mandatory. For relatively simple claims under a certain threshold, it could legitimately be questioned whether mandating some form of adjudicative ADR would not be more appropriate. It would free up judicial time that could be used for other cases.

17.2.2.2 Admission of part of the claim

One possibility is that the defendant admits part of the claim but not all of it. In these circumstances the defendant explains to the court what part of the claim he admits and what part he is contesting and why. The defendant would normally pay the amount admitted although this need not be done at once. The claimant will then be asked whether he accepts the partial admission as full settlement or whether he wishes to pursue the matter for the remainder.

> **Example** Smoke in the kitchen
>
> Susan purchases a new saucepan but when it is first used it burns badly causing intense smoke damage to the wall by the cooker. Susan believes that the whole kitchen should be repainted because painting only one wall would not look right. The sellers of the saucepan believe it is possible to paint one wall.

Here, the seller may well admit liability but contest the damages that are being asked for. In this case a partial admission will be made whereby the seller accepts to refund the cost of the saucepan and for the work involved in painting one wall. They deny that it is necessary to pay for full redecoration.

Susan would have to decide whether to accept this partial admission or seek a hearing to decide whether her full claim would succeed.

17.2.2.3 Denying the claim

Where the defendant contests the entire claim then he must tender a defence which is a formal statement saying *why* he contests the claim. This is also part of the response form. In the small claims court it is usual for the defence to be supplied at the time of acknowledging the service of the claim but this need not occur and it is possible to acknowledge receipt of the claim within fourteen days and serve a defence within twenty-eight days.[84]

17.2.2.4 Defendant does not respond

It is possible that the defendant will simply fail to respond. Although the claim form is a formal document issued by the county court it is surprising how many people, firms, and companies will simply ignore the form hoping that 'it will go away'. In fact it rarely does and refusing to respond to a claim can cause significant complications, allowing the claimant to seek 'judgment by default'.[85]

---

84. CPR, r 15.4.
85. ibid, r 15.3 when read in conjunction with pt 12.

A judgment by default is where a court rules on the matter without considering any evidence. Indeed, it has been noted that it is a purely administrative exercise that takes place when no defence is filed.[86] In straightforward cases such as the one in Amy's example, the matter would not be put before a judge. The court staff would check that the procedural steps have been completed appropriately and would then simply enter judgment on behalf of the court.

There is the power to set aside a judgment in default. Where the judgment was entered incorrectly (eg because the claim was not served in time) then the court *must* set aside the judgment.[87] These situations are, however, comparatively rare because most people take care to ensure that claims and documents are served appropriately.

The court has discretion to set a judgment aside if:

(a) the defendant has a real prospect of successfully defending the claim; or

(b) it appears to the court there is some other good reason why—

    (i) the judgment should be set aside; or

    (ii) the defendant should be allowed to defend the claim.[88]

Paragraph (a) is considered the issue that the courts will focus most directly upon; they will require considerable persuasion to allow a case to be reopened where judgment is likely to be given against the defendant thereafter.[89] Examples could include situations where a defendant did not receive the claim forms. Service can be to the last-known address of an individual[90] but if no forwarding address or service was active, it is quite possible the defendant did not know about the proceedings. It is notable that this is *discretionary* rather than mandatory. As service can be to the last-known address, a court could decide that the proceedings took place appropriately. However, it is more common for them to set aside a judgment in this instance.[91]

Judgments are public documents and a county court judgment can cause significant problems to a credit rating of either an individual or company. It has been suggested therefore that where an unaware defendant applies for a judgment to be set aside because he would have otherwise settled the case without the need for a judgment, this could be a reason for setting the judgment aside.[92] It is to be hoped that such applications are tested, however. A person should not be allowed to set aside the judgment to save embarrassment save where he was not aware of the claim, since otherwise the person is being rewarded for his lax conduct.

A fee is payable by the defendant to set the judgment aside (currently £255) and if there are costs incurred by the claimant (unlikely in the small claims track) then these would be payable by the defendant.

17.2.3 Track allocation, management, and mediation

When the defence is received, a court officer will make a preliminary assessment of the track that the case should be assigned to. In a case such as Amy's, there is no doubt that it would be the small claims track. It was noted earlier (17.1.4) that for non-personal

---

86. Stuart Sime, *A Practical Approach to Civil Procedure* (19th edn, OUP 2016) 137.
87. CPR, r 13.2.
88. CPR, r 13.3.
89. Stuart Sime, *A Practical Approach to Civil Procedure* (19th edn, OUP 2016) 144.
90. CPR, r 6.9.
91. See, for example, *Akram v Adam* [2004] EWCA Civ 1601.
92. Stuart Sime, *A Practical Approach to Civil Procedure* (19th edn, OUP 2016) 144.

injury cases under £10,000 there is a clear presumption that the small claims track will be used.

The court will send a directions questionnaire to both the claimant and defendant. A copy of the questionnaire for the small claims track can be found with the online resources. The questionnaire asks to confirm the personal details of the parties, the proposed court centre that the matter will be heard at, whether experts are to be present, and the number of witnesses to be heard.

Perhaps one of the more important questions is whether the parties are prepared to consider mediation. This is part of a recent trend to encourage alternative forms of dispute resolution (discussed further in Chapter 19). If both parties consent, then the case will be stayed and sent to the small claims mediation service.[93] This is a service that is operated by HM Courts and Tribunal Service where court staff act as mediators to try and settle the dispute. The mediation usually takes place via a teleconference. If mediation fails, then the stay is lifted.

Before the hearing takes place, a further fee has to be paid. This is known as the 'hearing fee' and the current level is set as in Table 17.8.

It should be noted that whilst these costs are relatively modest, it does mean that even a small claims track case can cost a relatively significant amount of money. Amy will now have had to pay £50 or £60 in court fees to recover £150, although this will of course be reimbursed if she is successful.

Whilst the hearing will usually be in public,[94] it will generally take place not in a courtroom but in a judge's room. Whether this is truly 'in public' is therefore open to question. Theoretically, there is nothing to stop someone going to the court and saying that they would like to watch proceedings, but how many people will know this and/or want to do so?

Table 17.8 The current fee to be paid for a hearing

Claim value(£)	Fee(£)
Up to 300	25
300.01–500	55
500.01–1,000	80
1,000.01–1,500	115
1,500.01–3,000	170
3,000 or more	335

Whilst the small claims track is civil litigation, the hearing will usually differ from the formality inherent in other forms of civil litigation:

1. The court may adopt any method of proceeding at a hearing that it considers to be fair.

2. Hearings will be informal.

3. The strict rules of evidence do not apply.

4. The court need not take evidence on oath.

93. CPR, r 26.4A.
94. PD 27, para 4.1.

5. The court may limit cross-examination.

6. The court must give reasons for its decision.[95]

The judge will normally take the lead in small claims track cases and it will usually have the feel of an inquisitorial approach or even be more akin to adjudication, where the judge will ask questions of the parties to understand what is at the heart of this dispute. This is partly because lawyers within the small claims track are relatively unusual, not least because the costs of representation are not normally recoverable in the small claims track.

The attendance of the parties is usually necessary but it is possible to provide written notice to the court and other party at least seven days in advance that they will not be present.[96] If this is done and all other documents are submitted in the usual way, the court will take account of those documents (eg the statement of claim or the statement of defence). If they do not provide the relevant notice and submit the appropriate documents and do not attend, then summary action can be taken. This means that where it is the claimant who does not turn up, the case can be struck out (meaning the action fails).[97] Where it is the defendant who does not turn up then the case will be decided solely on the claimant's evidence (if the claimant appears or has given the necessary notice not to attend),[98] meaning in all likelihood that the action will succeed.

The judge will normally pronounce judgment immediately after the conclusion of the hearing. This will not be in the form of a usual judgment and will instead be a simple explanation of his decision.[99] Ordinarily the judgment will be given verbally rather than in writing. However, hearings are recorded and therefore if a transcription is required then this can be arranged.

17.2.4 Remedies and appeal

Obtaining a judgment by itself is not sufficient, a remedy must be sought. The remedies and avenues of appeal will be considered in Chapter 18.

17.3 Judicial review

The second form of litigation to consider is judicial review. This is an area of civil litigation that is very different from the previous example. Instead of two sides arguing over money or some other form of dispute, judicial review is about holding the state to account. It is arguing that a decision that has been, or will be, made is legally impermissible (whether through illegality, irrationality, or procedural impropriety[100]). Many challenges under the *Human Rights Act 1998* (HRA 1998) are judicial reviews, in part because the 1998 Act states that a public body acts unlawfully if it acts contrary to a Convention right,[101] which is a ground for judicial review.

This section will not consider the substantive law relating to judicial review as that is a matter for other texts and modules.[102] Instead, this section will be similar to the

---

95. CPR, r 27.8.
96. ibid, r 27.9(1).
97. ibid, r 27.9(2).
98. ibid, r 27.9(3).
99. PD 27, para 5.3(1).
100. *Council for Civil Service Unions v Minister for the Civil Service* [1995] AC 374.
101. HRA 1998, s 6(1).
102. You are likely to cover this in your Public Law module.

previous section in that it will take a hypothetical case study and walk through the stages of the hearing. Judicial review has increased significantly in recent years and this has proven a thorn in the government's side. The government sought to make changes to judicial review, although in the end relatively modest changes were introduced by legislation.[103]

Unlike the previous example, we have shifted from the Crown Court to the High Court of Justice. Save for a few issues that are not relevant to us, claims for judicial review are brought in the Administrative Court,[104] which forms part of the Queen's Bench Division of the High Court. Traditionally, claims for judicial review took place in a Divisional Court (ie two or more judges, usually presided over by a Lord Justice of Appeal) but recently there has been an increase in single-judge hearings.

Let us now consider our hypothetical example.

> **Example** A mother's march
>
> Matilda wishes to campaign against the decision of the (fictional) Rutland County Council to close a nursery she uses in Smallville. She has organized a number of parents and they wish to march two miles down the centre of Smallville to the offices of Rutland County Council where they will make speeches and wave placards. The protest is planned to take place the day a Home Office minister is due to visit Smallville and so the chief constable of the (fictional) Rutland Police has decided to ban the march because he doesn't want the town to look unruly. Matilda wishes to challenge this decision. She visits the chief constable but he refuses to back down and thus she wishes to take action in court.

17.3.1 **Pre-action protocols**

As with other types of civil litigation there are procedural steps that must be considered before a claim for judicial review can proceed.

17.3.1.1 **A public function?**

The first point to note is that a judicial review can only be brought against a public body. The rules state that 'judicial review' means:

> . . . a claim to review the lawfulness of—
>
> i. an enactment; or
>
> ii. a decision, action or failure to act in relation to the exercise of a public function.

Thus judicial review is an action against an organ of the state. Whilst it is traditionally said that the English Legal System differs from certain continental jurisdictions (most notably France) in not having a separate court system for public matters, this is arguably no longer true with the advancement of judicial review and the creation of the Administrative Court.

Quite what is a public function is the subject of some debate and it is outside the scope of this book. It can be summarized as a function that the public would ordinarily

---

103.   *Criminal Justice and Courts Act 2015*, pt 4.
104.   PD 54A, para 1.1.

be expected to be delivered by the state, even if it is not actually doing so. For example, the incarceration of prisoners would be a function of the state even if they are being incarcerated in a private prison. However, for more detailed reference it is necessary to refer to texts that consider this in more depth.[105]

17.3.1.2 *Locus standi*

The first issue that must be considered is whether the claimant has the right to issue judicial review proceedings. There is not an absolute right to begin proceedings, and only persons with 'standing' (the anglicized meaning of *locus standi*) can bring proceedings. The test for this is set out in statute:

> No application for judicial review shall be made unless the leave of the High Court has been obtained in accordance with rules of court; and the court shall not grant leave to make such an application unless it considers that the applicant has a sufficient interest in the matter to which the application relates.[106]

Two issues arise from this. The first is that there is not an automatic right to judicial review, permission must be sought (discussed later at 17.3.2) and the second is the test of standing, that is 'sufficient interest'. Rather unhelpfully neither the Act nor the CPR define what 'sufficient interest' means but it has been considered to mean that a person has a genuine interest in seeking a remedy and can show they are, or are likely to be, affected by the issue to be reviewed.[107] The essence of the test is to prevent purely theoretical disputes from arising or to prevent people who will not be affected by the decision challenging it for non-legal reasons.

≣ Example More about the march

If we refer back to our example of Matilda, it would be extremely difficult to argue that Matilda does not have standing in this matter since she uses the nursery the protest relates to. If, however, Hazel, who lives 200 miles away, wishes to challenge the decision because she objects to 'police suppression of the right to march' then it is unlikely that she would have standing because she cannot show a link to the action.

That said, it has been suggested that some abuses of power are so widespread that any citizen would have the right to intervene.[108]

Arguably standing can be dealt with at one of two stages; either the permission stage or at the actual hearing. The general rule is that it will be dealt with at the permission stage although in exceptional cases the courts have said that the decision can be postponed so that they can reflect on standing in light of the evidence adduced.[109] However, arguably this does not breach the general rule since such instances are known as 'rolled up' hearings, ie ones where the permission and merits are dealt with at the same time.

---

105. See, for example, Hilaire Barnett, *Constitutional & Administrative Law* (9th edn, OUP 2016) Part IV.
106. *Senior Courts Act 1981*, s 31(3).
107. See *Halsbury's Laws*, vol 61, 656.
108. See, by way of discussion, *R v Somerset County Council and ARC Southern Ltd, ex parte Dixon* [1997] COD 323.
109. *R v Inland Revenue Commissioners, ex parte National Federation of Self-Employed and Small Businesses Ltd* [1982] AC 617

Section 31 is clear that permission is required in order to bring a review and that permission can only be given if the person has standing. In a rolled-up hearing a court will consider all the evidence and either allow the application and grant relief (subject to their discretion) or, instead of rejecting the case, often state that permission was refused even though the effect is the same.

Human rights

A slight issue arises in respect of applications under the HRA 1998. Section 7(7) HRA 1998 expressly states that when deciding whether to permit someone to bring an action under s 7 of the Act (which permits someone to bring proceedings claiming a breach, or future breach, of their rights) the court must make reference to Article 34 ECHR. Article 34 defines a 'victim' and it has been suggested that the definition of victim under the ECHR is more restrictive than the test ordinarily adopted by the courts when making decisions under Part 54. However, it is not necessarily easy to identify any practical issue because many issues raised as human rights issues would also be relevant under the grounds of judicial review.

Example Matilda and her human rights

If we refer back to our example Matilda's application may, or may not, raise human rights issues. On the one hand she could use s 7 HRA 1998 because the right to protest is contained within Articles 10 (freedom of expression) and 11 (right of assembly) of the ECHR. However, she could also complain about the decision using only domestic law (that it was irrational).

In fact, in this scenario it would make no substantive difference since Matilda would be considered a victim under Article 34 as well as having ordinary standing under s 31.

Exhaustion of alternative remedies

As part of the decision about whether a person has standing to bring an action in judicial review the courts will consider whether all alternative remedies have been exhausted. Judicial review is considered to be an action of last resort and therefore where there is, for example, an internal complaints or review system by a public body this should be exhausted before judicial review proceedings are brought. That said, the courts are willing to relax this where alternative proceedings would not be 'so convenient, beneficial and effectual' or where the alternative will not provide an effective remedy.[110]

In our example, it is unlikely that this would cause any real difficulty. There is no statutory or alternative appeals process where a chief constable decides to ban a march.

17.3.1.3 **Timing**

Judicial review actions are supposed to be timely: they are designed to review either decisions made recently or decisions that are about to be made. Save for planning and procurement cases, which were the subject of control as part of the 'reforms' to judicial review,[111] a claim for judicial review must be lodged 'promptly' and, in any event, not less than three months from the date of the decision to be challenged.[112] It should be

---

110. *Halsbury's Laws*, vol 61, 657.
111. See CPR reg 54.4(5) and *Public Contracts Regulations 2015*, SI 2015/102.
112. CPR, r 54.5(1).

noted that 'promptly' and 'three months' are not part of the same test: it is quite possible that waiting three months to judicially review a decision is considered not to be prompt, meaning that the application is dismissed.[113]

> **≡ Example** Returning to the march
>
> Let us assume that the march was organized two months before it is due to commence. The chief constable within the first three days said that he would ban the march. If Matilda left it until the week before the march then the court may decline to give permission.
>
> What if Matilda had actually been in discussion with the chief constable for four weeks in an attempt to reach a conclusion? If, after these talks, the final 'no' arrives then there would be little difficulty in showing the timeliness of the action because any delay was incurred by trying to resolve the dispute.

17.3.1.4 Exchange of letters

Save where time prevents it, a potential claimant should ordinarily send a letter to the defendant, stating why they are seeking to challenge the claim and asking for it to be resolved. The defendant should ordinarily acknowledge this letter and state a brief summary of why they contest the issue.[114]

17.3.2 Applying for permission

Unlike most forms of civil litigation, pursuing judicial review is not a matter of right. An applicant must first seek the permission of the High Court to do so.

A specific form exists to begin a claim for judicial review (N461 which can be found with the online resources) and this must be used. Along with the personal details of the claimant, proposed defendant, and any interested parties, it includes a request for details of the decision that is to be judicially reviewed and also the date the decision was made. Details of the proposed remedy sought must also be included, together with details of any other decisions that are to be made.

The form must also be accompanied with the relevant documentary evidence that is to be relied upon to justify the decision. This is because the initial application for permission will ordinarily be done on papers, and therefore sufficient evidence must be submitted to show that there is a case to answer. In Matilda's case, it is quite likely that the chief constable will have written to her, explaining why he will not permit a march. This, together with the letters she sent requesting permission etc, would form part of the documentary evidence. A fee is to be paid when the form is lodged (currently £154).

Once the form is served (and unlike the county court proceedings discussed before, the claimant will be responsible for service rather than the court), all parties must acknowledge service, using the appropriate form. This must take place within twenty-one days of service[115] and should include a summary of his grounds for contesting the claim or indeed contesting that permission should be given.[116]

---

113.   See, *Senior Courts Act 1981*, s 31(7).
114.   Stuart Sime, *A Practical Approach to Civil Procedure* (19th edn, OUP 2016) 556.
115.   CPR, r 54.8(2).
116.   ibid, r 54.8(4)(a).

The matter then proceeds before a 'single judge' (who is ordinarily a puisne judge). This judge will consider the evidence placed before him and decide whether to give permission for a judicial review to proceed. The test for whether judicial review should proceed was summarized as raising 'an arguable ground . . . having a reasonable prospect of success'.[117] Where it is thought that a successful claim would have no practical effect, permission can also be refused.[118] As part of the 'reforms' to judicial review, an additional threshold was introduced that may be considered by a court on its own motion or must be considered if the defendant so requests.[119] This additional threshold is that the court must refuse leave if 'it appears to the High Court to be highly likely that the outcome for the applicant would not have been substantially different'.[120] This is a higher threshold than the 'no practical difference' adopted by the Supreme Court, but it is designed to ensure that the cost of judicial review is avoided where the proceedings would, in essence, be theoretical.

17.3.2.1 Challenging a refusal

If the single judge refuses to grant leave, a person can seek to renew permission before a hearing.[121] This allows them an opportunity to persuade the judge that there is an arguable case or that the outcome would be 'substantially different' where the s 31(3C) test is considered. A fee of £385 must be paid to renew permission.

If permission is again refused, the only opportunity is to appeal to the Court of Appeal (Civil Division).[122]

Where the single judge decides that an application is 'without merit'[123] then it is not possible to seek a hearing to renew permission,[124] and instead the only avenue will be an appeal to the Court of Appeal (Civil Division). That said, such a challenge is unlikely to succeed.

17.3.2.2 Success rate

Although it was said earlier that the threshold for permission would seem relatively low (an arguable case) it is clear that a substantial number of cases fail to gain permission. The latest statistics show that of 1,400 applications made in the first half of 2020, 650 cases reached the permission stage, and of these 170 received permission to proceed.[125] Eighty-eight cases were found to be totally without merit.[126]

The relatively low success rate is one reason why governments have sought to restrict judicial review. The 1,400 applications lodged in the first half of 2020 require a public authority to respond in some way to the application, incurring cost and effort. However, as problematic as the government may view judicial review to be, it is now clearly considered an important constitutional safeguard that allows the state to be held to account.

---

117.   *Sharma v Brown-Antoine* [2007] 1 WLR 780, 787.
118.   *R (on behalf of O) v Secretary of State for the Home Department* [2016] UKSC 19.
119.   *Senior Courts Act 1981*, s 31(3C).
120.   ibid, as inserted by the *Criminal Justice and Courts Act 2015*, s 31(3D).
121.   CPR, r 54.12(3).
122.   CPR, r 52.15.
123.   CPR, r 23.13.
124.   CPR, r 54.12(7).
125.   Ministry of Justice, 'Civil Justice Statistics Quarterly: April to June 2020' (Ministry of Justice 2020) Section 8.
126.   Ibid.

17.3.3 **The hearing**

Assuming that permission is granted then the matter will begin to proceed towards a hearing. A fee of £770 must be paid at this stage, although this is halved to £385 if the claimant required a hearing to gain permission.

17.3.3.1 **Courts hearing judicial review claims**

As already noted, it is the Administrative Court that hears applications for judicial review, but that does not mean it sits in one place. The majority of judicial review proceedings continue to be heard in London but they are increasingly being heard in the regions too, either by puisne judges or acting judges of the High Court.[127] The principal courts where it sits include Cardiff, Bristol, Birmingham, Leeds, and Manchester. That said, as it is part of the High Court of Justice, it can sit anywhere and can certainly sit in any other court if it is convenient for the parties and/or judiciary to do so.

17.3.3.2 **Pre-hearing matters**

Once permission has been granted, the court will issue directions that will set out the timescale of proceedings and indicate who is going to hear the case (including whether it is necessary for the matter to be heard by a Divisional Court).

Theoretically judicial review cases could be decided without a hearing[128] but this is likely to be extremely rare and would be where the dispute is minor. Such cases are now more likely to be resolved through the use of ADR and therefore a hearing is more likely.

The claimant must submit, at least twenty-one days before the hearing, a skeleton argument outlining their case.[129] This must be served on all parties and include:

(a) a time estimate for the complete hearing

(b) a list of issues

(c) a list of the legal points to be taken (together with any relevant authorities with page references to the passages relied on)

(d) a chronology of events

(e) a list of essential documents for the advance reading of the court

(f) a list of persons referred to.[130]

'Skeleton arguments' are a misleading term as they can be extremely comprehensive. In judicial review hearings (and indeed in appeals), they are a written explanation (fully referenced) of the submissions of the individual. Whilst they will be expanded upon during the hearing, they are also used by the court to identify what issues they do not want to discuss in the hearing.

The other parties must file and serve a skeleton argument no less than fourteen days before the hearing, ie they will have sight of the claimant's skeleton argument for seven days and they should ordinarily address any area of the skeleton argument that they disagree with in their own skeleton argument.

---

127. *Senior Courts Act 1981*, s 9 permits a circuit judge or recorder to sit as a judge of the High Court for a particular case.

128. CPR, r 54.17.

129. PD 54, para 15.

130. ibid, para 15.3.

633

17.3.3.3 **Oral hearing**

The hearing itself will take place in open court and it will, unlike the small claims track cases which were discussed in the previous section, take place in a courtroom. The court itself can decide on the format of the hearing but ordinarily the claimant will open proceedings, followed by the defendant and then any interested parties.

Hearings on judicial review do not generally involve hearing testimony from witnesses, although the court does have a discretion to hear witnesses if they believe it would be helpful.[131] In practice, it is generally rare for witnesses to be heard as judicial review is rarely about the facts, it is normally a question of law, ie whether the decision complained of is illegal, irrational, or one that was reached in a procedurally improper way. The documentation that is submitted to the court is normally sufficient to reach the decision.

17.3.4 **Decision and remedy**

The verdict will either be given at the conclusion of the hearing or may well be reserved. Where it is given at the conclusion of the hearing it will be given *ex tempore* but where it is reserved then ordinarily a full judgment will be prepared that will then be handed down later. Where it is a Divisional Court (two or more judges) then a single judgment may be given or all judges may speak. Where a two-judge court is divided then technically the case is resolved against the defendant.[132] That said, the court does have discretion to re-list the matter before a three-judge panel before judgment is given, although it is likely that this will only be considered in exceptional circumstances.

The remedies available for a successful claim for judicial review will be considered in the next chapter.

17.4 **The Family Court**

The third, and final, example of civil litigation looks at a completely different issue, that of family law. As was discussed at 6.3.4, this is now the province of the Family Court and the court has its own procedure rules (*Family Procedure Rules*).

Family justice is a very broad type of civil activity that encompasses numerous different types of litigation. Some are akin to ordinary litigation (eg, partners seeking to dispose of property) whereas others are more specialist. Public childcare proceedings involve the state seeking to exercise its powers to protect children and can include, for example, decisions whether to remove a child from its parents.

As with the other two types of litigation we will start with an example.

> **Example** Increased contact
>
> Deborah and Joshua were married for eleven years and had one child, Sarah, who is aged 6. When they divorced, Deborah obtained a residence order for Sarah meaning that she stays with her. Joshua was granted a contact order that says that Sarah will see her father on

---

131.   CPR, r 54.17.
132.   See *Cambridgeshire CC v Associated Lead Mills Ltd* [2005] EWHC 1627 (Admin) [14].

certain days. During school term-time the contact is Tuesday evenings and all-day Saturday. During school holidays he can see her on Tuesday afternoons and all-day Saturday.

Joshua wishes to increase the amount of time he spends with Sarah as she grows up. He requests overnight contact on Friday evenings (so that she would stay with him on Friday evening through to Saturday evening) and the right to take her on holiday for one week a year.

Deborah is happy to allow for the holiday but she thinks Sarah is too young for overnight contact away from her at the moment.

This is what is known as a private child-law dispute. It is characterized as a private dispute because, by itself, it does not involve the state. It is for Joshua and Deborah to settle the matter although, as will be seen, this is not strictly true as the interests of Sarah are directly relevant to this dispute. In terms of law, contact arrangements are dealt with under s 8 *Children Act 1989* and it is under this section that Joshua will apply to the court.

17.4.1 Beginning the claim

As with other forms of litigation, there are procedures that must take place before proceedings can commence. The main issue is the desire to avoid litigation. It was seen earlier (and will be seen more clearly in Chapter 19) that the courts seek to avoid litigation more generally, but this is certainly the case in respect of family disputes, particularly those involving a child. Litigation is undoubtedly disruptive to family life, particularly when it is seen as a 'battle' over the upbringing of children which has the danger of spilling into the child's consciousness.

Part 3 of the *Family Procedure Rules* refers to non-court dispute resolutions. The rule is clear:

> The court must consider, at every stage in proceedings, whether non-court dispute resolution is appropriate.[133]

This rule is followed by a requirement that, for certain applications, non-court disposals must be considered. The detail of these rules will be considered in Chapter 19 but we can note at this point that private-law proceedings relating to children are one of these cases. Therefore, before Joshua can apply for a court order, he will first need to either attempt mediation or be given a waiver.

For our purposes, let us assume that Joshua and Sarah try mediation but it becomes clear that neither side is willing to 'budge' in terms of what they wish. Therefore, mediation has been tried but ultimately fails and only a court will be able to settle the dispute.

17.4.1.1 Claim form

As with other forms of litigation, the first step to litigation is to complete the claim form. The Family Courts have their own forms, and the relevant form to be used in this instance is form C100. A copy of this form can be found with the online resources. The form is more detailed than the other claim forms that have been examined. However, the

---

133. FPR, r 3.3(1).

form is also accessible, with the sections being phrased as questions, generally without the use of legalese. This is a reflection of the fact that legal aid is not normally available for private family-law disputes, and therefore there is an increase in litigants in person who are pursuing applications themselves. A dispute such as the one in our example between Deborah and Joshua could easily be completed without the need for a lawyer.

The form asks the claimant to say what the application is about. Section 8 of the *Children Act 1989* permits the making of various orders in respect of the upbringing of a child, but the one that we are concerned with is a 'child arrangements order' which deals with who has residence of the child, and at what point in time etc. The claimant is also to indicate whether there are any potential risks of harm (so that these can be investigated by the appropriate authorities), including issues relating to the history of the case and whether the court is being invited to ratify a consent order. Full details of the child must be given and information provided about whether they are known to the local authority social services department.

Section 2 of the form requires details about the mediation attempted. The most common answers here are that either the parties have attended mediation (as in our example), or that they have a mediation exemption. This is where the mediator accepts that mediation would not be appropriate (and they must sign the relevant part of C100 to indicate that). As will be seen from Chapter 19, there is some concern that mediators are allowing too many people to escape the requirement to attend a mediation hearing. There is some anecdotal evidence that the courts are beginning to take a harder line and are not accepting a wish not to pursue mediation. However, practice is not consistent as some courts do allow this.

Later sections of the form require details of the claim and details of the remedy sought (ie if the object is to settle the arrangements for access to the children, what pattern of contact will be used etc).

As with the other forms, there is a requirement that the claimant signs a statement of truth, with the usual consequences for any misleading statements.

A fee is payable at the time the application is lodged. This fee is currently £215 which is a not insignificant sum. There are real concerns about the costs of family law cases,[134] and whether this puts people off going to court. Where there is a disparity between incomes, it can also mean that a party could misuse the cost of litigation to benefit themselves unreasonably.

17.4.2 **Allocating the judge**

Whilst the Family Court is one joined-up court, it encompasses three levels of existing courts; the magistrates' court (where it used to be known as the *Family Proceedings Court*), the county court, and the High Court. It would not be appropriate to talk about where the case goes in terms of these courts because the Family Court is truly a joined-up court. However, this also means that cases are heard by magistrates, district judges (including deputy district judges), circuit judges (including recorders), and puisne judges. The judge should be allocated for the right seriousness of case. The Family Court is under considerable pressure in terms of the amount of people seeking

---

134.   Joshua Rozenberg 'Dramatic Increase in Court Fees Causing Deep Concern, Say Senior Judges' *The Guardian* (19 January 2015) <https://www.theguardian.com/law/2015/jan/19/dramatic-increases-court-fees-deep-concern-senior-judges>.

to use its services, so it is important that circuit and puisne judges are only used where their judicial experience truly warrants it. As with other forms of civil litigation, the 'workhorses' of the court are district judges, but with magistrates playing a surprisingly intensive role within the Family Court.

Upon receipt of the claim form, it shall be sent to a 'gatekeeper'. This is a nominated legal adviser or district judge[135] whose job it is to make an initial allocation to an appropriate judge of the Family Court. Guidance has been issued by the President of the Family Court[136] to determine the allocation but this must also be read in conjunction with the allocation order.[137] There appears a presumption that private family-law matters such as the one that Joshua wishes to initiate should be heard by lay justices,[138] and certainly this seems to be the default these days. The exceptions are where it is considered too complex or it is likely to take more than three days.

For our purposes, however, we will assume that the case will proceed as normal and will therefore be allocated to magistrates sitting in the Family Court. Ordinarily this should mean a bench of two or three magistrates, ordinarily including both a man and woman.[139] The magistrates are all specially trained and the presiding justice must be someone who has been approved to chair family proceedings.

17.4.3 **The hearing**

Hearings of family matters, including private family-law disputes, are ordinarily held in private, even if the courtroom is being used. Thus the general public will not be entitled to attend the court, although the parties will normally be allowed to bring a person to accompany them for moral support.

As a hearing in the magistrates' court, only the presiding justice or the legal adviser will speak. The chair will usually be addressed as 'Sir' or 'Madam'. Much of the formality of court proceedings is abandoned because the intention is to get to the truth of the matter. Known as the 'welfare principle', the overriding concern of a court when dealing with matters relating to children, is to do what is in the best interests of the welfare of the child.[140]

It is unlikely that the strict rules of adversarial trial will be adopted and instead it will be more quasi-inquisitorial. The justices (or their legal adviser) are likely to ask questions of each party, to try and understand their position. In many instances they will try to get both sides to agree a way forward as this is preferable to a court-ordered settlement, since both parties consider themselves to have a 'stake' in what has been agreed.

In matters such as the example involving Joshua, it is likely that judgment will be given on the day of the hearing. The justices, or their legal adviser, will summarize what the court has decided and why. Ultimately an order of the court will be produced, but this may not follow for a few days. The judgment, however, is usually in force from the time that it has been pronounced in court.

The remedies and avenues for appeal are considered in the next chapter.

---

135.   PD 12B, para 9.2.
136.   Judiciary.uk, 'President's Guidance on Allocation and Gatekeeping for Proceedings under Part II of the Children Act 1989' (22 April 2014). Available online at: <https://www.judiciary.uk/wp-content/uploads/2013/02/private-law-allocation-and-gatekeeping-guidance.pdf>.
137.   *The Family Court (Composition and Distribution of Business) Rules 2014*, SI 2014/840.
138.   *Presidents Guidance*, para 23.
139.   *Family Court (Composition and Distribution of Business) Rules 2014*, SI 2014/840, r 3(2).
140.   *Children Act 1989*, s 1.

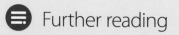

Summary

This chapter has introduced some of the concepts of civil litigation and, in particular, how a case proceeds through the small claims court, Administrative Court, and the Family Court. It has also:

- Identified that a single set of rules now govern most civil litigation (the *Civil Procedure Rules*).

- Identified that the family system has its own set of rules known as the *Family Procedure Rules*.

- Noted that the judge has specific responsibility for ensuring the case management of trials within the civil justice system.

- Noted that a wide variety of judges can sit on civil matters and their powers differ.

- Identified that there are three 'tracks' through which civil litigation ordinarily proceeds. These are the 'small claims track', 'fast track', and 'multi-track'.

- Demonstrated how a case would proceed through the fast track and noted that the procedure is more informal than in many other proceedings.

- Noted that costs can be used as a negotiating tool to allow cases to be settled.

- Demonstrated how a judicial review case would begin and proceed through the Administrative Court.

- Demonstrated how a private child-law matter is heard in the Family Court.

- Identified that family proceedings are often more inquisitorial than adversarial.

End-of-chapter questions

1. Read Hazel Genn, 'Do-it-yourself Law: Access to Justice and the Challenge of Self-representation' (2013) 32 *Civil Justice Quarterly* 411–14. Is it right that decisions about the welfare of a child, albeit in a private-law context, are left to litigants in person? Is there not a danger that emotion means that disputes are litigated beyond their limit?

2. Read Pablo Cortes, 'The Online Court: Filling the Gaps of the Civil Justice System?' (2017) 36 *Civil Justice Quarterly* 109–26. To what extent do you think it is possible to look at alternative forms of litigation in order to ease the pressure from the courts?

Further reading

Koo AKC, 'Ten Years after Halsey' (2015) 34 *Civil Justice Quarterly* 77–95.

This looks at how the decision in *Halsey v Milton Keynes NHS Trust*[141] has influenced the conduct of litigation and, in particular, the use of Alternative Dispute Resolution.

---

141.   [2004] EWCA Civ 576.

Lightman G, 'The Civil Justice System and Legal Profession' (2003) 22 *Civil Justice Quarterly* 235–47.

The (then) Lightman J discusses civil litigation and he suggests that much of the blame for the systemic delays in litigation can be laid at the door of lawyers.

Sorabji J, 'Part 36: A Rule in Need of Reform' (2015) 34 *Civil Justice Quarterly* 11–28.

This is an interesting article that suggests that Part 36, which was designed as a simple procedure to help encourage disputes to be settled quickly, has become overly technical and now instead leads to satellite litigation, meaning that litigation is an even longer process.

For self-test questions, flashcards, and links to useful websites, please visit the **online resources** at: **www.oup.com/he/gillespie-weare8e/**

18

Remedies and Appeals

By the end of this chapter you will be able to:

- Understand what the key remedies available in civil litigation are.
- Identify the key differences between pecuniary and non-pecuniary damages.
- Understand when equitable remedies may be used.
- Identify the correct route for a civil appeal.
- Understand the circumstances under which leave for appeal will be given.
- Identify the correct tests for granting leave and allowing or refusing an appeal.

Introduction

Chapter 17 presented how civil cases progress through the courts and focused on three different examples of civil action. Where it ended was the trial but what was not discussed, except in the context of costs, was what happens if the claimant succeeds. This is known as remedies and it is the order of the court as to what the losing side should do in respect of the claim. As will be seen there are different types of remedies that can be ordered and all are subject to certain rules and discretion. This chapter will also discuss what happens when a party disagrees with the ruling of the judge, ie appeals. The issue of criminal appeals was discussed in Chapter 16 and this, the second chapter on appeals in this book, allows you to compare civil and criminal appeals.

This chapter will follow the same structure as Chapter 17; ie at the beginning some brief general comments will be made but it will then return to the three case studies that were presented in Chapter 17. It will be remembered that this consisted of:

- Amy Daventry's faulty television where action was brought in the small claims court (technically the small claims track of the county court)
- Matilda's proposed march against the closure of a nursery, where the action was for judicial review before the Administrative Court of the High Court
- Joshua's application for extra contact with Sarah, his child, where the action was brought in the county court under the *Children Act 1989*.

For each of these examples a discussion will be made of the potential remedies and what the rules governing the remedies are. In the second half of the chapter the same studies will be used to understand how an appeal would be brought against the decision.

18.1 Civil remedies

The first issue to examine therefore is civil remedies. A difficulty with discussing remedies is that there are so many different types and that they are contingent on what the type of case is. Generally the claimant will indicate what remedy they wish but the court is able to grant such remedy as it considers appropriate. This section will consider some of the key types of remedies and, in essence, this will be under three broad headings:

- damages (ie financial compensation to remedy a wrong)
- equitable remedies (including specific performance in contractual disputes and injunctions)
- public law remedies (ie that which can be expected from a judicial review).

Each of these types of remedy will be discussed briefly although after the general issues have been discussed we will return to the case studies presented in Chapter 17 and discuss what remedy each claimant can expect.

18.1.1 Interim remedies

Whilst we tend to think of remedies as being something that occurs at the end of proceedings this is not always the case and sometimes a remedy will be sought at the beginning of, or during, proceedings. This is known as an interim remedy. In essence an interim remedy is supposed to secure the position so as to ensure that the full matters can be heard.

18.1.1.1 Identifying the defendant

One of the more unusual interim remedies is an action to identify the actual defendants. Whilst it may be thought that the identity of a defendant is always known this is not necessarily correct. One of the most important remedies here is the *Norwich Pharmacal* order.[1] This is a remedy that is designed to discover the identity of the defendant since in some instances the true identity may not be known. Where a third party is aware of the identity of the defendant and has in some way facilitated the wrong that the claimant is seeking to remedy then they are able to bring an action to discover the identity of the true person although it must only be done where it is contemplated that judicial or other proceedings will be instigated,[2] the latter potentially including employee misconduct proceedings.[3]

---

1. This is named after the resolution of the case *Norwich Pharmacal Co v Customs and Excise Commissioners* [1974] AC 133.
2. *British Steel Corporation v Granada Television Ltd* [1981] AC 1096.
3. *Ashworth Hospital Authority v MGN Ltd* [2002] 1 WLR 2033.

A contemporary example of when a *Norwich Pharmacal* order may be sought is in respect of computers. There may be a number of instances where someone wishes to allege that, for example, a person has posted defamatory postings or postings that could amount to harassment. A user who connects to the Internet has an IP address which is assigned to them by their Internet Service Provider. By using a *Norwich Pharmacal* order on the site hosting the relevant site (should it be based within the jurisdiction of England and Wales (so it can be enforced)) and the relevant Internet service provider it would be possible to identify the names of the posters, allowing a civil action to be brought against them. Examples of their use would include *Applause Store Productions Ltd v Raphael*[4] and *Patel v UNITE*.[5]

18.1.1.2 Interim injunction

Perhaps the most common type of interim remedy is that known as an interim injunction. The essence of an interim injunction is that it allows for the status quo to be maintained pending the full proceedings being heard. In some instances the fact that an interim injunction is made may suffice to resolve the whole proceedings but generally it will simply be a way of ensuring that the state of affairs continues pending litigation.

Example Interim injunction

Peter is a property developer and he is intending to build on some land that adjoins Rebecca's house. As part of the development he has decided to block off a path that leads from Rebecca's house that skirts Peter's land and leads to a stream. Rebecca may bring an action against Peter to prevent him from blocking off the land and where the block was to be semi-permanent (eg the building of a wall) it is possible that Rebecca may seek an interim injunction that prevents the block occurring until the final proceedings have been resolved.

Rules exist over when interim injunctions can be made[6] but also which judges are able to make injunctions (ordinarily only circuit judges and puisne judges). Also, it is likely that as injunctions are complicated (in that breach of an injunction can have significant consequences as it may be viewed as contempt of court and so breach could lead to detention) it is probable that they will lead to a matter being listed on the multi-track meaning that there are costs implications. One important aspect of an interim injunction is that ordinarily there will be an undertaking by the applicant to pay damages to the defendant if the case is ultimately resolved against them.[7] The reasoning behind this is that an interim injunction is ordinarily preventing a person from doing something and this may incur a cost. Where it was shown that there is no cause of action then that

---

4.   [2008] EWHC 1781 (QB).
5.   [2012] EWHC 92 (QB).
6.   CPR, pt 25.
7.   Stuart Sime, *A Practical Approach to Civil Litigation* (19th edn, OUP 2016) 469.

cost was, in effect, accrued inappropriately and the respondent should not have to pay for trying to do something they were entitled to.

> ### ▤ **Example** Undertaking as to damages
>
> Let us return to the position earlier in respect of Rebecca and Peter. Let us assume that Peter had arranged for contractors to begin blocking the path. Rebecca's interim injunction will almost certainly cost Peter money since he may have to pay the contractors during the period the litigation is ongoing or pay a penalty fee to defer the work. If it turns out that Rebecca is wrong and that Peter was entitled to block the path then Rebecca will probably have to pay these extra costs that were incurred by Peter.

18.1.2 **Final remedies: damages**

The more traditional forms of remedies are those that are made after the conclusion of successful litigation and it is to this that we now turn.

Perhaps the most obvious form of remedy is that of damages. This is the collective term that is given to financial compensation to remedy a wrong. It may be a contractual dispute where party X claims that they have suffered financial loss from party Y, or it may be a tort claim where X is claiming that he has been injured by Y (the tort of trespass to the person) or that X has invaded his property and caused damage (the tort of trespass to land).

Damages vary widely and in this section it will only be possible to describe some of the key rules in respect of their award. The first issue to note is that there are some differences in the way that damages can be awarded. So, for example, damages in contract are ordinarily assessed on the basis of the actual loss suffered[8] and it will be for the claimant to prove (to the civil standard) that these losses have been incurred. Damages for tort, however, may include general damages based on suffering, and this may be particularly true in personal injury claims.

If we look at damages for tort (and for these purposes we will consider a personal injury claim as being typical) then it is possible to distinguish between 'pecuniary' and 'non-pecuniary' damages. Pecuniary damages relate to identifiable sums of money that can be quantified as an actual loss. The general rule of pecuniary damages is that a person should be placed in the position that they would have been had the injury or loss not occurred.[9] How this is done will be discussed later but it will mean that all direct losses will ordinarily be covered, including expenses and loss of earnings. However, in line with this principle deductions will be made for any benefit that is received because of the injury (eg disabled living allowance) since to do otherwise may mean that the victim benefits from the injury.

Non-pecuniary damages are those that cannot be quantified as a direct loss but instead attract compensatory awards. Classic examples of this include damages for pain and suffering, loss of amenity, and psychological distress. Both pecuniary and non-pecuniary damages are divided into past and prospective damages. Past damages relate to the loss of suffering that a person has suffered already and prospective damages involve that which will occur in the future, including any future pain and suffering.

---

8. *Slater v Hoyle & Smith* [1920] 2 KB 11.
9. *Livingstone v Raywards Coal Co* (1880) 5 AC 25.

> ### ☰ Example An injured pedestrian
>
> Robert is an employee of a leading supermarket chain. Robert is employed as a store assistant. Whilst Robert is crossing a road (on a pelican crossing) he is struck by Wayne, who was driving negligently. Robert suffers a broken back and is hospitalized for four months. It is thought that when he recovers he will only be able to stand for no more than twenty-five minutes at any one time.
>
> Robert will be entitled to various types of compensation. The first is pecuniary damages. This will, for example, include his loss of earnings. This would include any loss of salary he has suffered as a result of being in hospital for four months. It will also include any loss of salary that he will accrue if he is not able to return to his job because of his reduced mobility. If he is required to pay for ongoing medical treatment (either for a determinate or indeterminate period of time) then this will also be classed as pecuniary damages since its cost can be calculated or estimated.
>
> Robert will also be eligible to receive non-pecuniary damages. In this example the most obvious reason for receiving non-pecuniary damages will be as a result of pain and suffering. How these are calculated will be discussed later but it is clear that he is eligible to receive this category of damages.

The primary test for deciding what should be recovered in tort is that of foreseeability[10] meaning that a person is liable to pay damages for loss or injury that is foreseeable by his actions that caused the harm. Perhaps the key example of this is a personal injury case. Let us assume that D injures V in a car accident. It is foreseeable that claims could arise for pain and suffering, expenses incurred, damage to property, loss of earnings etc.

Damages for claims arising out of an incident should ordinarily be dealt with by one action. All forms of awards (loss of earnings, future loss of earnings, pain and suffering, medical expenses etc) should be calculated at the one time and a person will not be able to reopen the litigation even where further loss was unexpected.

18.1.2.1 Pecuniary damages

As noted earlier pecuniary damages will include quantifiable damage. In a road traffic accident this would include damage to the car and any other property (including clothing if this is damaged by blood or because it had to be cut open), other expenses (including medical expenses (prescription charges, physiotherapy costs, etc)), and loss of earnings.

Perhaps the classic example of pecuniary damages is loss of earnings but this is not always easy to quantify. Courts do not order periodic payments (ie a sum to be paid as an annuity) but rather order a lump sum. However, it is too simplistic to say that if it could be proven that X could lose £10,000 per year for the next ten years then he should be awarded a lump sum of £100,000. This is because compensation is supposed to leave you in the position you would have been in. If X is given £100,000 but invests that money then after ten years he will have received more than £100,000 because of interest etc. Therefore the courts adopt a discounted multiplier to take into account the investments that a person can be expected to make. Traditionally it was thought that a

---

10. *Halsbury's Laws*, vol 29 (Damages) 408ff.

claimant would invest any compensation in the equity markets but the volatile nature of the stock market in recent years led to a re-think and it has now been decided to use a safer investment multiplier.

Even if the multiplier is resolved there are still difficulties in identifying loss of earnings. For example, how does one deal with the issue of possible promotion. For example, if V is a lecturer in a higher-education establishment when he is struck down by a motor vehicle and left with cognitive injuries that make it difficult to work as a full-time academic should he be compensated on the basis of his salary as a lecturer or the fact that he may become a professor at some point in his academic career? How does one decide the probability (or otherwise) of that? Where it is possible to assess the chances of a promotion then the courts will take this into account[11] but where it is not then they will consider a lump sum.

A particularly difficult issue, however, is where it involves a child who has never worked. How can one estimate what the loss of earnings for that child is? The starting point appears to be to use a sum that equated to the national average earnings in early working life[12] but this will change where a child is particularly intelligent[13] or there is other evidence to suggest that the child would be otherwise very successful.[14]

18.1.2.2 **Non-pecuniary damages**

Alongside pecuniary damages there will sometimes be non-pecuniary damages, particularly where it is a personal injury case. Perhaps the classic example of this will be compensation for pain and suffering. This is a compensatory award that is not based on actual losses but rather is designed to provide an award that reflects the pain and suffering a person will suffer. It is separate from the amount of award that will be paid to reflect ongoing medical bills since this is quantifiable and is therefore a pecuniary, rather than non-pecuniary award. Pain and suffering will also include any emotional harm that is caused either by the illness itself or by awareness of the harm, for example, where a young person suffers significant facial scarring, the award should not only be for the pain involved in the actual injuries but also include a factor for the emotional distress that may be caused by a realization that his face is permanently scarred and he may therefore attract unwelcome attention from members of society.[15] Where the injuries reduce the life expectancy of the victim the courts must also take this into account.

Identifying the level of compensation for pain and suffering is not easy. The usual approach is to look at past awards and try to find a comparable case, adjusting it for inflation etc. One of the more interesting legal texts that is available is *Kemp & Kemp: Quantum of Damages* (published by Sweet & Maxwell). This an updatable reference work that lists previous cases and awards given for damages. Each case will discuss the injuries that were received, the compensation awarded, and a brief summary of how that award was reached. A judge will consider these previous awards in deciding at what level to set the compensation for this aspect.

11.   *Doyle v Wallace The Times*, 22 July 1998 (CA).
12.   *Croke v Wiseman* [1982] 1 WLR 71.
13.   *Almond v Leeds Health Authority* [1990] 1 Med LR 370.
14.   For a discussion see *Halsbury's Laws*, vol 29 (Damages) 445.
15.   See *Dimmock v Miles* (1969, unreported) cited in *Halsbury's Laws*, vol 12(1) 883.

Separate to any amount of compensation for pain and suffering, a person who receives a loss of amenity (eg a sense, or a limb, or the ability to walk) can expect to receive a compensatory award for this. As with compensation for pain and suffering this is a non-pecuniary award that is designed to reflect the additional suffering involved in this. This loss of amenity can also be extended to other forms of foreseeable yet unquantifiable situations such as the loss of marriage prospects etc.[16] As with pain and suffering assessing the quantum of such damage is difficult and it is often said that the starting point is to look at previous cases to identify the likely award and to update this for inflation where appropriate.

18.1.3 Final remedies: equitable remedies

After damages, equitable remedies are perhaps the most common. There are a variety of different types of equitable remedies but two are of particular importance here. The first is specific performance, a particular equitable remedy in respect of contract disputes, and the second is injunctions. Injunctions were mentioned briefly earlier in the context of interim remedies but they can also feature in the Family Court. These are the two remedies that will be discussed briefly in this section.

18.1.3.1 Specific performance

Perhaps one of the better-known equitable defences is that known as specific performance, which applies to relationships bound by a contract. The essence of the defence is that the court will 'enforce against a defendant the duty of doing what he agreed by contract to do'.[17] The remedy differs from damages in that the latter will compensate a person for not fulfilling their contract whereas specific performance requires that the contract *will* be performed. It is possible that damages can also be awarded where, for example, the delay in fulfilling the contract has led to pecuniary losses being incurred.

646

> **Example** Selling on products
>
> Arnold has an agreement with Peter to purchase four miles of cabling for £2,500. Arnold has a separate agreement with Telly Communications Ltd to supply them with three miles of cables for £4,500. The agreement with Peter is that the cable will be delivered to Arnold by 3 February 2016 and the agreement with Telly Communications Ltd is that Arnold will supply them the cable by 5 February 2016. The contract with Telly Communications Ltd states that Arnold will be liable to pay £50 per day that the contract is unfilled because this offsets additional charges that Telly Communications Ltd will occur in their building project.
>
> On 3 February Peter contacts Arnold and says that he is not going to supply any cable because he can sell the cable to a building developer for £1,000 more. He says it will be at least four weeks before he gets any more cable. Arnold immediately tells Peter that he will instigate legal proceedings. The matter is heard on 8 February.
>
> The judge hearing the case identifies that Peter has not yet sold on the cable. He makes an order of specific performance which will require Peter to supply Arnold with the cable. He separately makes an order for damages to cover, in part, the late penalty charges.

16. See *Halsbury's Laws*, vol 12(1) 884.
17. *Halsbury's Laws*, vol 95 (Specific Performance) para 301.

As an equitable remedy it is discretionary, ie the court does not *have* to make the order but the fact that it is discretionary should not be taken to mean that the circumstances when it could be used are vague as it is subject to precise rules and regulations and it has been suggested that 'if the contract is within the category of contacts of which specific performance will be granted, is valid in form, has been made between competent parties and is unobjectionable in its nature and circumstances, specific performance will be granted as a matter of course'.[18] There are some equitable defences that can be pleaded but the action has, over the years, been refined until the point when it has become a standard remedy in breach of contract cases.

The relationship between equitable remedies should be understood. Where a person is aware that a contract is likely to be breached in the future (eg in the example earlier relating to Arnold and Peter, Peter tells Arnold on 1 February that he is not going to adhere to the contract) then the correct remedy is probably an injunction rather than specific performance,[19] the injunction restraining a person from breaching the contract. An advantage that this would bring of course is that it is possible to gain an interim injunction and so when the possibility of breach is first raised it may be possible to prevent that breach at the earliest opportunity.

As an equitable remedy it would ordinarily be used where common-law remedies, ie damages, will not suffice. There will be occasions where the breach of a contract does not require the specific performance of a contract (because, for example, goods can readily be obtained in another way) but rather the award of compensation. Where the court decides that a monetary payment will suffice then the courts will ordinarily decline to order specific performance.[20] It does not seem to matter whether the contract stipulates the quantum of damages in breach or whether damages are liquidated or unliquidated.[21] Some contracts will make clear that the remedy for breach is financial compensation and whilst this may lead the court to decide that it will not enforce specific performance it would seem that the court is more concerned with the intentions of the parties. Where the items which are the subject of the contract are hard to obtain or are of particular significance then it is likely that damages would not be appropriate and specific performance would be exercised.

647

☰ Example The rare vase

Veronica agrees to purchase a rare, twelfth century vase from Dianne for £25,000 and transfers the money to her. When she goes to collect the vase Dianne refuses to hand it over and says that she is going to sell it to another person who has offered her £10,000 more.

Veronica had also ordered a set of china plates from Edwina. These plates are sold in lots of shops but Edwina sold them to Veronica for £100 whereas the next cheapest seller sold them for £225. When Veronica goes to collect them Edwina refuses to hand them over, and says she is going to sell the plates to another customer who wants to order a lot more china at the same time. Edwina says she can't get any more of the plates because she has decided not to sell that range anymore.

---

18.   ibid, para 301.
19.   See *James Jones & Sons Ltd v Earl of Tankerville* [1909] 2 Ch 440.
20.   *Adderley v Dixon* (1824) 1 Sim & St 607.
21.   *Halsbury's Laws*, vol 95 (Specific Performance) para 313.

If Veronica was to bring an action against Dianne it is likely that the courts would order specific performance as the vase is very particular and can, in essence, only be obtained from Dianne. In respect of the plates, however, the courts may well take the approach that specific performance is not required. Veronica could buy the plates from another seller and if, as seems likely, she pays more than she paid Edwina then she can simply claim that additional sum as damages.

The most obvious example when specific performance will not be ordered is where it is no longer possible to do so.[22] There may be a number of reasons why this is the case, including the possibility that factual circumstances have changed or even that the property is no longer available. For example, in the earlier example of the vase, if Dianne had accidentally dropped the vase and destroyed it then there can be no specific performance—which would, in essence, require Dianne to somehow procure another vase (which may be impossible)—and instead the dispute would be settled with damages. The same could be true of the example of cabling presented earlier. If Peter has no cable because, for example, his supplier has none or it is stolen then it would not be possible for the court to order specific performance. That is not to say there is no breach in the contract because clearly there is but it is an example that would be best resolved by damages and not specific performance.

18.1.3.2 Injunctions

The other classic equitable remedy is that of an injunction. The issue of interim injunctions was considered earlier but they can also be a final remedy, either as an alternative to or in combination with damages. It should be noted that whilst there are some statutory provisions that allow a county court to make an injunction, the vast majority of injunctions are part of the inherent jurisdiction of the court and thus only actionable by the High Court. Only High Court injunctions will be considered in this section.

An injunction is normally used in contractual disputes where the breach, or anticipated breach, is negative in character (in *Evening Standard Co Ltd v Henderson*[23] an injunction was used to restrain an employee from working for a competitor in circumstances where their employment contract indicated that they could not do so). An injunction is also common in tort claims, for example, where a person is illegally trespassing on land they may ask a court to issue an injunction requiring that person to leave the land.

There are two types of injunction; an order that prohibits someone from doing something (a prohibitory injunction) and an injunction that requires a person to do something (a mandatory injunction). These are in essence two sides of the same coin and there is no real difference in how they are granted or what their effect is. The prohibitory injunction is the more usual, in part because the nature of many types of civil litigation is such that what is feared is somebody doing something that they should not do which causes harm or loss.

648

---

22.   *Watts v Spence* [1976] Ch 165.
23.   [1987] ICR 588.

As with specific performance, the injunction is an equitable remedy and therefore it is used where damages by themselves would not suffice.[24] There will be circumstances where financial compensation suffices and in those cases the court will decline to act although where it believes that there is the potential for future damage then this may provide a reason to use its equitable powers to grant an injunction.

The consequences of breaching an order can be severe and accordingly it has been said that the wording of an injunction must be very clear so that the person it is served upon knows exactly what he is expected not to do (or to do, depending on the type of injunction).[25] Where a mandatory injunction is used then the injunction will ordinarily include a time by which it must be complied with. Prohibitory injunctions ordinarily come into force immediately but do not need to and the court may give the defendant(s) time to comply with the order.

Breach of an injunction is a serious matter; it amounts to contempt of court, something that is stated on the face of the injunction. There are two types of contempt: criminal contempt and civil contempt. Refusing to obey an injunction is civil contempt but the consequences can be just as serious and may even lead to imprisonment. The burden is on the person served to understand the means by which they can obey the order[26] (although, as noted earlier, the actual injunction should be written in a manner that makes it readily understood). The responsibility for showing contempt is the plaintiff's, and they would return to the court to allege that the side who has breached the injunction has done so and seek an order for committal for contempt.[27]

Whilst it is possible to imprison for civil contempt it has been stated that this power should only be exercised with great care.[28] The maximum term for which a person can be committed to prison (technically it is not imprisonment which is a criminal sanction) is two years.[29] The actual term should depend on how serious the breach is; the more blatant the breach, and the greater the challenge to the court's authority, the longer the committal. There is no power to commit a person to prison pending the determination of sentence meaning that a person will either be committed immediately or will be at liberty while the court investigates the breach and considers sentence. If the court decides not to commit a person to prison it could issue a fine. Technically there is no upper limit to any fine[30] although realistically the court will take account of factors such as the gravity of the breach, previous instances, and the particular circumstances of the person.

Section 13 *Administration of Justice Act 1960* permits an appeal against a decision that a person is in contempt of court and any sentence imposed. Appeal from contempt in the High Court is to the Court of Appeal and, as it is civil contempt, it will be heard in the Civil Division even where a person has been committed to prison.[31]

649

---

24. *Attorney-General v Sheffield Gas Consumers Co* (1853) 3 De G M & G 304.
25. *Attorney-General v Staffordshire County Council* [1905] 1 Ch 336.
26. *Attorney-General (at the relation of Leyton Essex Urban District Council) v Walthamstow Urban District Council* (1895) 11 TLR 533.
27. See *Halsbury's Laws*, vol 22 (Contempt of Court) 98 for a discussion of the procedure.
28. ibid, 112.
29. *Contempt of Court Act 1981*, s 14(1).
30. *Halsbury's Laws*, vol 22 (Contempt of Court) 114.
31. For an example of this, albeit an unusual one, see *Slade v Slade* [2009] EWCA Civ 748.

18.1.4 **Final remedies: public law remedies**

Public law remedies are those that can be awarded after a claim for judicial review. Whilst it is possible that damages will be awarded it is more likely that a public law remedy will be made. It is important to note that in public law the court has complete discretion as to whether to grant a remedy.[32] This means that even if the court decides that a judicial review should succeed it may decline to grant any relief because it believes it is not in the interests of justice to do so. Indeed some applicants may not even seek a remedy but instead just want a ruling that a public authority has acted in an inappropriate manner.

Example Use of a leisure centre

Let us assume that Peabody District Council operate a leisure centre and they wish to restrict the opening hours. In order to do this, they need to seek permission from (a) the Council Leader, (b) the Mayor, (c) the Leader of the Council of the neighbouring district council, and (d) the (fictional) Department for Administrative Affairs.

For some reason, although all bodies were contacted, the Department for Administrative Affairs' reply was not received. A judicial review is brought by Jim Naseum, who uses the leisure centre after work. The court finds that the Department's permission was not granted because it was not received (and to that extent the decision to restrict opening hours was procedurally flawed) but this was simply because the letter was lost in the post. The Department had intended to grant permission.

In this example the court may well deny relief even though Jim Naseum will succeed in his application for judicial review. The court may well consider that there is little point in granting relief because the Department intended to give permission and when a copy of the letter is sent to the Council the decision can then be retaken lawfully.

There are four principal remedies that are available in judicial review proceedings:

- quashing orders
- mandatory (and prohibiting) orders
- injunctions, and
- declarations.

It is quite possible that there will be a combination of two or more remedies. So, for example, it is quite possible that a court may declare that there has been a breach of the law and quash the decision. Alternatively, it may quash a decision but then mandate that an authority acts in a particular way. In this section the four orders will be briefly discussed.

18.1.4.1 **Quashing orders**

Perhaps the most common public law remedy is that of the quashing order. Until the *Woolf Reforms* and advent of the Civil Procedure Rules banished Latin from civil

---

32. See *Glynn v Keele University* [1971] 1 WLR 487.

proceedings this was also known as a *writ of certiorari*. The effect of the remedy is that it quashes whatever decision has been made and returns the position legally to what it was before the order was made.

> ### Example Quashing a decision to refuse bail
>
> A slightly unusual, but certainly illustrative, example of a quashing order can be found in *R (on the application of S) v Newcastle Crown Court*.[33] S had been charged with a series of rapes relating to a complainant that he had purported to marry. S was a final year student and had been denied bail by a circuit judge sitting at the Crown Court at Newcastle-upon-Tyne. The ruling by the judge denying bail had the appearance of the judge adopting the wrong test for bail and Foskett J, whilst believing that an experienced judge was unlikely to have made such an error (as he will deal with bail decisions daily) decided that the appearance of the wrong test justified the use of a public law remedy. He therefore directed that the decision was quashed and remitted the matter back to the Crown Court for a new decision but before a different judge.

The effect of a quashing order will depend on the circumstances of the case. Elliott and Thomas distinguish between two types of situations: those where the decision was made in an inappropriate way and those where the decision itself was inappropriate.[34] Where the decision was reached in an inappropriate way then the quashing order will quash that decision but there is nothing to stop the authority from reaching the same decision again, albeit by adopting the correct process. Where the decision itself is wrong then the quashing order will mean that the authority must reconsider the matter and identify a different decision.

A quashing order is most effective when it is prospective action, ie the alleged illegal act is to occur in the future. In these cases the quashing order will almost certainly be the sole remedy as by quashing the order the status quo returns meaning the illegal act should not occur. Where it is in respect of a past matter it can be more complicated as the court may need to consider whether it is necessary to award compensation for the consequences of that unlawful decision etc.

18.1.4.2 Mandatory and prohibiting orders

Technically these are two distinct types of remedies but they are, in essence, two sides of the same coin. Before the abolition of Latin they were known as a *writ of mandamus* and a *writ of prohibition*. As with a quashing order, the name of the order accurately describes what the consequences of the action are. Given the nature of these orders they can only be used in respect of prospective decisions (since if it has already happened there is nothing to mandate or prohibit).

A mandatory order simply requires an authority to do a particular act. They therefore have no option but to do what is ordered by the High Court. If they do not do this then they are not only acting unlawfully but are arguably in contempt of court because

---

33. [2012] EWHC 1453 (Admin).
34. Mark Elliott and Robert Thomas, *Public Law* (OUP 2011) 555–6.

they have failed to follow an order. A mandatory order will require a body to do something that they have legal power to do but that does not mean that it is restricted to situations where an authority *has* to do something, it is simply that an order will require them to do something that is lawful.

☰ **Example** Holding an inquest

In *R (on the application of Medihani) v HM Coroner for Inner South District of London*[35] the High Court was asked to rule on the issue of whether an inquest into the death of a 15-year-old girl should resume. A person was charged with the murder of the girl but he attempted to commit suicide while in detention and suffered brain damage as a result of hanging himself. At a pre-trial hearing a judge held that he was unfit to tender a plea in respect of the charge of murder and a jury was then empanelled to decide whether he had, in fact, committed the *actus reus* of the crime.[36] They decided that he had committed the act of killing and he was detained in a secure institution.

The Administrative Court considered that Article 2 ECHR required an inquest to be held in these circumstances and therefore they made a mandatory order requiring (a) that an inquest be held, and (b) that the inquest be held before a different coroner than the one who declined to reopen the inquest.

A prohibiting order is the exact opposite. Instead of requiring a person to do something it prohibits them from doing it. The principal use of these orders is where an authority intends to do something and a claimant believes that this would be illegal. By seeking a prohibiting order (rather than a quashing order) it makes clear that the authority *cannot* do as it intended (whereas a quashing order may mean that the authority considers the matter again, reaches the same conclusion, and therefore further judicial review proceedings are required).

18.1.4.3 **Injunctions**

Injunctions have already been discussed in the context of private law remedies (in that they are an equitable remedy considered in 18.1.3.2). Elliott and Thomas believe that it may be advisable in some instances to seek an injunction rather than seek, for example, a prohibiting order. That said, at least part of the logic is that injunctions can be obtained in ordinary litigation[37] which, whilst correct, means that the litigant would not engage in a public law action but instead ordinary principles of litigation.

An advantage of injunctions is that, as seen earlier, it is possible to receive an interim injunction. Therefore where time is of the essence it is possible to obtain an interim injunction while the arguments are decided by the courts whereas public law remedies can only be granted at the end of proceedings. Whilst this is true, it should be noted that the courts are able to expedite matters, including hearing proceedings and applications by telephone (something quite common in the Family Division of the High Court).

---

35. [2012] EWHC 1104 (Admin).
36. See *Criminal Procedure (Insanity) Act 1964* and David Ormerod, *Smith & Hogan's Criminal Law* (13th edn, OUP 2011) 288–93 for a discussion on how this operates.
37. Mark Elliott and Robert Thomas, *Public Law* (OUP 2011) 558.

There may be some logic to the argument of Elliott and Thomas, however, especially, as they note, it is now clear that a public body, including a minister of the Crown, can commit contempt of court[38] meaning they will almost certainly obey an injunction.

18.1.4.4 Declarations

The final remedy is arguably not a remedy at all, it is merely a statement of the court as to what the legal position is. They do not carry any requirement or sanction but instead it is just a judicial statement about the legality, or otherwise, of a proposed decision. It was noted earlier that sometimes a claimant themselves may decide that they do not wish to seek a remedy because the mere statement of illegality will suffice.

One point to note is that even though there is no remedy attached to a declaration, a court will not use this to permit purely hypothetical cases to be raised.[39] The courts are clear that they are there to resolve disputes between parties and, in public law, to ensure that actions that have, or potentially have, an impact on individuals are reviewed. Where there is no impact or real dispute then the courts are reluctant to become involved, in part as a matter of public policy since there are already significant delays in the court system, a problem which could be exacerbated by permitting hypothetical questions to be raised.

Sometimes the courts will use a declaration as part of their discretion over remedies. For example, they may believe that a mandatory order is not required because a public body (particularly a court) would simply follow the logic of the declaration made and does not require the compulsion inherent in an order.

18.1.5 Applying the remedies

The preceding section has explained many of the basic principles of remedies but it is necessary very briefly to look at what remedies would be likely in the examples first introduced in Chapter 17. These case studies will then be carried forward to the second part of the chapter which discusses appeals.

18.1.5.1 Small claims track

The first example that we considered was that of Amy who purchased a television set that proved to be faulty. This is therefore a contract claim and it is arguably one of the easiest to consider.

It will be remembered that Amy purchased the television for £250 and only six weeks later it blew up and the retailer simply offered to put her in contact with a repairer who will charge her £150. This will be a contractual dispute so that we will be considering the issue of damages. As noted earlier, there are some restrictions on what can be claimed in contract but realistically in a claim as small as this it is unlikely this is going to be problematic.

Amy has two options; the first is to sue initially for £150 (the cost of the repair) but, more probably given the fact that the television is only one month old, the request would be for £250, the cost of the television itself. This is obviously known as pecuniary damages.

---

38. *Re M* [1994] 1 AC 377.
39. See, for example, the comments of Lord Hutton in *R (on the application of Rushbridge) v Attorney-General* [2004] 1 AC 357, 371.

In addition to this Amy will be able to claim for other pecuniary losses. This will include the cost of the litigation, any expenses incurred in the court proceedings (eg travel to court), any costs incurred in attempting to resolve the dispute (telephone calls etc), or other identifiable and foreseeable losses (eg if she hired a television set while this matter was in dispute). Amy will also be able to claim interest as identified earlier.

18.1.5.2 **Judicial review**

The second example was that of Matilda who was challenging the decision of the chief constable to ban her march. It will be remembered that this action was brought by way of judicial review and so the issue is one of public law remedies.

As Matilda wishes the march to go ahead there are, in essence, two options open to her. The first is a quashing order which would quash the decision of the chief constable to ban the march. The second option is to seek a mandatory order—requiring the chief constable to allow the march—but this would need to be in combination with a quashing order as this will always be required since to do otherwise would leave the chief constable's decision to ban the march in force.

The question is whether the High Court is likely to issue a mandatory order. Realistically there are a number of arguments to suggest that they would not. First, it could be argued that if the High Court declares that Matilda has the right to hold a protest, the police, as a public authority bound by s 6 *Human Rights Act 1998*, would recognize this and allow the protest. However, the stronger argument is that the High Court may not wish to rule on whether Matilda has the right to hold a protest. It is more likely that they would simply restrict their review to the question of whether it should be banned because the Home Secretary is also visiting the county at the same time. It is difficult to see how the court would construe this as anything other than an irrational decision. However, there may be other reasons for restricting a march, including the route of any march, and the court is not the best place to consider these issues: that is something that, under statute and common law, is the role of the chief constable. Accordingly, it is more likely that the Administrative Court will exercise their discretion to quash the decision of the chief constable but make no further order. This would mean that the chief constable would have to consider the issue again with the benefit of the decision of the judge in terms of understanding the importance of the right to protest.

18.1.5.3 **Children's contact**

Our final example was that of Joshua who wishes to see his child Sarah. Family remedies have not been considered before now because there are so many different examples of remedies within family law, partly due to the wide range of proceedings that exist within this area. As was noted in Chapter 17 the application Joshua made was under s 8 *Children Act 1989* (CA 1989) and the Act itself makes clear what remedies are available.

Section 10 CA 1989 permits the Family Court to make a s 8 order when certain persons apply for it. Obviously here Joshua has made an application and it was seen in Chapter 17 that he is permitted to apply for an order. A consequence of s 10 is that the court can make *any* order under s 8 once an application has been made for *any* s 8 order although in a matter such as the one presented in Chapter 17 it is highly unlikely the court will consider making any other form of s 8 order (eg revisiting who has residence ('custody') of the child). Section 11 permits the court to make directions on how any order is to be implemented and to impose conditions on any order. This could, for example, be used to phase in any change in contact regimes etc.

In essence the judge has three options open to him:

- allow the application by Joshua and alter the s 8 contact arrangements
- reject the application by Joshua meaning that the arrangements remain the same
- partly allow the application by making an order different to that sought by Joshua.

The third option shows the flexibility of CA 1989 proceedings. Just because Joshua has requested a particular contact pattern does not mean that the judge should approve it. Indeed the judge should only accede to the application if he decides that it is in the child's best interests to do so.[40] It will be remembered from Chapter 17 that Joshua wished not only weekly overnight contact but also a one-week holiday. Deborah, his wife, did not object to the holiday and it is likely that the judge would be influenced by that and place this within the order, almost certainly stating that the parties are to agree a suitable week between them (so that the court is not involved in comparing diaries). What was contested was the overnight contact. One possibility is that the judge may decide, rather than ordering weekly overnight contact immediately, to phase it in. This could be done through the powers within s 11 or, perhaps more likely, he may decide to make a s 8 order that allows for overnight contact once a month and then adjourn the application for six months. After six months the judge (through the Children and Family Court Advisory and Support Service (CAFCASS)) would have more information about how Sarah has reacted to overnight contact and this is likely to influence his decision as to increased contact.

18.2 Appeals

As in criminal cases, not everyone will consider that the court has made the correct decision and thus it is also necessary to consider appeals. Unlike in criminal appeals where, it will be remembered, there are limitations regarding when one party (the Crown) may appeal, the same is not true in civil litigation and the general rule is that either party may appeal.

Civil appeals differ slightly from criminal appeals in that the avenues of appeal are slightly more complicated, partly because it is less clear where an appeal is heard.

18.2.1 Route of appeals

In civil cases it is necessary to distinguish between first appeals and second appeals. To an extent this is quite an easy distinction since it operates in the same way that it sounds. That is to say, in some matters it may be possible to appeal a matter more than once. The route that this takes will differ, as will be seen later.

As a general rule, with the exception of final decisions made in multi-track cases (which will be discussed later), in civil cases an appeal is made to the next most senior level of judge. So unlike in criminal appeals where the matter will ordinarily proceed to the next highest court (an appeal from the magistrates' court will proceed to the Crown Court or High Court; an appeal from the Crown Court will go to the Court of Appeal (Criminal Division));

---

40. *Children Act 1989*, s 1.

an appeal in civil matters tends to be in respect of the judge. Table 18.1 presents the general rule.

Where the matter relates to the final decision of a multi-track case then the rule is simpler, it reverts to the court-type route. Thus the final decision of a judge sitting in the county court (including a circuit judge) will *always* go to the Court of Appeal (Civil Division) as will a final decision on a multi-track case within the High Court. The rationale behind this is that the multi-track cases are the more serious and complicated cases and therefore appeals should ordinarily proceed to the principal appellate court.

The position in respect of second appeals adopts the same pattern. Instead of following the route already discussed it will return to the court-based system. If the route adopted in Table 18.1 was adopted then an appeal from a district judge sitting in the county court would go to a circuit judge within the county court and from there to a puisne judge. However, the rule states that this second appeal would actually go to the Court of Appeal (Civil Division). Again the logic behind this is that a second appeal is no longer just about whether a matter was wrongly decided but should be based on the ordinary principles of review that one would expect in the Court of Appeal (Civil Division).

Table 18.1 Appeals: the general rule

Trial judge	Appeal judge
District judge (county court)	Circuit judge (county court)
Master of the High Court	Pusine judge
Circuit judge (inc deputy)	Puisne judge
Puisne judge (inc deputy)	Court of Appeal (Civil Division)

18.2.2 **Leave**

The general rule of civil cases is that there is ordinarily a requirement that a person requires permission (leave) before bringing an appeal.[41] There are some exceptions to this rule but ordinarily it applies to all proceedings, including an appeal against interim matters and not just final decisions.

The general rule is that permission can be sought either from the judge that has made the ruling to be appealed (and it is more common for leave to be granted in this way in civil cases whereas it was seen in Chapter 16 that this was highly exceptional in criminal cases) or from the judge where the appeal will be heard.[42] So, for example, a circuit judge makes a ruling in a fixed-track case. The first appeal will be heard by a puisne judge (see Table 18.1). The person appealing can either ask the circuit judge who made the judgment for permission to appeal or he can petition the High Court for permission. The exception to this rule is where it relates to a second appeal. It will be remembered that second appeals go to the Court of Appeal and because there has already been an appeal then the rule is that leave must be sought from the Court of Appeal itself,[43] in part to ensure that it hears only those matters that it thinks are most relevant.

---

41. CPR, r 52.3.
42. ibid, r 52.3(2).
43. ibid, r 52.3(3).

18.2.2.1 **Test**

The test for granting leave for first appeals (irrespective of who grants it) is:

(a) the court considers that the appeal would have a real prospect of success; or

(b) there is some other compelling reason why the appeal should be heard.[44]

Ground (a) is the more usual one and it will be difficult to persuade a judge that ground (b) is satisfied, in part because that will ordinarily mean that the judge has decided that there is not a real prospect of success. Of course an example of where it may be used is where precedent is against an individual but it is widely accepted that the precedent is wrong. There would not be an arguable prospect of success in that the court will be obliged to follow the precedent but by granting leave it may be that the case proceeds to a sufficiently high court that can remedy the breach of precedent.

> **Example** Bad precedent
>
> A wishes to appeal against the final decision of a district judge in a fixed-track case. The district judge felt obliged to follow a precedent of the High Court although practitioners and academics have suggested that it was wrongly decided. The avenue for this appeal will be to a circuit judge sitting in the county court. That judge will similarly be bound by the High Court precedent and so it cannot be said that there is 'a real prospect of success' but the district judge believes that, once that appeal has been disposed of, the matter is likely to proceed to the Court of Appeal (Civil Division) who will not be bound by the High Court precedent and could, if it chose, overrule it.

The test of 'real prospect' is not supposed to be a statistical test but is simply supposed to weed out those cases where the prospects are fanciful.[45] Where there has been a material irregularity leave should ordinarily be given even if there is doubt as to whether the decision itself is wrong[46] which accords to the usual issue about justice being seen to be done.

The test for second appeals is more restrictive and is:

(a) the appeal would—

  (i) have a real prospect of success, and

  (ii) raise an important point of principle or practice; or

(b) there is some other compelling reason for the Court of Appeal to hear it.[47]

The rationale behind this tighter restriction is that the first appeal should have resolved most irregularities. It may include, for example, the fact that the litigants believe a precedent, which bound the lower court, is wrong and which can only be achieved through appealing to a senior court.

---

44.   ibid, r 52.6(1).
45.   *Swain v Hillman* [2001] 1 All ER 91.
46.   *Re W (Children)(Permission to Appeal)* [2007] Fam Law 897.
47.   CPR, r 52.7(2).

18.2.2.2 **Reconsidering permission**

It is not unusual for leave to appeal to be dealt with purely on papers, especially where it is a petition to the next most senior court (rather than judge) or to the Court of Appeal itself. Where the decision to deny leave is granted on an appeal then an appellant may request that a hearing takes place to determine leave.[48] Strictly speaking this is not an appeal since it will ordinarily be considered by a judge of the same level. Where, on papers, a judge decides that the appeal is 'without merit' then they can order that an appellant is not permitted to request a hearing.

18.2.3 **The hearing**

A civil appeal will ordinarily involve decisions of law and will not therefore amount to a rehearing. When granting leave it is open to the court granting leave to restrict leave to certain grounds[49] in which case only those matters should be raised with the court unless (exceptionally) the court hearing the appeal grants permission to go beyond those grounds.

Skeleton arguments are widely used in civil cases and counsel will be expected to file these in appropriate time. They will be read by the judge and the appeal will tend to be more inquisitorial than adversarial, in that the judge will almost certainly restrict himself to those aspects that he believes have some merit and may question counsel on the legal submissions that he has put forward. Although the term 'skeleton' is used they are not merely bullet-point summaries but are instead complex legal arguments. Within the Court of Appeal a skeleton argument should 'normally' be no more than twenty-five pages in length[50] which shows how long they can be. They summarize the key points that are to be argued but must show why a party is referring the court to a particular authority and what the effect of that authority is.

Where legal authorities are to be cited then ordinarily in the county courts and the Court of Appeal it will be for the appellant to file a bundle that contains photocopies of the authorities that *both sides* will rely upon. The Practice Direction makes quite clear that both sides are supposed to communicate about the authorities that they wish to rely upon and these will then be filed in the same bundle. The advantage of this system is that it ensures that it is easy to access the various authorities and to ensure that each person is looking at the same thing. In the High Court it is not usually necessary to provide photocopies of the legal authorities but it is necessary to list what the authorities are so that they can be laid before the judge before the hearing.

18.2.3.1 **Composition of the courts**

For first appeals that take place before a puisne judge or below (see Table 18.1) then ordinarily the court will consist of a single judge of the rank identified within that table. Where the appeal is to the Court of Appeal (because, for example, the matter is against a ruling of a puisne judge or because it was against a final ruling in a multi-track case) then ordinarily a two-judge panel will sit. It is comparatively rare (although not unheard of) for puisne judges to sit in the Court of Appeal (Civil Division) and accordingly the

---

48. ibid, r 52.4(2).
49. ibid, r 52.5.
50. PD 52C, para 31.1.

court will consist of two Lord Justices of Appeal. If a two-judge bench is equally divided then the matter should ordinarily be re-listed before a three-judge bench.

Where the matter is an appeal from a decision of the High Court, particularly where it entails a multi-track case, or where it is a second appeal from the High Court (ie a decision of a circuit judge was appealed to a puisne judge and from there to the Court of Appeal) then it will ordinarily be a three-judge panel.

18.2.3.2 Powers of the appellate court

The general powers of an appellate are the power to:

(a) affirm, set aside or vary any order or judgment;

(b) refer any claim or issue for determination by the lower court;

(c) order a new trial or hearing;

(d) make orders for the payment of interest; and

(e) make a costs order.[51]

Ordinarily the appellate court will not refer matters back to the lower court save where it believes that a matter of fact needs to be resolved (including through the hearing of witness testimony). Usually (and certainly where it is a first appeal before a judge not in the Court of Appeal) the court will deal with the matter itself.

> **Example** Appeals varying an order
>
> Thomas appealed the decision of a circuit judge in a fast-track case. He complains that whilst the judge gave judgment in his claim for damage to property and awarded £14,000 he wrongly excluded loss of earnings of £5,000. The puisne judge hearing the matter agrees. Rather than returning the matter to the circuit court and requiring the judge to alter the judgment the puisne judge hearing the matter will simply alter the judgment and order to state that the damages are now £19,000.

18.2.4 Appeals to the Supreme Court

As with criminal law there is an appeal from the Court of Appeal (Civil Division) which will lie to the Supreme Court. These will be exceptional cases—although the majority of appeals the Supreme Court hears are civil rather than criminal, they still account for a miniscule proportion of all the appeals heard by the Court of Appeal. Permission to appeal to the Supreme Court should initially be made to the Court of Appeal that determined the original appeal although it is not unusual for that court to deny permission. Irrespective of this it is possible to seek leave from the Supreme Court itself (which will be determined by three justices) and whilst it is not necessary to certify a point of public importance (as occurs in criminal cases) it is likely to be only those types of cases that would be selected by the Supreme Court to be heard.

---

51. CPR, r 52.20(2).

18.2.5 **Examples of appeals**

The final section of this chapter will return to the case studies that were first presented in Chapter 17. In each of the examples a brief synopsis will be presented which demonstrates how the appeal will take place, where, and how it will be resolved.

18.2.5.1 **Small claims track**

The first case study involved Amy, who purchased a faulty television. The small claims track is, as identified in Chapter 17, simply one of the three tracks that civil litigation is ordinarily assigned to. Accordingly, the general rules of appeals contained within CPR 52 apply. This means that Table 18.1 applies and since a small claims hearing is ordinarily heard by a district judge (see 17.1.6.2) this means that any appeal will be made to a circuit judge sitting in the county court. This is one of the reasons why it would be extremely rare for a circuit judge to sit on a small claims track hearing since then an appeal would be to a puisne judge and, given the delays that exist within civil litigation, there are better things for a puisne judge to sit on than a small claims hearing (although, in reality, such an appeal would almost certainly be heard by a deputy judge).

Leave

As noted already, it is necessary to seek leave to appeal. Given that lawyers rarely appear in the small claims court it is quite likely that leave will not be sought from the district judge that made the ruling. That said, after the district judge has explained the reasoning of his judgment it is quite possible that a litigant may ask how they appeal. In those circumstances it is possible that a district judge may allow for the request to be made at that time but it is more likely that he would recommend that the party goes away and considers it.

A special form exists for appeals in respect of small claims appeals (N164 available with the online resources) and this includes a section that allows a person to apply for permission to appeal at the same time as initiating the appeal. The form then asks the appellant to explain why they are appealing against the decision of the judge. This should allow the judge to decide whether to grant leave on papers but if there is insufficient detail then a judge may call the appellant into court so that a hearing can be held and the reasons better articulated.

Pre-trial matters

The process for small claims appeals is simplified in much the same way as the hearing itself is. Ordinarily a series of documents are required to be filed for appeals, but this does not apply to appeals on the small claims track. Indeed, a standard document that should automatically be submitted is a transcript of the judgment or hearing. However, a transcript is not required for a small claims hearing.[52] Similarly, more formal documents such as skeleton arguments are not required, with section 5 of Form N164 taking its place.

A fee is payable (currently £120) and the court will serve all the various papers on the respondent and if the respondent seeks to contest the appeal then they will serve the papers on the appellant.

Hearing

As with the small claims the key presumption is that the hearing of the appeal will take place without the use of lawyers. The case will probably still be heard in chambers and

---

52. PD 52B, para 6.2.

the judge is likely to take a proactive stance in identifying what the key issues are and identifying what, if any, grounds there are for the appeal to succeed. As litigants in person are common, part of the difficulty with the hearing will be ensuring that the appeal is restricted to legal issues rather than a person simply arguing that he did not like the result. An appeal is based on the argument that a judge made an error of law in reaching the decision that they did. Laypersons are unlikely to have researched the law, making the position more difficult for the judge who will not be an expert in each area of the law.[53]

The test that the judge must use to decide whether to grant the appeal is the same as discussed earlier, ie whether the judge at first instance was wrong or whether there was a procedural flaw that renders the case an injustice. Judgment will almost certainly be given immediately and it is highly unlikely that the judge would ever refer the matter back to a district judge and would instead simply exercise his powers to vary an order.

Costs

Until comparatively recently the small claims track contained a potentially disadvantageous system in respect of appeals. Whilst, as noted in Chapter 17, the small claims track limited the costs of litigation there was no cap in respect of appeals. Accordingly, in our example, if Amy had succeeded in her claim, Screens 'R' Us could have threatened to appeal and state that they would engage a barrister to represent them at the hearing. The potential costs for this are such that Amy might decide not to contest any appeal.

That is no longer the case, however, and small claims track appeals are dealt with in a very similar way. Indeed, the rules governing costs for the small claims track expressly include 'costs relating to an appeal'[54] and thus the same costs as identified in 17.2 can be claimed, with the court fee of £120 being one of these. No costs for legal representation will ordinarily be payable.

There is (theoretically) the right to appeal against the decision of the appeal, this lying to the Court of Appeal (Civil Division) as it is a second appeal. It would be extremely rare for an appeal to be granted leave, however. A rare case where a small claims track issue did arrive at the Court of Appeal was *Akhtar v Boland*[55] and to the surprise of even the court itself, it would seem that the costs protection applies to those proceedings too.[56]

18.2.5.2 Judicial review

The second case study was in respect of Matilda's claim for judicial review. It will be remembered from Chapter 17 that this is a matter that takes place before the Administrative Court in the High Court. Therefore any appeal will be direct to the Court of Appeal (Civil Division) even for a 'first' appeal.

Where the judicial review was heard by two judges in the Administrative Court (ie a Divisional Court) then the matter will be heard before a three-judge panel of the Court of Appeal but where it was heard only by a single judge then it is possible that it will be heard by a two-judge panel.

Leave

As noted earlier the first issue is that the losing party must seek leave to appeal. Let us assume that Matilda was successful and she received an order quashing the decision of

---

53. For an interesting discussion on this see Penny Darbyshire, *Sitting in Judgment: The Working Lives of Judges* (Hart Publishing 2011) 245.
54. CPR, r 27.14(2).
55. [2014] EWCA Civ 943.
56. See ibid, [7].

the chief constable to ban the march. The chief constable believes that the judge did not take account of the cost involved in providing security for two high-profile events (the march and the visit of the Home Secretary) and that the decision is irrational.

Here the chief constable will be the appellant and Matilda will be the respondent. The chief constable must seek leave to appeal. As identified earlier, this can be sought from the court of first instance (the Administrative Court) or, if this is refused, from the Court of Appeal itself. As with the small claims track there is a form (form N161 available with the online resources) and there is a section of this form that allows the applicant to seek the leave of the court. However, rather than just complete the form the person must file the appropriate documents that identify what the decision is and what grounds are relied upon for the appeal,[57] including identifying the grounds of appeal.

The respondent has the right to make representations to the court on why permission should not be allowed, although these will normally be confined to paper submission.[58] The statement should not be more than three pages long and ordinarily no costs can be claimed for doing so;[59] this is partly because the respondent does not *have* to answer the appeal at permissions stage: it is for the claimant to persuade the court that they should have the right to appeal so silence from the respondent would not realistically change their success.

The clear presumption is for leave to be considered on the papers (by a single (puisne) judge) but if leave is refused then the appellant has the right to ask for a hearing in respect of seeking permission unless the judge, who considers the papers, refuses a hearing. Such an appeal will take place in open court and will be before a normal bench of the Court of Appeal, ie two (or more likely three) Lord Justices of Appeal.

Regardless of whether permission is sought by papers or by hearing, the test remains the same. Leave shall only be granted if:

(a) the court considers that the appeal would have a real prospect of success; or

(b) there is some other compelling reason why the appeal should be heard.[60]

'Real' prospect means that the appeal must have a realistic chance of success and is not merely fanciful.[61] In essence this means that the threshold is higher than prima facie, but it will obviously not be so high as to amount to the hearing of the appeal. Only the judge(s) can predict how the court will act, but there must be sufficient reason to believe that the grounds of appeal could be successful.

⚡ APPEAL AGAINST PERMISSION FOR JUDICIAL REVIEW

It was noted at 17.3.2 that permission was required before a judicial review could proceed. If permission is refused (even after a renewed hearing) then this can be appealed to the Court of Appeal (Civil Division) but only on the ordinary grounds of appeal. An appeal must be made within seven days of permission being refused, and where the Court of Appeal allows the appeal they have the power to grant permission for judicial review rather than remit the matter back for reconsideration.[62]

The fee for seeking permission to appeal is currently £528.

---

57. PD 52C, para 3.
58. ibid, para 18.
59. ibid, para 19.
60. CPR, r 52.6(1).
61. *Swain v Hillman* [2001] 1 All ER 91.
62. CPR, r 52.8.

Pre-trial matters

Assuming that leave has been granted then there are a number of matters that must be adhered to. As with the High Court, the Court of Appeal will not serve papers on any party and will expect the parties to use the usual rules of service, so that the court and all parties receive everything.

The appellant must complete the 'appeal questionnaire' that will be distributed by the court.[63] This will ask a series of case-management questions, including providing a time estimate. If the respondent disagrees with this time estimate, they must notify the court within seven days of this decision. Providing an unrealistic time estimate can disrupt the listing of the appeal but also lead to costs sanctions.

A core bundle must be compiled. This should include:

- the notice and grounds of appeal sealed by the court
- skeleton argument
- chronology of relevant issues
- transcript of the first-instance judgment
- written permission from first-instance decision (if applicable)
- the original claim form for judicial review
- the (original) acknowledgment of service and defence.

Details of any other information or evidence that is to be relied upon should be included as a 'supplementary bundle'.

It has been suggested that there are three types of respondent:

1. Those who are seeking to uphold the first-instance decision for the reasons set out in the judgment.

2. Those who are seeking to uphold the first-instance decision but for reasons that differ from the judgment.

3. Those who are seeking a variation of the first-instance decision.[64]

The most common respondent is #1 but then probably #3. An example of #3 may be where, for example, a judge made a finding of contributory negligence against the respondent, or where they believe the damages should have been greater or, perhaps more commonly, where they disagree with a costs order.

A respondent in position #3 is cross-appealing and therefore must submit a notice of appeal in the same way as an appellant, albeit after the appeal has been lodged. A respondent in #2 is not cross-appealing but he must issue a respondent's notice.[65] A respondent's notice is similar to an appellant's notice of appeal and sets out the reasons why the respondent is disagreeing with the reasons at first instance. A respondent in position #1 does not need to file a respondent's notice.

Where a respondent wishes to make representations to the court then they must submit a skeleton argument, which should also be filed on the appellant.

A fee (currently £1,199) must be paid before the hearing can take place.

663

---

63.   ibid, PD 52C, para 23.
64.   Stuart Sime, *A Practical Approach to Civil Litigation* (19th edn, OUP 2016) 571.
65.   CPR, r 52.13.

Hearing

Usually an appeal from the Administrative Court will take place before three judges and ordinarily these will be Lord Justices of Appeal rather than including puisne judges. For judicial review cases, it is usual for an appeal to be heard by a three-judge panel, but this has to occur when the first-instance decision was a Divisional Court (ie two or more judges sitting together).

Where the bench consists of Lord Justices of Appeal then the administrative head of civil appeals will ordinarily not only decide the constitution of the panel but also decide who will be the 'lead' judge, ie the one who is identified as probably giving the judgment of the court.[66] This will not necessarily be the judge who presides over the court as that is decided purely by seniority (ie date of appointment). Where the Lord Chief Justice, Master of the Rolls, or Head of Division sits then they would ordinarily preside (again, in seniority, so where exceptionally both the Lord Chief Justice and Master of the Rolls sit, the Lord Chief Justice would preside as he is President of the Courts of England and Wales which trumps the Master of the Rolls even though the latter is head of civil justice). Where the Lord Chief Justice, Master of the Rolls, or Head of Division sits, they would ordinarily decide who will give the lead judgment. Increasingly the Court of Appeal (Civil Division) has attempted to move towards single judgments;[67] although a number of cases will still involve different judgments, especially where the bench is divided, unlike the position in the Criminal Division, there is no custom that prohibits the issuing of minority judgments.

Whoever is the 'lead' judge will ordinarily take the lead on asking the questions of counsel although the other judges can contribute as they wish. As the skeleton arguments will have been read and digested by the court the judges will ordinarily focus only on those aspects that they believe have merit. For example, it will not be unusual for counsel to be told that of three grounds of appeal they are only interested in hearing ground 2. It would be a very brave (and in legalese 'brave' means 'stupid') counsel who would ignore such statements and seek to go beyond that ground.

One interesting practical point to note for the law student is the fact that counsel for the appellant is rarely asked to open the appeal. When a student moots, they are invariably told that they must introduce everyone, provide a summary of the first-instance decision and the grounds for appeal. Whilst this may have been common practice in the appellant courts some time ago, it is not the practice now. The judges will have read the skeleton arguments and digested the bundle, and so they do not want the court's time wasted by telling them things that they already know. To that extent, whilst it remains adversarial in that there are two sides trying to persuade neutral umpires of their case, it is perhaps more inquisitorial in terms of judicial control and interaction.

Judgment will either be given *ex tempore* (ie immediately and without being typed up verbatim) or will be reserved. Sometimes the reservation may only be for a short period of time, including overnight. All judgments, even *ex tempore* ones, are recorded and may therefore be transcribed or reported for the law reports. The Court of Appeal has the same powers as identified earlier. This can include, for example, remitting the matter back to the court of first instance. In judicial review cases it is unlikely that they will do this, not least because there may be questions of timing, save where it is necessary to hear factual evidence. It is more likely that the Court of Appeal will adopt its powers of endorsing, varying, or quashing the order.

---

66.   Penny Darbyshire, *Sitting in Judgment: The Working Lives of Judges* (Hart Publishing 2011) 245.
67.   ibid, 343.

Subsequent appeals

As noted earlier there is technically a further appeal but only to the Supreme Court. This is exceptional. Whilst the Court of Appeal can give permission to appeal, in civil matters it usually leaves the issue of leave to the Supreme Court itself.

18.2.5.3 Children's contact

The third example was Joshua's application under the *Children Act 1989* to see Sarah, his child. It will be remembered from Chapter 17 that specific rules exist for family proceedings—the *Family Procedure Rules* (FPR)—and these apply also to (some) appeals. Appeals within the Family Court are dealt with by the FPR but appeals to the Court of Appeal (Civil Division) are dealt with under the CPR as the Court of Appeal is not part of the Family Court.[68] Thus the procedure discussed earlier would apply to family appeals. Appeals within the Family Court ordinarily take the approach of escalating an appeal to the next level of judge. This is set out in Table 18.2.

Separate to this, however, both the Family Court and the High Court have discretion to decide that the matter should instead be dealt with by the Court of Appeal (Civil Division) but they should do so only when:

(a) it raises an important point of principle of practice; or

(b) there is some other compelling reason for the Court of Appeal to hear it.[69]

The position of a circuit judge is slightly complicated as it depends on the matter they ruled. The general rule is that an appeal from a circuit judge is to a puisne judge, even where it is a final decision (cf the position for general civil litigation discussed earlier). However, for certain categories of appeal, an appeal goes to the Court of Appeal (Civil Division). These include:

- decisions relating to public childcare proceedings, orders relating to the protection of children or children abroad

- decisions relating to adoption

Table 18.2 Route of appeals

Justices of the Peace sitting in the Family Court	Circuit judge
District judge of the county court sitting in the Family Court	Circuit judge
District judge of the High Court sitting in the Family Court	Puisne judge
District judge of the principal registry of the Family Division	Puisne judge
Costs judge	Puisne judge
Circuit judge or recorder sitting in the Family Court	Puisne judge or Court of Appeal.
Puisne judge (inc deputy) sitting in either the Family Court or the High Court of Justice	Court of Appeal

---

68. FPR, r 30.1 makes clear the extent of the rules.
69. FPR, r 30.13.

- a decision to hold a party in Contempt of Court, or an order following the finding for contempt
- a decision that was made on appeal.[70]

This is a relatively restricted list and it means that for most private-law proceedings, a decision of a circuit judge will go to a puisne judge.

If we refer back to our example of Joshua, it will be remembered that the decision was heard by justices of the peace, and therefore the appeal will go to a circuit judge (or a recorder).

Leave

As with the ordinary civil rules, there is not ordinarily an absolute right. That said, the FPR make clear that no permission is required to appeal a decision of lay magistrates to circuit level.[71] Presumably the logic of this is similar to the logic for appeal in criminal cases, ie that the magistrates are not legally trained and that justice requires the right of access to a legally qualified judge. However, given that a legal adviser will always be present in the Family Court and the justices are given specialist training, it must be questioned whether this is overly generous and that leave should be required for all cases.

For our example, if we assume that Joshua does not agree with the decision of the justices not to increase contact with the child, then it would seem that he can take this to a circuit judge without permission. That said, unlike a Crown Court appeal, the matter will not be a rehearing, it is an appeal and the same test will be adopted (see later).

Pre-trial matters

Joshua has submitted his appeal. He must now adhere to several pre-trial matters before his appeal can be heard, the most notable being the preparation of an appeal bundle.[72] As with other appeals, a skeleton argument is usually required. Where it is 'an appellant who is not represented [they] need not file a skeleton argument but [are] encouraged to do so since this will be helpful to the court'.[73] Even if a skeleton argument by a litigant in person is not as detailed or polished as one prepared by an advocate, the reason for requesting one is that it will help the judge in the pre-reading. An appeal is a review of a decision, not a rehearing, and thus the judge hearing the appeal will wish to concentrate on the key issues, and a skeleton argument can assist with this.

In many family matters there will not have been a written judgment *per se*. In the original hearing of Joshua's application it is likely that the district judge will simply have stated why it was that he refused to make the order that he did. It is quite possible, and indeed likely, that he would do this verbally. How can this be adduced before the circuit judge for consideration on appeal? The Practice Direction states that the parties should attempt to agree a version of the ruling and to submit that before the judge who made the decision.[74] Interestingly where an advocate was used in the proceedings then the Practice Direction *expressly states* that their fee for appearing in the original matter includes remuneration for taking a note of the judgment, transcribing it, attempting to reach an agreed version, submitting it to the judge, and making any amendments

70. FPD 30A, para 2.1.
71. FPR, r 30.3. The rule is by omission: the rule states that permission is required to appeal a circuit judge, recorder, district judge, or costs judge. Thus a decision by justices of the appeal must not require permission.
72. FPD 30A, para 5.8 sets out what is required.
73. ibid, para 5.15.
74. ibid, para 5.23.

required by the judge.[75] Where, therefore, a different barrister is engaged for the appeal or the litigant decides to represent himself, the original advocate is under a duty to supply their note of the judgment.

Once these documents are prepared they must be served on all other parties[76] and ultimately a date will be set for the appeal, including any procedural hearings that may be required (although in a matter as simple as this one it is likely that the only hearing will be the appeal itself). The court will request a time estimate for the appeal (which is easier to gauge when professional advocates are used but even litigants in person will be required to give an estimate) as this will assist the court in listing the appeal.

The respondent(s) to the appeal will also be required to prepare a bundle and skeleton argument and this will then be served on the court and the appellant.

Hearing

As this appeal will be to a circuit judge, the Designated Family Judge[77] will assign a judge to the appeal at a relevant and convenient court.

The actual hearing is a 'review of the decision';[78] in other words it is not a rehearing but an appeal. It will concentrate on whether the first-instance decision was (legally) wrong. The fact that it is a review and not a rehearing is emphasized by the fact that ordinarily evidence (including witness testimony) will not be adduced[79] and this is because it is not its decision to reach matters of fact but rather to conclude whether the judge of first instance erred in reaching his judgment.

The test for allowing the appeal is if the court believes the decision was:

(a) wrong; or

(b) unjust because of a serious procedural or other irregularity.[80]

Most appeals will be decided on ground (a) and it is notable that the test is that it is *wrong*. It is not enough that a judge may have decided differently, it must decide that the decision was wrong meaning, in essence, that it should not have been reached. As with main civil litigation appeals the appellate judge has the same powers as the original judge[81] and has the power to affirm, set aside, or vary an order or alternatively order a new hearing etc.[82] In the example of Joshua the circuit judge would decide what to do. It is highly unlikely that he would refer it back for a rehearing and would instead just make a revised order if he believes it appropriate to do so. Alternatively, he would dismiss the appeal.

Subsequent appeals

As the decision was in respect of an appeal, any subsequent appeal would go to the Court of Appeal (Civil Division) rather than to a puisne judge. The permission of the Court of Appeal would be required to do this and it would only succeed if the grounds set out earlier (at 18.2.2.1) were to be met.

---

75. ibid, para 5.25.
76. ibid, para 6.2.
77. A senior circuit judge who has judicial management control for family proceedings in their area.
78. FPR, r 30.12.
79. ibid, r 30.12(2).
80. ibid, r 30.12(3).
81. ibid, r 30.11(1).
82. ibid, r 30.11(2).

‹› Summary

This chapter has introduced the concept of civil remedies and then presented the different methods of appeals from decisions of the civil courts. This allows you to draw comparisons to the avenue of criminal appeals in Chapter 16. It has also:

- Identified that there are many different types of remedies that a court can award to a successful litigant.

- Demonstrated that the most common form of remedy is that which is known as 'damages' and that there are various heads of damage that can be claimed for, but that the main distinction is that between 'pecuniary' and 'non-pecuniary'.

- Equity has a number of remedies and these will only ordinarily be used where damages by themselves will not suffice but they can be combined with damages.

- It is possible to obtain remedies before the conclusion of a trial and these are known as interim remedies. Perhaps the most notable of these is the interim injunction but for this to be granted a claimant must give an undertaking to compensate the defendant if the claim is resolved against him.

- Appeals in the civil courts follow a slightly more complicated structure than in criminal cases.

- Save where it is a final decision in a multi-track case, the usual rule is that the appeal will be heard by the next most senior judge.

- It is possible to have a second appeal but the courts are reluctant to allow this except in the most serious cases.

- In order to appeal in civil cases it is usually necessary to seek permission before proceeding with a civil appeal.

? End-of-chapter questions

1. Should a court discount an award to take account of the fact that damages can be invested? What kind of investment should they base their decision on? Is this not risky given that even bank interest rates have been stagnant for the past few years?

2. Read Penny Darbyshire, *Sitting in Judgment: The Working Lives of Judges* (Hart Publishing 2011) 251 where she states that circuit judges do not like sitting on the appeals of district judges who sit in the same building as them. Is there not a danger of apparent bias (even if there is no actual bias) that a judge who works with the judge whose decision he is reviewing will uphold the ruling 'for a quiet life'? How does this differ, however, from puisne judges sitting in the Court of Appeal (Criminal Division)?

3. Is it fair that the costs for small claims track appeals are restricted? If an appeal concerns points of law should it not be appropriate that lawyers are allowed to be used?

For self-test questions, flashcards, and links to useful websites, please visit the **online resources** at: **www.oup.com/he/gillespie-weare8e/**

19

Alternative Dispute Resolution

By the end of this chapter you will be able to:

- Understand why the pressure for ADR arose.
- Define ADR and explain the three principal forms of ADR.
- Identify how the courts are able to persuade litigants to use ADR.
- Appreciate some of the advantages and disadvantages of ADR.

Introduction

It has been seen in the previous chapters that there are several different ways in which disputes can be resolved formally through the invocation of the judicial or tribunal system. However, court proceedings are not the only ways in which disputes can be resolved and in recent times there has been a push towards Alternative Dispute Resolution (ADR). As has been seen, the courts are expensive and therefore there is an argument for suggesting that disputes should only reach the courts or tribunals if there is no other alternative. Certainly, as will be seen, the courts are increasingly adopting this approach and are using their powers to encourage attempts at settling the dispute before a formal judicial resolution is sought.

This chapter will examine how ADR has grown and consider its application and some difficulties that may arise through its use.

19.1 What is Alternative Dispute Resolution?

There is no single definition of Alternative Dispute Resolution (ADR). Whilst there are agreed types of ADR, the term just realistically means a way of resolving a dispute without formally invoking the courts or tribunals. Thus ADR could range from an agreement by the parties (eg, party A deciding to forgo x per cent of a disputed bill because they accept that they did not perform the contract adequately) to a third party intervening in the dispute to make findings of fact, in which case it may look not dissimilar to a court case.

It is widely accepted that ADR involves two distinct types of resolution. These are known as adjudicative options and non-adjudicative options.[1] 'Adjudicative' means that a person sits as an adjudicator, ie a person independent of the parties will hear from the other parties and reach a conclusion on the dispute and, in most instances, decide upon the remedy. To that extent, as has been noted already, it could be questioned what the difference is between an adjudicative resolution and litigation. The answer lies primarily in the lack of formality, speed, and cost.[2] The legal process is complicated. As was seen in Chapter 17, there are rules governing how litigation is conducted within the courts. Alongside these procedural rules are rules of evidence. They will limit the types of evidence, or the circumstances in which the evidence can be presented to the courts. However, ADR operates outside of the legal system and therefore the parties themselves can decide what the rules are, without being bound by traditional understandings of the law and process.

Non-adjudicative forms are much broader. They tend to rely on facilitating an agreement. A third party may still be present, but their role is not to be determinative, but rather to try and bring the two sides together, to understand the point of view of the others, and to work towards a settlement that both are happy with. Non-adjudicative forms can therefore sometimes create situations where a party does not think that they have 'won' or 'lost' because it is about identifying a compromise that both are happy about and which avoids the requirement to spend considerable sums of money on litigation.

At the outset, it is important to understand the scale of ADR. It is tempting to think of ADR as being 'local' resolution of small-scale disputes. Whilst undoubtedly this will sometimes be the case, ADR can involve vast sums of money. For the reasons that are set out more fully later, it is increasingly common for commercial cases to be settled via ADR. This means that it is not uncommon for multi-million pound disputes to be settled through adjudicative ADR. Indeed the popularity of ADR, particularly arbitration, has caused the current Lord Chief Justice to speculate whether there is a danger that it will stifle the development of the common law since disputes that would otherwise be adjudicated by the courts, allowing precedent to develop, are now being dealt with outside of the judicial process.[3]

It is equally important to recognize a second truth of ADR. That it is not new. By bringing together all the forms of dispute resolution under the title of 'ADR' it is sometimes possible to believe that ADR is a modern concept. Indeed, it was realistically not until the twentieth century that 'ADR' became a popular concept, it largely centring on the work of Frank Sander, a professor of law at Harvard University.[4] However, some forms of ADR are much older. Arbitration, a form of arbitrative justice, has been in existence for hundreds of years, having existed in (English) ecclesiastical law since the seventh century.[5] In the 1920s, English commercial arbitration was lauded as being the exemplar that other countries, most notably the USA, should follow.[6] There is no doubt, however, that in recent years ADR has enjoyed a renaissance where its popularity has increased and where the judiciary encourage it to be tried as an alternative to litigation.

---

1. See, for example, Susan Blake, Julie Browne, and Stuart Sime, *The Jackson ADR Handbook* (2nd edn, OUP 2016) 13, 16.
2. ibid, 13.
3. Lord Thomas of Cwmgiedd, 'Developing Commercial Law through the Courts: Rebalancing the Relationship between the Courts and Arbitration' 2016 BAILII lecture. Available online at: <https://www.judiciary.gov.uk/wp-content/uploads/2016/03/lcj-speech-bailli-lecture-20160309.pdf>.
4. An illuminating history of the development of ADR and the place of Frank Sander can be found in Michael L Moffitt, 'Frank Sander and His Legacy as an ADR Pioneer' (2006) 22 *Negotiation Journal* 437–45.
5. Paul L Sayre, 'Development of Commercial Arbitration Law' (1928) 37 *Yale Law Journal* 595, 597.
6. ibid, 595.

19.2 **Why use ADR?**

Some of the reasoning behind this has already been discussed: it can be a cheaper, less formal, and quicker way to resolve disputes. It can operate in a more flexible way than the law, particularly the English law.

19.2.1 **A shift away from combat?**

It has been noted numerous times in this book that the English Legal System is based on the adversarial system of litigation. In essence this means that both sides separately prepare their respective submissions and then they arrive in court and participate in a quasi-gladiatorial contest until the tribunal of fact (in civil trials this usually being a judge) pronounces the winner. The manner in which this contest occurs was seen in Chapter 17 and even in tribunals, a system of justice that is usually considered to be more informal, the adversarial system remains intact with both sides still competing against each other (discussed in Chapter 7).

Yet in recent times there has been an increasing debate as to whether the adversarial system is the appropriate way of resolving all disputes. To an extent this was realized in specialist proceedings, perhaps most notably in proceedings relating to the welfare of a child. The *Children Act 1989* makes clear that the best interests of the child must be the court's paramount consideration[7] and this has led to the conclusion that in certain proceedings, most notably child protection proceedings, the full adversarial system is unhelpful and that making the proceedings more inquisitorial can be of assistance (see the discussion on family litigation at 17.4).

Even within ordinary litigation it is now becoming increasingly accepted that the adversarial system is not always of assistance and that it inherently involves both extensive cost and delay.[8] It has also been suggested that it involves two further disadvantages: an imbalance of power (which could be likened to the 'equality of arms' principle contained within Article 6 *European Convention on Human Rights* (ECHR) (see 5.4.5.4)) and the restriction of civil legal aid (see Chapter 11) means that the adversarial system allows the rich to exploit the law.[9] It is difficult to argue against these and although Article 6 will try to level the 'battleground' so far as possible, eg through exchange of documents (although this is not an automatic right: see for example *Secretary of State for the Home Department v MB*[10]) or the provision of legal assistance (see, for example, *Steel and Morris v United Kingdom*[11]) it is simply a fundamental part of the legal system.

Wider concerns exist over the adversarial system, not least being whether it encourages the resolution of disputes and the discovery of the facts or merely seeks to identify who has the better advocate. The advocate in adversarial systems, while being under a professional duty not to mislead the court, owes a duty to his client and will act in a partisan way before the neutral umpire, seeking to exploit the weaknesses of the opposing side while at the same time trying to hide their own weaknesses. Not only are the lawyers inherently partisan but most witnesses almost certainly will be, not least by

---

7. *Children Act 1989*, s 1(1).
8. Geoff Davies, 'Civil Justice Reform: Why We Need to Question Some Basic Assumptions' (2006) 25 *Civil Justice Quarterly* 32.
9. ibid.
10. [2006] EWCA Civ 1140.
11. (2005) 41 EHRR 22.

the labelling of witnesses as being 'for' or 'against' a side. A witness will not be called unless it is thought that they would assist the argument being put forward by the party, regardless of whether or not the person has anything to contribute to the finding of fact.

The adversarial system ensures that lawyers are central to the process. Since the analysis and presentation of evidence is key to the adversarial approach, one requires a lawyer who is able to assimilate the facts quickly and apply them with an appropriate knowledge of law. This by itself is not sufficient, however, since a lawyer must also advocate the points, ie use persuasion to encourage the tribunal of fact to make the appropriate rulings. In a market society such as England and Wales, this means that the best lawyers will always be in demand and can therefore charge significant fees. This not only makes litigation expensive but also creates a power imbalance between those who can afford these fees and those who cannot.[12]

19.2.2 Advantages of ADR

The shift away from the adversarial system must undoubtedly be considered a key advantage of ADR. However, there are more tangible advantages in its use.

As was noted in Chapter 17 the courts are beset by delays. Whilst procedure rules seek to try and improve the situation, it must be accepted that litigation can take a considerable length of time. This is particularly true of complicated cases. For the quarter January to March 2020, it was reported that the average length of time between claim and hearing in fast- or multi-track claims was 59.6 weeks.[13] This is the *average* length of time, meaning that for many cases it took considerably longer. Even simpler cases took time. The average length of time between claim and hearing was 39.7 weeks for small claims actions,[14] yet these are supposed to be the simplest of cases. In both instances it should be noted that this is the time between claim and the *main* hearing. There will then be a further hearing before the judgment is given.

In many instances, waiting over a year for a resolution to a dispute is simply not possible. For example, if the dispute is over a crucial factory part or the performance of a contract, considerable losses could be incurred if the status quo continues for the year it takes for the matter to proceed before the courts. ADR can be much quicker as it is, in essence, a case of ensuring that the parties agree and that a suitable time can be found with the person who facilitates ADR. As there are a considerable number of these, it is possible to move very quickly. Indeed, some forms of ADR now take place online, meaning that the process is even quicker.[15]

It is not just about speed, however. The costs of ADR are usually much cheaper than litigation. While this year-long trial process has been going on, there will have been considerable work undertaken by barristers and solicitors. Indeed, even prior to the court action being commenced there will have been considerable legal costs incurred. Where a dispute is over not very much money, it is quite possible that the costs of litigation will take up most of, or indeed exceed, the money being disputed. The *Money*

---

12. Geoff Davies, 'Civil Justice Reform: Why We Need to Question Some Basic Assumptions' (2006) 25 *Civil Justice Quarterly* 32, 37.

13. Ministry of Justice, 'Civil Justice Statistics Quarterly, England & Wales: January to March 2020 (provisional)' (MoJ, 2020) 1 available at <https://assets.publishing.service.gov.uk/government/uploads/system/uploads/attachment_data/file/889851/civil-justice-statistics-quarterly-Jan-Mar-2020-accessible-.pdf>.

14. ibid.

15. Julia Hörnle, 'Online Dispute Resolution: The Emperor's New Clothes?' (2003) 17 *International Review of Law, Computers & Technology* 27, 28.

Advice Service, a governmental website that helps provide financial advice, notes that a *negotiated* financial settlement in a divorce could cost upwards of £3,000.[16] That is where there is agreement. Where the divorce is contested, it states that costs of £36,000 are not unusual.[17] In many instances it will be more. The average family will probably not have much more than that in savings or indeed equity, and what equity there is in property should ideally be used to allow both parties to gain alternative property rather than paying for lawyers. Mediation, a form of ADR, however, may only cost £100 per hour, and if the parties are capable of being sensible and compromising, it is possible that agreement on the way forward could take place in four to six sessions.[18]

The informality of ADR also means that it is sometimes possible to go to the heart of the dispute, whereas the adversarial nature of litigation requires each side to establish their case. Indeed, adversarial systems tend to encourage so-called 'satellite litigation' where minor disputes start off and encircle the principal dispute, causing additional costs and delays. ADR can puncture this by encouraging people to concentrate on what is important to both parties.

A final and yet very important advantage, in some cases, is that ADR is generally confidential. As it is, in essence, an agreement between parties, both can assist on confidentiality. This can be important where the dispute is sensitive or where the issue at the heart of the dispute may cause reputational damage to one or other of the parties. Whilst it is possible in some cases to have confidentiality within litigation, the clear presumption is that litigation is public.[19] This may be uncomfortable for either or both parties, meaning that ADR becomes attractive.

19.2.3 Disadvantages of ADR

It is easy to get caught up in the enthusiasm of ADR but there are disadvantages too. ADR requires a degree of consent. In the absence of any law or rule to the contrary, both parties must agree to use ADR rather than litigate.[20] This is not always possible, particularly where disputes seem personal. In the raw emotion of feeling 'wronged', people do not often want to think rationally and instead prefer the idea of 'vengeance', even when the courts are not interested in that as a concept. A good example of this is divorce. As will be seen later, ADR is strongly recommended in family matters, but when a marriage has broken down it is not uncommon for the parties to want a fight rather than a compromise. Where, for example, adultery is admitted, the courts do not care about the circumstances of the adultery and the hurt that this may have caused a party. Legally it is irrelevant once admitted[21] and it is not relevant to the dispersal of assets. Yet the 'wronged' party is likely to believe it is material and therefore may be less willing to compromise in ADR.

There is also the disadvantage that it might end up in court in any event. Whilst it will be seen that some forms of ADR are protected by the courts, in that they will not

---

16.   Money Advice Service, 'How much does divorce or dissolution cost?' (MaS, n.d.) <https://www.moneyadvice-service.org.uk/en/articles/how-much-does-divorce-or-dissolution-cost>.

17.   ibid.

18.   Of course, there would be the formal costs of applying to the court for a divorce. A petition for divorce costs £550 to file and an application for a financial order costs £255. Applications in respect of children will be in addition to this (if required).

19.   See CPR, r 39.2.

20.   An example of where a law may provide a requirement would be a clause within a contract that required disputes to be settled by way of arbitration. The *Arbitration Act 1996* will enforce this as a contractual term and a court, faced with an attempt to litigate the dispute, will stay proceedings in the courts until the adjudication has happened.

21.   It would be relevant if not admitted because adultery is one of the grounds for divorce (*Matrimonial Causes Act 1973*, s 1(2)(a)) and therefore a party seeking to prove adultery would need to be able to prove it happened.

readily interfere with the ultimate decision, that is not the case with all forms. It is quite possible that in non-adjudicative forms of ADR, time and expense are incurred trying to identify a solution, only for it to collapse at the last minute or be rejected. It will be seen that the courts may take notice of this (when, for example, determining costs: see 17.1.5.3), but ultimately they are unlikely to reject litigation on this basis alone.

One of the advantages of ADR—informality—can also be a disadvantage. Whilst the legal system can be overly prescriptive and traditional, it does have the advantage that there is an established set of rules (both procedural and evidential) that neither side can influence. With ADR, the rules are generally agreed between the parties and thus if there is any power imbalance, it is possible that they may become skewed. Also, as ADR sits outside of the legal system, it is not affected by precedent. Therefore, the mere fact that a similar case had resolution x before does not necessarily mean that the second case will have the same resolution. Therefore, there is perhaps a degree of uncertainty with ADR.

Finally, some of the advantages are arguably over-stated. Whilst it is said that ADR is quick and cheap, it need not be. For example, for relatively minor disputes, the costs of ADR are likely to be more than the costs incurred under the small claims track in the county court (where costs are fixed: see 17.2). Also, ADR usually involves more work than for minor disputes. The small claims procedure requires the filing of the claim form, acknowledgement of service (and submission of defence, where appropriate, although that tends to be on the same form), and then the hearing. Some forms of ADR will require several steps, meaning that even if the process is quicker, it may seem more protracted.

That said, it should be recognized that in many cases ADR is likely to be an appropriate alternative to litigation, particularly where disputes are greater than the small claims track. The courts welcome ADR as the civil courts are overwhelmed with work and struggle to process the volume of cases that come before them. If they can encourage ADR, then this lightens the load before the courts. Where the dispute is either minor or simple, the courts will often view this as a more preferable outcome.

19.3 **Types of ADR**

It has been noted that there are two broad classifications of ADR; adjudicative and non-adjudicative, but what are the common forms of ADR? Table 19.1 summarizes the most common forms that are found within the UK.[22]

Table 19.1 Types of ADR in the UK

Adjudicative	Non-adjudicative
Arbitration	Offer and Acceptance
Adjudication	Negotiation
Expert determination	Mediation
	Neutral/Expert Evaluation
	Conciliation

22.   Table 19.1 is based on Chapter 2 of Susan Blake, Julie Browne, and Stuart Sime, *The Jackson ADR Handbook* (2nd edn, OUP 2016) which is published on behalf of the *Judicial College, Civil Justice Council*, and the *Civil Mediation Council* and which is widely considered to be the most authoritative statement of ADR in England and Wales.

19.3.1 **Adjudicative forms**

Adjudicative forms of ADR are those where the process does not lead to an agreement but instead somebody makes a decision as to the dispute.

19.3.1.1 **Arbitration**

Perhaps the most common form of adjudicative ADR is arbitration. As noted earlier, this is one of the oldest forms of resolving disputes, and it remains one of the most common forms of ADR. It is also the most formal of the forms, being very similar to a court process.

Arbitration is one form of ADR that is expressly recognized by the law. The *Arbitration Act 1996* sets out the three principles under which arbitration must take place:

1. The object of arbitration is to obtain the fair resolution of disputes by an impartial tribunal without unnecessary delay or expense.

2. The parties should be free to agree how their disputes are resolved, subject only to such safeguards as are necessary in the public interest.

3. The courts should not intervene save where prescribed by the *Arbitration Act 1996*.[23]

These principles encapsulate what arbitration is about. It is about the resolution of a dispute and it must be done fairly. As an adjudicative form of ADR, a person (or persons) is appointed to be the arbitrator and they must decide what the outcome of the dispute is. To that extent, they are analogous to a judge. The second principle demonstrates the flexibility of the arbitration, in that the parties can form their own rules on how the arbitration will take place (including ascertaining what is, or is not, part of the dispute) or they could delegate this to the arbitrator to decide.

The final point is an important one. The *Arbitration Act 1996* is very clear that the courts will be very slow to interfere with arbitration. Where a contract stipulates that disputes will be resolved through arbitration, or where the parties have reached an agreement to arbitrate, the courts will stay any proceedings brought before them that seek to litigate the dispute which is supposed to be the subject of arbitration.[24] Similarly, it is only possible to appeal a decision of an arbitrator under exceptional circumstances, usually a serious irregularity[25] or where there has been a material breach of law.[26] The courts are very slow to entertain any appeal because they fear that to do so would lead to the re-litigation of the dispute and would undermine the principle of arbitration.

Arbitration has also been used as a form of permitting religious tribunals to adjudicate on trials. In recent years there has been much media attention paid to the growth of so-called 'Sharia courts' where disputes are resolved under the principles of Islamic law. Other religions also have religious tribunals, including the Beth Din for Judaism. Do they have any legal force? The answer would seem to be both 'yes' and 'no'. Formally, religious tribunals do not form part of the English Legal System (save for the ecclesiastical courts of the Church of England (known as consistory courts) which do form part

---

23. *Arbitration Act 1996*, s 1.
24. ibid, s 9.
25. ibid, s 68, although it is possible to exclude this right of appeal under the arbitration agreement or contract.
26. ibid, s 69.

of the legal system due to the establishment of the Church of England[27]), however, there is no reason why they cannot act as a form of ADR. In *Al v MT (Alternative Dispute Resolution)*[28] the High Court stayed private family law proceedings to allow the matter to be the subject of arbitration in the Beth Din. The court ultimately upheld the ruling of that tribunal, although it noted that family law matters are not covered by the *Arbitration Act 1996* and thus the court could refuse to implement a decision. However, it demonstrated that the courts are willing to allow Alternative Dispute Resolution by religious arbitration, and this is one manner in which religious tribunals can be used to settle some forms of dispute.

⟳ QUESTION FOR REFLECTION

Should the English Legal System recognize the resolution of a dispute by a religious tribunal? Is this not permitting religious law to enter into the English Legal System via the 'back door'? However, if arbitration—and indeed most ADR—is about encouraging people to resolve their disputes on their own terms, why should it be any different if the parties wish to resolve their dispute according to the religious principles they believe in?

19.3.1.2 **Adjudication**

Adjudication is very similar to arbitration, in that it involves a specialist person adjudicating on a dispute.[29] It is arguably more specialist than arbitration in that it is often used to resolve very technical disputes rather than a wider dispute. It is often to be found in contracts where questions as to performance will be determined by an adjudicator. A failure to use the adjudicator would be considered a breach of contract and thus could be litigated in the courts.

19.3.1.3 **Expert determination**

In some cases the dispute will be about something extremely technical, which can realistically only be resolved by an expert. Litigation involving expert witnesses can be particularly expensive and therefore where the sole dispute concerns something resolvable by an independent expert, it is sometimes preferable to refer the matter to an expert to resolve the factual circumstances. The parties would need to agree to be bound by the decision of the expert and also agree what the consequences of that expert determination are. It differs from arbitration and adjudication in that the expert is not resolving a dispute *per se* but rather providing an independent (binding) opinion of a fact.

19.3.2 **Non-adjudicative forms**

Offer and acceptance and negotiation have, to an extent, already been covered as these are traditional forms of resolving a dispute. Technically neither require any sort of third-party intervention and it can be done by the parties themselves through the exchange of communications.

---

27. See the *Ecclesiastical Jurisdiction Measure 1963* which reformed the ecclesiastical courts and the work before them.
28. [2013] EWHC 100 (Fam).
29. Susan Blake, Julie Browne, and Stuart Sime, *The Jackson ADR Handbook* (2nd edn, OUP 2016) 14.

19.3.2.1 **Mediation**

Mediation is arguably a form of facilitated negotiation. A third party acts as a facilitator but, unlike arbitration, the third party has no role in determining issues and they instead simply try to encourage the parties to see things from the other's point of view. Mediation, as will be seen, is strongly encouraged within the family arena (where the justice system has a vested opinion in trying to ensure that disputes, particularly relating to children, are resolved in as amicable a manner as possible) and a number of not-for-profit bodies exist to facilitate family mediation.[30]

Mediation will frequently not involve both parties being in the same room at the same time initially. A typical mediation process may involve pre-sessional contact, so that the mediator understands the respective positions of the parties. The parties will then be placed in different rooms and the mediator will discuss matters with the parties and then start to shuttle between the two locations. In fact, in some instances the parties may never be in the same room: the mediator simply relays positions to each party until agreement is reached. In other situations, once the positions have been narrowed, the two parties will be brought together to try and resolve the dispute.

As with other non-adjudicative forms, mediation is relatively high-risk in that an uncooperative party is unlikely to engage with the process and therefore it could be considered a waste of time. A party that refuses to budge from their position is likely to mean that mediation collapses. Indeed, there is a danger that it does more harm than good, as the other party entrenches their position in response and because they feel that they 'did their bit' by trying to engage in mediation.

19.3.2.2 **Neutral/expert evaluation**

This is similar to expert determination (see 19.3.1.3) but is non-adjudicative. It is quite possible that the dispute is based on the opinions of the parties in respect of a factual circumstance. That being the case, sometimes bringing in a neutral expert to evaluate that issue can help resolve it. Unlike adjudicative expert evaluations, the parties will not be bound to accept the view of the expert, but instead it is used to encourage the parties to negotiate an appropriate settlement based on the viewpoint of the third party.[31]

19.3.2.3 **Conciliation**

Identifying what conciliation is, and how it differs from mediation, is extremely difficult.[32] It realistically must be considered a branch of mediation and so may not exist in its own right. Conciliation is sometimes referred to as the 'shuttle' form of mediation presented earlier, with 'mediation' being restricted to those situations where both sides are together. However, in many other contexts, this is called 'mediation'.

One potential difference is that in conciliation, the mediator might propose a solution independent of the parties.[33] This would differ from arbitration in that it is non-binding. Realistically, it is more that the third party is putting forward a suggestion to try and break an impasse between the parties. This is not uncommon in mediation either but, admittedly, some mediators see their role as being completely neutral and simply convey positions rather than put forward their own, so perhaps this is where conciliation may differ.

677

30   ibid, 17.
31   ibid, 19.
32   ibid.
33   ibid.

⚡ **CONCILIATION**

Conciliation is often used in industrial disputes. A good example would be where trade unions and employers disagree over work conditions, health and safety, etc. It is often used to try to settle disputes before strike action takes place. The alternative is either lengthy industrial disputes or litigation being brought where an employer seeks to interfere with strike action or where the trade union seeks declarations regarding health and safety legislation. By using conciliation, however, both sides can understand what the other's position is and try to reach a compromise that is suitable to both sides. A key to the success of conciliation is that the conciliator must be completely impartial. ACAS is often used in this role because of the reputation it has accrued over the years.

19.4 ADR and the courts

It may seem strange to think of the courts as wishing ADR to be used, but this must be placed into the context of extreme pressure being placed on the courts. Also, judges are realistic about litigation and the policy of the courts is that litigation is a measure of last resort.[34] How is this approval of ADR shown? The most notable shift in recent years is that the courts are using their powers to ensure that ADR is, at the very least, considered as part of the process of litigation.

19.4.1 Family law

Perhaps one of the best-known examples of how the courts encourage ADR is in respect of private family law, ie divorce and issues relating to the upbringing of children.[35] The *Family Procedure Rules* (FPR) place a positive duty on both the courts and the parties to consider the applicability of ADR. Rule 3.3 requires '[t]he court [to] consider, at every stage in proceedings, whether non-court dispute resolution is appropriate'. Where a court considers that ADR is appropriate, the court can order the adjournment of proceedings or a hearing in order to facilitate these approaches.[36]

More than this, however, the courts require parties to, at the very least, consider ADR before commencing litigation in respect of private family disputes. Rule 3.7 of the *Family Procedure Rules* requires an application for a private family law matter to enclose a form that says a person has attended a MIAM (Mediation Information & Assessment Meeting[37]) or that one of the exemptions for attending a MIAM applies. Rule 3.7 is an important provision but it could be suggested that it is too tame. Whilst Rule 3.8 appears to limit the circumstances under which mediation need not be sought, the reality is perhaps different. One of the grounds for not requiring mediation is that the proceedings would be for a financial remedy,[38] which is a very broad exemption. Given that ADR is perhaps most commonly used in respect of financial

---

34.   See the speech by Lord Justice Jackson 'Civil Justice Reform and Alternative Dispute Resolution' (20 September 2016). Available online at: <https://www.judiciary.gov.uk/wp-content/uploads/2013/03/lj-jackson-cjreform-adr.pdf>.

35.   Public family law is primarily focused on situations where the state is trying to intervene. So, for example, a local authority trying to take a child under supervision or into care, decisions as to the welfare and upbringing of vulnerable members of society.

36.   FPR, r 3.4(1).

37.   In essence, MIAM is a session with a mediator that is authorized to provide private family mediation services (see FPR, r 3.9).

38.   ibid, r 3.8(h)(ii).

disputes—particularly commercial litigation—it is perhaps surprising that a financial remedy should be exempting proceedings.

However, the more significant failing is in respect of mediators themselves. A mediator is entitled to certify that 'mediation is not ... suitable as a means of resolving the dispute'[39] and many mediators will sign the waiver form if the claimant turns up and says that he will not participate in mediation. Whilst this probably does meet the threshold—in that mediation is required to be consensual—it does give people a 'cop out'. Perhaps a better position would be to require at least one round of mediation (in that if people are required to attend, a mediator may be able to engage with them in order to persuade them that ADR is the best solution for everyone) or indeed to require other forms of ADR. For example, should an adjudicative form of ADR be required for some forms of private family law? Whilst it would not be suitable for all forms of disputes, it is not necessarily clear that the courts are the best location for all disputes. For example, under the *Children Act 1989*, if a parent wishes to take their child outside of the United Kingdom, they need the consent of the other parent or a court. Parents can often abuse this to cause difficulties for a parent who wishes to take the children abroad with a new partner. Does this really require the time of a court, or could this be dealt with by arbitration? The fact parents do not like the idea of a child having a foreign holiday is not a reason to prevent it or a reason for occupying the time of a salaried judge.

Rules 3.7 and 3.8 should be placed in the context of rule 3.3 discussed earlier. So, for example, the mere fact that an individual has sought to circumvent mediation does not mean that it cannot happen. If one party says they wish to participate in mediation and the other party does not, the judge would have the right under rule 3.3 to adjourn proceedings to give the parties time to think whether ADR is appropriate. In these situations they also have the power to take cooperation into account when determining costs (discussed later).[40]

19.4.1.1 **Civil disputes**

ADR is designed to facilitate the resolution of civil disputes. Historically it was thought that this meant private disputes, but in 2001 the government conceded that ADR could have a role in public-law matters too.[41] The courts enthusiastically supported this. In *Cowl v Plymouth City Council*[42] the then Lord Chief Justice (Lord Woolf) stated that:

> ... even in disputes between public authorities and the members of the public for whom they are responsible, insufficient attention is paid to the paramount importance of avoiding litigation whenever this is possible.[43]

The case concerned residential care for the elderly and the decision of Plymouth City Council to close two care homes. There existed a complaints process, by which grievances could be submitted that demonstrated that a decision would be reconsidered if considerable hardship was shown. The Court of Appeal believed that judicial review

---

39.   ibid, 3.8(2)(c).
40.   ibid, r 28.1 states that 'the court may at any time make such order as to costs as it thinks just'. Where a party has deliberately tried to circumvent ADR then the principles identified by the civil courts could easily be applied within the Family Court.
41.   See the speech by Lord Justice Jackson 'Civil Justice Reform and Alternative Dispute Resolution' (20 September 2016). Available online at: <https://www.judiciary.gov.uk/wp-content/uploads/2013/03/lj-jackson-cjreform-adr.pdf> 2.
42.   [2001] EWCA Civ 1935.
43.   ibid, [1].

was inappropriate until the complaints procedure had been exhausted, partly because they believed that this provided a cheaper, faster, and more appropriate disposal than litigation.

Since that time, the courts have readily applied this principle to other forms of judicial review[44] and so it would seem that ADR is not restricted to private disputes, although it would be fair to say that this is the most common position. However, the commitment to allowing ADR to be used in public disputes demonstrates that they are committed to ensuring that it is used to encourage the settling of disputes.

In terms of wider civil litigation, the *Civil Procedure Rules* (CPR) mirror the *Family Procedure Rules* in ensuring that ADR is actively considered. However, as will be seen, the civil courts are perhaps more robust than the family court, partly to take account of the fact that the disputes in the civil courts rarely involve matters concerning the welfare of a vulnerable person where other interests must take precedence.

Initially the rules are somewhat obscure about the place of ADR, with a reference to the court having the power to 'take any other step or make any other order for the purpose of managing the case and furthering the overriding objective, including hearing an Early Neutral Evaluation with the aim of helping the parties settle the case'.[45] Whilst express reference is made to Early Neutral Evaluation, a form of non-adjudicative resolution identified at 19.3.2.2, this rule gives wider authority to the courts to make orders to facilitate the early disposition of the case. Indeed, in determining the compliance of the overriding objective, the rules state that the court has a duty to encourage the parties to use ADR where the court believes this is appropriate.[46]

Perhaps the strongest, and clearest, encouragement comes from a Practice Direction that accompanies the rules. The *Pre-Action Protocols* apply to all civil litigation and 'explain the conduct and set out the steps the court would normally expect parties to take before commencing proceedings for particular types of civil claims'.[47] Importantly, it includes specific reference to ADR:

> Litigation should be a last resort. As part of a relevant pre-action protocol or this Practice Direction, the parties should consider whether negotiation or some form of ADR might enable them to settle their disputes without commencing proceedings.[48]
>
> If proceedings are issues, the parties may be required by the court to provide evidence that ADR has been considered. A party's silence in response to an invitation to participate or a refusal to participate in ADR might be considered unreasonable by the court and could lead to the court ordering that party to pay additional court costs.[49]

These are powerful statements and show that the courts are prepared to treat ADR seriously. Along with the general powers of the court to adjourn a matter, the CPR specifically provides that a party may seek a stay of proceedings while ADR is attempted.[50] If both parties agree to this request, then the stay is automatic, but the court retains discretion to stay proceedings if it 'otherwise considers that a stay would be appropriate'

---

44. See, for example, *R (on the application of Crawford) v Newcastle-upon-Tyne University* [2014] EWHC 1197 (Admin).
45. CPR, r 3.1(2)(m).
46. ibid, r 1.4(2)(e).
47. *Practice Direction: Pre-Action Conduct and Protocols*, para 1.
48. ibid, para 8
49. ibid, paras 9 and 11.
50. CPR, r 26.4.

to permit ADR.[51] This provides the court with the power to put pressure on the parties to consider ADR. The courts can go further, however, including through the use of the so-called 'Ungley Order'. This is an order named after QBD Master Ungley who pioneered its use.[52] The order, in essence, requires the parties to meet to discuss whether mediation (or other ADR) could solve their dispute. It does not require them to use ADR, it requires them to meet to discuss whether ADR is appropriate. This can be particularly useful where a party is equivocal about using ADR.

Can the courts go further and mandate that ADR takes place? In *Halsey v Milton Keynes General NHS Trust*,[53] the (then) Dyson LJ held that it would not be compatible with Article 6 ECHR to compel a party to undertake ADR.[54] The logic is that Article 6 safeguards the right to a fair and public hearing by an independent and impartial tribunal, which is considered to mean a court. However, not everyone agrees with this premise. It has been noted that other signatories to the ECHR have compulsory ADR and they have not attracted criticism for this.[55] It is also notable that in certain other common-law jurisdictions, where the right to justice is considered equally important, compulsory ADR can be found. A good example of this is Canada, where in Saskatchewan, litigants must attend a mediation session immediately after the initial papers have been filed.[56] This can be contrasted with the position in England which requires the parties to *consider* mediation, but it does not compel attendance. Perhaps the English position is based on the premise that non-adjudicative forms of ADR (which is what the courts appear to prefer in terms of encouraging ADR) can only work if both parties wish to cooperate, meaning mandating ADR would not work.

Whilst the English courts cannot mandate ADR, it is clear that by using their discretion over costs they can do the next best thing. It was seen from Chapter 17 that costs are now increasingly used by the courts in civil proceedings as a tool to persuade parties to do something. This is particularly true of ADR. The *Civil Procedure Rules* provide considerable flexibility in respect of costs[57] and in recent years, they have been prepared to use these.

One of the key landmarks was the decision in *Halsey v Milton Keynes General NHS Trust*[58] where the Court of Appeal held that unreasonable refusal to engage in ADR could be dealt with by a costs order. The court did note that the parties were free to engage with ADR in the manner that they wished, and thus the court will not look at the strategy they adopted.[59] In deciding whether there has been an unreasonable refusal, the court said that factors would include, but were not limited to:

(a) the nature of the dispute

(b) the merits of the case

(c) the extent to which other settlement methods have been attempted

(d) whether the costs of the ADR would be disproportionately high

681

---

51. ibid, r 26.4(2A).
52. Susan Blake, Julie Browne, and Stuart Sime, *The Jackson ADR Handbook* (2nd edn, OUP 2016) 96.
53. [2004] EWCA Civ 576.
54. ibid, [9].
55. Susan Blake, Julie Browne, and Stuart Sime, *The Jackson ADR Handbook* (2nd edn, OUP 2016) 96.
56. Barbara Billingsley and Masood Ahmed, 'Evolution, Revolution and Culture Shift: A Critical Analysis of Compulsory ADR in England and Canada' (2016) 45 *Common Law World Review* 186, 192.
57. CPR, pt 44.
58. [2004] EWCA Civ 576.
59. ibid, [14].

(e) whether any delay in setting up and attending the ADR would have been prejudicial

(f) whether the ADR had a reasonable prospect of success.[60]

Perhaps predictably, a solution to *Halsey* was for a party to maintain silence upon a request. If an unreasonable refusal could limit costs, then one strategy for parties was to neither accept nor refuse ADR. In *PGF II SA v OMFS Company 1 Ltd*[61] the Court of Appeal held that silence in the face of a request to engage in ADR was *by itself* unreasonable. Briggs LJ stated:

> In my judgment, the time has now come for this court to endorse the advice given in Chapter 11.56 of the ADR Handbook,[62] that silence in the face of the invitation to participate in ADR is, as a general rule, of itself unreasonable, regardless whether an outright refusal, or a refusal to engage in the type of ADR requested, or to do so at the time requested, might have been justified by the identification of reasonable grounds.[63]

This is tough language from the Court of Appeal and it is notable that Briggs LJ states that it should be regarded as unreasonable even if a refusal would not have been. The logic of this is undoubtedly that a party has the right to know whether their offer of ADR is to be accepted and, if not, why not. This is partly to ensure there is no loss of time, but also so that the case can be prepared in an appropriate way. The court believed that silence is not an option in civil litigation and there is an expectation that both sides will try to avoid litigation and ensure that any differences they may have are narrowed.[64]

Whilst *PGF* could be taken to be a sensible step forward from *Halsey*, it is notable that it is now recognized as a 'landmark' judgment.[65] It demonstrates, quite clearly, the importance that the courts place on ADR and they will not allow 'gameplay' to try and skew the results of ADR. In other contexts this can be seen where the courts have reacted to cases where a person seeks to litigate midway through an (unfinished) ADR process.[66] This is undoubtedly an attempt to frustrate the process of ADR and the courts are, quite correctly, likely to consider such activities unreasonable.

Costs orders are sufficiently flexible to ensure that either party can bear the costs irrespective of the general principle that the losing party bears the costs of the winning party. As litigation, particularly in multi-track cases, can be extremely expensive, the ability to order costs should focus the minds of the parties.

▌ Case Box *Laporte & Christian v Commissioner of Police for the Metropolis*

Two claimants had sought to argue that their arrest had been unlawful.[67] Whilst commencing their action, they indicated that they would be prepared to participate in ADR. The Metropolitan Police did not answer many of their queries and was equivocal as to whether they would participate in ADR.

---

60. ibid, [16].
61. [2013] EWCA Civ 1288.
62. This being Susan Blake, Julie Browne, and Stuart Sime, *The Jackson ADR Handbook* (2nd edn, OUP 2016) (note this footnote does not appear in the judgment).
63. [2013] EWCA Civ 1288 [34].
64. ibid, [37].
65. See the speech by Lord Justice Jackson 'Civil Justice Reform and Alternative Dispute Resolution' (20 September 2016). Available online at <https://www.judiciary.gov.uk/wp-content/uploads/2013/03/lj-jackson-cjreform-adr.pdf> 5.
66. Susan Blake, Julie Browne, and Stuart Sime, *The Jackson ADR Handbook* (2nd edn, OUP 2016) 134.
67. [2015] EWHC 371 (QB).

During the substantive hearing, the Metropolitan Police Commissioner won on all grounds. He sought costs from the claimants and asked for them to be on the indemnity basis.[68] Turner J refused to do this and applied *Halsey v Milton Keynes General NHS Trust*.[69] His Lordship held that the Metropolitan Police had been unreasonable in not participating in ADR. On that basis, he ordered that only two-thirds of the costs claimed by the Metropolitan Police should be payable by the claimant. The costs were in excess of £200,000 so the one-third loss demonstrates how seriously the courts take these issues, even against public authorities.

19.5 Online court

A recent innovation has seen the judiciary once more seeking to invoke ADR in place of litigation. Lord Justice Briggs was asked by the Lord Chief Justice to examine the structure of the civil courts. In his final report,[70] he recommended the creation of an 'online court'.[71] Whilst called 'a court', it is clear that Lord Justice Briggs intended that it would primarily be a dispute resolution service.

The online court (which is a name that Lord Justice Briggs wishes changed although there is no consensus to what[72]) would differ from the traditional courts in that, as its name suggests, it would take place entirely virtually. It is envisaged that there will be three stages to any dispute.

Stage 1. This would be the lodging of the claim. An online portal would facilitate this. Unlike traditional claim forms (which provide very generic questions), this portal would ask targeted questions so that the issues at the heart of any dispute would be identified. Where a matter is not disputed, it would be identified at any early stage and sent down a different path (ie to enforcement rather than adjudication). A degree of ODR (online dispute resolution) would be used at this stage.[73] This is where electronic communication is used to try and resolve the dispute. This would, in essence, be very similar to the position used by Amazon, eBay, and PayPal where there is a dispute. The various positions and offers would be put to the parties by an online facilitator (with parts of it potentially being automated) to see whether this could be resolved. In essence, this is not dissimilar to the offer/agreement or negotiation forms of non-adjudicative ADR identified earlier.

683

---

68. Indemnity costs are, in essence, more severe than normal costs and mean that where there is a dispute as to costs, the party gaining indemnity costs gets the benefit of the doubt, meaning that their claimed costs are payable. In standard costs situations, it is not unusual for a judge to summarily assess costs, ie decide himself how much should be payable for certain actions.

69. [2004] EWCA Civ 576.

70. Lord Justice Briggs, *Civil Courts Structure Review: Final Report* (Judiciary of England & Wales 2016).

71. ibid, ch 6.

72. ibid, 61.

73. See <https://www.judiciary.gov.uk/reviews/online-dispute-resolution/> for the website of the 'Online Dispute Resolution' Advisory Group, set up by the Master of the Rolls. This website provides comprehensive information about ODR and how it works.

Stage 2. This would be a compulsory form of ADR, probably conciliation. The online court is designed to simplify procedures and try to avoid cases proceeding to court. As part of this, there would be a requirement that the parties try to identify a solution. It has been suggested that the conciliation is likely to take place by telephone, but it could also conceivably be dealt with via Voice over Internet Protocols (VoIP) services (Skype, Facetime, etc) or even chat-based services.

Stage 3. Assuming that the dispute has still not been settled, the matter would proceed to trial. Depending on the issue, this would either be a decision on the papers, with both sides providing their written arguments, or alternatively an online trial, where the parties would participate. It could also be a hybrid, where a judge considers the papers but if he has any questions, he telephones either party to ask for further information or clarity.

The proposal seems quite radical, although, as Lord Justice Briggs himself notes, such courts are commonplace elsewhere in the world. Perhaps predictably the reaction of the legal profession was somewhat mixed. The chairman of the Bar Council was particularly lukewarm, suggesting that it would create a 'two-tier' justice system, arguing that those who can afford lawyers will continue to litigate whilst others will need to go through this process.[74] However, that rather neglects the point that if this is how two-tier justice is defined, that is already the position: cuts in legal aid have meant that those who cannot afford to litigate are arguably in a much poorer position. Indeed, it could be argued that if this online court is accessible for litigants in person, then a person seeking compensation would be better off using this than pursuing a conditional fee arrangement, as they are likely to lose less money.[75]

A more pertinent criticism was that if the costs of legal advice and limited representation were not included, that could mean that people rely on non-legal experts to decide the merits of their claim.[76] The judiciary have previously shown concern at so-called 'McKenzie friends' who charge payment for their services and are, in essence, becoming faux-lawyers.[77] If legal advice or legal representation is not permitted for claims of up to £25,000,[78] then such services may become more prominent. Lord Justice Briggs conceded that this could be right and there may be an argument for recovering some types of legal advice and services, although in a fixed way.[79] That has to be right: £25,000 is a serious amount of money and the suggestion that, for example, personal injury litigation could be pursued without any recourse to lawyers is perhaps unlikely. The online court should allow for the cost of initial legal advice to be provided and some form of representation at stage 3. That said, as with fast-track cases, these costs should be fixed to encourage settlement and proportionality of litigation.

---

74. Chantal-Aimée Doerries, 'Too Much, Too Soon' (2016) 166 *New Law Journal* 7692.
75. As fees would be recoverable and the matter may be solved more quickly through compulsory conciliation. In many personal injury cases, it is the damages that are being contested, not liability. A conciliator could suggest an appropriate award and see what both parties make of that.
76. Chantal-Aimée Doerries, 'Too Much, Too Soon' (2016) 166 *New Law Journal* 7692.
77. See 'Reforming the Courts' Approach to McKenzie Friends: A Consultation' (Lord Chief Justice of England & Wales 2016).
78. The level proposed for the online court.
79. 'Reforming the Courts' Approach to McKenzie Friends: A Consultation' (Lord Chief Justice of England & Wales 2016) 43.

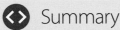 ## Summary

This chapter has examined the use of ADR within the civil justice system. In particular it has:

- Identified that there has been a shift away from the 'pure' form of an adversarial trial, although not to a full inquisitorial system.
- Noted that ADR is often cheaper and more informal than civil litigation, meaning disputes can sometimes be resolved more quickly and more amicably than through litigation.
- Discussed the three principal forms of ADR: arbitration, mediation, and conciliation.
- Noted that some contracts will now include an arbitration clause within them, meaning that disputes must proceed through arbitration first.
- Discussed the merits of the ACAS employment arbitration scheme, including noting that it potentially reduces the legal avenues open to someone claiming a breach in employment rights.
- Noted the finality of arbitration where courts are reluctant to interfere with the decision of an arbitrator.

 ## End-of-chapter questions

1. Read Geoff Davies, 'Civil Justice Reform: Why We Need to Question Some Basic Assumptions' (2006) 25 *Civil Justice Quarterly* 32–51. Is there a case for moving away from the adversarial system of justice? What would the difficulties be with such an approach?

2. Read Roberts 'Family Mediation After the Act' (2001) 13 *Child and Family Law Quarterly* 265–73. Why were the mediation proposals in the 1996 Act dropped? With many divorces is there not a danger that clients are arguing over relatively small assets, leading to acrimony and high legal bills? Would mediation not ensure a smoother transition through divorce?

3. Why do you think there is no right of appeal against the decision of an arbitrator? Is there a danger that by allowing an appeal to take place it would detract from the whole point of arbitration? It could allow an unhappy side simply to engage in expensive litigation after deciding that they did not like the decision of the arbitrator. Could an appeal be restricted to errors of law? One difficulty with this presumably must be the fact that arbitrators are not legally qualified so would they understand the legal principles they would then have to uphold? If only legally qualified arbitrators were used, how would this differ from a tribunal?

 ## Further reading

Davies G, 'Civil Justice Reform: Why We Need to Question Some Basic Assumptions' (2006) 25 *Civil Justice Quarterly* 32–51.

This an excellent article by a former Australian judge that questions many of the basic premises over the place of ADR in civil litigation.

Genn H, *Court-based ADR Initiatives for Non-Family Civil Disputes* (HMSO 2002).

This presents the report of Professor Genn who was examining the use of ADR in non-family civil disputes. It makes some interesting points about the perceptions of counsel and the judiciary over the use of ADR in complex commercial cases.

Koo, AKC 'Ten Years after Halsey' (2015) 34 *Civil Justice Quarterly* 77–95.

This looks at how the decision in *Halsey v Milton Keynes NHS Trust*[80] has influenced the conduct of litigation and, in particular, the use of Alternative Dispute Resolution.

For self-test questions, flashcards, and links to useful websites, please visit the **online resources** at: **www.oup.com/he/gillespie-weare8e/**

---

80. [2004] EWCA Civ 576.

PART V
THE FUTURE

20

The Future in a Post-COVID World

This chapter traditionally looks forward and identifies what likely changes can be foreseen in the coming years. This year, the chapter is slightly different although its emphasis is still the future. As noted in the introduction to this book, the writing of this edition has taken place during the COVID-19 crisis. In common with nearly everybody else in the United Kingdom, we have been working remotely from our respective homes, something true of those who work in the courts.

COVID-19 has undoubtedly had a major effect on the English Legal System during 2020. It provides us with a dilemma too though. As we are writing this chapter, the second-wave is emerging but the first vaccines have also been announced. By the time this book come out, COVID-19 may be beaten. Or it may have morphed. Such is the joy of writing a book that comes out some months after the manuscript is delivered!

We could have inserted references to COVID throughout the whole book. However, we thought if we did this and COVID-19 is beaten, then it could be frustrating for the reader. Similarly, however, we cannot ignore the fact that COVID-19 has had a major impact on the legal system. So, we are using this chapter to do both things. In this chapter we will be setting out the impact COVID-19 has had on the English Legal System, and what the consequences of those are.

However, we will still be looking to the future because there can be no doubt that COVID-19 will have long-term implications for the legal system. The justice system was already the subject of delays. Justice has been much slower as a result of COVID-19, and there are now significant delays. There needs to be a plan to deal with this, particularly if, as is possible, the virus mutates or a vaccine does not prove effective.

This chapter will follow the structure of the book. Each section will consider the impact on part of the English Legal System. At the end, we will consider what the future is likely to bring.

20.1 England and Wales

One notable feature of the COVID epidemic was that the four nations of the United Kingdom operated very differently, particularly in late 2020. As it is primarily a health matter, it is a devolved matter. Instead of a coordinated national response, significant regional variations have arisen, with some questioning whether the approach will hasten the break-up of the Union.[1]

As will be seen, many of the measures adopted, have the force of criminal law (see 20.4.2). England and Wales ordinarily do not have any different criminal laws but that was not true during the pandemic. In the Autumn of 2020, Wales entered a period of 'full lockdown' whereas England did not. A fortnight later, the position was reversed, with England in lockdown and Wales not.[2] This marks one of the first occasions when the criminal law of the two countries diverged.

It perhaps also demonstrates a weakness of our current system. If there was ever a time for a simple message and agreed actions, a global pandemic would be that time. Instead, what we have seen is the four nations acting independently and, in both Scotland and England, individual counties were, at one point, subject to different restrictions. That is something that the law has not had to experience before, and it raises interesting questions about whether the justice system, including the police and judiciary, were prepared for this.

20.2 Sources of law

It may be thought that the one area where COVID-19 would not have an impact would be sources of law. However, it impacted even them. While precedent has not changed, the role of both the executive and Parliament has been impacted. This includes the greater use of secondary legislation, ie legislation that is in effect made at the will of the government (the executive) and not Parliament.

20.2.1 Parliament during COVID-19

One of the surprising things about both chambers of the Houses of Parliament, particularly the House of Commons, is how small the chambers are. Before the coronavirus epidemic, this was perhaps best seen at Prime Minister's Questions. This weekly event, usually saw standing-room only for Members of Parliament.

Of course, such a small chamber is not helpful for social distancing. Many MPs (and, certainly the Lords), were also in vulnerable categories. Parliament was initially suspended for approximately a month, and then returned in a 'hybrid' mode. This saw a very small number of members in the chamber, with the majority being based at home and up to 120 MPs asking questions via Zoom. Not all business could be conducted in this way, with it initially being restricted to questions to a minister, the Prime Minister, and asking urgent questions.

Eventually, the hybrid Parliament was extended to select committees and the passage of legislation. However, it was a slow process and it is undeniable that Parliament could not proceed as quickly or efficiently as it used to. Controversially, the government announced that it was going to end the hybrid Parliament and require MPs to return to the chamber. However, this led to disquiet because many MPs felt unable to return for health reasons. Similarly, it was not business as usual, as the Speaker of the House

---

1. See, for example, 'How the COVID crisis is changing minds on Scottish independence' (2020) *The Guardian*, 13 September.
2. See *The Health Protection (Coronavirus, Restrictions)(No 3)(Wales) Regulations 2020* (SI 2020/1149 (W.261)) and *The Health Protection (Coronavirus, Regulations)(England)(No 4) Regulations 2020* (SI 2020/1200).

made clear that he would not relax social distancing. Thus, only fifty MPs were in the chamber at any one time, severely limiting the number of members who could speak in debates or seek to amend legislation.

Voting was also problematic. Parliamentary rules require in person votes, meaning that MPs were required to process through the chamber. The voting lobbies could not be used as they were too small. This meant that a vote took considerably longer than normal, again reducing the amount of parliamentary business that could be undertaken. Eventually, the Speaker announced that voting would take place in the lobbies but using a card-reader to automatically tally the results, meaning MPs were not required to wait to be counted.[3]

There is no doubt that Parliament has not been as effective as normal during its response to COVID-19. The amount of legislation that it passed was significantly reduced. There is also some concern that its ability to scrutinize legislation is not as effective as it would otherwise be. Of course, the extent to which parliamentary scrutiny is important when the ruling party has a sizeable majority has always been questioned, but it is less than ideal.

However, it should be recognized that some important legislation was passed. For example, the *Divorce, Dissolution and Separation Act 2020* received Royal Assent in June 2020. This Act will change the law of divorce, including introducing so-called 'no fault divorce'. Another piece of legislation passed was the *Sentencing (Pre-consolidation Amendments) Act 2020*. This Act will eventually lead to a 'sentencing code', ie a single document that sets out the rules to be adopted by courts when sentencing an offender. This will simplify sentencing.

20.2.2 **Secondary legislation**

691

A consequence of Parliament's limited ability to function has been a significant increase in the use of secondary legislation, particularly in respect of responses to COVID-19. Hansard, the publishers of the official business of the Houses of Parliament, established a website that tried to track the use of secondary legislation for COVID.[4] By November 2020, 297 statutory instruments had been laid before the House of Commons relating to COVID alone. They noted that this accounted for one-third of all statutory instruments. The rush to regulate, however, also caused problems as the site notes that:

> some Coronavirus-related SIs (which have not always been immediately withdrawn or revoked) have had omissions, technical mistakes and drafting shortcomings. As a result, others of the Coronavirus-related SIs have been made, at least in part, in order to correct these errors by amending the earlier instruments.

This raises serious questions about the extent to which Parliament is properly scrutinizing legislation. As was noted in Chapter 2, the courts will follow the wording of Parliament because it trusts that those words are the definitive statement of its intentions. The number of mistakes, however, suggests that this confidence may be misplaced.

While much of the attention on statutory instruments is focused on the restrictions that were introduced, and the penalties for non-compliance (discussed at 20.4.2), the

3. See <https://www.parliament.uk/about/how/covid-19-hybrid-proceedings-in-the-house-of-commons/remote-voting/>.

4. See <https://www.hansardsociety.org.uk/publications/data/coronavirus-statutory-instruments-dashboard>.

range of subjects covered by the statutory instruments was extremely broad. Figure 20.1 shows the departments that have put forward the most statutory instruments.

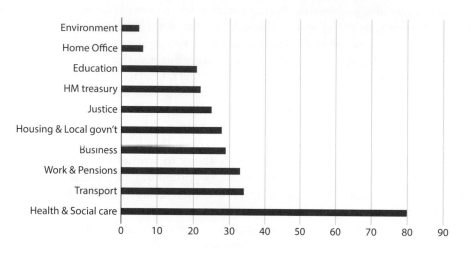

Figure 20.1 Departments passing the most statutory instruments.[5]

It is perhaps unsurprising that the Department for Health and Social Care was responsible for the most instruments as it was the lead agency responsible for dealing with the pandemic. Traditional boundaries between the departments altered as a result of the pandemic response. So, for example, the Home Office or Ministry of Justice would ordinarily be responsible for passing criminal law. However, the COVID-19 pandemic was a global health emergency, and many of the restrictions (backed by criminal penalties) were issued by the Department for Health and Social Care rather than other ministries.

☰ Example First Lockdown

The Health Protection (Coronavirus, Restrictions)(England) Regulations 2020[6] was the measure that introduced the first so-called lockdown in March 2020. It required certain businesses to close,[7] and placed restrictions on movement and gatherings.[8] These measures were enforced by prosecution[9] or the imposition of a Fixed Penalty Notice.[10]

This statutory instrument was made by the Secretary of State for the Department of Health and Social Care rather than the Home Secretary or Justice Secretary.

---

5. Adapted from <https://www.hansardsociety.org.uk/publications/data/coronavirus-statutory-instruments-dashboard> (data correct at the time the chapter was written).
6. SI 2020/350.
7. ibid, reg 4.
8. ibid, regs 5 and 6.
9. ibid, regs 8 and 10.
10. ibid, reg 9.

One of the controversies around the making of statutory instruments was the extent to which Parliament was said to have a role in the restrictions that were imposed. Figure 20.2 shows that the overwhelming number of statutory instruments was passed using the negative affirmation procedure, ie the law comes into effect unless Parliament objects. A much smaller proportion used the positive procedure whereby Parliament must vote on the proposed measure. Of course, it was noted earlier (20.2.1) that Parliament itself was affected by the requirements for social distancing, and the refusal to use remote hearings in any extensive way, may explain why so many instruments were passed in that way.

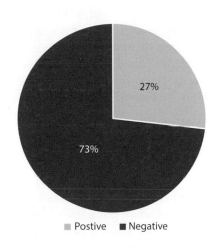

■ Postive   ■ Negative

Figure 20.2 Parliamentary scrutiny of COVID-related secondary legislation[11]

By convention, a statutory instrument passed by negative affirmation does not come into force until twenty-one days have elapsed since it was laid before Parliament. However, one-third of statutory instruments[12] passed by the negative affirmation procedure breached this convention, coming into force immediately.[13] Parliament could still choose to annul the instrument, but it is obviously politically more challenging to do so, as it is reversing a law rather than simply refusing to pass it.

The imposition of the second national lockdown period in November 2020 saw pushback from some within the Conservative Party. A number of members felt that national lockdown was unnecessary and could damage the economy.[14] While there was a backbench rebellion, it stood no real chance of changing the result as the opposition voted with the government. What it did do, however, was lead to political change. The PM realized that he needed the support of his party, and several key measures (such as lockdowns) were then passed by the affirmative procedure.

11.   This data is correct at the time the chapter was written.
12.   This data is correct at the time the chapter was written.
13.   See <https://www.hansardsociety.org.uk/publications/data/coronavirus-statutory-instruments-dashboard>.
14.   See, for example, Steven Swinford 'Theresa May leads critics as dozens of Tories vote against lockdown' (2020) *The Times*, November 4,

20.2.3 **Brexit**

We cannot really talk about the future without mentioning that Brexit will be a significant issue in life after COVID. In terms of being a legal source, COVID has not made any difference regarding Brexit. While there were delays in securing a Brexit agreement this does not affect the status of EU law as a source of English law.

One of the issues that is still being discussed is the intent of the EU to have the Court of Justice of the EU superintend any agreement. The UK Government is unhappy with this and, certainly, it would be unusual in international law for the court of one body (the EU) to have oversight over the agreement instead of either arbitration or an international court.

As set out in this book in Chapters 2 and 4, EU law will remain an important source of law for some time. In the short-term it is unlikely that we will notice any difference in terms of the law, save that there is no opportunity for the courts to refer a matter to the Court of Justice of the EU. It is likely to be some time before the courts face a decision about whether to follow EU law or to desire. The first move will undoubtedly be made by Parliament, but it is difficult to predict what issue it will concern.

It is inevitable that there will be a clash between politicians and the judiciary over the status of EU law. The courts tend to be conservative, and they are likely to recognisze that the judgments of the CJEU will remain an important source of interpretation of the texts that now form part of English law. It is unlikely that they will diverge as quickly as some politicians are likely to require. It was seen in Chapter 4 that there has been political concern over the extent to which it is perceived that the English courts follow the European Court of Human Rights, and it is likely the same charge will be directed towards the courts in respect of EU law.

20.3 **The courts and the practitioners**

Perhaps the biggest impact within the legal system has been in respect of the courts and practitioners. Courts are not designed for social distancing. The average courtroom is surprisingly small, meaning that the work ground to a halt very quickly once the pandemic worsened. Other courts had to quickly adapt to new ways of working. It is likely that some of these changes will continue in the post-COVID world.

20.3.1 **Remote hearings**

In the initial stages of the COVID crisis, when the United Kingdom entered a prolonged period of lockdown, the courts could not function. Quickly, however, a system of remote hearings began to be developed.

While remote hearings had been used in some courts (for example, the Judicial Committee of the Privy Council sometimes used remote hearings to save counsel the expense of travelling across the world to make submissions), they were not used routinely in all courts. As noted in Chapter 6, apart from when sitting in specific courts, eg the Family Court, an inferior judge cannot sit outside of a designated courtroom (cf a superior judge of the rank of puisne judge or above) without statutory approval. Remote hearings would see, in some instances, judges based at home.

The *Coronavirus Act 2020* anticipated the need for remote hearings. It allowed remote hearings to be used in a range of proceedings, particularly criminal matters.[15] Importantly, it recognized that justice must still be seen to be done, and it allowed for journalists and other members of the public to petition the courts to witness proceedings through accessing the live link.[16] The statute provided for both live audio (most likely telephone) and live video (including videoconference technology).[17]

The Act did not simply authorize the use of technology but tidied up ancillary issues. So, for example, it ensured that evidence that was given via a remote link would still be subject to the laws of perjury, something that would not necessarily be the case otherwise.[18]

That said, not all criminal proceedings could be conducted either by audio or video. A hearing could only be conducted entirely by telephone if it were incidental to a trial or appeal, or it was an application around bail.[19] A video hearing could similarly only be for ancillary matters in the Crown Court of Court of Appeal, although a full summary trial and an appeal to the Crown Court from a summary trial could take place remotely.[20] However, the restrictions in the Crown Court, particularly the absence of remote trials (which would be extremely difficult to hold), meant that very quickly there was a backlog of trials to be heard, with the numbers increasing each month.

20.3.1.1 Supreme Court

The Supreme Court was remarkable in that COVID appeared, at least in public, to make very little difference to its work.

When the country first entered 'lockdown' in March 2020, the Supreme Court ceased to sit in its court buildings in Westminster. However, very quickly, it started to use video conferencing. What was equally impressive about this, is that they continued to allow people to watch the proceedings by streaming those video conferences. It provided an insight into the houses of the various judges, and the locations they chose to sit while hearing the submissions. It also meant the judges needed to be more careful because any gesture is amplified when the camera is fixed on the face of the judge rather than looking at all of the judges on the bench.[21]

The advocates joined via video link. As they were not sitting in open court within the building itself, custom and practice requires that the advocates were not robed although, of course, they were dressed formally.

When a case started, or where a decision was given, the presiding judge would often provide an informal introduction to the case. Again, it shows the extent to which the court is prepared to try and make their decisions accessible, even to lay members watching the stream.

20.3.1.2 High Court and Court of Appeal

The High Court, as with other civil courts, quickly responded to remote hearings. Telephone hearings have already been used quite effectively in the High Court, as they

---

15. *Coronavirus Act 2020*, s 53 and sch 23.
16. ibid, s 55 and sch 25.
17. ibid, sch 23, para 2.
18. ibid, sch 23, para 4.
19. ibid, sch 23, para 8.
20. ibid, sch 23, para 8.
21. The recordings are archived on their page (<https://www.supremecourt.uk/>).

are used when someone needs an out-of-hours injunction, or a judge needs to make an urgent ruling.[22] However, other platforms were quickly used. Skype began to be used, and then Zoom and Microsoft Teams. The government had developed a cloud-based video platform for the criminal courts,[23] and this began to be used for some civil trials too, although Microsoft Teams began to become more common.

The Court of Appeal differed slightly between the divisions. The Civil Division tended to hear more matters remotely, whereas many of the Criminal Division matters were initially postponed.[24] This was perhaps because of the belief that an appellant in a criminal matter should be able to observe the proceedings, something difficult if they are in gaol. Even the Civil Division only dealt with urgent issues, and they tended, at least initially, to do such matters via teleconference rather than remote hearings. The success of the Supreme Court remote hearings demonstrate that the technology can be used, but it is perhaps easier to do in a single court rather than a court where several different constitutions sit at the same time. The cost of doing so could also be significant, although whether it is more expensive than a court room is perhaps debatable.

The Royal Courts of Justice (RCJ) is an impressive structure at any time. Finished in the late-nineteenth century, it has the appearance of a Gothic cathedral in places. It has a warren of corridors and courts. Some of the courts are surprisingly small, but others (for example, the Lord Chief Justice's court) are not. Quite quickly, once able to return to physical hearings, the Court of Appeal started to re-occupy the RCJ, particularly for criminal appeals, but increasingly for civil matters too. Several of the courtrooms are sufficiently large enough to allow social distancing. Benches for counsel, which tend to be ordered in seniority,[25] are being used to allow multiple counsel to sit socially distant, with solicitors and others sitting elsewhere in the court, including the public galleries, as members of the public cannot attend at present.[26]

However, even when the courts have returned to physical rooms, elements of remote hearings remain. For example, it is not unusual for counsel to appear remotely rather than in person, particularly where it would involve long travel (something that is discouraged during the lockdown periods). In the Court of Appeal (Criminal Division), the appellant would invariably be produced remotely, particularly where they were serving a custodial sentence.

One slight oddity in the Court of Appeal (Criminal Division) occurred in October 2020. Prior to this, counsel would appear unrobed when they joined remotely. This followed the convention that one does not wear robes out of court. However, in October it was decided that advocates appearing before the Court of Appeal should be robed, irrespective of whether they were appearing remotely. The idea that a barrister should sit in front of his or her webcam while wearing a wig, bands, and robes seems somewhat absurd. There has always been strong support for retaining traditional court dress in the criminal courts, but to require it of someone sat at home seems odd.

---

22.   This not infrequently happens to puisne judges assigned to the Family Division where they may be asked to make rulings about emergency medical treatment, often late at night.

23.   See <https://www.gov.uk/guidance/hmcts-rollout-plans-for-cloud-video-platform-for-video-enabled-criminal-hearings>.

24.   The Court of Appeal (Civil Division) operates a YouTube channel where live streamings of the court are broadcast. An example of a remote hearing where only the Master of the Rolls was present in court, can be found at: <https://www.youtube.com/watch?v=azxALiMetxE>. This video is also notable because comments have not been disabled, so there is a series of comments about the case from those who have later watched the video.

25.   QCs sit in the first row, junior barristers in the row(s) behind, with solicitors a row further back.

26.   If you want to see what a socially distant Court of Appeal looks like, see *Wingfield v Canterbury City Council* at <https://www.youtube.com/watch?v=QR2fHPXD1AU>.

When a judgment of the High Court or Court of Appeal is reserved, it is later 'handed down'. Traditionally, this is done in open court. Sometimes the judge will read the whole judgment out, but, more often than not, they will provide the decision and a brief summary of the reasons, stating that the definitive reasons are produced in the written judgment which is then handed to the parties. COVID changed this and, not unreasonably, the judgments were simply emailed to the parties and placed on the BAILII website. A time and date was notionally assigned for the handing down of the judgment, but the judgment was typically sent earlier than this.

It is to be hoped that this becomes the default in many instances. There are many cases where it is unnecessary for the parties, lawyers, and the judge to be present when the judgment is given. Yes, in some instances it will, and that can carry on, but it would make more sense for delivery of judgments to continue to be electronic. While it would only free up a small amount of judicial time, judicial time is precious and even a small saving could assist in reducing delays.

20.3.1.3 Crown and county courts

The Crown Court was affected quite early on, in part because the nature of the Crown Court does not lend itself to social distancing (discussed further at 20.3.2). On 17 March 2020, the Lord Chief Justice directed that no new jury trial should begin unless it was to last less than three days, and was listed to start before the end of April 2020.[27] In essence, this meant the simple cases, and would mean that if the pandemic situation worsened, there would be ways of drawing these cases to a close.

The next week it became apparent that the country was going to enter lockdown. On 23 March 2020, the Lord Chief Justice directed that no new jury trials were to start from that day.[28] Existing trials were permitted to continue, but only where the court staff were satisfied that arrangements were in place to keep jurors safe, and a short adjournment could facilitate putting those arrangements in place.

Where a jury was not required then some aspects of the Crown Court's work continued. As with civil matters, procedural issues were dealt with remotely, including by telephone or video conference. In many instances these were case-management hearings, where a defendant would not be required to attend. However, some sentencing hearings were conducted remotely, with the prisoner typically appearing via video-link from gaol. Some of these hearings took place with everyone being remote (including the judge), but in some instances they took place with the judge in the courtroom but the advocates and defendants appearing remotely.

The fact that no new jury trials could commence after 23 March was put forward as a potential avenue for appeal in *R v GP*.[29] A short-trial (two-and-a-half days) ended on the Friday before restrictions were put in force. Counsel sought to argue that media reports about jury trials ending, and the lockdown restrictions coming into force, meant that the jury may have felt under pressure to return a verdict. The Court of Appeal were unimpressed with the argument. They noted that it was purely speculation (although, to be fair, as noted in Chapter 14 we can usually only speculate as to why a jury reached a particular verdict) and that this was a short trial. The amount of time the jury spent deliberating was not inappropriate for a case of that length.

---

27. See <https://www.judiciary.uk/announcements/coronavirus-jury-trials-message-from-the-lord-chief-justice/>.
28. See <https://www.judiciary.uk/announcements/review-of-court-arrangements-due-to-covid-19-message-from-the-lord-chief-justice/>.
29. [2020] EWCA Crim 1056.

The Court of Appeal ended by noting that two of their number sat in the Crown Court during that period (although not that particular Crown Court), and it was their experience that 'jurors have invariably treated their public duty with enormous conscientious and have stepped up to the mark by ensuring that justice is properly and fairly done'.[30] Given the anxiety that existed during this period, this testifies to the resilience of jurors and their understanding of civic duty.

County court

The county court operated largely remotely. It was noted in Chapter 17 that some county court matters are now dealt with wholly electronically, and this undoubtedly helped preparation. As with the other courts, the early hearings were conducted by telephone but, quite quickly, remote hearings began to be used.

The Lord Chief Justice noted that some civil jurisdictions had been working at a near-normal pace,[31] although some judges believed that this perhaps better reflected the (well-funded) High Court, rather than the county court. Many county court buildings are old and do not have appropriate technology to allow for video-conferencing, although telephone hearings are possible.

20.3.1.4 Magistrates' courts

The magistrates' court did not stop its work during the COVID-19 pandemic, but they did have to adapt. Like the other courts, there was increased use of remote hearings, and it appears that the bulk of the work was undertaken by District Judges (Magistrates' Court) rather than the lay magistracy.[32] One reason for this, of course, is that the DJMCs can sit by themselves, meaning social distancing is much easier than with a lay panel of three. This would mean that the court may continue to sit in a building, with the defendant appearing remotely. That said, some courts did allow for social distancing, meaning that lay magistrates could sit.

COVID-19 saw an increase in the use of the 'single justice procedure' whereby a single magistrate, including a lay magistrate, can sentence a person in non-contentious matters that will not require a sentence of imprisonment. Typically these would be dealt with by way of a fine, with the magistrate identifying the appropriate amount. A lay magistrate and legal adviser would sit together, sometimes remotely, to go through these cases.[33] The use of this procedure meant that these matters could be kept out of the physical courts, meaning that the courts could be used for trials.

Even using the single justice procedure and increasing the number of district judge sitting days, the magistrates' court, as with the Crown Court, started to experience significant delays, with the backlog of cases being worse than at any other previous recorded time.[34] Of course, the number of magistrates as compared to judges does mean that when social distancing is relaxed, the magistrates' court is likely to be able to clear the backlog quicker than the Crown Court.

---

30. ibid, [41].
31. Justice Committee, *Coronavirus (COVID-19): The Impact on Courts* (HC 2020–21, 519) [28].
32. ibid, [18].
33. An explanation of how the process works is presented by a lay magistrate at <https://www.judiciary.uk/announcements/supporting-the-justice-system-from-home/>.
34 Justice Committee, *Coronavirus (COVID 19): The Impact on Courts* (HC 2010–21, 519) at [20].

20.3.1.5 Do remote hearings work?

While remote hearings became routine, questions began to be asked about whether they were an appropriate way of administering justice. Where the telephone is being used, it restricts the ability of the media to report on cases. The same is not true of remote hearings where accredited journalists were allowed to petition the court to be allowed to access the footage.

There is no doubt that courts have got used to technology, but there remain challenges. It has been noted that within the criminal courts, the biggest issue is seeking instructions, particularly where the client is in gaol. Prisons are not routinely allowing visitors, and there are limits as to the amount of time a prisoner can spend on the telephone or in front of a video-link. Indeed, one report noted that prisoners were reduced to one hour every five weeks, when ordinarily a visit would last nearly three hours per time, with repeated visits being possible.[35] Clearly, there have to be limits as every prisoner on remand will seek access to a lawyer, but it is important that a trial does not become unfair because the lawyer does not have access to their client.

Indeed, access to clients is something that is noted throughout research on remote hearings. The *Nuffield Family Justice Observatory* conducted research on remote hearings within the Family Court, and they noted that several respondents disclosed a difficulty in giving or receiving instructions, particularly during a hearing.[36] This is obviously problematic as the lay client should be able to ask questions, challenge assertions, and provide assistance to their lawyers. That said, this research covered the early stages of remote hearings, and features such as 'breakout rooms' have been added to most conference facilities. The technology should also allow the client and lawyer to use 'digital chat' that only they can see.

One difficulty with remote hearings is that there are sometimes assumptions that everyone knows who everyone is when they do not, particularly when they are speaking.[37] This could be because sometimes people joined video conferences as audio-only (particularly where there were bandwidth problems, or because they didn't have the right technology), or because the judge failed to ensure that all parties identified themselves when speaking. The latter is perhaps particularly pertinent. In some areas of the country, the judge will be used to hearing the same counsel, solicitors, or social workers. They may, therefore, inadvertently think that everyone has that knowledge, whereas a parent or other party to the case might not.

Access to technology is the biggest obstacle in remote hearings. There is an assumption that people have appropriate access but the reality is that is not always the case. One barrister noted:

> Many of my clients may not have WIFI, no credit on their phones, phones that are infrequently charged and no access to laptops nor iPads. They live in social deprivation . . .[38]

This will be the reality for many people. While many of us live in situations where there is ubiquitous WiFi or unlimited data packages on our smartphones, that is simply not

699

---

35. *Law Under Lockdown: The Impact of COVID-19 measures on access to justice and vulnerable people* (Law Society 2020) 27.

36. Mary Ryan, Lisa Harker, and Sarah Rothera, *Remote Hearings in the Family Justice System: A Rapid Consultation* (London 2020) 11.

37. *Making Family Justice Clearer* (Transparency Project 2020) at 6.

38. Mary Ryan, Lisa Harker, and Sarah Rothera, *Remote Hearings in the Family Justice System: A Rapid Consultation* (London 2020) 25.

the reality for many. Pay-As-You-Go telephones can be a lifeline to people, but it is likely that such people will not have sufficient money pay for extensive data usage, or to allow them to dial-in to a hearing that could last several hours. Simple things like ensuring that a freephone number is provided or the court calls the lay party instead can be important, but can easily be forgotten.

It has been reported elsewhere that for lay participants the telephone remains the most common device to be used,[39] which is a key lesson for the use of remote hearings. While rolling out advanced technology can appear beneficial, it could lead to a situation where a participant feels out of the loop, and unable to participate. It is incumbent on the judge to ensure that this does not happen. She should identify what technology the parties are able to access or use effectively, and ensure that all parties, particularly unrepresented parties, are able to follow and access the proceedings. It has also been reported that not infrequently parties were dropping off the call, but people were not noticing, meaning that either they could not rejoin, or time needed to be spent catching them back up again on what they had missed.[40]

Merely accessing the hearing is also not sufficient. It has been noted that most professional participants suggest it is necessary to have more than one device, particularly as most documents are now electronic. It is impractical to read the documents on the same device that the hearing takes place, meaning that participants ideally need two devices.[41] The lockdown meant that where a party had no electronic device, there was no opportunity for them to gain physical copies of the paperwork. In one study, 63 per cent of respondents did not have copies of the paperwork relating to their case.[42] That is unacceptable as it means that there is no realistic chance for them to participate in the proceedings, even if they are represented by a lawyer.

Do remote hearings work? The answer must be a qualified 'yes'. It is tempting to focus on the negatives and problems, but this must be put into context. The widespread use of remote hearings happened in the middle of a global pandemic and an unprecedented national lockdown. We have not been subject to the restrictions that were necessary to tackle COVID-19 before. Thus, the fact that the justice system continued to operate must be considered remarkable. Considerable effort has been put in to ensure trials can happen. Yes, there will be lessons learned, but as an emergency measure, remote hearings have worked.

20.3.2 'Nightingale courts'

While remote hearings allowed some of the business of the courts to continue, the reality is that they are less than ideal. As you may have experienced from your studies, watching a screen is a very different experience to watching something in-person. It can be more tiring, and it can look slightly disconnected. There can be a problem with connectivity, but the technology can be problematic too. It was noted earlier that there has been a shift away from telephones to visual technologies. However, while it may be reasonable to expect lawyers to acquire devices to participate in such hearings, it would not be appropriate for lay parties or witnesses to be required to do so.

39. *Making Family Justice Clearer* (Transparency Project 2020) at 6.
40. Mary Ryan, Lisa Harker, and Sarah Rothera, *Remote Hearings in the Family Justice System: A Rapid Consultation* (2020, London) 28.
41. ibid, 26.
42. *Making Family Justice Clearer* (Transparency Project 2020) at 7.

Certain types of hearings cannot take place remotely. Jury trials are perhaps the best example of this. It would be unfair to expect jurors to purchase IT equipment, and it would be too expensive to issue it to every juror, not least because of the costs of transporting it, reclaiming it, and cleaning it. The Crown Courts stopped sitting for jury trials in March 2020, and so a significant backlog was created.

In addition, not all civil trials could be heard remotely. Where witnesses, particularly lay witnesses are to be used, then it could be difficult for them to participate effectively. Telephone-only hearings would not allow the judge to consider, for example, non-verbal communication tells but also it would not be possible to identify whether someone was in the same room as the witness, potentially interfering with their testimony. Video-conferencing can assist with this, but it equally has limitations, not least where there are multiple parties, and so bandwidth and technology availability become problematic.

The increasing backlog of cases led to calls for alternative thinking to solve the problem, particularly in the Crown Court. Three principal ideas were advanced:

1. Diplock courts.

2. Auld courts.

3. Nightingale courts.

Diplock courts were referred to at 14.5.1. They were used extensively in Northern Ireland during the troubles due to fears about jury tampering. They saw a judge hearing Crown Court matters without a jury, with the judge serving as both the tribunal of law and fact. While some were in favour of this approach, it has been noted that not everyone agreed that Diplock cases were either fair, or perceived as fair.[43] The Lord Chief Justice, while not ruling it out (which would be unwise at a time when it was not known how long the pandemic will last) stated that their introduction would be undesirable.[44]

The government mooted the possibility of a judge sitting with two lay magistrates.[45] This occurs during an appeal to the Crown Court from the magistrates' court (see 16.2.1), and it will be remembered from Chapter 16 that it was also proposed by Lord Justice Auld in his review of the criminal justice system. Proponents argue that it is fairer than Diplock courts because it involves lay representation. However, it will be remembered from Chapter 14 that there is some doubt whether magistrates are as impartial as juries. From the same chapter it will be remembered that the magistracy are largely elderly, which is the highest-risk group for COVID. Delays are increasing in the magistrates' court and thus removing magistrates to sit in the Crown Court would simply displace one problem for another.

When it was feared that NHS hospitals would be overwhelmed by the number of patients suffering from COVID, 'Nightingale' hospitals were established. These were makeshift hospitals that were created in sports arenas and other large spaces. The army converted them into working hospitals, boosting capacity significantly. As the principal difficulty with the courtrooms is space, attention quickly turned to how additional capacity for courts could be introduced.

---

43. Mike McConville and Luke Marsh, 'The COVID blame game' (2020) 170 *New Law Journal* 7906 at 7. Also see Hannah Quirk 'Covid-19 and jury-less trials?' [2000] *Criminal Law Review* 569.

44. Jonathan Ames, 'Lord Burnett, the Lord Chief Justice, hails courts' tech solutions to coronavirus crisis' (2020) *The Times*, April 9.

45. Justice Committee, *Coronavirus (COVID-19): The Impact on Courts* (HC 2020–21, 519) at [77].

The first stage was to use multiple courtrooms. Jury trials resumed using three courts. The first contained the judge, counsel, and jury. All are socially distant (with counsel spreading across all benches) and the jury occupying seats ordinarily reserved for other people within the court. The second courtroom contains the solicitors, media, and others required to be present (probation officers etc). The third courtroom is used as the jury deliberating room. Most jury rooms are too small to contain twelve people socially-distanced. A courtroom obviates that requirement.

Initially only a small number of courts were authorized to operate in this way, including the Old Bailey, Cardiff, and Manchester Crown Courts. The larger court centres (Newcastle, Sheffield, Preston etc) followed quickly, with other courts joining. Of course, occupying multiple courtrooms within a building heavily limits the number of trials that can take place, and also displaces other activity. While civil court business could largely be held remotely, it was noted earlier that remote hearings are not suitable for all matters.

In order to expand court capacity, the Ministry of Justice decided to borrow the idea of Nightingale buildings.[46] Courts would be established in ordinary buildings. Initially, universities were approached about using their mock courtrooms (those that have them) but, generally, these were too small to occupy. Instead, large open spaces were sought that could be adapted for use as a courtroom. Conference facilities in hotels and conference centres were quickly booked. One of the more notable examples is the Salford Nightingale Court, which occupies the Lowry Theatre.

Some of the Nightingale courts are for civil business only, allowing the Crown Court to occupy the courtrooms that would otherwise be used by the county court. Other Nightingale courts undertake criminal trials, although usually only where it is unlikely that a custodial sentence would be imposed, or where there is no need for additional security. These temporary courts are authorized as courtrooms. It will be remembered from Chapter 8 that while a senior judge can sit anywhere, a circuit judge must usually sit in a designated courtroom, unless legislation says otherwise (8.1.2).

The Nightingale courts look different.[47] Everyone is at the same level, including the judge. Tables and chairs are set out for counsel and solicitors to sit. Jurors sit two metres apart and, in some courts, effectively partially encase the courtroom. The witness box is usually just another table and chair.

So, the courts are rudimentary. Does that matter? No. It is what happens inside that is relevant rather than how they look. Yes, a fully functional, purpose-built courtroom has advantages. Modern courtrooms are designed to ensure the views and acoustics are helpful to users. However, as an emergency measure these are undoubtedly helpful, and can assist in tackling the backlog that has arisen as a result of the pandemic. However, the size of the Nightingale courts, and the multi-room courts, mean that far fewer cases are being heard than normal, meaning that delays continue. This will be considered further later (see 20.4.4).

20.3.3 **The professions**

COVID has not only affected the courts, but also the professions.

---

46.   Originally these courts were to be referred to as 'Blackstone courts' but the name never caught on, and so they became 'Nightingale courts'.

47.   A view of the Nightingale Lowry Crown Court is available at <https://www.judiciary.uk/announcements/the-nightingale-court-at-the-lowry-theatre/>. The resident judge, His Honour Judge Potter, discusses how the court is operating.

20.3.3.1 **The Bar**

As the work of the courts slowed, this created problems for the independent Bar, particularly the common-law bar where advocacy is the key part of their role.[48] Research conducted by the Bar Council suggests that 75 per cent of chambers had their work halved, with over half of chambers questioning whether they can remain viable over the next twelve months.[49] The position outside of London appears marginally worse, although this could be reflected by the fact that the Royal Courts of Justice began hearing cases quite quickly.

The government has offered economic support in the form of loans to the self-employed, including barristers. However, it has been reported that few barristers have taken this up, in part because there is concern about bankruptcy.[50] While it is no longer the case that a barrister made bankrupt cannot practice, it would invariably lead to investigations about their propriety, and some chambers agreements would require them to leave, particularly where the set owns the building. Given this, it is easy to see why some barristers would be slow to accept a loan that they may find difficult to pay back.

Of more concern, is the future. With chambers seeing a reduction in work, it is likely that fewer pupillages will be offered.[51] This causes difficulties as there are already more students who pass the BPTC than there are pupillages. The restriction of pupillages could harm efforts to widen the accessibility of the profession, with those who cannot afford to take a year or more out more likely to seek an alternative career, potentially returning the Bar to the preserve of the independent wealthy.

20.3.3.2 **Solicitors**

Solicitors were affected in much the same way as many other professions. An immediate move was the switch to working from home. Instead of the major city law firms having thousands of staff in showcase, expensive properties, solicitors and paralegals were suddenly expected to work from home. It has been noted that this can be particularly hard on young professionals in expensive cities (such as London), where their accommodation is frequently a single room.[52] Carving out a 'professional-looking' workspace in such an environment is difficult.

That said, it has been suggested that some firms will begin to focus more on a virtual presence.[53] Many law firms have moved away from the high street and conduct business largely through telephone or the Internet. Using video technology, instructions could be received remotely. Even if a physical space is necessary, it would be more cost effective to have a small, shop-sized unit than an office block.

Larger firms are likely to require some form of physical infrastructure, not least for teamwork. However, it is likely that we will see more flexible working. It is unlikely that every employee will be required in the office each day. Again, this could provide

---

48.   Those at the commercial or chancery Bar were arguably less affected because requests for advice and opinions would continue.

49.   'New research reveals full impact of Covid-19 restrictions on the self-employed Bar' (<https://www.barcouncil.org.uk/resource/new-research-reveals-full-impact-of-covid-19-restrictions-on-the-self-employed-bar.html>).

50.   Jan Miller, 'COVID-19: Bar Council survey shows full extent of damage to the Bar' (2020) 170 *New Law Journal* 7897 at 5.

51.   A Pinto, 'Challenging but privileged times' (2020) 170 *New Law Journal* 7898 at 7.

52.   Kath Scanlon, Fanny Blanc, and Beth Cranshaw, 'Sharing a home under lockdown' (https://blogs.lse.ac.uk/lselondon/sharing-a-home-under-lockdown/).

53.   Veronica Cowan, 'After lockdown – more virtual law firms?' (2020) 170 *New Law Journal* 7904 at 19.

considerable cost savings for firms. If one-third of employees was to rotate their presence within a building, then the firm could operate on a smaller footprint.

Are there advantages to the employees? While there is some concern that remote working has led to an increase in people feeling lonely,[54] a mixture of in-person and remote working would solve this. Travelling to the office for shorter periods of time may also mean that employees can live further from the office, which may mean that they are able to afford better houses. It could also help in terms of work/life balance, including helping solicitors with young families.

However, the counter to this positive news is that obtaining work is likely to be challenging. The economic downturn means that potential customers could become insolvent (although, ironically, that is a legal process, requiring the use of lawyers). Even larger firms or firms who have managed to weather the pandemic are likely to be in no rush to engage in complicated deals. For personal work, the loss of employment seen nationally may mean that there are less private clients. That said, family work is likely to increase, with it being suggested that divorce rates may increase with partners realizing that they don't like spending lots of time with each other as much as they thought they would.[55]

20.3.3.3 Representation

An interesting question arose in *Re C (Children: Covid-19: Representation)*.[56] The Court of Appeal was asked to consider the implications of hearings where counsel was unavailable. A hybrid hearing had taken place whereby some parts of the court were heard remotely, but other parts were to be heard live in a (physical) courtroom. The mother of four children subject to care proceedings had engaged a QC who could not attend the physical hearing because she fell within the government guidance for 'shielding'.

The mother sought a six-month adjournment to allow counsel to attend in-person. At the time of the hearing it was thought that this would be a time when the virus would be under control although, as this would be late-September/early-October 2000, that would have proved, in hindsight, to have been optimistic. The judge at first instance dismissed the application, suggesting that the interests of the children required a quicker trial.

Counsel for the mother participated, but remotely. The judge accepted that this:

> is likely to impact how the mother feels at court, it will mean interactions between the mother and [counsel] will not be immediate but will be filtered . . . [by] a remote application, and it will mean [counsel's] physical presence in court to cross examine the father and paternal grandmother will be replaced by a remote presence . . .[57]

The judge, however, ruled that Article 6 did not require the physical presence of counsel, and that it was in the best interests of the child for the trial to progress.

The Court of Appeal upheld the decision of the judge. They noted that '[i]t is in the public interest and the interests of the children and families that, wherever it can

---

54. Syed Ghulman Sarwar Shah et al, 'The COVID-19 Pandemic: A Pandemic of Lockdown Loneliness and the Role of Digital Technology' (2020) 20 *Journal of Medical Internet Research* e22287.

55. See, for example, Helen Rumbelow, 'Can your relationship survive the second wave?' (2020) *The Times*, October 29.

56. [2020] EWCA Civ 734.

57. ibid, [11].

happen in a safe and fair manner, the work of the courts should continue'.[58] It will be remembered from Chapter 17 that the family courts put the interests of the child first (see 17.4), so this is an unsurprising statement. The Court of Appeal recognized that the mother could be seen to be disadvantaged by not having counsel present, but noted that this was not a situation where counsel would not be participating, they would simply not be appearing in-person.

It is worth noting that the QC had offered to return the brief (ie withdraw from the case) when it became known that it was an in-person trial. It was noted in Chapter 10 that it is quite rare to return briefs. COVID-19 no doubt provides a new right to do so. This may have been a reason why the courts ruled in the way that they did. If the mother had wanted in-person counsel then she could have sought alternative representation.

20.3.3.4 Solicitors Qualifying Exam

At the end of October 2020, after considerable consultation and debate, the Legal Services Board provided consent for the Solicitors Qualifying Exam (SQE). This marks a significant change in the way that solicitors can qualify for practice. No longer is there a need for a law degree or the Graduate Diploma in Law, indeed, there is no longer a requirement for anyone to hold a degree, although it is highly likely that most entrants will.

It is not yet certain how the SQE will change legal education. The profession tends to be conservative and, therefore, for some time it is highly likely that law graduates or graduates of conversion courses will be preferred.

What may happen is more diversity within the academe. The 'foundations of legal knowledge' requirement of the old Qualifying Law Degree limited the opportunities of law degree providers to be too radical. The SQE is likely to see some divergence. Some providers are likely to adapt the degree to become more vocational. The curriculum is likely to either prepare students for SQE 1 or, perhaps more likely, teach the subjects required for SQE 1. There can be benefits in doing this. It is perhaps more cost effective for the student, and it means that the student has the best preparation.

However, many universities will not alter their curriculum. A vocational degree has advantages, but it also has disadvantages. University is not just about learning the subject that one is reading. It is about the wider educational and life skills that are developed. Law is an academic discipline in its own right and, increasingly, those who teach law in universities are not qualified to practise law, but instead provide academic critique and insight in the same way as any other social science or humanities discipline. On that basis, some providers will decide that their role is not to train prospective lawyers, but to offer a rigorous curriculum that provides students with a critical insight into the law.

At present, less than half of law graduates will enter the legal profession. Therefore, adapting the curriculum to focus solely on preparation to be a lawyer could be seen as a risky proposition for institutions. The SQE also differs from how the Bar trains barristers. While there will undoubtedly be similarities, it does create the potential that a student may need to decide early on whether they wish to be a barrister or solicitor, something that does not happen now.

That said, it is undoubtedly the case that some providers will wish to incorporate the SQE into their curriculum. The tension between academic and vocational legal

---

58. ibid, [22].

education has existed for a long time,[59] and so the SQE could simply be another chapter in this debate. There is no doubt that the SQE will lead to diversification, and probably innovation.

However, with this innovation comes uncertainty, as it means that a prospective student will be faced with lots of choice to navigate. If, as seems likely, some institutions fully incorporate the SQE and others do not, then this is a big difference for someone who, in many instances, will be 18 when making their choice. People change their minds, with many people joining university thinking that they would become *x* only to decide to become *y* when they leave. The SQE could potentially complicate this depending on how institutions react.

20.4 Criminal justice system

Changes to the criminal courts have already been noted, but the criminal justice system carried most of the controversy in respect of the approach to COVID-19. This is, in part, because the statutory instruments put considerable power in the hands of the police.

20.4.1 Law vs Police

A criticism that has been levelled during the pandemic response was that the rules were confused. This was, in part, because the police often seemed to misunderstand the role of the law. Admittedly, they were put in an unenviable position because the government used 'guidance' and the law interchangeably. Often a message that was put out by the government was not actually a statement of law, but a request. But by not differentiating between them, the position became complicated and the police were in the firing line.

Perhaps the classic example of this was during the first period of lockdown in March 2020. Derbyshire Police used a drone to take footage of a couple walking their dog in the Peak District.[60] The police stated that this was 'not essential' travel, echoing the government advice at the time that only essential travel should be undertaken. However, the statutory instrument that imposed the lockdown did not restrict the type of exercise that a person could undertake. It stated that a person could only leave their house with reasonable excuse,[61] but the list of reasonable excuses included, 'to take exercise either alone or with other members of their household'.[62] The SI did not restrict how far someone could travel to take this exercise. It may have been intended that a person must act reasonably when taking their exercise (which could have included being sensitive to how far they travelled), but that is not what the instrument said. Accordingly, the people walking their dog were acting completely lawfully.

Sections of the press, particularly those who were sceptical of the restrictions, started to point to other examples that they perceived as police overreactions. However, in some instances the stories were inaccurate. For example, some papers referred to the police putting dye into a pool of water to discourage visitors who would be breaching

---

59. An interesting, albeit slightly provocative, history is presented by Anthony Bradney, 'Ivory towers and satanic mills: Choices for university law schools' (1992) 17 *Studies in Higher Education* 5.

60. Robert Mendick, 'Fed-up police take more extreme measures to ensure the public follow lockdown rules' (2020) *Daily Telegraph*, 26 March.

61. *The Health Protection (Coronavirus, Restrictions)(England) Regulations 2020* (SI 2020/350), reg 6(1).

62. ibid, reg 6(2)(b).

the COVID regulations.[63] In fact, the dye had been used in previous years because the water was not safe.[64] The dye had proven a consistent deterrent to visitors risking their lives by swimming in unsafe water. Thus, it had nothing to do with COVID, but the stories became linked.

The police were placed in an unenviable position. The government expected them to enforce ever-changing rules. But without giving them either the training or powers to do so. The public messaging of the government did not reflect the laws passed. This put the police in the almost impossible situation of being expected to enforce rules at a time when there was widespread confusion, not helped by the fact that the rules frequently changed.

20.4.2 Fixed Penalty Notices

One notable aspect of COVID-19 restrictions was the use of Fixed Penalty Notices (FPNs). From the beginning of the initial lockdown period, the police were empowered to issue a FPN for breaches of the restrictions.[65] Initially the FPN was for the sum of £60, and this was reduced to £30 if it was paid within fourteen days.[66] Repeated breaches saw the FPN doubling, up to a maximum of £960.[67]

Concern arose as to whether these powers were sufficient to deter people from breaching the restrictions, and quickly the financial element of the FPN began to rise. In July 2020, a person issued with a FPN for a first offence would be required to pay £100 (£50 if paid within 14 days), with repeated notices increasing to £3,200.[68] By October this had increased to £200 (£100 if paid within 14 days), and a maximum of £6,400. This was, however, simply for breach of the general regulations. There were higher fines in other circumstances.

The requirement to self-isolate when a person tested positive, or where they travelled into the country, was also backed by the FPN scheme. Here, the initial FPN was £1,000, rising up to £10,000 for repeated breaches.[69] Similarly, in a bid to stop large gatherings, the government required FNPs of £10,000 to be given where thirty or more people gathered illegally,[70] which led to people, including students, being fined for house-parties.[71]

It can legitimately be questioned whether an FPN amounting to £10,000 is an appropriate administrative response. There is no appeal as such from the imposition of an FPN. The only recourse a person has is to refuse to pay, and to be then prosecuted for breaching the regulations. Persuading the magistrates' court to impose a lower penalty is not too difficult because the court is required to consider the financial circumstances of the offender, and to take this into account when determining the fine.[72] This inevitably means that a fine of less than £10,000 would be imposed.

63. See, for example, Ewan Somerville, 'Police dye beauty spot "Blue Lagoon" black to keep lockdown-flouting tourists away' (2020) *Evening Standard*, March 28.

64. See, for example, 'Toxic Derbyshire "Blue Lagoon" dyed black' (2013) *BBC News Online*, June 10, showing that the police carried out the same action seven years before the COVID-19 pandemic.

65. *The Health Protection (Coronavirus, Restrictions)(England) Regulations 2020* (SI 2020/350), reg 10.

66. ibid, reg 10(6), (7)(a).

67. ibid, reg 10(6), (7)(b).

68. ibid, reg 9.

69. See, for example, *The Health Protection (Coronavirus, Restrictions)(Self-Isolation)(England) Regulations 2020* (SI 2020/1045), reg 12(4).

70. *The Health Protection (Coronavirus)(Restrictions on Holdings of Gatherings and Amendment)(England) Regulations 2020* (SI 2020/907).

71. See, for example, Vincent Wood, 'Four students fined £10,000 each for house party on eve of tier 3 lockdown' (2020) *The Independent*, October 21.

72. *Criminal Justice Act 2003*, s 164(1), (3).

Of course, that is not to say that there are not consequences of seeking to dispute the fine in court. An FPN is not recorded as an offence. Therefore, a person subject to an FPN does not have a criminal conviction. For the magistrates' court to impose a fine, it is necessary for the person to either plead guilty, or be convicted, of the relevant offence (breaching the regulations). At that point, the person will have a criminal conviction. This could have consequences for an individual, particularly in respect of employment or for their character if they were accused of another offence.[73]

It was seen in Chapter 14 that there are major concerns about the use of FPNs and, in particular, the fact that the evidence has not been tested. It is simply a police officer's opinion that the grounds for an FPN has been met. The government was clearly concerned about the fact that the courts would struggle to operate in a COVID environment. Prosecuting breaches would overwhelm prosecutors and the police. FPNs resolve some of this. However, it should not be one or other. FPNs could be used for minor breaches, with prosecution being used for more serious breaches or repeat offenders. In this way, the most serious breaches would be imposed by the magistracy or judiciary rather than by the executive.

20.4.3 **Flawed prosecutions**

While FPNs were used to great effect, the initial approach of the police was to arrest and prosecute suspects. Unfortunately, it became clear quite quickly that mistakes had been made, in part, because the authorities were trying to apply new rules in a challenging environment, and with little guidance.

Forty-four cases were prosecuted under the *Coronavirus Act 2020*, with all of them subsequently either being withdrawn at court or later set aside.[74] This was because the offences under the CA 2020 relate to those who were potentially infected,[75] and not the general restrictions of movement etc. Both the police and CPS had not appreciated this and, in many instances, had prosecuted people for an offence under the Act when, instead, it should have been under the regulations.

The CPS also noted that twelve cases under the statutory instruments (ie self-isolation, breach of lockdown etc) had been withdrawn or set aside. These cases were typically set aside because the police had not appreciated the regulations differed between jurisdictions. So, for example, the police prosecuted someone under the English regulation, when the Welsh regulation should be used, or vice-versa. It was noted earlier in this chapter (20.1) that the pandemic emergency led to divergence of the criminal law for the first time. Unfortunately, the border between England and Wales is not as easily demarked as elsewhere, with even towns straddling both countries.[76] This confusion is unfortunate, and perhaps demonstrates a difficulty if the laws in England and Wales continues to diverge.

---

73. A person who pays a FPN would be of good character if they had not been previously convicted of a criminal offence, whereas a person convicted in the magistrates' court would not.

74. *CPS announces review findings for first 200 cases under coronavirus laws* (see <https://www.cps.gov.uk/cps/news/cps-announces-review-findings-first-200-cases-under-coronavirus-laws>).

75. *Coronavirus Act 2020*, s 51 and Sch 21.

76. For example, the village of Llanymynech straddles the border, with the western half being in Wales, and the eastern half being in England. Depending on which side of the village an offence was committed, would depend on which regulation should be applied.

20.4.4 **Custody time limits**

It was noted earlier (20.3.1.3) that the Crown Court is suffering extensive delays. While Nightingale courts are making some difference, many of these temporary courts cannot hear trials where a custodial sentence is required, or where security is required. Some of those cases are heard in the ordinary Crown Court buildings but these are operating at much reduced capacity due to social distancing. This inevitably means that delays are increasing.

In Chapter 14 it was noted that a defendant will await trial either on bail (ie in the community) or on remand (ie in a gaol). Where a defendant has indicated that he will plead not-guilty then, as a matter of law, he remains innocent due to the presumption of innocence. A delay before trial can cause real problems for defendants. Some defendants will find that they are shunned socially, with people arguing that there is no smoke without fire, or their bail conditions will restrict their ability to carry out a normal life, including limiting their travel, overnight accommodation, and, potentially, who they can meet. The position is even worse for those who are remanded into custody, where they are deprived of their liberty while awaiting trial.

For this reason, there are maximum periods under which a person can be kept in custody, known as a 'custody time limit' (CTL).[77] The limits apply from the date of first appearance until the date at which the trial begins. For summary offences, the maximum period is fifty-six days.[78] For either-way offences triable in the magistrates' court it is seventy days, unless the mode of trial decision is made within the first fifty six days, when the limit becomes fifty-six days.[79] Given the maximum period of imprisonment the magistrates' court can impose on someone for a single charge is six months' imprisonment, fifty-six days is actually a long time. A person sentenced to imprisonment is typically eligible for release after serving 50%. Thus, fifty-six days is the equivalent of a 112 days sentence (with the maximum being 182 days for a single offence).

In the Crown Court, the maximum period of detention is usually 182 days,[80] either from the date when an either-way case is sent from the magistrates' court, or the date when an indictable-only case is sent to the Crown Court under the *Crime and Disorder Act 1998*, s 51 (see 12.3.2). In many cases, the parties will not be ready within such a time, and it is possible to seek an extension to the CTL by making an application to the Crown Court before it expires, and upon providing notice to the parties.[81] This is a formal application that will be heard in open court by a Crown Court judge who will decide whether it is appropriate for the CTL to be extended. This, in essence, provides additional case-management powers for the judge.

The delays in Crown Court trials have meant that there is little prospect of a trial being held before the initial CTL expires. The government responded by amending the Crown Court CTL to increase it to an ordinary period of 238 days instead of 182.[82] This is approximately an additional six weeks in custody, and this is only the initial CTL. Further extensions are inevitable.

709

---

77. *Prosecution of Offences Act 1985*, s 22 and see the *Prosecution of Offences (Custody Time Limits) Regulations 1987* (SI 1987/299) as amended.
78. SI 1987/299, reg 4(4A).
79. ibid, reg 4(2),(3).
80. ibid, reg 5.
81. ibid, reg 7.
82. *The Prosecution of Offences (Custody Time Limits)(Coronavirus)(Amendment) Regulations 2020* (SI 2020/953), reg 2.

In September 2020, a remarkable row broke out concerning CTLs. His Honour Judge Raynor, a circuit judge at the Crown Court in Woolwich, refused to extend a CTL because he believed that the efforts into creating the Nightingale courts etc were not effective, and not enough was being done to clear the backlog in the Crown Court. This would have been remarkable enough, but within the judge's powers. However, he alleged that the resident judge, His Honour Judge Kinch QC, had put pressure on him to extend the CTL. He further alleged that after making his ruling, the Senior Presiding Judge (Thirlwall LJ) removed the right of HHJ Raynor to reach a decision on the CTL in another case.[83]

If true, this would be a remarkable state of affairs. As was noted in Chapter 9, judges are supposed to be independent in how they conduct hearings, including independent from each other (9.1.3). Clearly, their orders can be appealed, but it would be inappropriate for judges to be put under pressure to a rule a particular way. The presiding and senior presiding judges have the power to decide how cases can be allocated (see 6.2.2.1), but they are not supposed to exercise these powers in a political way. Of course, the counter argument is that Thirlwall LJ did not do this. Some would argue that it was HHJ Raynor who acted improperly. The legislation had extended CTLs, and judges should accept that the requirements for social distancing will inevitably mean delays in the system. Perhaps it was HHJ Raynor who was trying to make a political point?

As ever, it is impossible to know who is right. There is undoubtedly a need to extend CTLs to ensure the public are safe where it is thought necessary to remand someone in prison. But, similarly, the requirement for a judge to scrutinize extensions for CTLs must mean that judges are expected to continue to balance the need to remand a person in custody against a likely custodial sentence and decide when remand becomes oppressive or inappropriate.

20.4.5 Sentencing

In *R v Manning*[84] the Lord Chief Justice said the following:

> We are hearing this [case] at the end of April 2020, when the nation remains in lockdown as a result of the Covid-19 emergency. The impact of that emergency on prisons is well-known. We are being invited in this Reference to order a man to prison nine weeks after he was given a suspended sentence, when he has complied with his curfew and has engaged successfully with the Probation Service. The current conditions in prisons represent a factor which can properly be taken into account in deciding whether to suspend a sentence. In accordance with established principles, any court will take into account the likely impact of a custodial sentence upon an offender and, where appropriate, upon others as well. Judges and magistrates can, therefore, and in our judgment should, keep in mind that the impact of a custodial sentence is likely to be heavier during the current emergency than it would otherwise be. Those in custody are, for example, confined to their cells for much longer periods than would otherwise be the case – currently, 23 hours a day. They are unable to receive visits. Both they and their families are likely to be anxious about the risk of the transmission of Covid-19.[85]

---

83. Catherine Baksi, 'MoJ's judicial critic complains of "improper and undue pressure"' (2020) *Law Society Gazette*, September 10.
84. [2020] EWCA Crim 592.
85. ibid, at [41].

It is certainly true that conditions in prisons are more draconian than they were prior to the pandemic. Prisons have the potential for exponential spreading of Covid-19 due to the close proximity of prisoners. This meant that in most gaols, inmates were kept in their cells for considerably longer than normal to minimize transmission. Illness of prison staff or requirements to self-isolate also meant that prisons were short-staffed, again requiring inmates to spend additional time in their cells.

In *Manning*, the LCJ recognized that the harshness of prison is a factor that can be taken into account when deciding whether to impose a custodial sentence. This is probably correct and could be welcomed by the Prison Service who may not be keen for a large influx of prisoners to arrive, each potentially carrying the virus.

Should the virus also lead to a reduction in sentence? The LCJ thought the answer is 'yes':

> Applying ordinary principles, where a court is satisfied that a custodial sentence must be imposed, the likely impact of that sentence continues to be relevant to the further decisions as to its necessary length and whether it can be suspended. Moreover, sentencers can and should also bear in mind the Reduction in Sentence Guideline. That makes clear that a guilty plea may result in a different type of sentence or enable a Magistrates' Court to retain jurisdiction, rather than committing for sentence.[86]

This is more controversial. The LCJ is clearly stating that sentencers should consider the impact of COVID-19 when deciding how long a sentence should be imposed, but is that fair? Admittedly, we are writing this six months after this judgment, at a time when the United Kingdom has entered the second 'lockdown' period. However, the virus will eventually come under control. Either through medicines or through learning to live with it. Taking the virus into account could lead to injustices. Take this example:

> Arnold and Charlie (separately) commit domestic burglary. Both have an extensive history of previous burglaries. Arnold was sentenced in February 2020 to five years' imprisonment. Charlie, in May 2020, is sentenced to four years' imprisonment due to the current harsh penal conditions.

Both Arnold and Charlie will serve their sentence at the same time. They might even serve it in the same gaol. Yet, Charlie will serve less time even though Arnold will be incarcerated in the same conditions as Charlie. That cannot be right.

Where there is greater justification for differences may be with shorter sentences. For example:

> Bobbie and Daniel have (separately) both been convicted of occasioning actual bodily harm. They have previous criminal convictions. Bobbie was sentenced to twelve months' imprisonment in 2019. Daniel is sentenced in June 2020 to nine months' imprisonment.

This is perhaps easier to justify because the conditions when Bobbie serves his six months' imprisonment,[87] would arguably be less onerous than the conditions that Daniel serves his four and a half month's imprisonment. However, if the harshness of conditions are to be taken into account, does that mean that defendant x should get a lesser sentence where it is likely that he will serve it in a gaol rated inadequate or seriously overcrowded?

---

86. ibid, at [42].
87. Automatic release would be granted after serving 50 per cent of time. It is possible that even earlier release could be granted if he was released on a tag.

QUESTION FOR REFLECTION

Taking account of COVID-19 when deciding whether to suspend a sentence of imprisonment would seem fair. However, is it appropriate for an offender to get a 'discount' where they are sentenced to immediate custody? What about, for example, when they are sentenced to a long term of imprisonment, where the current conditions may only form a small part of their overall sentence?

Conditions in gaol will vary out with COVID. Can the courts really take account of the 'harshness' of regimes when determining the length of a custodial sentence?

20.5 **Civil justice**

The civil justice system will be dealt with relatively briefly because it has already been discussed, particularly in the context of remote hearings (see 20.3.1). As a jury is the exception in civil matters, it was perhaps easier for many trials to go online. Where there were witnesses, particularly lay witnesses, this could be a reason for a trial not proceeding wholly online, but in such instances they tended to use hybrid hearings (some online, some in-person). In other cases, particularly commercial cases, witnesses would have adequate technology, or could attend solicitors offices in a socially-distanced way, to allow for remote hearings.

Much of the research on remote hearings (20.3.1) concerned proceedings in the Family Court. Much of its work is not the kind of proceedings that can be adjourned for a lengthy period of time. If a child is at risk of harm, then it is incumbent on the courts to ensure that it can adjudicate on such matters quickly, allowing the child to be safeguarded (where necessary) or returned to its parents (where appropriate). Sadly the pandemic led to an increase in private-law disputes. Even though the regulations permitted children of shared residences to travel between their houses, some parents simply refused to allow it.[88] Others refused contact visits, again, suggesting that the risks were too great. Such disputes clog up the family court. Even though most could probably be dealt with quickly, including over telephone, it undoubtedly wasted the court's time which could have been used for better purposes.

The coronavirus pandemic has led to major economic shocks throughout the world, including in the United Kingdom. Businesses has been closed for two extended periods of time (at the time of writing), with many workers being furloughed (temporary removed from jobs but receiving reduced wages) or made redundant. As was noted in Chapter 11, legal aid has been heavily restricted. The financial pressure can mean that there is increased likelihood that access to justice will be difficult. People losing their jobs will find it more difficult to challenge such decisions before the employment tribunals. Those who have been wronged, will find it more difficult to access the courts.

It was noted in Chapter 11 that, for many, it is now the free sources of advice, such as Law Clinics and Citizen's Advice, that people turn to. However, university campuses

---

88. See, for example, Helen Pidd, 'UK lawyers inundated by divorced parents arguing over lockdown custody' (2020) *The Guardian*, April 7.

are generally operating in blended mode, with restrictions as to the number of people allowed in. Similarly, many of the Citizens Advice buildings are not capable of operating in a socially distant way. Free services continue, but they are often being run online or by telephone. This can be challenging for those without Internet or smartphone access (for online services), and telephone-based advice is challenging where a person needs to see documents. Places where free access to technology was provided (libraries, community groups etc) are also affected by the restrictions and, in many instances, were not operating because of the costs that enhanced cleaning brought.

20.6 The future

What then will be the impact of COVID-19? Even with a vaccine imminent, it is thought that there is a risk that the virus will continue for several years, with fears that there may be mutations. It is unlikely that sustained periods of lockdown as seen in 2020 can continue. Neither is it likely that life will return to normal. While it is easy to be pessimistic and to look to what went wrong during the pandemic, there were some positive changes.

20.6.1 Alternative working

There appears to be a sustained call for more flexible working. People have realized that in the digital era, working from home is possible. It is unlikely that people will only work from home, not least because there are concerns about mental wellbeing where people do not physically meet. However, digital technology has shown that it is possible to work remotely, including collaboratively. It is likely that firms, including large solicitor firms, will embrace elements of this. It is unlikely that staff will be required to work five days a week in offices. That not only changes the dynamics of productivity, but it is also likely to bring economic benefits, particularly in places where travel is expensive.

Remote technology has clearly been a significant winner from COVID-19. If this pandemic had occurred twenty years ago, it is difficult to see how much of business, including the law, could have continued. Digital communication technologies have allowed contact, both professionally and socially. Many have adapted to the technology impressively. It has become second-nature to conduct meetings using Microsoft Teams, Zoom, or other platforms. Universities use the same platforms to conduct teaching and, as noted earlier, courts have used it too.

The Lord Chief Justice stated:

> What has to happen . . . is that information will be gathered about the experience of the use of these [video and audio] facilities so that careful decisions can be made about where they work, where they are good, where they do not work so well and where they do not really work at all.[89]

It has been noted already that increased technology was being sought by the courts. Clearly, there will be a need for digital technology to remain within the judicial process. Some hearings were probably more productive through the use of technology. It was noted that lawyers believed that there was less 'waiting around' and business was conducted efficiently. This was particularly true in civil matters but also criminal procedural matters.

713

---

89. Justice Committee, *Coronavirus (COVID-19): The Impact on Courts* (HC 2020–21, 519) at [61].

There is undoubtedly a case for certain procedural matters to continue to be dealt with remotely. At present, lawyers travel all over the country for hearings that last a few minutes and deal with non-contentious matters. It would surely be more appropriate for these now to be heard through video-technology?

Trials are unlikely to be heard remotely because of the need for witnesses etc. Jury trials will certainly not be conducted remotely, and, thus, the Crown Court is likely to return to normal practice quite quickly. What of the Court of Appeal and the Supreme Court? These are not trials *per se*. Where a party from Newcastle, Manchester, or Penzance have a matter listed in the Court of Appeal or the Supreme Court, they and their counsel must travel to London to participate in the hearing. Is that truly necessary?

This might be the litmus test for the appetite of the courts to embrace technology. The courts of England and Wales prioritize oral advocacy over anything else. Will they accept remote advocacy? Doing so would save money and help the environment. It would arguably make listing cases easier, but it is difficult to see the courts accepting remote advocacy as normal practice. They are too conservative and put too much reliance on physical attendance. It will be remembered that the Court of Appeal in *Re C (Children: COVID-19: Representation)*[90] accepted that the mother would be at a disadvantage by her mother not being physically present. That thinking is likely to be entrenched within the judiciary and the legal profession, meaning that radical reforms such as remote advocacy may not become routine for some time yet.

20.6.2 Clearing the backlog

The criminal justice system has suffered delays for many years, and COVID has brought these to a head. Interestingly, crime rates have fallen during the pandemic,[91] perhaps because in many situations alcohol has been restricted. Had crime remained the same, the backlog would probably be insurmountable.

As it is, the Lord Chief Justice has estimated that the backlog of jury trials is accumulating at approximately 1,000 cases per month.[92] Social distancing is unlikely to be reduced until a considerable proportion of the population have been vaccinated. One proposed solution is to reduce the number of the jury to a minimum of seven,[93] with an ordinary jury perhaps being nine or ten. That would be controversial, but less controversial than abolishing trial by jury and moving to either trial by judge alone, or by judge and two magistrates. However, it would only be worth doing if it was clear that this would allow more court or jury rooms to be available. If it does not, then there is no point.

In terms of routine trials, testing those involved for COVID-19 may help the Crown Court to resume. Tests that produce quick results have now been developed so it is perhaps possible to envisage a situation whereby the participants in a trial are tested daily. This may allow for reduced social distancing, meaning that the courts could be used as they were intended, allowing more trials to take place. Mass testing of all participants would be expensive, but probably less expensive than prolonging the backlog of cases.

How will that backlog be tackled? The Nightingale courts were introduced as a temporary measure, but the Justice Committee recommended the use of such courts

90. [2020] EWCA Civ 734.
91. See <https://www.ons.gov.uk/peoplepopulationandcommunity/crimeandjustice/bulletins/coronavirusandcrimeinenglandandwales/august2020>.
92. Justice Committee, *Coronavirus (COVID-19): The Impact on Courts* (HC 2020–21, 519) at [16].
93. ibid, at [78].

beyond the current emergency.[94] The actual temporary courtrooms will, of course, at some point be repurposed to their original purpose. Theatres would prefer people to watch a play than a Crown Court hearing. However, it would seem that the concept has worked. Delays in the criminal justice system are rarely spread evenly throughout the country. Pressures will be placed on certain parts of the country for relatively short periods of time. Deploying Nightingale courts to ease the pressure and prevent a backlog of cases could lead to sustained progress on reducing delays in the criminal justice system.

Nightingale courts could also be used to allow the Court of Appeal to sit outside of London more frequently. That would undoubtedly be useful for improving the transparency of the justice process.

20.6.3 Funding

The pandemic has led to a sustained period of economic difficulties. The government has had to spend vast amount of money propping up the economy. It has been estimated that the UK government will need to borrow £372bn for the 2020/21 financial year, as compared to the £55bn that had been planned.[95] That needs to be paid back at some point. While it is likely to be spread across multiple years, that means that unless there are significant tax increases, there will need to be spending cuts.

The government has conceded that in order to clear the backlog that has accrued in the criminal courts, they will need to spend more money on the courts. This means increasing the number of sitting days in the Crown Court.[96] However the Justice Select Committee noted that the government did not commit to doing this over multiple years, despite this undoubtedly being necessary. If crime is a priority of the government, they will not want to be perceived as harming the criminal justice system.

The difficulty is that the justice system budget covers the courts, probation, the prison service and legal aid (amongst other things). It is highly likely that this overall budget will be under extreme stress and the most likely area that will be squeezed is legal aid. As was noted in Chapter 11, legal aid is complicated and yet can easily be presented politically as the state making lawyers rich. That is not true, but newspapers are unlikely to man the barricade of truth to defend lawyers.

Of course, the economic fallout of COVID-19 is likely to mean that there is greater need for legal aid. Unemployment is rising, and there will always be concerns that not everyone let go will be given the appropriate notice. Similarly, those in employment risk being exploited as it becomes a 'hirers market' and increased threats of dismissal. Domestic abuse is thought to have risen during the pandemic,[97] and legal aid should be provided to help such victims escape from the abuse. Accommodation always suffers in economic drops, with unlawful evictions an ever-present danger. This is just a small list of problems that require a properly-funded legal aid system, but, unfortunately, it is highly unlikely that resource will follow such problems.

94.   ibid, at [93].
95.   Ben King, 'Coronavirus: How much will it cost the UK?' BBC News Online (<https://www.bbc.co.uk/news/business-52663523>).
96.   Justice Committee, *Coronavirus (COVID-19): The Impact on Courts* (HC 2020–21, 519) at [88].
97.   See <https://www.ons.gov.uk/peoplepopulationandcommunity/crimeandjustice/articles/domesticabuseduringthecoronaviruscovid19pandemicenglandandwales/november2020>.

20.6.4 **The legal system of England and (not necessarily) Wales**

The final point to note is that the divergence of English and Welsh law is likely to continue. It was noted in Chapter 1 that the government has not followed the recommendations of the former Lord Chief Justice (Lord Thomas) to establish a separate Welsh justice system. However, it is likely that the Welsh government will have noted that COVID gave them the ability to write their own laws, and the pressure will no doubt grow for that to occur more frequently.

If the Kingdoms are to remain united—and Scottish independence is very-much a live issue once more as it is believed the devolved nations handled the crisis better than Westminster—then a more federalized structure to the United Kingdom may be needed. This would see each of the four countries being given greater control of their own territory, albeit subject to oversight of the federal government on issues of common purpose. This may mean that the government's rejection of a Welsh justice system may yet prove premature.

Index

Note: Italic 'b', 'f', and 't' following page numbers denote boxes, figures and tables.

729